Tr

9

THE CAMBRIDGE ANCIENT HISTORY

EDITORS

Volumes I–VI

J. B. BURY, M.A., F.B.A.

S. A. COOK, LITT.D.

F. E. ADCOCK, M.A.

Volumes VII–XI

S. A. COOK, LITT.D., F.B.A.

F. E. ADCOCK, M.A., F.B.A.

M. P. CHARLESWORTH, M.A.

Volume XII

S. A. COOK, LITT.D., F.B.A.

F. E. ADCOCK, M.A., F.B.A.

M. P. CHARLESWORTH, M.A.

N. H. BAYNES, M.A., F.B.A.

VOLUME XII

LONDON
Cambridge University Press
BENTLEY HOUSE, N.W. I
TORONTO
BOMBAY · CALCUTTA · MADRAS
Macmillan
TOKYO
Maruzen Company Ltd

THE
CAMBRIDGE
ANCIENT HISTORY

VOLUME XII

THE IMPERIAL CRISIS
AND RECOVERY

A.D. 193—324

EDITED BY

S. A. COOK, Litt.D., F.B.A.

F. E. ADCOCK, M.A., F.B.A.

M. P. CHARLESWORTH, M.A.

N. H. BAYNES, M.A., F.B.A.

CAMBRIDGE
AT THE UNIVERSITY PRESS
1939

PRINTED IN GREAT BRITAIN

PREFACE

THE *Cambridge Medieval History* takes its beginning from the triumph of Constantine over his latest rival and the foundation of that city which for sixteen centuries was to be known by his name. This fact suffices to explain why this, the last volume of the *Cambridge Ancient History*, ends where it does. The volume is concerned with the evolution of the Imperial autocracy, the crisis that beset the Empire and threatened its dissolution, and the resolute recovery and reconstruction which made it possible for the Middle Age of Europe to inherit much that had been the possession of the Ancient World. It further describes the economic, intellectual and artistic character of that world in the closing phase, and the contemporary growth of the Christian Church within the Empire until, after conflict, it was taken into partnership by the Roman State. What the Ancient World owed to the past and could transmit to the future is indicated in the Epilogue which follows the final chapter of the volume and marks the completion of the work.

The period under review has a lasting monument in the work of Gibbon, but since his day the progressive criticism and appraisement of the literary sources and the wealth of fresh material both epigraphic, and still more numismatic, have combined to make corrections and new interpretations possible. Much still remains only half known or in dispute—and that fact has not been concealed in these pages—but the main outlines become sharper and firmer with each decade of scholarship. Yet it is not in details only that there remain pronounced differences of historical judgment: there is no agreement over important general questions such, for instance, as the relations between the Empire and the Christian Church. The testing of each strand of evidence demands the services of experts which are enlisted in this volume, and an attempt has been made to weave the strands together.

The Table of Contents reveals how many countries have played a part in this historical reconstruction of the period, and the bibliographies show the varied literature which in comparatively recent times has grown up to help the student. Continental scholarship is represented by chapters from Professor Alföldi of Budapest, Professor Bidez of Ghent, Professor Christensen of Copenhagen, Professor Ensslin of Erlangen, Professor Halphen of Paris, Professors Lietzmann and Rodenwaldt of Berlin and Professor Oertel of Bonn. Professor Nock and Professor Rand write from Harvard. The British contributors are Professor Baynes, Professor Collingwood, Mr Mattingly and Mr Miller. Two chapters (xiii and xiv) were written by the late Professor Burkitt shortly before his death in 1935. He did not live to revise them or to consider their contents in relation to other parts of the volume, which were then not written. These chapters needed to receive some revision and addition, and for this the volume is indebted to Professor Creed. An indication of these additions is given in the Table of Contents, but it is in place to say here that the account of Marcion, the gnostics, Syriac Christianity and the teachings of Mani are almost entirely as Professor Burkitt wrote them. The two chapters will be welcomed as a last example of the author's scholarship and intuition.

The volume begins with two chapters which give the political history of the period to the death of Philip the Arabian. By this time the Empire was faced by the new power of Sassanid Persia and the invasions of peoples from the Rhine to the Black Sea, whereas behind these the world of the Far East was in a turmoil from which were to emerge later even more far-reaching and disastrous movements of peoples. These are the subjects of chapters iii, iv and v. The great immediate crisis which threatened the dissolution of the Empire and its underlying causes are then described. At this point comes a review of the economic life of the Empire in the second and third centuries, which gives the background for the Imperial reconstruction that is to follow. A special problem in this field is that of Britain. The military history of Britain under Septimius Severus has already been treated. Now, as is appropriate in a work primarily intended for English readers, a brief review is given of the later development of Roman Britain. Next comes the description of the Imperial recovery, which was primarily the achievement of the Illyrian emperors. These more narrative chapters are followed by the systematic discussion first, of the transition from the Principate to the full Autocracy and secondly, of the reforms of Diocletian. The Great Persecution under Diocletian and the career of Constantine are reserved for the end of the volume, where they introduce the transition from the ancient to the medieval order. After the survey of the political and economic history of the period, there follows the second part of the volume; this is concerned with the religious, artistic and literary tendencies of the age. First comes a chapter on Pagan development in cults and religious thought.

The next three chapters deal with Pagan Philosophy and the Christian Church, together with the progress of the Church in the Eastern and Western halves of the Empire. These complete the picture of Christianity as a religious movement. At this point the transition of art from the classical to the late-classical is described. Next Latin literature is taken up from the point at which it was left in Volume XI, and in the survey are included the works of Christian authors writing in Latin. The second part of the volume is completed by a review of the philosophy and letters of the Greek-speaking parts of the Empire. There follow two closing chapters; in these the Great Persecution under Diocletian and its antecedents are considered and then the career of Constantine is outlined up to the Council of Nicaea, the point at which the *Cambridge Medieval History* opens. The volume ends with a short Epilogue.

It has already been pointed out that the advance in the study of this period has been due to criticism of sources and in particular to the use of numismatic evidence. The literary sources are briefly indicated in an Appendix to which Mr Mattingly has contributed a review of the evidence that is supplied by the study of coins. In three Notes the authors of chapters V–VI and VII treat of particular problems, and then follow the bibliographies, which are the work of the authors of the several chapters, except for the General Bibliography and that to chapters XIII–XV in which, in the absence of a bibliography from Professor Burkitt, will be seen the co-operation of several scholars besides Professor Lietzmann, the author of chapter XV. To these scholars, as indeed to all the writers who have taken great pains with the bibliographical material, students will, we hope, be grateful. Between the several bibliographies there has been a certain amount of interlocking, as also between these and the General Bibliography, which precedes them. Here and there a very recent book or an article about to be published may fail to be entered in a bibliography, though additions have been allowed as late as possible.

The varied character of the sources for this period has presented formal difficulties in the methods of reference, and we are indebted to the contributors for their willingness to see their own practice modified to secure such uniformity as is possible. If any form of reference is not immediately clear to the reader, assistance will be found in the details given in the Index of Passages. In the use of capitals and italics in the text of the chapters the practice of former volumes has been followed, and lack of uniformity is rather apparent than real.

On the title-page of this volume appear not three but four names arranged in the order dictated by the conventions of the University. The fourth name is that of Professor N. H. Baynes, who has the chief responsibility for the planning of the volume, though in this, as in earlier volumes, we have always had before us the original scheme as drafted by Professor Bury. The part Professor Bury played in the editing of the first half of this work and the width and depth of his historical judgment have not been forgotten by us, and we wish to take this final opportunity of placing on record our sense of his services to this work. The *Ancient History* has been an enterprise of the University through its Press, but it has been helped by many scholars of many Universities. Only the Editors know how greatly this help has exceeded the sum of the chapters which appear under the names of the several contributors. What is true of the whole is true of this volume, and we are also much indebted to contributors for their readiness to adapt their work to its needs. On the other hand, especially in a period when so much is in dispute, there would accrue more loss than gain from a forced uniformity of outlook or the suppression of conflicting views, when the same topics are bound to be discussed by more than one contributor. We have endeavoured to secure that where there must be such differences, the reader should know of their existence and their causes. We believe, however, that the volume possesses the unity that comes from the application of the same principles of criticism to all the problems which it presents.

Mr Miller wishes to acknowledge the help he has received from Professor F. de Zulueta, Mr I. A. Richmond, Mr E. B. Birley and Miss Anne Robertson. Professor Halphen has to thank Monsieur R. Grousset and Monsieur O. Jansé for their collaboration. Professor Alföldi and Mr Mattingly wish to thank each other for the benefit of much discussion on the problems connected with their chapters. Professor Nock also wishes to record his indebtedness to Mr Mattingly and to Monsieur F. Cumont and Professor W. S. Ferguson. Mr J. S. Boys Smith has earned the especial gratitude of Professor Lietzmann and the Editors for the pains he spent on the text and notes to chapter xv. Professor Rand wishes to thank his friends Mr B. M. Peebles and Mr A. B. Lord for assistance in the preparation of his bibliography and the correction of proofs. Mr C. R. C. Allberry has given valuable help with the bibliography and text of chapter xiv so far as Manichaeism is concerned.

The maps have been prepared by Mr Charlesworth with the help of the contributors whose chapters they illustrate. This is their purpose, and it is not claimed for them that they make reference to an atlas superfluous. Care has been taken to secure, as far as possible, a convenient grouping of the geographical material, and attention is called to the consolidated Index to the maps which appears at the end of the volume. Map 2 is based upon the Ordnance Survey Map of Roman Britain, with the permission of the Controller of H.M. Stationery Office. For the plans which accompany this volume we acknowledge the courtesy of H. Lamartin, Brussels, for Plan 1; Propyläen Verlag, Berlin, for Plan 2; Verlag Heinrich Veller, Berlin, for Plan 3; Verlag R. Oldenbourg, Munich, for Plan 5. Plan 4 is taken from D. S. Robertson, *Greek and Roman Architecture*.

We have once more to thank Mr C. T. Seltman for his assistance with the plans and for his co-operation in settling the illustrations. These, together with those to Volume XI, appear in Volume of Plates V, which he has prepared for publication at the same time as the present volume. Our debt to him is not limited to this, and we would acknowledge his generous help, especially in numismatic questions, throughout the whole of our task. For translations in this volume we have to thank him, and also Mr Boys Smith, Professor Fletcher, Mr H. P. W. Gatty, Mr G. T. Griffith, Mr R. D. McLellan, Mr Mattingly and Mr D. E. W. Wormell. Professor G. B. A. Fletcher has once more prepared the Chronological Table to the volume, and we are again indebted to him for his vigilant reading of the text. The General Index, Index to Maps and Index to Passages are the work of Mr J. Stevenson of St John's College, whose knowledge and watchfulness have been of great assistance to us in helping to control the many details both of form and substance that appear in a book of this complexity. We have advised him to omit from the General Index certain classes of items which appeared to us to be of no practical value, and for any such omissions we accept the responsibility.

In the prefaces to previous volumes we have expressed our thanks to the Staff of the University Press. A composite work of this kind gives rise to problems which may make demands on the resourcefulness of a Press, and this has been especially true of the present volume. We have therefore good reason to appreciate the unfailing helpfulness of the Staff of the Press, in this as in other volumes, and we take our leave of them with a due sense of gratitude.

The figure that best marks the transition from the ancient to the medieval world is that of Constantine, and for this reason we have chosen to place on the cover his portrait from a medallion, which is reproduced by the kind permission of the Director of the British Museum.

S.A.C.
F.E.A.
M.P.C.
N.H.B.

December, 1938

TABLE OF CONTENTS

CHAPTER I

THE ARMY AND THE IMPERIAL HOUSE

By S. N. MILLER, M.A.

Lecturer in Roman History and Archaeology in the University of Glasgow

CHAPTER II

THE SENATE AND THE ARMY

By W. ENSSLIN, Phil.Dr.
Professor of Ancient History in the University of Erlangen

CHAPTER III

THE BARBARIAN BACKGROUND

By L. HALPHEN

Membre de l'Institut de France, Professeur à la Sorbonne
(with the collaboration of R. Grousset and O. Jansé)

CHAPTER IV

SASSANID PERSIA

By ARTHUR CHRISTENSEN

Professor of Iranian Philology in the University of Copenhagen,
and W. ENSSLIN [1]

[1] Sections I–V are by Professor Christensen; section VI is by Professor Ensslin.

CHAPTER V

THE INVASIONS OF PEOPLES FROM THE RHINE
TO THE BLACK SEA

By A. ALFÖLDI

Hon. Phil.D. (Utrecht), Professor of the Ancient History and
Archaeology of the Hungarian territory in the University of Budapest

CHAPTER VI

THE CRISIS OF THE EMPIRE (A.D. 249–270)

By A. ALFÖLDI

CHAPTER VII

THE ECONOMIC LIFE OF THE EMPIRE

By F. OERTEL, Phil.Dr.

Professor of Ancient History in the University of Bonn

CONTENTS

CHAPTER VIII

BRITAIN

By R. G. COLLINGWOOD, M.A., F.S.A., F.B.A.

Waynflete Professor of Metaphysical Philosophy in the University of Oxford

CHAPTER IX

THE IMPERIAL RECOVERY

By H. MATTINGLY, M.A.

Formerly Fellow of Gonville and Caius College, Assistant Keeper
in the Department of Coins and Medals, British Museum

CHAPTER X

THE END OF THE PRINCIPATE

By W. ENSSLIN

CHAPTER XI

THE REFORMS OF DIOCLETIAN

By W. Ensslin

CHAPTER XII

THE DEVELOPMENT OF PAGANISM IN THE ROMAN EMPIRE

By A. D. NOCK, M.A., Hon. LL.D. (Birmingham)
Frothingham Professor of the History of Religion in Harvard University

CHAPTER XIII

PAGAN PHILOSOPHY AND THE CHRISTIAN CHURCH[1]

By the late F. C. BURKITT, D.D., Hon. D.Litt. (Oxon.), Hon. D.D. (Edinburgh,
Dublin and St Andrews), Hon. D.Theol. (Breslau), F.B.A.
Norrisian Professor of Divinity in the University of Cambridge

CHAPTER XIV

THE CHRISTIAN CHURCH IN THE EAST[2]

By F. C. BURKITT

[1] Additions to sections I–III of this chapter have been made by Professor J. M. Creed.
[2] Additions to section I of this chapter have been made by Professor Creed.

CHAPTER XV

THE CHRISTIAN CHURCH IN THE WEST

By HANS LIETZMANN, Hon. D.Theol. (Bonn), Hon. Dr.Phil. (Jena, Athens)
Professor of Church History in the University of Berlin

CHAPTER XVI

THE TRANSITION TO LATE-CLASSICAL ART

By G. RODENWALDT, Phil. Dr.
Professor of Classical Archaeology in the University of Berlin

CHAPTER XVII

THE LATIN LITERATURE OF THE WEST FROM THE ANTONINES TO CONSTANTINE

By E. K. RAND, A.M., Ph.D., Hon. Litt.D. (Manchester, Trinity College, Dublin,
Western Reserve), Hon. LL.D. (Glasgow)
Pope Professor of Latin in the University of Harvard

CHAPTER XVIII

LITERATURE AND PHILOSOPHY IN THE EASTERN HALF OF THE EMPIRE

By J. BIDEZ

Membre de l'Académie Royale de Belgique, Hon. D.Litt. (Athens, Brussels, Lille, Paris, Utrecht), F.B.A., Professeur émérite de l'Université de Gand

CONTENTS

CHAPTER XIX

THE GREAT PERSECUTION

By N. H. BAYNES, M.A., Hon. D.D. (St Andrews), F.B.A.
Professor of Byzantine History in the University of London

CHAPTER XX

CONSTANTINE

By N. H. BAYNES

CONTENTS

LIST OF MAPS AND PLANS:

CHAPTER I

THE ARMY AND THE IMPERIAL HOUSE

I. THE ACCESSION OF SEPTIMIUS SEVERUS

COMMODUS had left no heir behind him, and with his death[1] the line of the Antonines came to an unworthy end. As the conspirators had anticipated, the Senate promptly annulled his acts and condemned his memory. Nor did the Praetorian Prefect Laetus misjudge senatorial feeling when he induced the Guard to proclaim as successor the City Prefect, P. Helvius Pertinax. An Italian of humble origin, Pertinax had won his way into the Senate after a varied military experience as an *eques*. Under Marcus Aurelius he had commanded a legion on the Upper Danube, and for distinguished service there had been rewarded with the consulship. After holding consular commands under Marcus in Moesia and in Syria, he had been sent by Commodus to govern Britain, where he had sternly repressed a mutiny of the troops, and thereafter he had been appointed proconsul of Africa, where an outbreak of disorder called for a strong hand. It was not a career that gave the Praetorians any reason to expect a continuance of the licence which they had recently enjoyed, but they had no candidate of their own, and the promise of a donative of twelve thousand sesterces apiece overcame their hesitation. By the Senate Pertinax was at once accepted as a man who seemed likely to resume the policy of the earlier Antonines, while his military achievement and reputation commanded the respect of the frontier armies.

At sixty-six years of age he could not be expected to have a long reign, but there was the hope that if he took advantage of the

Note. To the principal literary sources, Cassius Dio, Herodian, and the Scriptores Historiae Augustae (S.H.A.), references are given in the footnotes only where it is desired to emphasize a piece of evidence or to draw attention to the terms in which it is expressed. The references to Dio follow the book-divisions as given above the left-hand pages of Boissevain's edition. For Latin inscriptions references are given to *C.I.L., Eph. Ep.,* or *Ann. épig.,* only for inscriptions not contained in Dessau. In coin references M.-S. indicates Mattingly and Sydenham, *The Roman Imperial Coinage.* See for coins Volume of Plates v, where also will be found (186, 230) portraits of Severus, Caracalla and Elagabalus.   [1] On 31 December 192 (vol. XI, p. 383).

general goodwill to secure a settlement of the succession, he might introduce a period of stable government, as another sexagenarian emperor had done, after the assassination of Domitian, by the adoption of Trajan. Unlike Nerva, Pertinax had a son of his own, and the Senate itself proposed that he should be given the title of Caesar. But the lad was young, and Pertinax did not feel that his own position was yet assured, and he rejected the proposal as premature[1]. On 6 March 193 the Prefect of Egypt, L. Mantennius Sabinus, issued orders for a general festival of fifteen days to mark the accession of the new imperial family[2]. The belated celebration can hardly have run its course, at least in the remoter parts of Egypt, before the Emperor was dead, with the succession still unsecured, and, judged by what followed, he must be likened not to Nerva but to Galba.

Between the reigns of Pertinax and Galba there is a resemblance also in the causes which cut them short. The follies of Commodus had been as serious a drain upon the imperial treasury as the extravagance of Nero, and that at a time when the sources of revenue were tending to shrink. An attempt made by Pertinax to stimulate commerce by lightening the customs duties and to encourage the cultivation of waste land by granting titles of ownership, with exemption from taxation for ten years[3], appears to indicate a positive and comprehensive policy to increase, or restore, the resources of the Empire. But a scheme of this kind required time, whereas the personal and public economies by which he endeavoured to relieve the immediate situation made themselves unpleasantly felt at once by those who were directly affected by them, notably the personnel of the palace. To the Praetorians he seems to have paid the promised donative[4], but he put a stop to practices of petty plundering in which they had been indulged by Commodus, and he attempted to enforce a strict discipline. Laetus, still Praetorian Prefect, was chagrined to discover that he had chosen a master instead of a tool, and he so worked upon the misgiving of his men that, on 28 March, a party of them marched

[1] Dio LXXIV, 7. At the same time he refused the title of Augusta for his wife, Flavia Titiana. Neither wife nor son figures in the Roman coinage, but both appear in the coinage of Alexandria, the one as Augusta, the other as Caesar (Vogt, *Die Alexandrinischen Münzen*, I, p. 158). Cf. Dessau 410.

[2] Wilcken, *Chrest.* 490.

[3] Known only, however, from Herodian II, 4, 6. In the reign of Severus the occupation of waste land, at least on imperial domains in Africa, was still regulated by the *lex Hadriana de rudibus agris et iis qui per X annos continuos inculti sunt* (Bruns, *Fontes*[7], 115).

[4] Dio LXXIV, 5, 4.

to the palace, and presently descended into the City streets displaying the head of the Emperor whom they had proclaimed eighty-seven days before. In spite of the brevity of his reign, Pertinax had made a lasting impression as a model of a constitutional ruler, and in the confused movements that followed his death his name became the symbol of a policy.

The Prefect of the City, T. Flavius Sulpicianus, who had enjoyed a brief experience of palace life as the father-in-law of Pertinax, was intriguing with the Praetorians for the succession when a rival presented himself in another elderly senator, M. Didius Julianus, a man of more dubious reputation but greater wealth. This was an opportunity which the Praetorians knew how to exploit. They put the Empire up to auction between the two until they had extorted from Julianus the promise of a donative of 25,000 sesterces apiece. It was a simple matter to intimidate the Senate into ratifying the bargain. The City populace resented being so disposed of, but they were a helpless mob, and their only hope was that the Praetorians' behaviour would remind the frontier armies that 'an emperor could be made elsewhere than at Rome.'

Their expectations were centred chiefly in the governor of Syria, C. Pescennius Niger. They were not disappointed; he was proclaimed emperor by his legions as soon as the situation at Rome was known in the East. But by this time the governor of Upper Pannonia, P. Septimius Severus, had already got himself proclaimed by the troops at his headquarters at Carnuntum (13 April)[1]. The conflict of ambitions was reinforced by the mutual jealousy of the two armies, confirmed by a long period of local recruiting. A repetition of the disaster of A.D. 69 seemed inevitable.

Since that date, however, the distribution and composition of the frontier legions had changed. With nine legions, including the legion in Egypt, the army of the East remained much the same, but the Rhine army had been reduced from seven legions to four, and its unity had been affected by the closer association of the legions on the Upper Rhine with the troops on the Upper Danube since the construction of the *limes* between the two rivers. On the other hand, the Danube army had been increased from seven to twelve legions by the frontier policy of successive emperors, and whereas in the first century it had been drawn partly from Italy and the Latin West, partly from the Greek-speaking

---

[1] *Idibus Aprilibus*, a correction generally accepted for the impossible *idibus Augustis* of S.H.A. *Sev.* 5, 1.

population of Macedonia and the Asiatic provinces, it was now recruited almost entirely from the Danube area. The legions from end to end of the river were united in the support of Severus[1], and their strength and position put the initiative in their hands.

At the time of his proclamation Severus took the name of Pertinax as a cognomen, and represented himself as his avenger. This was intended to conciliate the Senate, as a preliminary to the attainment of his first objective, which was to take advantage of his proximity to the capital to secure constitutional investiture and to gain control of the central machinery of administration and finance. By the time news of his departure from Carnuntum reached Rome he had already advanced by forced marches into North Italy. Julianus thereupon induced the Senate to proclaim him a public enemy, and attempted to put the City into a state of defence. But he had not the power to command obedience or enforce discipline, and in desperation he prepared to barricade himself within the palace. He put Laetus to death, and with him Marcia (vol. xi, p. 383), on suspicion of favouring the enemy, and then himself opened negotiations with Severus. But by now Severus was master of the situation in Italy. At Rome itself the Praetorians made it known to the Senate that they were in correspondence with the man whom it had just declared a public enemy, and the Senate, which had hitherto been content to watch the despairing efforts of Julianus with a malicious aloofness, now judged it opportune to condemn him to death and to recognize Severus as emperor. On 1 June Julianus was killed in the palace by a soldier. Soon after Severus entered Rome with his entire force in full armour. It was a ceremonial announcement of the power and spirit that were now to direct the government.

As part of the manifesto, however, Severus himself, in conformity with the ancient rule, had dismounted at the City gates and changed into civil dress. This was a display of deference to the Senate and People of Rome. Besides granting a donative to his troops, he sought to win the favour of the populace by a liberal distribution, and at a meeting of the Senate he took an oath, as Nerva, Trajan and Hadrian had done, not to put any of its members to death without bringing the case before it, and even had this procedure formulated as a rule in a *senatus consultum*. His policy, he promised, would be that of Marcus Aurelius: informers would not be encouraged; and he would be a Pertinax not only in

---

[1] All the Danube legions figure in Severus' coinage of 193 except the Vindobona legion, X Gemina. If this legion hesitated to follow the lead of Carnuntum, its hesitation can only have been momentary.

name but in goodwill to their order. It was a kind of ritual sanction to this declaration that he then celebrated in full form the
apotheosis of Pertinax, which the Senate had decreed when it
condemned Julianus to death.

Some of the older senators, who had long known Severus,
doubted his sincerity. At all events, his professions are an indication of the importance which he attached at this time to the civil
power. He had heard the expected news that Niger had been proclaimed emperor by the Syrian legions, and Niger, he knew, was
popular in the City. During the absence in the East which he now
anticipated, he had no desire to see turned against him the organs
of the central government which he had marched into Italy to
secure. But he did not rely entirely upon conciliatory methods.
He put to death, or proscribed, those who had been active partisans of Julianus, and in acting through the Senate in this matter
he was not only fulfilling his promise but was bringing home to it
a warning of what his enemies might expect.

He knew, however, that his position in the capital depended
less on the Senate than on the troops stationed there. Before
entering the City he had summoned the Praetorians to meet him
unarmed, had surrounded them with his legionaries and dismissed
them with ignominy. That he was not simply punishing the
murderers of Pertinax was presently shown by the manner in
which he reconstituted the Guard, now increased to 15,000 men.
Hitherto admission to its ranks had been a privilege confined to
natives of Italy and of the romanized communities of Spain,
Noricum and Macedonia; henceforth it was to be recruited from
the frontier legionaries, and in re-forming it Severus selected the
pick of the men from his own Danube legions[1].

Outside Italy there were two formidable groups of legions in
the West. These were the four legions stationed on the Rhine and
the three legions which formed the garrison of Britain. By this
time the Rhine legions had declared for Severus[2], but in Britain
the situation was still doubtful. The governor there, D. Clodius
Albinus, was suspected of entertaining ambitious hopes with which
his army was believed to sympathize; and it was known that there
were many in the Senate who would welcome his intervention. An
agreement was reached by which Albinus accepted from Severus
the position of Caesar, which was formally conferred upon him

---

[1] See the lists of Praetorians in *C.I.L.* VI, 32533 (A.D. 209)—36–38
(A.D. 212–4).
[2] All four are included in the legionary types of the coinage of 193. They
must be the *Gallicani exercitus* of S.H.A. *Sev.* 5, 3.

by the Senate and commemorated on the coinage[1]. Severus must have had reason to suppose that this arrangement, which carried with it a presumptive right of succession, satisfied Albinus, for his own immediate design was to have his hands free to meet the challenge in the East, where Niger had now had two months to make his preparations.

But before leaving Rome there was another precaution to take. So long as Niger had the support of the Egyptian army, he was in a position, like Vespasian in 69, to restrict the corn-supply, and if he were able to extend his control to the corn-growing districts of Africa, the capital would be in a serious position. To prevent this, Severus seems to have ordered detachments of the legion III Augusta to proceed from the Numidian frontier to the more eastern parts of the African province[2], where their presence would not only protect the corn-supply but also, by threatening Egypt, prevent the legion there, II Traiana, from sending any effective help to Niger.

II. THE CIVIL WARS AND PARTHIAN EXPEDITIONS

Early in July 193 Severus left Rome by the Flaminian Way to follow the road that led to the Danube at Singidunum and Viminacium and thence through Upper Moesia to Thrace. He selected this northern route in order to keep in touch with the forces disposed along the Danube, and to call out the full strength they could mobilize for the Eastern campaign. But it was not the shortest route to the East, and there was the danger that Niger might block his passage to Asia by occupying Byzantium, and even turn his whole position by moving upon Rome along the Via Egnatia, the direct route from Byzantium to the Adriatic. To meet this danger orders were sent to the legions in Moesia to march direct into Thrace, while part of the Illyrian army which had been led into Italy may have been shipped across the Adriatic to Dyrrhachium to advance eastwards by the Via Egnatia[3]. As it happened, the governor of Asia, Asellius Aemilianus, had already

---

[1] M.-S. IV, i, pp. 40–2; Herodian II, 15, 1–5. An offer of the position of Caesar may well have been sent to Albinus, as Dio implies (LXXIV, 15, 1), before Severus reached Rome. For the position of Albinus after his recognition as Caesar, see C. R. Van Sickle, *Class. Phil.* XXIII, 1928, p. 123.

[2] This appears to be the meaning of S.H.A. *Sev.* 8, 7. The legion III Augusta is not given a place in the legionary coin-types, but it had probably received the title 'pia vindex' by 194–195 (*C.I.L.* VIII, 17726).

[3] For the transport of a force of legionaries by sea cf. Herodian II, 14, 7; III, 1, 1. In S.H.A. *Sev.* 8, 12, Graecia may mean Macedonia.

occupied Byzantium for Niger, and was advancing upon Perinthus, when the first of the Severan troops arrived[1]. These were defeated with heavy loss, but Aemilianus was not in a position to maintain control of the straits, and he withdrew to Byzantium. To mask the stronghold a siege corps was detached under the command of one of the legionary legates of Lower Moesia, Marius Maximus[2], while a force was transported across the Propontis to Cyzicus. There Aemilianus, who had recrossed the Bosporus to intercept it, was defeated and killed.

Having thus gained a footing in Asia, the Severan army advanced eastwards into Bithynia, whence the main roads crossed the peninsula to Cilicia and Syria. The news of the battle of Cyzicus had made the province waver in its support of the Eastern claimant, and Nicomedia declared for Severus, while its neighbour and rival, Nicaea, became the headquarters of Niger. A force sent forward from there to hold the pass that ran along the southern shore of the Ascanian lake between Cius and Nicaea was decisively defeated. It was now the beginning of 194[3].

The victorious army was commanded by Severus' general, Tiberius Claudius Candidus[4], and it would appear that the force led by Severus himself through Pannonia and Upper Moesia had not reached Bithynia in time to take part in the battle. Its arrival not long after is the probable explanation of a sudden move on the part of Niger; he withdrew to Syria to raise reinforcements, making no further attempt to hold the route across Asia Minor beyond leaving a force to defend some fortifications which he had already erected on Mt Taurus in the narrow pass of the Cilician Gates. The Severan army, now at full strength, must have arrived there by March (194). Swollen by the spring rains and the melting of the snow, the stream which flowed through the defile swept away the fortifications. The position was at once abandoned by its defenders, and the Severan army descended into the plain of Issus.

In Syria, Niger had found that his retirement was regarded as an acknowledgment of defeat, and he was distracted there by the dissensions and jealousies that discover themselves in a failing cause. Laodicea, envious of the favour enjoyed by its rival ·Antioch as the headquarters of Niger, declared for Severus,

1 Presumably the advance-guard of the Moesian army, perhaps to be identified with the *vexillationes Perinthi pergentes* of Dessau 1141.

2 Dessau 2935.

3 With the victory at Nicaea Severus becomes *Imp. III*. He is so styled in a military diploma of 31 January 194 (*Ann. épig.* 1908, no. 146).

4 Dessau 1140; cf. Dio LXXV, 6.

and by the same venture Tyre sought to win a future advantage over its rival Berytus. Both cities were heavily punished for anticipating the course of events. But by now misgiving had spread to the troops, or their commanders, in more than one of the Eastern provinces, and Niger could no longer count on the legion in Egypt or on the legion in Arabia.[1] For reinforcements he had to look to Syrian volunteers, and especially to the townsmen of Antioch, and it was with a motley host that he set out for the north on hearing that Severus had passed the Cilician Gates. His army did itself no discredit on the plain of Issus, where the final battle of the war was fought, but in the end victory rested with the Illyrian legionaries. It would now be about April of 194[2]. Niger rode back to Antioch, but fled from the city when it surrendered. According to Dio, he was making for the Euphrates in the hope of finding refuge with the Parthians when he was overtaken and killed. By the order of Severus his head was sent to Byzantium to be displayed to the townsmen as an invitation to cease fighting for a cause already lost, but they continued to man their walls and for two years more postponed their punishment.

Meanwhile Severus was in Syria distributing rewards and penalties. Laodicea becomes a 'colonia' with the *Ius Italicum*. The elevation of Laodicea was the humiliation of Antioch, which was indeed 'attributed' to the rival city[3], which now displaced it, though not for long, as the official capital of Syria. The Palestinian city of Neapolis forfeited its political existence for its support of Niger. Cities which had supplied him with funds had to pay a fine of four times the amount, while those which had suffered by resisting him, such as Laodicea and Tyre, were handsomely indemnified. Senators who had favoured his cause had their property confiscated and were banished, while his adherents in general were treated with merciless severity, until it was found that refugees from his army were being driven across the Tigris to take service with the barbarians, whereupon a general amnesty was declared. Many of these refugees were skilled mechanics who

---

[1] For the recognition of Severus in Egypt by February, cf. Wilcken, *Chrest.* 96, pag. iv, l. 6; *B.G.U.* 326. *C.I.L.* III, 6580, shows him (as *Imp. III*) in control of the Egyptian legion, II Traiana, before the battle of Issus. L. Mantennius Sabinus, who had been Prefect of Egypt since 193 (*Chrest.* 490), was continued in his office by Severus (*I.G.R.R.* I, 1062). The same is true of the governor of Arabia, P. Aelius Severianus Maximus (Dessau 5842; *C.I.L.* III, 13612, etc.).

[2] On this vexed question see G. A. Harrer, in *J.R.S.* x, 1920, pp. 162–8, whose conclusions are here adopted.

[3] Herodian III, 6, 9.

taught their new masters the use of armour and the manufacture of arms. By such instruction, Herodian notes, the Romans made the barbarians more formidable enemies. It is a remark that admits of a wide and various application to the history of the Roman frontiers, but the incident has more than a military significance: it shows that the imperial frontiers, long before they failed as military lines, were ceasing to be spiritual boundaries. There had been correspondence between Niger and the Parthian king, one of whose vassals, Barsemius of Hatra, had sent Niger a force of archers. It was not only the military integrity of the Empire that Severus was vindicating when, after his triumph over his rival, he led an army across the Euphrates.

There were indeed good military reasons for the expedition. The Parthian king, Vologases IV, had held out promises to Niger, but had not sent him any actual help. Apparently he saw another way of profiting by the civil war, and we may recognize his influence at work in an attempt made by certain of his vassals to shake off the control which the Roman government had exercised in Mesopotamia ever since the expedition of Lucius Verus. Roman garrisons in Mesopotamia had been taken prisoner, the important stronghold of Nisibis had been besieged, and Osrhoëne had renounced Roman suzerainty. Severus decided to take advantage of the occasion, and of the internal weakness of Parthia at this time, to make a settlement of the Eastern frontier by resuming, in some measure, the annexationist policy of Trajan. He may have crossed the Euphrates about September[1] (194). By the early part of 195 he had punished Osrhoëne for its defection by reducing it to a province under the charge of a procurator[2]. Having advanced eastwards to Nisibis, he ordered his generals to overrun the territory of the Skenite, or Mesopotamian, Arabs, and then sent them upon an expedition across the Tigris into Adiabene. Before the end of August he had assumed the titles of Arabicus and Adiabenicus[3].

Besides making Osrhoëne a province, he had prepared for the formation of a province between Osrhoëne and the Tigris by the erection of Nisibis into a colony and the establishment there of a resident procurator; and the fact that the titles Arabicus and Adiabenicus, when first conferred, were each combined with the

[1] The dry season; cf. Dio LXXV, 2 (p. 339 Boissevain).
[2] This would be the occasion of his assumption of the style *Imp. V*, the first of three salutations of 195. For a *proc. provinc. Osrhoënae* in the reign of Severus cf. Dessau 1353.
[3] Dattari, *Num. Aug. Alex.* 3986.

title of Parthicus (Parthicus Arabicus, Parthicus Adiabenicus) indicates that the operations of 195 were regarded as steps towards a settlement of the whole problem of Parthia and the Eastern frontier. But before the end of the year 'Parthicus' disappears from each of the titles, as if the Emperor thought it politic to withdraw the implied threat to Parthia[1]. He even gives up the idea of holding the newly added province of Osrhoëne, which he restores to the native ruling family of the Abgars. The reason of this sudden suspension of his plans was that all available troops were wanted for the West, from which he had received disquieting reports of Albinus.

To Severus, who had two sons and a wife as ambitious as himself, the arrangement by which the governor of Britain became Caesar and presumptive successor can only have been a temporary device to ensure himself against a challenge in the West while he carried on his Eastern campaigns. Albinus, on the other hand, appears to have hoped that Severus would not go back on their agreement, which he himself seems to have accepted from a genuine desire to avoid an appeal to arms; and he would probably have allowed Severus to continue undisturbed to complete the settlement of the Parthian problem if he had been left to his own devices. But the very qualities which inclined him to accept the position assigned to him by Severus invited interference by the Senate. The two men were both Africans, but with a difference. Severus, though he had senatorial connections, was of a native family of no more than equestrian rank, and he himself had aroused misgiving in the Senate by his character and pretensions, whereas Albinus belonged to the senatorial nobility by descent, and he had been an obedient pupil in the school of Marcus Aurelius, whose policy of deference to the Senate he might be expected to resume. And intervention by the Senate was encouraged by the knowledge that the British legions, as they had shown in the reign of Commodus, were ready to proclaim a candidate of their own[2]. It soon became known to Severus that leading senators were in correspondence with Albinus, and were urging him to march to Rome. Before the end of 195 Albinus himself had realized that Severus had no intention to abide by their agreement, and he committed himself to a declared hostility by taking

---

[1] Cf. S.H.A. *Sev.* 9, 11. Parthicus Arabicus and Parthicus Adiabenicus reappear in the inscription on the arch of Severus at Rome, dedicated in 203, but there the Imperial titles are peculiar in this respect as in others. Cf. Dessau 425.

[2] See Vol. XI, p. 384.

INDEX TO NAMES

measures to secure his position. Severus' reply was to have him proclaimed a public enemy by the army in Mesopotamia. With this act a new civil war begins. The news had reached Rome by 15 December, when the people assembled in the Circus made an organized demonstration against the prospect that now confronted them. It cannot have been long after this that Albinus was proclaimed Augustus by his troops.

It was probably during this first period in the East[1] that Severus took the precaution of dividing Syria with its army of five legions into two provinces, Syria Coele (north Syria, including Commagene) with two legions, and Syria Phoenice (south Syria) with one. Before he left for the West he received the news that Byzantium had fallen. This was not now a very important event in itself, but it gave him an opportunity of displaying to his army a good omen for the success of the coming campaign against Albinus and of giving to his enemies a conspicuous warning. In 193 Byzantium had opened its gates to Aemilianus, and Severus now ordered its magistrates, as well as the soldiers within its walls, to be put to death; and besides confiscating the property of its citizens, he deprived it of its 'free' status, and indeed 'attributed' it to Perinthus as he had 'attributed' Antioch to Laodicea. To complete its humiliation he razed the principal buildings and demolished its walls. By this, Dio complains, he 'destroyed a Roman stronghold and base of operations against the barbarians from the Pontus and from Asia.' But no one knew better than Severus the military value of Byzantium, and the restoration of the city was begun as soon as the demonstration of ruthlessness had served his turn.

The long siege and defence of Byzantium impressed the imagination of contemporaries. 'For three whole years,' says Dio, 'it had resisted the armaments of almost the whole world.' It would appear that the historian exaggerates in time as well as circumstance. The siege, which had begun in the autumn of 193, must have ended well before the autumn of 196 if Dio is right in saying that the news of its fall reached Severus while he was still in Mesopotamia; for he had recrossed the Euphrates on his way to the West in time to be in Thrace by 27 May, the birthday of his younger son Geta[2].

He celebrated the occasion ceremonially with military games,

---

[1] See H. Ingholt, *Syria*, XIII, 1932, pp. 282–6.
[2] Jordanes, *Get.* xv, 84 M; cf. S.H.A. *Max. duo* 2. See G. A. Harrer, in *J.R.S.* x, 1920, pp. 163–4.

as became a formal act in a dynastic programme. This programme was carried further when he reached Viminacium, the capital of Upper Moesia. The previous year, when he was still in the East, he had announced himself to have been adopted into the family of Marcus Aurelius, so entering a line of deified emperors; and he had made good an awkward gap in the series by causing his army to proclaim the deification of his Antonine predecessor and 'brother,' Commodus[1], whose memory had been condemned by the Senate. The dynastic legitimation and religious sanction which he had thus associated with his rule were now formally communicated to his elder son, Septimius Bassianus, known as Caracalla[2]; he was proclaimed Caesar by the army in place of Albinus under the name of Marcus Aurelius Antoninus.

Meanwhile Albinus had crossed the Channel with the bulk of the British garrison—three legions and auxiliaries—and had gained a victory over a Lupus[3] who was apparently legate of Lower Germany. This would bring a great accession to his strength, for the Lower Rhine and Belgic Gaul seem still to have been the chief recruiting-ground for the auxiliaries of the British army. But Gaul was not unanimous in his support[4], and Trèves appears to have been held against him[5] as he passed south into the valley of the Saône. He established himself at Lyons, where the garrison, the Thirteenth Urban Cohort, came over to his side, though the governor of Lugdunensis refused to recognize him and quitted the province[6]. On the other hand, he had the support of the governor of Hispania Tarraconensis, L. Novius Rufus[7], who had a legion, VII Gemina, at his disposal. And in the West generally, the prevailing opinion was ready enough to credit him with the political virtues set forth in the coinage which he now issued from a mint at Lyons.

But Severus knew that the real field of political action was the

---

[1] For Severus as *divi M. Pii f.* in 195 cf. M.-S. IV, i, p. 99, no. 65; p. 185, no. 686. For the deified ancestry in the same year, with Commodus as *divus* and *frater*, cf. *C.I.L.* VIII, 9317.

[2] For convenience this name is used throughout, though it was not applied to him until after he became Emperor (p. 48). At this time he was eight years old.

[3] Dio LXXVI, 6, 2. Presumably he is the Virius Lupus who appears presently in northern Britain (p. 38).

[4] Cf. the escapade of Numerianus related by Dio LXXVI, 5.

[5] This is probably what is referred to in Dessau 419.

[6] For his restoration by Severus cf. Dessau 1152.

[7] *C.I.L.* II, 4125. He was later put to death by Severus (S.H.A. *Sev.* 13, 7). For opposition to Severus in Spain cf. Dessau 1140.

Senate House at Rome, where the party of Albinus was predominant and only awaited a favourable occasion to avow itself and assume control. He therefore decided, probably at Poetovio, to leave his army and to hasten south to Rome. At the same time he detached a force to hold the western passes of the Alps, so closing to Albinus the direct routes from Gaul into Italy and keeping open for himself communication between Rome and the main body of his own army, which he sent forward into Gaul through Noricum and Raetia. At Rome he obtained from the Senate a denunciation of Albinus as a public enemy. A dedication by himself to the deified Nerva as his ancestor[1], and the issue of a coinage which was not content to proclaim conventional virtues but advertised the gifts and games with which he now gratified the populace, were further moves in a political campaign which closed before the end of the autumn with a ceremonial departure, preceded by public vows for his safe return. Taking the available strength of the City garrison with him, he set out to rejoin his army, which by now had advanced into Gaul.

From Poetovio westwards the army seems to have followed a route through Noricum and Raetia along which Severus, with cynical calculation, had put the roads into good repair the previous year; this crossed the Noric Alps to Salzburg, from which it ran by Augsburg to Windisch. From Windisch the direct route to Lyons ran by Avenches to the valley of the Upper Rhône, but the strategy of the Severan army seems to have been to envelop Lyons by striking northwards into the Sequani country and following the valley of the Doubs by Besançon to the Saône at Châlon, for the first indication of its presence in Gaul points to Tournus, only some fifteen miles down stream from Châlon and about sixty miles north of Lyons.

At Tournus (Tinurtium) the *Life* of Severus places a first victory won against Albinus, and the fact that Severus assumed two imperial salutations (the ninth and tenth), apparently in close succession, before he left for the East on his second Parthian expedition[2], implies that an important success had preceded the concluding battle at Lyons. It is in itself improbable that his army would be allowed, without a struggle, to take command of the valley of the Saône, for this meant the almost complete envelopment of Albinus, who was already shut out from Italy by the occupation of the Alpine passes and now found himself cut off from his base in

[1] Dessau 418.

[2] Cf. J. Hasebroek, *Untersuchungen zur Geschichte des Kaisers Septimius Severus*, p. 98.

northern Gaul and Britain. He was, in fact, virtually shut up in Lyons, and it was in the immediate neighbourhood of the city, presumably on the line of the road from Tournus, on the right bank of the Saône[1], that the final battle took place on 19 February 197. It ended in the decisive defeat of Albinus, who put an end to his life when he found that he was surrounded and escape cut off.

It was hardly to be expected that his army would be able to withstand the solid strength of the Danube legions. Like the Syrian legions in the army of Niger, the British garrison can only have been the nucleus of a composite force, if Dio[2] is right in saying that in numbers the army of Albinus equalled that of Severus. Large contingents must have been raised in Gaul. Since the civil wars of 69 the localization of the several army groups had been so intensified by local recruiting that each of them now carried with it, in any political action which it might take, a large civilian population, not only from the neighbourhood where it was stationed but from the wider area whence it drew its recruits. If such regional feeling encountered resistances within its own range, these were not due to any attachment to the centre but were merely symptoms of a smaller within a larger particularism[3]. Neither Dio nor Herodian emphasizes the wars of 193–7 as a violation of a common patriotism, and Herodian presents the combatants rather as regional or racial groups than as members of the same State[4]. Native of a Punic town in Africa, Severus would be no less conscious than an Eastern like Herodian of the strength and danger of regional feeling, and he must also have been aware of the absence of any Roman patriotism powerful enough to react against it effectively. Both in the East and in the West he had seen individuals and communities favour the nearest claimant to the throne from no motive but self-interest, or acquiesce from mere supineness. If he treated them with much the same severity as the active combatants, they had given him reason to believe that the only means of holding the Empire together was military constraint, and even, in the immediate circumstances, a systematic terrorism.

Lyons was handed over to the soldiers, who sacked and burned it, while the cohort on garrison there, XIII Urbana, was replaced by detachments from the four legions on the Rhine[5]. The head of

---

[1] Cf. C. Jullian, *Histoire de la Gaule*, IV, p. 516, n. 1.
[2] Dio LXXVI, 6, 1.
[3] Cf. Herodian III, 2, 7, and 3, 3.
[4] Cf. Herodian III, 2, 2; 4, 3; 7, 2.   [5] Dessau 9493.

Albinus was sent to Rome, as Niger's had been sent to Byzantium, as a warning to those who persisted in their hostility. The warning would be addressed particularly to the senators, upon whom it seems to have produced an immediate effect, for an inscription proves that they sent an embassy to Severus at this time[1]. The embassy was sent to Germany, which shows that Severus himself was in the north directing the measures being taken against those who had favoured Albinus in Britain and in Gaul. It is to this period that Herodian assigns the division of Britain into two provinces[2]. The fact that these were so delimited as to divide the garrison between them (p. 36) indicates that the object aimed at was the same as in the partition of Syria—the prevention of a military challenge such as had come from Albinus and Niger. Since the Rhine legions had long been divided between two provinces, there was now no formidable army in the West under a single command.

Master of the West as well as of the East, Severus proceeded to carry on a systematic persecution of his political enemies, which was continued all over the empire for ten years with a relentlessness that provoked grave disorders. But the principal object of his resentment was the Senate. He had taken a considerable risk to secure its decree of investiture, and with that he believed he had the right to expect that opposition anywhere would be discountenanced. Yet an actual majority of its members had continued to favour Niger or Albinus, and by this hostility had negatived the effect of the official decree upon the general opinion.

Early in June he rode into Rome[3] at the head of a large body of troops. There was no surprise when he took the occasion of the first meeting of the Senate to address to it an oration in which he announced his own policy by commending the severity of Marius, Sulla and Augustus. He put the policy into action by sentencing to death twenty-nine of the senators who had supported Albinus. The confiscated estates of these and all other political enemies, in the East as well as in the West, passed into a newly instituted exchequer, the *res privata*, which was at the personal disposal of the Emperor (pp. 27–8). He had need of abundant funds; besides making another distribution to the populace of the capital, he gave a donative to the army and increased the pay by one-third. To the legionaries he granted also a formal recognition, hitherto denied them, of unions contracted with local women while on active

---

[1] Dessau 1143.
[2] Herodian III, 8, 2.
[3] Cf. Dessau 2185.

service, and he extended to the under-officers (*principales*) as well as the centurions the privilege of wearing the gold ring, which had been the badge of the equestrian order. This did not now confer upon them equestrian rank, but it was a mark of the Emperor's intention to make the army a recruiting-ground for the order, and therefore for the imperial civil service. The scheme of government which he had in mind was one which should be based upon the army and should rise through the equestrian hierarchy to find its point of unity and control in the emperor's sacrosanct authority, derived from a series of deified ancestors and transmitted by dynastic descent. He compelled the Senate to decree the deification of Commodus which the army had proclaimed in 195, to confirm the title of Caesar and the Antonine name conferred upon Caracalla by the army in 196, and to add the title of *imperator destinatus*[1].

Before the end of the summer of 197 the Eastern campaign was resumed. Vologases, seeking to recover the ground lost to the east of the Euphrates and to placate the resentment of his vassals at the Roman encroachment, had overrun Mesopotamia and laid siege to Nisibis, and Severus had decided to complete the settlement of the Eastern frontier. Part of his army, no doubt the main body, would have been sent on from Gaul to follow the line of the Danube. The force which he had led to Rome was transported by sea from Brundisium. On the approach of the Roman army, Vologases raised the siege of Nisibis and withdrew. Thereupon Severus returned to the Euphrates, down which he proceeded south-eastwards. The advance had now assumed the character of a triumphal procession; Seleuceia and Babylon were entered without challenge, while the feeble resistance which Ctesiphon offered merely gave an occasion for plunder to the troops and for a massacre of the inhabitants.

This unresisted advance into the heart of Parthia, a region which there was no intention of occupying permanently, was in reality a demonstration, which reached its visible conclusion when the Parthian capital lay in ruins. It was a demonstration intended to impress not only the Oriental princes but also the population of the Empire. By the title of Parthicus Maximus which he now assumed Severus announced to the Roman world a military triumph such as might be expected to obliterate the memory of the civil wars, and he made use of this auspicious moment, with his customary sense of the occasion, to accomplish the last act of his dynastic programme. The army proclaimed Caracalla joint

[1] Cf. Dessau 8914.

Augustus with himself, and tranferred the title of Caesar to his younger son Geta[1].

It was now early in 198. In a region where supplies for an army were hard to find, it was advisable to return by a different route from that by which he had advanced; he led his troops northwards for some distance up the Tigris, and then struck westwards into Mesopotamia. Here he encountered unexpected resistance at Hatra, which he made two unsuccessful attempts to take, the second in 199. In the course of that year, however, the campaign as a whole was successfully concluded[2]. By impairing the prestige of the Arsacids, as it turned out, he had prepared the way for the more formidable power of the Persian Sassanids, who were soon to displace them on the throne of Parthia. But at least he now made good a claim which Dio attributes to him in 195; he created a great bulwark to the Euphrates frontier of Syria. Osrhoëne, it is true, he was content to leave in the grateful hands of Abgar IX as a client kingdom, but he enclosed it within a province of Mesopotamia so delimited as to provide an outer line of defence which left the Euphrates at Circesium to follow the valley of the Chaboras to its junction with the Djaghdjagh at Thannuris, whence it ran eastwards by Singara to the Tigris, the upper course of which it then followed north-westwards. Resaina, where the routes from the Euphrates crossings at Zeugma and Nicephorium converged on the way to Nisibis, became a 'colonia.' Nisibis itself, a 'colonia' since 195, was the capital of the new province. The procurator there was presently succeeded by an equestrian prefect who was governor of the province, and *equites* also were given command of the two recently enrolled legions, I and III Parthicae, which formed the garrison.

Meanwhile Severus himself must have left Mesopotamia, after the second siege of Hatra, about the middle of 199, for by the end of the year he was in Egypt, after having spent some time in Syria, Palestine and, perhaps, Arabia. On this journey he pursued his policy of conciliating provincial opinion, but, now as always, policy was combined with personal considerations. Tyre, which was raised to a 'colonia' with the *ius Italicum*, and the 'colonia' of Heliopolis which was now given the same fiscal privilege if it had not already received it in 195, were both cities which had declared

---

[1] Parthicus Maximus seems to have appeared on the coinage about the turn of 197–198, occurring first with *Imp. X*. For Caracalla as Augustus before 3 May 198 cf. Dessau 2485; for Geta as Caesar before 29 August, cf. Dattari, *op. cit.* 4081–2.

[2] Cf. *Ann. épig.* 1916, no. 46 (1 Jan. 200); Dessau 2186.

for him in the civil war. If in his treatment of Syria as a whole he was able to forget that it had supported Niger, it was because, with the removal of his rival, he became conscious of the claim it had upon him as the native land of his wife Julia Domna. The remains of imposing buildings, both sacred and secular, testify that it entered now upon a new period of prosperity (p. 551). From Syria he may have gone to Arabia by Palmyra, which probably received its rank as a *colonia iuris Italici* in this reign. He visited Palestine, and there also he gave the cities reason to be grateful. Sebaste (Samaria) was made a 'colonia,' while in Judaea Eleutheropolis and Diospolis (Lydda) date the beginning of their era as cities from 199, and on the coinage which they now issue bear the Emperor's name as an honorary title. And this was a flourishing period for the synagogues.

From Palestine Severus went by sea to Egypt. It would be in obedience to his instructions, or in deference to his known wishes, that Arrius Victor, the *epistrategos* of Lower Egypt, instructed the *strategoi* of the nomes to see that the burden of maintaining the Emperor's suite and soldiers should not fall unfairly upon the native population[1]. Severus recognized that the condition of the villagers at this time was bad enough without the addition of a fresh burden owing to exactions and violence on the part of imperial officials, and he issued regulations to protect them against such abuses in future[2]. On the other hand, the institution of a council in the metropolis of each nome seems to have been intended primarily to make a larger number of the richer class liable for the performance of local and imperial liturgies[3]. It was now also that Alexandria was given a council of the municipal type. Another episode in the history of Alexandria that is associated with the name of Severus is the departure of Clement, the head of the Christian catechetical school there, as the result of action taken against the Christians in Egypt, as elsewhere, in accordance with an imperial constitution, or constitutions (201–2), which sought to put a stop to Jewish and Christian propaganda by making converts liable to severe penalties (p. 481). In 201 the Emperor sailed from Egypt to Antioch[4], where he gave the *toga virilis* to his son Caracalla, now in his fourteenth year, and designated him consul with himself for 202. When they entered upon office at the beginning of the year, they were still at Antioch, which was restored to its former dignity in commemoration of the event.

---

[1] *P.S.I.* 683. [2] Preisigke, *Sammelbuch*, 4284.
[3] For this reason the institution of βουλαί did not contribute to local harmony; cf. P. Oxy. XII, 1406. [4] *I.G.* XIV, 917.

Soon after, Severus set out upon the return journey to the West, following in the reverse direction the route by which he had come east to the victory at Issus. We know from Herodian that he visited the legionary headquarters of Moesia and Pannonia. An inscription recording that he and Caracalla reconstructed the *canabae* of the legion VII Claudia at Viminacium[1] suggests that he was especially interested in the remodelling of the civil settlements attached to the legionary camps which would now be necessary as the result of his grant to the legionaries of legal recognition of the unions they contracted with native women, and the permission this carried with it to live with them and their families[2]. The increased importance of such settlements is seen in the fact that, in the reign of Severus, two of them, those at Carnuntum and Aquincum, both previously 'municipia,' received the status of 'coloniae.' His movements in this region are reflected also in an improvement of the road-system, especially in Pannonia, Noricum and Raetia. One of the stretches of road now repaired, that from Celeia to Aquileia, would be on the route by which he entered Italy. Since he had reached Sirmium by 18 March[3], he had time to be in Rome by 13 April, the anniversary of his proclamation at Carnuntum, and presumably the opening day of the festival of his Decennalia, which he celebrated this year (202).

III. THE PERSONALITY AND POLICY OF SEVERUS

His entrance into the city, like all the more public acts of his reign, was well timed. His impressive achievement in the East, soon to be commemorated by the arch which still looks down upon the Forum[4], enhanced the celebration of his Decennalia, while the stability which nine years of success had given to his rule seemed to be projected into the future by the marriage of his son Caracalla to Plautilla, the daughter of his Praetorian Prefect, C. Fulvius Plautianus, like himself an African. But if the seven days festival of April 202 was the culminating point of the reign of Severus, it also brought the career of Plautianus to a climax which challenged the eminence of the Emperor. Plautianus had been Prefect, and almost continuously sole Prefect, since 197 (or earlier). After being honoured by Severus with the consular insignia, he was

---

[1] Dessau 9105. [2] Herodian III, 8, 5. For the effect of this indulgence at York and Caerleon see p. 42.

[3] If the date and place of the rescript in *Cod. Just.* II, 31 (32), 1 are genuine. [4] Dedicated in 203 (p. 10, n. 1).

given a seat in the Senate and obtained the consulship itself in 203, with the Emperor's brother, P. Septimius Geta, as his colleague. He now exercised a power unequalled even by that held under Tiberius by Aelius Sejanus. The fact that his enmity drove Severus' masterful wife, Julia Domna, to take cover in the company of philosophers is a measure of the influence he had asserted over Severus himself by an overpowering force of personality. And if relations between the two men became strained, and not for the first time, yet the Emperor does not appear to have been able to treat his Prefect with decision, and an occasion which presented itself in 203 for his personal intervention in Africa may have been welcomed as offering an escape from an ascendancy which he was unable to confront.

Ever since the time of Marcus Aurelius the desert tribes had been seriously troubling the African provinces and had even carried their raids into Spain. To ensure a stricter policing of the frontier, Severus had been developing in Tripoli the system, begun by Commodus, of establishing outposts beyond the *limes* on oases commanding the caravan routes from the interior. On the Numidian frontier also outposts were being established, probably as a preliminary to extending effective control to the line of the Oued Djedi (Nigris), while in eastern Mauretania (Caesariensis) a new *limes* was formed by a line of forts along the rim of the high plateaux dominating the province on the south[1]. In Tripoli the extension of the frontier system seems to have involved operations against the desert tribes[2].

The military base for Tripoli as well as Numidia was the headquarters of the legion III Augusta at Lambaesis. A number of inscriptions which indicate the presence of Severus there in 203[3] testify to his concern to improve the amenities of military life and to his interest in the erection or reconstruction of buildings by which camp and *canabae* were being adapted to the changed conditions[4]. Already the settlement had received a municipal constitution; under Severus or Caracalla it becomes a 'colonia,' like the settlements at Aquincum and Carnuntum on the Danube. And it was in the reign of Severus that the military area of

[1] E. Fabricius in P.W. *s.v.* Limes, cols. 665–9; see also the articles of J. Carcopino in *Revue archéologique*, vme sér. xx, 1924, pp. 316 *sqq.*, and *Syria*, vi, 1925, pp. 30 *sqq.*

[2] Aurelius Victor, *Caes.* xx, 19.

[3] For this and other evidence for a journey to Africa in 203–204 see Hasebroek, *op. cit.* pp. 132–5.

[4] See above, p. 19.

Numidia was separated from proconsular Africa and made an
independent province, of which the legate of the Third legion was
henceforth governor. Civil life also benefited by the Emperor's
personal interest in the African provinces[1]. Many communities
became cities of municipal or colonial status, while others which
were already *coloniae* received the privilege of the *Ius Italicum*.
Among these was the Emperor's birthplace, Leptis Magna, which
he also adorned with new buildings. And cultural life was, no
doubt, stimulated by the presence of the distinguished intellectuals
whom he assembled from every land[2].

By the end of May 204 he had returned to Rome to be present
at a celebration of the Secular Games[3]. To inaugurate the new era
thus announced Caracalla and Geta were nominated consuls for
205. The first notable event of the year was the work of the elder
brother. Jealous of the power of Plautianus and impatient of his
control, he produced evidence, probably concocted, of a plot
against the Emperor and himself. Summoned to the palace on
22 January[4], Plautianus indignantly denied the accusation, and
Severus was not unwilling to believe him; but Caracalla intervened, and the Prefect was killed by an attendant. His daughter
Plautilla was banished to Lipari, where she was put to death on
her husband's accession six years later.

Even after the removal of Plautianus, Severus did not assume
such a rôle in the life of the capital as to recover the attention of
the historians. In the narrative of Dio the most prominent figure
between the years 205 and 208 is a certain Bulla Felix, the leader
of a gang of six hundred bandits who waylaid travellers on the
roads of Italy for two years (206–207). Bulla himself was no
ordinary brigand, but his trade at this time was all too common.
During the civil wars the mobilization and dispersal of large
armies had flooded the empire with deserters and refugees, while
the subsequent persecution by Severus of his political enemies had
driven many of its ruined victims to desperation. Tertullian's
reference to the tracking down of brigands throughout all the
provinces[5] seems to have been suggested by the circumstances of

---

[1] It would appear that trade with the interior was not only encouraged by
the policing of the caravan routes beyond the *limes* but greatly extended by
the use of the camel (S. Gsell, *Mém. Ac. Inscr.* LXIII, 1933, p. 149), a matter
in which Syrian troops stationed by Severus on the Numidian frontier may
have had a hand (J. Carcopino, *Syria*, VI, 1925, p. 148, n. 5).

[2] Philostratus, *Vit. Soph.* II, 20, 2.

[3] Dessau 5050 *a*; *Not. degli Scavi*, 1931, p. 313.

[4] *Chron. Pasch.*, ed. Dind., I, p. 496; cf. Dio LXXVII, 3, 3.

[5] Tertullian, *Apol.* 2, 8.

the time. In the East the imperial police-gangs (κολλητίωνες) so harried poor and rich alike, innocent as well as guilty[1], that they soon found themselves confronted by brigands of their own making. In Egypt their activity aggravated evils caused by an oppressive system of liturgies and requisitions, which was driving the inhabitants of the villages to abandon their homes and take to brigandage; nor had the measures taken by Severus when in Egypt (p. 18) provided an effective remedy, for successive Prefects continued to issue edicts directed against brigandage and against exactions which provoked it[2]. In Baetica and Mauretania the procurators had been given special powers to facilitate confiscation[3]. It is not surprising that from regions as far asunder as Africa, Asia, and the Rhineland there is evidence of disorder still more serious than brigandage[4].

The interior condition of the empire must have given Severus more concern at this time than the safety of the frontiers. The East had been made secure against the Parthians. On the Rhine and Danube there was no immediate prospect of trouble, and we learn of no activity on either frontier more serious than an adjustment of the eastern boundary of Dacia by which the Trajanic *limes* along the Aluta to the Red Tower pass was replaced by a more easterly line, reinforced by a wall, which left the Danube below the junction of the Aluta and ran to the Transylvanian Alps at Brasso[5]. In Britain, it is true, the defensive system had collapsed after the withdrawal of the garrison by Clodius Albinus, but order was now being restored there by Alfenus Senecio (p. 38), and it was not till 208 that the Emperor himself set out for the island to crown the work of his legate by a punitive campaign.

Meanwhile he spent most of his time in Campania, for the life of the capital was demoralizing for his sons and probably distasteful to himself. He busied himself, we are told, with jurisdiction and affairs of State. The chief member of his council was

---

[1] For Asia cf. the Lydian inscriptions, Keil and Premerstein, *Dritte Reise*, in *Denkschriften der Wien. Akad.* LVII, 1914–15, nos. 9, 28, 55.

[2] For the activity of the *Kolletiones* in Egypt and an edict of the Prefect, Subatianus Aquila, see P. Oxy. VIII, 1100. This dates from 206. Cf. P. Oxy. XII, 1408 for an edict against brigandage issued by the Prefect, Baebius Juncinus, in 210–14.

[3] Dessau 1406; *C.I.L.* VIII, 9360.

[4] Cf. Dessau 429 (from Sicca Veneria in Africa) and 430 (from Ephesus). The African inscription dates from 208. From *ib.* 1153 we learn that about the same time detachments of all the four legions on the Rhine had to be mobilized to suppress disorder.

[5] Fabricius, *op. cit.* col. 645.

Papinian (Aemilius Papinianus), one of the two Praetorian Prefects whom he had appointed in place of Plautianus. Other members of the council were Paul and Ulpian. The association of the Emperor with these great jurists enriched the law with numerous constitutions[1] which made many of its rules more equitable and reinforced the humanitarian tendency which had shown itself under the Antonines and which was to influence the growth of the law throughout the whole period of the Severan dynasty; for although Papinian, on the death of Severus, was dismissed by Caracalla, who soon afterwards had the satisfaction of seeing him killed by the Guard, Paul and Ulpian survived into the reign of Severus Alexander to give continuity to the imperial legislation.

The humanitarian tendency of the jurists, as we shall see, was so directed by the Emperor as to serve a political policy. There was a political motive also when he chose to indulge his native taste for cruelty. If the execution of certain prominent senators like Quintillus and Apronianus showed him to be ready, during these last years in Italy, to give audience to dubious informers and to listen to stories of dreams and magical practices as evidence of treasonable ambition, this was not malice looking for pretexts but a credulous apprehension of opposition to his rule. And more than any of his predecessors Severus regarded his own authority as the guarantee of political unity. For, with a fateful harmony, his own nature and experience had conspired with the necessities of the time to suggest to him a structure of the State in which the keystone was the religio-dynastic power of himself and his family.

The picture of Severus which has been transmitted by the historians is made up of qualities which they have occasion to remark upon in their narrative of his wars, but they are the qualities discernible also in his civil policy. Like the conduct of his wars, this bears the impress of a single personality, which found in its associates, even in the least tractable among them, congenial influences and appropriate agents. It is noted by Dio that, until the decisive encounter at Lyons, Severus had not been present at any of the battles of the civil wars. But he was always the motive and directive force. The rapidity and range of the movements of his troops reflected his own decision of character and his power to plan with foresight and upon a large scale. When he took command himself, as at Lyons and in his foreign wars, his presence was the more felt because he expressed a dynamic personality with a

---

[1] See A. de Ceuleneer, *Essai sur la vie et le règne de Septime Sévère*, pp. 271–290.

conscious sense of effect. There was calculation even in his vices—his cupidity, his unscrupulousness and his vindictive cruelty.

Cruelty as well as perfidy was commonly attributed to the race from which he was sprung, and there were some who called him a 'Punic Sulla.' The African town of Leptis Magna, where he was born in 146, was a Phoenician foundation which still put up Punic inscriptions in the Imperial period; and he himself spoke Latin with a Punic accent. His consciousness of his origin and his race is proclaimed in his coinage and is evident in his policy. To such a man the Roman tradition was alien. He was possessed of great intellectual energy and curiosity, and he had acquired, in his provincial fashion, a considerable degree of Latin culture, but he did not comprehend Roman institutions in their rooted complexity, as these were understood by men who were themselves part of the same growth. He judged the Roman world of his day by his native instincts and his personal experience, and with a realism unembarrassed by historical sympathies or scruples he developed certain tendencies which he found there into a simplified and logical scheme of government.

The privileged position of Italy as the historic nucleus of the Roman State he disregarded as an anomaly. He assimilated the troops there to the frontier garrisons by establishing a legion, II Parthica, on the west bank of the Alban lake at Albano, by recruiting the Praetorian Guard from legionaries, drawn mostly from the Danube, the East and Africa, and by reinforcing the *equites singulares*, a personal bodyguard of the emperor instituted by Domitian or Trajan and composed of men chosen from the auxiliary cavalry regiments. With the exception of the Urban Cohorts and the City Watch, the army in Italy no longer represented Italy in arms, but composed an external coercive force at the disposal of the emperor.

In carrying out this levelling policy, however, he did not proceed merely by depressing the status of Italy but also by elevating that of the provinces. He particularly favoured Syria, the home of Julia Domna, and his own native Africa; but for the provinces generally he displayed a solicitude which awakened in the local communities a revival of activity expressed and commemorated by the erection of monumental buildings, commonly dedicated in his honour. It was not that he simply continued the Antonine practice of requiring from the officials of the central government a high standard of administration: certain of his measures were designed to place the provinces on the same level as Italy. The rule that Punic or Celtic, or indeed any native language, could be used in legal documents is known to us from a jurist of this period[1]. To provincials Severus granted a larger measure of the relief from the burden of maintaining the imperial post which the Italian towns had enjoyed since the time of Nerva. In allowing, or confirming, to the *collegia tenuiorum* in the provinces[2] permission to associate without special authorization he was extending to them a privilege which those of Italy had possessed at least since the time of Hadrian. If he revived in Italy the alimentary institutions, which had been neglected or suspended under Commodus, he gave to those in the provinces, which had hitherto been of a purely private character, an official recognition and protection by placing them under the charge of the provincial governors[3]. But his policy showed itself especially in grants to many local communities of citizen status, which placed them politically on the same level as the Italian towns, while to some of them, notably in Syria and Africa, he gave the *Ius Italicum*, which assimilated their territory fiscally to the soil of Italy[4].

The same policy is seen at work at the centre of government. For his own major officials the Emperor looked by preference to Syria and other Eastern provinces and to Africa; it was usually natives of these and the Illyrian provinces who were now selected for the equestrian commissions, and it was mostly soldiers from the same provinces who were promoted to the higher grades of the legionary centurionate, which now qualified, like the equestrian commissions, for entrance into the imperial civil service. The composition of the Senate was similarly affected. The sons of *primipili* received senatorial commissions as *tribuni laticlavii*[5], and the provincial element in the Senate was so increased, mostly by the introduction of Orientals and Africans, that the Italian members were reduced to a decided minority[6]. But the effect of this change was social and cultural more than political, for the Senate had already been brought effectively under imperial control in the

---

[1] Ulpian, *Dig.* XXXII, 11. An official recognition of Celtic is seen also in the use of the *leuga* as a measure of distance not only on the roads repaired in Gaul, where it had already been displacing the Roman *mille passus* (A. Grenier, *Archéologie gallo-romaine*, II, pp. 97–101), but also in the Rhine area (K. Schumacher, *Siedelungs- und Kulturgeschichte der Rheinlande*, II, pp. 228, 230).   [2] *Dig.* XLVII, 22, 1.   [3] *Ib.* XXXV, 2, 89.

[4] This policy showed itself also in the position now assigned to provincial mints. See H. Mattingly, 'The Coinage of Septimius Severus and his Time', *Num. Chr.* 5th ser. XII, 1932, pp. 178, 185–6; M.-S. IV, i, pp. 58–9.

[5] A. v. Domaszewski, *Die Rangordnung des römischen Heeres*, p. 172.

[6] To about one-third. See P. Lambrechts, *La Composition du Sénat romain de Septime Sévère à Dioclétien*, pp. 79 *sqq.*

exercise of such functions as it still retained, and it was now to
be eliminated as far as was possible from the scheme of government.

Even a senator so solicitous of the dignity of the order as
Cassius Dio has only an historian's reason to offer for the continuance of the senatorial magistracies—a regard for tradition
and constitutional continuity[1]. So far as administration was concerned, it had long been recognized, even by those who belonged
more fully than either Dio or Severus to the central tradition, that
with the growth of an imperial civil service the survival of senatorial privilege involved a complicated and clumsy dualism, and the
unification of administration through the displacement of senators
by equestrian officials was a process that had been going on since
the time of Augustus. This process was continued by Severus
systematically.

He broke with the established practice of confining legionary
commands to senators by placing the three newly enrolled 'Parthian' legions under the command of equestrian prefects. We have
seen that one of these legions, II Parthica, was stationed in Italy
at Albano, and with the Praetorian Cohorts, the associated *equites
singulares*, the City Watch and the Urban Cohorts, there was now
an army of over 30,000 men in Italy commanded entirely by
equestrian officers of the Emperor with the exception of the
Urban Cohorts, which, as the police of the capital, remained under
the charge of the City Prefect, who was a senator. The two remaining 'Parthian' legions were stationed in Mesopotamia, and
this reconstituted province, like its legions, was entrusted to an
equestrian prefect instead of the usual senatorial legate, on the
model of the system which Augustus had applied to Egypt and its
legionary garrison as 'one of the secrets of despotism.' And the
practice was now begun of sending a procurator as acting governor
(*vice* or *agens vices praesidis*) to Imperial provinces which had
hitherto been governed by a senatorial legate[2], a far-reaching extension of the existing practice by which the senior procurator of
a province, senatorial or Imperial, was occasionally appointed to

---

[1] Dio LII, 20, 2, where he speaks in the person of Maecenas.
[2] *C.I.L.* III, 1625; cf. 7901; cf. *Cod. Just.* IX, 47, 2 (Caracalla). The
procurators in charge of the Maritime, Cottian and Poenine Alps, and of
Sardinia and the two Mauretanias, which had all been procuratorial provinces
in the first two centuries, are now commonly given the title of *praeses*, which
comes into official use in this period as a general term for a provincial governor,
especially the governor of an imperial province, whether of senatorial or
equestrian rank (*Dig.* I, 18, 1).

act temporarily as governor when the proconsul or legate was absent or died during his term of office.

A complete elimination of senators, however, from provincial commands which had long been reserved to them was not at once possible, and elsewhere Severus contented himself with reducing the importance of such functions and the freedom of their exercise. He resumed the policy of breaking up provinces into smaller units: we have seen that Syria and Britain, the provinces from which Niger and Albinus had made their challenge, were each divided into two commands, and that the military area of Numidia was separated from proconsular Africa and erected into an independent province governed by the legate of the legion which garrisoned it (III Augusta). And in all provinces alike the freedom of the senatorial governors was restricted by the activity of imperial procurators[1].

The increased activity of the imperial procurators in the provinces was especially due to an enlargement of the imperial sources of revenue and a re-organization of the financial administration. To meet the difficulties bequeathed to him by Commodus and to cover his own lavish expenditure Severus had tried the usual expedient of debasing the currency, the silver content of the denarius being reduced to about 50 per cent. That this fresh debasement, when exploited by speculation, was liable to provoke local crises is proved by a decree of the Senate of Mylasa (in Caria)[2], which shows that there it drove the undepreciated local currency out of circulation and caused a sharp rise in prices; and Mylasa cannot have been alone in this experience. But a rise in prices does not seem to have become general[3], and Severus did not find it necessary to have recourse to large or frequent emissions of coinage, partly because improved material conditions increased taxable capacity, partly because of the wealth that passed into his hands from a new source. This was the confiscated property of those who had supported Niger and Albinus. For its administration a new treasury was instituted, the *res privata principis*. The *patrimonium* had long tended to become confused with the *fiscus*, and now it gradually ceased to have a separate administration. The new treasury enabled

---

[1] Thus, in Britain the procurator now appears alongside the governor in inscriptions recording the restoration of military buildings. Cf. *C.I.L.* VII, 1003 (from Risingham) and *Arch. Ael.* 4th ser. XVI, 1939 (from Chesters) for the association of the procurator, Oclatinius Adventus, with the consular legate, Alfenus Senecio.   [2] *O.G.I.S.* 515.

[3] F. Heichelheim, in *Klio*, XXVI, 1932–3, pp. 102–4, and *Economic History* (suppl. to *Econ. Journ.*), III, 10, Feb. 1935, pp. 7, 10.

Severus to restore the *fiscus* to solvency by relieving it of certain burdens, notably the increased pay now given to the soldiers, but administratively it was sharply distinguished from the *fiscus* by being treated, as its name indicates, as the private property of the emperor. The procurator in charge of it took rank alongside the *rationalis* of the *fiscus*, and such was its importance that its institution was a decided step, in one department, towards identifying the State with the person of the ruler. And finance was a department which impinged everywhere on other fields of administration. Drawing its revenues from estates in all parts of the empire, the *res privata* gave employment to an army of procurators whose functions, with those of the fiscal procurators, encroached from all sides upon the sphere of the senatorial governors.

A more direct encroachment by the imperial civil service is seen in the enlarged powers given to the Praetorian Prefects, a matter in which the ambition of Plautianus may have done much to draw out the policy of the Emperor. The control now exercised by the Praetorian Prefecture over the Prefecture of the Annona for the better provisioning of the army was a re-adjustment within the civil service itself. It was by the extended jurisdiction assigned to it that the Praetorian Prefecture encroached on the functions of the senatorial magistrates. The ordinary jury-courts (*quaestiones perpetuae*), which had continued to meet under the praetors or other senatorial presidents since the Republican period, now ceased to be held. Since the jurisdiction of the Senate itself was in practice confined to cases remitted to it by the emperor (mostly cases concerning its own members), the higher jurisdiction passed almost entirely to the imperial tribunal. To deal with the increased jurisdiction the circuit within which the City Prefect tried cases as the emperor's representative was limited to Rome and one hundred miles around, and the rest of Italy was subjected to the jurisdiction of the Praetorian Prefects. Hitherto they had exercised a summary jurisdiction in cases arising out of their duties of police. Now they had delegated to them, in civil as well as criminal cases, a general jurisdiction which not only covered Italy, outside the sphere of the City Prefect, but also included the hearing, *vice imperatoris*, of appeals from the provinces. After the death of Plautianus, Severus returned to the practice of appointing two Praetorian Prefects. The fact that one of these was the jurist Papinian indicates the new scope of the office. By this change juristic science was made more directly than before an instrument of imperial control and justice was assimilated to *castrensis iurisdictio*.

Papinian succeeded Plautianus as vice-president of the emperor's council (the *consilium principis*). The *senatus consultum* was now rarely employed as an instrument of legislation, and the jurists of the council therefore sought to give to the imperial constitutions something more than the validity as interpretations of the law which had always been accorded to them by a clause of the law of investiture. Ulpian was a native of Tyre, and Papinian also was perhaps an Eastern, but in asserting that the decisions of the emperor had 'the force of law' (*legis vigorem*) they contrived to find justification for the doctrine within the limits of the Roman constitution by discovering legislative power to be inherent in his *imperium*[1]. By its influence upon the imperial constitutions, which were framed in accordance with its advice, the council not only guided the growth of private law but did much to shape public policy and direct administrative action.[2]

The emperor and his council, in fact, now resembled a general and his staff, with the equestrian civil servants as their executive officers. This simplification of government on a military model was accompanied by a militarization of the civil service itself. It was recruited not only from men of equestrian family or of the upper class in the municipal towns, as under the Flavian and Antonine emperors, but also from professional soldiers who had risen, mostly from the ranks, to one of the higher grades of the legionary centurionate. Both elements were now mainly of provincial origin, chiefly Illyrian, African or Oriental, but the administrative service, working by established rules, was not easily deromanized, and those who passed into it through the centurionate—and this was the element which tended to predominate—had been formed through long years in a traditional discipline. Raised above the humble class in which they were born by some capacity for civil administration, such men fitted into, and indeed consolidated, the hierarchic structure of Roman official life, and if, in their uncultured hands, the administration lost finesse and flexibility, the military qualities and summary methods which it now acquired were not unsuited to the conditions of the third century.

The absorption of legionary centurions of the higher grades into the equestrian service, military or civil, and their increased

[1] Ulpian, *Dig.* I, 4, 1. Gaius (I, 5) had pointed the way to this doctrine.

[2] For the *adlectio inter comites Auggg. nnn.* of an *eques*, C. Iulius Pacatianus, procurator of the Cottian Alps (Dessau 1353), a special reason can be given (Hirschfeld, *Untersuchungen*, p. 271, n. 2; Hasebroek, *op. cit.* p. 95), but it still illustrates Severus' readiness to disregard senatorial privilege.

employment in extraordinary commands, created a new demand for these officers, which was met by freer promotion from the ranks of the legions themselves. This was not the least of the favours by which Severus improved the conditions of military life. The story is told by Dio that on his death-bed he advised his sons to enrich the soldiers and disregard all others. But this expresses the mind of Caracalla better than the larger policy of Severus, which identified the army with the more virile elements throughout the empire and aimed at a stricter regimentation of the population as a whole. It was a population too large and various to be capable of the patriotic devotion necessary to support a burdensome political system by voluntary energy, and the citizenship, so far from awakening such energy by its progressive extension, had lost its virtue by expansion and had ceased to animate in provincial life a directing element attached to the centre. It is significant that the discrimination which the Roman law had always observed as between privileged and unprivileged persons was ceasing to be a distinction between citizens and non-citizens, and was being reformulated, under the terms *honestiores* and *humiliores*, as a distinction between the upper official class and the mass of the population. Besides senators and equestrian civil servants, the *honestiores* included the decurions and magistrates of the cities, whose obligations, local and imperial, were now exacted with a methodical rigour[1], which was directed especially against the more wealthy among them. Citations in the Digest from the jurists of this period relating to the municipal *dekaprotoi* (*decemprimi*)[2], and the more frequent mention of them in Eastern inscriptions dating from the early third century onwards[3], indicate that the change was now taking place by which, from being the occasional recipients of burdensome honours, they became personally responsible, as representing the council, for the regular financial obligations of their community.

In the West as well as the East municipal administration had long been an increasing burden for a restricted number because of the exemptions granted by successive emperors to certain classes; but whether exempted by imperial constitution or simply by their lowly social condition, the *humiliores*, with the exception of the proletariate of the great cities, who had little or nothing expected of them but goodwill, had had public duties and obligations of their

[1] *Dig.* L, 2–4, which is drawn mainly from the writings of jurists of this period.

[2] *Ib.* L, 4, 3, 10 (Ulpian); L, 4, 18, 26 and L, 12, 10 (Herennius Modestinus).

[3] Cf. *I.G.R.R.* III, 60–1, 63, 64–5, 67, 69, etc.

own to fulfil; and it is to the Severan jurists that the Digest refers for their systematic formulation[1]. A stricter control was exercised by government officials over the guilds of merchants and shippers who did service for the *annona* (*mercatores frumentarii, olearii; navicularii*)[2], while the guilds which undertook to provide a fire-brigade in their city (*fabri, centonarii, dendrophori*) were reminded that their exemption was confined to working members, and did not apply to wealthy *adlecti* seeking an escape from municipal burdens[3]. If exemption from such burdens was now extended by Severus to soldiers who had served their time[4] and to the *coloni* on imperial domains, the veterans had military obligations imposed upon them (p. 32), while the relief granted to the *coloni* was to ensure that the imperial treasury should receive its full share of the fruits of their labour[5]. And the peasantry in general, besides providing labour, had to support requisitions in kind and, in the imperial provinces, especially in the frontier areas, had to supply the recruits for the army, and in particular for the garrisons of their own neighbourhood.

It was indeed upon a militarized peasantry that this structure of the State was based. The documents which attest the emperor's concern to protect the rural population from the oppression of officials only serve to show the variety of obligations for which it was made liable; and if he encouraged it, by grants of political status, to form itself into communities, that was because the communal organization provided a means of exacting these obligations[6], just as the collegial organization was now being employed to ensure the services due to be rendered by the trading and industrial population. Many of the peasant communities, indeed, were assimilated to military garrisons; such were the Thracian foundations which, like Forum Pizi, served as stations for the *cursus*

---

[1] *Dig.* L, esp. 5 and 6, mainly drawn from the writings of Ulpian, Papinian, Paul, Modestinus and Callistratus.

[2] *Ib.* L, 6, 6, 3–9. Dessau 6987, which shows friction between the *navicularii* of Arles and the officials of the *annona*, dates from 201.

[3] *Ann. épig.* 1920, nos. 69–70, set up in 205. The rescript of Severus and Caracalla cited in this inscription relates to the *centonarii* of Solva in Noricum, but it states the rule as applicable to all *collegia* of the kind. Cf. Callistratus *ap. Dig.* L, 6, 6, 12.

[4] *Dig.* L, 5, 7.

[5] *Ib.* L, 6, 6, 11. Under Marcus Aurelius the rule for such *coloni* had been *muneribus fungi* but *sine damno fisci* (*ib.* L, 1, 38, 1).

[6] That these communal obligations included the garrisoning of forts in the neighbourhood is implied by the constitution of Forum Pizi in Thrace; see M. Rostovtseff, *J.R.S.* VIII, 1918, p. 26.

publicus or for the *annona*[1], and the fortified *castella* in which the peasantry were being grouped in the frontier area of Numidia[2]. And in resuming the earlier practice of founding settlements of veterans[3], or of settling veterans in existing cities, he gave to these new or reinforced communities, along with the colonial name, much of the military character and function which the name had originally implied, either as elements in the frontier system or as supports to the central authority, now represented by himself and his dynasty.

To soldiers on active service, on the other hand, Severus gave something of a civil capacity by permitting under-officers to form *collegia*, by regularizing the unions formed by the men with local women, by permitting them to live with their families in settlements attached to the camps (pp. 19, 42), by stabilizing such settlements and giving to some of them colonial status, and by extending the practice of assigning land to frontier units to be given out to the men in allotments[4]. By this assimilation to one another of the rural population and the troops, frontier defence was passing into the hands of a peasant militia, and the difference between the military and civil elements of the State was defining itself territorially as a division, and in some measure an hostility, between the rural areas near the frontiers and the urbanized regions of the interior.

Severus is censured by Herodian for destroying military discipline by pampering the soldiers. It is true that, in spite of his personal hold over them, he occasionally had trouble with his troops, but there is nothing to prove that the army lost in efficiency during his reign. Modern historians, judging the Severan system by the military anarchy which followed upon the end of the dynasty, have been inclined rather to blame it for confirming the localization of the frontier armies and so facilitating usurpations. But no one had better reason than Severus to balance the political danger

---

[1] For Forum Pizi see Ditt.³ 880; *I.G.R.R.* I, 766. See also D. van Berchem, *Mémoires de la Société des Antiquaires de France*, LXXX, 1937, pp. 182–4.

[2] J. Carcopino, *Syria*, VI, 1925, pp. 145–7.

[3] Rostovtzeff, *Soc. and Econ. Hist.* pp. 378, 609–10. For Mesopotamia see F. Cumont, *Syria*, V, 1924, pp. 351–2. For the settlement of veterans in κολωνίαι in Egypt, without urbanization, see J. Lesquier, *L'armée romaine d'Égypte*, pp. 330–2.

[4] For a legionary as *conductor prati* at Carnuntum, the land being allotted to him by a *primipilaris*, cf. Dessau 9103. This dates from 205. The system had been applied in Egypt since the first century (Wilcken, *Grundzüge*, p. 397).

of military particularism against the exigencies of frontier defence. That he judged it expedient in the circumstances of the time to follow a dual policy appears from a comparison of his treatment of the army in Italy with his treatment of the frontier garrisons.

The forces in Italy, as now represented by the reconstituted Guards and by the legion stationed at Albano, he had changed from an Italian army to a denationalized army, with no attachments except to his own person, and organized in counterbalancing units commanded by his equestrian officers. The increase in the number of the Guards and the addition of the legion not only reinforced the military support of the imperial authority at the centre of the Empire but raised to a formidable strength the force now available to accompany the emperor when he took the field; and the extensive repairs which Severus and Caracalla carried out on the imperial road-system improved communication between Italy and the northern frontier as well as between the frontier garrisons[1]. But though provision was thus made for military concentrations in emergencies, Severus confirmed the existing system by which, in normal circumstances, localized provincial armies, now limited, with one exception (p. 48), to two legions, were responsible for the guard of their own sector of the frontier.

In increasing the employment of the small, highly nationalized units described as *numeri*, and in adding especially to the number of those levied in the East, Severus did not change the practice of sending them to serve on frontiers distant from their place of recruitment. For the formation of such units, largely by forced enlistment, and the maintenance of their native composition and character were a means of removing from certain unromanized areas disorderly or quarrelsome elements, or of employing at suitable points troops with special aptitudes, such as the Syrian *numeri* to which he entrusted the guard of the Saharan frontier of Numidia[2]. And there was an obvious military reason why some of the regular auxiliary units also, such as the various corps of Syrian archers, should continue, in spite of their wide distribution, to draw their recruits from the area where they were originally

[1] As indicated by the distribution of their milestones in Gaul and Upper Germany, the Alpine region, the Danube area, Cappadocia, Syria and Africa. Besides the numerous milestones of Severus and Caracalla, there is the *Antonine Itinerary*, which takes its name from Caracalla, to testify to the concern shown at this time for the road-system of the Empire; and the Tabula Peutingeriana also may date from this period.

[2] J. Carcopino, *Syria*, VI, 1925, p. 118.

raised. But for all other units, legionary as well as auxiliary, he developed the existing practice of recruiting for local service. The recent increase of the soldiers' pay may have been found necessary, especially since a general rise in prices seems to have occurred in the reign of Commodus[1], to attract recruits in sufficient number to maintain the system of voluntary enlistment, and for the same reason it may have become more necessary than ever to offer local service as an inducement. But in associating the frontier garrisons more closely than before with the land in their neighbourhood and its native population, Severus may not have been thinking merely of the effect upon recruiting. When Severus Alexander continued the policy of transforming the frontier troops into a peasant militia, one of his reasons, according to his biographer, was that the men would fight the better for having land of their own to defend. Septimius Severus seems to have believed that such local attachments would also stabilize the frontier garrisons, and make them less ready than a purely professional army to be marched off upon distant political adventures. If the military anarchy that followed the death of Severus Alexander belied this anticipation, it must be remembered that the system by then had maintained internal peace almost unbroken for nearly forty years, and that, with the end of the dynasty, it lost its principle of unity. For, more than any of his predecessors, Severus made the imperial house, as a *domus divina*, the centre of the religion and discipline of the army and indeed of the whole militarized structure which the State had now become.

As an African who had forced his way to the throne of the Caesars by a military pronunciamento and two civil wars, after well over a hundred years of a regular succession, Severus was conscious of the need for a legitimation more potent with public opinion than the reluctant recognition he had extorted from the Senate. It was for that reason that he had professed himself to have been adopted into the Antonine family as son of Marcus Aurelius. It was in the tradition of his race that even a fictitious genealogy, such as he and Caracalla are given in inscriptions, could make a man a true member of a kin, and if there was no precedent in Roman practice for a posthumous adoption, that would be no great difficulty when it was the emperor and *pontifex maximus* himself who was the subject of it. The support which the Antonine name gave to his dynasty throughout its history is a proof that, in

---

[1] F. Heichelheim in *Klio*, xxvi, 1932–3, p. 102; *Economic History* (Suppl. to *Econ. Journ.*), iii, 10, Feb. 1935, pp. 7–8, 10. See below, p. 262.

popular opinion at all events, the adoption produced all the effect of a valid act. It made Severus the heir and continuer of a line of deified emperors. This character he assumed with the conviction of a man who regarded himself as predestined to rule. If he did not commission a work which Cassius Dio wrote on the dreams and portents which foretold to him his future greatness, he must have supplied the material for it. He had accepted an assurance that he had a royal horoscope, and he had married Julia Domna as his second wife because she was similarly favoured.

This conjunction of the stars brought together a native of a Phoenician colony and a Syrian who was the daughter of the hereditary prince-priest of the *baal* of Emesa; and with their accession a Semitic dynasty came to occupy the throne for over forty years. It was as if the spirit of ancient Assyria had taken possession of the palace to make the Empire subject to a bureaucracy which should be the executive of a divine authority transmitted through a dynastic succession. In such a system there would be no place for a Senate or for the principle of delegation by the State, and it was a sign that this notion of government now tended to prevail that the title *dominus* came to be generally applied to the emperor. For this term, when given its full value, implied an authority which was undelegated, and which, therefore, as the contemporary Tertullian insisted, presented itself as divine[1].

Because of this implication, Tertullian notes, the title had been rejected by Augustus when he founded the authority of the Roman ruler on the magisterial *imperium* delegated by the State. In practice, however, he and his successors had permitted or contrived that it should appear as a power emanating from a *domus dominorum* to those of their subjects who were accustomed to such a form of government, and it was this notion that tended to become predominant with the Severan dynasty. But the original character of the imperial authority was not easily eliminated. The jurist Ulpian, whose political opinions were formed as a member of Severus' council, in the very act of asserting the authority of the ruler to be absolute, describes it as conveyed to him by delegation from the State; and this principle implied that the Senate, as the only regular organ of delegation, should survive as an essential element of the constitution, however reduced its administrative

[1] *Apol.* 34. For the divinization of Severus and Julia as Sol and Luna on the coinage cf. M.-S. IV, i, p. 75 and p. 162, no. 522; pp. 218, 220 *sq.*, nos. 36, 52, 59, etc. *Ib.* pp. 208–9, nos. 858–9, for the assimilation of Julia as *mater Augg.* to Cybele as *mater deum*. For the dynastic propaganda on the coinage cf. J. Vogt, *Die Alexandrinischen Münzen*, I, pp. 166–7.

rôle might be. If Severus himself made his army the mouthpiece of his dynastic scheme in the early part of his reign, he took the precaution of having the military proclamations formally confirmed by the Senate; and even the army spoke, in theory, for the State. And it was anxiety about the general assent to the dynastic succession on which he had set his heart that made him seek to cover up the mutual animosity of Caracalla and Geta with protestations of 'Concordia' on the coinage, and finally decide to remove them, with their mother, from the temptations and gossip of the capital to the discipline of the camp. He looked to Britain for a military success which he might use for political purposes, as he had used his Parthian triumph ten years before. By the prominent place given to his sons and especially to Caracalla, the coin-issues commemorating the British campaigns agree with Dio[1] and Herodian[2] in suggesting that in his personal intervention there the ageing emperor was thinking more of his dynastic project than of conditions in Britain, where his legate, Alfenus Senecio, seems to have had the situation well in hand before he himself crossed to the island in 208.

IV. SEVERUS AND BRITAIN

The withdrawal of the British garrison by Albinus in 196, besides precipitating a civil war, had left the province at the mercy of its enemies, who did not fail to take advantage of the opportunity. The activity of Severus and his legates in Britain was therefore directed to two ends—the lessening of the danger of another challenge from a British governor, and the restoration of the defensive system.

Herodian's statement that Britain was divided into two provinces is confirmed by Dio and a number of inscriptions[3], where the provinces appear as Britannia Superior and Britannia Inferior and as so delimited that the legion II Augusta, which had its headquarters at Caerleon in South Wales, and XX Valeria Victrix at Chester were in Upper Britain, while the York legion, VI Victrix, was in the Lower province[4]. As in the later arrangement represented by the *Notitia Dignitatum*, York would be the

---

[1] Dio LXXVII, 11, 1 (cf. 14, 1).

[2] Herodian III, 14, 2 (cf. III, 5, 1).

[3] Dio LV, 23; *C.I.L.* III, 6995; VII, 280 (cf. 281); VIII, 1578, 2080, 2766, 5180; *Ann. épig.* 1922, no. 116 (cf. *J.R.S.* XI, 1921, p. 102). In the *Antonine Itinerary* the heading of the British section, 'Iter Brittaniarum', may be due to a later recension.

[4] Dio LV, 23; *C.I.L.* VIII, 2080, 5180.

base for the system of the Wall and the supporting forts behind it[1], except that those in south Lancashire, as far north perhaps as the Ribble, would no doubt be controlled from Chester. As Lincoln was included with York in Lower Britain[2], the boundary between the two provinces seems to have run north-westwards from a point south of Lincoln to a point north of Chester. This division would imply that Lower Britain would normally be a praetorian province governed from York by the legate of the Sixth legion, who would henceforth rank as a provincial *legatus pro praetore*. Such seems to have been the position of the Claudius Paulinus who appears in an inscription from High Rochester as *legatus pro praetore* in 220[3], whose headquarters are given elsewhere as *ad legionem sextam*[4], and who was apparently of praetorian rank[5].

But if the immediate sphere of the consular legate was now defined as Upper Britain, with its two legions, he would exercise some measure of control over the praetorian province[6], where detachments of his legions were always liable to be employed, and he would presumably take command there when circumstances required a large legionary concentration in the north. Such circumstances prevailed more or less continuously throughout the reign of Severus, and this would account for the fact that the two legates of Severus whom our evidence proves to have been active in the north, Virius Lupus and Alfenus Senecio, were both consulars and must therefore be presumed to have been legates of the upper province, if Herodian is right in attributing the division of Britain to the year 197 and if the arrangement indicated by Dio and our epigraphic evidence was the original one[7].

---

[1] *C.I.L.* VIII, 2766 (Dessau 2762), mentions a prefect who commanded Coh. II Asturum in Lower Britain. This cohort was in garrison at Aesica on the Wall in the Severan period (*C.I.L.* VII, 732, dating from 225). The evidence of inscriptions proves unity of command in the early third century over the whole system of the Wall and its outposts from east to west, and over supporting forts behind it. See E. B. Birley, *Arch. Ael.* 4th ser. XI, 1934, p. 132.

[2] *Ann. épig.* 1922, no. 116 (cf. *J.R.S.* XI, 1921, p. 102).

[3] *J.R.S.* XXVII, 1937, p. 247, no. 7.　　　　[4] *C.I.L.* XIII, 3162.

[5] For his career see also *Eph. Epig.* IX, 1012.

[6] Cf. *C.I.L.* VII, 280, for the presence at Greta Bridge, which must have been in Lower Britain, of a *beneficiarius consularis provinciae superioris*.

[7] The passage (LV, 23-4) in which Dio describes the distribution of the legions in his day was written, or revised, after the death of Severus, as is shown, for example, by its placing the Brigetio legion, I Adiutrix, in Lower Pannonia, an arrangement which did not come into effect until the reign of Caracalla; and none of the epigraphic evidence for the division of Britain

Virius Lupus appears in Dio as dealing with the tribes beyond the northern frontier and he is mentioned in two inscriptions from Yorkshire[1], one of which dates from 197 or the early part of 198. The situation which confronted him was a serious one. The whole military system in the north, from the Wall and its outposts to the legionary bases of York and Chester, had been laid in ruins. The Yorkshire inscriptions tell of repairs done at Ilkley and at Bowes, and it would be under Lupus that the headquarters at York were restored. But it would appear that the depleted units of his province had not yet been brought up to normal strength, for Dio[2] tells us that he was reduced to purchasing peace from the Maeatae, a name by which the tribes of southern Scotland were collectively known at this time.

After 204, the year in which Severus returned to Rome from Africa, there is more evidence to show that active measures were being taken to deal with the situation. An inscription of 205 tells of successful operations in Brigantian territory[3], and Dio, writing of the year 206, alludes to victories in Britain[4]. This activity is reflected in the coinage of 206–7, in which it is especially connected with Caracalla, who seems to have been in Britain at this time[5]. But the restoration of the defensive system appears to have been mainly the work of Alfenus Senecio, who is mentioned as consular legate in a dedication to Victory[6] and is known from other inscriptions, one of which dates from 205–7[7], to have rebuilt forts over a wide area in the north.

Two of these come from the Wall forts of Birdoswald and Chesters[8]. Housesteads, also on the Wall, has yielded fragments of an inscription which mentions the name of Severus[9], while on can be dated earlier than that relating to Claudius Paulinus, whose governorship falls within the reign of Elagabalus. There is thus room for the possibility that, when Britain was first divided, an arrangement different from that indicated by Dio and the epigraphic sources may have been in force until the events now to be described had run their course and the situation in North Britain had defined itself.

[1] *C.I.L.* VII, 210, 273.   [2] Dio LXXV, 5, 4 (p. 346 Boissevain).
[3] *C.I.L.* VII, 200.   [4] Dio LXXVII, 10, 6.
[5] M.-S. IV, i, p. 225 *sq.*, nos. 84, 85 A (both of 206); p. 227, nos. 96, 98 (both of 207). It would seem to have been now that Caracalla assumed the style *Imp. II.* Cf. *C.I.L.* x, 5909 (of 207).
[6] *C.I.L.* VII, 513 (*Eph. Epig.* III, p. 132).   [7] Dessau 2618.
[8] *Trans. of the Cumberland and Westmorland Antiq. and Arch. Society*, N.S. XXX, 1930, p. 199 (cf. *J.R.S.* XIX, 1929, p. 214, no. 3); *Arch. Ael.* 4th ser. XVI, 1939. The dedication to Victory referred to above comes from the Wall fort of Benwell.
[9] *Arch. Ael.* 4th ser. IX, 1932, pp. 233–4.

a rock near Brampton legionaries have recorded that they were quarrying stone there in 207[1]. Together, these inscriptions indicate that Severus was responsible for the restoration of the Wall and its stations which excavation has shown to have followed upon a wholesale destruction. Dio complains of Severus that he associated with his own name buildings which he had merely repaired[2], and the vanity of the Emperor and his dynasty in this regard, or the desire to flatter it, may well have left some trace in the historical tradition. At all events, Aurelius Victor and Eutropius found it stated in the source which they employed that Severus was the actual builder of a wall in Britain, and from Victor it passed into the biography of the Emperor in the *Historia Augusta*, to recur in later allusions to Britain in ancient writers and to misdirect in modern times, from Camden onwards, the interpretation of the Roman remains between Tyne and Solway. It is known now that the building done there in his reign was a work of restoration. In this Senecio included the outpost of Risingham in Redesdale[3]. Bewcastle also, some six miles north of Birdoswald, and High Rochester, on the southern margin of the Cheviots, were reconstructed about this time. In southern Scotland an outpost to the western end of the Wall was provided by a restoration of the fort at Birrens[4], in Dumfriesshire, though this may not have taken place until after Senecio's departure.

The restoration of the defensive system was not confined to the northern area. The walls of Chester were now rebuilt, and Wales was partially re-occupied after having been virtually evacuated for more than half a century. There was much reconstruction at Caerleon. On the north-west coast the fort at Carnarvon was restored, and repairs were done to the road from Carnarvon to Chester. At Caersws, in Montgomeryshire, and perhaps at Brecon, both key positions on the lines of communication from the coast to the interior, there is some evidence of habitation in the Severan period, too meagre to indicate a re-garrisoning of the forts, but enough to suggest that they may have served as stations for road patrols. There is no reason to believe that the Welsh tribes had been giving trouble, and the distribution and character of the evidence points rather to a measure of vigilance which anticipated possible raids from the Irish, who may indeed have taken a hand in the recent disorder.

But it was in the north, beyond the Maeatae, that Severus be-

---

[1] *C.I.L.* vii, 912.   [2] Dio lxxvii, 16, 3.
[3] Dessau 2618.
[4] *Proc. Soc. Antiq. of Scotland*, lxxii, 1937–8.

lieved the ultimate source of trouble to lie, and he decided to make Caledonia his objective when he crossed to Britain in 208 to take command in person. Herodian tells us of bridge-making and other preparations for the campaign[1]. That these involved some preliminary operations in the field can be inferred from the coinage of this year. There Caracalla still plays the leading rôle, but in the issues of 209 Severus himself comes into the foreground[2] with the actual advance into the north. He is said by Dio to have approached the extremity of the island, which may well mean that he reached the Moray Firth, but though Dio and Herodian both magnify the difficulties of the campaign, they have nothing definite to say of the movements of his army. No trace of them is discernible until the estuary of the Forth is reached[3]; there the coin-finds from Cramond tell unmistakably of activity in the early third century[4]. It has therefore been suggested that Severus moved his troops to the Firth of Forth by sea. Confirmatory evidence comes from the mouth of the Tyne at South Shields, where it has been found that the fort which protected the harbour was developed in the reign of Severus into an important store-base[5]. Denarii of Severus of this year figuring Neptune and Triton may refer to the transport of an army by sea[6]. We are on surer ground when we turn to the evidence of Severan coins found in Scotland. Outside Cramond, these consist of a few hoards from Fife, Kinross and Kincardine-shire[7]. They seem to indicate an advance into the Aberdeen low-lands from the Firth of Forth. Indeed, they suggest that Severus may not have followed the route that ran north from Camelon, but may have crossed the Forth from Cramond into Fife and Kinross, and joined the Agricolan route about the Tay, or at some point between there and Camelon, by crossing the Ochils or rounding their western flank. Whichever route we suppose him to have followed to the Tay, the view that he transported his troops by sea to a base on the Forth suits the narrative of Dio, who

[1] Cf. the 'Bridge' type on the coinage of 208 (M.-.S. IV, i, p. 120, no. 225, p. 198, no. 786) and 209 (ib. p. 284, no. 441, where for tr. p. xi should be read tr. p. xii).   [2] M.-S. IV, i, p. 121, no. 231, p. 198, no. 788.

[3] Birrens as an outpost to the Tyne-Solway Wall does not come into the reckoning in this connection. The same is true of Risingham and High Rochester. From High Rochester the main land-route northwards ran by Chew Green, Cappuck and Newstead. The negative evidence of excavation on these sites, especially at Newstead, must be regarded as significant.

[4] G. Macdonald, *Proc. Soc. Antiq. of Scotland*, LII, 1917–8, pp. 213–6.

[5] I. A. Richmond, *Arch. Ael.* 4th ser. XI, 1934, pp. 98–9.

[6] M.-S. IV, i, p. 120, nos. 228–9; see Volume of Plates V, 230, c.

[7] Macdonald, *op. cit.* pp. 264–76.

gives Caledonia as his immediate objective, and refers operations against the Maeatae to a subsequent campaign.

When the operations of 209 were over, Severus raised Geta to the rank of Augustus[1], and all three Augusti assumed the title of 'Britannicus[2],' as if they regarded the Caledonian campaign as decisive. It resulted, Dio tells us, in the Britons being compelled to cede a considerable part of their territory[3]. This suggests that from a base at Cramond troops may have been stationed along the line of the Wall from Forth to Clyde, which had been evacuated a generation before[4]. If none of the excavated forts on the Wall has yielded coins or other objects of Severan date, this negative evidence is hardly conclusive against an occupation which cannot have lasted much more than a year (p. 42); and it is possible that the second, and more perfunctory, of the two restorations which have been noted in these forts, and which has been explained as a mere episode in their abandonment early in the reign of Commodus[5], may in reality represent a brief re-occupation in 209–211. If there was some re-occupation of the Forth-Clyde line at this time, the territory which would thus be cut off would be that of the Maeatae, and we know from Dio[6] that for some reason they suddenly awoke from the quiescence into which they had been bribed by Virius Lupus. In 210 Severus sent a force into their territory upon a campaign of merciless repression. Caracalla must have been in command to judge by his prominence in the coinage which commemorated it.

In 211 the Emperor apparently looked forward to an immediate return to Rome[7]. But the trouble in Britain was not yet over. The Caledonians had decided to come to the aid of their kinsmen, and the Emperor made up his mind that he must once more take the field himself. While he was busy with preparations, he died at York on 4 February. Caracalla at once made peace with the enemy. If Severus' design was to conquer the whole island, as Dio says, it had come to nothing. It did not even result in an occupation of

---

[1] *I.G.* III, ed. min. 1077. The occurrence of the title on the coinage of Geta with his first *trib. pot.* (=209) is infrequent.

[2] Not on the coinage till 210, but Severus is given the title in an inscription of 209 (Dessau 431). 　　　[3] Dio LXXVII, 13, 4.

[4] The latest coins from the Wall are of Marcus Aurelius and Lucilla with the exception of two doubtful attributions to Commodus (G. Macdonald, *The Roman Wall in Scotland*, ed. 2, pp. 463–4).

[5] Macdonald, *op. cit.* p. 479. 　　　[6] Dio LXXVII, 15, 1–2.

[7] M.-S. IV, i, p. 122, nos. 246, 247 A ('Fortuna Redux'). The 'Adventus Augusti' type on a denarius of 210–1 (*ib.* p. 133, no. 330) appears also to have anticipated a return to Rome.

any part of enemy country, for Dio tells us that any troops that had been posted there were withdrawn[1]. On the other hand, the long freedom which the province was now to enjoy from barbarian inroads must be attributed in a large measure to the effect produced by the northern campaigns of the last years of Severus. Some credit must be allowed also to the vigilance that was exercised under his immediate successors[2]. And this was a time when a new development was taking place in Britain, as elsewhere, at the legionary fortresses. Excavation at York has indicated that the troops there were ceasing to be quartered in the barracks, and similar evidence has come from Caerleon[3]. The disuse of the barracks would mean an access of importance for the adjoining settlements, and it will have been in the Severan period that the settlement at York received the status of a 'colonia[4].'

V. CARACALLA

In the coinage of 211 Caracalla and Geta are still connected with military events in Britain, and it would seem to have been late in the year before they left the island for Rome, where they deposited the ashes of their father in the mausoleum of the Antonines and celebrated his deification. Caracalla's passion to be sole ruler, which had made him await his father's death with impatience, now made intolerable to him the nominal equality which

[1] Dio LXXVIII, 1, 1. The history of Birrens would seem to run parallel with that of the stations on the Tyne-Solway Wall, to which it served as an outpost. As part of the Wall system it would not be regarded as in enemy country, and a continued occupation there would not be a contradiction of Dio's statement, which is borne out by what is known of the other Roman sites of Scotland.

[2] Besides evidence for a rebuilding of the amphitheatre at Caerleon under Caracalla or Elagabalus (see below, n. 3), there is the evidence of inscriptions for road repairs under Caracalla in Wales and in the neighbourhood of the Wall (C.I.L. VII, 1164, 1186) and of the restoration of fort buildings in the north under both Caracalla (ib. 351, 1002, 1042) and Elagabalus (ib. 838, 964, 1044-5 = J.R.S. XXVII, 1937, p. 247, no. 7).

[3] For York see J.R.S. XVIII, 1928, pp. 95-8; for Caerleon, Arch. Camb. June 1931, p. 155. At Caerleon the evidence for the disuse of the barracks c. 200 is the more significant by contrast with the evidence of an inscription from the site of the headquarters building recording restoration under Severus (V. E. Nash-Williams, Catalogue of the Roman Stones found at Caerleon, p. 5, no. 2 = C.I.L. VII, 106), and with the evidence for a rebuilding of the amphitheatre under Caracalla or Elagabalus (R. E. M. Wheeler, 'The Roman Amphitheatre at Caerleon', Archaeologia, LXXVIII, 1928, p. 154).

[4] It was a 'colonia' before 237 (J.R.S. XI, 1921, p. 102).

Geta enjoyed by his recent elevation to the rank of Augustus; nor did the brothers require the added motive of jealousy for hating one another. Such was their mutual dread and animosity that they themselves proposed, according to Herodian, that they should be separated by the waters of the Propontis, with Europe and North Africa to be ruled by Caracalla, the Asiatic provinces and Egypt by Geta[1]. But this was not to the mind of their mother, who felt their proposed partition of the Empire like a threat of personal mutilation to herself, and who seems to have believed that she could maintain between them some semblance of the 'Concordia' which the coinage still proclaimed. Her sons were under no illusion as to each other's intentions, and they took their precautions accordingly. At the end of February[2] 212, however, Geta was persuaded to meet his brother in their mother's apartment in the palace, where Caracalla, by pretending a desire for reconciliation, had induced Julia to call them together. Centurions whom he had instructed entered the apartment, and when Geta ran to his mother for protection he was murdered in her arms. If any of the frontier armies were inclined to show hostility to Caracalla, they soon thought better of it[3]. In Italy the Alban legion threatened trouble for a moment, but it was quieted by a promise of increased pay. It would be influenced also by the decided attitude of the Praetorians, who were persuaded by a liberal donative to recognize Caracalla as sole emperor. The Senate could do nothing but accept Caracalla's story of a plot formed against his life by Geta. To celebrate his escape from this alleged plot he issued an edict of amnesty in favour of all who, for whatever reason, had been condemned to exile[4], but Geta's associates, and many who were merely suspected of looking upon his murder with disfavour, were treated as his accomplices and put to death. Among them was the jurist Papinian. The agents of the imperial secret service, the *speculatores* and *frumentarii*, spread everywhere a sense of insecurity by an assiduous espionage[5]. Geta's name was ordered to be erased from all monuments[6], and the surviving inscriptions of the period testify by their mutilation to the rigour with which the order was executed.

[1] Herodian iv, 3, 5–9   [2] Dio lxxviii, 2, 5 with S.H.A. *Geta* 3, 1.
[3] In inscriptions of 212–3 there are protestations of loyalty from several frontiers, including the British frontier, for which see E. B. Birley, *Arch. Ael.* 4th ser., xi, 1934, pp. 127–31.
[4] Dio lxxviii, 3, 3; Mitteis, *Chrest.* 378; *Dig.* L, 2, 3, 1; *Cod. Just.* x, 61, 1.   [5] Dio lxxviii, 17, 1–2.
[6] See Volume of Plates v, 230, *g*.

Julia accepted the situation, and endeavoured to control and direct the behaviour of her elder son. We are told that he had been tractable as a boy, but he was not now easily advised. Though he was only twenty-five years of age when his father died, he had already been Augustus for thirteen years, and this premature possession of power had nourished a despotic temper which a natural shrewdness and a sharp tongue made the more formidable. After the murder of Geta his degeneration was rapid. Along with cruelty and duplicity he had inherited, in an exaggerated form, the religiosity of his family, and the consciousness of his unnatural act afflicted him with superstitious terrors, which drove him to have recourse to dubious sophists, whose prescriptions encouraged an addiction to magical practices. Ill health contributed to the nervous apprehension in which he lived. His mind became unbalanced. His habitual mood of sullen and suspicious moroseness would sharpen into a craving for bloodshed which the slaughter of the arena could not appease and which would drive him into a homicidal fury in which revengefulness appears to have been confusedly combined with religious and moral motives. From a megalomania in which he saw himself as another Achilles or Alexander the Great he would fall into a childish preoccupation with trifles which held up the course of ordinary business.

It was fortunate that his interest in government was fitful, and that he was inclined to leave practical matters to his mother or to his council[1]. The council continued to direct government according to the principles in which its members had been trained under Septimius Severus. Western Hispania Citerior, including the headquarters of the legion VII Gemina at Leon, appears to have been made a separate province[2]. It was probably also before the end of Caracalla's reign that a consular was appointed, virtually as governor, *ad corrigendum statum Italiae*[3], and if the office was still a temporary one for which occasion had been given by the prevalence of brigandage, it anticipated the regular institution of the *correctura*, and therefore marked an important stage in the assimilation of Italy to a province. In continuing the levelling policy of Severus the council would meet with no opposition from Caracalla, who himself reproduced the paternal type as in a distorted mould[4]. The father's dislike of the Senate showed in the son as an open contempt. He affected the blunt speech as well as the dress and

---

[1] Caracalla's dependence upon those about him may explain the emergence about this time of the freedman remembrancer of the palace as an equestrian *magister* with an *officium*. Cf. P.W. *s.v.* Scrinium, col. 897 *sq.*

[2] Dessau 1157; M. Marchetti, *Diz. epig. s.v.* Hispania, p. 807 *sq.*

[3] Dessau 1159.

[4] Eutropius VIII, 20.

habits of a plain soldier, and to the militarist policy which he
inherited he gave a more brutal form. 'No one ought to have
money but myself,' he is reported to have said, 'and I must have
it to give to the soldiers.' Actually, he raised the pay of the
legionaries from 500 to 750 denarii, with corresponding increases
for the other branches of the service (see below, p. 262).

This increase of fifty per cent. in the pay of the soldiers, along
with the frequent donatives with which Caracalla indulged them,
soon turned the surplus which Severus had left in the treasury into
a deficit. He followed his father's example of depreciating the
coinage. The weight of the aureus was reduced, and alongside the
denarius a new silver coin was put in circulation, the 'Antoninianus,' which appears to have been rated as a double denarius,
though it weighed little more than a denarius and a half, and contained no higher a proportion of pure metal than the older coin
now did (p. 262). Demands upon the rich and upon the cities for
aurum coronarium and other extraordinary contributions became
more frequent, and he increased the regular taxation, raising from
five to ten per cent. the duties on manumissions and inheritances,
and suppressing in the case of the latter the exception in favour of
near relatives[1].

Since its imposition by Augustus the duty on inheritances had
been payable only by those who possessed the Roman citizenship.
According to Dio[2], it was in order to increase the revenue from this
duty that the citizenship was extended by the 'Constitutio Antoniniana' of 212. Dio writes as if this conferred the citizenship
upon the whole of the free population then inhabiting the Empire,
but a mutilated text of a Greek translation of the edict mentions a
class of *dediticii* as being in some way excluded[3]. The retention of
the Latin term in a Greek version current in Egypt implies that
it had a recognized technical meaning, defining a political category not primarily Eastern. That there was such a category or
status is shown by the fact that the Lex Aelia Sentia of A.D. 4
(Vol. x, p. 433) placed certain freedmen 'dediticiorum numero.'
A mark of this status was incapacity to rise to the citizenship, and
this disability, and the desire to maintain it, would account for

[1] That these measures were not ineffective is shown by Dio's admission
(LXXX, 12, 2[2]) that at his death he left a large sum in the treasury.

[2] LXXVIII, 9, 4–5.

[3] P. Giessen 40. Before the words χωρ[ὶς] τῶν [δε]δειτικίων in l. 9 of the
papyrus there is a lacuna too long (19–22 letters) for any restoration to claim
more than a slight degree of probability. For the most recent attempt at a
restoration of the text see A. Wilhelm, *Amer. Journ. of Arch.* XXXVIII, 1934,
p. 179 *sq.* For the literature on this whole matter see the bibliography to
this chapter, B (*d*).

the express exclusion of *dediticii* from the benefit of the edict. We know of no class of this status at the time of the issue of the edict except the freedmen of the Lex Aelia Sentia, but the retention of the status or category meant that new classes could be assigned to it subsequently; and, in fact, we encounter at a later date a non-citizen class of *dediticii* other than the freedmen referred to[1], as well as a non-citizen class which continued to arise as the result of defective manumission (the Junian Latins; see Vol. x, p. 431; xi, p. 829).

But those immediately excepted from the benefit of the edict as *dediticii* (whether or not they included others than the freedmen of the Lex Aelia Sentia) were apparently few, and Ulpian[2], like Dio, can describe the edict as applying generally to the (free) population of the Empire. Caracalla announces in the preamble that he is showing his gratitude to the gods of the State for their protection (in the alleged conspiracy of Geta) by bringing them new worshippers on a scale worthy of the divine majesty[3]. The notion of the *cives Romani* as a body which perpetuated the worship of the tutelary gods of the State had been weakened by the vogue of more personal cults. In the re-assertion by Caracalla of a mutual bond between deity and the recognized members of the community we may suspect the influence of the Semitic idea, especially as the official religion, as the coinage shows, was now being given the Syrian, or Semitic, form of solar worship.

But Caracalla is presenting as a thanksgiving to the gods a measure which recommended itself on other grounds. Naturally no financial motive is mentioned, especially as money was a matter which he was secretive about; he professed, Dio tells us, to be doing an honour to the subject population of the Empire. The grant of the citizenship would indeed be little more than an honour. Though it opened the way into government service for an increased number of provincials, especially Easterns, it can have had little other practical effect. In criminal law the privileges that had once distinguished the citizen from the non-citizen were now confined to one class of citizens—the *honestiores*, and even they could no longer claim as a right to be referred from the courts of provincial governors to the tribunal of the emperor[4]. Neither in criminal

---

[1] As early as A.D. 232; cf. Dessau 9184.   [2] *Dig.* I, 5, 17.

[3] Cf. Wilcken, *Chrest.* 96, which dates from 215, for the introduction of the cult of Juppiter Capitolinus into Egypt at Arsinoë. For its probable connection with the edict see Wilcken, *Grundz.* p. 116.

[4] That is, as judge of first instance. This resulted from a delegation of *ius gladii* by the emperor to all provincial governors, the limits of a governor's competence now depending upon the terms of delegation.

nor in private law was there any abrupt movement towards a unitary system[1], a tolerant accommodation between the Roman rules and non-Roman institutions in their local varieties continuing to be the practice of the provincial governors, as directed by juristic opinion embodied in Imperial instructions.

It is true that by approximating the Empire formally to the politico-philosophical ideal of a universal community of equal men the edict impressed the imagination of later ages, but even in the political sphere it merely marked the end of a process. In practice it made so small a change that it was not much noticed by contemporaries, and officially it was made so little of that it has left hardly any trace upon the coinage. No doubt the very slightness of its effect testifies to the magnitude of the development of which it marked and symbolized the completion. But the policy of enfranchisement, once the controlled instrument of a liberal statesmanship, had come by now to express merely an inevitable recognition of the increasing preponderance of the provinces over a dwindling Italy. The citizenship had long been ceasing to serve as the repository of a national (Italic) sentiment, and the levelling of its boundaries came easily under an Oriental dynasty to which Roman institutions, seen from the outside, presented themselves as facile elements for the play of grandiose conceptions.

Although the name of Caracalla is thus associated especially with a memorable act in the civil history of Rome, his personal ambition was directed rather to the achievement of military glory. He was obsessed by the memory of Alexander the Great, of whom he believed himself to be a reincarnation[2]; he assumed the title of 'Magnus,' and dreamed of Eastern conquests which should show his affinity with the great Macedonian. But an immediate summons to military action came from nearer home. Between the Upper Danube and the Upper Rhine the debris of tribes which had once dwelt about the Elbe had recently formed into a confederacy, known as the Alemanni, which now began to threaten the Roman frontier. Caracalla crossed the Raetian *limes* in August of 213[3], and by the following month he had concluded a successful

---

[1] See E. Schönbauer, *Z. d. Sav.-Stift.* Rom. Abt. LVII, 1937, p. 309. The slightness of the immediate effect of the Constitution in unifying the law is against the view that its real authors were the jurists. Both in idea and in the actual terms of its preamble as given in P. Giessen 40, it is characteristic of Caracalla. To the jurists, on the other hand, it may well have been a disconcerting enactment, and they may have set themselves to minimize its effects. [2] See Volume of Plates v, 168, *b*.

[3] Dessau 451.

campaign by a victory on the Main[1], which he commemorated by assuming the title of 'Germanicus Maximus[2].' Besides building or restoring forts and repairing roads and bridges, he constructed (or completed) the stone wall (the 'Teufelsmauer') which replaced Hadrian's palisade on the Raetian *limes*, and the mound and ditch (the 'Pfahlgraben') which supplemented the palisade along the Upper German sector.

It was probably now that he took a liking to the *caracalla*, the garment from which he got the name that he is known by[3]. This was a Celtic (or German) tunic, which he lengthened and wore as a close-fitting skirted coat. He insisted with such effect upon its use among the populace of the capital that from this time onwards it plays a continuous part in the history of Roman costume. It was also in this campaign apparently that he acquired, probably at Baden Baden, his faith in the potency of Apollo Grannus, the Celtic god of healing, whom it was his practice to invoke in the ill health which afflicted him.

Ill health, so far from keeping him inactive, provoked him to restlessness, and in the spring of 214 he was again on the move. He seems to have spent some time on the Danube, and it was probably now that he carried to its completion his father's policy of limiting the larger military commands to two legions (p. 33) by so re-adjusting the boundary between Upper and Lower Pannonia as to bring Brigetio, the headquarters of the legion I Adiutrix, into the lower province, which was henceforth governed by a consular legate, whose two legions balanced the reduced command of the consular legate of the upper province[4]. There was the more reason for this precaution that the Danube was merely a stage on a march to the East. Vologases V, who had succeeded his father in 208/9, was threatened by his brother Artabanus, and the situation appeared to Caracalla to offer an opportunity for effective intervention. When he passed into Thrace and found himself near the borders of Macedonia, at once, we are told, 'he was Alexander,' carrying the impersonation so far as to enrol a corps of Macedonians, whom he armed like

---

[1] Aurelius Victor, *Caes.* XXI, 2.   [2] Dessau 451 (October, 213).

[3] The familiar form of the name, Caracalla, is that used by Eutropius and Aurelius Victor. In Dio and S.H.A. the form is Caracallus. The name does not occur in Herodian nor does it appear on coins or in inscriptions.

[4] τὰ παρὰ τῷ Ἴστρῳ στρατόπεδα διῴκησε (Herodian IV, 8, 1). For I Adiutrix in Lower Pannonia in 228 cf. Dessau 2375. For a consular legate of the province before the end of the reign of Caracalla cf. *ib.* 1159. On the other hand, Dessau 2382 shows I Adiutrix still in Upper Pannonia in 212 or 213.

Alexander's spearmen. The winter he spent in Nicomedia, training his Macedonians in the formation of the phalanx and carousing in a fashion that accorded better with the tradition of his hero than with the state of his own health. Julia Domna, watching the behaviour of her son from under cover of her coterie of philosophers, emerged to take charge of official business. By the time they arrived at Antioch, about May of 215, Caracalla was in a condition of nervous agitation which unfitted him for serious military operations[1]. As it happened, Vologases, conscious of the precariousness of his own position, was careful to avoid giving a pretext for hostilities. Sending an expedition into Armenia under his freedman Theocritus, who led the troops to disaster, Caracalla himself left Antioch for Alexandria, where he directed personally a carefully contrived massacre of the inhabitants. According to Dio and Herodian, they had incurred his displeasure by certain pleasantries at his expense[2], especially on the forbidden subject of the death of Geta. This may have sharpened his exasperation, but the nature of the measures which he took to ensure their good behaviour while he carried on his projected campaign in Parthia indicates that there had been a serious outbreak of sedition, aggravated by the turbulence of fugitives from the villages (p. 22)[3].

The winter of 215–216 was again spent at Antioch. About May 216[4] Caracalla sent the kings of Osrhoëne and Armenia friendly invitations to visit him, and, when they complied, kept them prisoners; and Osrhoëne was then incorporated in the province of Mesopotamia. By now the situation had changed in Parthia, where Vologases had been displaced by Artabanus (V). At the moment the new ruler was in no better case than his brother had been to oppose invasion. He had no choice, however, but to refuse a demand from Caracalla for the hand of his daughter, since this was only another way, as he knew, of demanding his kingdom[5]; for Caracalla, in his rôle as a second Alexander, indulged the ambition of uniting Romans and Parthians under a single diadem[6]. In the summer of 216 he marched through Mesopotamia, crossed the Tigris, and advanced to the eastern borders of Adiabene. He never saw an enemy, Dio tells us, and the only effect of his demonstration was to provoke preparations for resistance. He retired

---

[1] Dio LXXVIII, 20, 1.   [2] Dio LXXVIII, 22, 1; Herodian IV, 9, 2–3.
[3] For the expulsion of native Egyptians, καὶ μάλιστα ἄγροικοι, cf. Wilcken, *Chrest.* 22; Dio LXXVIII, 23, 2.
   Cf. G. F. Hill, *J.R.S.* VI, 1916, pp. 160–1; Dio LXXIX, 27, 4.
[5] Dio LXXIX, 1, 1.   [6] Herodian IV, 10, 2–4.

into winter quarters at Edessa to organize an expedition for the following year, but his influence with the troops was waning, and the knowledge of this not only gave heart to the enemy but encouraged conspiracy among his officers. In the spring of 217, when he was in the neighbourhood of Carrhae visiting a sanctuary of Luna, he was assassinated (8 April) at the instigation of one of his Praetorian Prefects, M. Opellius Macrinus, who had good reason to fear for his own safety since a prophecy that he was to become emperor had reached the suspicious ears of Caracalla.

VI. MACRINUS AND ELAGABALUS

As it happened, the prophecy came true. For want of a better candidate Macrinus was proclaimed emperor by the troops engaged in the Eastern expedition, and accepted by the other armies. He was at once recognized by the Senate, which, at the moment, was too much relieved by the removal of Caracalla to look closely into the qualifications of the man who had supplanted him. In reality Macrinus had much to recommend him to the Senate. He was known as a conscientious lawyer with a regard for precedent, and if he was the first *eques*, and the first Mauretanian, to become emperor, these disabilities, along with his personal diffidence, seemed to promise that he would be amenable to senatorial influence. This anticipation he confirmed by his attitude to the Senate and to Italy[1], while at the same time he sought to win the general goodwill by annulling the changes which Caracalla had made in the duties on inheritances and manumissions. This conciliatory policy was not without its effect upon civilian opinion, but with the troops he was not so successful. It was as a lawyer that he had been appointed Praetorian Prefect, and he had no capacity or taste for military operations. He forestalled a threatened outbreak in Dacia by returning hostages who had been taken by Caracalla[2], and put an end to the Armenian war by granting the diadem to one of the sons (Tiridates) of the king whom Caracalla had imprisoned[3]. In Mesopotamia, which the Parthians had invaded, he met with a reverse near Nisibis in the summer of 217, and after protracted negotiations he had to pay a considerable sum to Artabanus to obtain peace. Though the troops had no more stomach for fighting than he had himself, they resented

---

[1] The *iuridici Italiae*, whose activity had been encroaching upon the autonomy of the Italian towns, were now restricted to the legal functions assigned to them by Marcus Aurelius (Dio LXXIX, 22, 1). He even sent a senator on official duty to Egypt (Dio LXXIX, 35, 1; cf. P.S.I. 249)—the first breach of the Augustan rule.   [2] Dio LXXIX, 27, 5.   [3] *Ib.* 27, 4.

this ill-success against an enfeebled enemy, and their dissatisfaction was aggravated by their being deprived of privileges which they had enjoyed under Caracalla and by the cutting down of the rate of pay to that fixed by Severus, a reduction which was to apply to future recruits only, but which aroused the suspicions of the men on service. With so many units concentrated in the East, in close touch with one another, disaffection had the means to spread, and it communicated itself the more easily that the troops were predisposed to it by their veneration for the Severan dynasty and for the Antonine name borne by Caracalla, to whom they now looked back with regret. Macrinus had to comply with their demand that Caracalla should be deified; he himself took the name of Severus, and in proclaiming as Caesar, and soon after as Augustus, his nine-year-old son, Diadumenianus, he conferred upon him the cognomen of Antoninus.

But there were representatives of the Severan household living who would not allow the Antonine name to be so easily wrested from them, and who saw in the feeling of the troops an opportunity to recover the imperial dignity. Julia Domna had not long survived her disappointment at the apparent ruin of the dynasty brought about by the death of Caracalla, but her sister, Julia Maesa, had two grandsons to sustain a desperate hope. By her marriage to a consular of the name of Julius Avitus (now dead) she had had two daughters, Soaemias and Mamaea, each of whom had a son. The elder of the two boys, Varius Avitus, then fourteen years of age, was the son of Soaemias and a Syrian, Varius Marcellus, who, after a distinguished equestrian career, had been made a senator[1]. The younger, Gessius Bassianus Alexianus, ten years of age, was the son of Mamaea and a Gessius Marcianus, also a Syrian, who had held various procuratorships. Maesa had been ordered by Macrinus to retire with her daughters to her home in Syria. She could hardly have wished for a better base of operations. Here she enjoyed to the full the prestige which her family derived from its hereditary priesthood of the venerated *baal* of Emesa, an office now discharged by Soaemias' son, Varius Avitus, known henceforth as Elagabalus by identification with the god[2]

[1] Cf. Dessau 478.

[2] Cf. Aurelius Victor, *Caes.* XXIII, 1 and S.H.A. *Hel.* 1, 6, where the name, applied to both god and Emperor, is given as Heliogabalus through a confusion with the Greek ἥλιος. The same form of the name is used for the god by Eutropius. On the coinage and in military diplomata the god appears as Elagabalus, and similar forms are used by Dio and Herodian. Neither of these contemporary writers applies the name to the emperor, nor does Eutropius. On the coinage also and in inscriptions it invariably indicates the god.

and credited[1] with a personal beauty which enabled him to look the part. With the soldiers he had additional recommendations in the wealth of his grandmother and in the rumour, which she herself spread about, that he was in reality the son of Caracalla; and not far off, at Raphaneae, was the headquarters of the legion III Gallica. The boy was taken to the camp by night through the contrivance of Comazon Eutychianus, who was apparently Prefect in charge, and on 16 May 218 at sunrise, the auspicious hour for the young priest of *baal* and his Syrian followers, he was proclaimed emperor under the name which his reputed (now to be his official) father had borne, Marcus Aurelius Antoninus. Under the command of his tutor Gannys a considerable force marched upon Antioch. Twenty-four miles to the east of the city, on 8 June 218, it defeated Macrinus, who had been deserted by most of his troops. He attempted to make his way in disguise to Italy, but was arrested at Chalcedon and soon afterwards was put to death. The same fate befell more than one legate in the East who ventured to challenge his youthful successor[2].

The events which led to the proclamation of Elagabalus display at work the influences which were now controlling the government of the Empire. From the confused interplay of circumstances and personal motives two forces disengage themselves as decisive —the army and the Severan household. The assertion of the dynastic principle in an Oriental form had secured for the women of the imperial family a power more unchallenged than had been allowed to a Livia or an Agrippina under the Julio-Claudian emperors. Augusta, *mater patriae, mater senatus, mater castrorum,* Julia Domna had accumulated more titles of dignity and devotion than any empress before her, and she had represented her son in affairs of State. Soon her sister, Julia Maesa, also Augusta, will be acting officially for her grandson, Elagabalus, and even intervening in the deliberations of the Senate. But their private action was more important than their public activity, now that the concentration of government within the palace had subjected it to the play of personal influences.

If these Syrian women knew how to enjoy and indeed (by all accounts) to abuse their opportunities, they knew also how to suffer, and the pliancy and tenacity of personal ambition were

[1] Herodian v, 3, 6–8; S.H.A. *Op. Macr.* 9, 3; Vol. of Plates v, 168, *c, d.*

[2] Dio LXXX, 7, 1–3, where mention is made of III Gallica, in Syria Phoenice, the legion which had taken the lead in proclaiming Elagabalus, and of IV Scythica, one of the legions in Syria Coele. III Gallica was disbanded (cf. Dessau 2657 with 2314–5).

strengthened in them by their attachment to their dynasty. The dynasty which they held together not only maintained internal peace almost unbroken for nearly forty years, but gave to those years a character in which it both expressed itself and drew out the logical consequence for Roman culture of the imperial achievement and policy. The palace where they held court at Rome was a meeting-place of East and West, and the Oriental element, now entrenched within the Roman citizenship and government, invaded also the whole field of Roman culture and religion. This is a matter to be dealt with elsewhere in this volume (pp. 417, 613), though there is one incident in the religious interchanges which must be given a place here because it is almost the whole story of the reign of Elagabalus.

In letters written from Antioch to Rome in his name Elagabalus was made to assume the various imperial titles without waiting for the decree of the Senate, but the implied denial of the Senate and People as the source of his authority was modified by conciliatory promises. Here we may recognize the hand of Julia Maesa, despotic by policy as by family tradition, but experienced and wary, with two astute advisers in Gannys and Comazon. By the middle of July Elagabalus had been recognized by the Senate[1], and with this the stage was set for his appearance at Rome.

The following month Maesa and Soaemias sailed with the young emperor to Bithynia, where they spent the winter (218–219) at Nicomedia. Here Elagabalus insisted upon celebrating in public the bizarre ritual of his cult, in which he made a resplendent but very un-Roman figure. This perturbed Maesa, who knew the capital and could judge how such performances were likely to be received there. Remonstrance only provoked a furious resentment which resulted in Gannys being killed.

A slow progress through the Danubian provinces brought the procession to the gates of Rome in the late summer or the autumn of 219[2]. The imperial family was accompanied by a troop of expectant Syrians, not many of whom can have been disappointed. Some of them entered the Senate to reinforce the Oriental element already preponderant there, and to help to justify the Emperor's description of its members as his *mancipia togata*[3]. Comazon, Praetorian Prefect in 218, was consul in 220 with the Emperor as his colleague, and more than once was Prefect of the City. For his

---

[1] Cf. *C.I.L.* VI, 2001, 2009 (Dessau 466).

[2] Eutropius VIII, 22, with Dessau 2188, which implies that his arrival was earlier, though not much earlier, than September 29.

[3] S.H.A. *Hel.* 20, 1.

career there was no precedent[1], but about precedent the Emperor cared nothing. He bestowed equestrian and even senatorial offices upon his favourites without any regard to the qualifications required by Roman administrative rules[2].

The Western provinces, it is true, appear to have suffered little. There was peace upon the frontiers, which suggests that the military command was vigilant, and there are many inscriptions which tell of activity in the construction of roads and the erection of buildings, civil as well as military. In the East the provinces benefited more by the favour of an Oriental emperor than they suffered from any defects in his governors; and in any case the Eastern cities always felt the Roman method of efficiency as a constraint and responded with resiliency when the tension was relieved. A great abundance of local coinage shows that their economic activity was never more lively than in this reign[3].

It was within Rome itself that the Orientals looked mostly for their opportunities, and it was the central administration that suffered. Within the palace the imperial freedmen wielded a power such as they had not possessed since the first century, and offices were systematically sold. A barber, we are told, became Prefect of the Annona; the department had to be re-organized by Elagabalus' successor. The same appears to have been true of the financial system[4]. But though the *fiscus* was put in charge of an Emesene of low character, the confiscations which Dio complains of, the increased exaction of crown gold[5], and the general disorder into which the imperial finances fell may have been due less to the rapacity or incompetence of officials than to the foolish liberality by which the Emperor sought to win popular applause.

To Elagabalus Rome was merely a more conspicuous field for his accustomed activities. He had his priesthood formally recognized by the Senate, included it among his official titles and proclaimed it upon his coinage[6]. The black conical stone which was the material embodiment of his god was brought from Emesa to the capital, where it was enthroned in a shrine erected on the Palatine alongside the imperial residence. Rumours of secret

---

[1] Dio LXXX, 4, 1–2.
[2] For a characteristic career of this period cf. Dessau 1329.
[3] E. Babelon, *Rev. Num.* IVe sér. III, 1899, pp. 274–7.
[4] Cf. Cohen[2] IV, p. 453, no. 516 for Severus Alexander as *restitutor monetae*; cf. *ib.* p. 420, no. 180; S.H.A. *Alex. Sev.* 16, 1; 39, 9. For the Annona, *ib.* 21, 9; 22, 1–2; 39, 3.
[5] P. Oxy. XII, 1441, intr.; XIV, 1659.
[6] Cohen[2] IV, pp. 347–8, nos. 246–253; p. 350, nos. 276–277.

sacrifices there and ritual murders were willingly believed by
many who regarded with a suspicious distaste the chants and
ceremonies with which the god was honoured in public, notably
on the occasion of a procession at midsummer, when he was
conveyed to a temple in the outskirts of the city in a chariot
devoutly led by the Emperor himself and accompanied by a magnificent cortège, in which senators and knights were expected to
consider it an honour to take part. Presently a female companion
was found for him, first in Minerva, and then, more conformably
to his character and to the family tradition of his priest, in the
Punic Tanit[1], and the nuptials were duly celebrated as a public
festival. The Emperor himself divorced a Julia Paula to marry
the Vestal Virgin, Aquilia Severa, excusing the sacrilege by
claiming for the marriage a religious function[2]. In effect, he
appears to have thought of it as an earthly rendering of the
celestial union. This notion of ritual analogy, of evoking by
representation the energies of the powers that controlled nature,
was nowhere more active than in the cult of the Syrian *baalim*
and their female counterparts, and the boy's function as priest
would stimulate and indeed consecrate the sensualities and
perversions which we read of in Cassius Dio and in the biography in the *Historia Augusta*. Rome was not now unfamiliar
with the naturalistic religions of the East nor incredulous of the
efficacy of their rites, but it was not prepared to see its emperor
serve as their minister. The incongruity of a circumcised Augustus,
who abstained from the flesh of swine to perform with a ritual
purity the obscenities of a Syrian cult and who paraded in public
tricked out in the effeminate finery prescribed by its ceremonial,
offended a public opinion which was not exacting in morals but
expected a traditional decorum from its rulers.

The offence was aggravated by Elagabalus' claim of supremacy
for the provincial cult of which he was priest, and his placing in
the shrine of his god, as tokens of sovereignty, the symbols of other
deities. The acceptance of the sovereignty of the god would have
given a powerful religious sanction to his own rule, but to attribute to him a policy of strengthening the imperial authority by
attaching it to a solar monotheism would be to magnify and indeed
invert the significance of his action, which was little more than an
exhibition of childish egotism and of the contentiousness of Syrian
baal-worship. Nor was the tendency for the solar cults to become

---

[1] See Volume of Plates v, 156, *b*.

[2] ἁρμόζοντά τε καὶ σεβάσμιον εἶναι γάμον ἱερέως τε καὶ ἱερείας,
Herodian v, 6, 2; cf. Dio LXXX, 9, 3.

unified directing itself to a true monotheism, but rather, through syncretism, towards an abstraction or a pantheism; and it was an intellectual movement. Among the mass of solar devotees the recognition of an affinity between their cults did not diminish mutual jealousy or local exclusiveness. Not even a priest who was also Roman emperor could identify the solar religion with one of its local forms. Still less could he make his *baal* ruler of the Roman pantheon[1]. The established religion was too closely interconnected with official and popular life for any serious displacement or re-adjustment to be made without such a disturbance of rooted institutions and inveterate habits as would not be supportable without a profound change of the general conscience. So far from inducing such a change the *baal* of Emesa by its pretensions pro-voked a reaction of traditional feeling which expressed itself in the nickname of 'the Assyrian' contemptuously applied to the emperor who was its priest.

The women of the imperial family became aware of an ap-proaching crisis. Julia Maesa, resolved to save the dynasty if anything should happen to Elagabalus, played upon his impatience of affairs of State as distracting him from his priestly preoccupa-tions to induce him to adopt his cousin Alexianus under the name of Marcus Aurelius Alexander and to associate him with himself in the government as Caesar[2]. He soon became aware that the effect of the adoption was to organize against himself the favour with which his cousin was generally regarded, and twice he attempted to procure his assassination. This aroused the Prae-torians to action, not perhaps without the instigation of Mamaea and the connivance of Maesa, and on March 11, 222[3] he and his mother were killed in the palace. His body was dragged through the streets to the Aemilian bridge, where it was thrown into the Tiber with a weight attached to it. The god was involved in the condemnation of the Emperor's memory and the annulment of his acts. In the form of the black stone he was sent back to his home, where, however, his prestige was apparently undiminished, and perhaps enhanced, by his Roman adventure[4].

[1] Such evidence as there is for the worship of Elagabalus indicates a local, or at least a purely Oriental cult (Dio LXXIX, 31, 1; Herodian v, 3, 4; *Ann. ép.* 1910, nos. 133, 141). There is nothing to show that the Emperor enlarged its vogue. With three doubtful exceptions (Dessau 4329, 4330, 4332) all occurrences of the name in inscriptions after 218 are in the imperial titles, where it was erased along with the Emperor's name after his death.

[2] Not later than 10 July (cf. *C.I.L.* vi, 2001; Dessau 466), and apparently before 1 June 221 (*C.I.L.* vi, 3069).

[3] Dio LXXX, 3, 3, confirmed by *C.I.L.* vi, 1454.

[4] Cf. S.H.A. *Aurel.* 25, 3–6.

CHAPTER II

THE SENATE AND THE ARMY

I. SEVERUS ALEXANDER: DOMESTIC POLICY

THE new emperor, Alexander, was born in the Phoenician town of Arca Caesarea. 1 October 208 is usually given as his birthday. It is true that he, like his predecessor, was dedicated to the service of the Sun God of Emesa, but his mother, Julia Mamaea, who had gone to Rome with her imperial nephew, had been sensible enough to keep her son away from the practices of his cousin. Julia Maesa was therefore able to play him off against Elagabalus, when the Augustus had fallen into contempt and the position reached its crisis. The over-tension of a despotism that was alien in character led to Elagabalus' bloody end, but this was not due merely to race-hatred, for Rome was already permeated with Oriental elements and was used to them. By intelligent management the Syrian princesses achieved their purpose: Alexander was proclaimed Augustus, and was accepted without protest by the Senate.

Marcus Aurelius Severus Alexander, as he was now called, ascended the throne in his fourteenth year (6 or 11 March 222). It is certain that his mother, in view of his expected succession to the Empire and because of her active interest in the spiritual currents of the time, had given her son the best of educations, and the Emperor doubtless continued to receive her maternal care. He may indeed have been a well-brought-up and charming youth, with a great desire to learn, and matured at an early age. However, what his later biographer in the *Historia Augusta* has to say

Note. The main literary evidence for the reigns described in this chapter is to be found in Dio LXXVII–LXXX (Boissevain), Herodian V–VIII, Orosius VII, Zosimus I, and Scriptores Historiae Augustae, *Alexander Severus, Maximini duo, Gordiani tres, Maximus et Balbinus*. On the value of this last source in particular see below pp. 58 *sqq.* and the Appendix on Sources at the end of the volume. More incidental references in ancient writers and relevant Papyri are given in the Bibliography to the chapter.

The most important inscriptions are cited in the footnotes to the chapter together with passages from the *Codex Justinianus* and the *Digest*. The coins supply at times important evidence, on which see the footnotes and the Bibliography A (2).

Coins of these reigns are illustrated in Volume of Plates v, 168, 230, 232, where also will be found portraits of Severus Alexander and Gordian III.

on details of his manners and character is not to be used as a really historical account. For in this account Alexander's permanent lack of independence is ignored, and the picture is drawn of the ideal *restitutor rei publicae*—a picture which made such an impression on Jakob Burckhardt that to him 'this person so incomprehensible against the background of his times' could appear as 'a true St Louis of antiquity[1].' But there was no Life of a Saint in the mind of the biographer: for, as has been shown[2], it is the picture of Julian which is reflected in the *Life of Alexander*. When, further, the writer of the *Vita*, like other sources, infers from the name Severus the Emperor's especial severity towards the soldiers, he contradicts his own observations upon his hero as a friend of the military. But, above all, this interpretation misunderstands the point in the programme of the government which seems bound up with the choice of this name—the linking of the régime with the founder and the good times of the Severan dynasty. Alexander meets us in inscriptions as 'Divi Severi nepos,' 'Divi Magni Antonini Pii filius,' and in his decrees he speaks of 'divi parentes mei' and calls Caracalla 'pater meus[3].' Passing over Elagabalus, he deliberately proclaims himself the youngest and true scion of the dynasty of the Severi. Herein we see the influence of the two Augustae— for Mamaea also had by now been elevated to that rank.

Now that they had so plainly set this end before them, the imperial princesses, Mamaea in particular at this time, shrewdly recognizing the demands of the age, were able to steer the ship of State upon a changed course towards the desired goal. The new government broke with the challenging religious policy of its predecessor, which had awakened disgust and loathing even in the altered Roman character, and went back to the traditional religious practices. It also made an attempt to allow the senatorial class, whose position in the State was threatened, to play once more, at least in appearance, an honourable rôle, and this without any change of the dynastic purpose and without any diminution of the historically established authority of the emperor and its sole prerogative. But whether the young emperor's Council of Regency, entrusted to sixteen chosen senators of high standing, or even the Council of State (*consilium principis*), to which, besides men of equestrian rank, many senators were summoned, could effectively throw their weight into the scales, remains an open

[1] *Die Zeit Constantins des Grossen*[3], p. 14.
[2] By N. H. Baynes, *The Historia Augusta, its date and purpose.*
[3] Dessau 479, 480, 8920-1. *Cod. Just.* IV, 1, 2; cf. Ulpian, *Dig.* XII, 2, 13, 6. *Cod. Just.* II, 1, 8; XII, 35, 4.

question. Still, Herodian received the impression that under
Severus Alexander's government the People and the army and
even the Senate were content with the form of the imperial rule,
which from a disgraceful tyranny had assumed the appearance of
an aristocracy. This judgment, which already overstressed the
goodwill of the new régime to the senatorial order, then became
the point of departure for a valuation which saw in the government's actions, not only the expected opposition to the indefensible
conditions of the immediately preceding years, but also a yet more
significant opposition to the policy inaugurated by Septimius
Severus, who, realizing the practical needs of the Empire, had
sought to conciliate and favour both the army and the equestrian
class. Thus the impression is in fact created that through a
thorough-going reform the re-establishment of the Augustan
principate was being attempted, while in many modern accounts
this fiction is carried to such lengths as to give rise to a belief in
the revival of senatorial supremacy.

But the only basis for this view is, unfortunately, the *Vita Alexandri*, a biography which has been described as a historical novel[1].
For apart from the Regency Council of Sixteen already mentioned,
nothing is said by Herodian or Cassius Dio about changes in the
established governmental order. It is true that the historian Dio
can show us how, in the mind of a man who was an active politician
and was permitted to hold along with the Emperor a second
consulate in 229, facts and wishes combined to shape his thoughts
on the relation of the monarchy and the Senate. The beginning of
Augustus' principate gave the historian an opportunity for having
the question of a re-establishment of the Republic or a creation of
a monarchy discussed by Maecenas and Agrippa in set speeches
before Augustus. In this discussion Dio reveals his own attitude
on the question. Agrippa defends the re-establishment of the
Republic with ideas and phrases borrowed from the language of
the schools of rhetoric; but the possibility of their practical
realization can at most have played a part only in the dreams of
incurable romanticists. Maecenas, however, advocates the monarchy as a necessity, and, furthermore, his monarchy bears the
features of the time when the second century was passing into the
third. It is true that no mention is made of the actual power of
the armies. Yet the monarchy does not figure as dependent on the
Senate. A demand is indeed made for the honours due to this
corporation, based on the reflection that 'it is in the nature of men

---

[1] By so high an authority on the *Historia Augusta* as E. Hohl. See
Propyläen-Weltgeschichte II, p. 422.

to find pleasure in being reckoned by the more powerful as of equal rank[1].' If the Senate thus remains—to quote another of Dio's phrases—'the ornament of the State[2],' the noble gesture may suffice which leaves to it the appearance of an extensive authority[3]. But this only strengthens the other demands that the emperor should have the sole right of appointing officials and that a larger sphere should be given to the equestrian order in the administration of the empire. While fully safeguarding their high dignity, Maecenas is yet willing to see the old magistrates treated as hardly more than municipal officials. He even speaks in favour of the assimilation of Italy in administration to the provinces of the empire. Since Dio can hardly be considered an opponent of the Senate, his Maecenas speech indicates the highest rôle which an intelligent senator could at that time expect his order to fill. Thus where the *Vita Alexandri* exceeds these limits in describing the Senate's power, its credibility is in any case poor. And not much more effective are the arguments for the theory that the speech of Maecenas is a criticism of the actual or contemplated reforms of the Emperor. This is so even if allusions are made in Dio's programme-speech to matters which were actually handled differently by Severus Alexander's government.

It is of little importance that a change was made in the *cursus honorum* of the senators, and that the number of those who after the quaestorship could omit the tribunate or aedileship and rise at once to the praetorship appears to have been now considerably increased, so that these two intermediate stages soon vanished completely. But the burdening of the quaestorship with the expenses of the games prevented this abridgment of the *cursus honorum* from being a relief. It may, however, be regarded as an increase in prestige that the *curatores regionum urbis sacrae*, who were associated with the City Prefect, had now to be of consular rank[4].

A reform that cut deeper may be detected in the biographer's account of the change in the position and rank of the Praetorian Prefects[5]. In this very confused report, which does not do justice to the previous exceptional cases and confounds the granting of the *ornamenta* with the real *adlectio inter senatores*, we must attribute an increased importance to the sentence, 'praefectis praetorii suis senatoriam addidit dignitatem, ut viri clarissimi et essent et dicerentur.' The epigraphical material shows, indeed, for the

---

[1] Dio LII, 32, 1.   [2] Dio XXXVII, 26, 3.   [3] Dio LII, 31, 1.
[4] S.H.A. *Alex. Sev.* 33, 1; cf. Dessau 1209 and E. Kornemann, P.W. *s.v.* Curatores, col. 1797.
[5] S.H.A. *Alex. Sev.* 21, 3–5.

period after Severus Alexander, that the incompatibility of the
position of Praetorian Prefect with actual membership of the
senatorial order did, in fact, no longer exist; but it is still true that
this Prefecture continued to be in the majority of cases the crown
and consummation of an equestrian career. For the reign of
Severus Alexander there exists only one piece of trustworthy
evidence in a papyrus of A.D. 232[1], bearing an official character,
in which the prefects, whose names are not mentioned, are termed
lamprotatoi, that is, *viri clarissimi*. On the other hand, we find that
the title *eminentissimus vir* was still retained. This title had been
reserved solely for the Praetorian Prefects, and they may have
continued to use it, to show their exceptional position, even when in
virtue of the imperial decree they were ennobled as *viri clarissimi*[2].
Further, when one sees that Ulpian, even before his Prefecture,
was concerned with the rank of the Praetorian Prefects and considered it correct that a *vir praefectorius* who had not yet been
granted the consular *ornamenta* should have precedence over the
wife of a *consularis vir*[3], the conclusion may be drawn that this
influential man had endeavoured to obtain a rise in rank in the
sense indicated. Furthermore, the biographer claims to know that
the Emperor, the friend of the *patres*, took this step in order to
prevent a non-senator from sitting in judgment on a senator.
Actually, however, with all respect for the wishes of the senators,
the result of this change could only be to enlarge the judicial
powers of the Praetorian Prefects and at the same time to
strengthen the authority of the emperor. The composition of
the *consilium* which was summoned by the emperor may also reflect a concession to the Senate. Nevertheless, in the inclusion of
the *iuris consulti* we may recognize the co-operation of the equestrian officials in the central administration, admitting, however,
the possibility that those jurists, especially, who came from the
equestrian order such as Ulpian, for example, and probably
Paulus too, could play a leading rôle thanks to their superior
knowledge of business methods.

Thus we can accept the fact that a change did occur in favour
of the Senate, but not to the extent that the *Historia Augusta* would

---

[1] U. Wilcken, *Phil.* LIII, 1894, p. 81 = *Chrestomathie* I, no. 41, col.
III, 13.

[2] This view has already been advocated, as against A. Stein (*Der römische
Ritterstand*, pp. 252, 254 *sq.*, 260 *sq.*), by E. Stein, *Geschichte des spätrömischen
Reiches*, I, p. 53 n. 3, and recently by P. Lambrechts, *La Composition du Sénat
romain de Septime Sévère à Dioclétien*, p. 107.

[3] *Dig.* I, 9, 1 pr.

lead us to believe. It is certain that there was a desire to make concessions to the prestige of the Senate. The government might even hope thereby to gain an increase in strength and to create or to preserve a certain counterweight against the excessive demands of a pampered army. With all this the *patres* could naturally indulge the hope of better times; but, with the complete collapse of such hopes in the confusions and crises which followed, the memory of Severus Alexander's reign was likely to be coloured with the rosy tints of a dream. And although the young emperor, under the influence of his entourage, appears to have been neither desirous nor, because of his lack of force, capable of turning back the wheel of history, yet, while the Empire continued its ever-advancing development towards autocratic absolutism, Alexander's reign shows one more endeavour to let the Senate play its rôle within the limits of possibility as 'the ornament of the State.'

The accession of Alexander had been accompanied by the *damnatio memoriae* of Elagabalus with all its consequences. Sure proof of this is found in the erasure of his name from the inscriptions. But the change of personnel in the government was not so important as the biographer asserts, if even a Comazon Eutychianus, to whom Elagabalus owed his accession to the throne, became *praefectus urbi* once more. Cassius Dio was, it is true, not subject to the same odium, but he had been in the previous reign *curator* of Pergamum and Smyrna, and now he was made proconsul of Africa and afterwards governor first of Dalmatia and then of Upper Pannonia. On the other hand, L. Marius Maximus appears to have been rewarded with the consulate of 223 because he had not served under Elagabalus. The Praetorian Prefecture was given to Flavianus and Chrestus, who had both probably taken part in the overthrow of Elagabalus and of their predecessors in this office. The jurist Domitius Ulpianus was promoted as early as March 222 to be *praefectus annonae*, and was already Praetorian Prefect before 1 December[1]. The empress-mother had seen in him the man who, thanks to his legal knowledge and his experience of affairs since the reign of Septimius Severus, could in this office render the best service to the Empire, and one who also appeared willing to keep the insolent Praetorians in check. In this policy, however, he does not seem to have received from his two colleagues the support that was expected; for, when an attempt on his life was discovered, Ulpian believed that both were implicated in the

---

[1] *Cod. Just.* VIII, 37, 4; IV, 65, 4, where he is termed by the Emperor *'praefectus praetorio et parens meus.'*

plot and in consequence both were put to death. Nor was he capable, as events proved, of mastering the Guard. For trivial reasons street-fighting broke out in Rome between the soldiers and the populace and lasted for three days, when the people were forced to give up the conflict for fear the troops might set fire to the whole city. Finally the man whose intelligent and far-sighted rule might have brought further blessings to the Empire fell a victim to his Praetorians in the very palace of the Emperor, who was unable to protect him. Whether Ulpian had up till then been sole Prefect cannot be safely affirmed or denied from our sources, although the subsequent history of his office rather points to a negative conclusion[1]. Nor is the date of his death recorded. There is no reason to put it very near the beginning of his Prefecture[2]; but one might well be tempted to connect the bloody riot of the Praetorians with the difficulties and dissensions in the imperial household.

Mamaea had married her son in 225 to a woman of a senatorial family, Cn. Seia Herennia Sallustia Barbia Orbiana, the daughter of Seius (?) Sallustius Macrinus[3]. Orbiana received the rank of Augusta, and her father became Caesar. But good relations did not long continue in the imperial house. Even in the lifetime of her mother Maesa, Mamaea had obtained the predominant influence, and, when her mother died and was consecrated Diva, she saw that the time had come for her to exercise as 'mater Augusti et castrorum' a quasi-autocracy. Ambitious as she was, she now became jealous of the real or supposed influence of her daughter-in-law. The masterful and imperious conduct of the empress-mother caused the Caesar to turn with complaints to the Praetorians; but this only cost him his life on the ground of attempted revolution, and his daughter was forced to go into exile in Africa (227/8). From this time onwards Severus Alexander remained unmarried; for Mamaea guarded against a repetition of this experiment. Coins of the Emperor with the legends 'Salus' and 'Felicitas Augusti' and those of Mamaea with 'Felicitas

---

[1] Zosimus (I, 11, 3) describes Ulpian as sole Prefect after the removal of his two colleagues. A final decision depends on the chronology of the Prefecture from the time of Domitius Honoratus; cf. Lambrechts, *op. cit.* p. 105 and A. Jardé, *Études critiques sur la vie et la règne de Sévère Alexandre*, p. 39. The fact, also, that there were two Prefects after 241 (p. 82) suggests that Ulpian did not remain alone in that office.

[2] Jardé, *op. cit.* p. 39 n. 1.

[3] Cf. A. Stein, P.W. *s.v.* Sallustius (4), col. 1910; M. Fluss, P.W. *s.v.* Seius (22), col. 1128.

publica' proclaim the success and desires of the empress-mother.
Soon after this, her title was enlarged to that of 'mater Augusti et
castrorum et senatus atque patriae,' and finally she is even likened
to the mother of the gods with the addition of 'et universi generis
humani[1].' One may presume that the Praetorians, who with the
collapse of the Caesar Sallustius had lost an opportunity of showing
their power, now became refractory. Their anger was finally
discharged upon Ulpian, whose death may thus be placed in the
year 228. This may also explain why the Emperor suggested to
Cassius Dio, his colleague in the consulship for 229, that he
should spend his consulate outside Rome; for Dio had gained the
dislike of his Pannonian troops by his strict enforcement of
military discipline, and thus was rendered suspect to the Praetorians also. Dio's proud resolution is proved by his showing
himself nevertheless to the soldiers in Rome and in Campania in
the company of the Emperor before leaving for his Bithynian
home. Small wonder, then, that he concluded his history with
the words of the Iliad:

'And Zeus drew Hector to safety from the shafts and dust, from bloodshed, slaughter, and the din of strife.[2]'

Examples of this sort prove the weakness of the Emperor in the
face of the soldiers. He did not even venture to proceed directly
against Epagathus, the chief culprit in the murder of Ulpian, and
he was only brought to book when Alexander had got him out
of the way by promoting him to the governorship of Egypt.
But the tension between the soldiery and the government could
not be lessened, since the imperious Mamaea, who doubtless
knew how to appreciate the power of money, was suspected of
having become miserly to the detriment of the troops.

Disorder in the finances assuredly demanded the cutting down
of expenses to bare necessities. But recognition of the crisis and
efforts to meet it could do but little to better conditions as a whole.
Many taxes may have been abolished, or at least reduced; but
whether the *aurum coronarium* was among these must remain
uncertain[3]. In any event, in view of the needs of the State, no

---

[1] Dessau 485. She appears as Dea Panthea with the attributes of Diana,
Victoria and Felicitas on a medallion in the British Museum. See Volume
of Plates v, 230, *i*.

[2] Ἕκτορα δ' ἐκ βελέων ὕπαγε Ζεὺς ἔκ τε κονίης
        ἔκ τ' ἀνδροκτασίης ἔκ θ' αἵματος ἔκ τε κυδοιμοῦ.   *Iliad* xi, 163–4.

[3] So long as the attribution of P. Fayûm 20 (Bruns[7], no. 96) to Severus
Alexander is not proved beyond doubt. For references see W. Ensslin,
Klio xviii, 1923, p. 129 *sq.* and M. Rostovtzeff, *Soc. and Econ. Hist.* p. 611,
n. 56; Germ. Ed. ii, p. 350, n. 56.

reduction of taxes can have been made to the extent asserted by the *Historia Augusta*. And if in some rare instances a shifting of obligations from the traders to the producers was attempted, this did not reduce the burden of taxes sustained by the general public. The government persisted in the further collection of an additional tax (*anabolikon*) on raw and manufactured products from Egypt, since the free market was unable to satisfy particular requirements, especially those of the imperial capital. It is true that the fiscal administration was ordered to deal justly and moderately with the subjects, but at the same time there can be traced an intelligible anxiety to secure that the taxes prescribed by law were in fact duly paid. Forced labour and liturgies, that is to say compulsory service of all kinds, remained as formerly a heavy burden on the lower classes of the population. In this connection it is possible that the relations of the State with the *collegia*—the various guilds of ship-owners, merchants and craftsmen—were subjected to a revision. There was no nationalization, but there may well have been a more rigorous control of those corporations whose services were of paramount importance to the State. From this time onwards the old formula 'permitted by decision of the Senate' (*quibus ex S.C. coire licet*) disappears, and we may see therein a cessation of private enterprise in the formation of such guilds, the place of which may have been filled by some intervention on the part of the State. A better employment of State-industry to repair the finances is shown, for instance, in the creation of the *ratio purpuraria*, which appears under Severus Alexander and is probably to be connected with sale of purple from imperial factories[1]. On the other hand we cannot speak of a reform of the monetary system; only the extensive minting of a copper currency of good quality seems to point to some effort at improvement. The legends on the coins, 'Moneta Restituta' and 'Restitutor Monetae,' refer only to the recoining of the *dupondius*[2]; the coins in precious metals are no better than they were under Alexander's predecessors. It appears, however, that there were discussions at this time of projects prompted by the extensive depopulation of important areas. Thus Dio, through the mouthpiece of Maecenas, advocates the founding of a State mortgage-bank[3], and the beginnings of a State credit policy towards owners of land can still be traced in our sources.

The government, too, despite the weakness of the financial position, maintained the traditional expenditure. Five *congiaria*

[1] Cf. M. Bang in L. Friedländer, *Sittengeschichte Roms*, IV, 1921, p. 54.
[2] K. Pink, *Num. Z.*, N.F. XXVIII, 1935, pp. 13, 16.
[3] Dio LII, 28, 3 *sqq.*

were made in cash payments to the Roman populace on the
occasions of the three consulates of the Emperor, perhaps at the
consecration of the temple of Juppiter Ultor and after the Persian
war. Rome was embellished with magnificent buildings. On the
Campus Martius the Baths of Nero were enlarged to create the
Thermae Alexandrianae, equipped with a separate water-supply
and a library, in the construction of which Sextus Julius Africanus
assisted (p. 477). Also the Baths of Caracalla were completed and
the Amphitheatrum Flavium was restored. In Italy and the
provinces works of public utility, such as bridges, aqueducts and
baths, were undertaken, and to meet the cost of these part of the
revenue of the cities was placed at their disposal. The building and
improvement of roads, especially in the Danubian provinces,
served at the same time the special purpose of increasing Rome's
military preparedness. There was further undertaken an extension
of the frontier defences in the direction begun by Septimius Severus
(p. 32), whereby in certain provinces the peasants of the frontier
districts were concentrated in fortified places; and thus was
pressed forward the assimilation of the rural population to the
frontier troops now transformed into settlers. With this went the endeavour, not exactly to urbanize that part of the population which
was important for military purposes, but as far as possible to render
it more civilized. The literary papyri which have been found are
evidence for the spread of school education; and we know from
a passage in Ulpian[1] that there were elementary teachers even in
the villages. In this passage the principle is maintained that these
teachers should not be exempt from the services required by the
State, but that the amount of such services should be fixed by
agreement with the provincial governors. There is reason to think
that Ulpian was in general keenly interested in the provincial
administration: he had devoted a part of his extensive writings to
the duties of its officials. We can hardly therefore assume that
during his prefecture administrative practice was in essentials
altered from that which prevailed before the reign of Elagabalus.
There is certainly no reason to think that a beginning had already
been made in the separation of civil and military authority in the
provincial administration. As one special case, it is worth observing that, in spite of the extension of the citizenship by Caracalla, a decree of 224 enjoined on the provincial governors the
duty of keeping to the existing customary law[2]. A comparison

---

[1] *Dig.* L, 5, 2, 8.

[2] *Cod. Just.* VIII, 52, 1: '*nam et consuetudo praecedens et ratio quae
consuetudinem suasit custodienda est, et ne quid contra longam consuetudinem
fiat, ad sollicitudinem suam revocabit praeses provinciae.*' Cf. *Dig.* I, 3, 33, 34.

with two passages from Ulpian's *de officio proconsulis* reveals the author of the decree.

The other legislation affords evidence of some improvements in the civil law, but it still follows the trend of those legal conceptions which the jurisprudence of that epoch had developed. In his handling of the criminal law Severus Alexander deliberately sets his own age in opposition to the régime of his predecessor, especially as regards the Lex Iulia maiestatis, where a tendency to lessen the harshness of the law can be observed. The Emperor himself says 'etiam ex aliis causis maiestatis crimina cessant meo saeculo[1].' On the other hand he speaks in the Lex Iulia de adulteriis of the 'castitas temporum meorum,' and demands a stricter enforcement of penalties[2]. An identification with the prevailing juristic trend can perhaps be seen in a rescript on the Lex Cornelia de falsis in the formula 'secta mea non patitur[3].' In any event the proceedings against the Christians under this government were not conducted in accordance with the letter of the existing regulations. If it is true that in the seventh book *de officio proconsulis* Ulpian adopted a codification under the *lex maiestatis* rather than under the *sacrilegia*[4] of the penalties prescribed against the Christians, reason for this procedure could be seen in the more lenient application of the former law. But to this the will and desire of the empress-mother may have contributed with even greater force. However strong the endeavour to wipe out the memory of the invasion of unmixed Orientalism into religious worship, the fact of a far-advanced syncretism remains. The increasing permeation of religion with the philosophy of the time, or, perhaps more correctly speaking, the permeation of this philosophy with religious elements is reflected in the attitude of the circles interested in matters of the spirit. Mamaea was no Julia Domna; still she was acquainted with the spiritual currents of her day, and she may have concerned herself with the 'new philosophy.' Hippolytus of Rome could thus dedicate to her a treatise on the Resurrection, and later, during the Persian war, she summoned Origen to the imperial headquarters in order to acquaint herself with his theology. But all this, in spite of the Christian tradition from the time of Eusebius, does not make Mamaea a Christian.

The same is true of her son, even if there is nothing extra-

[1] *Cod. Just.* IX, 8, 1; cf. IX, 8, 2 and IV, 1, 2.
[2] *Ib.* IX, 9, 9.
[3] *Ib.* IX, 22, 5; cf. IX, 8, 2.
[4] P. Jörs, P.W. *s.v.* Domitius (88), col. 1453.

ordinary in the account given by his biographer of the erection of a statue of Christ together with other figures worthy of reverence in the imperial *Lararium* or house-chapel[1]. Benevolent tolerance of the Christians[2], which was probably affected by an increasing number of believers in the imperial household, is the kernel round which the later legend was able to grow. It, however, is quite understandable that the Christians in the Emperor's entourage should have made use of the change in the administration of the law of treason to improve the lot of their brethren, since in general the reign propagated the idea of a State ruled by law. For this one has only to read the ordinance on the possibility of direct appeal to the emperor, which was intended to meet the excesses of the procurators and governors, who, it is true, felt in their turn the pressure of the fiscal authorities[3], or the preamble to a decree by which not even the emperor could become an heir if a will were not formally completed[4]. Here it is expressly stated that 'even though the law conferring the imperial authority (*lex imperii*) may have released the emperor from the ordinary formalities of the laws, there is nothing which would be so peculiarly characteristic of the imperial power as to live according to the laws.' Perhaps we have here a personal expression of opinion by Alexander, since Ulpian had, for certain cases, laid down the principle that the emperor is above the laws—'princeps legibus solutus est[5].'

II. SEVERUS ALEXANDER: FOREIGN POLICY

The reign began with a few years of relative quiet, and there was reason to hope that the tasks of internal reconstruction could be advanced in peace. Riots of the Mauri in Tingitana, campaigns against the Isaurian hill-tribes and a single inroad by some Germans did not give rise to any serious alarm[6]. But towards the end of this decade a threatening storm arose from the east. The Parthian empire had succumbed to the attack of the

[1] Cf. G. Wissowa, *Religion und Kultus der Römer*, p. 92. A. Momigliano, *Athenaeum N.S.* XII, 1934, pp. 151 *sqq.*, attempts to support the account of Severus Alexander's philo-Semitism, but cf. E. Hohl, *Bursian*, 256, 1937, p. 156.

[2] The attempt of G. Krüger (*Die Rechtsstellung der vorkonstantinischen Kirchen*, pp. 273, 292) to infer more than this from our sources must fail by reason of its defective criticism of the statements of the *Historia Augusta* (cf. especially p. 247, n. 4). [3] *Dig.* XLIX, 12, 5 = P. Oxy. XVII, 2104.

[4] *Cod. Just.* VI, 23, 3 of the year 232. [5] *Dig.* I, 3, 31.

[6] Cf. H. Nissen, *Bonner Jahrb.* CIII, 1898, p. 114 with J. Vogt, *Die alexandrinischen Münzen*, I, p. 186, and Ritterling, P.W. *s.v.* Legio, col. 1429, ll. 68 *sqq.*

Persians under Ardashir (Artaxerxes) the son of Pabak. After
the overthrow of the Arsacid Artabanus V, Ardashir had become
King of Kings by the grace of Ormuzd (see below, chap. iv).
A pronounced national sentiment, supported by intense religious
feeling for the possession of Zarathustra's teaching in what they
thought was its old purity, animated the king and his fellow-
warriors. With the coming of this new Persian empire of the
Sassanids—as they are called after the grandfather of the first
king—the East laid aside its defensive policy for an offensive.
Ardashir already envisaged as his political goal the re-establishment of the old empire of the Achaemenids. Rome's claim to
universal empire was now matched by that of a new and powerful
State. By the issue of a gold coinage the king opposed to the
hitherto unchallenged prerogative of the Empire a claim to an
equality of rights. In the year 230 alarming news reached Rome.
Ardashir had broken into Mesopotamia and was besieging
Nisibis; his horsemen were already endangering Syria and Cappadocia. Diplomatic action led to no result. War was inevitable and
demanded the use of strong forces. The supreme command must
be assumed by the Emperor in person—the need was admitted
by Mamaea, concerned though she was for her son. Wide and
careful preparations were made for the campaign. Troops were
raised in Italy and the provinces. It is possible that the legion IV
Italica was recruited on this occasion. Detachments (*vexillationes*)
were summoned from the legions on the Rhine and the Danube.
P. Sallustius Sempronius Victor[1] received an extraordinary command of the fleet to secure the seas and protect the dispatch of
reinforcements.

In the spring of 231 Severus Alexander left his imperial capital
accompanied by his mother. On his overland route to the East
he collected an army which, consisting of picked troops, seemed
equal to the task which lay before it. It was not clear, however,
what was the temper of these forces, in spite of the repeated
minting of coins with the legends 'Fides exercitus' and 'Fides
militum.' The repetition of this rallying-cry rather gives one the
impression that desire and reality did not correspond. Not long
before, the legions in Mesopotamia—Parthica I and III—in spite
of the dangers of the hour had mutinied and killed the governor
Flavius Heracleo[2]. And when the Emperor had established his
headquarters at Antioch, and from there had sent a second
embassy to Ardashir, with, it is true, no better result, riots had

[1] Stein, P.W. *s.v.* Sallustius (21), col. 1958.
[2] Ritterling, P.W. *s.v.* Legio, col. 1331.

to be suppressed among the Eastern contingents. A usurper, named Uranius Antoninus, whose name and coins[1] suggest a reaction of the admirers of Elagabalus, had risen in Edessa with the support of Syrian troops, perhaps legio III Gallica. There was also a mutiny among the detachments summoned from Egypt, who certainly belonged to the II Traiana[2].

These unwelcome events were the prelude to the opening of the Persian war in 232. The army of operations was divided into three parts. In the north the division of the left marched towards Media by way of Armenia, where Rome's allies the Arsacids still maintained their resistance. The division of the right advanced in a south-easterly direction over the route taken by Septimius Severus in 197 (see above, p. 6). The main army, under the command of the Emperor himself, was intended to advance eastwards through North Mesopotamia. But the excessive caution of Alexander prevented these latter troops from ever engaging the enemy. Ardashir was thus able to concentrate superior forces and annihilate the right wing as it was operating on the Euphrates. Thereupon the Emperor, who with all the European soldiers was suffering severely from the climate, withdrew his own forces and ordered the northern division also to retreat to Antioch. This division had successes to record in Atropatene, but during its retreat it suffered severely in the Armenian highlands from the inclement weather. In spite of all this the enemy themselves must have sustained no inconsiderable losses; for the Persian king nowhere pressed the pursuit, and even remained inactive for four years. The Roman offensive had failed. Its net result was the doubtful success of seeing the frontier for the time being still intact. And now a new peril threatened in the West. The removal of strong forces stirred up the Germans. The danger of a war on two fronts, which Augustus had sought to avoid by a diplomatic solution of the Eastern question, and which later had proved no real danger because of the growing weakness of Parthia, remained from now onwards an anxiety and heavy burden on those who directed the foreign policy of the Empire. The news from the West caused the *vexillationes* drawn from that quarter to demand their immediate return. Herein was shown the disadvantage of making the soldier a settler. The Persian war was therefore broken off in 233 without the conclusion of peace. Before his return to Rome the Emperor took measures for the defence of the frontier in the East. At Rome he was received with the honours of a

---

[1] See Volume of Plates v, 230, *m*.
[2] Cf. Ritterling, P.W. *s.v.* Legio, cols. 1331, 1528.

conqueror and celebrated a triumph as 'Parthicus Maximus' or as 'Persicus Maximus[1].'

The return of the European contingents seemed to have removed the worst danger on the Rhine and on the Danube; but an ambitious campaign was prepared against the Alemanni. On this occasion Pannonia furnished most of the recruits, who were collected on the Upper Rhine in 234. Their training was entrusted to C. Julius Verus Maximinus. The Rhine army was strengthened by detachments from other legions; besides the II Parthica from Italy, special contingents of light-armed auxiliaries were dispatched; these had returned from the East with Severus Alexander. In the same year the Emperor, again accompanied by his mother, proceeded to join his army, which was concentrated at Mainz. The passage over the Rhine had already been secured by a pontoon bridge[2]. But instead of giving battle Alexander, still swayed by the Augusta, began to negotiate. He hoped to maintain peace by cash-payments. But in this policy he failed to take into account the fighting spirit of his troops, who misconstrued his conduct as cowardice and who also perhaps thought that the Roman money would be better expended on themselves. Dislike for Mamaea with her supposed avarice, and antipathy towards an emperor who could never show a will of his own, led to a revolt. The Pannonian recruits proclaimed their commander Maximinus as emperor. In vain did Severus Alexander hope for the support of the other troops, especially those from the East. When Maximinus advanced against him he found himself deserted, and in mid-March 235 he was killed in Vicus Britannicus (Bretzenheim near Mainz). His mother shared the same fate.

They both fell victims to those forces in which the founder of the dynasty had seen the surest defence of his house, and they paid with their lives for the failure of their attempt to reach the goal of the first Severus by other means than his. The plan of serving the interests of the Empire and of the dynasty by winning the support of the upper classes for a régime based on military supremacy was bound to fail if it did not succeed in mastering the unruliness of the armies. But as soon as the danger from without the empire had strengthened the self-consciousness of the soldiery through the feeling that they were indispensable, as soon as they had begun to desire a soldier for their emperor, there was no hope left. For precisely those qualities which this hour demanded were just those which Severus Alexander lacked, however well-meaning

---

[1] Jardé, *op. cit.* p. 82.   [2] See Volume of Plates v, 230, *l.*

and sensible of his imperial duties he may have been. The last of these Syrian emperors could not fulfil his rôle, since he was neither a Severus nor an Alexander.

III. THE FIRST SOLDIER-EMPEROR AND THE SENATORIAL OPPOSITION: MAXIMINUS THRAX, THE GORDIANS, PUPIENUS AND BALBINUS

Maximinus was the first representative of a new type of ruler. The son of a Thracian peasant—only a falsification of history has made him a Goth—a man who attracted attention by his extraordinary strength and size, he had risen from the ranks, and when admitted into the equestrian order he had made a career for himself. As legionary prefect he commanded the legio II Traiana in Egypt in 232[1], and at the time of the Persian war he was governor of Mesopotamia (*praefectus Mesopotamiae*). His soldierly qualities and his skill in handling troops were the reasons for entrusting the training of the recruits to him in 234 as *praefectus tironibus*. He was a man after the soldiers' heart: he shared their sentiments; he knew what they wanted. It is no wonder that shortly after his elevation he doubled their pay.

The news from the Rhine soon reached Rome. We know nothing of the manner in which Maximinus obtained his recognition from the Senate; but the *patres*, thus surprised, could do nothing else than bow to the inevitable and confirm him as emperor. Proof of this is found in the co-option of Maximinus into the priestly colleges on 25 March 235. In any case the Senate, in order to maintain its position, had taken the customary constitutional steps[2]. The *patres*, it is true, may have given vent later to their rancour and their aversion to the hated upstart by denying the ratification by the Senate, thus preparing the way for the conception of an immediate open opposition of that body, which even is supposed to have raised Alexander to the gods. But the erased inscriptions tell another story. Not until the period of overt rebellion against Maximinus was the Senate able to act as it may well have desired to act at the time—for there was resentment right from the beginning. This and the fact that Maximinus, occupied with the

---

[1] Accepting the very probable supplement in P. Par. 69 by U. Wilcken, *Phil.* LIII, 1894, p. 95 = *Chrestomathie* I, no. 41, col. III, 14.

[2] It is useless to speak of the nullity of an enforced legal transaction by pointing to paragraphs of modern criminal law, as is done by O. T. Schulz, *Vom Prinzipat zum Dominat*, p. 54 *sq.*

urgent tasks on the frontier, did not visit Rome either at this time or later were bound to prejudice his popularity, even though he made the expected gesture to the inhabitants of the capital by granting them a donative on taking over the government.

The prosecution of the war against the Germans appeared to Maximinus to be his first and most important task, but before he joined battle he had to deal with opposition in his own army. A number of centurions and senatorial officers had planned his removal. It was their intention to deliver the Emperor into the enemy's hands by breaking down the bridge after he had crossed to the right bank of the Rhine. A distinguished senator named Magnus was to take his place. The plot became known, and Maximinus had the real or suspected culprits put to death without trial. The historian Herodian[1], who is biassed against this emperor, attempts, without good reason, to make his readers believe that the plot existed only in the imagination of Maximinus. He does, however, mention other men who could not reconcile themselves to the *fait accompli*. The Osrhoënian archers forced the purple on Quartinus, a man of senatorial rank and a friend of the murdered Augustus. This movement must have been prompted by the jealousy of the Oriental troops towards those of the West. But Quartinus had hardly been raised to this dignity when he fell by the hand of Macedo, the former commander of the Osrhoënians, who had himself provoked the mutiny. His double game brought him the punishment of death instead of the reward he expected. But it is no wonder that the Emperor's suspicions could never afterwards be allayed. By nature rather brusque and in no way sympathetic towards the senators, who prided themselves on their rank and education, Maximinus used these revolts as an excuse for removing the senatorial officers and replacing them by professional soldiers. But this was still in the future. For the Osrhoënians took part in the fighting against the Germans, and it was only after this that they were punished[2]. It is hardly to be assumed that Maximinus should have given this heavily compromised contingent an opportunity of rehabilitating themselves only to disband them after their victories.

The Emperor crossed the Rhine near Mainz and led his army far into the enemy's country, following an opponent who retreated before his superior forces. The light troops, the Oriental archers and the Mauretanian javelinmen, proved their skill in skirmishes with the Germans, to whom their tactics were unfamiliar. It was not until they reached marshy country that the enemy took their

[1] VII, I, 8.   [2] A. v. Domaszewski, *Rh. Mus.* LVIII, 1903, p. 543.

stand for a decisive battle. The bravery of Maximinus fired his troops to attack, notwithstanding the difficulties of the ground. Despite heavy losses they inflicted a crushing defeat on the Germans. The field of battle must be sought in the frontier district of Northern Württemberg and Baden, and thus we may conclude that the enemy were Alemanni[1]. With justifiable pride the Emperor could accept the triumphal title of Germanicus Maximus and commemorate the 'Victoria Germanica' on the coinage of the following year. A picture of the battle which was publicly displayed before the Curia in Rome spread the fame of the victorious emperor. This energetic advance re-established peace for some time along the Rhine and Upper Danube. Additions to the *limes* forts show the strong interest taken in the maintenance of the frontier defences. Maximinus could consider this victory over the Germans as confirming his title to the throne; accordingly he now (in 235) raised his son C. Julius Verus Maximus to the rank of Caesar[2], the ceremony possibly forming part of the festival of victory held at Sirmium, where he had taken up his winter quarters. If he had in fact projected a new attack upon the Germans for 236 and planned conquests on a large scale, such schemes had perforce to be abandoned, for the Sarmatians and Dacians gave him trouble. The triumphal titles Sarmaticus and Dacicus Maximus and tombstones of soldiers who fell in the Dacian campaign are the only evidence of these struggles in the years 236 and 237. In the spring of 238 we find the Emperor again in Sirmium.

The subject peoples of the empire soon came to feel that a keener wind was blowing. It is true that the practical recognition of the right of the Praetorian Prefect to make general decrees, provided only that these did not modify the existing legislation[3], was implicit in the previous development. Further there are inscriptions which give evidence of expenditure on public works, one of which expressly praises the Emperor as 'Aquileiensium restitutor et conditor,' while road-building[4] especially was continued with undiminished energy. Yet the increasing claims of military requirements were ever more markedly felt. Moreover,

[1] P. Goessler, 'Eine Alamannenschlacht des Jahres 236 (*sic*) n. Chr.' *Forsch. u. Fortschr.* VII, 1931, p. 109; id. *Germania* XV, 1931, p. 8.

[2] C. Bosch, *Die kleinasiatischen Münzen*, II, I, I, p. 53.

[3] *Cod. Just.* I, 26, 2 of 13 Aug. 235, which is erroneously ascribed to Severus Alexander.

[4] Cf. G. M. Bersanetti, 'Massimino il Trace e la reta stradale dell' impero,' *Atti III Congresso di Studi Romani*, I, 1934, p. 590.

through the Emperor's distrust of a covert opposition, the followers of the last dynasty were continually exposed to threats and police spying. Herodian[1] recounts all the evil consequences of the wide-spread activity of informers, including confiscations, which reduced many rich families to beggary, and an organized Terror maintained by the barbarian tyrant, whose persecution of the upper classes is notably exemplified in his cruel treatment of high senatorial officials. The wife of the Emperor, Caecilia Paulina, tried to exercise a restraining influence upon him. But she must soon have died. She was consecrated Diva, so that the later Christian tradition that Maximinus had his wife executed can therefore be explained only through the hatred felt by the Christians for an emperor who, after a period of quiet, had initiated a fresh persecution.

This new persecution of the Church began soon after the Emperor's accession; it sprang, according to Eusebius[2], in the main from political considerations; it was a reaction against the régime of the last emperor, who had been friendly to the Christians. Maximinus feared hostility on the part of the Christians, and, to prevent possible difficulties, began at once to enforce against them the existing regulations, but only to the extent of ordering that, in special cases, proceedings should be taken against the clergy. This was a measure of domestic security, and not a systematic persecution for religio-political reasons, as happened later under Decius. In 235 Pontianus, bishop of Rome, and with him Hippolytus, were deported to Sardinia; and Origen's *Exhortation to martyrdom*, addressed to Ambrosius and Protoctetus, in which he contemplates a threat to his own safety, further shows the effect of the imperial edict in Palestinian Caesarea. In the cases of Hippolytus and of Origen we may, in view of their relations with Mamaea, see action against or at least a threatening of men politically suspect. On the other hand, in Cappadocia and Pontus a purely local persecution of Christians broke out which had no connection with the imperial instructions of 235. Here it was the governor Serenianus who intervened at the instance of the pagan population, the atheistic Christians being held responsible for the devastating results of an earthquake. We may, however, note the perspicacity of the Emperor in appreciating the importance of the clergy in the structure of the Christian communities and thus of the Church as a whole. It appears that the threatening danger passed quickly and harmlessly by. Political caution on the part of the Christians must have

---

[1] VII, 3.   [2] *Hist. Eccl.* VI, 28.

contributed to this outcome. For this reason Maximinus does not figure in the list of persecutors given by Lactantius, though he does appear in the tradition of Eusebius and probably also in the Apocalypse of the so-called *Testament of our Lord*[1], where he is described, in traits which we also find in Herodian, as an emperor from a foreign people, a murderer of men and a grasper after gold.

Ancient critics constantly harp on the avarice of Maximinus. He is said to have confiscated even the public moneys of the municipalities, endowments of all kinds, votive-offerings from the temples and the ornaments of public places in so far as these last were made of mintable metals. It is possible that this generalization is exaggerated and that the critics wilfully overlooked the fact that the defence of the empire required a large part of the means thus provided; nevertheless the statement is a faithful echo of the feeling of those who in all this wished to see only a means to the end of enriching the soldiers at the expense of all the other subjects of the empire. Whether the soldiers really became dissatisfied with these proceedings, as Herodian asserts[2], under the influence of reproaches which are said to have been made to them by their relatives and friends, it is difficult to decide. But at least the action of the Emperor cannot be explained as the result of the hatred of the townsfolk felt by a peasant soldier, since in the last resort the peasants certainly suffered no less than others under the harsh pressure of the taxes. We may, however, conclude from the analogy of other experience that the severe screwing up of taxation not only made the propertied classes nervous but very seriously damaged the public spirit that had expressed itself in voluntary services, the more as the State exchequer now and later became increasingly like the sieve of the Danaids. It was therefore this unconscionable financial policy, the result of the pressure of circumstances, which gave the signal for a new rising.

The imperial procurator in Africa, under the compulsion of the government, proceeded in the collection of taxes without mercy or regard for justice. This drove a number of rich young nobles, who saw their inherited possessions thus endangered, into armed resistance. They mobilized their tenants and servants, and killed the procurator in Thysdrus (the modern El Djem). This done, the only means of securing themselves was to proclaim a rival emperor. The proconsul M. Antonius Gordianus Sempronianus

---

[1] K. J. Neumann, *Hippolytus von Rom*, p. 138; but cf. E. Fascher, P.W. *s.v.* Testamentum dom. nost. col. 1019.
[2] VII, 3, 6.

permitted himself to be forced to accept the purple. On or about 19 March 238 this eighty-year-old proconsul became Augustus. He was said to be descended on his father's side from the Gracchi and on his mother's side from Trajan. He was a rich landed proprietor, interested in literature—he had studied with Philostratus—but had become *consul suffectus* only late in life and had not taken a prominent part in politics. Maximinus had therefore left him in the position which he had occupied under Severus Alexander. He was a personality whose qualities would recommend him as a rival to a hated emperor, and he was ambitious enough to feel flattered at the thought of ending his days in the imperial dignity. After a few days the new Augustus made his entry into Carthage together with his son of the same name, whom he had appointed co-emperor. An embassy, headed by the quaestor, now left for Rome with a proclamation to the Senate and the People, while Gordian I appealed in private letters to his fellow nobles. Vitalianus, the commander of the Guard, as a supporter of Maximinus, must first be removed. The envoys obtained an introduction to him by a ruse, alleging that they had been sent by Maximinus on a secret mission, and killed him.

The programme of the new government could now be published. It promised to stop the informers' activities, to make losses good and to recall the exiles. The Senate went over to the Gordians' party and confirmed their imperial titles (2 April). They voted the *damnatio memoriae* of Maximinus, and perhaps at the same time consecrated Severus Alexander[1]. The Roman populace gave vent to its feelings in wild excesses: the images of Maximinus were destroyed, his followers hunted out and killed. The City Prefect Sabinus also fell a victim to the popular anger. Meanwhile the Senate had acted with extraordinary energy. A committee of twenty consulars—'vigintiviri rei publicae curandae'—was constituted and charged with securing the defence of Italy against the expected attack of the deposed emperor. Then an appeal was made to the provinces, calling upon them to make common cause with the Senate's emperors, each of whom received, in addition to the title Africanus, the other significant name of Romanus. However, the Roman mint had no time to take up these new titles on the coinage, for the fall of the dice had already gone against the Gordians. Capellianus, the governor of Numidia, remained faithful to Maximinus. Fighting against his well-armed

---

[1] He is designated Divus for the first time in an undated decree of Gordian III (*Cod. Just.* IX, 51, 6). Cf. Dessau 1315, 9221.

troops, the legio III Augusta and its auxiliaries, Gordian II fell at the head of his poorly armed militia. His father thereupon committed suicide, and their African followers were visited with terrible punishment. But with this episode, which had ended in a trial of strength decided in favour of the army, the game was by no means over.

With the recognition of the Gordians the Senate had once more assumed a political rôle, and it could not now retreat. The senators assembled in solemn session in the temple of Juppiter on the Capitol. None could or wished to think of a restoration of a Republican régime. But an attempt was made to set up a principate in conformity with the revived prestige of the Senate. Thus the two most highly respected members of the Committee of Twenty, M. Clodius Pupienus Maximus and D. Caelius Calvinus Balbinus, were elected to the imperial dignity. Pupienus had climbed the ladder of office from humble beginnings, and had made a reputation as an efficient officer and provincial governor. He had twice been *consul suffectus*, and as City Prefect he had displayed both prudence and firmness. It was the irony of fate that the Senate, to defend itself against the soldier-emperor, should have required the services of a man at whose birth also there had been no dream of his elevation to the imperial throne. Balbinus was of noble birth: he was quite young when he became a member of the Salian priesthood of the Palatine. He too had been twice consul, and in 213 was even *consul ordinarius*. This double election of two emperors was a new departure constitutionally. In their complete equality of rights—so that on each of them was bestowed for the first time even the hitherto indivisible dignity of Pontifex Maximus (vol. XI, p. 415)—we see, not so much an indication that the Senate considered the double principate as the general rule[1], but rather a memory of the duality and equality in power of the highest magistracy of the Republic. The close relation of the new Augusti to the Senate can be seen in the legend on the coins 'patres senatus'—though this, it must be admitted, was not its first appearance—and still more in the retention of the Committee of Twenty[2]. But the proceedings of the Senate met with no undivided approval. The election of Pupienus, who since his City Prefecture was anything but liked by the populace, was answered with rioting. And followers of the Gordians, relying on the dynastic tradition, demanded and forced the elevation to the Caesarship of M. Antonius Gordianus, a

[1] For another view see E. Kornemann, *Doppelprinzipat und Reichsteilung im Imperium Romanum*, p. 96.   [2] Dessau 8979.

grandson of Gordian I by the marriage between his daughter Maecia Faustina and Junius Balbus. Both the Gordians were now consecrated. A donative of 250 *denarii* per head contributed to the further appeasement of the people's temper. Pupienus set about gathering an army in North Italy, while Balbinus stayed in Rome. But it is an error to see in this an endeavour to separate civil and military power even as between the two emperors.

Maximinus had received the news of the African rising while he was at Sirmium. After two days' consultation with his intimates he addressed the army in a speech which had been prepared for him. He described the impotence and the military weakness of his opponents and uttered violent threats against Rome and the Senate. A generous donative did not fail of its effect. The following day the whole army began its march, in its ranks being many Germans, for the most part cavalry, with which the tribes on the right bank of the Rhine had furnished him either voluntarily or under compulsion. The unforeseen departure and the huge baggage-train were hindrances to his progress. On the fall of the Gordians, the situation remained unaltered, but that fall at least disclosed the fact that the appeal made by the Senate to the provinces had not met everywhere with approval. Thus, besides the provinces whose defence he had secured, Dacia and Spain and, according to the inscriptions on coins, Asia Minor also, stood firmly by Maximinus. The Pannonian regiments, which formed the advance guard, found Emona evacuated. All supplies had been carried away or destroyed in accordance with orders. This action on the part of the enemy, which was repeated as the army progressed, led to a shortage of food with its unfavourable consequences. Aquileia was the first town to offer resistance, which had been organized, on the instructions of the Senate, by the consulars Crispinus[1] and Menophilus. An attack by the advanced guard was repelled. Negotiations, which were conducted by Maximinus through a tribune who was a native of the town, came to nothing. The Emperor then ordered a general attack, which was, however, delayed because floods from the melting snows had destroyed the bridge over the Isonzo. Not until a pontoon bridge had been improvised from casks was it possible on the third day to force the passage. In spite of the energy of Maximinus, all efforts were in vain. The defenders maintained a stubborn resistance, inspired by their confidence in their local patron deity,

---

[1] Cf. R. Paribeni, *Not. degli Scavi*, 1928, p. 343; A. Stein, 'Bellum Aquileiense,' *Hermes*, LXV, 1930, pp. 228 *sqq.*

Belenus. Increasing losses, the threat of hunger, and resentment at the Emperor's unjustified severity towards some officers, whom he accused of failing in their duty, undermined the discipline of the besiegers. The fate of the undertaking was finally decided by the soldiers of the second Parthian legion, whose families and goods in Alba were held by their opponents. On 10 May they murdered Maximinus and his son. But the besieged did not as yet open the gates to them, although the army had rendered homage to images of the senatorial emperors which were shown to them from the city-wall. Only a market outside the wall was granted to the half-starved troops.

Mounted envoys from the army, now tired of war, bearing the heads of the slain emperors as their bloody credentials, met Pupienus in Ravenna, where he was concentrating the volunteers and the levies from Rome and Italy. He hastened to Aquileia, where the leaderless army did him homage. After offering sacrifice in thanksgiving for this victory Pupienus addressed the troops, stressing their obligation of faithfulness to the Senate and People of Rome and to the emperors elected by them. He then dismissed the troops to their permanent stations. At the head of the Roman garrison troops and the Germans, whom he had taken into his service in reliance on their loyal spirit, which he knew from the time of his German command[1], Pupienus returned to Rome. Everywhere he was greeted with enthusiasm as victor. In Rome the news of Maximinus' death had been hailed with frenzied joy. Amid general jubilation Pupienus entered the capital in state accompanied by his co-Augustus and the Caesar. The power of the senatorial emperors—and therewith a new phase in the constitution of the Empire—appeared secure. Men forgot and wished to forget that a short while before a bitter struggle had been raging in Rome. The Praetorians who had remained there, provoked by the conduct of two senators, had waged a savage battle against the populace, which had attacked them; during this, before calm was restored, large districts of the City had gone up in flames. The government was undoubtedly at fault in not at once clearing up its attitude towards the Praetorians, all the more so since the excessive exultation over the fall of Maximinus and the preferment of the German life-guards did not allow the disaffection to be healed. Soon the legends on the coins which declared the wishes of the government, such as 'Concordia,' 'amor mutuus,' 'fides mutua Augustorum,' were powerless to conceal the fact that

[1] Cf. Ritterling, P.W. *s.v.* Legio, col. 1335; and, for another view, M. Bang, *Die Germanen im römischen Dienst*, p. 61.

jealousies were rife. Pupienus stressed his peculiar merits by using the name Maximus on a series of coins[1]. Balbinus repaid the upstart with a haughty demeanour. The common task of defending the empire against external foes might perhaps have brought about a change. Pupienus was to have proceeded against the Persians, who had again broken into Mesopotamia, and Balbinus against the Goths, who had crossed the lower Danube. But the Praetorians had decided otherwise. During a festival they seized Pupienus, who had in vain asked the mistrustful Balbinus to intervene with the Germans, and then they captured Balbinus. Both were brought amid ignominy and mockery into the Praetorian camp, and there were murdered. Then at last the Germans showed a desire to hurry to their assistance, but on receiving the news of the two emperors' deaths they took no action. The rebels proclaimed the Caesar Gordianus as Augustus. By this proclamation (July 9) the hopes of the Senate were, after ninety-nine days, shattered by the self-will of the soldiers. Once more it could only submit to the compulsion of force, though its disappointment may have been lessened by the fact that the young Augustus came from one of the most distinguished senatorial families.

IV. GORDIAN III

Gordian III became Augustus at the age of thirteen[2]. This was a grave reaction against the attempt to entrust the Empire to the best citizen. Who conducted the business of State for the dependent emperor? Whereas from the year 241 we can recognize in the Praetorian Prefect Timesitheus the real controller of the Empire we can draw no sure conclusion for the first few years. Gordian's father must have died before 238, and even the influence of his mother Maecia Faustina is mentioned only in highly suspect passages of the *Historia Augusta*; the epigraphical and numismatic evidence which we should expect for an influential empress-mother is entirely lacking. However, the efforts of members of his mother's household to use the situation for their own advancement may have given a handle for the malicious tradition of an administration run by eunuchs and court-favourites in these early years. The assured facts rather point to a continuance of senatorial influence. Thus, for instance, L. Caesonius Lucillus Macer Rufinianus, proconsul of Africa and later City-Prefect, and Menophilus, governor of Lower Moesia, were both previously members

---

[1] See Volume of Plates v, 232, *a*, *c*.　　[2] For his portrait *ib.* 186, *c*.

of the Committee of Twenty. A certain Annianus, who under the senatorial régime had been charged with holding the levy in North Italy, was later made commander of the legion stationed at Mainz, the XXII Primigenia. The Praetorian Prefecture was held by Aedinius Julianus, a man of equestrian rank who had previously risen to be prefect of Egypt, and then, after admission to the Senate, had become governor of Lugdunensis. Domitius is mentioned as holding this office in 240 either with Julianus or after him. Further, it is certain that after 241 two Praetorian Prefects still held office together[1]. The advisers of the Emperor were apparently desirous of shaping the imperial administration, if not in the spirit of the last reign, at least in continuation of the régime of Severus Alexander.

Many decrees published in the first years of the reign, although they deal for the most part with questions of civil law, permit us to perceive certain general directions of policy which were retained even after 241. The nefarious activities of the *delatores* were combated according to the promise of Gordian I. A decree published 6 September 238 orders the provincial governors to see that nothing should happen which is not in accordance with the principles of the age[2]. In the administration of the provinces the position of the governor was reinforced, especially in its judicial authority. Unjustified decisions of military judges in civil matters were forbidden[3], and efforts were made to restrict the encroachments of the financial procurators in cases where they had not to administer the law as deputies of the governors (*vice praesidis*), a practice which became in course of time more frequent. Only when they were so deputed could they in private lawsuits appoint the judges or hear cases reserved for the governor[4]. One may recognize a certain strengthening of the central administration conducted by the Praetorian Prefect in the right of appeal to the Prefect against a decision of the governor[5], or in the fact that an official who did not fulfil his duties was to be dealt with either by the Prefect or by the governor[6]. In fiscal matters the rights of the *fiscus* and its administration were often emphasized, but there were also proceedings against breaches of the law, and particularly

---

[1] Dessau 2159; *Cod. Just.* IX, 2, 6 (April 243).
[2] *Cod. Just.* X, 11, 2; cf. P. W. Townsend, *Yale Class. Stud.* IV, 1934, p. 65 *sq.*
[3] *Cod. Just.* VII, 48, 2.
[4] *Cod. Just.* III, 3, 1; IX, 20, 4; cf. Townsend, *op. cit.* pp. 66 *sqq.* and on this W. Ensslin, *Phil. Woch.* LVI, 1936, col. 1314.
[5] *Cod. Just.* IX, 2, 6.   [6] *Cod. Just.* VIII, 40, 13.

precautions against straining the law in favour of those who were in the employ of the State[1]. Among other things steps were taken against attempts to obtain the support of the *fiscus* by the cession to it of part of any property in dispute[2]. A significant case of governmental intervention has been preserved in the inscription of Scaptopare[3], commemorating a petition of the inhabitants of this and another village in the territory of Pautalia in Thrace. Their complaints were directed against the oppression and extortion of soldiers, minor imperial functionaries and others. The local hot springs and the proximity of a much-frequented market had previously in times of peace brought a good income to the villagers. Conditions were now entirely changed; they were so impoverished by excessive billeting and requisitions that they threatened to leave their homes. The Emperor ordered an examination of the case, and the erection of the inscription proves that the villagers of Scaptopare were satisfied with the success of their appeal. Also the repeated reminders of the prohibition against money-lending by imperial officials, either in their own names or through men of straw, point again to the beneficent aims of the government[4]. Under Severus Alexander the right of inflicting punishments had been withdrawn from the financial procurators, and now it was also taken from the supervisors of municipal administration called *curatores rei publicae*[5]. To lighten the burdens of town-councillors a period of respite was decreed between the taking over of the separate offices and duties[6]. At the same time it is clear that the honour of belonging to the municipal council (*ordo*) was accompanied by a certain compulsion: for men who were condemned to exile for a period were to be ordered on their return to resume membership of the *ordo*, and were to be excluded from its honours only for as many years as their exile had lasted[7]. In other respects, too, the government was little disposed to free men from services and duties. For instance, of the freedmen in the service of a senatorial *patronus* only one was released from the obligation of taking over the duties of guardian and tutor[8]. Care for public education is shown in the decree allowing the municipalities to dismiss the *grammatici* and rhetors appointed by them, if they were proved incompetent[9].

---

[1] *Cod. Just.* II, 50, 4 and 5. [2] *Ib.* II, 17, 2.
[3] Ditt.³ 888; cf. M. Rostovtzeff, *Social and Economic History*, pp. 427, 559 n. 89, 621 n. 18; German ed. II, pp. 186, 363 n. 18, 365 n. 27.
[4] *Cod. Just.* IV, 2, 3. [5] *Ib.* I, 54, 3.
[6] *Ib.* X, 41, 2. [7] *Ib.* X, 61, 2.
[8] *Ib.* V, 62, 13; cf. X, 46, 1. [9] *Ib.* X, 53, 2.

The populace of Rome were amply supplied with donatives and games. There was however a decline in building activity; for we are informed only of the reconstruction of the Balneum Surae and the enlargement of the barracks of the marines who had been detached for service in the amphitheatre. It may be, however, that the government co-operated in the removal of the damages caused by the street-fighting. The finances of the Empire must have been subjected to heavy strain, and the government was compelled to reduce the State grants made to the priests; at least, the last entry of payment preserved in the Arval *Acta* of 241 shows that the usual *sportula* of 100 *denarii* had been reduced to 25[1].

The soldiers received the customary donatives. Also numerous decrees show that, as under Severus Alexander, efforts were made to secure their legal position, especially under the law of inheritance. One gains the impression that, in spite of the attempt to maintain discipline, a far-reaching and prudent compromise was practised as before. It is true that as early as 238 Gordian had disbanded the legio III Augusta for its share in the overthrow of the first two Gordians. Its officers and soldiers, apart from those who were more heavily punished, were transferred to other corps—a considerable number of them are found fifteen years later in the formations concentrated in Raetia—and it was intended that their place should be supplied by a regrouping of African *auxilia*[2]. But this action proved a source of weakness: for when Sabinianus' rebellion broke out in Carthage in 240 the governor of Mauretania, probably Faltonius Restitutianus[3], had to be called up with his troops. The usurper's attempt soon failed. It is possible, however, that on this occasion detachments from the Rhine frontier were sent to Mauretania for additional security[4].

On the Rhine there was still peace resulting from the German victory of Maximinus. But the departure of his army had once more set in motion the enemy on the Danube. Attacks by the Goths and their neighbours, the Dacian Carpi, probed the weakness of the defence. In 238 Istros was pillaged. The peril was not averted until Menophilus, as governor of Lower Moesia, had intervened with a large army. Negotiations with the Goths and

[1] Cf. G. Wissowa, P.W. *s.v.* Arvales fratres, col. 1467; id. *Religion und Kultus der Römer*, 1912, pp. 93, 500 n. 2.

[2] Cf. the '*vexillatio militum Maurorum Caesariensium Gordianorum*' in C.I.L. VIII, 2716; R. Cagnat, *L'armée romaine d'Afrique*, p. 207.

[3] Cf. A. Stein, P.W. *s.v.* Faltonius, col. 1976.

[4] So with Cagnat, *op. cit.* 222 *sqq.*; for another view see Ritterling, P.W. *s.v.* Legio, col. 1336.

the grant of annual payments induced them to withdraw, first handing over their prisoners[1]. A similar demand by the Carpi was put off until Menophilus, supported by a reinforced and well-drilled army, was able to decline it. For three years the enemy remained quiet, while the defence was strengthened by the building of roads and the erection of new fortifications in the towns. Upper Moesia received the right of coinage in order to supply the new requirements. According to the coins minted at Viminacium they now reckoned there by a provincial calendar which began on 1 July 239[2].

The revolts in Africa and the increasing burden of military problems, which was especially due to the renewed danger upon the eastern frontier, may have created the desire to have in charge of the central administration a man who was equal to these demands. We do not know who brought Timesitheus to the Emperor's notice. In 241 Gordian appointed him Praetorian Prefect and himself married Furia Sabinia Tranquillina, the daughter of Timesitheus, perhaps as early as May, but certainly before 23 September[3]. C. Furius Sabinus Aquila Timesitheus, whose name is transformed in Greek sources to Timesikles or Timesokles, and in the *Historia Augusta* is contracted, perhaps in derision, to Misitheus, had acquainted himself by personal experience with a great part of the empire. An inscription from Lyons[4] gives us his career. He served in Spain as prefect of an auxiliary cohort. As financial procurator in the administration of the imperial treasury and domains he served in the provinces of Belgica and Arabia, where he was twice deputy governor. He then came to Rome and there held the office of manager of the imperial stage (*logista thymelae*) and later that of chief of the Inheritance Tax Office. He next went as procurator to Syria and Palestine, charged with the collection of the outstanding special taxes arising out of the Persian war of Severus Alexander. Returning to Belgica as deputy of the *procurator patrimonii* he became at the same time vice-governor in Lower Germany. Then followed a procuratorship with increased powers in Bithynia, Pontus and Paphlagonia, a similar post in Asia as deputy governor for the proconsul, and finally the procuratorship of Lugdunensis and Aquitania. A man who, without

---

[1] Cf. L. Schmidt, *Geschichte der deutschen Stämme*, I[2], *Die Ostgermanen*, p. 204.

[2] G. Elmer, *Num. Z.*, N.F. xxviii, 1935, p. 36.

[3] Bosch, *op. cit.* p. 56; cf. A. R. Bellinger, *Yale Class. Stud.* v, 1935, p. 147 n. 29.

[4] *C.I.L.* xiii, 1807; Dessau 1330.

prejudice to his career, had weathered the storms of repeated changes of emperor was certainly a capable administrator, concerned with affairs and not with persons. His ambition, which cannot be denied, was satisfied with the position of Praetorian Prefect. For some three years this man of outstanding culture and eloquence was the real controller of the Empire, a faithful servant of the State and an expert adviser of his imperial son-in-law. An apocryphal inscription to his honour in the *Historia Augusta* lauds Timesitheus as Father of the Emperor and Protector of the Empire, thus truly rendering the real significance of his person and his position.

How much of the manifold efforts in road-building to serve the peaceful, and in time of need, the military communications of the empire, can be attributed to Timesitheus, is uncertain; but the least that can be said is that he continued what others had begun. In Africa the construction of a *limes* gave security to Numidia[1]. The advanced post of Msad was withdrawn, and the course of the *limes* was fixed on the line from Thabudis following the Oued Djedi, then bending in a north-westerly direction to El Gehara, with covering forts at Gemellae in the oasis Ducen and Ausum (Sadouri). The reinforced *numerus Palmyrenorum* here guarded the frontier. In Mauretania the completion of the fortified settlements of frontier peasants and military settlers, begun under Severus Alexander, was pushed on under the governor, Faltonius Restitutianus, especially supervised by Felix, the procurator of the imperial domains[2]. But the main military efforts were concentrated on the campaign against the Persians, which the Emperor inaugurated in the spring of 242 by the solemn opening of the temple of Janus, the last observance of this ceremony.

While Maximinus still reigned, Ardashir had captured Nisibis and Carrhae. Shapur I, the son who succeeded him in 241, pursued his father's plans of conquest (p. 130). A renewed thrust into Syria seriously endangered Antioch on the Orontes. Meanwhile Gordian, accompanied by Timesitheus, had joined the army, which on its passage overland to the East was to gather up the mobilized contingents of the Danubian army. The removal of these troops, and also, perhaps, the previous recall of Menophilus, tempted the enemy to the attack. Bands of

[1] Cf. E. Fabricius, P.W. *s.v.* Limes, col. 667; J. Carcopino, 'Le Limes de Numidie et sa garde Syrienne', *Syria*, VI, 1925, pp. 30–57, 118–49; Townsend, *op. cit.* IV, 1934, pp. 109 *sqq.*

[2] Cf. Carcopino, 'Les Castella de la plaine de Sétif', *Rev. Africaine*, LIX, 1918, pp. 5 *sqq.*; Townsend, *op. cit.* p. 113 *sq.*

raiders, especially of the Carpi, pushed forward as far as Thrace. But the intervention of Timesitheus soon re-established peace. After this success the army was transported from Thrace to Asia. In 243 Timesitheus, who had also shown his mettle as organizer of the campaign, through his skilful leadership—one blow following rapidly upon another—succeeded in freeing Syria from the Persians and in retaking Carrhae. A decisive battle near Resaina secured to the victorious Romans the whole of Mesopotamia with Singara, and even Nisibis became theirs once more. Edessa in Osrhoëne, where previously under king Abgar X an Osrhoënian client State had been once more set up[1], became again a Roman colony. A further advance was contemplated, leading along the Chaboras to the Euphrates and then following the latter river towards Ctesiphon. Suddenly Timesitheus was cut off by illness. His successor was the forty-five year old M. Julius Philippus, the son of an Arab sheikh from Trachonitis named Marinus. The career of his brother C. Julius Priscus does not correspond with the tradition of his lowly origin. Philip had probably already risen to the position of deputy Prefect. His burning ambition did not allow him to rest content with the place of most influential subject: he wished to wear the purple himself. Disaffection was aroused among the soldiers by difficulties purposely created in the commissariat, the fault of which was attributed to the Emperor's incapacity. If Gordian really did attempt to compound for the position of co-emperor, or at least for the Caesarship, he had not realized the true character of the Arab. In the neighbourhood of Zaitha, between Circesium and Doura-Europus, Gordian's fate was sealed: he was murdered by the soldiers. Philip became emperor (end of February or beginning of March 244). As late as the Persian campaign of the Emperor Julian the cenotaph of Gordian III still stood near Zaitha, at once the record of the successes gained under his name and a memorial which showed what forces were in fact at that time determining the Empire's fate.

V. PHILIP THE ARABIAN

Once proclaimed Augustus, Philip endeavoured to obtain as soon as possible his recognition by the Senate. To this body he reported that Gordian had succumbed to an illness, and succeeded, through his subsequent conduct, in getting this official version accepted by the public, since he steadfastly paid the utmost respect

---

[1] Cf. Bellinger, *op. cit.* pp. 142 *sqq.*

to the memory of his predecessor, to whom the Senate was compelled to render the supreme honour of consecration among the Divi. The mortal remains of Gordian were taken to Rome, and, as we have seen, a cenotaph was erected near Zaitha. Without any hesitation the Senate recognized the new Augustus, and confirmed the appointment as Caesar of his son M. Julius Severus Philippus, who was at most but seven years old. Philip had already concluded peace with the Persians. His desire to gain personal contact with Rome with all possible speed may have been increased by the memory of the fate of Maximinus. By the terms of the peace the Empire retained possession of Lesser Armenia and Mesopotamia. We cannot accept the report of Zonaras[1] according to which the Emperor first ceded Armenia and Mesopotamia, only to withdraw from this compact under the pressure of the ill-feeling thus created. For this must have meant the renewal of the war, and of that we have no record. On the other hand a criticism by Zosimus[2] of the consequences of the peace may find its justification in the fact that henceforth relations with Greater Armenia became less close. Philip returned home to the West as 'Parthicus' and 'Persicus Maximus'. He left his brother Priscus behind as governor of Mesopotamia; Nisibis and Singara each received the additional name of Julia; the old Sichem-Neapolis was dignified as 'colonia Julia Sergia Neapolis'; at the place probably where Philip was born in Trachonitis near the Shuhba of to-day, was founded the town of Philippopolis with the rights of a *colonia*, and Bostra received the distinguishing title 'colonia metropolis.' The Thracian Philippopolis also received from this emperor the status of a *colonia*, possibly on his return march from the East. Coins give evidence of the celebration of games on this occasion at Beroea in Macedonia[3]. On 23 July, 244, at the latest, Philip entered Rome[4]. A first donative, to be followed by three more, proves that he felt the traditional anxiety to win the good will of the citizens. His relations with the Senate seem to have developed favourably from the beginning. What was expected of the new ruler is shown in the encomium of a contemporary rhetorician, entitled *Eis basilea*, which is preserved in the collection of Aelius Aristides' orations[5]. In this pamphlet is sketched, in clear contrast with the abuses of recent times, the ideal picture of the just ruler, equipped with the Stoic virtues,

[1] XII, 19 (p. 583).   [2] III, 32, 4.
[3] See Volume of Plates v, 232, d.   [4] Dessau 505.
[5] E. Groag in *Wien. Stud.* XL, 1918, pp. 20 *sqq.*; Rostovtzeff, *op. cit.* pp. 397 *sqq.*, 614 *sqq.*; Germ. ed. II, pp. 159, 165, 354 *sqq.*

who should be above all a benevolent prince (φιλάνθρωπος
βασιλεύς): the best man should be emperor: he should be the
master, not the servant, of the soldiery. How far the reality
corresponded with this ideal it is impossible to say; but at least
it is certain that the reality fell short of the ideal in one respect:
for Philip sought to found a dynasty. Marcia Otacilia Severa, the
mother of his little son, was raised to the rank of Augusta; his
brother was advanced to an important office, and soon afterwards,
in the spirit of this family policy, Severianus, the Emperor's
brother-in-law, was honoured with a high command. Philip
even had his father Marinus consecrated, in order to procure for
his family a further title to legitimacy[1].

Zealously and earnestly the Emperor devoted himself to his
imperial duties. A touch of clemency may be seen in the decree
declaring a general amnesty for those suffering exile or relegation[2].
A number of decisions in the Codex Justinianus, especially those
which date from the beginning of the reign, are concerned with
questions of civil rights. A noteworthy ordinance provides that
appeal could be made only to the emperor against a decision which
had been given by an official acting for the emperor (vice principis),
i.e. the Praetorian Prefects or their deputies[3]. The co-operation of
the consilium principis is also mentioned once in the Code of Justinian[4]. Philip also had to intervene against the injustice of the
Treasury administration[5]. Yet on the other hand his government
could not waive the legal claims of the State against its subjects,
in view of the heavy demands upon its finances. For instance,
the fact that a son was a prisoner of war was not to be an excuse
for his father's failure to fulfil his obligations[6]. Though poets
were expressly forbidden to claim immunity from taxation[7], there
is no need to infer from this that Philip was a man of no education
or that he was hostile to culture. As ambassador of Athens, his
birthplace, the sophist Nicagoras presented an address to the
Emperor. Some would see in Nicagoras the author of the Eis
basilea; but in that case it cannot be identified with his Pres-
beutikos or ambassadorial address, for that must have referred to
the purpose of his mission and no such reference is to be
found in the Eis basilea[8]. The position of members of the
municipal councils is illuminated by the fact that sons of the
decuriones were compelled to undertake posts of honour and fulfil

[1] See Volume of Plates v, 232, f.
[2] Cod. Just. IX, 51, 7.   [3] Ib. II, 26, 3.   [4] Ib. VII, 26, 6.
[5] Ib. IX, 49, 5.   [6] Ib. X, 52, 2.   [7] Ib. X, 53, 3.
[8] Cf. W. Stegemann, P.W. s.v. Nikagoras (8), cols. 217 sq.

public duties in their fathers' communities[1]. For the rest, Philip
was a good enough soldier to continue on his part the building
of roads[2]. But with all his good will he was not able everywhere to remove the prevailing abuses. It is thus a bad sign
for the security of communications that in Petra Pertusa in
Umbria a company of marines from Ravenna had to be called up
to combat brigandage[3]. An example of oppression of the worst
type is contained in a petition addressed directly to the Emperor
from imperial *coloni* of the Phrygian village Araguë (before the
summer of 247) complaining of unprecedented extortion at the
hands of officers and soldiers, municipal officials and imperial
functionaries[4]. Whether imperial subjects elsewhere really enjoyed
that peaceful and quiet life which was praised by the petitioners
in contrast with their own unhappy experiences may fairly be
doubted, for, from the second year of this reign at latest, the empire
had to suffer from war and soon from riots also with all their
consequences.

Perhaps as early as 244 the Carpi threatened the frontiers, and
when in 245 neither Prastina Messallinus, governor of Lower
Moesia, nor Severianus, who commanded a still larger force, was
able to drive the enemy back over the Danube, Philip himself
took over the supreme command before the end of the year. By
this time however Lower Moesia, Thrace and Macedonia had
been extensively ravaged, as is proved by the cessation of the
coinage. In the summer of 246 the Emperor was in Dacia, where
he granted to the sorely afflicted province the right of coinage.
The provincial Era which is reckoned from this grant begins
about 20 July in this year[5]. The triumphal title 'Germanicus
Maximus' is our only evidence for successful conflicts with the
Germans, presumably the Quadi. In the next year Philip was able
to add with pride the title 'Carpicus Maximus.' After winning a
battle he drove a body of the Carpi to shut themselves up in a
fortress. A sortie and an attempt at relief were both repelled,
thanks to the valour of his troops, the Moors in particular, and
he was able to force the weakened enemy to conclude peace. He
then returned to Rome, and there, availing himself of the impression produced by this victory, raised his son to the rank of

[1] *Cod. Just.* x, 39, 3.
[2] Cf. E. Stein, P.W. *s.v.* Julius (Philippus), col. 766.
[3] Dessau 509.
[4] *O.G.I.S.* 519, cf. Rostovtzeff, *op. cit.* pp. 426, 621; Germ. ed. II, pp.
185, 364 with a new attempt at restoring the inscription.
[5] Cf. F. S. Salisbury and H. Mattingly, *J.R.S.* XIV, 1924, pp. 21 *sqq.*

Augustus (before June 247)[1]. The empress Otacilia now received the honorific appellation of 'mater Augusti et castrorum et senatus et patriae[2].' By the imperial dignity of the young Philip a real double principate was again created, for the son was also Pontifex Maximus. It is noticeable too that hereafter on inscriptions and coins his *tribunicia potestas* is so reckoned as if he had already received it while he was as yet only Caesar. It is reasonable to see in this, as well as in the use of the title Sebastos before the actual promotion to Augustus, nothing else than an attempt to give more than his legal due to the son of the emperor and the heir to the throne[3]. But the practice of Philippus himself must have inspired this attitude, since even from the beginning of the reign his decrees were published in the joint names of himself and his son the Caesar[4]; and this again may be connected with his dynastic policy.

Meanwhile the year had dawned which, according to the Varronian calculation, concluded the first millennium from the foundation of the City of Rome. At the beginning of this year of jubilee on 21 April 247 the Emperor was in the field, and so the secular games and millenary celebrations had to adorn its close. With impressive magnificence the two Augusti, as consuls of the year, the father for the third and the son for the second time, fulfilled the traditional religious ceremonies and presided over the splendid games in the Circus Maximus, for which had been preserved the many wild beasts collected in expectation of Gordian III's triumph over the Persians. The new dynasty was thus able to regard itself as the starting-point of a new saeculum and was celebrated as such. In these exuberant festivities the favour of the Roman populace could be wooed; for Philip's government had otherwise been able to spend but little on the capital. We hear only of the building of a water reservoir (*lacus*) in Transtiberim[5]. But what a change had come over the Roman world in the two hundred and fifty years since Augustus had celebrated the birth of a new saeculum—nay, even in the century

---

[1] Bosch, *op. cit.* p. 57 n. 284.   [2] Dessau 513.

[3] Cf. Schulz, *op. cit.* p. 246; Kornemann, *op. cit.* p. 98.

[4] Cf. the inscription of Araguë cited above (p. 90, n. 4); *Cod. Just.* IV, 29, 10 (of 15 Aug. 244) and often elsewhere. That in the only dated Codex passage after the appointment of the son as Augustus (IX, 32, 6) this title is not expressed is explicable on the ground that (in 32, 5) 'Imp. Philippus A. et Philippus C.' was correctly given and then was mistakenly followed by 'Idem A(ugustus) et C(aesar).'

[5] Aurelius Victor, *Caes.* XXVIII, 1.

which had elapsed since the ninth-centenary festival of Antoninus
Pius! He who now bore the name of Augustus was an Arab, and
however closely he may have identified himself with the duties of
his imperial station, yet the true Rome and the Roman character,
to which men thought that in those days of festival they were
doing homage, remained for him, and must remain, alien and
foreign. But where in Rome were these things then to be found?
A strange dispensation of fate had decreed that this millenary
jubilee was to be the last secular celebration. This changed world
is strikingly exemplified in the work of the Christian historian
Orosius[1], who, by a misreading of the facts, makes Philip celebrate the festival in honour of Christ and of the Church.

There were, however, counter forces still at work which sought
to maintain the old order. Now begins the period when the
Danubian troops, especially the Pannonians, feel themselves to be
the representatives and guardians of the true Roman *virtus*. Thus
the same army with which Philip had won his victories, already
perhaps in reaction against the new Oriental dynasty, set up a rival
emperor in Ti. Claudius Marinus Pacatianus, an officer probably
of senatorial birth. Not long after the millenary festivities, which
Pacatianus commemorated on his coinage with the legend 'Romae
aeter(nae) an(no) mill(esimo) et primo[2],' the recently gained security
of the provinces on the lower Danube was again endangered. The
sequel to the revolt of the army was an invasion of the Goths, to
whom the annual allowances had recently not been paid, or rather
could not be paid. Under Argaithus and Gunthericus the Goths
broke into Roman territory. The Carpi, Taifali, Asdingian Vandals
and Peucini followed their example in large numbers. Marcianopolis was besieged, but the city stoutly resisted, thanks to its
renovated walls and the valour of its inhabitants who were led by
a Thracian called Maximus. After a second vain assault the enemy
withdrew with heavy casualties. Even before the usurpation of
Pacatianus had produced its fatal consequences, revolts broke out
in the East, the cause of which is to be found in the far too strict
régime which had been enforced by the Emperor's brother
Priscus. After serving as governor of Mesopotamia he had been
entrusted, as 'praefectus praetorio rectorque orientis,' with supervision of the general administration of the East. The excessive
pressure of taxation led to disturbances in which one Jotapianus
assumed the purple in the border territory between Cappadocia
and Syria. In Syria itself appeared a third usurper, Julius Aurelius
Sulpicius Uranius Antoninus, in whom we should doubtless see

[1] VII, 20, 3.
[2] See Cohen², v, p. 182, no. 7.

a relative of the Uranius of Severus Alexander's reign. This latter pretender was able to hold out, in the critical time which followed, until 253/4.

These repeated blows of misfortune, threatening the dissolution of the Empire, shook Philip's self-confidence to such a degree that in the Senate he offered to abdicate. Decius, who was then probably City Prefect[1], was the only member who opposed this offer. His reference to the weakness of these usurpers was justified in the case of Jotapianus and of Pacatianus; for the latter was soon afterwards killed by his own soldiers, and the former also met his end before the close of Philip's reign. And now the Emperor, in attempting to clarify and secure affairs in the Danubian provinces, pursued a course which was destined to lead to his own downfall. In Decius he recognized the man who could re-establish order there. It was with reluctance that Decius, who foresaw the result of a military success, allowed himself to be persuaded into accepting this commission which gave him the supreme command in Moesia and Pannonia. If we may believe the account of Jordanes in his *Getica*[2], a part of the soldiers had made common cause with the Goths. However, before the year 248 had reached its close, Decius must have succeeded in discharging his mission by some means or other; for an inscription of this year from Romula (now Rečka on the right bank of the Alt), which had been fortified and probably made a *colonia* at this time, speaks of Philip and his house as 'restitutores orbis totius[3].'

The energetic action of Decius seems to have repressed the Goths and their allies, for in spite of the turmoil of the following year they kept peacefully within their own territory. But the more the general succeeded in getting his troops in hand and in winning their confidence, the more worthy they thought him of the imperial power. In June 249 they compelled him to assume the purple. He sought an understanding with Philip and promised to lay aside his imperial insignia on arrival in Rome. His sincerity may be gauged from the fact that he did not at first have his name and image stamped on the coins: he may perhaps have even continued to coin money in the name of Philip[4].

---

[1] Johannes Antioch. frag. 148, *F.H.G.* IV, 598. Cf. Wittig, P.W. *s.v.* Messius (9), col. 1250, who, on insufficient grounds, assumes the year 249.

[2] XVI, 90, p. 81, 9 *sq.* Mommsen.

[3] Dessau 510; cf. E. Stein, *op. cit.* col. 763.

[4] So we may interpret the coins of Upper Moesia from Viminacium carrying the year XI for Philip and Otacilia. G. Elmer, *Num. Z.*, N.F. XXVIII, 1925, p. 39, regards these coins as genuine. For another view see Wittig, *op. cit.* col. 1267.

The latter, however, did not trust Decius, and gathered an army. The Emperor had already stationed auxiliary troops in the fortified Concordia in Venetia[1] and a strong detachment of the legion XIII Gemina at Aquileia[2]. Apart from the troops in garrison in Italy we have no information about the composition of the army at whose head Philip, now in ill health, marched to meet Decius. But numerically it is said to have been superior to that of his opponent when the two forces met in September near Verona. Philip met his death in the battle, and the fortune of war decided in favour of the Pannonian Decius. On receipt of this news in Rome the Praetorians put the young Philip to death in their camp. A late tradition declares that the Philips were deified[3]; but the fictitious claim of the Emperor Licinius Licinianus to be related to the house of Philip may have given rise to the story. The erasure of their names from inscriptions proves the contrary for the time of their downfall.

But in the Christian tradition the fact that Philip fell at the hands of Decius has brought him the place of honour as the first Christian emperor. It is true that at the beginning of 249 a pagan mob attacked the Christians in Alexandria (p. 520 *sq.*); but for this there was certainly no official responsibility. Thus Dionysius, the contemporary bishop of Alexandria, could call the conduct of the Emperor a benevolent toleration. That Philip observed such a principle is shown by the fact that in his reign the bishop of Rome, Fabianus, could transfer to the capital the bones of Pontianus, who had died in exile in Sardinia. Letters which Origen sent to the Emperor and his wife prove only that they took an interest in religious questions; and from the fact that Eusebius knows of these letters but does not use them in proof of Philip's Christianity it is clear that the Emperor was not a Christian, neither baptised nor catechumen. But to a generation of the faithful who had witnessed the horrors of the persecutions and who could, not wholly without reason, see in Decius' persecution a reaction against the policy of Philip, the benevolent tolerance of the latter was a sufficient proof of an inner inclination towards Christianity. The time, however, had not yet come when a Roman emperor was to fill with new life the universal claims of the Imperium Romanum by uniting them with the equally universal

---

[1] Dessau 9479.

[2] *C.I.L.* v, 808; cf. H. M. D. Parker, *A History of the Roman World from A.D. 138 to 337*, pp. 156, 341, n. 25.

[3] Eutropius, IX, 3; cf. E. Stein, *Hermes*, LII, 1917, pp. 571 *sqq.*, who would attribute the consecration to Constantine I.

claims of the Christian Church. Those threatening years still lay ahead in which Church and Empire alike were to undergo the severest trials. The fall of Philip was the preface to this period of distress. His rise as well as his overthrow had shown once more in the sharp illumination of inexorable facts that 'an emperor could be made elsewhere than at Rome.' And, for those who had eyes to see, it could no longer remain a secret that the army created the emperors. Harsh reality had trampled underfoot the swelling ambitions of the Senate. What was left to it was merely the right, uncontested indeed but hardly ever in the future freely exercised, to co-operate in conferring that legal sanction which established a new master of the Roman world.

CHAPTER III

THE BARBARIAN BACKGROUND

I. THE LANDS BETWEEN THE ROMAN EMPIRE AND CHINA

ROME was not overthrown in a day. It was the work of centuries that produced the great tidal wave which in the dawn of the Middle Ages was to sweep away those solid barriers (as they seemed) which the Roman Empire had erected wherever its frontiers stretched. For centuries before this decisive event, the great plains of Eastern Europe and the steppes or high plateaux of central Asia, which one day were to impart the final impetus, obscure as they are and often silent, were in fact the scene of vast upheavals of peoples which presaged ruin for distant lands. It is truer to say that one knows that it happened than how it happened, for certainly the scanty archaeological or historical evidence at our disposal for the period before the middle of the fourth century (the subject of this chapter) for the most part is neither very clear nor very conclusive. The task is to bring order out of this chaos as best one can, and to elucidate the handful of facts which represents the sum of our present knowledge.

There is one fact, however, which should be made clear from the first. The many territories comprised in the area between the Roman and Chinese Empires, though they lack unity either geographical or political, were nevertheless engaged throughout their whole extent in a perpetual travail which reacted on almost every one of their peoples, diverse as they were in origin and language, since almost all experienced indirectly the effects of events in which one or other of them was directly involved. Each impulse starting from one end of this immense 'entre-deux' passes from group to group and produces adjustments which affect the whole mass.

One group alone seems to stand as an exception to this rule, and watches the passage of the centuries unmoved, namely the central group of peoples of Indo-European language already long settled as farmers on the narrow strips of alluvial land which they inhabit to this day, extending round the inner circumference of the Tarim basin and as far as the northern slopes of the T'ien-shan in Dzungaria. These interesting peoples, industrious and not unskilful, have watched the conquerors pass, and a succession of conquerors has, in effect, passed along the edges of the neighbouring deserts. But they themselves have cared for none of these things, indifferent to everything except the cultivation of their soil and always ready to accept any overlord whose demands did not exceed the act of submission and the payment of a tribute: even had they had the will to resist they lacked the power, scattered as they were in their little cities on an attenuated line more than a thousand miles long.

This group is to-day one of the best known of any, thanks to the notable discoveries of Aurel Stein, Grünwedel, A. von Le Coq, Pelliot and Hackin, who have excavated considerable remains of their ancient civilizations (though none, unfortunately, belonging to the period now under review), and have drawn from their hiding-places very many precious manuscripts[1] which illustrate the intellectual side of their culture. Here indeed, in the very heart of Asia, survived the culture of the ancient Sacae from beyond the Oxus, of whom the most westerly branches spoke the East-Iranian language, while their kinsmen in the North-East, at Kucha, Karashahr and Turfan, spoke a different language formerly known as Tocharish but now more correctly called the Kuchean or Turfanese language, which seems to be nearer to the pure Indo-European group. But this interesting group of peoples does not itself play any active part in our period. Extraordinarily impressionable as it is, it engages our interest here only because it helps us to reconstruct some of the links in the long chain which runs over great deserts and high mountain-passes, and joins together the different populations scattered over those vast lands between the two Empires of Rome and China. For the Indo-Europeans of this central zone, which corresponds roughly to Chinese Turkestan, form a stable mass which hitherto has defied alike the nomads of the steppes and the armies of China; but they are also a pole of attraction, because the great routes across Asia go through their lands, and thus, while they lose nothing of their own individuality, they are a possible connecting-link between the Western and Eastern civilizations.

The chief of these Asiatic routes is the famous 'Silk-route,' known to us mainly through what is said of it by the Greek geographer Ptolemy in the second century of our era, a route which for some time linked up the Chinese Empire with the world of Parthia and Rome. Starting in Syria it climbed to the Iranian

[1] As an example of this may be cited the Manichaean documents referred to below, p. 504 *sq.*

highlands by way of Edessa, Nisibis, Ecbatana, Rhagae, Bactra and the mountains of the Comedae (the modern Kumedh, in the Pamirs), to reach, between Roshan and Ferghana, the silk-market at the spot that bore the name of the 'Stone Tower' (λίθινος πύργος), where the caravans from the Levant exchanged their wares with the caravans from China. Ptolemy, relying on Marinus of Tyre, even relates how a Graeco-Syrian merchant (whom some take to have been a subject of the Parthian Empire[1]), Maes Titianus by name, had dispatched agents along this route as far as the city of the 'Seres.' This city may belong to Kan-su, whether Si-an-fu, or even the capital of the Later Han, Lo-yang or Ho-nan-fu. About its identity geographers are not yet agreed, as is true also of the Roman names of the places which marked the course of the 'Silk-route,' Issedon Scythica and Issedon Serica, which may be Kashgar and Kucha, or Kucha and Lou-lan, north of the Lop-Nor. It was along this route that Buddhist missionaries from North-West India and Afghanistan, which then formed the Indo-Scythian Empire, brought to the Tarim basin the elements of what is called the Graeco-Buddhist civilization. From the first century to the fifth, Indian monks, in fact, unceasingly made their way by the passes of the Pamirs from Kashgar to Tun-huang, whether by Yarkänd and Khotan on the south or by Kucha, Karashahr and Turfan on the north, as they pressed on to preach the gospel of Buddha, at first in all the Indo-European oases of the Tarim and later in China itself. These brought with them, as they had brought to the Indo-Scythian Empire of the Punjab and Afghanistan, that Graeco-Roman art in which they then found their means of expression.

It may, moreover, be observed how other elements of Graeco-romanization became added at the same time to the Graeco-Roman images of Buddha that were imported into this Tarim region. These elements were brought by trade all along the route from Antioch to Si-an-fu. Sir Aurel Stein, in his exploration of the oases mentioned above, has found—though for a period earlier than the fourth century—striking evidence of this double influence. At Rawak, near Khotan, he has discovered bas-reliefs of the first century of our era carved in stucco with figures of bodhisattvas, notable for their truly hellenic nobility and harmonious proportions[2]. At Rawak, too, and also at Yotkan (formerly Khotan) and in the valley of the Niya between Khotan and the Lop-Nor, he has found Roman sealings of the same period representing Pallas Athena armed with the thunderbolt and wearing the aegis[3] and also

[1] Vol. XI, p. 122.   [2] Volume of Plates v, 132, a, b, c.   [3] Ib. 132, d.

Zeus, an Eros, a Heracles, and four-horsed chariots, finally Indo-Scythian coins from Afghanistan. At Miran, south of the Lop-Nor, classical influence is yet more clearly visible and displays the particular effect of Roman Asia Minor. Among the fragments of frescoes brought from this region by Sir Aurel Stein may be noted a Buddha followed by his monks which is in a purely Roman tradition, beardless 'angels' or genii, some winged some wingless, in red mantles that recall the art of Pompeii, and figures also beardless and wearing on their heads the Phrygian cap which gives them the appearance of Mithras. These frescoes, which belong to the third century of our era, afford striking analogies with the painting of Roman Syria and the Fayûm of Imperial times. One of them bears an inscription in Indian characters which gives the name of the painter Tita, which may well be an indianized form of Titus.

II. THE CIVILIZATION OF THE STEPPES

Noteworthy as are the facts that have been described, it would doubtless be rash to regard them as the dominating factor in deciding what were the influences that counted for most in the history of the relations between Asia and Europe in the period under review.

Indeed, the lands between China and the Roman frontiers are, above all, the meeting-point of two great streams of culture: on the one hand the Sarmatian, certainly the stronger of the two, rising near the Roman frontiers or, more exactly, from the regions occupied by the nomad Goths, and on the other hand the Turko-Mongol stream, rising near the frontiers of the Chinese Empire or, more exactly, from around the modern Ordos in lands occupied at that time by the eastern Hsiung-nu. The meeting of these two streams, reinforced by tributaries which in the same way rose either in the West or in the East, produced a kind of hybrid civilization common, as it seems, to all the nomads between the Roman Empire and China; and this, in fact, is an early symptom, and a clear one, of that close intercourse between widely differing peoples which has been suggested above, and which may be emphasized here.

To get a clear view of it, one should turn to this same central region of Asia, not indeed to the settled Indo-European population of the Tarim, which remained unaffected by the various nomad civilizations, but to the Turko-Mongol peoples who frequented the high pastures round or between the upper Irtysh and the Tarbagatai Mountains on the one hand, and the upper Orkhon and the northern bend of the Huang-ho on the other. It is here that one can get the best impression of that art which for want of a better name is called or miscalled 'the art of the steppes[1].' In the period under review, it had long since acquired its essential character; but it continued to develop in matters of detail, for the sufficient reason that the nomads who were its exponents were always on the move. It appears most plainly in bronze plates for harness or armour, standard-staffs with the most interesting stylized animal decoration depicting, among other things, in arresting foreshortening, deer (*cervidae*) or wild beasts, strangely entwined in mortal combat[2]; and finally, jewels and ornaments originally encrusted with glass beads, though usually only the sockets still survive. Naturally the products of this art are nearly always very difficult to date, but there seems very little doubt that in the third and fourth centuries it was still very far from being worked out, and throughout this period we encounter it constantly, with local variants or perhaps with one or other of its component elements predominating, over the length and breadth of the regions between China and the Roman Empire. The discoveries of the last fifty years, some of them very recent, allow us now to define, though still very imperfectly, some of its typical manifestations, and they fall into four main groups.

The Sarmatian group, which comes first, is close to the lands inhabited by the Goths or by peoples of Graeco-Roman civilization, and hence naturally shows clear traces of having been directly influenced by Hellenistic art. Iranian art, too, made its influence felt upon it, but in spite of the combination of influences this group furnishes (in the south-west) the farthest outpost of 'the art of the steppes.' This point has been developed in another chapter devoted to the Sarmatian peoples[3], both those of them who became amalgamated with the Goths and those who, farther East, kept their independence under the name of Alans; but it will perhaps be useful to emphasize the great interest of some of the treasures found at Novocherkask and now thought (with high probability) to belong to the third century of our era[4]. One of the most interesting is a diadem of gold, with decoration in pearls, garnets and amethysts: in the centre is a large Hellenistic or Roman cameo, but on the upper rim are *cervidae* and trees showing the taste and manner of all the ornaments which are most characteristic of the art of the steppes. The thighs of the animals are hollowed into pear-shaped sockets intended for precious or semi-

[1] The nomads, of course, frequented the high plateaux as well as the steppes themselves.   [2] Volume of Plates v, 134, *a, b*.
[3] Vol. xi, chap. iii.   [4] Volume of Plates v, 136, *a*.

precious stones in a style that appears again on a silver belt from
Maikop and on a number of objects worked in precious metal
from Siberia and especially from the region of Lake Baikal. Other
Sarmatian objects of the second and third centuries which have
been found in proximity to these, such as scabbard-ornaments in
the form of sledges or ringed sword-pommels, have been matched
by similar discoveries in Eastern Asia, which indeed are no doubt
their prototypes.

The second group of discoveries belongs to the countries on
both sides of the Ural Mountains, in the neighbourhood of Perm
and notably at Kachka in the heart of the Finno-Ugrian country,
or, again, farther south in the province of Orenburg, or finally on
the other side of the pass of Ekaterinburg near Shadrinsk. The
finds in these parts, some of them at least dating from the third
and early fourth centuries, are closely related to the products of
Sarmatian art; they include buckles, necklaces, gold and silver
rings, fibulae, swords, filigree earrings and enamelled glass beads[1].
Comparable with these finds are those of Pianibor near Sarapul
about two hundred and twenty miles below Perm on the River
Kama, where the conical earrings (made of a metal thread wound
into spirals), the pendants in the shape of bird or horse, or the
bronze brooches shaped like epaulettes, characteristic as they are,
have points in common with the finds of the Ural district.

Much farther east, on the upper Yenisei and more particularly
near Minusinsk, various excavations, unhappily without method,
have brought to light incidentally a respectable number of objects
that can be assigned probably to the second, third and fourth centuries of our era. Especially noteworthy are knives of bronze or
iron, excellent bronze bowls, and pieces of armour or harness
decorated in the animal style so characteristic of the civilization of
the steppes.

Finally, on the borders of China round the bend of the Huang-
ho and in Ordos, a fourth group, closely related to the third,
shows more perfect and more highly developed examples of this
same animal style of art, and among them excellent plaques with
polycephalic animals and with human heads, to be dated probably
to the third century, and also bronze or iron knives and cylindrical
bowls not unlike those of Minusinsk[2].

To this highly schematic picture should be added some mention
at least of various sporadic groups such as that revealed by the
finds at Kosibejevo in the province of Tambov to the east of the
upper Don, or the group from the province of Kaluga on the River

---

[1] Volume of Plates v, 136, b.   [2] Ib. 134, c, 138, a—d.

Oka south of Moscow. Both yield a great number of objects belonging almost certainly either to the third century or perhaps (in Kaluga at any rate) to the fourth, and introduce us to an art which stands between the Sarmato-Gothic and that of the countries occupied by the Germans south of the Baltic. Fibulae from Kosibejevo, or those in the shape of triangles or horseshoes from Kaluga, necklaces with perforated terminal discs (at Kosibejevo), or enamelled jewels, bracelets and crescents—all these things, and others, make up a curious hybrid art that certainly implies a regular traffic across the barbarian hinterland between the Baltic provinces and the countries of the Black Sea.

It is this that gives to certain products of the art which the Russian excavations are slowly bringing to light their air of belonging together in a way that often seems disconcerting. But through all this tangle of interacting influences one thread can be followed by the most casual eye: no one can deny the extraordinary continuity of an art of which on the one hand the manifestations appear sufficiently varied to prevent confusion (the Ural and Minusinsk groups, for example, are perfectly distinct), while, on the other hand, its extremes, so to speak, meet in the oddest way, as one can see in the Sarmatian group and the group from Ordos, where the same armour-plates and lance-handles repeat themselves in the same animal style.

The first general impression that one gets from this common art is that it is a stereotyped art. In our period its subjects seem already fixed and time-honoured, the result of the meeting and blending of many ancestral influences. It has been affected, or even shaped (in degrees and proportions varying with place or period), by the ancient civilizations of Greece and Iran and China; yet it is perhaps in our period most of all that it shows itself as at once homogeneous and mature. It has its realism, but above all it relies on simplification, as can best be seen from a glance at those little heads of foxes or asses reduced to their essential features, or at the pole-tops in the shape of *cervidae* that are so common in our museums. Moreover, its principal aim is decoration. Even in those dramatic contests of animals in which some of the artists excel, even when they portray the terrifying spectacle of these ferocious creatures tearing their prey with sharp fangs or twisting their bodies with all the power of their muscles, still they cannot resist the temptation to frame the scene, or even to obscure it, with a regular network of curved lines. The antlers of the *cervidae* or the horses' manes issue in spirals or ringlets; horns and tails merge into foliage or into heads of birds or gryphons; the nostrils curl round in spirals. The animal loses itself in its own decoration, dense as of tropical undergrowth. Decorative indeed is this art of the steppes, in its very essence, decoration is its one purpose, and one must admit that it succeeds. Even the stylization in which it takes such delight is only another means to this end.

It may well be asked whether there is no other conclusion to be drawn from a study of the works which it has produced, whether the historian is not justified in trying to look beyond the passive material of the archaeological finds to a glimpse of that life itself which he is denied by the absence of contemporary texts, though the want is satisfied in the periods immediately before and after. If it is true that a particular type of art reveals a particular type of culture, one can see reflected here the features of those motley hordes of nomads, sprung from different stocks but leading the same kind of life, the peoples who in the third and fourth centuries roamed the wide steppes between Rome and China. They are horsemen, tireless horsemen, like the nomads who for centuries are to pour into China and Europe: always and everywhere pieces of harness are among the objects that meet our eye. Nomads and drovers with no fixed abode (and consequently no cities), they drive before them their herds of horses, cattle and sheep, from the steppe to the hills and from hills to steppe in time with the seasons. They are bandits, like all their kind, and they go armed, as ready to attack others as to defend themselves, with their bows and keen arrows—arrowheads are plentiful among the finds—with their swords and their long lances, decorated with these stylized animals which were used perhaps as insignia or as totems. They live by hunting the wild beasts that abound in the desert, they pitch the tents of felt used by Turko-Mongol peoples from time immemorial, they are followed by their women wearing gay dresses and ornaments sparkling with glass beads (those beads which we know to-day only by their empty sockets) and no doubt riding with their children and belongings in the same chariots in which they are to appear later. From the picture of the Hsiung-nu of Mongolia which survives from the second century B.C. in the Chinese chronicle of the Han dynasty to the picture of the Huns of the Danube frontier in Ammianus Marcellinus at the end of the fourth century of our era, the same character lives and survives, as does the art which is its product.

III. THE WESTWARD EBB OF THE BARBARIANS OF THE STEPPES

Among and between these nomads, then, there were perpetual eddies. Asia was in flux, and the nations of the steppes were ever ready to take the tide in their affairs which might lead them on to better lands and to booty. The stronger hordes, those with a more energetic ruler to bring them to greater victories, succeeded in subduing the weaker one by one, and enrolling them in their turn to join in assailing fresh tribes or winning fresh booty unless there arose, from China, a strong power to impose order on all alike.

To keep out all these nomads the Chinese emperors had reared a whole system of defences, a veritable *limes*, which was initiated, in 121 B.C., by the great Han monarch Wu-ti. This *limes*, which in more than one feature recalls some sectors of the Roman *limes*, *e.g.* in the area of the Agri Decumates, had been formed, since 108 B.C., of a continuous line of small forts and military colonies from the present city of Su-chou, in Kan-su, as far as Tun-huang, on the border of modern Chinese Turkestan, in the direction of the Tarim. Along this line the Chinese were thenceforward incessantly engaged in holding in check the barbarians, whose chief element was the Turko-Mongol nomad tribes whom they called without distinction by the name Hsiung-nu, probably the same tribes who were called Huns by the people of the West. It was at the western end of this line, on the other hand, that they strove to secure the control of the 'Silk-route' and the suzerainty over the Tarim basin, which the Hsiung-nu had never ceased to challenge. They, therefore, sent expeditions, of which the most famous had been under the second—the 'later'—Han dynasty, when two great Chinese generals, Tou Ku and Pan Ch'ao, had been enabled to crush the Hsiung-nu in A.D. 73 near Lake Barköl and then in 75 near Yar, some distance from Turfan, after a counter-offensive of the barbarians who had succeeded in conquering Kashgaria. The last quarter of the first century had been filled with unceasing struggles of the two generals, above all of Pan Ch'ao, to keep the 'Silk-route' free and to control it. Indeed, when Pan Ch'ao was made governor-general at Kucha in the closing years of the century, he seems to have turned his eyes to the countries of the West, beyond the Tarim, if it is true that he sent his lieutenant Kan Ying to make a reconnaissance to the borders of the Parthian Empire and charged him in A.D. 97 to collect information about the distant Ta-ts'in, the Roman Empire.

But despite the efforts of Pan Ch'ao and, later, those of his son

Pan Yong to maintain the Chinese positions in these regions, the troops of the Celestial Empire were compelled, in the course of the second century, to make a deep withdrawal from the Tarim and then from the *limes*, in order to return to the defensive, and even this defensive was maintained with difficulty when, in the last quarter of the century, the Han dynasty, weakened by risings of which the most serious was that of the 'Yellow-hats' that broke out in Chihli and Ho-nan in 184, sank into anarchy. Throughout all the closing years of the century and the beginning of the third century rebel military chiefs were making themselves masters in the northern, southern and western provinces. It was the beginning of the unhappy period known as 'the Three Kingdoms' (Wei, Wu and Shu), and for nearly a century China was a prey to civil war and consequently unable to police the steppes. The nomads, also, had a free field in Central Asia. This was the great period of the Tungus-Mongol (or Mongol-Tungus) hordes called the Sien-pi, from the middle of the second century masters of Mongolia proper, where they had overwhelmed most of the Hsiung-nu. From there they had succeeded in extending their power by degrees from the peninsula of Liao-tung (north-east of the gulf of Chihli) as far as the Gobi desert, driving back such of the Hsiung-nu as refused to submit to them, some towards the Altai Mountains, others to the borders of China (of which some of these Hsiung-nu had for quite a time become the more or less loyal allies) hard by the Great Wall, in Ordos and to the north of the province of Shan-si.

These very troubled times, in which one gets the impression that the whole of Asia was in ferment, lasted into the second half of the third century. Then the unity of China was restored after a fashion by the Ssu-ma family, who usurped the imperial throne under the name of the Chin dynasty. Once again, as in the Han period, the prestige of China began to make itself felt in Central Asia, where, in their anxiety to escape conquest by the Sien-pi, the Indo-European princes of the Tarim basin did homage to the Celestial Empire (A.D. 285)—their saviour, as they hoped. There was also a tendency for diplomatic relations to be formed at that time between the Chinese Empire and Rome by way of the Tarim region. The annalists, at least, indicate that in A.D. 284 the Chin emperor received presents sent by the Ta-ts'in (the Roman Empire). But this was only a pause. The Celestial Empire, so far from saving others, could only save itself at the cost of admitting within the Great Wall as *foederati* those of the Hsiung-nu who had retired southwards before the Sien-pi. They settled more especially to the north of Shan-si, and, as in the Roman Empire, these foreign protectors were apt to be dangerous if the central government should weaken again, inasmuch as the Chinese, like the Romans, in the course of the third century were obliged to strengthen their army with a number of Hsiung-nu chiefs or generals, who received Chinese titles.

At the beginning of the fourth century the decline of the Chin dynasty hastened the catastrophe. One of the Hsiung-nu generals who had been admitted into the Empire, Liu-yüan, established his authority over all the Hsiung-nu *foederati* and installed himself in A.D. 303–4 at T'ai-yüan, the capital of Shan-si, where he proclaimed himself Emperor in 308. In 311 his son Liu-ts'ung, a kind of ferocious genius, invaded the province of Ho-nan, sacked the Imperial capital Lo-yang, captured the feeble Emperor Chin Huai-ti himself, and had him executed two years later. This was the signal for barbarians from near and far to fall upon China as their prey and to fight over her provinces and her plunder: among the most formidable were the Hsiung-nu, Sien-pi and T'o-pa (another group of Turk or Mongol tribes). The details of this struggle are both bloody and obscure, but they are of much less importance than the stark developments which they produced: the Chinese Empire was systematically dismembered, and its northern provinces Chihli, Shan-si, Shen-si, Shan-tung and Ho-nan were torn from it. This vast and brutal operation served to occupy all the forces of the steppes, a fact which probably explains the temporary lull in the movements of peoples on the eastern frontiers of the Roman Empire in Europe.

During the fourth century, however, the situation gradually changes, and becomes more complex. On the one hand, the wars of neighbouring ethnic groups, and within the groups themselves, started fresh movements which had their repercussions in the steppes; but also the tracts of Mongolia, partially emptied of Sien-pi when they conquered Chihli and Shan-tung (where they split up in exhaustion), were now occupied by new hordes, probably of Mongols, and doubtless from the extremities of the modern Manchuria. They were the Juan-juan, whose swift expansion in Mongolia became in less than fifty years a serious threat to all the Hsiung-nu who still remained: these remnants had breathed more freely since the descent of the Sien-pi upon China, but they now began to feel the pressure of the new arrivals, whose chiefs asserted their superiority by rejecting the Hsiung-nu title of *shan-yü* in favour of the purely Mongol title of *khan*, and proceeded to make themselves masters of all Mongolia and extend their power from the gulf of Corea to the Altai Mountains. Moreover, they drove before them to the south-west, so as to press upon Sogdiana and Bactria, other peoples who now enter the stage of history, notably a group nearly related to the Juan-juan, the Hephthalites (the *Yeta* of the Chinese), who, under the name of Huns which they shared with the Hsiung-nu, were destined to cross swords with Persia and India. Similarly some of the barbarians established in Shen-si in north-western China, seeing no easy conquests in the eastern provinces, set out again in the direction of Central Asia, where one of their chiefs, Fu Chien, later (in A.D. 382) ruled over lands extending to Karashahr and Kucha. In this way the passage became barred on every side.

It was at this time that the groups of the Hsiung-nu, who at the beginning of the third century had been pushed back by the Sien-pi towards the Altai Mountains, advanced towards the extreme west of Asia. The details of the fearful struggle of nomads that ensued are obscure; but its consequences are clear. Driven from the Altai range the Hsiung-nu ended by crossing the steppes which extend to the north of Lake Balkash and the Aral Sea. There two choices lay before them, the route to the south-west towards the Jaxartes valley and the rich lands of Sogdiana and Bactria, or that to the west straight on towards the Volga. But actually at this time their freedom of choice was restricted. The Jaxartes valley had been occupied for more than three centuries by the Yüeh-chih (the Indo-Scythians mentioned by Greek historians), who had been driven from Mongolia or near it about 170 B.C., and after a rough passage had finally settled here, where they acquired a veneer of Greek and Hindu culture and founded a powerful State which at one period, in the first century of our era, had for a time extended beyond the upper Jaxartes valley itself over the valley of the Oxus and the Hindu Kush, the lands watered by the Indus, Pamir, Kashmir, the Panjab, and the plain of the Ganges above Benares. Certainly this was already ancient history, and partially effaced by their reverses from the beginning of the third century onwards in obscure wars against the Sassanids of Persia and the Gupta princes of India; but hard pressed as they were by their enemies in the south, the Yüeh-chih could still hold the regions of the Jaxartes securely enough, and this being so the western Hsiung-nu had no alternative but to keep straight on. About A.D. 355 they advanced westwards with the intention of forcing their way at all costs across the great plain of Russia.

This was the date at which the 'great invasions' of the West begin. The Hsiung-nu, who had hitherto made history exclusively in the East, now suddenly proceeded, under their new name of Huns, to contribute their chapter to the history of Europe.

To study the nations of the steppes, though it may set us more problems than it resolves, does answer some questions. The barbarian invasions of the early Middle Ages are in a sense no more than a sequel of the struggles which for so long had had the steppes of Asia for their main battlefield, or at any rate the only battlefield of which historical texts (the Chinese annalists) have anything to tell us. Our literary sources in general tell us of the developments in Mongolia and on the Yellow River and of those on the banks of the Danube; but between the two tales there is a gap. Here archaeology comes to our aid and supplies the missing link in our chain of evidence: it is certainly not pure coincidence that the early medieval art in Europe known as 'barbarian art' is really only the continuation, almost without change, of what we have hitherto called 'the art of the steppes.'

It is impossible without going far beyond the chronological limits of this chapter to give this fact its full and proper emphasis, though the researches of the experts increasingly illustrate it. But one need only remember that it is from the soil of Hungary and Wallachia, from tombs in the lands occupied by our European Huns after they had broken down the barrier of the Goths, that perhaps the most numerous and certainly the most characteristic specimens have been recovered of an art that, with different manifestations and traditions, reappears in the tombs of the Goths, Franks, Burgundians, Vandals, Lombards, and of all the Germanic peoples of the West. Bronze cauldrons of the Huns identical with those of Minusinsk and Ordos have been found by the River Kapos in the heart of Hungary; the same knives also; and the jewels in glassware, the fibulae, the clasps, the perforated baldric-plates, the pins with animal heads which characterized the art of early medieval Europe are nothing if not the ancient art of the steppes. The steppes, it seems, have overflowed over Europe. The historian is thus justified in crossing the arbitrary boundaries of two so-called continents which are really the complement of each other, in quest of the principle of continuity without which history itself becomes a riddle without an answer.

CHAPTER IV

SASSANID PERSIA

I. THE SASSANIAN EMPIRE: POLITICAL HISTORY

TOWARDS the close of the Second Century of our era the king of Persis, a vassal of the Arsacid Great King, had his capital at Stakhr (Istakhr) not far from Persepolis. The ruling dynasty was that of the Basrangi, but the province of Persis contained local principalities most of which were more or less independent. Gochihr, the king at Stakhr, was attacked and put to death by Pabhagh, son of Sassan, a high dignitary at the Temple of Anahita in Stakhr, and of a Basrangian princess, whose name seems to have been Denagh[1]. The successor of Pabhagh as king of Persis was his eldest son Shapur, but Ardashir (Artakhshatr, Artaxerxes), brother of Shapur and lord of Darabgerd with the exalted military title of *hargobadh* (p. 114), rose in revolt against him and became king in A.D. 208[2], Shapur having died suddenly, in consequence of an accident, if the tradition may be trusted[3].

After having reduced to submission all the local princes of Persis, Ardashir seized the neighbouring province of Kerman, next Ispahan, Susiana and Mesene. At this point the Great King Artabanus V marched to attack in person this dangerous rebel, but was defeated and killed, in A.D. 224[4], in a great battle which was fought according to Tabari in a plain called Hormizdeghan, the whereabouts of which cannot be fixed. After conquering the western provinces of the Arsacid Empire, Ardashir had himself crowned in due form (A.D. 226) and took the title of King of Kings (*Shāhānshāh*) of Iran[5]. Later expeditions won by arms the eastern

---

[1] *KbZ* ll. 27–28. *KbZ* = the new inscription of the 'Ka'ba of Zoroaster,' on which see the Bibliography to this chapter I, 1, E.

[2] The date is made certain by the inscription recently found at Shapur (Sh. Shap.). See the comments of A. Christensen in the article of R. Ghirshman, *Rev. des arts asiat.* X, 1936, p. 127 *sq.*

[3] The chronicle of Tabari is here the chief source. The genealogy of Ardashir which it gives is found also in the inscriptions. According to *KbZ* l. 28, the mother of Ardashir was named Rodhagh. A popular legend makes Ardashir, as formerly Cyrus, of humble origin; the Kārnāmagh, Agathias II, 27: see Christensen, *Les gestes des rois dans les traditions de l'Iran antique*, pp. 78 *sqq.*

[4] Or 227 if the second Sassanian epoch year is followed (see above, vol. XI, p. 111); the year 224 is implied by the inscription (Sh. Shap.) mentioned above (note 2). [5] See Volume of Plates V, 234, *a.*

countries Seistan (Sacastene), Gurgan (Hyrcania), Abharshahr (the modern Khorassan), Merv (Margiana), Balkh (Bactria), Khvarezm (Chorasmia). Ardashir also seized Bahrein, and finally the King of Kushan, ruler of the Valley of Cabul and of the Panjab, and the Kings of Turan (Quzdar south of Quetta) and of Makuran (now Mekran) recognized him as suzerain[1]. The war of conquest which Ardashir waged against Rome is described later in this chapter.

According to a tradition of doubtful value, Ardashir had taken to wife an Arsacid princess, who was the mother of the prince Shapur. At all events, Shapur, whom his father named heir to the crown, was a grown man in 224, when he fought in the battle against Artabanus. Ardashir's consort was probably that Adhur-Anahid whose name is found[2] with the title of 'Queen of Queens' (*bānbishnān bānbishn*). Her name—the 'Fire of Anahita'—may have been given to her to commemorate Ardashir's coronation at the fire-temple of Anahita at Stakhr. For this city remained the holy city of the dynasty: four centuries later, according to Tabari, the last Sassanid King, Yazdgard III, was crowned in that same temple. But the capital of the Empire and the seat of the new dynasty, as of its predecessor, was Ctesiphon.

Ardashir adopted, in its main lines, the organization and administrative institutions of the Parthian State, as is attested by the survival under the Sassanids of political and bureaucratic terminology in the north-western dialect (Arsacid Pahlavi). What differentiated the new Empire from that of the Parthians was, first of all, a strong centralization, which substituted a unified State for a loose congeries of vassal kingdoms. Such of its governors as were of the royal stock bore the title of *shāh*, but were none the less no more than high officials in the Great King's service. The feudal system did not cease to exist. The *vāspuhrs*, the chiefs of the feudal nobility, marched to war at the head of the levy of their subjects, but these armies of peasants were ill organized and of slight military value. Mercenaries also became more important. The aristocratic mail-clad cavalry, which formed the élite of the army, was probably recruited from the lesser feudal nobles who were directly dependent on the crown. Furthermore, the fiefs of the great families were scattered throughout all the corners of the Empire. The administrative division into cantons was not organically connected with the several kinds of provincial govern-

---

[1] The account in Tabari is confirmed by the evidence of coins and by a bas-relief at Salmas. See E. Herzfeld, *Paikuli*, pp. 36 *sqq.*

[2] In *KbZ* l. 24.

ments, which were all rather military in character. This was aimed at preventing the governments from being feudal in tradition and from becoming hereditary principalities.

The second characteristic of the Sassanid State is the creation of an official Church resting on Mazdean doctrine, which had been for centuries the common faith of the Iranian people and which the Parthian kings had followed with a zeal that grew as iranism prevailed over hellenism. The organization of the Mazdean—or, one may say, Zoroastrian—religion into a State Church, like the centralization of the royal power which it completed, was doubtless an innovation, but one which consummated a slow evolution. This powerful Church was a very distinctive element in the civilization of the Sassanian period. The *Avesta*, the Holy Writ of Mazdeism, had probably been set down in Aramaic characters in the Arsacid period. According to the Zoroastrian tradition Ardashir I caused a high clerical official (*ēhrbadhan ēhrbadh*), Tansar, his chief helper in the task of organizing the Mazdean Church, to have the scattered texts of this Arsacid *Avesta* collected and to produce a new edition of it which was authorized and made canonical[1].

Ardashir, who died in A.D. 241, was followed by his son, Shapur I, who was not formally crowned till 242[2]. It seems that the peoples of the Caspian provinces in the northern and eastern marches had taken advantage of the change of kings to rise in rebellion, for the Chronicle of Arbela states that Shapur, in the first year of his reign, fought against and reduced to obedience the Chorasmians, the Medes of the mountains (*i.e.* of Atropatene), the Gelae, the Dailamites and the Hyrcanians. Furthermore, the Pahlavi work 'The cities of the Iranian Empire' (*Shahrestānēhā ī Ērānshahr*)[3] relates that he defeated a king named Pahlezagh in Khorassan, the eastern area of the kingdom, where he proceeded to found the strong city of Nev-Shapur (Nishapur). He took the title of 'King of Kings of Iran and Non-Iran.'

The war against Rome ended with the peace of A.D. 244 (p. 131). The Arab fortress of Hatra, south of what had been Nineveh, which had held out against the attacks of Ardashir, was reduced by Shapur. In Armenia the king Tiridates of a collateral

---

[1] Prof. H. S. Nyberg, in a recent work, *Irans forntida religioner* (Stockholm, 1937), adopts a highly sceptical view of the details of the traditional narrative concerning the composition and collecting of the *Avesta*.

[2] Volume of Plates v, 234, *b*.

[3] J. Markwart—G. Messina, *A Catalogue of the Provincial Capitals of Eranshahr*, pp. 12, 52-3.

branch of the Arsacid dynasty fled in 252 or 253 on the appearance of a Persian army, which occupied the country. Then followed a new Perso-Roman war, in which the Emperor Valerian suffered a complete defeat and was taken prisoner (p. 135). This triumph was immortalized by a series of Persian reliefs[1]. But Odenathus the king of Palmyra, the great trading city in the Syrian Desert, joined forces with what remained of the Roman troops and harried the Persian army till it was driven beyond the Euphrates. Though Shapur repeatedly attacked Palmyra it was without success. Later, Tiridates returned to Armenia and once more ruled that country.

The statesmanship and military qualities of Shapur I marked him out as the worthy son of his father, and like his father he made the succession secure by nominating the prince who was to follow him. The Chronicle of Arbela describes him as harsh and stern. But hard as he was to enemies within and without, he displayed a notable tolerance in matters of religion. It is a well-attested fact that he showed goodwill towards the great heretic Mani, whose teaching was anathema to the Mazdean clergy, and Mani dedicated to the king one of his chief works, the *Shāhpuhraghān*[2]. According to the Armenian Chronicle of Elisaeus Vardapet, a chief of the Magi, in a speech to the Armenians two centuries later, related how Shapur, after vainly attempting to stamp out Christianity, changed his policy and forbade the Magi and chiefs of the Magi to continue their persecution, and proclaimed that 'Magi, Manichaean (*Zandīgh*), Jew, Christian and all men of whatever religion, should be left undisturbed and at peace in their belief in the several provinces of Persia[3].' In this connection may also be remembered the part played by Shapur in the story of the composition of the Sassanian *Avesta*.

According to the Parsee tradition, the king caused to be included among the holy books secular works on medicine, astronomy and metaphysics found in India, Greece and other countries. It is probable that these were really works compiled by Iranians

[1] See below, p. 123. It is also, perhaps, the subject of a battle-scene on a fresco at Doura (M. Rostovtzeff, *Caravan Cities*, pp. 210 *sqq.*) and it is mentioned in the inscription *KbZ* l. 13 in connection with the city of Urhai (Edessa).

[2] For Manichaeism, see below, pp. 504 *sqq.*

[3] See V. Langlois, *Coll. des historiens de l'Arménie*, II, p. 203 *sq.* E. Herzfeld has called attention to a passage, unfortunately mutilated, in the inscription of Kartēr Hormizd, in which there may be a reference to this edict of toleration. It refers to 'Zandīghs, Jews, Shamans, Brahmans, Nazaraeans, Christians and what other religions there are.' See *Arch. Hist. of Iran*, p. 101.

with the use of foreign sources. But, in any event, the inclusion of treatises of this kind among the sacred writings at Shapur's orders is evidence of his broadmindedness[1].

After Shapur's death in 272, the crown passed to his son Hormizd I, who had been governor of Khorassan with the title of Great King of the Kings of the Kushans. He died after reigning a year. His brother Vahram I (273–276)[2], who abandoned Mani to the mercy of the Mazdean clergy (p. 513), and the next King Vahram II (276–293)[3], son of Vahram I, had also been governors of Khorassan before ascending the throne of Iran. Vahram II was at once valiant and energetic. There was again a war with Rome, and the Emperor Carus advanced as far as Ctesiphon, but his sudden death ended the triumphal progress of the Roman army. None the less, a rising in the eastern parts of the Empire drove Vahram in 283 to make peace with Rome, which gained possession of Armenia and Mesopotamia. Hormizd, the Great King's brother, who was then Governor of Khorassan, sought to create for himself an independent kingdom in the east, and had gained the help of the Sacae, the Kushans and the Gelae. Vahram took the field against his brother; crushed the revolt and, after reducing Sacastene to submission, he set up as its governor his son the future Vahram III with the title of King of the Sacae (*Saghān-shāh*). For the prince designed to succeed was always named governor of whatever province was at the moment the most important and the most exposed to attack. The Sassanid Empire now included Hyrcania, all Khorassan, perhaps Chorasmia and Sogdiana, and Sacastene with Makuran and Turan, the countries of the Middle Indus and its delta[4].

Vahram III, after a reign of only four months, lost his crown in 293 in an insurrection staged by his great-uncle Narsah (Narses)[5], son of Shapur I. In the great inscription of Paikuli Narses recounts in detail his triumph and the homage paid to him by the grandees of the Empire and the vassal kings. He began a war with Rome and drove Tiridates from Armenia (p. 132). But the war

---

[1] These parts, as many others, of the Sassanian *Avesta*, which after its completion by Shapur I and revision and final authorization under Shapur II, comprised 21 books or *nasks*, perished during the centuries that followed the fall of the Sassanid Empire. In the eighth and ninth books of the *Dinkart* we possess an epitome of the 21 *nasks*.

[2] Volume of Plates v, 234, *c*.   [3] *Ib.* v, 234, *d*.

[4] So Herzfeld, *Paikuli*, pp. 35–51, who, by means of such inscriptions as were known when that book was published (1924) and of coins, has contributed to elucidate the rather obscure early history of the Sassanid Empire.

[5] Volume of Plates, v, 234, *e*.

was not attended with success and the peace that was made in 298 restored Tiridates to his throne and cost Persia five cantons of Lesser Armenia.

Narses died in 302. The reign of his son, Hormizd II[1] (302–309) passed without great events and was followed by internal wars which ended in the accession of Shapur II, Hormizd's infant son. During his minority his mother ruled jointly with the great nobles, whose power notably increased at the expense of the royal prerogative. But when the young king came of age, he displayed remarkable strength and vigour and contrived to check the ambitions of the feudal notables. Already well advanced in middle life, after subduing with merciless harshness the rebellious Arab tribes, he began in 356 the war of revenge upon Rome.

II. ORGANIZATION AND ADMINISTRATION OF THE SASSANIAN STATE

Sassanian society was marked by the feudal structure which it inherited from the preceding period[2]. Four classes were distinguished: the clergy (*āsravān*), the warriors (*artēshtārān*), the bureaucrats (*dibhērān*, the secretaries) and the commons (*vāstryōshān*, the peasants, and *hutukhshān*, the artisans or workmen). The three first classes formed the aristocracy, which was very firmly marked off from the plebeians. But this division was in theory rather than in fact. The inscription of Shapur I at Hajiabad gives the names of the four classes of the Sassanian high society. The most exalted of these was that of the *shahrdārs*, which, in all probability, comprised the vassal kings of foreign origin and the governors who belonged to the royal family and bore the title of *shāh*. The chiefs of the great feudal houses formed the second class, that of the *vāspuhrs*. Seven families enjoyed peculiar privileges. The first of these was that of the Sassanids[3]. Certain high offices, military and civil, were hereditary in these houses, but little is known of the true character of these offices. The dignity of *hargobadh*[4] belonged by right of birth to the family of the Sassanids.

---

[1] Volume of Plates v, 234, *f*.   [2] See Vol. XI, pp. 120 *sqq*.

[3] Among the others are known the *Kārān Pahlav*, the *Sūrēn Pahlav*, the *Aspāhbadh Pahlav*, the *Spendiyādh* and the *Mihrān*. Kārān (written k.a.r.n. or k.a.r.n.i.), not Kārēn, is the form attested by the inscriptions; *Pahlav* signifies 'Parthian.' A considerable number of eminent families and of names of individual *vāspuhrs* are found in the inscription of the 'Ka'ba of Zoroaster.'

[4] Pronounced *argobadh*. This title, like so many others, is inherited from the Parthian State. A relief of a certain 'Vorōd, the argabad' has been found at Palmyra. See H. Ingholt, 'Inscriptions and Sculptures from Palmyra I', *Berytus*, III, 1936, p. 93.

The third class, the *vuzurgān*, 'the Great Ones,' comprised the Ministers and other heads of the Administration, and the fourth, the *āzādhān*, 'the Free Men,' the lesser nobility, which, scattered through all the Empire, acted largely as inferior functionaries in provincial government. The military aristocracy being also a civilian aristocracy, the *vāspuhrs* were often also members of the class of the *vuzurgān*.

Little is known with precision about this complicated hierarchy. The gradation of society showed itself at every turn, in clothing, the form of the headdress, personal ornaments (rings, girdles, diadems) and in the horses they rode. There were titles of honour, as for example those which gave the name of the king in whose service the bearer of the title had distinguished himself[1]. The wife of a *shāh* was *bānbishn*, the title *Mēshān-bānbishn* (Queen of Mesene) corresponding to *Mēshān-shāh*. The consort of the King of Kings was named Queen of Queens (p. 110).

The inscriptions, especially those previously mentioned, give a large number of titles of high State functionaries. The Chief Minister still had the old title of *hazārobadh*[2]. The 'Chief of the Husbandmen' (*vāstryōshān* [or *vāsrōshān*] *-sardar*) was Minister of Finance, the *spāhbadh* was General of the Army, the *dibhērobadh* Chief of the Secretaries[3], the *handarzbadh* was something like a Minister of Public Instruction. The *kartēr*[4] was beyond doubt one of the most exalted dignitaries but his functions cannot be defined. The title of *ganzobar* 'treasurer' has recently been discovered in an inscription[5]; hitherto this title had not been known in Pahlavi texts. The *mōbadhān mōbadh* was the supreme head of the Mazdean Church. He controlled the priestly dignitaries, the *mōbadhs* and the great body of the inferior Magi (*mōgh*). The superior of all the fire-temple priests (*ēhrbadhs*) had the title of *ēhrbadhān ēhrbadh*. Other high functionaries of the Church were the *dastvar* and the *vardabadh*, the 'Master of Observances[6].' Some titles of court-officials are also known, such as those of the 'Chief of the Court,' the 'Chief Huntsman' and the 'Chief of the

---

[1] Thus the inscriptions (*Paik.* and *KbZ*) give several *Tahm-Shāhpuhr*, a *Shāhpuhr-shnūm* and a *Nokhv-Hormizd* (*tahm* = 'strong'; *shnūm* 'joy'; *nokhv* 'first').

[2] Old Persian *hazārapati*, Greek χιλίαρχος.

[3] The Secretaries (*dibhēr*) were a very important element in the administration. They drafted and registered the royal edicts, conducted the State correspondence and were experts in diplomacy.

[4] See Herzfeld, *Paikuli*, Glossary No. 558. The word is also found in *KbZ* l. 33.   [5] *KbZ* l. 33.

[6] This title is found in *KbZ* l. 32.

Servitors[1].' A curious title is that of the 'sword-wielder' (*shapshērāz*)[2].

In the Parthian period there was a division of the Empire into four toparchies, those of the north, south, east and west[3]. This is found again in the latest phases of the Sassanian period, the toparchs being then designated by the name of *marzbān* (the great *marzbāns* with the title of *shāh*), later by the name of *pādhghōspān*. It may be assumed that the four-fold division of the Empire also existed in the first phase of Sassanian history, but we possess no definite information about it. The title of *marzbān* is not found in the inscriptions of this period, and the existence of the title of *pādhghōspān* in the inscription of Paikuli is not certain[4]. Most probably the four toparchs, during the reigns of the earliest Sassanid Kings as in the age that preceded them, were called *bidhakhsh*[5].

In the two inscriptions referred to above[6] there are also found the titles of a number of vassal kings and governors of royal blood which are made up of the name of the people or province and the word *shāh* (*Armenān-shāh*, *Marv-shāh*, *Kermān-shāh*, *Saghān-shāh*, etc.), and then certain analogous titles ending in *-khvadhāy* ('Master'). The latter inscription gives a series of titles of satraps (*shatrap*) who governed a city with the district round it, such as the satraps of Hamadan, of Gadh or Ispahan and of Nayriz[7]. A little later, under Shapur II, the word *bidhakhsh* was used to designate all the governors of the great provinces[8], and finally, from about the beginning of the fifth century, this title was replaced by that of *marzbān*. Several other titles of administrative officials for the provinces are found in the inscriptions of the third century: for example, a *Saghastān-handarzbadh*, 'Director of Education in Sacastene,' and a *shatrpav-āmārkār*, 'Superintendent

---

[1] *Darbadh, nakhchīrbadh, parastaghbadh.*

[2] Found, like the preceding titles, in the *KbZ*.

[3] Despite the observations of M. Pagliaro in the *Rivista degli studi orientali*, XII, 1929, p. 160 *sq.* the present writer is inclined to believe that the title of the toparchs, in that period, was *bidhakhsh* (*bdeashkh* among the Armenians, who had borrowed their administrative system from the Parthians).

[4] Herzfeld, *Paikuli*, Glossary no. 798.

[5] In the inscription of Paikuli (*ib.* Glossary nos. 214 and 780–1) the *bidhakhsh* is named after the *hargobadh* and the chief of the Sassanid clan and before the *hazārobadh*; the *KbZ* gives the names of a *bidhakhsh* and a *bidhakhshān*, in both instances immediately before the name of a *hazārobadh*.

[6] *Paik.* and *KbZ.*

[7] *Ahmadān-shatrap, Gadhē-shatrap, Nagrīch-shatrap.*

[8] See the list of 'vitaxes' in Ammian. Marc. XXIII, 6, 14.

of accounts to the satrap.' As to the internal administration of the cities during the period in question we are completely without information, though a *vāzārbadh*, 'head of the bazaar,' a high police official, is mentioned in an inscription[1].

III. SOCIAL AND ECONOMIC CONDITIONS

The *Avesta* glorifies agriculture as the best form of livelihood: by working the land man assures himself of all kinds of divine rewards. But though agriculture always enjoyed high esteem, though good kings and good governors always paid attention to the irrigation system, upon which the cultivation of a land as arid as Iran primarily depends, the lot of the peasant, under the feudal system, was not enviable. He was tied to the soil, bound to furnish statutory labour, and to serve as a foot-soldier in war; in addition he was liable both to a personal tax and to a land tax. The personal tax was fixed at a yearly sum, which was divided out among the taxpayers by the authorities: the land tax, before the fiscal reform of the sixth century, was so arranged that after an assessment of the harvest each canton had to pay from a sixth to a third, according to the fertility of the soil. The lot of the city-dwellers was more pleasant: they had to pay the personal tax, but were probably relieved of military service, and they controlled commerce and other profitable professions.

Ctesiphon, the capital of the Empire, was an aggregate of two large fortified cities on the east and west of the Tigris, Ctesiphon proper, and Seleuceia, which had been destroyed by Avidius Cassius in A.D. 165 and was rebuilt by Ardashir I under the name of Veh-Ardashir. This double town lay outside Iranian territory proper, and its populace was a mixture of differing races, but it held a central position in international commerce. At Ctesiphon caravans coming from the west through Edessa and Nisibis (for the route through Palmyra and Doura was given up after the fall of the Palmyrene kingdom) could meet caravans that had come from India by the Cabul Valley, or from China along the Tarim basin, and then through Turkestan, Khorassan, Raï (Rhagae) and Hamadan (see above, p. 98). Other great routes linked Raï with the Caspian provinces, and Hamadan with Susiana and the Persian Gulf, crossing the kingdom of Persis. One provision in a treaty that Diocletian offered the Persians in 298 (p. 336), which would have restricted communication between Persia and Rome to Nisibis only, was firmly rejected by Narses. In Iran the Chinese

---

[1] *KbZ* l. 34.

bought Babylonian carpets, precious stones from Syria, Iranian rouge for the eyebrows, and textiles from Syria and Egypt; their principal export was silk, above all raw silk, which the Iranians re-exported, sometimes in the raw, sometimes after working it up. The sea-borne commerce of the Persians was concentrated mainly on the old harbours and those new ports recently constructed by Ardashir I within the Persian Gulf, at Mesene and at Charax; here the Arab population made splendid sailors.

Among the industries of the Persian Empire the making of textiles reached a high pitch of perfection. The Sassanid kings, like their Persian and Parthian predecessors, spared no pains to create new industries, for which they could call on the technical knowledge of their prisoners of war. Thus Shapur I exploited to the full the engineering skill of the Romans by making the prisoners from Valerian's army build the great dam at Shoshtar, a fine piece of construction that has survived to this day.

IV. THE STATE-RELIGION AND FOREIGN RELIGIONS

The *Gathas*, that is the metrical preaching of Zoroaster, expound the doctrines of the prophet in their original purity. The more recent parts of the *Avesta*, where older deities, rejected or ignored by Zoroaster, make a re-appearance, represent a compromise between Zoroastrianism and popular belief. In the last centuries before Christ two different systems of Mazdeism had sprung into being: one sect regarded Space, the other Time, as the original Principle, which produced the Good and the Bad Spirit (Ormuzd and Ahriman)[1]. Of these rival systems the second, 'Zervanism' (*zervān* = Time), was ultimately triumphant, and 'Vayism' (*vayu* = Space) has only left faint traces in the tradition. The Zervanist teaching, popularized in a creation-story in which first Ahriman and then Ormuzd were born from the bosom of the primordial god, Zervān (or according to other accounts, of his wife), in time prevailed completely, and this view breaks through in Mithraism as later in Manichaeism; indeed, the official Mazdeism of the Sassanid era is frankly Zervanist. But the Parsees after the fall of the Sassanids gave up Zervanism: the cosmogony myths of the Sassanid *Avesta* have disappeared, and the Pahlavi religious books have been so recast and edited that but few traces of Zervanism survive.

But it is not only the Zervanist view which differentiates Sassanid Mazdeism from medieval and modern Parseeism. Occa-

[1] Eudemus Rhodius (Damascius, *de primis principiis*, ed. Ruelle 1, p. 322).

sional hints dropped by foreign writers—Armenian, Syrian, or Byzantine—which are confirmed here and there by survivals of the native tradition, reveal the religious beliefs of the Sassanids in an unexpected guise. True that Ormuzd was always revered as the divine head of all good creatures, and those peculiarly Zoroastrian abstract deities, the *Amesha-Spenta* (*Amahrspand* in Pahlavi), as his chief helpers. But sacerdotal lore was particularly busy with such deities as *Mihr* (Mithra), originally a god of the morning light, who became a sun-god, *Ādhur*, god of fire, *Dēn Mazdayasn*, 'Mazdean Faith' personified (also called *Bēdukht*, 'Daughter of God')—and these three deities formed, together with Ormuzd, a tetrad of creative powers. Or by associating the primordial god, Zervān, with these four, a man had five supreme deities to worship. The *magi* apparently even took over some gods and goddesses who were not originally Iranian: *Nānā* or *Nānāī* (who was identified, probably, with the ancient goddess *Anāhīd*), *Bēl* and *Nabhō*.

Finally, Sassanid Mazdeism included some features which clashed curiously with the original spirit of Zoroastrianism, and which were undoubtedly due to the pessimistic mentality which dominated Western Asia during the first centuries of our era. According to the Zervanist view, Ahriman, the elder of the twins, held by right, from the very beginning, control of the world, and so the life of the universe, which is to last in all for 9000 years (after a preliminary stage of 3000 years), is filled throughout by a fight between the two Spirits, though it is true that the fight is to end in the victory of Ormuzd. Another Zervanist myth told how woman fell because Ahriman seduced her, and how in consequence she became his natural ally[1].

Fire-worship is one of the elements of the ancient Aryan religion to which the *magi* gave new life. There were house-fires, village-fires, and provincial-fires. The most sacred of all were the *Farrbagh* or Priest's fire, the *Gushnasp* or Warrior's fire, and the *Burzēn Mihr* or Farmer's fire. The exact position of the first is still disputed[2]. Gushnasp had his temple at Ganzak in Azerbaijan; it was the fire of the Kings too. The temple of Burzēn Mihr rose

---

[1] The most recent researches on the ideas and doctrines of Sassanid Mazdeism are: H. S. Nyberg, *Journ. Asiat.* 1931, ii, pp. 1 *sqq.* and 193 *sqq.*; E. Benveniste, *Monde Orient.* 1932, pp. 170 *sqq.*; Christensen, *L'Iran sous les Sassanides*, pp. 136–54, and Nyberg, *Irans forntida religioner* (1937).

[2] See A. V. Williams Jackson, *J.A.O.S.*, 1921, pp. 81 *sqq.*; E. Herzfeld, *Arch. Mitt. aus Iran*, i, pp. 182 *sqq.*; A. Pagliaro, *Orient. Stud. in Honour of C. E. Pavry*, p. 383.

amid the mountains of Revan, to the north-west of Nishapur; the name (meaning 'Mithra the Lofty') betrays a close connection with *Mithra*, just as the common name for the provincial fires, 'Vahram-fires,' shows that these fires were dedicated to the god of the victorious assault and of war, *Vahrām* (*Vrthraghna*). The present writer inclines to the view that the Gushnasp fire had special connections with Ormuzd—for in the rock sculptures it is Ormuzd who invests the king with power—and the Farrbagh fire with the *Dēn Mazdayasn*.

Sassan, the grandfather of Ardashir I, was, as has been observed (p. 109), the head of the temple of Anahita at Stakhr. It was a temple towards which the Sassanid family showed great devotion throughout, and it has recently[1] been identified with the 'Ka'ba of Zoroaster,' an Achaemenid building, at the foot of which has been discovered a long Pahlavi inscription, telling of the institution of fires for the souls of princes and of other great personages[2].

Both the Arsacid and the Sassanid fire-temples conform to one type: a square building, surmounted by a cupola, within which the sacred fire was kept burning upon an altar in a room that remained completely dark, so that it could not be touched by the light of the sun[3]. Excavations carried out by the French at Shapur in 1935–1936 have brought to light the ruins of a fire-temple, which dates probably from the first century of the Sassanian era. It is a square building with an external vaulted corridor: four bull-headed corbels, two of which still survive upon the north-east wall, most of which is preserved, appear to have acted as supports for the roof-beams. Inside, a square flagstone was perhaps the base for the fire-altar[4].

From the pictures given on the reverse of Sassanian coins we can recognize the different types of the fire-altar. On those of Ardashir I is depicted a fire burning upon a tripod, which stands upon a column[5]. Coins of later kings show us the altar, in the form of a column and without tripod, flanked by two men holding in their hands some rod-like object. Running round the coin is frequently found the legend 'Fire of. . .,' followed by the name of the king who issued it. Upon the votive monument of Shapur I,

[1] By M. Sprengling.
[2] See the Bibliography to this chapter, I, E.
[3] Herzfeld, *Arch. Hist. of Iran*, pp. 88 *sqq.*
[4] Volume of Plates v, 140, *a.* See G. Salles and R. Ghirshman, *Rev. des arts asiat.* x, 1936, pp. 117 *sqq.*
[5] Volume of Plates v, 234, *a.*

discovered not far from the above-mentioned temple, the words 'fire of Ardashir' and 'fire of Shapur' give the date of the coronation of these two kings. From this the present writer draws the conclusion that the fire shown upon the coins is the one that the king consecrated at the ceremony of his coronation, to be the symbolic protector of his reign[1].

Each of these great temples and of the fires of Vahram, which were established in the provinces, had a considerable body of priests under the direction of a '*mōbadh*' or of a '*mōghān mōgh*' ('Magus of the magi') to serve it. '*Ēhrbadhs*' kept watch over the ceremonies of divine worship, assisted by lower clergy, each of whom had his special task.

In addition there were several foreign religious communities in the Sassanid Empire. Jews were numerous, above all in the cities of Mesopotamia and of Babylonia, particularly at Seleuceia-Ctesiphon; here dwelt their civil and religious head, the *Rēsh Gālūtā*, whose election had to be confirmed by the Great King. At Doura *graffiti* and some short inscriptions in Sassanian Pahlavi have been found in the ruins of a synagogue[2]. Even in the purely Iranian territory there existed Jewish colonies in the cities.

Christianity first began to spread in Western Iran towards the end of the Arsacid era, thanks to the zeal of the missionaries of Edessa[3]. East of the Tigris there was a bishopric of Arbela. Then later the transplantation of prisoners of war, in obedience to the orders of Shapur I and of his successors, helped towards the propagation of Christianity even in the more distant provinces. Bishoprics were created, and in spite of internal dissensions a Christian Church, with Syriac for its language, was gradually organized in Iran under the primacy of the Bishop of Seleuceia-Ctesiphon (the *katholikos*). In Armenia King Tiridates introduced Christianity towards the close of the third century.

In the eastern regions of the empire Buddhism claimed many followers. Paintings, which recall the style of the reliefs of the time of Shapur I, discovered in the niches of the colossal statues of Buddha at Bamiyan, to the east of Cabul[4], and coins issued by 'the worshipper of Mazdah,' the famous *Kūshānshāh* Peroz (brother of Shapur I), figuring the image of Buddha, bear striking testimony to a peaceful rapprochement between the two religions.

Apart from this the Mazdean clergy were somewhat disdainful

---

[1] See the Bibliography to this chapter, I, E.
[2] A. Pagliaro, *Excavations at Dura-Europos*, VIth *Rep.* 1932–33, pp. 393 *sqq.*
[3] See below, p. 493.
[4] See below, p. 124.

in their relations with non-Mazdeans, and to a certain extent intolerant, especially towards dangerous innovators such as the Manichaeans[1]. But the adherents of foreign religions were able to live in peace, their organizations and their religious laws were respected, so long as they did not set themselves up against the authority of the State or conspire with its enemies. It was political reasons more than religious intolerance that brought about the first great persecution of the Christians under Shapur II.

V. THE ARTS

Practically nothing is known of any literary activity during the first century of the Sassanian era. The only fact that demands notice is the reshaping and editing of the *Avesta*, which has already been mentioned (see above, p. 112).

In architecture, the ancient Sassanid palaces preserved the arrangement of the rooms practically as it had been under the Achaemenids. But the exterior of the buildings was entirely altered. The essential features of this new architecture have been briefly summarized thus[2]: 'The pillared halls, with a flat roof, were henceforth and for ever replaced by vaulted and domed rooms. The Sassanids transformed the square and octagon in their rooms into the round and the cupola by introducing for this purpose in the four corners pendentives, angle-brackets which are equally adapted to the square and to the dome. This profound talent for construction enabled them to create new proportions: the great hall at Ctesiphon has a diameter of nearly eighty feet.'

There still exist considerable remains of two large palaces, which allow us to form some idea of this third-century architecture; one, the palace at Firuzabad (Ardashir-Khvarreh), south of Stakhr, built by Ardashir I, the other the palace at Ctesiphon, now called the Taq-e-Kesra, which Herzfeld regards as the work of Shapur I[3]. The outer walls of Firuzabad were windowless, but furnished with blind arcading and lofty attached columns. At Taq the north wing collapsed in 1888; in the centre of the façade of this was a lofty arch that opened on to a huge elliptical vault extending over the whole depth of the building, which formed the hall of audience[4]; here, too, the outer wall was windowless, but ornamented with niches, attached columns, and blind arcading in four storeys. Herzfeld regards this as an imitation of a Roman

---

[1] See below, pp. 504 *sqq.*
[2] See L. Morgenstern, *Esthétiques d'Orient et d'Occident*, p. 91.
[3] See Herzfeld, *Arch. Hist. of Iran*, p. 94.
[4] Volume of Plates v, 140, *b.*

theatre. None the less, this colossal ruin, rising in the midst of the desert, produces an overwhelming effect.

The rock-hewn sculptures of the first Sassanid kings usually represent the investiture of the king by Ormuzd or depict scenes of triumph or battle. The arrangement of the figures is formal. Some reliefs have an accompanying inscription: in others the shape of the crown affords us a means of identifying the king, since each king had a crown peculiar to him, and the shape of these crowns is known from coins. The king's hair falls in regular ringlets and the end of the beard is knotted into a ring; behind his head pleated ribbons float out; he usually wears a necklace, earrings and other ornaments. If he is on horseback the harness of the royal mount is furnished with various ornaments, and a large pear-shaped ball, attached to the horse's flanks by chains, hangs loosely down.

In most of these investiture reliefs Ormuzd is seen, in archaic dress, a mural crown on his head, stretching out to the king the ribboned ring, symbol of royal power. Ardashir I has left two such reliefs; one, in a poor state of preservation, at Naqsh-e-Rajab, where both god and king are on foot; in the second, at Naqsh-e-Rostam[1], they are both on horseback[2]; the same attitude is found in the relief of Shapur I at Naqsh-e-Rajab and that of Vahram I on the rock of Shapur[3]—one of the finest works of art of this whole period. On the relief of Narses at Naqsh-e-Rostam, the king and the goddess Anahita, who is bestowing the royal ring on him, are both on foot[4].

The triumph of Shapur I over Valerian is depicted no less than five times, at Naqsh-e-Rostam and at Shapur[5]. In the rock-hewn carvings at Shapur, the chief scene, common to all these reliefs, showing the Roman Emperor throwing himself on his knees before the Great King on horseback, forms the centre of a vast composition in which Persian soldiers and Roman prisoners are depicted in several ranks one above the other. The workmanship of these

[1] The cliffs of Naqsh-e-Rajab and of Naqsh-e-Rostam are in the neighbourhood of Stakhr and Persepolis; those of Shapur more to the south-west, near Kazerun.

[2] See Sarre and Herzfeld, *Iranische Felsreliefs*, Pls. 12 and 5; Volume of Plates, v, 142, *a*.

[3] *Felsreliefs*, pls. 13 and 41. It should be observed that the relief of Vahram I has an inscription of Narses, who annexed this monument for himself: Herzfeld, *Paikuli* p. 173. See Volume of Plates v, 142, *b*.

[4] *Felsreliefs*, pl. 9.

[5] *Felsreliefs*, pls. 7, 44, 45 and 43; Herzfeld, *Arch. Hist. of Iran*, pp. 83–86, pl. 11 below and 12 above; see Volume of Plates, v, 148.

carvings differs greatly, and this difference in style proves, as has been observed, 'how strongly not only foreign influences but foreign hands must have been at work in Sassanian sculpture[1].'

A relief carved on the cliff at Shapur, representing the triumph of a king (possibly Shapur I) over an Indian people[2], is of great interest because it depicts the king seated in the centre with legs crossed, in that position of frontality which stresses the imposing figure of the monarch[3]. In a relief at Naqsh-e-Rajab Shapur I is shown on horseback, in front of a gathering of notables of the Empire[4].

Vahram II had carved on the cliff at Shapur his triumph over some tribe (probably Arabian)[5], and is perhaps the hero of a battle-scene; here the king, on his horse, with the royal banner flying, is shown galloping at full speed upon an enemy, whose lance drops broken before his victorious onslaught[6]. A similar scene is met earlier in a relief of Ardashir I at Firuzabad, where the foe overthrown by the king's lance is probably Artabanus the Arsacid[7]. At Naqsh-e-Rostam, on the right of the investiture-scene of Ardashir I, Vahram II had himself depicted in peaceful guise in the bosom of his family[8].

The effect of these Sassanid reliefs is pictorial rather than sculptural; they are paintings reproduced in stone. We can recognize some elements of this style in wall-paintings and in Arsacid and Sassanid *graffiti* at Doura[9] and in three *graffiti* discovered at Persepolis[10]. A wall-painting, partially preserved, at Dokhtar-e-Nushirvan, to the north of Bamiyan in Afghanistan, shows us a Sassanid prince, governor of the country, seated on his throne in a frontal position[11]. Some Manichaean paintings from the caves of Khotcho[12], and some delicate Manichaean miniatures, depicting a concert and a group of Manichaean priests, pen in hand, seated at

---

[1] *Arch. Hist. of Iran*, p. 83.

[2] *Felsreliefs*, pl. 40; *Arch. Hist.* pl. 12.

[3] See below, p. 558.   [4] *Felsreliefs*, pl. 11.

[5] *Ib.* pl. 42.   [6] *Ib.* pl. 6.

[7] Herzfeld, *Arch. Hist. of Iran*, pl. 11, above.

[8] *Felsreliefs*, pl. 5.

[9] Fr. Cumont, *Les Fouilles de Doura-Europos*, ii, Atlas, Paris, 1926, pls. 98 and 99; M. Rostovtzeff and A. Little, 'La maison des fresques', *Mém. de l'Ac. des inscriptions*, XLIII, 1932, pp. 167 *sqq.*; Rostovtzeff, *Caravan Cities*, pp. 194–5, 211, and pl. 35.

[10] Herzfeld, *Arch. Hist. of Iran*, p. 80.

[11] A. and Y. Godard and J. Hackin, *Les antiquités bouddhiques de Bāmiyān*, pp. 65 *sqq.* and pl. 42.

[12] A. von le Coq, *Chotscho*, Berlin, 1913, with plates (esp. pl. 5).

their desks, furnish us with some further ideas upon this branch of Sassanid art[1].

The French excavations at Shapur have brought to light a hitherto unprecedented piece of work. It is a monument dedicated in honour of Shapur I, and clearly carried out by Roman workmen[2]. So far there have been uncovered the lower part of two columns, on the shaft of one of which is a Pahlavi inscription (referred to as *Sh. Shap.*), two Corinthian capitals which crowned these columns, a knee in marble (probably the remains of a statue of Shapur, of which the inscription speaks), and the torso of a woman, dressed in antique costume, also in marble[3].

Carved and chased silver cups were a speciality of the Sassanid Empire. Among existing examples two at least belong to the early period of Sassanian art[4]. One, in the British Museum, represents Shapur I hunting deer; the other, in the Hermitage Museum at Leningrad, shows us Vahram I hunting wild boars[5].

Society in Sassanid Iran rested on three pillars: the monarchy, the aristocracy, the Zoroastrian clergy. These three factors worked together or strove against each other according as the central power was strong or weak. In this play of forces the personality of the king was all-important. In the first century of the Sassanid period the royal power was, during most of the time, strong enough to unite the higher classes in a common task, which resulted in the strengthening of the State against foreign enemies and the consolidation of the social structure. From the achievement of this task the period derived its characteristic spirit and style. The seeds of Sassanian civilization had begun to germinate in the soil of Iran before Alexander, but hellenism continued to influence it across the national and religious consciousness which was made active by the first Sassanid kings. Upon this union of iranism and hellenism was built up the imposing edifice of the Sassanian State and society, that Empire which was a worthy antagonist of Rome in the wars to be described in the following section.

[1] See Volume of Plates v, 144, *a*.　　　　[2] *Ib.* 144, *b*.
[3] G. Salles and R. Ghirshman, *Rev. des arts asiat.* x, 1936, pp. 117–129.
[4] Volume of Plates v, 146, *a*, *b*.
[5] K. Erdmann, *Jahrb. der preuss. Kunstsammlungen*, LVII, 1936, p. 197, figs. 1 and 2.

VI. THE PERSIAN WARS WITH ROME

The rise to power of Ardashir, the first king of the Sassanid dynasty, and his conquest of the provinces of Parthia have already been described. It was the extension of this power to the west of what had been Parthia that led Persia to a clash with Rome.

After the fall of Ctesiphon Ardashir extended his authority over Assyria—the land on the upper Tigris, the later Mosul, for in after years the official name of this province was Budh-Ardashir[1]. But an attack on the strongly fortified desert city of Hatra was a failure. The king, however, succeeded in reducing Greater Media whose principal city Ecbatana-Hamadan he captured. Under the impression produced by this success Parthia also, it would seem, came over to his side[2]. A further attack on Lesser Media— Atropatene (Azerbaijan)—and Armenia met with a resolute resistance. The Armenian king, Chosroes I[3], was an Arsacid, a near relative, though hardly blood-brother[4], of the dethroned Parthian king, Artabanus. It was with him that the sons of Artabanus had found an asylum and support. A tetradrachm of Artavasdes of the year 227–8 was probably minted in Atropatene and from it we learn of the rule of one of the sons of Artabanus in this district. Though a bas-relief of Ardashir in Salmas may represent the homage of an Armenān-shāh[5], considering the evidence derived from our other sources we have no ground for inferring at the most more than a partial success. For the king of Armenia reinforced by contingents from the tribes of the Caucasus[6] was able to hold up the advance of Ardashir's armies in Atropatene and, if we may trust the Armenian authorities, also in Adiabene, and compelled the Persians to retreat. It is possible that Chosroes also appealed for support to Severus Alexander, though it is certain that at that time no help of any importance was given him. In Rome, it is true, as reports came in from the frontier provinces, the new situation in the East was watched with anxiety, but it was still hoped that peace could be maintained. But Ardashir might reasonably suspect in the unyielding

---

[1] E. Herzfeld, *Paikuli*, p. 37.

[2] Dio LXXX, 3, 2 *sq.* (p. 475 Boissevain).

[3] Cf. Baumgartner in P.W. *s.v.* Chosroes (3), col. 2445 and F. Justi, *Iranisches Namenbuch*, p. 134 *s.v.* Husrawanh, no. 8.

[4] So the Greek Agathangelus 1, 9 (*F.H.G.* v, 2, p. 115a).

[5] Cf. Herzfeld, *op. cit.* p. 37.

[6] Cf. P. Asdourian, *Die politischen Beziehungen zwischen Armenien und Rom*, p. 122 *sq.* with Von Gutschmid, *Z.D.M.G.* XXXI, 1877, p. 47 *sq.*

resistance of Armenia, Rome's ally, the influence of the Roman government; it is therefore not surprising that his next attack was directed against the Empire itself. In 230 the Sassanid invaded Mesopotamia. He besieged, though without success, the fortress of Nisibis, while his cavalry already threatened Cappadocia and Syria. The watchword of the campaign was restoration of the ancient frontiers of the Persian Empire—the frontiers which had formerly been held under the Achaemenids. It was an expression of that strong national feeling with which Ardashir had inspired his followers and which, united with the conviction that possessing the true and genuine religion they might rest assured of the divine favour, gave alike to the King and to his army a new enthusiasm.

In Rome men had still not realized, they had not even dreamed, that the new master of the neighbouring Eastern Kingdom was a man of a different mould from that of his Parthian predecessors. Only thus is it conceivable that a reference to former victories of Rome should be thought sufficient to drive him back to his own land. Indeed he was the less likely to be impressed thereby since the last engagement of the Romans under Macrinus with that Artabanus whom Ardashir had conquered was in no wise such as to suggest the superiority of the imperial forces (p. 50). The Roman embassy thus returned without success. In A.D. 231, while Severus Alexander was mobilizing his army, it would seem that further attacks of the Persians were made on border fortresses[1], although with no more favourable result for Ardashir than in the preceding year. The Roman army of the East received its marching orders, and the Emperor in person brought up considerable reinforcements from the West. The troops which were at his disposal in the East, at least as far as the legions were concerned—to which their auxiliary regiments must be added— can be determined from a list given by Cassius Dio[2]. According to that list there were in Cappadocia the legion XV Apollinaris with its principal garrison in Satala in Lesser Armenia and XII Fulminata in Melitene. I and III Parthica were in Mesopotamia at Singara and perhaps at Resaina. In Syria XVI Flavia was in garrison at Samosata, IV Scythia probably at Zeugma. In Syria Phoenice III Gallica was in Raphaneae. In Palestine VI Ferrata was at Caparcotna or Legio in Galilee and X Fretensis in Jerusalem. In Arabia III Cyrenaica was at Bostra, and finally in

---

[1] Herodian VI, 2, 5.
[2] Dio LV, 23 sq.

Egypt II Traiana was at Nicopolis in the neighbourhood of Alexandria; from this last legion detachments were certainly drawn (see p. 70). A late Armenian source (Moses of Chorene[1]), in spite of its very confused statements, is thus to this extent accurate in affirming that the Emperor had raised troops from Egypt to the Black Sea and then adds 'and from the desert,' for one may safely presume that reinforcements composed of auxiliary troops—especially light cavalry and bowmen—drawn from Osrhoëne and Palmyra were added to those contingents from these districts which had certainly been recruited under Septimius Severus for the protection of the Eastern frontier. At this time the twentieth cohort of the Palmyrenes was in garrison at Doura[2], and it may be that the defences of the town were now strengthened[3]. Indeed it is probable that the Palmyrenes were the more ready to place their troops and their resources at the Emperor's disposal since through the more rigorous governmental control within the new Persian Empire their trade connections with the Persian Gulf were if not completely interrupted yet at least seriously interfered with. Further, the Romans could rely upon the co-operation of Armenia. What forces Ardashir could oppose to the legions we cannot determine in detail; it is however certain that for the time being the Persian army did not differ in composition or in armament from that of the Parthians (cf. vol. XI, p. 119 *sq.*). But his troops had been well trained in the recent campaigns; the King could rely upon their loyalty and they were inspired by a new spirit.

In the winter of 231–2 the Roman headquarters were in Antioch. But Severus Alexander was compelled to settle difficulties which had arisen in his own army (see p. 69 *sq.*) before he could advance with the three columns into which his forces were divided. A renewed attempt to establish peace through negotiation had failed, since Ardashir had declined to discuss terms. The plan of campaign as laid down by the headquarters staff included a left wing column which was to march through Armenia, perhaps led by Junius Palmatus, and a right wing column which was to follow the Euphrates down to Ctesiphon, while the main army led by the Emperor in person was to hold a middle course through northern Mesopotamia. It remains doubtful whether the two last mentioned armies were to advance together as far as

---

[1] II, 72.
[2] F. Cumont, *Fouilles de Doura-Europos*, pp. liv, lix and 357. Cf. M. Rostovtzeff, *Yale Class. Stud.* v, 1935, p. 202.
[3] Cumont, *op. cit.* p. lix.

Palmyra, where an inscription attests the presence of the Emperor[1]. If this were so, the aim might have been to camouflage the Emperor's real intentions, as Julian on a later occasion sought to disguise his plan of campaign[2]. Or should it be supposed that Severus Alexander at the outset accompanied the right wing column in order to persuade the enemy that it was on this line that the main army was to attack? It is probable that the former alternative should be adopted, for the statement that soldiers—especially the European troops—suffered severely from ill health caused by the climate is more easily explained on the supposition of such a march. In this case, the Emperor's advance must have led by Nicephorium, not by Doura[3], which will have lain upon the route of the right wing column. Rutilius Pudens Crispinus, who later defended Aquileia (see p. 79 *sq.*), will have belonged to this column and was perhaps its leader: he is named as commanding the legionary *vexillationes* in the inscription from Palmyra which has been previously mentioned. Ardashir first marched against Armenia and met the enemy while still in Media Atropatene. He contrived though not without difficulty to bring the Roman advance to a halt. Receiving information of a threatening attack upon his capital, he left only an observation corps in Atropatene and led his main army southwards. We do not know where he came up with the Roman right wing column. That column suffered a severe defeat. But the Persian losses also cannot have been inconsiderable, for Ardashir did not pursue the Romans. And it is further worthy of remark that later Persian tradition is completely silent on Ardashir's wars with Rome, perhaps because they did not lead to any decisive result. When after this reverse Alexander brought the campaign to an end and in the following year left the East (see p. 70) no formal peace was, it is true, concluded, but the position occupied by the Empire before the war was restored. In detail we can trace the efforts which were made to strengthen the defences of the threatened areas. The legion III Gallica was now moved to Danaba to cover the road leading from Damascus to Palmyra: perhaps the legion VI Ferrata was also moved—from Palestine to Phoenice[4]. And if not previously, it was assuredly at this time that the walls of Doura were strengthened under an order of general application directing the further development of defensive fortifications[5].

[1] *O.G.I.S.* 640.
[2] Cf. *Cambridge Medieval History*, I, p. 81.
[3] So Cumont, *op. cit.* p. lix.
[4] Ritterling in P.W. *s.v.* Legio, col. 1594.   [5] Herodian VI, 7, 5.

Ardashir's action, we must suppose, was further determined by conditions in the east of his empire. Although we cannot recover the immediate reason for the shift of his interest, it is certain that from the year 233 it is in the east that his forces are engaged (see above, p. 109 *sq.*). A series of conquests confirmed his power in these regions and increased the strength with which Ardashir could turn against the West, and in the last year of Maximinus Thrax (A.D. 237–8) Mesopotamia was overrun; Nisibis and Carrhae fell. The rare coins of Ardashir which show him adorned with a mural crown may perhaps commemorate this success[1]. When word reached Rome of the loss of the two cities and of the perilous position on the Euphrates frontier which was thus revealed it is possible that Gordian III, in order to save all that could still be preserved, once more revived the client state of Osrhoëne under Abgar X in Edessa[2]. For the succeeding period we have no information. But towards the end of his reign the first Sassanid king is said to have created his son Shapur co-regent. A rare coin-type that represents Shapur with a helmet of which the crest ends in an eagle's head proves that he had been declared the successor to the throne[3] and on coins of Ardashir his portrait appears together with that of his father[4]. Since the capture of Hatra is ascribed in tradition both to Shapur and to Ardashir it is reasonable to conclude that Shapur overcame the resistance of the fortress as co-regent with his father, consequently in A.D. 241. Towards the end of this year Ardashir died and then on 20 March 242[5] under favourable auspices Shapur was crowned king.

With Shapur I there had come to the throne a man who represented even more energetically than his father and with more resolute determination the imperialism of the New Persian Empire. The struggle with Rome was immediately resumed. The enthusiasm of the first onset carried the Persians far into Syria; even Antioch was threatened[6]. At this time the Osrhoënian

---

[1] Volume of Plates v, 234, *g*. A. D. Mordtmann, *Z.D.M.G.* xxxiv, 1880, p. 10 thought that these coins belonged to the latest period of the Arsacids or to the time of the war against Severus Alexander. Cf. F. D. J. Paruck, *Sasanian Coins*, p. 77.

[2] Cf. A. R. Bellinger, *Yale Class. Stud.* v, 1935, p. 146.

[3] Volume of Plates, 234, *h*. So Herzfeld, *op. cit.* p. 37. Cf. Paruck, *op. cit.* p. 322, no. 97.

[4] Paruck, *op. cit.* pp. 78, 315, nos. 58 *sqq.*

[5] Nöldeke, *Tabari*, p. 412 *sq.*

[6] M. Fluss in P.W. *s.v.* Sapor (I), col. 2327, ll. 45 *sqq.* dates to the year 224 the siege and capture of Nisibis. That, however, is inconsistent with the testaments of Syncellus and Zonaras, who place the capture of the city under

kingdom of Abgar must have come to an end. In the following year Gordian III or rather his father-in-law and Praetorian Prefect Timesitheus (see p. 87) restored the honour of the Roman arms. Antioch was secured, Carrhae recovered, while a decisive victory at Resaina opened up the way to Nisibis which once more became Roman. But at this time Timesitheus died (before October 243)[1]. The ambition of his successor in the Praetorian Prefecture, Philip the Arabian, led in the end to the fall of Gordian and to the termination of the campaign which had opened with such success. Philip, now emperor, concluded a treaty of peace with Shapur I; which secured to the Roman Empire its former frontiers. There was no talk of a cession of Mesopotamia and Armenia (which must here mean Armenia Minor), though this is asserted in a late source. The Armenian kingdom cannot have been expressly surrendered under the terms of the treaty, although in the further course of events the condition of the Roman Empire hindered any consistent support of the Armenians. This fact naturally caused them to think that they had been sacrificed and the Roman failure to render them effective assistance was the more bitter since the Armenians up to A.D. 243 had loyally fulfilled their duties as allies of Rome. For we must conclude from Agathangelus that Chosroes I had intervened with success in the war under Gordian: according to Agathangelus[2], indeed, the Armenian king after a victory against Persia continued the war for another ten years until he was dethroned.

It would further appear that quite apart from the defeats which he had suffered Shapur needed peace for other reasons. According to the Chronicle of Arbela[3] Shapur was forced to fight with the Chorasmians and then with the Medians of the mountains. The chronicler, it is true, is in error when he dates these operations to the first year of Shapur's rule; but from his account we may conclude that they fall early in the King's long reign. After his victory Shapur could maintain a firm hold upon Atropatene and

---

Maximinus Thrax, and fails to recognize the significance of Tabari's dating, whose account (Nöldeke, *op. cit.* pp. 31 *sqq.*) connects this event with the victories of Shapur which led up to Valerian's capture, but is once more silent as far as the initial successes and the setbacks are concerned.

[1] *O.G.I.S.* 640 already names Philip as Praetorian Prefect in the year 554 of the Seleucid Era (October 242–October 243).

[2] II, 12 (*F.H.G.* v, 2 p. 118a), where indeed the chronology is not distinctly marked, but it is clear that the Persian king is Shapur.

[3] Ch. 8 in E. Sachau, *Berl. Abh.* 1915, Nr. 6, p. 64; cf. Christensen, *L'Iran...*, p. 214 and above, p 111, for a different dating of these operations.

the districts which lay to the north-east and to the east. Thus the way was opened for operations against Armenia. At first Shapur was content to seek to remove Chosroes, whose courage and energy had created difficulties in the past and were still to be feared in the future. In this he was successful and Chosroes was murdered. Tiridates, a minor, succeeded his dead father as king of Armenia shortly before A.D. 252. For in this year a Persian army appeared in Armenia and compelled Tiridates to take flight into Roman territory: in this expulsion relatives of the young king were implicated. Whether one of these was Artavasdes, king of the Armenians, who is mentioned in the *Historia Augusta*[1], cannot be determined, but it is certain that this king owed his throne to Shapur's favour. The attempt[2] to see in this Artavasdes the saviour of Tiridates who bore the same name, and therefore to regard him not as king but as regent is unsatisfactory, since Artavasdes could hardly have been permitted to play such a part under Persian supremacy.

The loss of Armenia meant for Rome the collapse of the one bulwark of the Empire's eastern defences. The Persian king had in any future war with Rome secured his right flank, which had hitherto always been threatened. And it would seem that forthwith in the same year Shapur attacked Mesopotamia and thus once more created a grave danger for the Empire. According to Tabari[3], he appeared before Nisibis "after the course of eleven regnal years", which would bring us to A.D. 252; and when a Syriac source[4] mentions an attack on Syria and Cappadocia under the year 563 of the Seleucid Era, i.e. A.D. 251/2, this would, despite the anticipation of later events, point to the year 252 as the date of the resumption of the war with Rome. But the king was forced to raise the siege of Nisibis before any success had been won. New disturbances had broken out in the east of his empire. In this time probably fell the war against the 'Turian king' Pahlezagh[5] mentioned above (p. 111). The next attack on Nisibis which ended in the capture of the town may thus be dated to A.D. 254. To what extent Shapur may have in this year followed up his success it is difficult to say, for our scanty sources for the most part give us only the general course of this new war without any details of its separate phases and without any certain chrono-

---

[1] S.H.A. *Trig. tyr.* 3, 1.
[2] Made by Asdourian, *op. cit.* p. 128.
[3] Nöldeke, *op. cit.* p. 31.
[4] Land, *Anecd. Syr.* I, p. 18.
[5] Christensen, *op. cit.* p. 214 *sq.* Cf. Herzfeld, *op. cit.* p. 41.

logical indications. Perhaps if one uses with caution a passage in the Chronicle of Malalas[1] it may be suggested that at this time or in the following year Persian squadrons in their further advance were beaten back before Emesa. Here the usurper Uranius Antoninus (p. 92 *sq.*) had maintained his position as Roman emperor; and from the dating of the coinage he would seem to have held out until the year 565 of the Seleucid Era, i.e. until A.D. 253/4. It is thus to his efforts that this partial Roman success must be attributed. But his rule must have been brought to an end in the storms of the following years. His final overthrow should perhaps be connected with the intervention of Valerian: the reports from the East had become so threatening that the Emperor decided to take action in person. But we must assume that now in accordance with Persian military usage the attacks upon the Roman eastern provinces were made continuously every year and thus gave to Shapur the opportunity to enlarge his father's title of *Shāhānshāh ī Ērān* (King of Kings of Iran), which he too always bears on his coinage, to that of *Shāhānshāh ī Ērān u Anērān* (King of Kings of Iran and Non-Iran) which he employs on his inscriptions[2] (p. 111).

Previous attempts to understand with closer accuracy the situation in the Roman East before the arrival of Valerian are based upon a passage in Zosimus, which places the capture of Antioch before Valerian's arrival, and further they rely for the time of the city's capture on a year-date of the Antiochene Era preserved in Malalas[3]. But Zosimus in this passage[4] is clearly giving an anticipatory survey of all the losses suffered by the Empire through the weakness of Roman emperors up to the capture of the Syrian capital, while the year-date as given in the text of Malalas cannot be retained. Consequently the tradition must be followed which speaks of Persian successes before the intervention

---

[1] Malalas, XII, p. 296, 12 *sqq.* (ed. Bonn). Cf. A. Schenk Graf von Stauffenberg, *Die römische Kaisergeschichte bei Malalas*, p. 372 *sq.*

[2] Christensen, *op. cit.* p. 215.

[3] Malalas, XII, p. 296, 9 (ed. Bonn; I, 391, n. 1, ed. Oxford), where the δτι′ of the MSS. is corrected into τιδ′. Since, however, the 314th year of the Antiochene Era would bring us to A.D. 265–6 C. Müller in *F.H.G.* IV, 192 emended to τδ′ and in this he is followed by A. Schenk Graf von Stauffenberg (*op. cit.* p. 366, n. 89) reading δτ′. This would give A.D. 255/6. But if we see in the δ a misunderstanding of an original ∠, the sign for 'year', we might rather emend the text to τι′ and this 310th year would then correspond to A.D. 261/2, which at least agrees better with the account of Malalas, who also places the fall of Antioch after the capture of the Emperor.

[4] I, 27, 2.

of Valerian, yet does not place the fall of the city of Antioch until after Valerian's overthrow[1]. According to this tradition the Persians spread devastation throughout Syria up to the walls of Antioch, while Cappadocia was likewise overrun. The leadership in the latter campaign was in the hands of Hormizd[2], the son of Shapur, who was supported by a Roman deserter from Antioch with the Syrian name Mariades, i.e. Mâryâd'a, 'My Lord discerns,' a name which in half-graecized form becomes Kyriades[3]. Tyana was captured at this time, and Caesarea (Mazaca) may already have had to endure the Persian onset. By the time that Valerian reached Antioch (probably 256) the Persians had conveyed the booty won in these campaigns across the Euphrates. The fall of Doura must also be placed in this or the following year, when the town fell after a formal siege through the undermining of part of the city-wall, as the excavations have proved[4].

From his headquarters in Antioch in A.D. 257 the Emperor successfully met a renewed Persian invasion. It is to this that the coin legends *Victoria Parthica*[5] and *Restitutor Orientis*[6] must refer. Valerian then summoned to his support Successianus, who had victoriously defended the town of Pityus, far distant on the east shore of the Black Sea, against the attacks of the Borani, the neighbours of the Goths in the Crimea[7]. Successianus was created Praetorian Prefect. The view that the attacks of these barbarians, which were shortly after repeated in alliance with the Goths, were instigated by Shapur has little probability[8]. They can be adequately explained by the difficult position of the Empire at this time of which these tribes can hardly have remained in ignorance. Another Gothic foray into Asia Minor caused Valerian together with his main army to march northward to

---

[1] Georg. Syncellus, p. 715, 16 *sqq.* (ed. Bonn). *Orac. Sibyll.* XIII, 89 *sqq.* and XIII, 119 *sqq.* (ed. A. Rzach). Zonaras XII, 23 (p. 594).

[2] Cf. S.H.A. *Trig. tyr.* 2, where an Odomastes is mentioned in whom Nöldeke (*op. cit.* p. 43, n. 2) recognized an Oromastes, i.e. Hormizd.

[3] Cf. A. Stein in P.W. *s.v.* Mariades, col. 1744.

[4] A. R. Bellinger, *The Excavations at Dura-Europos, Prelim. Report of Third Season* 1929–1930, 1932, p. 163 *sq.*; C. Hopkins, ib. *Prelim. Rep. of Fifth Season* 1931–1932, 1934, pp. 10 *sqq.*; R. Du Mesnil du Buisson, ib. *Prelim. Rep. of Sixth Season* 1932–1933, 1936, pp. 188 *sqq.*; M. Rostovtzeff, *Yale Class. Stud.* v, 1935, p. 202.

[5] P. H. Webb in M.–S. v, i, p. 104, no. 453; cf. p. 33.

[6] *Ib.* p. 60, nos. 286–7; p. 103, no. 448; cf. p. 33.

[7] Cf. L. Schmidt, *Geschichte der deutschen Stämme*, I²: *Die Ostgermanen*, pp. 210, 212 *sq.*

[8] Asdourian, *op. cit.* p. 128.

repel the invaders. But he got no farther than Cappadocia. A plague decimated his army and reduced its military efficiency. After the departure of the troops a new Persian attack had to be met. Coins of A.D. 259 with the legend *Victoria Parthica*[1] are evidence for a further victory of the Emperor, but whether the victor engaged the enemy on the soil of Cappadocia or whether he met the Persians only on his return march to Antioch, or indeed whether these events both fall in one and the same year it is not possible to determine.

In A.D. 260 Shapur none the less once more took the field and encamped before Edessa which defended itself with resolution. Finally the Emperor decided to attack the enemy. But sickness still prevailed in his army, and the spirit of his men was depressed. He, therefore, sought to negotiate and to induce the Persian king to conclude peace by the offer of a large payment in money. Shapur had, however, learned the reasons for this submission; at first he declined the offers and then expressed his desire for a personal interview with Valerian. The Emperor agreed: in fatal confidence he met the Persian king and was taken prisoner. On the fact of the capture our sources are in complete accord, but they disagree in their accounts of the manner in which it was effected. While Zosimus represents it as a treacherous breach of faith on the part of Shapur, others would place it after a battle with insufficient forces against the superior strength of the enemy, others again—and this must certainly be false—will have it that Valerian had fled from beleaguered Edessa to the Persian king in face of a mutiny of his own starving soldiers[2]. In one way or another, a Roman emperor had become a Persian captive. The very foundations of the Roman world seemed shaken, and it is no wonder that Shapur commemorated the event on rock reliefs, which still survive (see above, p. 123). There also appears three times on these representations another Roman whom once Shapur even leads by the hand: he has been rightly identified[3] with Kyriades (Mariades); we must therefore conclude that he was still co-operating with the Persians at the time of Valerian's capture. This event is to be dated to midsummer 260, since the mint of Alexandria issued coins of the eighth year of Valerian, which

---

[1] M.–S. v, i, p. 39, no. 22; p. 58, no. 262; p. 60, no. 291.

[2] For references see L. Wickert in P.W. *s.v.* Licinius (Valerianus), col. 492.

[3] F. Sarre, *Die Kunst des alten Persien*, p. 41; see Volume of Plates v, 148.

began on 29 August 260[1], whereas a papyrus of 29 September 260[2] is already dated under Macrianus and Quietus[3].

With Valerian a captive, Shapur for a time had no more serious opposition to fear. It is true that the Roman troops were united in Samosata under the command of Macrianus, but it would seem that the army retreated into Asia Minor. Edessa maintained its resistance, but the way to the west was open. Shapur with the help of Kyriades (Mariades) whom he had probably created Roman emperor was now able by a surprise attack to gain possession of Antioch[4]. (The traitor Kyriades later fell into disfavour with Shapur and was burnt to death.) But before this, it would seem that a part of the army under Spates[5] had been dispatched against Cilicia; Tarsus and other cities were captured at this time. The main Persian force, however, marched into Cappadocia, where Caesarea (Mazaca) fell through treachery after a heroic defence by Demosthenes. Meanwhile in Cilicia opposition began to be organized through the efforts of a Roman general Callistus who is probably to be identified with the Ballista known to us as Praetorian Prefect under Macrianus and Quietus[6]. The Persian forces were scattered, aiming at different objectives, and thus Callistus could successfully surprise Soloi (Pompeiopolis) and win further successes in Cilicia Trachea at Sebaste and Corycus. Shapur then led back to Persia his army together with much booty and many captives. But already a foe had arisen in Odenathus of Palmyra

[1] J. Vogt, *Die alexandrinischen Münzen*, p. 204.

[2] P. Oxy. XII, 1476. Cf. Wickert in P.W. *loc. cit.* col. 493.

[3] After the foregoing account was in print Professor Alföldi kindly informed the present writer that reasons will be given for a different chronology in his forthcoming article in *Berytus*, which adduces the evidence of a hoard of coins recently found in Northern Syria and placed at his disposal by Professor H. M. Ingholt. If the results of this paper are accepted, it must be supposed *inter alia* that Valerian came to the East as early as A.D. 253 and that Antioch was taken three times by the Persians, twice before and once after, the capture of the Emperor. This proposed course of events is adopted by Professor Alföldi in the narrative of chapter VI (pp. 170 *sqq.*).

[4] Ammian. Marc. XXIII, 5, 3 says expressly *et haec quidem Gallieni temporibus evenerunt*, therefore only after Valerian was taken prisoner.

[5] Malalas, XII, p. 297, 19 *sq.* (ed. Bonn). For the name cf. F. Justi, *Iranisches Namenbuch*, p. 308. It might perhaps be suggested that the name Spates represents a corruption of *spāhbadh* (cf. Christensen, *op. cit.* p. 125), the title of the General of the Army (see above, p. 115).

[6] Cf. Henze in P.W. *s.v.* Ballista (2), col. 2831; A. Stein in P.W. *s.v.* Fulvius (74), col. 257, ll. 45 *sqq.*

(cf. p. 172) who in the sequel was to rob the Persian king of the fruits of his victory.

Whether Valerian lived long enough to see this we do not know; the Emperor died in captivity, probably at Gundeshapur. The statements of Christian sources with their story of a cruel and humiliating treatment of the captive Emperor inflicted by God as punishment for his persecution of the Christians must be accepted with great reserve. It is more certain that Shapur settled the Roman prisoners of war in the district of Gundeshapur and Shoshtar and through their labour built the dam in the neighbourhood of Shoshtar (p. 118) which still bears the name of the Emperor's Dam (*Band-e-Kaisar*) and thus preserves the memory of an achievement which signified a unique victory of the East over the West. The youthful vigour of the Sassanid Empire had become a real danger for the East of the Empire: to repel that danger greater forces were necessary and that at the very time when from Rhine to Danube and to the shores of the Black Sea the newly increased strength of the Germanic peoples was surging against the northern frontiers, while soon within the Empire itself there was to begin a period of revolutions which hopelessly divided the imperial forces and wore them down in murderous battles. But even when these domestic difficulties were overcome the powerful pressure which was the consequence of a defensive on two fronts was bound to strain the resources of the State and thus considerably to increase the burdens laid upon the subject population. That defensive on two fronts, which since the rise of the New Persian kingdom had become a vexatious necessity, thus exercised also upon the internal development of the Roman Empire a manifest and permanent influence.

CHAPTER V

THE INVASIONS OF PEOPLES FROM THE RHINE TO THE BLACK SEA

I. THE MOVEMENTS OF THE PEOPLES ON THE BLACK SEA, DANUBE AND RHINE

IT was not only in Europe and Asia Minor that the provinces were swept by ever recurring waves of destructive invasion, as, time and time again, the barriers of the *limites* gave way. Africa and Egypt, too, suffered under the plundering raids of the neighbouring peoples, though, despite considerable devastation, the damage done by these inroads was mainly of a local character. Again, the assaults of the New Persian Empire must definitely be counted among the barbarian invasions. Shapur might claim to be the heir of the great and highly-civilized empire of the Achaemenids, but his imperialism was predatory. His savage devastations disqualified him from putting himself at the head of the anti-Roman reaction in the East; one has only to remember the case of Mariades (p. 171). This was indeed a great piece of good fortune for Rome. But the Persian wars have already been described; the movements of peoples in the Danube basin must now be considered[1].

Note. The excellent contemporary sources, above all Dexippus, for the period covered by this and the following chapter are almost all lost. A comparison of the secondary sources shows that the more detailed Byzantine authors (Zosimus, Zonaras, Syncellus) go back to the same sources as the Latin *compendia* of the fourth century (Aurelius Victor, the *Epitome de Caesaribus*, Eutropius, Rufius Festus and the *Chronicon* of Jerome; further the *lives* in the *Historia Augusta* from Gallienus to Aurelian). The order of events in the Byzantine authors is decisive (see, for an example, Note 1 at the end of the volume). The Latin *compendia* have mainly been used to check and supplement the gaps in the Byzantine writers, also the fragments of Dexippus and Petrus Patricius, the statements of Cedrenus and other Byzantine writers and scattered observations in Ammianus Marcellinus, and the rest of Latin literature. The evidence of coins is most important. For these see the bibliography, where also will be found relevant collections of inscriptions and archaeological publications, etc. For portraits of Decius and Gallienus see Volume of Plates, v, 186, *d*; 196, *a, b*.

[1] For all details reference should be made to A. Alföldi, *Die Gotenbewegungen und die Aufgabe der Provinz Dacien*, which is to appear in a volume entitled *Die Römer in Ungarn*, published by the Römisch-Germanische Kommission of the German Archaeological Institute.

Of the older neighbours of Rome on the frontiers it was not the Germans that were the most dangerous. We hear, however, under Valerian and Gallienus, of the plundering of Pannonia by the Quadi in concert with the Sarmatae Iazyges. The Marcomanni, too, at the beginning of the same reign (254) penetrated into Pannonia and, finding no resistance, pushed their raid as far as Ravenna[1].

As the forces of the Empire were tied down by other military tasks, Gallienus could only bring the Marcomanni to a halt by ceding to them a part of Upper Pannonia—doubtless on the frontier—while he sealed the treaty of peace by taking to himself as secondary wife the beautiful daughter of their king. It is notable how little is heard of the Asdingian Vandals, who, from the time of Marcus Aurelius, had been settled in the east of Hungary. It is likely enough that they often joined in the Gothic invasions of the Danube provinces, but the fact is expressly recorded on one occasion only (under Decius); later, in 270, after a raid on Pannonia they suffered a hard blow from Aurelian on the bank of a river in Pannonia. Equally secondary is the part played by the Bastarnae, from their settlements in the delta of the Danube; they are only mentioned quite occasionally as participants in raids, until, under the pressure of new Germanic peoples, they were finally settled by the Emperor Probus in Thrace.

Far more serious was the aggressive spirit of the free Dacian peoples (that is, peoples settled outside the province of Dacia). Disturbed by the displacements of groups of Germanic tribes under Marcus Aurelius, they were never afterwards completely pacified. In the reign of Commodus and at the beginning of the third century these Dacian peoples were the really formidable aggressors; nothing is heard as yet of the Goths and their companions in migration. To these free Dacians belong, among others, the Carpi[2] who are often heard of from the time of Caracalla[3] and whose defeats were celebrated by the emperors by

---

[1] This Italian raid as far as Ravenna is usually attributed to the Alemanni (cf. e.g. L. Schmidt, Gesch. der deutschen Stämme, II, 3, p. 248 sq., also M. Besnier, L'Emp. rom. p. 180). But the compendia of the late fourth century show the two invasions as quite distinct from one another (cf. Eutropius IX, 7; Jerome, Chron. p. 220, 24 Helm); only Orosius (VII, 22, 7) and Jordanes (Romana, 287 M) confuse them. It may be added that Ravenna lies on the natural continuation of the imperial road from Pannonia to Aquileia.

[2] Cf. C. Patsch, P.W. s.v. Carpi, cols. 1608, 1610.

[3] Dio LXXVIII, 16, 7 (p. 395 Boissevain); C.I.L. III, 14416; A. von Domaszewski, Westd. Zeits. Korr.-Bl. 1900, p. 147.

the adoption of the title of Dacicus Maximus[1]. Maximinus, for example, took this style as early as 236 (p. 74). In the lost *Scythica* of Dexippus the Carpi played a leading part[2]. In the fateful year 236 they gave the Romans their share of trouble, but the new governor of Lower Moesia, Tullius Menophilus, succeeded in holding them in check during his term of office (p. 84 *sq.*). It is to be observed, however, that despite their pretensions to be stronger than the Goths, they were more lightly esteemed by the Roman government: the Goths received annual subsidies, while they did not. Besides Moesia, Dacia was the chief object of their visitations; the task of curbing them was rendered ever more difficult by the contemporary inroads of the Goths. Philip succeeded in defeating them after extensive devastations in 245 and the years following, but in 248 they broke out once more (pp. 90 *sqq.*). On this occasion the main stroke was delivered by the Goths: while they turned to the wealthier provinces of Moesia and Thrace, the Carpi poured over unhappy Transylvania; again in 250 under Decius and once again under Gallus and Valerian they continued restless. When Aurelian in 271 marched eastwards, their robber-bands again appeared in the Danube provinces. The title of victory, Dacicus Maximus, borne by Decius and Gallienus, indicates that the free Dacian peoples were still being successfully repulsed; Aurelian himself routed them and was honoured by the title of Carpicus Maximus (272)[3]. It seems as if they were now being roughly handled by intrusive German neighbours. To secure peace Aurelian settled large parts of this people within the Empire south of the Danube; and, when the residue joined with the neighbouring Bastarnae in giving further trouble under Diocletian, they too were transferred to Pannonia and other provinces, after Probus had already settled great masses of Bastarnae in Thrace. It was precisely these peoples that found the pressure of the Gothic tribes too much for endurance.

It is clear that it was these Dacian neighbours of the Roman province, together with the other peoples near the *limes*, who were

---

[1] This title must refer to successes over free Dacians and not to victories in Dacia; as is shown by the fact that victories over the barbarians in Pannonia or Moesia were never marked by such titles as Pannonicus or Moesiacus.   [2] Frag. 6 (Jacoby, *F.G.H.* II, p. 456).

[3] Philip, too, was called Carpicus; it is impossible to say with certainty whether this title and that of Dacicus refer to the same Dacian peoples, or whether the latter does not rather arise from the repulse of other free Dacians, for example, from the Bukovina.

first invited by the weakening of the Roman frontier defence to undertake continuous raids for plunder; it was only by slow degrees that this rôle passed to the Goths and the other Germanic peoples, who now begin to make their appearance. The advance of the Goths from East Germany must, it is true, have occurred somewhat earlier, but the occupation of the rich lands of South Russia is bound to have taken up some time, and it was only the rumours of the booty of the Carpi and their companions that brought the Goths to the Danube provinces.

Dexippus begins his description of the invasions of all these peoples, whom he lumps together under the classical name of 'Scythians,' with the year 238[1]. But that was not the first time that the Goths had entered the Roman field of vision. When the Illyrian troops were with Severus Alexander in 231–2, fighting the Persians, 'Germans' broke into the Danube provinces[2]. By 'Germans' are meant not Western Germans only, as has been supposed; for the Goths as early as 238 were receiving annual subsidies from Rome[3], and must therefore have been already responsible for serious inroads, so that it is probably they who are meant here. Under Maximinus Thrax the Gothic danger must have been acute, for the great campaign, prepared by the Emperor in the winter of 237–8 and frustrated by his rivals, against the German peoples 'as far as the Ocean[4],' can only have been aimed at them[5]. Perhaps it was Gothic invasions that were responsible for bringing the autonomous coinages in Moesia and Thrace to an almost complete standstill under Maximinus[6].

The plundering of Istros (not far from the mouth of the Danube) by the Goths, reported by Dexippus, did not involve the final destruction of the city[7]; the other Greek cities of the Black Sea

[1] S.H.A. *Max. et Balb.* 16, 3.

[2] Herodian VI, 7, 2.

[3] Petrus Patricius, frag. 8 (*F.H.G.* IV, p. 186 *sq.*). This passage appears to imply that subsidies had already been paid in the past. For another view see B. Rappaport, *Die Einfälle der Goten*, p. 29 and Schmidt, *op. cit.* I[2], p. 204.

[4] Herodian VII, 2, 9. The phrase cannot refer to tribes who had long been on the frontier.

[5] The fact that operations were to start from Lower Pannonia supports this view. How far the Goths may have been included, together with the Western Germans, under the title Germanicus Maximus of Maximinus Thrax is not clear.

[6] B. Pick, *Die antiken Münzen Nordgriechenlands*, I, p. 187. The continuation of the city-issues under Gordian III shows that the gap is not due to political or economic reasons.

[7] Cf. S. Lambrino, *Rev. des ét. lat.* XI, 1933, p. 457.

likewise continued to maintain themselves. The coinage of Olbia and Tyras ceased, it is true, under Severus Alexander, and the reason may well lie in the difficulties occasioned by the Goths, but inscriptions both of Istros and of Olbia attest the presence of Roman troops as late as 248 under Philip; in Olbia, traces of Roman life have been found as late as Valerian[1]. But the Gothic raid of 238 certainly did serious damage in Moesia; the sources unfortunately fail to reveal how it ended.

How important the control of this people appeared to the victorious senatorial party is revealed by the fact, that, to replace Decius, the future emperor, their best general, the hero of Aquileia (p. 79), M. Tullius Menophilus was sent as governor to Lower Moesia; in his three years of office (238–241) some degree of peace reigned in these lands on the frontier. The fortifications and city-walls were reconditioned, the troops were trained to discipline (p. 85). It seems that Gordian III on his expedition against the Persians in 242 was compelled to halt at this point to drive bands of Goths[2] from Moesia and Thrace; and the Gothic King Argaithus took advantage of the absence of the Emperor in Asia to make a serious raid on the provinces adjoining the Lower Danube[3].

The tide of the Gothic offensive rose higher still in the Danube lands under Philip. Its history depends solely on the confused account in Jordanes[4]. He speaks of two inroads under this emperor and his account can hardly be rejected. If Philip in 246 and at the New Year of 248[5] is called Germanicus Maximus as well as Carpicus Maximus, the former title may refer to the defeat of the Goths in their first invasion[6]. Perhaps it was only after this attack by the Goths that their annual subsidies were withdrawn. Defensive works on the fortified road that, running along the river

---

[1] Cf. M. Ebert, *Südrussland im Altertum*, p. 228.

[2] S.H.A. *Gord. tres*, 26, 3–4 speaks only of '*hostes*'; the Alani, *ib.* 34, 4 are an invention; cf. E. Stein, P.W. *s.v.* Julius (386) Philippus, col. 761.

[3] S.H.A. *Gord. tres*, 31, 1 and *ad loc.* P. v. Rohden, P.W. *s.v.* Argaithus, col. 685. The passage seems to the present writer to represent a contemporary account and not to be a duplicate of the later activities of Argaithus (Argunt). For another view see Rappaport, *op. cit.* p. 33, and Schmidt, *op. cit.* I², p. 205 and above p. 86 *sq.* On the occasion of this raid a coin-hoard (Săpata-de-Jos) seems to have been buried in a fort of the Wallachian *limes*; cf. V. Christescu, *Istros*, I, 1934, p. 72.

[4] *Getica*, XVI, 89 *sqq.* M.

[5] Cf. *Röm. Mitt.* XLIX, 1934, p. 96 *sq.* with illust. 6.

[6] For a different view cf. Schmidt, *op. cit.* I², p. 205 and II, p. 244, and above, p. 90

Aluta, united Moesia to Dacia, and the fortification of Philippopolis in Thrace, prove that Philip did not look on helplessly while
the storm broke[1].

The year 248 brought with it another exceptionally heavy
Gothic attack under Argaithus and Gunthericus[2], with the assistance of their companions in migration, the Taifali, who appear
now for the first time, and also in association with the Asdingian
Vandals, Carpi and Bastarnae (p. 92). It is possible that the pretender, Pacatianus, was proclaimed about May 248 in Upper
Moesia[3], partly in consequence of having gained some passing
success over them; but according to Jordanes the finishing off of
the war was reserved for Decius, who was sent into the Danube
lands with full powers, probably before the end of the year (p. 93).
The activities of Decius must have met with some success, as the
confidence that the Danube army reposed in him suggests; but
his success consisted rather in confirming the discipline of the
troops, in spite of desertions to the enemy, than in actually defeating the Goths[4]. The only recorded detail is that Marcianopolis, a great city of Lower Moesia, west of Odessus (Varna), was
blockaded, but saved from worse harm by the inexperience of the
assailants in siegecraft; the terror of the inhabitants is attested by
the numerous hoards of coins that were buried on that occasion.

The departure of the Danube army for Italy in the summer of
249 brought the Goths back to Moesia. Their king, Kniva, who
led the campaign, set to work in the next year with a deliberation
that betrays at every point a strategy on the truly grand scale. The
main army, which, as it finally retired towards South Russia, must
likewise have come up from the Black Sea, nevertheless makes its
break through the Moesian *limes* far to the west at Oescus; the
crossing at this point implies a command of the fortified line of
the Aluta, which guarded one of the most important entrances
into Transylvania (see Map 5, facing p. 164). It is clear, then,
that Kniva maintained tactical contact with the hordes that broke
into Dacia—according to Lactantius, Carpi. A detachment of
the army broke at the same moment into Lower Moesia and
pushed on as far as Philippopolis in Thrace; Kniva himself
pressed eastward against Novae and was compelled to withdraw by
Trebonianus Gallus, the governor of Lower Moesia. This, however, was no real success for Rome, for the Gothic leader had no

---

[1] As Zosimus (I, 23, I) maintains.
[2] On the mythical king Ostrogotha, cf. Schmidt, *op. cit.* I[2], p. 201 *sq.*
[3] See Alföldi, *Num. Chron.* 1924, p. 11.
[4] Jordanes, *loc. cit.*; cf. *C.I.L.* III, 12351.

thoughts of flight, but quietly turned to the interior of the province. He moved south down the valley of the Iatrus and besieged
Nicopolis, where a large part of the population had taken refuge.
Meanwhile, the Emperor had his son Herennius Etruscus ap-
pointed Caesar, in order to be able to send him in advance as his
responsible representative with the detachments of the Danube
army, which had been brought into Italy to overcome Philip[1].
Very soon afterwards Decius himself hastened from Rome to
Moesia, and, near Nicopolis, gained a considerable victory over
Kniva, who is said to have lost over 30,000 men. The energetic
Emperor further succeeded in clearing Dacia of the Carpi; a
Spanish inscription[2] names him Dacicus Maximus as early as the
autumn of 250, and before the year was out, he was honoured in
Apulum as *restitutor Daciarum*[3]. But the leader of the defeated
Goths was again quick to find the right move. He turned south
to unite with his second army. Decius moved after him, but was
too slow; the Goths already had the 4000 feet high plateau of the
Balkans behind them, when Decius in his turn climbed the
Shipka pass. He was hoping to be able to relieve Philippopolis in
a few days[4], but was compelled after his forced march to rest his
men and horses at Beroea at the southern foot of the mountains.
Here he was taken unawares by Kniva and so completely beaten
that he could barely make his escape over the Balkans.

Decius had already had reason to fear that his Thracian troops
might mutiny[5], and it was probably this rebellious spirit in the
army that led T. Julius Priscus[6], the governor who was besieged
in Philippopolis, to have himself proclaimed emperor and to join
the Goths. It may be that, in return, the soldiers were promised a
safe-conduct. But this desperate step failed to save the besieged;
thousands of them were butchered at the taking of the city and
great numbers of men, including many of senatorial rank, were
taken prisoner[7]. Priscus disappears from history; he cannot long
have survived his treachery.

Decius fled with the remnant of his army back to the Danube

---

[1] Wittig, P.W. *s.v.* Messius (9) col. 1269. The coins with *Exercitus Inlyricus*, etc. do not belong to this context, cf. p. 166, n. 2.
[2] *C.I.L.* II, 4949.   [3] *C.I.L.* III, 1176.
[4] Dexippus, frag. 26, 8–10 (*F.G.H.* II, p. 469 *sq.*).
[5] Dexippus, frag. 26 *ad init.* (*F.G.H.* II. p. 468).
[6] The correct form of the name is given in the *Ann. épig.* 1932, no. 28; Aurelius Victor, *Caes.* XXIX, 2, calls him Lucius Priscus in error.
[7] The siege of Philippopolis in Dexippus, frag. 27 (*F.G.H.* II, p. 470), which ended without success, must be placed later, perhaps in 268.

at Oescus, where Gallus stood with his corps still intact, and prepared to renew the war. It was still the summer of 250, but Decius was so weak that for nearly a whole year, up to his tragic death, he was not in a position to cross the mountains, but was forced to leave the Goths to wreak their fury on Thrace. He restricted himself from the first to the task of awaiting the withdrawal of the enemy, in order to beset them on their return. Yet he failed even to hold the Balkan passes—obviously the most advantageous course—but sent Gallus to the mouth of the Danube, in order to prevent the Goths from crossing, if they took that route; he himself probably remained farther upstream, in order to keep a watch on the western crossings. It must not be forgotten, that it was scarcely possible for him to bring up troops from other parts of the Empire; the risings of pretenders in Rome, Gaul and the East made such a course inadvisable if not impossible.

In May 251, when Herennius Etruscus was made Augustus, new and notable coin-types suddenly appear on the Antoniniani of the mint of Rome[1], one for Decius, the other for his elder son, both celebrating a 'Victoria Germanica.' These must refer to the Gothic war[2]. The victorious engagement thus celebrated can, as things lay, only relate to battles north of the Balkan range. The Goths chose the shortest and most convenient road to the Black Sea and, in view of the defensive attitude of the Romans[3], must have reached the Dobrudja before it came to a battle.

The Romans had the better of the fighting, but the Goths still retained all their booty and captives[4]. Kniva once again displayed his talent for command when, a month later (June 251), the decision fell. He succeeded in luring the Emperor, who walked incautiously into the trap laid for him[5], into a marshy place near Abrittus (Aptaat-Kalessi) in the Dobrudja and in inflicting upon him a decisive defeat. After Herennius Etruscus had died bravely, Decius fought on, until he too fell on the field of honour.

The Illyrian provinces had already suffered terribly from these invasions. There is no record of the number of cities that perished. It is probable that Marcianopolis, for example, met its fate. On

[1] On the determination of the mint see Alföldi's comments in *Num Közlöny*, XXXIV, 5, 1938, p. 66.

[2] Hitherto misunderstood. But Wittig, *op. cit.* col. 1269 expresses doubts about the previous explanations.

[3] Zosimus I, 23, 1; Syncellus, p. 705, 10 *sqq.* (Bonn).

[4] It is to this that Zonaras XII, 20 (p. 589) must refer.

[5] This is admitted by Zosimus (I, 23, 2) despite the partiality he shows for Decius at this point.

this site has been found an enormous hoard of silver[1], and nothing but a general catastrophe can have made men forget such a gigantic fortune.

But the failure of the gallant Decius had not only set his crown on the hazard; any barrier that could hold back the barbarian flood was now swept away. Trebonianus Gallus, now proclaimed emperor, found himself compelled, in his desperate plight, to consent officially to the Goths' quietly carrying off with them their rich booty and their hosts of captives.

The history of the subsequent Gothic raids has been obscured by the fact that the Byzantine writers have run together under Gallus all those later incursions of these peoples that demonstrably took place in later reigns. The reason may be that Dexippus at this point gave in advance a comprehensive survey of the story of raids that were now becoming a matter of course[2]. But we must not infer that the Goths now kept quiet for two whole years[3]. On the contrary, the superior strategy of Kniva and the booty taken, not to speak of the acquiescence of Gallus, were only too calculated to raise the martial spirit of the Germans to the pitch of arrogance[4]. They do, indeed, appear, in return for the annual subsidies that they exacted, to have left Moesia in peace for a time, but they sought compensation elsewhere. In 252[5] other Goths[6] together with the Borani—apparently a Sarmatian people from South Russia—the East German Burgundians[7] and the Carpi broke

[1] N. Mouchmoff, *Le trésor numismatique de Réka Devnia*, Sofia, 1934.

[2] As Rappaport, *op. cit.* pp. 43 *sqq.*, well suggests. Confusion of the names 'Gallus' and 'Gallienus' probably contributed to making the Byzantine authors enter under earlier years these expeditions that really fell under Valerian and Gallienus.

[3] When Orosius (VII, 23, 1) and Jordanes (*Romana*, 288 M) maintain that the Goths continued their devastations for 15 years until 269, that is a subsequent calculation based on the years of the reign of Gallienus, who is made the scapegoat.

[4] Zosimus I, 24, 1.

[5] The thread of the history is given by Zosimus, who returns three times under Gallus to the Gothic inroads. In I, 26, 1 he gives the general, anticipatory, description which has been mentioned above; in I, 27, 1, with αὖθις he marks the invasion of the Goths and their comrades in the following year, an invasion which spent its fury on the mainland, and finally, in I, 28, 1, he describes the first expedition by sea in the next year to that. The correctness of the continuation after 253 (see Alföldi in *Berytus*, IV, 1937, pp. 53 *sqq.*) confirms the earlier date also.

[6] That it was actually a different group of Goths—perhaps, the later Ostrogoths—that made these expeditions, cannot be strictly proved, but appears a necessary assumption.   [7] Cf. Schmidt, *op. cit.* I², p. 130 *sq.*

into the European provinces, and in 253 made a first expedition by sea to Asia Minor[1], which spread fire and sword as far as Ephesus and Pessinus. In the spring of the same year the Goths under Kniva stirred again and demanded an increase of their subsidies. But the governor of Lower Moesia, Aemilius Aemilianus, succeeded in inducing his troops by liberal promises to undertake a counter-attack on the Gothic territory north of the Danube; success brought him proclamation as emperor, and death.

But this bold stroke had no lasting effects. Aemilianus was not even able to clear Thrace of the hostile bands[2]. In 254 the Goths again crossed the Danube, 'as is their custom,' laid waste Thrace, and pushed on to Thessalonica, but were driven off with heavy loss[3]. Greece was seized with panic; Thermopylae and the Isthmus were fortified; the walls of Athens, which since Sulla's time had fallen into decay, were restored. But there was no one able to curb the robber bands in the field. For at the same time the Marcomanni made havoc of Pannonia, while, of the two emperors, one had perforce to take the field against the Germans on the Rhine, and the other was tied down in the East. The position in Illyricum was terrible enough[4]. The details cannot be followed in the authorities. The activity of the mint of Viminacium between 253 and 257 points to some degree of order in Upper Moesia during this period; but the transference of its activity to Cologne shows that the Rhinelands were regarded as of more importance than the payment of the Danube troops. The Gothic peril became so constant that the glacis of the Balkan range was fortified in order to observe and fend off the raiders ('latrunculi')[5]. The usurpations of 260, in which the desperation of the Danube population expressed itself, only made a weak position weaker still. But from 261 onwards there was some relief; the undisturbed activity of the mint of Siscia points to a re-organization beginning in 262.

Not less terrible were the sufferings of Asia Minor[6]. The Borani succeeded in inducing the Roman vassal-king of Bosporus to put his fleet at their disposal, and, even if they had little success in 254,

---

[1] It must be assumed that the description of the Gothic expedition by sea in 256 as 'second invasion' (Zosimus I, 35, 2) implies the reckoning of the expedition of 253 as 'first.'

[2] Zonaras XII, 22 (p. 591).

[3] It is not known when the capture of Dyrrhachium by the Goths, mentioned in Dexippus, frag. 3 (F.G.H. II, p. 456), took place.

[4] Zosimus I, 37, 3.   [5] C.I.L. III, 12376 (Kutlovica).

[6] For the chronology of these expeditions, cf. Alföldi, op. cit. p. 57 sq.

they conquered Pityus and Trapezus in the next year; in 256 followed a great naval expedition, undertaken by their Gothic neighbours, accompanied along the west coast of the Black Sea by their land-army. After the garrison of Chalcedon had basely left its post despite its superior numbers, that wealthy city fell into the hands of the Goths and was followed by Nicomedia, Nicaea, Prusa and other cities in the neighbourhood; the unresourceful Valerian could do nothing to check them. The anarchy and misery that these raids brought in their train are depicted with all the vividness of actual experience in a pastoral letter of the Bishop of Neocaesarea[1]. And yet Valerian had the effrontery to celebrate the great event as a *Victoria Germanica* on his issues of Antioch in 257—a boast as well grounded as the parallel announcement of a *Victoria Part(hica)*[2]. If in the next decade no further expeditions by sea followed, the credit must be assigned to the efforts of Gallienus[3]; the reputation of Odenathus may have contributed something to the result.

If in the years following 260 the restlessness of the East Germans seems to some extent to have died down, new and more violent waves broke on the Empire at the end of the reign of Gallienus, most probably set in motion by the arrival of new bands of Germans in South Russia and in the northern Danube-basin. First of all, the whole of Asia Minor was swept by marauding bands of warriors brought by sea (267)[4]. They were Goths, who, making their way through the Bosporus, laid waste Chalcedon and then plundered the rich city of Nicomedia. There was, it appears, no one to say them nay, when they sailed through the Hellespont and fell upon the cities of Ionia. They reduced to ashes the famous temple of Diana at Ephesus and, on the return, the time-honoured site of Troy. No less wide were their depredations on land; the west of Asia Minor was the first to suffer (Lydia and Phrygia are expressly named after Bithynia); they then passed on to Cappadocia and Galatia. But, when Odenathus, shortly before his death[5], advanced with his army against them as far as Heraclea Pontica, they were already again on board, carrying

---

[1] Migne, *Patr. Graec.* x, pp. 1037 *sqq.*: cf. A. Draesecke, *Jahrb. f. prot. Theol.* VII, 1881, pp. 730 *sqq.*

[2] It is to be observed that the Goths once again are called Germans. *Victoria Guttica* or *Gothica* does not appear until under Claudius.

[3] On building of walls in Miletus in 263, cf. Th. Wiegand, *Sitz. Ber. Berl. Akad.* 1935, p. 205.

[4] On the criticism of the sources and the chronology of the next three great invasions, see Note 1 at the end of the volume.

[5] This gives the date.

with them a booty that included many prisoners, among whom may have been the grandparents of Wulfila, the apostle of the Goths[1].

This great success stirred up the Black Sea peoples to further endeavours and in the next year they mustered in numbers as yet unparalleled at the mouth of the Dniester; 500 ships, on the most modest estimates, according to others, 2000, put to sea, and, even if the number of 320,000 warriors for the land-army that accompanied the fleet along the coast is grossly exaggerated, it was probably the strongest German army that trod the soil of the Empire in the third century. The fleet was mainly supplied by the sailor-folk of the Heruli, who seem to have been newcomers to the shores of the Black Sea; the mass of the land-army was formed by bands of Goths, but Bastarnae and fragments of other peoples joined the expedition and spread over Thrace. Byzantium and Chrysopolis were ravaged by the sea forces; but on the Propontis many of their ships were wrecked, and the imperial fleet also attacked with success. Even if an occasional enterprise miscarried—the invaders failed, for example, to take Tomi and Marcianopolis—they overran all Greece as far south as Sparta, with fire and sword, and Athens fell to their arms. Here the imperial commander Cleodemus assailed them with his fleet, and bands of Athenian volunteers under Dexippus, whose admirable *Scythica* and *Chronica*, the best accounts of the history of the period, have unfortunately been lost, inflicted on them considerable losses. Through Boeotia, Epirus, Macedonia they made their way back, aiming for Moesia. The unsuccessful siege of Philippopolis[2] (which is not to be confused with the siege under Decius) may have happened at this time. It seems to have been another detachment of the fleet that pushed through the Hellespont, repaired the ships at Athos and besieged Cassandreia (Potidaea) and Thessalonica. On the news of the approach of the Emperor Gallienus and his army, this force advanced to meet him through Doberus and Pelagonia. The advance guard of Dalmatian cavalry cut to pieces 3000 barbarians; then the mass of the army crossed swords with the imperial forces at Naïssus. In the grim battle that followed the Romans were at first driven back, but they were skilfully rallied to a surprise attack on the enemy, who left 50,000 men on the field and crowded into a fortified laager. The Herulian chieftain, Naulobatus, who surrendered to Gallienus, was rewarded with the consular insignia, and, perhaps, given employment with his followers in the Roman service. The victory, however, was not

---

[1] Schmidt, *op. cit.* 1[2], p. 234 *sq.*
[2] Dexippus, frag. 27 (*F.G.H.* II, p. 470).

exploited to the full because Gallienus was compelled to withdraw the greater part of his army post-haste, to defend himself against the treachery of Aureolus. But in the meantime his general Marcianus successfully prosecuted the operations against the Germans. After the death of Gallienus Claudius came in person to take up the struggle. When the Germans, dying like flies from lack of provisions, withdrew from their laager on Mount Gessax to Macedonia, they were twice defeated by the newly established corps of cavalry and pursued by their opponents, though it appears that early in 269 fresh bands of considerable size crossed the Danube to the assistance of their compatriots. Assailed by famine and plague, the survivors were taken prisoner and made use of as soldiers and farmers. The Herulian fleet, which undertook a fresh expedition in 269, likewise failed to achieve any great success, as the cities, it appears, were well guarded, though the countryfolk were harried far and wide.

II. THE ABANDONMENT OF DACIA

From these locust-swarms that had for so long been devouring the Danube provinces year by year Dacia had been the worst sufferer. Even before the Gothic storms, she had been vexed by the free Dacians (see above), and, from her geographical position, she was most exposed of all provinces to attack: the Transylvanian Alps simply form one great bridgehead in advance of the Danube front and this projecting semi-circle lacked an extended connection with the *limes* of Moesia and Pannonia, being separated from both provinces by the vassal-states of the Sarmatae Iazyges and Roxolani, originally created to separate the powerful kingdom of Dacia from the Roman boundaries. After the conquest of Trajan these buffer-states had lost their *raison d'être*; the fortified roads and regular patrols, that crossed and controlled these strips of land, were not calculated to hold up the drive of powerful peoples. Marcus Aurelius had intended at least to get rid of the gaps to the north and west of Dacia (vol. xi, pp. 350 *sqq.*), but the senseless Commodus again left these inlets unstopped, and the north of Hungary kept filling up with fresh arrivals from East Germany, while from the east and south of Transylvania came the heavy pressure of the Goths. The situation of the province was rendered even more difficult by the change of strategy that aimed at parrying hostile offensives not by the cordon on the *limes*, but by a disposition of the troops in depth. Under this system such an advanced frontier-position as Dacia lost its strategic importance, and stress was no longer laid on its adequate garrisoning. In the process of concentration to the rear the *élite* corps were withdrawn from the actual frontiers and transferred to important road-junctions in the interior, while the gaps came more and more to be filled with barbarian *foederati* or militia of inferior quality.

The ancient literary authorities declare that Dacia was lost under Gallienus, but this simply reflects the general tendency to make that emperor responsible for all the evils of his times, a tendency zealously promoted by the hostile party of the Senate. But the discussion of the movements of the Goths has already revealed the fact that the invasions reached their zenith not under Gallienus, as the late Roman historical compendia of the second half of the fourth century maintain (they depend on a literary scheme, that sketches the type of the tyrant in its progressive degeneration), but rather in the years from Decius to the death of Valerian, and that any state of anarchy that the fearful aftermath of 267–269 might produce was nothing new. The evidence of epigraphy and numismatics permits the reconstruction of some such picture as the following.

The normal circulation of coinage was indeed seriously reduced from the time of Philip onwards, but it was still generally active as late as 253. In the summer of 256 bronze issues for the *provincia Dacia* were still being struck at the mint of Viminacium. The last surviving official inscriptions fall between 256 and 259. But, where systematic excavations have been made, for example, in Apulum, the chief stronghold of the province, it has become clear that the provision of pay for the troops was still maintained and had not ceased before the beginning of the reign of Aurelian. The road from Orsova to Karánsebes, uniting Moesia and Dacia, was held, as late as Gallienus, even more firmly—as the coin-hoards show—than the mountainous country proper; the fact is confirmed by inscriptions of the years of his sole rule.

It has been noted (p. 94) that from the time of Philip *vexilla-tiones* drawn from the frontier legions were permanently stationed in North Italy; among them were the detachments of the two legions of Dacia, which seem to have gone over in 268 to Postumus with other *vexillationes* stationed there (see, however, below, p. 214). But the parent legions themselves were also set in motion. At a date soon after 261 the commander of the Legio XIII Gemina appears in Mehadia, at the southern gateway of Dacia—together, it must be supposed, with his corps, which seems as early as 260 to have taken part in the revolts of Ingenuus and Regalian. Later under Gallienus both legions are found in Southern Pannonia,

where the road to Italy crosses the Drave, as a regular garrison for
Poetovio. What other troops there may have been in Transylvania,
and whether detachments of legions were among them, is unknown. But there is first-hand evidence to prove that until the
beginning of 270 the abandonment of the province was not even
considered. Types of the very first issue of Aurelian, on the model
of Decius, represent the reliance of the Emperor on the might of
Illyricum; among them is a *Dacia Felix*[1]. Then comes a sudden,
unexpected change, necessitated by events of a novel character.

The facts are clear. Aurelian after his proclamation hastened
to Rome[2], thence to fight in Pannonia, only to return to North
Italy for a severe campaign against the invading Juthungi. In the
winter of 270–1 he arranged affairs in Rome and Italy and prepared for an expedition against Palmyra. On his way to the East
he first cleared the Danube lands and Thrace of marauding bands[3],
then crossed to the northern bank and swiftly defeated the
Goths in a series of great battles, in the course of which the
chieftain Cannabaudes lost his life[4]. The importance of the victory
is underlined in what Ammianus Marcellinus says of the Goths
'per Aurelianum, acrem virum, et severissimum noxarum ultorem
pulsi, per longa saecula siluerunt immobiles[5].' The victorious
Emperor, then, was complete master of the situation; how came
he to the sudden resolve to abandon Dacia ('desperans eam posse
retineri')?

The explanation is to be found in the general position. Zenobia
controlled Egypt, the chief granary of the Empire. The corn-fleets
in 271 were no longer reaching Italy from Alexandria; the
decision must not be postponed, if Rome was not to go short. As

---

[1] This first issue appears to have been planned under Quintillus (himself
an Illyrian), because the reverse *Pannonia* appears with the same *officina* mark
from the same mint in the latest of his issues.

[2] The sequence of events in Zosimus 1, 48 *sq.*, to which the statements of
the *Vita Aureliani* stand in a somewhat similar relationship to that shown
in Note 1 at the end of the volume, is here followed. It appears to the present
writer that considerations of time exclude as many wars in 270 as are usually
assumed.

[3] Perhaps they were Carpi, for the Emperor was already Carpicus
Maximus in 272 (*C.I.L.* III, 7586). But cf. S.H.A. *Aurel.* 30, 4.

[4] S.H.A. *Aurel.* 22, 1–2: *contra Zenobiam. . .iter flexit. multa in itinere
ac magna bellorum genera confecit. nam in Thraciis et in Illyrico occurrentes
barbaros vicit, Gothorum quin etiam ducem Cannaban sive Cannabauden cum
quinque milibus hominum trans Danuvium interemit*; Orosius VII, 23, 4:
*expeditione in Danuvium suscepta Gothos magnis proeliis profligavit dicionem-
que Romanam antiquis terminis statuit*, cf. also Eutropius IX, 13, 1 and Jordanes,
Romana 290 M.   [5] XXXI, 5, 17.

the Gallic Empire was still independent, it was only by the army of the Danube that the East could be subdued. If the Illyrian troops, already weakened by losses, were to be withdrawn (and they did in the sequel bear the brunt of the fighting against Zenobia[1]), without surrendering the Danubian provinces to the mercy of the Goths, there was but one course open and that Aurelian took. He ordered the withdrawal of the Roman population ('Romanos') from Dacia, transferred the legions of Dacia to Moesia, to the two gates of Gothic invasions, Ratiaria and Oescus, and named the country Dacia Ripensis. Behind it he carved out of Moesia and Thrace a Dacia Mediterranea, the capital of which, Serdica, received a great new imperial mint. This organized migration of Romans from Dacia to the south side of the Danube, where farmers and recruits for the army were much needed, a migration protected by the prestige of Aurelian's victories, removed Roman civilization from Dacian soil as completely as Trajan had driven out the earlier Dacian inhabitants of the land[2] (vol. xi, p. 553).

This strategic withdrawal re-established the Danube frontier for a considerable time, while it also supplied a home to a large section of the Goths, in which they succeeded in forming an independent State as the Visigoths, destined thereafter to be ousted by the Huns and to exercise a deep influence on the fortunes of France and Spain. The other Goths in the Black Sea area, probably ancestors of the Ostrogoths, stirred again in 276; Tacitus, Florian and Probus were to be much plagued by their naval expeditions. From the West Goths, too, came isolated plundering raids southwards. But the great movement was at an end, and the East German Gepidae, who had meanwhile pushed into Eastern Hungary and had fought bitterly with the Goths and Vandals for their settlements, were not in time to share actively in the invasions[3].

III. THE ATTACKS OF THE WEST GERMANS

It is under Caracalla that the name of Alemanni first occurs. It appears that this people is identical with the Semnones, who lived to the west of the Elbe[4] and, encroaching on the lands where

---

[1] Zosimus I, 52, 3.

[2] For another view see C. Patsch, *Sitz.-Ber. d. Wien. Akad. phil.-hist. Kl.* 217, 1. Abh. 1937, pp. 176 *sqq.*; Besnier, *op. cit.* pp. 243 *sqq.*; C. Daicoviciu, *La Transylvanie dans l'Antiquité*, Bucharest, 1938.

[3] It appears to the present writer that the mentions of them in S.H.A. are additions by the compiler of the work.

[4] Schmidt, *op. cit.* II, pp. 236 *sqq.*

the more gifted and civilized Hermunduri had been settled, exercised a dangerous pressure on the *limes* of Upper Germany and Raetia. Caracalla inflicted a serious defeat on them in 213 and protected the military frontier opposite them with new works of defence (p. 48). But, twenty years later, they started a destructive offensive against the frontier-districts of Upper Germany and Raetia. The coin-hoards attest the destruction of very many forts in these years (A.D. 233–234). The Raetian *limes* in what is now Bavaria seems to have been badly shaken over considerable sections at that time, whereas the stretch towards Upper Germany was successfully restored[1]. The gentle Severus Alexander failed against them in 234, and it was left for Maximinus Thrax to punish them effectively in the following years (p. 73 *sq.*). Again there was a temporary relief; everywhere the fortifications were repaired and strengthened. The continuity of coin-hoards in the region of the German *limes* down to the joint rule of Valerian and Gallienus, together with the inscriptions, shows that life was going on normally in these parts. But the general convulsion of the Empire gave these peoples, too, their chance. They certainly made raids under Gallus, for the expeditionary force concentrated in Raetia in the early autumn of 253 was doubtless intended to avenge their devastations[2]. The sudden withdrawal of the army to Italy had the natural effect of heightening the offensive spirit of the Alemanni. Besides minor incursions, of which our meagre sources preserve no record, they carried out a terribly destructive raid on Gaul and pressed on through Switzerland into Italy[3]. One band made its way as far as Rome itself, but was frightened off by a numerous army, which the Senate had hastily assembled and armed. Gallienus himself now hurried over the Alps. He brought with him the legion VIII Augusta from the Rhine and, on his way, drew the I Adiutrix and II Italica from Pannonia and

---

[1] Cf. Schmidt, *op. cit.* II[1], pp. 246 *sqq.*; P. Goessler, *Germania*, xv, 1931, 12; W. Veeck, 'Die Alamannen in Württemberg' (*Germ. Denkmäler der Frühzeit*, I), 1931, pp. 97 *sqq.*, E. Fabricius, P.W. *s.v.* Limes, col. 611; E. Norden, *Altgermanien*, p. 24 *sq.* The rest of the literature is cited in these works.

[2] Aurelius Victor, *Caes.* XXXII, 1.

[3] Schmidt, *op. cit.* II[1], pp. 248 *sqq.* It must be supposed that this is the invasion, described in Zosimus I, 37–38, 1 (cf. Norden, *op. cit.* p. 25), when the Emperor was actually north of the Alps (Zosimus I, 37, 1) and Rome itself was threatened. This identification is supported by the fact that the invasion of the Marcomanni in 254 (cf. p. 139) did not get farther south than Ravenna, and can therefore be left out of account.

Noricum; his army, including the Praetorian Guard and the II Parthica (from Albano), had not exceeded some ten thousand men. Yet it sufficed to inflict a crushing defeat on the vastly superior numbers of the Alemanni near Milan[1]. The exact year is not certain, but it must have been either 258 or 259[2]. That Gaul had been visited more than once by these invaders in the years preceding is a very probable assumption[3].

The blow thus sustained by the Alemanni certainly weakened them and drove them from Italy; but none the less it was soon found impossible to restore and defend the *limes* area in the angle formed by the upper waters of the Rhine and Danube. Gallienus did, indeed, refortify Vindonissa in 260, to bar the way southward to the Alemanni[4], and other forts were built at the same time[5]. But the revolt of Postumus, at the end of 260[6], set the Rhine frontier and the Upper Danube in hostile opposition to one another, and the intervening district along the *limes* between the two fronts became a no man's land. The latest inscription from the Raetian *limes* dates from 256–7[7]; it is to these strips of land along the frontier that the notice, 'sub principe Gallieno...amissa Raetia'[8] must apply. The loss is likewise recorded[9] of 'the districts round the Lahn as far as the Sieg, or even perhaps as the Ruhr, that is to say, the Roman sphere of influence extending from the most northerly part of the frontier barrier[10].' The evidence of

---

[1] See *Num. Chron.* 1929, pp. 232 *sqq.*

[2] This victory was numbered as the fifth German victory of Gallienus and was followed by the suppression of Ingenuus and Regalianus, autumn 260. See p. 184 *sq.*

[3] The exploits of Chrocus (Gregory of Tours I, 32–4) may not be wholly legendary (cf. Schmidt, *op. cit.* II¹, p. 249, n. 1 and C. Jullian, *Hist. de la Gaule*, IV, p. 566): at least his name is good Alemannic.

[4] *C.I.L.* XIII, 5203.

[5] G. Bersu, *Schwäbischer Merkur*, 8 Jan. 1927 (Isny).

[6] For this, the precise date, see the forthcoming article of the present writer, 'The year-reckonings of the reigns of Valerian and Gallienus', in *J.R.S.*

[7] *C.I.L.* III, 5933; cf. Fabricius, *op. cit.* col. 611.

[8] *Paneg.* VIII (v), 10; cf. H. Zeiss, *Bayr. Vorgeschichtsbl.* X, 1931/2, p. 45.

[9] *Laterc. Veron.* 15 (in *Not. Dign.* ed. Seeck, p. 253): *trans castellum Mogontiacense LXXX leugas trans Rhenum Romani possederunt, istae civitates sub Gallieno imp. a barbaris occupatae sunt.* Cf. E. Ritterling, *Bonn. Jahrb.* CVII, 1901, pp. 116 *sqq.*; Norden, *op. cit.* pp. 24 *sqq.* Further details in J. Steinhausen, *Arch. Siedlungskunde des Trierer Landes*, 1938, pp. 375 *sqq.*; J. Hagen, *Zeitschr. d. Aachener Geschichtsvereins*, LI, 1930, pp. 344 *sqq.*

[10] Ritterling, *loc. cit.*

archaeology and coins suggests that the *agri decumates* were over-run at the same time[1].

That Gallienus in 268 still meant to hold Raetia in strength is shown by the evidence of Aurelius Victor[2]: Aureolus, the commander of the new cavalry corps, stationed in Milan, at the time of his revolt was in Raetia 'in command of the army.' Obviously he had called the troops from that province to join him, for the Alemanni immediately afterwards broke through[3] and advanced over the Brenner as far as Lake Garda. After the murder of Gallienus the new emperor Claudius marched against them and dealt them a heavy blow, though unable to exploit his victory strategically, for he was already compelled to turn his arms against the Goths, who had flooded into the Balkans. So it came about that the half of the Alemanni who survived[4] were able to escape homewards, as it seems with no great difficulty. The gate had not been barred and bolted against their invasions. They were not even deterred from invading Italy once again in the very next year. Aurelian was engaged in mastering the Vandals in Pannonia, when he received the tidings that the Alemanni, with their kinsmen, the Juthungi[5], were plundering the fields round Milan (see below, p. 298 *sq.*). One band was actually in possession of Placentia when he arrived. Near this latter city the Emperor sustained a defeat brought about, it appears, by a surprise attack by night from Alemannic forces hiding in the woods. The Via Aemilia in the direction of Bologna-Ancona was laid open to the foe, and it was not till they had reached the key to Rome on the Via Flaminia that Aurelian overtook them and defeated them decisively on the Metaurus near Fanum Fortunae. As the enemy streamed back northwards, he pursued and defeated them a second time near Ticinum, not far from Milan. The vagrant remnant seems then to have been wiped out[6]. These blows, it must be presumed, fell mainly on the Alemanni; the Juthungi withdrew in an orderly column to the Danube, where they were overtaken and defeated by the Emperor. This severe, but victori-

---

[1] The coin-finds (cf. *e.g.* Schmidt, *op. cit.* II[1], 1, pp. 245 *sqq.*) have not yet been arranged under dates and mints according to the results of the most recent research.

[2] Aurelius Victor, *Caes.* XXXIII, 17.

[3] P. Damerau, *Kaiser Claudius II Goticus*, p. 52 *sq.*, where further literature will be found.   [4] [Aurelius Victor], *Epit.* XXXIV, 2.

[5] They were living at the time somewhere between Nuremberg and Regensburg, north of the Danube: cf. Schmidt, *op. cit.* II[1], pp. 251 *sqq.*

[6] S.H.A. *Aurel.* 18, 6.

ous campaign had the effect of finally frightening off the Alemanni
and their comrades, at least from Italy. But Raetia was not
secured against them until Aurelian, on his way to fight Tetricus
in Gaul, cleared Vindelicia of their marauding bands (p. 309).
Probus later threw back the Alemanni over the Neckar on to the
foot-hills of the Swabian Alps, a success that marked the complete
efficiency of the Roman defensive at least (p. 315)[1]. Raetia could
at last draw breath[2].

In a rapid glance over the raids of the Germans of the Rhine,
the remarkable fact emerges that it was not any movements among
the German peoples themselves, but simply and solely the loosening of the Roman power that occasioned the storm on the *limes*.
The Franks are no newcomers to the Rhine[3] but only a new league
of Bructeri, Chamavi, Salii and others, who had united in order
to make head more easily against Rome. This banding together on
a considerable scale had in point of fact strengthened them considerably and had laid the foundations of the rôle they were afterwards to play in history. They became active rather later than the
Alemanni. As early as 231 they were giving trouble to the Legio
I Minervia[4], but the operations against the Alemanni by Severus
Alexander and Maximinus must have had their effects on them as
well. It is, however, chiefly the coin-hoards that show how fast
and far the sense of insecurity spread along the Rhine and in
Gaul[5]. From 253 onwards the situation became difficult in the
extreme. It is significant, indeed, that Gallienus thought less of
the raids of Marcomanni and Quadi, that even extended to Italy,
or of the imperilling of Greece by the Goths, than of the danger
on the Rhine[6]. It is at this point that the authorities first mention
the Franks as the opponents[7]. In 254, at the latest, the Emperor

---

[1] S.H.A. *Prob.* 13, 7. Cf. Norden, *op. cit.* p. 31.

[2] S.H.A. *Prob.* 16, 1. Cf. also Zeiss, *op. cit.* p. 45.

[3] Schmidt, *op. cit.* II[1], p. 433.

[4] *C.I.L.* XIII, 8017; Schmidt, *op. cit.* II[1], p. 242.

[5] This material was first used by A. Blanchet, *Les trésors de monnaies
romaines et les invasions germaniques en Gaule*, 1900; cf. also his latest work,
*Les rapports entre les dépôts monétaires et les événements militaires, politiques
et économiques*, Paris, 1936. Further references to literature will be found
in I. J. Manley, *Effects of the Germanic Invasions on Gaul, 234–284 A.D.*
Evidence from the Dutch frontier districts is collected in H. Brunsting, *Het
Grafveld onder Hees bij Nijmegen* (Allard-Pierson Stichting, Arch. Hist.
Bijdragen, 4, 1937, pp. 198 *sqq.*).   [6] Zosimus I, 30, 2.

[7] Zonaras XII, 24 (p. 596); Aurelius Victor, *Caes.* XXXIII, 3. On these
invasions see also Schmidt, *op. cit.* II[1], pp. 437 *sqq.* and A. Vincent, *Mélanges
Pirenne*, II, pp. 669 *sqq.*

seems to have reached Gaul. Arrived there, he guarded the Rhine crossings and ejected the scattered bands of invaders[1]. He even crossed the river to punish the raiders; an expedition of this kind seems to have occurred in 255—its successful termination was celebrated by an inscription of the Twentieth legion[2]. But, as Gallienus had few troops at his disposal and was almost crushed by the vast hordes of the enemy, he eased the situation by concluding an alliance with one German prince against the rest—an alliance that actually put a stop to the raids.

Two, or perhaps three, major campaigns fell to the Emperor's lot before 258[3]. He did not hesitate to set up his headquarters on the front itself in Cologne[4]. Thence he hurried (258 or 259) to Italy against the Alemanni and again (in 260) to Pannonia against Ingenuus; at his departure he left his son, Saloninus, in Cologne. At this moment, in the autumn of 260 (p. 185), his general Postumus succeeded in disposing of an invading band of Germans and used his success to secure his own proclamation as rival emperor. It must be admitted that Postumus defended the Rhine frontier with the same energy as Gallienus and developed the defence further by fortifications and the erection of bridge-heads[5]—depending no less than Gallienus on the aid of German against German. His coins and inscriptions announce German victories in 261 and 264. But the division caused by his proclamation sealed the fate of the *agri decumates*. Even so, his forces were frequently and severely hampered by the need to arm against Gallienus and by heavy fighting against him. That he was not even wholly successful on the defensive is illustrated by the numerous hoards of coins buried in his reign on French soil[6]; they show that the general insecurity rather increased than

[1] Zosimus *loc. cit.*

[2] *C.I.L.* XIII, 6780. Cf. A. von Domaszewski, *Phil.* LXV, 1906, p. 350. The inscription, *C.I.L.* XI, 2914, to judge from the tribunician power, should also date from 255.

[3] Among the five German victories, which he counted (cf. *Num. Chron.* 1929, pp. 218 *sqq.*), the defeat of the Alemanni was included, as were certainly also the wars with the East Germans, so far as they were successful; the exact attributions are thus rendered more difficult. As the war with the Alemanni was *victoria quinta* (cf. *Num. Chron., loc. cit.*) the successes on the Rhine must all fall before it.

[4] This is proved by the transference of the imperial mint of Viminacium to Cologne. On the place of the mint, see G. Elmer in the *Bonn. Jahrb.* CXLIII, 1938.

[5] See Schmidt, *op. cit.* II[1] p. 250; Steinhausen, *loc. cit.*

[6] Cf. the sketch map in Manley, *op. cit.* p. 64 (fig. 2).

diminished, as compared with the previous years (see, however, below, p. 314).

All that he actually achieved was completely lost under his weak successors. Aurelian brought some relief, but it was reserved for Probus to restore order and stability. Under Gallienus and Postumus the Franks took to the sea and plundered, among other places, Tarraco in Spain; under Probus himself one roving band carried out a romantic expedition of exploration and robbery in the lands of the Mediterranean (p. 314 *sq*.). That the examples cited were not isolated is everywhere shown by the coin-hoards, that were buried at that time along the English Channel and right down the coasts of France.

IV. THE EFFECTS OF ROME'S STRUGGLE WITH THE GERMANIC WORLD

The movement of the East Germans, thanks to the advances in excavation, is to-day completely intelligible (cf. vol. XI, chap. II). A general view can be gained of the process by which, in a comparatively short time, they pushed on from their tiny settlements in Scandinavia to possess a vast area in the east of Europe. Their new settlements were in the main fertile and thinly populated, and so it is evident, that it was not hunger and need or lack of land to cultivate that led them southwards, but sheer excess of youthful energy and love of adventure—just as in the '*Sturm und Drang*' period of the Celtic race many centuries earlier.

The Goths were men of a mighty stamp; their warriors were giants indeed[1]. Sometimes it happened that the attacking Germans were few in numbers and only able to gain the upper hand through the effeminate cowardice of the garrisons of Asia Minor or of the civil population[2]; but even when the Germans came in mass the emperors could usually only lead inconsiderable expeditionary forces against them[3]. There is probably no great exaggeration in the statement that the Juthungi alone possessed 40,000 cavalry and 80,000 foot[4].

Apart from this wealth of numbers and vitality on the German side, the main cause of their successes lay in the decline of the Empire and the acute crisis on which it had now entered. War on several fronts at once and, still more, the constant risings of pretenders drew the armies from the frontiers; it can often be shown

---

[1] Dexippus, frag. 26, 6 (*F.G.H.* II, p. 469).   [2] Zosimus I, 34, 3; 37, 2.
[3] See, for example, Dexippus, frag. 6, 10–11 (*F.G.H.* II, p. 459); Zonaras, XII, 24 (p. 596); Zosimus I, 68, 1.
[4] Dexippus, frag. 6, 4 (*F.G.H.* II, p. 457).

that the withdrawal of troops from a section of the frontier immediately provoked a German invasion. Under such conditions with pestilence and war decimating the population, with the citizen body lacking all military efficiency, ready to stand by and watch the raging of these children of nature, with an unexampled financial crisis and revolution of ideas convulsing the world, it was an amazing achievement to be able to ride out the German storm at all. When one remembers that the army even in normal times was too small for its tasks, and that the Empire's man-power was now terribly on the decline; when one adds that in these times of terrible pressure the whole organization and tactics of the army were remodelled and that a new class of professional commanders had to be trained to replace the dilettanti of the Senate, the achievement, due above all to the soldier-sons of Illyricum and a few gifted personalities, must be rated very high indeed.

It was a great piece of good fortune for Rome that her adversaries were so primitive. Instead of fighting in numerically fixed tactical units, the Germans took the field in bands formed through kinship or neighbourhood[1]; discipline in any real sense there was none. After a stout resistance on the field of battle they often collapsed from defective organization of supply, as, for example, in the Balkans in 269. Inferior equipment and a reluctance to wear helmets were serious handicaps. Furious, unconcerted attacks often led to disaster[2], and of the siege of cities they could make nothing[3].

The waves of the mighty inundation did, indeed, slowly subside. But the devastation that they left behind them was terrible. The masses of the cultivated classes, who at this time lost their lives or were carried off as slaves, could never again be replaced. Hundreds of cities were taken, and the terrors of those years are attested not only by coin-hoards all over the Empire, but also by the burnt layers turned up everywhere by the archaeologist's spade as the hall-mark of the epoch. Along with countless treasures of art Rome's store of gold went as booty, ransom or tribute to the Germans. The export trade from the Rhine to the Danube lands, which, as recent research shows, had attained serious economic importance (p. 242), was completely checked by the constant threat to the river-frontier, while trade by sea suffered from the raids of the pirates.

[1] Schmidt, *op. cit.* 1[2], pp. 55 *sq.*, 60; H. G. Gundel, *Unters. zur Taktik u. Strategie der Germanen*, Diss. Marburg, 1937, p. 21.
[2] Dexippus, frag. 6, 10 (*F.G.H.* II, p. 459).
[3] Dexippus, frag. 25 (*F.G.H.* II, p. 466).

Even in modern times war lets loose the basest passions. What wonder, then, if those children of nature revelled in sheer destruction[1]? If they deliberately burn cities after sacking them[2], or murder such prisoners as are sick or decrepit[3]? It would not be wholly just to charge them with the moral guilt for all this. The tragedy was not brought about by any ethical inferiority of the German race, but by the clash of two worlds at different levels of culture. As long as the Germans remained in their primitive environment, it was natural that they should earn their daily bread, not in the sweat of their brow, but in blood: 'volenti non fit iniuria.' But when they turned this law of violence against the world-State, which was adapted for peace and had based its whole mighty organization on a humane mode of life, their primitive morality proved disastrous to the higher morality of the Empire, little as they can be blamed for it.

It is an observed fact that, the greater the friction, the greater the assimilation to one another of two surfaces in contact; and so even these destructive wars produced a pronounced assimilation of the opposing parties, which, for the Germans, acquired a decisive historical importance.

In order to compete with the armies of Rome, East and West Germans alike united in considerable leagues, which in several instances, such as the Alemanni or the Franks, became the basis for States destined to survive. The rise of this class of leaders is illustrated by the appearance of such personalities as Kniva, the great opponent of Decius. In the later campaigns it becomes plain how quickly the East Germans had assimilated the military technique of the classical world[4].

The gold extorted from the Roman State or from individuals produced a major economic change in the German world. Gathered at first in mere greed and employed as ornament, this valuable form of property gradually became a regular medium of exchange and was the chief factor in raising the Germans to an advanced stage of money economy[5]. The finds make it possible to follow the process by which gold coinage, streaming into Germany,

[1] Cf. Zosimus I, 33, 3.   [2] Zosimus I, 35, 2.
[3] Dexippus, frag. 27, 10 (*F.G.H.* II, p. 472).
[4] Cf. Dexippus, frag. 29 (*F.G.H.* II, p. 474). The siege of Philippopolis, described by that writer, frag. 27 (*F.G.H.* II, p. 470), must have occurred in a later invasion, if only because it shows a highly developed technique; the probable date is 268 or 269.
[5] Alföldi, 'Nachahmungen der röm. Goldmedaillons als germ. Halsschmuck,' *Num. Közlöny*, XXVIII/IX, 1933, pp. 10 *sqq.*, where the literature is collected.

reached the North and, as early as the fifth century, filled the whole of Scandinavia.

Even stronger in its effects on Germany than the rivalry of opposition was the slow and barely perceptible radiation of the forms of ancient civilization. It will always be remarkable, that this form of peaceful penetration, while beginning much earlier with the West Germans, took a much firmer hold of the East Germans, as the later history of the Goths and Vandals shows. It is not possible here to describe the great influx of Roman export-trade into free Germany, its passage as far as Scandinavia, and the lively circulation of Roman money in the German sphere[1]; but one fact can be stressed, that the definite settlement of the Goths on the Black Sea and in the basin of the Danube had an extremely invigorating effect on the trade-routes leading from these directions northwards. Plundering raids had already brought great wealth from the Roman provinces to the Germans; but the regular influx of gold, coined or in bars, was first due to the relation of the tribes to the Empire as *foederati* and to the employment of individual Germans in the imperial army (see below, p. 219).

The years spent in such service gave an education that could not fail to have its consequences. German nobles now began to reach high posts as officers, even if, in the first place, it was only as leaders of their own people serving with Rome. Naulobatus, the Herulian chieftain, who in 268 received consular insignia from Gallienus, doubtless gave in return his services in the army[2]; the 'Pompeianus Dux, cognomine Francus,' for example, who played a part in the capture of Zenobia, was certainly a Frank[3]. How rapidly these sturdy warriors made themselves at home at imperial headquarters is illustrated by the anecdote about the Herulian Andonoballus[4]; the debate as to which is preferable—the old hostility or the friendship of the emperor—reminds one at once of the contest of Eriulf and Fravitta at the court of Theodosius the Great. How the spirit of the ancient world came thus to permeate the Germans cannot be shown in detail here. To this must be added—as early as the third century and with increasing force thereafter—the Christian missions in West and East.

---

[1] For a survey of the scattered literature and its results see O. Brogan, *J.R.S.* XXVI, 1936, pp. 195 *sqq.*; cf. also the review by H. J. Eggers, *Germania*, XX, 1936, pp. 146 *sqq.*

[2] For a different view see M. Bang, *Die Germanen im römischen Dienst*, p. 92.   [3] For a different view see Schmidt, *op. cit.* II[1], p. 439 n. 4.

[4] Petrus Patricius, frag. 171 (Cassius Dio, ed. Boissevain, III, p. 745).

Such contacts as these encroached more and more on the original civilization, Celtic in colouring, that the Germans had hitherto possessed. No less influential in this direction than the civilization of Rome was the Graeco-Sarmatian civilization of South Russia, which not only succeeded in transfusing the Gothic peoples, but finally extended as far as the Ugrians in the zone of the wooded steppes and took possession of the Huns as they thrust forward from Asia into a region between the Caucasus and the Caspian (pp. 100 *sqq.*). This cultural influence can only be grasped to-day from the material remains, above all, from the characteristic gold jewelry with inlaid stones, which subsequently became so fashionable among the Franks and Anglo-Saxons (p. 108). The fact that the ugly Sarmatian habit of deforming the skull succeeded in establishing itself among the East Germans may, indeed, attest the taking over of deep-seated religious and other ideas over and above the borrowings of art. In all this we can detect the historical preparation of the German peoples for the rôle that they were destined to play in the Middle Ages.

This will be better understood from a brief survey of the other side of the picture. It has been seen that Rome was unable to make a complete settlement with the intruders. She was glad enough to be able to deflect their hordes or secure their withdrawal by payments of money. These payments developed into a regular system, which, under the decent cover of the old scheme of subordinate *foederati*, led on to the new and superior warrior-caste found in the later Germano-Roman States[1]. As early as Caracalla the budget was seriously burdened by the annual subsidies paid to barbarian peoples[2]; the movements of the Germans in the third century simply compelled the Empire to include the whole of the surrounding world of the Germans in this system of subsidies, which led directly to the interdependence of the two great powers on one another. It can only be hinted in passing, how many distinct gradations of assistance were possible; conquered princes had to render actual service, others took over the defence of sections of frontier as allies of equal status, under Gallienus, or remained in their own lands to help the emperor against his enemies[3]. It is further to be observed, how varied and

---

[1] Cf. E. Kornemann, 'Die unsichtbaren Grenzen des röm. Kaiserreichs' (in *Staaten, Völker, Männer*, pp. 96 *sqq.*); Th. Mommsen, *Ges. Schriften*, VI, p. 229 *sq.*; A. Graf Schenk v. Stauffenberg, *Die Welt als Geschichte*, II, 1936, pp. 159 *sqq.*

[2] Dio LXXIX, 17, 3 (p. 421 Boissevain).

[3] Zosimus I, 30, 3.

extensive were the employments of German material both in regular Roman troops and in national formations in the imperial army (p. 211 *sq.*). The serious lack of farmers led, from the time of Marcus Aurelius and, more particularly, from the middle of the third century[1], to the transplantation of ever-increasing masses of Germans to the soil of the Empire as free or half-free farmers.

While this intermixture of the peoples thus permeated the lowest strata of the population, it also extended upwards into the highest. The grandees of Rome might find it absurd that Caracalla should appear in public in German dress[2]: but it was at least a foreshadowing of what was to be. The Marcomannic secondary wife of Gallienus, in her position of high honour, and the German princes on the council of war of the soldier-emperors illustrate once again the incipient germanization of the court.

A far-reaching process of ancient history moved thus towards its consummation. Rome was first compelled to draw the men to maintain her world-empire from Italy instead of from the capital; the exhaustion of Italy next transferred this rôle to the civilized provinces of the interior, and, after them, to the rough sons of the frontier-lands. Even these could not for ever bear the brunt of the ceaseless wars of the third century. Rome was now driven to go beyond them to the barbarian world. What she sought was just human raw material, and no more, but the political centre of gravity shifted naturally to the new forces beyond the frontiers, and thereby rendered inevitable the birth of the Germano-Roman States.

[1] *E.g.* Zosimus 1, 46, 2; 68, 3; 71, 1–2; S.H.A. *Prob.* 18, 1–3. This is becoming clearer from the results of excavations also in the Danube provinces.
[2] Dio LXXIX, 3, 3; Herodian IV, 7, 3.

CHAPTER VI

THE CRISIS OF THE EMPIRE (A.D. 249—270)

I. INTRODUCTION: THE AGE OF DECIUS,
GALLUS AND AEMILIANUS

A BRIEF survey of the period is necessary at the outset, in order to indicate who were the chief actors in the moving drama that was played in this brief span of time, what were its essential features and on what lines the action proceeded. Even this preliminary view enables one to recognize the special character of these two decades by one of its essential traits—by the amazing acceleration of the rhythm of events. Under Antoninus Pius the solidarity and inner strength of the Empire had been so great that its stability seemed to reduce every movement to insignificance and the whole period took its character from conditions, not from events. Then ensued blows of unexpected violence, but still quite isolated blows, like the Marcomannic War, or sudden revolutions like the *coup d'État* of Septimius Severus. Such decisive events then follow more and more closely on one another; in each and every department of life the pulse accelerates till about the middle of the century, and then, gradually and with many a relapse, it resumes its regularity. Not till Diocletian has life become calm enough for us to be able to recognize its essential conditions.

In the opening sections no appraisement of values will be given. It is first necessary to fix the course of events. We observe these at first from a great distance, so that the main contours may stand out more clearly while the details disappear, and the great movements show themselves plainly, but the din of battle and the voices of individuals are no longer heard. Only when the external order of events has been determined as precisely as possible, we may approach the tumult of wars and the life of every day, the headquarters, armies and masses, so as to determine the forces that were at work, and appreciate the historical evolution which kept these forces in play and the effect of individuals.

How do matters stand when this period begins? The two Philips are dead; the victorious pretender, C. Messius Quintus Decius, approaches Rome. The Senate welcomes him on his arrival with extravagant honours and bestows on him the name of

Traianus, the ideal model of the emperor 'by grace of the Senate[1]'. Decius, however, at once emphasizes his absolute dependence on the army of Illyricum,[2] which had clothed him with the purple. Decius had overcome Philip near Verona in September 249 (p. 94). In Rome, soon after the customary celebration of his arrival and the solemn vows for the long continuance and happiness of his rule, he initiated that campaign against Christianity that threw large sections of the population into panic and misery (see below, pp. 202 sqq.). He had still a short time left him for buildings in the capital and for other occupations of peace. From Syria was brought, according to the fashion of the times, the head of the usurper, Jotapianus[3], and as late as the end of December it was still possible to discharge time-expired soldiers[4]. But signs of disturbance soon appeared. In Gaul a civil war broke out, only to be suppressed—whether the Emperor himself visited the province cannot be decided[5]. Thereupon followed the tidings of the inroad of the Goths into the Balkans (see above, p. 143). About April or June 250 Decius made his elder son, Herennius Etruscus, Caesar, a youth who, to judge by his portraits, had hardly reached man's estate—and sent him with an armed force to Moesia. Soon afterwards he himself set out. Probably to ensure the loyalty of the capital by a representative of his house he appointed his second son, Hostilianus, Caesar[6]. P. Licinius Valerianus, a respected member of the Senate, was, it appears, set at the boy's side, to direct the civil administration for him during the Gothic war. The wife of Decius, Herennia Cupressenia Etruscilla, now raised to the rank of Augusta, may well have lent her help and counsel to the young prince. Simultaneously with the war the persecution of the Christians proceeded on a grand scale. Towards the middle of June the required sacrifices began, and the authorities, during some

---

[1] The name Traianus only appears after the entry of Decius into Rome (cf. K. Wittig, P.W. s.v. Messius (9), cols. 1247 sqq.). But, as there was no justification for the adoption of the name by Decius himself (such as the motives that prompted Severus to take the name of Pertinax, or fictitious relationship, as in the case of the adoption of the name of Antoninus by Caracalla, Elagabalus, etc.), it is evident that this title of honour was voted by those same people, who greeted the new emperor with the cry 'felicior Augusto, melior Traiano.'

[2] Cf. Alföldi, Fünfundzwanzig Jahre Röm.-Germ. Komm. p. 12 sq.

[3] Aurelius Victor, Caes. XXIX, 2; Zosimus I, 20, 2 (under Philip).

[4] Wittig, op. cit. col. 1267 sq. Whether these veterans were still kept on the roll is another matter.   [5] Eutropius IX, 4.

[6] Wittig, op. cit. col. 1262. For another view see G. Elmer, Num. Zeitschr. 1935, p. 40 and K. Pink, ib. 1936, p. 19.

weeks, gave certificates of compliance to the loyal who sacrificed and began to persecute the recalcitrant (see p. 202). But the effects of the long drawn-out war soon began to be acutely felt. The mob of Rome, in its desire for a new régime[1], went to the length of proclaiming a rival emperor: the name of Decius was erased from many inscriptions. But the pretender, Julius Valens Licinianus, a man, it would appear, of senatorial rank, was soon crushed[2]. In May 251, the two sons of the Emperor were proclaimed Augusti. But, very soon after the joyful celebration of that event[3], the whole Empire was shaken by the news of the destruction of the Roman expeditionary force (about the beginning of June), and the heroic deaths of Decius and his elder son at Abrittus in the Dobrudja.

It was some slight consolation that Julius Priscus, the governor of Thrace, who had surrendered with his mutinous troops to the Goths at Philippopolis and had been proclaimed emperor, had in the meantime vanished from the scene. The wrecks of the defeated army in the Dobrudja proclaimed the legate of Lower Moesia, C. Vibius Afinius Trebonianus Gallus, second emperor, as the surviving son of Decius was still a child[4]. Gallus, in the disastrous position in which he stood, had lost the power to dictate to the enemy the terms of peace. The flower of the population of Thrace—so far as it still survived—was carried off by the Goths, and with it went the wealth of the provinces; besides all this, the raiders received annual subsidies, to induce them not to return.

Gallus treated his fallen predecessors with all respect and had them consecrated by the Senate; Hostilianus he adopted as his son. Only Etruscilla was forced into retirement, but the wife of the new emperor, Afinia Gemina Baebiana, did not become Augusta, so as not to encroach on her prerogative.[5] Gallus, however, at the same time made his own son, Volusianus, Caesar and, not long afterwards, Augustus; had not the son of Decius died of the plague,

---

[1] Aurelius Victor, *Caes.* XXIX, 3.

[2] Certainly before the election of the Pope Cornelius, March 251; cf. Cyprian, *Ep.* 55, 9.

[3] The appointment only took place very shortly before Abrittus; the mint of Antioch had not time to strike for Herennius Etruscus as Augustus, but only the mint of Rome. Cf. also J. Vogt, *Die Alex. Kaisermünzen*, p. 198.

[4] For another view see Wittig, *op. cit.* col. 1273 and elsewhere.

[5] The type of *Iuno Martialis* may refer to the wife of Gallus; this new goddess may be the deification of the *mater castrorum*.

complications must soon have arisen.[1] Although enough remained to be done in the devastated lands on the frontier, Gallus
hastened to Rome to ensure his position by showing his respect
to the Senate.[2] Gallus seems, in fact, to have concentrated his
entire attention on Rome[3], and it appears that it was at Rome
that Gallus and his son provided decent burial for the poor who
had been carried off by the plague[4]. It was just at this moment
that a fearful plague broke out, which for fifteen long years was
to rage over the whole Empire. Apart from this, the two rulers
were incapable of any kind of energetic action; the inroads of the
East Germans not only continued, but rose to the pitch of an
appalling disaster—to say nothing of the complete neglect of the
East (see p. 169). The persecution of the Christians, which
began again in 253, did not reach any serious dimensions, for
the reign of Gallus and his son lasted only two years.

The successor of Gallus as governor of Lower Moesia, M.
Aemilius Aemilianus, had succeeded early in 253 in putting an
end to the devastation of his province by the Goths and had even
carried to a victorious conclusion a punitive expedition north of
the Danube. He was now proclaimed emperor. Though Goths
were still running wild in Thrace, Aemilianus turned in haste to
Italy to catch Gallus unprepared. The surprise succeeded, and he
had reached Umbria before Gallus and Volusianus encountered
him. Their army was so inferior in numbers to that of their
adversary, that their own troops chose to make away with them
rather than hazard a hopeless battle—at Interamna, or, according
to another tradition, a little farther north at Forum Flaminii.

After Gallus had thus been disposed of, Aemilianus was recognized in Egypt[5] and throughout the East, and plentiful issues
from the Imperial mint attested his confirmation by that same
Senate that had so recently condemned him as *hostis publicus*[6].
His wife, Cornelia Supera, was made Augusta. But all these
glories lasted no more than three or four summer months[7]. For,
when Gallus gave orders to P. Licinius Valerianus to bring up the

---

[1] The combinations suggested by Elmer, *op. cit.* p. 41, break down on the
fact that the activities assumed by him for a 'Moneta Comitatensis' simply
represent the latest issues of the mint of Rome; cf. Alföldi in *Num. Közlöny*,
XXXIV, 5, 1938. The suspicions suggested in Zosimus I, 25, 2 seem to be
unfounded.   [2] Zonaras XII, 21 (p. 589); Zosimus I, 25, 1.
[3] Zosimus (I, 27, 1) writes: τῶν κρατούντων...πάντα δὲ τὰ τῆς Ῥώμης
ἔξω περιορώντων.   [4] Aurelius Victor, *Caes.* XXX, 2.
[5] Vogt, *op. cit.* p. 201.   [6] Aurelius Victor, *Caes.* XXXI, 3.
[7] For a different chronology see H. Mattingly, *J.R.S.* XXV, 1935, pp.
55 *sqq.*; cf. A. Stein, *Laureae Aquincenses*, 1938.

Rhine legions to his aid, Valerian, instead of doing so, had himself proclaimed emperor. He had a strong army, which had been collected in Raetia, no doubt to fight the Alemanni; he, too, now turned with it towards Italy. Aemilianus met the fate of Gallus, for, as he marched north, he was murdered, not far from the place where his predecessors had met their death (near Spoletium or perhaps between Ocriculum and Narnia). The army of Valerian was felt to be the stronger, and Valerian himself was an imposing figure, in virtue of his birth and his career, and so the troops of Aemilianus chose to kill their own lord rather than face a new civil war. It must have been out of respect to the authority of the Senate that the new ruler did not leave it to the army to proclaim his son, P. Licinius Egnatius Gallienus, as his colleague, but requested the *patres* to appoint his son a second Augustus about September 253[1].

While the best corps of the Roman army were tied down to Italy by the civil wars, the frontier-guard was everywhere being shattered by the encircling pressure of the neighbouring peoples. Valerian now resolved to entrust the conduct of the wars in the West to his son, while he himself very soon afterwards went to the East, which, since Philip, had not set eyes on any emperor.

II. THE ROMAN EAST FROM VALERIAN TO THE ACCESSION OF AURELIAN

The harsh rule of Philip's brother Priscus had at once produced a violent reaction. Jotapianus, who was perhaps descended from a branch of the family of Severus Alexander, was raised to the throne in Syria (or, perhaps, in Cappadocia) but he was quickly crushed (p. 92 *sq.*). As neither Decius nor Gallus was in a position to appear in person in the East, the danger abroad and the demoralization at home continued alike to increase. The peoples of South Russia, who had by this time sucked the Danube provinces dry, began to organize great sea-raids to plunder Asia Minor (see p. 147). In 253 came the first sea-raid by the Goths of the Black Sea which reached Pessinus and Ephesus. Armenia was too weak to defend herself without vigorous assistance from Rome against the New Persian Empire (see p. 131) and the friends of Persia succeeded in murdering the excellent king, Chosroes. Soon afterwards (under Gallus) his son Tiridates was compelled to flee from his country, and now began that new Persian offensive

---

[1] Cf. L. Wickert, P.W. *s.v.* Licinius (84), col. 352 *sq.*

against the Roman provinces of the East that was to last nearly a decade[1]. Early in 253 the Persian bands swarmed over Mesopotamia and Syria, captured Antioch and made good their retirement with an immense booty and a countless host of captives. When Valerian hastened to the spot in the winter of 253–4, he was already too late. But the priest-king of Emesa, Sulpicius Uranius Antoninus, who, owing to the impotence of the central government, had been set up as a pretender and had successfully organized the defence of his own small home-land, now vanished from the scene at the Emperor's approach. The gallant commander of Pityus, the Successianus who had conducted an admirable defence of that city against an assault of the Borani early in 254, was appointed Praetorian Prefect and joined the Emperor in rebuilding Antioch from its ruins.

Egypt, too, gained a moment of relief. How loosely the government had been holding the reins can still be seen from the decay of the coinage of Alexandria under Decius[2]. In the second Egyptian year of Gallus (August 30, 251–August 29, 252) no coins were issued—an omission without parallel between 216 and the end of the autonomous issues in 296[3]. But even the presence of Valerian failed to bring any real stabilization. In 255 Pityus and Trapezus fell victims to an unexpected renewal of the attack of the Borani by sea, and in 256 the Goths launched their second great naval expedition, which, having sailed along the west coast of the Black Sea, scared the demoralized garrison out of Chalcedon. The conquest of this key-position placed the great cities of Bithynia at the mercy of the Goths (see above, p. 148).

In this crisis Valerian proved utterly incompetent. Out of dread of usurpations he could not bring himself to entrust any of his generals with an expeditionary force against the Goths; all he did was to send a certain Felix to Byzantium to direct the defence of that important strategic centre, preparatory to undertaking the campaign himself. Setting out from Antioch, however, he got no farther than Cappadocia, while the passage of his army proved a sore burden to the cities. As his general headquarters he chose Samosata, a fortress in a commanding position on the Upper Euphrates, covered against Persian attack by the strong advanced bastion of Edessa. But even from this favourable position he was unable to prevent the renewal of the Persian invasions. Hormizd,

---

[1] For details in the account that follows, see A. Alföldi, in *Berytus* IV, 1937, p. 53 *sq.* For a somewhat different chronology see above, pp. 133 *sqq.*
[2] J. G. Milne, *Catalogue of Alexandrian Coins...*, p. xxiv.
[3] Id., *A History of Egypt under Roman Rule*[3], p. 71.

son of Shapur, first led an army against the frontier of the Euphrates. The recent excavations at Doura-Europos, the point at which he broke through, have given us an amazingly vivid picture of the siege and of the mine-warfare that shattered the nerve of the garrison of the fort. The latest coins found in the purses of the soldiers who fell in this underground war can be dated to the year 255, and appear to show that the fortress fell in that year (see, however, p. 134).

Under these catastrophic conditions the spirit of hostility to Rome in the East found violent expression. Mariades, a Syrian noble of Antioch, led Shapur in 258 or 259 against his native city. The local knowledge of the traitor led to a complete surprise. The well-to-do were able, it is true, to escape; the officials saved the mint and the State treasure, but the masses, who shared the sympathies of Mariades, stayed on the spot. It must have been through treachery that the range of hills near the city fell without a blow into the hands of the Persians. Shapur made good his retirement a second time unscathed with his booty, after burning the city and laying waste the surrounding country.

In this fearful crisis Valerian found a vent for the general embitterment. Since August 257 he had been engaged in persecuting the Christians with a success denied him against his foreign enemies (see below, p. 205 *sq.*), and he now proceeded to intensify the harshness of his measures against them. Hatred was again allowed to run riot against a background of general disaster and danger, exactly as under Decius.

The surprise attack on Antioch was followed by an even more terrifying and devastating invasion by Shapur in 260. He had pushed past Commagenian Antioch as far as Cappadocia, before the fatal clash with the ageing Emperor took place. The Roman army was decimated by the plague; it was even more seriously depressed by the complete inertia and feebleness of its commander-in-chief. In his lack of all resolution he seems to have postponed the actual decision; it looks as if he shut himself up behind the walls of Samosata. Finally he risked an engagement in Mesopotamia, only to suffer defeat. The Persians then beset Edessa, where the starving garrison, mutinous though it might be, still gallantly repelled the enemy. Then, of a sudden, came the terrible tidings that the Emperor had fallen into the hands of Shapur. A whole series of picturesque and even fantastic stories was spun about Valerian's capture and the humiliations to which he was subjected. When the Emperor died is not recorded. The jubilation among the Persians was immense (see pp. 135 *sqq.*).

The disaster itself occurred in the second half of June, 260[1]. The Persians followed hard on the Roman army as it fled in utter confusion, laying waste the cities as they went. For the third time Antioch was visited by the tide of plunderers. Many other flourishing centres of civilization in Syria, Cappadocia and Cilicia were destroyed. Lycaonia, too, had been drawn into the vortex, when at last a counterstroke came from the side of Rome.

Mesopotamia itself had been occupied by the Persians, but, while Nisibis and, as it seems, Carrhae also were taken, Edessa defied their attack. Its valiant defenders were actually able to give sufficient trouble to Shapur on his return to induce him as he passed the fort to surrender the treasure captured in Syria, rather than expose to their attacks an army that had lost its formation and had ceased to care for anything beyond securing its booty. Behind the cover of this bulwark Macrianus, who had been *praepositus annonae expeditionalis* and, at the same time, *procurator arcae expeditionis*, or, in other words, Quartermaster General, was able in Samosata to take in hand the whole task of re-organization. The enemy had scattered over the east of Asia Minor to plunder and thus facilitated the Roman counter-stroke. A certain general Callistus (nicknamed Ballista) had put on shipboard the troops that he had collected in concert with Macrianus, and had surprised and defeated the Persians at more than one point on the Cilician coast; he even succeeded in intercepting the baggage-train and concubines of the Great King. This loss impelled Shapur to retire, driving before him his hordes of captives. But he was thankful enough to regain the Euphrates, for, as he passed Carrhae on his way to Ctesiphon, he was again attacked, this time by Odenathus, prince of Palmyra, and suffered such fresh losses that his victorious homecoming still left him crippled for a long time to come.

Macrianus had renounced his allegiance to the captive Emperor when Shapur tried to negotiate with him in his name. That is the reason why the obverse types of Valerian disappear at this moment from the issues of the imperial mint at Samosata and the coinage is continued solely in the name of Gallienus. But in September, when the successes above chronicled had brought a first interval of peace, Callistus and Macrianus broke with Gallienus. Callistus and Macrianus were both barred from the throne—the former, perhaps, by his low birth, the latter by his lameness. They therefore proclaimed as Augusti the two sons of

---

[1] The election of the Pope Julius on July 22nd, 260, seems to be connected with the arrival of the news of the death of Valerian.

the latter, T. Fulvius Junius Macrianus and T. Fulvius Junius Quietus. Callistus was named Praetorian Prefect.

Conditions were not unfavourable for this rebellion[1]. The much suffering East greeted the young pretenders with enthusiasm; Gallienus had his hands fast tied in the West, while Shapur was completely crippled. But Macrianus would not confine himself to one section of the Empire and soon set out with his elder son, of the same name, to conquer the West. In the spring of 261 the Eastern army reached the Danube provinces, where Aureolus, the gifted but unscrupulous general of Gallienus, awaited it. The regiments of Pannonia, which cherished a bitter spite against Gallienus for putting the defence of the Rhine frontier before the protection of Illyricum and had already twice risen against him (see p. 184), joined the Eastern army. But these Oriental troops had little stomach for civil war. When the battle began and a standard chanced to fall with its bearer to the ground the other *signiferi* hastened to lower their standards, in token of submission. Both of the Macriani met their death. Callistus, who had stayed behind in the East with the younger pretender, Quietus, was unable now to sustain his position. On the news of the fall of the Macriani many cities revolted against him and Gallienus adroitly directed Odenathus, prince of the desert-city of Palmyra, to attack him. Odenathus assailed Callistus in Emesa and slew him, while the inhabitants of the city, in their hard plight, executed Quietus, about November 261.

The complications and abuses that these revolutions occasioned can to some extent be realized from the one example of Egypt. The mint of Alexandria, as late as August 260, was preparing coins of Valerian for the Egyptian New Year (August 30); the capture of the Emperor was not yet taken to involve the loss of his imperial rights; the contrary view taken by Gallienus was obviously not yet known. But as early as September Macrianus and Quietus were recognized in Alexandria as in most other parts of Egypt. After the defeat of Macrianus in Illyricum the mint of Alexandria resumed its allegiance to Gallienus, whereas other parts of the country, as the papyri show, remained true to Quietus up to the moment of his death. In Alexandria itself these changes were attended by bloody fighting. The city split into two hostile camps; the testimony of the Bishop Dionysius shows that the feud was still alive about the Easter of 262. The head of the opposition party was L. Mussius Aemilianus, who since 257 had been prefect of Egypt. As he was still there in 262, there can be no

[1] For details see Alföldi in *Berytus* v, 1938.

doubt that he had first taken the side of the Macriani and only raised his own flag of revolt after their fall. As the mint of Alexandria lay in the quarter that resumed its allegiance to Gallienus, it was not at his disposal, but it is quite possible that he took the purple. It may be that he was encouraged to do so by a successful blow at the Blemmyes on the southern frontier of Egypt; Odenathus was unable to attack him, as he was at that very moment advancing into Persia (see below).

The detachment of Alexandria was highly dangerous to Italy: it seems as if Rome looked in vain for the Egyptian corn-fleet. It was probably by a naval expedition that Gallienus succeeded in ridding himself of the rebel: Aurelius Theodotus, the general of Gallienus, successfully carried out the *coup*, while the Emperor himself, it seems, advanced by land to Byzantium, ready to intervene, if need arose. Theodotus, who now became prefect of Egypt, succeeded a little later in crushing a fresh rebellion, led by a Moorish officer, Memor.

In the years that followed, Septimius Odenathus, prince of Palmyra, came to be the most important political factor in the Roman East. It will be seen later how important a part the Palmyrene archers played in this period in the military history of Rome. But, besides archers, Odenathus had excellent heavy mailed cavalry on the Persian model. Nor did he fail to profit by the luck of the moment. He had little difficulty in surprising Shapur's rabble army; the defeat of Quietus was made easy by the withdrawal of the main army under Macrianus, while Gallienus, until his hands were free, was only too glad to find so effective an ally.

Odenathus had originally sought closer touch with Shapur, whom he had esteemed far more highly than he had the Romans, but he was rudely rebuffed. This left him no choice but to draw closer to Valerian. As early as 258 he enjoyed the high distinction of becoming *vir consularis*. His successful attack on Shapur on his march homewards reveals the relentlessness of his opposition to that prince—an opposition perhaps intensified by the Sassanid conquest of Characene and the closing of the caravan route to the Persian Gulf. Gallienus bound him to himself in the service of the Empire by high titles of honour, and, after the removal of Quietus in 261, entrusted him with the counter-offensive against the Persian Empire. Odenathus was able to supplement the remains of the Roman army of the East with a strong native levy from Syria and in 262 opened his first counter-attack, which he began by regaining the great Mesopotamian fortresses, such as Carrhae and Nisibis, and then defeated the Persians in battle. Shapur was besieged in his own capital, and Gallienus could receive the title of Persicus Maximus. Some years later, early in 267, in a campaign in which his son and co-ruler, Septimius Herodes, shared, Odenathus again marched to the gates of Ctesiphon. He then turned back to meet the invasion of the Goths in Cappadocia, and advanced as far as Heraclea Pontica; but he came too late, and, not long afterwards, was murdered together with his son (p. 176).

These victories produced a decisive change in Rome's relation to Persia. Chance has preserved the record of the execution of great works of fortification in Adraha by the governor of Roman Arabia in the years 261–2 and 262–3, and this is doubtless only a reflection of a more general activity. In Doura, one of the most important points at which Shapur had broken through, a Roman-Palmyrene garrison was again stationed as early as 262. Armenia, too, must have returned to its allegiance to Rome, even if our sources only suggest it indirectly.

The relation of Odenathus to Gallienus is precisely defined by the titles which the Palmyrene prince received from his overlord. On his first expedition against Persia he had already at his disposal the remains of the Roman army; he must then have held the title of *dux Romanorum*. This is an exceptional position, in which the exact powers are deliberately left undefined, as is likewise the case with the civil titles of this prince. The competence of the Roman governors was not meant to be undermined by this new dignity, which was intended to have a purely personal significance. After his victory over Persia Odenathus received the title of *imperator*. Besides the diadem of the king, Odenathus now wore, as did his son after him, the laurel-wreath of the imperial Imperator. Such an honour was barely reconcilable with the subordinate position of a vassal-prince, and already foreshadowed the struggles for the prestige of Empire that were to ensue. Nor did the civil distinctions bestowed on Odenathus represent any steps in the normal official career. As early as the second century the special commissioners to restore order in the cities of the Roman East had been designated *legati Augusti ad corrigendum statum civitatium liberarum* (vol. xi, p. 558). Now, when exceptional conditions were the rule, this function was further developed. Thus arose the position of a *corrector totius Italiae*, held by the distinguished Pomponius Bassus (p. 391); Odenathus similarly became *corrector totius Orientis*. This did not imply that the civil and financial administration was allotted to him, only that he enjoyed a certain right of supervision. Apart from the Roman titles of honour the dignity of the Palmyrene ruler is now described by the new title 'King of Kings.' This was not incompatible with his subordination to his Roman suzerain, for the same title had long been allowed, together with the absolute grant of independent sovereignty, involved in a separate coinage in gold, to the kings of Bosporus. But what the name did emphasize the more strongly was a rivalry with the Great Kings of Persia.

The boundaries of the realm of Odenathus in his new position were to the north the Taurus mountains, to the south the Arabian Gulf; it extended also to Cilicia, Syria, Mesopotamia and Arabia. Asia Minor and Egypt were not included and had to be seized by force later, as will soon appear.

More particularly after the conferment of the title of *imperator* the position of the mighty sheik fell little short of imperial autocracy. From the Roman point of view, therefore, it could only be regarded as a temporary concession, demanded by the necessities of the moment. Friction with the governors must have been an everyday occurrence. Two significant cases are known. A Roman official, Quirinus by name[1], could not stomach the fact of Odenathus' conducting the war of Rome (against Shapur); Odenathus, in revenge, sought to put him to death. It is not impossible that this 'Quirinus' is the same as Aurelius Quirinius, who is recorded as head of the financial administration of Egypt in 262. The second instance was far more serious in its effects. A Rufinus is mentioned, who had had the 'elder Odenathus' put to death and was called to account for it before Gallienus by 'the younger Odenathus.' In the 'elder Odenathus' we must, with Mommsen, recognize the prince of Palmyra; in the younger Odenathus, his son falsely so-called, Vaballathus Athenodorus— the more so as another tradition makes the Emperor get rid of our Odenathus[2]. In that case, the instigator of the murder would be the Cocceius Rufinus, who is known as governor of Roman Arabia at this time, and the political character of the deed is further to be seen in the fact that the eldest son of the king, Hairanes-Herodes, was killed along with him[3]. It is known from other sources that the murderer himself was a kinsman of the prince, who, of course, may have been prompted by personal rancour; but behind him stood the plotter, who imagined himself to be acting in the interests of Rome.

With Odenathus vanished from the scene yet a third leading personality of Palmyra—and this, too, can be no mere coincidence.

[1] Not Carinus, cf. Petrus Patricius, frag. 168 (Cassius Dio, ed. Boissevain, III, p. 744).
[2] Johann. Antioch. frag. 152, 2 (*F.H.G.* IV, 599).
[3] See Note 2 at the end of the Volume.

It was Septimius Vorodes, who had received from Gallienus the dignity of a *iuridicus* and a *procurator ducenarius* and who had stood at the side of his king as military governor (*argapetes*) of Palmyra. The latest inscription that mentions him was set up in April 267; it was just about that time that Odenathus was stabbed. In one way or another he seems to have been involved in the plot.

Odenathus, indeed, was originally no convinced adherent of Rome. But, grievously insulted by Shapur and at bitter war with him, and loaded by Gallienus with unprecedented distinctions, he maintained a firm loyalty to Rome. Yet, after all, it appears as if the second victory over Persia widened the horizon of his ambition and as if he were meditating a breach with Rome[1]. For this he had to pay with his life, as had many another barbarian king in the course of the Empire.

There are many other indications which suggest that Gallienus intended to make a thorough settlement with Palmyra immediately after the death of Odenathus. In the year 267 a new mint was established in the west of Asia Minor, the die-engravers of which were in part detailed from Siscia, and so attest the initiative of the Emperor. As in this period the foundation of mints was without exception designed to provide pay for the troops, this new mint points to the establishment of a base of operations in Asia Minor. Further, the new issue of 268 at Siscia has the reverse type *Oriens Augusti*, which sounds like an advertisement of the claim to the East (p. 187). The *Vita Gallieni*[2] also reports that Gallienus sent Heraclianus with an army to the East, but that the Palmyrenes defeated him. Even if this goes too far and an open clash cannot yet have occurred, it is clear that Gallienus was only prevented by the terrible raid of the Goths on Asia Minor in 267 and the great Herulian invasion of 268 (p. 149) from making a final reckoning with Zenobia, the wife of the dead prince, who carried on the government in the name of her son, Herodianus, a minor, and, after him, of her third son, Vaballathus (p. 178).

The complete failure of Valerian, the inability of Gallienus to transfer his activities to the East, the terrible German invasions of 267 and 268, must all have fostered the conviction in Palmyra that Rome was no longer capable of holding the reins of the East. The important part that the soldiers of Palmyra had for decades maintained in the Roman army must have heightened their consciousness of their native worth. The achievements of Odenathus followed, to confirm the conviction that it was the mission of

---

[1] In the episode of Rufinus (Petrus Patricius, frag. 166 (Cassius Dio, ed. Boissevain, III, p. 744)) this is twice emphasized.   [2] 13, 4–5.

Palmyra to rule the East, a mission that Zenobia set to work to realize with all the ambition and capacity of a Julia Domna.

It was most fortunate for Rome that Palmyra could find no support against her in Persia. It was not only the senseless folly of Shapur or the adroit diplomacy of Gallienus, not even the entanglements of the last years that compelled the Queen to fight out the battle for the East in a Roman setting and under Roman forms. Not that the strength of Iranian influence in this environment need be denied. Odenathus, it is clear, was regarded as a pure barbarian, not only by the Roman commanders who were active in the East, but by the Syrians of Emesa themselves. More than this, it is obvious that the rise of the Palmyrene power was favourable to the elements that hated Rome. But, on the other side, it must not be forgotten that Palmyra had not only been illumined by the setting sun of Roman civilization, but had already experienced the warmth and brilliance of Rome's noonday prime. The long service of her young men in the Roman armies in Africa and Europe must have done much to promote assimilation to Roman ways. Even the Palmyra that, as a new Great Power, refused to serve Rome any longer, could not get clear of the Roman track, on which she had so long been running.

It was not the title of Great King, but that of Augustus, with the rest of the full imperial title, which was the final goal of the ambition of Vaballathus; Zenobia too, after the break with Rome, adopted the style of Pia and Augusta. Instead of the Persian tiara Vaballathus wears on his coins the laurel-wreath of the Imperator, as does his mother likewise. Moreover, these new aims of Palmyrene ambition were fixed by men who represented the highest classical culture of the age, above all, by the philosopher Longinus[1]. At the court of Palmyra assembled the Neoplatonists, who, fleeing from Italy after the murder of Gallienus, continued to dream of the rule of philosophy in the State.

It has been supposed that the Palmyrenes, in the years 267–9, quietly and gradually absorbed the whole East, without disowning the Roman government. But so well disguised an acquisition of sovereign rights is hard to imagine. There is no evidence for a separation of Syria from Rome in these years, nor is there any support for the supposition that Zenobia then attached herself to Persia in place of Rome. It could hardly be reconciled with such

---

[1] The political connections of Zenobia with Bishop Paul of Antioch seem to the present writer to be even less real than to Fr. Loofs (*Paulus von Samosata*, pp. 17 *sqq.*, 31 *sqq.*). For another view, cf. *e.g.* G. Bardy, *Paul de Samosate*[2], pp. 260, 275 (with references to literature).

a direction of policy towards Persia, that Vaballathus should still have borne the title of 'King of Kings' in 270 and that, even after his ensuing revolt, he should have been called Persicus Maximus. That Mesopotamia was abandoned to Persia at the time is a mere baseless hypothesis: when Aurelian appears in Asia, Mesopotamian troops join him—a clear proof to the contrary (p. 303).

On the other hand it can be shown that Zenobia only resolved to refuse obedience to Rome at a later date, on receiving the news of the death of Claudius. To take Asia Minor first, it is known[1] that the power of Zenobia there till the death of Claudius extended no farther than Ancyra. West of this point, the cities of Pisidia did in fact continue their issues of coin in the names of Gallienus and Claudius, and one is inclined to place somewhere in this region the new imperial mint, mentioned above; it continued to function without change under Claudius. The statement that Claudius was planning to transplant the Isaurians to Cilicia may also be historical[2]. All the more surprising is the fact that both the new imperial mint and the autonomous issues of Pisidia no longer mention Quintillus. In point of fact it was just at this time (beginning of 270) that the Palmyrene troops began to conquer the west of Asia Minor; when the news of the elevation of Aurelian arrived, they were just trying to occupy Bithynia, though they did not succeed[3]. That is why the mint of Cyzicus, founded at the beginning of the reign of Claudius with die-engravers from the mint in the west of Asia Minor[4], continued to strike for Quintillus and, after him, without delay, for Aurelian.

As regards the spread of Palmyrene power in Syria, the position is cleared up by the activity of the mint of Antioch. It works without a break to the end of the reign of Gallienus and even dispatches workers to the new mint in the west of Asia Minor. It then continues its striking for Claudius; the numerous types of its two issues are certainly quite enough to fill the eighteen months of this ruler[5]. But the coinage of Quintillus of this mint is to seek. Just as the accession of Aurelian brought a change in Asia Minor, so too in Syria. Zenobia re-opens the mint of Antioch and strikes coins at once for Vaballathus, with the titles which Gallienus had given his father, but with the bust of Aurelian on the reverse. She was therefore aiming at an understanding with the famous general, but she had already gone too far to obtain it (p. 301 *sq.*).

---

[1] Zosimus I, 50, 1–2.　　　　　　　　　[2] S.H.A. *Trig. tyr.* 26, 7.
[3] Zosimus *loc. cit.*; cf. also *I.G.R.R.* III, nos. 39–40.
[4] A fact that implies that the Emperor had full control of it.
[5] For another view see H. Mattingly, *Num. Chron.* 1936, p. 101 *sq.*

Palmyrene activity following on the death of Claudius probably extended to the province of Arabia[1], and also to Egypt. In the latter country the bitter feeling against Rome had been steadily rising since the suppression of the revolts described above. Yet another revolution in Alexandria followed, in which many members of the Council joined in the breach of loyalty; for several years the rebels were besieged in the suburb of Bruchium, until at last they were starved out and forced to surrender, apparently in the autumn of 268. It was no long time, however, after the awful havoc of this war, that the anti-Roman party shouted in triumph as the Palmyrene troops marched in.

Many writers, it must be admitted, have set this conquest under Claudius. But, as the mint of Alexandria belonged to that emperor till the end of his reign and was even able to inaugurate an issue for Quintillus, it is clear that it was only just at that moment, about February 270, that the troops of Zenobia arrived. The prefect, Tenagino Probus, was actually on the seas, engaged in the subjection of the Gothic pirates and, in his absence, the Palmyrene army under Zabdas, 70,000 strong, defeated the weak Roman levies; Probus returned in haste and threw back the foe, but soon lost his life by the treachery of the leader of the Palmyrene party in Egypt.

Tenagino Probus served under Claudius first as *praeses Numidiae* (end of 268), then as prefect of Egypt, and in that capacity— doubtless in 269—he chastised the Marmaridae, situated between Egypt and Cyrene. From thence he was called to Carthage to quell a revolt[2]. The year must have been nearing its close when he returned with his army to Egypt and then took to the sea, the Gothic pirates having got as far as Cyprus (p. 150). Then, early in 270, followed his return and his death fighting against Palmyra. As at Antioch, so at Alexandria, the coins reflect the new turn taken by events on the proclamation of Aurelian. Here again appears the portrait of Vaballathus as *imperator dux Romanorum* with the bust of Aurelian on the other side. Here again a compromise was proposed and supported by the despatch of the corn-fleet in this year to Rome. But at the same time[3] Aurelian was proclaiming his resolve to be *Restitutor Orientis.*

---

[1] Malalas XII, p. 299, 4 (Bonn). Cf. A. Graf Schenk v. Stauffenberg, *Die röm. Kaisergeschichte bei Malalas*, p. 379 *sq.*

[2] *S.H.A.* Probus, 9, 1. For another view see A. Stein, in *Klio*, XXIX, 1936, pp. 237 *sqq.*

[3] On the first issue of his own reverse types at Rome as distinct from those of Quintillus which continued till then, at latest, the summer of 270.

III. THE WEST FROM THE JOINT REIGN OF VALERIAN AND GALLIENUS TO THE PROCLA- MATION OF AURELIAN

While his father betook himself to the East, Gallienus was left with the task of ordering the affairs of the West. It was perhaps at this moment that his mother, Egnatia Mariniana, died and was consecrated; in her place his wife, Cornelia Salonina, received the rank of an Augusta.

Now that the invasion of the Empire by its neighbours, Dacian, Sarmatian and, above all, German, had become endemic, wars threatened on every hand. It is not possible to determine precisely where and in what order the five German wars of Gallienus between 254 and 259 ran their course. What is certain is that he was constantly and completely engaged in war, prepara- tions for war and measures of defence against the invasions, and must have done much more work at fortification than is directly recorded.

It is clear, however, that he regarded the position in Gaul and on the Rhine as the most critical and therefore undertook the conduct of war on that front in person, while entrusting to his generals the defence of the Danube lands. There, too, there was mischief enough. In 254 the Goths were already threatening Greece and the Marcomanni drove through Pannonia into North Italy; Pannonia had also to suffer in these years from her neighbours, the Quadi and Iazyges, and could only be defended effectively by the settlement within it of a Marcomannic king and his tribe. Dacia was sorely harassed by the Carpi, but the title of Gallienus, Dacicus Maximus, in 257 points to their defeat. The despair of the population of Illyricum at an emperor who would not come to their help, broke out during the ensuing years in a succession of rebellions.

In order to have yet another representative of the reigning house, whose presence might check usurpations if it did nothing else, the Emperors early in 256 raised to be Caesar the elder son of Gallienus, P. Licinius Cornelius Valerianus. He was still a boy, unable to direct wars in person; it is probable, then, that he remained chiefly in Rome. He soon died, early in 258, apparently from natural causes, whereupon his younger brother, P. Licinius Cornelius Saloninus, was at once proclaimed his successor. But the difficulties produced by the incessant wars fanned such a flame of hatred and desperation, that the government, towards the autumn of 257, no doubt on the initiative of the elder Emperor, resumed the persecution of the Christians and further intensified it in the following year (see p. 205 *sq.*).

The same year (257) brought with it an important change in the government. Gallienus numbered the victories he had won under his own auspices and not those of his father, beginning with the war against the Alemanni; on issues of Cologne he now appears *cum exer(citu) suo*, clearly emphasizing his independent command-in-chief. A definite separation of Eastern and Western armies must have occurred, probably not unconnected with an estrangement between the two rulers that had consequences beyond the military sphere. Gallienus now had his hands free to carry out the reforms that he desired. It is certain that he now called into being his new central cavalry corps, henceforth stationed at Milan (see p. 217). It had soon to be tested in battle against Ingenuus.

The imperial mint of Viminacium was in this year transferred to Cologne, where Gallienus mainly resided and directed the repulse of the German invasions from the Rhine. Nor did he fail to show his energy in the building of fortifications. In fact he did his utmost to earn the title of *restitutor Galliarum* that his issues of Cologne give him. Either in 258 or the following year he had to leave the Rhine to combat a serious invasion of Italy by the Alemanni. With a small army he succeeded in defeating and ejecting a greatly superior force, and returned forthwith to Germany.

The next year was one of catastrophes unexampled in Roman history. Early in 260 the governor of Numidia successfully repulsed a number of attacks by the Bavares and Quinquegentanei, in one of which the historian Q. Gargilius Martialis, after greatly distinguishing himself, met his death on the field of honour[1]. This campaign seems to mark the end of a series of disturbances of longer standing.

Then, towards the end of July, came the news of the tragedy in the East (p. 171 *sq.*); the whole Empire was in confusion, and conditions moved rapidly towards anarchy. But Gallienus kept his head. Father and son had from the first been set in opposition by fundamental differences of temperament and this had led on, no doubt owing to Valerian's failure, to an effective separation of East and West in 258. In this moment of peril the benefits of the change were realized. Gallienus was able to break the last ties that bound him to the policy of his father. The captivity of the elder

---

[1] Dessau 1194, 2767; Cyprian, *Ep.* 62, 1 *sqq.*

Augustus was naturally felt as an unprecedented disgrace to the Roman name; even the late historians with senatorial sympathies record their verdict that it was an *ignobilis servitus*. This was the view that Gallienus himself adopted. Far from considering any steps for the recovery of his unhappy father[1], he even went so far as to deny, by a kind of *damnatio memoriae*, any connection with his fatal régime. Hitherto the imperial coins of Egypt had invariably given Gallienus himself the added name of Valerianus; now all of a sudden this stops[2]. Saloninus, too, in the short span of life yet allotted to him, ceased to be called Valerianus and was named Gallienus—at least in such places as Asia Minor[3], where the Emperor's orders could still reach the officials. Gallienus would not even tolerate further mention of the great victories that he had himself won under his father's auspices and insisted on the numbering of his military successes from the separation of 258. More than this, he prescribed the beginning of a new count of his regnal years. This order reached Egypt in early summer 261 (p. 173) and the new regnal year one was placed besides the old year eight[4]. Here the new count was afterwards abandoned, but in the West it continued in use[5]. But the reaction against the old régime went still further. Gallienus broke with the policy of Valerian, who had steadily leaned on the Senate, and, by a polite but definite exclusion of the senators from all high commands in the army (p. 220), dealt a sore blow to the dignity and status of the senatorial career. It is part of the same policy that his colleague as *consul ordinarius* in 261 was no senator, but a distinguished *eques*, L. Petronius Taurus Volusianus[6], a man high in his confidence, who had already been *praefectus vigilum* and Praetorian Prefect. The opposition of this man to the *nobiles* is also reflected in the fact that he was not co-opted into the high priestly offices; but, in 267–8, he was *praefectus urbi*, and protected the interests of the Emperor during his absence. A further evidence of the break with the policy of friendship to the Senate is to be seen in the

---

[1] Lactantius, *de mort. pers.* 5, 6.

[2] A. Barb, *Num. Zeitschr.* 1925, p. 114; Wickert, P. W. *s.v.* Licinius (84), col. 351.

[3] Alföldi, *Num. Chron.* 1929, p. 264; Cohen[2] v, p. 529, no. 101; Mionnet, *Suppl.* II, p. 433, no. 1421 *sq.*

[4] H. Feuardent, *Numismatique de l'Égypte ancienne*, II, p. 238 *sq.* For another view see J. G. Milne, *Anc. Egypt*, IV, 1917, p. 155 *sq.*; L. Laffranchi, *Aegyptus*, XVII, 1937, pp. 25 *sqq.*

[5] Eutropius IX, 11, 1. So too Aurelius Victor, *Caes.* XXXIII, 35; S.H.A. *Gall. duo*, 19, 5.

[6] E. Groag, P.W. *s.v.* Petronius (73), cols. 1225 *sqq.*

suspension, soon after the beginning of the sole rule of Gallienus, of the bronze coinage with the signature s(enatus) c(onsulto), a formal but tenderly cherished symbol of the authority of the *patres*. This bronze coinage had, it is true, lost its meaning through the complete devaluation of the double denarius; but none the less its disappearance was tantamount to a grave infringement of the sovereign rights of the Senate (see below, p. 220). From the middle of 261 the revolution in policy was felt in every department of life. Its full import is further seen in the complete reversal of the imperial policy towards the Christians (p. 206 *sq.*).

This change of direction and organization was carried out under the most unfavourable conditions imaginable. Before the autumn of 260 was past, two dangerous revolts broke out in quick succession in the Danube lands. If the conjecture, that the election of Pope Julius followed on the news of the capture of Valerian, is correct, the rebellion of Ingenuus also broke out in the second half of July, for it was 'comperta Valeriani clade'[1] that he raised the standard of revolt. He was governor of Pannonia, and, despite the misgivings of the Empress[2], enjoyed the confidence of Gallienus[3]. Moesia also joined him. He chose as his residence Sirmium in the south of Pannonia, a city that was often to serve as imperial headquarters. Not far from it, at Mursa, his troops encountered Gallienus as he hastened to the spot. The new cavalry corps and its commander, Aureolus, came out of the test with flying colours; the Moorish javelin-men, too, had their share in the victory that Gallienus gained. Ingenuus was captured as he fled and was put to death.

The Emperor had no wish to punish the rebels severely[4]; but none the less the rebellion was renewed by the same troops. They proclaimed emperor Regalianus, the governor of Upper Pannonia, who had a number of old billon coins overstruck with his own portrait at his improvised mint of Carnuntum[5]. Parallel issues reveal the fact that he was married to a daughter of an influential family of the Senate, Sulpicia Dryantilla[6]. Regalianus probably had his adherents also in the Senate. It can be shown that, besides the two legions of Upper Pannonia (X Gemina and XIV

---

[1] Aurelius Victor, *Caes.* XXXIII, 2.
[2] Petrus Patricius, frag. 162 (Cassius Dio, ed. Boissevain III, p. 743).
[3] *Chron. min.* I, 525, 45 Mommsen.
[4] Ammian. Marc. XXI, 16, 10; Petrus Patricius, frag. 163 (Cassius Dio, ed. Boissevain III, p. 743).
[5] The doubts of B. Saria in *Klio* xxx, 1937, pp. 352 *sqq.* do not appear to the present writer to be justified.   [6] See Volume of Plates v, 232, *j, k*.

Gemina), the XIII Gemina (which can hardly have been still at its old post in Apulum) and the garrison of Durostorum in Lower Moesia were implicated in the revolt. But the reign of Regalianus cannot have lasted more than a few weeks. Gallienus returned in haste and made an end of him.

Meanwhile (in September), Macrianus had broken with Gallienus, had proclaimed his sons emperors and drawn the East to his side (p. 172 *sq.*). This was yet another immediate result of the catastrophe of Valerian. But the general consternation thus produced had further, indirect consequences. Just before the end of 260 followed a fourth usurpation. M. Cassianius Latinius Postumus, who was possibly governor of one or other Germania[1], had quarrelled with another high officer, Silvanus. Silvanus was in Cologne directing the government in the name of the Caesar Saloninus (who, capable and attractive, was still quite a boy), and even issuing commands to Postumus himself. The quarrel was about the booty taken from German invaders, which Postumus wished to distribute among his soldiers, but which Silvanus sought to have delivered to the court of the Caesar,—probably to secure the return of the stolen property to its owners. It is a pretty picture of demoralization. Postumus marched on Cologne and invested the city. While the siege was still in progress, the mint went on striking large gold pieces in the name of Gallienus for the New Year of 261[2] and, in defiance, the young Caesar was proclaimed Augustus[3]. But not long afterwards the garrison surrendered both the prince and his tutor, and Postumus had them put to death. The usurper then succeeded in occupying the passes of the Alps[4] and any thought of crushing him was frustrated by a new threat. Macrianus was advancing with an army, 30,000 strong[5]. Aureolus defeated this force in Pannonia[6], where Gallienus, the persistent absentee, was held responsible for the desperate misery of the times and where the garrisons again joined this new rival; but the Oriental troops soon abandoned the contest and the two Macriani both fell (summer, 261). Meanwhile yet another rebellion, the fifth in a few months, had been disposed of. A certain Valens, probably proconsul of Achaea[7], who had

---

1 Cf. Petrus Patricius, frag. 165 (Cassius Dio, ed. Boissevain III, p. 743).
2 See Alföldi in a forthcoming number of *J.R.S.*
3 M.-S. v, i, p. 123, nos. 3, 14.
4 Petrus Patricius, frag. 165 (Cassius Dio, ed. Boissevain III, p. 743).
5 S.H.A. *Gall. duo,* 2, 6. The number is exaggerated, *ib. Trig. tyr.* 12, 13.
6 Zonaras XII, 24 (p. 599): cf. Alföldi, *Berytus* v, 1938.
7 A. Stein, P.W. *s.v.* Fulvius (82), col. 261.

assumed the purple, met his death at the approach of Macrianus—
if any conclusion can fairly be drawn from the confused account
in the *Augustan History*. In 262 the former prefect of Egypt,
Aemilianus, spread consternation in Italy by detaining the corn-
fleet, and had to be removed (p. 173). It is possible that Gallienus
pushed forward to Byzantium, to restore order in those regions
(p. 174). It seems that on this occasion Pannonia, too, was re-
organized; the establishment and undisturbed activity of the
mint of Siscia from A.D. 262 onwards may count as evidence of
the fact[1]. Early in autumn at the end of the ninth year of his
reign, Gallienus was certainly in Rome to celebrate his *decennalia*,
with a magnificence still attested by an exceptionally rich issue of
coins. The panic of 260 and the usurpations attendant on it were
for the moment overcome.

It was now possible to attempt a reckoning with Postumus[2].
In all probability Gallienus took the field against him early in
263. The passes of the Alps were either already in his hands or, if
not, were now captured. The first encounter brought defeat, but
it was followed by a decisive victory. The pursuit of the beaten
enemy was entrusted to Aureolus, the commander of the new
corps of cavalry; but Aureolus was meditating treason and
allowed Postumus to slip through his fingers. There was a general
conviction of his guilt; the Emperor alone gave credence to his
excuses—it was one day to cost him his life. Postumus, escaping,
succeeded in re-assembling his army—he could call upon large
bands of free Germans—but suffered a second severe defeat. He
threw himself into a fortified city in Gaul and was besieged there
by the Emperor. Luck again came to his aid. Gallienus was
seriously wounded by an arrow and was incapacitated from
directing the operations. He was presumably carried back to
Rome; the foothills of the Alps in the South of Gaul seem to
have remained in his hands, or at least the most important
passes.

The attempt to re-unite the whole of the West in one hand had
failed, and the failure involved a terrible weakening of the armed
forces of the Empire. The continuance of the conflict meant that
a large part of the troops on both sides was directed inwards,
whilst the frontier-defence suffered enormously; the district
along the *limes* of Raetia and Germany was doomed to perish
between the rival powers (p. 155). The lasting sense of insecurity

[1] See Alföldi, *Siscia* i.
[2] For criticism of the sources and the details of this war see Alföldi,
Zeitschr. f. Num. XL, 1930, pp. 1 *sqq.*

in Gaul itself is attested by countless coin-hoards buried in those
years. Postumus, who, after his exploits as general in 260, had
again in 261 to parry a German invasion[1], must undoubtedly have
been often compelled to defend himself against such attacks.
Even his boasted victory of 264[2] was certainly the outcome of a
defensive campaign. On the other side, the forces of Gallienus
were insufficient to provide Dacia, that great advanced bridgehead of the Danube front, with a full complement of garrisons
(see p. 151); even the Danube front itself had to be strengthened
by settlements of barbarians. Finally, this inner cleavage robbed
Gallienus of his last chance of ordering the affairs of the East in
person; to guard against the Persian danger, he was compelled to
feed the rank growth of Palmyra.

Postumus did not content himself so exclusively with the
mastery of his Gallic realm as has been supposed. That he was
mainly restricted to it was more due to Gallienus than to himself.
It is true that at his proclamation he protested before his former
master that his only intention was to protect and prosper Gaul,
the task assigned him by Gallienus, and that he would shed no
drop of Roman blood. His coins, too, at the outset speak only of
the salvation of the Rhine provinces and represent him as
Restitutor Galliarum and as Hercules of Roman Germany
(*Hercules Deusoniensis*). But after the consolidation of his rule in
the West his ambitions increased out of all measure. He succeeded in forcing Britain to his side and visited the island in
person[3]. It has long been known from inscriptions that Spain
went over to him. After all this, he came to feel himself the
protector of *Roma Aeterna*, a new *Hercules Romanus*—as coins
attest—and, indeed, fears of his advance were entertained in
Italy while Gallienus was fighting against the Goths in 268[4]. In
fact, he even succeeded, if only for a short time, in bringing North
Italy on to his side, as will shortly appear. That Postumus even
dreamed of ruling the East is shown by his coin-types (continued
by his successors) with *Oriens Aug(usti)*. His aspirations to
world-rule are further illustrated by the legend on the reverse,
Restitutor Orbis.

To this general attitude the organization of his new State
corresponds. He certainly set up a new Senate, because he also
appointed consuls independently of Rome. He himself held the
consulship five times,—the fourth time as colleague of his future

[1] Dessau 561.   [2] M.-S. v, ii, pp. 336 *sqq.* nos. 3, 14–15, 97.
[3] A. Stein, P.W. *s.v.* Cassianius, col. 1663 *sq.*
[4] Zosimus I, 40, 1.

successor Victorinus[1], the fifth time just before his death in 269.
His bronze issues often bear the formula S(enatus) C(onsulto); one
of his senators, as is well known, was Tetricus, whom he entrusted
with the governorship of Aquitania and who afterwards sat on his
throne. He had his own Praetorian Guard, stationed in Trèves[2],
for he had chosen that city as his residence and adorned it with
buildings[3]. Here, too, under his care, a new imperial mint was
established[4]. Both at this mint and at Cologne a precisely regulated coinage in gold was produced, clear evidence of an efficient
economic administration, while his small change was just as bad
an inflation-coinage as that of his antagonist.

What Gallienus was doing in the years from 263–267 is
unknown. There seems to have been no serious warfare, and the
effects of that inner consolidation that has been observed in the
empire of Postumus were not unfelt on the other side. The epidemic of usurpations of 260 had been mastered, and, until the
new flood of German invasions (in 267), there was a respite that
made progress possible. These short years, indeed, permitted the
ripening of that reaction of the ancient spirit, whose very soul
Gallienus was[5], a reaction that even found expression in the art
both of his court and that of Postumus. Under the patronage of
Gallienus the circle of Neoplatonists that gathered about Plotinus
succeeded in framing a philosophy suited to an educated man and
in finding an expression for the political and patriotic necessity
of polytheism which remained valid to the end of paganism. In
art, again, the reaction of the classical antique against the modern
primitivism breaks for a brief moment of high intensity and significance into flower; the observations on aesthetics found in
Plotinus show how close must have been the connection between
the Neoplatonists and this new bloom of art. The whole movement
had a pronounced hellenic character; was not the court of Gallienus crowded with Greek men of letters?[6]

[1] The fact that Postumus and Victorinus were colleagues in the consulship has misled the author of the S.H.A. into regarding Victorinus as co-
regent with Postumus. (Gall. duo 7, 1; Trig. tyr. 6, 1–3.) The truth is
given by Aurelius Victor, Caes. XXXIII, 9–12; Eutropius IX, 9; cf. Epit.
XXXIV, 3. The same order of events is reflected in the coins; cf. P. H. Webb
in M.-S. v, ii, p. 324 sq.

[2] C.I.L. XIII, 3679; cf. E. Krüger, Arch. Anz. 1933, cols. 687 sqq.

[3] O. Hirschfeld in C.I.L. XIII, p. 584 b; R. Rau, P.W. s.v. Treveri, col. 2340.

[4] C.I.L. VI, 1641; cf. G. Elmer, Bonn. Jahrb. CXLIII, 1938.

[5] See below, p. 231.

[6] Alföldi, Fünfundzwanzig Jahre Röm.-Germ. Komm. p. 29 and also
C.I.L. XIV, 5340 (M. Aur. Hermogenes, procurator a studiis).

It was in definite harmony with these cultural endeavours that Gallienus strove to lead the masses away from the mystery-religions to the cult of Demeter of Eleusis[1]. It was perhaps while engaged in measures of defence against the new German peril in the Aegean that he journeyed to Athens, allowed himself, like Hadrian, to be elected as eponymous archon and received initiation at Eleusis. On the aurei of Rome appears at this time the solemn religious type that represents Gallienus in the guise of Demeter—a combination that strikes the modern mind as ridiculous, but that is not so alien from ancient sentiment or unfamiliar in the speculation of the mystics and gnostics; it bears the name *Galliena Augusta*[2]. The return of Gallienus to his capital was celebrated with extravagant honours—G(*enius*) P(*opuli*) R(*omani*) int(*ravit*) urb(*em*).

Apart from this, Gallienus is known to have been occupied with the putting of the fleet on to a war basis and with the fortification of the coast cities of Asia Minor. At the new year of 268 he experienced the joy of seeing his third son Marinianus solemnly inaugurate his public career as consul[3], but in the spring he was compelled to hasten to the Balkans to counter an exceptionally serious invasion of the Heruli and Goths. He had already won a decisive victory at Naïssus, when a veritable Job's message called him suddenly back to Italy.

Aureolus, who had from the first commanded the *equites*, the new 'flying army' of Gallienus and was now entrusted with the troops of Raetia and other subalpine districts, in order to prevent the invasion of Italy by Postumus, now changed sides. He had already once, in the previous offensive, frustrated the complete success of Gallienus by his ambiguous conduct. The coins, which he struck in Milan in the name of Postumus, all glorify the virtues of the cavalry under his command, who were the mainstay of his rebellion. Gallienus handed over to Marcianus the prosecution of the Gothic war (p. 150) and soon appeared in the plain of the Po. Aureolus was defeated in a pitched battle near Milan. He withdrew into the city and was besieged by Gallienus. While the siege was in progress he was proclaimed emperor[4]—an advancement that was to cost him his life. Meanwhile a conspiracy had been formed by the leading personalities in the entourage of Gallienus. The Praetorian Prefect Heraclianus, the Emperor's

---

[1] Alföldi, *op. cit.* p. 22 *sq.* and *Zeitschr. f. Num.* xxxviii, 1928, pp. 174 *sqq.*　[2] See Volume of Plates v, 236, *k*.

[3] Alföldi, *Num. Chron.* 1929, p. 266 *sq.*

[4] For details see Alföldi, *Zeitschr. f. Num.* xxxvii, 1927, pp. 198 *sqq.*

deputy in the chief-command, M. Aurelius Claudius[1] and L. Domitius Aurelianus, the new commander of the cavalry[2], were the ringleaders of the plot. On a false report of the approach of Aureolus with his army the unsuspecting Emperor rushed out without helmet and cuirass, to meet him and received the fatal thrust. The fact that the siege proceeded without interruption after the murder of the Emperor argues strongly for the complicity of the whole staff. Great, however, was the indignation of the army over the loss of its brilliant commander; it was only the secret understanding between the chief officers that made it possible to still the storm. To facilitate the prearranged proclamation of Claudius, the story was put abroad that Gallienus, as he lay dying, had solemnly appointed him his successor[3]; at the same time, the State-chest, which in those evil days was always carted round with the Emperor, so as to be available at need, paid out twenty aurei to each man, the time-honoured method of winning over the army[4]. But the demand of the army that the kindred of the dead should be spared came too late. The Senate, bitterly offended by its exclusion from the high commands, and the mob of Rome, that made Gallienus the scapegoat for all the sorrows of his time, murdered his relations and confidants, above all, his brother Valerian (consul in 265) and his little son, Marinianus. Claudius could do no more than hinder further bloodshed. The Senate, however, had to consent to consecrate Gallienus; the temper of the army was such as to commend the step to Claudius, and the *patres*, naturally, followed his lead.

It was in vain that Aureolus now surrendered to Claudius: he was at once put to death. All these tragic happenings fell in the August of 268[5]. It was a piece of good fortune that the new emperor was in Northern Italy, for he was thus enabled quickly

[1] Zosimus I, 40, 2.

[2] Zonaras XII, 25 (p. 601); Aurelius Victor, *Caes.* XXXIII, 21, S.H.A. *Aurel.* 16, 1–2.

[3] Aurelius Victor, *Caes.* XXXIII, 28; *Epit.* XXXIV, 2; cf. P. Damerau, *Kaiser Claudius II Gothicus*, p. 45. G. Barbieri, *Studi ital. di filol. class.* XI, 1934, pp. 329 *sqq.*

[4] The parallelism of Zosimus I, 41 τῶν δὲ στρατιωτῶν κελεύσει τῶν ἡγουμένων ἡσυχασάντων with S.H.A. *Gall. duo* 15, 3 *sic militibus sedatis Claudius* etc. shows the common source, and makes the narrative of the *Vita* credible apart from such fictitious additions as the meaningless condemnation of Gallienus' memory—*tyrannum militari iudicio in fastos publicos rettulerunt.*

[5] A. Stein, *Arch. f. Pap.* VII, 1923, pp. 30 *sqq.*; Wickert, *op. cit.* col. 362; for another view see Damerau, *op. cit.* p. 27.

to bring to action and repel the Alemanni (p. 156), who had already reached Lake Garda. It is probable that he then went to Rome to pay his respects to the Senate and People[1]. Certainly at this stage—if not an even earlier one—an alliance was concluded between emperor and Senate. After the measures taken by Gallienus, there must be some real significance in the reappearance of the type of *Genius Senatus* on issues of Rome with the Emperor's titles at the New Year of 269. The extravagant honours paid to Claudius after his death[2] and the choice of his insignificant brother by the Senate to succeed him are clear witnesses to a strong bond between emperor and Senate. The lost biographical history of the emperors, of the middle of the fourth century, sought to explain the enthusiasm of the *patres* by the legendary account of the solemn devotion by Claudius of his own life to the service of the State, on the model of the heroic sacrifice of the Decii[3]. But, in point of fact, that enthusiasm had a far more prosaic foundation.

Claudius had now a splendid opportunity to attack Postumus. A little time back, Italy had been exposed to the usurper by the adhesion of Aureolus; now Postumus, in his turn, found his rear exposed to Claudius. The fact that he did not come to the assistance of Aureolus is indeed remarkable. He was beyond doubt prevented from so doing. For, although it was not till some four or five months later that he was able finally to dispose of his rival, Ulpius Cornelius Laelianus, the revolt of the latter may well have begun earlier. Some idea of this clash of forces is given by the fact that the mint of Cologne was still striking a plentiful issue for Postumus for the New Year of 269, while the legion XXX Ulpia of Vetera (Xanten) went over to Laelianus and both Mainz and the capital Trèves, where his coins were struck, also joined him[4]. Laelianus was shut up in Mainz and died when the city was taken; but Postumus himself, when he denied his barbaric troops the satisfaction of sacking the city, had to pay for his refusal with his life. It is remarkable that at so appropriate a moment the legions of the Rhine did not return to their allegiance

---

[1] Damerau, *op. cit.* p. 58. *Cod. Just.* III, 34, 6 does not imply that Claudius was still in Rome on April 25, 269.

[2] Damerau, *op. cit.* p. 81.

[3] Aurelius Victor, *Caes.* XXXIV, 3–7; *Epit.* XXXIV, 3–4. The emphasis on the effective consultation of the *libri Sibyllini* belongs to the anti-Christian polemic of the Senate in the late fourth century, overstressed in the *Historia Augusta*.

[4] See *Germania* XXI, 1937, pp. 95 *sqq.*, where the name of the mint is to be corrected.

to Claudius, but preferred to set up M. Aurelius Marius and, after his death in a few months, M. Piavonius Victorinus.

In Rome, the plan of recalling Gaul to its obedience was for a moment debated, but Claudius decided, rightly, that the extermination of the East Germans in Illyricum was a more serious duty[1]. So to Illyricum he went. But he thrust into the south of Gaul an expeditionary force, commanded by Julius Placidianus, who soon afterwards was made Praetorian Prefect. The *vexillationes* and cavalry serving under him maintained their position near Grenoble, doubtless in order to facilitate the hoped-for advance of Claudius with the main army. They actually succeeded in restoring communications with Spain, which, on the evidence of inscriptions, acknowledged Claudius. But when Augustodunum (Autun), not far to the north, closed its gates and called on Claudius for aid, Placidianus could not save the city; after a siege of seven months it was forced to surrender at discretion to Victorinus[2]. By that time Claudius was probably already dead.

Claudius gained one more decisive victory over the Goths, who after the victory of Gallienus had continued to be hard pressed by Marcianus, and then directed the 'mopping-up' process from the imperial palace in Sirmium, until early in 270 the plague took him from the Empire's service.

The Senate, reawakened to energetic action by the policy of Gallienus (p. 183), anticipated the army in its decision. The authorities deserve full belief when they tell us that the brother of the dead Emperor, M. Aurelius Quintillus, was chosen emperor by the Senate. He seems to have been in command of the flying column which had to protect North Italy against the German invasions. It might be supposed that he went direct to Rome, to present himself before the Senate; but he never reached the point of distributing the promised largesse to the people of the capital, and the actual news of the proclamation of Aurelian found him in Aquileia.

The armies had at first accepted the election of Quintillus, as the issues of the mints of Milan, Siscia and Cyzicus show; only Palmyra broke away (see p. 179). But he was a very insignificant person, entirely unversed in State affairs, and his collapse at the first shock proves that he would never have had the energy on his own initiative to grasp at the purple. The common soldiers hardly knew him and abandoned him the moment that a popular general became a candidate for the throne; it was soon revealed, too, that the generals could not have backed his proclamation. All the

[1] Zonaras XII, 26 (p. 604).   [2] For details see Damerau, *op. cit.* pp. 76 *sqq.*

more remarkable in its contrast is the praise of the pro-senatorial historians of a later age: 'Unicae moderationis vir et civilitatis, aequandus fratri vel praeponendus'[1]; but even they had to admit that owing to the shortness of his reign he did not amount to anything. He was in fact intended to be a tool of the Senate.

Quintillus was, of course, anxious to win the favour of the Danubian troops and, as an Illyrian himself, he had the personifications of the warlike *Pannoniae* placed on his issues of Milan; the types of *Genius Illy(rici)* and *Dacia Felix* likewise seem to have been prepared for him at the same mint, but never actually issued by him. His dependence on the memory of his elder brother is shown by his assumption of the name of Claudius; the issues in honour of *Divus Claudius (Gothicus)* at Milan and Rome began in his reign and served the same purpose.

When Aurelian rose against him in Illyricum in April 270, his armies at once abandoned him and he was driven to commit suicide. Aurelian spread the report that Claudius had designated himself and not his brother as successor[2] and, soon after his proclamation, had coins of *Divus Claudius* struck in Siscia and Cyzicus for purposes of propaganda, a clear evidence of the same intention. In actual fact Aurelian, and not Quintillus, stood in the succession of Claudius as representative of that *Virtus Illyrici* that was destined to save the Empire.

IV. THE CHIEF POLITICAL FACTORS

The general development of the imperial autocracy has been described elsewhere (chap. x), but it is here in place to note how the consummation of a long process, which was bound to be reached in the third century, was hastened by successful or unsuccessful usurpations and the violent deaths of emperors. It became clear that the Senate could no longer secure stability for the throne, and that it must have another foundation than legalistic traditions, highly as these continued to be regarded. What was first needed was a religious basis, and as Juppiter Optimus Maximus became dim, men turned to this or that Eastern God temporarily in the ascendant, until at last, under Aurelian, 'Sol dominus imperii Romani' embodied the idea of a unifying deity to correspond to the sole earthly ruler of the world (p. 309). A dangerous rival to this claim was the equally monarchical and

1 Eutropius IX, 12, reflected in S.H.A. *Claud.* 12, 3 and Orosius VII, 23, 2.
2 Damerau, *op. cit.* p. 90.

universal idea of the God of the Christians. Decius and his successors had striven to place in the foreground, not the divinity of the emperor but the divine power that shielded him, and with this came the possibility that the idea of the divine favour might remain, but that the pagan gods might give place to the one true God.

It is, however, important to realize that the extraordinary emphasis given in these disastrous times to the fabled bliss of the Golden Age which the emperor brings with him is closely connected with the struggle of the State against Christianity. This becomes at once clear when one considers the overstressing in the official propaganda of the blessings conferred by the *restitutor orbis* and by the emperor, as *salus generis humani*, and to the emphatic protests raised in the other camp[1]. The *saeculum novum* with all its glories, advertised by the issues of Decius and Gallus from Antioch, was, in fact, a pitiful age of disasters; yet, if these issues are to be believed, each ephemeral emperor was destined to bring in a Golden Age, in which peace eternal reigns; the hapless sons of Gallienus must each be the leaders of the new age, as 'novum Iovis incrementum'[2], and, during the terrible invasions of the end of the reign of Gallienus, 'ubique pax' the coins say[3]. The Christians, however, needed to be recalled to the enjoyment of this marvellous age of bliss[4]. This doctrinaire creed was, of course, a blank contradiction of the hard reality, but there was no other redeemer who could be matched against the Christian. When, under Gallienus, Augustus is called 'deus', instead of 'divus', as before[5], the meaning is that Augustus really is a god, not a dead man, as the Christians say. This theological transfiguration of the person of the emperor and, even more so, his direct deification, had originally been in sharp conflict with the old humanistic conceptions and, above all, with the mentality of the Senate. Now, however, the opposition of Christianity made the worship of the emperor a part of the policy of the patriotic conservatives, and so it remained until paganism had drawn its last breath.

The absolutist Empire never allowed its subjects to share in real political or constitutional decisions. At best, complaints might be brought before the All-Highest by the Senate in the

---

[1] Alföldi, *Siscia*, 1, 1931, pp. 20 *sqq.*
[2] Id. *Num. Chron.* 1929, pp. 266 *sqq.*
[3] Id. *Zeitschr. f. Num.* XXXVIII, 1928, pp. 183 *sqq.*
[4] *Acta Cypr.* 1. (R. Reitzenstein, *Sitz. d. Heid. Akad.* 1913, no. 14, pp. 22 *sqq.*). [5] See Volume of Plates v, 236, *l.*

Curia or by the masses at the games, in the gentle disguise of a formal litany[1]; decisions were taken in the 'silentium' of the palace by a court clique. But, as the autocracy still rested, however much by anachronism, on the fiction of a conferment of official competence by the Senate and as this conferment could obviously only happen after the pretender to the throne had proved his claim by success, the real choice must first of all be left to the free play of forces. Thus the retention of the old political forms, with their Republican colour, at the changes of emperor left considerable room for the conflict of political forces in the Empire,—especially as, in the twenty-four years between the deterioration of the situation at the end of the reign of Philip and the beginnings of Aurelian, there were some thirty proclamations of emperors.

No separation of these risings into legitimate and illegitimate can be made. For from the very first the act by which the supreme offices of State were conferred was of minor importance when dealing with the candidates backed by the armed forces. And, as often as continuity had not been secured by the advancement of the emperor's real or adoptive son, difficulties inevitably arose. Dynastic sentiment, developed by transference of this kind, had been strong enough to guarantee the succession by fictions of a pious or even of a repellent character (as in the cases of Hadrian, Elagabalus and Severus Alexander)—and could guarantee it even to children like Gordian III; in our period, too, there was still recourse to it[2]. But the storms of the age would not permit of the introduction of a sure, dynastic succession. The decisions lay with those who carried the sword. Thus the *patres* had been forced to declare Decius a *hostis publicus*, for only so could Philip protect his rear when he marched out against him; but the tables were soon turned, and Decius was welcomed with an extravagance of delight as 'optimus princeps'—a Trajan come again (p. 166). The same thing happened once more with Gallus and Aemilianus[3]. Nor had the Senate even to pay for its change of tone; its recognition was regarded as a mere formality. Never once did the Senate protest when the man whom it had legitimized was killed, but prudently consulted the wishes of his successor. The strict adherence to principle shown by a Senate uncompromisingly true to Republican tradition in the third century, is no more than a fond illusion of the partisans of the Roman

[1] Alföldi, *Röm. Mitt.* XLIX, 1934, pp. 79 *sqq.*
[2] So Aemilianus, *Joh. Antioch.* frag. 150. (*F.H.G.* IV, p. 598.)
[3] Aurelius Victor, *Caes.* XXXI, 3.

aristocracy of the late Empire, as mirrored with peculiar clarity in the *Historia Augusta*.

But it would certainly be a grave mistake to deny to the Senate of the period under review any kind of political importance. It not only reacted with notable energy against the attempts to thrust it aside and appointed emperors of genuine senatorial sympathies on other occasions than in 238, but it was able, in 270 and 275, to command even greater authority and consent than before, because the anarchy and bloodshed caused by the violent changes on the throne had taught the army the useful lesson that the maintenance of continuity in the constitution must be shielded and respected. Not only did the solemn election of Tacitus fall to the lot of the Senate but Quintillus, before him, was the Senate's tool. One may even go further and say that the close sympathy between the *patres* and Claudius (p. 191) seems to have had a history behind it; not without reason does Orosius[1] say of him: 'voluntate senatus sumpsit imperium.'

Nor must it be forgotten, that the candidates whom the soldiers raised to the throne, who, after all, were almost without exception senators down to 260, were quite capable of maintaining a completely senatorial programme and temper, as, for example, did Decius and Valerian. Most of the other creatures of the army, too, were full of expressions of respect and reverence for the Senate. Philip in a moment of discouragement wished to return his authority to the Senate, though he had not received it from them (p. 93). The example of the disaster of Maximinus Thrax likewise played its part in putting the fear of the Senate into the soldier-emperors. They made all haste after their proclamation to make pilgrimage to Rome and to pay their respects to the *patres*. Aemilianus, for example, represented himself as executor of the Senate's will.[2] When in this age the stamp of senatorial authority (s.c.) appears on gold and silver coins where the right of issue had from the first been reserved to the emperor, as for example, under Gallus, Tacitus and the Tetrarchy or when under Gallienus and Claudius in the issues of small change in Cyzicus and the still unnamed mint in western Asia Minor the four proud letters s.p.q.r. are advertised with full official approval, the facts tell their own story.

The contrast between the enhancement of honour and the decline of actual power is highly significant of an age in which symbolical and abstract values prevailed over reality. In this case, for example, the more than ornamental part played by the Senate as a supreme authority at the election of Emperors was

[1] VII, 23, 1.   [2] Zonaras XII, 22 (p. 591).

questioned by no one, least of all by the soldiers of Illyricum, who felt themselves to be carrying on the traditions of old Rome; but all its other political functions had been completely lost. As a constitutional instrument it had been treated with tact and tenderness by the emperors from Augustus onwards, but its participation in State affairs had been continually whittled down and its functions transformed into formalities. Unimpaired, however, stood the reputation and influence of its members as governors and generals, until Commodus began to have them represented by knights in the provinces and a practice, begun as an exception, became the rule. Gallienus excluded senators from the high commands by his permanent *agentes vices*[1] and restricted their employment as civil governors: he thus appears in this field, as elsewhere, as completing a long process of evolution. It was not the soldier-emperors, it was the incapacity of the senators that accelerated the process: 'militiae labor a nobilissimo quoque pro sordido et inliberali reiciebatur'[2]. The permanent state of war called for hard professional soldiers at the head of the troops, not spoilt gentlemen of the capital.

If in spite of this exclusion the Senate still remained something more than a relic of ancient glories, the fact must be credited to the great landed possessions of the senatorial families, which were not so completely ruined by the bankruptcy of the State and by the inflation as were the money fortunes of the middle classes. The *album senatorium* of the late Empire shows an uninterrupted high position of many of the great families of the third century. It was obviously this economic strength that nerved the Senate to a new political effort in defence of Italy and its heritage of culture in the fifth and sixth centuries. Even in the crisis of the third century it was due to these wealthy lords, that in Rome itself the continuity of the traditions of classical art was not broken and that important treasures of literary and philosophic humanism were handed on to the next age. Again, it is to the reaction of the Senate against revolutionary Christianity that the visible quickening of the old Roman religious sentiment in Rome itself in that dark time was due.[3] It was the emperors of genuinely senatorial temper, like Decius and Valerian, who were the natural enemies of the Church.

But it was not to the Senate alone that the emperor was bound by the ties of an honoured tradition: the idle mob of the capital

---

[1] P. Lambrechts, *La Composition du Sénat romain...* (Diss. Pann. i, 8) pp. 98 *sqq.*, with references.

[2] *Paneg.* III (XI), 20, 1. Cf. also O. Seeck, *Gesch. des Untergangs der antiken Welt* II², pp. 26, 478.

[3] A. D. Nock, *Harv. Theol. Rev.* XXIII, 1930, pp. 251 *sqq.*

must receive the customary tokens of respect and favour. With what care the precise scope of imperial generosity in Rome was recorded in our period is still shown by the exact list of *congiaria* in the Chronographer of A.D. 354. But, under the sole rule of Gallienus (and, simultaneously, under Postumus), the systematic count of the benefactions of the Augusti on the coins ceases, and the representation of 'liberalitas' only continues for a time as an empty form, to disappear almost completely after Aurelian. The attempt to win the favour of the citizens now recedes behind the bid for the support of the soldiers by *largitio*[1]. It was the abrupt changes on the throne rather than the old importance of the capital that still enabled Rome to witness brilliant festivities, such as the processions that glorified the advent of the god-emperor or the dazzling shows at the periodic imperial festivals. The accounts in the *Historia Augusta* of the pomp and glory displayed at the *decennalia* of Gallienus may not all be true, but they certainly preserve many genuine characteristics[2].

Decius in his day beautified the capital by his completion and dedication of the Thermae of Commodus[3]; he may also have built a portico[4] and restored the Colosseum[5]. But even then the fortification of the City demanded first attention. There is no reason to question the statement[6], that he was busy on plans for the fortification of Rome. Any considerable building activity was then interrupted by the plague that began under Gallus, by the constant absence of the emperors and by financial distress and war. The Arch of Gallienus of 262, erected after the custom of the age to celebrate the *decennalia* of the emperor, was a private dedication of a simpler character[7].

Despite all this, the wars of these decades hastened a change in the function of Rome in the State, that had long been preparing. Now that the emperor must be near the field of war, permanent imperial residences grew up at or behind the front so that Rome ceased to be the centre of political life. The free development of the conception of the emperor had as its corollary: 'where the ruler is, there is Rome.' Hand in hand with this final loss of political privilege went the crystallization of the abstract idea of the eternal supremacy of Rome. It is no accident that at this very moment the idea of the primacy of the Roman Church received

---

[1] See below, p. 221 *sq.*

[2] A. von Domaszewski, *Rhein. Mus.* LVII, 1902, pp. 510 *sqq.*

[3] G. Costa, *Diz. Epig.* II, p. 1488. Platner-Ashby, *A Topographical Dictionary of Ancient Rome*, pp. 525 *sqq.*

[4] Platner-Ashby, *op. cit.* p. 421.   [5] *Ib.* p. 6.

[6] Aurelius Victor, *Caes.* XXIX, 1.   [7] Platner-Ashby, *op. cit.* p. 39.

its final shape from Cyprian who voiced the idea of the 'Cathedra Petri'[1]; the guard at this shrine of human culture was already being relieved.

Beside this decline in power of the old vital centre of the world-state stood the rise of the army as a factor in politics. Its right to share in the election of the emperor had long been established by custom, and it now found vigorous expression in the ceremonial of inauguration. But from the time that Septimius Severus and Caracalla shortsightedly abandoned the traditional reliance on the Senate and proclaimed their dependence on the soldiers, it was the temper and will of the army that must prove decisive in filling the throne. But as the Italians had long since disappeared from the army and the educated classes in the inner provinces had likewise ceased to take any serious part in its recruitment, the word now rested with the sons of the border-provinces. What, in the end, determined their attitude was not really the military point of view, but the atmosphere of their native lands, their nationality and the degree in which they were permeated by Roman influences.

A notable rôle was played by the Osrhoënian archers, who from the time of Caracalla formed a regular part of the Imperial forces (p. 216). The proclamation of the first Uranius under Severus Alexander[2] rested on their support; but, on the other hand, they with the other Syrian archers formed a strong backing for the Syrian emperors[3] and for Philip the Arabian, and, after the death of Severus Alexander, tried to displace the candidate of the Pannonians by an emperor of their own (p. 73). When a special issue of coinage under Gallus celebrates the chief god of the Osrhoënians Aziz[4], who was identified with Apollo Pythius, it was in honour of this important arm of the service. The valour of the Osrhoënians in 260 in battle with Shapur enables us to realize clearly their military, and consequently their political, value. The whole career of Odenathus and his family is but one reflection the more of the might of these Oriental archers.

Another important corps d'élite consisted of the Moorish javelin-men, who had given open support to the elevation of their countryman, Macrinus; and the proclamation of Aemilianus, too, a Moor of Girba,[5] must have stood in some relation to the rising

---

[1] E. Caspar, Geschichte des Papsttums, I, pp. 77 sqq.
[2] Syncellus, p. 674 (ed. Bonn).   [3] Herodian VIII, 1, 9.
[4] Alföldi, Vjesnik hrv. arh. društva, n.s. XV, p. 223 sq. For another view see K. Pink, J.D.A.I. LII, 1937, p. 104 sq. See Volume of Plates V, 234, j.
[5] [Aurelius Victor], Epit. XXXI, 1 (wrongly referred to Gallus, cf. von Domaszewski, Die Daten der S. Hist. Aug. p. 14, n. 4).

reputation of his fellow Moors. The usurpation of the Moorish officer, Memor, under Gallienus and of the Mauretanian Saturninus under Probus are further practical examples of the same thing.

But the armies of the Western provinces took a much more serious part in the making of emperors in this period. The notion of the *Historia Augusta*,[1] that it was the civilian Gauls (Gallicani, Galli) who were the originators of the separate empire of Western Europe, though still deeply rooted in the historical literature of to-day, finds no support in the genuine tradition. The civil population of that age was not at all inclined to risk its life for a separate Gallic Empire; and it was a Roman and not a Gallic programme that Postumus and his successors announced (p. 187). But the army, to which they owed their rule, was not disposed to leave unguarded the Rhine frontier, which was its home, and to fight in distant lands; it was for that reason that it repeatedly elected emperors of its own. The bitter results of this separatism have already been seen.

The real decision in the election of emperors lay, from Severus onwards, with the Danube army, of Illyro-Celtic stock. From the time of Decius the sons of Illyricum themselves often reach the throne, until with Claudius it became the rule for more than a century that the emperors shall hail from the Danube countries. It was the supreme good fortune of the Empire that this folk was completely romanized (vol. XI, pp. 550 *sqq.*) and, despite the fearful devastation of its own lands, was resolute to fight for the majesty of Rome in all quarters of the Empire. Beginning with Decius and continuing down the line of his Pannonian successors, the Genius Illyrici is displayed as a new revelation of Roman patriotism, Roman virtue and Roman self-sacrifice,—as was only just, for it was Illyricum that restored the unity of the Empire. This Illyrican supremacy represents at the same time a last advance of the West against the preponderance of the East. If the Latin language could make itself at home in the East, if the Roman conception of the State could take firm root, and if a new Rome could be founded there, it was the efforts of the new ruler-caste of Illyricum that deserve the credit. This rôle fell, above all, to the Pannonians as can still be recognized, though the Dacian regiments played a distinguished part, while Moesians and Thracians had their share in the great task of restoration.

On the other hand it must not be forgotten that the encroachment of army influence on political life involved pernicious consequences. Apart from the fact that the movements of the army

[1] S.H.A. *Gall. duo*, 4, 3; *Tyr. trig.* 3, 3–4, 6, 9; *ib.* 5, 2, 5.

in themselves produced severe pressure and serious disturbance in the life of the civil population involved, apart, too, from the heavy financial burden of the chronic state of war, an original error of the Principate had bad results. From the Julian house onwards, at every change of emperor gifts of money were made to the troops to secure their loyalty and, after 193, these developed into a systematic purchase of military fidelity, which contributed largely towards a revolution of economic life (cf. p. 221). The large gold pieces of Gallienus, with the legend 'ob fidem reservatam'[1], express only too clearly the purpose for which they were issued.

Such were the forces that determined who should be made emperor. But it would be a grave mistake to see their effects in isolation. They crossed one another in a hundred different ways. Decius, the Pannonian, was the pride of the senatorial party; other Illyrians, like Claudius and Quintillus, though plain soldiers and not senators themselves, were nevertheless helped on their way to the purple by the complicity, or, it may be, by the direct will of the Senate. Valerian, Regalianus[2] and other men of consular rank owed their elevation to the army, and that same army remained unswervingly loyal to the high-born Gallienus in his later years. Nor did the high birth of Gallienus prevent him from cutting down the privileges of his senatorial peers.

The Praetorian Prefects still played their ominous part in the rise and fall of emperors, as, for example, Heraclianus in 268. But this position was now only exceptionally a step to the throne, as earlier with Macrinus, and later with Florian and Julianus. Until the year 260 it was an apple of discord between the senatorial governors; after that date one commander of the new cavalry corps after another—Aureolus, Aurelian and Probus—grasped at the succession. It is easy to understand why Diocletian abolished a position of such dangerous strength.

Yet another force that raised up pretenders by the score or brought about their overthrow lay in the psychological *malaise* of despairing mankind, seeking its redeemers and hurling its scapegoats to destruction. The aspirants to the throne showed neither scruples nor any sense of responsibility. Decius, the conservative senator, cannot be cleared of this reproach by all the tendencious stories of heathen literature (cf. p. 222 below), any more than can the other 'constitutional' rulers, like Valerian. They were as guilty when they clutched at the purple as were the rough soldiers who rose from the ranks, or the men of the Eastern border-lands. In revolt against Gallienus rose his own creatures and familiars,

[1] Alföldi, *Zeitschr. f. Num.* XXXVII, 1927, p. 210.
[2] H. Dessau, *Zeitschr. f. Num.* XXII, 1912, p. 201 *sq.*

like Ingenuus, Postumus, Aureolus, Claudius and Aurelian—all highly-skilled soldiers, or, finally, his father's confidant, Macrianus. The loyal spirit of an Agrippa was for ever lost. Only very slowly was the balance against this wild orgy of personal ambition and adventure restored by the sound political sense and earnest Roman sentiment of the Illyrian peasants. When after the exclusion of the senators, in 260, the officers from the Danube countries following the equestrian career came more and more to monopolize the highest commands, the election of an emperor was gradually restricted to them.

V. THE STATE AND THE CHURCH

Soon after his accession Decius took in hand a persecution of the Christians. In this there were several stages. First came measures against the leaders of the Church, beginning with the imprisonment of the Bishop of Rome, who was put to death on January 20, 250. There is evidence to show that the persecution was pressed more severely in March, but the third stage of more decisive action must be placed in June, since the many certificates of having made sacrifice to the pagan gods that have been found in Egypt were all issued between June 12 and July 15. This reflects the carrying through of a new measure providing that all subjects of the Empire, from small children to the priests of the pagan cults, must be registered as making an offering, and the enforcement of this order was controlled by the whole machinery of the Roman administration. The penalty for recalcitrancy was death, though the magistrates only imposed it where they failed by persuasion or threats to secure obedience. The *acta* of the martyrs compiled for the purpose of edification and in a set literary convention do not afford, in general, trustworthy evidence, but there is no reason to doubt that the number of those who suffered for their faith was large (see below, p. 521). Porphyry, a pitiless enemy of Christianity and a well-informed contemporary, declares that in the persecutions of the middle of the third century thousands were put to death[1]. That a still larger number of *confessores* were left alive is to be explained, not only by the leniency of the magistrates but by the dying down of the persecution due to the Gothic war about the end of the year 250. The firm stand of these *confessores* greatly impressed the Christians who had yielded, and the organizing skill, political tact, and determination of the clergy in the restoration of the Church was a potent factor in

[1] Cf. P. de Labriolle, *La réaction païenne*, p. 285 *sq.* On the number of the martyrs see P. Allard, *Rev. des questions hist.* n.s. xxxiv, 1905, pp. 235 *sqq.*

recovery. But it cannot be doubted that the general result might have been far different had Decius not met his death in battle and had he been able, with iron hand, to persecute not for a year but a decade, and leave no breathing-space to the Church.

It is in place here to consider what motives impelled the Emperor to turn executioner. It is true that the Christians were exposed to penalties before Decius, if they were denounced, and that before his time there had been sporadic persecutions (pp. 515 sqq., 654 sqq.). The hatred of the mob against Christianity was of old standing, and if the Christians saw in the worship of the heathen gods the cause of the troubles and evils that beset the world, it cannot be doubted that the pagans repaid them in their own coin. At the end of Philip's reign Origen could declare that wars, famines and plagues were attributed to the increasing number of the Christians[1], and even that the cessation of persecution was made responsible for the disorders that followed. The feeling of the mob was whipped up by agitators from the lettered classes as in Alexandria and elsewhere. Thus there was a widespread popular hostility to the Church which might well induce Decius to act. It is also not impossible that the Emperor bore in mind that the strongest supporters of his predecessor had been the Eastern archers, among whom the partly Christian Osrhoënians played a leading rôle. His own power rested on the soldiery from Illyricum where Christianity had made hardly any progress. Finally, his good relations with the Senate urged him along the path of persecution. Thus to other motives may be added the general direction of policy that followed his accession.

It may further be pointed out that the Christian community was ever more strongly claiming to be an *imperium in imperio*. Despite the humanity and tolerance of the Roman State, the Church was resolute to yield no whit of its ideals in order to obey the Roman laws. Thus was removed the possibility of an understanding, and the claims of the Church to dominion, illustrated by the illusion that certain recent emperors had even been Christians, were too high to admit of reconciliation. Immediately before the Decian persecution Origen had declared that Christ (and therefore also His followers) was stronger than the emperor and all his officers, stronger than the Senate and the Roman People[2]. He looked for a day when the heathen cults should disappear and loyalty to the sovereign be no longer attested by pagan cult-acts. This does not, he argues, mean anarchy as even the barbarians will lose their savagery through the teaching of the Church. It is

----

[1] *Contra Celsum*, 2, 79.   [2] *Ib.* 3, 15.

thus true of Decius that his opponents prescribed for him in full measure the principle of his action[1].

Finally, the change that had converted the Principate based on Republican and juristic concepts into an absolutism which rested on a theological basis made the claim of the emperor to worship wholly irreconcilable with the claim of the Christians. In the view of the present writer, the offering demanded of the Christians by Decius was something other than an expiatory supplication of the gods, and its purpose was not to restore the *pax deorum* but to attest loyalty to the Emperor, whose reign was assumed to bring divinely-ordained happiness in which an attempt to deprecate disaster had no place (p. 194). Indeed, to declare the need for world-wide offerings to appease the gods would refute the courtly insistence on the Golden Age which the ruling emperor was supposed to restore to earth. For in this period the sane logic of mankind had yielded to such idealizing theories. The primary purpose of the offering was the welfare of the emperor and it was a matter of subsidiary importance what god received it; this was no innovation but was in the tradition of the Empire[2]. Only the precise registration of those who make offerings and the certificates were new. Furthermore, the anniversary of Decius' proclamation as emperor fell about the middle of June, and the offering ordered about that time (p. 166) may be regarded as the traditional expression of loyalty on this occasion. In the early Empire, needless to say, such offerings to the Emperor-Saviour were spontaneous, and compulsion was employed only in the absence of goodwill or in times of great danger. But what was once offered in gratitude from below was later on commanded from above. This test of loyalty, as the sources show, was eagerly welcomed by the pagans, who might well regard refusal as a denial of the general goodwill to the sovereign inspired by the occasion. The idea of the renewal of felicity on earth by the Saviour-ruler clashed with the Christian doctrine—'tempora Christianis semper, et nunc vel maxime, non auro sed ferro transiguntur'[3]. It seems, therefore, that by such action Decius was determined to demand religious ways of expression of loyalty towards the emperor, and this is further emphasized by the appearance on coins of Decius of the busts of all the consecrated emperors[4].

---

[1] H. Lietzmann, *Gesch. der alte Kirche*, II, p. 165.

[2] Reasons for this view, which goes beyond the scope of the present chapter, are given in *Klio*, XXXI, 1938, pp. 323 *sqq.*

[3] Tertullian, *de cultu fem.* II, 13, 6. The direct reference is to women's ornaments, but he plays upon the idea of the imperial Golden Age.

[4] See H. Mattingly in *J.R.S.* XIV, 1924, p. 9 and *Num. Chron.* 1924, pp. 210 *sqq.*; Volume of Plates V, 236, *a–i*.

Under Decius' successor, Trebonianus Gallus, there were signs of an approaching persecution, but hardly had the new emperor decided upon it than he died. Gallus, too, began with proceedings against the Bishop of Rome, Cornelius, who was arrested and banished, as was, soon after, his successor Lucius. He too next proceeded with measures against the clergy, but did not reach any general persecution[1]. It can be asserted with confidence that Gallus did not renew Decius' order for a universal act of sacrifice, and what traces of such an act there are must be attributed to the local initiative of a governor[2]. It has been pointed out that such an order need not be regarded as exceptional, and may, as that of Decius, have been connected with some imperial anniversary[3]. It is, thus, at least hazardous to regard Gallus as having simply continued the policy of his predecessor and his death left unrevealed how far he intended to carry his attack upon the Church.

It was not until 257 that a new persecution was launched, this time by Valerian. The bishop Dionysius of Alexandria in laudation of Gallienus[4] set himself to find a foil to that emperor as the author of the later toleration, and chose for this purpose the rebel Macrianus rather than Valerian, who after all was Gallienus' father. Yet Valerian had been Decius' chief lieutenant, and it is hardly probable that he did not share his hostility to the Church, so that it may be conjectured that it was only his pre-occupation with the dangers of the Empire that delayed his action. Macrianus' part in the persecution may be reduced to his activity as chief finance minister (*curator summarum rationum*), whose administrative machinery was involved particularly in the confiscation of Church property (p. 207). If then the decision really lay with Valerian, the reason for it is not far to seek. August 257 found him with a whole series of defeats to his discredit, and he sought to turn popular indignation against the Christians and avert it from himself. The *acta* of Cyprian and works of Dionysius of Alexandria afford excellent evidence for the character of Valerian's actions. The State demands no more than the minimum of obedience, not that the Christians should abandon their faith but that they should add to it a willingness to respect old-established religious formalities. In the words of the governor of Africa—'qui Romanam

---

[1] Statements of Cyprian which have been taken to refer to such a persecution are to be interpreted rather as a call to resistance should it be demanded.
[2] Cyprian, *Ep.* 58, 9; 59, 6.
[3] The view that there was a general order which took the form of a supplication to Apollo salutaris because of the pestilence that had broken out is not here accepted.
[4] See Eusebius, *Hist. Eccl.* VII, 10, 2–9 and 22, 12–23, 4.

religionem non colunt, debere Romanas caerimonias recognoscere.' And it was made clear that this recognition is imperative because it attests loyalty to the sovereign. The defence of the Christians takes up this point—the Christians do not cease to pray for the welfare of the emperors, but can only do so to the one true God. In the words of Cyprian—'nullos alios deos novi, nisi unum et verum Deum—huic Deo nos Christiani deservimus, hunc deprecamur diebus et noctibus—et pro incolumitate ipsorum imperatorum'[1].

The persecution began, as under Decius, with the arrest of the leading churchmen, but then followed a different course. The main body of believers was not called to book, but meetings for religious purposes and entry to the cemeteries were forbidden under pain of death. Around these cemeteries, particularly in the Catacombs, workshops and rooms had been formed for the social life and administration of the Church, and it was here that in Rome the bishop Xystus and his deacons together with many clergy and laity were arrested and then put to death. It is surprising that Dionysius of Alexandria and Cyprian, despite their manful recalcitrancy, were at first visited only with exile or at worst, *deportatio*, but their reprieve was short. In a year came a new rescript ordering the immediate execution of the clergy; highly-placed Christians who clung to their faith suffered confiscation as well as death, while the Christians of the imperial household and domains were punished with *deportatio*[2]. The humbler folk, so long as they did not disobey the former edict or provoke the magistrates to action, were left untouched. The persecution cost many lives and continued till the death of Valerian[3]. But, though it lasted three years, it did not overthrow the Church. The *disciplina Romana*, which for centuries had held in its grasp the civilized world, could not prevail over the *divinitus tradita disciplina*[4] of Christianity. Herein was to be the secret of victory—in the iron calm and Roman pride with which a Cyprian faced death, in the resolution with which the Roman see claimed to lead the whole Church amid the terrors of persecution, in the unswerving discharge of spiritual duties and the care for the oppressed and the poor in days of constant peril.

When Valerian was taken prisoner by the Persians, Gallienus, in this as in all else, broke with his father's policy (p. 184 *sq.*). His

---

[1] *Acta Cypr.* 1, 2.   [2] Cyprian, *Ep.* 80, 1.

[3] The news of Valerian's capture could have been known in Rome by July 22, 260 (see above p. 172). In the East the persecution continued somewhat longer till the fall of Macrianus, cf. Eusebius, *Hist. Eccl.* VII, 10, 9.

[4] Cyprian, *de lapsis*, 5.

first decree has not come down to us, but only the Greek translation of a rescript to the bishops of Egypt[1] in which he extended his concessions to that country after the fall of Macrianus (A.D. 261) and of Aemilianus (262). The imperial decree which gave freedom and security to the Faith and its adherents and restored to the communities their places of worship and cemeteries was of fundamental importance. Christianity was now pronounced neither outside the law nor against the law. When the Emperor acted on a petition from the bishops, he admitted that they possessed a legal status, and in giving back the property of the Church he confirmed the legality of its possession. It is true that his murder was followed by a violent reaction, but his action pointed the way to the final solution. The organization of the Church was able to advance, and in a favourable moment an emperor like Aurelian was prepared to admit the competence of the bishops of Rome and Italy in an ecclesiastical question (see p. 303).

When Gallienus decided to end the policy of persecution and the tradition it implied, it was not that he failed to recognize the danger to the Empire of the Christian movement or that he lacked the will and ability to carry through a Roman policy of restoration planned by Decius and Valerian. Such a judgment of his capacity is the fiction of late historians. The explanation of his action is rather that he realized that Christianity could only be cured by treatment, not by the knife, and it was his hope that in the anti-Christian polemic of Neoplatonism, the outcome of the intellectual circles in which he moved, might be found the antidote that was needed to bring about the cure[2].

In the short reign of Claudius II there are recorded a host of martyrdoms. The *acta* that tell of these are late and not above suspicion. But they are not to be wholly set aside, for they are concerned with executions in Italy and it was here that the reaction against Gallienus was most violent, so that a change of policy towards the Christians was to be expected. Claudius, who enjoyed the confidence of the Senate, was for that very reason inclined to persecution, even though the Gothic war and his own death hindered him from taking part in it. Although he and his immediate successors did not resume the policy of persecution on a large scale, they preferred to ignore Christianity in a hostile spirit, rather than to continue Gallienus' real toleration of the Church. Yet it was not in their power to undo what he had done or to counter its consequences.

---

[1] Eusebius, *Hist. Eccl.* VII, 13.
[2] See A. Alföldi, *Fünfundzwanzig Jahre Röm.-Germ. Komm.* pp. 17 *sqq.* See also below, p. 230.

VI. THE ARMY AND ITS TRANSFORMATION

Until the middle of the third century and even for a time thereafter, the legions remained the backbone of the Roman army, and their number was increased by Septimius Severus (p. 17) and, though less notably, by some of his successors[1]. More than half the army, to the number of 200,000 men, consisted of legionaries, and throughout the century the best of these were drafted into the *cohortes praetoriae*. The most valiant and warlike soldiers of that time were the Illyrians, and these supplied the majority of the legionaries, and, after Septimius Severus, of the Guard. Their political predominance reflects that of the legions, which, as the use of *vexillationes* became the rule instead of the exception, provided the best infantry and a part of the cavalry for a new mobile army, so that in the wars of Aurelian and even somewhat later the great military creation of Rome still brilliantly proved its worth, though indeed it no longer was the sole decisive factor.

Although Septimius Severus confirmed the right of the soldiers to a family life and allowed them to lease the *prata legionis* (p. 32) it would be a mistake to suppose that thus early the legionaries became settlers by compulsion like the barbarians who were then planted behind the *limites*. The Illyrians were, indeed, a peasant stock, yet they left their farms to become soldiers and fought the battles of the Empire from end to end of it, especially in the many campaigns of the middle of the century. But before the reforms of Constantine the legionaries, like the frontier cavalry, had come to be regarded as peasants tied to their farms[2], and this implies that in the preceding decades the legions had been transformed into a settled and hereditary frontier guard. The great wars of the middle of the century, the pestilences that visited the Empire and the loss of men carried off in the widespread barbarian invasions had exhausted in the Illyrians the last source of romanized man-power, so that Constantine no longer relied upon them. Further, with the constant withdrawal of the best troops to serve in the mobile army, the garrisoning of the frontier sank to a secondary rôle that was entrusted to barbarians and semi-barbarians.

In the period of the great military crisis Rome had to meet enemies who had shown superiority in the field, and the need to match their methods undermined the tactical supremacy of the

---

[1] H. M. D. Parker, *J.R.S.* XXIII, 1933, p. 176.
[2] *Ann. épig.* 1937, no. 232; S. Paulovics, *Archaeol. Hungarica* XX.

legion. This was not due to any failure of the Illyrians, who were
no less suited to maintain the Roman art of war than the Italians
had been. They were simple peasants, but the fact alone that they
supplied most of the centurions of the army at this time shows
that they were well able through years of service to train themselves in Roman discipline and skill of manoeuvre, and they were
inspired by the spirit of Rome (vol. xi, pp. 540 *sqq.*). But the
countless forced marches of great range were merely hindered by
the old Roman practice of fortifying camps at the end of each day.
Caesar had long before realized how hampering the heavy
legionary armament could be in the face of a nimble and mounted
enemy[1], and now, in the third century, the infantry tactics and
weapons of the legions were clearly shown to be out of date. A
hint of this may be found in the fact that Macrinus had sought to
increase the mobility of his troops by taking away their breast-
plates and heavy shields[2]. Further, now that the enemy, both in
East and West, trusted to long-distance missiles or sudden cavalry
attacks, the *pilum*, which was designed for use against close and
comparatively immobile masses, lost its effectiveness and disappeared in the third century, and with it the short sword, which
was replaced by the long *spatha* of the auxiliaries and the German
enemy, together with the lance[3]. But new equipment, suited to
the fighting of the time, had already been supplied to other
formations, as was indeed inevitable now that cavalry was becoming more important than infantry.

As the old tactics lost their hold, discipline naturally declined.
But more grave was the effect of the disappearance of suitable
personnel. The level of education began to sink during the third
century, especially among the officers, where it is more dangerous. The exclusion of senators from a military career did more
harm to the civil service than to the army, but the disappearance
of the Italian officers of equestrian rank in this period meant an
irreparable loss, and inevitably lowered the cultural standard of
the whole hierarchy. Whereas earlier the *principalis* marked out to
be centurion had already in the bureaux of his superiors acquired a
thorough knowledge of all sides of the service and had also proved
himself in military administration, the army officer in this epoch
was a mere man of his hands[4], and in the fourth century often
an illiterate.

[1] *Bell. Gall.* v, 16, 2–4.   [2] Dio LXXIX, 37, 4.
[3] P. Couissin, *Les armes romaines*, pp. 471 *sqq.*
[4] A. von Domaszewski, *Die Rangordnung des röm. Heeres*, p. 42; cf. G. L.
Cheesman, *The Auxilia of the Roman Imperial Army*, p. 99.

Next come the regular *auxilia*. In order to understand the later development it is important to stress the fact that in the second century these had not so wholly lost their national character as might be thought. Though Trajan's Column shows many auxiliaries in uniform Roman equipment, advantageous as that could be, their organization and way of fighting were less assimilated to those of the legions than has been supposed. Such an assimilation was hardly possible for the cavalry, which in the legion played a subordinate rôle, and it is not an archaism when Vegetius[1] declares that there was a marked difference between *auxilia* and legions—'alia instituta, alius inter eos est usus armorum.' The motley groups of fighters with their special kinds of dress and arms that also appear in these reliefs are not all to be regarded as 'irregular' formations.

In the second century national peculiarities in the practice of war were highly appreciated,[2] and barbarian formations had even been made out of romanized personnel. To take one instance, the *ala Ulpia contariorum civium Romanorum* used the long thrusting spear of the Iranians[3] to meet the Quadi who fought in the Sarmatian way, and the tactics of the Sarmatians and Alani, together with their use of the wedge-formation in attack, were practised in the army[4], and there was even made an *ala I Gallorum et Pannoniorum catafractata* for use against these enemies. Hadrian, in particular, who had studied the barbarian ways of fighting, will not have contented himself with allowing the use of national war-cries by the *auxilia*. This is obvious so far as the numerous cavalry regiments and infantry of the Oriental bowmen are concerned; nor can Rome have dispensed with the admired dexterity of the Batavians, the much-copied cavalry manoeuvres of the Spaniards or the skill of the Moorish javelin-men. National methods of fighting became even more important in the third century. There are new archer formations and an *ala nova firma milliaria catafractaria* in competition with the Parthians and Persians. To the variously equipped troops that have been mentioned may be added, for instance, the *ala* of camelry, the *cohortes scutatae Hispanorum* and other formations, even cavalry[5] armed with the *scutum*. It is even possible that the half-naked Germans on Trajan's Column were regular troops like those cohorts which were disbanded after the rebellion of A.D. 69— 'Germanorum...nudis corporibus super umeros scuta quatientium'[6].

[1] Vegetius, *de re milit.* 2, 2.   [2] Arrian, *Tact.* 33, 2.   [3] *Ib.* 4, 4.
[4] *Ib.* 4, 3; 7; 44, 1.   [5] *Ib.* 4, 4.   [6] Tacitus, *Hist.* II, 22.

The practice of filling up the *auxilia* with recruits from the region in which they were stationed militated against the maintenance of their national character, but the practice was far from uniform. It has been shown that in the third century the Oriental bowmen received recruits from their home countries[1] as also the *ala nova* of cataphracts[2]. At the beginning of that century the *cohors III Batavorum milliaria*, which had been stationed in Pannonia for a long while, still made dedications to its tribal goddess Vagdavercustis[3], and so must have retained its national character. Soldiers' sons joined their fathers' formations and thus assisted a continuity of race that must not be underrated. However much the *auxilia* might be romanized, there were openings for national characteristics, especially when, as early as Hadrian, arose the fixed institution of the *numeri*, which were separated off, not because of their alien character but because of their special functions in the strategy of that emperor.

Hadrian's strategic conception, that is, the police supervision and fixing of the frontiers in the unyielding line of a single cordon instead of a defensive battle-zone in depth, was inspired by high civilizing ideals; but it failed to meet the military needs of the Empire and led directly to the collapse of the defence in the stern times of the third century. The Roman army was far too small to guard the whole line that encircled the world-empire. To fill up the gaps Hadrian created the *numeri* as a kind of militia which cost less than the troops of the line, were worse equipped and not trained to equal efficiency.

For a while these served their purpose and their presence was attested on almost all the frontiers, sometimes supported by first-line troops. But the peoples within the Empire soon failed to supply men to hold the gaps in the defences, the more as invasions, especially those of the Germans, ever more often broke into it. At the same time, the constant elaboration of the defensive lines called for more garrison troops. The result was that the late second century already saw the first settling of barbarians from without the Empire, who were no longer organized as *numeri*. It was still possible to follow the old pattern and place these new settlers under officers such as *praefecti gentium*[4], as for example the *gens*

---

[1] G. Cantacuzène, *Mus. Belge* XXXI, 1927, p. 159 *sq.*; H. van de Weerd— P. Lambrechts, *Laureae Aquincenses*, 1938.

[2] P. Goessler, *Germania* XV, 1931, pp. 10 *sqq.*

[3] Alföldi, '*Pannonia*' I, 1935, p. 184 *sq.* A. W. Byvanck, *Mnem.* Ser. III, vol. V, 1937, p. 320.

[4] R. Cagnat, *L'armée romaine d'Afrique*[2], pp. 263 *sqq.*

Onsorum who have been newly posted under a *praepositus* in Lower Pannonia at the end of the second century[1], and the *dediticii Alexandriani* settled at Walldürn on the Rhine under Severus Alexander.[2] The like control was exercised over the Chatti who at the end of the second century were transplanted to the *castellum* at Zugmantel in the Taunus with their families and goods[3]. In the third century, too, the frontier troops were often reinforced by prisoners of war and fugitives from enemy countries, but at times it became necessary simply to admit a client State within the frontier line, as is shown by the settlement under Gallienus of a king of the Marcomanni on the *limes* of Upper Pannonia.

The *numeri* gained little from this barbarization of the frontier garrisons. Despite their entire or partial lack of romanization they were put under Roman commanders and officers[4], yet the soldiers who served in them were not only *dediticii* and *gentiles*, but, unlike the other Imperial troops, they did not receive citizenship after the completion of their years of service. None the less, they became romanized to a considerable extent[5], and this process was assisted by their later recruitment from the inhabitants of the part of the front allotted to them. The rise in their status (from the Roman point of view) is reflected in the fact that as late as the third century several *numeri* were advanced to be cohorts and *alae*. On the other hand the value of the citizenship had so fallen that men from Emesa and Palmyra who had become *cives Romani* could be used to form *numeri*[6]; even among the *gaesati* of Tongres citizens are found[7].

As early as the end of the second century bounties were provided for those auxiliaries whose sons carried on their trade of arms[8], and in the third this duty was imposed on them. Even earlier than the *auxilia* the soldiers of the *numeri* were tied to the soil. It has already been noted how this military peasantry[9] became barbarized both in and after the ravages of the years of

---

[1] Ritterling, *Germania*, I, 1917, p. 132.

[2] *C.I.L.* XIII, 6592. E. Fabricius, *Hist. Zeitschr.* XCVIII, 1907, p. 22 *sq.*

[3] R. von Uslar, *Saalburg-Jahrbuch*, VIII, 1934, pp. 61 *sqq.*; id. *Klio*, XXVIII, 1935, pp. 294 *sqq.*; W. Schleiermacher, *Germania*, XXI, 1937, pp. 22 *sqq.* Cf. the German officer Leubaccus at this place, *C.I.L.* XIII, 7613 a.

[4] von Domaszewski, *op. cit.* pp. 59 *sqq.*; Rowell, P.W. *s.v.* Numeri, col. 1336 *sq.*

[5] E. Stein, *Beamten und Truppenkörper*, pp. 236 *sqq.*

[6] J. Carcopino, *Syria*, VI, 1925, p. 127, XIV, 1933, pp. 20 *sqq.*; Rowell, *op. cit.* col. 1334.

[7] *C.I.L.* XIII, 3593.   [8] *C.I.L.* XVI, 132 and H. Nesselhauf, *ib.* p. 118.

[9] Rostovtzeff, *Soc. and Econ. Hist.* pp. 375 *sqq.*

crisis. Under the Tetrarchy it was a matter for congratulation if by any means men could be found to continue this service[1]. Their fixed settlement and the principle of local defence, to which they owed their existence, used up the *numeri*. They disappear from the military system after Diocletian, having either perished or else been changed into other formations. The new strategy demanded instead of the Hadrianic *numeri* the revival under another name of Trajan's irregulars.

The system of the inelastic frontier cordon and the ranging along it of the whole military strength of the Empire broke down as often as serious attacks were launched upon it. But this second-century idea was too deeply rooted in the whole conception of the State for it to be abandoned. That would have meant the sacrifice of the Roman element in the frontier provinces, which at that time did most to uphold the Empire and so could not be reduced to a mere glacis or field of operations. As early as the second century there were efforts to make good the exhaustion of man-power by the strengthening of the frontier fortifications[2], and after the German and Persian invasions there was fresh activity in improving the *castella* and building new defences. In this Gallienus was as active as Postumus and, later, Diocletian and his successors. But though they clung to the traditional method of defence the emperors could not evade the demands of a new situation. If the Empire was to be kept secure, it was necessary to return to a grouping of the armies in depth, and the constant wars of movement made indispensable an army that was ever ready to take the field and was independent of the frontier line. These two needs led to the creation of a new mobile army which was normally posted at important points behind the frontiers. As the new conception of defence prevailed, it conferred increased importance on the significant strategic points of Italy, especially on Aquileia[3], Milan[4] and Verona, the two latter receiving under the sole rule of Gallienus the name of *colonia Gallieniana* on the score of the building of new fortifications[5]. The minting of money and manufacture of arms were removed to these or other great military centres, as also troops including newly organized corps.

About the middle of the century *vexillationes* from Danube legions are found in Aquileia[6], where they formed a standing

---

[1] *Paneg.* VIII (v), 9, 3–4.   [2] Carcopino, *Syria*, VI, 1925, p. 143 *sq.*
[3] A. Calderini, *Aquileia Romana*, 1930, pp. 52 *sqq.*
[4] *C.I.L.* XIII, 6763: cf. Ritterling, P.W. *s.v.* Legio, col. 1336; Dessau 1188 (A.D. 242).
[5] Dessau 544, 6730.   [6] von Domaszewski, *op. cit.* p. 187.

camp. This appears to have been a defensive measure taken by Philip, who in other respects also strove to protect North Italy[1]. Mobile detachments of the Upper Pannonia legions stationed at Aquileia later became regiments of the field-army and were transferred to the East[2]. The commanders of these mobile units were called *praepositus* or *dux*[3]: thus the *ducenarius* Aurelius Marcellinus, who directed as *dux* the work on the fortifications of Verona in 265, was also the commander of such detachments. *Vexillationes* of the Eastern legions came to North Italy in consequence of the victory over Macrianus (p. 185) and when Aureolus went over to Postumus in 268, they seem to have been detached by the latter to Gaul (possibly against Laelianus), as their names appear on the gold struck at Trèves by Victorinus[4].

Gallienus posted mobile troops not only south but north of the Alps. *Vexillationes* from Germany and Britain are found at Sirmium in Pannonia in the period of his sole rule[5]. At the same time, the two legions withdrawn from Dacia (p. 151) were established in Poetovio at the crossing of the Drave, thus barring the road that led to Italy[6]. In like manner a detachment from the legions at Albano and Lambaesis was posted at Lychnidus on one of the chief roads that lead to Greece[7]. Thus there can be no doubt that Gallienus went beyond what had hitherto been attempted and devised a far-reaching strategic scheme to break the waves of the barbarian invasions. It may be that the *vexillationes* from Lower Moesia and Pannonia that are found in Dalmatia in the third century belong to the same setting. The

---

[1] Parker, *A History of the Roman World*, p. 156.

[2] *Ann. épig.* 1912, no. 89; *Not. dign. Or.* VII, 7 (=42), *Or.* VIII, 7 (= 39): cf. Ritterling, *op. cit.* col. 1686 *sq.* The corresponding positions of both legions in the *Notitia* show, as Ritterling has pointed out, that they originally made up a double formation. They can therefore only be the detachments from North Italy. Cf. also Dessau 1332.

[3] *C.I.L.* VI, 1645. N. Vulić, *Spomenik of the Serb. Acad.* LXXV, Class II, 58, 1933, p. 58, no. 176. Cf. also L. de Regibus, *Historia* IX, 1934, pp. 456 *sqq.*

[4] P. H. Webb, M.-S. V, ii, pp. 386 *sqq.*; cf. Ritterling, *op. cit.* cols. 1344, 1375. For other views see J. de Witte, *Rev. num.* 1884, pp. 293 *sqq.*; A. Blanchet, *Mus. Belge*, XXVII, 1923, pp. 169 *sqq.* and *Rev. num.* 1933, p. 228; Sir C. Oman, *Num. Chron.* 1924, pp. 53 *sqq.*; H. Mattingly, *Trans. Int. Num. Congr.* 1936, pp. 214 *sqq.*

[5] Dessau 546; cf. *C.I.L.* III, p. 2328[182].

[6] B. Saria, *Strena Buliciana*, pp. 249 *sqq.* Further literature is given in Alföldi, *Die Gotenbewegungen und die Aufgabe der Provinz Dacien*, see above, p. 138 n. 1.

[7] Vulić, *op. cit.*; for another view, Saria, *Klio*, XXX, 1937, pp. 352 *sqq.*

troops on this mobile footing were of course used also in offensive operations, as for instance the advance to Southern Gaul under Claudius II.

Some emperors after Gallienus may have regarded this separating off of mobile troops as a transitory innovation, but he can hardly have done so. At all events, the continuous state of war often prevented the *vexillationes* from returning to their parent legions on the frontier, and what began as exceptional continued till it was confirmed in the definitive new organization of Diocletian and Constantine when the detachments became *legiones comitatenses* or *palatinae* in the mobile army (p. 398)[1]. The general rule of having two legions in each province, to which Severus and Caracalla gave effect, brought it about that these legionary *vexillationes* appear in pairs as a combined unit; this practice, also applied tactically, remained an essential part of the late Roman army organization.

Whereas this system was defensive in motive and was still half based on the infantry of the old order, the frequent wars of movement caused cavalry to come more into favour. It is true that at the beginning of the century it was firmly and widely held that the strength of the Roman army lay in its infantry and close fighting with spears, whereas the Parthians were distinguished by their cavalry and long-range archery[2]. As late as 238 Maximinus drew up his army for battle with the square of legions and *auxilia* as its main strength. But even the cavalry had come to play a more decisive rôle than his *ordre de bataille* would suggest.

The Moorish javelin-men with their small shields, riding barebacked, had already become famous in Trajan's wars, and in the third century from Caracalla onwards they once more came to the front[3]. Under Macrinus or Elagabalus they are commanded by a tribune of the Praetorian Guard[4]; being thus regarded as *élite* troops, they can hardly have been reduced to the grade of *numeri* but remained irregular formations. Under Macrinus they were effective against the Parthians[5] and in combination with the Oriental archers they contributed greatly to the successes of Severus Alexander and Maximinus against the Germans of the Rhine. The former brought large forces of them to the West[6].

---

[1] E. Fabricius, *op. cit.* p. 28.   [2] Herodian IV, 10, 3
[3] Dio LXXIX, 32, 1 (p. 440, Boissevain).
[4] *C.I.L.* VIII, 20,996; cf. Ritterling, *op. cit.* col. 1327.
[5] Herodian IV, 15, 1.
[6] Herodian VI, 7, 8; VII, 2, 1–2; VIII, 1, 2–3; Zonaras XII, 15 (p. 573);
S.H.A. *Max. duo* 2, 7–9.

Philip's defeat of the Carpi was due to their impetuous attack, and then they appear with Valerian against the Persians, though at the same time Gallienus used a Moorish corps against Ingenuus. Finally, they fought with success against Palmyra under Aurelian (p. 303).

The other important specialist troops of this period, the Oriental archers, seem to have been mainly cavalry, armed with the most dreaded weapon of antiquity, the composite bow of the Iranian and Turkish nomads[1]. The best archer regiments after Caracalla's annexation of their country were the Osrhoënians. Caracalla used them against the Germans, probably as irregulars[2], and so too Severus Alexander and Maximinus: they distinguished themselves in the war against Shapur. Finally, the heavy cavalry of the Iranians, with their long spears and armour both for man and horse[3], were used in the Roman army especially after the increasing conflicts with Persia, in which, indeed, the enemy, too, were driven to adopt Roman tactics[4]. Orientals were used as *catafractarii* because of their long familiarity with this kind of fighting[5].

Such were the new kinds of troops which were at Gallienus' disposal when he decided to break with tradition and bring cavalry into the foreground instead of infantry. But it is significant that he did not rely primarily on these when he organized mounted regiments on a new model[6]. Doubtless he realized the danger to the State if he placed this new instrument of war in the hands of the Moors and Orientals, and so he had recourse to the unexhausted man-power of Dalmatia and created the *equites Dalmatae*. Since, after this army had been disbanded, the *Notitia Dignitatum* always mentions the *equites Mauri*, the *equites promoti* and *equites scutarii* with the Dalmatian regiments, it is fairly certain that Gallienus grouped them together, converting into new *corps d'élite* the Moorish javelin-men, and also the concentrated legionary cavalry (*promoti*)[7] and the *scutarii*, who must

---

[1] J. Werner and K. Stade, *Germania* XVII, 1933, pp. 110 and 289. This bow is described in Ammian. Marc. XXII, 8, 37.

[2] *C.I.L.* XI, 304; but see Dessau 2540, where a '*numerus Hosroenorum*' is mentioned.

[3] See vol. X, p. 61, vol. XI, p. 119 *sq*. Volume of Plates IV, 26 *b* and V, 150. Cf. F. Altheim, *Epochen der röm. Geschichte* II, p. 198 *sq*.

[4] Herodian III, 4, 9.

[5] Goessler, *op. cit.* pp. 8 *sqq*.

[6] Cedrenus, p. 454 (Bonn): cf. Ritterling, *Festschr. für O. Hirschfelds 60. Geburtstag*, pp. 345 *sqq*.

[7] Ritterling, *op. cit.* p. 348.

have used a distinctive way of fighting. This far-reaching re-organization was made in A.D. 258 (p. 182). The coin-issues show that the official designation of this whole cavalry force was simply *equites* and that it was posted at Milan under Gallienus, as also under Aurelian[1]. At the *decennalia* of Gallienus it is put on a par with the Praetorian Guard, and this shows that it was a real house-hold corps under the direct command of the emperor. From this time onwards its commander was the most powerful subject of the Empire, though only of equestrian rank. Claudius seems to have held this post after the rebellion of Aureolus[2], and this agrees with the fact that he is described as second only to the emperor. After him Aurelian and then Probus (who was called Equitius) used this position as a jumping-off place to the throne.

It is important to observe that this cavalry army acted as a unit wholly independent of the infantry: thus it won the victories over Ingenuus and Macrianus. But even later this separation continued, as in 269 against the Goths, where friction between the two arms almost led to a serious disaster. Here, too, the Dalmatians did much to secure victory, as later in the Eastern wars of Aurelian. In the battles before Antioch and near Emesa the *equites* played their independent rôle. Once the cavalry army had so brilliantly proved its worth, and while so much remained for it to do, Aurelian can hardly have broken it up and distributed its units over the East. It is more probable that this was done by Diocletian[3], to destroy the central political importance of their commander. At some time before A.D. 293 the name *vexillationes*, which had been used of legions of the mobile army[4], was trans-ferred to mounted detachments[5], which may be regarded as being parts of the cavalry army. Diocletian also restored the con-nection of the *promoti* with the legion, but this only lasted for a time[6].

After Gallienus Aurelian doubtless did much for the re-organization of the army. It seems, he strengthened the *catafractarii*, who are also called *clibanarii*. For on the Arch of Galerius at

---

[1] Alföldi, *Zeitschr. für Num.* XXXVII, 1927, pp. 198 *sqq.*

[2] Zonaras XII, 26 (p. 604).

[3] von Domaszewski, *Westd. Zeitschr.* XXI, 1902, p. 188 *sq.*; id. *Die Rangordnung*, p. 192, note 1. For another view Ritterling, *op. cit.*

[4] So late as 269; see Dessau 569 '*vexillationes adque equites.*' *C.I.L.* VIII, 9045, 9047 do not refer to these. Cf. Carcopino, *Syria* VI, 1925, p. 141.

[5] *Cod. Just.* X, 55, 3: cf. E. Stein *op. cit.* I, p. 92, n. 1; Parker, *J.R.S.* XXIII, 1933, p. 188.

[6] R. Grosse, *Röm. Militärgeschichte* p. 36; M. Besnier, *L'Empire rom.* p. 190, n. 289.

Salonica the emperor's bodyguards wear the scale-armour of the cataphracts[1] and the conical helmet (*Spangenhelm*) typical of the Iranians, which was then inherited by the Germans of the middle ages. Their standards are the Iranian *dracones*—serpents flying and hissing with the gaping jaws of a wild animal. These may have been used before by the Thracian auxiliaries[2] and were employed in manoeuvres to mark enemy positions[3], but they had earlier been regarded as foreign and barbarian[4]. It may be taken as certain that this Persian equipment had established itself before Galerius' victories and no emperor had had so much to do with enemy cataphracts as Aurelian. He had, indeed, discovered the right tactics and weapons to use against them (p. 303 *sq.*), but he doubtless learned to respect the *clibanarii* of Zenobia and introduced such regiments into his army on a large scale.

Another innovation with far-reaching consequences has been attributed to Aurelian[5]. He apparently formed *auxilia* of Vandals, Juthungi and Alemanni, and this meant a quite new access of Germans to the army. There are now found wholly non-Roman formations, as even earlier a *cuneus Frisiorum* in Britain. But the new German *auxilia* also kept their ancient national standards, shield-devices and dress, which, as ever more Germans were enrolled, spread so quickly that by the early period of Constantine they became regular in the whole army[6]. As early as the Tetrarchy the emperor himself wore even in peace time the long trousers, the once despised *bracae* of the Celts and Germans. It is probable that before the century ended the customs of the German warriors, as the raising on a shield and the crowning with a torque, appeared at the proclamation of the emperors. All this did not happen suddenly and without precedent. Caracalla created a privileged *élite* force of Germans, the *leones*, which lasted on, it may be as a special kind of bodyguard[7]. Germans had done this service to the first emperors and the third-century rulers from Caracalla

---

[1] See Volume of Plates v, 150, *b*.

[2] Because they are carried by Thracian horseman-gods; cf. D. Tudor, *Ephem. Dacor.* VII, 1937, pp. 209, 217.

[3] Arrian, *Tact.* 35, 2 *sq.*

[4] For the literature concerned with these standards see J. Dobiáš, *Trans. Int. Num. Congr.* 1936, pp. 169 *sqq.* and F. Sarre, *Klio* III, 1903, p. 359. The mention of the *dracones* in S.H.A. *Gall. duo* 8, 6 is an addition by the compiler. For another view see von Domaszewski, *Rhein. Mus.* LVII, 1902, p. 513 *sq.*

[5] Cf. Th. Mommsen, *Ges. Schriften* VI, p. 282 *sq.*

[6] Alföldi, *Germania* XIX, 1935, pp. 324 *sqq.*

[7] Dio LXXIX, 6, 4 (p. 409 Boissevain).

certainly had German bodyguards. The reliefs of the Arch of Galerius show these as typical.

But the emperors of the third century, though they could not do without this excellent fighting material, strove as far as possible to keep the Germans in a subordinate position, as half-free *coloni* or third-line soldiers in the *numeri* or at least attached to other troops under Roman supervision. It may be that it was Philip, in whose reign recruits were already notably scarce, who first admitted them to the regular *auxilia*. Claudius certainly did so. But the wearing down of the Empire's own resources is shown by the handing over of part of the Upper Pannonian *limes* to a German prince under Gallienus or the alliance in the same period with German kings on the Rhine outside the frontier. The contingents bought from the Germans under the cloak of a *foedus* gradually became indispensable. No hesitation was felt about enlisting great numbers of irregulars from free Germany. This had been the practice of Trajan and Marcus Aurelius, as of Caracalla, Maximinus and Pupienus. It was followed by Gallienus on the Rhine and after him by Postumus. By keeping these irregulars it was possible to isolate these alien elements and in fact the Germans did not come to the front politically in this period because their isolation was effective. But this procedure meant that the Empire's gold was constantly drained away. And as the troops of the line were used up, the irregulars became ever more predominant and finally became regulars. The world was upside-down. Yet the guiding of the increasing flood of Germans in the army into Roman channels marks an achievement of the third-century emperors.

The great changes in the army were reflected in its hierarchy and it was Gallienus who made the decisive alterations in its organization. There is one institution which seems to date from the beginning of his reign, which was to lead to important developments, that of the *protectores divini lateris*. The model for these may have been the *somatophylakes* of the Hellenistic Kings (vol. VII, p. 9). The Hellenistic ideas that underlay the autocracy were salient in this period, and Gallienus, though he showered distinctions on the Germans, still excluded them from the regular service of the State. This suggests that the first institution of the *protectores* is to be distinguished from its later development in which the direct personal relation of the *protectores domestici* to the monarch became tinged with the idea of loyal retainership familiar to the germanized officers of the court. Another sign of the change in the position of the *protectores* is to be seen in the fact that at first the name marked a distinction reserved for the tribunes of the Praetorian Guard, the prefects of the legions and the commanders of the mobile units, whereas later it was applied to the whole body of centurions[1]. The essential feature of the institution was residence at the Imperial camp as a kind of training as staff-officers (p. 378).

Gallienus' exclusion of senators from military service had important consequences. The creation of so eminent a position as that of the general of the new cavalry army foreshadowed the office of *magister militum* under Constantine. This general, and no less the army-commanders in the provinces, the *praefecti legionis*[2] and the *praepositi* or *duces* of the *vexillationes* were *equites* (p. 377). But the equestrian order was no longer the old social class of Rome and the Italians. Even under the early Empire centurions had been promoted to this rank and Septimius Severus granted all under-officers the privilege of wearing the gold ring which was the badge of the equestrian order (p. 16). This process continued, and Gallienus bestowed this rank on the sons of *principales* and centurions at their birth.[3]

As this development broke down the old class-distinctions, so the new strategy deprived Rome of its central importance in favour of the Imperial headquarters. To these were also removed the arms-factories[4] and the decentralization of coining worked in the same direction. In this, too, Gallienus broke with tradition. But the army not only lost its connection with the capital but was wholly divorced from old ideas of the State. It no longer stood for the Roman citizen body, and had no feeling for ancient prerogatives, but depended simply on the will of the monarch. This personal attachment to the Imperator had also much to do with the change that came over the economic life of the Empire.

The Roman denarius had for centuries possessed a value based not on State regulation but on its intrinsic worth, and though since Nero its silver content imperceptibly decreased, it was the foundation of the prosperity of the Antonine period. But in the reign of Septimius Severus the debasement of the currency was already so advanced that either it must be checked or account must be taken of its consequences. Severus adopted the second alternative. He

---

[1] E. Stein, *op. cit.* I, p. 81 *sq.* The literature of this subject is to be found here and in Schenk von Stauffenberg, *Die Welt als Geschichte*, I, 1935, p. 81 *sq.* n. 24.

[2] Grosse, *op. cit.* pp. 3 *sqq.*; L. de Regibus, *op. cit.* pp. 451 *sqq.*

[3] von Domaszewski, *Die Rangordnung*, pp. 34, 42 *sq.*, 54, 61, 80 *sqq.*

[4] *Ib.* pp. 25, 46, 109.

allowed the process to continue, but was able to compensate the soldiers, apart from an increase in their pay, by granting them the benefits of a new taxation in kind, the *annona*[1]. This new levy bore hardly on the provincials and induced a far-reaching system of requisitions. From Septimius Severus onwards the silver content of the currency fell though gradually, until in the lamentable conditions of A.D. 253 Valerian and Gallienus found themselves forced to resort to a more drastic debasement of the currency to get money for the State, and after the catastrophe of 260 the denarius was rapidly replaced by a silver-washed copper coinage. At the same time the imperial authority attached an arbitrary value to this inflation-currency, and compelled its acceptance at this rate; now that the value of money was fixed by authority, not by the free play of economic forces, the foundations of the old individual form of life were destroyed. But while no effort was made to do more for the silver currency than regulate the inflation-money, gold was issued and put into currency by a new method. By substituting increases of pay[2] for military distinctions and developing the abuse of presents in gold Severus had inaugurated a process that was to have far-reaching effects. Apart from the facts that from his reign onwards the normal issues of gold were ever more often made to coincide with the periodic Imperial celebrations and that the gold reserve more regularly moved about with the imperial court and camp, there now further developed a peculiar system for the distribution of the gold coins (which never lost their full metal content). This change is best seen in the money struck for presents. These gifts became especially common since the reign of Hadrian and usually consisted in the second century of bronze pieces of no intrinsic value but well fitted by their high artistic execution to be presented to highly placed personages on great occasions. After Severus the 'medallions' suited to the taste of a cultivated upper class were gradually replaced by large gold pieces, which, in striking contrast to the poverty of the time, had become by the period of the Tetrarchy heavy lumps of gold. Their types displayed with growing emphasis their connection with the Imperial festivals.

These largesses, which were no longer designed for the citizens but for the soldiers, served not only to secure their loyalty but called forth the traditional religious and emotional expression of it. It was not undisguised bribery, but was allied with offerings

[1] D. van Berchem, *Mém. de la Soc. nat. des antiquaires de France*, LXXX, 1937, pp. 124 *sqq.*

[2] von Domaszewski, *Neue Heid. Jahrb.* x, 1901, pp. 230 *sqq.*

and solemnities as was demanded by the spirit of the age. 'Liberalitas praestantissimorum imperatorum expungebatur in castris, milites laureati adibant,' writes Tertullian[1]. This development of the system of presents gained a new impetus as the old conception of money died out in the second half of the third century. While the compulsory acceptance of the inflation-money and the growing contribution in kind deprived the civil population of money of intrinsic value, the soldiers were provided for not only by payments in kind but by the presents that accompanied the Imperial festivals, a process whereby the minister of finance became a *comes sacrarum largitionum*.

Despite all this, whoever would make the soldiers alone responsible for this development, should not forget how these men served the Empire with their lives. The millions of Italian and other citizens of the towns merely looked on at the wars, and had no desire to put themselves in peril for their country. They preferred to endure the crushing burden of taxation and the oppression of the autocracy.

VII. THE EMPERORS

First the picture, or rather caricature, presented by the ancient authorities must be considered. Of Decius there is no contemporary tradition apart from the Church Fathers, like Cyprian, who knew him only as *tyrannus ferociens*. For Lactantius, this persecutor of the Faith is an *exsecrabile animal*. The Byzantine tradition presents a view that looks like a direct answer to such slanders. That convinced heathen, Zosimus, maintains that he ruled most admirably and won all his battles. Again, in the story told by the late Greek sources of his accession, the same tendency is revealed: the intention is to clear him of the charge of usurpation. Actually, he had already been months in Illyricum, and had certainly got rid of the partisans of Pacatianus, when his revolt began; he could not therefore have been forced to assume the purple by those same soldiers, in dread of punishment. Nor does it appear to the present writer to be true that he intended to lay aside the purple, but that the evil, distrustful Philip would not credit his intention[2]. That would be to attribute to this man of iron a course of conduct actually followed a century later by the soft and servile Vetranio, or, before him, by the feeble Tetricus. Decius knew that the purple on his shoulders meant empire or death—in that knowledge he acted. The same tendency is even more crudely

---

[1] *de corona* I, I.   [2] See, however, p. 93 *sq.*

exaggerated in that pamphlet against Christianity, the *Historia Augusta*. For it Decius is the ideal champion of the old Roman position, an embodiment of true Roman virtues. But what is beyond all doubt is that the Senate always regarded him as flesh of its flesh and that his heroic death finally silenced all criticism in these circles and so prepared the way for his later transfiguration. To excuse the terrible disaster that befell this defender of the old national religion and morality the sources on which our Byzantine authorities depend sought a scapegoat to bear the guilt. They found one in the successor of Decius, the witness of his fall— Trebonianus Gallus. The treachery of Gallus, as alleged by our authorities, is an absurd invention. What was left for him to do, when all was lost, but to bow to the inevitable and let the Goths go their way?

Of the unhappy Valerian the heathen sources, truthfully enough, have almost nothing good to report; the Christians load him with abuse. But the *Historia Augusta*, in its hatred for the Christians, excels itself and makes this wretched figure a national hero. The whole *vita Valeriani* is a reply to Lactantius, who says of this persecutor—'deus novo ac singulari poenae genere adfecit.... Etiam hoc accessit ad poenam, quod cum filium haberet imperatorem, captivitatis suae tamen ac servitutis extremae non invenit ultorem, nec omnino repetitus est[1].' Forged letters are quoted to prove the contrary, and the biographies that follow Valerian's in this pitiful production swarm with praises of the persecutor. All this has no relation to reality.

Never were the historical features of an emperor so distorted as were those of Gallienus. Even in his lifetime, when despairing humanity demanded the causes of the fearful blows of fate, the short-sighted naturally sought to lay the blame on the man who held the rudder of State. Embitterment of this kind helped many an adventurer to rise against him. Then, when this *malaise* of the mind had been mastered, the resentment of the Senate against him grew ever fiercer. It was in vain that the army tried to repress the Senate's fury after his murder: 'patres...stimulabat proprii ordinis contumelia.' The fact that so few edicts from the sole reign of Gallienus are preserved in the law books of Justinian compared with the rather ample material from his joint reign with his father shows that the *patres* might tolerate the shame brought on the State by the father, but could never forgive their own humiliation by the son. A generation later, it is true, a panegyrist could still debate whether the instability of the

[1] *de mort. pers.* 5, 1; 5, 5.

Roman State under him came from 'incuria rerum' or 'quadam inclinatione fatorum[1],' but the attitude of the Latin writers was so completely determined by the views of the senatorial circles that the unjust verdict became ever more exaggerated as time went on. This state of mind is represented by the author of the lost biographical history of the emperors on which our later chronicles and compendia depend. He found in the sound tradition much that was favourable to Gallienus, and so he endeavoured to integrate and harmonize its self-contradictory verdict in a manner very natural to ancient thought. From the poems of Solon onwards we find recurring in ancient literature the ethical dogma that good fortune and prosperity bring men to destruction— 'mutant secundae res animos.' The Greeks themselves established the formal type of the tyrant, who, after good beginnings, 'secundis solutior,' is progressively corrupted: even an Alexander could not escape such reproaches from moralists. The theme was in due course inherited by the Romans, and the anonymous historian naturally followed this scheme in calumniating Gallienus. But the arbitrariness of his method is soon betrayed by the actual sequence of the events, which he forces into this artificial progression from good to evil[2].

There is a second literary motif that plays a part with our anonymous writer in his blackening of the character of Gallienus —that of the growing effeminacy of the luxurious tyrant; it passed into the *Caesares* of Julian and rises in the *Historia Augusta* to a veritable medley of ancient commonplaces: Gallienus has here become *sordidissimus feminarum omnium*[3]. There is yet a third tendency that starts with our anonymous historian: in contrast to Gallienus he eulogizes his opponents, in particular Odenathus and Postumus, who brought salvation where the profligate failed. That is why the chapter on the thirty tyrants is spun out in so romantic a style in the *Historia Augusta*.

In the Greek writers, on the contrary, we find only the favourable portrait of a humane and illustrious prince. Even if this may represent no more than the devotion of cultured Hellenists, such as Dexippus, Porphyry, Callinicus and Longinus, the popularity of Gallienus among the lower social circles of the East is still echoed in the fantastic stories told by Malalas. In the Christian literature of his own age Gallienus was greeted with high

---

[1] *Paneg.* VIII (v), 10, 1 *sqq.*; cf. *ib.* VI (VII), 2, 2 on the *soluta et perdita disciplina* of that time.

[2] For details see Alföldi, *Die Gotenbewegungen*, etc.

[3] See Alföldi, *Zeitschr. f. Num.* XXXVIII, 1928, pp. 156 *sqq.*

praises, or even with formal panegyrics. But this note grew fainter when emperors followed who had become Christians themselves and thus could easily overtrump the good will shown by Gallienus. St Ambrose, for example, already takes his full share in condemning him. The great historian of later Rome, Ammianus Marcellinus, found on the one hand the verdict: 'neque Gallieni flagitia, dum urbes erunt, occultari queant, et, quisque pessimus erit, par similisque semper ipsi habebitur'[1]; on the other, the praise of the Greeks. He took over the re-proaches[2], but also admitted, albeit with some embarrassment, the favourable judgments—in one case, indeed, where the Greek authority is still preserved[3]. Now that the research of recent years has cleared the memory of Gallienus of this coating of calumny, it can be seen that, this apart, the really weak sides of the man had been completely forgotten, even his natural failings can hardly be discerned.

The same senatorial reaction that created this dark picture tried to acquit Gallienus' successor, Claudius, of participation in his murder (p. 190) and to surround him with an atmosphere of glory and light. Even his insignificant and shortlived brother received the meed of unstinted appreciation.

Let us now see what the facts in their turn have to say. The tradition that survives from late antiquity would suggest that the emperors in these decades had the power to do good or evil, as their own natures dictated, to act of their own free will. But, in reality, the path they trod depended on a long and varied series of premisses. In all departments of life it may be observed how a secular evolution set the seal on that great crisis of the Empire, and how the new shape that things now took had had a long preparation behind it. A few examples must here suffice.

The development of art is particularly revealing for the history of civilized States. Here it is possible to trace very clearly the long lines of connection between the early and late Imperial period. For instance one can determine the road by which the chief characteristic of late Roman-medieval painting, the gold back-ground, was unobtrusively led up to through centuries[4]. The change of style in relief-sculpture has revealed how, as early as the second century, the inability to create new compositions resulted

---

[1] Aurelius Victor, *Caes.* XXXIII, 29.
[2] XXI, 16, 9; XXIII, 5, 3; XXX, 8, 8.
[3] XXI, 16, 10. Cf. Zonaras XII, 25 (p. 602).
[4] F. Bodonyi, *Arch. Értesitö,* 1932/3, pp. 197 *sqq.*

in the old scenes becoming over-crowded by the addition of new figures. This process means the disappearance of the background, and perspective loses its *raison d'être*. This 'anarchy of forms' reaches its climax in this period[1], while at the same time economic stress crushes the great sarcophagus workshops in Rome. The approaching new order of things can do no more than bring in a primitively schematic form of composition, and the exhaustion of the power of composition is followed, about A.D. 300, by the disappearance of technical virtuosity. But the art of portraiture shows, with peculiar clearness, that during the regression of the organically conceived portrait to a lifeless schematic generalizing likeness, there suddenly, about 260, appears a violent recoil to the classical. Since this reaction is found not only in Italy but simultaneously in the realm of Postumus, it is clear that it is widely based, and that, though the rulers might favour it and guide it to maturity, they did not initiate it[2].

Much light is thrown on these progressive changes of orientation by the unbroken sequence of the history of the monetary devaluation. This shows clearly that about 260 the manipulation of the silver content of the double denarius that had been going on for two centuries, accelerated and led to its complete destruction. Here again it is instructive to draw the parallels between the course of this process in the regions governed by Postumus and by Gallienus, as it demonstrates an essential similarity that did not depend on those two personalities. The career of this debased money is precisely similar in both areas; at about the same time it sank, on one side and the other, to be a mere copper piece, coated with silver. The only difference is that the inflation in Gaul brought with it a great outburst of private coinage (of a rude and barbarous character), intended to exploit for itself, instead of for the State, the difference between nominal and metal value. In the lands governed by Gallienus this mischief was successfully averted, except in Rome, where from 268 to 270 similar abuses flourished though on a more modest scale. On the other hand, Postumus continued to turn out his aurei at the normal weight, whereas the procurator of the mint of Rome let the weight of the gold coins fall so low, that in many issues they were disks as thin as paper. In other mints, on the contrary, order reigned in this field even under Gallienus. But the corruption now established was

<hr />

[1] H. U. von Schoenebeck, *Röm. Mitt.* LI, 1936, p. 256.
[2] Alföldi, *Fünfundzwanzig Jahre Röm.-Germ. Komm.* pp. 35 *sqq.*; G. Rodenwaldt, *Arch. Anz.* 1931, cols. 318 *sqq.* and *J.D.A.I.* LI, 1936, pp. 82 *sqq.*

terrible: despite the iron hand of Aurelian each issue of small change can be seen, for a century and a half, to be diminished in size in a few months, and there is no pause in the reforms that simply establish, under old or new titles and denominations, some normal weight for these coins.

It is possible, again, by following the changes in the representation of the monarch, to discern the earlier foundations on which the autocratic constitution was based. Step by step we can trace the process by which the old emphasis on organic function gives way to the new stress on outward form. Here again it becomes evident that the transition was actually made in this epoch of crisis, and that Diocletian and Constantine only gave clear definition to what was already accomplished. The displacement of the civil *princeps* by the military *dominus* is unmasked and seen as the production of a very long process of evolution.

The centrifugal tendencies that found expression in the rise of usurpers and undoubtedly slowly prepared the way for the later separation of East and West, had likewise a course of development proper to them. Not only does the need of a second ruler grow more acute and his competence come more and more to be associated with a division of territory[1]. Under Philip and Aurelian appear administrators of the East as *rector Orientis*, *praefectus Orientis*; Valerian had already his own Praetorian Prefect in the East and, as early as 258, the armies of East and West were separated—if only for a time. The new capitals of the Tetrarchy (Nicomedia and Antioch, on the one hand, Milan, Trèves and Sirmium, on the other) justified themselves in practice as early as our period. In contrast to all this, the process of the complete unification of religion[2], of politics, administration, political economy, etc. is at least as old: it begins to mature about the middle of the third century.

Military developments tell the same story, and it has been made clear that the invasions of the Germans were only a secondary result of this weakening. Like a human body that is ageing, the mighty organism of the Empire sank into a feverish condition, marked by that acceleration of the course of events that has been observed, and followed by heavy blows from every side. The movements of the army, famine and devastation brought on that fearful plague that raged from Gallus to the death of Claudius and contributed largely, with the wars, towards the destruction of such

[1] See E. Kornemann, *Doppelprinzipat und Reichseinteilung*.
[2] See the works of F. Cumont; cf. also W. Weber, *Die Vereinheitlichung der religiösen Welt* (*Probleme der Spätantike*, 1930).

romanized elements as might have had in them the power to survive[1].

There was often no scope for any really free initiative on the part of the rulers. To take, for example, the laws of the period, one finds nothing but regulations to alleviate the time's distress or the enforcement of compulsory rules, no independent legislation. The administration likewise was turned from its normal functioning by wars, requisitioning, or persecutions of the Christians. New milestones often reflect no lively activity in road-making, but simply advertise loyalty in the face of the constant pronunciamentos[2]. But it is no accident that Gallienus after 260 found himself obliged wholly to abandon road-making. Money and labour alike were monopolized by the wars.

But, despite limits set by the trend of things, the life and prosperity of millions still depended on whether the Emperor won or lost his battles, whether he adopted the necessary measures or not at a crisis: the part played by the individual must not be underestimated. The activity of the ruler was, indeed, at this time confined to the few main problems of existence[3]. Apart from Gallienus the emperors were no more than military adventurers, the rebels of yesterday. Yet, finding themselves faced by tasks that transcended normal human capacity, they lived at the highest tension and speed only to die, for the most part, by the sword.

In judging the achievements of the emperors, must be considered only those chief actors who had a real historical rôle and mission.

Decius was a native of Southern Pannonia. But he is not to be confused with his successors, who sprang from that province and were simple soldiers. His family had certainly owned great possessions; his wife came of a distinguished Italian family. Not only did he pass through the normal senatorial career, but he rose to its highest dignities, he was consul and City Prefect. His administration was not successful: rivals rose against him in Gaul, Rome and the East. As a general he was a failure—a failure that made possible and provoked the terrible invasions by the Germans.

[1] Zosimus 1, 26, 2; 37, 3; Zonaras XII, 21 (p. 590); Aurelius Victor, Caes. XXX, 2; XXXIII, 5; S.H.A. Gall. duo 5, 5; Eusebius, Hist. Eccl. VII, 21, 1 sqq.; Johann. Ant. frag. 151 (F.H.G. IV, p. 598); Cramer, Anecd. II, p. 289; Cedrenus I, p. 452, 14 sqq. (Bonn); Jerome, Chron. p. 219, 4 sqq. Helm; Orosius VII, 21, 5; 22, 2–3; 27, 10; Jordanes, Getica, XIX, 104, M.; Vita Cypr. 9; Cyprian, de mort. 14, 16; ad Demetr. 5, 10; K. Pink, Num. Zeitschr. 1936, p. 25. H. Oppermann, Plotins Leben, p. 51 sq.
[2] H. Nesselhauf, Germania XXI, 1937, p. 175.
[3] See the anecdote in Zonaras XII, 27 (p. 606).

His attacks on the Church were not such as to break its power, but only to shed blood and create mischief. And yet his whole activity shows his iron hardness, still seen in his portraits[1]. In his campaign against the Christians, in his persistence after his failures against Kniva, in his heroic death, the same abundant energy is revealed. It was not without good reason that he was named 'reparator disciplinae militaris.' His extraordinary force of will, his sincere loyalty to the Senate and his death on the field of honour have transfigured his person and ensured the vigorous survival of his conception of Roman conservatism and of his political methods. His reliance on the Illyrians, as representatives of a constructive patriotism, was justified by the future.

Trebonianus Gallus came of an old Etruscan family of Perusia and, as governor of Lower Moesia, was assisted by accident to the throne. His slackness must have been in part responsible for the ill-success of the campaigns of Decius after whose death he seems (to judge by what Dexippus tells us) to have taken no serious steps to check the German invasions. His listless reign contributed largely to mature the ill results of the disaster of Abrittus. Nor did the revolt of Aemilianus have any other result.

It was a further misfortune for the Empire that Valerian was now able to seize the throne. He had already (in 253) had a brilliant career; in 238 he had been a notable defender of the Senate and, later, as confidant of Decius, had taken a share in administration at Rome during his absence. His rule was generally acclaimed with high hopes. At the beginning he did indeed strive to restore order and it seems that he really was a good administrator; the whole management of the persecution of the Christians suggests the skilful politician. It is probable enough that history would have had much good to say of him, had his feeble hands held the reins of power in a time blessed with peace. But the ageing Emperor was quite unequal to those military tasks that faced him. For eight years in the East he had no triumphs to chronicle save over the Christians,—against Germans and Persians he was too irresolute and weak; in the end, his own hesitancy and impotence betrayed him into the hands of Shapur.

His antithesis—and the contrast grew more and more pronounced—is to be seen in his son Gallienus. At the age of about 35 Gallienus was raised by the Senate to the rank of Augustus at his father's request. But his greatness was first seen when he succeeded in mastering the chaos that followed on his father's captivity. Nor did he stop there: with sure hand he gripped the

[1] See Volume of Plates v, 186, *d*.

mechanism of State and society, to carry through those essential reforms that secured their continuance. Though himself of high birth he had the courage to make a clearance of the *desidia* of the senators. It was no accident that the Pannonians, who till 261 had been obstinately disloyal to him, thenceforward served him faithfully to the grave and after; he opened up to them the road to the highest positions. Even earlier than this began his far-reaching re-organization of the army, in which like a pioneer he showed the way for the future. With unerring insight he chose out and promoted the great generals of the next age. At the same time he deliberately furthered the reaction that was setting in to defend the ancient culture. As for the Christians, his intention was to fight them with the weapons of enlightenment; in Rome, Athens and Syria philosophers and men of letters are encouraged by him to work to this end. Art turns back, if only for a moment, from its modern primitivism to the classical tradition of the Antonine period.

He had certainly enjoyed a good education. His amazing energy and readiness, which was acclaimed as 'alacritas Augusti,' carried him again and again over a succession of terrible blows and alarms to a swift and right decision. It was the same elasticity and energy that made him leap up and rush out, when his murderers lured him out ôn the pretext that the enemy were at hand. His achievements as general were above the ordinary. For seven years he beat back the attacks of the Germans of the Rhine; he repelled the hordes of Alemanni from Italy and checked the Heruli and Goths in 268. He overcame his own talented but disloyal generals, such as Postumus and Aureolus, and also Ingenuus and Regalianus.

In chivalrous fashion he challenged Postumus to a duel, so that, instead of thousands, only one of the two should fall. 'I am no gladiator' is the answer of Postumus. But Gallienus could not be as merciless as his successors, the soldiers, who ruled 'manu ad ferrum' (p. 297). He called a halt to the massacre of the Christians. Ever benevolent and ready to help, he never repulsed a petitioner; he even forgave those who little deserved it[1]. Yet this leniency had its evil consequences; such as the abuses of the *monetarii* in Rome. His dearly loved wife, Salonina, the patroness of Plotinus, accompanied him wherever he went. Even up to the death of her husband she was with him in his camp.

Augustus was his model. But, just as the artistic reaction of his

[1] Zonaras XII, 25 (p. 602); Petrus Patricius frag. 163 (Cassius Dio, ed. Boissevain, III, p. 743).

age failed to achieve the imitation of Augustan art and could get no farther back than the baroque of the Antonines, so did the spirit of the Rome of Augustus at which he aimed end in the Hellenic patriotism of those Greek men of letters who based themselves on ideas current in the second century. Amidst bloodshed and dissolution he sighed for the glories of the older days: Athens was his Mecca. His contemporaries did not understand him. His kindred and friends were butchered when he fell. Even before his death misfortune had ever attended him. But through a crisis of supreme terror he ensured the continuity of the development of the Empire. He is no type, like the rest, no mere representative of a kind, but an individual. Between Hadrian and Julian he stands as a pillar of Greek culture, which thanks to him still exerts its influence on us. Like Caesar and Augustus, like Trajan and Hadrian, like Diocletian and Constantine, Decius and he form a pair of opposites, who together point the way to the future. As Diocletian returned to the principles of Decius, so did Constantine realize the ideas of Gallienus, even if unconsciously drawing the same consequences from a more advanced stage of the historical development.

Claudius, whose heroic qualities were highly esteemed by Gallienus and whose career was advanced under him up to the supreme command of the *equites*, already belongs with his successors to those great soldiers of Illyricum, who with unprecedented energy won back the peace and unity of the Empire. His supreme achievement was the final repulse of the Gothic onslaught in 268, after chequered fighting. This simple, but intelligent and experienced, man had no time in his short period of rule to display any ideas of his own. His co-operation with the Senate alone indicates to us a general direction in his policy.

CHAPTER VII

THE ECONOMIC LIFE OF THE EMPIRE

I. GOVERNING TENDENCIES

The first century of our era witnessed a definitely high level of economic prosperity, made possible by exceptionally favourable conditions (see vol. x, chap. xiii). Within the framework of the Empire, embracing vast territories in which peace was established and communications were secure, it was possible for a bourgeoisie to come into being whose chief interests were economic, which maintained a form of economy resting on the old city culture and characterized by individualism and private enterprise, and which reaped all the benefits inherent in such a system. The State deliberately encouraged this activity of the bourgeoisie, both indirectly through government protection and its liberal economic policy, which guaranteed freedom of action and an organic growth on the lines of 'laissez faire, laissez aller,' and directly through measures encouraging economic activity. In fact, the State did all in its power to facilitate an increase in the numbers of the bourgeois population and of the cities throughout the Empire. In consequence, the productive economic centres became more numerous, and under conditions of free competition economic activity itself advanced, and achieved, on occasion, forms of large-scale production which approximated to monopoly. The large number of separate economic centres within a world-wide Empire in which busy highways bound the whole together resulted in a marked interdependence between the various parts of the Empire, and also between the Empire and foreign countries. Regions of primary production (raw materials) on one side, and regions where the processing of raw materials was systematically organized on the other, with different kinds of economic specialization at different centres, led to a lively reciprocal interchange and interpenetration, which, in their turn, caused a high degree of prosperity especially in the cities. There was thus a vigorous, if limited, economic development—limited both by an ultimately agrarian character and by a capitalism whose nature was non-progressive. These limits had been fixed by the decentralization that began as early as the first century of our era, by the difficulties inherent in the problem of labour resources, by the permanently unstable character of non-agrarian economy owing to the inadequate development of large-scale credit institutions, and also by the outflow into foreign lands of precious metals in large quantities, and, to some extent, by the first beginnings of State-socialism, which slowly gain a footing during the first century.

The economy of the second and third centuries is the continuous organic development of the features observed in the first, including both the actively progressive and the retarding elements.

There was further advance especially in the liberal economic system, based on private enterprise, and rooted in city-bourgeois culture. This development is connected with the fact that external conditions remained constant. Indeed, the field open to economic enterprise actually grew larger towards the close of the first century and during the second. New territories in Britain, on the eastern bank of the Rhine, on the lower Danube and beyond that river (Dacia), in Asia Minor (in the direction of Commagene and Armenia) were annexed. The line of the Euphrates was reached and crossed, Transjordania and Arabia Petraea were incorporated in the Empire, and the frontier in north-west Africa was advanced southwards. Moreover, in other regions, where direct occupation was not attempted, the Empire was suzerain, as in the Bosporus (Crimea), and in Palmyra, where Roman troops were stationed in the second century to guard the interests of Rome. For a time this extended empire was still mostly at peace, and its communications secure. The numerous colonial wars of the period, one of whose effects was in fact to extend the sphere of economic activity, caused no particular disturbance, nor did the minor and occasional political complications. The elaborate system of communications was enlarged as new territory was occupied, old and new roads were maintained, improved, and extended, as the numerous milestones show. Garrisons protected the key-points on the lines of communication, police-troops guarded travellers by land, river, and sea. 'Iter conditum per feras gentes, quo facile ab usque Pontico mari in Galliam permeatur' are the words used of Trajan's achievement in the field of foreign policy[1], and it was Trajan, in all probability, who created the Red Sea Fleet. Nomad tribes on the borders of Africa and Transjordania were induced to settle down and so become peaceable. Thus the imperial coinage, and writers such as Dio Chrysostom or Aelius Aristides could repeatedly celebrate the world peace, and its effects on economic life and well-being, and

---

[1] Aurelius Victor, *Caes.* XIII, 3.

Aristides is not far from the truth when (in his encomium of Rome, delivered in 156) he declares that 'every Greek and barbarian can easily travel to whatever destination he chooses, and that neither the Cilician Gates nor the tracks of the desert need make him afraid[1].'

Moreover, the long peace continued not only beyond the frontiers but also within the Empire and thus maintained, especially under the 'constitutional monarchy,' the social and economic position of the bourgeoisie. For economic policy remained liberal. If we pass over the normal State-socialist element and the normal intervention of the State for purposes of control (see p. 255 *sq.*), such as are to be found under the most liberal régimes, and if we disregard the special position of the emperor, who as the private owner of domains and of large-scale concerns manufacturing bricks and textiles, occupied an intermediate position, the old basic principle that the chief economic unit was not the State but the individual remained for the time being true, and was applied *mutatis mutandis* even in Egypt. Free trade prevailed in actual fact, as what custom dues there were did not hamper commerce. The State indirectly protected, and directly encouraged, economic progress.

The reasons for the expansion of the Empire were not wholly military, but partly economic. Just as the possibilities of exploitation had been among the motives behind the Nubian and Arabian expeditions of Augustus and the occupation of Noricum, so now British lead and tin, Dacian gold, and the rich land in Africa, in the Decumates agri, and in the Wetterau, drew the Romans on. Commercial interests had their say in the incorporation of Transjordania and Arabia Petraea, in the conversion of Doura into a fortress (by L. Verus), and even in the rivalry with Parthia. The Roman garrisons which were posted to protect Olbia, Chersonesus, and Palmyra were designed largely to further a commercial policy. The construction of several roads or canals in Egypt, in the approaches to the Caspian, in Bithynia, in Africa, and in Britain were inspired by the same motive. In this connection Trajan's canal linking the Nile and the Red Sea is very important; and the improvement in harbour facilities (another reform with which Trajan is specially connected), and the creation of a fleet on the Red Sea have also a background of economic policy. The circumnavigation of the Black Sea by Arrian acting under Hadrian's orders continues the earlier series of similar

---

[1] XXVI K, 100. Cf. Irenaeus, *adv. Haer.* IV, 46, 3; Ps.-Aristides XXXV K, 37 (A.D. 247, see above, p. 88 *sq.*).

exploratory voyages. When the Chinese general Pan Ch'ao, as Chinese annals tell us, dispatched agents in A.D. 97 on a mission of exploration from Turkestan to Ta-ts'in[1] (though this venture met with no success), and when, conversely, Marcus Aurelius sent a mission, starting in all probability from Ctesiphon, to China which arrived there in 166[2], it was once again commercial policy which inspired these efforts.

With the government adopting this attitude, the bourgeois population could, and necessarily would, grow in numbers in the regions already available. And in districts freshly opened to exploitation a new bourgeoisie came into being consisting of immigrant foreigners or of members of the indigenous population who acquired Mediterranean culture. Urbanization advanced in Gaul, Germany, Britain, the Danubian regions, including Dacia and Thrace, and also in Spain and Africa. Even Egypt received a city in due form (Antinoopolis); and the bourgeois of the Egyptian *metropoleis*, among whom we must reckon the landowning veterans, only became important in the second century, when, after the re-partition of the great *ousiai* of the magnates in the second half of the first century (vol. x, p. 293), still more of them found a livelihood as farmers and landowners. Vespasian, Trajan, and Hadrian, influenced in part by the recruiting problem, namely the difficulty of securing adequate enlistment in Italy, strongly encouraged this development. It is at least clear that the power of assimilation possessed by the Graeco-Roman city-culture was not weakened until the time of Hadrian, and in some cases not even after him, though the bourgeois population never formed the majority, which was always and unquestionably composed of workers on the land. Thus while the increase in the number of cities meant a further rise in consumption and in the demands resulting from city-culture, the increase in the numbers of the bourgeois population meant an extension of economic activity and of an order that was capitalistic in method. Again, primitive forms of economy which were based on hunting, pasturage and unorganized corn-growing, gave place to systematic agriculture and horticulture and the production of wine and oil. The vine was cultivated more and more on the Moselle and in the Wetterau, the olive in

---

[1] See above, p. 104, and the translation in F. Hirth, *China and the Roman Orient*, pp. 39 and 42, cf. pp. 214 *sqq.* and 175 *sq.* Which part of the Roman world is Ta-ts'in is in dispute. Perhaps Syria. For the identification with South Arabia see A. Herrmann, *Die Verkehrswege zwischen China, Indien, und Rom um 100 n. Chr.* p. 8.

[2] See Honigmann in P.W., *s.v.* Ctesiphon, Suppl. iv, col. 1111.

Africa, and both in Transjordania, also, in old-established agricultural regions such as Egypt. Barren districts were brought under cultivation by the institution of *emphyteusis*. Also the army played its part by the development of the territories it garrisoned, and through the settlements of veterans on the land.

decentralize

The tendency to decentralization already noted naturally would be of effect no less in regions which had begun, or continued, to be developed, than elsewhere. The negative side of this tendency has already been stressed. There was, however, a corresponding positive side, and this is what concerns us now. For decentralization meant not only that the centre declined in significance, but also that the peripheral regions became more self-dependent, and economic activity increased. Indeed, the result was, in the last resort, that regions which had relied substantially on primary production and had imported manufactured articles processed by a skilled technique, now themselves worked up and finished the raw materials, thus developing special capabilities of their own, until in the end they imported raw materials from abroad to be processed at home. No doubt the characteristic ambition of colonial regions to emulate the achievement of the colonizing centre was a contributory factor. This ambition had an excellent chance of being realized—since the military and political importance of these border countries meant that they offered the best economic prospects, if only because of the increased demand, for which the armies were largely responsible. Yet another consideration—even more valid then than to-day— was the transport difficulty, as has been emphasized in an earlier volume (x, p. 422). For although the technical improvements in travel and communication were relatively great, yet, judged by absolute or rather by modern standards, transport remained primitive, and travel by sea was dangerous even between Italy and Gaul[1]. Aelius Aristides for instance, who loudly praises the general security of communication, gives a glimpse of the truth in the preamble to his encomium of Rome[2], when he says that a sea voyage involves such great risks that it is wise to guard against them by vows to the gods, and he himself composed a hymn to Sarapis after rescue from peril at sea[3]. Journeys by land are also not wholly safe, and before them, too, men offer their vows to the gods. And transport overland at its best is slow and relatively dear. Thus costs and risks combined to bring about the trans-

---

[1] Suetonius, *Claud.* 17, 2.   [2] XXVI K, I.

[3] XLV K (εἰς Σάραπιν); cf. *c.* 33 *sq.* It should be remembered, however, that Aristides was a constitutionally nervous man.

ference of production to the region of consumption—a phenomenon not peculiar to the ancient world. Branches are established,
and there is a migration of industrialists and industries, of agriculturalists and agricultural enterprise. The important part played
by internal trade, and by the progressive secondary decentralization (see below, p. 241), is proof of all this. Problems connected with adequate labour resources are another factor in the
situation (see below). To sum up: the tendency to decentralization,
together with the increased demand in the frontier territories,
determines, positively no less than negatively, the development
of economic life, including production and exchange.

II. PRODUCTION

We consider production first, but begin with an illustration of
its negative side, since Italy was affected by this. An inevitable
result of decentralization was that Italy, originally the chief productive centre, whose period of greatest prosperity in the early
years of the Empire has been described[1], suffered a recession,
though Northern Italy was not affected like the rest. So many
causes contributed to this process that it is not easy to determine
which was the most decisive. The growing independence of the
provinces, and their emancipation from the domination of a single
economic centre are doubtless an important factor, especially in
the West; but it can hardly have been crucial, since, as we shall
see, Gaul (together with Germany) and Northern Italy in some
sense took the place formerly occupied by peninsular Italy. There
must then have been other contributory forces at work. The
problem of recruiting labour should be mentioned here. It has been
suggested elsewhere that Italy was dependent on slaves to a very
large extent for her resources of labour. The imperial peace,
however, was unfavourable to the import of slaves in large
numbers, and they became dearer. Hence, Italian production for
export was handicapped by comparison with many provinces,
such as the Three Gauls, Germany, Asia Minor, and Egypt,
where the problem was simpler, since the lowest class of the indigenous population provided an abundant reservoir of labour.
Northern Italy and Istria also enjoyed more favourable conditions
on the whole than the rest of Italy. A further important factor is
the depopulation of Italy, which manifested itself in the shortage
of recruits, and in the well-known remedial legislation of Nerva,

---

[1] See vol. x, pp. 392 *sqq.*

Trajan, and other emperors. It is not only a sign of degeneration in a culture that had outlived its vitality, but is also connected with the outflow of the population from Italy into the provinces. Better prospects were to be found there, so that farmers and contractors emigrated, and soldiers at the end of their military service preferred not to return home.

Thus the old flourishing export of industrial and agricultural products slowly declined. Italy began to lose her dominating economic position, just as she gradually lost her political pre-eminence. She became part of the Empire, no whit superior to the other parts, some of which (Gaul for example, see p. 242) out-stripped her economically. It is true that Italian woollens, Italy's excellent wine and oil long continued to be bought and exported, while in the second century Capuan metal vessels still maintained their position in the markets of the West. But Italian industry no longer kept its lead. The great manufactories gave way to small concerns of the artisan type working for the home market, and even these were hard hit by imports from Gaul. The manufacture of glass, pottery, and metal vessels for large-scale export gradually ceased, and local production took its place. The 'world monopoly' of Fortis lamps was broken in the second century.

There was a corresponding decline in Italian agriculture, formerly organized systematically for export. Thus during a widespread temporary crisis in production, connected with an excessive cultivation of the vine and a deficient cultivation of corn, it was not necessary in Italy, as it was in the provinces, for Domitian to impose special restrictions on vine-growing[1]. For although under the Antonines viticulture was specifically encouraged along with corn-growing[2] and undoubtedly paid, yet the rural economy of Italy progressively deteriorated into a more extensively organized production of corn, which was now mostly supplied by *latifundia* with *coloni* (i.e. by a technique of production which included small holdings), and which still sufficed to cover demand under such conditions as had prevailed hitherto[3]. The causes of this process are not easy to explain, but it was

[1] Suetonius, *Dom.* 7, 2. Whereas in the provinces existing vineyards were to be reduced by at least a half, in Italy only new vineyards were prohibited.

[2] Fronto, *ad M. Caes.* ii, 5 (p. 29 N.).

[3] The production of corn may have declined as well as of wine and oil. The great estates may to some extent have reached the previous quota of grain, but not more, for Italy continued to need a supplement from abroad. But the amount produced had fallen, since not so much was needed. The old quota of wine and oil was not even reached. For the internal supply of corn see Dessau 3696 (A.D. 136).

doubtless due in large measure to the drop in population and to the transference to the provinces of that activity, capitalistic in its methods, which was specifically bourgeois. Big capitalists must have hastened to fill the gaps, high officials who were anxious to invest in land the profits saved or perhaps extorted during their careers, and who were persuaded by the artificial means of imperial decrees to spend their wealth in Italy[1]. Thus conditions came into being which resembled those of the second century B.C. Free and unfree, agricultural and non-agricultural labourers, and also small peasant farmers, who had before been ruined by the new big agricultural capitalists (so that here the factors at work have a reciprocal action)—such were the men who may have furnished material whence the *coloni*-tenants were drawn. The development was unhealthy, as was that of the second century B.C.; the emperors from Claudius to Marcus Aurelius fought it, but the forces at work were stronger than the power of the emperors, and it was the destiny of Rome, as of so many other victors in history, to be ultimately destroyed by the results of her own victory.

The positive side of decentralization is almost more important than the negative. The north-eastern region of Upper Italy, and the more recently civilized areas profited most. Upper Italy (including Istria) differs from the rest of the peninsula[2] because of its proximity to the Danubian lands. There the demand for the amenities of civilization was so great, that despite the beginnings of emancipation and self-sufficiency (pp. 240 *sqq.*), and despite Gallo-German competition, which was very fierce from the second century onwards, there was still an opening for North Italian export. So the production of wine and oil (the latter especially in Istria) flourished here, being carried on in large-scale agricultural productive units, like the *villa* of Brioni Grande. There was also a vigorous industry producing articles for large-scale export, comprising pottery and bricks, textiles (mass-produced in the time of Pertinax)[3], and the traditional metal, amber, and glass wares, for which Aquileia remained the unchallenged centre throughout her history.

Among the more recently civilized regions Gaul marched in

---

[1] Pliny, *Ep.* VI, 19, 4; S.H.A. *Marcus*, 11, 8.

[2] This is only generally true: an exact geographical delimitation is not possible. Cf. what is said of the Fortis lamps (of Mutina) above, p. 238, and the wool-weaving business of Pertinax (in Liguria); see below, n. 3.

[3] S.H.A. *Pert.* 3, 3 *sqq.* The Emperor's father had a private *taberna coactiliaria* in a *villa* in Liguria, which was greatly enlarged by Pertinax.

the van, because in that country the cultural advance had long since been relatively great; and this activity presently extended to Roman Germany and Raetia. Other regions, such as the Danubian provinces (including Dalmatia and Thrace), Britain, Africa, and Transjordania, developed along similar lines, though now, as formerly, progress was conditioned by geographical and political factors, so that marked differences appear in the speed, degree, and individual peculiarities of the growth and spread of economic development. Thus Britain begins her economic development in the second century, and reaches peak production in the third and fourth centuries. Dalmatia and Noricum advance more rapidly than Pannonia and the provinces on the Lower Danube. Dacia's development had to start from the beginning. The newest colonial territories (Britain, the more recently acquired regions on the Danube, the new districts in Africa, and Transjordania) at first still continued in the old economy of their barbarian past, concerning themselves with primitive primary production of articles which they exchanged for wine, oil, and agricultural products of more civilized areas, and this primary production was, as it seems, so increased as to yield a yet greater surplus[1]. Then, however, forces came into play which, as we have seen, were conducive to methodical exploitation of the existing local possibilities and to self-sufficiency. Agriculture was intensified, and sufficed to meet the needs of the influx of immigrants from abroad. The productive unit of the *villa rustica* became more general; viticulture and olive-growing spread. Germany west of the Rhine became increasingly independent of the wines of southern Gaul and of Italy. From Hadrian's time especially oil production advanced in the south-west of Africa[2]. Wine and oil were also produced in Dalmatia and in Transjordania, and sufficient wine for local needs in Africa. The mines in Britain and Dacia were worked more actively. In the industrial field (in pottery, glass, metal, and textile wares for everyday use) Gaul reached an unexpectedly high level of production, and from the reigns of Vespasian and Trajan Germany west of the Rhine gradually followed suit. A similar progress occurred in the Danubian regions, especially in Noricum, and, later, in Pannonia. Africa supplied her own needs. So did other lands, though to a lesser degree. Britain made within her own borders the pottery and metal wares in daily use. Special capacities, such as the Celto-

---

[1] For a brisk private traffic with Britain in the middle of the second century see Aelius Aristides, XXXVI K, 91.

[2] See the inscriptions (Bruns, *Fontes*[7], 115, III, 6 *sqq.*, 116, III, 9 *sqq.*) and archaeological evidence dating from the second to the fourth century.

Germanic gift of artistic creativeness, the joy in craftsmanship which finds vivid expression in the Gallo-German monuments, and the business ability which is manifest and striking, entered into happy partnership with the economic methods introduced by the lands possessing a long tradition of civilization.

The ramifications of the general decentralization, and the secondary decentralization which ensues, can be clearly seen in the special history of Gallo-German manufacture of *terra sigillata* in the period from the first to the second century. The chief centres of manufacture split off and move from the South of France to the Allier basin (Lezoux), eastern Gaul, Raetia, and Alsace, and finally to Rheinzabern. Similarly in the African lamp industry Italian wares gave place to Carthaginian, which themselves lost the market to lamps of purely local manufacture.

The tendency here described was due primarily to the supplying of local needs and production for a neighbouring market, yet the economic development of the newly civilized territories did not stop short at this stage, but they frequently advanced, as North Italy had done, to production for distant consumers. In this connection it was of minor importance that articles of primary production, such as African corn (now cultivated in larger quantities) of which Italy stood in need[1], or British lead and tin, increasingly competing in the second century with the Spanish lead and tin, or Dacian gold, found a distant market, since these were vital commodities with a certain rarity value or in mass-demand, and markets always have a welcome for objects of this kind. Nor should we stress the supply of oil from southern Gaul to the German provinces and to Britain, or of Gallo-German wine to Britain[2], since here the climate made import inevitable. The rapid emergence of a trade in finished articles to neighbouring technically underdeveloped and culturally backward regions is of secondary importance too; thanks to imperial expansion these regions had come within the sphere of influence of the newly civilized territories, so that Gallo-German products were sent to Britain and free Germany, or Norican wares to Pannonia and the lands beyond the Danube, or, later, Pannonian wares to Dacia.

Such a development was bound to happen, and under similar circumstances would always recur, and the influence of transport conditions on such exchanges is very slight. It is, on the other hand, of primary importance that some of the recently developed

[1] For the African corn-fleet see S.H.A. *Comm.* 17, 7.
[2] Notwithstanding S.H.A. *Prob.* 18, 8.

economic areas succeeded, despite decentralization and difficulties of transport, in winning the imperial, and, in a certain
sense, even the world market. Such was the case with Gaul and
Germany. Gallic wine, for example, was exported from Arelate
and Narbo to the East, and Gallic pottery, until the middle of
the third century, when the great crisis came, possessed a kind
of world monopoly such as had previously been enjoyed only by
the most highly developed countries with a long tradition of
civilization. Pottery from Gaul is found during this period in
Italy, Spain, Africa, and even in Egypt and Syria. *Terra sigillata*
from Rheinzabern is found on the lower Danube and in Britain[1];
Gallic fibulae in the Danubian regions, in free Germany (where
they are copied) and in eastern Europe. Cologne glass practically
dominates the Western market. Belgian cloaks were still in
demand during the third century, and served as models for the
woollen weavers of Phrygian Laodicea under Diocletian[2]. Most
of the industries in these new regions did not attain world-wide
significance, and hence did not develop forms of mass-production.
The high level of output achieved by the Gallo-German industries,
a level approximately equal to that reached in Italy in earlier
times, was due to exceptionally favourable predisposing conditions. These were the fact that in culture these districts had
the start over the other frontier provinces, further, the presence
of raw materials locally in large quantities, good conditions of
labour, fine achievement in the field of skilled craftsmanship and
marked business ability, and good internal transport along rivers
or canals, which facilitated the building up of an extensive local
trade, and so made it possible that large-scale production for local
demand should be developed into mass-production for distant
markets. Finally, we must not underestimate the influence of the
Rhine army with its great demand resulting in a corresponding
supply, so that when, in the second century, the military
centre of gravity swung over from Rhine to Danube, it set free
considerable surplus production.

    In the older provinces of the Empire there was no development
which advances so far beyond the previous level. Yet in these
provinces, too, the general conditions (lasting peace, spread of
civilization, urbanization, formation of bourgeoisie and *possessores*,
and cessation of the Italian ascendancy) acted as a steady stimulus,
so that for the time being at least the standard achieved in the first

[1] See vol. XI, p. 539.
[2] S.H.A. *Gall. duo*, 6, 6; *Car.* 20, 6; *Ed. Diocl. de pretiis*, XIX, 27.

century was still maintained. Thus Spain presents much the same picture as in the first century. The sherds from the 'Monte Testaccio' in Rome, which suggest that Spain produced a surplus of oil, wine, and fish, mostly date from the second and early third centuries. There was also a large export of corn, and after the Neronian confiscations it was also grown on the great estates of the imperial *Patrimonium*. Mining, the organization of which is well known from the lex metalli Vipascensis[1], dating from the time of Hadrian (the beginnings perhaps go back to the Flavians), is probably already declining somewhat by the second century, owing to partial exhaustion of the veins of silver; and tin production also appears to have receded. But these were hardly crucial changes, and on the whole the old industry maintained its former position.

In Sicily, Sardinia, and Corsica, Macedonia, Greece, Crete, and Cyrenaica, things remained essentially unaltered.

The East gained rather than lost, especially Eastern industry. For although the market was somewhat contracted through the tendency to independence and the competition of the West[2], this was amply compensated by the cessation of Italian predominance and by the possibilities of export to the East, where the frontiers had been advanced, and to the lands beyond the frontiers in the South-east, where trade was protected. Indeed the East as a whole gained in importance from Trajan's time and from the organization of peace under Trajan and Hadrian. The traditional production of Asia Minor and Syria flourished, and was further stimulated by the proximity of the armies. Even Egyptian industry on occasion—as in A.D. 138—was drawn upon for military supplies in the form of textiles for the Cappadocian army[3]. The agricultural produce of Asia Minor (corn and wine) continued to be exported and the fisheries, the quarries, in fact industry in general, especially the manufacture for export of its famous woollen goods with its subsidiary of purple dye works, maintained production. In Syria also the old-established centres flourished. The strong impulses which affected trade here (p. 246) naturally benefited also the old-established Syrian industries (linen, silk, glass, and dyed woollens). Similarly, Egypt maintained its level of activity in agriculture and industry: indeed, the fact that the bourgeoisie did not achieve its full development until the second century must have especially accelerated economic development

[1] Bruns, *Fontes*[7], 112; E. Schönbauer, 'Beitr. zur Geschichte des Bergbaurechtes,' *Münch. Beitr. z. Pap.-Forsch.* XII, 1929, pp. 33 *sqq.*
[2] Cf. the supersession in the Rhineland of Alexandrine glass by that of Cologne (vol. XI, p. 539).　　　[3] *B.G.U.* 1564.

at that time. Agricultural export from Egypt remained on the whole unimpaired in the second century, and the better manufactured articles of Alexandrine industry flooded the Empire in the old way with textiles, leather goods, papyrus, glass, artistic metal wares, spices, and perfumes. Alexandria still remained the industrial city par excellence.

In the North-Eastern area, South Russia, if this may be reckoned as part of the Empire, flourished by virtue of its corn-export to the Roman army until just before Trajan's reign, and, to some extent, later, when the Cappadocian army at any rate was supplied.

The conclusion is that production on the whole had increased and that productive centres had multiplied. New agricultural and industrial magnates[1], and new producers of raw materials, amongst whom must be counted the *conductores* of the imperial mines, sprang up like mushrooms. New or extended large territorial units for primary production or processing raw materials emerged, partly in competition with one another, and at the same time there was an abundance of specialities of both kinds connected with particular localities, all of which invited trading interchange. For decentralization had as its goal the cheap and profitable supply of local demand, but emphatically did not aim at self-sufficiency, still less at a closed system. Similarly the capitalistic producer aimed at the maximum possible profit, implying the maximum possible turnover and interchange.

III. INTERCHANGE AND COMMERCE

Admittedly, interchange, like production, was characterized by decentralization. The negative effect was here discernible in two ways. First, some of the old trading countries played a more passive part. Secondly, the commercial interdependence of the Empire became less close owing to the marked advance in the internal trade of the provinces. Italy again (except in the north) is the country most subject to the greater passivity and contraction[2] which affect both commercial enterprise and the balance of trade. In both spheres the situation became increasingly unfavourable, so that Italy came more and more closely to resemble one of the purely military regions (excluding, of course, their hinterlands). Trading activity, however, in and for Italy, just as

---

[1] Often the same persons are both: those concerned with industry (as with commerce) are found as owners of the *villae rusticae, e.g.* at Trèves.

[2] The old-established trading communities of the East also suffer in some degree through the rise of a strong competition from the traders of the West.

in the military districts, was by no means small. The large-scale organization of the *annona civica* by the emperors, the massive ruins of Ostia, and, to some extent, the remains of the 'Monte Testaccio,' the frequent evidence of import to Rome and Italy from the provinces and from regions outside the Empire, which supplied Italy with the necessities of life, raw materials, and manufactured goods, articles of mass consumption and luxuries, all emphatically prove the contrary. In contrast, however, with earlier conditions more non-Italians than Italians were responsible for the commercial activity. Moreover, imports were paid for to an even greater extent by the proceeds of taxation both direct and in-direct (*e.g.* converted into officials' salaries) drawn from the Empire as a whole, or by non-Italian sources of revenue (*e.g.* from the revenues accruing to the emperor, which were spent in Italy), than by income derived from the export trade. Hence the balance of trade was definitely more unfavourable than it had been at the beginning of Imperial times—if, indeed, it was then unfavourable at all[1]. The rise of Ostia (an importing harbour-town), which was enlarged by Trajan and equipped with great new warehouses, may be contrasted with the decline of Puteoli (traditionally an exporting harbour-town) in the second century[2], to illustrate the change.

The second factor, the new part played by internal trade (*i.e.* by provincial and local trade), which now might become the most important branch of trade as a whole, and whose advance is one of the most striking features of the age, affects the whole Empire. That was the effect of the improvement and extension of the transport system, which now reached remote districts by water and by land. In the older regions, such as Italy and the chief countries of the East, there had always been considerable internal trade. This still maintained itself, and became more extensive so as to include within its scope the other parts of the East. A similar development occurred in the provinces of the West, where Gaul had already led the way. Here again, as in the East, river or lake transport was more important than road traffic. Lyons and Trèves are perfect illustrations of this. The silver patera of Capheaton is meant to depict the interconnection be-tween road, river, and sea transport in Britain[3], and an African mosaic is crowded with river vessels as well as sea-going ships[4].

If in these factors certain negative sides of decentralization

[1] See vol. x, p. 397.　　　　[2] *O.G.I.S.* 595 (A.D. 174).
[3] See Volume of Plates v, 152, *a*.　　[4] *Ib.* 152, *b*.

find expression, these are amply compensated by the positive sides. The developing internal trade is itself to be set down on the credit side in the last analysis, since it came into being alongside inter-provincial and international trade, without exterminating or weakening them. In fact they too developed at the same time. The conditions of production and transport, the further enlargement of the area open to trade, and not least the scale on which supplies for the army were needed in the North-west, the North, and the East, all contributed to this end. Thus the passivity of which we spoke was balanced by an increased activity on the other side. Whereas the Italian dealers (except those from North Italy) disappeared to an ever greater degree from the markets, adaptable Orientals, who had always known how to outwit their Italian rivals, remained, commerce was conducted, as before, by Syrians and their companions from Antioch and Tyre, from Palmyra and Doura, from Petra, Philadelphia, Gerasa, and Bostra, by Egyptians from Alexandria, and by Levantines from Amisus, Sinope, Nicomedia, Ephesus, and the like. Their ranks were swelled by the descendants of the old Greek traders, not so much from the motherland, though Corinth and Patrae still play some part, but colonial Greeks. Apart from Asia Minor, already referred to, Dalmatia, where Salonae was the commercial capital, supplied its quota; as did places adjoining to the south, such as Dyrrhachium; so too Thessalonica in Macedonia, Mesembria and Abdera in Thrace, Tomi and Istros in Lower Moesia, and Olbia, Chersonesos, and Panticapaeum in South Russia, which were helped to importance by the enhanced significance of supplies to the army, and so on. The true heirs of the old Italian dealers were, however, Occidentals—Upper Italians from Aquileia, Gallo-Germans from Narbo and Arelate, and from Lyons, Trèves and Cologne (these three not merely centres of internal trade and army supply), together with Britons from Londinium—to mention only a few of the most important. The volume of trade, in which foreigners were also engaged, especially in the West (Danubian regions, Africa, Britain), may well have increased by comparison with earlier times. That is the conclusion to be derived from authors, inscriptions and papyri, from finds of goods, from coinage, and architectural monuments, such as the '*Piazzale delle Corporazioni*' in Ostia, dating from the second and third centuries. The distribution of the traders indicates a lively commercial activity and a still greater intercourse than before. Oriental traders are found not only in the Roman and non-Roman East, but also in the West, in Rome and Italy, in Sicily, Gaul, the Rhineland, Britain, the

Danubian provinces (including Dalmatia and Thrace), and in south Russia. And Occidental traders, especially the Gallo-Germans, are met with not only in Italy and throughout the West, but also in the foreign countries of the North, and, on occasion, in the East of the Empire. New competition spurred them on. Gallo-German, Istrian or North-Italian, and Dalmatian dealers fought one another for the chance of supplying the Danubian provinces[1], which were so important in the second and third centuries; and for the lower Danubian area there were further competitors from Asia Minor and Syria. Cologne was a trade rival of Aquileia and Alexandria (see above, p. 243, n. 2).

A further indication of the development lies in the geographical advance not only of intermittent but also of systematic trade within the Empire, and in the fact that the outposts of the export trade were constantly moved forward. Thus Gallic trade advances to the Rhine, Gallo-German to the Danube, to Britain and free Germany, Norican trade to Pannonia, the Pannonian to Dacia, and the Syrian to the Euphrates. In the North, Scotland and Ireland were reached. The increasing finds of articles and coins show that trade grew with free Germany, not only from the Rhine valley, or by way of the north coast of Germany, but also from the Danube and South Russia. A like advance marks the trade with Scandinavia and Central Russia. Knowledge of India became increasingly evident; Trajan, Hadrian, Pius, and Elagabalus, received Indian embassies, and the coin-hoards in India, and the residence of Egyptian traders in India, and Indian traders in Egypt, show how close the connection was. The Indian trade, however, pushed farther forward to Sumatra, Indo-China, and finally, by way of Annam, to China itself. Commerce with China was not only through a series of intermediaries, but from 166 (according to the Chinese annals) there was also direct trade[2].

Further evidence is provided by the specialization of the profession of dealer (in corn, wine, oil, wood, pork, etc.), which suggests intense activity. The wide distribution of wholesale trading concerns, and of the retail businesses dependent on them, points in the same direction, as do the numerous warehouses and storage-rooms, the bazaars, markets, and fairs, the import and

---

[1] See vol. XI, p. 549.

[2] See above, p. 235 n. 1. A direct connection between Tyre and Lian-shu by way of Kashgar seems to have been established as early as A.D. 100 (perhaps through the use of Parthian agents) according to the report of Marinus in Ptolemy (*Geogr.* I, 11, 7). A. Herrmann, *Mitt. d. geogr. Gesellsch. Wien*, LVIII, 1915, pp. 480 *sqq.* See, however, vol. XI, p. 122.

export firms with their branches, dock-warehouses, and counting-houses, ships and caravans, the freighters and overseas merchants who 'travel widely'[1], and the business men who travel by land. There were also trading corporations and associations, on the lines of the 'Chamber of commerce' at Ostia for the branch of the *annona civica*, the Gallic trading companies, the Alexandrine associations of *naukleroi* and *emporoi*, and the societies of Palmyrene merchants with their communal caravans organized on Oriental models. The law governing commercial transactions was worked out in the minutest detail and implies complicated trading negotiations such as are exemplified in the Egypt papyri and the legal documents from Doura. Token money[2] also appears, indicating that the pressure of monetary transactions was such that the ordinary coinage of Empire, province and city proved insufficient. Finally, the general prosperity, to which we recur later, is a striking testimony to the flourishing condition of trade. If we attempt to make a list of countries according to their trading activity, the following order may be tentatively suggested. Gaul and Germany west of the Rhine, with North Italy, Syria, and Egypt stand first. In the second category come Asia Minor, Dalmatia, South Russia, Italy, Spain, the Danubian lands, and Britain. Africa (with Numidia and Mauretania) and Sicily perhaps come only in the third class together with the remaining territories.

With trade at this level, the former interdependence of the Empire internally and with the external world naturally remained unaltered. The character of the goods exchanged also underwent no change, whether we consider interprovincial or international trade. This means that interprovincial trade continued to supply not only various specialities, which will have been handled by moderate-sized trade organizations and by itinerant vendors[3], but also large quantities of the most vital necessities, which constituted wholesale trade. Among these necessities were food-supplies, metals, woods, textiles, and pottery metal and glass utensils of everyday use, so that this trade was clearly of basic importance in the economic scheme. International commerce was complementary to interprovincial trade, and supplied the same products as before[4], namely mass-produced articles and luxury specialities, not of immediate vital importance. There was still a great demand for both types, and in view of the permanently unfavourable foreign trade balance this resulted in a vast drainage of money

---

[1] E.g. *I.G.* XII, (9), 1240.
[2] Rostovtzeff, *Soc. and Econ. Hist.* pp. 172, 542, Germ. Ed. I, pp. 150, 319.
[3] Philostratus, *Vita Apoll.* IV, 32, 2.   [4] See vol. X, pp. 412 *sqq.*

abroad. The special products of particular regions, and the conditions of demand were, it is true, somewhat different from what they had been in earlier times, through the increase in the cultivation of the olive and the vine, and as a result of local manufacture and the new configuration of the industrial export trade—a change which results from what has already been said about production. There remains, however, a sufficient degree of local specialization and also of differentiation between regions of primary production and those processing raw materials to cause interreliance and commercial interdependence. The inscriptions of the second century furnish a large number of interprovincial trade connections, mostly on a reciprocal basis, which are not only of an occasional, but also often of a permanent character. Thus Aelius Aristides speaks specifically of a steady flow of traffic between Gaul and Britain[1], and the merchant Flavius Zeuxis from Phrygian Hierapolis travelled seventy-two times between Asia Minor and Rome[2].

IV. PROSPERITY: PROGRESS AND RETROGRESSION

The picture as a whole is one of a more lively and flourishing economic activity, reaching its zenith in the age of the Antonines, and finding its reflection in the widespread city prosperity of the times, a prosperity for which the *nouveaux riches*, naturally enough, claim most of the credit[3]. The ruins of the cities, frequently still magnificent, and of the luxurious aristocratic residences in the country, the funeral monuments and the inscriptions in stone which record the munificence of wealthy citizens, and also the large and small farms in purely agricultural districts, all have the same clear tale to tell. Fortunes were made in a multitude of ways. Sometimes systematically organized agriculture brought wealth, as in Africa, where the tenants of the imperial domains, a numerous class since the Neronian confiscations, must be reckoned amongst the other large agriculturalists. Sometimes wealth had a mercantile origin, as in Palmyra, Doura, Petra, and also in Ostia. Sometimes its causes were both agricultural and mercantile activity, as in South Russia, sometimes mercantile, industrial, and agricultural, as in Gaul, Germany, and North Italy, or in the East. Prosperity grew not only in the cities of world-significance, but also in the thousands of medium-sized and small cities, such as Thamugadi and Lambaesis in Africa, Heddernheim in Germany east of the Rhine or Smyrna and Assos in Asia Minor, or

---

[1] Aelius Aristides, xxxvi k, 91.　　　　　　[2] Ditt.[3] 1229.

[3] *E.g.* the Secundini of Igel, *Germania Romana*[2], iii, pp. 49 *sqq.* (cf. pp. 24 *sqq.*).

Hermupolis Magna in Egypt. This wide diffusion of prosperity is, indeed, its characteristic feature; there is a decentralization of property corresponding to the economic decentralization. The huge fortunes concentrated more especially in Rome and Italy at the end of the Republican era and in the opening years of the Empire shrank or disappeared if we except the fortune of the emperor. The confiscations under emperors such as Nero and Vespasian indirectly assisted this process. Prosperity was now spread throughout the Empire—indeed, the change in the economic situation was mostly due to this one cause, namely a more equable distribution, and the middle class, under the direct encouragement of the emperor, shared to a considerable extent in the wealth of the Empire as a whole. This is but another aspect of the levelling process which manifested itself in very similar fashion in other spheres, such as those of nationality, of constitutional law, of defence policy, and of culture.

In view of this evidence it cannot be denied that an increase in economic activity took place, but on closer examination it appears that this increase was only in quantity not in quality. In other words, it was a matter of greater extension not of greater depth; the level of organization already reached in the Hellenistic age was not surpassed. There was merely a constant expansion of the existing economic system to embrace territories of the Empire newly opened to development. Hadrian marked a clear-cut break, as he was responsible for checking the expansion of the Empire, though by doing so he admittedly made it possible for the seed which had been previously sown to come to full maturity in the early years of the Antonines. A glance at the forms of production shows that there was no qualitative economic advance. In agriculture the *villa rustica* of Brioni Grande, and the luxury estates, the manors, and the farms of Gaul, Belgium, Germany, or Africa, surpass the Pompeian villas in size alone, not in organization, whereas the provincial villas, especially the larger ones, on the whole hardly approached the Pompeian standard, if, indeed, they had any desire to do so (see below, p. 274). In the industrial sphere it is true that in connection with the great estates of the emperors and of private citizens in Italy as in the provinces (Gaul, Germany, Belgium, Britain, Africa) new large-scale concerns producing for export on the model of the Egyptian *ousia*-manufacture did come into being, this process being encouraged by the fact that raw materials, such as clay and wool, could be processed by agricultural labourers during the winter. These forms of production, however, did not cause an advance in the essential character of industry, any more than did the large concerns run by specialists in some particular line of business (brickyards, potteries, builders' and glaziers' workshops), in the cities or the countryside of the new or old provinces. The step from the manufactory to the factory (see vol. x, p. 391, n. 1) and the machine as the fundamental means of production was still not made. In businesses the personal element predominates throughout. Often every imaginable form of business activity is united in one hand—industrial, commercial, agricultural, and banking. A crucial piece of evidence is that 'large-scale' industry practically never succeeded in exterminating, or even in markedly limiting, skilled craftsmanship, least of all in the West. The craftsman remained, not as a mere survival, but really independent and capable of competition, side by side with the rival form of production[1]. It follows that even now there was no 'large-scale industry' in the technical sense of the word, in spite of all approximations to division of labour and specialized manufacture of the parts (which, however, are not inconsistent with skilled craftsmanship[2]), but only highly organized production by skilled craftsmanship, a point to which we shortly return. The mining industry also introduced no new form of organization. So too, trade and banking provide no evidence which would point to an advance beyond the stage reached in the first century of our era or in the Hellenistic age. The arrangements at Doura, which we now know extremely well, are typical. Their subdivision, the limited scope of their transactions, their linking of shops for assorted commodities with pawnbroking all show a form of organization based on the small-scale unit[3]. The 'trading companies' (*societates*) everywhere remain mere associations of dealers for business purposes, and do not lose their personal character. It is not surprising, therefore, that the economic picture appears fundamentally unchanged. Agriculture, not industry, is of prime importance, and has actually gained in relative significance (see below, p. 274). Fortunes are made either by the traditional means of a political career (emperor, favourites, senators, knights), or else by trade and speculation[4], rather than by industrial enterprise; and surplus profits from every type of undertaking, the industrial included, are still constantly invested in land[5].

---

[1] The Gallic funeral *stelae* showing craftsmen may therefore partly reflect real small-scale industry and need not be for the most part merely evidence of large-scale production.   [2] Augustine, *de civ. Dei*, VII, 4.

[3] Cf. the trading firm of Nebucelus and Co. (in the first half of the third century). *Rep. Dura*, IV, p. 142 *sq.*   [4] Galen, *protrept.* 1, 38.

[5] Cf. the merchants of the Moselle and their *villae rusticae*.

What were the underlying causes of the absence of development in technique? The economy of the second and third centuries was a continuous organic development of the features observed in the first century, including both the actively progressive and the retarding elements (p. 233). The actively progressive elements, whose ramifications continued into the third century and later, and are exemplified at the close of that century in the planting of vineyards held on an emphyteutic tenure in the large Egyptian estates[1], have now been analysed. The retarding elements, where the old and the new are closely intertwined, now demand attention.

Among the old factors is the unstable character of ancient private economy, which is connected with the absence of extensive financial operations and of wide credit facilities for productive enterprises[2]. In agriculture we may indeed call to mind the *alimenta* of Nerva and his successors (although considerations connected with the birth-rate and social reform rather than with economic policy were decisive here), the measures of relief for land-owners ascribed to Severus Alexander (see above, p. 65), Hadrian's[3] remission of rents, and the rebates in taxation on land held on emphyteutic tenure. There is nothing corresponding to this in industry. Indeed the financial resources brought into play by emperors (on the model of Hellenistic rulers) or by great land-owners for their own industrial purposes constitute a movement away from the bourgeois system of economy, which is what we are considering here, and can thus be considered in another connection. State protection of industry is also absent.

A second retarding factor, also of long standing, which Rostovtzeff has emphasized[4], is that consumption remained low despite the progress made. The purchasing power of the very large lower class was small. The circle of buyers for wares of somewhat superior quality derived accordingly from the middle and upper classes, and from the army, which for this reason had unusual economic significance. So long as industry, keeping pace with the political expansion, could steadily enlarge and extend its field of custom from the buying capacity of the newly-acquired lands, there was no difficulty. When, however, the limits of the *oikoumene* were reached, and the external market in consequence grew weaker, industry should have exploited the internal market more actively, and should have extended its scope to include the lower

[1] *E.g.* P. Oxy. xiv, 1631 (A.D. 280).   [2] See vol. x, p. 422.
[3] P. Giess. 4–7; P. Ryl. ii, 96.
[4] *Soc. and Econ. Hist.* pp. 303 *sqq.*; Germ. Ed. ii, p. 67 *sq.*

classes. This, however, would have required a modification in the social structure of the Empire.

Here a third factor emerges, the legacy, from the Hellenistic era, of slave labour in manufacture as the most efficient form of industrial production. Although that era was the technical age of the ancient world, the evolution of the factory remained incomplete, not because of any technical or intellectual deficiency, but because the slave was a unit of labour which could be exploited to the full, so that the problem of economizing labour never became pressing. In Hellenistic, and even in early Imperial, times it was possible to manage tolerably well with a form of production that fell short of real intensity, first because the demand was still sufficiently large, secondly, because the nature of the ancient civilization, based on coastal and river communications, remained to some extent unaltered, so that the question of transport costs was not yet so acute, thirdly, above all because there were still sufficient slaves or substitutes for them. All three premises had now been more or less invalidated. Demand could not be increased under present methods. Slavery, on which the activity of even the smaller workshops was still chiefly dependent, diminished, and free labour gained in consequence, especially in the West. This necessarily implied greater emphasis on individual skilled craftsmanship, whereas the half-free labour of the East still remained as a factor favouring the larger type of organization, though at the same time perhaps favouring strikes of workmen[1]. The question of transport costs became more difficult. The old system should have been jettisoned, the technical side perfected, and so the whole problem of communication, and, ultimately, the structure of society, would have been altered.

But the creative energy necessary for such a radical change was lacking. Instead, the problems at issue, including that of providing as cheap articles as possible for the lower classes, were solved by ever greater decentralization, in other words by retrogression instead of progress. Manufacture on the large estates is one of the symptoms of this decentralization. The striking provincialization and deterioration of industrial products, which constituted a bad, and at times a mechanical, copy of the material side of Mediterranean culture, is a consequence alike of decentralization and of the demand for cheaper articles. It was, however, inevitable that the constant attempts to eliminate or reduce the

[1] *I.G.R.R.* iv, 444. (Pergamum, about the time of Hadrian.) Even in this instance, which is relatively the most certain, it is not beyond all doubt that a genuine strike of workers is meant.

costs of transport would act as a deterrent to the development of large production into a genuine large-scale system, and would cut short approaches to this development, such as we encounter in the Fortis lamp-business or the Graufesenque potteries[1]. A fourth new factor specially affecting agriculture should be mentioned. In the previous period Italian agriculture had become more intensive owing to a relative shortage of land. With the end of his shortage, and a shrinkage in the supply of labour (slaves), the change was made, as we saw, to a less intensive type of cultivation, which prepared the way for a revival of feudalism. In the provinces there was no land shortage for the ruling class. In view of the survival of the indigenous aristocracy down to this time (e.g. in Gaul and Britain) intensive cultivation had, in any case, only advanced to a limited extent. It was accordingly possible for the Roman or romanized bourgeoisie to make a fortune through non-specialized agriculture, which involved far less trouble, and was the natural choice for the man who only resided partially on his estate, or for the absentee landlord. The system of small tenancies subject to the payment of a rent was in some cases simply the continuation of older conditions; elsewhere it arose since the native population was not forthwith enslaved but merely degraded to the condition of tenants or again native peasants who were heavily in debt were, it is true, deprived of their land but allowed to cultivate it on payment of a rent. Thus the approach was made to a system of cultivation which was securely based on the model of the working of the domains and on Italian prototypes. At any rate, sufficient forces were in operation to frustrate the methodical and intensive economy of the capitalistic system, and to prevent a more highly organized production even in agriculture.

A fifth factor, however, perhaps the most important of all, was the promotion of State-socialist tendencies that were opposed to the individualistic principle of economic theory. The gradual whittling-away of the dominant people by colonization and romanization, and in addition the defective 'political' will of a middle-class which, despite all constitutionalism, was more governed than

---

[1] Rostovtzeff (loc. cit. above, p. 252 n. 4) attributes the weakness of ancient industry entirely to the smallness of the consuming body in antiquity, and so to a social cause. He regards an expensive machine-industry as not capable of being supported, and refuses to recognize the significance of slave-labour as an essential factor. To the present writer, it does not appear impossible that the Ptolemaic paper-industry, flourishing under a mercantilistic system, and possessing almost a world-monopoly, should have been able to support rationalization by the introduction of machinery.

governing, whose interests were economic rather than political, and whose response to the demands of military service for defence and to the need of maintaining the numbers of the population was conditioned by the fatal consequences of over-civilization, resulted in a state of affairs terribly like conditions in Greece during the Hellenistic age. Thus after Vespasian Italy slowly relinquishes the leadership, until under Septimius Severus and Caracalla[1] she becomes politically insignificant. With the army drawing its recruits increasingly from the lower classes, especially of the peasant type, the centre of gravity shifts to these classes more and more, and in consequence to the provinces also. The old traditional culture of the ancient world had lost its power of resistance and could build no barrier against the irruption from the East and from the strange ('barbarian') North of foreign cultures and ideas, and of different forms of State and society. The situation was fraught with danger for the existing economic system, and the danger came from outside. The menace was magnified, however, by an internal danger arising out of stagnation. For life—including economic life—is movement. Every historical process from its earliest beginning carries within itself the counter-forces making for its own destruction. While progress is being made, they are kept under or even absorbed; but with stagnation they rise to the surface. Thus the economic system based on a private economy and tending to individualism and freedom concealed within itself the germ of the counter-movement in the sense of a controlled State-socialism which was now inevitably stimulated by the changed situation in the whole field of civilized life.

State-socialism is here taken in the widest possible sense as an orientation imposed from above of the whole social and economic order based on the interests of the State and not of the individual. We are not here concerned (see above, p. 234) with the normal restrictions of the liberal system by State economic intervention[2], nor yet with occasional incursions of the State into private economy for reasons of economic or social policy, incursions intended for purposes of relief, which do not really abrogate the principle of *laissez faire*[3]. We are considering rather State-capitalism and

---

[1] The *Const. Antoniniana* marks just as much the decline of the Romans as a raising of the provincials (see above, pp. 45 *sqq.*).

[2] Cf. the Imperial domains, mines, fisheries; the provisioning of the great cities and the army in connection with the earlier treatment of the problem of the food-supply (*euthenia*) by the *polis*.

[3] For economic-political measures see vol. x, p. 386 and above, p. 238. For social-political measures see above, pp. 239, 252 and below, p. 261.

State-socialism of the type which Augustus had formerly resisted, but which from the second century onwards advanced inexorably, characterized by State egotism rather than altruism, by regimentation, standardization, and a dictatorial attitude rather than by control and paternal beneficence. Within this framework the idea of the omnipotence of the State, which had already evolved from the organic conception of the Polis, changed more and more under the influence of orientalizing-hellenistic and other theories of the State which still survived within the frame of the Empire. This new political and social form was bound ultimately to reshape economic life also, the more so since an economic question—that of the public finances—played a decisive part in the change. The replacement of one economic system by the other, and the substitution of a new civilization and attitude to life for the old took more than a century and a half. It was completed by the end of the third century, but the beginnings go back to the earliest years of the second century.

V. THE BURDENS OF STATE DEMANDS

This tendency towards State-socialism grew the stronger through the emergence of the first great crisis of the Empire's foreign policy caused by the attack alike from North and East upon a Roman world which was internally growing weaker and by Trajan's tremendous efforts to master these difficulties. At that time it became evident that even the financial system of the mighty Roman Empire was not sufficiently strong and elastic to maintain enhanced expenditure on defence, or to hold out for any great length of time in wars which did not finance themselves without being rudely shaken. Although the State from the early days of Nero and Domitian had steadily increased its possessions of territory and mines (see below, p. 272), yet large reserves were lacking. It was a hand-to-mouth existence. War loans, such as had been seen from time to time in the Republic, were unknown[1]. Hence the burden could not be spread over a number of years, but immediate needs demanded extraordinary taxation or increased rents. Moreover, in view of the inadequate transport system (witness the constantly recurring famine[2]), the burdens were not evenly enough distributed from a territorial point of view, and the war zones and adjoining regions were dispro-

[1] On the disappearance of great fortunes see above, p. 250.
[2] Inscr. *B.S.A.* xxiii, 1918–9, nos. 67 *sqq.*, ed. Tod (Macedonia A.D. 121–3); Pliny, *Pan.* 29 (by contrast).

portionately hard hit by levies of corn paid for at a fixed rate below the market price—perhaps, on occasion, not paid for at all—by other contributions of natural products, and by expenses connected with transport and road-building. Admittedly these were regarded as emergency measures. But Trajan's wars lasted for year after year. In consequence the burdens imposed on the population and on certain regions (e.g. Macedonia and Bithynia) were very great, and had disastrous economic consequences. When Hadrian and Pius, in view of these facts, abandoned attack as a means of defence and fell back on the defensive, the financial pressure diminished, debts were cancelled[1], and economic life could revive; yet in the last resort this recovery was superficial, the more so since Hadrian's policy of strengthening the Empire internally also cost money, so that no savings were made. For the problem of foreign policy, which Trajan attacked with such striking energy, was not solved, but only kept in suspense, so that presently Marcus Aurelius and other emperors had to face it again, the sole difference being that the situation had meanwhile grown more dangerous.

Thus the question of army supplies and the whole problem of finance became cardinal from the second century onwards. The government oscillated between increased taxation and remission of debts. Then the currency was tampered with. Following Nero's precedent, Trajan, despite his large supplies of gold—mainly the booty from his Dacian conquests—and other emperors debased the denarius, presumably at the same time increasing the amount in circulation. The stability of the currency was not immediately threatened, since the prestige of the Empire was still sufficiently high. In foreign countries, however, where the coins were accepted according to their metal content, it seems that already under Marcus Aurelius the denarius, whose proportion of precious metal had been reduced by twenty-five per cent., encountered difficulties[2]. Corresponding with the slow decline of the currency there was a gradual weakening of economic principles. The needs of the government had to be met promptly and cheaply, and in consequence the tendency towards State-socialism and compulsion grew more and more marked.

The financial system and, as part of it, the method of meeting

---

[1] Hadrian's remission of debts of A.D. 118 (900 million sesterces for citizens' debts alone to the treasury), *C.I.L.* VI, 967; for coins P. L. Strack, *Untersuch. zur röm. Reichsprägung*, II, p. 60 *sq.*; Dio LXIX, 8; S.H.A. *Hadr.* 7, 6. For remissions of rent see above, p. 252, n. 3.

[2] See Note 3 at end of volume, p. 724.

the costs of local administration, had the most diverse origins, Oriental, Greek (these had already coalesced in the Hellenistic age), and Roman. Direct taxation, forced labour, serf or half-free labour in State concerns, the provision of transport at the order of the State (*angareiai*), the responsibility of professional groups for meeting the State's demands, personal responsibility of salaried officials for a regular and punctual payment of revenue from taxation and other sources of income—these were Oriental traits. Of Graeco-Roman origin were, apart from indirect taxation, extraordinary capital levies and compulsory services in time of emergency, the following: the almost, or wholly, unpaid tenure of administrative office (as an honorary position), salaried subordinate officials, State leases, and contracting for the State. A Greek conception was the property-liturgy undertaken once only, or at most at long intervals, from a sense of duty, a conception which gradually extended to include the holding of a magistracy. Finally, it was an idea peculiar to the Roman Empire to draw on the cities (or quasi-city communities), or on their *honoratiores* and *possessores* as agents for the distribution, raising, and guaranteeing, not only communal but also imperial demands and for producing men on whom obligations fell.

There were, accordingly, numerous institutions in existence whose scope could be extended. As the demands of the State grew, not only was the number of irregular impositions increased, and more frequent *angareiai* and compulsions imposed, but also existing remunerations were reduced or abolished, while the more normal taxes and rentals were at least maintained at their former level. Moreover, in difficult times the guarantee especially of the leading city officials was more frequently realized. The advantages which the smaller positions in the hierarchy of officialdom, with their modest revenue and modest glory, or the places of honour with their relative splendour originally had to offer soon came to be less than the disadvantages. The consequence was that there gradually arose a reluctance to undertake activities on behalf of city or State of one's own free will or because it was the traditional or natural thing to do[1]; and the lack of enthusiasm was most marked when the times called for the relief of economic burdens and the reduction of trouble to the bare minimum. The crisis had come. The omnipotent State could find no resource by which to surmount it but brute compulsion, and so, at the close

---

[1] Cf. the struggle of an Egyptian nome-strategos against the opposition, Wilcken, *Chrest.* 35 (A.D. 135)

of the first and beginning of the second century, the hated 'liturgization' came increasingly into evidence. By means of forced labour and compulsory supply it came to encroach more and more on the preserves of the State contract, and to some extent also of the transport system, though the *navicularii* (p. 31) were still immune, because their interests were still sufficiently linked with those of the State as a result of privileges and compensation. The liturgy of office came into being or was at least more firmly rooted, and the compulsory decurionate, the compulsory decemprimate, and compulsory magistracy appeared. In this change, city self-government, the special symbol of life as it was lived in the world of classical antiquity, was attacked.

It is interesting to observe that the change to State-compulsion was made by none other than Trajan and Hadrian. Self-government was restricted by Trajan (anticipated to some extent by Nerva) so that the control of city finances might give the State greater opportunities of making inroads on their funds[1]. Compulsory State leases, and compulsory recruiting for the lower and middle grades of local officials, reached an advanced stage during his reign. The problem of filling the office of Gymnasiarch, and the question of high prices are agitating the citizens of the Egyptian quasi-city Hermupolis Magna in the year 115[2]. The earliest evidence for the 'inviti decuriones' is found in a letter of Pliny to Trajan (113). Methodical organization of the liturgy-system goes back to his successor, whose reign also marks an important stage in the development of the imperial bureaucratic State. The *frumentarii*, introduced as secret police and informers to watch a recalcitrant populace, already have a certain significance under Hadrian. Yet Trajan and Hadrian are avowedly constitutional and enlightened emperors. Indeed, Trajan had his qualms about the compulsory decurionate, as his reply to Pliny shows. The inevitability of the development, and the exigence of foreign policy and of the self-preservation of the State could not find a better illustration.

VI. THE GREAT CRISIS AND THE RESTORATION

The economic advance under the early emperors was based on the peace and strength of the Empire. The results of a change in these essential conditions can easily be imagined. They have already been touched on. The falling-off in that bourgeois muni-

[1] Cf. Trajan's interest in the finances of the Bithynian cities in his correspondence with the younger Pliny.   [2] Wilcken, *Chrest.* 149.

ficence, by whose aid the first periods of crisis in the second century had been surmounted, foreshadows the decline. Nevertheless the level of economic activity was more or less maintained down to the time of the Antonines. There were two reasons for this. First, the bourgeoisie, which was responsible for meeting the many demands, was temporarily able to shift a sufficient part of its burden on to the lower class and lower middle-class, a process which gave rise to revolutionary movements, peasant revolts, and what may have been strikes, or something like them[1]. Secondly, the capital resources, into which the State on occasion made inroads with scant ceremony, were dissipated only by slow degrees. It becomes increasingly clear, however, once we have grasped the obstacles with which economic activity had to cope, why it was inevitable for the above-mentioned stagnation to ensue and by a gradual process, though already as early as the second century, to merge into retrogression, which is in fact inherent in stagnation.

The progressive change in agricultural production from the middle-sized specialized farm to the diffusely organized large-scale unit, the frequent nationalization of landed property, dating from the end of the first century, and the coming into being of the colonate, all testify to such a retrogression. The decline in achievement in the industrial and technical spheres (p. 253), and the gradual spread of *oikos*-economy on the great estates, point in the same direction. The development of State-controlled commerce and the withdrawal of ships from service crippled free trade, and the intellectual and spiritual deficiency which became marked in cultural life as a whole during the second half of the second century affected the economic life of the community just as profoundly as it did the other branches of human activity. Whole regions began to go out of cultivation, not only in Italy and Greece, but also in Spain under Marcus Aurelius[2]. Wars, especially with the Marcomanni and Parthians, military conscription (as in Spain), and the great plague brought by troops from the East in 165, accentuated the loss of land to cultivation. Clearly things could not long continue so without the gravest danger to economic life and to the Empire itself. It was urgently necessary to check the tendency; and far-sighted emperors tried time and again to do so. Reference has already been made to Hadrian's new direction of policy. Subsequently Pius, and Marcus Aurelius in particular,

---

[1] See above, p. 253, n. 1. A by-form of strike is found in the simple flight (ἀναχώρησις), as it is known in Egypt, but also elsewhere (see the petitions mentioned below, p. 264).   [2] S.H.A. *Marcus*, 11, 7.

began seriously to economize. The constantly recurring social-political measures for the benefit of the lower class (including freedmen and slaves) which had been especially hard hit, the concern to secure an equitable administration of justice, and the attempts in Italy to revive agriculture, and to convert *coloni* into peasant farmers all point in the same direction, as do the increased urbanization under Trajan and Hadrian, the cancellation of debts, and the edicts against extortionate rates of interest and profiteering. But such palliatives were not enough. What was needed was a complete change of the old order on which civilization was built. But for this, as for so much else, the necessary vigour was lacking.

So events followed their inexorable course, and after the reign of Marcus Aurelius the threatening storm broke. During the third century external dangers became steadily more pressing. From almost all sides came attacks on and invasions of the Empire: Franks and Alemanni, Vandals, Goths and Sarmatae, Persians, Blemmyes, and the peoples of Libya and Mauretania all burst into the Empire and plundered it; Italy herself was not immune. The catastrophe was the greater because many of these invasions occurred simultaneously. Cities were sacked; whole provinces or quasi-provinces, such as the Bosporan kingdom, were lost. In the middle of the century the Empire split asunder. It is true that, now, too, the internal crisis was primary; but the situation now was such that the external pressure gave the impulse which accelerated the process of internal disintegration. For the army, which since Marius might always play a part in politics, and whose numbers had steadily increased through forced levies, gained enormously in significance, as it was now more indispensable than ever, and traded on this indispensability. Then was accomplished that dangerous modification in the structure of the army whose nature has already been described (p. 255): it amounted to a provincialization and barbarization of the soldiery, its conversion into a peasantry and a proletariate. The result was the emergence of a soldateska which ultimately seized all power for itself, swept aside hampering constitutionalism, the last attempt at compromise by the old cultured bourgeoisie, and set up in its place a constitution so reformed as to be adequate only in the eyes and to the mind of the class from which the soldiery was drawn, and which was for the most part convenient and profitable to them. The emperors could not or would not check this development towards a military absolutism. Even good and energetic rulers such as Gallienus were powerless here, because in the last resort such centralized power was the only means of holding together a crumbling Empire. Thus there came into being the State of the third century, for which the great jurists duly created its own theoretical basis at the beginning of the century.

The ordinary and extraordinary demands which this State made on its citizens were far greater even than those of the second century. The wars with their losses, the struggles between pretenders, and the extravagant outlay on soldiers and favourites cost vast sums. So did the expenditure on the army which numbered (at the time of Caracalla) some 400,000 men; and the soldiers' real wages had risen somewhat above their already high level[1]. The menacing spectre of State bankruptcy drew ever nearer. The old remedy was prescribed: reduction in value of the currency and increased taxation. The aureus was reduced in size—in the years down to A.D. 256 to approximately a third of its original form—while the silver coins were reduced in purity and size. The denarius of the Severi retained only about half the silver content in comparison with the Neronian standard, and the double denarii under Caracalla and the later emperors (Antoniniani) were an overvalued fiduciary issue, which, in the same period of time, ultimately contained only about a third the silver content when compared with two Neronian denarii. These measures were to a large extent inflationary[2] in character, and in the case of silver ended in disguising the true character of the coin; as they were not merely temporary measures, they caused a rise in prices, henceforth, after Commodus, to twice and almost three times their former level[3]. The rise in taxation consisted for the time being (p. 269) not in an increase in the normal items of taxation (land-taxes, poll-taxes, trade-taxes, etc.) corresponding to the devaluation of the currency—which such a step would have made plain to see—but in supplementary taxation. Thus there was levied a supplementary tax in gold, the *aurum coronarium* (originally a gold crown as a testimony of loyalty to the new ruler, but a regular exaction from Elagabalus' time onwards)[4]. Roman

---

[1] On the question of pay see Note 3, p. 724. They were also paid off in land after Septimius Severus (Rostovtzeff, *op. cit.* p. 378 and, further, Germ. Ed. II, p. 141). On the claims of the soldiers see Ps.-Aristides XXXV K, 30.

[2] On insufficient production of silver as a further factor see p. 277, but that is also a sign of the failure of the State economy.   [3] See Note 3.

[4] On Roman taxes and the *Const. Antoniniana* see Dio LXXVIII, 9, 4 *sq.* On Roman trade-taxes, S.H.A. *Alex. Sev.* 24 (A. W. Persson, *Staat und Manufaktur im röm. Reiche*, p. 58 *sq.*). A general lowering of taxes under Severus Alexander is most improbable (see above, p. 31). One

taxes were now levied on provincials and provincial taxes on
Romans. Above all there were the requisitions in kind, and among
those imposed on the landholder, so far as he did not substitute
a money payment, was the provision of soldiers from among his
coloni. It was just the financial and monetary difficulties that forced
the State to raise the supplies it needed in kind instead of using
for their purchase the declining revenue from taxation, and this
change again favoured to some extent the establishment of a
natural economy. The *annona*-corn was now demanded without
payment offered, and the same applies to soldiers' clothing and
to the wares which from about the beginning of the third century
were extorted from the Egyptian producers, the *anabolicae species*;
these were at first distributed among several of the chief cities of
the Empire, but from Aurelian's time were set aside for the sole
benefit of the city of Rome. The irregular impositions for troops
on the march remained, and in view of prevailing conditions
became heavier.

The State's demands were the more oppressive because the
taxable resources had shrunk in the previous century, and from
the time of the Severi onwards more and more land passed out of
cultivation. Hence the claims of the State were fundamentally
incapable of fulfilment. Yet the very existence of emperors and
Empire alike depended on their being fulfilled. Thus began the
fierce endeavour of the State to squeeze the population to the last
drop. Since economic resources fell short of what was needed,
the strong fought to secure the chief share for themselves with a
violence and an unscrupulousness well in keeping with the origin

would expect an increase in the rates of taxation in view of higher
prices, and the beer-tax in Egypt seems to have increased in A.D. 238 as
compared with the second century (so editors to P. Oxy. XII, 1433, 52).
On the other side, it looks as if the Egyptian trade-taxes in 276 were
still the same as in the time of Marcus Aurelius and L. Verus (P. Tebt. 11,
287; B.G.U. 9=Wilcken, *Chrest.* 551, 29 *sq*.). This still remains a
problem which it would be easier to solve if the thesis of A. C. Johnson
(*Amer. Journ. of Arch.* XXXVIII, 1934, p. 53 *sq*.) is accepted that Egypt as
a 'self-contained country' had 'a fiduciary currency' till the reign of
Gallienus, that the debasement of this currency had no influence on the
price-level and that the rise of prices is to be attributed to bad harvests or
bad management. But any such explanation has in turn to meet serious
reasons for doubt (see Heichelheim, *Econ. Hist.* III, 10, Feb. 1935, p. 7, n. 3).
Money penalties also, despite the devaluation of the denarius, remained unchanged under Severus Alexander as under Antoninus Pius and Marcus
Aurelius. *Dig.* II, 4, 24 compared with Gaius IV, 46 (G. Mickwitz, *Geld
und Wirtschaft im röm. Reich des 4 Jahrhunderts n. Chr.* p. 37).

of those in power and with a soldiery accustomed to plunder. The full rigour of the law was let loose on the population. Soldiers acted as bailiffs or wandered as secret police through the land. Those who suffered most were, of course, the propertied class. It was relatively easy to lay hands on their property, and in an emergency they were the class from whom something could be extorted most frequently and most quickly. Consequently, by the system already in force in the previous two centuries, they had been held ultimately responsible and liable for providing taxes and other impositions. For the same reason they were now the first to suffer from the exactions of the State. At the same time, quite apart from questions of finance, there was a purely political motive at work—the desire to shatter the privileged position of the bourgeoisie. A bitter resistance was put up by the bourgeoisie, supported as it was by some of the emperors, especially in lands such as Africa and Spain which were far removed from the war zone, and in which the bourgeoisie was economically still relatively intact. The civil wars of the third century and the frightful period of anarchy after Severus Alexander were the result, in the course of which the infuriated soldateska and its leaders indulged in orgies of brutality. We gain a vivid picture of the assassinations and confiscations, the terrorism and spying, and the sacking of cities from Herodian, the speech of pseudo-Aristides addressed to the Emperor Philip, and also from Cassius Dio, the *Historia Augusta*, and other sources.

There is no doubt that the inhumanity of the struggle was due in part to the hatred which the peasant soldiery, drawn from the lowest class, felt for the bourgeoisie, but it would be mistaken to over-stress this factor, to regard class hatred as the sole motive, and the civil war as a purely social revolution, which aimed at establishing the dictatorship of the proletariate. Such a view is disproved by the fact that not all the soldiers were members of the proletariate, some of them owned property[1]; and moreover the poor suffered at least as much, perhaps more, than the rest from the general economic pressure resultant on unsettled conditions, and in particular from the violence of the soldiery. The petitions of Scaptopare (A.D. 238; p. 83) and Araguë (A.D. 244–247; p. 90), and above all Herodian's narrative in Book VII show this quite clearly. The proletariate may, it is true, look on with malice at attacks on the bourgeoisie, and the mob may join in plundering them, small folk who are oppressed by soldiers may

[1] Rostovtzeff, *op. cit.* pp. 376 *sqq.*, Germ. Ed. II, pp. 137 *sqq.*

appeal to soldiers who are their relatives or friends and beg for a kind of protection—but that does not provide any proof in social revolution from below. And if villagers in their appeals to the emperors declare that they cannot endure their present vexations and if the emperors confirm what they say, the conclusion cannot be drawn that the emperors had made the lower classes their one political support[1].

In connection with all this, compulsion and State-socialist regulation had established themselves more firmly. These had gradually come into being, their first beginnings dating back to the time of Trajan and Hadrian, when they had been applied with moderation, but now they had developed into an established system, and hence had been incorporated in the final synthesis devised by the new political theorists at the beginning of the third century (cf. *Dig.* L). He who was not especially privileged, or who was not excepted for the performance of other services to the State—as imperial official and soldier, or, again, as lessee on a large or small scale of the emperor's estates and mines, as *navicularius*, *mercator*, *faber*, *centonarius*, etc.[2]—had to undertake the municipal *munera* according to his powers, financial, intellectual or physical. Since the population had declined, and the number of those who might be called upon for services was still further reduced through privilege and exception, whereas more and more land had gone out of cultivation, the demands made successively on the remaining men of means were ever more quickly recurrent, the land remaining untilled was forcibly attached to the communities or the neighbouring landowners[3], and the financial guarantees of the *decaproti* and *curiales* were more and more frequently realized. Arrest, confiscation, and execution hung over their heads like a sword of Damocles[4]. The proceedings of the city councils (which in the year 199 were set up also in the Egyptian *metropoleis* on the model of the rest of the Empire), councils which did not know how they were to meet the old and the newly imposed burdens, and whom they were to find to act as *archontes* and to undertake the liturgies of office, grimly illustrate the growing misery of the age[5].

---

[1] See N. H. Baynes in *J.R.S.* xix, 1929, p. 299 *sq.*
[2] It is doubtful if these compulsory associations go back to Severus Alexander despite S.H.A. *Alex. Sev.* 33, 2.
[3] P. Thead. 16 (A.D. 307); P.S.I. 292 (third century); *Cod. Just.* xi, 59, 1 (Aurelian).
[4] Cf. P. Oxy. xii, 1477 (third-fourth century).
[5] P. Oxy. xiv, 1662 (A.D. 246); xii, 1413 (A.D. 270–5).

Even the *navicularii* complained and at times threatened to strike, as at Arelate in 201[1].

Yet the vicious circle, or rather spiral, could not be broken. If the propertied class buried their money, or sacrificed two-thirds of their estate to escape from a magistracy[2], or went so far as to give up their whole property in order to get free of the domains rent[3], and the non-propertied class ran away, the State replied by increasing the pressure. It demanded from the bodies liable (p. 258) that they should produce and identify those who had to undertake liturgies, and enrolled on occasion (as in Egypt under Probus) the whole remaining population of the villages for extraordinary manual labour in helping to maintain the irrigation system[4]. Moreover, in view of the steady drop of revenue from taxation, and the decline in the production and supply of gold and silver, the State resorted to repeated debasement and increase of the currency in circulation. The mints worked with feverish activity[5]. The gold coinage remained pure, but the coins became smaller and smaller, and in the end they were only accepted by weight. After 256 the silver currency of the Empire in its chief denomination, the Antoninianus, lost 75 per cent., and ultimately 98 per cent., of its silver content; in other words it became silver-washed copper. The Egyptian provincial currency, which itself was of lower grade than the Imperial, followed suit though less drastically and rapidly. The mistrust of the 'new coinage' was general: in 260 the Egyptian money-changers of Oxyrhynchus refused to accept it at its official valuation[6], though the State itself seems to have made its demands in accordance with the old scale of values (see above, p. 263, note). In Egyptian contracts the parties preferred to reckon on the basis of the 'old Ptolemaic coinage[7].' Prices in Egypt rose after about 280 to from fourteen to twenty times their original level.

In these disturbed and catastrophic decades of the third century countless people, especially of the bourgeois middle-class, were ruined and impoverished, and these were precisely the men who had brought into being and maintained the economic pro-

---

[1] Dessau 6987.

[2] Wilcken, *Chrest.* 402 (A.D. 250).

[3] P.S.I. 292 (third century).

[4] P. Oxy. XII, 1409.

[5] S.H.A. *Aurel.* 38, 2 for the number of workers at the mint.

[6] P. Oxy. XII, 1411; it is uncertain whether the devalued billon Antoniniani or the devalued billon tetradrachm is referred to. See Mickwitz, *op. cit.* p. 52.

[7] Stud. Pal. XX, 71, 11 (A.D. 268–270).

sperity of former times. The wasteful policy of the State, the constant interference with private economic life, and the inflations, amounted to a landslide beneath which a vast amount that was of value was crushed out of existence. How great a part was played by the spread of the system of liturgies is shown by the abundance of Egyptian papyri bearing on this theme. Admittedly conditions were not the same everywhere. Africa, the home of Septimius Severus, and Syria, the home of his wife, enjoyed a privileged position. So too did Germany and the Danubian regions because of the soldiers who came from them. And Britain, which lay far from the centre of things, and where city life was less of a determining factor than elsewhere in the Empire, actually enjoyed a relative prosperity in the third century (see below, p. 278), though here too after the middle of the century the cities declined. Moreover, it remains true that the bourgeoisie was not wholly destroyed; otherwise Diocletian could never have maintained the *curiales* as servants of the State with property to pledge, and the completion of the municipalization of Egypt at the beginning of the fourth century would have had no meaning. But the bourgeoisie, which had been the typical representative of a wholly different age, was broken; spiritually and materially it had received a mortal blow. The well-to-do bourgeois is now the exception, not the rule. The 'abundantia' on which the emperors had once prided themselves, which they had promised to maintain, and which they had proclaimed on their coinage, appears under Probus as a Utopian aspiration[1].

Yet although the bourgeoisie had lost incalculably, this does not mean that the position of the lower classes had in consequence improved. They too suffer and complain, strike and revolt; and this ill-will took highly dangerous forms on occasion, as is shown, for example, by the rising of the Bagaudae in Gaul in the second half of the third century, or the strike of the *monetarii* at Rome in Aurelian's time. Since, however, the masses turned upon the well-to-do alone as those who were squeezing them to the last drop[2]—to turn upon the soldiery who did the same they were too weak—the ruin of the bourgeoisie was hastened in this way too. Thus the end of it all was discontent, depopulation, flight, and banditry among those who had been uprooted, and together with this a shortage of labour. It is estimated that the numbers of the population fell by approximately one third, from seventy to fifty

[1] S.H.A. *Prob.* 20, 6; 23, 2 *sqq.* See Rostovtzeff, *op. cit.* pp. 416 *sqq.*, Germ. Ed. II, pp. 176 *sqq.*

[2] For an illustration see the late parallel in Libanius, *Or.* XLVII (*c.* A.D. 395).

millions[1]. Pestilence and a growing reluctance to have children contributed to the decline. Documents from the Egyptian village of Theadelphia dating from the late third and early fourth centuries give appalling glimpses of the desertion of farms and depopulation[2]. The State, which addressed its demands to the villagers as a body, by its own act drove them one after the other on to the streets. The resultant banditry, which the State in turn tried to meet by a special police force, took fantastic forms. In the petitions to the emperor the threat of flight is the 'ultimum refugium' and among the common questions which used to be put to an oracle in Egypt three standard types were: 'Am I to become a beggar?' 'Shall I take to flight?' and 'Is my flight to be stopped?'[3]

When things had gone so far, it was impossible to turn back; all that remained was to follow the road to the end. This meant guarding against a general flight, announcing compulsory labour, and binding all classes—or at least all who did not belong to a privileged caste—to their professions, the peasant farmer to his land and forced labour, the State-employed worker (p. 272) to his workshop, the trader, including the *navicularius*, to his business or his corporation, the small property-owner to his duties in connection with liturgies, the large property-owner to the *curia*, the soldier to his military service, and so on. By one means or another the development had to reach its conclusion in other respects also. Much was achieved in this direction, after Gallienus and the Illyrian emperors (Aurelian in particular) had shown the way, by the far-reaching reforms of Diocletian and Constantine. With these emperors we rightly begin a new era, even though much was not really completed until the fourth and fifth centuries.

The ancient world did not retire from the arena without a struggle; the history of the third century shows how it fought for what remained of political and spiritual freedom against the constraints of tyranny and dogma. But the same century shows how urgent was the need for peace, a need which ultimately led to acquiescence in Diocletian's régime, the more so since the external dangers continued undiminished. From the reign of Gallienus onwards the army had been re-organized; it had become less national, but readier for action, politically more trustworthy, and a more efficient instrument of power. The unity of the Empire was restored by Aurelian, the internal chaos became less pronounced. The organization of

---

[1] E. Stein, *Geschichte des spätröm. Reiches* I, p. 3.   [2] Cf. P. Thead. 16.
[3] Ditt.[3] 888 (A.D. 238); *O.G.I.S.* 519 (A.D. 244–7); P. Oxy. XII, 1477 (third-fourth century).

the corporations on a basis of compulsion goes back in essentials to Aurelian[1]. The stabilization of the currency, which was in complete disorder, and hence of the revenue from taxation, was taken in hand. Aurelian, cautiously feeling his way, renewed the gold issues, and by some means or other (the details are controversial) fixed a value for the very debased billon coins (p. 307). Diocletian began again to coin in pure silver, reviving the Neronian standard, even though the extent of this coinage was limited after the 'thorough discrediting' of the currency in the third century[2]. He also organized a regular system, governed by the gold pound, with gold, silver, and large or small billon or copper issues (p. 403 *sq.*). It is possible that on this occasion the Aurelian billon piece, which was continued in the Diocletian petty cash issues, was again devalued to correspond to its actual buying power, a reform whose immediate result was a further unsettlement of the market, which in its turn occasioned Diocletian's famous edict in 301 regulating prices and wages[3], though it may be admitted that as regards economic policy the value of this edict must have been very limited. At any rate, in spite of the new copper inflation of the fourth century[4], the currency was on the whole pretty well stabilized, especially after the solidus had been linked in A.D. 307 with the gold pound at a fixed ratio of seventy-two to one.

The price paid for the restoration of the Empire was twofold. First, the absolute State had come, catering for the population at large, schematic, appealing to mass-intelligence. Secondly, a complete State-socialism was in force, which with its terrorism by officials, its over-emphasized restrictions on the individual, its progressive State-interference, and its burdensome taxation and liturgies, previously not so clearly defined, and its methods of

---

[1] E. Groag in *Vierteljahrsch. f. Soz.- und Wirtsch.-Gesch.* ii, 1904, p. 493.

[2] Purchase of gold under compulsory powers by the State is attested by P. Oxy. xvii, 2106 (beginning of the fourth century). The fixed price is 100,000 for a pound. If these are denarii (as the editors take it), whereas the edict of Diocletian (xxx, 1) provides for 50,000 as the maximum price, this reflects the recent inflation (see n. 4).

[3] See p. 338. If, on the other hand, the theory of Giesecke (*Antikes Geldwesen*, pp. 180 *sqq.*) is accepted, the complete devaluation of the billon-double denarius goes back not to Diocletian but to Aurelian, who had made it equal to $\frac{1}{20}$ of the Septimius Severus denarius, which still contained 50 per cent. of silver. Giesecke thus interprets the much debated legend xx. 1.

[4] This inflation goes back to Constantine and was about sixfold in the Empire in the years 310–335. It then once more died away. In Egypt, which suffered exploitation, it continued and rose by the year 400 to 45,000 times.

realizing its demands, acted very much as before, except in so far as the union with the Christian Church, from the time of Constantine, gave the system a religious veneer, and stamped subjection as resignation to the will of God. Those to whom this development does not appeal must reflect that, despite all the complaints and opposition, which still continued, this was the only way, under the circumstances, in which the Empire could survive, and remnants of the old bourgeois society, of the old culture, and incidentally of the old economic system could be saved. Finally, as we shall see, this was the only way in which a new culture could mature, though in a greatly changed form and realizing itself perhaps in opposition to the State rather than through it.

VII. ECONOMIC SYSTEM IN THE STATE-SOCIALISTIC ERA

If we seek within the framework of the stricter State-socialist system, in the more rigid form which it assumed during the third century, to gain an impression of the economy itself, especially after the middle of the century, it is by no means easy to reconstruct a clear picture. The *Historia Augusta* needs checking by other evidence. The dated documentary material is not very plentiful, except for Egypt. Diocletian's edict 'de pretiis' dates from the year 301, which is late for our purpose, though the conditions during the second half of the third century are necessarily also mirrored in it. The '*Expositio totius mundi et gentium*', and the '*Notitia dignitatum*', both of which, especially the first, give abundant material, are later still, dating from a time when the reforms made under Diocletian and Constantine had already had their effect. Statistics, which alone would give us a solid basis on which to work, are lacking for this as for other periods. The danger is great of over-stressing the darkness, or, alternatively, the high lights in the picture. Hence it is necessary to proceed deductively—as was done above—and to base our judgments on the general conditions of the age in the first instance.

If the available evidence for the production of commodities in the several countries at particular times is set out[1], it will be found that the products of the various regions, including those in excess of local needs, are hardly different, apart from a few instances, from those established above with special reference to the second

[1] As will be found in the general works of Gummerus, Charlesworth, Rostovtzeff or the monographs of Collingwood, Persson and others cited in the bibliography to this chapter.

century. Individual exceptions occur: thus during Aurelian's reign[1] the vine was apparently cultivated less in Italy than it had been previously so that viticulture had to be assisted by the emperor; thus too Probus once more permitted the cultivation of the vine in Gaul and Spain, and in the other provinces, without limitation[2]. Similarly in the middle of the century the output of Gallic pottery and Spanish minerals declined, with a compensating increase of British products, and the textile and arms industries appear to have increased production. Interchange of goods occurs. Provincial (i.e. internal) trade on a smaller or larger scale prevails in many parts, especially now in Britain, where there were local fairs (p. 293), as also at the Thracian city of Scaptopare (in 238) and at Baetocaece in Syria[3] (sometime between 253 and 259) according to immemorial custom. Interprovincial trade also continued in being (see below, p. 276). There remains for consideration commerce with the outside world along four main trade-routes. One led to central Africa, though since the decline of the kingdom of Meroë it passed via Adulis instead of Meroë. A second stretched to the South-east, starting in Egypt and travelling via the Red Sea to Arabia and India[4]. There was also the route to China[5], starting from Syria and passing through Palmyra, Doura, and Parthia, or alternatively from South Russia. Fourthly, there was the route to the North, which led to free Germany, beginning on the northern or north-western frontier.

Nevertheless production and interchange were profoundly altered. This alteration is most clearly visible if we survey the constituent elements making up the sum total of economic activity, which show a marked shift in the centre of gravity accompanied by a corresponding change in productive methods. Thus State enterprise was a sphere of economic life which increased in importance; after the State had succeeded in securing control over private economy as described above, it was but a step to its direct participation in the economic field. In view of the growing

[1] S.H.A. *Aurel.* 48, 2.

[2] S.H.A. *Prob.* 18, 8; Eutropius ix, 17; Aurelius Victor, *Caes.* xxxvii, 3.

[3] Ditt.[3] 888; *I.G.R.R.* iii, 1020. Cf. *Dig.* l, 11, 1 (Modestinus).

[4] For Indian embassies Stobaeus, *Ecl.* i, 3, 56 (of the reign of Elagabalus); S.H.A. *Aurel.* 41, 10 (to Aurelian, together with Bactrians, Seres, Axumites and other envoys); Eusebius, *Vita Const.* iv, 7 (to Constantine, together with Blemmyes and Ethiopians).

[5] Sixteen Roman coins of the time from Tiberius to Aurelian have been found in the province of Shan-si (*The Academy* xxix, 1886, p. 316). The Chinese annals (see above, p. 235, n. 1) speak of connections also in the third century.

identification of emperor and State, the economic activity of the emperor, which in the early years of the Empire can still be regarded as the private activity of an individual (p. 234), must now be considered a form of State enterprise. Septimius Severus marks an important stage in this development (see above, p. 27 *sq*.). State-ownership of land, which had already been increased by confiscations in the second half of the first century, was again extended by him and the military anarchy. The working of imperial domains had been practised in the Hellenistic age, especially under the Ptolemies: that model was followed by Rome and this in its turn generally encouraged the adoption of the system of the colonate. In the second and third centuries, however, not only was the State (or the emperor) the largest landed proprietor, it was also the biggest owner of mines and quarries, and in course of time came to be the greatest industrialist, having gained control of a specific category of industries. This last development results from an extension of organizations which had existed from the beginnings of imperial times to supply the needs of the court, the army, and the State (such as mints, builders' yards, brick-kilns, textile-mills, iron-foundries, and occasionally armourers' workshops). Governmental arms-manufactories in great numbers were now erected in the proximity of the emperor and his army, and there was an increase in the imperial production of wool and linen, of low and high grade textiles and clothing which involved an expansion in the purple dye-works. Though we have evidence for this process in the opening years of the third century (p. 273), it presumably falls in its more intense form in the second half of the third century and reaches its final development in the fourth. As a result the State could more and more provide for its own needs and so could substitute the compulsory contributions in kind which were supplied by private skilled labour[1]. A system of forced labour was imposed on the workers in the manufactories, in much the same way as on workers for the Ptolemaic State-monopolies or on *coloni*, and they were organized on a semi-military basis. They were employed either in imperial workshops, or, as in the case of the weavers, at home. The materials were furnished to them, being partly procured through taxation in kind; a fixed amount of work was allotted to them and duly collected.

It has already been mentioned that trade—wholesale and retail—became increasingly subject to governmental control. Severus

---

[1] See above, p. 263. P. Lips. 57 (A.D. 261); P. Oxy. XII, 1414 (A.D. 270–5), 1–16.

Alexander and Aurelian by this means, together with the quicken-ing of the old idea of *euthenia*, put the supply of vital necessities to Rome, which had been threatened, on a secure basis[1]. The same is true of other cities, as those of Egypt[2]. This develop-ment could link up with the remains of hellenistic retail trade-monopolies (*e.g.* of oil in Egypt[3]), and also with the old production-monopolies—both of which in the intervening im-perial era had been modified into a system of concessions[4]. Supply by means of *anabolicae species* meant nationalization. Transport was also largely nationalized[5]. All this intervention, and the direct participation of the State in economic activities with the aid of forced and often highly recalcitrant labour[6], represents a drift towards Oriental forms of economic organiza-tion. Yet they arose, not from any ideological considerations (for such considerations were not in fact primary at all in the emer-gence of State-socialism), but from the struggle with the problems of finance and employment. This is why limits were fixed to direct State participation in economic activity, so that this, generally speaking, went no further than was dictated by the need to secure essential supplies for the army, the court, and the imperial officials, and thus, to take a single example, the organization of the textile industry as a whole was neither nationalized (*i.e.* made into a monopoly), nor was nationalization intended[7]. That no principle was involved is shown by the fact that denationalization is also to be found in both agriculture and industry. Thus State-owned land in the neighbourhood of the German *limes* was allowed to relapse into private ownership in the third century, and State-owned land lying barren and uncultivated in Egypt was offered for sale. Corroborative testimony is to be found in the supplanting of the State enterprise in the British mining industry by private contractors (p. 291).

A second characteristic feature of the age is the advance of feudal economy. We are dealing here partly with the maintenance and further development of conditions which prevailed in the

---

[1] S.H.A. *Alex. Sev.* 33, 2; *Aurel.* 46–8.

[2] *E.g.* P. Oxy. XII, 1455 (A.D. 275).

[3] Stud. Pal. XXII, no. 177 (A.D. 137); P. Oxy. XII, 1455 (A.D. 275). Cf. P. Gnomon (probably of the reign of Antoninus Pius), §102.

[4] See vol. X, p. 386 *sq.*

[5] S.H.A. *Aurel.* 47, 3.

[6] S.H.A. *Aurel.* 38, 2.

[7] For a private weapon-manufactory worked by slaves as late as the end of the fourth century see Libanius, *Or.* XLII, 21 and *passim*.

first and second centuries. Hence we find *latifundia* on the Italian model, such as have been described above (p. 238 *sq.*), besides indigenous great estates among the Celts, in South Russia and elsewhere, and landed property which the city bourgeoisie acquired or the veterans earned and which they exploited at first as 'agricolae boni' by intensive cultivation, but gradually came to run by non-specialized large-scale production (pp. 250, 254). Those of this old-established wealthy class who were adaptable and knew how to move with the times were able to maintain themselves in the face of the difficulties of the third century, and actually gained more than they lost. In the third century there appeared beside them the class of *nouveaux riches*. It was composed of men who had understood how to turn the troubled times and their position in the new State to their own advantage, and to secure immunity from economic burdens for themselves. They rose to power not so much as *homines oeconomici* by virtue of their commercial ability and business energy, as the old bourgeoisie had done, but rather by unscrupulousness, extortion, bribery, and exploitation of the political constellation of the moment, though it is true that business initiative was united to those qualities. Soldiers and officers, officials, large contractors, profiteers, and speculators of every kind made up this category. In Italy, Gaul, Germany, Britain, the Danubian regions, Africa, Egypt, Syria and Palestine, the province of Asia, and, in fact, throughout the Empire, large estates became increasingly common in the third century, whether the property was long in the same hands or newly acquired, whether the land was public or private in origin, whether the soil was good or bad, and they gradually imprinted their mark on the age. The feudalism, which had been predominant at the end of the Republican era, began to return; the chief change being that this new feudalism was not so much a city phenomenon as the old, but began to withdraw more and more to the land. The owners lived with increasing frequency amidst their *coloni* and the artisans of the estate in the villas themselves, as the splendid remains in the Moselle valley, in Britain, and in Africa show. In the villas goods were produced in the first instance to meet the producers' own needs (in providing the essentials of food and clothing and material for building and packing), but there was also production for the State (as taxes in kind), and for the market. Manufactories for processing the wool, brick-works and potteries for utilizing the clay, had associated themselves with agriculture as subsidiary forms of production. Mines were also in the hands of the great landlords, and on occasion they held fairs in the villages they owned[1]. The period of anarchy and of the crisis in currency encouraged *oikos*-economy and the industrialization of the villas, together with the abandonment of the cities and their unpleasant atmosphere, so that in the fourth and fifth centuries a closed house-economy became ultimately the customary system.

The greater the spread of State and feudal economy typifying the new system, the greater the decline in an economy based on a free peasantry and on the city. Yet decline did not mean destruction. There was a free peasantry in the third century, as also at a later date[2]—quite apart from the soldier peasantry created under the Severi—and city life also continued. Yet both cities and peasantry suffered appallingly for reasons that need not be repeated here. The economic structure as a whole was even more affected by the fatal decline of city economy than by the dying out of the free middle-class peasantry. The storm of political disasters which burst over those who had no political power, the intervention of the State and its use of compulsion, the general insecurity[3] affecting currency and communications in particular, the deterioration and closing of roads, the commandeering of shipping by the State, the permanent contraction of the available market through the decay of the consumer class in the cities, through provincial 'autarky,' and through the State and the feudal landlords meeting their own needs in their own closed system, and, last not least, the contraction in the resources of unfree labour—such are the factors which undermined the foundations of the old city economy, which crippled enterprise and initiative, and which prevented the growth of capital. Where urbanization had set in relatively late (as for instance in Britain), it was more and more rapidly reversed than elsewhere, yet there too in the course of the third century city economy (in the East to a less, in the West to a greater degree) was forced to give ground to such an extent that the part it plays in the fourth century is only of minor importance. This economy could not be wholly destroyed simply because the cities, though impoverished, continued in being, and accordingly there still existed a demand on the part of the city population, though admittedly it was for cheap articles. Moreover, the *oikos*-economy of the feudal landlords never became complete, so that they (like the wholesale dealers, to whom we shall return presently) stood in need of luxuries which naturally

---

[1] *I.G.R.R.* iv, 1381 (*c.* A.D. 260); cf. Bruns, *Fontes*[7], 61 (A.D. 138).

[2] Cf. the Egyptian peasantry; M. Gelzer, *Stud. zur byz. Verwaltung Ägyptens*, p. 75.

[3] S.H.A. *Prob.* 20, 5 (*mox secura res p.*); 23, 3.

could not be manufactured in the *oikos* but called for specialists who would normally live in the city. So city production of a kind remained, those responsible for it being on the whole of the artisan class. Even more indispensable was the part played by the city through retailers and pedlars, and above all in the wholesale trade, which, indeed, no longer dealt in mass-produced articles but in luxuries, for which there was a considerable demand from the feudal landlords and potentates, a demand met not only by the neighbouring city, but also by remote parts including foreign countries. These facts explain why a respected independent bourgeois class of wholesale merchants could maintain itself in the cities, especially in the old commercial centres of Gaul, Syria, Egypt, and Asia Minor (but also in Britain and Germany), even though the significance of the country markets for the supply of local needs increased.

Another very important change in the economic system concerns its methods and concentration. A more primitive economy emerges. There is a decline in bourgeois intensive capitalistic production, while older forms indigenous to the land reappear. Full capitalistic development—if we survey the whole field of ancient economic history—was only an interlude. The State and feudal organization of agriculture was less thorough and hence less productive. Industry relapsed into small-scale production (work in the home, work for wages, skilled craftsmanship which was practised also by itinerant craftsmen[1]). An exception is to be found in the industry of the large estates on occasion, and more especially in State industry, which offered serious competition to private industry in supplying the demands of the government and the army, and which necessarily involved a curtailment of the part to be played by the private producer. There is a further decline in quality, except for articles which are definitely to be regarded as luxuries for the upper class. As with quality so with quantity: production becomes less intense. Arable land lies fallow, not only in Italy but also elsewhere—in Egypt, for example, where land belonging to the State was forced upon cities to secure its cultivation (p. 265). The land was exhausted by over-cultivation, but the chief trouble was the lack of labour. Egyptian vineyards fall into decay[2], and at the end of the third century the Egyptian irrigation system has ceased to function[3]. In the mines, as on the

---

[1] Many examples in *Ed. Diocl. de pretiis*, on which see Gummerus in P.W. *s.v.* Industrie und Handel, cols. 1527 *sqq.*

[2] Stud. Pal. xx, no. 58, col. II, ll. 11 *sqq.* (A.D. 266).

[3] P. Oxy. XII, 1409 (A.D. 278); P. Thead. 16 (A.D. 307).

land, there is a shortage of labour, with which the monetary crisis of the third century may perhaps be connected. An actual exhaustion of the mines themselves (as happened to some extent in the Spanish tin-workings) is secondary by comparison. A marked gap was naturally left by the loss from Aurelian's time of the output from the Dacian mines. Under these circumstances the encouragement by the emperors of mining for precious metals is comprehensible.

The position of industry was unfavourable. We have already referred to the weakness of Italian industry, and of the Gallic potteries. In this connection the German invasions did incalculable damage. Egyptian industry, which through forced contribution had been further limited and regulated, also suffered. Like the Shepherds' revolts in earlier times, the invasion of the Blemmyes in the third century and later and the risings of Firmus under Aurelian and of Achilleus under Diocletian did immense harm. Devastations, and decline in production, naturally had repercussions on commerce. The destruction of Palmyra (273) dealt a fatal blow to that city's famous trade. At an even earlier date the Gothic invasions of the Crimea were similarly destructive to the South-Russian trade. In these chaotic conditions 'autarky' spread. Britain emancipated herself. The obstacles to the interchange of goods did not yet affect internal trade—which entered on a decline in the fourth and fifth centuries in the course of the development of oikos-economy—but their consequences were marked in the interprovincial and export trades. The preferential treatment accorded to the interests of the army and the State endangered in Italy and elsewhere the import of supplies from other parts of the Empire, and created conditions of famine[1]. The Indian trade deteriorated, as the coins show, trade with Germany suffered as a result of the depreciation of the currency (see above, p. 257), and the Eastern trade was further handicapped by the elimination of Palmyra. Thus there was a quantitative decline in trade. Moreover, its forms grew simpler; barter and natural economy became commoner in view of the calamities which befell the currency in the second half of the century; and the fact that the commercial centres were frequently transferred into the country (see pp. 271, n. 3, 293) hardly suggests enhanced commercial activity. There was thus a marked retrogression in the former commercial interdependence which had been so strikingly characteristic of earlier times. It gave place to a resolution into individual lands and

---

[1] S.H.A. *Aurel.* 48, 1 (Rome). Cf. Rostovtzeff, *op. cit.* p. 618, n. 39; Germ. ed. II, p. 359.

regions which desired to achieve a substantial degree of self-sufficiency. Throughout the Empire a state of crisis made its presence felt, gradually arising and becoming increasingly acute down to the time of Aurelian and Diocletian, and affecting economic life in Egypt, Syria, Asia Minor, the Danubian region, Gallo-Germany, Spain, and Africa, just as profoundly as in Cyrene, Greece, or Italy.

Yet exaggeration must be avoided; and these statements require qualification at numerous points. Thus the recession was not universal, nor was its incidence everywhere on the same scale. The chief exception is Britain, whose peak of development, as we have seen (p. 240), was attained precisely in the third and fourth centuries. This paradox is connected with the country's situation on the periphery of the Empire, and with the fact that its economic development is, relatively speaking, deeply rooted in indigenous forms. British agriculture, pottery, mining, iron and textile industry were flourishing, as was the trade within the province, so that in addition to owners of large estates, wealthy and independent business men and tradesmen were seen. African agriculture with its fields of olives and corn was by no means ruined in the third century, even in its second half, and Egyptian agriculture also survived (p. 252). The Syrian-Palmyrene trade maintained itself in a critical era under the protection of the Palmyrene kingdom[1], and Antioch remained a prosperous city even after the abandoning of Doura and the capture of Palmyra (p. 305). The Alexandrine usurper Firmus was a very well-to-do wholesale trader, who dispatched his ships to India, and who appears also to have had connections with the paper industry[2]. Diocletian's edict de pretiis, which in the version known to us was meant to apply to the Eastern half of the Empire, also fixes the prices for a series of Western textile products, and this evidence allows us to infer that some degree of interdependence between the various parts of the Empire still continued in existence. There are further considerations to be entered on the credit side. The development of land on an emphyteutic tenure is found (p. 252). Moreover, the system of State economy with planned production cannot be arbitrarily condemned as primitive and inefficient in view, for example, of hellenistic evidence disproving this verdict, though it is undeniable that the best age of the Ptolemies

---

[1] For a Palmyrene trading association *I.G.R.R.* III, 1045 = *O.G.I.S.* 646 (between A.D. 263/4 and 266/7).
[2] S.H.A. *Quad. tyr.* (*Firmus*, etc.) 3, 2 *sqq.* For Indian embassies see p. 271, n. 4.

introduced the private initiative of high capitalism to bolster up the system. Indeed, the State manufactories at the close of our period can point to a high level of achievement. Moreover, the system of payments in kind, which comes into evidence in the course of the century and has attracted much attention, has recently been shown[1] to have been by no means general, and furthermore not to be regarded as primitive without qualification, since it originates in the conscious attempt to secure a sufficiency of the necessities of life for State functionaries while temporarily dispensing with a coinage whose values fluctuated so violently.

So we come to the decisive witness. If after the political re-consolidation at the end of the third and the beginning of the fourth century, and after the social-political re-alignments in the fourth century, there was a relatively quick economic recovery, this implies that during the time of the great crisis enough must have been preserved for it to be possible to take up the threads anew, in much the same way as Attic economy took up the threads after the crisis of the Peloponnesian War. There can be no denying the upward trend in the fourth century. Gaul and Germany flourished, especially after Trèves became an imperial residence. The wealth of the Gallic and German, and also of the British, African, Syrian, and Egyptian great landed proprietors was enormous. The Egyptian irrigation system began once more to function. The Gallo-German industry, which met the demands of the army, was expanding. Industrial production in Syria reached a high level, as a glance at Diocletian's edict or the *Expositio totius mundi* shows[2]. Interprovincial and international trade revived with the restoration of security, though in accordance with the evidence cited above it was essentially a speculative luxury trade. In the ports of Gaul, Asia Minor, Syria, and Egypt, activity returned in the fourth century. The trade with the East and the South-east, which had not wholly died out in the third century, along the routes to Persia, Abyssinia, Arabia, India, and China, increased in volume despite the destruction of Palmyra and Doura. Admittedly the standard of the second century was not reached again. Fiscalism, *angareiai*, and inflation had remained; and the generally primitive character of the forms of production was a further legacy from the past. Moreover the economic system was unbalanced, in marked contrast to the previously prevailing conditions. It was unbalanced territorially, because the countries, if we disregard the demand for luxuries, had resolved themselves into separate economic

---

[1] Mickwitz, *op. cit.* pp. 165 *sqq.*   [2] Cf. also Libanius, *Or.* XLII, 21.

organisms to a far greater extent than was previously the case. And it was unbalanced socially because a large number of poor or impoverished and oppressed peasants and townspeople, whose feelings found expression on occasion in revolts (such as African Donatism at the beginning of the fourth century), stood opposed to a much diminished group (when compared with its previous size), made up of exploiters and also partly of speculators.

Such were the consequences of a system called into being by State-socialism. Yet during this historical process, as even the last piece of evidence indicates, a revolt makes itself felt against the economic principles around which the system was constructed. Every age contains within itself both the old and the germ of the new (p. 255). As State-socialism had been a reaction against exaggerated individualism, so now in opposition to exaggerated State-socialism a new individualism arose represented by the feudal landlords. Among this class were to be found not only those who had derived their strength from the State, but also others who had grown strong partly by opposition to it. How many of the great landed proprietors on the borders of Germany, Mauretania, Syria, Asia Minor, and even of Italy itself, when the Empire proved incapable of defending them, had been forced, like the estate owners of South Russia in the face of the onslaught of the Goths[1], to fight for their lives with the aid of the levies raised from among their own *coloni*! In fact, they acted in the same way with their limited resources as a Postumus or a Zenobia had done on a grand scale. Naturally such action increased their power. It is interesting, however, to observe that even those who exploited the State-socialist system for their own benefit, when they had become powerful enough, appeared in the ranks of the State's opponents. For this is what it amounts to when the powerful feudal landowners exploit the superiority of their economic position *vis-à-vis* to subordinate State officials in order to escape from the taxation and services due to the government. The result was to make still more marked their economic advantage, and to make still heavier the burdens of the weak, who had finally no other resource but to take refuge from the State in the *patrocinium* of the potentates (including the Church) and thereby still further enhance the patron's prestige. This tendency made its appearance in the third century[2] and reaches its

---

[1] Rostovtzeff, *op. cit.* pl. xxxvi, Germ. Ed. ii, pl. xxxviii.

[2] *E.g.* for Egypt: Preisigke, *Sammelb.* 4284 (A.D. 207); Heroninus correspondence, P. Flor. ii (see the Introduction), middle of the third century; P. Oxy. xii, 1424 (*c.* A.D. 318).

full development at the end of the fourth century and the beginning of the fifth.

Such, then, were the imperious barons who could and did set themselves up in opposition to State-socialism. The large estates, as we saw, owed their origin not only to pressure from the government but also to private initiative. Moreover it was the individualistic aristocratic class which salved a considerable part of the ancient culture, whose traditions were still maintained on the estates (as also in the Christian Church), and with it some part of the ancient economic system. Accordingly this class undertook the rôle played by the old bourgeoisie to a greater degree than did the survivors of that bourgeoisie themselves. It must be admitted, however, that in the course of this process there was an increasing tendency to pass from bourgeois city culture and economy to their feudal-rural equivalents. This change, however, in spite of a certain limited return to an age in which individualistically-minded feudal landlords and the Roman State had once held the balance between them, and in spite of all survivals down to the Turkish era—marks the real end of the ancient world.

CHAPTER VIII

BRITAIN

I. CITIES, VILLAS, VILLAGES

IN this chapter an attempt is made to sketch the state of Britain, apart from political and military affairs, in the third and fourth centuries. It would be unnatural, in the case of Britain, to follow rigidly the rule of this volume and end with Constantine the Great; enough is therefore said about the later fourth century to indicate the general lines along which events were moving at the close of the Roman occupation; but there is no need here to discuss the social and economic conditions of early fifth-century Britain in detail.

The close of the Antonine age divides the history of Roman Britain into two parts, each with a well-marked character of its own. Thanks to Haverfield's collection and sifting of evidence concerning villas[1] it has long been known that, so far as these are concerned, the graph of British prosperity was rising throughout the third century to a climax in the fourth; and as lately as the time when Rostovtzeff wrote his *Social and Economic History of the Roman Empire*[2] it could be argued on this ground that Britain formed an unexplained exception to the general rule, according to which the third century was an age of depression and bankruptcy all over the Empire. Since then, the excavations carried out at Verulam, one of the chief towns of Britain and in the heart of its most peaceful district, have altered the perspective in which the evidence of the villas must be placed.

Verulam, when its magnificent walls were laid out under Hadrian, was a large and rapidly-growing town[3]. It continued to grow for some time, but reached its high-water mark about the end of the second century, and a decline set in. By the middle of the century, the process of decay has become evident. By about 275 the walls were to some extent in ruins, the theatre had fallen into disuse and was being quarried for building-materials, and so severe was the general dilapidation that, as the excavator writes,

---

[1] In the various Romano-British chapters of the *Victoria County Histories*; cf. especially those on Hampshire and Somerset.

[2] See chaps. IX–XI for that author's general view of the third century. For the statement quoted about Britain, see p. 422.

[3] R. E. M. Wheeler, *Verulamium*, pp. 26–28.

Verulam 'must at this time have borne some resemblance to a bombarded city.' The proximate cause of this condition can hardly have been foreign invasion or civil war: it must have been sheer economic exhaustion.

In the light of these new facts, others long familiar gain fresh significance. At Wroxeter the great Hadrianic forum was burnt down about 160 and rebuilt[1]. About the end of the third century it was burnt down again, and lay thereafter in ruins. Here, as at Verulam, the third century saw prosperity give place to exhaustion. Evidence of a similar kind, but undated, has been found elsewhere. At Silchester, some of the best houses fell at some time into slum-conditions, when people lit their cooking-fires on tessellated pavements. At Caerwent, the sites of deserted and ruined houses were used for the erection of an amphitheatre within the walls. It is tempting to conjecture that the decay of Silchester and Caerwent may have happened, like that of Verulam and Wroxeter, in the third century; but even without this conjecture the evidence of a catastrophe affecting town-life during that century is clear. Britain was not exempt from the 'rapid and disastrous decay' which elsewhere overtook the cities of the Roman world.

The ultimate causes of this decay are a matter of general Roman history and lie outside the subject of this chapter. But there is evidence from Britain supporting Rostovtzeff's view that it was connected with a reversal of Imperial policy: that whereas earlier emperors had subsidized and protected urban life, Severus and his successors looked upon towns as convenient reservoirs of wealth, easily tapped to defray the general expenses of the Empire. The evidence consists of certain small inscriptions on Hadrian's Wall, implying that parts of it were built at their own charges by the tribal authorities of Britain and that these parts belong to the Severan reconstruction rather than to Hadrian's original work. The tribes named are the Catuvellauni whose capital was Verulam, the Durotriges, and possibly (the stone is lost and the reading corrupt) the Brigantes. The demand for such contributions towards the defence of the country must in any case have borne hardly on the tribal cities, whose prosperity had depended more on official encouragement than on spontaneous growth; and it was even more significant in what it ultimately implied than in what it immediately entailed. For ultimately it implied that the central government was tired of fostering an urban civilization; and, in Britain at least, town-life was not strongly enough rooted to survive

[1] The excavations (1924–7) are still unpublished; but see Sir G. Macdonald, *Roman Britain* 1914–1928, pp. 89–97.

the change. The first phase of romanization, when romanization meant urbanization, was over. The history of the third and fourth centuries is the history of a second phase, when Britain was evolving a new form of civilization, Roman or Romano-Celtic in style, but no longer urban in structure.

As thus stated, the position is no doubt over-simplified. The cities did not cease to exist; politically and juridically they still served as centres of local government, and they even retained some economic importance as centres of industry. Here and there, especially in outlying regions, there was actually an increase of urban prosperity, as in the little frontier-town of Corbridge[1], whose industrial activity mainly dates from after the time of Severus. And the general decay of town-life was not uniformly accepted by the central government as inevitable: on the contrary, we find Constantius Chlorus making heroic efforts to restore Verulam[2] to its earlier grandeur, and similar efforts were made elsewhere; but their effects were not proportionate to the labour and cost expended. The days when the city was economically and culturally the focus of civilization were gone for good.

In the second phase of romanization, the centre of interest lies in the villa. This was an isolated farm-house standing in the middle of its own land, a block of dwelling-house and outbuildings, generally more or less rectangular in shape, enclosing a farm-yard, not unlike the farm-steadings that exist to-day in parts of England where the population is not concentrated in villages. The isolated farm is typical of Celtic agriculture, and there is reason to think that the Romano-British villa-system owed some of its characteristic features to the scattered farms of the pre-Roman country-side. In certain cases, such pre-Roman farms have been transformed into villas by a process of architectural and cultural romanization; evidently their owners, substantial and independent yeomen, were ready to welcome Roman ways of living and rich enough to pay for their fancy without government subsidies. In that sense the rise of villas was a more spontaneous movement than the rise of towns; and because more spontaneous, it proved more lasting. Sometimes no doubt a villa was the bailiff's residence on an Imperial domain; sometimes it was built by a speculator taking up uninhabited land on favourable terms; but these were the exceptions. As a rule, villa-dwellers were British farmers, large or small, who romanized their houses and themselves of their own free will. The largest among them were

[1] Cf. G. S. Keeney, 'Corstopitum as a civil centre,' *Archaeologia Aeliana*, ser. 4, xi, 1934, p. 158.   [2] Wheeler, *op. cit.* p. 29.

no doubt also those same tribal grandees who carried out the public business of the tribe in the cities, and these would presumably have town-houses as well as their villas in the country.

The rise of the villa-system, or perhaps we should say the systematic romanization of the British farm, was a thing of slow growth. It began very soon after the Claudian invasion, but throughout the second century it was only gathering momentum; even in the fourth, new villas were being built and old ones enlarged. There is some evidence of a special boom in the early third century, and it is difficult not to connect this with the simultaneous check in the growth of towns. If, as has been suggested, the government's new predatory attitude induced the higher classes to conceal their wealth as far as possible, they would live more on their country estates, and allow their town-houses to fall into disrepair and use them as little as possible; while those whose duties did not call them to the town would retire to the country altogether.

This movement into the country must have been further stimulated by the monetary crisis of the late third century[1]. The violent rise of prices accompanying that event must have made the ordinary operations of household marketing all but impossible. In towns, food and all kinds of necessaries must have become unprocurable; but families living on their own estates could keep themselves in almost all the necessaries of life independently of fluctuations in prices, and this was an additional motive for living in the country. For the villa was to a great extent self-supporting; and what it could not produce for itself (pottery, window-glass, ironmongery, and so forth) it could probably at a pinch obtain by barter, exchanging its own surplus produce. This may partially account for the way in which many villas tended to develop into small industrial establishments, smelting lead, working iron, fulling cloth, making tiles, and so forth. This industrialization of the villa was never so widespread and seldom so thoroughgoing in Britain as it was in Belgium, but it was far from rare, and must have been valuable when money became an insecure means of exchange.

When the Diocletianic re-organization of the Empire introduced a new age of peace and prosperity, within whose radius Britain was drawn by the work of Constantius Chlorus, a fresh attempt was made to stimulate the moribund cities, but the villas could profit by the new conditions without any artificial aid. The stormy times of the third century had taught the Britons how to

---

[1] Rostovtzeff, *Soc. and Econ. Hist.* pp. 419–21.

live quietly and comfortably on the land; now that times were better, the chief difference was that they lived more luxuriously. This seems to have been the age when villas were largest and most sumptuous. In some, there are as many as thirty or forty living-rooms, surrounding an inner courtyard away from the noise and smell of the farm-buildings; these larger villas are placed with a keen appreciation of the value of soils, slopes, and exposure to sun, and planned with a degree of spaciousness and elegance not to be matched again until the eighteenth century; while their decoration is up to the highest standards of Roman Imperial art. This prosperous country-house life was much promoted by the establishment of a sound currency; in many Romano-British villas the Constantinian coins outnumber all the rest put together. It was also promoted by the financial policy of the age, which favoured large estates at the expense of small, and tended to make rich men richer. But it was not created by these conditions. It was the farm-system of the pre-Roman Britons, passed through a triple process of change: first, owing to its adaptability, acquiring a romanized form; secondly, owing to its solidity, surviving the economic crisis of the third century; and thirdly, left now alone in the field, profiting by the new prosperity of the Constantinian age.

The history of the villa-system after the middle of the fourth century is obscure. In a great many villas, the coins found cease between 350 and 370. It has been argued that this points to a widespread destruction of them—in fact, the virtual extinction of the villa-system—in the invasions of which the most severe was perhaps the barbarian incursions of c. 367. But certain recent excavations suggest that, had the majority of our villas been more expertly dug, evidence of a much longer occupation might have been found; while the autobiography of St Patrick strikingly shows how such invaders, in a long-continued series of raids, may avoid killing the goose that lays them the golden eggs. Alternative hypotheses are therefore, in the present state of our knowledge, worth considering.

Even if the invasions of the late fourth and early fifth centuries did not destroy the villas, they certainly made the roads unsafe and so did much to ruin the system of trade which (as we shall see later) had grown up on the decay of the town markets. The effect of this would be to intensify the self-supporting character of the villa, and teach it to do without many things which hitherto carters and pedlars had brought to its doors. In consequence it would stand less and less in need of money, and would tend to revert towards an altogether moneyless economy.

The same consequence would be produced by something for which we have abundant evidence in Gaul and which can hardly have been absent from Britain, namely brigandage by revolted peasants and broken men. These Bagaudae (as they were called in Gaul) were an inevitable product of fourth-century economic conditions. Every recruit to their bands meant another man withdrawn from productive labour and living henceforth by robbery; and where they were numerous the wealth of the villas, and in particular their trading capacity, must have suffered proportionally. The cessation of coins in villas can thus be accounted for without assuming either violent destruction or even disastrous impoverishment. All that need be assumed is that, owing to foreign invasion and civil disorder, the villas were being reduced to the economic status of self-supporting households.

After the decay of the towns, the villas, even including their entire staff of labourers and their families, can hardly have contained five per cent. of the population, and of the rest the great majority must have been agricultural peasants. Originally these may have been to a great extent members of legally and economically independent village-communities; but the changes of the Imperial age, especially in its later phases, must have reduced them to a servile status, dependent on wealthy landowners, speculative capitalists, or the managers of Imperial domains. They lived in villages, amorphous clusters of one-roomed huts, fenced against wild animals; their main occupation was mixed farming, the cultivation of crops (mostly wheat) in little rectangular or irregular fields and the pasturing of livestock in the open country beyond. Here and there, especially in the well-known Cranborne Chase villages dug by Pitt-Rivers, they were a good deal influenced by Roman ways of living; but for the most part their romanization was hardly above the vanishing-point, and they lived, so far as material civilization was concerned, much as their prehistoric ancestors had lived before them. In certain districts, especially the Fens, there was a great rise of peasant population during the Roman period, due in this case to large-scale drainage which can hardly have originated in anything but capitalistic enterprise. Elsewhere, notably in Wiltshire, whole villages died out in the fourth or even the late third century, perhaps through the deliberate transplantation of their inhabitants. This again may possibly be connected with the growth of the woollen industry, to which we shall return. Arable land cannot be turned into sheep-walks without depopulation.

We have seen that the third and fourth centuries were an age of individualistic farming, which tended to the creation of larger and larger estates. We shall see that the same tendency is visible in the sphere of industry. Under these conditions, the wealthier individuals reached a high degree of comfort and prosperity. But the smaller men, and especially the old village-communities, paid the price for these developments by being reduced to the status of a proletariate. Not only was their condition unimproved by the general prosperity, it was depressed by it. The contrast between rich and poor was not only a contrast in wealth and comfort, it became increasingly a contrast between security and insecurity. It was not enough to be poor; the poor were exploited and oppressed in a thousand ways, which the Gaulish writers of the late Imperial age have described in burning phrases. They took their revenge by revolt and brigandage, and thus joined hands with the barbarians in overthrowing the civilization that had oppressed them.

The chief conclusion which has emerged from this survey is that the replacement of the town by the villa as the main vehicle of romanization really means the replacement of State initiative by individual initiative in the promotion of civilized and romanized life. The towns represent romanization as the central government wished to have it; the villas represent it in the shape in which it commended itself to the individual British landowner. If we turn to industry, we shall see a similar change going on.

II. INDUSTRIES AND TRADE

To begin with mining and metallurgy. The gold-mine of Dolaucothy, the only one of which we know, belongs to the early part of the Roman period; there is no indication that it continued to be worked during the later centuries. Perhaps the payable deposits were by then exhausted. The same cannot be true of the argentiferous lead-ores in the Mendips and elsewhere; for these have had a great history since Roman times; but it is a curious fact that all the lead pigs, which are the chief testimony to the Roman working of these ores, belong to the first and second centuries. Did lead-mining cease after that time?

The mining-settlement at Charterhouse-on-Mendip has yielded relics of the first and second centuries; in the third, they become rare. Similarly, the lead-working village at Pentre in Flintshire seems hardly to have lived beyond the second century. On the other hand, the Roman objects found in connection with lead-mines in the Matlock district become commonest in the fourth century, though there are no pigs of that time. The inference seems to be that after the Antonine period lead-mining went on, and in some districts with increased intensity; but that in some way the organization of it was modified. During the early period, to judge from the pigs, it was a State monopoly; but the Derbyshire pigs show that in some cases the industry was leased to *conductores*; and it is at least possible that the total lack of pigs dating from the third and fourth centuries indicates a still further development by which the mines came into the hands of comparatively small lessees, no longer important enough to issue pigs stamped with their own names, but carrying on the industry, effectively enough, by independent work at scattered sites all over the lead-fields. It has been suggested[1] that the numerous and large hoards of late fourth-century silver coin found in and about the Mendips are a testimony (despite the absence of confirmation from Charterhouse) to continued prosperity among the lead-miners of that region down to the last phase of the Roman occupation, the coin flowing into the mining-district in cash payment for lead produced there; and this would suit well with the hypothesis that centralized State exploitation had been superseded by a system in which small miners or groups of miners worked for their own hand.

Iron-mining, too, went on. The slag-heaps of the Weald show evidence of working throughout the Roman period: in some there are signs of renewed and intensified activity, perhaps after a gap, in the third and especially the fourth centuries. In the Forest of Dean mining went on until early in the fourth century: the one excavated iron-mine, however, on the hill of Nodens at Lydney (p. 296), was not worked after the third, and seems to have been occupied by a very primitive community dealing little in coin and doing its trade by barter. On the whole, the evidence suggests that iron-working continued to flourish in one district or another throughout these later centuries, but was in the hands of independent miners and metallurgists working for the most part on a small scale and in somewhat primitive conditions.

The case of tin is peculiar. Early in the Roman period, a few short-lived and isolated attempts were made by Roman settlers to exploit the Cornish ores, but this had come to an end before the middle of the second century. About 250, however, the Spanish tin-mines closed down, and supplies had to be sought elsewhere. A boom in Cornwall was the almost immediate result. Roads were built by the emperors of the late third and early fourth

---

[1] By [Sir] Arthur J. Evans, 'Notes on the Coinage and Silver Currency in Britain,' in *Num. Chron.* ser. IV, XV, 1915, p. 433.

centuries; Roman coin flowed into Cornwall in large quantities; and dinner-services of tin and pewter began to be fashionable in British villas. How was this revived industry organized? An ingot of tin from Carnanton was thought by Haverfield to bear the stamped letters DD NN, which would indicate State property[1]; but metallurgical experts who have re-examined it lately are unable to see the letters, nor are they visible to the present writer in Haverfield's photograph; and unless the reading can be verified we should be wise to assume that here, too, the ores were worked by independent miners, operating by themselves or in small groups, whose sale of their produce (as in the case of the Mendip hoards) would account for the influx of Roman coin.

Another industry of which something is known during this period is pottery. In the first and second centuries the pottery of ordinary domestic use in Britain falls almost without residue into two classes: the high-class 'Samian' ware imported from Gaul, and the coarse pottery of local manufacture. As long as the Gaulish factories supplied the luxury demand, little was expected of the local potters except cheap and serviceable goods; but the collapse of the 'Samian' industry in the third century gave an opening to any British potter who could put on the market something rather more ornamental and refined. For the most part, the local potters failed to take their opportunity; to do so implied special conditions in the shape of good clay and high technical skill; but here and there such conditions were present, and industries grew up capable of supplying the demand for dinner-table wares. The two best-known examples are those of the Nene valley and the New Forest[2]. In the Nene valley, the industry goes back to the late second century, but its great period is the third and fourth, and during the greater part of that period its prosperity was steadily increasing. Excavations at Castor and elsewhere give us a picture of a society of master-potters, men of some wealth, living in genteel houses with good tessellated pavements and the furniture of ordinary well-to-do provincial life, close beside the kilns which were doubtless worked by hired or servile labour under the immediate supervision of its employers. The favourite metallic lustre-ware of the Nene valley works travelled all over the country and did much to replace the vanished 'Samian.'

In the New Forest an equal degree of technical success was accompanied by an altogether different type of organization. Small independent potters lived a semi-nomadic life in the woods,

---

[1] *Proc. Soc. Ant.* XVIII, 1900, pp. 117–22, with plate; *Eph. Epigr.* IX, 1262.   [2] See Volume of Plates v, 154, *a*.

building themselves temporary kilns and sleeping in huts like those of charcoal-burners; each working for his own hand, though in a common tradition, and each peddling his own goods or entrusting them to a middleman hawker. The hard, durable, well-fired pots from these New Forest kilns, often effectively decorated with lustrous glaze or painted patterns or stamped designs[1], circulated widely over the southern districts, though unlike the Nene valley wares they hardly touched the north.

Here, as in the case of mining, we seem to trace in the third and fourth centuries a widespread and flourishing industry based entirely on individual enterprise; sometimes developing features akin to those of a factory-system, but mostly remaining at the level of artisan production. In mining, this individualistic system appears to have superseded the earlier system of State exploitation; in pottery, it developed a new degree of technical skill, concentrated production, and wide distribution, through the breakdown of the Gaulish factories. In order that such a system should be possible, communications must have been good and transport cheap all over the country; for the essence of the system is that certain districts specialized in the kind of products to which they were best adapted, and sold them in a market scattered very widely over the country-side. One result was that the less progressive local potters in face of this competition were either restricted to the production of very cheap and inferior goods or else put out of business altogether. By the fourth century, a large and increasing proportion of the pottery in ordinary use appears to have been thus made by specialists and distributed over wide areas.

One striking example is provided by the blackish, hand-made, calcite-gritted ware which was used in enormous quantities at military sites in the north during the last quarter of the fourth century. It is in many ways primitive, almost prehistoric, in technique, though quite good enough for rough domestic service. The quantities of it that have been found imply a colossal output, and its uniformity suggests a single place of origin: and in recent years one place of origin has been identified at Knapton in Yorkshire. It looks as if, owing to special conditions of market and distribution, a local industry preserving certain very ancient methods of manufacture had suddenly acquired almost a monopoly of providing coarse pots to the northern garrison-troops[2].

The textile industry was developing at the same time along lines to some extent similar. We know of three villas in the south

---

[1] See Volume of Plates v, 154, b.　　　[2] P. Corder and J. L. Kirk, *A Roman villa at Langton, near Malton, E. Yorkshire*, pp. 96–99.

of England which, at some date subsequent to their original building, and therefore probably not earlier than the third century, have been wholly or partly converted into fulling-establishments. The scale of these establishments is far too large for satisfying the needs of a single estate, or even of a single small district. The cloth treated in them must have come from large areas and must have been widely distributed after treatment; in fact we have here archaeological confirmation of the entry about 'British woollen cloaks' in Diocletian's Edict of Prices, implying that the products of the British woollen industry were a staple article of trade in the Empire at large. So far, the industry was presumably run by private persons; but the *Notitia Dignitatum* mentions a *praepositus gynaecii Ventensis* in Britain, that is, the manager of a State cloth-mill presumably at Winchester; which indicates that side by side with the privately-owned industry there was also a State-owned industry, no doubt making up the wool grown on Imperial domain-lands.

The history of trade during these centuries is not unlike that of industry. The early importation of luxury-articles and of things necessary to a romanized life has dwindled to a mere fraction of its former self. Glassware and a certain amount of pottery are coming in from the Rhineland; and a good deal of wine and oil are perhaps still being imported, although home-grown tallow, beer and even (after Probus) wine are much used as substitutes. By the third century, and still more by the fourth, imports would seem to have become quite inconsiderable. Exports consisted, we must assume, mainly of raw materials like iron, lead, leather; also, increasingly, of woollens, and apparently of dogs and perhaps still slaves and cattle on the hoof. The use of British artisans by Constantius Chlorus in Gaul does not indicate an economic demand there for British technical skill, it was doubtless an ordinary administrative *corvée*; and Julian's shipment of British wheat to devastated areas on the Rhine comes similarly under the heading not of trade but of forced levies in kind. In short, apart from a steady trickle of goods across the northern frontier into Caledonia, we have as little reason to think that Britain now exported much as to think that she imported much. She was, in all essentials, self-providing.

Internal trade, however, was very active indeed. The distribution of Castor or New Forest pottery would by itself be sufficient proof. Coal, no doubt from the Somerset mines, freely reached the native villages of Wiltshire. The centralization of such processes as fulling proves either that weavers sent their own cloth

long distances to be fulled or (more likely) that the fullers bought
it up and re-sold it after treatment. All this implies a good and
well-maintained system of communications. Milestones show
that in the third and fourth centuries much care was bestowed on
road-maintenance; and the Fenland waterways carried a heavy
barge-traffic handling pottery from the Nene valley.

But here too there is evidence that the system operating in
the third and fourth centuries differed from that of earlier times.
At first, the chief instrument of internal trade was the town with
its market-place and shops. No doubt, this urban retail trade
required supplements of another kind. We can hardly suppose that
every 'Samian' cup in a Wiltshire village was brought there by a
villager who had ridden or driven to the nearest town to get it.
There must have been itinerant salesmen even when the towns
were at the height of their prosperity. But when the towns de-
cayed, from the early third century onwards, the increasing
volume of internal trade must have flowed almost entirely
through channels which left the town on one side. One of these
was doubtless the itinerant hawker, whether a whole-time middleman or an artisan peddling his own goods: another was the country
market or fair, of which an example has been identified with much
probability at Woodeaton close to Oxford[1]. Thus the failure of the
official Roman urbanizing policy, although that policy was conceived partly in the interests of commerce, did not injure Britain
commercially; a spontaneous growth of independent traders,
small and large, arose all over the country, developing with the
development of individualistic manufacture, and satisfied all the
requirements of internal trade so long as the roads were well kept
and safe for peaceful travellers.

III. ART AND RELIGION

Art in Britain, during the later Roman period, presents a very
curious problem. After the first generation or two from the conquest, the hope of a flourishing Romano-British style, comparable
with those of regions no farther away than the Moselle valley,
died away and vanished for ever. In sculpture, apart from a few
official monuments probably made by foreign workmen, there is
practically nothing after that date except the most barbarous and
incompetent prentice-work. In metal-work, where the Britons
had once been so successful, the remnants of Celtic taste which
still lend interest to the products of the second century disappear

[1] J. G. Milne, 'Woodeaton Coins,' *J.R.S.* XXI, 1931, pp. 101–109.

almost entirely, swamped by the mass-production of goods imitating Continental models. In pottery, the Castor factories have been hailed as repositories of a surviving or reviving Celtic spirit: but their designs are in no sense properly British; they are merely an offshoot of the Romano-Celtic Rhineland style. There is more real spontaneity and charm, less that is merely imitative and sophisticated, in the New Forest designs, but even here it would be an exaggeration to speak of a school of Romano-British art. In a word, the spirit of early British art seems to have been altogether crushed by the uniform culture of the Western Empire. The works of art which the standards of that culture demanded, such as tessellated pavements and painted walls, nowhere show any trace of the ancient Celtic tradition.

None the less, the end of the Roman occupation saw that tradition re-asserting itself and building up a new school of design which was to have a glorious future in the early Christian art of the British Isles. This Celtic revival was not due to the invasion of Britain proper by Picts and Scots free from the contamination of Roman taste; it originated inside the romanized area, and first manifested itself in the celticizing of decorative motives drawn from Roman art. The fact is clear, however we may try to explain it, that the tradition of pre-Roman art was still alive, although submerged. And, paradoxical though it may seem, there is reason to suspect that the vitality of this tradition accounts for the badness of the art which the Britons produced under Roman rule. Celtic art had always been abstract, an art of pure linear pattern; Roman Imperial art was naturalistic, based on representation of human and other natural forms. The Britons, unable to combine these opposite tendencies, never so far forgot their own tradition as to adopt the other with success; when the reason for trying to adopt it was removed, they went back to their own traditional style and were henceforth free to go wherever it led them.

In any attempt to study the religious life of a Roman province, it is necessary to distinguish between the official cults, to which everyone was expected to conform, and the spontaneous practices of the people. Intermediate between these two were cults neither official nor popular, but sectarian: propagating themselves by proselytizing, and demanding of their votaries no mere conformity but a sincere and lively faith.

The official cults, to judge from inscriptions, were kept up throughout our period by military and other officials with singularly little effect on the general habits of the people: little, indeed,

even on those of the army itself. In Gaul, a certain absorption of
the Roman pantheon by the natives is attested by modern place-
names. The lack of any such evidence in Britain may no doubt be
due to the replacement of Celtic place-names by Germanic; but
in Gaul the evidence of place-names is supported by that of
epigraphy, and evidence of this kind, though not wholly absent, is
in Britain rare. There are very few cases in Britain where we have
reason to think temples existed to Juppiter or Mars or Minerva or
Apollo, other than those serving official purposes.

The real religion of the British people was a system of local
cults by which the divinities dwelling in certain places were
worshipped at these places themselves. Originally such a place
was not a built temple, it was (to quote an inscription from Bath)
a *locus religiosus*; and offerings made there were not of such a kind
as to preserve for posterity the name of the god inhabiting it. But,
as time went on, a few of these cults acquired in externals a
certain degree of romanization. During the third and fourth
centuries there arose at many sacred places in the south and south-
east of Britain temples of the kind known as Romano-Celtic: a
small square building surrounded with a portico and having
annexed to it a house for the priest or hermit who tended it. In the
north they do not occur; but we find a parallel phenomenon,
small rudely-made altars after the Roman fashion, dedicated to
this or that local Celtic god: the distribution of the altars enables
us to guess the neighbourhood in which the god's home lay, and
we can thus locate a dozen or more cults. Sometimes the worshippers who dedicated these altars went a step further, and identified the god with some member of the Roman pantheon. But this
can hardly be called romanization in religion; it was a give-and-
take process by which local Celtic worships increased their
celebrity and their following among soldiers and officials, accepting in return certain outward features of Roman religious
practice. Side by side with these local cults there was a system of
rites and festivals based upon the calendar; but for these our
evidence is mostly indirect, gleaned partly from the later institutions of the un-romanized Celtic fringe, and partly from their
survivals in English folk-lore. Of a Celtic pantheon or group of
gods worshipped *semper, ubique, ab omnibus*, Britain yields no trace.
What uniformity these cults possessed was due, not to the existence
of dominating figures like the Juppiter Optimus Maximus of Rome,
but to family likeness among the cults and festivals themselves.

The sectarian religions of Mithras, Sarapis, Isis, Cybele and the
rest can be traced as passing fashions affecting the military and

cosmopolitan elements in the population. Mithraism, the most important of them, became popular among the frontier garrisons in the third century. To suppose that it ever influenced the civil population, or became part of the general religious tradition of the country, is quite unwarranted by what we know of it. (See further below, p. 428.)

From the historian's point of view the appearance of these sectarian cults is interesting chiefly as a *praeparatio evangelica*. Like them, and in competition with them, Christianity began as an Eastern sectarian cult. Statements of Tertullian[1] and Origen[2] imply that it was making headway in Britain in the first half of the third century, and there is no reason to doubt them. At the beginning of the fourth, we have the names of three Britons (Alban of Verulam and Aaron and Julius of Caerleon) who suffered in the Diocletianic persecution, and of three British bishops who attended the Council of Arles in 314. By the time Christianity ceased to be a sect and became the official cult of the Empire, there was thus an organized system of Christian communities in Britain, having in many towns little churches like that which has been excavated at Silchester. It was still the religion of a minority, and a poor minority at that. Even late in the fourth century, the forces of wealth and social rank were still on the side of paganism, and were producing such things as the splendid temple of Nodens on the hill-top of Lydney. The ultimate triumph of Christianity owed nothing to the secular arm; it was achieved after Britain had parted from the Empire, and was the work of churchmen and missionaries, recapturing for Christ what Caesar had already lost.

[1] *adv. Judaeos*, 7.   [2] *in Lucam hom.* 6.

CHAPTER IX

THE IMPERIAL RECOVERY

I. AURELIAN 'RESTITUTOR ORBIS'

WHEN plague laid low the conqueror of the Goths at Sirmium in the January of A.D. 270,[1] his task was still far from ended and the choice of a successor was of vital importance. Quintillus, own brother of Claudius, was the nominee of the Senate, supported no doubt by that part of the army that was with him at Aquileia. But neither legitimacy of succession nor integrity of character could long sustain his position. After a reign of a very few months, of which we know as good as nothing, he succumbed to the man of destiny, Aurelian, who had only to show himself at army-headquarters at Sirmium to secure the voice of the troops. At the death of Claudius he had been engaged in the operations against the Goths, and this preoccupation gave Quintillus time to issue coins in all the imperial mints except Antioch, which, under orders from Zenobia, suspended issue. The news of Aurelian's elevation was the death-warrant of Quintillus, whether or no the sentence was carried out by his own hand.

The new Emperor was of humble birth, perhaps a native of Sirmium, a tough soldier of the new school, trained in the camp and imbued with its ideals. His nickname, 'Hand on hilt' ('Manu ad ferrum'), gives a vivid idea of the impression that he made on his contemporaries. A man of great strength of body and mind, a fine soldier and disciplinarian, he was as deficient in

Note. The main literary sources for this chapter are: the Lives of the several Emperors in the *Historia Augusta*, Aurelius Victor, *Caesares*, the *Epitome de Caesaribus*, Eutropius, Lactantius, *de mortibus persecutorum*, the Panegyrists, Zonaras and Zosimus. Among the fragments some of Dexippus and Petrus Patricius are important. For the evidence of coins, which is especially important in view of the defects of the literary tradition, see in particular, Mattingly and Sydenham, *Roman Imperial Coinage* (M.-S.), vol. v, parts i and ii (by P. H. Webb) and Volume of Plates v, 238, 240, 242. The most important inscriptions are cited in the notes.

[1] Claudius died in January, A.D. 270, and Quintillus reigned for some three months, up to about April 270. Cf. Zosimus, I, 47 (ὀλίγους τε βιώσαντος μῆνας). Are the seventeen days, given by some historians, a confusion with seventy-seven days (Chronographer of A.D. 354)? The coins, which are not uncommon, suggest that the reign lasted months rather than weeks.

tact and flexibility as he was firm in courage and purpose. The long account of his early career in the *Augustan History* makes heavy demands on our credulity,[1] but certainly by the end of the reign of Gallienus he was a leading figure among the Illyrian officers and took a prominent part in the plot against Gallienus and the subsequent execution of Aureolus. Appointed master of the horse by Claudius, he distinguished himself in the great Gothic war and, whether or not marked out by him for the succession,[2] had, as we have seen, no difficulty in securing it after his death. The task awaiting him was one to tax even his powers. The restoration of the Empire, begun by Claudius, was as yet far from complete. The Gallic Empire in the West, the Palmyrenes in the East still marred the imperial unity. If the Danube front was assured, Italy was still exposed to invasion from north and north-east. Behind the problems of military recovery lay those of political and economic life. The government of the provinces, the relation of Emperor and Senate, the ruined coinage—all these demanded attention, as soon as a breathing-space could be obtained from war. The Empire was in a state of transition. The old Empire of the *princeps* and Senate, of Rome and Italy as queens of the provinces, was dead or dying; a new society, with new social and new religious ideals, was being born. If Aurelian was only partially successful, the wonder remains that in so few years, with such limited natural gifts, he could accomplish so much.

For the moment it seemed doubtful whether the new emperor was to be allowed to approach his major tasks. The Juthungi (Scythians) had invaded Italy through Raetia, and Aurelian had to march direct from Sirmium against them. He caught them on their retreat and defeated them as they crossed the Danube. They then sent envoys to minimize this reverse and to demand the customary subsidies. Dexippus well describes their reception in state by Aurelian, in the presence of statues of the deified emperors and of the insignia of the Roman army, and the resolute answer given to their elaborate and sophisticated pleadings. In the end, it seems, they were glad to return home without further

[1] S.H.A. *Aurel.* 3 *sqq.* The passage is in the author's most suspect vein, tendencious and thickly sown with forged documents, *e.g.*, those relating to the supposed adoption of Aurelian by Ulpius Crinitus and his nomination to the consulship. It is of small value for history.

[2] Coins of Aurelian showing him TR. POT. VII. COS. II (M.-S. v, i, p. 285, no. 186) apparently belong to A.D. 274, as in 275 Aurelian was COS. III. The high tribunician count looks like a continuation of the count of Claudius II.

loss. It appears that Aurelian now visited Rome and received
the recognition of the Senate, but that almost immediately afterwards an invasion of Vandals called army and emperor to Pannonia. Over this enemy Aurelian gained no uncertain victory.[1]
An embassy was heard by Aurelian and peace was granted by
the will of the army; but, to secure supplies and safe return, the
Vandals bound themselves to give 2000 cavalry to the Roman
service. A body of 500 that broke faith was summarily destroyed[2]. Meanwhile the Juthungi ('Marcomanni'), uncon-
vinced by Aurelian's arguments or arms, again invaded Italy,
and, this time, the danger was acute. Aurelian, coming on them
near Placentia, dared to propose their capitulation, but was
caught in an ambush and so heavily defeated that his cause
seemed almost hopeless. The barbarians, however, scattered to
plunder, while Aurelian put the cities of Northern Italy in a state
of defence and concentrated his forces. Three striking victories—
on the Metaurus, at Fanum Fortunae and near Ticinum—completed their discomfiture, and all that was left of the great host
wandered home. The favour of the gods, sought by the consultation of the Sibylline books, had again saved Rome[3]. Aurelian
was to have time to show his true worth.

The Senate had looked on without enthusiasm at the first
labours of an emperor who was not of its own choice. Some
of its members had even ventured to conspire against him.
Now it could only accept him for better or worse: thanks-
givings were decreed for his victories, and none dared
question the stern revenge which he took on his enemies.

---

[1] Dexippus, frag. 6 (Jacoby, *F.G.H.* II, pp. 456 *sqq.*) is the main authority.
See also Zosimus I, 48–9; Petrus Patricius, frag. 12 (*F.H.G.* IV, p. 188);
S.H.A. *Aurel.* 18 *sqq.*; Orosius VII, 23, 4. The narrative in the text gives
what appears to the present writer to suit the sources best, but it is possible
to maintain that Aurelian was engaged with the Juthungi once only in this
year, viz. in the campaign of North Italy (see above, p. 152).

[2] Petrus Patricius frag. 12 (*F.H.G.* IV, p. 188). According to Zosimus I,
48 the result of this battle was doubtful.

[3] S.H.A. *Aurel.* 18 *sqq.* has much to tell of the campaign; he calls the
invaders Marcomanni. Aurelius Victor, *Caes.* XXXV, 1 *sqq.*, places the
campaign after that against the 'Persians.' According to Anon. Dionis
Continuator, frag. 10, 3 (*F.H.G.* IV, p. 197), the barbarians had taken
Placentia. [Aurelius Victor], *Epit.* XXXV, says that Aurelian *tribus proeliis
victor fuit, apud Placentiam, iuxta amnem Metaurum ac fanum Fortunae,
postremo Ticinensibus campis.* Placentia, however, was a defeat; *iuxta amnem
Metaurum ac fanum Fortunae,* perhaps, represents two actions. For the
defence of Pisaurum cf. Dessau 583.

The one challenge to his authority came from a different quarter. The mint-officials, who had 'debased the coinage,' rose in revolt under Felicissimus, the master of the mint. If the story of the 7000 soldiers[1] lost in the bitter fighting on the Caelian Mount is even remotely true, we must suppose that the grievances of the moneyers were shared by many outside their ranks and that Aurelian had to deal with something like a civil war[2]. The mint of Rome was reduced in size and, perhaps, for a short time even closed, while something was done to improve the faulty coinage, though it hardly merits as yet the name of a reform. One step now taken by Aurelian gave evidence of his sound judgment and care for the State. To guard Rome against any repetition of such a threat as the invasion of the Juthungi, he surrounded the capital with new walls. The work, undertaken in consultation with the Senate and with the assistance of guilds of City workmen, was begun in 271 but only ended under Probus. The new walls were not elaborate fortifications designed to stand a long siege, but a barely adequate defence against sudden barbarian attack. The total length was twelve miles, the normal height twenty feet, the width twelve. There were eighteen gates, single or double, frequent sally-ports and towers for artillery. The walls in general followed the old Customs boundary. The plan of the work shows clearly that it was built by civilian labour: the hands of the soldiers were needed for other tasks[3]. Meanwhile the authority of Aurelian was challenged abroad. Septimius in Dalmatia, Urbanus and Domitianus in places unknown, revolted, but were speedily crushed[4].

---

[1] 'bellatores,' Aurelius Victor, Caes. xxxv, 6.

[2] Aurelius Victor, Caes. xxxv, 6, speaks of monetae opifices who auctore Felicissimo rationali nummariam notam corrosissent. Eutropius ix, 14, monetarii rebellaverunt vitiatis pecuniis et Felicissimo rationali interfecto, might seem to make Felicissimus their victim. But was his real meaning that Felicissimus was executed because of the debasement and that the monetarii then revolted to save their own skins? S.H.A. Aurel. 38 develops the tradition of Victor in rhetorical style, embellished with a forged letter of Aurelian to Ulpius Crinitus. The offence of the moneyers was certainly debasement of the coinage, not uttering coins with treasonable legends (as suggested in Rev. Num. 1891, pp. 105 sqq.). The nummariam notam corrodere of Victor suggests a clipping of the edge of the struck flan. Malalas xii, p. 301 (Bonn) records a revolt of moneyers at Antioch—perhaps only a false version of this.

[3] All necessary information will be found in I. A. Richmond's The City-Wall of Imperial Rome.

[4] Zosimus i, 49; he gives Ἐπιτίμιος for 'Septimius' (Septiminus; codd. [Aurelius Victor], Epit. xxxv, 3). A coin of a Domitianus, in the style

On the Danube frontiers an important change was made during this year. Aurelian withdrew Roman troops and civilians from Dacia, 'desperans eam posse retineri,' and formed a new province of Dacia on the right bank of the Danube, comprising parts of Moesia, Dardania and Thrace and with its capital at Serdica. Allusions to 'Dacia Felix' on coins of Milan and the coinage of a new mint at Serdica itself prove the date A.D. 271 to be preferable to 275[1] (see above, p. 152).

Aurelian was now free to turn his attention to the major problems of imperial restoration. The Gallic Empire, under Tetricus I, was pacific and threatened no immediate danger: it was essentially Roman and its interests in the main were those of Rome. But the Palmyrenes, even if nominally loyal subjects, were in fact a foreign people, threatening, under diplomatic forms, to undermine all Roman authority in the East. The concordat between Zenobia and Claudius had broken down even before his death (see however, p. 179). The Palmyrenes had gained a hold on Egypt, even if not full control of Alexandria, and Zenobia was pushing her occupation of Asia as far north as the Hellespont. The coins that appear in the first year of Aurelian both at Antioch and Alexandria, with head of Aurelian on one side balanced by head of Vaballathus on the other, have been claimed as evidence of the recognition of the Palmyrene prince by Rome. The titles 'vir clarissimus rex imperator dux Romanorum' define the place of Vaballathus under the new concordat[2]. When we reflect, however, that this 'Concordia' coinage leads on directly to independent issues of Vaballathus and Zenobia, that the mint-mark below the head of Aurelian marks his as the reverse (secondary) side of the Antioch coins, and that there are no certain allusions to Vaballathus on the coins of any of Aurelian's own mints, we are led to a different view. The concordat represents either a one-sided offer on the part of Palmyra alone, or, at most,

of the Gallic Empire, was found in France in the Department of Loire-Inférieure (*Rev. Num.* 1901, pp. 319 *sqq.*; 1930, pp. 7 *sqq.*). Perhaps he revolted in the south of Gaul, where Aurelian held sway.

[1] S.H.A. *Aurel.* 39, 7; Malalas XII, p. 301 (Bonn); Eutropius IX, 15. The date 275 is proposed by L. Homo, *Essai sur le règne de l'Empereur Aurélien*, pp. 313 *sqq.* The historians do not give a precise date, but the coins should be decisive. It is conceivable that abandonment took place in stages, some preparatory withdrawals by Gallienus, the main evacuation in 271, its completion in 274.

[2] Coins of Antioch (M.-S. v, i, p. 308, no. 381) and Volume of Plates v, 238, *b.* Cf. Homo, *op. cit.* pp. 66 *sqq.*

a grudging concession by Aurelian, like the brief toleration extended later as a temporary necessity by Diocletian and Maximian to the British Empire of Carausius (p. 331). No sooner was Aurelian free in Italy than he produced his own solution of the Palmyrene problem.

In the summer of A.D. 271 Aurelian marched by land through the Balkans, collecting his forces as he went and stopping for a moment to destroy a Gothic raider, Cannabas (Cannabaudes), and 5000 men on the far side of the Danube[1]. The outlying provinces added by Zenobia to her Empire were soon recovered. Egypt, too, returned to her allegiance, whether coerced by a separate expedition or not. The joint coinage of Aurelian and Vaballathus at Alexandria was struck in two years, 269–70, 270–1; early in 271—after March 11th—followed the independent coinage of Vaballathus and Zenobia, but, before the end of August, the mint was again striking for Aurelian alone. As Aurelian advanced, the Palmyrenes withdrew from the Hellespont. He moved from Byzantium to Ancyra and found none to challenge him till Tyana closed her gates against him. A short siege was ended by the treachery of a native, Heraclammon, and Aurelian, moved even more by motives of State than by a vision of the seer, Apollonius, spared the city[2]. The serious fighting was still to come.

Zenobia is one of the most romantic figures of history. As consort of Odenathus and then as regent for her little son, Vaballathus, she showed the spirit and courage of a man in the great crisis of her country's destiny. She had a taste for Greek culture, drew such a famous rhetorician as Longinus to her court, and sought to win the favour of the Greek element among her subjects. To Egypt she was attached not only by political and commercial connections, but also by a deep knowledge of Egyptian letters and a special devotion to Cleopatra, whom she set before her as an example. Through her patronage of Paul of Samosata, who contended with Domnus for the possession of the see of Antioch, she could bid for the support of the Christian population. Now, as Aurelian approached, the fear of his wrath and the example of his mercy at Tyana drew the Greeks from her cause.

---

[1] S.H.A. *Aurel.* 22, 2. It has been conjectured that this Cannabas was the same as the Kniva of the Gothic list of kings (P.W. *s.v.* Domitius (36), col. 1378). For Aurelian as Gothicus Maximus (TR.P. III—A.D. 271–2) cf. Dessau 8925.

[2] S.H.A. *Aurel.* 24, 2–9, where much is made of the apparition of the pagan saint.

The oracles of Seleuceia and Aphaca returned discouraging answers to her inquiries. The priests were probably good judges of politics, and condemned Zenobia for her rashness in challenging rather than conciliating her great antagonist[1].

Egypt had surrendered without a blow, and it was at Antioch in Syria that Zabdas, Palmyra's best general, had concentrated his forces. Now, as Aurelian approached, he marched out northwards to meet him on the banks of the Orontes. Aurelian brought with him troops from Raetia, Noricum, Dalmatia, Pannonia and Moesia, with barbarian auxiliaries, while local levies, including 'clubmen' from Palestine, joined him later. Zabdas had the remains at least of two Roman legions among his infantry, but rested his hopes even more on the Palmyrene archers and the heavy cavalry, the *clibanarii*—mounted on huge horses, in armour that covered man and beast. Aurelian himself was a professional commander of cavalry and disposed of an excellent corps of Moorish and Dalmatian light horse. At his express orders, these gave way before the first onslaught of the mailed knights. Only when these were exhausted by their exertions did they turn back on them and discomfit them. The decision thus won, Aurelian sent his infantry across the Orontes on the left flank of the enemy and completed the rout. Zabdas retired to Antioch, parading a false Aurelian as his captive, evacuated the city without further disaster and left a small garrison in a strong post at Daphne[2]. Aurelian was welcomed by the Antiochenes and requited their surrender with mercy. He confirmed the claims of Domnus as against those of Paul, on the ground that it was he who was endorsed by the bishops of Rome and Italy, and thus won the goodwill of a part at least of the Christian community (see p. 491). Aurelian then stormed the post at Daphne, and followed Zabdas, by way of Apamea, Larisa and Arethusa, to Emesa, whither Zabdas had withdrawn, instead of by the direct route to Emesa, in order to gain time for Persian assistance to arrive. The Emperor was now joined by troops from Mesopotamia, Syria, Phoenicia and Palestine and in the plain before Emesa repeated his victory of the Orontes over a force estimated at

---

[1] Zosimus I, 57 *sq.*

[2] Zosimus I, 50 *sqq.* is our main authority—an excellent one—for the war. He gives three main battles: (1) on the Orontes, (2) capture of the post at Daphne, (3) Emesa. S.H.A. *Aurel.* 25, 2–3, gives only the last decisive battle. Eutropius IX, 13 writes *Zenobiam...haud longe ab Antiochia sine gravi proelio cepit.* Jordanes, *Romana*, 290 *sq.* M., puts the main battle at Hymmae near Antioch.

70,000 men, using similar tactics, but incurring even greater risks than before from the Palmyrene *clibanarii*. Palestinian 'clubmen' played an important part in the victory, beating down the riders whose armour they could not pierce. While the issue still hung in the balance, Aurelian, we hear, was conscious of a divine helper in his army, whom he afterwards recognized as the Sun-God, Elagabalus, of Emesa[1].

Zenobia's wider ambitions had sustained a decisive check, but she could still claim that 'almost all the fallen were Romans'[2] and might even hope to tire out her conqueror, till he should be recalled by troubles on the Danube and North Italian front. She withdrew 80 miles to Palmyra and prepared for a siege. An expeditionary force from Egypt may now have joined Aurelian, while Persian assistance may have attempted to reach Zenobia[3]. Aurelian, in his pursuit, was harried by the nomads of the desert, and was himself wounded in the fighting round the walls of Palmyra. For a moment he hesitated and offered moderate terms of surrender which Zenobia was unwise enough to decline in undiplomatic language. He now bent his will to the task. The desert tribes were beaten or bribed into submission; Aurelian seems to have entrusted them with the profitable task of furnishing his army with supplies. The Persian relief force did not appear— perhaps it was actually defeated by the Romans. Zenobia herself escaped on a dromedary to seek the hoped-for help, but was overtaken by Roman cavalry at the Euphrates and brought back captive. The peace party in Palmyra gained the upper hand and opened the gates of the city. Its imperial power was, of course, at an end, but it was spared from pillage and had only to receive a garrison of 600 archers under Sandarion. An able officer, Marcellinus, was left in general control as prefect of Mesopotamia and governor 'totius Orientis.'

Aurelian, now adding the title of 'Parthicus Maximus' to those of 'Germanicus' and 'Gothicus Maximus' that he already bore, moved to Emesa and there held a trial of Zenobia and her counsellors. The Queen, humbled at last, condescended to save

[1] This story, occurring only in S.H.A. *Aurel.* 25, 4–6, should be treated with due reserve.

[2] Anon. Dionis Continuator, frag. 10, 5 (*F.H.G.* IV, p. 197).

[3] S.H.A. *Aurel.* 27, 4 makes Zenobia boast in a letter to Aurelian *nobis Persarum auxilia non desunt*; again, *ib.* 28, 2, Aurelian *auxilia quae a Persis missa fuerunt intercepit*. According to Zosimus (I, 55) Zenobia fled to secure the Persian help. The title Parthicus Maximus, borne by Aurelian (TR.P. III–C.I.L. VIII, 9040) suggests actual fighting with Persians. The titles Palmyrenicus (Dessau 579) and Arabicus (*ib.* 576) were perhaps unofficial.

herself by casting the blame on her advisers, and the noble
Longinus met his death with a courage that shamed his mistress.
With a long train of captives, Aurelian retraced his steps to the
Propontis, but, in the crossing, lost most of the Palmyrenes, but
not their queen, by accidental drowning[1]. By the autumn of 272
Aurelian had moved north to the Danube to repulse an invasion of
the Carpi and gain the new title of 'Carpicus Maximus.' It was
there that ill news from Palmyra reached him. The city had risen
under a certain Apsaeus and set up a king Antiochus, who claimed
kinship with Zenobia, after an attempt to induce Marcellinus to
betray his master had failed. Sandarion and his archers were
massacred. Aurelian from the first had relied on speed of movement, and this resource did not fail him now. He marched post
haste to the rebel city and struck down resistance before it had
had time to take root. Judgment this time was stern and final.
Antiochus was spared, more in contempt than mercy, but Palmyra
was pillaged, its treasures carried off, its walls dismantled, and it was
left to relapse into a little desert village.[2] It had flashed like a meteor
across the political firmament and like a meteor it passed into night.

Egypt, meanwhile, had felt the impulse of the revolt. A certain
Firmus, a man of great wealth and wide commercial connections,
whose personality seems to have made a great impression on his
age, established himself for a moment less as emperor than as
governor in another's interest—perhaps for Marcellinus, should
he desert Aurelian, or, failing him, for Antiochus. His aim
certainly was 'to defend what was left of the cause of Zenobia.'
The troublesome tribe of the Blemmyes lent some support to his
revolt. Aurelian moved at once against this new enemy, besieged
him at Bruchium and forced him to commit suicide[3]. The first
part of Aurelian's programme was at last complete. The 'restitutor
Orientis' could now think of completing his claim to be 'restitutor
orbis,' by bringing the West back to its allegiance.

Little is recorded of the Gallic empire from the death of
Postumus in A.D. 268[4] to the defeat of Tetricus in 274. There may,
indeed, have been an unwritten compact between the Roman and
Gallic rulers to maintain the *status quo* while Claudius dealt with

---

[1] According to Zosimus (1, 59) Zenobia died by illness or by voluntary
starvation; this conflicts with the general tradition and should be rejected.

[2] S.H.A. *Aurel.* 31 (he gives Achilleus instead of Antiochus): Zosimus 1,
60 *sq.*

[3] S.H.A. *Aurel.* 32, 2–3; *Quad. tyr.* (*Firmus etc.*) 1–6. Zosimus 1,
61 simply records a revolt of Alexandria. Groag (P.W. *s.v.* Domitius
(36), col. 1390) thinks that his relations with the Blemmyes were confined
to trade.   [4] Or 269; see above, p. 191.

the Goths. Victorinus, the successor of Postumus, issued, apparently towards the close of his reign, a series of coins commemorating legions of the Rhine, Danube, Palestine and Egypt but not of Italy or Raetia, and these may reflect a definite move not against Claudius but against his successor Quintillus and an offer of friendship to Aurelian and the Palmyrenes[1]. Quintillus' short reign may well have been taken up with steps to meet the new menace. The barbarian invasions of Italy by way of Raetia may even have been instigated by the Gallic emperors. But, even if this reading of the coins is correct, Victorinus had miscalculated. Aurelian would hear nothing of a divided Empire, and the death of Victorinus, which probably followed close on that of Quintillus, may have been due to something more than private vengeance.

Of the mysterious Victoria or Vitruvia, mother of Victorinus and maker of the new emperor, Tetricus, sober history has hardly a word to say[2]. Tetricus, formerly governor of Aquitania, was a mild and pacific ruler who was content to hold his Empire in quiet, while Aurelian safeguarded Italy and recovered the East. He had a son of the same name, who was first Caesar and then, for a very short period, Augustus. It was his fate to see Gaul harried by barbarian invaders by land and sea, and to suffer much from the insubordination of his troops and the machinations of one of his governors, Faustinus. Only the coins, with their references to the 'Pax' and other virtues of the Emperor, suggest that his reign had a more satisfactory content than this. Judging the future of the Gallic Empire to be desperate, he appealed to Aurelian to resume control—'Eripe me his, invicte, malis.' Aurelian was not slow to respond. Early, it would seem, in A.D. 274, he marched into Gaul, encountered Tetricus in the 'campi Catalaunii' near Châlons, and, when Tetricus came over during the battle, broke the gallant but hopeless resistance of the Gallic army[3]. Gaul returned to her allegiance and the mint of Lugdunum celebrated the 'Pacator Orbis' and his mercy to his

---

[1] Cf. H. Mattingly in *Trans. of Numismatic Congress*, 1936, pp. 214 *sqq.* For other views see C. Oman, *Num. Chron.* 1924, p. 59; A. Blanchet, *Musée Belge*, XXVII, 1923, pp. 169–171, and above, p. 214, n. 4.

[2] For Victoria, S.H.A. *Tyr. Trig.* 31; Aurelius Victor, *Caes.* XXXIII, 14.

[3] Aurelius Victor, *Caes.* XXXV; *Epit.* XXXV; Zosimus I, 61; Eutropius IX, 13; Orosius VII, 23, 5; S.H.A. *Aurel.* 32. The date is probably early 274 rather than late 273. The *vota* coins of Tetricus I and II probably imply that Tetricus at least began a fifth year of rule; the celebration of *vota quinquennalia* could regularly begin with the end of this fourth year of a reign. This would take us into 274. For the titles of Tetricus I as known from coins (A.D. 270–274) see M.-S. V, ii, pp. 399 *sqq.*

defeated rivals, while some provision was made for the future government of the province as well as of Britain. Britain, from its position, seems bound to have followed in the main the fortunes of Gaul, but the fact that coins of Claudius II and Quintillus reached the island without delay, suggests that it may, to some extent, have pursued a course of its own[1].

Aurelian could now return to Rome to celebrate a magnificent triumph as 'restorer of East and West.' While the crowds applauded the procession, in which Zenobia walked in golden chains, the senators groaned to see their fellow-senators, Tetricus and his son, submitted to the same indignity. Aurelian, however, was magnanimous in his victory. He settled Zenobia at Tibur and gave her in marriage to a senator—a strange end to a strange career—and 'promoted' Tetricus to be 'corrector Lucaniae[2].' For the rest of the year 274 Aurelian could devote his energies to internal reform. The coinage had sunk into the deepest degradation, and the first reform of 271 had hardly gone below the surface. Aurelian now called in the old money and issued new.[3] The new billon piece, superior in appearance, but little better in its metal than the old, received a definite value—xx or xx. 1—perhaps 2 sestertii of 10 'libellae' each. There was a subsidiary coinage of bronze, no longer bearing the mark of the senate, S.C., but issues of gold were relatively scanty and of pure silver there was none at all. The reform, therefore, was from the first imperfect. The new billon did indeed receive a fixed value and was more securely based on the old unit of reckoning, the sestertius, than on the ruined denarius. But what guarantee was given, that the new coinage had a solid backing and that the old evil of the issue of masses of almost worthless billon would not again bring chaos into commercial life?

In other ways Aurelian showed his regard for the material well-being of his subjects. He punished with exemplary severity informers and peculators and burned the bonds of masses of old debts in the Forum of Trajan. He controlled the price of bread in Rome and, for the old distribution of corn, he substituted a

---

[1] British hoards occasionally show Quintillus without Tetricus I; cf. the Selsey Hoard, *Num. Chron.* 1933, pp. 223 *sqq.*

[2] S.H.A. *Aurel.* 33; [Aurelius Victor], *Epit.* xxxv; Eutropius ix, 13.

[3] Zosimus i, 61. Cf. *Num. Chron.* 1927, pp. 219 *sqq.*; a different view in M.-S. v, i, pp. 10 *sqq.* The sestertius, in the coinage of the Empire, contained four *asses*; its division into ten *libellae* belongs to accountancy (cf. Volusius Maecianus, *Distributio*, 65 *sqq.*). The theory of the reform here adopted is not yet to be regarded as in any way certain; it seems to meet the known facts more nearly than any other.

dole of two pounds of baked bread, adding one ounce to the ration from a special tax on Egypt. He made also free distributions of pork, oil and salt, and is even credited with a scheme for distributing free wine as well, and with planning extensive plantations in the east and north-east of Italy to supply it[1]. On three occasions he gave largess, to the value of 500 denarii in all[2]. The clearing of the bed and the repair of the banks of the Tiber and the building of new barracks—perhaps for the 'collegia suariorum'—in the 'Campus Agrippae,' all attest the same range of interests. Two lasting effects of these policies were the extension of the powers of the 'praefectus annonae,' and possibly the establishment on a public footing of such guilds as the butchers and bakers of Rome and the 'navicularii' of the Nile and Tiber[3].

It is definitely stated that Aurelian consulted the Senate about the building of the walls of Rome (p. 300). But the senators, excluded from the camps by Gallienus, were losing their grip of public life, while, in the provinces, knights were replacing them not only in the command of the army, but also in the civil government. Perhaps Aurelian, busied as he was with wars, simply allowed these tendencies to follow their natural course. Of the defence of the frontiers again only too little is known. Though Probus was left in Gaul in A.D. 274, the Alemanni again appear in the *agri decumates* in the following year. The 'limes Raeticus' was apparently restored and Vindelicia, as we hear vaguely, was freed from 'obsidio barbarica.' On the Danube old Dacia had been abandoned as a dangerous liability and the legions, XIII Gemina and V Macedonica, went to their new stations at Ratiaria and Oescus. As late as 274 Aurelian had to drive back barbarians from the Danube. To the East two new legions, I Illyricorum and IV Martia, were sent, the one to Syria Phoenice, the other to Arabia, to strengthen the Roman grip on lands where the old corps had suffered heavily under the Palmyrene rule and the war of recovery[4]. Egypt continued restless to the end of the reign and in 275 Probus was dispatched to deal with a new incursion of the Blemmyes.

[1] As the story of free wine occurs only in S.H.A. *Aurel.* 48, we should probably regard it as an interpretation of Aurelian's actual encouragement of viticulture.   [2] S.H.A. *Aurel.* 48; Chronographer of A.D. 354.

[3] This is only a reasonable guess; cf. J. P. Waltzing, *Étude historique sur les corporations*..., II, pp. 268 *sqq.*: Groag in P.W. *s.v.* Domitius (36), col. 1410.

[4] E. Ritterling, 'Zum römischen Heerwesen des ausgehenden dritten Jahrhunderts,' in *Hirschfeld's Festschrift*, Berlin, 1903, pp. 345 *sqq.*

Of the dangers arising from the arrogance and insubordination of the armies Aurelian seems to have been fully conscious, and it may well be that he anticipated Diocletian in the attempt to remove them. It is said that Aurelian began to introduce the Eastern forms of royalty and roundly told his troops that it was not they, but the god who assigned the imperial power. Herein may be seen one of the springs of that religious policy which Aurelian followed throughout his reign and crowned in 274 by the erection in Rome of a magnificent temple to the Sun-God and the establishment of a new college of senators as *pontifices dei Solis*[1]. Sol 'dominus imperii Romani' was to be the centre of revived and unified paganism and the guarantor of loyalty to the Emperor, whose companion and preserver he was. So far as he can be identified with any one figure of worship, the Sol of Aurelian was the Elagabalus of Emesa, who had helped him in his decisive battle and now returned, after the tragic fiasco of the Emperor Elagabalus, to enjoy the reverence of Rome. But it was clearly the intention of Aurelian to make the most of the breadth and inclusiveness of his worship, in which Greek and Roman worshippers of Apollo might unite with Eastern devotees of Mithras or Elagabalus, while, on the other hand, the form of the cult was Roman. The inauguration of a State cult of the 'Genius Populi Romani' shows the development of religious ideas which reached their full development under Diocletian. Towards Christianity Aurelian maintained a negative attitude which was passing at the time of his death into positive hostility. His whole experience of life must have inclined him rather to the persecuting policy of Decius and Valerian than to the 'universal peace' of Gallienus (p. 194). Persecution of the chief enemies of paganism might well seem to be the necessary counterpart to the establishment of the new solar monotheism. But the trial of strength against the new foe was reserved for a later Emperor: Aurelian 'inter initia sui furoris exstinctus est[2].'

Late in 274 Aurelian was called to Lugdunum to suppress some obscure disorders and turned an invasion of Juthungi and Alemanni from Raetia. His eyes were however set towards the East, where the conquest of Mesopotamia was still to be accom-

---

[1] Zosimus I, 61; Aurelius Victor, *Caes.* xxxv, 7; S.H.A. *Aurel.* 39. Dessau 1210 is the earliest known inscription of a 'pontifex dei Solis.' For the evidence of the coins, which is important, see M.-S. v, i, pp. 265 *sqq.* and especially Volume of Plates, v, 238, *c, d.*

[2] Lactantius, *de mort. pers.* 6; Constantine, *Oratio ad Sanctorum Coetum* 24; Zonaras xii, 27 (p. 606).

plished and at the end of the year he set out on his last journey. At Caenophrurium, between Perinthus and Byzantium, Aurelian's confidential secretary, Eros, incurred the displeasure of his master by a lie, and, to save his skin, forged a list of prominent soldiers, who with himself were marked for execution, and showed it to the supposed victims[1]. The threatened men knew only too well the merciless severity of Aurelian and proceeded direct to his murder, only to find out the deception when it was too late. The guilty Eros was executed, but his crime could not be undone. In a fit of penitence and self-distrust, the army refused to appoint any of Aurelian's murderers to succeed him and referred the choice of a new emperor to the Senate. For some six months, from about April to September 275, embassies passed to and fro—the army appealing to the Senate to resume its old function, the Senate shrinking from so perilous a responsibility. At last in September the aged Tacitus was induced to accept an honour that was almost a sentence of death. The fact of any interregnum of more than a few weeks has been disputed by many modern authorities, but the coinage shows clearly that for some considerable period government was carried on in the name of the Empress Severina for the dead Aurelian, and that the five years and six months of the reign are reckoned not to the death of Aurelian, c. April, but to the accession of Tacitus in September[2]. Coins of Severina struck in all *officinae* of several mints, with types of 'Concordia Augg.' and 'Concordia Militum,' bear witness to the conditions of the interregnum. It was yet to be seen how this 'Concord of the troops' would stand the test of time.

The defects of the literary tradition for a remarkable reign are partly remedied by the evidence of a large and varied coinage[3]. Aurelian strikes at the mints of Rome, Milan, Siscia and Cyzicus, though in 274 Ticinum takes the place of Milan. It is thus possible to trace the decline of the mint of Rome after the revolt of the moneyers, the concentration on military interests at Milan and Siscia, the extensive issues at Cyzicus to meet the needs of Aurelian's Eastern campaigns. At Milan the types (c. 271) 'Dacia Felix,' 'Genius Illurici' and 'Pannoniae' attest the interest in the

[1] Zosimus 1, 61 *sq.*; S.H.A. *Aurel.* 36 gives the name of the secretary as Mnesteus (perhaps an error arising out of μηνυτής).

[2] Aurelius Victor, *Caes.* XXXVI, 1 (interregnum of about six months); S.H.A. *Tac.* 1–2. The coins are decisive in favour of an interregnum of some length. The 'Divus Aurelianus' of the S.H.A. implies consecration, but coins are lacking.

[3] M.-S. v, i, pp. 248 *sqq.* See also Appendix on Coins.

new order on the Danube. In 271, indeed, Serdica comes into activity as a mint for the new Dacia and thereafter shows its devotion to the Emperor and Sol, his divine patron. In the east new mints were opened at Tripolis in Phoenicia and at an unknown city with a dolphin as mint-mark. Lugdunum in 274 honours the restorer of the West, while Antioch strikes first for Vaballathus and Aurelian, then for Vaballathus alone, and finally for Aurelian alone, the restorer of the East (p. 302). More than all this, the coins reveal the emotional background of the reign. After a short first period in which the tradition of Quintillus prevails, the dominant notes of Aurelian's own coins ring clear in the 'Concord of the Armies,' 'the restoration of the world,' the 'lordship of Sol,' master of the Roman Emperor and protector of his chosen, the Emperor.

II. TACITUS AND FLORIAN: SENATORIAL INTERLUDE

The appeal of the army to the Senate to nominate Aurelian's successor might conceivably have led to a serious revival of senatorial influence. Aurelius Victor asserts that the edict of Gallienus (p. 197) could have been revoked, and that the senators could have recovered their place in the camps[1]. The army, in a mood of self-restraint and self-denial, would have raised no objection, had the Senate only acted with sufficient firmness. But the condition was unfulfilled. Such honours as military command had to offer were too perilous to tempt men who attached more and more value to the uninterrupted enjoyment of their hereditary dignity and wealth. The *Augustan History* enlarges on the rejoicings of the Senate, both in private and public, over the universal right of hearing appeals now granted to the *praefectus urbis* and the recovery of the *ius proconsulare*[2]. How much is really implied in these high claims it is not easy to gauge. The new emperor himself was a senator, so too, no doubt, was his half-brother, Florian, whom he made Praetorian Prefect, and his kinsman, Maximinus, whom he appointed governor of Syria. But we have no real evidence of any general restoration of senatorial privilege. To take one small test, the mark of senatorial control, S.C., does not appear at all on the bronze coinage of Tacitus and not always on that of Florian.

It was in September 275 that Tacitus at last yielded to pressure and accepted nomination as Emperor. He was seventy-five years

---

[1] Aurelius Victor, *Caes.* xxxvii, 6, reading '*amisso.*'
[2] S.H.A. *Tac.* 18–19.

of age, a heavy handicap even for a man who was 'egregie moratus
et rei publicae gerundae idoneus[1].' He had already been consul
under Aurelian in 273. Of his short reign we know little of any
moment. He asked for divine honours for Aurelian[2], punished
some of his murderers, and built a temple of the deified emperors.
He himself held the consulship for the second time in 276;
when he requested the same office for Florian, the Senate refused
his request and he expressed himself delighted with its independence. He made over his own 'patrimonium' to the State,
but, in the six months of his rule, 'congiarium vix dedit'—whatever that may mean. He set a good example in his private life and
attempted sundry reforms which tended to improve morals and
restrict extravagance. The statement that he forbade the debasement of the metals—gold, silver and bronze—perhaps veils a
policy which had real economic importance[3]. Old as he was,
Tacitus showed himself ready to bear the burdens of his office.
The Maeotidae, the Goths from the northern shores of the Black
Sea, who claimed to have been called in to assist Aurelian in his
campaign against Persia, invaded Asia Minor and penetrated as
far as Cilicia. Tacitus took the field against them and actually
reached Tyana, while Florian gained a victory ('Victoria Gothica'),
which is commemorated on coins[4]. But the indulgence of Tacitus
to his kindred, already shown in his favouring of Florian, bore
evil fruit. A kinsman, Maximinus, appointed to the governorship
of Syria, made himself hated by his oppressions and was murdered.
The discontent spread to the entourage of Tacitus. We must
suppose that the army was already repenting of its moderation
and turning its eyes towards Probus, the natural successor of
Aurelian, who held a high command in Syria and Egypt. The
strain was too much for the aged Emperor, who collapsed and
died at Tyana, c. April 276[5].

Florian, without waiting for the approval of the Senate,
snatched the Empire as his natural inheritance[6], and was generally

---

[1] Eutropius IX, 16; Aurelius Victor, Caes. XXXVI, 1; Epit. XXXVI.

[2] According to S.H.A. Aurel. 41, 13 he did this before he was emperor,
on the first news of Aurelian's death.

[3] We depend mainly on S.H.A. Tac. 9 sqq.; we have no serious means of
checking the statements of the Vita.

[4] Cf. S.H.A. Tac. 13; Zonaras XII, 28 (p. 608); Zosimus I, 63.

[5] That he died of disease seems to be better attested than that he was
killed by his troops.

[6] Aurelius Victor (Caes. XXXVI, 2) makes Florian seize Empire nullo
senatus seu militum consulto. S.H.A. Tac. 14, 1, says that he seized Empire

recognized, except in Syria and Egypt, which now came out
openly in defence of their own candidate, Probus. The usurpation
of Florian was necessary if he was to have any chance of holding
power, and would no doubt have been condoned had it been
successful. He led his army to Tarsus, in the hope that the
numbers and quality of his troops would be decisive. But Probus
cleverly delayed the decision, and the soldiers of Florian, suffering
severely from an uncongenial climate, began to waver in their
loyalty. After a bare three months of rule, during most of which
Probus had contested his claim, he died at Tarsus, betrayed by
his own men (c. end of June, 276)[1].

The coinage of these two short reigns, which seemed little
more than an interregnum between Aurelian and Probus, has
a life and colour of its own[2]. The Golden Age, always hoped for
and never realized, is characterized in new terms. The Sun-God
is less prominent than under Aurelian, though he still appears as
the director of the loyal troops in their allegiance. The stress falls
more on the old divine protectors of Rome, and particularly on
'Roma Aeterna' herself. 'Clementia Temporum,' a watchword of
the two reigns, perhaps alludes directly to the influence of the
'clemency' of the Senate. The coinage of Florian, with its emphasis
on 'Perpetuitas,' 'Securitas' and 'Victoria Perpetua,' betrays some
anxiety about the durability of the 'gentle times.' Of neither
emperor can we form any very clear conception. Whatever their
personalities and policies, they were not given opportunity to
translate them into lasting fact.

III. PROBUS: 'PACATOR ORBIS'

With the accession of Probus the Senate sank into the background and the balance of power shifted again to the camps.
However loyally Probus might seek the approval of the Senate
and deplore the precipitancy of Florian, which had driven him to
seek a decision by force, it was on the consent of the armies that
his rule actually rested. A native of Sirmium, trained like
Claudius II and Aurelian in the school of war, he is said to have
been foremost in the service of Aurelian against Palmyra and
Tetricus, and had, according to one account, been appointed by

quasi hereditarium, although Tacitus had promised that the 'best man'
should succeed him.

[1] For the war with Probus cf. [Aurelius Victor], *Epit.* xxxvi; Zosimus i,
64 (the best account).   [2] M.-S. v, i, pp. 319 *sqq.*

Tacitus to be 'dux totius Orientis[1].' Aurelian had restored the Roman Empire. Probus conceived it to be his task to complete the restoration by re-establishing order throughout the provinces, and, at the same time, by bringing the troops back to a proper discipline and love of hard work. In this task he was brilliantly successful and deserves a large measure of the praise which our authorities lavish on him. Almost the equal of Aurelian in military capacity, his superior in balance and moderation of character, he holds an honourable place among those who paved the way for the great re-organization of the State by Diocletian.

A settlement with Persia was still to be made, but for the moment no danger threatened from that quarter, while the presence of the Emperor was urgently demanded in the Western provinces of the Empire. After executing vengeance on such as still survived of the murderers of Aurelian, Probus moved northward and then westward, perhaps defeating the Goths in Illyricum on the way[2], and paid a short visit to Rome to receive the approval of the Senate. He then led his army into Gaul. Hordes of Germans—Franks in the north, Longiones (Lugii) and Alemanni in the south—had burst over the Rhine frontier and penetrated into the whole of Gaul. The story of the invasion in its detail is entirely lost. There may not have been one sudden incursion so much as a gradual worsening of an evil, which had begun soon after the strong hand of Postumus was removed and now only reached its crisis. The burial of hoards of coins of Gallienus, Claudius II and the Gallic emperors, which are commonly attributed to the German terror, may perhaps represent rather the ineffectual protest of the provincials against the unpopular reform of Aurelian. Such hoards occur too freely in Britain to be attributed to a cause that operated only in Gaul, and the fact that the Gallic coins of Aurelian's reform do not bear his mark of value, xx. 1, suggests that the reform was not as fully carried through in that province as it was in the rest of the Empire[3].

---

[1] The *ducatus totius Orientis* only in S.H.A. *Prob.* 7, 4; whether or not Probus fought against Tetricus I, we hear of him in Gaul just after the war. All the exploits attributed to Probus before he became emperor are suspect, since it has been proved beyond all reasonable doubt that the victory over the Marmaridae in Africa (S.H.A. *Prob.* 9, 1) belongs to the other Probus, Tenagino Probus, who died in Egypt in battle against the Palmyrenes under Claudius II: see A. Stein in *Klio*, xxix, 1936, pp. 237 *sqq.*

[2] Cf. *C.I.L.* xi, 1178; Probus is already Gothicus in 277.

[3] The mark of value, xx. 1., probably implied as a corollary the surrender-value of the old coinage (p. 11). Its absence perhaps means that the old coinage was allowed to find its value in terms of the new.

In the course of little more than a year's hard fighting, Probus completed the deliverance of Gaul. He himself took the field against the Longiones and captured Semnon, their chief, and then, when his lieutenants had defeated the Franks on the lower Rhine, he joined them in a victorious attack on the Burgundians and Vandals. Sixty famous cities of Gaul were freed from the barbarian, tens of thousands of Germans were killed, forts were established across the Rhine 'in solo barbarico,' and Probus could even play with the idea of establishing a new province of Germany. Nine chiefs knelt for mercy at his feet, hostages were demanded and 16,000 Germans were distributed in small bodies over the Roman army[1]. The Germans had to supply corn and cattle and submit to disarmament; it was for the Roman Empire that they were now to till their soil, to Roman arms that they were to look for protection and the decision of their internal quarrels[2]. One body of prisoners was sent to Britain, where they were later to render valuable service to their captor (p. 316 *sq.*).

Early in 278 Probus could regard the Gallic danger as ended and turn his attention to other problems[3]. He pacified Raetia, and repulsed an invasion of Vandals from Illyricum[4]. A rebellion in the East was already over before Probus himself could arrive to suppress it. A certain Julius Saturninus, an able soldier, who is said to have held high command under Aurelian and to have enjoyed the full confidence of Probus himself, was forced by his troops in Syria to assume the purple, and, after a brief usurpation, perished at Apamea[5]. Troubles in the south of Asia Minor now claimed the attention of Probus. Lydius (or Palfuerius?), a brigand of daring and capacity worthy of a better cause, seized

[1] Zosimus I, 67 *sq.*; S.H.A. *Prob.* 13 *sq.*; in a letter to the Senate Probus (*ib.* 15, 3) speaks of *septuaginta urbes nobilissimae captivitate hostium vindicatae* (for the number, as against the sixty given elsewhere, cf. Julian, *Conv.* [*Caes.*] 314, A–B, possibly significant for the date of the biography); Orosius VII, 24; Zonaras XII, 29 (p. 609). 　　　　[2] S.H.A. *Prob.* 14.

[3] The order of events is far from certain: fighting was perhaps going on at the same time in Gaul, Raetia and Illyricum.

[4] Zosimus I, 68, 2; ποταμοῦ Λίγυος has been thought to indicate Augsburg on the Lech as the scene of the battle.

[5] S.H.A. *Quad. tyr.* (*Firmus etc*). 7 *sqq.* says that Aurelian had given him *limitis orientalis ducatum* and describes his visit to Egypt; Jordanes, *Romana*, 293 M, says that he was *magister militum*, sent to restore Antioch, and that he rebelled there. Zonaras XII, 29 (p. 609) calls him a Moor; Zosimus I, 66 agrees and says that he was governor of Syria. Two gold coins of Saturninus, apparently of the mint of Antioch, are known: cf. Babelon, *Mélanges*, sér. 3, pp. 167 *sqq.* and *Bull. de Num.* 1895, p. 107.

Cremna and held it till his death in a long and desperate siege[1]. The unruly Isaurians were kept in check by fortresses, and were perhaps recruited into the new legions, I to III Isaura[2]. Ptolemais revolted in alliance with the Blemmyes and attacked Coptos; but the revolt was suppressed without the personal intervention of Probus[3]. Against Persia the Emperor made no move as yet, but he haughtily declined presents from the Persian king (Vahram II) and may perhaps have granted a truce on terms favourable to Rome. In the course of 279–80 Probus returned homewards, by way of Illyricum, and, as he passed through Thrace, settled 100,000 Bastarnae within the Empire[4], a policy convenient for the moment but fraught with peril for the future.

The closing years of the reign were marred by military insurrections which perhaps testify to deeper discontents and more serious ills than the disordered ambitions of a few generals and the dislike of the troops for too firm a discipline. Proculus, a native of Albingaunum (Albenga), south-west of Genoa, a hardy but licentious soldier, was spurred on by his virago wife, Samso, to assume the purple. Lugdunum, moved by unknown grievances, abetted his revolt but was powerless to sustain him. The Franks, to whom he tried to flee, with their native perfidy betrayed him to Probus[5]. More serious was the revolt of Bonosus, the commander of the Roman fleet at Colonia Agrippina. Married, it is said, to a Gothic wife, he was in close touch with the barbarians and used his unrivalled powers of drinking to extract secrets from his booncompanions. He was born in Spain of a Gallic mother, but traced his descent from Britain. Now, having by his carelessness allowed the Germans to burn some ships of his fleet, he took refuge in revolt, but, after serious fighting, he despaired of success and hanged himself[6]. The whole West seems to have been in a state of unrest. The deletion of the name of Probus on an inscription of Valentia[7] suggests some trouble in Spain, while in

---

[1] S.H.A. *Prob.* 16, 4; Zosimus I, 69 *sq.*
[2] E. Ritterling in P.W. *s.v.* Legio, col. 1348.
[3] Zosimus I, 71; S.H.A. *Prob.* 17, 4–6.
[4] Zosimus I, 71, 1; S.H.A. *Prob.* 18, 1.
[5] Despite the evidence of our authorities, the rebellion of Proculus seems to have been distinct from that of Bonosus and not to have begun at Cologne. [Aurelius Victor], *Epit.* xxxvii, 2 puts the rising of both Proculus and Bonosus at Cologne, and he is supported by Eutropius ix, 17, Orosius vii, 24, 3 and S.H.A. *Prob.* 18, 5; S.H.A. *Quad. tyr.* (*Firmus etc.*) 13, 1 says 'hortantibus Lugdunensibus...in imperium vocitatus est.'
[6] S.H.A. *Quad. tyr.* (*Firmus etc.*) 14 *sq.*   [7] Dessau 597.

Britain a governor who threatened rebellion was forestalled by the mission of Victorinus, a Moor, the very man who had recommended him to Probus. By the help of the German captives who had been sent to the island he nipped the revolt in the bud[1]. In default of precise evidence, it may be suspected that economic causes were at the root of these troubles. Coins of the reform of Aurelian are definitely rare in British deposits and, when Carausius seized the island in 286, he began by overstriking coins of the Gallic emperors. This seems to suggest a disinclination on the part of the province to accept the new coinage, with all that it implied[2].

Reaching Rome at the turn of the years 281–2, Probus celebrated a magnificent triumph, which made a vast impression as much by the ingenuity of its display, as by the variety of conquered enemies that it paraded for the delight of the mob of Rome.

Peace seemed now to be assured within the empire, and Probus could at last turn his attention to the war against Persia. But he had erred in judgment, if not in intention, in his treatment of the troops. Not only had he made heavy demands on their services in war, but he had not even allowed them to relax in the intervals of peace. Everywhere they were set to useful work, and, in the West particularly, where Probus wished to encourage the culture of the vine, they had been employed on clearing the ground for new vineyards. Even worse than this, perhaps, Probus had pacified the empire and, in his delight at the success achieved, had spoken too optimistically of a time when an army would no longer be required[3]. Such remarks could very easily be misunderstood. All these discontents grew to a head and culminated in one final revolt that proved fatal to the Emperor. He had gone forward to Sirmium to superintend the recovery for cultivation of the 'Mons Alma,' when his own soldiers suddenly turned against him and killed him in the 'iron tower,' to which he had fled for refuge. The movement was not so local as some authorities incline to represent it. Carus, Prefect of the Guard, who had been left to muster the troops in Raetia, was pressed by his men to revolt. Like Decius with Philip he seems to have tried to keep faith with Probus. But the troops sent by Probus against him deserted, and

---

[1] Zosimus I, 66; cf. Zonaras XII, 29 (p. 609), which explains the account of Zosimus.

[2] Cf. the great Blackmoor hoard (*Num. Chron.* 1877, pp. 90 *sqq.*), apparently buried after the rout of Allectus, but still consisting mainly of coins of the Gallic Empire.

[3] S.H.A. *Prob.* 20, 3 (*brevi milites necessarios non futuros*); *ib.* 22, 4 and 23, expands the theme in rhetorical vein.

Carus was then forced to assume the purple. The death of Probus removed the occasion of a civil war. Our tradition, out of kindness to the memory of both men, tries to veil the tragedy, but there can hardly be a doubt that the 'Concordia Militum' had once more failed in the moment of crisis[1]. Senate and People mourned their loss and awarded to Probus the posthumous honour of consecration[2]; but the decision of the troops could not now be questioned and Carus was accepted as the new ruler of the Roman world.

Of few reigns of such note as that of Probus have we so slight and unsatisfactory a record. A little longer than that of Aurelian and almost as notable, it can be told to-day in half the space. The eulogies lavished on Probus are poor compensation for the lack of detailed account of his administration. To the Senate Probus from the first showed all possible respect. He sought its approval for his elevation, and, if his biographer is correct, allowed it to hear appeals from the more important provincial governors, to appoint proconsuls, to assign legates from among the consulars, to bestow the *ius praetorium* on equestrian governors and to set the seal of its own decrees on the laws which he himself proposed[3]. It seems probable that the *Historia Augusta* preserves, with a false show of precision, some memory of an actual attempt by Probus to obtain assistance from the Senate in governing. It is likely enough that Probus was sincere in his wish to strengthen the civil government and that he conceived of himself, as Aemilian had done before him, as general of the State, not as the autocrat, free to deal at will with all problems of administration. But as regards the final issue, the judgment of Aurelius Victor stated in a highly significant passage of his *De Caesaribus* is certainly correct[4]. The Senate, partly by its own fault, failed to regain its place in the camps and the 'militaris potentia convaluit.' The senators, over-fond of luxury and security, 'munivere militaribus et paene barbaris viam in se ac posteros dominandi.' Helpers in his labours Probus must have had, but they will have been soldiers and knights rather than senators.

The four rebellions that marred the reign are certain evidence

---

[1] S.H.A. *Prob.* 21, Jordanes, *Romana*, 293 M, [Aurelius Victor], *Epit.* XXXVII, 4 and Eutropius IX, 17 simply record his death in a mutiny. The true account is given in Zonaras XII, 29 (p. 610); S.H.A. *Carus*, 6, 1 knows it, but rejects it.

[2] Probus is not 'divus' in the *Historia Augusta* and has no 'consecration' coinage. But cf. 'sub divo Probo,' *Pan.* VIII (v), 18, 3 and *C.I.L.* I², p. 255.

[3] S.H.A. *Prob.* 13, 1; these rights are said to have been given by Probus in his *secunda oratio* to the Senate. [4] *Caes.* XXXVII, 5 *sqq.*

of something rotten in the state of the army. Probus may have
been unwise to re-impose discipline too suddenly and unre-
mittingly on troops that had half forgotten how to obey: it is
possible that he was not quite fortunate in the choice of his
assistants. In the main, however, the difficulties lay beyond his
control and were only capable of solution by the drastic reforms
imposed later by Diocletian. The Emperor's policy of settling
barbarians in the Empire had its dangers as well as its advantages,
as was instanced by the exploit of Franks, thus settled, who broke
loose and after plundering Greece, Sicily and Africa, finally made
their way safely home[1]. A gladiatorial revolt of some magnitude
also disturbed the peace of the reign.

The coinage offers some compensation for the defects of the
literary tradition[2]. The market continued to be flooded with the
base billon of the reform, still marked xx, xx.i, and the vast
issues were used to present to the public a wealth of reverse types
and an unprecedented richness of variety in the presentation of
the Emperor himself. 'Virtus Probi Aug.' is freely used as a sort
of alternative to the normal title. Dated coins are rare, but
establish one detail of interest—that Probus could reckon his tribunician power 'a die in diem,' from the date of its first conferment, and not renew it on December 10th[3]. Lugdunum
strikes in great abundance, celebrating the divine powers
Hercules, Mars, Sol, Victoria and Virtus, that bless the Emperor's
labours, and the new Golden Age of peace, assured by his triumphs
in the field. The gods come more and more to be viewed as the
divine 'protectors' or 'companions' of the Emperor—a heavenly
'comitatus' analogous to the earthly. The mint of Rome concentrates attention on the personality and achievement of Probus,
the universal victor crowning the 'restoration of the world' that
had been won by Aurelian. The symbolism of the Golden Age
is employed with even more than the customary fervour. The
Empire has recovered faith in its destiny, in its emperor and his
divine helpers. The loyalty of the army is, as ever, a keystone of
the Imperial system; but the insistence on it suggests an ardent
hope rather than a settled confidence. Sol still enjoys a large
measure of the honour to which he had been advanced by Aurelian
and still directs the loyalty of the troops, but he has already lost
his primacy in the Pantheon. The mint at Ticinum, as usual,
has much to say of the loyal and harmonious army and strikes the
type of 'Princeps Iuventutis,' which seems to emphasize the

[1] Zosimus i, 71.   [2] M.-S. v, ii, pp. 1 *sqq.*; Volume of Plates v, 238, *i–k.*
[3] A. Alföldi, *Blätt. für Münzfreunde*, 1923, pp. 352 *sqq.*

relation of the Emperor to the Imperial cavalry. In loyalty to the Emperor, a native of Sirmium, the mint-city of Siscia, throned between her two streams, boasts herself as 'Siscia Probi Aug.' Hercules, who laboured in the service of Juppiter for the good of the human race, supplies a series of symbols fit to represent the work of the new Hercules, the Emperor: an old theme of the Imperial coinage, brought to the fore by Postumus in Gaul, is now taken up by the Imperial mints and prepares the way for the Herculian dynasty of Maximian. Types of imperial virtues, such as Abundantia, Felicitas and Ubertas, probably reflect the policy of land-reclamation and planting of vineyards. Serdica distinguishes itself, as under Aurelian, by a certain exuberance of feeling acclaiming the 'Invictus,' the 'Bonus,' the 'Perpetuus imperator Probus.' Probus, like Aurelian, is even hailed as 'Deus et Dominus.' In religious fervour and devotion to the person of the Emperor this mint stands out above all the rest. Late in the reign its staff was transferred to Siscia, not to Rome by Carus, as was once supposed[1]. At Cyzicus the themes of loyalty and discipline in the army are very fully handled[2]. Antioch and Tripolis have a much narrower range than the other Imperial mints, and concentrate on a few main themes—the Victory of the Emperor, the Sun-God his preserver, the restoration of the world and the 'Clemency of the Times.' There is clear reflection of a difference in temper in the public that used the coins. Other provinces claim from the coinage a detailed comment on each single aspect of the Emperor's activities, the East is content to contemplate him under a few aspects that know no change.

The coinage proves beyond doubt that the panegyrics of the historians have their foundations in fact. The personality of the Emperor stands out as the vital factor in the recovery of Rome[3]. The moods of depression and uncertain hope are over. As the forces inimical to the Empire ebb, the forces of recovery flow in an ever increasing tide. Greater triumphs are still in store, if the soldiers can but be taught to use their swords only in their country's service, if their 'Concord' and 'Fidelity' can be so assured, that they will not need to be invoked unceasingly on the coinage.

[1] See *Blätt. für Münzfreunde*, 1923, p. 313 *sq.* against M.-S. v, ii, pp. 123 *sqq.*
[2] Whether its issues are limited to two occasions, one in A.D. 276, one in A.D. 278–9, is hardly certain as yet.
[3] For the tradition concerning the character of Probus, cf. Zonaras XII, 29 (p. 609): ἐφιλεῖτο δὲ παρὰ πάντων ὁ Πρόβος ὡς πρᾷος καὶ εὐμενὴς καὶ φιλόδωρος.

IV. CARUS AND HIS SONS: 'PRAESIDIA REIPUBLICAE'

The new emperor was emphatically a creation of the army, nor did he deny the source of his power. In reporting to the Senate his elevation by the troops, he was nominally asking for its approval, but in reality presenting it with an accomplished fact. There are so many accounts of his birthplace that we might suspect it to be entirely unknown, but it is probable that he was a native of Narona in Illyricum[1]. Like most of his immediate predecessors, he was a soldier by education and trade. His conduct of the Persian War, which seemed to him the main object of his reign[2], proves that he was no mean general. Apart from that, we have no material for judging his character as emperor, beyond the general opinion of our authorities that he stood 'medius,' between good and bad emperors. One great natural advantage, denied to most of the emperors just before him, he certainly enjoyed; he had two sons of full age, capable of receiving at once the rank of Caesar and of sharing in some measure in the burden of Empire. Carinus, the elder, was left as virtual governor in the West and was sent in the first place to defend Gaul. Supreme power brought out all the baseness and meanness of his character, but it is hardly probable that Carus really thought of substituting his younger son Numerian or Constantius Chlorus for Carinus or even of putting the latter to death[3]. Numerian had an excellent reputation as a poet, an orator and a man of the best intentions. Whether he was in any way fitted to rule the State must remain uncertain.

It was early in the autumn of 282 that Probus had met his death. Preparations for the Persian war were at once pushed forward, but some delay was caused by an incursion of Quadi and Sarmatae across the Danube. Carus at once showed his professional ability by defeating the invaders with heavy loss in killed and captured and thought fit to advertise this initial success by some notable coin-types[4]. It was early in 283 that Carus marched east to take the field against Persia, but of the details of his journey we know nothing. Persia had declined while Rome had recovered and Vahram II, who now sat on the throne, was no Shapur. Carus crossed the Euphrates, defeated Vahram, took Seleuceia and was

[1] The question is in itself of no great moment, but it illustrates most aptly the uncertainties of our tradition; see *Pros. Imp. Rom.*[2] 1, p. 299, no. 1475.
[2] Cf. Anon. Dion. Continuator frag. 12 (*F.H.G.* iv, p. 198). Carus declared that ἐπὶ κακῷ Περσῶν εἰς τὴν βασιλείαν ἦλθεν.
[3] S.H.A. *Carus*, 7, 3 and 17, 6.
[4] For the coins cf. G. Elmer, *Der Münzensammler*, 1935, pp. 11 *sqq.*

accepted throughout Mesopotamia. He then crossed the Tigris and crowned his triumph by taking the capital, Ctesiphon, and thus fairly earning the title of 'Parthicus Maximus[1].' It is noteworthy that Rome still applied the old name to the new enemy, even as she continued to call the Goths Germans. The Persians were distracted by factions, and Carus, urged on, it may be, by the perfidious advice of Aper, his Praetorian Prefect, who nursed his own secret ambitions, refused to rest on his laurels and tried to pass the bounds set by fate for Roman conquest eastward. Near Ctesiphon he met his death under circumstances that arouse grave suspicion—according to the official version, by a stroke of lightning, more probably by the treachery of Aper[2]. Carus has no Alexandrian coins of the year 283–4, and his death must, therefore, fall at about the end of July 283. He had reigned a little over ten months.

The two Caesars, sons and natural heirs of Carus, succeeded unopposed, the one in the East, the other in the West. The Persian war was brought to an end, possibly after a minor reverse[3]; Mesopotamia, at least, remained under Roman rule. Numerian, who appears to have been entirely under the influence of his father-in-law, Aper, had no thought but to bring his army safely home. On the journey, he began to suffer from an inflammation of the eyes, which gave an excuse for conveying him in a closed litter. When the army had reached the neighbourhood of Nicomedia, the stench of corruption from the litter betrayed to the troops the fact that their young Emperor was dead[4]. Aper had no doubt hoped that the death would be attributed to natural causes and that he would succeed to the vacant throne. But the officers of the Eastern army had other views. On Carinus they based no hopes—now, if not earlier, his true character as an emperor was fully realized. But they had a rival claimant to Aper in their own midst in the person of Diocles, commander of the *protectores domestici*. A council of the army appointed him its emperor to avenge the death of Numerian, and his first act was to brand Aper as the murderer and strike him down with his own hand—'Gloriare, Aper, Aeneae magni dextra cadis[5].'

[1] Zonaras XII, 30 (p. 610); Aurelius Victor, *Caes.* XXXVIII; *Epit.* XXXVIII; Eutropius IX, 18; S.H.A. *Carus*, 8, 1.

[2] His death was attributed to *fulminis ictus*; to disease S.H.A. *Carus*, 8, 2; 8, 7. [3] Zonaras XII, 30 (p. 611).

[4] Aurelius Victor, *Caes.* XXXVIII, 6; *Epit.* XXXVIII; Eutropius IX, 18; S.H.A. *Carus*, 12, 2; Jordanes, *Romana*, 295 M; Zonaras XII, 30 (p. 611 *sq.*).

[5] S.H.A. *Carus*, 13, 3.

Diocles had many years before received an oracle from a Druidess in Gaul that he would be emperor, 'when he had killed his boar.' Superstitious as he certainly was, he may have brooded long over the oracle and come to the conclusion that the 'fatalis aper' was none other than the Praetorian Prefect. In striking him down he fulfilled the omen of his rule[1]. The date will be late in the autumn of 284—probably November 17.

Carinus in the West had ruled with little opposition from home or abroad, but had alienated men's sympathies by his cruelty and lust[2]. The magnificent shows with which he delighted the mob of Rome were a poor substitute for sound government[3]. The new threat to his position roused him to a display of unexpected energy and resource. Even before the elevation of Diocles, Julianus 'corrector Venetiae' had revolted and extended his power as far as Siscia. His coins of that mint promise 'Libertas Publica,' constitutional government in place of the tyranny of Carinus, and acclaim the 'Happiness of the Age,' 'the Victory of the Augustus,' 'Juppiter the Preserver,' and 'the Pannoniae of Augustus.' He fell without any serious struggle in the fields of Verona and left the stage clear for the clash of two mightier rivals[4]. Diocles marched west and encountered Carinus in the valley of the Margus. The decisive battle was fiercely contested and the advantage rested with the troops of Carinus, but the Emperor was killed in the hour of victory by an officer whose wife he had seduced, and Diocles was accepted by the leaderless army[5]. The war had been difficult and laborious, and Diocles was politic enough to avert further bloodshed by a generous pardon of the hostile faction (spring 285). The dynasty of Carus, surely founded as it seemed on his two sons, had passed away, and the fate of the Empire was in the hands of an almost unknown officer. But the Roman destiny was making no mistake. The man had at last been found with the right qualities of mind and character to set the seal of completion on the great task of restora-

---

[1] *Ib.* 14, 3.

[2] S.H.A. *Carus,* 16 *sqq.*; *Epit.* xxxviii, 7; Eutropius ix, 19, 1; Eunapius, frag. 4 (*F.H.G.* iv, p. 14). No doubt the fact that Carinus was the rival of Diocletian caused his memory to be treated with scant respect.

[3] S.H.A. *Carus,* 19.

[4] Aurelius Victor, *Caes.* xxxix, 10; Julianus revolted *Cari morte cognita*; *Epit.* xxxviii. For his coins cf. M.-S. v, ii, pp. 579, 593 *sq.*

[5] Aurelius Victor, *Caes.* xxxix, 11, at Marcus in Moesia; *Epit.* xxxviii, no site given; S.H.A. *Carus,* 18, 2, '*apud Marcum*' (read *Margum,* so Hohl after Casaubon); Jordanes, *Romana,* 295 M, '*apud Margum.*'

tion for which Claudius, Aurelian and Probus had spent their last breath.

The coins of the dynasty of Carus[1] hold out to the world a new vision of the Golden Age, blessed in the plenty and security of its peace and safeguarded by the valour and victory of the emperor, and the loyalty of his troops. Lugdunum, Rome, Siscia and Cyzicus, each presents its own picture of the promise of the reign. The mint of Serdica, which had already been closed towards the end of the reign of Probus, strikes no coins. Antioch and Tripolis celebrate the new dynasty with a narrow range of types. The coinage of Carinus and Numerian as Augusti—Carinus seems to have borne the title a little before his father's death—continues to celebrate the same themes, with increasing stress on the winning of universal peace by the victories in Persia and on the eternity of Rome assured by the dynasty. The last phase of Carinus, when threatened by the elevation of Diocles, is marked by an insistence on the 'Loyalty of the Troops' and the 'Peace of the Army.' An 'adventus' type at Ticinum may mark a stage of his advance to take the field against his rival[2]. Perhaps the most marked feature of the whole coinage is the stress laid on the security of the house of Carus, with his two young sons, the hope of the State and the *principes iuventutis*. Diocles, as he pondered the problems of imperial government, will not have failed to contrast the strength of Carus, with his two heirs, with the loneliness of Claudius, Aurelian and Probus, and, when the time came, found means to provide himself with a like protection.

V. DIOCLETIAN: 'PARENS AUREI SAECULI'

The new emperor Diocletian, as he now chose to call himself, was a Dalmatian by birth, of humble parentage. A persistent tradition makes him originally the son of a 'scribe' or a freedman of a senator named Anullinus[3]. He had risen like most emperors of the age through service in the army, and had served, we are told, in minor posts in Gaul under Aurelian and as governor in Moesia under Carus, before he was called to the command of the Emperor's bodyguard. He had also held the office of consul. His service had hardly trained him in the arts of generalship and his military talents when tested proved to be respectable rather than brilliant. But he had a sound knowledge of the requirements of the army and a good eye for the larger aspects of strategy.

---

[1] M.-S. v, ii, pp. 122 *sqq.*   [2] *Ib.* v, ii, p. 175, no. 294.
[3] Zonaras XII, 31 (p. 613); Eutropius IX, 19.

Perhaps his training, as contrasted with that of an Aurelian or a Probus, had helped to develop in him that subtlety, which, as Tacitus has reminded us, is often lacking in the born soldier[1]. Yet if he ranks in history as statesman more than general, this is due rather to his eminence in the former capacity than to his weakness in the latter.

To his contemporaries he was an object of intense admiration, tinged with a certain uneasiness and distrust. It was certainly by divine favour that he had been elected by the army. He was a notable personality, wise and subtle, but, withal, a man who would satisfy his own severity, while leaving its cost in unpopularity to be paid by his assistants[2]. A judgment in the *Historia Augusta* strikes a truer note than is usual in that work: 'consilii semper alti, nonnumquam tamen ⟨ferreae⟩ frontis, prudentia et nimia pervicacia motus inquieti pectoris comprimentis.[3]' Though he decked himself with kingly display and hung about his person a religious awe and sanctity, his busy brain was ever scheming for the welfare of his Empire, and the lord and master conducted himself as a father of his people[4].

During the long years through which he had been waiting for the 'fateful boar' (p. 323), he had clearly pondered the problems of his age and had reached certain conclusions, which, as emperor, he was quick to put to the proof. The Empire was too heavy a burden for any one man to bear. Diocletian therefore took care to provide himself with helpers, and nothing showed his genius better than his power to choose them well. The men of his choice accepted his moral ascendency and did his work. Again, the emperor was continually exposed to the jealousy of his generals. Diocletian made his helpers actual partners in the imperial power and, by multiplying the imperial persons, left no prospect of final success to any local rebellion. The Empire had been passing by a slow transition from the old Augustan order into something of a very different character. Diocletian saw that the time had now come to abandon the old and to accept the new with all that it might imply.

This principle extends over the entire life of the State and conditions the whole of Diocletian's work. The Empire was too large for one emperor to administer: there must, then, be several rulers, each with his own administrative staff. The provinces had been unwieldy and, at times, dangerous in the hands of ambitious

[1] Tacitus, *Agric.* 9.　　　　　　　[2] Eutropius ix, 26.
[3] S.H.A. *Carus*, 13, 1.　　　　　　[4] Aurelius Victor, *Caes.* xxxix, 8.

governors. They must be divided into smaller units. The civil
and military commands had begun to be separated, and knights
had been replacing senators in camp and court alike. In both
these cases, the new idea must be allowed free development. In
all but a few provinces equestrian 'dux' and 'praeses,' now
entirely distinct in function, replace 'proconsul' or 'legatus.' The
frontier armies had given way repeatedly under the great barbarian invasions, and the emperors had been compelled to scrape
together a field-army, with cavalry as an important and independent arm. This essential force must be strengthened and made
permanent. The 'loyal and harmonious' troops had come to be a
menace to peaceful society. They must be brought back to the
old Roman discipline. Emperor after emperor had fallen by the
swords of his 'commilitones.' His person must be withdrawn
from all vulgar contacts, and surrounded with the outward
prestige of kingship and the mystical sanctity of religion. The
basis of authority in the State had come to be questioned. The
Senate had outlived its ancient dignity and worth, but the Imperial
office had not been strong enough to dispense with its moral
support. For the Empire, at large, then, not for the army only,
the Imperial office must be reinterpreted and re-established as
the centre of the national life. Neglect of the gods had brought
down their displeasure, attested by many a national disaster.
Rome must return to that reverence for the divine which had
made her great. The meaning of the name 'Rome' was no longer
centred in the capital or even in Italy. The provinces, then, and
the great provincial capitals must receive equal recognition.
Economic life and the State 'annona' had been subject to serious
disturbances. In both spheres, order and balance must be restored. Taxation, based on an obsolescent system, had ceased to
yield the necessary quota. A new basis for a sufficient revenue
must be discovered. The old system of one imperial mint, with
occasional auxiliaries in the provinces, and a multitude of local
mints for token-money, was already almost superseded. The
change must be completed and the needs of the Empire must be
met uniformly by local mints, all striking the same Imperial
coinage. The detail of all that makes up the new constitution of
Diocletian is reserved for special treatment elsewhere (chap. XI),
but without some mention of it here the external history of the
reign could not be understood.

The prospects of the reign might at first seem favourable, if
Diocletian could quickly heal the wounds of civil war. What
he could do, he did—as it seems with good effect. He showed

mercy to the friends and adherents of Carinus and actually continued in office his Praetorian Prefect, Aristobulus[1]. After some fighting on the Moesian and Pannonian front, which earned him the title of 'Germanicus Maximus,' he may have visited Rome as some think in the summer of 285[2] and received the recognition of the Senate. But the apparent calm of the Empire was not yet to be trusted, and Gaul at once offered an ugly problem in the revolt of the Bagaudae, bands of peasants, who, driven from their homes by the double terror of barbarian and tax-collector, had set up two emperors of their own, Aelian and Amandus. Here was the first opportunity for Diocletian to test his new plan. He had at his side Maximian, an old comrade in arms, brave and vigorous in action, lacking in originality but entirely loyal. He now gave him the commission to pacify Gaul. Maximian more than fulfilled the hopes set on him. The Bagaudae were no match for a skilled general, and were quickly tamed in a series of light skirmishes, but the rapid victory was more merciful than a protracted war would have been[3]. Maximian seems to have received at first the title of Caesar, or second in command, but certainly for no long time, as it is never found on the coins[4]. Early in A.D. 286 Diocletian advanced him to the rank of Augustus, perhaps subject to some restriction that we cannot precisely define, which was only removed at the appointment of the Caesars in 293[5]. Maximian had excelled all expectation and his troops were no doubt forward in pressing his claims to reward, but it is unlikely that Diocletian acted on anything but his own better judgment.

The Empire now rested on the 'Concord' of its two emperors and each found his own sphere for service. In defeating the Bagaudae, Maximian had gained some successes over the Franks and directed Carausius, who distinguished himself in the war, to take over command by sea against Frankish and Saxon pirates. Carausius revolted and, as we shall see later, gave Maximian full occasion to be busy in the north of Gaul and Britain. Meanwhile in 286 and 287 Maximian had to repel an incursion of Alemanni

---

[1] Aurelius Victor, *Caes.* XXXIX, 14 *sqq.*

[2] There is no certain evidence of this visit.

[3] Aurelius Victor, *Caes.* XXXIX, 16 *sqq.*; Eutropius IX, 20; Orosius VII, 25, 2.

[4] Zonaras XII, 31 (p. 614). Maximian was adopted as κοινωνός in the fourth or second year of the reign; M.-S. v, ii, p. 204; G. Costa, *Diz. Epig. s.v.* Diocletianus, pp. 1796 *sqq.*

[5] Costa, *loc. cit.* p. 1798; there were at first two years, later only one year, between the two emperors in their tribunician count.

and Burgundians on the Upper Rhine and, two years later, found the Alemanni again troublesome. In 288 Maximian, by the victory of his Praetorian Prefect, Constantius, pushed the Franks back to the ocean and concluded a treaty, restoring to their king Gennoboudes his kingdom[1]. A revolt of the Moors in Africa in 289–90 was suppressed by Maximian's generals. Diocletian was more diversely employed. In 286, if not earlier, he won the title of 'Germanicus Maximus' on the borders of Pannonia and Moesia. In 288 he induced the Persian king, Vahram, to surrender all claim to Mesopotamia, perhaps also to Armenia, and became 'Persicus Maximus[2].' In the same year he set up his nominee, Tiridates III, as king of Armenia. In the same year again he was in Raetia, aiding Maximian against the Chaibones and Heruli[3]. In 289 and again in 292 he fought the Sarmatians, in 290 he turned back a Saracen invasion of Syria, in 291 he put down a revolt of Coptos and Busiris in Egypt[4]. In all these years the Augusti had met but once, at Milan, in the winter of 289 to 290 when their arrival drew envoys from Rome to congratulate them on their concord and their triumphs[5]. An 'adventus imperatorum' at Massilia, spoken of in the *Acts of the Martyrs*, cannot be identified and may be entirely unhistorical[6].

Diocletian had by now matured his schemes for the division of imperial power and chosen the right men for his purpose, perhaps as early as 292, or even 291, though the formal act of investiture seems to have fallen in 293. Constantius Chlorus, a Dardanian nobleman of high repute and tried merit, was appointed Caesar to Maximian in the West, while Galerius, a rough but able soldier, took the same rank under Diocletian in the East. To bind both Caesars to himself and his colleague, Diocletian required them to put away their wives and marry the crown princesses. Constantius put away Helena, mother of Constantine, and married Theodora, daughter of Maximian, while Galerius gave up his former wife to marry Diocletian's daughter, Valeria[7]. Thus was established the famous Tetrarchy

---

[1] *Paneg.* x (ii), 10, 3.   [2] Costa, *op. cit.* p. 1801.

[3] *Paneg.* x (ii), 5, 1; xi (iii), 7, 2.   [4] Zonaras xii, 31 (p. 614).

[5] *Paneg.* xi (iii), 10 *sqq.*; for the view that there was also a meeting in 287–8 see p. 385 n. 1.

[6] *Acta Martyrum (Passio SS. Victoris etc.* ed. Ruinart, p. 333 s.f.).

[7] Aurelius Victor, *Caes.* xxxix, 24 *sqq.*; Eutropius ix, 22; Orosius vii, 25, 5; Zonaras xii, 31 (p. 614 *sq.*). This tradition of the noble descent of Constantius may prove in the end to be no more than part of the legend of the house of Constantius: Aurelius Victor, *Caes.* xxxix, 26 *sqq.* makes Constantius a rude countryman like his colleagues.

of Diocletian. One Augustus, Diocletian, held the East with Egypt, Libya, Arabia and Bithynia under his own hand, and Illyricum and, it would appear, the western part of Asia under the care of his Caesar, Galerius. The other, Maximian, held the West, with Rome, Italy, Sicily, Africa, and perhaps Spain under his control, while Gaul and rebel Britain were assigned to the Caesar, Constantius. Each Caesar held the tribunician power, but was subject in all things to his own Augustus, while Diocletian, by his wisdom and 'auctoritas,' dominated all alike. Our authorities, throwing the history of many years together, represent the choice of Caesars as due to a dire conjunction of present perils—Narses in Persia, Achilleus in Egypt, Julianus and the Quinquegentanei in Africa, Carausius in Britain. It has been well observed that there is serious confusion here[1]. The appointments were actually made in an interval of quiet, when the first problems of the reign were well on the way to settlement and others had barely risen on the horizon. The main crisis of the reign fell in the years 295 to 298, and by that time the Tetrarchy was in full working order and was ready to give a dazzling proof of its worth.

The team of four was finer than its individual members. It was strong in union and deserved the eulogy pronounced on it in the *Historia Augusta*: 'quattuor sane principes mundi, fortes, sapientes, benigni et admodum liberales, unum in rem publicam sentientes, perreverentes Romani senatus, moderati, populi amici, persancti, graves, religiosi, et quales principes semper oravimus[2].' In the end, it is true, the expenses of four courts proved a heavy burden, but in the first stages it was mitigated by the moderation of the rulers. Diocletian came more under the reproach of avarice than Maximian, who held the wealth of Rome and Italy, while Constantius enjoyed a unique reputation for restraint and generosity.

Omitting nothing that could strengthen his work, Diocletian consecrated the Tetrarchy by placing it under the direct protection of the great gods—his own dynasty, the Jovian, under Juppiter, that of Maximian, the Herculian, under Hercules. Élite corps of Illyrian troops bore the proud names of 'Iovii' and 'Herculii.' In Diocletian resided the divine wisdom, the 'providentia' of the supreme god, in Maximian the willing obedience and heroic energy of his great coadjutor in the service of men. If we may hazard a guess at the exact sense in which Diocletian and Maximian were related to their divine patrons, we may say that

[1] Costa, *op. cit.* pp. 1805 *sqq.*; cf. passages collected above (p. 328, n. 7).
[2] S.H.A. *Carinus*, 18, 3.

the Genius of each emperor, itself divine and an object of worship, was now declared to be the very Genius of Juppiter and Hercules themselves. Juppiter and Hercules are actually at work, as Victoria and Virtus had long been, in the spirits of their earthly representatives[1].

Although we are still three years short of the reform of Diocletian, this is probably the best place at which to review his pre-reform coinage[2]. It was essentially a continuation of the previous reign. The mints were the same, except that Heraclea and Treveri were added just before the reform. The main issue was still that of the base billon xx. 1 piece. No silver was struck, but gold appeared in moderate quantities, at first on the standard of 70 to the pound, later at 60. For a very short period at the outset there is one Augustus, Diocletian, alone; of Maximian as Caesar there is no trace. Then come the two Caesars in 293, commonly acclaimed as 'Principes Iuventutis' or 'praesidia reipublicae.' While the types still bear on such natural themes as the imperial vows, the Golden Age, the eternity of Rome, the virtues and exploits of the emperors, the religious interest is definitely to the fore, and, as we should expect, is focussed on the two figures of Juppiter and Hercules. Other deities—Mars, Minerva, Sol—have their honours, but of a lower order. The labours of Hercules are once more used as symbols of the exertions of Maximian for the good of the Empire, and Juppiter and Hercules are commonly associated in a single type, as the divine patterns of the two Emperors on earth. Not far behind in importance is the 'Concordia Augustorum,' the keystone of Diocletian's building—a legend especially common in the Eastern mints, which prefer to concentrate on a few themes of central importance. The unusual type of the three Fates, 'Fatis Victricibus[3],' reflects the superstition which lay deep in the character of Diocletian. He had a firm belief in divination, he loved to probe into the future and he attributed his own rise to the mysterious workings of destiny. The divine world is related very closely to the human, and the divine powers appear again and again as 'Preservers' or 'Companions' of the Emperors. The old paganism had always been weak in theory, and even the elaborate reinterpretation which the new Pythagoreans were applying to it could hardly produce a satisfactory system of thought. It was not on its intellectual side a creed for which any sensible government would

[1] Cf. Mattingly, 'The Roman "Virtues,"' *Harv. Theol. Rev.* xxx, 1937, pp. 103 *sqq.*   [2] M.-S. v, ii, pp. 204 *sqq.*; see Volume of Plates v, 240, *a–f.*
[3] See Volume of Plates v, 240, *d.*

persecute. But paganism as a background to the historical mission of Rome and her emperors had an altogether different power. For this paganism the most religious emperors might one day strike a blow.

VI. 'QUATTUOR PRINCIPES MUNDI'

Armed with the strength of the two new Caesars Diocletian could face with confidence the trials that yet awaited him. The problem for the moment was that of Carausius in Britain. A Menapian of the lowest birth[1], but of an ability and energy quite above the average, he had won distinction in the wars with Bagaudae and Franks in 286 (see p. 327) and had been appointed by Maximian to command the Channel fleet and clear the seas of the Frankish and Saxon pirates. Suspected of being less anxious to check the pirates than to relieve them of their plunder and to convert it to his own uses, he was sentenced to death by his master, but, receiving timely warning, revolted together with his fleet and maintained a hold on the north coasts of Gaul, while the island of Britain hastened to welcome him as a deliverer (late 286 or early 287)[2]. Maximian was still on the Lower Rhine in 287 to 288, and, by April 21, 289, was in readiness to deliver a decisive blow against the 'arch-pirate.' But the attack was launched in vain on an admiral 'perfectly skilled in the art of war.' Carausius seems to have gained a decisive victory at sea. But he aspired to something more than a precarious independence as a rebel. He offered and obtained peace and celebrated a triumph, greater than any success of his arms, by striking coins for 'Carausius and his brothers,' Diocletian and Maximian[3]. As a token of reconciliation he abandoned his first irregular coinage on the model of the Gallic Empire and struck the base billon xx. i piece like the rest of the Empire. Aurelius Victor tells us that he was permitted to rule Britain, because he seemed fit to deal with the warlike nations that threatened the island[4]. The peace, however, though loyally celebrated by Carausius with British issues for his colleagues, was not acknowledged on the coins of any Imperial mint. The Empire was only biding its time. In 293 Constantius set to work and blockaded Gesoriacum (Boulogne) by a great mole drawn across its harbour. Carausius

---

[1] But cf. E. Janssen in *Latomos*, I, 1937, pp. 269 *sqq.*, who makes him a native of Britain.

[2] Aurelius Victor, *Caes.* XXXIX, 19 *sqq.*; Eutropius IX, 21; Orosius VII, 25, 6.   [3] See Volume of Plates, v, 240, *h.*

[4] Aurelius Victor, *Caes.* XXXIX, 39 *sqq.*

was powerless to protect the town, and Gesoriacum fell; but victory was won by a mere hair's breadth, for the first tide after its capture broke the mole and opened it once more to the sea[1].

Gaul was now lost to the rebel and, even in Britain, the authority of Carausius was severely shaken. Allectus, his chief minister, killed his master (293) and took over the defence of the island realm[2]. Constantius was resolved to make no mistake. He spent two full years on his preparations, subduing the sympathizers with the rebels among the Menapii, while Maximian brought up an Illyrian corps, the 'Virtus Illurici,' to prevent any possible diversion on the Rhine[3]. In 296, the Roman fleet was ready for action. It put to sea in two detachments, under Constantius himself and his Praetorian Prefect, Asclepiodotus. A fog that separated the two squadrons enabled Asclepiodotus to slip past the main fleet of Allectus, which was waiting for him near Clausentum (Bitterne by Southampton). Asclepiodotus landed near the Isle of Wight, burnt his boats to commit his troops to the adventure, and encountered and routed Allectus somewhere in Hampshire. Allectus, flying from the lost battle, was killed and only the wrecks of his army succeeded in reaching London. The city was in danger of being sacked by this rabble, when the fleet of Constantius, which had been lost in the fog, sailed up the Thames and delivered the port of London from this peril. Constantius was hailed as the 'restorer of the eternal light' of Rome, and extended his mercy to the repentant Britons[4]. The attempt to make Britain an independent power, behind the wall of its fleet, had ended as it was bound to end, in failure, but it had been a gallant adventure.

The coinage of the British Empire throws some light on the character and policy of its rulers as well as on the spirit and hopes of the ruled[5]. Carausius is revealed as a man of original genius. He began by striking base billon, like that of the Gallic Empire, without the mark of value, xx. i, but struck beside it the first good silver to appear from any Roman mint for many a long day. Diocletian paid him the compliment of borrowing this change in his reform of 296. Britain, it seems, was unwilling to accept the coinage of Aurelian's reform, and Carausius yielded to its wishes,

---

[1] *Paneg.* VIII (v), 6–7 (cf. VI (VII), 5, 2).

[2] Eutropius IX, 22; Aurelius Victor, *Caes.* XXXIX, 40–41.

[3] See Volume of Plates v, 240, *g*.

[4] *Paneg.* VIII (v), 14–20; M.-S. v, ii, pp. 429 *sqq.* and references there given.

[5] M.-S. v, ii, pp. 426 *sqq.*

but, under the peace of 290, sacrificed financial independence and came into the general Imperial system. Carausius struck at a number of British mints—Londinium, Clausentum and probably Rutupiae (Richborough). On the continent, he struck at Gesoriacum and, perhaps, even inland at Rotomagus (Rouen). Considering himself a true Roman, he maintained the Roman tradition and claimed to be a restorer of Rome. He honoured legions under his command and others, stationed in the Empire, from which he can hardly have had actual support. He dwelt with justifiable pride on his fleet, claimed the protection of Juppiter, Mars, Minerva and Neptune, boasted of his victories but, even more, of his most glorious achievement, the honourable peace with the Empire. It is a notable fact that the only quotation from Virgil on a Roman coin occurs on the issues of this low-born Menapian rebel—'expectate veni' are the words of welcome with which Britain greets her deliverer[1]. The coinage of Allectus is less varied and interesting. It is confined to the two British mints, Londinium and Clausentum, and is mainly concerned with the virtues of the Emperor, notably his 'Pax' and his 'Providentia,' and the prowess of his fleet. A remarkable series of coins of the fleet, 'Laetitia Augusti' and 'Virtus Augusti,' with the type of a galley—perhaps the very names of Allectus's flagships—is struck in a much smaller size than the xx. i pieces of Carausius and bears the signatures, q.l. and q.c. This perhaps represents an attempt to launch a new denomination, the 'quinarius,' beside the larger piece. But even on that larger piece, the mark of value, xx. i, had disappeared with the breach with Rome, and the British coinage was again independent[2]. The smaller piece, which seems to belong mainly to the end of the reign, may be due to a reform and reduction of the coinage, possibly in some relation to the reform of Diocletian. The great gold hoard of Arras has recently revealed something of the impression made by the triumph of Constantius and his merciful restoration of the blessings of Roman rule to a humbled and contrite province[3].

Maximian, as has been said, had appeared in Gaul to ensure its peace while the great expedition sailed to Britain. After success in Britain was assured, the Emperor was called away on an errand of his own. In Africa a troublesome confederacy of Moorish tribes, the Quinquegentanei, had risen in revolt, and the local forces proved insufficient to suppress them. Late in 297

[1] M.-S. v, ii, pp. 439, 510, nos. 554 *sqq*.
[2] *Ib.* v, ii, pp. 438 *sqq*.
[3] *Aréthuse*, 1924, pp. 45 *sqq*.: see Volume of Plates v, 240, *k*.

Maximian marched to Africa by way of Spain, and made a speedy end of the rebellion[1]. He was in Carthage on March 10, 298 and, later in that year, seems to have visited Rome for the first time in his reign. Constantius was for a while detained by the affairs of Britain: indeed, it is obvious that after the ten years of the British Empire there were many things that needed attention and correction. He re-organized the defences of the island and laid the foundations of a new age of prosperity. The Saxon pirates in particular, who had been allied to the British emperors, were now fended off by a Count of the Saxon Shore with an efficient fleet and strong, well-distributed forts behind him. It must have been in this new settlement of Constantius that Britain was divided into the four provinces of Flavia Caesariensis, Maxima Caesariensis and Britannia Prima and Secunda. In 297 the Western Caesar established the Salian Franks on the island of the Batavians. A little later, perhaps in 298, Constantius is found again in Gaul, heavily engaged with a marauding horde of Alemanni. He ended the campaigns by a brilliant and spectacular victory near the 'city of the Lingones,' made all the more notable by a sudden reversal of fortune. Beaten at first in the field and narrowly rescued by ropes thrown down from the walls of the city, he received reinforcements the same day and led them out to break and scatter the enemy. After this exploit, the West enjoyed some years of uninterrupted peace.

Diocletian and his Caesar had been equally busy in Illyricum and the East. Galerius was set to serve his apprenticeship on the banks of the Danube, warding off invaders and clearing ground for cultivation by deforestation and irrigation. In 294 and 295 he had to deal with Goths on the move westwards towards the territory of the Burgundians. At about this time forts were built at Aquincum and Bononia on the Danube. In 296 or 297 there was fighting against various peoples—Marcomanni, Sarmatae, Bastarnae and Carpi—and the whole of the last-named people was transferred to settlements within the Empire[2]. It was no doubt to make room for such new immigrants as these that Galerius spent his labours on land-reclamation[3] that does honour to this rough soldier, but seems to have embittered his spirit, as he saw others enjoying higher honours at less cost.

Diocletian, no doubt, was in the background, directing and

[1] Orosius VII, 25, 8; Eutropius IX, 23.
[2] Aurelius Victor, *Caes.* XXXIX, 43.
[3] Aurelius Victor, *Caes.* XL, 9 *sqq.* (reported at the end of his life, but obviously to be referred to an earlier date).

encouraging his Caesar: we find him wintering at Nicomedia, 294–5. In 296–7 Egypt demanded his personal intervention. That turbulent province had already needed correction earlier in the reign; now, the capital, Alexandria, broke out in revolt and created an emperor of its own. The Achilleus of our literary authorities is undoubtedly the Domitius Domitianus of the coins, who interrupts the coinage of Diocletian in its twelfth year, 295–6, and strikes in two distinct years himself, 295–6 and 296–7. His revolt is not clearly distinguished from the earlier revolt of Coptos and Busiris, and it is, of course, possible that the same man was concerned in both. But it is hardly to be imagined that there was actually rebellion in Egypt from 293 to 296; it is far more probable that the events of several years have been carelessly thrown together. Diocletian invested Alexandria and forced its surrender after eight months, c. November 296–June 297[1]. The exact causes of the rebellion are unknown, but they presumably had something to do with economic discontents in connection with the monetary reform of Diocletian (p. 338). That reform had not been long in working when Domitianus revolted, and he himself struck coins of the old Alexandrian pattern as well as the new. Those of the old pattern he may have issued to please the Alexandrians, those of the new were needed to keep in touch with the rest of the empire: on them he seems to have struck for Diocletian, Maximian and the Caesars, claiming a partnership in Empire as Carausius had claimed it in Britain[2]. After his first anger had abated, Diocletian spent some time in Egypt, re-ordering its affairs and making useful arrangements, which were still in force when Eutropius wrote his 'Breviarium[3].' It is probable that Diocletian drew some ideas to be applied more generally throughout the Empire from Egypt, the most highly organized of all the provinces.

In the summer of 296 a more dangerous enemy threatened the Empire. Narses of Persia, succeeding Vahram III in 293, brought back something of the spirit and energy of the great Shapur to the Persian kingdom. Weary of subordination to Rome and at

---

[1] Jordanes, *Romana*, 298, 300 M; Orosius VII, 25, 8; Eutropius IX, 23; Malalas XII, p. 308 *sq.* (Bonn); Zonaras XII, 31 (p. 614). For the coinage of Domitius Domitianus, see Cohen, VII, pp. 53 *sqq.*; W. Kubitschek, 'Zur Geschichte des Usurpators Achilleus', *Sitz. d. Ak. d. Wiss. Wien*, 1928, pp. 1 *sqq.*; U. Wilcken, *Sitz. d. Ak. d. Wiss. Berlin*, 1927, pp. 270–276. There seems, on the whole, to be no sufficient reason for associating the revolt of Achilleus at all closely with the earlier revolt of Coptos.

[2] Kubitschek, *op. cit.* pp. 21 *sqq.*   [3] Eutropius IX, 23.

variance with Tiridates, the vassal king in Armenia, he took advantage of Diocletian's preoccupation in Egypt and invaded Syria. Galerius was called up from Illyricum and forced the invader to retire towards Carrhae, but, following up his success too impetuously, he was caught in an ambush at Callinicus and heavily defeated. Diocletian had moved up to Antioch to support his Caesar, and it will have been at this time that factories of arms were established in Antioch, Edessa and Damascus[1]. He received Galerius with a scorn deliberately calculated to inflame his proud spirit, and made him follow on foot behind his chariot. At the same time he accorded him the opportunity to repair his fault. Galerius brought up reinforcements from the Danube countries, veterans of such legions as V Macedonica and XIII Gemina and Gothic auxiliaries from Dacia. Confident in his new strength, he marched into Greater Armenia and, by strategy as able as it was bold, outgeneralled and routed Narses and captured a huge booty, including the wives and children of the Great King[2]. Narses retired into the heart of his kingdom and Galerius pushed on and captured Ctesiphon.

Galerius was in a mood to exploit his success to the full and establish a new Roman province, but Diocletian 'cuius nutu omnia gerebantur' prepared a less showy, but more permanent settlement. The captives, hostages of the highest value, were treated with all honour and lodged at Daphne near Antioch. Narses renounced his ambitions and bent his policy to the recovery of his wives and children. His envoy, Appharban, pleaded for a joint recognition of Rome and Persia by one another as co-ordinate great powers. He was roundly rebuked by Galerius for a false moderation of tone that accorded ill with the violently aggressive policy of Persia. But, in the end, he was sent back with some hope of a friendly settlement and, not long afterwards, an Imperial Secretary, Sicorius Probus, met Narses on the river Asprudas and concluded peace. The great difficulties raised by the terms of this treaty cannot be discussed here; it must suffice to say that Mesopotamia was definitely surrendered and a Roman protectorate over Armenia was acknowledged. Five small provinces across the Tigris were ceded to Rome—Intilene (Ingilene), Sophene, Carduene, Arsanene, and Zabdicene—and Nisibis was fixed as a centre for the commercial relations between the two empires. In return for all these concessions Narses received back

---

[1] Malalas XII, p. 307, last four lines, p. 308, l. 1 (Bonn).
[2] Eutropius IX, 24; Jordanes, *Romana*, 301 M; Orosius VII, 25, 9 *sqq.*

his captives, but nothing more. In order to avoid the appearance of complete surrender, he raised objections to the clause touching Nisibis, but here too, after mild pressure, he gave way[1]. The triumph of Roman arms and diplomacy made an immense impression. 'Circenses Adiabenicis victis' were celebrated at Rome, from May 13 to 17, and an arch, that still stands, was erected at Thessalonica, to immortalize the victory. Galerius boasted himself a son of Mars and, forgetting something of his old subservience to Diocletian, began to force his claims and policies on the senior Emperor. The Persian victory was to bear fruit in other fields.

The middle period of the reign of Diocletian (c. 293 to 299) saw the crucial test of his policy and administration. The Tetrarchy sustained the trial as perfectly as its author could have desired. Augusti and Caesars loyally supported one another in all difficulties, distributing labours and covering one another's rear during campaigns. The recovery of Britain, the crushing of revolts in Mauretania and Egypt, and the crowning victory over Persia, established confidence in the government and raised Roman prestige to a height which it had not reached since the days of Septimius Severus. The divine splendours of Juppiter and Hercules already invested the two imperial houses. To these were now added the glories of the kingdoms of this earth. Though, as has been recently shown[2], Oriental forms had already invaded the Roman court, Diocletian took some decisive step in this direction which struck the imagination of his own and later times. He appears against a background of ceremonial and adoration as of the Persian palace, arrayed in garments embroidered with gold and jewelry, and gives full official recognition to practices which before had been experimental. Persian kings were not as readily murdered by their bodyguards as the Roman *imperatores*, who were only marked out by the purple cloak and mixed freely with their comrades. Diocletian was astute enough to be taught by an enemy and to add to the mysterious awe of religion the splendours of Persian royalty.

Even before the conclusion of the great wars those changes in administration which support Diocletian's claim to be the second founder of the Empire had begun to take shape. These changes are described and discussed elsewhere in this volume (chap. XI), but it is to be remembered that they were the constant preoccupation of the Emperor. One side of this activity

[1] Petrus Patricius, frags. 13, 14 (*F.H.G.* IV, p. 188 *sq.*).
[2] A. Alföldi, in *Röm. Mitt.* XLIX, 1934, pp. 1 *sqq.*

was directed towards the economic problems besetting the Empire which were a legacy from his predecessors. It is for this reason that they are reviewed in a separate chapter VII, together with the epidemic of high prices which Diocletian sought, though with small success, to remedy by his famous Edict *de maximis pretiis*. It may not, however, be out of place to point out here the possibility that the Emperor himself had unwittingly helped to produce the disease for which he sought to find a remedy. Towards the end of A.D. 295 he added to the aureus a coin of pure silver. He further made a billon piece, usually called a *follis*, which was superior in size and weight to the xx. I coin of Aurelian and his successors. The *follis* was now the first coin below the precious metals, and may be regarded as equivalent to the old sestertius, one-fourth of the silver piece. On the other hand the xx. I coin was now to be reckoned at a half-sestertius. Thus there was created a stable currency, but at the cost of a very drastic devaluation of the xx. I piece, the coin with which the market had been flooded during the past reigns. If we may apply to this date the evidence of an important papyrus[1] this measure had an unexpected, but not unnatural result. The news that the old coin was to be reduced in value led to a rush to exchange it for commodities at any price, and in view of the vast masses of it in circulation it is easy to see why there was a great rise in prices which continued, only partly checked by the Edict, until the effect of the devaluation had worked itself out. The Edict was issued in A.D. 301. Two years later other forces challenged his statecraft, and claim some attention here.

Diocletian's name has been traditionally associated with the last and greatest persecution of the Christians, and his evil reputation has been only partially redeemed by his fame as administrator and reformer. That persecution is considered elsewhere in this volume (chap. XIX), but its place in the political history of the Empire must here be briefly defined. During the years which followed the attempt of Decius and Valerian to break the strength of the Church the Christian faith had secured its position: it was now 'a State within the State,' too strong and too well disciplined to be ignored. Could Diocletian in his devotion to the old sanctities of public life and in his revival of pagan worship maintain a strict neutrality in face of a growing and ambitious Church?

At first the problem was not urgent: the Church had lost something of its fighting spirit and was not quick to give provocation. When about 295 Diocletian began something like a purge of the

[1] P. Ryl. Inv. 650.

army, seeking to remove from it its Christian elements, it was still doubtful whether that repression would be further extended, though it may be suggested that the coinage of the reform with the type of Genius Populi Romani on its commonest denomination, the *follis*—a type which continued unchanged into the period of the persecution—shows the presence of ideas which were later to declare themselves in action.

If it is sought to find reasons for the violent change in policy which was effected by the edicts of 303 it can be urged that in the early years of the reign military problems perforce took precedence: the religious issue was deferred till the end of the great wars. Peace with Persia once concluded, Diocletian was free to turn his mind to the completion of his task of internal re-organization. Anxious to secure the foundations on which imperial authority was in future to rest, he may well have come slowly to the conclusion that the Christian Church must bow to his will. The Emperor's personal conviction inspired the edict against the Manichaeans (p. 668): the gods of Rome had made Rome great; senseless innovation might bring divine wrath upon the Empire. The Christian in thought and social custom was a revolutionary, regarding as evil demons the gods of the Empire's worship. Diocletian might thus with reason come of his own accord to the reluctant conclusion that the peace of Gallienus had conceded too much, that the Church must be coerced. And yet the suddenness of the change in policy can hardly in this way be adequately explained: pressure must have been brought to bear upon the Emperor by representatives of a more aggressive and intolerant type of paganism, and of these the leader was undoubtedly the Caesar Galerius. His influence vastly strengthened by his Persian victory, Galerius, with the enthusiastic support of Neoplatonist champions of the older faith, compelled Diocletian to admit that the challenge of the Christian Church must be boldly met. Diocletian yielded to the insistence of his Caesar; his efforts to prevent the shedding of blood proved fruitless, and at length the task of suppressing the Church was left to those whose heart was set upon the bloody work. Amongst the Christians there were countless defections, but those who withstood the will of the rulers of the Roman world were numerous enough to defeat the imperial purpose. Diocletian found, like many a statesman both before and after his day, that he had entered into conflict with forces which did not obey the laws with which statecraft had made him familiar[1].

[1] See, for a somewhat different interpretation, below, pp. 665 *sqq.*

VII. 'PROVIDENTIA DEORUM, QUIES AUGUSTORUM'

On November 20, A.D. 303 Diocletian appeared in Rome with Maximian to celebrate his *vicennalia*, give largesse to the people and enjoy the acclamations of the old capital on his accomplished work. He was uneasy, however, in mind and found the licence of the Roman mob little to his taste. Even before the end of the year he withdrew to Ravenna and entered on the consulship of 304 in that city[1]. Early in 304, on his journey to Nicomedia, he suffered some form of nervous breakdown, which incapacitated him for all public duties and seemed likely at one time to end in death. Presently he recovered health, but let himself be convinced that the State needed the services of younger men[2]. On May 1, 305 he made a solemn act of abdication at Nicomedia, while Maximian, from whom he had extracted a promise to retire with him, abdicated at Milan. Constantius succeeded in the West, as senior Augustus, Galerius as junior in the East. For the vacant posts of Caesars, there were two natural claimants, Constantine, son of Constantius, and Maxentius, son of Maximian. Both, however, were passed over, on whatever pretext, and Severus and Maximin Daia, both protégés of Galerius, the latter a relative also, were appointed, the one for the West, the other for the East. These two appointments must have excited comment, not all of a favourable character. But of definite opposition there was none. The system of Diocletian had sustained its decisive test; the transition from First to Second Tetrarchy was accomplished without hindrance. Diocletian withdrew to his palace at Salonae to grow vegetables, Maximian to a life of self-indulgence on his country estates in Lucania. The gods had watched faithfully over the succession, and our 'lords and masters, the most happy and blessed senior Augusti,' could enter on their well-earned rest.

These events, if accepted at their face value, imply that Diocletian was carrying out in its due time a scheme pre-arranged many years before, when the Caesars were first appointed. That abdication had been considered as a possibility from the outset need not be denied. The whole purpose of the office of Caesar was to train men for the chief rank, and such training would lack half its meaning if promotion were to be indefinitely deferred. Galerius, too, an even more ardent supporter of the scheme of the Tetrarchy than its founder, contemplated retirement at the completion of his own *vicennalia*. But it is improbable that any special terminus was fixed in advance. The most natural, the *vicennalia*

---

[1] Lactantius, *de mort. pers.* 17, 3.　　[2] Lactantius, *de mort. pers.* 18.

of Diocletian, passed without a change, and there is much to show
that the actual occasion was rather forced on Diocletian than chosen
by him. For several years before 305 Galerius had been claiming
the full recognition of his great services. He had forced on
Diocletian the dangerous step of persecuting the Christian Church,
and had set up internal conflicts in his mind which must have
contributed to his collapse of 304. The choice of the new Caesars
has no meaning except as an illustration of the personal likes and
dislikes of Galerius. Christian writers concluded that Diocletian
abdicated because he despaired of success in the struggle he had
forced on the Christians. Aurelius Victor records that Diocletian,
'imminentium scrutator,' sought to escape that internal discord
and general crash, which, as he learned from his researches, was
impending. Some modern scholars have supposed that he would
have repented at the last of his original intention to abdicate, had
not Galerius brought such pressure to bear as his weary mind
could not resist[1].

The verdict of history on the character and achievement of
Diocletian has on the whole been favourable. He vindicated the
majesty of Rome and carried her arms victoriously into every
quarter of the empire. He rebuilt the State on new foundations
and gave her under changed forms a new lease of life. He contrived an ingenious system of government which successfully
escaped the dangers to which his predecessors had succumbed.
He established a new basis of authority which finally ended
military anarchy. His one conspicuous failure lay in his religious
policy which may be contrasted with what Constantine achieved.
But nothing less than a deep change of heart could have turned
Diocletian from his innate conservatism and love of the old
religion to a frank acceptance of the new, and for such a change he
was too old. Constantine came to the task in the freshness of
youth, and he had Diocletian's failure before him as a guide and
as a warning. Here, as elsewhere, it was given to him to complete
the work that Diocletian had begun. But the Empire had cause
to be thankful for Diocletian, as one 'born for the good of the
State.' He had served Rome loyally according to the light that
was in him, and he had fulfilled the tasks to which he had set his
hand; he was able to commit the burden of Empire to a system
of his own making and to carry into retirement the love and
admiration of his subjects. It is a wonderful path that leads from
Diocles, the low-born freedman, to Diocletian, 'Iovius,' 'felicis-

---

[1] Lactantius, *de mort. pers.* 18. The theme has been much debated in
modern times; see the works cited in the Bibliography and below, p. 667.

simus senior Augustus.' Even if much of his building collapsed
in that fatal crash he had foreseen, there was that in his work that
had the quality to endure.

VIII. THE SECOND TETRARCHY: GALERIUS IN POWER

The abdication of Diocletian, even if pressed on him at the
last against his own will, must have appeared to his subjects an
act of noble renunciation which set the seal on his life-work. The
Empire was still under the system that he had devised, and
Diocletian could hope to spend his declining years as most
honoured of 'Elder Statesmen,' watching it enjoy the peace and
security that he had won for it. Maximian laid aside the purple
in quite another mood, loyal to the last to his great colleague, but
openly fretting at the unwelcome necessity. His talents and
inclinations were all for an active life: retirement for him meant
stagnation. There seemed to be little danger, however, that, after
once having been persuaded to enter on his rest, he would force
a way back into public life.

Constantius Chlorus, Augustus of the West, was now senior
emperor, though Galerius, his colleague of the East, assumed the
leading position in all but name. The sons of Constantius himself
and of his former senior, Maximian, had both been passed over,
and Severus, the new Caesar of the West, no less than Daia in the
East, was Galerius' man. Constantius held only Gaul, Britain
and Spain, while Severus held Italy, Africa and Pannonia. In
the East, Maximin governed Egypt and the provinces as far
north as Taurus, while Galerius himself held the rest of Asia,
Greece, and Eastern Illyricum. The facts are too eloquent to be
misunderstood. The actual arrangements represented the interests
and wishes of Galerius, and of Galerius alone. Constantius found
himself in a position where he must either accept virtual subordination to his junior or hazard a civil war. It was not merely
his gentle and merciful disposition, but also sound judgment
that made him hold his hand.

The new Augusti were men tried and approved by long and
successful service. Both were distinguished soldiers and administrators, both loyal adherents of the new imperial system.
Beyond this the resemblance ceases, even if we make allowance for
the strength of the Christian tradition which glorifies Constantius,
the friend, and blackens Galerius, the enemy. Constantius was a
man of breeding and culture, of strong and refined religious

sense, with more of the old Roman *humanitas* than the ordinary Illyrian captain. Galerius, though himself 'probe moratus,' was uncompromising, merciless and excessively ambitious; a more fatal defect was his false standard of values as seen most tragically in his religious policy (chap. XIX). The new Caesars were both unknown to the world at large. Severus was a good soldier but nothing more, if we rule out his notable qualities as a boon-companion. Maximin was a half-barbarous lad, a kinsman of Galerius, who perhaps thought to use him as Diocletian had used Maximian, as a clumsy but effective tool. He was afterwards to reveal qualities, if not virtues, that surprised his maker.

Whether the unbroken peace of the new régime would have endured for long cannot be decided, for, after little more than a year of rule, Constantius died at York on July 25, 306. Signs of troubles to come were not wanting. Early in the year Constantius, who was preparing an expedition against the Picts, sent a direct request to Galerius to dispatch Constantine to his assistance. Constantine, the son of Constantius by Helena, the low-born wife[1] whom he had put away to marry Fausta—according to some born out of wedlock[2]—had been brought up in the East at the courts of Diocletian and Galerius and had shown early signs of ambition and energy. Diocletian may have seen in him a kindred spirit and trained him for future service. But this is nowhere recorded and is certainly not proved merely by the fact that Constantine lived to complete the reforms of Diocletian; the completion too often looked like drastic revision. To Christians writing at a later date Constantine's boyhood seemed comparable to that of Moses among the Egyptians, while Galerius appears as the brutal tyrant who tries him with dangerous ordeals from which only divine grace and his own courage deliver him[3]. After the abdication of Diocletian, his position, however honourable in name, was that of a hostage. The story of the flight of Constantine to his father, travelling by forced marches and killing the post-horses behind him to defeat pursuit, is undisputed. The secret history of the event is less certain. Galerius may have suggested delay, but he certainly did not refuse the request of Constantius outright and finally gave Constantine his passport. Yet Constantine flies like an escaped convict. The true explanation can be

---

[1] *Origo Constant. imp.* (Mommsen, *Chron. Min.* I), p. 7; Zonaras XIII, I (p. 1); Eutropius X, 2.

[2] Zosimus II, 8, 2; II, 9, 2; Zonaras, *loc. cit.* alternative account πάρεργον ἐρωτικῶν ἐπιθυμιῶν.

[3] *Origo Constant. imp.* p. 7; Zonaras XII, 33 (p. 623).

guessed, if not proved. Constantius, in demanding back his son on a colourable excuse, was trying to recover his freedom of action. Galerius, if he refused point-blank, would put himself completely in the wrong in any quarrel that might arise from his refusal. But between Galerius and Constantius lay Severus, through whose territories Constantine must travel, and Severus, the natural rival of Constantine, would hardly need a hint to detain him on any excuse that might be found. Galerius would be able to profess complete innocence and readiness to negotiate, but Constantine would remain a hostage[1]. This was the subtle design that was defeated by Constantine's amazing energy and foresight. He found his father still at Bologne and crossed with him to Britain, where he conquered 'Britannicas gentes in intimo oceani recessu sitas.' Very soon afterwards Constantius died.

The meaning of the diplomacy of Constantius was now revealed. Without thinking of waiting for the decision of Galerius, the army, largely swayed by the counsels of the German allied king, Crocus, acclaimed Constantine as its new ruler of the West. His age and even more his abilities demanded that the defence of the house of Constantius should be entrusted to him rather than to his half-brothers, the sons of Theodora. Laureate images of Constantine were sent to Galerius, to announce what had taken place and to ask for his approval. The implications of the mission were obvious to Galerius—'We recognize your supremacy, we accept the requirements of the imperial system, we want no civil war: but we will not submit to complete elimination.' Galerius was statesman enough to curb the paroxysm of anger into which the news threw him, before he gave his reply. He accepted Constantine as Caesar and advanced Severus to be Augustus of the West[2]. He may have hoped thus to render Constantine harmless, until he could be dealt with later; he may even have made an honest sacrifice of his personal resentment, in order to maintain the order of the Tetrarchy without a civil war.

IX. CONSTANTINE AND MAXENTIUS: FILII AUGUSTORUM

The elevation of Constantine may have shaken, but certainly did not overthrow the system of government by tetrarchy. It had, however, an immediate consequence which at once had that effect. There was living in the neighbourhood of Rome one who had

---

[1] Lactantius, de mort. pers. 24; Origo Constant. imp. p. 7; Zosimus II, 8.
[2] Lactantius, de mort. pers. 25; Eusebius, Vita Constant. I, 22.

even better claims to the succession than Constantine—Maxentius, son of Maximian, born of no dubious or morganatic match, but in lawful wedlock. It was only later that rumours spoke of him as a supposititious child. If Constantine was to be placed in his lawful position by the troops, why should not Maxentius hope for the same justice? Had there been no public wrongs to reinforce a private grievance it is doubtful if Maxentius would have had the energy to enforce his own claim. But Rome and southern Italy were already bitter over their loss of privilege and subjection to taxation, and, above all, over the suppression of the Praetorian Guard—a step taken by Severus at the instigation of Galerius[1]. A conspiracy led by Marcellianus, Marcellus and Lucianus, the officer in charge of the pork market, was supported by the Guard and gained immediate success. There was little resistance, but Abellius, the 'vicarius' of the City Prefect, lost his life. Maxentius was proclaimed *princeps* and acknowledged in Rome and South Italy, while the North still held to Severus, who had his seat at Milan. Africa at once joined Maxentius and relieved him of anxiety about the food-supply. But his position was precarious and, with the approval of the Senate, he sent the imperial insignia to his father, who left his retirement in Lucania to rally the army in his support[2]. But it was in vain that Maximian tried to draw Diocletian with him into the vortex.

Galerius had accepted one compromise, but he was in no mood to accept a second. Apart from his personal aversion to Maxentius and Maximian, he saw in the new move a deadly threat to the whole imperial system for which he stood. He declined to recognize Maxentius and ordered Severus to march against him. Severus, like a loyal colleague, obeyed and led his army up to the walls of the capital. But from this point the campaign would not go according to plan. Rome kept her gates stubbornly shut, and secret agents were soon at work in the ranks of Severus, whose soldiers had served long under Maximian and felt the call of the old loyalty. Judicious bribery completed what diplomacy had begun, and Severus had no choice but to retire rapidly on Ravenna. Maximian, who had by now resumed his position as Augustus, followed him and succeeded in inducing him, on the promise of his life, to commit himself into his hands (early 307)[3]. Severus was imprisoned and kept as a hostage against Galerius,

---

[1] Lactantius, *de mort. pers.* 26, 2–3.

[2] *Ib.* 26; Eutropius x, 2, 3; *Origo Constant. imp.* p. 8.

[3] Eutropius x, 2, 4; Lactantius, *de mort. pers.* 26; *Origo Constant. imp.* p. 7; Zosimus ii, 10, 2.

while Maxentius assumed the title of Augustus. But Galerius still remained to be dealt with. It could not be hoped that he would tolerate the indignities that Severus had suffered, and it became necessary to seek all possible reinforcement against him. While Maxentius stayed in Rome, Maximian travelled to Gaul to sound the intentions of Constantine, who was already showing great vigour in his administration. Maximian offered him in marriage his own daughter, Fausta, to whom Constantine had already been betrothed some years earlier. The two motives—to secure his own position and to weaken the dangerous might of Galerius—proved sufficient. Constantine received Fausta in marriage, acknowledged Maxentius as Augustus and himself accepted promotion to that rank at the hands of Maximian[1].

Meanwhile the storm broke on Italy. By the summer of 307 Galerius had completed his preparations and, leaving his comrade Licinius to hold Illyricum for him, he marched into Italy and reached Interamna without a battle. Much to his surprise and dismay he soon detected symptoms of that same disaffection among his troops that had been the undoing of Severus. Giving up the countryside of Italy to his men to plunder, he withdrew in baffled rage to Pannonia to reconsider his plans[2]. The invasion of Galerius had been fatal to Severus. Probably during the absence of Maximian in Gaul he was put to death at Tres Tabernae in defiance of the agreement[3]. The hold of Galerius on the West was completely lost. What part Constantine played in these machinations remains uncertain, but he certainly refused the opportunity to join in crushing Galerius on his retreat.

Late in 307 Maximian re-appeared in Rome and proceeded to embroil matters still further by a *coup d'État* of his own. For whatever reason—personal ambition, anger at the treachery shown to Severus, or intrigue in the interests of Constantine, now his son-in-law—he summoned the troops to a meeting and tried to tear the purple from the shoulders of his son. But the scheme miscarried. Maxentius took refuge with the soldiers, who refused to listen to the father and drove him out, 'like a second Tarquin,' to seek refuge in exile at the court of Constantine[4].

Galerius then proceeded to seek a solution on his own lines. The whole system of Diocletian was threatened, now that the West had broken away under two Augusti and one senior

---

[1] Lactantius, *de mort. pers.* 27.
[2] Zosimus II, 10; *Origo Constant. imp.* p. 7 *sq.*   [3] Zosimus II, 10.
[4] Lactantius, *de mort. pers.* 28; Eutropius X, 3, 1.

Augustus of its own. What more fitting than that the authority and wisdom of 'Iovius' himself should be called in to safeguard what he had built? Diocletian was nominated to the consulship of 308 with Galerius and was called to a conference at Carnuntum at which Maximian also was present. Diocletian would neither return to the helm himself nor suffer Maximian to remain there. Licinius, a trusted comrade-in-arms of Galerius, was set up as the second Augustus at his side; Maximin Daia was still to be the Caesar of the East, while Constantine was reduced to the same rank in the West. Maxentius was declared a public enemy (November 308)[1]. The forms of the Tetrarchy were thus restored, but the restoration was as short-lived as it was artificial. Maximian fled once more to Constantine in Gaul. Maxentius maintained himself in Rome and Italy. Constantine refused to submit to degradation, and Maximin Daia, hitherto a submissive follower of Galerius, protested against the promotion of Licinius over his head. Galerius tried to satisfy their claims by bestowing on them the title of 'filii Augustorum' in place of that of Caesar. The concession was only accepted as a step to full recognition, and both Constantine and Maximin are soon found claiming the title of Augustus[2]. The system of two Augusti and two Caesars was at an end, and six Augusti together divided amongst themselves the rule of the Roman world. The primacy of Galerius, it is true, remained unquestioned, but the new system, resting on no general basis of agreement, was obviously unstable and only needed some slight shift of the balance of power to break down completely. The 'fatal crash' that Diocletian had foreseen was impending; it was not merely the love of the simple life that made Diocletian prefer to cultivate his garden at Salonae.

It was rapidly becoming clear that Diocletian's elaborate scheme to subordinate persons to his system must ultimately prove a failure. The marvellous 'Concordia' of the First Tetrarchy had been a lucky accident. The system was too complicated to escape disturbance from conflicting claims of heredity or service and clashes of temperament and will. It was on the personalities of its six rulers that the future of the Empire now mainly depended. Increasing years and responsibilities did something to steady and deepen Galerius' character, but nothing to enlarge his sympathies or his understanding. He was loyal to what he knew, but incapable of fresh learning. The old Maximian returned to Empire worse than he had left it. He was almost purely mis-

---

[1] Zosimus II, 10; Lactantius, de mort. pers. 29, 2.
[2] Lactantius, de mort. pers. 32, 5–6.

chievous and destructive, 'vir ad omnem acerbitatem saeviti-
amque proclivis, infidus, incommodus, civilitatis penitus expers[1].'
Maxentius, his son, was apparently a man of no especial force of
character. Under the influence of supreme power he seems to
have yielded to licentiousness and cruelty, and to have alienated
the personal sympathy he had once enjoyed. His real importance
lay in the fact that he represented the old claim of Rome to
especial honour. When men could hope for a better champion of
the same claim in Constantine, they soon abandoned Maxentius.
Maximin Daia developed a strength and independence of character
that could hardly have been expected of him. His personal
character was bad and he bears the same stigma of cruelty as the
other persecutors. But there are still left one or two indications of
a more favourable side to his character, and it was something that
a persecutor should advance as did Maximin from mere repression
to a deliberate attempt to reform paganism on lines suggested by
the persecuted religion[2]. Licinius appears first as a mere piece
in the game of Galerius, a good soldier devoted to his cause. But,
as his later career was to show, he was perhaps the most detestable
of all the hard men of his age, self-seeking, unimaginative and
coldly cruel.

Finally, in Constantine we meet one of those rare personalities
who leave a decisive mark on history. His great vigour of mind
and body, his personal courage and soldierly ability were in themselves enough to bring him to the fore. But to these were added
gifts of a rarer quality. He was a born organizer and leader of
men, with an immense capacity for forming schemes and finding
the means of carrying them out. It is with full justice that he
ranks with Diocletian as joint founder of the new Empire. But
he had something beyond this that Diocletian never had. Like
Diocletian, he could meditate on the causes of social and political
events and devise new solutions for old problems. Unlike him,
he could submit to the influence of new ideals on his own inner
thought and life. All this still lay in the future, but as early as
308 he was marked out as the coming man on whom rested the
hopes of the many who had seen the promise of Diocletian's
Golden Age recede and die away.

For a time the six Augusti ruled side by side, untroubled by
any serious disturbances from without—so sure was the peace
that Diocletian had established. Constantine in Gaul had campaigns to fight against barbarians on the Rhine and gladdened the
hearts of his subjects by exhibiting captive Germans as gladiators

---

[1] Eutropius x, 3, 2.   [2] Lactantius, de mort. pers. 36, 4.

in the arena[1]. But the initiative, as it seems, lay with him. He was practising his soldiers and training his own vast energies for greater tasks to come. After Carnuntum the old Maximian returned to his court, still in name senior Augustus, but without any real imperial function. Restless and ambitious to the last, he sought means to overthrow Constantine and tried in vain to use his daughter, Fausta, against her husband. Finally, when Constantine was marching Rhinewards he revolted and seduced a body of troops; but he was besieged and captured at Massilia and died by his own hand (early 310)[2]. It was a serious step for Constantine to take—to be consenting to the death of the once great 'Herculius,' the father of his wife and the first bestower of the Augustus title on himself, but it is hard to see how he could have escaped the necessity. The link with the Herculian dynasty was now broken and Constantine, to find a new basis for his authority, encouraged the legend that his father, Constantius, was descended from Claudius II. Sol Invictus was adopted as the patron deity of the dynasty and began to appear in great prominence on Constantine's coins.

Maxentius meanwhile remained in undisturbed possession of Italy, expressing himself according to his own ideas of government. Though no persecutor on principle he made himself hated by his cruelty, lust and greed, but the Praetorians were committed to his cause so that no attempt to dislodge him without external aid could hope to succeed. His ambitions to found a dynasty, however, were blighted by the death of his son Romulus in 309. On one occasion when a great fire broke out in the city and, in the confusion, the soldiers came to blows with the people, a serious massacre was only narrowly averted by the intervention of the Emperor[3]. A rebellion in Africa threatened the corn-supply of Italy and might have proved fatal to Maxentius had any of his rivals chosen to abet it. The details are obscure. A body of troops favouring Galerius deserted the service of Maxentius. Maxentius, in alarm, demanded as hostage the son of Alexander, who was acting for him as prefect in Carthage. Alexander, a Phrygian by birth, an old man of weak and irresolute character, still found the courage to refuse this demand and declared himself emperor. Rufius Volusianus was sent to Africa by Maxentius with a few cohorts and soon made an end of Alexander and his cause, the city of Carthage paying heavily

[1] *Paneg.* vi (vii), 12.
[2] Lactantius, *de mort. pers.* 29–30; Zonaras xii, 33 (p. 622).
[3] Zosimus ii, 13.

for her treason (311)[1]. It was not in Africa or by Alexander that Maxentius was to be overthrown. Now that Maximian was dead and disowned by Constantine, Maxentius re-discovered his filial loyalty and struck coins in honour of him as 'Divus.' What is even more remarkable, he struck also in honour of 'Divus Constantius Cognatus,' seeking thus to establish a double claim to the Empire of the West.

Galerius was now looking forward to his *vicennalia*, the celebration of which was due to begin on May 1, 311, and was levying taxes unmercifully to fill his coffers. It had been his intention earlier to use the occasion for his own abdication and to hand over the government to Severus and Licinius as Augusti, and Candidianus, his son, and Maximin Daia as Caesars[2]. But circumstances had proved refractory, and retirement now would have meant the death-blow to that system of government to which he still clung as an ideal. But the solution of the problem was taken from his hands. He fell ill of a terrible and disgusting malady and died within a month of the celebrations on which he had expended so much anxious care. The death of the first Augustus was bound to have serious consequences, and did in fact almost lead to a direct outbreak of civil war. Maximin Daia, who from 308 had been asserting his individual rights against Galerius, occupied Asia and marched north to the Bosphorus. Licinius hastened to meet him on the other side of the Straits, but, at the last moment, the two rivals agreed to accept the delimitation of their powers as actually determined at the moment[3]. But a decisive struggle was impending. The four Augusti were no longer bound together in one system of loyalty, and their number was not a strength but a weakness. Constantine began to turn decidedly against Maxentius, branding him as a tyrant and seeking the support of the Christians in his dominions. Licinius, who had at least some sense of political strategy, drew closer to Constantine and became betrothed to his sister, Constantia. It was inevitable that Maxentius and Maximin should seek alliance to protect themselves against a coalition that threatened them both[4]. The invasion of Italy, and the battle of the Milvian bridge were soon to free Rome of her tyrant, and Maximin was to die soon after a broken fugitive from Licinius at Tarsus. A few more years and Constantine was to be ruler over a united Empire.

The coinage of the period has a double interest apart from the economic (p. 338)[5]. The history of its mints illustrates the

[1] Zosimus II, 14.   [2] Lactantius, *de mort. pers.* 20.   [3] *Ib.* 36.
[4] Lactantius, *de mort. pers.* 43.   [5] See Volume of Plates v, 242.

political quarrels and alliances, the return of Maximian as senior Augustus, the new mint of Maxentius at Ostia, the coinage of the pretender, Alexander, at Carthage. The types throw light on the last phases of dominant paganism, with Juppiter and Mars still high in honour, Hercules, receding with the collapse of the Herculian line, Sol returning to supremacy in the coinage of Constantine. Maxentius, as might be expected, concentrates attention on the old sanctities of Roman religion and particularly on the worship of Roma herself. But it was under the concept of Genius, in his various aspects, that paganism fought its decisive battle with Christianity. 'Genius Populi Romani,' 'Genius Imperatoris,' 'Genius Augusti'—these are the types that fill the token coinage which passed through all men's hands. It was the creative spirit, immanent in ruler and people, that was set against the spirit of Christ, working through the Church. The 'Sol invictus comes' of Constantine was carried over from his pagan to his Christian period. Sol might become to the world, as he had become to Constantine himself, a symbol of Christ.

Diocletian, watching from Salonae the final breakdown of his system after the death of Galerius, may well have felt that his life-work had been in vain. Nor would such a feeling have been without its deeper justification. However much of the body of his reforms might be carried over into the system of Constantine, the spirit was changed. A new conception of the relation of the temporal world to the divine had won its way to triumph. The gods were no more to be mere expressions of the forces that moved in human government. The eternal was now recognized to be the real, of which even the majesty of eternal Rome was but a reflection. Christianity had proved its power of disruption in shattering the old foundations of the Roman State. Would it now prove equally capable of providing a new spiritual basis for the secular power, or was the strife of Church and State henceforward to be a constant factor of political life? Here were questions to stir the passionate interest of the new generation of Constantine. The older generation, with its great representative, Diocletian, must have closed its eyes wearily on a new world that it could no longer understand.

CHAPTER X

THE END OF THE PRINCIPATE

I. FOUNDATIONS AND DEVELOPMENT
OF THE ABSOLUTE MONARCHY

CASSIUS DIO tells us (LIII, 28, 2) of a decree of the Senate, of the year 24 B.C., promulgated in favour of Augustus, by which he was freed from the compulsion of the laws and received full liberty of action; and he sees in this the foundation for a real absolutism. The so-called *lex de imperio Vespasiani*[1] contains the same clause and points to the same conclusion, although it includes the restrictive provision: 'uti quaecunque ex usu rei publicae maiestateque divinarum humanarum publicarum priva-tarumque rerum esse censebit, ei agere facere ius potestasque sit.' Recent penetrating research[2] has, in the opinion of the present writer, removed the doubt (vol. XI, p. 407) whether this right had in fact been expressly granted at the very beginning of the Principate. We can now look beyond the wholly personal *auctoritas* of the first *princeps* and see the constitutional *auctoritas* upon which Augustus could pride himself as the essential basis of his power[3]. Particularly in the case of Vespasian, this *auctoritas* was created for a new ruler by the powers conferred through the *lex de imperio*: at the moment it was in no way merely personal. The emperor received, now and for the future, full freedom of action; and the limitation that he should rule in accordance with the interests of the State, lost importance, inasmuch as he was left to judge whether the condition was fulfilled. This legal formulation and foundation of the emperor's power had done all that a law could do to make the Principate an autocracy (vol. XI, p. 408). For, indeed, the provision, that State interests should be regarded, which was still maintained to debar the Principate from becoming an open absolutism, was not a barrier strong enough to prevent self-willed men from setting up an autocratic *régime*[4]. At all events, it seemed later that the *lex de*

---

[1] Dessau 244; Bruns, *Fontes*[7] 56, ll. 21 *sqq.*

[2] A. von Premerstein, *Vom Werden und Wesen des Prinzipats*, aus dem Nachlass herausgegeben von H. Volkmann, Bay. Abh. N.F. Heft 15, 1937, pp. 176 *sqq.*   [3] von Premerstein, *op. cit.* pp. 187 *sqq.*

[4] von Premerstein, *op. cit.* p. 192.

imperio or *lex regia* marked the transference of full sovereignty to the emperor. Even Ulpian[1] in his day declares that what the *princeps* has decided has the force of law, because, by the *lex* (*regia*) concerning the imperial powers, the People has transferred to him all its own power and competence. And such a champion of unlimited absolutism as Justinian I could still recognize in this law the foundation of the imperial sovereignty, when he declared that by the old law, described as the *lex regia*, all the rights and powers of the Roman People had been transferred to the emperor[2]. If we turn back to Cassius Dio, even for him the position of the first *princeps* is already a complete monarchy, just because People and Senate have made over all power to him[3]. The systematic description of the imperial power which he gives in this connection contains in a different form a similar statement of the unlimited power of the monarch[4]. When we take the words which Dio uses to express the significance for his own day of the Senate's decree in favour of Augustus, we find that for him the emperor is 'truly absolute' ($\alpha\dot{v}\tau o\tau\epsilon\lambda\dot{\eta}s$ $\ddot{o}v\tau\omega s$) and 'not subject even to his own decrees or the laws' ($\alpha\dot{v}\tau o\kappa\rho\acute{a}\tau\omega\rho$ $\kappa\alpha\grave{\iota}$ $\dot{\epsilon}\alpha v\tau o\hat{v}$ $\kappa\alpha\grave{\iota}$ $\tau\hat{\omega}v$ $v\acute{o}\mu\omega v$). For Dio, the emperor's supremacy is no longer founded on the outstanding personality of the ruling *princeps*: the institution of monarchy had long been taken for granted as indispensable, so that any and every occupant of the throne is regarded as representative of this form of government.

The *auctoritas* of the first *princeps* was not merely founded on his political supremacy, but was supported by the attribution to him of innate supernatural and superhuman capabilities and characteristics, which made him seem god-sent and his actions divinely inspired. His authority had a religious as well as a political sanction, already apparent in the very name Augustus (vol. x, p. 483). It has been called 'charismatic *auctoritas*'[5]. With the inheritance of the political form created by the authority of the first *princeps*, with the name of Augustus, borne by his successors to mark their exceptional position, with the imperial cult, the outcome of the 'charismatic' *auctoritas* of the first Augustus, remained inseparably bound up the idea of the ruler's 'charismatic'

---

[1] *Dig.* 1, 4, 1, pr.; cf. Dio Chrys. *Or.* III, 43, ὁ δὲ νόμος βασιλέως δόγμα; von Premerstein, *op. cit.* p. 177.
[2] Const. Deo auctore § 7 = *Cod. Just.* I, 17, 1, 7.
[3] Dio LIII, 17, 1; cf. vol. x, p. 589.
[4] Dio LIII, 18, 1; cf. LXXVI, 14, 6.
[5] M. Weber, *Wirtschaft und Gesellschaft* (Grundriss der Sozialökonomik, III. Abt.), p. 140; cf. pp. 753 *sqq.*

character. But in place of the real *charisma* attaching to one peculiar supreme personality, an institutional *charisma* was substituted.[1] Although it could obviously only be spoken of in connection with the individual ruler, the *auctoritas* granted by law and confirmed by force of religion really attached to the institution of the emperor. Thus Pliny, in his Panegyric on Trajan, could put forward the idea: 'the gods have given thee supreme power and control over all things, even over thyself'[2]. The consciousness of an imperial power created and blessed by the gods grew continually stronger, and made it possible for good and bad rulers, forceful, ambitious men and weak youths in need of guidance, the well-born and parvenus, all to represent this imperial power, and for all alike to be recognized as the instruments of a divine guidance and providence manifested in their elevation to the throne[3]. Coins with the legend *Providentia Deorum* are rightly pointed out as the expression of this conception[4]. The picture of the 'exalted one' (*der Erhabene*) endured, of the *iure meritorum optimus princeps*, the ideal ruler who knew how to combine *auctoritas* and *libertas*; and its glory was never wholly lost, even in the period of naked absolutism after Diocletian[5]. But the possibilities of opposition which were latent in the defence of *libertas* by the Senate[6], the repository of ancient traditions, must not be overlooked (see below, pp. 372 *sqq.*). First we must follow the course of developments in the position of the emperor, which led at last to absolute autocracy in the fullest sense of the words.

The limitation by tradition of the monarchy, which had grown up in the course of two centuries, is apparent in the passage of Dio from which we have already quoted: 'the names Caesar and Augustus give him no new powers, but the first shows his right to the succession, the second the splendour of his position'[7]. Dio may have been thinking primarily that Septimius Severus, by

---

[1] Weber, *op. cit.* p. 774. F. Schulz, *Prinzipien des römischen Rechts*, p. 124 *sq.*

[2] 56, 3: *ad te imperii summam et cum omnium rerum, tum etiam tui potestatem di transtulerunt.*

[3] A. Alföldi, *Röm. Mitt.* L, 1935, p. 75 *sq.*

[4] A. D. Nock, *Harv. Theol. Rev.* XXIII, 1930, p. 266 *sq.*; M. P. Charlesworth, *ib.* XXIX, 1936, pp. 118 *sqq.*

[5] See the references in U. Gmelin, *Auctoritas. Römischer Princeps und päpstlicher Primat* in *Geistige Grundlagen römischer Kirchenpolitik*, Forschungen zur Kirchen- und Geistesgeschichte 11, 1937, pp. 69 *sqq.*, 77 *sqq.*

[6] Cf. E. Kornemann, *Die römische Kaiserzeit*, p. 72 *sq.*

[7] Dio LIII, 18, 2.

his fictitious adoption into the family of Marcus Aurelius (see above, p. 12), hoped to appear as the chosen successor of the imperial line. He did officially so appear when he dedicated a memorial to Nerva, 'Divo Nervae atavo,' as the ancestor of his family[1], and his purpose is clearly reflected in the numerous inscriptions in honour of Severus and his sons that emphasized this relationship[2]. The ruling emperor wished to be able to look back upon a long line of divine forbears, and he did so; he got a share of the glory that radiated from them. But his attempt to build up a legal foundation for his position can also be seen— the conception of a hereditary dynastic title to the throne. We may see in Dio's words the idea of the unbroken, and for him natural, succession of emperors, and his equally natural acceptance of the institution. 'The splendour of his authority' ($\tau\grave{\eta}\nu$ $\tau o\hat{v}$ $\mathring{\alpha}\xi\iota\acute{\omega}\mu\alpha\tau o\varsigma$ $\lambda\alpha\mu\pi\rho\acute{o}\tau\eta\tau\alpha$) Dio connects with the name Augustus. It is accidental, but significant, that he uses the same word for this *auctoritas* as that used in the Greek version of the *Res Gestae Divi Augusti* at the words 'auctoritate omnibus praestiti[3].' Dio finds an addition to *auctoritas* in the name Augustus, though he does not define in what this addition consisted. It is, however, easy for us to recognize in this the supernatural splendour of the emperor's position; emperor-worship, which is treated of else-where[4], was the worship of this godlike element. Here we shall adduce only such facts as made a significant contribution towards the changes, or rather the development, in the position of the emperor. It should be said at once that it is often hard, when dealing with the marks of deference and the ceremonial by which the emperor was set apart from all other men, to distinguish be-tween what was still the honour done to a human being and what was already the worship of a divinity[5]. It is true to say, in general, that spontaneous respect for an outstanding personality gave place to an obligation to respect the idea of a ruler, personified in the holder of the office; an obligation that found justification in philosophy and theology[6]. We hardly ever meet with anything entirely without precedent; but the tendencies of earlier times are fixed and potentialities become certainties. Hellenistic in-

[1] Dessau 418.
[2] *E.g.* Dessau 420, 422, 431, 448 *sq.*, 454, 458. Cf. Alföldi, *op. cit.* p. 82 *sq.* J. Hasebroek, *Untersuchungen zur Geschichte des Kaiser Septimius Severus*, p. 88 *sq.*		[3] V. Ehrenberg, *Klio*, xix, 1925, p. 210.
[4] Vol. x, pp. 481 *sqq.*; below, pp. 412 *sqq.*
[5] Cf. Nock, *Harv. Stud.* xli, 1930, p. 50 *sq.*
[6] Alföldi, *Röm. Mitt.* xlix, 1934, p. 67.

fluences, rooted in an Oriental past, had already caused much of this development, and closer contact with the East was bound to bring about further progress in the same direction.

II. THE DIVINITY OF THE IMPERIAL OFFICE: GOD-EMPEROR AND EMPEROR BY THE GRACE OF GOD

The curious adoption-decree of Septimius Severus marks, as we saw, a step in the direction of emphasizing the divinity of the ruling emperor. With him and his successors there are ever clearer signs of an increasing prominence given to the divine nimbus. For some time, indeed, *adoratio* had been paid to the likeness of the emperor (and in law the original and the likeness were identical), for instance in the army[1]; and there not merely the portraits regarded as standards, the *imagines*, but also the statues in the shrine where the standards were kept were worshipped. It was in keeping with the general policy of the Severi that emperor-worship was made prominent in the camps. This is true, although the imperial portraits did not yet bear the titles of gods. The inscription on an altar from the Raetian *limes*, which the prefect of the cohors III Britannorum set up in honour of Caracalla, Geta and Julia Domna, 'mater Augustorum et castrorum,' as well as to the Capitoline Trinity and the *genius cohortis*[2], names the emperors before the gods, thus indicating their full divinity. It is equally noteworthy that, at the erection of a shrine in the camp at Lambaesis, statues and likenesses of members of the imperial house, the *domus divina*, are mentioned first, before their tutelary deities[3]. We may see in these examples both the desire of Septimius Severus to exalt and assure his own position by divine consecration, and also the influence of his Syrian consort on the development of the imperial cult. Her title 'mater castrorum' had indeed been already created by Marcus Aurelius for Faustina[4]. But it had a new emphasis, and its ultimate expansion into 'mater castrorum et senatus et patriae' was bound everywhere to connect it closely with emperor-worship; while the more frequent use of the phrase *domus divina*, with its stress on divine origin, also bears witness to the same tendency. The desired deification is unmistakable on a coin showing Geta crowned

---

[1] Alföldi, *op. cit.* pp. 67 *sqq.*; and see vol. x, p. 483 *sq.*

[2] *C.I.L.* III, 5935. A. von Domaszewski, *Die Religion des römischen Heeres*, p. 76, no. 163.

[3] Dessau 2445; von Domaszewski, *op. cit.* p. 85, no. 180.

[4] Dio LXXII, 10, 5 (p. 261 Boissevain); Alföldi, *op. cit.* p. 69.

with rays as the Sun-god and his right hand raised in the act of benediction, which bears the legend: *Severi invicti Aug. pii fil(ius)*[1]. This shows him as the offspring of the unconquered Sun-god and Sun-emperor. The intention and thesis is plain, allowance being made for its appearance on a coin officially produced by the State mint. Coins with the image of the empress are less discreet, as is shown by the changes in the form of her diadem under the Severi. For the diadem, which became the attribute of the Augusta in the second century, develops into something like a sickle moon. Together with the emperor's halo of sun-rays, the sickle moon, used below the bust of the empress, is the unmistakable sign of divinity. Emperor and empress appear as sun and moon, symbols of the Oriental *aion* idea in reference to the *aeternitas imperii*[2]; and the third-century emperor is on the way to become 'partner of the stars, brother of the sun and moon' like the Sassanian king[3]. Julia Domna, 'mater Augustorum,' is undisguisedly portrayed as Cybele[4], while coins with the image of Cybele and the legend *Mater Deum* or *Matri Magnae* may have been intended to hint at the same idea[5]. The empress is also depicted sitting on the throne of Juno, as *mater Augustorum*, *mater senatus* and *mater patriae*[6], while Julia Mamaea is similarly represented[7]. The emperors, indeed, refrained from appearing, as Commodus loved to do, in the dress of the gods and did not emulate his appearance on the coins (vol. XI, p. 389 *sq.*)[8]. Only in the second half of the century, since Gallienus and Postumus, does this tendency become stronger until it reaches its culmination in Jovius Diocletianus and Herculius Maximianus.

Parallel with this development, the world of gods was revalued in honour of the emperor as *numen praesens*[9]. The gods became, so to say, helpmates of the emperor, as the epithets *custos* and *conservator*, *sospitator* and *tutator* indicate, until, with the designation of a divinity as *comes Augusti*, Heaven appears as the copy of the imperial court[10], and an inscription *Herculi Aug. consorti d. n.*

---

[1] Alföldi, *Röm. Mitt.* L, 1935, p. 107 *sq.*

[2] Cf. E. Norden, *Die Geburt des Kindes*, p. 137 *sq.*; Alföldi, *op. cit.* pp. 124, 143. See Volume of Plates, V, 230, *a*.

[3] Cf. Ammian. Marc. XVII, 5, 3; A. Christensen, *L'Empire des Sassanides*, p. 88.

[4] Cohen[2] IV, p. 114 *sq.*, nos. 116 *sqq.*; Alföldi, *op. cit.* p. 109, n. 3.

[5] Cohen[2] IV, pp. 115 *sqq.*, nos. 122 *sqq.*, no. 140 *sq.*

[6] Cohen[2] IV, p. 114, no. 110 *sq.*; Alföldi, *op. cit.* p. 115.

[7] Cohen[2] IV, p. 494, no. 43 *sq.*; Alföldi, *op. cit.* p. 126.

[8] Cf. Alföldi, *op. cit.* pp. 104, 106.   [9] Cf. Dessau 453.

[10] See above, p. 319; Alföldi, *op. cit.* p. 98; cf. Dessau 3811.

Aureliani invicti Augusti was possible[1]. In the matter of oaths, too, the State gods lost importance in comparison with the emperor, for to swear by the imperial *genius* was legally more binding than to swear by them[2]. In addition, the emperor whom the world obeyed received ever new attributes, which connected him with the heavenly lord of the Universe whose divine power was all-embracing. Septimius Severus and Caracalla are compared on coins to Sol, the *rector orbis*[3]; and *fundator pacis* was added on an inscription[4] under Diocletian in 290. The latter formula alone appears already on the coins of Septimius Severus[5]. Since Valerian this is matched by *pacator orbis*[6], *restitutor generis humani*[7] and *restitutor orbis*[8], since Aurelian by *restitutor saeculi*[9]; and this latter title points to the emperor as the inaugurator of a new Golden Age. This official acceptance of theocratic claims on the part of the reigning Augustus, as the restorer of the happiness of his age (Commodus had once caused his own reign to be proclaimed as 'the Golden Age')[10], is also traceable in the names *Pius* and *Felix* commonly given to the emperors from the time of Commodus. There may have been in these still some idea of the piety of the favoured of the gods; but *invictus*, first assumed by Commodus and invariably used after the second half of the third century, is thereafter to be connected with the Oriental Sun-god[11]. *Aeternitas Augusti* is regularly used on coins from the reign of Gordian III, together with *perpetuitas* from that of Severus Alexander[12]; and both imply not only a claim to divinity hereafter but also the recognition of the true divinity of the living emperor, who is 'deus et dominus natus.' This appears first on the imperial coins of Aurelian either in the dedicatory form of words '*deo et domino nato Aureliano*' or even more simply in the form *Imp(eratori)*

[1] Dessau 583.

[2] *Dig.* XII, 2, 13, 6 (Ulpian); Tertullian, *Apol.* 28; Minucius Felix, *Octav.* 29, 5; cf. H. Kruse, *Studien zur offiziellen Geltung des Kaiserbildes im römischen Reiche*, p. 59.

[3] Cohen[2] IV, p. 63, no. 596; p. 200, nos. 541 *sqq.*   [4] Dessau 618.

[5] Cohen[2] IV, p. 25 *sq.*, nos. 202 *sqq.*

[6] Webb in M.-S. v, i, pp. 55, 91, nos. 218, 294; cf. Index v *ib.* v, i, p. 410 and v, ii, p. 678.

[7] M.-S. v, i, p. 55, no. 220; p. 91, no. 296; the Emperor with right hand raised in blessing and with the globe in his left hand. Cf. Dessau 510, 577 *sq.*

[8] M.-S. Index v in v, i, p. 412; v, ii, p. 682.

[9] M.-S. v, i, p. 290, no. 235; cf. Alföldi, *op. cit.* p. 99.

[10] Dio LXXIII, 15, 6 (p. 297 Boissevain); S.H.A. *Commod.* 14, 3.

[11] Alföldi, *op. cit.* p. 89 *sq.*

[12] Cohen[2] IV, p. 421, no. 190 *sq.* and v, p. 26, nos. 36 *sqq.* Cf. *perpetuus* M.-S. v, ii, p. 679; Dessau 613; with *aeternus* Dessau 614.

deo et domino Aureliano, with *restitutor orbis* on the reverse[1], and after him also for Probus and Carus[2]. From the time of Caracalla coins often bore, besides the official titles of the emperor, the lion of the Sun,[3] indicating the theological derivation of the imperial régime from the Sun-god; and finally the divinity of the emperor was made plain by putting busts of the emperor and a god side by side. Thus Hercules appears with Postumus[4] and on the reverse of some coins Mars or Juppiter with the same ruler[5]; Hercules again with Probus and Maximian[6]; Mars with Victorinus[7]; Sol with the same[8] and also with Probus, sometimes in the form, *Sol comes Probi Aug.*, which ignores the emperor's titles and only stresses his divine aspect[9]. The preponderance of the emperor is plain at last, when Carus is represented with Sol and the legend is only: *Deo et domino Caro invic(to) Aug(usto)*[10].

It was taken for granted, especially from the reign of Septimius Severus onwards, that in imperial dedications such phrases as *devoti numini eius*[11] or *devotus numini maiestatique eius*[12] should appear. That this common formula should have lacked a religious significance seems very unlikely[13]. For even if we are unable to say whether or when the conception that the emperor himself was a *numen*, a divinity, and not merely the wielder of a godlike power[14] was read into this formula, there must have been a religious significance attached to it. Indeed, one may say that in the phrase *numen maiestasque* both the 'charismatic' and the constitutional *auctoritas* were comprehended; and this fact helped the emperor's *maiestas* by reinforcing it with the divinity attributed to him, as the *divina maiestas* of Diocletian shows[15]. In the same way, it became the certainly commanded rule in the third century

---

[1] M.-S. v, i, pp. 264, 299, no. 305 *sq.*

[2] *Ib.* v, ii, pp. 19, 109, no. 841; p. 114, no. 885; pp. 133, 145, no. 96; p. 146, no. 99 *sq.*

[3] *E.g.* Cohen² iv, p. 179, no. 335; p. 182, no. 366; p. 184, nos. 401 *sqq.*; v, p. 110, no. 157; p. 165, no. 42; M.-S. Index iv in v, i, p. 383; v, ii, p. 633. Cf. Alföldi, *op. cit.* p. 85.

[4] M.-S. v, ii, Index iv, p. 630.

[5] *Ib.* v, ii, p. 358, no. 264; p. 360, no. 283.   [6] *Ib.* v, ii, p. 630.

[7] *Ib.* v, ii, p. 389, no. 30; p. 394, no. 90.

[8] *Ib.* v, ii, p. 388 *sq.*, nos. 12, 21, 25.

[9] *Ib.* v, ii, p. 644 and especially p. 108 *sq.*, nos. 829, 835.

[10] *Ib.* v, ii, p. 146, no. 99.   [11] *E.g.* Dessau 421, 426, 547.

[12] Dessau 431, 470 and 482 including the empresses; 552 for the Empress Salonina; 568 *sqq.*

[13] So D. M. Pippidi, 'Le Numen Augusti,' *Rev. des ét. lat.* ix, 1931, p. 103, n. 2.

[14] Cf. F. Pfister, P.W. *s.v.* Numen, col. 1285 *sq.*   [15] Dessau 627.

(though there are earlier examples of its tentative use) to speak of the emperor in inscriptions as *dominus noster* (*d. n.*)[1]. Here, too, religious motives are at work[2].

Once the emperor had grown god-like, and emperor-worship, originally provincial, had become universal, so that an African citizen colony could dedicate an inscription to the 'God Aurelian[3],' that other tendency, to acknowledge his position as superhuman, to see in him the medium of divine intervention and to recognize him as divinely favoured, could lead men to admit and to demand an especial position for the sole master of all. How these two tendencies could both lead up to the deification or sanctification of the ruler is shown by two inscriptions dating from Diocletian, the first of which is a dedication to the *diis genitis et deorum creatoribus dd. nn. Diocletiano et Maximiano invictis Augustis*[4], the other to the *diis auctoribus ad rei publicae amplificandae gloriam procreato......
Iovio Maximo*[5]. Of Aurelian, who let himself be worshipped as a god, the writer who continues Dio tells us[6] that he informed mutinous soldiers that they were mistaken if they believed that the fate of the emperor was in their hands, for God alone could bestow the purple and determine the length of a reign. Cassius Dio puts comparable words into the mouth of Marcus Aurelius[7]. We have spoken above (p. 354) of the meaning of the legend *Providentia Deorum* for this conception. Here we can add that even Balbinus and Pupienus, who were nominated by the Senate[8], and also Tacitus, used this symbol on their coins. And anyhow we may interpret also *Providentia Augustorum* as another expression of the idea of rule 'by the grace of God.'

This idea of divine favour is especially noticeable on coins which occur earlier but become ever more common in the third century, on which a divine patron gives the emperor the globe, the symbol of his power over the world[9]. Roma still appears

---

[1] Cf. M. Bang in Friedländer, *Sittengeschichte Roms*[9] iv, p. 82; Alföldi, *op. cit.* p. 81 *sq.*   [2] Alföldi, *op. cit.* p. 92, n. 2.

[3] Dessau 585; cf. 5687.   [4] Dessau 629.

[5] *C.I.L.* iii, 12326; cf. N. H. Baynes, *J.R.S.* xxv, 1935, p. 84; Alföldi, *op. cit.* p. 84.

[6] Petrus Patricius frag. 178 (Boissevain, Cassius Dio, iii, p. 747. *F.H.G.* iv, p. 197).

[7] Cf. on the question of a possible connection of the two accounts, Rostovtzeff, *Soc. and Econ. Hist.* p. 617, n. 37.

[8] Cohen[2] v, p. 11, no. 23 *sq.*; p. 17, no. 33 *sq.*; M.-S. v, i, pp. 345, 348, nos. 195 *sqq.*, 212.

[9] Cf. A. Schlachter, 'Der Globus,' *Stoicheia* viii, 1927, pp. 64 *sqq.*; Alföldi, *op. cit.* pp. 117 *sqq.*, especially p. 119.

with Gordian III and Florian[1], as she frequently did earlier. More often, Juppiter performs the investiture, as on the coins of Severus Alexander, Gallienus, Aurelian and Probus, Carus, Carinus and Numerianus[2]. In the case of the last two, the investing figure may also be their father Carus; and it is certainly Diocletian, who receives himself[3] the globe from Juppiter and hands it to Maximian[4]. Sol appears in this rôle on the coins of Gordian III and Aurelian[5]. Coronation by a god may be explained in the same sense. Thus Sol crowns Probus; Sol and Hercules crown Carus and Carinus; Hercules crowns Postumus[6]. Where Mars appears in this capacity there may also be a reference to those by whom the emperor was chosen (see below, p. 369).

Whether men believed in the revealed divinity of the emperor or in a divine favour upholding him, there was always something divine about his person and his office. It was just this idea of divine favour which made it possible later for the Christian emperors to express the peculiar sanctity of their position in the traditional ceremonial, to receive the due expressions of reverence and to retain the imperial insignia and dress[7].

III. THE COURT AND ITS CEREMONIAL. DRESS AND INSIGNIA

The character of the sources for the decisive period of transition in the third century rarely enables us to describe with confidence the external setting of the imperial power. For it is just in such matters that the *Historia Augusta* generally gives only the facts of the time of its composition. Characteristic features due to adulation and the growing pre-eminence of the *princeps* had their tentative beginnings in the first two centuries of our era. But it is almost impossible to say how far and when they reached fixed and obligatory forms. The habit of calling everything to do with the emperor *sacrum* (so that the word finally came to mean 'imperial') is apparent *e.g.* in the phrase *cognoscens ad sacras appellationes*[8],

---

[1] Cohen[2] v, p. 48, no. 269; p. 51, no. 284; M.-S. v, i, p. 358, no. 90.
[2] Cohen[2] iv, p. 421, no. 190; M.-S. v, i, p. 103, no. 440; Index iv, p. 375; v, ii, p. 640; pp. 163 *sqq.*, nos. 202, 206, 209; p. 177, no. 314; p. 191, nos. 376, 380; p. 202, nos. 466, 470.
[3] M.-S. v, ii, pp. 255 *sqq.*, nos. 321 *sqq.*, 328 *sq.*
[4] *Ib.* p. 288, no. 583.
[5] Cohen[2] v, p. 66, no. 496; M.-S. v, i, Index iv, p. 375.
[6] M.-S. v, ii, p. 61, no. 404 *sq.*; p. 167, no. 225, p. 338, no. 17.
[7] Alföldi, *Röm. Mitt.* xlix, 1934, pp. 1 *sqq.*; *ib.* l, 1935, pp. 1 *sqq.*
[8] Dessau 1190 *sq.*

which dates from the middle of the third century; and the holder of the court office *a cognitionibus* is sometimes called *procurator sacrarum cognitionum*[1] from which, even before Diocletian, the title *magister sacrarum cognitionum*[2] is probably derived. But this use of the word may not yet have been strictly official. In the same sense, the description of an imperial rescript of 204 as *sacrae litterae*[3] may be mentioned; as also the use of *theia epistole* by the proconsul of Asia[4]; and as early as the reign of Commodus a procurator speaks of the *sacra subscriptio domini nostri*[5]. In view of this, the passages quoted in the *Digest* from Ulpian, Paul and others, mentioning the *sacrae constitutiones*[6], are not to be regarded as interpolations. As so often happens, unofficial and semi-official usage probably preceded the official. As another example of this, we may mention the imperial mint, *sacra moneta*, so called once in an inscription dating from the reign of Hadrian[7], but first used on gold coins by Carus and his sons, in *S(acra) M(oneta) A(ntiochensis)*[8], and on consecration coins of Carus from the mint of Siscia in the form *S(acra) M(oneta) S(isciensis)*[9]. In view of these developments, it is probably correct to say that the term *sacrum palatium* was not an innovation of Diocletian[10], especially since Rome had been called *urbs sacra* in official documents from the time of the Severi and had thus become the 'imperial city[11].'

The emperor, dwelling in the *sacrum palatium*, must be approached by those deemed worthy of the honour in the humble attitude of *proskynesis*. This attitude was derived from a mixture of the gestures of supplication and prayer with Eastern practices. As the source is untrustworthy, it is impossible to decide whether there was really a greater insistence on *proskynesis* under Elagabalus which Severus Alexander then forbade[12], or whether we should

[1] Dessau 9021.
[2] *Ib.* 1459; cf. O. Hirschfeld, *Die kaiserlichen Verwaltungsbeamten*[2], p. 330; A. E. R. Boak, *Harv. Stud.* XXIV, 1915, p. 98.   [3] Ditt.[3] 881.
[4] Abbott and Johnson, *Municipal administration in the Roman Empire*, p. 466; cf. *Rev. des étud. grec.* XIX, 1906, p. 86 *sq.*
[5] Dessau 6870. Bruns, *Fontes*[7] 86, col. 4, ll. 12 *sq.*
[6] E.g. *Dig.* XXIII, 2, 60 *pr.*; XXVI, 7, 5, 5; XL, 1, 5 *pr.*; XLII, 1, 27.
[7] Dessau 1638; Hirschfeld, *op. cit.* p. 186, n. 3.
[8] M.-S. v, ii, p. 149, no. 122; p. 201, no. 464 *sq.*
[9] M.-S. v, ii, pp. 129, 147, nos. 108 *sqq.*
[10] Alföldi, *Röm. Mitt.* XLIX, 1934, p. 32.
[11] H. Jordan, *Forma urbis Romae regionum XIV*, p. 8; cf. Hirschfeld, *op. cit.* p. 284, n. 3; Dessau 98, where Caracalla *aquam Marciam ...in sacram urbem suam perducendam curavit*; cf. Dessau 1128, 1370, 8979. Friedländer, *op. cit.* 1[10], p. 32, n. 7.
[12] S.H.A. *Alex. Sev.* 18, 3.

interpret this alleged prohibition only as a misunderstood report of an alteration in the form of the ceremony. Such a change is attributed to the younger 'Maximinus,' who sometimes expected his foot and not his hand to be kissed[1]. In any case, *proskynesis* was taken for granted by Cassius Dio, by Herodian and by the panegyrist of Philip (see p. 88 *sq.*)[2], although we cannot be sure exactly what form the ceremony took at the courts of the Severi and their successors. Adoration of pictures of the emperor may have influenced the development, but again there is no clear evidence. Herodian[3] tells of homage done to the pictures of Balbinus, Pupienus and Gordian on their accession. A gold coin of Postumus shows us for the first time a representative of the People, on his knees before the enthroned emperor, receiving a benefaction[4]. Under Gallienus we hear of those who met the emperor performing *proskynesis* even in the streets of Rome[5]. When, moreover, Caracalla is reported at a reception to have been merely 'greeted' (*salutatus*)[6], it is perfectly possible that the ceremony of *proskynesis* is meant; for later sources, in which only *proskynesis* can be intended, give the name *ordo salutationis* to the order of precedence in which it was to be carried out[7]. The description of Caracalla's reception also gives the order in which the various ranks performed the ceremony: Praetorian Prefects, *amici* (vol. XI, p. 425), heads of court offices, members of the Senate and *equites*. It is uncertain whether precedence was then arranged at the will of the ruling emperor, or whether it was already fixed by rule. The latter seems more probable, and must then have gone beyond the long-standing division of the 'friends' into the first and second *admissio*. With the stricter regulation of the *admissio*, a department of the court, the *officium admissionis*, which was known to Suetonius[8], grew in importance. As early as the third century its president ranked as *eques* and had the title of *magister*. Probably the *velarii*, who drew the curtains (*vela*) of the audience-chamber, belonged to this office[9]. Even if we can believe that Severus

---

[1] S.H.A. *Max. duo*, 28, 7.

[2] Dio LXV, 5, 2 (p. 121 Boissevain); cf. LVIII, 11, 2; Herodian III, 11, 8; Eἰς βασιλέα 19 = Ps. Aristides II K, 257 *sq.*

[3] VIII, 6, 2; cf. S.H.A. *Max. duo*, 24, 1 *sq.*

[4] M.-S. V, ii, p. 359, no. 276; Alföldi, *op. cit.* p. 58.

[5] Plotinus, V, 5, 3; Alföldi, *op. cit.* p. 101 *sq.*   [6] *Cod. Just.* IX, 51, 1.

[7] *Cod. Theod.* VI, 22, 7, *pr.* (of A.D. 383); cf., for the etiquette of greeting, Alföldi, *op. cit.* p. 28; Friedländer, *op. cit.* pp. 90 *sqq.*

[8] Suetonius, *Vesp.* 14.

[9] *C.I.L.* XIV, 3457; cf. Hirschfeld, *op. cit.* pp. 310, n. 2, 314, n. 3. Boak, *op. cit.* p. 111.

Alexander showed consideration to the senators in the rules for their visits to him[1], we none the less get a general impression that the emperor was becoming increasingly remote and etiquette increasingly stiff, so that in the end not only ordinary visitors but also advisers had to remain standing in the imperial presence. It has been rightly concluded from the types on coins which show the emperor seated and surrounded by standing allegorical figures, and at a later date on his throne in the presence of standing gods[2], that the custom of standing before the emperor is earlier than the reign of Diocletian, in which it is first certainly attested[3], though the term *consistorium* instead of the earlier *consilium* is possibly not older than this period. Since the above-mentioned coin-types begin with the reign of Severus Alexander[4], it seems unlikely that he made a rule of allowing every senator the right to sit in his presence after saluting him[5].

As regards dress and insignia, fixed forms to distinguish the unique position of the emperor had also developed. Although Septimius Severus, at his entry into Rome, exchanged his military dress for the toga[6], the wearing of uniform in the City, which indicates the progressive militarization of the régime, became increasingly common[7]. Up to the end of the third century the *toga praetexta* was still worn, it is true; but the emperors tended more and more, on festive occasions, to wear triumphal costume as their gala dress, while for empresses gold-embroidered robes of State were already the fashion[8]. The *vestis alba triumphalis*, a variation of the triumphal costume, can be seen on a painting of Septimius Severus and his family[9], in which golden garlands set with gems show a tendency to over-elaborate Oriental pomp; and this style of ornament became commoner, until it finally assumed the form of a diadem set with precious stones, which is only a garland translated into jewelry[10]. From the beginning, however, military dress was always better suited to show rank and superior position. The Imperator alone had the right to wear the *paludamentum* or the purple mantle, and even in his day the historian

[1] S.H.A. *Alex. Sev.* 4, 3.

[2] Alföldi, *op. cit.* p. 43 *sq.*   [3] *Cod. Just.* x, 48, 2.

[4] Cohen[2] iv, p. 442, no. 406; p. 481, no. 5 *sq.*; p. 491, no. 15.

[5] S.H.A. *Alex. Sev.* 18, 2.

[6] Dio lxxv, 1, 3 (p. 325 Boissevain).

[7] Alföldi, *Röm. Mitt.* l, 1935, p. 8.

[8] Alföldi, *ib.* p. 26.

[9] K. A. Neugebauer, *Die Antike* xii, 1936, Pl. 10; p. 157 *sq.*; Alföldi, *op. cit.* p. 32 *sq.*

[10] So R. Delbrueck, *Spätantike Kaiserporträts*, p. 59 *sq.*

Tacitus saw in it the symbol of sovereignty[1]. This idea is yet more marked, when from Pescennius Niger onwards[2] donning the purple becomes more and more prominent at the assumption of imperial power. The purple (*purpura*) thus became the mystic symbol of power, and men could suppose that the dying Gallienus wished to single out Claudius as his successor by sending him the imperial mantle[3]. Gold embroidery appears in regular use on the imperial purple from the time of Commodus, and the setting of *fibulae*, belts and so on with precious stones, which was still thought by the soldiery to be 'unroman' in Macrinus, and must have met with opposition in other cases, was eventually accepted. So too, the elaborate ornamentation of the imperial chariot and harness, had become regular distinctive marks of the emperor by the beginning of the third century[4].

As the triumphal robe became the gala dress of the emperor and as at the same time he himself became divine, the sceptre with the eagle, generally used with civil costume, became part of the insignia perhaps even before the reign of Diocletian. The long sceptre, symbol of the power of the father of the gods, which already appears in the painting of the Severi and which third-century emperors mostly carried when wearing military costume[5], indicates the divinity or the divine investiture of the emperor; so that Constantine and his successors, who ruled 'by the grace of God,' could retain it. When the globe changed from being the symbol of the universe to being that of sovereignty is not certain; but the fact that Caracalla as 'junior Augustus', and Philip the younger as Caesar, are both represented with it[6] makes it probable that the change had taken place by their time. It can be shown that from being an emblem in the portrayal of emperors, it had become a real part of the insignia from the fourth century, though coins which show the Augustus giving it to his co-regent may point to an earlier date[7]. Nor was the wearing of the diadem, in which the change to autocracy is most emphatically expressed, a use regular since Constantine,

---

[1] Tacitus, *Ann.* XII, 56.

[2] Herodian II, 8, 6; V, 3, 12; VI, 8, 5.

[3] Aurelius Victor, *Caes.* XXXIII, 28; *Epit.* XXXIV, 2; cf. Alföldi, *op. cit.* p. 50 *sq.*

[4] Alföldi, *op. cit.* p. 58 *sq.* with *Röm. Mitt.* XLIX, p. 108.

[5] Alföldi, *op. cit.* pp. 112 *sqq.*

[6] Cohen[2] IV, p. 186, no. 411 *sq.*; V. p. 165, no. 46; cf. Alföldi, *op. cit.* p. 120.

[7] *E.g.* Tetricus to his son, M.-S. V, ii, p. 416, no. 204 *sq.*; cf. for Carus and his sons and for Diocletian see above, p. 361, nn. 2 *sqq.*

wholly without precedent in the third century. Apart from the coin-types that show the emperor with the headband of the sun-god, there are many others that show the radiate diadem, that is the royal diadem with rays attached, which indicated the sovereign, and the Romans thus grew accustomed to the sight of the once forbidden royal headgear. The first known official use of the diadem without rays is on a commemorative medal of Gallienus[1]; according to the literary sources Aurelian wore the diadem[2]. Finally, besides the chair of office, the *sella curulis*, which the emperors as consuls still retained in later times, the throne had become a special mark of distinction. This sign of monarchy, too, had a religious origin; and as the court took on a sacral colouring, it became so integral a part of the imperial splendour[3] that this chair, originally the seat of the gods, was innocently adopted by the Christian emperors as a symbol of their power.

Torchbearers accompanied the emperor on his public appearances; and they were an essential part of the honours paid to him[4]. Cheering by the populace as the emperor passed by, which had begun even earlier, was prescribed and ceremonially regulated before the beginning of the third century. By the same period, acclamation in the Senate had also become the rule[5]. The protocols of the Arval Brothers for 213 show how firmly established this mode of addressing the emperor in a kind of litany had become[6]. Of the examples of acclamations by the Senate given in the *Historia Augusta*, only the single example in the *Vita Commodi* may be accounted genuine[7]. Dio tells us of the hymn of praise to the emperor which culminated in the description of the emperor as a deity[8].

The marks of honour which the emperors inherited from the consuls were also maintained. Lictors carrying fasces decorated with laurel-leaves accompanied Gordian I at his entry into Carthage[9]; lictors are depicted at sacrificial ceremonies under Trebonius Gallus. None the less, this train of lictors was not

---

[1] Alföldi, *op. cit.* p. 148.

[2] [Aurelius Victor], *Epit.* xxxv, 5; Malalas xii, p. 299, 20 (Bonn).

[3] Herodian ii, 3, 3 *sq.*; iii, 8, 6; iv, 5, 1; cf. Alföldi, *op. cit.* p. 125 *sq.*

[4] Herodian i, 8, 4; 16, 4; ii, 3, 2; 8, 6; vii, 1, 9; 6, 2; cf. Dio lxxii, 35, 5 for Marcus Aurelius; Alföldi, *Röm. Mitt.* xlix, 1934, p. 117.

[5] O. Hirschfeld, *Kleine Schriften*, pp. 691 *sqq.*; Alföldi, *op. cit.* pp. 83 *sqq.*

[6] Dessau 451.

[7] S.H.A. *Comm.* 18 *sq.*; cf. J. M. Heer, *Der historische Wert der Vita Commodi*, pp. 187 *sqq.*

[8] Dio lxxvii, 6, 2 (p. 361 Boissevain); lxxviii, 5, 1 (p. 378 Boissevain); cf. Herodian ii, 3, 3.

[9] Herodian vii, 6, 2.

always present, and its appearances were probably confined to the occasions on which the emperor performed certain acts as magistrate or *imperator*[1]. For long before, besides or often without the civil attendants, the military escort (βασιλικὴ πομπή) had become the most distinctive feature of imperial processions. As early as Caracalla adverse comment was aroused when the Praetorian Guards, fully armed, accompanied him into the Senate, contrary to previous custom[2]. In this action, too, we may note the progressive militarization which went hand in hand with the transformation of the first citizen into an autocratic monarch. It is usual to distinguish this new form of the monarchy from the Principate under the name of Dominate. But it may be observed that, just at the period of greatest absolutism, *dominus* becomes the ordinary form of address, and *dominus noster* is no longer reserved exclusively for the emperor. It would be better to adopt the words of Dio about the monarch 'autocrat over his own decrees and the laws' (αὐτοκράτωρ καὶ ἑαυτοῦ καὶ τῶν νόμων) as giving the essence of this later unveiled and avowed absolutism; and to use this term 'Autocracy' to distinguish the later absolutism from the Principate of the early Empire[3].

IV. THE APPOINTMENT OF THE EMPEROR: ELECTION AND DYNASTIC EXPERIMENTS

However far above his subjects the emperor might be, he owed his position to the expression of the popular will. Even though he and the theorists might see in this expression the divine providence and the favour of Heaven at work, constitutional considerations were not forgotten. Through its representatives the People chose the *princeps*; but the consummation of popular sovereignty was at the same time its destruction[4]. At first, the Senate voiced the People's will. But after the death of Commodus the secret, which Tacitus at Nero's fall could still call the *arcanum imperii*, namely that a *princeps* could be made elsewhere than in Rome[5], was a secret no longer. Indeed it was soon almost the rule. It is proper to speak of this period as one of military monarchy, or even military anarchy, in so far as this indicates who were the most prominent agents in deciding who should mount the throne. But so long as the emperors had to reckon with the prestige and resistance of the Senate and while the senators held fast by their admitted claim, the right of the

[1] Alföldi, *op. cit.* p. 102.		[2] Herodian IV, 5, 1.
[3] Cf. above, vol. XI, pp. 400, 417.
[4] So Mommsen, *Röm. Staatsrecht*, II[3], p. 1133.		[5] Tacitus, *Hist.* I, 4.

Senate and the Roman People to take part in appointing the emperor remained undisputed. But the *populus Romanus* found that almost the only right left to it was the modest rôle of acclaiming the new ruler. Only in the elections of the two emperors created by the Senate and in that of Gordian III as Caesar did the People play a part, and that more by way of riot than in form of law[1]; yet special reference was made to the People, acting with the Senate[2]. But normally, the People's functions remained purely ornamental. Yet even in the late fifth century, at the election of Anastasius, allusion is made to the consent of the People, as well as of the Senate and the army[3].

The regular practice in the third century was for the army to proclaim the new emperor, after which the Senate gave its formal agreement either at the request of the emperor himself or else on being merely informed. We cannot say how often the *patres* bowed to hard necessity in the exercise of this right to which they clung; for only once, at the election of Maximinus, is it reported that they approved the actions of the legions because it was dangerous for the unarmed to oppose the armed forces[4]. It is not surprising that the accumulated hate felt for the Thracian trooper elevated to the throne should have moved the senators at the first opportunity to carry on the struggle begun by their election of the Gordians with men of their own choice, Balbinus and Pupienus. But their real power was small; so small that they then had to accept a boy as Caesar and later to acknowledge as Augustus Aemilianus, whom they had formerly proclaimed a traitor[5]. Indeed, after the murder of Aurelian, when his army turned to the Senate for the appointment of his successor, the *patres* answered that this was the army's duty, so that it was only after some interchanges that the Senate decided to elect Tacitus[6]. A remark of the biographer of Aurelian[7] gives the right explanation of their diffidence, namely that the Senate knew very well that the soldiers did not take kindly to an emperor chosen by itself. But though the choice of Tacitus may be fairly cited to show the constitutional position of the Senate[8], it would be illogical to ignore the evidence that choice provides of the army's right to have a say in the matter. From the beginning, the military basis of the imperial power was only partly hidden by the civilian forms of the

---

[1] Herodian VII, 10, 5 *sqq.*   [2] Herodian VIII, 6, 2 with 7, 4.
[3] Constantin. Porphyr. *De caeremoniis*, I, 92, p. 424, 7 *sq.* (Bonn).
[4] Aurelius Victor, *Caes.* XXV, 2.   [5] Aurelius Victor, *Caes.* XXXI, 3.
[6] Aurelius Victor, *Caes.* XXXV, 9 *sqq.*   [7] S.H.A. *Aurel.* 40, 3.
[8] So O. Th. Schulz, *Vom Prinzipat zum Dominat*, pp. 145 *sqq.*

constitution of the Principate. At his accession, Nero could refer
both to the *auctoritas patrum* and to the *consensus militum*[1]; and on
coins of Vitellius and Vespasian mention of the *consensus militum*
also appears[2]. Perhaps we should not see in this the assertion of
a right; but it is clear from the coins of the third century that the
emperors then thought of election by the army as a necessary legal
preliminary to their assumption of office. Leaving out of consideration the fact that *fides* or *concordia militum* or *exercitus* is referred to over and over again, it is noteworthy that soldiers are
depicted as present when Severus Alexander receives the orb from
Juppiter or when Gordian is invested by Roma[3]. Finally, it is
a soldier who proffers the orb[4]; for though we may see in the
'soldier' the god Mars, the god is only a symbol for the army[5]. It
is significant for the election of Tacitus that this type first appears
on one of his coins; while another shows his coronation by
Mars[6], although on this the *genius* of the Senate re-appears, after
having been absent since the time of Valerian[7]. That man was
legally emperor who had been elected either by the Senate or the
army and then recognized by the other partner. But the words
used by Eutropius to describe the election of Claudius give the
best picture of the reality: 'a militibus electus, a senatu appellatus
Augustus[8].' Decius, like Vespasian, in spite of the deference
which he otherwise paid to the Senate, dated his reign from the
day of his proclamation by the army, thus admitting its right to
share in his elevation[9]. External events, too, decreased the
importance of recognition by the Senate. Postumus and other
separatist emperors, who, despite all their claims to the whole
Empire, never were so recognized in Rome[10], ruled with no less
actual authority for all that. The unsuccessful rival was *hostis* or,
by official usage after Constantine I at the latest, *tyrannus*[11]; but
the history of the so-called 'thirty tyrants' shows with distressing
clarity what a misuse of the right of election might bring about.
Aurelius Victor associates the end of the Senate's right of election

---

[1] Tacitus, *Ann.* XIII, 4.   [2] Alföldi, *Röm. Mitt.* L, 1935, p. 44 *sq.*
[3] Cohen[2] IV, p. 421, no. 190; cf. p. 482, nos. 9 *sqq.*; V, p. 48, no. 269;
p. 51, no. 284.
[4] M.-S. V, ii, p. 49, no. 310; p. 117, no. 909.
[5] So Alföldi, *op. cit.* p. 119.
[6] M.-S. V, i, p. 339, no. 127; p. 337, no. 109.
[7] Alföldi, *op. cit.* p. 17.   [8] Eutropius IX, 11, 1.
[9] Cf. Schulz, *op. cit.* p. 271 and pp. 225 *sqq.* Wittig, P.W. *s.v.* Messius
(9) Decius, col. 1254 *sq.*
[10] So rightly O. Th. Schulz, *op. cit.* pp. 98 *sqq.*
[11] Cf. *Cod. Theod.* XV, 14, 1 *sq.*

with the death of Probus and Carus' election[1]. Carus seems to
have contented himself with an announcement of his election
without any formal request for confirmation by the Senate (see
above, p. 321). This does not mean that the announcement might
not be received with acclamation signifying consent; but any
initiative on the part of the Senate was done away for good. A
formal right to share in the election, often not unlike that of the
People, must have survived. Only on some such hypothesis can
we explain the first fifth-century utterance of a newly-elected
emperor that has survived in his own words; here the army and the
Senate (by now a totally changed body) are named as electors, but
the greatest emphasis is laid upon the divine favour. When
Marcianus announced his assumption of office to Pope Leo I,
he said he had come to it 'by God's Providence and the choice of
the Senate and the army[2].'

Although the idea that the ruler was elective survived into
the days of the autocracy 'by the grace of God,' an idea that the
succession might be passed on to the emperor's heirs was also
current from the very first[3]. Septimius Severus, by means of
his fictitious adoption, endeavoured to make his sons heirs in a
dynastic succession (see above, p. 12), while he singled out
his elder son by creating him Caesar and Princeps Iuventutis
and having him named *imperator destinatus*[4]. A year later, Caracalla
became Augustus and Geta became Caesar. This public settlement of the succession was designed to win support among the
populace, by familiarizing them with the idea of a dynasty; and
all the propaganda-value of the coinage and of Emperor-worship
was exploited to this end[5]. One success of the campaign may be
seen in the ever greater frequency of the words *domus divina* in
inscriptions[6]. The effect of legitimacy is shown by the succession
of Elagabalus and Severus Alexander and by the influence which
the princesses of the imperial house, from Julia Domna to Julia
Mamaea, could acquire. Even the ephemeral reign of the first
two Gordians was long enough to arouse sentiments favourable

[1] Aurelius Victor, *Caes.* XXXVII, 5.
[2] Ep. Leonis 73 = Migne, *Patr. Lat.* LIV, p. 900.—Mansi, *Conciliorum
Collectio*, VI, 93 B; cf. the similar utterance of Justin I in *ep. Hormisdae* 41.—
A. Thiel, *Epistolae Roman. pontificum*, 1868, p. 830 = Mansi, *op. cit.* VIII,
434 A.   [3] See vol. X, p. 151; vol. XI, pp. 410, 415.
[4] The evidence is collected in E. Kornemann, *Doppelprinzipat und
Reichsteilung im Imperium Romanum*, p. 86.
[5] J. Vogt, *Die Alexandrinischen Münzen*, I, p. 166 *sq.*
[6] R. Cagnat, *Cours d'épigraphie latine*[4], p. 168. Rostovtzeff, *op. cit.*
p. 598, n. 31.

to Gordian III as the legitimate heir[1]. It thus became the rule for the sons of the emperor to be created Caesar and finally Augustus. There was in general no real co-regency, although all the imperial honours, almost always including even the pontificate since Philip and his son[2], were conferred upon the junior, thus creating a kind of fictitious co-regency or rather partnership. This practice seemed to secure the succession; this combination of dynastic successor with partner was intended to ensure that, when the Augustus-father died, the Augustus-son should pass automatically to the throne[3]. Though, indeed, stern reality often refuted this doctrine. The idea that membership of the imperial family gave a man some claim to the throne induced Florian to put himself forward as Augustus after the death of his step-brother Tacitus, and he was recognized even though his predecessor had declined, in accordance with the older usage, to nominate his successor; and this holds good even if we doubt the truth of Tacitus' solemn renunciation in favour of a free election by the Senate[4].

The idea of a division of the Empire appears once during the joint rule of the hostile brothers Caracalla and Geta (p. 43) and it might appear that a necessary connection between dual rule and such division should be presumed[5]. But the idea of the unity of the Empire was too strong, even in this case of bitter enmity[6]; and there was in fact no division when circumstances necessitated the separate action of the co-rulers in the East and the West, as with Valerian and Gallienus or Carus and Carinus[7]. What this does show is that it might be necessary, both for the safety of the Empire and of the emperors personally, to mark out separate spheres of activity, while maintaining without limitation the Augustus-father's authority over the whole. This was a precedent that could be used by Diocletian in his re-organization of the Empire, especially in the form devised by Carus[8], when he left Carinus behind as Caesar in the West with extended powers which approached joint-sovereignty. But there was still a difference between Augustus and Caesar; and there was thus no question of a division of the Empire.

[1] Herodian VII, 10, 6.　　　[2] Schulz, op. cit. p. 258.
[3] Kornemann, op. cit. p. 92. E. Stein, Geschichte des spätrömischen Reiches, I, p. 48.
[4] S.H.A. Tac. 14, 1.　　　[5] Cf. Kornemann, op. cit. pp. 88 sqq.
[6] V. Ehrenberg, Deutsche Lit. Zeitung, 1931, p. 559.
[7] Kornemann, op. cit. p. 102 for Valerian-Gallienus, whereas in the case of Carus-Carinus (p. 109) he speaks of division of the Empire.
[8] Kornemann, op. cit. p. 108.

V. EMPEROR AND SENATE

The survival of the Senate's constitutional share in electing the emperor was matched by the continuance of its right to judge the deeds of the dead Augustus and so decide the consecration of the *divus*. But Septimius Severus first told the army of his intention to deify Commodus and then left the Senate to bring it to pass[1], while the Senate itself deified Gallienus in deference to the will of Claudius, but against its own convictions[2]. This function of the Senate, which belongs to the original form of the Principate, was thus only exercised, in fact and possibly in law, at the instance of the emperor and its significance was thus seriously diminished[3]. Initiative declined into co-operation whereby the traditional respect still felt for the *patres* was brought in to add honour to the dead emperor. Thus the principle, that no deification could take place without the Senate's approval[4], could remain unchallenged, while the idea of the power of the emperor to command this action could arise side by side with it[5]. Even if we admit that the Senate, in passing judgment on a dead emperor, was using the power of making laws which it had acquired[6], we must be cautious in our use of this fact when estimating its constitutional position. For, in legislation, the Senate was gradually being reduced to the position of an imperial publicity department.

The jurists ever more frequently quote the imperial *oratio* instead of the *senatus consultum* which was founded on it[7]; and this must mean that the former was adopted without discussion or amendment. The force of law which the imperial *constitutiones* were recognized to have[8] tended further to limit senatorial legislation. But for measures introducing some radical change, later to be known as *leges generales*, the more solemn form of the *senatus consultum* was retained, even as late as the fifth century[9]. Moreover, the emperors almost managed to turn the old rule that it was for the Senate, as representing the People, to give dispensation from the laws, into an exception[10]; and the axiom that 'the *princeps* is freed from the laws[11]' is definite proof of this. The emperor

---

[1] S.H.A. *Sev.* 11, 4; Dio LXXV, 7, 4 *sq.*; Schulz, *op. cit.* p. 36 *sq.*

[2] Aurelius Victor, *Caes.* XXXIII, 27; Schulz, *op cit.* p. 93.

[3] Mommsen, *op. cit.* II³, p. 886.

[4] Tertullian, *Apol.* 5.   [5] Cf. S.H.A. *Op. Macr.* 6, 8.

[6] O'Brien Moore, P.W. *s.v.* Senatus, Suppl. VI, col. 779.

[7] Cf. vol. XI, p. 420; O. Karlowa, *Röm. Rechtsgeschichte*, I, p. 643 *sq.*; for this form of citation in imperial rescripts cf. *Cod. Just.* V, 71, 9.

[8] *Dig.* I, 4, 1 with I, 2, 2, 12.   [9] *Cod. Just.* I, 14, 3.

[10] Mommsen, *op. cit.* II³, p. 884.   [11] *Dig.* I, 3, 31 (Ulpian).

could justify himself by appeal to the *lex de imperio*[1], a fact which
reveals the legal basis from which the emperor could at any time
undermine the surviving rights of the Senate. Thus he could himself grant privileges which had formerly needed to be confirmed
by a dispensation from the Senate[2], though that did not prevent
him from declaring himself bound, of his own free will, by the
relevant laws in a civil case (see above, p. 68). We have also
seen (p. 65) how the Senate lost importance, from the time of
Severus Alexander onwards, in the administration of the laws
affecting the *collegia*. Formally the granting of pardons and
quashing of undetermined cases were prerogatives of the Senate;
but in fact and even by law the former right was exercised by the
emperor. Co-operation of emperor and Senate, whereby the Senate
probably acted on the emperor's suggestion, still existed under
Pertinax[3] and was known to Ulpian[4], although in a later work he
speaks of the *princeps* only[5]; the emperor's sovereignty in such
cases was fully admitted by the reign of Caracalla[6]. The judicial
competence of the Senate continually lost importance in face
of imperial competition. Even the right of the Senate to be
sole judge of its own members in criminal cases, legally secured
under Septimius Severus, was precarious (vol. xi, p. 422), since
even Severus did not consider himself bound to respect it[7]. But
the emperors continued to send cases to the Senate for trial; and
even after Diocletian the Senate still pronounced judgment, when
thus invited to do so[8].

Turning to financial matters, the independent importance of
the senatorial *aerarium* as a separate institution was already so reduced (vol. xi, p. 423) that according to Dio the emperor's power
over it was as unlimited as over the *fiscus*[9]. But as late as 204
the Senate voted the funds for the Secular Games[10]; and in spite
of the curtailing of its right, the *aerarium* lasted until it became a
municipal instead of a State treasury[11]. It is very uncertain how
far, if at all, the continued minting of bronze coins with the Senate's

---

[1] *Cod. Just.* vi, 23, 3; cf. above, p. 352 *sq.*; D. McFayden, 'Rise of the
Princeps' Jurisdiction,' *Washington Univ. Stud.* x, 1923, p. 262 *sq.*
[2] *Dig.* i, 3, 31.
[3] Dessau 1127 with S.H.A. *Pert.* 6, 8.
[4] *Dig.* iii, 1, 1, 10.   [5] *Dig.* xlviii, 23, 2.
[6] *Cod. Just.* ix, 51, 1; cf. 51, 7 (Philip the Arabian).
[7] Dio lxxiv, 2, 1 *sq.*; Herodian ii, 14, 3 *sq.*
[8] Mommsen, *op. cit.* ii[3], p. 125; Stein, *op. cit.* i, p. 52.
[9] Dio liii, 22, 3 *sq.*   [10] *C.I.L.* vi, 32326, 29.
[11] Mommsen, *op. cit.* ii[3], p. 1013. Hirschfeld, *Die kaiserlichen Verwaltungsbeamten*[2], p. 17. O'Brien Moore, *op. cit.* col. 791.

mark, S.C., denotes a survival of the independent *aerarium*[1]. On the coins attributed to the interregnum after Aurelian's death[2], S.C. may only mean that the Senate remembered its ancient rights in exceptional circumstances. But it is significant that, after the minting of such coins ceased under Claudius II and (in spite of larger striking of money) under Aurelian (see above, p. 307), there was no resumption of it even under Tacitus and only a partial one under Florian (see above, p. 311). The bronze coins of Postumus with the Senate's mark have nothing to do with its rights of minting, and rather express the claim to a legitimate title to the whole Empire, including Rome and its Senate[3]; this is true also of types of coin, over which the Senate never shared control, where the legend appears as a peculiar sign of legitimacy[4].

The right of the Senate to appoint the Roman magistrates was so whittled away by the *princeps*' nomination and commendation that little remained of it; and in the third century the appointment to all offices in the capital was attributed to the emperor[5]. Of these offices, the consulate, the praetorship and the quaestorship survived, and there were always plenty of men ready to undertake the duties, in spite of the demands which they made on their holders' private fortunes, so long as important posts in the administration of the Empire were filled by ex-consuls and ex-praetors. In many ways the activity of the Senate seems to have been that of a municipal council, as when Aurelian charged it with the rebuilding of the City walls[6]; and the organization of defence against the Alemannic invasion about 260[7] signifies little more from a constitutional point of view. None the less, the Senate had a prestige founded not only on the splendid traditions of several centuries, but also on its close connection with Rome. In comparison with the idea, noticeable as early as the first days of Commodus, that Rome was where the emperor was[8], the conception of Rome as the seat of the emperor was not less widespread[9]. However much, in a State which had greatly advanced

---

[1] W. Kubitschek, P.W. *s.v.* Aerarium, col. 670.

[2] So doubtfully P. H. Webb in M.-S. v, i, p. 361; for another view Alföldi, *Röm. Mitt.* XLIX, 1934, p. 91.

[3] M.-S. v, ii, p. 332 *sq.*

[4] M.-S. v, i, p. 320; Alföldi, *Röm. Mitt.* L, 1935, p. 15, n. 1.

[5] *Dig.* XLII, 1, 57 (Ulpian); XLVIII, 14, 1 (Modestinus); cf. Dio LII, 20, 3; Mommsen, *op. cit.* II³, p. 928.

[6] S.H.A. *Aurel.* 21, 9; L. Homo, *Règne de l'empereur Aurélien*, p. 221 *sq.*

[7] Zosimus I, 37, 2.   [8] Herodian I, 6, 5; cf. VII, 6, 2.

[9] Herodian II, 10, 9.

towards civic equalization, the emperor might become the personification of the Empire, and the political significance of Rome and its Senate fall into decay, Rome's splendour as the capital of the world could not be dimmed. In spite of political set-backs and of the change in the Senate's personnel, tradition was not forgotten, and as the scanty historical writings that have survived indicate, the Senate continued to claim its share in this splendour. A coin-type of Tacitus which depicts the emperor offering the orb to Roma[1] may indicate a desire to counteract by propaganda a threatened disappearance of the significance of Rome; politically speaking, the type soon proved to be no more than a pious hope. But the tradition was so strongly rooted that it was vigorous enough to survive the removal of the emperor from Rome and the foundation of a second Senate in the new imperial city in the East. It was, indeed, in making a Senate out of the municipal council of Constantinople that the emperors of the unconcealed autocracy showed their respect for this tradition. Thus the Senate, as an imperial assembly with the remains of its privileges, became part of the State in its final transformation.

The composition of the Senate, which the emperors controlled by admitting the sons of senators to the magistracy and also by means of the *adlectio* (vol. XI, p. 419), had altered, since the reign of Septimius Severus, to the disadvantage of the Italian element, which till then had had a small majority[2]. Italians now occupied hardly more than a third of the places and many of them had only recently become members at all. Apart from Africa, the birthplace of Severus, it was mainly the Eastern provinces, especially Asia Minor and Syria, that provided the newcomers; even Egypt contributed its representatives for the first time[3]. They were mostly sprung from the provincial aristocracy first receiving equestrian rank. Only by degrees were men admitted from other classes, and those generally by way of advancement in the army. That there was a change of personnel in favour of Italians under Severus Alexander cannot be proved. But the decline in the number of senators from the Western provinces, Gaul and Spain, is remarkable, and also the fact that so few are known to have come from the Danubian provinces; and this in spite of the increasing importance, and, ultimately, domination, of the Pannonians, though the latter only became really marked at a time when senators were excluded from those military offices

---

[1] M.-S. v, i, p. 339, no. 126; see Volume of Plates v, 238, g.
[2] Cf. P. Lambrechts, *La composition du sénat romain de Septime Sévère à Dioclétien*, pp. 79 *sqq*.   [3] Dio LXXVII, 5, 5 (p. 360 Boissevain).

(see p. 377 *sq.*) that appealed so strongly to the martial nature of the Illyrians. Men from the provinces were seldom allowed to become patricians. On the other hand, although Italian patricians were preferred as consuls, they were mostly excluded from influential posts in the imperial administration. In spite of the many newcomers, the emperors could never completely carry out their intention of suppressing opposition, although they were to some extent successful. The reason for this lies in the traditional influence of the Italian senators, which became all the stronger as the obligation to reside in Rome, which had already been but lightly enforced, was less and less observed[1]. The growing preference shown for the *equites* was a more effective weapon. A fusion of classes was prepared by the approximation of the rank of many equestrian offices to that of the senators, by the ever increasing inclusion of *equites* in the Senate, and by the abandonment of the rule that Praetorian Prefects in office might not be senators. The fusion was complete when it was admitted that the administrative service of the Empire could only be staffed by imperial officers. The senators were still distinguished by the title of *clarissimus* and they ranked first in the Empire after the emperor and his family, while the Caesars from Geta onwards bore the special title of *nobilissimus*. The *equites* were never given a special title as such. But they could achieve, in the imperial service, the successive ranks of *vir egregius*, *vir perfectissimus* and *vir eminentissimus*; and the last was finally reserved for Praetorian Prefects (see above, p. 61)[2].

VI. CHANGES IN THE ADMINISTRATION OF THE EMPIRE AND IN THE ARMY

The attempt to find more and more officials and officers in the class of *equites* becomes marked under Septimius Severus. Following the precedent of Egypt an equestrian prefect is appointed to govern the new province of Mesopotamia and, at the same time, the commanders of the two legions stationed there, I and III Parthica, as well as of II Parthica (then in garrison in Italy), became equestrian prefects (see above, p. 24). From this time on, equestrian procurators are frequently appointed deputies of the governor not only in imperial but also in senatorial provinces[3]. Such deputy governors in senatorial provinces,

---

[1] *Dig.* L, 1, 22, 6 (Paul).　　[2] Hirschfeld, *Kleine Schriften*, p. 654.
[3] The references for this and for what follows are collected in C. W. Keyes, *The Rise of the Equites in the Third Century of the Roman Empire*, pp. 1 *sqq.*, and in Lambrechts, *op. cit.* pp. 96 *sqq.*

apart perhaps from Timesitheus in Asia (see above, p. 85), were still only made to meet some temporary emergency as when a proconsul died in office. But the intention by this device to supersede, for political reasons, senators by *equites* in the imperial provinces is plain; and it was carried out by uniting two functions in the hands of the *procurator vice praesidis*. (*Praeses* in this context is a general name for governor[1].) Under Gallienus, the 'independent vicariate' appears[2], and the *agens vices praesidis*, who held no other office, could act as governor and finally be spoken of simply as the *praeses*[3]. But not all senatorial governorships were thus transformed, and not all under Gallienus; the incomplete sources that we have do not allow a precise chronology. The traditional system was probably altered in Numidia only after 268, in Pontus et Bithynia certainly after 269, when a senator was still governor, and at latest in 279. In Pannonia Inferior, the change made by Gallienus was annulled and a senator appointed before 283. In Britain, Hispania Tarraconensis, Moesia Inferior and Syria Coele, the governors never ceased to be senators. Only in Baetica, among the senatorial provinces, do we hear, under Florian or Probus, of a *v(ir) p(erfectissimus) a(gens) v(ices) p(raesidis)*. We do not know whether the other provinces administered by ex-praetors were treated in the same way; but there is some probability that they were, in so far, that is, as the threatened situation of the province makes the presence of troops likely in troublous times. The provinces administered by consulars, Asia and Africa, still had their senatorial proconsuls; but it is uncertain whether they were appointed by *sortitio*[4] or by the emperor's direct nomination[5].

These developments are connected with the exclusion of senators from military command by Gallienus. Aurelius Victor tells us[6] that this emperor forbade senators to serve in the army or have access to it, in order to prevent the *imperium* from falling into the hands of the high aristocracy. In fact, since the sole rule of Gallienus the *legatus legionis* disappears; and in his place is the *praefectus legionis*, at first with the suffix *agens vices legati*, though this hardly serves to disguise the definitive change. The title of *egregius* marks the new commanders as *equites*. Probably centurions qualified for appointment by twice achieving the rank of *primus pilus*, thus becoming, so to speak, chief of staff in their legion. At

---

[1] *Dig.* I, 18, 1.
[2] von Domaszewski, *Rhein. Mus.* LVIII, 1903, p. 228.
[3] Cf. Hirschfeld, *Die kaiserlichen Verwaltungsbeamten*[2], pp. 385 *sqq.*
[4] Lambrechts, *op. cit.* p. 103.   [5] O'Brien Moore, *op. cit.* col. 795.
[6] Aurelius Victor, *Caes.* XXXIII, 34.

the same time, as a matter of course, the senatorial *tribuni laticlavii* also disappear. The way to the highest command was now open to the man who could rise from the ranks. Aurelius Victor[1] thought that the senators might have recovered their position under Tacitus, in view of the accommodating disposition of the army. But no known attempt was made, and the situation remained as it had been under Gallienus. This had the further result that in the provinces governed by *equites* where there was an army, civil and military authority was concentrated in one man's hands, whereas in the imperial provinces, which were still governed by senators, there was of necessity a division of powers. It seems that a unified command was not necessarily created where more than one legion was stationed. The men who were given a general command in times of crisis were called *praepositi* or *duces*[2]; but their title was not officially fixed. *Dux* does not yet indicate a man in the same position as the later *dux limitum*, even though that title certainly looks back to earlier precedents.

Another military reform of Gallienus may be connected with his anxiety to strengthen his own position as emperor, namely the institution of the *protectores*[3]. The title of *protector lateris divini* was at first only conferred on high officers[4]. It is also doubtful whether under Gallienus centurions and cavalry decurions, who ranked with them, could become *protectores* as well as legionary praefects and tribunes of the troops centred at Rome. The duties of the *protectores* lay in the imperial headquarters, for the most part in the immediate neighbourhood of the emperor's person (they are the *protectores domestici* of later times). Others served with the Praetorian Prefects though they were later dispatched to special service with the troops in the provinces. Their corps became a kind of staff-college and membership of it opened the way to greater things. Many were Illyrians, as we should expect in view of the composition of the army[5]. Whether or not the *comitatus* of the Germanic tribes provided the model for the system is disputed[6]. But the attempt was made to attach the *protectores* to the emperor by a special kind of personal loyalty.

Otherwise, the organization of the army remained unchanged

[1] *Caes.* xxxvii, 6.
[2] Cf. Ritterling, P.W. *s.v.* Legio, col. 1340, l. 36 *sq.*; O. Seeck, P.W. *s.v.* Dux, col. 1869.
[3] Dessau 2785, 4002, 5695, 9204.
[4] R. Grosse, *Röm. Militärgeschichte*, p. 13; Stein, *op. cit.* i, pp. 81 *sqq.*
[5] Cf. Stein, *op. cit.* i, p. 80 *sq.*
[6] For recent support of this view see A. Graf Schenk von Stauffenberg, *Die Welt als Geschichte*, i, 1935, p. 82 *sq.*; see, however, above, p. 219.

until the middle of the third century. Provincialization advanced (vol. xi, p. 311). The troops gradually took root, as it were, in the regions where they were stationed, until they were eventually turned into frontier settlers under an hereditary obligation to serve in the army. This might lead to difficulties when they were required to fight on battlefields far from home (see above, p. 70). Yet, while wars in and outside the Empire were never-ending, a multitude of separate detachments had to be moulded together to form a single mobile fighting force. It is possible that sometimes even detachments appeared as full legions, only to be merged in the mother-legion in the frontier provinces if they were not broken up for other reasons[1]. The cavalry was increased to meet the mobility and new tactics of the enemy, especially the Persians, by the new organization of mounted *auxilia* and the strengthening of the cavalry attached to the legions. In this, as in other things, Gallienus was the innovator[2]. Legionary cavalry were often especially used as *vexillationes*; this is suggested by the later use of the word to denote a cavalry regiment. From the time of Gallienus onwards, the independent cavalry general like Aureolus and Aurelian stood highest in prestige; and the latter, when he became emperor, seems to have encouraged this development and for tactical purposes to have separated the legionary cavalry as *promoti* from the legion itself, although even under Diocletian they continued to be united for administrative purposes[3]. Peoples not subject to the Empire, especially the Germanic races, had been received into the army, at first as irregular auxiliaries. But from the reign of Claudius II onwards German prisoners of war were included in the regular *auxilia*[4], an anticipation of the recruitment of free Germans which was later extensively practised especially under Constantine.

This increasing tendency to centralize imperial administration in the hands of the emperor led to a development and re-organization of the machinery of the government devised under the Principate[5]. The Praetorian Prefect constantly appeared as the chief agent of the change[6]. His office, generally shared with a colleague, was usually the culmination of an equestrian career; but

---

[1] Ritterling, *op. cit.* col. 1338.

[2] Cedrenus I, p. 454 (Bonn); cf. L. Wickert, P.W. *s.v.* Licinius (84), col. 364. Alföldi, *Zeitschr. f. Num.* xxxvii, 1927, pp. 128 *sqq.*; see also p. 216 *sq.*   [3] Cf. Stein, *op. cit.* I, p. 92, n. 1.

[4] Cf. M. Bang, *Die Germanen im röm. Dienst*, p. 61 *sq.*; Graf Schenk von Stauffenberg, *op. cit.* p. 79 *sq.*   [5] Vol. xi, chap. x, vii.

[6] Cf. Stein, *op. cit.* I, pp. 53 *sqq.*

from the time of Severus Alexander its holders were *ex officio* senators (see above, p. 61). These Prefects commanded the Praetorian Guard and the troops garrisoned in Italy; as members of the imperial staff, they controlled recruiting and armament; they were the officers responsible for the commissariat; and they thus had a share in the collection of the special contribution which had become necessary for this purpose. As they stood in a peculiar sense in the emperor's service, special duties could be laid on them. Their jurisdiction, as representatives of the emperor, often in a sense competed with his, since appeals could be addressed to them, so that in practice they often were an ultimate court. Appeals to the emperor were still possible; but the right was disputed and they were forbidden by Constantine[1]. The Prefects were criminal judges for the whole of Italy with the exception of the area within a hundred miles of Rome, which was subject to the City Prefect, and of persons who were exempted from the jurisdiction of the provincial governors. Their right to condemn prisoners to *deportatio* proves most clearly that they represented the emperor[2]. To help them carry out their constantly increasing duties, the emperor appointed deputies for them, *vice praefectorum praetorio*, later *vicarii*, at first probably with roving commissions, but in particular cases with fixed areas to look after[3]. The Prefects also had, as representing the sovereign, a general oversight over the State post and the political and financial mechanism of government[4]. From the reign of Maximinus Thrax onwards (see above, p. 74), they had the right to publish ordinances binding on everyone, so long as they did not modify existing laws; and although this was not quite the same as a secondary right to make laws[5], it yet gave them power to issue general instructions that must be obeyed. Finally, they were the most important members of the permanent imperial *consilium*, which advised the emperor in his legal decisions. It is not surprising that this diversity of duties, not to mention the danger likely to arise from putting so much power in one man's hands, caused the office to be divided between colleagues; and that, besides soldiers, we find lawyers and experts in administration being appointed to this post.

In these troublous times, much was demanded of the State finances. But the economic system was breaking down largely under the pressure of taxation, and money could only be raised by

---

[1] *Dig.* I, 11, 1, 1; Mommsen, *op. cit.* II[3], p. 974.
[2] *Dig.* XXXII, 1, 1, 4 (Ulpian); Mommsen, *op. cit.* II[3], p. 973.
[3] Cf. Stein, *op. cit.* I, p. 55.　　　　[4] Mommsen, *op. cit.* II[3], p. 1120.
[5] So Stein, *op. cit.* I, p. 55.

the most drastic methods. This process led to a more wide-spread resort to compulsion and to an increase in unpaid services, *munera* and *liturgiae*, which gives the impression that State-socialism was developing; but for the details we must refer to the chapter on economic history (chap. vii). The financial administration was radically altered when the Praetorian Prefect was made responsible for the assessment and collection of the increasingly numerous payments in kind destined for the support of the army (the *annona militaris*), which circumstances made it necessary to exact more and more often. With this responsibility, an important part of the financial administration had come into the hands of the Prefect[1]; and the change was made at the expense of the chief financial officer of the State, the *rationalis* (vol. xi, p. 430), who was responsible for the normal taxes and duties, administered by his procurators and for the enterprises that belonged to the *fiscus* such as mines, mints and factories. The *rationalis* also had to meet competition in the shape of the office set up by Septimius Severus to look after the *res privata* (see above, p. 27 *sq.*). The income from this emperor's private fortune was mostly spent on public services. The *res privata* was administered by a *pro-curator*, later *magister, rei privatae*, who had in practice the same privileges as the *rationalis*[2]. As a result of the frequent changes of ruler, no distinction seems to have been made between the emperor's private lands and his crown lands, although the *patri-monium* existing before Severus as crown property in a special sense and administered separately was only later merged into the *res privata*. Procurators of the *res privata* were active in the different regions of Italy and in the provinces; and in some cases they represented the interests of the *patrimonium* as well[3]. The Finance Minister and the Minister of imperial domains, both ultimately *viri perfectissimi*, had perhaps become, next to the emperor, persons to whom appeals could be addressed in trials on matters falling within their sphere of duty. But as a natural consequence of the fact that these duties had been originally en-trusted to members of the imperial household, these officers always ranked as court-officials, as is most clearly reflected in the name given to their subordinates, *palatini*, after Diocletian.

The equestrian chiefs of the different departments of the imperial cabinet[4] had also taken the places of former members of the emperor's household (vol. xi, p. 427). Answers to deputations from the Empire and to foreign ambassadors,

---

[1] Stein, *op. cit.* i, p. 62.   [2] *Dig.* XLIX, 14, 6, 1 (Ulpian).
[3] Dessau 1330.   [4] Hirschfeld, *op. cit.* pp. 318 *sqq.* Stein, *op. cit.* i, p. 57.

directions for the civil service, remained under the *ab epistulis*, in whose department all official correspondence had earlier been concentrated. The numerous private appeals to the emperor were dealt with by the *a libellis*. The legal decisions to be delivered by the sovereign himself were referred to the *a cognitionibus*. Research on complicated legal problems and questions of cults was the business of the *a studiis*. The activities of the *a memoria* were the most loosely defined, but in general they were concerned with the exercise of clemency and the bestowal of favours by the emperor; and the officials of this department thus became the most influential of all. They ranked with the most highly-placed procurators and were perhaps distinguished by the title of *magister* even before the reign of Diocletian (cf. p. 389)[1]. In the reforms of Constantine, the *a studiis* disappeared as did the *a cognitionibus*, whose duties were taken over by the *a libellis*. A man always needed high attainments to hold one of these offices; and they were purely civil. Civilians could also rise to other procuratorships, usually starting as *advocatus fisci*, legal representative of the imperial treasuries. But most third-century procurators were ex-soldiers who, from being officers, were singled out for employment in the imperial administration.

The inferior staff of the *officia*, as the bureaux of the more important departments of State were called, was often composed of soldiers detailed for the purpose. This was the result of the long-standing identification of civil and military powers and of the progressive militarization of the whole State; and the survival of the titles which betray their military origin, even after the separation of the civil and military administration, is significant[2]. Militarization must have been almost complete when the *officiales* could also be called *milites*, and their service, as indeed all official service, could be known as *militia*, so that a new name, *militia armata*, had to be found for military service in order to distinguish it. It is true that there were also many clerks (*exceptores*) and account keepers (*tabularii*) who had never been in the army. But their profession was not yet promoted to be an office. They followed it as a kind of trade; they were members of guilds (*scholae*) which even before Diocletian were partly State-recognized and attached to the several *officia*; and they were paid direct by those who claimed their services. In this practice we may see the beginnings of that shifting of the cost of government on to the subject which was later to lead to the system of *sportulae*[3].

[1] Hirschfeld, *op. cit.* p. 330, n. 3.
[2] Boak, P.W. *s.v.* Officium, col. 2047.   [3] Stein, *op. cit.* I, p. 69.

CHAPTER XI

THE REFORMS OF DIOCLETIAN

I. THE SAFEGUARDING OF THE IMPERIAL THRONE·
THE SUCCESSION AND CEREMONIAL

DIOCLETIAN had entered upon rule over a State that was, in general, again unified within and made safe without by the military prowess of his Illyrian predecessors. As one who had watched with open eyes the threatened collapse and the recovery, he came to the throne when he was of ripe years and we may assume that he had, before he began to rule, thought over the ways and means to become master for good of that critical situation. This need not imply that he must have come to power with a plan of re-organization already fully worked out, but he may have had, in connection with tendencies which had become apparent earlier, a goal before his eyes, which, in the last resort, envisaged the securing of the position of emperor as the firmest support of the unity of the Empire. The experiences of the last decades had shown, more clearly than ever, that the emperor must be, so to say, present everywhere at once and immortal[1], if all the duties connected with the maintenance of the State were to be performed. In the first place, the imperial power had to be protected from the interference of the armies, carried out by means of usurpations. But, as almost all experience had shown that the victory of a general in the absence of the emperor led to the elevation of the victor to the throne, this must be guarded against. For this reason, Maximian was sent as Caesar to the West to solve particularly pressing problems. With the title of Caesar, the reversion of the succession was given to him, but not yet the co-regency that was conferred on him with the title of Augustus[2]. But even then the leadership of the whole remained with the Senior Augustus, who still set himself apart, as Jovius, from

---

[1] Cf. L. Ranke, *Weltgeschichte*, III, p. 471; K. Stade, *Der Politiker Diokletian*, p. 35.
[2] Cf. W. Ensslin, P.W. *s.v.* Maximianus (1) Herculius, cols. 2489 *sqq.*; E. Kornemann, *Doppelprinzipat und Reichsteilung im Imperium Romanum*, p. 114 *sq.*

Maximian as Herculius[1]. Pressing new problems and, at the same time, anxiety about the succession, led to the further step of the appointment of two Caesars as helpers and chosen successors: and this body of four emperors, this Tetrarchy (see above, p. 328 *sq.*), was to remain, according to Diocletian's plan, the constitutional practice for the future, as Lactantius puts it: 'ut duo sint in re publica maiores, qui summam rerum teneant, item duo minores, qui sint adiumento[2].'

Thus two pairs of rulers were to fulfil the vast task of defending the State and of administering it, wherein the Caesars were to have a full share of the imperial honours, but were to be a step lower in rank by comparison with the Augusti and, at the same time, the authority of the 'senior Augustus' was to guarantee unified conduct of affairs[3]; for in him alone was vested the power of legislation for the whole Empire[4], with a supreme right of supervision, for instance over the administration of finance[5], and certainly also the final decision in the appointment of successors. As Diocletian had no male heirs of his body, it was not difficult for him to fall back upon the basic principle of the choice of the best man. That these 'best men,' in the pressing circumstances of his times, must be, before all else, distinguished soldiers, may have been intended to flatter the ambition of the generals, for whom, through this method of choosing, a legal expectation of the very highest position in the Empire seemed to be reserved. But in this the initiative remained with the emperor alone. Army and Senate were to play no part, even though we see that the appointment to the position of Caesar took place before the assembled soldiery[6] and even if we must assume that the customary acclamation, the empty shell of an earlier right, followed on an imperial message to the Senate. The adoption of the Caesars by the Augusti, who appeared as *fratres*, connected up with the rules for the succession of the Antonine period, and thus created an artificial imperial family. It also raised, at the same time and in a special sense, the designated candidates for the succession into the sphere of the superhuman that attached to the position of emperor.

---

[1] Stade (*op. cit.* p. 36) would not admit that this expresses the superiority of the Jovius, but his objection that the later senior Augustus Constantius became by adoption Herculius is not decisive, for no such consequences were thought of when these names were chosen.   [2] *de mort. pers.* 18, 5.
[3] Aurelius Victor, *Caes.* XXXIX, 36, *cuius nutu omnia gerebantur.*
[4] Stade, *op. cit.* p. 50 *sq.*   [5] Eusebius, *Vita Constant.* I, 14, 1.
[6] Lactantius, *de mort. pers.* 19, 1 *sqq.*

The assignment to them of territorially defined areas of administration (see above, p. 329), under the superior guidance of the
Augusti, was designed to prepare the Caesars for their career
as rulers. The right to intervene still rested with the Augusti,
as Diocletian had already intervened earlier in the West (see
p. 328)[1], and, as occasion arose, the Caesar was employed in the
immediate area ruled by his Augustus (see p. 336). The Caesar,
chosen with the best knowledge and sense of responsibility and his
capacity proved under the observation of his Augustus, was to
succeed him automatically. When Diocletian then decided to abdicate along with Maximian (see p. 340), he seems to have made,
by his rules for the succession, the abdication of the Augusti in
some sense obligatory also on his successors in order to prevent
the holder of the highest position in the State from growing too
old in office. For this idea, the plan of abdication of Galerius[2] is
evidence, while we may recognize a connection with the rest of
Diocletian's dispensation in the fact that this same Galerius,
without violating the scheme of Diocletian's Tetrarchy, could
recognize Constantine as Caesar (see p. 344), but, in his refusal
to accept Maxentius, might conceal his personal dislike for him
behind the constitutional doctrine that he was legally unable to
create three Caesars[3]. But it is not likely that Diocletian should
have fixed the term of abdication at the twentieth year after a
man's elevation to the position of Caesar[4]. The new arrangement
passed over, at the first change of rulers, the natural heirs of
Maximian and of Constantius. Diocletian's personal dislike of
hereditary dynastic claims may have helped to bring this about.
But Galerius' readiness to give way in the case of Constantine
still leaves the conclusion possible that heirs of the body were not
in principle excluded. At the first opportunity an attempt to
form a dynasty met with widespread support; here, indeed, was
a danger to the system of Diocletian, but its main principle, that
of a division of responsibilities, continued to operate even after
the later dynastic remodelling of the constitution.

The original division of responsibilities certainly took place
mainly with military ends in view, and thus it is understandable
that, at first, since each of the rulers held the supreme command
in his own area, none of them should have been tied down

---

[1] Cf. Stade, *op. cit.* p. 50 *sq.*; Ensslin, *op. cit.* cols. 2498 *sqq.*

[2] Lactantius, *de mort. pers.* 20, 4; 35, 4.

[3] *Ib.* 26, 4; cf. E. Stein, *Geschichte des spätröm. Reiches*, 1, p. 100, n. 1.

[4] So O. Seeck, *Geschichte des Untergangs der antiken Welt*, 1³, p. 36, with
J. Burckhardt, *Die Zeit Constantins des Grossens³*, p. 42 *sq.*

to a fixed capital. Even if, in the end, Trèves and Milan by the side of Aquileia, and also Sirmium and Nicomedia were preferred as imperial headquarters, all the same, the mobility of the court was in principle maintained. If men had already, earlier, as occasion arose, called the residence for the time being of the emperor *castra*[1], the imperial camp, as well as *palatium*, the imperial palace, the former term, as *stratopedon*, seems to have established itself more and more in the Greek-speaking world[2] and simultaneously the court became the *comitatus*, the retinue[3]. Rome, it is true, remained the Empire's capital, with all the attendant privileges and expenditure for its inhabitants, and the imposing ruins of the Baths of Diocletian still proclaim that nothing was spared in the external embellishment of the City[4], while *Roma aeterna* still appears, even if more rarely, in the legends on coins, though the *palatium* in Rome was deserted. The consciousness that, in times not long past, the idea that he who has Rome has the Empire was still powerful, may have helped to produce the result that the City did not in any sense become the preferred residence of the Augustus of the West. At the same time, the influence which the Senate had ever and again brought to bear was thus most readily set wholly aside. Now it really became true that Rome was where the emperor was. We may still, to be sure, read in a panegyric of the time, written in connection with the meeting of the emperors in Milan (p. 328), that sovereign Rome had gladly granted, by sending the bright luminaries of her Senate to Milan, the semblance of her majestic splendour to that city, so that the seat of the imperial government seemed to be there, whither both emperors had come[5]. But in this connection, we must not forget that it is said, in another panegyric, that Rome herself would appear more reverend ('augustior') if the emperors were present in the City[6].

Emperor and court were now, for good and all, surrounded by the ceremonial forms which, reaching far back in their origins, at this time received the final shape that was to continue into the future. The authority of the imperial office was to be raised into something inviolate and sacred and thereby to be secured from attack. Without actually calling himself a god, Diocletian

---

[1] Cf. O. Hirschfeld, *Die kaiserlichen Verwaltungsbeamten*[2], p. 313; A. Alföldi, *Röm. Mitt.* L, 1935, p. 46.

[2] See the evidence in Seeck, *op. cit.* p. 445, note to p. 22, l. 23.

[3] *Cod. Just.* VII, 67, 1.

[4] Chronographer of A.D. 354, in *Mon. Germ. Auct. Ant.* IX, p. 148, 21 *sqq.*

[5] *Paneg.* XI (III), 12, 2.   [6] *Ib.* X (II), 13, 4.

emphasized this unapproachable and superhuman quality of his authority, not least, be it said, by the name Jovius, which necessarily surrounded the person of the emperor with an especial aura of sanctity. In this connection it is a matter of no importance whether the adoration which was expected from the subject took the traditional forms of the imperial cult, which saw a god in the ruler of the world, or whether it was directed to the genius of the emperors as the very genius of Juppiter and of Hercules working in them (p. 330) or whether, finally, in the Jovius and Herculius only the divinely-favoured agents, chosen by the gods to re-establish the Roman Empire, were to be recognized and revered[1]. The assumption by Diocletian of the name Jovius resulted not only in fixing firmly and in a lasting form the Juppiter-like equipment of the *imperator*[2], but, in addition, it also, in the long run, allowed the desired sanctification of the imperial power and of its holder so firmly and completely to root itself that even the invasion of a new religion could not dislodge the idea of his divine consecration. Here we may mention that, on occasion, in this period the halo, the *nimbus*, appears as the outward expression of the inward glory of the divine illumination residing in the emperor's person[3]. In thus giving its final and obligatory form to court ceremonial, and only in this, can be seen some justification for the verdict of those authors[4] who make Diocletian responsible for the introduction of this ceremonial, the characteristic which marks the fundamental division between the *princeps* and the autocratic emperor. The fact that both contemporaries and men who lived later saw parallels to this manifestation of developed autocracy in Persia, cannot, it is true, be used, after what has been said earlier (see above, pp. 361 *sqq.*), to prove that Diocletian took over these arrangements directly from the court of the Sassanian kings, but it suggests the presumption that, however many approximations were already present, the Oriental model influenced his decision to create a fixed order of ceremonial (see p. 337 *sq.*)[5]. It would not be the only example in history of the victor taking over something from the vanquished.

[1] Cf. N. H. Baynes, *J.R.S.* xxv, 1935, p. 84.

[2] Alföldi, *op. cit.* p. 104.

[3] *Ib.* p. 144; Ensslin, *op. cit.* col. 2499; K. Keyssner, P.W. *s.v.* Nimbus, col. 622. *Ib.* col. 617 for the Nimbus in Sassanid art.

[4] Eutropius, IX, 26; Aurelius Victor, *Caes.* XXXIX, 2–4; Ammian. Marc. xv, 5, 18; Jerome, *Chron.* p. 216, 10 *sqq.* (Helm).

[5] Alföldi (*Röm. Mitt.* XLIX, 1934, pp. 6 *sqq.*) sees in the reference to Persia no historical fact at all, but a literary commonplace in the representation of a tyrant.

The seclusion of the sacred person of the ruler is marked by the greater difficulty of gaining admission to him, apparent in the limitation of the *adoratio* to a strictly defined circle of persons, in which we may see a precursor of the future higher classes of rank. According to the Panegyrist, the *adoratio* took the form, at the meeting of the Emperors at Milan, of 'an act of adoration like that performed in the holy of holies, which filled with wonder those to whom the rank of their dignities gave the right of admission to the rulers.' What in this particular case brought the performance of this customary form of adoration (which was at once a duty and a coveted right) into some confusion, was the presence of two Augusti, for which the regulations for the order of precedence at court provided, it would seem, no ruling[1]. It is worth observing that *proskynesis* was demanded even from the blood-relations of the emperors[2]. The tradition that Diocletian introduced this ceremony may well contain a measure of truth so far as it was he who prescribed the procedure which was followed in the fourth century, namely, that of kneeling down and kissing a corner of the imperial robe. The emperor seldom showed himself in public; and his rare appearances became festive occasions. The overloaded splendour of the dress and the jewellery used as the expression of absolutist state then received their firmly fixed fashion. The diadem alone was not worn by Diocletian as a regular part of the insignia, if he ever wore it at all. That was reserved for Constantine[3]. It is possible that, besides regulating the court ceremonial, in which the *admissionales* were employed (see p. 363), Diocletian also drew up new rules for the other court servants and among them for the chamberlains whose duties lay in the *sacrum cubiculum*, the *cubicularii*[4]. Yet such hints as we possess for the development of the position of the highest chamberlain, the *a cubiculo*, into that of *praepositus sacri cubiculi* point to Constantine as the innovator[5]. In any event, there is no reason to ascribe to Diocletian the introduction of eunuchs as chamberlains[6].

---

[1] *Paneg.* XI (III), 11, 1–3.
[2] Lactantius, *de mort. pers.* 18, 9.
[3] [Aurelius Victor], *Epit.* XLI, 14, *caput ornans perpetuo diademate*.
[4] J. E. Dunlap, *Univ. Mich. Stud. Hum. Ser.* XIV, 1924, p. 182.
[5] Cf. Stein, *op. cit.* p. 169, n. 1.
[6] So Hug in P.W. Suppl. III. *s.v.* Eunuchen, col. 452.

II. ADMINISTRATIVE REFORMS

The central administration remained in essentials unchanged. The Praetorian Prefects, who were still two in number[1], retained their spheres of duty, except that the new taxation system considerably increased their influence in the administration of the State finances, and except that, through personal attendance on the Augusti and the resultant absence from Rome, they lost the immediate command of the Praetorian Guard, which Diocletian finally degraded to being a garrison of Rome and of which he reduced the numbers very greatly[2]. The frequent changes of residence on the part of the emperors had been the cause of making the personnel of the imperial chancery also, with its archives, easily movable. From the boxes to hold the documents, the *scrinia*, it seems that, under Diocletian, the designation *scrinia*, used for the separate departments of the chancery, arose[3]. The heads of the departments were now certainly *magistri*. They belonged to the circle of those who made up the imperial *consilium*. There was also the permanent body of legal advisers and those summoned to the council from time to time for other affairs of State[4]. Besides the designation of the body of advisers as *consilia sacra*, it seems that, as early as Diocletian, *consistorium* also arose as a name for it, although the earliest evidence of its use has been doubted[5], because the advisers who were members of the civil service were still called *a consiliis sacris*. But it is not rare to find examples, even in the usages of official speech, of a variation in such designations, until one of them finally becomes the definitive form. In the career of a certain C. Caelius Saturninus the position of *a consiliis sacris* is followed by that of *magister libellorum*, that of *magister studiorum* (see p. 382) and then that of *vicarius a consiliis sacris*[6]. The last seems to be the name for the position of deputy for the absent, or over-burdened Praetorian Prefect, who was also perhaps not learned in the law. This *vicarius* might therefore count as the predecessor of the *quaestor sacri palatii* of Constantine. It remains doubtful how far he, at the same time, while deputizing for the Prefect, exercised some kind of supervision over the whole of the imperial *scrinia*, that is to say, a function of the later *magister officiorum*[7]. The

---

[1] Zosimus II, 32, 2; Dessau 8929, 8938.
[2] Lactantius, *de mort. pers.* 26, 3; R. Grosse, *Röm. Militärgeschichte*, p. 58 *sq.*
[3] So first in *Cod. Theod.* VI, 35, 1 (of A.D. 313); cf. Seeck, P.W. *s.v.* Scrinium, col. 894.   [4] Lactantius, *de mort. pers.* 11, 5 *sq.*
[5] *Cod. Just.* IX, 47, 12; Hirschfeld, *op. cit.* p. 342, n. 1.
[6] Dessau 1214.   [7] Cf. M. Besnier, *Hist. Rom.* IV, p. 301.

frumentarii, who acted as couriers in the service of the central administration of the Empire and especially as secret police, were abolished by Diocletian on account of deeply-rooted abuses[1]. But, because, at least for the courier service, a substitute had to be created it is possible that he replaced them by the *agentes in rebus*[2], who, it is true, cannot be proved to have existed before 319[3]. The central administration of the finances, controlled as before (see above, p. 381) by the Finance Minister, the *rationalis*, and the Minister of Domains, the *magister rei summae privatae*, was so far extended that the *rationales vicarii*[4] were instituted, in connection with the regulations drawn up for the *dioeceses* which are to be described below. It is probable that the *magister summarum rationum* also, who was the immediate subdirector in the ministry of finance, now became the *vicarius summae rei rationum*[5]. That the parallel arrangements for the *res privata*, which can be found in the *Notitia Dignitatum*, also date back to Diocletian, is indeed very probable, but cannot be proved with certainty.

Diocletian's reform of the provincial administration went far deeper. The reform was intended to secure the position of the emperor from being assailed by officials who lusted after power, by a fundamental separation of civil and military authority and by a substantial reduction in size of the provinces. The reform had this problem to solve: how, in addition to the provision of the means for the defence of the Empire and for the carrying on of the internal administration, at the same time, to hold together, by the creation of a body of civil servants controlled down to the last detail, the heterogeneous elements in an Empire that was of great territorial extent, so as to form a unified State; and how to secure recognition for the imperial will which was the supreme representation of that unity. On the other hand the reduction in size of the provinces, and thus of the areas of jurisdiction, was to the advantage of the subject, in that Diocletian at once insisted on the regular exercise of their legal functions by the governors in person, and only granted them the right to appoint other iudges (*iudices*) to represent them on occasions when they were prevented by other official business from attending, and even then not for all kinds of legal cases[6]. At the beginning of Diocletian's

[1] Aurelius Victor, *Caes.* xxxix, 44 *sq.*; Fiebiger, P.W. *s.v.* Frumentarii, col. 123.

[2] Hirschfeld, *Kl. Schriften*, p. 625; A. E. R. Boak, *Univ. Mich. Stud. Hum. Ser.* xiv, 1924, p. 68. For another view, Stein, *op. cit.* p. 173, n. 2.

[3] *Cod. Theod.* vi, 35, 3.   [4] Cf. Dessau 1211.

[5] *Ib.*; cf. Hirschfeld, *Die kaiserlichen Verwaltungsbeamten*[2], p. 38 *sq.*

[6] *Cod. Just.* iii, 3, 2; cf. A. Steinwenter, P.W. *s.v.* Iudex, col. 2471.

reign there may have been, in round figures, fifty provinces in existence. By comparison with earlier conditions, Septimius Severus had already subdivided Syria and Britain (see above, pp. 11, 36 *sq.*) and Aurelian had carried through the transference of the province of Dacia to the left bank of the Danube, thus reducing in size the neighbouring provinces (see p. 301). In all probability, Novempopulana also had been separated from Aquitania before Diocletian's reign[1]. The innovations of Diocletian, if we may anticipate, were not introduced at one blow, but were only carried out gradually[2]. The separation into Imperial and senatorial provinces now ceased to exist, and therewith, for good and all, the Senate's show of sovereignty in provincial administration; so also the privileged position of Italy, which was now included in the system of provincial administration. In this, too, the emperor could point to precedents. Dio[3] had already pleaded (see p. 60) for the administrative assimilation of Italy to the provinces, in so far as it was not subject to the City Prefect within a hundred miles from Rome, and from as early as the second century areas where trials were conducted by imperial *iuridici*, men of praetorian rank, were instituted (vol. XI, p. 433 *sq.*), while *curatores* had been appointed for the supervision of the municipalities (vol. XI, p. 468 *sq.*). From the reign of Caracalla there were, in addition, at first special mandatories *ad corrigendum statum Italiae*, later mostly called *correctores totius Italiae*; but, all the same, there were already before Diocletian several *correctores Italiae* for particular areas, although these areas were not named in their titles, and so it still continued for a time until, for example, a *corrector Italiae regionis Transpadanae*, or a *corrector Italiae Transpadanae*, together with a *corrector Campaniae*, appears[4]. The final division into such areas seems to have been completed about A.D. 300[5]. For these, it is true, the designation *provincia* was at first avoided, but technically there remained no difference. Even now Rome and the area as far as the hundredth milestone remained excepted.

As in the case of the division of Italy, so also the subdivision of the provinces was carried out gradually. The division of Egypt into three and, at the same time, the complete assimilation of it

---

1 J. B. Bury, *J.R.S.* XIII, 1923, p. 139; who, however, goes too far in attributing the establishment of other provinces to Aurelius and Probus; cf. Stein, *op. cit.* p. 65, n. 3.

2 J. G. C. Anderson, *J.R.S.* XXII, 1932, pp. 24 *sqq.*

3 Dio LII, 22, 1.   4 *C.I.L.* VI, 1418 *sq.*; Dessau 1212.

5 A. von Premerstein, P.W. *s.v.* Corrector, col. 1654.

to the other provincial administrations only began after the suppression of the rebellion (see p. 335), and Numidia was first divided in the last year of Diocletian[1]. The list given in a manuscript from Verona, the *laterculus Veronensis*[2], comes nearest to the actual state of the division of provinces, as it was at the end of his reign. The details given in this manuscript, however, are not, as was long supposed, identical with the list in Diocletian's time; on the contrary, a comparison of it with the list of provinces represented at the Council of Nicaea and with the account of a Synod of Antioch in A.D. 328, shows that, for the Eastern provinces, the *laterculus* is evidence only for conditions after the changes introduced by Constantine when he had taken possession of the Eastern part of the Empire, while, for the West, it represents only the provincial divisions after the year 358, unless it is assumed that the arrangements made by Diocletian were in part abrogated and then later re-introduced[3]. But certainly the number of provinces increased, in round figures, to a hundred under the first Tetrarchy.

Of the former senatorial provinces, Africa and Asia retained a proconsul at the head of their governments, and were subject directly to the emperor, not to the Praetorian Prefects. A third proconsul was appointed for Achaea[4]. Further, the governors, after this, bore the titles, with their emphasis on rank, of *consularis*, *corrector* and *praeses*. It is usually assumed, and doubtless on the point of principle rightly, that the first two groups of offices were filled from men from the senatorial class and, indeed, of the rank of ex-consuls, whereas the positions of *correctores* were filled from men of the rank of ex-praetors, and, on the other hand, the *praesides* were *equites* and *viri perfectissimi*[5]. Whether Diocletian had in mind a rigid division between provinces governed by *equites* and by senators is not certain, but he may well have allowed senators, now as earlier, to reach high civil office. Moreover, this period affords but little certain evidence for the title *consularis*[6], as for instance the title of the governor of the still undivided Phrygia and Caria (ὑπατικὸς ἡγεμών), of which the literal translation would be *consularis praeses*, though there is also the evidence of another title for the governor of the

---

[1] Cf. G. Costa, *Diz. Epig. s.v.* Diocletianus, p. 1834.

[2] Mommsen, *Ges. Schriften*, v, pp. 561 *sqq.*; O. Seeck in his edition of the *Notitia Dignitatum*, pp. 247 *sqq.*

[3] Cf. E. Schwartz, *Bay. Abh.* 1937, pp. 79 *sqq.*

[4] *E.g.* Dessau 1217, 1220.

[5] At times even after A.D. 293 still *vir egregius* (Dessau 638).

[6] On the title *consularis* for governors before Diocletian cf. Dessau, Index VI, vol. III, 1, p. 356.

same province (πρεσβευτὴς καὶ ἀντιστράτηγος τῶν Σεβαστῶν ὕπατος), that is, *praeses Phrygiae et Cariae legatus propraetore Augustorum consularis*[1]. It almost seems as if only the title *consularis* was not yet firmly established, although it could be borne, in conjunction with another, by men of this rank even before Diocletian, as, for instance, also in the case of the *consularis vir corrector Campaniae*[2]. On the other hand, the career of L. Aelius Helvius Dionysius gives evidence pointing in the other direction, for he was City Prefect in 301 and, after he had been *corrector utriusque Italiae*, and had thus administered areas in both parts of Italy, became governor of Coele Syria, and bore as his title there only *praeses Syriae Coeles*[3], when we might have expected, in the case of this man from the senatorial class, *consularis*. Besides this, there already occurs, soon after the abdication of Diocletian, a *v(ir) p(erfectissimus) corr(ector) Apuli(ae) et Calab(riae)*[4], and probably also the career of a certain *eques*, named Caecilianus, who was *corrector* of the same provinces, belongs to the period before the reign of Constantine[5]. In any event, the differences of class cannot any longer have been so very keenly felt, when Constantine, even at the beginning of his reign, could ignore them.

In order better to control the provincial administration, the earlier extraordinary deputies of the Praetorian Prefects (p. 380) now became a permanent institution. The *vicarii praefectorum praetorio*[6], or simply *vicarii*, had a definite area assigned to them, which in general corresponded with the extent of one of the twelve *dioeceses* which were created at this time. These were: Oriens, the lands south of the Taurus with Isauria as far as Egypt and Cyrenaica; Pontus (Eastern Asia Minor); Asiana (Western Asia Minor); Thrace, with Lower Moesia; Moesiae, with Macedonia, Epirus, Achaea and Crete; Pannoniae, with Dalmatia and Noricum; Italia, with Raetia; Africa (west of the Great Syrtes); Hispaniae with Mauretania Tingitana; Viennensis (southern and western France as far as the Loire); Galliae (the rest of France and the lands as far as the Rhine); Britanniae, now sub-

---

[1] Anderson, *op. cit.* p. 24.

[2] Dessau 1212; cf. von Premerstein, *op. cit.* col. 1653, ll. 1 *sqq.*; col. 1654, ll. 32 *sqq.*

[3] Dessau 1211; Stein (*op. cit.* p. 103, n. 2) is of the opinion that this office existed before Diocletian's reform, but against this may be set the pre-existent subdivision of Italy into two larger administrative areas, the Vicariates; cf. von Premerstein, *op. cit.* col. 1654.

[4] *C.I.L.* ix, 687; cf. L. Cantarelli, *La Diocesi Italiciana*, p. 156.

[5] Dessau 1218; for another view Stein, *op. cit.* p. 185, n. 2 and Cantarelli, *op. cit.* p. 158 *sq.*   [6] Dessau 1214.

divided into four provinces. In addition, Italy was divided into two vicariates. The *vicarius Italiae*, with an official residence in Milan, had the districts north of the Apennines, *Italia annonaria* (see below, p. 400). Suburbicarian Italy, that is, the rest of the mainland and the islands, was subject to the *vicarius in urbe Roma*. The proconsuls were exempted from the supervision, which the *vicarii* had the right to exercise over the provincial administration; further, the *praefectus Aegypti* formed an intermediate authority between the *vicarius* of the *dioecesis Oriens* and the governors of the newly-created Egyptian provinces[1]. The activities of the *vicarii* meant a weakening of the Praetorian Prefecture, especially in that their jurisdiction competed with that of the Prefects in so far as appeals against their verdicts went direct to the emperor. The same intention of weakening the higher office may be recognized in the institution of a *vicarius praefecturae urbis*[2], side by side with the City Prefect. The *vicarii* were of the equestrian class and *viri perfectissimi*[3]. It has been suggested that we should see, in the setting-up of the *vicarii* even over the great majority of the senatorial governors, an important principle at work, namely the tendency to bring those of higher standing into dependence upon officials of lower rank[4]. And in fact, for the future, not only was the higher official responsible for the actions of his subordinates, but the latter also were responsible for the behaviour of their superior. In all this, however, there remains the doubt, whether the developments with regard to the vicariate did not arise from the intention to reserve these newly-created posts for *equites* who engaged in civil careers, in order not to make the latter too short in comparison with the military. Here also, it is wise to think of the difference as more closely connected with the real standing of an office than with the title of a class or rank, even if it did take some time before the designation of a class, *vir clarissimus*, could become that of a rank, which then, in its turn, stood higher than the designation *perfectissimus*. *Vicarii* and governors were purely civil officials, concerned with justice and administration; hence, generally speaking, the term *iudices* is used for such civil officials.

---

[1] M. Gelzer, *Studien zur byz. Verwaltung Ägyptens*, p. 5.

[2] Dessau 1214; cf. Ensslin, *Byz. Zeitschr.* XXXVI, 1936, p. 320.

[3] Helvius Dionysius once more provides an exception as *iudex sacrarum cognitionum totius orientis*, which describes the vicariate of the East (Dessau 1211).

[4] Cf. H. M. D. Parker, *A History of the Roman World from* A.D. 138 *to* 337, p. 264; Stein, *op. cit.* p. 104.

In the course of the reform, military authority, with a very few exceptions, was separated from the civil. Generals, as *duces* with the rank of *viri perfectissimi*, took command in the provinces that still had senatorial governors. As early as the year 289 we find a distinction made between *iudices* and *duces* in a Panegyric[1]. In the provinces under an equestrian *praeses*, who, at the outset, combined both powers, the separation was introduced only gradually as the reform was carried through[2] and it had become so far universal by the end of Diocletian's reign, that only in those provinces where the hostile character of the inhabitants or of the neighbours made a permanent state of siege necessary and those in which, because of their smallness, no danger of a pronunciamento was to be feared, as in Mauretania Caesariensis and Isauria, did the *praeses* remain at the same time the military commandant[3]. The *duces* were dependent upon the co-operation of the civilian officers for their commissariat, a fact which also gave the desired occasion for mutual supervision.

The increase in the number of official positions had as a result the setting-up of a great number of *officia*[4], and, even in the lower grades, a strict separation between the civil and military services was introduced. It is true that all officials were still called *milites*[5] and that the *cingulum militare* formed part of the official costume which the City Prefect, who performed his functions in the civil dress, the *toga*, alone among the higher officials did not wear[6]. The staff of a higher official could still be described as *cohors*[7]. Service, *cohortalis militia*, a designation that was only later restricted to that of the subordinates of the governors[8], still did not, even in the reign of the Emperor Licinius, create a claim to the privileges of a veteran, that is, of the *militia armata*[9]. Perhaps this happened on the analogy of the military career under Diocletian, who had not given to the veterans of the cohorts the same privileges as to those serving in legions and the *vexillationes*[10]. The recruitment of the personnel of the civil offices was from the civil population. But, conformably with military usage, a strict order of advancement by

---

[1] *Paneg.* x (ii), 3, 3.   [2] Anderson, *op. cit.* pp. 24, 29 *sq.*
[3] Cf. *Not. Dign.* Occid. xxx, where the title *dux et praeses* and the personnel of his *officium* show that the military side predominated; and Orient. xxix.
[4] Lactantius, *de mort. pers.* 7, 4.   [5] *Ib.* 31, 3 *sq.*
[6] Cf. Th. Mommsen, *Röm. Staatsrecht*, ii³, pp. 1067, 1069.
[7] Cf. *Dig.* xlviii, 11, 1.
[8] A. von Premerstein, P.W. *s.v.* Cohortales, col. 358; A. E. R. Boak, P.W. *s.v.* Officium, col. 2047.
[9] *Cod. Theod.* viii, 4, 1.   [10] *Cod. Just.* x, 55, 3.

seniority of service ruled also in the *officia*, and, as the general exercised jurisdiction over his soldiers, so the higher official became the regular judge of his staff. How far, moreover, the conception of *militia* could finally be extended beyond service actually rendered in the army, and in the *officia*, is shown by a quotation from St Ambrose[1]: 'omnes homines, qui sub ditione Romana sunt, vobis militant imperatoribus terrarum;' and we need not hesitate to apply this dictum to the period of Diocletian. And this obligation to serve the State must be considered to have been civil in character for the majority of subjects.

III. THE STRENGTHENING OF IMPERIAL DEFENCE

The fundamental principle of the universal obligation to serve in the army was not removed; but in fact recruitment was already before, and especially after the time of Diocletian, conducted by a mixture of conscription and enlistment. The method of finding men for the army, as we see it generally practised in later times, may be regarded as derived from a concentration and extension of existing conditions[2]. The levy, which took place under the direction of *protectores*, affected the sons of soldiers, who were subject to an hereditary obligation to serve which as early as 313 came to be regarded as a matter of course[3]; further, all those fit for service who, as *vacantes* or *otiosi*, belonged to no corporation that had obligations to the State or the municipality, or who, as *vagi*, men without a domicile, were not attached to a cultivable holding of land. An indirect form of levy existed in the obligation to provide recruits, laid upon the landowners by the State, which must have helped not a little to bind the *coloni* to the soil they cultivated. Owing to the scarcity of labourers it seems that this obligation was not without its hardships, although the *capitularis functio*, the duty of providing one recruit only, was mostly performed by several landowners together. As, with the increase in the numbers of the army made by Diocletian, this demand was also intensified, and gave rise to many abuses, the Emperor appears to have acceded more often than his predecessors to requests to commute the provision of recruits to the payment of money[4]. With the money thus obtained, volunteers could then be enlisted from the free peasantry of races skilled in warfare, especially, as heretofore,

---

[1] Ambrosius, *Ep.* 17, 1.
[2] Mommsen, *Ges. Schriften*, VI, pp. 246 *sqq.*; Grosse, *op. cit.* pp. 198 *sqq.*
[3] *Cod. Theod.* VII, 22, 1; cf. Stein, *op. cit.* p. 85, n. 3.
[4] Lactantius, *de mort. pers.* 7, 5.

the Illyrians (see p. 332), but also, and to an increasing degree, from tribes outside the Empire, later especially from Germans. The *laeti*, prisoners of war settled in separate, self-contained groups on the land of the Empire, took a special place among the elements of the population which were liable to military service, and so did also the *gentiles*, who came of peoples which acknowledged the sovereignty of the Empire but which were not subject to its administration.

Diocletian carried further the reform of the army begun by Gallienus (see above, pp. 377 *sqq.*), and greatly increased the numbers of troops under arms. Special attention was still paid to the system of frontier defence[1]. It is only necessary here to cite one particularly impressive example of the efforts made in the building-up of the frontier defences, the *strata Diocletiana*, that solid and fortified military road from Damascus by way of Palmyra to Sura on the Euphrates, together with the extension of the forts and watch-towers on the road from Petra by way of Palmyra to Circesium[2]. In connection with the gradual development of the division of the provinces, the frontier provinces, now made smaller, received, according to the practice developed in the course of the third century, in the ordinary way two legions each, under the *duces*. For the other bodies of troops also this formation in pairs was generally introduced. Thus the total number of legions, which is reported to have been thirty-three under Caracalla[3], and which, probably before the reign of Diocletian, had undergone a certain amount of augmentation, was increased to sixty, in round figures, and the total, also, of the *auxilia* connected with them, the cohorts and the *alae*, was similarly increased. Lactantius[4] blames Diocletian for having so multiplied the army that each of the four emperors had more troops under arms than the earlier *principes*. That is a gross exaggeration; for we can hardly suppose that the number of troops under arms had been even doubled. Although the newly-raised legions may perhaps have had at first the nominal strength of six thousand men, they must later have been much smaller, and can hardly have exceeded the strength of the original detachments from which, in part at least, the new legions had originated, as, for example, the legions of the same name which were created from the V Macedonica and XIII Gemina for service in Egypt[5].

[1] Zosimus ii, 34, 1; *Paneg.* ix (iv), 18, 4.
[2] Cf. E. Fabricius, P.W. *s.v.* Limes, cols. 653–9; further references in Parker, *op. cit.* pp. 275 and 367, n. 70; Besnier, *op. cit.* p. 309, n. 188.
[3] Dio lv, 23 *sq.*　　　　　[4] Lactantius, *de mort. pers.* 7, 2.
[5] E. Ritterling, P.W. *s.v.* Legio, col. 1356.

The aim of frontier defence is apparent also in the new distribution of the legions[1]. Thus there were now stationed on the Danube, from Noricum to its mouth, sixteen legions in place of eleven from the beginning of the century, in Egypt six, after this, in place of one; in the frontier provinces of the *dioecesis Oriens*, from Arabia to Mesopotamia, twelve instead of eight[2]. We may, perhaps, hazard a guess, that the increase set in earliest on the Danubian frontier; for detachments from each pair of the legions there, under *praepositi*, are found among the troops used to suppress the revolt in Egypt[3], and also the reinforcements employed to carry the Persian war to a successful conclusion (p. 336) were drawn by Galerius from that area[4]. We must assume, in this connection, without, it is true, knowing about the participation of more than one single regiment of cavalry, designated *comites*, and of one further *vexillatio* in the Egyptian campaign[5] ,that independent cavalry took part in it. For, even before 293, the tactically independent cavalry of the legions was known as *vexillatio* (see above, p. 379)[6]. And in an inscription from Noricum of the year 311 or 312, before Constantine had established his rule there, a *praepositus equitibus Dalmatis comitatensibus* appears[7]. Thus it is obvious that the separation of cavalry and infantry, which was to be the distinguishing mark of the late Roman army, was further advanced by Diocletian, and that, in this connection, at least a certain number of cavalry regiments, if not all already, were distinguished by the name of *comitatenses*. But as the Praetorians were no longer available as a reserve for use in emergencies (see above, p. 389), Diocletian needed a substitute for them. It has been conjectured that he retained a certain number of the detachments from the legions as permanent formations for special service, evidence for this being found in the presence in garrisons at Aquileia of a detachment of the XI Claudia[8], from which the later legion of *comitatenses*, the *undecimani*, may have sprung. In any event, however, the establishment of a *corps d'élite*, composed of veteran legionaries called *lanciarii*[9], marks a fully-authenticated step in the direction of separating off a mobile reserve. One of these legionaries is

---

[1] Parker, *J.R.S.* XXIII, 1933, pp. 175 *sqq.*
[2] Ritterling, *op. cit.* col. 1365 *sq.*
[3] P. Oxy. I, 43; cf. Ritterling, *op. cit.* col. 1359 *sq.*
[4] Ensslin, P.W. *s.v.* Maximianus (2) Galerius, col. 2522.
[5] P. Oxy. I, 43, col. II, 24 *sqq.*; col. I, 15.
[6] *Cod. Just.* VII, 64, 9; X, 55, 3.
[7] Dessau 664.   [8] Parker, *op. cit.* p. 272.
[9] Dessau 2045, 2782.

called *lectus in sacro comit(atu) lanciarius*[1]. In this case, the conclusion is permissible, that at least this troop of infantry should be considered *comitatenses*. And when the Caesar Julian extols Maximian Herculius, Constantius I and Constantine as the creators of the army stationed in Gallia, which he commanded[2], we may assume here too independent new formations, which later appear under the name of *auxilia palatina*. So much is certain, that the *comitatenses* were not first created, as a mobile fighting army, by Constantine[3], however much he may afterwards have done towards developing the organization which Diocletian had initiated.

IV. THE REFORM OF TAXATION AND THE REGULATION OF THE COINAGE

The carrying-on of wars and the increase in the size of the army, as well as the increase in the administrative apparatus, with the heightened expenditure of the court, and finally the cost of the new buildings put a very heavy burden on the finances. For, besides fortresses and other military buildings (see p. 397), Diocletian himself, and, in imitation of him or at his suggestion, his co-regents also, did much building, so that an unfriendly critic could even speak of Diocletian's 'building mania[4].' The palace near Salonae, the home of the Emperor's old age, in which the Old Town of Spalato fitted comfortably, and the vast ruins of the Baths of Diocletian in Rome, still to-day perpetuate the splendid ideas of their builder and at the same time give permanent expression to the effort, in taxes and labour-services, which his government demanded from the subjects for their erection. All this, which provoked Lactantius[5] to the criticism, that the number of beneficiaries had begun to grow greater than the number of tax-payers, demanded, in view of the precarious state of the finances, a reform of the system of taxation. Because of the terrible debasement of the coinage, the receipts from taxation could not cover the needs of the State, even when what had formally been regarded as the norm was no longer strictly observed[6]. As a result, special levies in kind, destined to secure the support of the army, became even commoner, and were raised by

[1] Dessau 2781.
[2] Julian, *Or.* I, p. 34 c; Mommsen, *Ges. Schriften*, VI, p. 236, n. 3.
[3] Zosimus II, 34, 2.
[4] Lactantius, *de mort. pers.* 7, 8; see p. 567.   [5] *Ib.* 7, 3.
[6] Cf. G. Mickwitz, *Geld und Wirtschaft im römischen Reich des 4 Jahrhunderts n. Chr.* p. 177 *sq.* with pp. 59 *sqq.* against Seeck, *op. cit.* II[2], p. 226 *sq.*

special order (*indictio*)[1] of the emperor from the provinces forming the area on the line of march. For these special levies, the designation *annonae* was already established[2]. The reform of Diocletian converted this extraordinary levy into a regular official tax. Its yield, the *annona*, formed for the future the chief foundation for the State economy. The tax was a payment made in kind, levied, as far as was possible, evenly over the whole Empire, and directly connected with the produce of agriculture. Town-dwellers who had no landed property were thus exempted from it. Italy was so far included in it, that the northern districts had to provide the *annona*, and were thus known as the *regio annonaria*. The rest of Italy, the *regio suburbicaria*, had, on the other hand, to undertake the provisioning of Rome with cattle, wine, wood and lime. For the carrying-out of the new tax-regulations, it was necessary to establish, by means of a State-conducted census, the number of the units, for purposes of taxation, which had to pay the *annona*. Every five years verifications took place, which were later consolidated into a cycle of fifteen years, and this was, in its turn, also called *indictio*. A unit for the purposes of taxation was an area of cultivable land (*iugum*) which could be worked by one man (*caput*) and which would provide him with the means of existence. The unit was thus both the land and the labour on it, in which connection a female worker counted as half a *caput*. The numbers of *iuga* and *capita* had therefore to correspond with one another. According to this method of assessment, the tax could also be designated *iugatio* or *capitatio*. The extent of the *iugum* was determined by its productivity and the type of cultivation it underwent. Thus, in Syria, the unit consisted, according to the quality of the land, of 20, 40 or 60 acres of plough-land, or of 5 acres of vineyard, or of 225 or, in mountainous districts, 450 olive-trees[3]. On the other hand, in Africa the unit remained fixed on the arrangement, which had existed up till now, of the *centuria* of 200 acres, whose basis was the obligation to make payment in kind for the victualling of Rome. Besides this, there was also the *capitatio humana* and, further, the *capitatio animalium*; in this way the poll-tax and animal-tax of the period previous to Diocletian were included in his new system[4]. A recently-discovered papyrus has furnished us with a copy of the edict, dated 16 March 297, of the Prefect of Egypt, which brought the new

---

[1] *Cod. Just.* x, 16, 3.   [2] *Ib.* x, 16, 2; cf. Dessau 1330.

[3] Bruns-Sachau, *Syrisch-römisches Rechtsbuch*, 1880, § 121.

[4] See Stein, *op. cit.* p. 109 *sq.* for the right interpretation; cf. id. *Gnomon* VI, 1930, p. 409, n. 2.

tax-regulations into force for that country[1]. With the words:
'therefore I have publicly set forth the quota of each *aroura*[2]
with respect to the quality of the soil, and the quota of each head
of the peasants,' the *iugatio* and the *capitatio humana* are introduced at the same time.

Commissioners for valuation (*censitores*) carried out the
assessment. The State had the greatest possible interest in the
maintenance of the units that had once been established. Thus, if
fields were abandoned by their cultivators, the government took
steps to grant them to others (*adiectio*), who would then be
responsible for the taxes. Once the census had been completed
it was only in exceptional cases possible to secure the sending
by the emperor of *inspectores* or *peraequatores* for the purpose of
a revision; for indeed, in such cases, a reduction of the number
of tax-units might have to be faced. The amount of the tax
demanded from the unit was, it is true, by no means always the
same. Every year, by the imperial *indictio*, the total needs of the
State were publicly announced; then the Praetorian Prefect's
office, which even now continued to have the administration of the
annona and remained, for the future, the most influential financial
authority, apportioned it among the provinces, where it was the
duty of the governors to take the necessary steps for the collection.
If, for whatever reason, the sum estimated by the *indictio* proved
not to be sufficient, an additional assessment, the *superindictio*,
was imposed[3].

The collection of the taxes had to be carried out by the governor's
subordinates, under his supervision, and, in particular, by the
members of the councils of the municipalities, as an obligatory
duty (*munus*). From among the latter the collectors (*susceptores*)
and the recoverers of arrears (*exactores*) were appointed. Those
responsible for the collection had to make good any deficits
resulting from uncollectable taxes, and in the event of their
inability to pay, the liability falls upon the whole body of coun-
cillors that had appointed them. It is not surprising that the
State, in face of the anxiety to escape such burdens, now first
fully and completely developed the hereditary fixation of individuals in a class. In just the same way, the tax-regulations must
have had as a result a growth of hereditary obligations and
the binding to the soil, first and at once, of the *coloni*, the

[1] P. Cair. Inv. no. 57074 ed. A. E. R. Boak, *Early Byzantine Papyri*
no. 1; *Ét. de Papyrol.* II, 1933, pp. 1 *sqq*.
[2] This may be an attempt to translate *iugum*.
[3] Ensslin, P.W. *s.v.* Superindictio, col. 933.

tenants[1] (in this case, perhaps, in connection with the effect of a system of tenure based on a fixed percentage of produce), and also of the small independent peasantry[2]. The landowner paid the tax for that part of his property the cultivation of which he managed himself; the *coloni* were responsible directly to the collecting authority for their share. Moreover, at first the *annona* had to be paid by all agricultural land, even by the imperial domains. It was reserved for later arrangement to break through the original intention to equalize the burdens of taxation, by means of privileged exemption. In the edict already cited, the reason for the new regulations is given as the desire to put an end to the former arbitrariness and inequality, with their disastrous results, and 'to give a saving norm to which the taxes shall conform.' And Aurelius Victor[3] thought, at its first application, that the reform was quite tolerable. Only Lactantius, whose hostility to Diocletian is plain to see[4], asserts that the heavy burdens of the *indictiones* had immediately broken down the strength of the *coloni* and, at the same time, caused a flight from the land. The attempt of Galerius to impose the *capitatio* and indeed the *capitatio humana* on the populations of the towns also, and even on Rome[5], which was in part the cause of the elevation of Maxentius to the throne, seems, after all, to have been confined to his own half of the Empire[6].

The fact that there was, in the re-organization of the administration of the State finances, a recognition of a fully-developed system of natural economy, has given rise to the opinion that, as a result of the disorganization of the coinage, a general retrogression to a natural economy set in. But an examination of the papyri has proved for Egypt that in contracts concerning future payments and also in those concerning leases of land, letting of houses, loans and service, the system of natural economy, during the inflation period, made only small headway, and even then only in cases where payments in kind were already usual. There are, too, enough examples of conditions in the rest of the Empire to prove that private transactions were in no way predominantly based on a natural economy; on the contrary,

---

[1] *Cod. Theod.* V, 17, 1 of A.D. 332 already assumes the compulsory attachment to the soil of the *coloni*.

[2] Mickwitz, *op. cit.* pp. 179 *sqq.*; Stein, *op. cit.* p. 22, n. 2.

[3] *Caes.* XXXIX, 32.

[4] Lactantius, *de mort. pers.* 7, 3; cf. Lydus, *de magistr.* 1, 4, p. 11, 11 *sq.* Wuensch.   [5] Lactantius, *de mort. pers.* 26, 2.

[6] Cf. *Cod. Theod.* XIII, 10, 2 with Seeck, *Regesten*, p. 52, 17 *sqq.*

money was still the chief medium of exchange[1]. But why then had the emperor given preference to a tax founded on payments in kind? Payments in kind were a direct guarantee of the supplies for the army and thus served to ensure the security both of the Empire and of the throne. And, in addition, it may well have been the case that those who were in receipt of salaries and wages, that is to say the influential members of the bureaucracy, with memories of unpleasant experiences during the period of inflation, saw in the fixing of their incomes in kind an assurance of their future stability. If, having established the system, the State wished to cover its other needs completely, it had to insist more than ever upon the performance of the unpaid services of its subjects, but this is treated of elsewhere (see chap. VII). Thus, as regards the membership of the municipal councils, Diocletian's rescripts show that an obligation to serve already existed, and it may be assumed that by now it was no longer an easy task to find the necessary number of persons to undertake such duties; in consequence reasons for being exempted from undertaking them, which had formerly been in force, such as illness, illiteracy and *infamia* (loss of honour), were not regarded now as valid; similarly the previous consent of the father was no longer necessary for the nomination of a son who was still subject to parental authority[2].

Diocletian's reform of the coinage proves that he did not intend to change the existing economic system, and it was much rather directed to making ends meet and to creating an easier circulation of money, with the security necessary for this. In the first place, his minting of coins was a continuation of the methods of previous reigns, although in the case of gold coins the standard used at the beginning, of 70 *aurei* to the pound, was soon set at 60 (see p. 330). After the naming of the Caesars, a reform of the coinage was planned and, even before 295/6, was so far carried into effect, that in Alexandria the new imperial coinage was already being minted, although the old provincial coins were not yet wholly given up[3]. Soon after this, the last relics of a local system were cleared away. The difficulty of changing money was to be disposed of by this means. All mints, of which the number was increased, struck, under a strict imperial control, Empire coins of uniform types. The separate mints distinguished their coins with the abbreviations of the names of the towns in which they were situated, together with special marks for the *officinae* and

---

[1] Mickwitz, *op. cit.* pp. 115 *sqq.*　　　[2] *Cod. Just.* X, 32, 4–13.
[3] J. Vogt, *Die Alexandrinischen Münzen*, I, pp. 225 *sqq.*

the issues. The distribution of mints, which was by no means uniform over all the *dioeceses* (Spain, for instance, had none at all), seems to have been determined by a consideration of the local needs of trade and necessity of assuring the supplies for the army. The reform[1] further raised the standard of the *aureus* to 60 to the pound, and also introduced a silver coin, of which 96 went to the pound and which thus resembled the *denarius* of Nero, but which was not given this name and was probably simply called the *argenteus*. In order to provide small change, Diocletian continued the minting of billon, of an alloy of copper with a very small addition of silver, and, to be precise, in three denominations: one, weighing about 150 grains (9.72 grammes), with the laurel-wreathed head of the emperor and the type 'Genius Populi Romani,' usually known as the *follis*; a middling-sized one, weighing about 60 grains (3.89 gr.), with the head crowned with rays (*radiati*); and a small one, weighing about 20 grains (1.3 gr.), again with the laurel-wreath. The second denomination was about the size and weight of the xx.i coins of Aurelian, which had passed as the equivalent of two sestertii of 10 *libellae* each (see p. 307). Diocletian also, in his turn, built on the foundation of the sestertius, although he identified the tenth part of it, the *libella*, with the *denarius communis*, of which no more than 50,000 might be paid for the gold pound (p. 269), whereas 40 were reckoned to the *argenteus*, 20 to the *follis*, which also had the mark xx.i, and 5 to the middling-sized piece. Thus the coin of Aurelian, which corresponded to the last of these, was devalued to one quarter. In this connection, we must assume that there was a valuation of the different coins of the separate denominations in relation to one another and the *denarii communes*, so that we get at least an approximation to the already-mentioned highest price of gold, reached in the maximum standard of Diocletian, namely: 60 *aurei*, = 1200 *argentei*, = 2400 *folles*, = 9600 *radiati*, = 24000 of the small coins, = 48000 *denarii* (see above, pp. 269, 338)[2].

It is possible that the revaluation of the billon coins, because of their nominal value being estimated too high in relation to their real, was the cause of a further disturbance of the markets (p. 338), which made itself especially strongly felt where troops passed on the march. The protection of the soldiery against an

---

[1] Cf. H. Mattingly, *Roman Coins*, pp. 217 *sqq.*

[2] See Mickwitz, *op. cit.* p. 70, n. 138, who admits this as a possibility, but also proposes other conclusions, rating the *follis* at 5 denarii, the radiate coin at 2, leaving the smallest unit quite out of account.

artificial raising of prices is the reason given, in the preamble, for the publication of the Edict on Prices of the year 301[1], together with the general intention to prevent a real rise in prices also. For food-stuffs and for the most varied kinds of merchandise, maximum prices are given in *denarii*. The price of bread-corn and luxury goods, the daily wages of artisans, as well as the authorized fees for the services of an advocate, all found a place here, and the whole offers to the economic historian an opportunity of deep insight into the commodities and the possibilities of employment in those days, and also, because of the fixing of the maximum price for gold, the possibility of obtaining an idea of relative values. We may say with confidence that this edict is by far the most consistent attempt to regulate prices and wages of which we know[2] and that it was therefore designed for the whole Empire[3]. As all the surviving fragments of the inscription have been found in the East, it may be inferred that Diocletian was concerned that its provisions should continue to be known, whereas, in the West, the customary form of announcement was considered sufficient. But in spite of threats and the imposition of the most rigorous sentences, the authority of the State found its match in the opposition of traders and merchants; and the Edict had to be revoked[4].

V. CONSERVATIVE TENDENCIES IN DIOCLETIAN'S GOVERNMENT

In spite of the many connections with earlier tendencies, we have, in general, had to deal with innovations in the administration of the Empire, in the reform of taxation and in the regulation of the coinage. But on the other hand, in one thing Diocletian followed wholly in the steps of his Illyrian and Pannonian predecessors and compatriots, namely, in his attempt to maintain and invigorate the idea of Rome. It would be wrong to believe that in this he was inspired by memories of the historical glories of Ancient Rome or that he was moved by a romantic passion for the past. He lacked almost all the qualities of a romantic. But

---

[1] Ed. Mommsen-Blümner (Berlin, 1893): for the fragments found later cf. Besnier, *op. cit.* p. 315, n. 225. Cf. Lactantius, *de mort. pers.* 7, 6; Aurelius Victor, *Caes.* xxxix, 45; Consul. Constantinop. in *Mon. Germ. Auct. Ant.* ix, p. 230; Malalas xii, p. 307, 3 *sqq.* (Bonn).

[2] Stade, *op. cit.* p. 64. [3] ii, 24 (p. 9, Mommsen-Blümner).

[4] Lactantius, *de mort. pers.* 7, 7. On the attempt of Stade (*op. cit.* pp. 62 *sqq.*) to prove that effect could be given to the Edict cf. Stein, *op. cit.* p. 113, n. 1 and Mickwitz, *op. cit.* pp. 70 *sqq.*

he had, in the long years of his service and in the course of his many journeys to and fro across the Empire, become imbued with the idea that the emperors, their army and their civil service, and so, also, the subjects were, or at least should be, Roman. True, it was a Roman-ness of his own day, with an Illyrian-Pannonian stamp[1], that had revealed itself to him, but one which none the less, conscious of the continuing influence of a great past and united by a momentous task to be performed in the present, displayed a vigorous self-confidence that could face the future without dismay. The various elements in the population of the Empire, often so markedly different from one another, were to be welded together into a unity by this idea of Rome, of which the emperors were reckoned the most impressive exponents, and which should find its expression in law and religion. As a result of such principles, the government of Diocletian, in spite of all its innovations, took on a markedly conservative aspect[2].

Besides the attempt to create for Roman law a larger sphere of influence, we encounter, in the many rescripts of Diocletian, again and again the endeavour to check the further infiltration of non-Roman, and especially of Greek, legal concepts into the law of the Empire. But even he was not able wholly to prevent this process. Moreover, the number of cases for which the imperial decision was invoked, shows, if not a lack of legal knowledge in the judges of the courts of lower instance, at all events at least a strong mistrust of their judgments in the parties seeking justice. On the other hand the members of the imperial *consistorium*, who must be regarded as the authors of the imperial rescripts 'the character of which is often reminiscent of classical jurisprudence,' are praised by a distinguished jurist for their knowledge, which was as clear as it was comprehensive[3]. Possibly we may perhaps see in this holding fast to the old a proof of a lack of originality, if it were not for the existence of certain innovations in private law, which the Emperor allowed as being in the spirit of the old, truly Roman law. His insistence, also, upon Latin as the official language, which was in itself promoted by the increase in numbers of the civil service, and also upon the spreading of a knowledge of Latin in general, points in the same direction[4], although, it is true, this belated attempt at romanization did not have any great success outside the circles interested in the civil

---

[1] Alföldi, *Fünfundzwanzig Jahre römisch-german. Kommission*, pp. 11 *sqq.*
[2] Cf. Stade, *op. cit.* pp. 66 *sqq.*
[3] L. Mitteis, *Reichsrecht und Volksrecht*, p. 199.
[4] Cf. Stade, *op. cit.* p. 67 *sq.*

service as a career or outside the offices themselves, and even here such success was not lasting.

Diocletian's religious policy was also conservative. Care for religion was one of the duties of the emperor. But, over and above this, he was concerned to win the protection of the gods by a revival of Roman piety and morals. If, in dedications, we encounter the old formulas, and if the Jovius laid great emphasis on the worship of Juppiter Optimus Maximus, we must not forget, in this connection, that we may indeed observe the form, but cannot be sure of the content. In all probability, Diocletian recognized in Juppiter, as Aurelian in Sol Invictus, only a manifestation of the one highest, supreme godhead, so that, here also, it is apparent that old ideas have changed. But, in spite of changed conceptions and of the greatest possible freedom in permitted modes of adoration, the intention remained fixed, to make plain in the State religion the unity of men of the same way of thinking and to release the forces, which tended to work in parallel directions, in the interests of the Roman world and its imperial master[1]. Ever since Decius, in view of the aggressive power of the Sassanian Persia, which was strengthened by its State religion, had tried to carry out a consolidation of forces on the same lines[2], the idea remained operative. It is true that Diocletian practised toleration for a long time, perhaps in conformity with the same train of thought to which he gave expression in his Edict on Prices, where he justified his forbearance on the ground that he cherished the hope that men would better themselves without compulsion[3]. But, in the long run, he could not avoid the cogent necessity of settling, once for all, this problem also among those which the emperor had to face. The execution of this very important section of his religious policy against the Christians is treated elsewhere[4]. Hence more or less clearly, we see the ultimate aim of the autocratic emperors: the will to make a single ruler, a single law and a single religion the firm bonds of imperial unity.

In conclusion, we may say that, however much may have been earlier achieved in most directions, Diocletian was the first to gather together into a completed whole the various experiments and

[1] M. Vogelstein, *Kaiseridee-Romidee*, pp. 50 *sqq.*, on which cf. Ensslin, *Zeitschr. d. Sav.-Stiftung*, LIII, Kanon. Abt. XXI, 1932, p. 402 *sq.*

[2] Cf. E. Meyer, *Blüte und Niedergang des Hellenismus in Asien*, p. 79; Ensslin, *N.J.f. Wiss.* IV, 1928, p. 403; Kornemann, *Die römische Kaiserzeit*, p. 144.   [3] I, 12 *sq.*

[4] See above, p. 338 *sq.*, and, for a somewhat different interpretation, below, pp. 662 *sqq.*

expedients of his predecessors, and that he thus created the firm
foundation for a new imperial system on which Constantine, in
particular, was destined to build. But, none the less, in spite of
changes and developments in details, his successors could not
deviate far from the main lines which he laid down. Thus it
comes about that the institutions of the late-Roman, or if we
prefer it, the early-Byzantine, State show a certain rigidity, which
was not so much the result of ingenious planning as the expression of an unavoidable development. When the very existence
of the Empire was at stake, autocratic absolutism became a necessity, while the external pressure, which hardly ever relaxed, and
the internal demands, made by the maintenance of the administrative machinery, led to a constant strain upon the resources
of the Empire and even to their exhaustion. In this sense,
Diocletian's financial policy, and the reform of taxation which
maintained that policy, were and remained the centre of his re-
organization of the Empire, round which was built up all the
inexorable fiscal system with all its consequences that in later
times was the hall-mark of this State. But, in spite of all, Diocletian did not succeed in training the subject, who became more
and more a mere carrier of State burdens, to take a personal
interest in the political life around him. And so the State created
by Diocletian resembled, not the new house that he intended to
build, but rather an emergency shelter, which could indeed offer
protection from the storm, but in which the lack of light and
warmth became more and more obvious. But, in spite of all,
we can understand why it was that, after all the miseries of a
period that was often anarchic, a writer of the fourth century[1]
could still call him 'the man whom the State needed,' 'vir rei
publicae necessarius.'

[1] S.H.A. *Carus*, 10.

CHAPTER XII

THE DEVELOPMENT OF PAGANISM
IN THE ROMAN EMPIRE

I. INTRODUCTION

THE interactions of Greek, Macedonian, and Oriental ways
and institutions and their consequences for religion have
already been described (vol. VII, pp. 1 *sqq.*). There was give and
take, but for a century and a half Hellenism predominated.
Oriental, and above all Egyptian, cults reached Greece in considerable volume, but in hellenized forms, and they were incorporated within the native framework of religious organization. We
may call this the first wave of Oriental cults, in contrast with what
we shall call the second wave (pp. 422 *sqq.*)—the wave which came
to the Latin-speaking world. The first wave lacks certain striking
features of the second. Mithraism seems to have been absent,
though indeed the Iranian rites from which it developed were
practised here and there within Asia Minor; Zeus of Doliche
was not known outside his native Commagene; the *taurobolium*
must indeed have existed, but was probably no more than a bull-
chase followed by a solemn sacrifice[1]; the priests of the Egyptian
deities as established in Greek cities were commonly annual
functionaries, comparable with the priests of Zeus and Apollo,
and not a professional clergy with a distinctive character.

Oriental cults sometimes came to Greece as a result of political
considerations, but in a far larger measure they were brought by
soldiers, trading groups or individuals, and slaves: then they
gained new adherents, not only among the unprivileged but also
among citizens of distinction. We can suggest reasons why the
ground thus gained was not lost. The traditional gods of the city-
state might, like the city-state itself, appear old and weary. The
novelty of the Oriental gods could be a virtue[2], and they might
well appear less parochial and more adapted to men's needs in the
new world of dynasts, and in the still larger *oikoumene* and *kosmos*
ruled by the decrees of Fate. They had also the prestige of the

[1] For a possible indication of the blood baptism in Phrygia of the eighth–
seventh century B.C. cf. G. Körte, *Ath. Mitt.* XXIII, 1898, pp. 97 *sqq.*

[2] Cf vol XI, p. 579 *sq.*, on the success of Alexander of Abonuteichos.

ancient East, and over and above this not only did their cult-dramas impress the eye and ear, but also their mythology echoed natural human emotions. Isis as wife and mother and widow, the mourning Attis, the young Adonis cut off in his prime—they need not avert their eyes, like Artemis, from the dying Hippolytus. The half-Oriental gods were credited with a great readiness to help their worshippers. They were *epēkooi*, 'ready to aid,' an epithet applied to them far more frequently than to the Olympians[1].

New religious forces came into play, and new religious forms were created. Nevertheless, the depth of the new development was not equal to its extension. Various reasons for this may occur to us. First, we have to reckon with the religious education which the average citizen underwent: as boy, as ephebe and as adult, he performed many functions in civic ritual, and they set their mark on him. Secondly, rulers rarely sought to make innovations in religion. Thirdly, the political world in which a man lived was not, as later under Roman rule, a large entity with a widespread social stratification, but an aggregate of civic and regional units. You were not a subject of a Seleucid or Ptolemaic empire; you were a citizen of Alexandria or Antioch, or a member of a Syrian *politeuma*, or a tribesman of the Trokondenoi. No centre sent forth impulses comparable with those to be exercised by Rome.

A static equilibrium was thus attained, more Hellenic in the older Greek cities, less Hellenic in the new Greek cities of Asia Minor and Syria, still less and sometimes progressively less Hellenic in the towns of the Fayûm and of the eastern frontier. The preservation of this equilibrium in the older Hellenic area was further ensured by a decline in the infiltration of new population elements. Till the middle of the second century B.C. the older Greek cities had kept some significance in politics and in trade; then the change was rapid and complete.

Rhodes was impoverished by Rome, Corinth destroyed; Delos, which had received Egyptian cults early and Syrian cults later, was ruined by Mithridates. The population dropped and was still too large. After Sulla Greece was a land for tourists, students, and antiquarians, Athens a university city with a starving proletariate. The tramp of soldiers seldom echoed south of the Egnatian Way; the Syrian trader would not come, for who could buy his wares? Foreign slaves could not be imported, save by the few who were very rich[2]. The three main avenues for new cults were closed; in

---

[1] O. Weinreich, *Ath. Mitt.* XXXVII, 1912, pp. 1 *sqq.*

[2] Note, however, Ditt.[3] 1042, where a slave founds a temple of Men Tyrannos at Sunium.

so far as Oriental worships flourished in Greece (outside the Roman colonies) it must, with very few exceptions, have been as survivals of the first wave. A partial prosperity returned in the second century of our era (vol. XI, pp. 555 sqq.), but it redounded to the benefit of local spirit and local institutions.

Rome was in a large measure isolated from Hellenistic evolution until the time when she came to play an important and soon a predominant part in this Graeco-Oriental world. It was all very sudden. Foreign merchants increased in numbers, as it were overnight; slaves came in masses from successful wars; soldiers spent long years in distant lands and returned to Italy with new beliefs and practices. The privileged position enjoyed everywhere by Roman citizens, and even by non-Roman Italians greatly encouraged migration (vol. XI, p. 441), and migrants were commonly exposed to new influences. Expansion and growth were in process or in prospect down to the end of the second century of our era. There was no chance of a static equilibrium; even Augustus could not achieve this, when he used his great skill to remedy the disintegration which came from wars and civil strife, from the resulting new wealth and new poverty, and from the new ways and new scepticism which had entered with such sudden violence.

The concentration of power at Rome caused her conquests to have domestic repercussions which had no analogy in Macedon, and the process of change was accelerated by various factors in the framework of Roman life.

Apart from domestic cult, Rome's worships were the care of the State, and those of importance were controlled by permanent boards composed of citizens of the highest rank. While local parish worships were administered by annual boards of *magistri* consisting of freedmen and slaves, no one other than the *nobiles* and a few paid subordinates had any real function in the worship of the great gods of the State. *Religio* and *pietas* were in the air, but the Greek schooling of citizens, irrespective of wealth and standing, in civic religious tradition was absent. Secondly, the gods were more abstract. Thirdly, the lower orders were apt, when things were going ill in this world, to think that the community's relations with the other world must be incorrect, and that something must be done to restore the *pax deorum*. The governing class met the situation by consulting Apollo, whether at Delphi or more often through the Sibylline Books, and incorporating one foreign cult after another in the worships of the State. Such cults were set under the care of the *quindecimviri* or commission for foreign worships, and, though fully incorporated in the Roman scheme, retained the Greek rite. Thus hymns to the Mother of the gods were sung in Greek. The hellenization of a worship was cultural; the romanization of a cult was political[1].

These measures met the needs of the moment, but did not transcend the limitations of official cult, and the urban proletariate was swelled by foreign elements. Its native members had not the Senate's contempt for unregularized alien worships, and Oriental cults soon had many adherents among the *plebs urbana*. The ruling class felt otherwise, and interfered repeatedly, often on the pretext of a fear, genuine or pretended, of immorality arising out of secret rites, sometimes from a feeling that the solidarity of the State was menaced.

II. OFFICIAL RELIGION

In a review of the attitude to religion of the Empire, as an institution, the character of official policy, in its varying phases of change and conservatism, requires definition. It is, indeed, governed by the *princeps*, as *pontifex maximus*, as member of all the priestly colleges, and as responsible for public morals and well-being. We learn it in the main from temple-foundations, from coin-types, from dedications by the *princeps* or the Arval Brothers, and from the actions of the *quindecimviri sacris faciundis*. The rule of Augustus and of the Julio-Claudian dynasty continued and reinforced *mos maiorum* as understood by the more serious spirits of the last generation of the Republic, but could not change existing trends except by adding the new religious sentiment towards the *princeps*. Cybele was well established, before her cult was magnified by Claudius: the cult-drama of Osiris was perhaps introduced at Rome under Gaius[2] (vol. x, pp. 496, 499 *sq.*) and Egyptian cults were acceptable not only to the demi-monde of Rome and the men of Pompeii but also to farmers in Italy[3].

The advent to power of the Flavian dynasty marks a new epoch, for the new ruling class, recruited in a considerable measure from the Italian municipalities, was very different in composition from the Augustan *nobiles* and marked by a greater simplicity of

[1] This is illustrated by the measure of liberty allowed in the *S.C. de Bacchanalibus*. Aurelian (p. 414) is an exception.

[2] A room, possibly a chapel, with Isiac decorations, has been found in his palace; see G. Rizzo, *Monumenti della pittura*... fasc. 2, F. Cumont in *Rev. hist. rel.* CXIV, 1936, pp. 127 *sqq.*

[3] Rustic calendars show this (vol x, p. 505 n. 2): A. L. Broughton (*Class. Phil.* XXXI, 1936, pp. 353 *sqq.*) argues that they come from North Italy.

living and a smaller degree of traditionalism. Sarapis was believed to have confirmed by miracle Vespasian's claim to the throne, and the precinct of Isis, which he shared, perhaps since the time of Gaius, was placed upon coins. Domitian, although his personal devotion was to Minerva and Juppiter, reconstructed the temple in the Campus Martius after a fire and was a benefactor of the temple of Isis at Beneventum (vol. XI, pp. 27, 33).

In the succeeding period, when the emperors were drawn from the Western provinces, Roman tradition was followed, and the rise to power of some individuals from the Near East had no striking consequences[1]. Hadrian, whose rule marked an epoch in government and art, acted significantly when in building the temple of Venus and Roma he introduced the point of view of the provinces. His personal predilection was for classical Greek ideas; while his favourite Antinous was deified in Egyptian style as Osirantinous, Antinoupolis (vol. XI, p. 650 *sq.*) and the art-type of Antinous (vol. XI, p. 791) were Greek. Nevertheless, this did not change religious policy in Rome, where Hadrian restored many temples, and his successor Antoninus Pius was honoured 'ob insignem erga caerimonias publicas curam ac religionem[2].' At the end of this epoch Commodus shows the weakening of tradition, while the *Historia Augusta*, for what it is worth, stresses his irresponsibility and cruelty, and not his piety, when mentioning his interest in Mithraic and other Oriental rites, and the most notable feature of his coins is an obsession with Hercules[3]. Nevertheless the coins do show novel concessions to alien religions.

The Severan dynasty brought more drastic changes than had the Flavian. Its members had policies, and, like Augustus, appreciated the support which writers could give. Temples were built in Rome to new gods—the African Bacchus and Hercules (who figure prominently on the coins commemorating the Secular Games of 204; see p. 21), Sarapis (on the Quirinal) and Dea Suria; the temple to the Carthaginian Caelestis, attested in 259[4], may well be due to Septimius Severus. Caracalla, who built the temple on the Quirinal, was known as 'lover of Sarapis.' Nevertheless, Roman feeling was not dead, and Elagabalus went too far when

---

[1] The appearance of RELIG. AVG. on a coin of Marcus Aurelius with a representation of Hermes, sometimes in a temple in Egyptian style (vol. XI, pp. 357, 365; Volume of Plates v, 130, *b*) is probably due to a supposed miraculous incident in the Marcomannic War.

[2] Dessau 341.

[3] Volume of Plates v, 130, *h, o*; M. Rostovtseff–H. Mattingly, *J.R.S.* XIII, 1923, pp. 91 *sqq.*   [4] Dessau 4438.

he glorified the fetich of Emesa and sought to mate it to Vesta and to make it the chief deity of the Roman world. He seems to have provoked even the champions of other non-Roman cults[1].

The Illyrian emperors stood for Rome: a peculiar devotion to Vesta in Roman dedications of their time[2] is one index of the reaction, and the Decian *libelli* (pp. 202, 521), which for the first time defined pagan loyalty, constitute another. Economic stringency curtailed expenditures on traditional worship, but this was not peculiar to such worship: throughout the Empire, dedications are very rare from the middle of the third century till the time of Diocletian[3].

Nevertheless, this period is marked by one innovation of the greatest importance—Rome had a Republican cult of Sol, but it had faded, and the importance of Sol in the City is due to Aurelian, who on his return from Syria built the great temple of Sol Invictus, introduced the celebration of his birthday (*natalis Invicti*) on December 25, and established the college of *pontifices Solis*. Liberal as Aurelian was to other cults in the City, he thus incorporated in Roman constitutional form emotions and ideas which had been constantly gaining in strength (see below, p. 417 *sq.*). It was a creative act, like the Ptolemaic creation of the cult of Sarapis: it made what was potentially a 'cosmopolitan religion[4],' and it gave a new concentration and emphasis to official piety. Thereafter Sol was very prominent.

Diocletian's main policy was Roman (see above, p. 407). While the Jovii and Herculii restored a temple at Carnuntum, probably in 307, D(EO) S(OLI) I(NVICTO) M(ITHRAE) FAVTORI IMPERII SVI[5], Diocletian and Maximian made a dedication at Aquileia DEO SOLI[6] and Diocletian built an Iseum and a Sarapeum in Rome[7]; nevertheless the very titles Jovii and Herculii for the rulers, Jovia and Herculia for legions, show the Roman emphasis of dynastic policy. Of course paganism as a whole was strengthened and deliberately given shape (as above all by Maximinus Daia): the revival of private dedications[8] may be ascribed partly to this, and partly (since it starts before the persecution) to improved economic conditions.

[1] F. Cumont, *Rev. instr. publ. Belg.* XL, 1897, pp. 89 *sqq.*

[2] A. D. Nock, *Harv. Theol. Rev.* XXIII, 1930, pp. 251 *sqq.*

[3] J. Geffcken, *Der Ausgang des griechisch-römischen Heidentums*, pp. 20 *sqq.*

[4] G. La Piana, *Harv. Theol. Rev.* XX, 1927, p. 321.   [5] Dessau 659.

[6] *C.I.L.* v, 803. For a temple erected at Comum to the same deity by these emperors see F. Cumont, *C.R. Ac. Inscr.* 1914, pp. 147 *sqq.*

[7] K. Stade, *Der Politiker Diocletian*, p. 107.

[8] Geffcken, *op. cit.* p. 29 *sq.*

Let us now turn to the evidence of coins and medallions for alien cults[1]. They cannot tell us the whole of official policy: we must not forget that, apart from the issue which shows the sisters of Gaius personified as Virtues, they give no sign of the eccentricities of that emperor. The Roman temple of Isis appears on coins of Vespasian, that of Sarapis and that of Cybele on those of Domitian. Attis is used by Hadrian, but only as a type for Phrygia: Isis and Sarapis are represented as welcoming Hadrian and Sabina, which is simply a record of their visit to Alexandria. Hadrian was interested in provinces and regions as entities, with their own traditions, as we see in his so-called 'province' series[2]. Medallions of Hadrian, on the other hand, and of both Faustinas[3] represent Isis, and medallions of Hadrian and of his wife Sabina show Cybele. So do medallions of Antoninus, the two Faustinas, and Lucilla; and Cybele assumes special importance in connection with the apotheosis of the elder Faustina, who is herself shown as riding, like the goddess, in a chariot drawn by lions. On some issues of this period Attis is associated with Cybele. These facts assume importance in view of the contemporary rise of the *taurobolium* (see below, p. 424 *sq.*). At the same time, while MATRI DEVM SALVTARI occurs on a consecration-coin of Faustina I and MATRI MAGNAE on coins of Faustina II and Lucilla, legends naming the deities represented are otherwise lacking.

This fact adds significance to certain issues of Commodus. Not only is he, in 192, represented as faced by Sarapis and Isis and again as clasping hands with them over an altar[4], but, at about the same time, coins with a type of Cybele bear the legend MATRI DEV(M) CONSERV. AVG., and others showing Sarapis have SERAPIDI CONSERV. AVG. These have no parallel under any earlier *princeps*. Contrast them with the conventional IVPPITER CONSERVATOR of 181 and 182. Even other legends of the end of Commodus' principate, I. O. M. SPONSOR. SEC. AVG. and IOVI DEFENS. SALVTIS AVG., imply a

---

[1] The evidence (when not cited) will be found in H. Mattingly–E. A. Sydenham, *Roman Imperial Coinage* (M.–S.) (pending the appearance of IV, ii, Cohen[2] is used); H. Mattingly, *Coins of the Roman Empire in the British Museum*; Fr. Gnecchi, *I medaglioni romani*. The official character of the religious interest of coins is strikingly illustrated by the nearly complete absence of Silvanus, who had no public worship in Rome: we have only a coin of Trajan's, where he apparently represents 'the great native deity of the woodlands of Illyricum' (H. Mattingly, *B.M.C. Rom. Emp.* III, p. xcix) and medallions of Hadrian and Antoninus—all uninscribed.

[2] J. M. C. Toynbee, *The Hadrianic School*, pp. 24 *sqq.*; Volume of Plates, V, 128, *a–i*.   [3] One such type of the older Faustina is listed in M.–S. III, p. 189, as a coin.   [4] Volume of Plates V, 130, *p*.

new directness of concentration upon his person. Previous rulers had their divine protectors, but they would have shrunk from the explicit HERC. COMMODIANO, which appears in 190, and from the contemporary HERC. COM(ITI), which is the forerunner of similar types on which Sol is the Imperial comrade. Again, IOVI EXSVP(ERANTISSIMO) in 186/7 and 188/9 implies the official recognition of a popular tendency to astral thought; other evidence records that Commodus named a month Exsuperatorius[1].

The coinage of Commodus, like his life, may seem to betray an eccentric megalomania comparable with that of Gaius, and yet he prefigures the future (vol. XI, p. 392). When we pass to the sturdy realism of Septimius Severus, his coins show a strong consciousness of his African origin. While the type of Dea Caelestis on his coins in 203/4 and Caracalla's in 203 to 210 or thereabouts is associated with the legend INDVLGENTIA AVGG. IN CARTH. and may be rightly regarded as no more than a religious symbol for Carthage, the appearance of Bacchus and Hercules with DIS AVSPICIBVS is significant, for they are clearly the African equivalents of those familiar gods. Their representation on coins commemorating the Secular Games of 204 means that the gods of the *princeps* ranked as gods of the Empire. Again, Septimius Severus, like Clodius Albinus (also an African), set SAECVLVM FRVGIFERVM on coins, and, though he never used the native type once employed by Albinus, this is no doubt the African god, a special interest of Albinus' home, Hadrumetum. Caracalla has also a type of Ammon, widely worshipped in Africa, with the legend IOVI VICTORI: but, since the god had appeared on some small bronze coins struck by Marcus Aurelius at Caesarea in Cappadocia, the reason for his emergence here may be not Caracalla's interest in Africa but his interest in Alexander the Great: other indications show that the Macedonian conqueror was again dominating men's imaginations (p. 550).

Sol without a legend was a Republican coin-type occasionally revived during the earlier Principate: sometimes he has the legend ORIENS and stands for the Eastern interests of a particular time, for instance Trajan's. On the coins of Septimius he appears, and between 202 and 210 has the striking legend PACATOR ORBIS on issues of both Septimius and Caracalla: some of the latter's, between 201 and 210, call him RECTOR ORBIS: one of Geta's appears to show him as in a special relationship to Sol[2]. Such

[1] F. Cumont, *Arch. f. Religionswiss.* IX, 1906, pp. 323 *sqq.*
[2] A. Alföldi, 'Insignien und Tracht der römischen Kaiser' (in *Röm. Mitt.* L, 1935), p. 107 *sq.*, an article which should be consulted for this whole range of ideas.

ideas were not wholly new, but their numismatic formulation anticipates the attitudes of Aurelian and of Constantine—the men with a mission and authority. This Imperial self-consciousness, in stronger men, was a major fact of history.

Cybele appears on Julia Domna's coins from 193–6 with MATRI DEVM and MATRI MAGNAE and Julia while still living was represented as Cybele. Cybele comes again on Caracalla's coins of 213 (MATRI DEVM), and thereafter nearly drops out of the repertory of Roman types into which influential empresses[1] had brought her. Isis is represented on coins of Julia Domna with the legend SAECVLI FELICITAS and on Caracalla's coins of 215, where she is shown welcoming him—a transparent allusion to his visit to Alexandria. Sarapis (without name) is frequent on Caracalla's probably contemporary issues, confirming the other evidence for his predilection.

In spite of Julia Domna's connections with Emesa, nothing Syrian appears on the coinage till we come to Elagabalus[2]. Elagabalus not only shows the sacred stone of Emesa on coins and medallions[3], but also uses the legends INVICTVS SACERDOS AVG., SACERD. DEI SOLIS ELAGAB., SANCT. DEO SOLI ELAGABAL., SOLI PROPVGNATORI, SVMMVS SACERDOS AVG. The literature has not exaggerated. In sharp contrast, Severus Alexander, while continuing normal solar types, has otherwise a neutral coinage. The succeeding years offer us nothing for our present purpose save the combination of a solar type with AETERNITAS AVG., AETERNITATI AVG. under Gordian III, with AETERNITAS AVG. and AETERN. IMPER. under Philip; the (unnamed) appearance of Sarapis on coins of Gordian III and Gallienus, one of whose medallions is inscribed SERAPIDI COMITI AVG.; issues of Claudius Gothicus showing Sarapis, both alone and with Isis, and having in each case CONSER. AVG.; issues of Claudius Gothicus showing Isis Faria with SALVS AVG. (a legend coupled also with an Apollo type), and a Cabirus with DEO CABIRO, which has been thought to refer to the repulse of the Gothic attack on Thessalonica, a seat of Cabiric cult.

Under Aurelian the pre-eminence of Sol, as the fountain-head

---

[1] The next was Helena.

[2] The reverse type of VENVS CAELESTIS on a coin of Julia Domna (Mattingly–Sydenham, *op. cit.* IV, i, p. 173) belongs to a coin of Soaemias and was wrongly combined with the present obverse.

[3] One medallion has the inscription CONSERVATOR AVGVSTI. The sacred stone appears also on Alexandrian coins (J. G. Milne, *Catalogue of Alexandrian coins in the Ashmolean Museum*, p. xxxviii), which is the more significant, since we do not see in them later any indications of Aurelian's policy.

of Imperial power, is strikingly illustrated by the coins and he is of course very often named. Sarapis, with the legend SERAPI (also SARAPI, SARAPIDI) COMITI AVG., makes an appearance under Postumus; thereafter, except for two types of Maximinus Daia, one with GENIO AVGVSTI and the Genius holding a hand of Sarapis, the other with SOLI INVICTO and the sun holding a hand of Sarapis[1], Sarapis is absent till the time of Julian. The coinage of Diocletian and his associates is primarily interested in Juppiter, Hercules[2], Mars and Sol, and their medallions show a notable narrowing of the range of gods represented. Thereafter few gods survive save Sol, the god of transition, whom Constantine would couple with a Greek cross[3].

That is what the coins tell us; we never see on them Attis by himself or named, and never Juppiter Dolichenus, Dea Suria, Adonis, Mithras, Osiris, or any of the Syrian Baalim. So if we look at the names of the ships in the Roman navy, we find Isis Pharia twice, but no Dea Suria or other Oriental deities.

III. THE EASTERN PROVINCES

The various cultural areas of the Greek-speaking half of the Empire were tenacious of tradition. During the Hellenistic age (see pp. 409 *sqq.*) Egyptian and Syrian cults had established themselves in numerous cities outside their lands of origin. Isis and Sarapis became civic deities, not only at many points in Greece and the Greek islands and the old Greek fringe in Asia Minor, but also in as much of Phoenicia as the Ptolemies had controlled: their worship, and that of Cybele, in Crete date from this period (vol. XI, p. 664). So again Syrian and Thracian cults reached Egypt. On the other hand, in the Roman period there does not seem to have been much interchange in the Near East of cults Oriental in origin. Developed Mithraism is attested in Egypt[4], Syria[5], Asia Minor, and Greece, but not on any large scale. The first Mithraeum at Doura was due to archers from Palmyra, the second to Roman

---

[1] J. Maurice, *Numismatique constantinienne*, II, p. 566, III, pp. xxiii, 20, 23 *sq.* etc.

[2] Cf. Milne, *op. cit.* p. xxxix, for coins with Zeus and Heracles as almost the sole output of the Alexandrian mint in Diocletian's seventh year.

[3] Maurice, *op. cit.* I, p. 247, cf. N. H. Baynes, *Constantine the Great and the Christian Church*, pp. 97 *sqq.*

[4] F. Cumont, *Harv. Theol. Rev.* XXVI, 1933, p. 158; E. Breccia, *Mém. inst. franç. Caire*, LXVII, 1934–7, pp. 257 *sqq.*

[5] F. Cumont, *Syria*, XIV, 1933, pp. 382 *sqq.*

legionaries[1]; in the same way, the sacred cave of Mithras on Andros was built by a veteran and three soldiers of the Praetorian Guard (A.D. 202–9). Attis, for whom the native Greek generally felt a certain repugnance, has left few traces in Egypt and apparently none in Syria[2]. The *taurobolium* was not celebrated at Athens till the fourth century (see below, p. 425); a ταυροβ(όλιον) is mentioned as part of a celebration, apparently of the Traianeia, at Pergamum in A.D. 105, but we may doubt whether it included the bath of blood[3].

All this is in striking contrast with the vitality of local cults, more or less hellenized, and of Greek cults. Dionysus was worshipped widely in Asia Minor and Syria and, it seems, at many points in Egypt; in Syria he appears well into the hinterland, as in the Druse country; he merges with the Arab god Dusares, and the god of some antipathetic Arab tribe was identified with his old enemy Lycurgus. The actors' guild (the holy synod of the craftsmen of Dionysus) was everywhere, and may have counted for something in this; but it is far from being the whole story. The only religious epics written under the Empire were concerned with the conquests of Dionysus, whose cult flourished strongly in the Western provinces also, and was closely linked to men's hopes of immortality. Heracles was found wherever there were Greeks and was identified with native gods at Tarsus, in Phoenicia, in Egypt, in Parthia; he, Aphrodite and Nike are the only Greek religious types in the art of Doura. The goddess between the two riders (Helen and the Dioscuri, or an equivalent) is found all over the Near East, appearing even at Palmyra; she had local affinities in Anatolia. Artemis Ephesia was worshipped at places widely distributed over Asia Minor and Syria, as well as in Crete.

In fact the static equilibrium described earlier (p. 410) was very generally maintained: local cults, whether purely Greek in origin or native with more or less Greek lacquer, were predominant, and the only universal phenomena were certain Greek worships, the cult of the emperor, Judaism, Christianity, and a moderate infiltration of philosophy. But the Near East, though retentive of tradition, was not stationary; intellectually and artistically it was the creative half of the Empire. It accepted but little from the

---

[1] M. Rostovtzeff, *Röm. Mitt.* XLIX, 1934, pp. 180 *sqq.*

[2] On the other hand, the art-type of Cybele appears in Alexandrian coinage and was copied in Syria; cf. H. Graillot, *Le culte de Cybèle*, p. 388.

[3] *I.G.R.R.* IV, 499. The ταυροβόλια recorded at Ilium, and probably of about the same date (J. L. Caskey, *Am. Journ. Arch.* 2nd Ser. XXXIX, 1935, pp. 589 *sqq.*) were clearly of the simple bull-chase variety.

West; the emergence of the Capitoline cultus in Egypt after the Edict of Caracalla[1], and the introduction in the fourth century of the Roman celebration of January 1[2], are of small moment when compared with what the East gave to the West. The religious developments which we shall study in the Western half of the Empire must in the main be creations of men in or from the Near East, which, like Christianity, acquired a following in new lands, where they were deliberately chosen techniques for dealing with the supernatural and not modifications of an inherited way of life.

Local spirit had its more active, outward-looking aspect, and its less active parochial aspect. Zeus of Panamara was the god of a union of cities in Caria, worshipped in annual festival with a liberal distribution of food and drink, and in the records he is described as inviting all the world to his banquet[3]. The worship of Sarapis at Alexandria was marked by a zeal for propaganda which appears in accounts of the god's miracles written down, not only to be preserved in archives but also to be recited to the faithful. Isis also had her literature, the so-called 'Praises,' a Hellenistic work extant in various copies[4], and a litany or list of titles and places of worship, in which, as in Apuleius, she is represented as the object of the adoration of all men[5]. Alexandria was marked by contentious piety, in the formation of which anti-Jewish feeling probably played a part.

On the other hand, if in Egypt we look beyond Alexandria to the countryside, we see what may be called inertia. The country-dwellers of the humbler kind were not bothered by fate, or intellectual curiosity, or the prestige of Isis throughout the world. They wanted safety in their limited horizon, and they hoped to get it by rite and charm; they wanted occasionally some refuge

---

[1] Cf. Wilcken-Mitteis, *Grundzüge und Chrestomathie der Papyruskunde*, I, i, p. 116.

[2] Cf. M. P. Nilsson, *Arch. f. Religionswiss.* XIX, 1918, pp. 50 *sqq.*; also vol. XI, p. 664 on Fortuna Primigenia in Crete.

[3] P. Roussel, *Bull. corr. hell.* LI, 1927, p. 129.

[4] W. Peek, *Der Isishymnus von Andros und verwandte Texte* (a new copy, not earlier than 100 B.C., at Thessalonica has been published by S. Pelekides, Ἀπὸ τὴν πολιτεία καὶ τὴν κοινωνία τῆς ἀρχαίας Θεσσαλονίκης. παράρτημα τοῦ δευτέρου τόμου τῆς ἐπιστημονικῆς ἐπετηρίδος τῆς φιλοσοφικῆς σχολῆς, 1933, published at Thessalonica 1934, p. 4 *sq.*).

[5] P. Oxy. XI, 1380, re-edited by G. Manteuffel, *De opusculis Graecis Aegypti e papyris ostracis lapidibusque collectis* (*Travaux de la Société des Sciences et des Lettres de Varsovie*, Classe I, xii, 1930), pp. 70 *sqq.* For four late Hellenistic hymns to Ermonthis identified with Isis, discovered at Medinet Mâdi, see A. Vogliano in *Pubb. della R. Univ. di Milano*, Cairo, 1936.

from their own littleness and they used magic for this, as also to secure the satisfaction of their loves and hates. Native Egyptian religion had always involved the assumption that there was an infallible procedure for getting what you wanted. So in the hinterland of Asia Minor and Syria men looked to the local gods for protection; that was sufficient; there was this difference from Egypt that the Semitic and Anatolian gods were more capricious, more to be feared, less completely to be controlled, and that the Semite was capable also of a strong sentiment of dependence on a hereditary god and of a passionate dogmatism best known in Judaism but occasionally approached at Palmyra. Christianity encountered this vigour and this inertia; the inertia lasted longer.

The spirit of these manifestations was strong. Against it we must set other factors in religious life—the philosophical trend to henotheism, powerful in East and West alike, the name of Zeus, the popular tendency to think of the gods as simply power, the importance of such figures as Nemesis and Tyche, and the disposition, old in the East, to invest the gods with celestial attributes and functions. As being behind phenomena in general and the stars in particular, they could give escape from the iron bondage of Fate's decrees. Fate and magic were part of a world picture which was nearly universal[1]. Furthermore, many gods were treated as solar. The philosophic theory which supported this has already been treated of (vol. XI, p. 646); further, in Asia Minor and the Near East as a whole, the Sun was widely regarded as the all-seeing god of justice, bringing light and avenging hidden deeds of darkness; in a hymn found at Susa, at latest of the first century B.C., he is identified with Dionysus and is the universal lord[2].

This mood was not confined to the educated, but it did not overshadow localism, and learned pagan polemic against Christianity, while allowing the unity of the divine nature, commonly stressed the inherent natural rights of national tradition. Such tradition increasingly asserted itself even against the old supremacy

---

[1] The power of astrological ideas is shown in the dissemination of the planetary week, on which cf. F. H. Colson, *The Week*. We see it spreading in the first century of our era, but in the third Cassius Dio (XXXVII, 18) thinks it in need of explanation. For Mithraism the week was linked to a doctrine of seven ages of the world (F. Cumont, *Rev. de l'hist. des religions*, CIII, 1931, pp. 29 *sqq.*); to people in general it was not as important as might appear.

[2] F. Cumont, *Mémoires de la Mission archéologique en Perse*, XX, 1928, pp. 89 *sqq.* and M. P. Nilsson, *Arch. f. Religionswiss.* XXX, 1933, p. 164, and cf. *ib.* pp. 141 *sqq.* for the thinking involved and for the importance of the solar calendar as making its diffusion possible.

of Greek culture. The East took its revenge for the conquests of Alexander. We see the rise of Syriac, which had become a literary language by the addition of Greek words to the vocabulary of Aramaic, the similar emergence of Coptic from Demotic, the use of Neophrygian as a language for inscriptions, and the birth, or at least the epigraphic self-expression, of that strange brotherhood known as the Xenoi Tekmoreioi[1]. Meanwhile Philo of Byblus, the writer of *Corpus Hermeticum* xvi, and the gnostics whom Plotinus attacked[2], professed to be in cultural rebellion against Hellas. We can hardly devise a formula to cover these various phenomena without becoming fanciful: but it remains true that a certain shift of balance had long been happening. From about 200 B.C. the native was asserting himself against the Hellene in Egypt; in the next century Rome's cynical *laissez-faire* in breaking the Seleucids and ignoring the Euphrates allowed Parthia to become an apparent counterweight; and then with Mithridates (and perhaps again with Cleopatra) the East was born as a cause if not as an entity[3]. In the third century the Empire found a rival in the Sassanian kingdom, militant in politics and in religion. Mani's disciples carried his words westwards, but his face was set to the East. The end of all this was Islam.

IV. THE WESTERN PROVINCES

We may now consider the spread of Oriental cults in the Latin-speaking half of the Roman Empire. Rome was from of old a borrower in religion, as in art and letters (p. 571 *sq.*), and the Roman West remained a borrower, for all its power of setting its own stamp on what it borrowed. Rome drew men by the opportunities which it presented; so did the Western provinces, with the new wealth and markets which they offered to traders. It is no accident that Mithraism was so strongly represented in the Danube region, which offered a rich field for exploitation; while the third Mithraeum at Poetovio was built by soldiers, the first and the second were built by slaves and freedmen in the tax-farming service[4]. The trader followed very close on the soldier's heels even in war, ready to buy slaves and other booty and to sell wine and oil. The introduction of cults by individuals and foreign groups was a different thing from the civic establishment of Egyptian and Syrian cults in the Hellenistic age, and from the quindecimviral

---

[1] Cf. W. Rüge, in P.W. *s.v.* Tekmoreioi.   [2] II, 9; see below, p. 627.

[3] Cf. E. Norden, *Neue Jahrbücher*, xxxi, 1913, pp. 656 *sqq.*; W. W. Tarn, *J.R.S.* xxii, 1932, pp. 135 *sqq.*

[4] M. Abramič, *Führer durch Poetovio*, pp. 162 *sqq.* and 172 *sqq.*

establishment of Cybele at Rome. There the community fixed the form in which a new worship should be celebrated. Here the worship came as it was, and could retain peculiar features. Another factor differentiating Roman from Greek culture was that in Roman practice a manumitted slave became a citizen of his town.

Account may now be taken of certain specific worships. The worship of Cybele spread apace in Gaul; it made headway also in Africa, in the frontier provinces, in ports, and along the great roads, and gained many adherents among provincial and municipal dignitaries (including not a few of Gallic and Spanish descent): at the same time, it did not prove equally attractive to men in the army and in the Imperial service.

Cybele's acceptance at Rome makes her dissemination in a measure a part of the spread of Roman culture, and this is the only Oriental cult for which municipalities constructed temples[1]. At the same time, her worship at Rome was not confined to the official cult, but was conducted also by confraternities, and, though it was controlled, it was not imposed by authority but carried abroad by devotees. Further, it did not lose one alien feature— the *galli* or men who had castrated themselves and thereafter, often as wandering mendicants, practised penances and mortifications. No Roman citizen had the legal right to enter their ranks, but the mood of devotion and submission was not confined to these eunuchs, and was fostered by the splendid ceremonies of March 15–27, which corresponded to Holy Week and Easter. Fasting and sorrow and the *dies Sanguinis* turned into the joy of the Hilaria, which commemorated the re-animation of Attis. At the end the Great Mother passed with silent blessing through the flower-strewn streets to her *Lavatio*[2]. The drama of nature's death and life has nowhere found a more moving expression in ritual.

The initiations which existed in this worship were private. On the other hand, the *taurobolium* and *criobolium* could be seen by all. The *taurobolium* was a ritual act originating in Asia Minor (p. 419) —bathing in the blood of a bull, which, as the name indicates, must originally have been captured after a solemn chase. The *criobolium*, which also had Hellenistic precedent at Pergamum[3], involved the

[1] The nearest approach to an exception appears to be the restoration in A.D. 194 of a temple to Juppiter Dolichenus by the *vicani Aquenses* (*C.I.L.* XIII, 7566ᵃ). Cybele's official standing is further illustrated by the fact that the guilds called *dendrophori*, who carried in procession the tree which was in a sense Attis, acted also as fire-brigades (see above, p. 31).

[2] Cf. Volume of Plates v, 158, *a, b.*

[3] *O.G.I.S.* 764, n. 36. (Some late inscriptions from mons Vaticanus speak of the rites as combined.)

use of a ram. In either rite the *vires* or testicles of the animal were preserved in a vessel called a *kernos*. The use and significance of this bath are so far known to us only from the Western half of the Roman Empire. At first it may well have been a rite regarded as effective in itself, and not attached to a particular deity. The earliest certain known instance in the West, dated in A.D. 134 and found at Puteoli, is associated with the Semitic Venus Caelestis[1]: here it is a private ceremony. In later years numerous commemorative altars dedicated to the great Idaean Mother of the gods and Attis describe the ceremony as having been performed on behalf of the Empire or the Emperor or both *ex vaticinatione archigalli* and indicate that it was under the authority of the *quindecimviri*[2]. The special connotation of the act as done for the public well-being[3] was perhaps due to a specific act of the *quindecimviri*, romanizing the practice just as Cybele's public ceremonies had been earlier adapted. There is no doubt of the official endorsement of the practice, for the legal provision is 'qui in portu pro salute imperatoris sacrum facit ex vaticinatione archigalli a tutelis excusatur[4].' Its frequent use may have been due to anxiety for the Empire and consequent *religio*.

The *taurobolium* was celebrated also for the benefit of individuals, who thereby acquired the status of *tauroboliati*[5]; the rite was sometimes repeated after twenty years[6], but in one of the latest texts, dating from the Julianic revival[7], a recipient appears as 'reborn for eternity': yet an elaborate inscription[8] of the late period in which the rite was much used at Rome does in fact suggest that the *taurobolium* and *criobolium* were even then thought of primarily as a 'thing done,' as a *dromenon* rather than a way of securing blessings for the individual. This is illustrated by the earlier phrase *taurobolium movit*[9], and by the performance of *taurobolium* or *taurobolium* and *criobolium* by pairs or groups of people and even by a city or a province[10]. In any case, this rite, which became notably

---

[1] Dessau 4271 (form used *Caelesta*). Graillot (*op. cit.* p. 159) is, however, probably right in interpreting *C.I.L.* II, 179 (Olisipo, A.D. 108) as the record of a woman's *taurobolium*.

[2] At Lyons it lasted more than a day: *C.I.L.* XIII, 1753 *sq.*

[3] But note the Pergamene precedent (p. 423).

[4] *Frag. iuris Rom. Vatic.* 148.   [5] *C.I.L.* VI, 1675.

[6] Dessau 4153 *sq.*   [7] Dessau 4152 (A.D. 376).

[8] H. J. Rose, *J.H.S.* XLIII, 1923, pp. 194 *sqq.*; XLV, 1925, pp. 180 *sqq.* The parallel which he notes to a Persian liturgical formula may be due to some Iranian apocryphal writing: the present writer cannot see, as many do, other Iranian influence in the rite.

[9] Dessau 4118, 4138.   [10] Graillot, *op. cit.* p. 165 *sq.*

popular in Gaul, reached Rome without leaving a trace in Greece
proper: an inscription at Athens, probably of the fourth century,
speaks of the *taurobolium* as having been celebrated for the first
time[1].

Taurobolic inscriptions show that Rome was thought of as
the centre of the cult. One records the transference of the rite
from Rome to Lyons; others indicate that local authority belonged
to the *archigallus*, who in the romanized cult need not be a eunuch
or a Phrygian by race: he might be consulted by a neighbouring
town which had no such dignitary, and had high standing as an
inspired person. There were also priests (one or more) elected by
the *decuriones*: we have a record of the quindecimviral permission
to one at Cumae in 289 to wear his priestly insignia within the
territory of the town[2]. Further, there were priestesses, sometimes
called *ministrae*, and confraternities, the *cannophori* and *dendrophori* (see above, p. 423).

Attis receives not a few other dedications, in some of which he
is identified with Men, another god from Asia Minor, in the form
Attidi Menotyranno[3]. Asia Minor gave also the war goddess Ma,
identified with Bellona, an old Roman goddess of whom we know
little. Her cult is said to have been brought back by Sulla's
soldiers. It was distinguished by the alien ministrations of her
priests, called *fanatici*, who cut themselves with knives and worked
themselves into frenzies, in which they prophesied. As a rule,
apparently they attracted alms rather than devout attention, but
we find at Mainz a cult-society devoted to the honour of the
Goddess[4]. In general Cybele and Attis were the predominant
divinities from Asia Minor.

We have seen how Isis and Sarapis gradually won official
sanction. From Flavian times onwards they were, in spite of
occasional expressions of contempt, safely entrenched in the exotic
dignity of their temples. These, like the other temples of the Near
East itself, were elaborate complexes of buildings fitted for the
permanent habitation of a professional clergy and the temporary
lodging of devotees and initiates. They had a daily service, the

---

[1] *I.G.* III, 172.

[2] Dessau 4131; A. D. Nock, *Conversion*, p. 285. In *C.I.L.* VI, 508
(dated 319) members of the college were present and made the *traditio*.
Graillot (*op. cit.* p. 229) remarks that there is no evidence that the *quindecimviri* thus supervised any of the other cults introduced in accordance with
the Sibylline books. (They can have had no concern with Oriental cults
independently introduced at Rome.)

[3] F. Cumont, *Religions orientales*[4], p. 58.

[4] Cumont, *op. cit.* p. 224.

opening of the shrines and awakening and clothing of the statues; they had the ceremonial holding up of a vessel containing the sacred Nile water for adoration; they had congregational singing and acclamations; they had sacred dances and processions[1], and the great public rite of Ploiaphesia or *Navigium Isidis*, intercessions for the Roman State and libation into the sea at the opening of the sailing season on March 5 (and we may recall that Isis and Sarapis had a special interest for sailors as their protectors); they had the mystery-drama of Osiris; they had, for the chosen few (and not necessarily in all temples), initiations. Our evidence suggests that the priesthood did not possess the civic tone of the worships of the Egyptian gods established in Greece during the earlier part of the Hellenistic period, but that it was professional and probably copied from Alexandria and, whatever the racial origin of its members, valued Egyptian appearances.

Inscriptions show that the dissemination of the cult was greatest in parts which had relations with Egypt or which had foreign and, in particular, military elements[2]: there is no evidence of a Western provincial city giving public homage: the known worshippers were men from Rome, officials, high or low, freedmen and slaves; unromanized provincials are hardly found. Tacitus[3], it is true, says that part of the Suebi, who dwelt beyond the range of Roman power, sacrificed to Isis, but this may be due to a misunderstanding of the ship's symbol associated with their goddess.

So much for the quantitative aspect of this cult. The qualitative aspect is even more remarkable. A peculiar degree of devotion is manifested towards Isis and Sarapis; liberality to the shrines (attested notably by the jewelry presented by a woman to Isis)[4]; penitence (shown by sitting before the temple and telling of the divine punishment for sins, or by such acts of reparation as breaking the ice on the Tiber and crawling round the Campus Martius); strange acts of piety (getting Nile water from Meroe at the command of Isis); contemplation of the ineffable beauty of the sacred face of Isis; preservation of the garment of initiation for one's burial; meditation on the meaning of initiation. Devotion to Isis made men call themselves *Isiaci*. The service of Isis was a

---

[1] Cf. Volume of Plates v, 160, *a, b*.

[2] In Africa, Carthage and Lambaesis were the great centres (Cumont, *op. cit.* p. 236).

[3] *Germ.* 9. Cf. F. Heichelheim in P.W. *s.v.* Nehalennia. On the identification of Isis with Noreia cf. vol. XI, p. 553 and v. Petrikovits in P.W. *s.v.* Noreia.   [4] Dessau 4422.

sacred war, entered with a soldier's undertaking of allegiance. Isis predominated; Osiris, Anubis, Horus were a divine setting for her achievements, and Osirian mummification did not travel with the cult; Sarapis was important, as a god of miracles; and from Flavian times he was commonly identified with the Sun.

One other borrowing from Egypt may be mentioned—the festival of the Pelusia on March 20, which was taken from the celebration at Pelusium, and included ritual bathing, like the Maioumas, which was carried from Antioch to Ostia.

The official acceptance of Syrian worships has been discussed earlier (see above, p. 417 *sq.*). What of the infiltration of Syrian cults in a private way? The Syrian slave came early to the West; the Syrian trader followed. We have remarked earlier on the particular attachment of the Semite to his ancestral worships; the Tyrian group at Puteoli retained its cults and its devotion to them and to Tyre in 174[1]. It is not surprising to find at Corduba an altar dedicated in the second century to Syrian deities by people of Syrian names[2]; a record of a Salambo procession at Seville[3]; a temple to the hereditary god of the men of Gaza (apparently Marnas) at Ostia[4]; Juppiter Damascenus and Dusares worshipped at Puteoli; Zeus Kasios at times in the West[5]; a dedication at Rome to Hypsiste Astarte[6]; successive temples to Syrian deities on the Janiculum, with an inscription perhaps rightly explained as referring to sacred communal meals[7]; a small area in Rome called Adonaea on a third-century plan; numerous dedications to Juppiter Dolichenus, including the description of the members of a guild of his as *fratres carissimi*, chosen by him to serve him[8], and the existence of a *cenatorium* of his at Bononia[9].

Dedications to the last-mentioned god are widespread and include many by soldiers; they may be regarded as in the main a result of the Flavian garrisoning of the Eastern frontier (vol. XI, p. 140). Formal cults of the Syrian deities in the Western provinces are in fact mainly confined to military regions, and their worshippers,

[1] *O.G.I.S.* 595; G. La Piana, *Harv. Theol. Rev.* XX, 1927, pp. 256 *sqq.*
[2] F. Cumont, *Syria*, v, 1924, p. 342 *sq.*
[3] *Ib.* VIII, 1927, pp. 330 *sqq.*
[4] *C.I.G.* 5892; Cumont, *Religions orientales*[4], p. 253.
[5] A. Salač, *Bull. corr. hell.* XLVI, 1922, pp. 187 *sqq.*
[6] *Not. degli scavi*, 1935, pp. 91 *sqq.*
[7] See Cumont, *C.R. Ac. Inscr.* 1917, pp. 275 *sqq.*
[8] Dessau 4316.
[9] Dessau 4313. For a recently discovered temple at Rome with important sculptures see A. M. Colini in *Bull. Comm. Arch.* LXIII, 1935, pp. 145 *sqq.*

when not of the army, are for the most part Oriental in origin. Of course, the eunuch priests who begged for the Syrian goddess circulated widely, and men gave to them fearing the power of their curse, perhaps hoping for a blessing[1]; but this did not establish cultus or religious habits, and this goddess does not seem often to have received from non-Syrians a devotion such as was paid willingly to Isis by non-Egyptians. Dacia has one inscription to Dea Suria, Germany none. An exception is the dedication to the Syrian goddess found by the Roman Wall in Britain, identifying her with Justice and speaking of the revelation by which the soldier responsible for the record had learned her might[2]; but the wording makes it clear that Julia Domna's prestige had opened the channel of grace.

We pass to Mithraism. Mithras, the Persian god of light, appears as the object of a special cult at Gurob in the Fayûm in the third century B.C. (doubtless at some shrine maintained by a group of Persians who had remained in Egypt after the end of their rule); the nature of this worship is unknown. Plutarch tells how the pirates, against whom Pompey warred, celebrated certain secret sacrifices to Mithras on the Cilician mountains. The cult, as we know it, certainly took its rise in parts of Asia Minor where Iranian elements had remained strong in the population, as in Cappadocia.

We learn something from allegorical explanations of Mithraism, as in Porphyry, and from Christian attacks on it, but our knowledge is in the main derived from the material remains of the worship; from the temples at Doura, at Rome, Ostia and other sites in Italy, in Britain, and along the Rhine and Danube frontiers. They are built in a shape intended to give the likeness of a cave, with a bas-relief on a pedestal in a niche at the end, benches for the worshippers to recline, sculptured and sometimes pictorial decorations, and a water-supply for purifications[3]. The iconography has local variations but is on the whole curiously constant. The bas-relief shows Mithras slaying the bull, from which comes the life of the earth's crops. The formal model is the earlier type of Nike sacrificing a bull, but the scene has a cosmic significance and its place in the centre of the shrine emphasizes that Mithraism had a mythical

---

[1] Cf. the collection box for 'lady Atargatis,' F. Cumont, *Aréthuse*, fasc. xxvii (1930), pp. 41 *sqq.*; P. Perdrizet, *Syria*, xii, 1931, pp. 267 *sqq.*; Volume of Plates v, 162, *a*.

[2] F. Buecheler, *Carm. Lat. epig.* 25. Cf. *C.I.L.* xiii, 6671, for what seems to be a dedication to Julia Domna, under Caracalla, as *Caelestis dea*.

[3] See Plan 1, facing p. 570.

cosmogony of its own and a content of ideas on which it was easy
to graft further interpretation. On either side stand Cautes and
Cautopates, attendant spirits of light, and the whole is framed in
a series of panels giving the god's *Vita*; his birth from the rock,
his shooting at a rock and production of rain, his chase and capture
of the bull, his reception of the Sun-god's homage, his sacred meal
with the Sun-god[1].

These impressive candle-lit shrines witnessed ceremonies of
initiation and ritual meals. Jerome describes seven grades of
initiation, the believer becoming successively *corax, nymph(i)us*[2],
miles, leo, Persa, heliodromus and *pater*. A statement in Porphyry[3]
suggests some local variation of terminology. We know a little
of the ceremonies, some of which are represented in drawings on
the walls of a Mithraeum at S. Maria di Capua[4]. There was at
some point a simulated death; at another the *miles* was offered a
wreath on a sword and refused it saying 'Mithras is my wreath,'
and thereafter refusing to wear wreaths at banquets. Furthermore,
the initiates shared in their sacred meals a continuing religious life;
and there was no professional priesthood, leadership being vested
in members who had reached the highest grade as *patres*. Men
alone were admitted; a possible exception, if it proves valid, will
represent one of the varieties of Mithraism[5].

Among the points in which Mithraism differed from the other
'mystery religions[6],' there is one of the greatest importance. For
the Egyptian, Syrian, and Anatolian cults of this type which
travelled westwards the primary ceremony was the cult-drama, re-
enacting what had happened and what in a sense annually happened to the god. This was open to all worshippers and not only
to initiates; initiations were something additional, not available
at all times, in all shrines or to any who could not pay enough[7].
In Mithraism the initiatory ceremonies were in the foreground
from the earliest phase of which we have knowledge, and there
was no annual rite of a dramatic kind. Mithras was not born
annually and did not die and he had a complete *Vita*. There was

---

[1] See Volume of Plates v, 162, *b*.

[2] Not, as emended, *cryphius*: cf. F. Cumont, *C.R. Ac. Inscr.* 1934,
p. 107 *sq.*; M. Rostovtzeff, *Röm. Mitt.* XLIX, 1934, p. 206. New light on
the terminology will be available when the *graffiti* of the Doura Mithraeum
are published.　　　　　　　　　　　[3] *de abstin.* IV, 16.

[4] A. Minto, *Not. degli scavi*, 1924, pp. 353 *sqq.*; Volume of Plates v, 164, *a*.

[5] Cf. Buckler-Calder-Cox, *J.R.S.* XIV, 1924, p. 31.

[6] Cf. A. D. Nock, *J.R.S.* XXVII, 1937, pp. 108 *sqq.*

[7] Cf. Nock, *Conversion*, pp. 56 *sqq.*

no ceremony which could be made into a public rite, and Mithras never became a civic god. Mithraea might, as at Augusta Treverorum and Poetovio, be built near other shrines[1]; they might be the object of devotion of a domestic[2] or military unit; but the cult and the temples were always private. This worship, by its own vitality, retained its forms over a wide range of space and time, without hierarchy or quindecimviral control.

Mithras was the god who, beyond all others, mattered most to the believer. He was a principal actor in the making of the world, and would be in its eventual re-making (an idea present in Mithraism though perhaps less prominent than in early Zoroastrianism), and, what was more, he was the protector here and now, and would be after death, of the man who received his rites and lived worthily of them: moral demands were stressed. Occasionally he was identified with Zeus and must therefore have been considered as the Supreme Being. In native Persian ideas, which appear to have predominated, he was neither the supreme nor the only god. Above him stood Ahura Mazda, who could be translated as Juppiter Caelus, a god too high for our common prayers, and now remote from the battle—not (as for Zoroaster) commander of the faithful. Behind Mithras stood Zervan akarana, infinite time, who may well be the subject of the representations (following an Orphic type) which we sometimes find in Mithraea; for a Greek he was probably Kronos[3]. Ahura Mazda had his opposite Ahriman, and this god—as god of death rather than of evil in any abstract sense—receives dedications in some Mithraea, just as earlier the Magi had made special sacrifices to him.

The worship of Mithras did not exclude other worships. A powerful impetus, such as that which manifests itself in the expansion of Mithraism, could not fail to make it for some adherents a focal point round which their other religious practices were grouped; and there was nothing to prevent individuals from indulging the deep-seated instinct for a diversification of forms. We see this instinct in Christianity; it had freer scope in Mithraism.

Mithraism had ideas, power and qualities which differentiated it from the other Oriental cults which were at the same time actively followed. It is small wonder if Justin Martyr and Tertullian

---

[1] But at Augusta Treverorum two altars have the phrase '*in suo posuit*' (S. Loeschcke, *Die Erforschung des Tempelbezirkes im Altbachtale zu Trier*, p. 36). Inferences from the juxtaposition of shrines are insecure.

[2] E.g. the *domus Augustana* whose *pater et sacerdos* is mentioned early in the third century; Dessau 4270.

[3] A. D. Nock, *Harv. Theol. Rev.* XXVII, 1934, p. 79.

regarded it as a diabolic copy of Christianity. Where it was powerful—as at Ostia, Heddernheim and Poetovio—it was very powerful. But it made its appeal only along certain lines; it omitted vast areas of the Empire: above all, it was weak in those very regions in which Christianity spread with particular strength. The absence of women deprived it of the support of what was in antiquity, as it is to-day, the sex more interested in religious practices of any and every kind. It lived on its ideas and its emotional force; it had not, like Egyptian and Syrian cults, local nuclei of men to whom it was a national religion.

V. TENDENCIES IN POPULAR PIETY

We have considered the two halves of the Empire in so far as they differed. Some things were common to both—the existence of private guilds, serving religious, funerary, and social purposes, the cult of the emperor, the astrological picture of the universe, the practice of magic, and philosophy. The cult of the emperor was in the East built upon earlier institutions, in the West it was deliberately introduced (vol. x, chap. xv). Yet in spite of this and in spite of local and temporal variation (e.g. vol. xi, p. 561), it remained a universal fact; everywhere men looked towards him who stood between humanity and the gods, everywhere he was at one and the same time the subject of innumerable vows and the object of an unmeasured homage which took the forms of divine adoration because there were none higher; everywhere the emperor's name was used in solemn oaths. The ruler of the world was associated with the gods; he was also chosen by the gods, or by the Sun in particular: they went with him on his ways. The intensity of this emotion deepened and found new expressions[1].

> mox crescit in illos
> imperium superis.

Everywhere, above the emperor, there was Fate and its decrees, written in or by the stars in their courses[2]. Everywhere there were similar attempts to break these decrees by magic—the same formulas in Syria and Egypt and Moesia and the Rhineland and Italy. Everywhere those who sought an interpretation of life looked to philosophy.

---

[1] Cf. A. Alföldi in *Röm. Mitt.* L, 1935, pp. 85, 94, 107, 119. The Christian emperors continued to hold this exalted position, and retained many of its expressions.

[2] See above, p. 421.

These things, and the local components in the piety of each place, made a constant background. In the provinces of Latin speech this was modified by the second wave of Oriental cults. Certain worships of Near Eastern origin proved able to bear a generalized significance and made a powerful impact. They spread above all among the mobile elements of the population and in cities and regions where mobile elements were strong[1]. Cybele and Isis apart, they made little impression outside those elements and cities and regions. The Western provinces had received ancient culture, as they received the worship of the emperor, ready-made. Accordingly, they combined Rome's worships, which came like Rome's language, with their native cults. The ignorant probably pursued their old practices, as is shown by later survivals: those of more wealth and cultivation, who could make dedications, gave to their ancestral gods Roman names, often made specific by the addition of local epithets (as for instance Mars Cocidius), and Graeco-Roman art-types suitably modified[2].

Some deities preserved their native entity. In Gaul (vol. XI, pp. 507 *sq.*, 518 *sq.*) and Britain the organization of Celtic religion by Druidism disappeared, but Epona and Rosmerta and the goddesses called *Matres* or *Matronae* were distinct in name as in art-type from the usual pantheon. In Africa (cf. vol. XI, p. 487 *sq.*) the Punic deities retained very considerable power, which corresponded to the age, tenacity, and development of the civilization to which they belonged. Saturnus was a native deity; Caelestis, whose native name was Tanit, was in fact the Carthaginian equivalent of the Dea Suria: the worship of Liber in this province appears to have been the romanization of a native god: the *Cereres* were perhaps also native[3]. Here as in Thrace native piety

---

[1] F. Cumont (*Les mystères de Mithra*[3], p. 64) has observed that the absence of clear evidence for Mithras at Puteoli can be explained from the fact that at the time when Mithraism was rising the commercial importance of Puteoli was declining; contrast the place which it occupied at Ostia. R. M. Peterson, *The cults of Campania*, p. 214, remarks on the smaller development of Oriental cults at Neapolis, which was not a great port in the late Republic and under the Empire, and which also had a firmly rooted Greek civilization. L. R. Taylor, *Local cults in Etruria*, p. 249, notes that the only Syrian worship represented in Etruria is that of Juppiter Dolichenus (on his dissemination cf. above, p. 427; Sol juvans at Pyrgi, Taylor, *op. cit.* p. 127, may be an old local indigenous cult). On the other hand, Mithraism was here more widely diffused than in Southern Italy.

[2] There was creativeness also: cf. M. P. Nilsson, 'Zur Deutung der Juppiter-gigantensäulen,' *Arch. f. Religionswiss.* XXIII, 1925, pp. 175 *sqq.*

[3] Cf. Cumont, *Religions orientales*[4], p. 200, on this and on Liber and Liber in Illyria as a native divine pair superficially romanized.

remained very strong in spite of the incoming of alien religious elements; Thracian piety, which had a notable power of fusion with alien elements, appears in Dacia and occasionally in Pannonia (vol. XI, p. 552). For Spain (vol. XI, p. 498) our evidence is scanty, but some indigenous cults are attested, although romanization was much older here than in Gaul outside Narbonensis. Otherwise Roman names and Roman forms seem to have been of the nature of a superimposed thing and primarily a cultural phenomenon. Mercurius in Gaul is essentially Celtic rather than Roman.

The vitality of native worships in the West is clear and did not wholly disappear when Christianity became the official religion. Roman soldiers, and even dignitaries (vol XI, p. 538) did not hesitate to make dedications to *Matres* and *Matronae* or Noreia, but neither in Gaul nor in Spain nor in Africa do such dedications bulk large numerically, and there is in general a marked divergence between the religious interests of provincials and of administrators[1]. Celtic and Germanic deities did not travel like those of the Near East[2]. Even the Celtic Epona, who had a foothold in the Celtic element in North Italy and whose guardianship of horses gave her a function of general utility, though worshipped by men who had no Gallic blood, did not develop into anything new and cosmopolitan. Once more, that is the difference between romanization and hellenization. Slaves, traders, officials, and soldiers brought influences from their original homes, and also from the capital. The halo around the Eternal City grew brighter in the years of stress; in religion, as in the Forma Orbis, all roads start in Rome.

No cultural factor was of more importance than the army. Something has been said of its religion in an earlier volume (vol. X, p. 483 *sq.*). We have there seen the difference between its fundamental institutions and those of city life. A Roman camp had its military *sacra*, its auspices, its observance of the Saturnalia. Nevertheless, it was originally no more than the place where an army halted. The situation changed when the system of frontier defences caused legions to be immobilized in *castra stativa* with dependent civilian settlements[3]. The troops, recruited on the spot,

---

[1] J. Toutain, *Les cultes païens dans l'empire romain*, I, pp. 466 *sqq.* Caracalla seems to have taken an interest in the Celtic Apollo Grannus (Dio LXXVIII, 15, 6).

[2] On the other hand, the Carthaginian cult of Caelestis, which was akin to Syrian piety, obtained a certain dissemination (F. Cumont in P.W., *s.v.*).

[3] Cf. vol. XI, pp. 442 *sqq.* and Toutain, *op. cit.* II, pp. 25 *sq.*, 62 *sq.*

had a local colour; they lacked the conservative factor of domestic cult, for they were officially celibate till the time of Septimius Severus, and it was natural that they should welcome religious groupings around new powerful divinities. Further, they received new impulses from the movements of *vexillationes*, from the transference of centurions on their promotion, and from the fashions of the Imperial house. Their habits, and the influence of their habits were perpetuated by the frequency with which, after serving their time, they settled near the camps in which they had been stationed (cf. vol. xi, p. 443). Military culture and military religion thus assumed a permanent condition[1].

Nevertheless, we must not exaggerate the extent to which the religion of the army and of other foci of mobile life diverged from native Roman practice. The *Feriale Duranum* mentions no festivals save those of old Roman deities and commemorations of the Imperial house.[2] In Mogontiacum, Heddernheim, Colonia Agrippinensis, and Vetera, dedications to Oriental deities amount to slightly more than 14 per cent. of all dedications—and that in spite of the fact that new cults were more apt than old cults to inspire permanent records of piety. Furthermore, while temples to the Capitoline triad were very common in the Latin-speaking provinces, private dedications to it come in the main from the military and from Imperial functionaries, and dedications to Juppiter Optimus Maximus are most frequent in the frontier provinces; among the dedicators soldiers predominate. As for Rome itself, dedications to Hercules and Silvanus, the latter of whom perhaps indicates by his popularity the rise of Italian countryside elements, considerably exceed in number those to any Oriental deities[3]. Both were notably popular with the army, and, in the West, with provincials. We must not forget the frequency of dedications by non-Romans to Roman deities or to fully romanized deities of Greek extraction[4]. Thus inscriptions from the Syrian shrine on the Janiculum[5] couple the Zeus Keraunios (here a Baal) with the Nymphae Forrinae (i.e. Furrinae). Receptivity was not on one side only.

Let us pass from the quantitative aspect of the spread of Oriental cults to its qualitative aspects. To many men to whom

---

[1] Cf. A. S. Hoey, *Harv. Theol. Rev.* xxx, 1937, pp. 15 *sqq.*
[2] To be published in *Yale Class. Stud.*
[3] V. Macchioro, *Rev. arch.* iv Sér. ix, 1907, p. 143.
[4] *Ib.* pp. 272 *sqq.*; cf. the Republican evidence from Minturnae discussed by A. D. Nock, *Amer. Jour. Phil.* lvi, 1935, p. 90.
[5] P Gauckler, *Le sanctuaire syrien du Janicule,* pp. 18, 57.

such practice was not hereditary and indigenous these worships may well have meant the satisfaction of their desires for immortality, for a more dignified status in the universe, for an escape from Fate, for the opening of windows in heaven; to some they meant vocation and divine guidance and *militia sacra*; to Lucius they meant a new life, with purpose and meaning[1]. But to most men who used them they were probably no more than an interesting extra, another and perhaps a more effective way of access to the supernatural; exacting penances[2], speaking with authority and differing from traditional worships in that they involved a chosen personal relationship with the deities concerned.

The cults had their myths, the appeal and significance of which must not be underestimated, as well as their rites, both subject to moderate change, and both were capable of interpretation in accordance with the philosophies of the time. Mithraism, indeed, had its cosmogony and its eschatology, but the cults in general had no theology in our sense of the word save what was read into them by educated devotees; Stoic physics and Orphic[3] and Pythagorean ideas of the soul and of its destiny as re-worked by Plato, were of particular influence; so was the notion that the level of the stars was the true homeland of man's spirit. Plutarch's *Isis and Osiris* (cf. p. 439) records interpretations of Egyptian myths as expressing intellectual and psychological experience. These have special interest because of their closeness to some of Philo's allegories; but they were not canonical interpretations, universally accepted, and 'physical' interpretations also existed[4]. Again, henotheistic tendencies in thought found expression in piety[5]. A modicum of philosophic ideas was a very common possession, and the cults, philosophically interpreted, could give supernatural authority to widespread notions, for the gods were 'guardians of the soul and mind[6].'

The priest's address to Lucius in Apuleius[7], with its severe condemnation of the hero's youthful self-indulgence and its call to self-dedication, shows that the cult of Isis could thus reinforce

[1] Apuleius, *Met.* xi.

[2] Cf. R. Pettazzoni, *Harv. Theol. Rev.* xxx, 1937, pp. 1 *sqq.*

[3] Orphic literature was much quoted, and there is an Orphic *lamella* of the second century (O. Kern, *Orphicorum fragmenta*, p. 108, no. 32 *g*), but whether actual Orphic communities existed under the Empire is very doubtful. The reference to a community in the Orphic Hymns may be a literary convention.

[4] Cf. H. R. Schwyzer, *Chairemon*; P. Oxy. xi, 1381, ll. 170 *sqq.*

[5] Cumont, *Religions orientales*[4], p. 270.

[6] Dessau 4147; cf. *C.I.L.* xii, 1277.   [7] *Met.* xi, 15.

morality: self-denial was exacted by other cults[1]. Mithras is usually thought to have set the highest standards and could be an example of vigorous combative action as well as of purity.

In general, the Oriental cults were symptomatic of change rather than productive of it. They have been supposed to have served the ends of autocracy: more significant, however, is the observed fact that some of their expressions of devotion appear to reflect the linguistic and artistic idioms of a loyalism already aroused on other grounds[2]. Solar theology did very possibly make a contribution to the complex of ideas and emotions tending to exalt the *princeps*, but solar theology had its roots in philosophy and, while reinforced by the piety of various cults, did not depend only on them. Again, the spread of the Oriental cults was probably a result rather than a cause, even a contributory cause, of inter-mixture and racial levelling; the most striking instance of this in the religious sphere is, after all, the second-century Dionysiac association at Tusculum, in the members' list of which freemen and slaves alike are described by their bare *cognomina*[3]. The sarcophagi of the period are a warning against exaggerations of the power of the Oriental cults: although in representations of the seasons Attis sometimes stands for winter, there are hardly any other traces of the Eastern deities[4]. The mourning Attis is common on other funerary monuments[5]: he could typify the fate awaiting all, even the young and lovely: perhaps there was also some hope that, like Attis, the dead man might not remain in the power of death. Otherwise, the appearance of the Oriental deities in art in general is all but confined to terracotta and bronze figurines and monuments definitely associated with their worship or presumably dedicated to the memory of their ministrants[6].

Novelty was not lacking, but it was in the main a matter of a change of atmosphere (see below, p. 448) or individual innovations or changes of emphasis, until we come to the latter part of the third century and the first part of the fourth, when we find certain attempts to strengthen paganism in the face of what had

[1] Cf. Cumont, *op. cit.* pp. 35 *sqq.*   [2] *Ib.* p. xi.

[3] Cumont-Vogliano, *Amer. Journ. Arch.*, 2nd Ser. XXXVII, 1933, pp. 215 *sqq.* (especially p. 234).

[4] See Cumont in *Bull. de l'Inst. archéologique liégeois*, XXIX, 1901.

[5] Volume of Plates v, 164, *b*; A. D. Nock, *Harv. Theol. Rev.* XXV, 1932, p. 338; F. Cumont (*C.R. Ac. Inscr.* 1906, p. 75, n. 1) regards the *polos* of the dead man on some Greek bas-reliefs as in effect assimilating him to Sarapis.

[6] For an exception see representations of Egyptian cultus as local colour in paintings.

become a tremendous opposition. Thus a pious individual at
Acmoneia in Phrygia founded a cult of the 'immortal gods[1].'
Nevertheless, the whole development of Imperial paganism has
only one feature as striking and significant as the spread of
Dionysiac religion or of Orphism—and that is the rise of solar
theology.

What then of the syncretism or *theokrasia* which has been so
often discussed? Some have suggested that the various deities of
paganism fused into a few figures or melted into a general nimbus
of orientalized godhead. In this suggestion there is both truth and
falsehood. Greek thinkers had from early times supposed that the
pantheons of all nations consisted of gods performing like functions
and that these divine persons corresponded to one another, that
Ammon was Zeus, and so forth. This theory did not in the
popular mind destroy differences of identity; Alexander paid a
visit to Ammon as Ammon and not as Zeus. Further, there had
been even earlier much give and take between kindred divine
figures in Syria and Anatolia, to an extent which makes it impossible for us, and probably made it impossible for ancient worshippers, to draw clear distinctions; such exchange sometimes
involved purely stylistic features, but could go deeper. Again, the
depth of emotion excited by Isis, *una quae es omnia*[2], *myrionyma*[3],
caused far-reaching identification (p. 420) and this was not peculiar to her; even Hermes or Priapus could be treated as a
universal cosmic god. In such identifications it was assumed that
the native name, whether Isis or Dea Suria, was the *verum nomen*,
the other divine titles being what we might call dialect variations.
Add to these factors the widespread generalizing trend noted
earlier, and the common tendency to invest any prominent god
with solar attributes, and you have enough to account for a
considerable blurring of the edge of divine personalities.

On the other hand, local pride and local devotion acted as
limiting factors, and the continued existence of the old names
and of individualized types meant the continued existence of
distinct entities. Isis and Magna Mater shared a temple at Lacus
Benacus[4], a priestess at Aeclanum, a priest at Ostia[5]; but they

---

[1] F. Cumont, *Cat. des sculptures et inscriptions des Musées du Cinquantenaire*, ed. 2, pp. 158 *sqq.*; H. Grégoire, *Byzantion*, VIII, 1933, pp. 49 *sqq.*
Cf. Buckler-Calder-Cox in *J.R.S.* XIV, 1924, p. 25; E. Williger, *Hagios*,
p. 95, on possible Christian influence on a cult in Isauria.

[2] Dessau 4362. 　　　　　　　　　　[3] *Ib.* note on 4361.

[4] *C.I.L.* v, 4007.

[5] L. R. Taylor, *Local Cults in Etruria*, p. 80 *sq.*

were distinct, and the result was not a composite product such as Hermanubis. Juppiter summus exsuperantissimus was highest, but that would for many imply gods, as well as men and things, below him. There are dedications (from the second century B.C. onwards) and art-types of a pantheistic kind[1]; some of these imply a concept of divine unity, but others involve no more than the old desire to ensure safety by neglecting no god; in a certain number we may suspect an element of *jeu d'esprit*[2]. The habit of grouping and identifying deities may have contributed to a decline in attention to the *minutiae* of the custom which assigned one victim to one god and one to another. Nevertheless, subordination and identification did not destroy the gods; sometimes in the last struggle with Christianity it supplied an apologia for their worship. The development at issue seems to have come from above; and such dedications in the Western provinces as are its expressions are predominantly from soldiers of the higher ranks or from their military dependents, and from Imperial slaves and freedmen[3].

VI. PAGANISM IN THOUGHT

When we look at literature after A.D. 69, we find in Pliny the Elder a hard rationalism with a deep-felt wonder at the universe, in Epictetus a naked morality invested with a warmth of theistic emotion (vol. XI, pp. 694 *sqq.*), in the Neopythagorean Apollonius of Tyana asceticism and piety, in Dio of Prusa deep moral earnestness and contemplative piety, in Statius and Martial awareness of Oriental cult. Juvenal, as a satirist, handles the traditional topic of women's superstition with special reference to these alien worships.

This is all fairly conventional. Nevertheless, a change of mood was taking place. Tacitus occupied a middle ground, interested in fate and freewill, ready to speak of a Parthian cult, concerned even with the past of the Judaism which he hated. Plutarch (vol. XI,

---

[1] V. Macchioro, *Rev. arch.* IV Sér., IX, 1907, p. 266, n. 1; R. Dussaud, *Monuments Piot*, XXX, 1929, p. 83 (on Graeco-Asiatic deities represented with the addition of busts from the Graeco-Roman pantheon); J. G. Milne, *Catalogue of Alexandrian coins*. . ., p. xxix; A. D. Nock, *J.H.S.* XLV, 1925, p. 90, and *Conversion*, p. 136 *sq.*; F. Cumont in Daremberg-Saglio, *s.v.* Panthea.

[2] Cf. the hymn to Attis sung in theatres and interpreted esoterically by the Naassenes (Hippolytus, *Refutatio*, V, 9), a *paignion* probably of Hadrianic date (see below, p. 446) and Ausonius, *Epigr.* 48 *sq.*

[3] Cf. Toutain, *op. cit.* II, p. 248; *ib.* p. 255 on the importance of Rome as a focus.

pp. 696 *sqq.*) stands on one side of this middle ground, Mesomedes further on the same side, Lucian thereafter on the other. Plutarch in his youthful essay *On superstition,* speaks of the two errors, atheism and superstition, with an inclination to regard the former as the less insulting to divinity; he mentions sabbath observance, but without any marked discrimination between it and some Greek practices. The main body of his work is inspired by a lofty piety, a faith in divine providence and justice as shown in reward and punishment; a dislike of crude and barbarous deeds, whether done in the name of religion or otherwise; a devotion to ancestral rites; an interest in the soul's destiny; and a questioning spirit which continually asks *why*—why are oracles silent? why do the Jews abstain from pork? is the god of the Jews identical with Dionysus[1]? Plutarch shows throughout a profound belief in the brotherhood of man and the unity of the divine; all men seeking the divine, all using symbols of various kinds. Thus in his work *On Isis and Osiris,* dedicated to a friend Clea who had been initiated in these mysteries as well as in those of Dionysus, he studies the names and myths and public ceremonies of these and other Egyptian gods, finding in them the same meanings as in Greek cults. He speaks of the believer as searching out afterwards by reason the meaning of that which he has received in mystery. Meanwhile Mesomedes showed his ingenuity in glorifying various deities including Isis for whom 'all things are danced[2].'

To Plutarch most Greek, Roman and Oriental rites were good, created in the mythical past by wise men whose insights included all the best that posterity later came to learn; and the science of god was the crown of philosophy. To Lucian Greek and Oriental rites were alike worthless survivals. Much of his writing is lighthearted fooling at the expense of myth and rite (including the scene of supposed Magian necromancy by the Euphrates); but in the *Philopseudes,* the *Alexander,* and the *Concerning the death of Peregrinus,* he speaks from the heart[3]. There is no gaiety, but the bitter seriousness of the Syrian who has found that nearly all his Greek contemporaries have forsaken reason[4]. Although he re-

---

[1] Cornelius Labeo, whose date is uncertain, represents a similar learned interest.

[2] K. Horna, 'Die Hymnen des Mesomedes,' *Wien. Sitz.* ccvii, 1928, i, p. 13. The *Pervigilium Veneris,* whatever its date (p. 586), illustrates the generalizing trend.   [3] Cf. vol. xi, pp. 686 *sqq.*

[4] Cf. a papyrus of A.D. 150–200 (W. Schubart, *Hermes,* lv, 1920, pp. 188 *sqq.*), in which Apollo's claims were apparently vindicated by miracle.

presents the gods as complaining of the new barbarian invaders of Olympus[1], he does not suggest that a particular credulity was connected with the cult of certain gods; apart from his Herodotean parody, *Concerning the Syrian goddess*, he had not much to say about the Oriental cults to which this chapter is devoted. His attitude is like that of Celsus, who in his *True Word*[2] compares the Christians with worshippers of the Great Mother, Mithras, and Sabazios.

The almost contemporary rhetorician Aelius Aristides is conspicuous for his attachment to the deities who delivered him from persistent ill-health, as also for a strong philosophic trend towards monotheism. He wrote a prose hymn to Sarapis, concerned with the god's miracles, but he shows no interest in the hereafter and does not mention other Oriental deities. Nor does Maximus of Tyre, whose reflective piety shows what his audience liked.

Lucian in his *Philopseudes* introduces a superstitious philosopher, and this may remind us that Apuleius thought of himself as *philosophus Platonicus* and is so described in a dedication by the men of his town[3]. His novel, the *Metamorphoses* (see p. 580 *sq.*), reveals the depth of devotion which could be excited by the goddess of many names: an ending in miracle and piety replaces the ironic humour of the Greek original. Its undeniable autobiographic note fits what we learn from the *Apologia*. There Apuleius defends himself against a charge of magic: he is obviously not too anxious to rebut the suggestion of occult interests, and happy to speak of how he had been initiated in a whole series of mysteries, *studio veri*[4]. He refers to a lost speech devoted to these initiations. His philosophic side appears in his other works (p. 581 *sq.*), and presumably he was not conscious of any marked inconsistency.

Philosophy became more and more linked to piety and revelations, and less averse from magic. Neopythagoreanism was the pioneer both in its asceticism and in this development (vol. x, p. 507), which at times brought the atmosphere of a *séance* into the philosopher's room, and Neopythagoreanism was succeeded by the revival of Platonism in the second century. This revival, commonly called Middle Platonism, regarded Plato's work in general and some treatises in particular (above all the Timaeus)

---

[1] *Deorum concilium*, 9; *Iuppiter trag.* 8 (where the alien gods are described as having much richer statues than the Greek gods).

[2] Cf. Origen, *contra Celsum*, I, 9.

[3] Apulée, *Apologie: Florida*, ed. P. Vallette, p. vii.

[4] Apuleius carried to considerable lengths a tendency for which there are parallels: cf. A. D. Nock, *Conversion*, pp. 107 *sqq.*

as a storehouse of inspired truth. Special emphasis was laid on his doctrine of the One, on his dualism of soul and body, on his myths of the after-life (taken as dogma), on his theory of *daimones* as beings intermediate between god and man, on his ideas of divine transcendence and inspiration, on his statement that man's goal is to become like god, on his doctrine of Ideas as involving the supposition of a whole world of objects above the world of the senses, on the contrast which he, like other philosophers, made between the few and the many.

Hard thinking and dialectics had a place in this philosophy, but much of its appeal was to the heart and to the soul rather than to the head. In influential circles an inturned piety which offered to the Supreme Being the 'sacrifice of reason,' and an ascetic salvationism overshadowed Greek self-sufficiency[1]. The inspired teacher and the divine revelation were in the foreground. As teachers we have Pythagoras, of whom various lives were written, and Plato and Apollonius as portrayed by Philostratus[2], largely in the image of Pythagoras. As revelations we have the Hermetic writings, which may be dated from about A.D. 100 onwards, the 'Chaldaic Oracles,' probably of the time of Marcus Aurelius[3], which introduced *theurgia* or philosophical occultism, and the Mosaic cosmogony, as used not only by Numenius of Apamea but also up and down the Hermetica, the theological oracles ascribed to Claros[4], the kindred oracles used by Porphyry, of whom we are about to speak, and the supposed revelations of Protesilaus to a vine-tender in the Troad, as described by Philostratus in his *Heroicus*[5].

Practical men, like Cassius Dio, clung to the gospel of action, and not all philosophers turned their gaze from the world. But creativeness, apart from the development of pagan henotheism[6], lay in this direction and produced in early Neoplatonism something which had an enduring influence. A young philosopher, Porphyry of Ascalon, who had been a Christian but returned to paganism, wrote a treatise *Philosophy from the Oracles* (see below, p. 632) in which various utterances, notably from shrines of

---

[1] Cf. A. D. Nock, *Gnomon*, XII, 1936, pp. 605 *sqq.*; *J.R.S.* XXVII, 1937, p. 112.

[2] Cf. the romance of Heliodorus (see below, p. 615).

[3] W. Kroll in P.W. *s.v.* Iulianos; F. Cumont, *Religions orientales*[4], p. 294.

[4] A. D. Nock, *Revue des études anciennes*, XXX, 1928, pp. 280 *sqq.*

[5] S. Eitrem, *Symbolae Osloenses*, VIII.

[6] Cf. above, p. 437 and E. Norden, *Agnostos Theos*, pp. 78 n. 1, 155 n. 1 (on Tiberianus), 233 *sqq.* (on Firmicus Maternus before his conversion).

Hecate, were set forth and interpreted. Later he met a man of very different temper who was to be his master—Plotinus, an Egyptian by birth but in the purest Greek tradition, a mystic with a hard analytic mind. Plotinus was interested in Oriental things; he accompanied Gordian's expedition in the hope of learning Persian and Indian wisdom at first hand. Nevertheless, his system is derived from Platonic thought[1] and it is on this basis that he attacked a school of gnostics: he could not allow of absolute and positive evil, in the universe or in the human body, although the relative valuation which he allowed to both makes the antithesis between the two views seem to us much less sharp than it seemed to him; he resented dogma, but he was above all the disciple of Plato and, after the flesh, of Ammonius Saccas. In particular, his hostility was aroused by attacks, which to him looked partly insincere, on Plato and by morbid animosity against the Greek tradition. Plotinus, like the Hermetists, counted piety among the greatest of virtues; but this piety was not, for either, the piety of the populace. Plotinus drew analogies and metaphors from worship, and clearly knew the structure of an Egyptian temple; but he did not haunt the sanctuary. 'The gods must come to me, not I to them.'

Under his influence Porphyry changed: like his master he remained interested in Oriental religious traditions and his demonology seems to show an Iranian element[2], but he rejected animal sacrifice, wrote polemics in defence of asceticism, developed a simple and touching religious ethic which, as we see it in the *Letter to Marcella* (his wife), reveals the influence of the New Testament, and in his *Letter to Anebo* (an Egyptian priest) criticized severely ritual of the type which we call magical. Since both he and the Neoplatonist Hierocles wrote against Christianity, and Julian and Sallustius used Neoplatonism to interpret paganism for the educated, and Neoplatonist pagans continued to exist till the beginning of the sixth century, it has been inferred that Neoplatonism and Christianity were opposing forces. This seems ill-founded[3]. From Plotinus—or from Amelius—the opposition of Neoplatonism and gnosticism was clear: and many of the arguments used would be applicable to Catholic Christianity. Further, in a time of stress the ablest writers of paganism rallied to its defence, and these writers included outstanding Neoplatonists; when the defence had broken, the last pagans numbered

---

[1] With indebtedness to Moderatus (E. R. Dodds, *Class. Quart.* XXII, 1928, pp. 129 *sqq.*) and Ammonius Saccas.

[2] F. Cumont, *Religions orientales*[4], pp. 279 *sqq.*   [3] See below, p. 632.

in their ranks those who cared for classical culture, and these naturally included Neoplatonists. That is all; Porphyry's arguments in his *Against the Christians*[1], so far as it is known to us, do not turn on Neoplatonist doctrine, and, although any idea of divine incarnation presented difficulties, Neoplatonism was not only for Augustine the bridge from Manichaeism to Christianity but proved to others capable of combination with Christian doctrines[2]. In any case, it did not and could not produce a mass movement.

Porphyry's defence of his standpoint against simple faith in cultus died with him, although the tendency to deprecate animal sacrifice, which we have noted earlier, did not, and Ammianus Marcellinus regarded the hecatombs of Julian as wasteful and foolish. Porphyry's influence was countered by Iamblichus, who wrote an elaborate answer to the *Letter to Anebo*, under the title *On the mysteries*, supplying in it an apologetic and rationale for the various methods of constraining the gods, of securing communion with them, of causing epiphanies and the like. His disciples, such as Maximus of Ephesus, busied themselves with techniques of this kind which were known as theurgy[3]; they found an apt disciple in Julian. We must not think hardly of these men. Some (as for instance Iamblichus himself) combined these interests with a sustained power of hard thought in other fields; all had an unquestionable devotion to something which is for us hard to seize but which was for them very precious; the high moral fervour of Julian was probably not peculiar to him. Quiet reasonableness is possible in times when there is quiet, and when reason seems to justify faith in itself.

VII. ORIENTAL CULTS AND CHRISTIANITY

It has long been asked, and with reason: how did Christianity as a sacramental religion develop out of legal and non-sacramental Judaism? Justin Martyr and others were struck by the existence of baptismal and communion ceremonies in various pagan cults, argued that the Devil had in advance counterfeited Christianity. Many modern students have preferred to suppose that Christianity borrowed its sacramentalism from the Oriental mystery-religions; —either directly and deliberately or (as is easier to suppose) as a result of the unrealized but irresistible influence of an environment saturated with such ideas.

[1] See further below, pp. 630 *sqq.*
[2] Cf. Augustine, *De vera religione*, iv, 7.
[3] See below, p. 638; J. Bidez, *La vie de l'empereur Julien*, pp. 73 *sqq.*

The teachings of Jesus involved no radical break with Palestinian Judaism, and the gradual separation of the growing Church was a matter of excommunication rather than of apostasy. The Christians outside Jerusalem, to whom Paul wrote, included many of Jewish antecedents or Judaizing affinities. Their Judaism had been that of the Dispersion and not that of Jerusalem, and they spoke Greek and thought Greek. Nevertheless, they were and had been in a very sharp antithesis to surrounding paganism; that was the legacy of Antiochus Epiphanes and of the Maccabees. Further, the early converts from a purely Gentile background severed themselves from their religious past when they joined the *tertius populus*.

What changed the character of the new movement, and gave to Christian sacramentalism its special features, was the discovery that Jesus would not after all return almost at once and bring in the Sovereignty of God. The Church ceased to be a band of travellers along a short and narrow isthmus and became a normal continuing society within the world. Accordingly, the ceremony of admission and the common meal of fellowship were related to the society as a society and assumed a position comparable with the rites of ancient religious groupings and mysteries. This being so, they came to be described in similar language.

There was a special reason for this. Hellenistic Judaism had not shrunk from the metaphorical use of mystery-terminology to describe religious experiences in which the individual, as member of the Jewish circle within the world and of a narrower concentric circle within Judaism, felt himself to be the passive recipient of a transforming grace. In this, as in so much, Hellenistic Judaism followed the precedent of Greek philosophy. So did Christianity, but with a significant difference[1]. This Judaism wove its web of metaphor and imagery around individual emotions and around facts in national tradition as viewed in the light of those emotions. Christianity followed this usage, and Paul's 'mysteries' are, like Philo's, secrets of God progressively manifested[2]. But Christianity also applied this idiom to its communal ceremonies. The sect of Therapeutae, as described by Philo, evolved a subtle allegorization of the crossing of the Red Sea; Paul utilized something of the sort to explain the implications of baptism (I Cor. x). Philo explained

[1] E. R. Goodenough, *By Light, Light*; with the modifications of A. D. Nock, *Gnomon*, XIII, 1937, pp. 156 *sqq*.

[2] '*mysterion*' is here simply 'secret,' as in the Septuagint and some popular Greek, and probably conveyed to Paul no immediate suggestion of pagan rites.

the Manna given to the Israelites as the Divine Logos bestowed on man for his sustenance; Paul and the Fourth Gospel applied similar exegesis to the Christian sharing of bread and cup.

The Christian sacraments had notable differences from their pagan analogues. In Greek mysteries ceremonial and moral purity was demanded as a prerequisite, and righteous conduct after initiation was expected[1], but in the Christian mysteries a greater emphasis was laid on the moral purpose of the recipient; it was in fact a *sine qua non*[2], and the Eucharist unworthily received was unto damnation. Further, in Christianity initiates were not, as in the Oriental mystery-religions other than Mithraism, an inner circle. Nor must we forget that, although the Church early gained great strength in Rome and Africa, its chief dissemination before Constantine was in Asia Minor and Syria— that is to say, in regions characterized by local cults far more than by the mystery-religions of the 'second wave.'

On the other hand, the spread of the Oriental cults and the spread of Christianity in spite of their differences (among which we must specially stress the contrast between the world-wide hierarchical organization of Christianity and the local and congregational basis of paganism) were conditioned by common emotional needs and by a common *Weltbild*. The desire for membership of a group affording mutual aid and support, which gave to ancient cult-associations much of their attractiveness, the anxiety for insurance against an uncomfortable or shadowy hereafter, the wish to secure a powerful supernatural protector who could bend for your benefit the decrees of fate, the craving for some sort of plus-value, the eager curiosity for revelation—all these were operative in both advances. So was the desire for some sort of effective rite, for some denial by act of man's helplessness. The men who used the Christian way were not so different from those who used the pagan, and approximation can be detected in the third century.

Christianity might have come much nearer to the course of the Oriental religions in Roman paganism. But for the establishment and acceptance of the principle of authority and a binding code of conduct, largely taken from the Old Testament, the way would have been open for every kind of compromise and for independent

---

[1] Cf. M. P. Nilsson, *Arch. f. Religionswiss.* XXXII, 1935, pp. 127 *sqq.* Under the Empire we seem to see an increase in the ethical emphasis of cults.

[2] In Jewish expiatory ceremonies 'without repentance no rites availed' (G. F. Moore, *Judaism*, 1, p. 505). A notion of intention was not foreign to Greek sacrifices, but the Jewish emphasis was far sharper.

divergent development such as we see in the Dionysiac cult-societies. But for the acceptance of the Old Testament and its interpretation as the spiritual heritage of Christianity, the new religion would have found itself curiously impoverished. These bulwarks were not built in a day or without a struggle. The various movements which we group under the name of gnosticism were attempts of freer spirits to build Christianity into schemes comparable in a measure with those which Plutarch described for Egyptian religion and Numenius for Platonism blended with Judaism; they satisfied a similar desire for abstraction and instinct for innovation. The Naassenes, who flourished near Hierapolis in Phrygia in the second century of our era, took a hymn to Attis, probably Hadrianic in date, sung in theatres in which Attis was identified with Adonis, Osiris, Men, and read into it their theology—a sort of religion of all educated men. A letter ascribed (doubtless wrongly) to Hadrian speaks of men at Alexandria who worshipped Sarapis and Christ alike[1]. People of education, Greeks and liberal Jews, came into Christianity or grew up within it. Their culture involved the philosophical interpretation of sacred story and also a deep dislike of intellectual isolation. If, they argued, intelligent men agreed that the various names and cults of deities must be regarded as appropriate to the masses and sanctified by antiquity and civic or national tradition, yet in reality enshrining truth in allegory, did not the Christians mean the same things, and why should men quarrel over terms? The enemy of orthodoxy was not paganism but sophistication. What is significant is not that this tendency appears, but that it was arrested. The Jewish strain in Christianity, with its abomination of Gentile worships and its assumption that they connoted immorality; the links of community to community, which prevented unfettered development; the hierarchic system; the principle of Apostolic authority and Apostolic tradition; the numerical preponderance of folk with the *foi du charbonnier* prevented what would in effect have been the absorption of Christianity in Graeco-Roman culture.

Christianity grew steadily. Paganism went its way, but economic pressure caused a diminution in sacrificial expenditure and perhaps helped the trend towards 'the sacrifice of reason[2].'

---

[1] S.H.A. *Quad. tyr.* (*Firmus*, etc.) 8; cf. W. Bauer, *Rechtgläubigkeit und Ketzerei im ältesten Christentum*, p. 51 *sq.*

[2] An inscription of the Julianic period (see above, p. 424) recording the revival of the *taurobolium* speaks of the man responsible as offering 'deeds, mind, good action' as a sacrifice.

The litany of Licinius' army before the defeat of Maximin[1] shows how near solar henotheism could come to Christian monotheism. Revivals and survivals of paganism after Constantine's death fall outside the scope of this volume, but certain features of them are instructive for our present purpose. The aristocratic group at Rome which clung to paganism as a thing inseparable from the classical culture to which they were devoted showed enthusiasm for Mithraism and the *taurobolium*, reviving them not only under Julian but also under Eugenius. These were in a sense the most emotional, extreme and exciting forms of the old religion: to Christians they were objectionable in a corresponding degree[2]. Nevertheless, when we turn to the edicts of Christian emperors for the suppression of paganism, we find no mention of these things, but prohibition of divination, sacrifices—specially nocturnal (and therefore *ex hypothesi* magical)—magic, and finally all temple cultus. Further, while Julian was himself devoted to Mithras, to solar worship in general, to Cybele, and to theurgy (p. 443), and not inattentive to the Egyptian deities, his religious policy was directed to the restoration of Greek traditional practice coupled with borrowed elements of ethical order, philanthropy, and organization, as effective weapons of Christianity. His friend Sallustius, in his treatise *Concerning the gods and the universe*, concerns himself with the gods as a whole: he refers to the (prehistoric) 'founders of the mysteries,' but just as a Hellenistic writer might have done, and, while he speaks of the myth of Cybele and its expression in rite, he confines himself to the dramatic ceremonial which Claudius had brought to Rome. Neopaganism was to Julian *hellenismos*. The local gods, as for instance Marnas of Gaza, lasted longest[3].

---

[1] Lactantius, *de mort. pers.* 46. See below, p. 687 *sq.*

[2] Firmicus Maternus, *De errore profanarum religionum*, has been regarded as indicating that its author singled out the 'Oriental mystery-religions' as the chief foes of Christianity. They receive most space in his work, but he is describing the religions of various *races*, Egyptians, etc. (alluding in chap. 9 to Adonis as worshipped in the West—in 5 perhaps to Mithras as so worshipped —but the text is fragmentary); he does not neglect ordinary Graeco-Roman cult and myth. Ambrosiaster alludes to the cults of Cybele, Isis, Mithras, when attacking paganism in general: but he, like the writer of [Cypr.] *adv. Senatorem*, had in view the Roman aristocratic group: in any case his polemic against astrology is much longer.

[3] Cf. Mark the Deacon's *Life of Porphyry of Gaza*; see S. A. Cook, *The Religion of Ancient Palestine in the Light of Archaeology*, p. 186.

VIII. CONCLUSION

We have considered the early wave which carried Egyptian and Syrian and Anatolian worships to regions outside their homes, and the later wave which carried similar worships (though in a somewhat different form) and Mithraism through the Latin part of the world. We have also sought to estimate the diffusion and intensiveness of these cults, and our observations have led us to reject any idea of a substantial concomitant orientalization of life. Two objections might be raised; first, is this likely in view of the Oriental influence which has been so often assumed in art, law, and political forms? Second, what of the enormous change in intellectual outlook and spiritual atmosphere between Augustus and Constantine? Is not the result something much more Oriental than Greek or Roman in type and temper? And could not a shift in religious ideas be at least a contributory cause for such a transformation?

As regards the first point, legal orientalization and political orientalization within the period down to Constantine are, in fact, at best highly doubtful[1]. The precise extent of Oriental influence in art is disputable (see p. 558 *sq.*), but that there was material influence is not open to question. Nevertheless, there is this crucial difference. In art we are dealing either with imported works or with works produced by artists who had left the Near East and settled in the West or with copies of these works. In cults it is not so. When a foreign group brought a strange cult, the ministrant or ministrants of that cult belonged to its racial background; the cult of Sarapis on Delos remained in one family for generations. Control would, however, often pass to citizens: thus after Claudius, the *archigallus* at Rome was a citizen, Rome became Cybele's holy city, so far as the West was concerned, and the cult was, so to speak, de-Anatolized. Mithraism had no professional alien priests. Under these conditions, however carefully forms were preserved, there was not a personnel with genuinely alien instincts, and this must have contributed powerfully to the absorption of the cults. The suggestion which is here examined involves a modern notion of religion as mainly a matter of a specific type of ideas, distinct from those of everyday life, and such that a change of these ideas will alter men's attitudes. Alteration is effected by conversion to the prophetic religions; but, even there, it is not as a rule thorough-going and here, it can seldom have resulted from adhesion to one of these cults.

[1] Cf. N. H. Baynes, *J.R.S.* xxv, 1935, pp. 83 *sqq.*

As for the second point, the crucial issue was again not cults or race but men. The Syrian Orontes did, as Juvenal says, flow into the Tiber, and even non-Oriental elements, as they entered the ruling class, did not show as sensitive a repugnance to Oriental cults as their predecessors had done. But race is not everything; Lucian of Samosata was probably a pure Semite—as much so as Elagabalus—and as a boy he did not talk Greek, and yet he clung to the old order at a time when many pure Hellenes had followed after other things. Intellectual and literary activity are largely determined by conventions and by a man's choice; Frederick the Great was as Prussian as his father, but he preferred to try to think and write in French.

The change in spiritual atmosphere between Augustus and Constantine is part of a long gradual transformation. Our fathers could quote Swinburne's

> Thou hast conquered, O pale Galilean; the world has grown grey from thy breath

and could think in terms of an antithesis between a free untrammelled Greek mind and a dogmatic medievalism, or between clean-limbed models for Pheidias and unwashed hermits. That is all past; we know now that paganism had of itself gone far in the direction of grayness and dogmatism and asceticism. Athens had known great days, when a brilliant minority had enjoyed the stimulus of an intelligent and well-integrated society, and when for minority and majority alike men's feet seemed surely set on paths which led to unlimited horizons. Humanity looked at the world, and found it good; and the Orphic insistence on a sense of sin, a hatred of the body, and a yearning for salvation was left to a hypochondriac few. Nevertheless, even before the end of the Periclean age, new forms of individualism and new external conditions threatened the old harmony. Great achievements and glittering prizes were still in store, but no new satisfying adjustment. The cosmopolitan minority of intellectuals were driven in on themselves. Philosophy could no more build a city; she did but strive to give man shelter under a wall, 'as in a storm.' The brilliant success of the Roman Principate in its first two centuries gave a new hope but did not kill a sense of futility and disintegration. After Marcus Aurelius the days were darkened; coarser natures and cruder ways had to serve the needs of harder times. Meanwhile a new order was coming to birth.

CHAPTER XIII

PAGAN PHILOSOPHY AND THE CHRISTIAN CHURCH

I. THE FORMATION OF THE CANON

AFTER the execution of Ignatius of Antioch, in the days of Trajan[1], the Christian Church enjoyed a long period of peace from persecution by the State. But the 'struggle for existence' never ends, and the period from about 120 to 190 shews us the new Society adapting itself to its environment in the Roman Empire. In the great work of Irenaeus *Against Heresies* (A.D. 186) we find a literary expression of the Catholic system, so complete and successful that the whole history of the Church from Irenaeus to the Reformation, and even later, may be viewed as a natural development of it[2]. Before Irenaeus, on the other hand, new factors were continually presenting themselves. Some of these the Church accepted; others it rejected, but in rejecting them the opinion of the dominant party was profoundly modified. At the end of the period the Church's face is definitely turned back to the infallible Past, to the tradition and memory of the days of the first apostles.

The Christian Church, at the beginning of the period considered in this chapter, was a somewhat loosely organized collection of local societies. They were held together mainly by a common Hope and a Holy Book. The Hope was that their Lord Jesus, who had been crucified in Judaea and yet had risen again, was coming very soon from heaven to judge the living and the dead and to renew the earth, and they believed that their Holy Book (which was also the Holy Book of the Jews) had foretold this of their Lord, as well as many details of His career when He lived on earth. Both these main Articles of Faith were encompassed with difficulties, both in themselves and as *credenda* for new converts.

The consideration of the Bible and its place in the Christian scheme is mainly an affair of ecclesiastical history and development, leading to the formation of the Christian Canon of the Old and the New Testaments, but it is necessary to have some idea of the trains of thought which led up to this conclusion and to con-

[1] See vol. XI, p. 292.   [2] See vol. XI, p. 253.

sider briefly some of the main personalities connected with it. We must, in the first place, dismiss altogether from our minds the modern evolutionary view which believes that truth and excellence of every kind have developed by a sort of organic process from small and perhaps unlovely beginnings, with fresh elements of real value coming in from time to time by what is not so much evolution as 'epigenesis[1].' Neither the Christians nor the pagans so regarded the Old Testament. It was true or false, enlightening or the reverse. There was, it is true, much in the Bible which was shocking to the would-be convert. It was not so much the miraculous element and the geocentric outlook that were a difficulty to the heathen, for these things they shared with the Christian, but they were deterred by the barbarous style of the Greek and by the presence of trifling regulations and taboos which seemed to be beneath the dignity of the Highest God. On the other hand, the Christians were able to argue that the whole Bible, i.e. the 'Old Testament,' was written long before Plato; and the 'argument from prophecy,' i.e. the assertion that this or that event in the career of Jesus Christ had been indicated by Hebrew Prophets long ago, seems to have had real weight.

The difficulty felt by the Christians was rather this: if the Bible was the very word of God, by what right did Christians disobey so many of the plain commands found in it? Christians ate pork and hare, and disregarded all the ritual laws of the Pentateuch: was the Pentateuch after all God's book? One answer to this question was given in the Epistle of Barnabas, a very early document, perhaps Alexandrian, which maintained that all the so-called food-laws were misinterpreted by the Jews and that they were really moral commands to avoid the society of various types of sinners. The Bible, on this view, was wholly moral, but obscurely expressed. Another view, given by one Ptolemaeus, a disciple of Valentinus the gnostic[2], was that we have to distinguish different elements in the Jewish code. There are elements which come merely from the 'tradition of the elders,' others that were added by Moses because of the hardness of the Israelites' hearts, others that are really divine. Of this last class, some were figurative, like the command to eat unleavened bread at Passover, now fulfilled in Christ; other things are permanent, like the Decalogue. A very similar theory to this is to be found in the Didascalia, a manual for Christians written somewhere in the East during the first half of

---

[1] See the note by G. Tyrrell in Christianity at the Cross-Roads, p. 18, on the significance of the concept of epigenesis for theology.

[2] In Epiphanius, Haer. xxxiii, 3 sqq. (known as the Epistle to Flora).

the third century. In this work we are taught that the good Law is the Ten Words and the Judgments, given before the Israelites made the golden calf and served idols. But the rest was given because the Lord was angry with them, and so He laid on the Israelites new and burdensome laws, from which Jesus has delivered Christians.

A more radical solution was championed by Marcion of Pontus. According to the Chronicle of Edessa he left the Catholic Church in A.D. 138, so that we may place his career between 100 and 170, during the first half of which he was not a declared heretic. He started from the kindness of the Father whom Jesus had announced, and whose gracious willingness to forgive freely was different in character from the severe justice of the God of the Bible. Marcion concluded that they could not be the same, and that the Gospel of Jesus was something wholly new. According to Marcion, the world set forth in the Bible, *i.e.* the Old Testament, is the product of Law acting upon Matter. Law cannot and will not forgive: the God of Law and Justice exacts 'an eye for an eye and a tooth for a tooth,' in other words 'action and reaction are equal and opposite.' Man was formed in the image of the God of the Bible, and when he, man, breaks the just laws of that God, God punishes him as he deserves. So the human race went on for many generations, till seeing their misery the Kind Father sent His Son to live among men and heal their sins and diseases. Jesus and His Father are nowhere clearly defined or differentiated. They represent Grace, a third Principle, distinct from Matter and its Laws.

To Marcion, Jesus was not born: He appeared in Judaea in the fifteenth year of Tiberius, as the Gospel says[1], and went about doing good among men. After a while the God of Law instigated Jesus's enemies to kill Him. But death had no power over Jesus. He appeared alive at the right hand of the God of Law and pointed out that He, Jesus, had only done good to men: the God of Law was guilty of His death. For this the God of Law, according to the Law itself, deserved to die, but Jesus agreed to take in exchange the souls of all those who accepted the Christian Gospel. So He descended again and revealed to Paul, the only true disciple, that we have been 'bought with a price[2].'

It is easy to pick holes in this fantastic scheme, as indeed Tertullian and Epiphanius and other Church writers did. But it is almost impossible to exaggerate the importance of Marcion for the development of the Church. In the first place, the rival Church

---

[1] Lk. iii, 1.   [2] 1 Cor. vi, 20.

that he founded lasted for centuries. Its organization was very much that of the Great Church, so like, in fact, that it is thought probable that he was a pioneer and that many features of the Catholic hierarchy were adapted from the Marcionite system. It is certain, at least, that the Marcionites produced their share of martyrs, for instance the presbyter Metrodorus, who met his death in the Decian persecution.

The sacramental theory of the Marcionites, which refused baptism and the Eucharist to married persons, we meet with again in the Syriac-speaking Church of Mesopotamia[1]. But some words must here be given to the Marcionite Bible, which is very closely connected with the origin of the Canon of the New Testament. Marcion rejected the God of the Jews as his God, and so rejected the Old Testament which told him of that God. He made great use of it, it is true, in his story of the formation of Adam, but it had for him no authority. He was left without a Bible. In its place he put an account of the words and deeds of Jesus, and a collection of the writings of His true apostle Paul.

The elaborate investigations, made during the nineteenth century, of the relation of the Marcionite 'Gospel' to the tale told by Luke in his First Volume (i.e. the gospel) have substantially confirmed the allegations of Tertullian and Epiphanius, that Marcion took 'Luke' and arbitrarily altered it, mostly by cutting out incidents which he regarded as Jewish perversion of the true Gospel[2]. Where the Church Fathers are wrong is in their natural assumption that Marcion chose out one of the four Canonical Gospels and mutilated it. In Marcion's day these works existed, but they were not yet 'canonical.' It is likely that Marcion regarded his procedure as that of extracting from a bulky historical work[3] those records of the Lord Jesus which seemed to him to be genuine.

Marcion's 'Apostolicon' consisted of ten letters of Paul, *i.e.* the collection familiar to us, *minus* the Pastoral letters (and of course Hebrews), but including Philemon. The earlier history of the Pauline Epistles is obscure and the occasion of their first collection as a Corpus is uncertain. Some of the Pauline Epistles were in general circulation before the end of the first century. Clement of Rome clearly knew and used Romans and at the appropriate moment[4] he bids the Corinthians 'take up the Epistle of the

---

[1] See below pp. 493 *sqq.*

[2] See particularly the telling appeal to the Concordance in Sanday's *Gospels in the Second Century*, pp. 222–230, an argument that has never been answered.

[3] Lucas, *ad Theophilum*, vols. I and II.   [4] *Ep.* I *ad Cor.* XLVII, I

blessed Paul the Apostle' in which the Apostle had charged them concerning the evils of partisanship (1 Cor. i. 11 *sqq*.). Ignatius, likewise, certainly knew 1 Corinthians; he probably knew Ephesians also, and he may have known other Pauline letters. Decisive evidence is lacking, but it is not unlikely that a collection of Pauline Epistles, of the same compass as Marcion's, was already in existence when Ignatius wrote. There is, at any rate, good reason to think that the compiler of the Pastoral Epistles was familiar with the rest of the Pauline Corpus in its entirety[1]. But for Marcion—now left without the Bible of the Church, that is the Old Testament—the writings of Paul the one true Apostle attained a new position of paramount authority. True they, like St Luke's Gospel, could not be accepted as they stood, but required to be purged of many a judaizing corruption. Thus purged, they were made to form a second constituent part of Marcion's new Canon of Scripture. Marcion was the first formally to 'canonize' the Pauline Epistles.

The Catholic Church could not fall behind the heretic in the authority which it bestowed upon the writings of the Apostle. For it too the Pauline Epistles became Scripture. Indeed, there is evidence that Marcion's edition of the Pauline letters directly influenced the New Testament of the Catholic Church[2].

A Life and Sayings of Jesus and a Collection of Pauline Letters —here we have the germ of a New Bible. The Church followed Marcion's lead. But whereas Marcion made his 'Gospel' and his 'Apostle' a substitute for the old Bible, the Church got its larger collection of apostolic writings as a New Testament alongside the Old Testament.

II. MONTANISM AND THE NEW PROPHECY

In the first Christian communities as we know them from the books of the New Testament we find prophets taking a leading part in the common life and holding a place second only to that

[1] P. N. Harrison, *The Problem of the Pastoral Epistles*, pp. 88–92; 167–175. An important witness for a full Pauline Corpus is Polycarp, who quotes from 1 and 2 Tim. as well as from 1 Cor., Gal., Rom., 2 Thess., Ephes., Philipp. But the date of this part of Polycarp's letter is under dispute. Dr Harrison assigns it to *c.* A.D. 136–137. (*Polycarp's Two Epistles to the Philippians*, p. 315. See below, p. 474.)

[2] This evidence mainly comes from the Latin *Argumenta* detected as Marcionite in 1907 by Dom de Bruyne. For the influence of Marcion upon the New Testament of the Catholic Church cf. A. von Harnack, *Die Briefsammlung des Apostels Paulus*, pp. 17–23.

of the Apostles. A prophet speaking under the direction of the Spirit has a recognized claim on the acceptance of the Church. The first Epistle to the Corinthians shews the Apostle Paul seeking to guide and control the enthusiastic utterance of the prophets. The prophetic ministry appears to have maintained its place in the succeeding generation: the Apocalypse is a literary movement of Christian prophecy in the closing years of the first century, and Ignatius of Antioch, himself a bishop, speaks under the influence of inspiration.

The writings of Irenaeus illustrate the changes which had passed over prophecy in the Church by the later decades of the second century. Irenaeus has very little to say about Christian prophets; his main task had been to stem the rising flood of gnostic heresy and for this purpose he relied upon the appeal to apostolic tradition. At the same time he has no doubt that the prophetic gift continues in the Church; he appeals to the now canonized texts of Paul which speak of men and women prophesying in the congregation, and finds it necessary to warn his readers of the danger of expelling prophecy from the Church[1]. Some time before Irenaeus wrote prophecy had ceased to occupy the place it once had held. Already in the *Didache* it is plain that while in principle the highest veneration and respect is still accorded to the prophet, the danger of imposture is acutely felt, and the local ministry is tending to take over rights and duties formerly associated with the prophet. The first enthusiasm has passed. In Hermas, the Roman seer, we can detect the gradual dying down of inspiration. It is difficult not to feel that his work known as *The Shepherd* covers more than half a life-time. In the first 'Visions' we have the experiences of an ecstatic, not always quite coherent; in the long 'Similitudes' at the end we have moral and dogmatic teaching set forth in wearisome and laboured parables, without literary charm and only redeemed by their obvious sincerity and their manful grappling with difficult problems[2].

It is likely that the decline in prophecy was not everywhere equally pronounced. There have come down to us from the earlier decades of the second century the names of an Asiatic prophet Quadratus, and a prophetess Ammia of Philadelphia[3], and this may indicate that the ministry of prophecy had maintained itself

---

[1] *adv. Haer.* III, 11, 12.

[2] See the appreciation in A. Schweitzer, *Mysticism of Paul the Apostle*, p. 289.

[3] Scriptor anon. *ap.* Eusebius, *Hist. Eccl.* V, 17, 3–4. Cf. *ib.* III, 37, 1.

more effectively among the churches to which the prophet John had once addressed the letters of the Apocalypse. It was at any rate in Phrygia that a new prophetic movement flared up in the latter half of the second century which set problems to the Church leaders in the chief centres of the Christian faith throughout the world. There can be little doubt that Montanus and his prophecy was in the mind of Irenaeus when he so plainly vindicated the legitimacy of prophecy within the Church. Not that Irenaeus was ever himself an adherent of the new movement, but he had taken part in an attempt at reconciliation in connection with Montanism[1], and his words shew that he was deeply concerned at the reaction which Montanism had provoked[2].

The 'New Prophecy,' as Montanism was often called, was generated in the vivid expectation of the coming of the Kingdom of Christ on earth, which filled the thoughts of many Christians of this period[3]. When Gratus was proconsul of Asia[4], Montanus, formerly perhaps a priest of Cybele, fell into a trance at the village of Ardabau in Mysia near Phrygia soon after his conversion, and prophesied in the power of the Spirit. Two women, Priscilla and Maximilla, were later likewise struck with the prophetic afflatus. These left their husbands and joined themselves to the mission of Montanus.

Our knowledge of the original Montanism is derived almost entirely from the hostile reports of contemporary Asiatic Church

[1] Eusebius, *Hist. Eccl.* v, 3, 4.

[2] The text of the passage in Irenaeus referred to above (p. 455, n. 1) is very obscure as it stands. If, with Ritschl, Bonwetsch, de Labriolle, and others, we accept the emendation '*pseudoprophetas quidem esse volunt*' for '*pseudoprophetae quidem esse volunt*' everything falls into place.

[3] Cf. the stories of the Syrian bishop who led out men, women and children of his flock to meet Christ in the desert, and of the bishop in Pontus who disorganized the life of many of his people by his confident prophecy that the Judgment would come upon the earth within a year, related by Hippolytus, *In Daniel.* IV, 18, 19.

[4] Scriptor anon. *ap.* Eusebius, *Hist. Eccl.* v, 16, 7. Unfortunately the proconsulship of Gratus cannot be fixed, and the date of the rise of Montanism is uncertain. Epiphanius would fix it in A.D. 156–7 (*Haer.* XLVIII, 1) and this date is adopted by Bonwetsch, Harnack and others; Eusebius in 172 in the Armenian version of the *Chronicon* under Olympiad 238, 1. (Cf. de Labriolle, *La crise Montaniste,* p. 570 and cf. *Hist. Eccl.* IV, 27.) The text of Epiphanius, *Haer.* LI, 33 as commented on by Holl, *Berlin Corpus* II, p. 307 would support the dating of Eusebius. Cf. the full discussion in de Labriolle, *op. cit.* pp. 569–89. It may be that the two datings refer to different events in Montanist history; so H. J. Lawlor and J. E. L. Oulton, *The Ecclesiastical History of Eusebius,* II, p. 180 *sq.*

writers from whose works Eusebius has happily preserved extensive extracts. Tertullian—the one convert to Montanism of first-rate importance—provides us with evidence of Montanist belief and practice in Africa at the beginning of the third century (p. 537 *sq.*). But except for scanty fragments preserved mainly in Tertullian and in Epiphanius, the collections of Oracles, which for Montanist believers had the authority of direct revelations, have perished. Slender as the sources of our knowledge are, they yet enable us to recover the main characteristics of the teaching and mission of Montanus and his associates.

The fundamental convictions of the New Prophecy in its earliest form were, first that the Heavenly Jerusalem was shortly to descend upon the earth—its arrival was expected at the little Phrygian township of Pepuza—and that Montanus himself was indwelt by that Paraclete of whom Jesus had promised that He should come after Him to carry on His work. Concerning the Paraclete Jesus in St John's Gospel had said: 'I have yet many things to say unto you, but ye cannot bear them now; but when he, the Spirit of truth, is come, he shall guide you into all the truth' (xvi, 12–13). These words afforded a scriptural basis for the Montanist claim, which so shocked the common sentiment of the Church, that the apostolic teaching—nay the teaching of Christ Himself—was incomplete and that a fuller revelation had now been vouchsafed which the Church was called upon to accept[1]. Yet bolder language is attributed to Montanus: Epiphanius quotes him as saying: 'I am neither an angel, nor a messenger, but I am come the Lord God, the Father[2].' There is probably some misunderstanding here. Montanus no doubt thought himself to be the medium through which God spoke, but it is unlikely that he thought himself to be personally God. His own view of the divine activity is expressed in another oracle: 'Behold man is as a lyre and I hover over him as a plectrum. Man sleeps, and I wake; behold it is the Lord who removes the hearts of man and gives them [other] hearts[3].' The leaders of the movement thought of their mission as the final phase of revelation. 'After me,' said Maximilla, 'there shall be no prophetess more; then will be the end[4].'

The tense expectation of the coming Judgment was associated in Montanism with an ascetic rigorism which accentuated tendencies already powerful in the Church. The martyr's death, though it was not to be directly courted, was not to be eluded by

[1] Tertullian, *de virg. vel.* 1.   [2] Epiphanius, *Haer.* XLVIII, 11.
[3] *ib.* XLVIII, 4.   [4] *ib.* XLVII, 2.

flight. With respect to fasting Montanus strengthened the prevailing requirement, making the Wednesday and the Friday fasts obligatory and extending their duration. Again, the Montanist Churches prohibited second marriages, agreeing in this with an earlier Christian tradition which regarded second marriage as 'fair-seeming adultery[1].' Of Montanus it is said by an early antagonist that he 'taught the dissolution of marriage[2],' and it seems likely that the movement in its early stages discouraged, if it did not actually forbid, married life. Maximilla and Priscilla had left their husbands. The strength of similar tendencies within the Church is well illustrated by the Apocryphal Acts of John, of Peter and of Paul, which emanated from Asia Minor in the second half of the second century.

In general the temper of the movement was conservative and orthodox. Enemies admitted that they held the articles of the common faith of the Church. If there was a tendency to Monarchianism (p. 533) among a section of the Montanists, this was no Montanist peculiarity. They venerated the same scriptures as the Church, and they had no quarrel with the Church's hierarchy as such. When they were forced into the position of a separate sect they appear to have carried on the threefold ministry of the Church while imposing upon it the superior orders of Patriarchs (resident at Pepuza) and Associates ($\kappa o \iota \nu \omega \nu o \hat{\iota}$)[3]. Yet to the great Church now organizing itself into a hierarchy of authority, the fundamental claim of Montanism inevitably wore the aspect of a challenge. If the Paraclete directly declared the will of Christ through Montanus, authority was powerless. Here is the historical significance of Montanism: it was this claim which more than anything else roused the episcopacy of Asia to a fierce condemnation of the New Prophecy. Montanism could not meet that attack: its power was broken in Central Phrygia but it may well be that withdrawing from the cities it strengthened itself among the peasantry. In the villages of the Tembris valley there are funeral monuments dating from the third century, which differ from other Christian monuments in Phrygia, whereas in other monuments Christians were content to veil their Christianity in

---

[1] Athenagoras, *Suppl.* 33.

[2] Apollonius *ap.* Eusebius, *Hist. Eccl.* v, 18, 2.

[3] These higher orders carried on, it may be presumed, the succession of the first originators of the movement. For the Montanist hierarchy see Jerome, *Ep.* 41, 3, and *Cod. Just.* i, 5, 20. The texts are discussed in de Labriolle, *La crise Montaniste*, pp. 495–507. The title $\kappa o \iota \nu \omega \nu \acute{o} \varsigma$ has been found in an inscription dated A.D. 514–15 from the neighbourhood of Philadelphia (*Byzantion*, ii, 1925, p. 330).

neutral formulae, the makers of these monuments boldly professed their faith as 'Christians addressing Christians.' It has
been conjectured that they were Montanists[1].

Montanism forced the Church to wrestle with the problem of
the legitimacy of ecstasy in prophecy and the place of prophecy
amongst orthodox Christians[2]; it contributed towards the establishment of a closed canon of scripture to which no new revelations could be added. This is an idea which in the last quarter of
the second century found expression in the works of Irenaeus and
the so-called 'Muratorian Canon,' which enumerates the books of
the New Testament and ends by condemning the 'Cataphrygians.'
Again, the wide sphere which Montanism had opened to woman
within the Church[3] led the Catholics anxiously to maintain the
restrictions which St Paul had set upon the public ministry of
women. Thus the challenge of the New Prophecy did but serve
to strengthen the hierarchical government of the Catholic Church.
It is in connection with the opposition to Montanism that we first
hear of the summoning of Church councils. The believers in Asia,
we are told, held frequent meetings with regard to the New
Prophecy, and after testing the utterances of the prophets agreed
to excommunicate its adherents[4]. This was a momentous innovation: through these assemblages guided by the Holy Spirit the
Church gained a new realization alike of its unity and its strength.

The strenuous opposition of the leaders of the Church pre-

---

[1] The view that these inscriptions were Montanist is not undisputed. See
Revue de l'Univ. de Bruxelles, XXXVI, Oct. 1930, p. 233, where Grégoire
gives reasons for withdrawing his acceptance of that view. But the use of
the word Χρειστιανῶν in an inscription which on other grounds has been
judged to be Montanist gives support to Calder's view that they are
Montanist (*Byzantion*, VI, 1931, p. 423 *sq.*).

[2] On this cf. de Labriolle, *op. cit.* pp. 555 *sqq.* At a later date the same
problem was raised for the Church by Priscillianism.

[3] The prophesying of Priscilla and Maximilla set a precedent which unquestionably influenced the later practice of the Montanist Churches.
According to Epiphanius (*Haer.* XLIX, 11), the Montanists admitted women
to be bishops and presbyters, but his statement is open to question. Cf. de
Labriolle, *op. cit.* pp. 507–12. It is not certain that the prophetess who
celebrated the Eucharist referred to by Firmilian (Cyprian, *Ep.* LXXV, 7)
was Montanist. It is in itself probable that women were eligible for the
higher orders of patriarch and κοινωνός. A Montanist inscription discovered in the neighbourhood of Pepuza, and assigned to the late third
century, gives the names of a man and a woman side by side on an official
marble cathedra. There can be little doubt that they both held high place in
the Montanist hierarchy. See *Byzantion*, VI, 1931, p. 423 *sq.*

[4] Scriptor anon. *ap.* Eusebius, *Hist. Eccl.* V, 16, 10.

vented the New Prophecy from winning the acceptance which it
sought of the Church at large. Against its own will and intention,
Montanism became a sect. As a sect it had a long history[1]. In the
West it appears to have declined rapidly in influence. After Tertullian not a word is heard of Montanism at Carthage. It may be that
here, as perhaps elsewhere, Montanists fused with the like-minded
Novatianists (p. 540 sq.). But later, in the fourth century, there
were Montanists at Barcelona as well as at Rome. The corporate
existence of the sect at Rome was probably ended by a decree of
Honorius in A.D. 407. In the East Montanism fought harder and
lived longer. Clement of Alexandria found it necessary to refute
the heresy, and Origen also takes occasion to discuss and repudiate
its claims. In the fourth century it counted many adherents in
Asia Minor and had found a foothold in Constantinople. Like
other heretical bodies it fell under the ban of the Christian emperors, and though a last echo is heard as late as the ninth century,
it was probably virtually extinguished by the persecuting legislation of Justinian, under whom the Montanists in Phrygia shut
their Churches with themselves inside and set fire to them over
their heads[2].

III. THE APOLOGISTS

Early Christian apologetic was the outcome of persecution: it
was because 'certain wicked men were endeavouring to molest
our people' that Quadratus presented to Hadrian the first
Christian apology. It is to protest against the injustice of the
Roman State in regarding the confession of the Christian faith
—the *nomen Christianum*—as a punishable offence, to meet the
popular charges of 'atheism,' cannibalism, and Thyestean orgies
that in succession the Apologists composed their defences of the
Christian revelation. In these writings the hated sect appeals
against the judgment of the Roman world.

The Christian Apologists of the second century thus possess a
significance out of all proportion to their intellectual ability or to
the intrinsic literary merits of their works. With them the Christian Church enters for the first time into the common world of
literature and culture. The writings of the first age of Christianity
were directed to the guidance and edification of the faithful: a
contagious missionary movement had spread itself in the main
centres of commercial and political life and won adherents chiefly,
though not exclusively, among the lower social strata of society.

[1] For the later history of Montanism, see de Labriolle, *op. cit.* pp. 469–536.
[2] Procopius, *Hist. Arc.* XI, 23.

Bound together by an intense and enthusiastic conviction, these
newly converted believers had not yet found it necessary to state
a case for their faith in order to conciliate the instructed opinion
of the unconverted world. It is indeed possible that some such aim
was not entirely unfamiliar to the author of the Third Gospel and
the Book of Acts. But even the Lucan writings, like all the rest of
the New Testament literature, and the writings of the Apostolic
Fathers, are primarily intended for, and would only be intelligible
to, a believing public. The Apologists, on the other hand, deliberately aimed at influencing the opinion of the world. A new
culture is beginning to take shape. The Christian Church has
become conscious of itself as a 'third race,' alongside pagans and
Jews; and it seeks to win public recognition and legal toleration
from the powers that be.

The Apologists presented their faith in the guise of a new and
superior 'philosophy' which claimed to supersede the rival and
contradictory philosophies of the pagan world. They address
themselves to the world at large, or—more frequently—to the
reigning emperor. Whether or not such writings ever reached
the hands of the emperor himself may be doubted. But even if
this style of address is to be regarded as mere literary form, it is
none the less significant of the apologetic aim. The Christian
Church is coming to think of itself as the bearer of a world religion, related to the world-wide empire of Rome. Thus, one of
the later Apologists, Melito of Sardes, addressing Marcus
Aurelius, speaks in these terms of the Christian faith: 'A philosophy which formerly flourished among the barbarians, but which
during the great reign of your ancestor Augustus sprang up among
the nations which you rule, so that it became a blessing of good
omen to your Empire.' 'To this power,' he continues, 'you have
succeeded as men have desired; and in this power you will continue with your son, on condition that you guard that philosophy
which has grown with the Empire, and which came into existence
under Augustus.' He affirms that Nero and Domitian alone of
the successors of Augustus had been misled into a policy of hostility to the Church[1]. Melito expresses a conviction of which the
writings of the Greek Apologists were at once a symptom and a
cause.

There is little that is original in these apologies. Christianity
was following in the wake of Judaism, and though actual dependence upon particular Jewish writings can seldom be established, certain main themes have been taken over from the

---

[1] *Ap.* Eusebius, *Hist. Eccl.* IV, 26, 7 *sqq.*

propagandist literature of Hellenistic Judaism. Christian and Jewish Apologists alike maintained the superior antiquity and originality of the Jewish scriptures as against the writings of the Greeks, and argued that the classical writers of Greece had borrowed from Moses. Christian Apologists, no less than Jewish, were concerned to pour scorn upon the idolatrous practices and the immoral mythologies of paganism. Again, Hellenistic Jews had anticipated Christians in drawing upon the language and ideas of current popular philosophy, to explain and commend their religious beliefs. But while the Christian Apologists laid under contribution the literature both of Jews and Greeks, they were not the less loyal to the main convictions of the primitive Christian faith. While the use of popular philosophical ideas enabled them to establish contact with the world at large, these ideas are never substituted for the tradition of the Church. The two streams run side by side. The ethical standard of the Christian Church is steadfastly upheld; there is no wavering in their conviction that the Old Testament Scriptures are directly inspired by the Divine Spirit, and that the prophecies contained therein have been fulfilled in the Life, Death and Resurrection of Jesus Christ; lastly, the general belief of the Church of the second century, that this same Jesus is to come again to judge the world, and to inaugurate a millennial kingdom upon earth, maintains its ground.

Indeed it is not in the inherited material, but in the faith which has turned this material to its own uses that the interest lies. Here is the triumphant proclamation of a new freedom—a liberation from the oppression which weighed so heavily upon the pagan world of that day. Man was no longer the victim of the malice of the countless demon powers which beset his life: the victory over the demons had been won once and for all time, and that victory could be appropriated by the humblest Christian through faith. The numberless gods of the pagan pantheon were but a demonic delusion: there was but one God, and the Divine Word issuing from that God offered to all men release from subjection to arbitrary and immoral deities. The message of Good Tidings came to the convert as a mighty liberation, precisely as it did in the beginning of the Church's history (vol. XI, p. 275 *sq.*). The stars in their courses (so pagans declared) determined the life of man and there was no escape from inexorable Fate: here again the Apologists can claim to bring to the pagan world release, for they can assure man that despite the stars he is the master of his own soul and that his will is free: with himself rests his destiny—whether he claim an immortality of bliss or choose a punishment which shall have no end. One can still catch the thrill of this declaration of independence, by which, through faith, the convert could pass from the prison of a determinist universe.

Through these early apologies there runs a democratic exultation: this gospel of liberation is not confined to the cultured few, it is no aristocratic *gnosis*. It appeals to women as well as men, to young and old alike, to rich and poor, to the slave as well as to the free man. It is indeed a catholic proclamation. As 'sisters' and 'brothers' all can find a place in the family of the Christian faith. It is easy to ascribe too great an importance to the terminology through which the message is expressed: naturally the Apologist employs the common language of the culture of his day. Some converts were formerly pagan philosophers, and philosophers they remained after their conversion. Christian theology was still in the making and the theological thought of the Apologists is tentative, exploratory. For the pagan of the second century his philosophy was essentially religious, and the motive force which drives the Christian convert to present his faith in philosophic guise is throughout a religious conviction. The modern reader misses a reference to the Gospels, but the 'memoirs' of the Apostles were but lately written: they lacked the authority which was generally attributed to antiquity. It was a far more cogent argument to appeal to those more ancient scriptures—the writings of the prophets confirmed as they were by the recent fulfilment of their prophecies. The faith which was born under Tiberius—a faith but of yesterday—had its roots in an immemorial past; before there was a Greece there was Christianity.

The earliest Christian apology—that of Quadratus—we no longer possess. Eusebius, indeed, declares that it was addressed to Hadrian, but its date and place of composition remain uncertain[1]. The earliest surviving apology is the recently recovered work of Aristides, a 'philosopher' of Athens, which Eusebius states was, like that of Quadratus, addressed to Hadrian[2]: many scholars have thought that in view of the Syriac translation's heading 'To Adrianus Antoninus' that it was to Antoninus Pius that the apology was presented. Aristides writes in an artless style, and his thought is as simple as his language. Beginning with a rational argument for the existence of God, he proceeds to review the three

---

[1] *Hist. Eccl.* IV, 3, 1. It was perhaps composed in Asia Minor: the Chronicle of Eusebius dates the apology to A.D. 124–126. Cf. O. Bardenhewer, *Gesch. d. altkirch. Literatur*[2], I, p. 184 *sq.*

[2] *Hist. Eccl.* IV, 3, 3.

great types of religion, Paganism, Judaism and Christianity[1]. The greater part of the book is taken up with a polemic against the false pagan cults of Chaldaeans, Greeks and Egyptians. In contrast to the polytheistic heathen the Jews recognize the One True God; yet they, too, have gone astray in the practice of their faith, which is rather a worship of angels than a worship of God. Aristides then turns to the Christian religion. He attempts no reasoned defence of the new faith, but is content to describe who the Christians are; whence they are derived; who Jesus Christ was, and what are the commands which He has 'graven in the hearts of Christians.' Finally, he proclaims the judgment which God is to bring upon the world.

The extensive genuine works of Justin give the best picture of the attitude of second-century Christians to their chief opponents. In his apology he begins by asserting that Christians are not 'atheists,' as was generally supposed; their morals are excellent, following the ethical teaching of Christ, which is illustrated by extracts from the Gospels (mostly from Matthew and Luke); Christ was spoken of by prophets who had lived centuries before Him. Those who are persuaded that the truth is with the Christians are admitted to their Society by a bath, called also 'illumination' and 'rebirth,' and are then allowed to partake of the Christian ritual meal called 'Eucharist,' which is described in general terms. It takes place on Sundays after they have read in their sacred books and heard a discourse from their president. Justin has already mentioned that they prayed for the Imperial power.

In the other chief work of Justin, the Dialogue with the Jew Trypho, we have Justin's attitude towards the Old Testament. At the opening of the first apology[2] Justin had expressed the main lines of his theology: Christians are not 'atheists,' they worship the Creator of all things, put their Master Jesus Christ in the second place, and the prophetic Spirit in the third. In the Dialogue this theory is expanded. Christ is the Word (*Logos*) of God, who sometimes appeared in various forms to Biblical heroes of old time, in the shape of a man to Abraham, as fire in the bush to Moses, and finally was born as a human being of the Virgin Mary,

---

[1] The view of J. Geffcken (*Zwei griech. Apolog.* p. 46), adopting the threefold classification of the Greek text as against the fourfold classification of the Syrian Version (Barbarians, Greeks, Jews and Christians) preferred by Seeberg and others, as the original, is here followed. This threefold classification answers to the prevailing conception of the Christians as 'The Third Race' already found in the early second-century *Praedic. Petri ap.* Clement Alex. *Strom.* VI, 5.   [2] § 13.

and was crucified and rose again. Before this the Divine Spirit, speaking by the Hebrew prophets, had predicted many of the events which were to happen in His earthly life. This 'Word' of God is distinct from the ultimate, invisible Creator.

Justin is here making use of a term current in popular contemporary philosophy, where it provided a mediating principle between the Supreme God, and the phenomenal world. By its means he is able to give an intelligible interpretation of the Biblical revelation, and supremely of the Person of Jesus Christ Himself; while at the same time he is able to explain the partial revelations, which, as he holds, have been made to other peoples. All good and holy men of whatever race have been inspired by the same Logos, and thus Justin is able to claim that whatever has been truly said by the sages of all peoples—Socrates and Plato, for instance—belongs of right to the Christians. The Logos doctrine as it appears in Justin is undeveloped. Justin is not a great thinker, and he does not see that his theory of the 'Spermatic' Word, present in some degree in all mankind, makes superfluous his alternative theory that Greek wisdom is historically derived from the Prophets of the Old Covenant. But though it is easy to point to inconsistencies and inconsequences in Justin's thought, it was none the less a momentous step when Justin raised for Christian theology—almost by accident—the perennial problem of the relations between faith and reason, 'natural religion' and revelation.

The long Dialogue with Trypho ends with friendly speeches; it is not stated that Trypho is converted to Christianity. The object of the work is mainly an expression in dialogue form of Justin's own theology, and thereby of the Church's attitude to paganism on the one side and to Judaism on the other. As against Judaism the Church was determined to hold on to the Old Testament, interpreting it from a Christian standpoint. The Christian's Master was born a Jew; Justin is persuaded that the Israelite sacred Book spoke of Him, it is therefore the sacred Book of the Christians; in fact, the Christians are the true Israel and the Jews are ignorant and blinded heretics. The sacred Book gives the true origin of man and the earth, and the true account of what will happen in the future. Justin is not afraid to find elements in the Graeco-Roman mythology which illustrate the relation of Christ to the Father of all[1], but in general he borrows little from heathen religion or heathen science. He holds firm to the original Christian expectation of the coming judgment, the coming resur-

[1] See *Apol.* i, 21 *sq.*

rection of the just and the coming thousand years of their glorious reign in Jerusalem.[1]

The 'Address to the Greeks' of Tatian (date uncertain, perhaps *c*. A.D. 165), Justin's disciple, is written in a different temper. Tatian was a Syrian by birth (p. 493); and he is animated by a hatred of the Greeks and of Greek culture. The barbarian origin of the Christian religion is in its favour. He convicts the Greek religion of immorality, and the Greek thinkers of error and radical inconsistency; at great length he establishes that Moses had lived before the Trojan War and the Heroic Age; and argues that the Greeks had misunderstood and misused the Old Testament revelation. The Logos doctrine is less prominent than in Justin and—here again unlike Justin—he manifests a rigorous, ascetic temper which led him eventually to break with the Great Church. From a literary point of view Tatian's work marks an advance upon his predecessors, since, for all his contempt for Greek culture, he knows how to use the arts of Greek rhetoric to confound his pagan adversaries.

Athenagoras of Athens, a contemporary of Tatian, in his Supplication concerning the Christians (πρεσβεία περὶ Χριστιανῶν) addressed, it would seem, to Marcus Aurelius and his son Commodus (date uncertain, but probably *c*. A.D. 177) sets himself to disprove the calumnies popularly believed of the Christians: in turn he rebuts the charges of atheism, cannibalism and incest. The work is better constructed than that of Justin and he writes far more temperately than does Tatian. He employs an atticizing Greek and makes some pretension to literary style. He is not unmindful of the virtues of the Greek sages, and argues that if Christians now are persecuted by their neighbours that is no more than befell Pythagoras, Heraclitus, Democritus and Socrates. But he, too, finds the Greek philosophers inconsistent: Christianity is for him the true philosophy which has superseded the confused speculations of the Greeks. The peculiar interest of his work lies in the picture of the life and character of the early Christian communities and the influence on both of a belief in a bodily resurrection. The tone of the Apology is well reflected in its closing words: 'For who are more deserving to obtain the things they ask than those who, like us, pray for your government that you may, as is most right, receive the kingdom son from father, and that your empire may extend and increase, all men becoming subject to your sway? And this is also for our advantage that we may lead a

---

[1] *Dial. c. Tryph.* 80 *sq.*, following Rev. xx, 4, 6.

peaceable and quiet life and may ourselves readily perform all that is commanded us.'

Last in the roll of the second-century Apologists is Theophilus, who held the see of Antioch in the reigns of Marcus Aurelius and Commodus. Of the many works which he is known to have written, the apologetic work *Ad Autolycum* alone has come down to us. This Apology, written in flowing and easy Greek, was composed some time after the death of Marcus Aurelius (A.D. 180). It is the longest and most ambitious of the second-century Apologies, but it adds little that is new in this type of literature.

IV. THE GNOSTICS

The future of the Christian Religion, and with it the future of civilization, was destined to go upon lines not very different from that of Justin Martyr's synthesis. But meanwhile other formulations of Christianity were being made, formulations which neglected the Old Testament and started from the current philosophy and the current science. Such were the speculations of Valentinus and Basilides and the other schools commonly known as gnostics.

Two theories underlie these theologies: one is the Ptolemaic system of Astronomy, the other is the belief in the immortality of the soul, imprisoned in a mortal body. The first of these led to belief in the various systems of Astrology, the second to the doctrine expressed in the Greek catchword *sōma sēma* 'the body a tomb.' These two theories are quite independent of Jewish and Christian ideas, but were widely spread in the classical world in the first two centuries of our era.

What is the shape of the World? The ancient view, attested among other authorities by the Old Testament, is that it was not unlike an old-fashioned trunk. Up above, covered by a curved top, was the Kingdom of Heaven. Below was the Earth, with pillars at the corners supporting the heavens, with the abode of the dead underneath. In modern days we believe in the Copernican system, in which the ball of the earth goes round the Sun, itself a mere member of the Milky Way. Neither Heaven nor Hell can be a part of the phenomenal universe, as they were to the ancients. Between these two views comes the Ptolemaic System. It still regarded the Earth as the centre of all things, but in so far as it differed from the old system it was founded upon scientific observation, upon agreement with observed facts[1]. Whatever men might believe, there remained always the impressive spectacle of

---

[1] On these theories see F. C. Burkitt, *Church and Gnosis*, pp. 30 *sqq.*

the fixed stars, revolving night after night round the Pole. These, once their invariable configuration had been noted, must be thought of as fixed in a rigid though transparent sphere rotating round the Earth. And if the stars are fixed in a sphere of this kind, it seemed reasonable to explain the more unaccountable movements of the other heavenly bodies in a similar way. There must be similar spheres for the Sun and for the Moon and for the Five Planets. If these were fixed in their spheres, their spheres must move irregularly.

The believer in the Ptolemaic astronomy had therefore come to regard the Earth on which he lived as surrounded by crystal, transparent, but rigid, spheres, as the heart of an onion is encased by its outer layers. This view immensely enhanced the importance of each planet. It was no longer a tiny point of light mysteriously wandering among the other heavenly bodies, but was the Lord of a Sphere which encased the Earth itself. If it was high or low above the ground, nearer or further from other heavenly bodies, it seemed reasonable to suppose that it exerted a special influence on the Earth and its inhabitants. And along with this belief there was another, intimately bound up with the scientific character of the Ptolemaic system. Whatever might be the rules of the courses of the planets, the very observations that had led to the construction of the system had taught the comparative regularity and inevitableness with which the heavenly bodies, planets included, do move. If then the planets (or their spheres) had an influence on men, that influence came inevitably and inexorably. 'Astrology,' the natural child of Ptolemaic astronomy, is a doctrine of Fate, of inevitable and inexorable Fate.

The *soma-sema* doctrine may be described as the reverse or back-view of 'the Immortality of the Soul.' The immortality of the human soul is not a doctrine taught in the Bible, either in the Old or New Testament. A vivid belief that the God of all the earth will in the end do right led most Jews to believe, from the time of the Maccabaean rising onwards, that martyred saints would not be unrewarded and that notorious sinners and persecutors, such as Antiochus Epiphanes, would receive in their own persons the due punishment for their evil deeds. So arose the belief in the Resurrection of the Dead. It is a moral doctrine, not a physical theory. The Greek notion of the immortality of the soul, on the other hand, is not in itself moral but logical and psychological. The soul of man, the *Psyche*, the queer inhabitant of the human body that in dreams seems to be able to wander outside at will, only to be imperiously called back on waking, was held by many

Greeks to be immortal. But it was imprisoned in a mortal body, like a bird in a cage. This body was of earth, of the same or similar substance as stones and mud and other inanimate things. The soul on the other hand was 'ethereal,' *i.e.* its true nature and abode was the Upper Air, in the pure region high above the clouds. The body enclosed it like a tomb: if only the body were dissolved, the immortal soul was free to mount up to its true home. But, as has been seen, the victorious Ptolemaic system with its attendant Astrology had brought in the Spheres, translucent walls of crystal cutting off Earth from Heaven beyond, cutting off the Soul in its upward flight. How could the Soul get through?

There is yet another problem with which thinkers of this period were occupied. If there be one God, the ultimate Source of everything, how does this variegated and partly evil world come about? How can One become Two, and part at least of the Two be in opposition to its original?

Christianity, the religion which is essentially a belief that 'Jesus appeared in Judaea' (to use the phrase employed by Mani [p. 508]) was a divinely-sent Deliverer of man, had first to explain how this Jesus was fitted to the Old Testament, the divine vehicle of truth. But when Christianity had become established in the Graeco-Roman world and was beginning to attract some of the educated classes who were uninfluenced by Judaism, it is the questions sketched above to which 'Jesus' required to be fitted. Was it not possible to set forth the rôle of Jesus in a way that satisfied the cultivated ideas of modern enlightened society? This is the setting in which the various Gnostic sects appeared.

The most famous of the gnostics is Valentinus, whose activity may be dated about 130–150. He had a number of disciples, who were divided into an Eastern and a Western school. His doctrine survived in Egypt, and both the document called 'the Apocryphon of John' and that called 'Pistis Sophia[1]' seem to be ultimately derived from Valentinus' construction. It is with a description of Valentinus' system, probably as set out by his disciple Ptolemaeus, that Irenaeus begins in his great treatise 'Against Heresies'; it is mainly from Irenaeus, rather than from the later 'Fathers' who used Irenaeus, that we are able to get a fair estimate of what Valentinus was attempting to enunciate by his curious mythology[2].

He taught that there was an original Forefather, called also The Deep (*Bythos*). With this primordial essence dwelt a Thought

---

[1] See below, p. 472.
[2] For the following paragraphs, see Burkitt, *op. cit.* pp. 42 *sqq.*

(*Ennoia*), called also Grace, for it was not conditioned, and Silence, for it made no sign of its existence. Somehow the immeasurable Deep made its own Thought fecund, and so Mind (*Nous*) came into being; and though it was called Unique it had a correlative side to it called Truth. It will be noticed that the Pairs are very much like the Hegelian Thesis and Antithesis that between them bring forth a Synthesis. In other words the Valentinian heavenly hierarchy, known as the *Pleroma*, is rather philosophical description than mythology. After all, human beings only know of two kinds of fresh production: there is the thought or idea that seems to be self-produced from a man's consciousness, and there is the new individual that comes from generation in plants and animals. By the first process the ultimate Forefather of Valentinian theology conceived His original Thought, and by something analogous to the second the dumb Thought produced what could be called *Nous*. In other words *Nous* was 'begotten, not made.' *Nous*, Mind, is an intelligent Understanding, the inevitable counterpart of which is Truth. For if there be nothing true to understand there can be no intelligent understanding.

It must also be pointed out that the original *Bythos*, the hidden Deep that produced the first Thought out of itself, corresponds in many ways to the Subliminal Self of modern psychologists. There is in the human personality an inner treasure-house within us, impulses good and bad which proceed not so much from our conscious reasoning powers as from what is called 'the abysmal depths of personality,' *i.e.* from something corresponding to the Valentinian word *Bythos*. It was by a process analogous to that by which new notions come into our minds out of the unknown activities of our unconscious selves that the Valentinian Forefather produced His first unexpressed Thought.

Many more pairs of Aeons, according to Valentinus, were formed by a process of a similar kind, the last of which was Design and Sophia. The last is usually translated 'Wisdom,' but a more appropriate English term is Philosophy. As we are soon to learn, *Sophia's* conduct was not marked by true Wisdom, *Sophia* took no pleasure in Design. The first Forefather could properly be perceived by *Nous* alone, by the pure Intelligence. But somehow *Sophia* had got a glimpse of this exalted Forefather, and she desired to have direct intercourse with Him. This was not designed for her: her search for the Unsearchable was labour and sorrow, and (to continue the tale) her unauthorized passion somehow made her fecund with a formless monster. In pain and terror *Sophia* cried out for help to be sent to her from the Father and all the

Aeons, and so the Father sent to her a new Being called *Horos*, who separated her from the monster that she had conceived, and restored her to her proper condition among the Aeons. Her monstrous offspring, on the other hand, fell outside the heavenly Society (the *Pleroma*), and became the cause of this sensible and material world.

It is evident that Valentinus' account of the origin of things and of the mixture of good and evil found in this our world was psychological, akin to the mental processes of our own mind, which are indeed the only mental processes we know of. 'Sophia' is Philosophy. Philosophy sometimes seems to have a glimpse of the Deep, that is, of Ultimate Reality: it desires to have direct touch with Ultimate Reality. The vision of what is ultimate is entrancing but intoxicating. Philosophy cannot conceive it intelligently and produces only disordered fancies[1]. What physician, or rather surgeon, can treat the disordered fancies of Philosophy? Valentinus' name for him is *Horos*, *i.e.* 'Boundary,' in other words true Definition.

Here we come to the most interesting, and at the same time the most Christian, feature of Valentinian doctrine. Horos, we are told, had other names meaning Emancipator, Redeemer, etc., but he is also called 'Cross' (*stauros*), because he 'crucified away' the disordered fancies of Philosophy. This is the Pauline doctrine that the believer in Christ Jesus has 'crucified' the flesh with the affections (*pathemata*) and lusts thereof[2]. It is expounded in the *Acts of John*, a second-century work with 'Gnostic' affinities, where we are told that the real effective Cross is the marking-off (*diorismos*) of all things, a figure not + but T, which divides everything below it into 'right' and 'left,' but above it there is no division[3]. The essence of Christianity is contained in the Cross and what Christians have associated with the Cross. No religious theory that does not contain a doctrine of the Cross has a right to the name 'Christian,' though from the beginning it was a stumbling-block, a 'scandal.' We have seen how Valentinus incorporates the Cross as the decisive factor in his drama of salvation: it is just this that makes his heresy, however erratic and however unorthodox, a *Christian* heresy.

The further ramifications of Valentinian cosmogony do not need to be given here in any detail, including the production of the heavenly pre-existent Jesus by all the Aeons, so that He has

---

[1] The word used by Valentinus is *Enthymesis*.   [2] Gal. v, 24.

[3] M. R. James, *Apocryphal New Testament*, pp. 254 *sqq.* ('Acts of John' xiii in *Apocrypha Anecdota* II).

the virtues of all of them, or again the stages in the production of
the visible world and the world of men, or the ultimate redemption
of 'Achamoth' (as they named the disordered fancy of Sophia)
and of those of her offspring who attained to some measure of
true knowledge (*gnosis*). In the evolution, the fall, and the subsequent reinstatement of 'Sophia,' or Philosophy, the essential
ideas of Valentinus are expressed. There is no intellectual necessity for the fall of Sophia, but both as a Greek and as a Christian
Valentinus believed in the empirical fact. As a Greek he held the
soma-sema theory, that the better, 'ethereal,' part of him was imprisoned in gross matter; while as a Christian he found a doctrine
of the Fall of Man, from the effects of which the Son of God had
come down to earth to deliver those who received Him. Like
Mani after him, Valentinus felt that the Fall must have happened
in essence before this world, this mixed world, came into being.
The world on this theory is the result of the Fall, the Fall is not a
regrettable accident which occurred soon after it came into being.
According to Valentinus pure Mind is clear, disordered Mind is
'foggy'; fog is the beginning of Matter!

The system of Valentinus, given above, is the most notable of
all the gnostic systems. But there were others, some elaborations
or modifications of Valentinian theory, others combinations of
parts of it with theories connected with the numerical values of the
Alphabet (similar to what Jews call Gematria), or with elaborations
of Christian ceremonies such as the Eucharist. These last are particularly connected with one Marcus, who appears to have combined the Valentinian mythology with various tricks of legerde-
main, rather resembling some of the séances of modern pseudo-
mediums. The Coptic treatises found in the Askew MS. in the
British Museum, known as *Pistis Sophia*, contain descriptions of
some of these pseudo-eucharists[1]. These Coptic tracts are later,
but they have some sort of connection with Valentinian doctrine:
they show the belief that through 'Jesus the Saviour' and the
mysteries which He institutes the true gnostic, when set free from
the body, becomes a ray which cannot be seized by the Archons
and rulers of the lower heavens, but passes direct to the regions
where it belongs and becomes a part of the One Ineffable itself.
'Such a man,' says the gnostic Jesus, 'is a man in the world, but
he is King in the Light. He is a man in the world, but he is not
one of the world, and Amen, I say to you, that man is I and I am
that man[2].'

[1] *Pistis Sophia* 373–6: monstrous varieties are referred to in *ib.* 387.
[2] *Ib.* 230.

Two other systems demand notice here, that given in the *Apocryphon of John* and that of Basilides. The 'Apocryphon of John' is the name of a work, fragments of which have been preserved at Berlin for nearly forty years.[1] What makes this obscure and fragmentary work particularly important is that it is obviously the exposition of a gnostic system described and controverted by Irenaeus at the end of his first Book against Heresies[2]. In the *Apocryphon* Jesus appears in a vision to John the Apostle and reveals Himself as 'the Father, the Mother, and the Son.' The original Source of all things, corresponding to the Valentinian *Bythos* or Deep, is depicted as dwelling in His own clear and tranquil Light, which is the Fountain of the Water of Life. Out of the depths of His own pure essence comes His own *Ennoia* or Thought, just as in the system of Valentinus, but She is given (without explanation) the name Barbelo. This All-Mother, which occurs in the *Pistis Sophia* tracts, is always represented as a kindly, sympathetic personage, unlike the oddly-named Demiurge or Archon who formed this material world, called *Sabaoth* or *Ialdabaoth* or similar names, which seem to have been derived or corrupted from the Greek Old Testament. Barbelo does not appear to have any Semitic derivation: it seems to be adapted from the Coptic *belbīle*, a 'seed' or 'grain.' Thus while Greek speculation traced the first beginnings of things to a Thought or Notion, the more concrete Egyptian mind thought of a Seed.

Basilides, a contemporary of Valentinus, produced an independent system, which seems to have made a certain impression, but attracted less followers or modifications than the Valentinian theology. Basilides conceived that there were 365 heavens, each superior to the other. Each was less concrete, less material, than the one below it, till at last in the ultimate region, the cause of all those below it, we arrive at what is altogether Nothing![3] No doubt this queer theory is an attempt to explain how diversity could come out of unity, or the concrete out of the undifferentiated, but the fact is that we do not know, any more than we know the real nature of our own consciousness of ourselves or of other things. The 365 heavens of Basilides seem to be nothing more than an attempt to acquit the Heavenly Power of responsibility for letting this material concrete world come into existence.

---

[1] It is not yet published, but a very full account of it is given by Prof. Carl Schmidt in *Philotesia, P. Kleinert zum LXX Geburtstag dargebracht*, pp. 317–56. Similar to the *Apocryphon of John* is 'Setheus,' an ancient Coptic text bound up in the Bruce Papyri at Oxford.

[2] *adv. Haer.* I, 27.   [3] Hippolytus, *Refut.* VII, 20.

V. IRENAEUS

Irenaeus, bishop of Lyons at the end of the second century, is a milestone in the history of the Christian Church. He was a native of Asia Minor and had in his youth known Polycarp, bishop of Smyrna, who was martyred in February, 155 or 156, at the age of 86[1]. This Polycarp is a link between the 'apostolic' age, which, so to speak, ended with Ignatius, and the age of Irenaeus, which marks the fully developed Catholic system. It seems that Irenaeus' statement that Polycarp was acquainted with the Apostle John is mistaken[2], but he may well have known the mysterious Elder John of Ephesus, who had 'seen the Lord.' He must also have known Ariston, first bishop of Smyrna, of whom the same is said, but Polycarp's immediate predecessor was one Bucolus.

The long period of Polycarp's episcopacy almost covers the period between the writing of the later books of the New Testament and their acceptance as canonical. This is why the theory that Polycarp's 'Epistle' to the Philippians consists of two letters run together is important. The last two chapters are a short letter written soon after Ignatius had passed through Philippi, before he had arrived in Rome for martyrdom: in the first twelve Polycarp is giving advice in answer to a request and the whole tone is far more appropriate to his venerable old age[3]. It is not surprising, therefore, that in this part Polycarp refers not only to 1 Corinthians but also to 1 Peter (possibly written by his predecessor Ariston of Smyrna), and probably to 2 Corinthians, Ephesians, 2 Thessalonians, 1 Timothy and 1 John, in other words to a body of writings not unlike the New Testament as finally accepted.

To come back to Irenaeus: he was chosen bishop of Lyons after the persecution there in 177, of which the account, preserved by Eusebius, may be from his pen. During the next ten years appeared his eminently successful treatise known as the *Five Books against Heresies*[4]. His main argument is that the teaching of the Apostles has been handed on by successors, whose names can be adduced, to the churches of his own time; in particular that the Church was founded in Rome by Peter and Paul and from that day onwards their successors are known,

[1] For the date, see C. H. Turner, *Studia Biblica*, II, pp. 128, 154.
[2] From the arguments of B. H. Streeter, *The Primitive Church*, pp. 186, 266.
[3] See P. N. Harrison, *Polycarp's Two Epistles to the Philippians*.
[4] So successful that a fragment of Book III, written *c.* A.D. 200, was found in the dust-heaps of Oxyrhynchus in Egypt (*P. Oxy.* III, 405, cf. *ib.* IV, p. 264).

without a break to Eleutherus the present bishop, that there
has been complete continuity, and that Matthew, Mark, Luke and
John, the fourfold Gospel of the universal Church, give the true
account of Jesus Christ. There is nothing in these of the doctrines
of Valentinus or any other gnostic. Along with the Four Gospels
Irenaeus appeals to the Acts and to the Epistles of Paul and of
John—in a word, to the New Testament. What, judged by these
authorities, is apostolic is right; what is not to be found in them
is wrong. The development of Christian ideas for the future will
tend to be an unfolding—an 'evolution' in the older sense of the
word as opposed to '*epigenesis*'—of dicta enunciated by apostles
and preserved in approved and therefore authoritative writings.

A word should be said here of the *Epideixis*, a work of Irenaeus
the full title of which is 'The Demonstration of the Apostolic
Preaching.' This work, mentioned by Eusebius[1], was long lost,
but turned up in an Armenian version in 1904[2]. It was written
about 190, after the *Against Heresies*, and gives the main beliefs
about God and human history held by Irenaeus. Apart from a few
curiosities of expression, such as describing the Word and the
Spirit as the 'hands' of the Father, it sounds commonplace now-
adays, but that is chiefly because the main lines of Christian theology and of Biblical interpretation followed the same course down
to a hundred years ago, down to such books as *Line upon Line*.
In Irenaeus Christian ideas about God and man had attained the
outline which later ages did little more than fill in and polish, and
the Bible is used to support these ideas by a system of allusion and
indication, which to modern notions of the interpretation of
ancient documents is strangely fanciful and unnatural.

[1] *Hist. Eccl.* v, 26.
[2] The best edition is the English version by Dr J. Armitage Robinson.

CHAPTER XIV

THE CHRISTIAN CHURCH IN THE EAST

I. GREEK-SPEAKING CHRISTIANITY

THE work of Irenaeus of Lyons *Against Heresies*, published about A.D. 188, is, as was said above, a milestone in the history of the Church[1]. Irenaeus had come from Asia Minor, he was in touch with Rome, he wrote in Greek in southern Gaul, and his work found an immediate public in Egypt. But after his time comes a change: the older centres of Greek-speaking Christianity declined in influence. In the West Latin became the vehicle of Christian thought and writing at Rome as well as at Carthage. The anti-Pope Hippolytus (who died in the persecution under Maximinus Thrax *c.* 236) is the last spokesman of Greek-speaking Roman Christianity[2]. Meanwhile from Syria and Asia Minor as well as from Greece nothing of importance appeared. But in the first half of the third century Greek-speaking Christianity found new centres in Alexandria and in Palestinian Caesarea, the influence of which was felt throughout the Churches of the East.

The prosperous age of the Antonines had closed in the reign of Marcus with war and pestilence, and thereafter there had set in a period of economic decline and of public disturbance threatening collapse to the civilization of the Empire. This deterioration and the Imperial recovery which came in the last quarter of the century are treated elsewhere in this history (chaps. v–vi, ix). Here we are concerned to notice that it was during this period of imperial disintegration that the Christian Church, in spite of persecution, firmly established itself in the society of the Empire and enlisted in its defence some of the leading minds of the age. There was no abrupt change from the Christianity of the Great Church of the second century, and the Alexandrian Fathers may be regarded as the successors of Justin and the Greek apologists. But the position of the leading writers of the Church in relation to the world about them became wholly different: the important part which Justin

[1] See above, p. 474.　　　　　[2] See below, p. 534.

played in the internal development of the Church cannot mitigate the judgment that he was a poor writer and a confused thinker very imperfectly abreast of the culture of his age; but in the third century there were scholars and thinkers within the Church who had learned most of what the culture of their age had to give, and who laid foundations on which a Christianized society could build in succeeding centuries. The Alexandrian Fathers, Clement and Origen, were the most illustrious representatives of this new Christian culture, but throughout the empire the social status of the Church was rising, and influential Christian writers in the Greek-speaking empire were not confined to Egypt.

To begin with the writing of history: the familiar apologetic contention of Jews and Christians that the Mosaic writings were anterior to the heroic age of Greece, and were a source used by Greek writers themselves, was now translated into a scientific form which was to provide the framework of historiography for centuries to come. Theophilus, Bishop of Antioch, already mentioned as the latest of the second-century Greek apologists, makes reference to an earlier work of his own (περὶ ἱστοριῶν) dealing with the early history of mankind[1]. This book has entirely disappeared and we know nothing in detail of its method. In the next generation, a Christian writer, Julius Africanus, produced a monumental work on world-history which attained a widespread and enduring celebrity. It is still known to us in part from surviving fragments, and also through the medium of the later *Chronica* of Eusebius, which were largely based upon it. Julius Africanus, born, it seems, at Aelia Capitolina (Jerusalem), had served for a time as an officer in the army of Severus, and was on terms of intimacy with the Christian dynasty at Edessa. Much of his life was spent at Emmaus (Nicopolis) in Palestine. His published writings included an encyclopaedic work entitled *Kestoi* dealing with a large variety of subjects ranging from military tactics to magic. From a papyrus fragment of the eighteenth book of this work, we learn that Julius was charged with the duty of constructing a library for the Emperor Severus Alexander at Rome in the Pantheon[2]. His *Chronicles* gave a synchronistic history of the peoples of the world. The Biblical chronology provided the cadre for the work as a whole, but for the later period he used the reckoning by Olympiads. According to Julius Africanus, the present world was to last in all for six thousand years. Of these six thousand years, three thousand carried the history down to Peleg

---

[1] *ad Autol.* II, 28 and 30.
[2] Grenfell and Hunt, *P. Oxy.* III, p. 39.

son of Eber[1] and 2500 from Peleg to Jesus Christ[2]. Thus when the book appeared in the fourth year of Elagabalus, A.D. 221, its readers were encouraged to look forward to a period of some three centuries before the coming of that last millennial period, the 'Sabbath' of the world, which was to succeed the six thousand years of history. If the interval seems short, yet the scheme shows that in the expectation of the author the millennial Kingdom of Christ had retired into a fairly distant future. Apocalyptic Christianity was accommodating itself to a world which was at least temporarily stable.

Together with a new scientific construction of world-history based upon the scriptures of the Christian Church, the first half of the third century witnessed the rise at Alexandria of a Christian philosophy of the universe, founded upon the same authority.

The origins of Christianity in Egypt are wrapped in obscurity. The earliest names associated with the new Faith at Alexandria are those of eminent heretics: Basilides, Valentinus, and the Marcionite Apelles. The Gospel of St John was certainly current in Egypt well before the middle of the second century[3]. Whether or not the other canonical Gospels were received at the same period is unknown. In any event, the Egyptian Christians had an indigenous Gospel of their own, *The Gospel according to the Egyptians*, and this was tainted with gnostic influence. It has been plausibly conjectured that the earliest Alexandrian Christianity was largely gnostic in character, and that this explains the meagreness of our information as to its history. In later centuries the patriarchal See of Alexandria unlike the other patriarchates maintained relations of close friendship and even a measure of subordination to the See of Rome, and the suggestion has been made that this relationship originated in help which the Roman Church supplied in freeing the Church of Alexandria from heretical domination, and that the later legend of the evangelization of Alexandria by St Mark (unknown to Clement and Origen and still absent from the earliest Latin Gospel prologues)[4] reflects the same mission from Rome to Egypt. Be this as it may, when the Alexandrian Church emerges into the light of history in the later years of the second century, we find its leading teacher Clement at one with the Great Church in

---

[1] Gen. x. 25. The name means 'Division' and is interpreted in Genesis of the division of the earth which is said to have taken place in the days of Peleg. Julius interprets it also of the division of time.

[2] Fragments in Routh, *Reliquiae Sacrae*[2], II, pp. 244, 245, 306.

[3] See C. H. Roberts, *An unpublished Fragment of the Fourth Gospel*.

[4] D. de Bruyne in *Revue bénédictine*, XL, 1928, pp. 196 *sqq.*

acknowledging the Rule of Faith, the fourfold Gospel and a Canon of other New Testament scriptures in the main identical with that received elsewhere. Again Clement and his successor Origen are at one with the Great Church in repudiating the aberrations of the gnostic systems and the gnostic attitude of exclusiveness in relation to the faith of ordinary Christians. But they stand for a new type of Christianity which is zealous to claim the title of gnostic for the fully instructed believer. With this goes a new attitude towards philosophy. Whereas the earlier apologists had written mainly in a polemical spirit to defend Christianity against attack and to expose the weaknesses of paganism, the Alexandrian Fathers tend quietly to assume the inherent superiority of the Christian dispensation and make constructive use of a Platonizing philosophy to expound and to elucidate the Church's faith.

These theologians gave their teaching in what came to be known as the Catechetical School. This was something more than a school of instruction for those seeking baptism. It probably grew up as an informal association of pupils around an illustrious teacher. At a later date it came to be a kind of Christian College or University in which oral instruction was given to inquirers of all kinds. Origen incorporated into his educational course the study of logic, dialectic, natural science, geometry and astronomy as a propaedeutic for the higher pursuits of ethics and theology. How far this comprehensive system of education is to be ascribed to Origen's own initiative, and how far it had its roots in earlier practice, it is scarcely possible to say.

The first teacher of the School to attain fame was one Pantaenus, who is said also to have gone on a missionary expedition to 'India,' but his works have not been preserved[1]. His successor, known as Clement of Alexandria, occupied the chair for about the last twenty years of the second century. He describes himself as an Athenian, was a pagan by birth and had picked up a varied knowledge of Classical lore (perhaps rather from extracts and florilegia than from a study of originals), and we have from him a very great part of a sort of Introduction to Christianity that throws a vivid light on the intellectual conditions of the age which witnessed a movement of Greek culture towards the new religion and an influencing of the new religion by Greek culture. The *Address to Greeks* sets forth the attraction of Christianity, the *Tutor* explains the general way of life and conduct appropriate for Christians, the *Misc-*

[1] Clement (*Ecl. Proph.* 56) says that Pantaenus taught that the Prophets used the present sometimes for the future and sometimes for the past.

ellanies is an unmethodical collection, mainly concerned with the portrait of the true 'gnostic,' *i.e.* the enlightened Christian who understands from philosophy and intelligence the reasons and true significance of the Christian life.

Clement takes over the familiar polemic against the old mythology and the current defence of the superior antiquity of the Old Testament. But in his hands polemic is subordinate to a quiet insistence upon the educative function of the Logos throughout the history of mankind. The process of revelation, fulfilled when the Logos appeared as man in Jesus Christ, is one in all its stages. Both the Jewish law and Greek philosophy were preparations for that fuller truth which was to come. In his conception of human nature Clement remains close to Platonic tradition. Man is a free being, bearing himself the responsibility for his destiny—Αἰτία ἑλομένου· Θεὸς ἀναίτιος. From the beginning of the creation man has received the breath of God's spirit. To train and perfect this divine gift is the function of the Logos. Deification or likeness to God is the final goal of human life, and in Christ the divine purpose expressed in the words 'Let us make man after our image and our likeness' has already been fulfilled.

Writing for a society more or less leisured and educated, Clement warns his readers at length and in detail against the perils of licence, luxury, and extravagance. Yet he is no foe to the refinements of culture, nor would he have his readers renounce the world. A genuine appreciation of the spirit of Greek culture is discernible in his writings. Christ, Clement teaches, does not exclude the rich man as such from the Kingdom of God; rather would he have him mortify his attachment to the goods of the world and use them for a worthy purpose. The common life is to be Christianized, not renounced[1].

Clement is weakest on the side of constructive thought. He had intended to complete his trilogy with a '*Didaskalos*,' expounding the fuller doctrine of the Revelation of the Word. This he was never able to achieve. His attempts at systematic doctrine are confused, and he habitually falls back in his discursive manner upon the practical duties of the Christian life and the apologetic presentation of the faith wherein his chief interest lay.

The real value of Clement's writing, apart from his citations of other authors, sacred and profane, consists in the picture that he unconsciously draws of a paganism attracted by the Christian system and willing to accept it if it can be shown to be not inconsistent with a cultivated and enlightened view of the universe, and

---

[1] *Quis dives salvetur*, 12–14.

on the other hand of a Christianity willing to express its beliefs in a way consistent with the best Pagan culture. Of the two beliefs with which we set out, viz. the Bible and the Second Coming of Christ, little is said of the latter, and with regard to the former the method of allegory in Clement's hands succeeds in making the natural meaning little more than a belief for those who have not attained to what Clement calls a 'gnostic' view.

Clement left Alexandria when the persecution of Septimius Severus broke out there (p. 18), and seems to have died in Palestine. He was succeeded in A.D. 203 in the headship of the Catechetical School by the youthful Origen.

Clement has been thrown into the shade by his successor. Where Clement was weak, Origen was strong. In him for the first time the Church found a theologian who united a firm adherence to the Rule of Faith with a mastery of Greek philosophical thought, and who knew how to blend these two strains into a single coherent system. This great achievement created the presuppositions of all the later development of Greek theology. The theologians who called Origen blessed and those who execrated his memory were alike the products of the new Christian world which he, more than any man, had brought into being. Between the age of the Councils and the rude beginnings of Christian theology in the first and second centuries there stands the achievement of Origen, believer, thinker and, albeit uncanonized, saint.

Origen was born in or about the year 185. His parents were Christian. His father, Leonidas, was martyred at Alexandria in the Severan persecution, and Origen was only prevented from joining him by his mother, who hid his clothes. The boy was well educated, and after his father's death and the seizure of his father's property by the State, he maintained himself by teaching; a couple of years later, when he was only nineteen, he had begun secretly to instruct pagan pupils in the Faith. Hearing of this, Demetrius, the bishop of Alexandria, appointed him head of the Catechetical School, now vacant through persecution, a post which he held for many years.

How Origen escaped the persecution is not known, but that is no more curious than the case of Tertullian, or of Ḳonna, bishop of Edessa during Diocletian's day[1]. His learning and Christian faith are undoubted. So is also his over-enthusiastic zeal, which led him to castrate himself, in a too literal following of Matthew xix. 12. This act was disapproved, but it did not diminish the affection with which his pupils regarded him, of which we have

[1] See below, p. 500.

a proof in the Panegyric addressed to him at a somewhat later time by Gregory known as Thaumaturgus, the Wonder-worker, afterwards the evangelizer of his native Cappadocia, who had come to learn law at Berytus, but, meeting with Origen, became a Christian scholar and eventually a bishop. A long and fruitful period of study and teaching at Alexandria ended in the tenth year of Severus Alexander (A.D. 232), when a quarrel with Demetrius his Bishop led to Origen's final removal to Caesarea, where he continued his work as a teacher. He died at Tyre in A.D. 253 at the age of sixty-nine, his health broken by imprisonment and torture during the Decian persecution of 250.

Of the immense body of Origen's writings but a fragment survives in the original. His great apologetic work, the eight books *Contra Celsum*, has come down to us intact; nine of the forty volumes of the *Commentary on St John* survive, and eight of the twenty-five volumes of the *Commentary on St Matthew* as well as some homilies on Jeremiah. We have, too, the *florilegium* of extracts from Origen compiled by St Basil and St Gregory Nazianzen, called the *Philocalia*; also treatises on Prayer and on Martyrdom. A larger proportion of his work is known to us only through the medium of Latin translations. Where these can be tested they are shown to have been seriously and frequently altered to suit the exigencies of a later standard of orthodoxy. Especially is this true of the great dogmatic work *de principiis* (περὶ ἀρχῶν), which is known to us as a whole only through the translation of Rufinus. This translation allows us to discern the plan and proportions of the original; but fragments of the original Greek extracted by Justinian as texts to be condemned, together with extracts from the accurate rendering by St Jerome preserved in his letter to Avitus, prove how seriously Rufinus tampered with the text. A restoration of Origen's own system, securely based upon surviving Greek material and upon Latin translations only where they can be controlled by Greek parallels, is an achievement which has been reserved for the scholarship of this present century.

While still a young man at Alexandria, Origen had attended the philosophical lectures of the founder of Neoplatonism, Ammonius Saccas, and thus gained a thorough knowledge of the philosophical thought of his age. This knowledge he applied to the elucidation of the faith which he had received, and to which he was whole-heartedly devoted. The means whereby he was able to co-ordinate his philosophical system with the faith of the Church he found at hand in the principle of allegorical interpretation of scripture, the method of which he expounds and justifies at length

in the last of the four books *de Principiis*. In the earlier books of this
work, he states his system constructively. For Origen as a Platonist
philosopher true being is incorporeal being, grounded in the one
Supreme God. Eternally with God Himself is the Logos, or Son
of God, who, though not God Himself (ὁ θεός), is yet truly, though
subordinately, God (θεός without the definite article). Along
with Father and Son, the Rule of Faith taught Origen to recognize
the Holy Spirit. These three Beings form a Trinity, but a graded
Trinity of three distinct Beings (οὐσίαι or ὑποστάσεις), not a co-
equal Trinity within a single οὐσία. Eternal existence is likewise
to be predicated of a number of dependent intelligences, endowed
with a freedom of choice, whom God eternally creates through His
Logos or Son. Origen then proceeds to deal with the visible
material world and the souls which inhabit it. The origin of this
world he traces to the falling away of created intelligences from
the God who made them in consequence of 'a satiety of the love
and contemplation of God[1].' Corporeal existence is a lower stage
to which minds (now 'cooled,' ἀποψυγέντα, into souls, ψυχαί) are
condemned in consequence of their apostasy. Thus, this our world
with its manifold grades of being—angels, the heavenly bodies,
men, beasts and demons—has issued from an antecedent fall.
From these conditions the Divine Logos, made one with an intelligence which had not swerved from God and which was the
human soul of Jesus, brings redemption. After passing through
death, Christ has opened to those who follow Him the way of
ultimate release from corporeal existence and of return to God.
This world of ours, as distinct from the eternal created world,
has had a beginning in time. There have been worlds before it,
and there will be worlds after it[2]. The endowment of free will, with
the possibility which it entails of alienation from God, may be
expected to issue in a new fall and a new world. But beyond the
temporal succession of worlds is the eternal living Purpose of
God, which will be realized in the final restoration of all living
souls (including the Prince of Evil himself) into union with the
Godhead when the hampering restrictions of bodily existence are
laid aside. We may here observe one great innovation upon the
Church's faith as it had been generally accepted in the second
century. Origen's system leaves no room for the expectation of a
millennial reign of Christ on earth.

It is plain that this great system is no mere development of
scriptural doctrines. Though Origen's doctrine is very far from

[1] *de Princ.* II, 8, 3, Koetschau, p. 159.
[2] *de Princ.* III, 5, 1–15, with note in Koetschau, p. 273.

being identical with the system of a gnostic such as Valentinus, yet there is a true analogy between Origen's doctrine of the ante-natal fall of intelligences as cause of the 'casting down' (so Origen interprets καταβολή) of the world, and the fall of *Sophia* with its outcome as taught by the great gnostic[1]. Again, Origen's leading doctrine of the Logos is one in fundamental principle with the mediator Logos of later Greek thought. The systematic applica-tion of this concept in Christian theology was to entail grave con-sequences, but these seem not to have become generally apparent when Origen wrote. For all its audacity, it does not appear that his system caused offence when he put it out. The troubles in which he was personally involved sprang from questions of Church order and personal jealousy rather than from doubts as to his doctrinal orthodoxy.

It is congruous with Origen's conception of the nature of theo-logy that the greater part of his writings took the form of scientific exegesis of the books of Scripture or of more popular scriptural homilies delivered in the congregation of the faithful. The greater part of the surviving Latin translations of Origen is of those works of biblical exegesis. Even where Origen's system was condemned and neglected, his contributions to exegesis maintained their place. Here too a word must be said. Like others who have been inclined to draw elaborate conclusions from the letter of a sacred text—the Jewish Rabbi Akība was an instance a century earlier—Origen devoted much attention to the wording of the Hebrew Bible and tried to correct the current Greek version, commonly known now as the Septuagint. He knew a little Hebrew, enough to appreciate the three later Jewish translators, Aquila, Symmachus and Theo-dotion. These he incorporated into a work known as the *Hexapla*, which exhibited in parallel columns the Hebrew Old Testament, the Hebrew transliterated into Greek, Aquila, Symmachus, the Septuagint and Theodotion. The Septuagint column was a revision made by Origen; he corrected certain things, mostly proper names, to agree with the Hebrew, and made certain transpositions with the same object. Besides these alterations he marked with an *asterisk* (*...) passages not in the Septuagint which he added from Theodotion or Aquila, and with an obelus (÷...[2]) pas-sages found in the Septuagint but absent from the Hebrew.

The *Hexapla* itself, a colossal work, six times the size of the Old Testament, has perished, but some manuscripts of the Greek Old Testament and some Church Fathers preserve extracts. Part of

[1] See above, pp. 469 *sqq.*
[2] The form ÷ also occurs, as well as other signs.

two vellum leaves, containing a copy of the Hexaplar text of
Psalm xxii, survive at Cambridge: they came from the lumber-
room (Genīza) of the Old Synagogue at Cairo, as a bit of a palimpsest with Hebrew medieval writing on the top[1]. A compendium
of the *Hexapla*, called the *Tetrapla*, with only four columns on the
open page (*i.e.* omitting the Hebrew), seems to have been made
by Origen, but that also is lost. Large portions of a Syriac translation of the Septuagint column, with many extracts of renderings
by Aquila, Symmachus and Theodotion, known as the *Syro-
Hexaplar*, also survive, but the main result of Origen's undertaking consists in corruptions and interpolations in the manuscripts of the Greek Old Testament, derived from consulting the
manuscript of the Hexapla, which for many centuries found a
home in Caesarea, in the library founded there by Pamphilus, the
patron of Eusebius the Church historian.

It is difficult for modern scholarship to assess Origen at his true
historical value. Modern scholarship is essentially critical, Origen
is both credulous and unhistorical. Every writing that Church
authority allowed him to receive he was willing to allegorize and
to interpret as teaching what he considered to be the Church's
doctrine. When a learned contemporary, Julius Africanus, put
before Origen serious and indeed incontrovertible arguments for
the Greek origin of the story of Susanna, Origen failed to feel their
force. Again, he said it would be a disgrace for the Church to
have to resort to the Jews for pure texts of the Scriptures!

In the *Contra Celsum* published in 248, on the eve of the Decian
persecution, when Origen was over sixty years of age, we have the
greatest of the Greek apologies for the Christian religion. Each
of the two antagonists who meet in this work is a worthy representative of his cause. The *True word* of Celsus had been written
under Marcus Aurelius contemporaneously with the earlier Greek
apologetic literature. Its author was a pagan imbued with a
Platonizing philosophy who was concerned at the rising power of
the Christian faith wherein he saw a threat to the stability of
society and the State. He rebuts the claims of the new religion;
sees in Jesus an impostor who relied on thaumaturgic powers, and
urges the complaint that Christianity makes its appeal to a blind
faith. He shows himself to be conversant with the Jewish and
Christian Scriptures and with the actual beliefs of Christians of his
time. He does not confine himself to attack, but ends with an
appeal to Christians to support the Empire, in whose welfare they

---

[1] There exists also a palimpsest of the Psalms in the Ambrosian Library
at Milan, with Greek writing above.

have no less interest than their pagan fellow-citizens. Why, he asks, should they not respect its religious observances, even if they are not willing to abandon their own? and why should they not take their share in its defence?

We have no means of knowing how this book was received when it was published, nor whether it had called forth attention among Christians at the time. Perhaps not. Origen, at any rate, seems not to have known the book until his friend Ambrosius prompted him to write a reply. Origen follows the argument of Celsus from point to point so closely that it is probably possible to reconstruct the original almost in its entirety from his refutation. In spite of a diffuse and somewhat laboured style, Origen's answer is a noble defence of the Christian faith. He shows himself to be learned in all the wisdom of the Greeks, and while he meets the anti-Christian polemic of Celsus with patience, courtesy and discernment, he does not fail to recognize that there is much in Celsus' own teaching of which he can approve. He shares his reverence for Plato and accepts the same fundamental conception of the Deity. Even in dealing with Celsus's criticisms of Christianity, Origen is himself sufficiently Greek in thought and feeling to admit implicitly the force of some of his antagonists' contentions. If Celsus points the finger of scorn at the crucified Jesus as an impossible Deity for a thinking man, Origen does not reply with a Pauline 'glorying in the Cross.' His own presuppositions are so far in harmony with those of Celsus that he takes the line of explaining that the sufferings were a part of the experience of the human body and soul of Jesus, and makes it plain that they are not to be thought to involve the Divine Logos Himself.

In the *Contra Celsum*, as elsewhere, Origen makes full use of Greek philosophical conceptions to elucidate the Christian faith. But he yields nothing to the spirit and the claims of the pagan State. First and foremost, he is a devout Christian, ready to suffer martyrdom for his faith. Plato himself falls under Origen's criticism for combining his philosophy with an acceptance of the gods of the State. He himself will make no compromise, and though, with Melito, he can recognize a Providential purpose in the world-wide Empire of Rome, in that it had facilitated the spread of the Christian faith into all lands[1], he will allow of no unqualified loyalty to the State. Prayers should be offered for a sovereign if he be good, and for soldiers if they are engaged in a just war. If, he further urges, the custom of the Empire exempts the holders of certain priesthoods from military service lest they

---

[1] *contra Celsum*, II, 30.

should incur the pollution of blood, it is not an unreasonable claim that a priestly people which offers pure prayers to God should be released from the same requirement. Their prayers, he argues, will be more beneficial to rulers than help in arms, for by prayer they will be able to confound the demons who are responsible for stirring up war. Nor will Origen make any response when Celsus exhorts Christians to undertake the duties of public office. Christians know of another corporate body (ἄλλο σύστημα πατρίδος) established within each city which has yet higher claims upon their services—a body which is governed by men chosen not for their ambition, but for their modesty.

The reconciliation of Church and State is not yet in view: for all Origen's knowledge of Greek literature and his indebtedness to Greek philosophy, he is alienated—more profoundly than his predecessor Clement—from the old pagan culture and its champion the pagan State. The spirit of the martyrs was in him, and inspired his life as it sustained his end.

After Origen left Alexandria, the headship of the Catechetical School was given to Heraclas, who afterwards became bishop of Alexandria. His successor in both posts was Dionysius (248–265), who demands mention as a characteristic representative of Alexandrian Christianity. He was an active and energetic bishop, who endured a persecution, and after returning from banishment found himself involved in the thorny questions of the readmission of penitents who had complied with the orders of the government[1]. From a tale told in Eusebius[2] we see that he was a believer in the almost magical virtue of the consecrated Eucharist. But how far the Church had now travelled from the point from which we started can be gathered from his treatment of the Apocalypse[3]. Dionysius had come across the work of one Nepos, an Egyptian bishop then deceased, called *A Refutation of Allegorists*; in this work Nepos had set forth the old belief in a Reign of Christ on this earth for a thousand years, attesting it by the witness of the Apocalypse of John[4]. That, or something differing from it only in minor detail, had been the Christian Hope; now it was fading away, and its supporters were held to have peculiar opinions and to interpret Scriptures 'after a somewhat Jewish fashion,' *i.e.* literally and not as an allegory. Eusebius tells us that Dionysius was not content with allegorizing. He was willing to admit that the writer of the Apocalypse had had a real vision and was named John, but he could not have been the John who wrote the Gospel

---

[1] See below, p. 521 *sq.*	[2] *Hist. Eccl.* VI, 44.
[3] Eusebius, *Hist. Eccl.* VII, 24 *sq.*	[4] XX, 4 *sqq.*

and the Epistles: the style of the Apocalypse (he says) is different, indeed barbarous, and the themes specially characteristic of the Gospel are absent from it. No more able piece of literary criticism is to be found in ancient Christian literature, except the critique of Susanna by Julius Africanus mentioned above. It shews the power of ruling ideas that Dionysius felt himself free to pass so sharp and scientific a judgment upon an early Christian work which had been definitely accepted by Justin Martyr and Irenaeus in the century before, but which, under the influence of teaching such as that of Clement and Origen, was now out of fashion.

The Churches of Asia Minor were amongst the earliest and most active centres of Christianity, and about the year 190 Polycrates of Ephesus maintained against Victor of Rome the Asiatic custom of celebrating the Lord's Passion by the days of the Jewish month, even if this custom made Easter to fall otherwise than on a Sunday[1]. Polycrates in his letter to Victor[2] enumerates the great stars of Asia, Philip of 'the twelve apostles,' John who lay on the Lord's breast, besides Polycarp and others.

It is clear that Anatolia (to use the most general term) was then a leading Christian region, but from that day its influence declined. This does not mean that Christianity ceased to be practised or even to spread there, but the epigraphical evidence suggests that it had taken on an unobtrusive form that refrained from offending heathen neighbours by stressing Christian symbols. A fish or a swastika inserted among the ornamentation of a tomb reveals to the modern archaeologist that the monument commemorates a Christian who reverenced 'Jesus Christ the Son of God' and His Cross, but to contemporaries it might suggest no esoteric meaning.

A remarkable instance of this tendency is to be found in the inscription of Avircius Marcellus[3], to whom was dedicated a work against the Montanists. A late and legendary life of St 'Abercius' tells how he went miraculously to Rome and healed the emperor's daughter, giving also the words which he set up on his gravestone. The whole tale seemed quite unworthy of serious notice, but in

---

[1] It should be noted that the view of the *Quartodecimans*, as the Asiatic Christians were called, was that the question at issue was the annual commemoration of the *Passion* of Jesus: the *Resurrection* was celebrated every Sunday.

[2] Eusebius, *Hist. Eccl.* v, 24. See on this N. Zernov in *Church Quarterly Review*, cxvi, 1933, pp. 24 *sqq.* and below, p. 532.

[3] See the text of Eusebius, *Hist. Eccl.* v, 16. On the spelling of the name see Sir W. M. Ramsay, *Cities and Bishoprics of Phrygia*, vol. i, pt. ii, p. 737. The inscription (*I.G.R.R.* iv, 696) with a commentary is on pp. 722 *sqq.*

1883 Sir W. M. Ramsay found, three miles south of Hieropolis in Phrygia, two pieces of the inscription itself, which therefore is to be regarded as genuine and was probably the source round which the hagiographer constructed his legend. It describes the journey of Avircius to Rome in the West and Nisibis in the East, being received everywhere and given a fish from the fountain and a drink of 'good' ($\chi\rho\eta\sigma\tau\acute{o}\nu$) wine with bread. The inscription Avircius set up in his lifetime at the age of 72, about A.D. 190.

Nearly all scholars are agreed that in this allusive language Avircius indicates to his co-religionists that in all his travels he had been received and admitted to the Eucharist. But the fact that the expressions which he uses are so vague and figurative, some persons even thinking he was a priest of Cybele, seems to go with the declining influence of Anatolia upon Christian thought in the period[1].

Farther to the East, Firmilian, bishop of Caesarea in Cappadocia during forty years of the middle of the third century, was one of the more prominent figures of his time. He was a friend of Origen, whom he induced to pay him a visit in Cappadocia after he left Alexandria. Presently he is prominent in the Council or Synod at Antioch, which was concerned with the conditions on which Christians who had recanted during persecution could be readmitted to the Church. In 256 he answered a letter from Cyprian of Carthage on the re-baptism of heretics (see below, p. 541).

This controversy has a peculiar interest for the ecclesiastical historian, as it reveals two great principles that had been growing up in the Church. Heretics who had been baptized in the Name of Jesus, who now wished to be reconciled to the Church, should they be baptized afresh? Yes, said Cyprian, and persuaded all his eighty-seven suffragans to say the same. Dionysius of Alexandria[2] agreed, and so did Firmilian. On the other side stood Stephen of Rome. He had on his side two things—the ancient custom, and therefore the authority, of the Roman Church, and the growing belief in the mysterious efficacy of sacraments. In an age when the baptism of infants was coming in, what was the good of it to infants, if it had to be repeated? If the child had died in the interval, its state would be the same as if it had never been baptized at all. It is to be remembered also that 'Baptism' and 'Confirmation,' i.e. reception into the fold of the Church and the gift of the Holy Spirit, are both administered by Eastern Christians in the rite known as baptism. Cyprian and Firmilian agreed that the heretics

---

[1] But for the practice of the Montanists, see above, p. 458.
[2] Eusebius, *Hist. Eccl.* VII, 5.

did not have the Holy Spirit; therefore, they maintained, their baptism should be repeated. Years later a compromise was reached: valid baptism must be in the name of the Trinity, not in the name of Jesus only; and the orthodox Church repeated the ceremony when heretics were admitted, not as a fresh baptism, but as a precaution in case some defect had been used by the heretical minister when the penitent was previously baptized[1].

Firmilian mentions in the course of his argument that he had known of a woman who had actually dared to consecrate the Eucharist with a not unworthy invocation, and had baptized many according to the legitimate rite. How could such baptism be accepted? He evidently considered such an unheard-of monstrosity must prove his case.

No Council or Synod was held in this affair. It was otherwise in the case of Paul of Samosata, in which Firmilian was also concerned. This episode is interesting, in itself, for its political accompaniments, and as a mark of the growing power of Rome. In itself it is interesting, for Paul of Samosata held a view about the nature of Jesus Christ and His relation to God, entirely alien from that held by Origen and Origenists who interpreted the Incarnation in terms of the Logos conceived of as a distinct Being or Person alongside the Being or Person of God the Father. Paul taught that the Logos (whom he seems to have identified with the Holy Spirit) was not a distinct entity, but rather the reason in God analogous to the reason in man. His doctrine of Jesus Christ resembled that of the Roman 'dynamistic Monarchian' Artemas, from whom indeed he was alleged to have derived it[2]. Jesus he held was a real man, miraculously born indeed, and deemed worthy to receive a fuller measure of the Divine Spirit than any other man, but essentially human as we are by nature. This type of Christology shocked the prevailing feeling of the age, and

---

[1] Archbishop Benson's remarks on this controversy in the Dictionary of Christian Biography (art. *Cyprianus*) are worth quoting: 'The unanimity of such early councils and their erroneousness are a remarkable monition. Not packed, not pressed; the question broad; no attack on an individual; only a principle sought; the assembly representative; each bishop the elect of his flock; and all "men of the world," often christianized, generally ordained late in life; converted against their interests by convictions formed in an age of freest discussion; their Chief one in whom were rarely blended intellectual and political ability, with holiness, sweetness and self-discipline. The conclusion reached by such an assembly uncharitable, unscriptural, uncatholic, and unanimous.' Cf. C. Dyovouniotes in *Church Quarterly Review*, CXVI, 1933, pp. 93–101.

[2] Eusebius, *Hist. Eccl.* VII, 30, 16.

induced Firmilian of Cappadocia and certain other bishops to assemble two synods and possibly more in order to condemn Paul's opinions, and to depose him from the venerable see of Antioch to which he had somehow attained. Unfortunately hardly a word of Paul's side has survived: it is only from his adversaries that we hear of his dangerous opinions, his arrogant behaviour, and of the scandal of the beautiful *subintroductae* whom he is alleged to have maintained. He managed, it is true, to avoid condemnation at the first synod in 264, but in 268—Firmilian died, apparently on his way to Antioch—Paul betrayed himself into a dispute with Malchion, a presbyter of Antioch hostile to him, and the bishops, all of them of Origen's school, pronounced him a heretic to be deposed.

It is instructive to observe that in condemning Paul the Council condemned the use of the very word which in the next century was to become the watchword of orthodoxy on the Person of the Son of God: *homoousios*. It was natural that they should do so. The Eastern Bishops present at the Council were as a whole Origenist, and as disciples of Origen they held the Logos to be an *ousia* distinct from, and subordinate to, the *ousia* of the Father. Paul's doctrine merged the Logos in the Godhead and the condemnation of *homoousios* was no doubt intended to rule out this tendency. The decision was to prove a cause of some embarrassment to the champions of Nicene orthodoxy. The fact is that in the next century the doctrinal issues had shifted. Danger then threatened from an accentuation of the subordinationist element in Origen's theology. The Logos was left so far distinct from—nay inferior to—the essence of the Godhead, that his true Divinity was imperilled or directly denied. Against such a tendency it seemed necessary to assert what the Council of 268 had denied—the *homoousion* of the Son with the Father. Neither in 268 nor in 325 had theologians hit upon the distinction in meaning between *ousia* and *hypostasis* whereby the later orthodoxy sought to satisfy the legitimate interests of both tendencies in theological doctrine.

Paul's deposition was not easily achieved. In 268 Roman writs did not run in Antioch. Power was in the hands of Zenobia[1], and Paul refused to give up the Church buildings. But four years later Aurelian had crushed Zenobia and on being petitioned he assigned ownership to those who could show that they were in communion with the bishops of Rome and Italy. No doubt in this Aurelian had in view the 'restoring and cementing the

---

[1] See above, p. 302.

dependence of the provinces on the capital,' to use the words of Gibbon, but his action marks an advance in the prestige of the Western church. The Western bishops prudently agreed with the decision of Eastern brethren in the deposition of Paul of Samosata from St Peter's former see, and accepted the elevation of Domnus, son of Demetrianus, Paul's predecessor, to be bishop of Antioch.

A word is due here on the slow but steady advance of an ascetic ideal and the exaltation of virginity among Christians in the ante-Nicene period before the conversion of the Empire. That this ideal had limitations is sufficiently proved by the choice of Domnus, just mentioned, to succeed his father Demetrianus, though there is nothing to suggest that Demetrianus during his sacerdotal career had lived with his wife. The exaltation of virginity is not a vital constituent of Christianity, though the tendency does shew itself here and there in the New Testament, e.g. 1 Cor. vii and Apoc. xiv. 4, as well as Matt. xix. 12[1]. But that is explicable by the early Christian idea that the world was just about to come to an end, so that no man, believer or unbeliever, would ever have any grandchildren.

In any case this tendency persisted, and the unmarried life, if strictly continent, became the ideal. 'It was not in *this* world that the primitive Christians were desirous of making themselves either agreeable or useful[2].' The further discussion of the question is a matter for ethics and philosophy. It is necessary to draw attention to it here, in order to render the organization of the early orthodox Syriac-speaking Church and of the heretical Manichees less extraordinary and fantastic.

II. SYRIAC-SPEAKING CHRISTIANITY

Christianity east of the Roman Empire dates from about A.D. 160–170. The Christian Religion started in an Oriental land, and during the period covered by the Book of Acts the Aramaic-speaking community at Jerusalem may have seemed as important as the little Greek-speaking communities founded by Paul in the maritime or quasi-maritime towns of the Mediterranean. But the Jewish War and the destruction of Jerusalem by Titus in 70 broke up Jewish Christianity for ever. Jewish Christians survived till the fourth century, but in obscurity.

[1] See above, p. 458.
[2] Gibbon, ed. Bury, II, p. 35. The final paragraphs about the virtues of the Christians in Gibbon's chapter xv (*ib.* pp. 34–38) deserve study.

Hence it came about that for eighty years—nearly three generations—from, approximately, 80 to 160, there were hardly any but
Greek-speaking Christians. At the end of that period are found
the first beginnings of Latin-speaking Christianity, and Syriac-
speaking Christianity began about that time also. Two traditions
of its first beginnings survive, neither entirely trustworthy, but by
combining them we may gain some idea of the course of events.
Epiphanius[1] declares that Tatian, the disciple of Justin Martyr,
went back to his native Mesopotamia after Justin's martyrdom
(perhaps A.D. 165), adding that it was Tatian who composed the
Diatessaron. The native Syriac tradition is that Addai, one of the
seventy-two disciples of the Lord, was sent to Edessa, converted
the king, Abgar the Black, and brought in the use of the *Diatessaron*. That this tradition places the conversion of Edessa far
too early is evident from other parts of the legend which make
Paluṭ, ordained deacon by Addai, to be consecrated bishop by
Serapion bishop of Antioch (about 180), but the use of the
Diatessaron as a substitute for the Four Gospels is confirmed by
the practice of the earliest Syriac ecclesiastical writers. Eusebius[2]
thought that Addai stood for Thaddaeus: a much more probable
conjecture is to identify Addai with Tatian, to regard them as the
names by which the same man was known to Greeks and Syriac-
speaking people respectively.

Edessa, called by the natives Urhai, the modern Urfa, was a town
refounded by Seleucus Nicator in northern Mesopotamia about
thirty miles north-west of Ḥarrān (Carrhae), and this in the time
of Tatian was the capital of an independent buffer-State (Osrhoëne)
between the Roman and the Parthian Empires. The State was taken
over by the Romans in 215, a few years before the collapse of
Parthia and the rise of the Sassanians, but when Christianity
reached it, it had a king and court who used the native dialect. This
dialect is commonly known as Syriac: it is akin to, but different
from, the Aramaic spoken in Palestine, that of Palmyra and that
spoken by Babylonian Jews and the Mandaeans.

The translation of the New Testament, or parts of it, into this
Semitic language is a very notable event. There were Egyptian
Christians in the second century, but Coptic translations of the
Bible were not made till the third. In the fourth century, as we
learn from Eusebius' account of the Martyrs of Palestine[3], the
Scriptures in Palestine itself were read in Greek and then orally
translated into the native dialect. Of the first rendering of any

---

[1] *Haer.* XLVI, 1.   [2] *Hist. Eccl.* I, 13.
[3] I, 1 (in the Syriac version A).

part of the Bible into Latin there is no record: it seems to have happened in the period 150–170, when Latin-speaking Christianity began to be important. In any case Latin was the Imperial language, and some sort of rendering of the authoritative Scriptures into it could not be indefinitely delayed. What is certain is that Latin and Syriac stood for a long while as the only languages into which the Bible had been translated. There was a colony of Jews at Edessa and the neighbouring city of Nisibis: the Old Testament had already been translated by them into Syriac before the days of Addai-Tatian. The Syriac Old Testament used by the Christians is this Jewish translation, slightly revised.

The *Diatessaron* may very well be regarded less as a last attempt at Gospel-making than as the first of the Versions. The Four Gospels had gradually become sacrosanct, at least at Rome, by about A.D. 150: at the same time, Latin-speaking Christians were beginning to form an increasingly large element in the Church there. Should the Gospels be translated for these? On the one hand, it might seem that translation might diminish the special value of the inspired words, on the other, it was obvious that a knowledge of the contents of the Gospel message was desirable for Latin-speaking converts, if not a necessity. A way out seems to have been found in the production of a Latin Compendium drawn from the Canonical Four, which was called *Diatessaron*, a musical term which indicated both the sources of the work and the essential harmony of the sources.

In its original form the *Diatessaron* is no longer extant. But a little before the year 546 Victor, bishop of Capua, happened to find an anonymous Harmony of the Gospels, which he rightly identified as akin to the Harmony of Tatian mentioned by Eusebius in his *Church History*. Victor incorporated this Harmony into a volume of the New Testament which he corrected with his own hand[1]; he mentions in a preface that he had added an adaptation of the system of parallel references known as the Eusebian Canons, and it is probably through Victor that the wording of the text has been assimilated to that of Jerome's Vulgate. But the harmonic arrangement is very well preserved[2].

Certain medieval Harmonies in Dutch appear to be based on an independent copy of the codex found by Victor of Capua. In them and in the text of the Codex Fuldensis itself there are

[1] Dated 21 April, A.D. 546.
[2] The Codex Fuldensis (as it is called) found its way to Jarrow or Monkwearmouth, and was subsequently taken by St Boniface to Fulda in Germany, where it is still treasured in the Cathedral.

surviving traces of the older pre-Vulgate text which characterized the original compilation.

When Tatian, then, returned to Mesopotamia, where he was known as Addai (p. 493), this Harmony was ready to his hand. He prepared a version of it in his native Syriac, making such changes and improvements as naturally characterize a second edition[1]. The work itself was suppressed by authority in the fifth century and no copy of the Syriac *Diatessaron* has survived, but Ephraim Syrus (died A.D. 373) wrote a commentary on it which is extant in an Armenian version, and an Arabic translation exists, in which the wording of the text before translation into Arabic had been assimilated to that of the Syriac Vulgate known as the Peshiṭta. From these, and some minor authorities, the order of the incidents can be securely made out, always with the same result: Ephraim and the Arabic agree together against Victor of Capua and the Dutch Harmonies, and practically in all cases the Latin order is more primitive (and less satisfactory) than that of the Syriac. The Syriac *Diatessaron*, indeed, has all the characteristics of a second and revised edition.

As mentioned above, the 'historical' work which embodies the native tradition about Addai, the founder of Christianity in Edessa, makes Paluṭ his priest or 'elder' to have been ordained bishop by Serapion about 180. 'Addai,' therefore, and his mission, cannot belong to apostolic times, but must be placed in the

---

[1] [Professor Burkitt's view, stated in the text, that the original *Diatessaron* was a Latin composition, is not accepted by all scholars. Since Professor Burkitt wrote this chapter, the discovery at Doura of a tiny fragment of the *Diatessaron* in Greek (describing the Burial of Christ) has established what had hitherto been uncertain, that the *Diatessaron* existed in Greek. (See *Studies and Documents*, III. *A Greek Fragment of Tatian's Diatessaron from Doura*. Edited by C. H. Kraeling, 1935.) It is also established that this Greek *Diatessaron* was in use at least as early as the first half of the third century—probably about 222. Further, it is hard to resist Dr Kraeling's argument (*ib.* pp. 15 *sqq.*) that the Greek should be regarded as the original of the Syriac and not *vice versa*. A similar type of argument to that advanced by Dr Kraeling against the conjecture that the Syriac is prior to the Greek, would militate against the conjecture that the Greek is based upon a Latin original. The textual problems call for further investigation in the light of this new discovery, but it seems highly probable that the Greek *Diatessaron* is Tatian's original *Diatessaron*, and that the versions, Latin and Syriac, depend ultimately upon the Greek. For Professor Burkitt's view of the new discovery and its bearing upon his theory of an original Latin *Diatessaron* reference should be made to an article published posthumously in *Journ. Theol. Stud.* XXXVI, 1935, pp. 255 *sqq.*, 'The Doura Fragment of Tatian.' J. M. C.]

last third of the second century. That is the decisive reason for rejecting the chronology assumed in the work of Meshiḥa-zeka, a chronicler of the early sixth century, who compiled a biographical list of the bishops of Adiabene from the earliest times. The names of these bishops may be genuine—the first was Peḳida—but the lengths of their episcopates and the serious gaps between them seem designed to bring up the establishment of the mission into early post-apostolic times, *i.e.* into the reputed date of Addai himself. That a Syriac-speaking Christianity was introduced into Adiabene and that there were bishops in Arbela before the collapse of the Parthian Empire (A.D. 226) may be granted, but it is all subsequent to the conversion of the king of Edessa[1].

No connected account of the early history of Eastern Christianity was written down. All that can be done is to emphasize what seem to be outstanding events. First of all comes the naturalization of Christianity in a Syriac-speaking land. Of the numbers of the converts we know nothing, but an accidentally preserved notice of a flood at Edessa in A.D. 201 mentions 'the temple of the Christians' as an important building. More significant is the fact of the conversion of the celebrated Bardaisan. Bar Daiṣān (in Greek, Bardesanes) was born in A.D. 154. He was a friend of the king of Osrhoëne, Abgar IX, and was known in his day as the Aramaean Philosopher. He is said to have been educated by a heathen priest at Hierapolis (Mabbōg) and to have become a Christian about 180. His works have mostly perished, for he came to be regarded as a heretic, but a *Dialogue on Fate* by his disciple Philip survives, in which Bardaisan is the chief speaker, from which many of his opinions can be gathered. This dialogue gives an attractive picture of him, answering at length the difficulties of his followers and showing a wide acquaintance with many departments of knowledge.

It was particularly as an astronomer and an astrologer that Bardaisan was famous. He was the author of a grandiose system of the universe, which is both striking in itself and further important as the basis on which Mani afterwards erected his construction (p. 510). To Bardaisan 'God' is not the Creator and

---

[1] Further light on the character of Syrian Christianity is afforded by the Christian church discovered at Doura. Built in A.D. 232 to succeed a place of worship in a private house, it has particular importance from its extensive mural paintings (Volume of Plates v, 166), which indicate a relation of parenthood to Western religious art. Further, the discovery at Doura of the fragment of Tatian's *Diatessaron* (see above) reveals the dependence of local piety on that of Edessa.

Source of the stuff of which the Universe is made, but the Arranger of it into an ordered Cosmos. God is not the sole *Ithyā*, the sole self-existent Being or Entity; besides God there are the four pure substances of Light, Wind, Fire and Water, and the foul Dark substance. All these are contained in Space, which appears to be the Seventh Entity[1].

Originally these Entities were in a happy state of equilibrium: then something occurred whereby they were hurled together and mixed, but God sent His Word and cut off the Dark from contact with the pure substances, and 'from that mixture which came into being from the pure substances and the Dark, their enemy, He constituted this World and set it in the midst, that no further mixture might be made from them and that which had been mixed already, which (mixture) now is being refined by conception and birth until the process is complete[2].' What this doctrine asserts, is that things were originally in equilibrium, that something then occurred to disturb this equilibrium, whereby general disaster was threatened, but that God came to the rescue and confined within certain limits the damage done and provided for its eventual reparation.

This corresponds in a sense to the ordinary Christian doctrine of the 'Fall,' but it differs from it inasmuch as it puts the Fall before the construction of our World—nay more, it makes the Fall to be the cause of this World, not a regrettable incident occurring after this World had been made. In this the Bardesanian doctrine agrees with Manichaeism[3]: in fact, the religion of Mani becomes more comprehensible if the ideas of Bardaisan are recognized as one of its formative elements.

The World and its inhabitants having been the result of a premundane accident, it is not surprising that Bardaisan did not believe in the resurrection of the body. Man, according to Bardaisan, is naturally mortal; it was Abel, not Adam, who died first. Our Lord only raises Souls: the effect of Adam's sin was to prevent Souls after death from what Bardaisan called 'crossing over,' while on the other hand the Life or Salvation brought by our Lord was that He enabled Souls to cross over into the Kingdom, or as Bardaisan also called it 'the Bridal-Chamber of Light.' The Body, he said, is incapable of thought, while the Soul is merely ignorant:

[1] For the cosmogony of Bardaisan, see C. W. Mitchell, *Ephraim's Prose Refutations*, 11, pp. cxxii *sqq.*: the leading text is Moses bar Kepha (died 903), given in F. Nau, *Bardesanes (Patrologia Syriaca* I, 11, pp. 513–515).

[2] Moses bar Kepha in Nau, *op. cit.* p. 514.

[3] See below, p. 510.

God places in the Soul the Leaven, *i.e.* the divine faculty of Reason, where it works by its inherent energy till the whole Soul becomes rational and therefore divine. This Reason he regards as a 'stranger' in the Soul, *i.e.* it is a gift from God, not a mere natural development[1].

Did Bardaisan know Greek? Or rather, seeing that Bardaisan lived part of his life at the court of Edessa and therefore probably could speak Greek, had he a first-hand knowledge of Greek literature and philosophy? It is difficult to say for certain, but it would seem that he had little or no first-hand knowledge of Greek writings, and that a good deal of the vaguely Hellenic air of the 'Bardaisanian' theories opposed by Ephraim, from whom we get most of our knowledge of them, is due to Harmonius, the son of Bardaisan, who is said by Theodoret[2] to have studied at Athens and become familiar with the language and philosophy of Greece. Harmonius adhered to his father's doctrines, and set them forth in 'Hymns'; the tradition runs that Ephraim took the metres which Harmonius is said to have introduced into Syriac literature, and turned them into vehicles for orthodox teaching.

That Bardaisan himself was a poet, and in particular that he wrote the splendid poem in the *Acts of Thomas* known as 'The Hymn of the Soul' is more than doubtful. In all that Ephraim quotes from Bardaisan there is a complete absence of the mythic and poetical element. In Ephraim's *Refutations* the Aramaean Philosopher appears as a matter-of-fact man of science, a teacher of positive doctrine about the physical constitution of the world in which we live. To us, no doubt, it is science falsely so called, speculations as groundless as his derivations of the names of some of the ancient months from the Syriac of his day. But such as it is, it is positive doctrine about matter and sense-perception; there is no parabolic setting-forth of the meaning of human life or the ways of Divine redemption. Moreover, the attitude of Bardaisan towards life is different from that characteristic of the *Acts of Thomas*, including the great Hymn. This, like Syriac ecclesiastical writing generally, sets forth an ascetic philosophy of life, and there is nothing ascetic in the attitude of Bardaisan. It is true that he regarded man as naturally mortal, and held that only the immortal soul is redeemed by Christ. But he did not reject marriage, as the *Acts of Thomas* does. In the Hymn itself there is nothing about marriage or generation, but the food and dress of 'Egypt' are regarded as unclean, and not merely as things temporary and perishable.

[1] Mitchell, *op. cit.* p. cxxv.   [2] *Haer. Fab.* I, 22.

We may fairly regard Bardaisan as a native product of Syriac-speaking Christianity, but the times were not propitious for free growth and development. A little before A.D. 200 may be placed the ordination of Paluṭ the disciple of Addai by Serapion of Antioch: there can be little doubt that this tradition signifies the incorporation of the mission of Tatian into the episcopal system of the Catholic Church. Probably also it was marked by the translation of the Four Gospels into Syriac, though the *Diatessaron* was still generally used for a couple of centuries.

In one important respect the custom of the Syriac-speaking Church retained till the fourth century the ascetic ideas of its founder. The heresy of which Tatian is accused is that of the Encratites, those who regarded the married state as incompatible with the Christian life. Except in the views of Bardaisan, just mentioned, this belief was dominant in the Syriac-speaking Church. The words 'holy' (*ḳaddīsh*) and 'continent' are synonymous. It must not be supposed that these Christians were a body of 'race-suicides.' Where they differed from the Christian of to-day was in their theory of the Sacraments. Aphraates, writing in 337, appears to divide Christians into the 'Sons of the Covenant' (*Bnai Ḳyāmā*) and the Penitents. The Penitent is the general adherent, who has as yet not volunteered for the sacramental life; the son (or daughter) of the Covenant is the baptized Christian, who is admitted to partake of the Eucharist. Those who volunteer for baptism are to be warned—'He whose heart is set to the state of matrimony, let him marry before baptism, lest he fall in the spiritual contest and be killed.... He that hath not offered himself and hath not yet put on his armour, if he turn back he is not blamed[1].' In other words, the average Christian of this community looked forward to becoming a full Church member only at a somewhat advanced age, and as a prelude to retiring morally and physically from the life of this world. In Aphraates, baptism is not the common seal of every Christian's faith, but a privilege reserved for celibates, or at least for those who intend to live a celibate life for the future[2]. We meet with a similar organization among the Marcionites and the Manichees.

The traditions current at Edessa contain memories of two persecutions, the martyrdom of Sharbil under Decius and of 'the Confessors of Edessa' under Diocletian. The martyrdom of Sharbil, high-priest of Bel and Nebo, though preserved in very

---

[1] Aphraates, *Hom.* VII, 20 (Wright, p. 147 *sq.*; Parisot, col. 345).
[2] See Burkitt, *Early Eastern Christianity*, pp. 125–142, where there is a full discussion.

ancient manuscripts, is almost wholly unhistorical. The date of Sharbil's martyrdom is put at A.D. 105[1], and the details of his conversion by Barsamya the bishop are fanciful in the extreme. What is important is that the worship of Edessa is still represented as that of Bel and Nebo, *i.e.* the Planets, as in the *Acts of Addai*: in the *Acts* which deal with the Diocletianic persecution, on the other hand, the official worship is of the Emperors and of 'this Zeus.' The inference to be drawn is that Christianity had in the interval ousted the old native cults, and that what was put before the people of Edessa in the Diocletianic persecution was a foreign official worship ordered by the Imperial authority.

The dates of martyrdom of the Confessors are, for Shmona and Guria, Tuesday 15 Nov. A.D. 309, and for Habbīb the Deacon, Saturday 2 Sept. A.D. 310[2]. The three Confessors were apparently the only victims in Edessa of the great persecution, not, it would seem, because the Christians of Edessa and neighbouring towns were few, but for the opposite reason that the Christians were very numerous, and the government was unwilling to proceed to extremities. In Nicomedia, where Diocletian had his court, the persecution broke out in 303[3] and it rapidly spread to Palestine, but it was six years before anyone was executed in Edessa.

In A.D. 312–13 Ḳonna, bishop of Edessa, began to build the great church which was finished by his successor Sha'ad. It is noteworthy that Ḳonna escaped the persecution. Nothing more is known of him, but he and Sha'ad and their successor Aitilāhā (*i.e.* 'Theodore') were honourably commemorated on Sept. 3.

From Ḳonna onwards the dates of the bishops of Edessa are duly given in the *Chronicle of Edessa*, a work which goes down to A.D. 540, but which was evidently compiled from contemporary official records. We learn that the city remained orthodox during the reigns of Arian Emperors, and finally under Rabbula, bishop from 411 to 435, old heretics, such as the Marcionites and the disciples of Bardaisan, were reconciled to the Church. The episcopate of Rabbula is the central point in the history of Syriac-speaking Christendom, the natural division between the ancient and medieval world. It will, therefore, be convenient to conclude this survey of the early period by an account of the two great writers, Aphraates and Ephraim, who belong to the age before Rabbula, and to indicate the main stages in the history of the New Testament in Syriac.

---

[1] 416 Sel. Era.   [2] See Burkitt, *Euphemia and the Goth*, p. 30.
[3] For this persecution in general see below, pp. 664 *sqq.*

Aphraates (in Syriac *Aphrahaṭ*) was the Principal—it is almost too early to call him the Abbot—of the Convent of Mar Mattai (*i.e.* St Matthew) near the modern Mosul. Between 337 and 345 he wrote a series of Discourses on the Faith in answer to an enquirer. The *Discourses* are twenty-two in number, the first words beginning with the successive letters of the Semitic alphabet, together with a final Discourse 'On the Cluster' or the descent of our Lord from Adam and Abraham, giving a kind of general view of religious history. The alphabetical arrangement of the *Discourses* was a method of preserving their proper order; what we have is no miscellaneous bundle of sermons, but an ordered account of the Christian Religion as understood by 'the Persian Sage,' as Aphraates was called.

The result is singularly different from the contemporary theology of the Greeks, both Athanasian and Arian. Aphraates is not unorthodox, but his mind moved along other channels than those of the Greeks. For instance, he treats the Holy Spirit as, at least grammatically, feminine. 'What father and mother doth he forsake that taketh a wife? This is the meaning: that when a man not yet hath taken a wife, he loveth and honoureth God his Father, and the Holy Spirit his Mother, and he hath no other love. But when a man taketh a wife he forsaketh his Father and his Mother, those namely that are signified above, and his mind is united with this world[1].' As we see from this quotation, the Christian community that Aphraates has in mind is unmarried, and he seems to know no other. His name for them is Sons and Daughters of the Covenant[2], a word which in later days became one of the many Syriac terms for monk or *kanonikos*, but with Aphraates is still the word for a baptized Christian.

At a later period the theory of the Christian life changed. In the Syriac-speaking Church, especially from the time that Christianity became the State religion of the Roman Empire, the mass of the adherents wished to make the most of both worlds. They wished to obtain the benefits of baptism all their lives, and had also their young children baptized in infancy. Thus a Christian community came into being, of which the greater number were actually baptized, though only a minority of them were specially addicted to religion. In this way the *Bnai Ḳyāmā* became a monastic order in the Society, instead of being the Society itself.

Ephraim, in Syriac *Aphrēm*, often called 'Ephrem Syrus,' is the

[1] *Hom.* XVIII, 10.
[2] For another view of the Sons of the Covenant, see R. H. Connolly in *Journ. Theol. Stud.* XXXVI, 1935, p. 234.

most widely famous of Syriac writers. His earlier life was spent at Nisibis, but after that town was abandoned to the Persians by Jovian in 363 he migrated to Edessa, and died there in 373. Vast quantities of extant literature are ascribed to him, and though much is spurious the genuine remainder is very voluminous[1]. Much of it is 'poetry,' i.e. works written in lines of so many syllables. Syriac poetry is even easier to write than 'blank verse' in English, for only the number of syllables need be counted; there is no accent, no quantity, no rhyme. And as Ephraim is extraordinarily prolix, and as when the thought is unravelled it is mostly commonplace, his poems make very heavy reading for us moderns. His prose is better, and in the treatises edited from a very illegible palimpsest from the Nitrian collection in Egypt[2] he shows real critical insight. At least, his theory that the Manichaean system is best explained as an adaptation of those of Bardaisan and of Marcion has much to recommend it. It is a pity that Ephraim's Commentary on the Diatessaron is extant only in an Armenian translation.

Rabbula, bishop of Edessa from 411, made it one of his first cares to undertake an authoritative revision of the New Testament in Syriac from the Greek, 'because of its variations exactly as it was[3].' This survives in many manuscripts, some of them as old as the fifth century, and is known as the Peshitta, i.e. the simple (version), so called to distinguish it from later learned translations which were embellished with critical marks. The Peshitta is used in the services of all existing sects of the Syriac-speaking Church, and the manuscripts all agree most wonderfully in text, so that there are hardly any variations. The New Testament books include the Four Gospels, Acts, the Pauline Epistles (including Hebrews), with James, 1 Peter and 1 John. The four minor General Epistles and the Apocalypse are not included. So far as we know, this was the first time any of the General Epistles had been translated into Syriac. Neither in Aphraates nor in the genuine works of Ephraim is there a single clear reference to any of the General Epistles, and the Doctrine of Addai says 'The Law and the Prophets and the Gospel...and the Epistles of Paul... and the Acts...: these books read ye in the Church of God and with these read not others.'

---

[1] See the list of genuine works in Burkitt, S. Ephraim's Quotations from the Gospel, p. 24 sq.

[2] By the late C. W. Mitchell, Brit. Mus. add. 14623, of the fifth or sixth century.

[3] Overbeck, Ephraemi Syri, etc., p. 172.

We need not ascribe to Rabbula an anachronistic interest in textual criticism. What he was interested in was to assimilate his Church to that of the Empire by substituting the 'Separate' Four Gospels for the *Diatessaron*. The Four were called in Syriac the Separated Gospel (*Evangelion da-Mĕpharshē*) as distinguished from the *Diatessaron* which was also called the 'Mixed' Gospel (*Evangelion da-Mĕhalṭē*). He was eminently successful; so much so, that no copy of the *Diatessaron* in Syriac is extant. But two copies of the pre-Rabbulan Syriac text of the 'Separate' Four Gospels have survived, known as the Sinai Palimpsest (Syr. *S*) and the Curetonian MS. in the British Museum (Syr. *C*). Both are extremely ancient: Syr. *S* belongs almost certainly to the fourth century, and Syr. *C* can be very little later. Of *C* a little less than half is preserved; *S* has lost only 17 leaves out of 159, but it is a palimpsest and some words and lines are here and there illegible[1].

S and *C* differ in text from each other as well as from the Peshiṭta, but they more often agree in characteristic readings, so that it is possible to gain a fair idea of their original. We may reasonably connect this with the tradition of the ordination of Palut by Serapion of Antioch, *i.e.* a little before A.D. 200 (p. 493). The *Diatessaron* was a whole generation earlier, and till the time of Rabbula (411–435) the separate Four never were much used in the Syriac-speaking Church. There are no marks of liturgical use either in *S* or in *C*, and their text has many harmonistic readings, which doubtless show the influence of the then better known text of Tatian's Harmony. Apart from this, this Old Syriac version (so called to distinguish it from Rabbula's revision) is a very valuable textual witness, having curious and still unexplained affinities with the text of Alexandria (generally considered by modern critical scholars to be the purest), with the Old Latin texts, and also with the texts now associated with Caesarea.

No manuscript of the Old Syriac except the Gospels has survived, but Commentaries or paraphrases of Ephraim on the Pauline Epistles and the Acts are extant in Armenian translations, which give some idea of what the text must have been. Hebrews

---

[1] Syr. *C* is called from Canon William Cureton, who discovered it among the MSS. which reached the British Museum from the Nitrian Library in 1842: he edited the fragment in 1858. Syr. *S* was discovered in the Convent on Mount Sinai by Mrs Lewis of Cambridge in 1892: the text was first published in 1894. Justinian's Convent on Mount Sinai is the same place where the famous 'Sinai Codex' (‫א‬) of the Greek Bible came from, but the Syriac MS. of the Gospels had been turned into a palimpsest somewhere in the district of Antioch in A.D. 778, and doubtless reached Sinai as a refugee with other Syriac books containing Georgian writing.

is there received but not Philemon, the number of Pauline letters being kept up by an apocryphal Third Epistle to the Corinthians, actually quoted in the ancient (but spurious) Acts of Sharbil[1].

III. MANI AND THE MANICHEES

The end of the third and the beginning of the fourth century saw not only the great and open struggle between the Christian Church and the Roman Empire, it saw also the beginning of the struggle between the Church and the strangest of all Christian heresies. The fight went on all through the fourth century, and it was not till the middle of the following century that Manichaeism, called by one of its earliest opponents, Alexander of Lycopolis in Egypt, 'the New Christianity,' was definitely worsted. For nine years, from 373–382, Augustine was a Manichee, and that period may be regarded as the high-water mark of the Manichaean religion in the Roman Empire. In the East it survived for a long time, and did not finally disappear till the age of Zenghis Khan.

It was on Sunday, 20 March A.D. 242 that the preaching of Manichaeism first began[2]. On that day a young man called Mānī began to announce at Seleuceia-Ctesiphon the capital of the new Empire of the Sassanians, and under the patronage of the king Shapur I, the new religion of which he was the prophet. Mani was executed by the order of another Sassanian monarch a little more than thirty years later (p. 513), but by the time of his death his religion had taken root all over the East, and in the succeeding century it had spread throughout the Roman Empire.

A few years ago our knowledge of Manichaeism was very scanty. Besides the writings of Augustine in Latin and other controversial writings in Greek we had an elaborate account of it in Arabic[3]. In 1912 and 1921 were published C. W. Mitchell's *Refutations of Ephraim*: Ephraim died only a hundred years after Mani and wrote in Syriac, the language in which Mani composed most of his works. More sensational than Mr Mitchell's decipherments have been the discoveries of Manichaean documents in Central Asia. Three or four scientific expeditions made in the early years of this century to Chinese Turkestan, north of Tibet, in the now desolate region north and south of Lop-Nor (see Map 7), brought to light thousands of written fragments, some hundreds of which were from Manichaean manuscripts. Un-

[1] W. Cureton, *Ancient Syriac Documents*, p. 56.
[2] Before this, according to the *Kephalaia* 15, 24 *sqq.* (Schmidt-Polotsky, *Mani-Fund*, p. 47), Mani had gone on a voyage to India and preached there.
[3] I.e. in the Fihrist: see G. Flügel, *Mani*, 1862.

fortunately they are all fragments, bits of torn books and rolls, but they are at least the writings of Manichees, not mere refutations. Some are in a sort of Persian, more are in a Turkish dialect, and it should be added that from the same region comes an account of the Manichaean religion written in Chinese. As recently as 1931 the yet more surprising discovery of a small Manichaean Library has been made in Egypt, from near Lycopolis, consisting of about half-a-dozen volumes in Coptic, containing hymns, letters, some historical accounts of the tragic deaths of Mani and his successor Sisinnius, and a lengthy work called the Chapters or First Principles (Κεφάλαια). Unfortunately the volumes are badly preserved: the papyrus leaves are stuck together, and the process of restoration, which is necessarily slow, has to precede decipherment and publication.

All our documents, however, tell very much the same story, they all give very much the same picture of the religion of the Manichees. We begin, as the Manichees themselves did, by the Two Principles and the Three Moments. The Two Principles, or Roots, are the Light and the Dark. The contrast between the Light and the Dark is the fundamental distinction for Manichee thought, more fundamental than that between Good and Bad, or God and Man. The Three Moments are the Past, the Present, and the Future. Light and Dark are two absolutely different eternal Existences. In the beginning they were separate, as they should be. But in the Past the Dark made an incursion on the Light and some of the Light became mingled with the Dark, as it is still in the Present, in this world around us; nevertheless a means of refining this Light from the Dark has been called into being, and of protecting the whole realm of Light from any further invasion, so that in the Future Light and Dark will be happily separated.

Light and Dark are the proper designations of the two Principles, but to Mani with the idea of Light was conjoined everything that was orderly, peaceful, intelligent, clear, while with that of Dark was conjoined everything that was anarchic, turbulent, material, muddy. The usual Manichaean presentation of the primordial condition of Light and Dark is that of two contiguous realms or states, existing side by side from all eternity without any commixture. Opposite the realm of the Light, in which dwelt the Father of Greatness, was the realm of the Dark, a region of suffocating smoke, of destructive fire, of scorching wind, of poisonous water, in a word, of 'darkness that might be felt'; for the Dark to Mani, as to Bardaisan, was not 'privation mere of light and absent day,' but a substantial entity. The denizens of this pestiferous realm suited its character: Mani represents them as groping about in aimless anarchy. They and their abode were pictured as in every way odious: the horrible Dark is peopled with a horrible race appropriate in character and habits to the place they live in. But in all this there is nothing evil. Evil began when the Dark invaded the Light.

Mani could not explain how this first disturbance of the eternal order took place, any more than Bardaisan could. He seems to have said that somehow the Dark smelt and perceived that there was 'something pleasant' beyond his region. It cannot well be doubted that Mani's point is that the beginning of evil is unregulated desire. But we must not regard Mani's cosmogony as a mere allegory: fantastic as his Gods and Angels may be, it is clear that he and his disciples did regard them as real. The modern investigator has to be clear on both sides: to be fair to the religion of the Manichees we need to remember that the fantastic myths which Mani taught correspond to a serious view of the strange mixture of good and bad which we feel within ourselves and see in other human beings; and on the other hand as historians we must not treat as allegories the tales of the Primal Man and the rest of the Manichaean mythology because to us, with our modern conceptions of the material universe, the tales sound silly and bizarre.

The tale of the Primal Man is fundamental to Manichaeism. He was called into being to repel the invasion of the Light by the Dark, and was clothed or armed with the Five bright Elements, with Light, Wind, Fire, Water and Air (as distinct from 'Wind'). But the result was disaster. The Primal Man was left lying unconscious on the field, and the Five Elements were swallowed up by the Dark. This combat corresponds to the Fall in Catholic doctrine, but, as has been said above (p. 497), it is still nearer to the doctrine of Bardaisan, in that it makes the Fall to be the immediate cause of the world in which we live.

The Primal Man recovered from his swoon and entreated the Father of Greatness for help, so a fresh evocation of Light powers came into being. One of these, the Friend of the Light, called to the Primal Man, and the Primal Man had power to answer him[1]. The Powers of Darkness were definitely mastered and their invasion of the Light was arrested. But victory is one thing and

---

[1] This Answer and the corresponding Call were hypostasized by the Manichees: they seem to correspond to the Call of the Missionary and the favourable Answer it is able to bring forth from the Soul, even when enmeshed in material surroundings.

reparations another. The dark Archons had absorbed, almost digested, the Five Bright elements, and the Realm of Light would be for ever poorer if these were not recovered. The problem was not only to turn the proper region of Darkness into a prison by encircling it with an impenetrable wall, but also to extract the absorbed Light from the Archons. According to Mani our world is the result of that process.

First of all, a great deal of the Light-substance was immediately disgorged, and out of this the two pure Luminaries, Sun and Moon, were made. But a great deal remained in the very frames of the Archons, so the Primal Man 'flayed them, and made this sky from their skins, and out of their excrement he compacted the earth, and out of their bones he moulded and piled up the mountains,' so that 'in rain and dew the pure Elements yet remaining in them might be squeezed out.' Thus to Mani our earth with the visible heavens above us is formed of the dismembered parts of the evil demons of Darkness. It is held together and guarded by five Beings, especially evoked for the purpose by the Light: these are the *Splenditenens*, who holds the world suspended like a chandelier; the 'King of Honour,' whose rays collect the fragments of emitted light; the 'Adamas,' with shield and spear driving off any rescue-party of the demons of the Dark; the 'King of Glory,' who rotates the heavenly spheres that surround the world; and the gigantic 'Atlas,' on whose shoulders the whole mass is supported.

Meanwhile the Archons, though fettered and dismembered, produced not only plants and animals but also a being made in the image of the Divine Messenger of the Light that had appeared to them. This was Adam, truly a microcosm, the image of the world, of God and matter, of Light and Dark. To him, as he lay inert on the ground, appeared Jesus the *Zīwānā*—exactly what this epithet means is doubtful, but in any case it denotes a heavenly Being— who roused him from his slumber and made him realise his true nature. 'Jesus,' says Mani[1], 'made him stand upright and taste of the Tree of Life...when he said "Woe, woe, to the creator of my body! Woe to him who has bound my soul to it and to the rebels who enslaved me!"' As Cumont remarks[2], by making Adam taste of the tree of knowledge Jesus, and not the Tempter, revealed to him the extent of his misery. But man will know henceforth the way of enfranchisement. By continence and renunciation he must set free little by little the Divine Substance

---

[1] Theodore bar Konai *ap.* Pognon, *Inscr. mandaïtes*, p. 193.
[2] *La Cosmogonie Manichéenne*, p. 49.

within him, thereby joining in the great work of distillation with which God is occupied in the universe. If only Adam had persevered all would have been well, according to the Manichees, but he forgot and knew Eve, an inferior being, formed by the Archons to entice him. So Seth was born, and in him and us, his descendants, the particles of the Light are still imprisoned.

This is the Manichaean teaching about the Past. In the Present the Powers of Light have sent Prophets—Mani names Buddha and Zoroaster—but till Mani himself appeared the only one that mattered was, to use Mani's own phrase, 'Jesus who appeared in Judaea.'

Jesus in Mani's system occupies a peculiar position, which suggests that Manichaeism must be classed as an aberrant form of Christianity rather than as an independent religion. He was the last of the Prophets before Mani, and Mani regarded himself as the apostle of Jesus, beginning all his letters with 'Mani, apostle of Jesus Christ.' So Augustine had told us, and it is now confirmed by a fragment from Turfan and from the finds in Egypt. The 'Jesus' revered by Mani has, it is true, a different nature from the Jesus Christ of orthodox theology, and also from the Jesus of the Four Gospels. But Mani does mean the same 'Jesus who appeared in Judaea,' and his followers, as the books of Manichaean hymns testify, revered him along with Mani himself. It was Jesus who, when sent on his message of salvation, had contrived the vast mechanism, which takes up the souls of men and the light-particles of their bodies to the Moon when they die, which thus waxes for fifteen days, and when the souls have been purged (by the Sun, apparently) they are emptied out from the Moon, which then wanes for fifteen days. The souls are gathered into the 'Column of Glory,' no doubt meaning the Milky Way, till at last the 'Perfect Man[1]' is reconstructed.

In accordance with the Gospel[2] human history will end with the second coming of Jesus, who will judge all men by their treatment of the Faithful—*i.e.* the Manichaean Elect. This piece of the early Christian Hope was attested by a fragment found at Turfan, and now it is found to be the very core of the first of the 'Homilies' in Coptic (called *The Discourse of the Great War*), published in 1934[3].

Thus according to Manichaean belief the particles of the Light, still enmeshed in this dirty world, are being gradually distilled out

---

[1] See Eph. iv, 13.   [2] See especially Mt. xxv, 31–46.

[3] By H. J. Polotsky, *Manichäische Handschriften der Sammlung A. Chester Beatty*, I. *Manichäische Homilien.*

of it. In the end nothing will be left but what is, literally, dust and ashes. Even this will be consumed in a great bonfire which is to last 1468 years, after which it will sink down into the Dark by its own weight, while all the heavenly material will have been refined out of it and taken to the realm of Light where it belongs. The Smudge—*i.e.* this world, in the Manichaean view—will have been completely erased. That is their hope for the Future. It is a striking instance of the definiteness of Manichaean doctrine, that this curious period for the duration of the Great Fire, viz. 1468 years, the origin of which has not been explained, has been found in the Turfan documents, though otherwise it was only known from the Arabic *Fihrist*[1].

The rôle of Jesus in Manichaeism deserves a paragraph. Before the discoveries at Turfan the general tendency had been to emphasize the Oriental element in Mani's system and to regard the Christian element, then known most from Augustine, as due mainly to the adoption of a Christian dress by Manichaeism in the West. The new discoveries have changed all that: they prove that the Christian element, though heretical, is fundamental to Manichaeism, and that Mani, who came from the land of Babylon and had travelled to India, drew most of his inspiration from the Christianity of Marcion and of Bardaisan.

A first difficulty in comparing Christianity with the Manichee Religion lies in a difference between their fundamental conceptions. Orthodox Christianity more or less starts with the religion of Judaism, the religion of the Old Testament. The primal antithesis is between 'God' and 'His Creatures,' of which the race of Men is the noblest species. The main question in Western Christology was whether, and to what extent, 'Jesus who appeared in Judaea' was to be reckoned as belonging to 'God' or to 'the Creatures.' But to Mani the ultimate antithesis was not between God and Man, but between Light and Dark. A Man was not a unit, but a particle of Light enclosed in an alien and irredeemable envelope: there is no hope for a Man as such. The hope is that his Light-particles, not his whole personality, may escape at death from the dark prison-house of the body. And 'God' also belongs to a conception quite different from the personal, transcendent, Yahweh of the Old Testament. As used by the Manichees 'God' seems to be a name for anything wholly composed of and belonging to the Light-substance. The 'Primal Man,' the 'Messenger,' and others of the heavenly hierarchy, are little more than manifestations of the energy of the Light. They are not even, properly

[1] Flügel, *op. cit.* p. 90.

speaking, eternal, for they seem to come into existence to meet a need, as occasion arises.

With this view of God and Man, it is no wonder that Mani thought of Jesus as human only in appearance. But Jesus occupies a peculiar position also in the hierarchy of Light. Full as our accounts are of the Manichee cosmogony, no tale of theirs purports to give the story of how he was 'evoked' or called into being. Alone among the heavenly denizens He has a personal name, is in fact a person, as Buddha is, or Hermes, or Mani himself. No doubt this is because Jesus, whatever Mani may have thought about Him, is ultimately a certain Person 'who appeared in Judaea' a little more than two hundred years before Mani began to preach.

It has been indicated above that many of the outstanding principles of Manichaeism are far more natural results of tendencies in the Christianity of the third century and of Mesopotamia than of its modern development. The Manichaean idea of this world as the result of an original catastrophe, so that 'the Fall' comes before 'this world' exists and is indeed the cause of its existence, is derived from Bardaisan, the Aramaean Christian philosopher of Edessa[1]. The Manichaean view of Jesus is doubtless akin to that of Marcion. The Manichaean church, which they themselves called *Ecclesia*, was also organized like the Marcionites: as was also that of the early Syriac church of the Euphrates Valley, otherwise orthodox[2]. Moreover the tendency towards Asceticism, as remarked above[3], was characteristic even of the Great Church within the Roman Empire.

The Manichees were divided into two main classes, the *Elect* and the *Hearers*. The 'Elect' alone was the true Manichee, the 'Hearer' was no more than an adherent, but the renunciations exacted of the Elect were severe and their numbers were comparatively small. All Manichees were vegetarians, but the Elect abstained from wine, from marriage, and from property. They were supposed to live a wandering life, possessing no more than food for a day and clothes for a year. Their obligation not to produce fresh life or to take it was so absolute that they might neither sow nor reap, nor even break their bread themselves, 'lest they pain the Light which was mixed with it.' So they went about, as Indian holy men do, with a disciple who prepared their food for them. 'And when they wish to eat bread,' we read in the *Acta Archelai*[4], 'they pray first, speaking thus to the bread "I neither

---

[1] See above, p. 497.   [2] See above, p. 499.   [3] See p. 492.
[4] Given in Epiphanius, *Haer.* LXVI.

reaped nor winnowed nor ground thee, nor set thee in an oven; it was another did this, and brought to me: I eat thee innocently." And when he has said this for himself, he says to the disciple "I have prayed for thee."' On the other hand, it was one of the first duties of the mere Hearers to provide food for the Elect, so that in a country where there were any Manichees the Elect were sure not to starve. Women as well as men entered the ranks of the Elect.

There is a difference between the inner attitude of the Manichee ascetic and the orthodox Christian monk. The latter, whether hermit or coenobite, had retired from the world with a consciousness of sin and a sense of personal unworthiness. It is not for nothing that 'mourner' is one of the Syriac technical terms for a Christian monk. The Manichee Elect does not appear to have been a 'mourner.' He was indeed fenced about with tabus, but by virtue of his profession he was already Righteous: he was called *Zaddīkā*, 'the righteous' (in Arabic *Zindīk*), by his co-religionists. And though he was forbidden to prepare his food himself, yet a sacramental, even physical, benefit accrued to the Universe through his eating it. This came to pass through the particles of Light contained in the food passing into his own pure body, which at his death would be conveyed somehow into the realms of Light. Exactly how this was effected our documents do not tell us: it may be doubted if Mani himself had a consistent theory about it.

The religious duties of the Hearers can best be inferred from the *Khuastuanift*, *i.e.* 'Confession,' a document which has been recovered almost entire from the finds in Chinese Turkestan[1]. It is written in Turkestan Turkish, and contains a preamble followed by confession of fifteen kinds of sins, each section ending with the Persian (not Turkish) formula *Manāstār hīrza*, which means 'O cleanse our spots!'

The *Khuastuanift* is more than a mere confession. Each section begins by formulating the true Manichee doctrine, and then goes on to say 'If we have neglected or denied this, we are sinful and must cry *Manāstār hīrza*.' It is thus a profession of faith also, the most instructive document we possess for studying Manichaean religion as a working system. But it must be borne in mind how ambiguous a term is 'God' when used by Manichees, for to them 'God' is rather a substance than a person. *Tāngri*, *lit.* 'God,' is

---

[1] Edited by A. von Le Coq in *Journ. Roy. Asiat. Soc.* 1911, pp. 277–314: a revised and improved translation is given by W. Bang in *Muséon*, XXXVI, 1923, pp. 137–242.

rather to be rendered 'divine' than 'God,' for the Supreme Being when thought of as personal is called *Azrua*, *i.e.* the Persian *Zrvān*, which practically corresponds to our use of 'the Eternal.' The Primal Man is here called *Khormuzta*, *i.e.* 'Ormuzd.' This does not imply an adaptation of Persian or Magian myth: it is merely the name used of the Manichaean figure, just as if one were to call the President of a non-Christian religion its Pope.

Further, we have to bear in mind the fourfold nature of God according to Manichee theology. 'Mani enjoined belief,' says the *Fihrist*[1], 'in four great things—God, His Light, His Power, His Wisdom. And God is the King of the Paradise of Light, His Light is the Sun and Moon, His Power is the Five Angels, viz. the Air, the Wind, the Light, the Water and the Fire, and His Wisdom is the Holy Religion', which last in the *Khuastuanift* is identified sometimes with the Prophets who announced it, sometimes with the ordinances themselves. This fourfold conception of the Divine determines a good deal of the structure of the document.

The Prologue sets forth that as the Divine Khormuzta with the Divine Five Elements came down to fight against the Demons of the Dark, but was overcome and temporarily lost his Divine Light, so we, the penitent Manichees, if we have erred and lost touch with Azrua the pure bright God and become mixed with the Dark, may nevertheless hope to be restored, even as the Primal Man was.

After treating of blasphemy against God, against Sun and Moon, against the Five Divine Elements, and against social offences and false religion, it deals with offences after entering true religion[2], the preamble to which forms a sort of Manichaean *Credo*. 'Since coming to know the True God and the Pure Law, we have learnt the law of the Two Roots and the Three Moments, that the Light-root is God-land, the Dark-root is Hell-land; yea, we learned what had been before land and sky existed, why God and Demon had battled against each other, how Light and Dark had intermingled, and who had created land and sky; yea, we learned in what way this land and sky will be annihilated, and how Light and Dark will be separated, and what will happen afterwards: to the divine Azrua, the divine Sun and Moon, the divine Power, and the Prophets, we turned, we trusted, we became Hearers. Four bright seals on our hearts have we sealed, (1) To Love, the seal of the divine Azrua, (2) To Believe, the seal of the divine Sun and Moon, (3) To Fear, the seal of the Five divine

---

[1] Flügel, *op. cit.* p. 95.
[2] Sections 1–8.

elements, (4) Wise Wisdom, the seal of the Prophets.' This Manichaean *Credo* is permeated by the four-fold conception of God's nature, which has been mentioned above. The section then goes on to say that if the penitents should have violated their faith, then——*Manāstār hīrza*!

The remaining six sections refer to various offences in fasting, almsgiving and other religious duties. It ends saying 'every day, every month, trespass, sin do we commit! To the Light-Gods, to the Law's Majesty, to the pure Elect Ones, from trespass, from sin escaping, we pray *Manāstār hīrza*!'

There is a real difference between Christian and Manichee ethics. It can be expressed in a single sentence: Christianity is concerned with persons, Manichaeism with things. Christian sympathy goes out to men and women, who even in a fallen state are regarded as the image of God, and for whom Christ has died. The sympathy of the Manichee was directed, not towards men, but towards the Light imprisoned in men. Men were, to some extent and at second hand, in the image of God, but they were only a sort of pirated copy, made by the evil dark Archons to imitate the Messenger of the Light who had appeared to them.

The third of the four Homilies (published in 1934[1]) is of historical interest. It gives an account of the 'crucifixion' (*i.e.* the martyrdom) of Mani by Vahram I (Varanes, Bahram), grandson of Shapur, Mani's patron. It mentions one Innaeus, chief of the Manichees after Mani's successor Sisinnius, who pleased Vahram II and secured for the Manichees some peace from persecution. There seems to be another part of this work at Berlin, so that we may hope in future to be able to know something of the course of Manichee history before Islam overwhelmed Manichaeism and Zoroastrianism alike.

Meanwhile perhaps the most instructive product of the wonderful recovery of specimens of Manichaean literature during the present century are the many examples of Manichee hymns, which, like Christian hymns, more accurately depict the hopes and aspirations of those who used them than books of formal instruction or controversy. No doubt the Manichaeans' ethic is ascetic, 'a fugitive and cloistered virtue,' but their hymns prove that their religion inspired in them genuine emotion, full of loyalty to Mani and to Jesus. 'Amen, to thee, first born Apostle, Divine Lord Mani our Saviour!' Or again: 'Thou art God and Full Moon, Jesus Lord, Full Moon of waxing glory!...Mani, new Full Moon!...Holy one, Jesu, cleanse my stains! Divine

---

[1] Polotsky, *op. cit.* pp. 42–85.

Lord Mani, deliver my soul!' Or again: 'O Jesu, Virgin of Light! O Lord Mani! Do Thou make peace within me! O Light-bringer, deliver my soul out of this born-dead life, deliver my soul out of this born-dead life!' We may quarrel with the form of expression, both from the literary and the theological point of view, but it is clear that the Manichees who composed these pathetic ejaculations must have been moved by genuine religious sentiment.

Such were the main characteristics of the religion, which challenged official Christianity all through the century in which the Orthodox and Arians were struggling for mastery. It failed in the end, but the fear and alarm the Manichaean propaganda excited was real: it can best be felt by us in reading the story of Porphyry of Gaza and his encounter with Julia, the Manichaean missionary[1]. It was a serious conflict. The religion of Mani, when we look below the fantastic mythology with which he clothed his ideas, is a serious attempt to explain the presence of evil in the world we live in, and it does combine immediate pessimism with ultimate optimism—perhaps the most favourable atmosphere for the religious sentiment. It is true that the Manichees thought of our world as the result of an accident, and that no true improvement is possible till it is altogether abolished. This world, they thought, is bad to begin with, and it will go from bad to worse. But they believed that Light is really greater and stronger than the Dark, that in the end all that was good in their being would be collected in the domain of Light, a realm altogether swayed by Intelligence, Reason, Mind, good Imagination, and good Intention. Though at the same time there would always exist another region, dark, and dominated by unregulated desire, it would only be peopled by beings for whom such a region was appropriate, and that they would be separated off for ever from invading the region of Light and so producing another Smudge, such as our world essentially is, according to the Manichaean view.

[1] See the account in the *Life of Porphyry, Bishop of Gaza, by Mark the Deacon*, trans. by G. F. Hill, pp. 94–101.

CHAPTER XV

THE CHRISTIAN CHURCH IN THE WEST

I. THE CHRISTIAN PERSECUTIONS

THE attitude of the Christian community to this world and to its political organization in the Roman Empire was already unambiguously defined in the Apostolic Age, and it remained unaltered in the period which immediately succeeded. Even when the Second Coming of the Lord no longer possessed the overwhelming imminence of the first age and the community had become accustomed to the thought that they must still long await the dawn of that epoch of glory and blessedness, the consciousness that they were strangers and pilgrims upon earth remained thoroughly alive. It is true that they prepared themselves for a continuing sojourn amidst the conditions of the present age, that they freely acknowledged the benefits of the civil order and in accordance with Paul's exhortation (Rom. xiii) rendered it the obedience that was due, while in their common worship they called upon God to grant his protection to Emperor and Empire; but they were conscious that they themselves already possessed full citizenship in the kingdom of the heavenly Christ, which at its full manifestation at the last day would put an end to the dominion of the Romans and establish upon a rejuvenated earth a new life in accordance with divine laws. The Imperium Romanum wore for the Christians the aspect of something temporary, to which they adapted themselves in the confident expectation of a better dispensation to come.

But in the practice of daily life this inward aloofness found little visible expression. In his spirited *Apology* Tertullian protests to his pagan readers that the Christians avail themselves of the good things of this world exactly like their opponents, that in common with them they make use of the legal and commercial system and of all the institutions of public life, and that they engage in the ordinary callings of men just as they do. And over and above this he boasts that they are honest taxpayers, who for their Christian conscience' sake disdain the usual deceits and evasions for defrauding the revenue. As the only point of difference, he names

Note: For Church institutions mentioned in the first section of this chapter see section II.

their refusal to join in the worship of the pagan gods[1]. Yet there was something further. Not all professions were permissible for the Christian. Not only were the trades of immorality or such activities as were connected with pagan worship forbidden to him, but also participation in public offices and military service, which meant that a considerable part of civic activity was denied to the Christian. In such things their inward indifference to the life of the State became outwardly perceptible too.

In personal intercourse the Christians' attitude to this world and all its might and splendour naturally showed itself in a thousand ways and soon gave rise throughout the world to fundamental mistrust and to illusions, born of hatred, which by degrees gained ever sharper definition. Not only were some of those tales of atrocities related of the Jews transferred to the Christians, but newly invented abominations were added to them. It was known that the Christian gatherings for worship culminated in a common meal which was called *Agape*, i.e. 'Love-feast,' and that no uninitiated person was admitted. And since it was also known that amongst themselves the Christians called each other brother and sister, it was easy for prurient imaginations to fabricate stories of secret nocturnal orgies, which in the loathsome darkness gave free rein to incestuous lusts and converted the horrible crime of Oedipus into an act of worship. It was also learned that at this sacred meal the flesh of the Son of Man was eaten and his blood drunk. From this arose, as may be readily conceived, the contention that the Christians slaughtered and devoured children. But even where such tales were not credited, the conviction of the hostility of Christianity to the State, indeed of its fundamental hatred of mankind and of its coarse superstition opposed to all culture, was firmly rooted. About the year 180 the Platonic philosopher Celsus gives well-considered and pointed expression to the repugnance felt by the educated classes of his time to Christianity.

These anti-Christian sentiments were the driving force behind all the Christian persecutions before the year 250: they exercised a decisive influence upon the attitude of the authorities and in consequence upon their estimate of the legal position. In general, the principle laid down by Trajan in his rescript to Pliny (vol. XI, p. 255 *sq.*)[2], that the Christians were not to be sought out, held good for the whole empire. But if valid accusations came before the authorities, the Christian had then to offer sacrifice or die. This seems strange, but it shows us clearly that the question of the

---

[1] Tertullian, *Apol.* 42.   [2] Pliny, *Ep.* x, 96 (97) and 97 (98).

toleration of Christianity was dealt with, not from a juridical, but from a political, point of view. The Christians' hostile attitude to the State was regarded as judicially well-established. But this attitude as such was not punished, and the authorities gave every Christian who was denounced the opportunity of giving evidence to the contrary by offering sacrifice before the statue of the emperor. Only when he would not obey the order to sacrifice, and thereby violated the reverence due to the majesty of the Empire and its tutelary gods, was he condemned to death.

Since, then, the State did not seek out the Christians, the Christians remained tolerated, and they made the fullest use of this situation: their uncommonly successful expansion, whether we reckon it in time or by its extent, affords clear evidence of this. Official action was only taken against the Christians when special provocation so roused popular feeling that it resulted in definable charges against definite persons: granted that those who made accusations were sometimes raving mobs who with howls of execration at last dragged the mishandled victim of their frenzy before the tribunal. The Christians vainly asked again and again that their legal position should be made clear, demanding proof of the atrocities or other crimes attributed to them by the populace. The authorities, as far as we can see, took no steps in the matter, and they likewise studiously avoided all discussion of religious questions. They were not conducting religious prosecutions, but using their powers to secure tranquillity, and punishing the provocative disloyalty of those who refused to offer sacrifice. Whoever offered sacrifice returned home unmolested, and the officials did not concern themselves with his Christian beliefs or his previous activities.

We hear repeatedly that special Imperial edicts had prohibited the profession of Christianity. But we never hear that these edicts had made it the duty of the officials to stage Christian persecutions. These edicts then were only repetitions of Trajan's directions. And the manner in which they were carried out was left as before to the political judgment of the provincial authorities. About the year 215 the famous jurist Ulpian prepared a collection of such anti-Christian edicts, not of course with an antiquarian or historical interest, but in order to clarify criminal procedure by systematization of the law[1]. As may be readily understood, this collection has perished without leaving a trace. But we have preserved in Eusebius[2] two Imperial edicts which deal with the Christian question in a manner that departs so widely from the uniform

[1] Lactantius, *Div. Inst.* v, 11, 19.   [2] *Hist. Eccl.* iv, 9 and 13.

attitude of the State as everywhere else attested that it does not seem possible to accept these documents as genuine.

The accounts of Christian persecutions came to take two literary forms in this early period. The first is that of the letter. In this form we have the Martyrdom of Polycarp of Smyrna (156) and the account of the martyrs of Lyons (177). The other form is that of the minutes (Acts) of the trial: and this later became the rule. But it would be false to assume that in Acts of this kind we possess shorthand reports, or even official records of the Roman authorities. They are literary productions no less than the accounts composed as letters. If they wear the garb of official minutes, this is merely an attempt to give them a form that will bring home the credibility of the account to the minds of their readers and hearers. The Alexandrian anti-Semites, too, honoured the memory of their champions, who were executed under Claudius, in the form of such minutes[1].

The first instances of this type date from the time of Marcus Aurelius (161–80). In Pergamum two Christians named Carpus and Papylus, the latter a councillor from Thyatira, were in vain put to the torture by the Proconsul who was staying in the city. They steadfastly refused to offer sacrifice and were finally burned alive. Then a woman named Agathonice ran forward out of the crowd and, overcome with longing for the glory of heaven, threw herself into the flames with the martyrs. In Rome at about the same date the Christian philosopher and apologist Justin was beheaded with six of his disciples. The most impressive document remains, however, the Latin Acts of the execution of the martyrs of Scilli in Africa: the unaffected directness of these simple people, and the conciseness of the narrative which accords so wonderfully with it, still produce the same effect on us to-day as once on the church of Africa. The minutes begin in correct style with the date, 1 August 180, the scene is laid in Carthage in the council chamber of the Proconsul Saturninus. And then in question and answer the melancholy drama is unfolded before us: confession of Christianity, refusal to sacrifice, rejection of time for reflection, sentence—and 'all said, "Thanks be to God!" and were immediately beheaded for the name of Christ.'

The counterpart to this is supplied by the letter[2] which the communities at Vienne and Lyons wrote to their sister communities in Asia Minor to acquaint them with what had befallen

[1] See vol. x, p. 683; U. Wilcken, 'Zum alexandrinischen Antisemitismus' (*Abh. sächs. Gesell. d. Wiss.* XXVII, 1909, 23, pp. 826 *sqq.*).

[2] Eusebius, *Hist. Eccl.* v, 1, 3–3, 3.

them[1]. In it we are given a full description, deeply moving in its terrible plainness, of a persecution which overtook the two communities in A.D. 177. What incident actually occasioned it we do not learn. But suddenly throngs of people rush through the streets, break into the houses, and drag the Christians together into the market-place with every kind of maltreatment, until the governor appears and so restores order to the proceedings. In these two cities there is a regular hunting-out of the Christians: they are thrown in crowds into the prisons, interrogated, tortured, and whoever denies Christ is set free. But the suspicion of the rabble remains alert, and so even these apostates are re-arrested and now regain their hold upon the faith and courage shown by their companions. They now confess steadfastly and suffer the same fate. Every torment that bloodthirsty imagination can devise is enacted in the darkness of the prison-cell or amid the hatred and publicity of the arena. Their mangled limbs are roasted to cinders on red-hot chairs, the brave slave-girl Blandina meets her end at the stake, the ninety-year-old bishop Pothinus, brutally mishandled, dies in prison, and round him rows of unfortunates gasp out their lives stretched in the stocks. But the communities of the two Gallic cities do not break down under this persecution. From the steadfastly endured sufferings of the martyrs they had won the assurance of heavenly succour and come to know how in the most fearful pains of death a heavenly radiance enlightens the eyes that have been granted the vision of the glory of God beyond the reach of human sight. When earthly torments threaten to overwhelm the body, then God's mercy lifts its witnesses above all such pains and makes them equal to the angels. He who has come victorious through this conflict is already here on earth transported into the world to come, bearing witness by his deeds, words, and looks to the truth of the living Christ.

What the communities of Gaul wrote to their fellow-Christians in Asia Minor was the universal experience of Christendom wherever martyrs won the crown of victory. And so every one of these testimonies in blood became a seed from which there sprang in a thousand hearts new fruit for Christianity. Thus in the martyr[1] the old enthusiasm of primitive Christianity revived, and the reverence which the community already paid to their bravery and contempt of death from purely human motives was united with the recognition of the holy Spirit who revealed himself in the

[1] On the connotation of 'martyr' see F. Jackson and K. Lake, *The Beginnings of Christianity*, vol. v, note v and H. v. Campenhausen, *Die Idee des Martyriums in der alten Kirche*.

martyrs. Thus too these men and women became authorities empowered to give a decisive ruling on important questions of the community. This became especially evident in the days of the Decian persecution, and in many places led to conflicts with the episcopate, which felt its authority impaired by the claims of the martyrs. A living picture of the enthusiastic temper of the martyrs is given us by a document from North Africa, which in its own way is unique, the Passion of Perpetua and her companions (see below, p. 594). In it the imprisoned Christians have themselves recorded their experiences, and the principal heroine, Vibia Perpetua, and one of her companions named Saturus give a full account of the visions vouchsafed to them, and in so doing they disclose quite naïvely their consciousness that a martyr has the right to demand such revelations from God, and that his intercession can procure the deliverance of departed souls in the world to come and his exhortation reconcile contending clerics upon earth. The appended description of their last agonies not only depicts the horrors that were devised for the entertainment of the multitude who filled the arena, but also enables us to trace the feelings of the victims and the ecstatic insensibility which raised them above the physical torments of these terrible scenes. This Passion was enacted in the reign of Septimius Severus in the year 203.

We hear at about the same time of a Christian persecution in Egypt, which drove the teaching of Christianity out of Alexandria and exacted as its victim amongst others Origen's father. No authentic Acts of the martyrs survive for the immediately succeeding period. That the emperors of the Syrian dynasty, with their leanings towards syncretism, took no great pleasure in themselves initiating Christian persecutions is intelligible enough, as it is also that the reaction under Maximinus Thrax carried off, along with many high officials of this period, a number of leading churchmen. And now too, when districts of Asia Minor were suffering from severe earthquakes, popular fury against the Christians blazed up fiercely once more: the Christians were held responsible for these terrible manifestations of the undisguised wrath of the gods, and in these years threatening clouds were indeed gathering over the Roman Empire. The Persians were pressing forward in Syria, and on the lower Danube the Goths broke across the frontier and threatened with dissolution an Empire already weakened by economic depression and ever recurrent disputes for the throne.

The year 249 again witnessed a persecution of the Christians by the excited mob in Alexandria, and then there began under the Emperor Decius the first systematic Christian persecution, organized for the whole Empire by Imperial command. The new Imperator was confronted with a task of unprecedented difficulty and wished to unite all the forces of the Empire for its achievement. He also called to his aid the hearts of his subjects by appointing a general sacrifice of homage and intercession before the images of the tutelary gods of the Empire. In all cities, villages, and hamlets sacrificial commissions were set up, which were to supervise its execution and to deliver to everyone who took part a written certificate of having performed the act of sacrifice. Thus would be achieved both the propitiation of the angry gods and the eradication of the hated Christians: for those Christians who obeyed the Imperial command thereby dissociated themselves from the Church as apostates from their faith, while those who steadfastly resisted were removed by death.

All the witnesses we have concur in their evidence that these measures for the first time seriously imperilled the existence of the communities. The Christians, when summoned to appear, yielded in great numbers to coercion and offered sacrifice. And the cunning persons who by bribery purchased evidence of their loyalty without really offering sacrifice were judged only a little more leniently by the Church, and in the end they too were reckoned among the lapsed[1]. The number of martyrs was large and at their head stand bishops Fabian of Rome, Babylas of Antioch, and Alexander of Jerusalem. But taken as a whole there were relatively few who remained constant by comparison with the many apostates. However, trustworthy Acts of the martyrs for the Decian persecution have hardly been preserved, and though it might seem as though Decius had attained his object, the facts that have been handed down are to us a proof to the contrary. The Church had been able to endure the occasional defection of individuals in the sporadic persecutions of the earlier period and to punish apostasy with irrevocable exclusion. The wholesale defection of the Decian persecution could no longer be met with the full rigour of the tradition that had existed hitherto. Even before the persecution ceased, the possibility was under consideration in the most widely separated Church provinces of admitting the lapsed to the penance of the Church and thereby opening the way for their restoration to the Christian fellowship (see below, p. 538 sq.).

[1] Cyprian, Ep. 30, 3; 55, 14; de lapsis, 27.

The first to be inclined to such leniency were the circles of enthusiastic martyrs who, with their inherent authority from the holy Spirit, granted pardon to their weaker brethren and urged upon the bishops, or even dictated to them, their admission to the fellowship of the Eucharist; and in many places their injunction found a ready acceptance. But even where such unrestrained readiness to pardon met with resistance from episcopal authority, it was not contested that in principle the restoration of the lapsed was possible, the only requirement being a properly regulated procedure for attaining this end. In one way or another the fruits of victory were snatched from the hands of the pagan State. The masses of the lapsed returned to the Church, and the steadfast confessions of the many martyrs served only to strengthen among Christians as a whole their sense of the invincibility of Christianity. The State itself shrank from pressing its policy to a logical conclusion against all who opposed it: it was simply not possible to exterminate the Christians by bloodshed, and thus by the spring of 251 the fury of the persecution abated, and in the summer it came to an end with the death of the Emperor, who lost his life on the Gothic front.

This, the most severe and widespread onslaught upon Christianity, was followed in the course of the next few years by a few slighter clashes, and in the summer of 257 the Emperor Valerian determined on a new assault upon the Church so displeasing to the gods. Again the blow was directed in the first instance against the leaders of the community: this time bishop Xystus of Rome suffered together with his deacons, at whose head stood Laurence, glorified by legend; and almost at the same time fell the head of Cyprian, bishop of Carthage (258). But two years later Valerian was taken prisoner by the Persians, in whose hands, to the dishonour of the Roman Empire, he died. His son and successor Gallienus had good grounds for putting an end to the Christian persecution. Indeed he even issued an edict of toleration, in which the Christians were granted the use of their places of worship and their cemeteries, and a general ordinance was issued that they were not to be further molested[1]. So ended the State action that began with Decius. The martyrs of this period of persecution won for the Church what hitherto she had never possessed, the recognition of her right to exist.

[1] Eusebius, *Hist. Eccl.* VII, 13.

II. THE INNER LIFE OF THE CHURCH

The earliest description of the Christian Sunday service comes from the pen of the apologist Justin (*c.* 150)[1] and may be regarded as evidence for the custom of the Roman church. The congregation assembles and listens first to a reading from the Gospels or the writings of the prophets, to which a fixed time is allotted. There follows a sermon of exhortation by the officiant. And then begins the second act of the service, to which only the baptized are admitted, whereas in the first part, not only the whole body of the catechumens may take part, but probably also non-Christians who are believed to have a serious interest in Christianity and perhaps also to be inclined to join the community. This second part, which consists in the observance of the Eucharist[2], begins with a common prayer of the congregation for the salvation of Christendom and its moral perfecting, that it may attain to eternal salvation. Then the members of the congregation salute each other with the kiss of brotherhood as the symbol of that common brotherhood in which all Christians are bound together. There follows the 'Offertory,' *i.e.* members of the congregation bring to the officiant bread, wine, and water, and he then recites over these gifts placed upon the table a prayer of thanksgiving, the *Eucharistia*, and at its conclusion the congregation responds with 'Amen.' This prayer contains also the invocation of the divine Logos, in which the officiant prays for his descent upon the bread and wine that to the Christians they may become the saving food of the body and blood of Jesus. After this supreme act of the rite the deacons distribute the consecrated gifts to those who are present and later they take them also to those who are absent, to the sick, and to those in prison. The conclusion of the service, however, consists in the collection of voluntary offerings, which are deposited with the officiant and enable him to succour the sick, the widows and orphans, those in prison, the needy, or strangers sojourning with the community.

We see therefore already contained in the Roman observance of the Eucharist at about the middle of the second century all the essential elements of the Sunday liturgy that still determine its course to the present day. At the same time, however, it is clear that here already a decided change has taken place as compared with the earliest times. The rite described by Justin corresponds to the type of morning service still familiar at the present day. In

---

[1] Justin, *Apol.* I, 65–7.

[2] 'Eucharist' is used throughout this chapter for the celebration of the Lord's Supper, the Greek '*Eucharistia*' for the prayer of thanksgiving alone.

the earliest period the Eucharist belongs to the late afternoon hours and is the climax of a common meal of ritual character in which the community, or in many cases perhaps only sections of the community (house-communities), are united in a celebration in which religious sociability is combined with the sacramental partaking of the body and blood of the Lord. By about the middle of the second century, the sacramental meal has developed into an independent rite and has been transferred to Sunday morning and joined with the service of reading and preaching.

The common fellowship meal of the community continued to exist alongside it and was still a regular practice about the year 200; but it then died out slowly in the course of the third century, and survived only in its formal rudiments. Tertullian tells us the form such a celebration took in Carthage at the end of the second century[1]. Rich and poor join together in this Love-feast. First a prayer is said standing, then all recline and the meal begins; but the food and drink are partaken of in moderation and conversation is kept within proper bounds; for they know that the Lord is with them at table. When the meal is ended, and at sunset the lights are lit, there are readings from holy scripture, or they listen to recitation or song by members of the brethren. A final prayer concludes the gathering. Just the same form is taken by a celebration of the kind at about the same period in Rome, and the description there given of it adds a few new details to the picture[2]. Here the rule is that a well-to-do host invites those who take part, and the celebration is held in his house. And it is strictly prescribed that a cleric must preside at the celebration and must break the hallowed bread, which, though strictly distinguished from the bread of the Eucharist, is distributed as consecrated food amongst those taking part. But here already the transformation of the *Agape* into a simple act of charity is discussed, and mention is made of the possibility of handing the guests provisions to take away with them, instead of sitting down with them to a common meal.

The source from which we derive this information is the *Church Order*[3] composed by Hippolytus, the rival bishop of Rome, which preserves for us also the oldest liturgical form for the Sunday celebration of the Eucharist, apart from the *Didache*, which belongs to a quite different type (vol. xi, p. 289). After the

---

[1] Tertullian, *Apol.* 39, 16–19.

[2] Hippolytus, *Church Order*, 48–50 Funk; Hauler, p. 113 *sq.*; Connolly, p. 187 *sq.* See following note.

[3] Hippolytus, *Church Order*. The principal texts are contained in: (1) for the Latin version, E. Hauler, *Didascaliae Apostolorum Fragmenta Ueronensia Latina, accedunt Canonum qui dicuntur Apostolorum et Aegyptiorum Reliquiae,*

kiss of peace, the deacons place the offering in the form of bread and wine and water upon the altar-table, the bishop lays his hands upon it, and the *Eucharistia* begins with the following dialogue:

Bishop: The Lord be with you.
Congregation: And with thy spirit.
Bishop: Hearts up (ἄνω τὰς καρδίας)!
Congregation: We have them to the Lord (ἔχομεν πρὸς τὸν Κύριον).
Bishop: Let us give thanks to the Lord.
Congregation: It is meet and right.
Bishop: We thank Thee, God, through Thy beloved Servant Jesus Christ whom in the last times Thou hast sent us as Saviour and Redeemer and Messenger of Thy counsel, the Logos who comes from Thee, through whom Thou hast made all things, whom Thou wast pleased to send from heaven into the womb of the virgin, and in her body he became flesh and was shown forth as Thy Son, born of the holy Spirit and the virgin. To fulfil Thy will and to prepare Thee a holy people, he stretched out his hands, when he suffered, that he might release from suffering those who have believed on Thee.

And when he delivered himself to a voluntary passion, to loose death and to break asunder the bands of the devil, and to trample hell and to enlighten the righteous and to set up the boundary stone and to manifest the resurrection, he took a loaf, gave thanks, and spake, 'Take, eat, this is my body which is given for you.' Likewise also the cup and said, 'This is my blood which is poured out for you. As often as you do this, you make my commemoration.'

Remembering therefore his death and resurrection, we offer to Thee the loaf and the cup and give thanks to Thee that Thou hast counted us worthy to stand before Thee and to do Thee priestly service.

And we beseech Thee, that Thou send down Thy holy Spirit upon this offering of the church. Unite it and grant to all the saints who partake of it to their fulfilling with holy Spirit, to their strengthening of faith in truth, that we may praise and glorify Thee through Thy Servant Jesus Christ, through whom to Thee be glory and honour in Thy holy church now and ever. Amen[1].

This prayer can be regarded as the pattern, and in a certain sense even as the foundation, of all Eucharistic prayers that have

Leipzig, 1900, p. 101, l. 31– p. 121; (2) for the Ethiopic, Arabic, and Coptic versions, together with English translations, G. Horner, *The Statutes of the Apostles*, London, 1904. See also F. X. Funk, *Didascalia et Constitutiones Apostolorum*, vol. 11, Paderborn, 1905, pp. 97–119; T. Schermann, *Die allgemeine Kirchenordnung*, Erster Teil, Studien zur Geschichte und Kultur des Altertums, Dritter Ergänzungsband, Paderborn, 1914.

For a critical discussion, see E. Schwartz, *Ueber die pseudoapostolischen Kirchenordnungen*, Schriften der wiss. Gesell. in Strassburg, Strassburg, 1910; R. H. Connolly, *The So-called Egyptian Church Order and derived documents*, Texts and Studies, vol. VIII, No. 4, Cambridge, 1916 (a continuous text is printed in Appendix B, pp. 175–194).

[1] Hippolytus, *Church Order*, 31, 11–21 Funk; Hauler, p. 106 *sq.*;

come down to us; and even in the modern liturgical forms of most of the Christian confessions its formulas or ideas can be clearly recognized, even though in varying degrees. The actual *Euchar-istia*, *i.e.* the thanksgiving of the person praying, relates to the benefits which God has bestowed upon mankind through the sending of His Son and through His passion. The mention of the suffering introduces the 'night in which the Lord was betrayed,' and leads on to the recitation of the words of institution, upon which, in expansion of the Pauline conclusion (1 Cor. xi, 26), follows the so-called *Anamnesis*, which gives expression to the consciousness of the congregation that they are celebrating the commemoration of the death and resurrection. And then there follows a formula praying for the descent of the holy Spirit upon the elements which seems to be the root of the later so-called *Epiclesis*[1].

These elements, bread and wine, are here described as the offering of the congregation, and the officiant thanks God that he is exercising the function of a priest. We here find it clearly expressed—and this was already indicated by earlier evidence—that the Christian church celebrates the Eucharist as a ritual sacrifice, and accordingly ascribes to the officiant the office of a priest. The celebration is here regarded as a sacrifice, because the congregation lays the elements of bread and wine as its gifts upon the altar. These, however, by the descent of the holy Spirit are filled with a wonderful divine power, and the congregation which partakes of this heavenly food presents a parallel with the members of cult-fellowships who partake of the divinely-imbued sacrificial meal: this idea too is already anticipated in Paul (1 Cor. x, 18–21). Alongside both these ideas of sacrifice goes also a third, and this is the earliest in the sphere of Christian thought. According to this idea, prayer is the only sacrifice worthy to be offered to God, and accordingly the sacrificial character of the Eucharist has its basis in the prayer of thanksgiving, *i.e.* the '*Eucharistia.*'

About the middle of the third century in Cyprian[2] an entirely new conception of sacrifice can be observed, which then developed rapidly and proved decisive for the Catholic interpretation of the Mass. According to this conception, the act of the priest is an imitation of the sacrifice of Christ, whose body and blood are

Horner, p. 139 *sq.*, p. 245, p. 307 *sq.*; Connolly, p. 176; and cf. H. Lietz-mann, *Messe und Herrenmahl, eine Studie zur Geschichte der Liturgie*, pp. 174 *sqq.* and also pp. 158 *sqq.*, p. 42 *sq.*, p. 57 *sq.*, p. 80 *sq.*
[1] Justin knows of a similar prayer for the descent of the Logos (*Apol.* 1, 66, 2). See above, p. 523.   [2] Cyprian, *Ep.* 63, 14.

again offered as once upon Golgotha. Here we have quite plainly before our eyes an idea of primitive religion transferred to a Christian cult. The solemn rehearsal or the dramatic re-enactment of some event from the history of the gods releases the same divine forces and produces the same effects as were once displayed at the time of the original occurrence. This view underlies many actions of the mystery religions, and it is found at the most varied levels of ritual practice down to ordinary healing-magic. It was under the influence of this idea that the community attempted to reach an understanding of the miraculous character of the Eucharist.

Ideas derived from primitive religion soon surrounded also the rite of baptism with ceremonial additions. The water is cleansed by solemn exorcism from the elemental spirits that dwell in it[1]; but the candidate too has had driven out of him the evil spirit which dwells in him in that he is a pagan[2]. As early as the beginning of the third century we find the custom by which the candidate in a solemn formula renounces Satan and all his service and all his works, and then gives his oath of allegiance (*sacramentum*) to his new lord Jesus by the recitation of the creed. After the baptism, which cleanses the pagan from his sins, he is anointed and receives the holy Spirit by the laying on of the bishop's hands. In this way he is finally received into the Christian fellowship and, immediately after his baptism, joins in the Eucharist[3]. In Egypt, Rome, and Carthage it was the custom to deliver to the candidates at their first communion, in addition to bread and wine, a cup of milk and honey, to give them a foretaste of the heavenly food of which the blessed partake in the Kingdom of God[4]. In this rite, too, borrowing from the ancient mystery cults springs to the eye. Along with these two great acts of the liturgical life, we find already at the beginning of the third century a number of special rites in process of development: thus the ceremonial of consecration for bishops, priests, and deacons, and many forms of blessing fruits and flowers[5].

---

[1] Hippolytus, *Church Order*, 46, 1 Funk; Connolly, p. 183; Cyprian, *Ep.* 70, 1; Clement of Alexandria, *Excerpta ex Theodoto*, 82. Tertullian, *de Bapt.* 4.

[2] Hippolytus, *Church Order*, 45, 9 *sq.* Funk; Connolly, p. 183.

[3] Hippolytus, *Church Order*, 46 Funk; Hauler, pp. 110–13; Connolly, pp. 183–6. Tertullian, *de Bapt.* 7–8; *de Res. Carnis*, 8.

[4] Hippolytus, *Church Order*, 46, 22 *sqq.* Funk; Hauler, pp. 111–13; Connolly, p. 185 *sq.* Tertullian, *de Corona* 3; *adv. Marcionem*, I, 14; Clement of Alexandria, *Paed.* I, 6, 45.

[5] Hippolytus, *Church Order*, 53–4 Funk; Hauler, p. 115 *sq.*; Connolly, p. 190.

Moreover the ordering of daily prayer also begins to make its appearance, and it prepares the way for the later hallowing of the canonical hours. In other respects the formation of a Christian church year still remains within very narrow limits. The most prominent division of time is still, as in primitive Christianity, the week, in which Wednesday and Friday are marked as days of fasting, while Sunday as the Lord's day is devoted to the service of the Eucharist. A survival of the Jewish Law appears in the widespread observance of the annual Passover, which is naturally observed on 14 Nisan, the day commanded in the Old Testament, or in other words on the day of the full moon of the spring month: consequently on the same day as that on which the Jews keep the festival. Only the content of the celebration is changed. Whilst the Jews keep the Passover as a festival of national rejoicing, it is for the Christians the day of the commemoration of the passion and crucifixion of Christ and is accordingly marked by fasting, till the first cock-crow announces the end of the night of suffering and the community can 'break the fast,' *i.e.* join together in the Eucharistic meal[1].

By the side of this original form of the Passover celebration, there arose as early as the second century another, which emphasized opposition to Judaism more strongly: from being a commemoration of the death it came to be a yearly celebration of the resurrection, in which as it were the weekly celebrations of the resurrection on Sundays reached their culmination. This was marked by the choice of the day. Instead of the night of the full moon of the Jewish Passover, the night preceding the following Sunday was chosen, and this Sunday with its celebration of the Eucharist was made into the Christian festival of rejoicing, preceded by the night of Christ's rest in the grave, which was kept with fasting and prayer. The custom also soon grew up of baptizing the catechumens of the year on this night of Easter Eve. The reason for this was that those seeking baptism were every year formed into a group and together instructed in the fundamental doctrines of Christianity.

In connection with this practice a tradition of instruction was developed, which took many varying forms in the different districts, but increasingly came to adopt the threefold creed, expounding the individual clauses in greater detail. In consequence, this confession became the rule of faith and could be treated as a secured formulation of the content of Christian truth; for in the minds of the community the interpretation given of its clauses in

[1] *Epist. Apost.* 15 Schmidt.

the instruction of catechumens was inseparably bound up with its wording[1]. In the conflict with gnosticism, this instruction in the Christian doctrine of the Church, thus linked with the baptismal confession, was of the greatest service.

The festival of Easter introduced a period of fifty days, which was observed as a time of Christian rejoicing, and concluded with the feast of Pentecost. Pentecost too was originally no other than the Old Testament day taken over from Judaism (Lev. xxiii, 15–21), but it was observed in the Church as the festival of the outpouring of the holy Spirit upon the Apostles (Acts ii). Beyond these two days, Easter and Pentecost, the Church year was not developed during the third century. The festival of Epiphany on January 6, which makes its appearance amongst the gnostic followers of Basilides in Egypt, remained for the time being unknown to the Church[2].

On the other hand, in the middle of the second century the custom was already growing up in the individual communities of celebrating the anniversaries of the deaths of their own outstanding martyrs[3]. In the third century this custom spread more widely and became established: the Decian persecution supplied abundant material for the development of these community celebrations, and thus arose within the churches the first beginnings of calendars of saints. Towards the end of the second century we can begin to trace also the Christians' peculiar style of burial, which, apparently under the influence of Jewish models, developed uniformly in different places, namely the burial of the dead in so-called catacombs[4]. These are underground cemeteries such as were frequently employed in the East and were not entirely unknown even in the West. But the Christians clearly extended them systematically under pressure of their distressed condition in relation to the State and developed them into immense constructions which in the persecutions of the third century could be used as refuges for the persecuted communities or as secret places for common worship. They always take the form of long horizontal galleries driven into the earth, sometimes in several storeys one above the other, and their walls are provided with rectangular recesses, in which the bodies were laid without

[1] Irenaeus, *adv. Haer.* I, 10, 1–2; I, 22, 1; III, 4, 1. Tertullian, *de Praescr.* 13; *adv. Prax.* 2 and 30.

[2] Clement of Alexandria, *Strom.* I, 21, 146, 1–2.

[3] *Martyrium Polycarpi*, 17–18.

[4] Herzog-Hauck, *Realencyklopädie*[3], x, pp. 804–13; Cabrol, *Dict. d'Archéologie Chrétienne*, ii, pp. 2441–7.

coffins and wrapped only in cloths. A slab fixed with mortar shuts off the grave from the corridor. Well-to-do families possessed rectangular burial chambers branching off from these corridors, and where the catacombs were constructed in particularly firm soil, or were bored into the rock, we find also larger chambers and hall-like structures, in which more spacious graves occur, with semicircular vaulting (Arcosolia), or canopied graves. In these chambers consecrated to the dead we meet also with the first certain traces of a peculiar Christian art, and the rich abundance of the catacomb pictures, found in various districts of the Roman Empire and extending over more than three centuries, affords information on the earliest motifs and their manifold developments in early Christian art. But we must always remember that owing to this limited nature of the material we know only one phase, though certainly an essential one, of the development of art, and that we have also to reckon with the growth of the Christian artistic impulse in the realm of the living (p. 565). This is brought vividly before our eyes in the period after Constantine by the surviving monuments.

III. THE ROMAN CHURCH

The Roman church became conscious at an early date that, as the community of the capital of the world, she occupied a special position in Christendom and must fashion herself accordingly. The First Epistle of Clement (c. 95), written in the name of the community, already expresses a lively sense of obligation to come to the aid of a sister community, threatened by internal dissension, with good advice and furthermore with authoritative direction. Naturally the authoritative character of its instruction is not made to rest upon appeal to the importance of the writer of the letter, but is given an objective basis in the word of the Bible and supported by emphasis upon the apostolic appointment of all leaders of the community (*episkopoi*) and their successors (vol. XI, p. 291). But the Roman community's sense of its own importance is nevertheless unmistakable and it finds expression in the whole tenor of the letter. Rome imparts profitable instruction to the Corinthian community and regards this as her right and her duty: but one gets the impression that the Romans would have been greatly surprised had Corinth, let us say, in similar circumstances dispatched such a letter of admonition to Rome.

Of the evolution of church order in Rome we have no precise information. Towards the middle of the second century a certain Hermas writes a book which bears the title *The Shepherd* and consists of a highly elaborated series of visionary scenes, inter-woven with lengthy exhortations to repentance. In it also appear incidentally the leaders of the community, the *episkopoi* and *diakonoi*, or presbyters, without any sharp differentiation between the titles being recognizable (vol. xi, p. 292). It is clear only that Hermas still knows nothing of a monarchical episcopate in Rome, but is thoroughly familiar with disputes about rank and honour within this circle. But the question must have been cleared up soon afterwards; for in the second half of the century, indeed soon after the year 150, we find single persons like Anicetus and Soter coming forward as responsible leaders of the community. We have indeed preserved in Irenaeus[1] a list of the Roman bishops from Linus, whom the apostles appointed, to Eleutherus. And as Irenaeus still knew the successor of Eleutherus, bishop Victor, this list may be appealed to as the ancient and official tradition of the Roman church (vol. xi, p. 291).

We have also, from fourth-century sources[2], lists of Roman bishops which agree with this ancient list, continue it, and even supply precise dates of the accession to office and day of death of the individual popes. That for the early period these precise dates are invented will not be seriously doubted. Many, however, are still to-day inclined to accept the years given, at least those for the second century, as trustworthy tradition. Unfortunately a critical examination of the material does not confirm this belief. The Roman list of popes was first supplied with trustworthy chrono-logical details under Fabian about the year 240, and the period of the rule of Pontian from 22 August 230 to 28 September 235 is the first tolerably assured date of the Roman papal chronology. All earlier dates assigned are guesses of later chronographers and can make no claim to rest upon ancient tradition. On the other hand, we have no reason for disputing the trustworthiness of the list of names itself, and we may see in the persons named the prominent men of the Roman college of presbyters from the days of the apostles to the end of the second century, though it is only after Anicetus that we can speak of monarchical government by one bishop.

We cannot doubt that this strengthening of the authority of the leader of the community was the outcome of the conflicts which that period brought to the Roman community. About the middle of the century both Marcion and his followers and the

---

[1] Irenaeus, *adv. Haer.* III, 3, 3.
[2] *Catalogus Liberianus* and *Index*; see C. H. Turner in *Journ. Theol. Stud.* XVII, 1916, pp. 338–53; H. Lietzmann, *Petrus und Paulus*[2], pp. 7–16.

Alexandrian gnostics, especially Valentinus, endeavoured to gain a footing in Rome and to win over the Roman community: but both assaults were repulsed with full and lasting effect.

From the same period we have the account of a visit which Polycarp, the aged bishop of Smyrna, paid to Rome. This was the occasion of a discussion of the fact that Rome kept no celebration of the Passover, and Polycarp did not succeed in persuading the Romans to adopt the custom of Asia Minor in keeping the Passover in association with the death of Christ. But this in no way disturbed the peaceful relations of the Church with Asia Minor, and Rome offered no objection when Christians of Asia Minor who were settled in Rome celebrated the night of the Passover in their accustomed way. But towards the end of the century the rapidly prevailing custom of celebrating the resurrection on Easter Sunday had been adopted in Rome, and now the difference between the two rites seemed to Victor the bishop intolerable.

It was probably the existence of both customs side by side in the city of Rome itself that finally determined him to turn against the church of Asia Minor as a whole[1], in order to strike at the root of the evil. He assured himself of the assent of most of the churches of the East, and of the church of Gaul, to the practice adopted in Rome of celebrating Easter on a Sunday, and then demanded of the church of Asia Minor that they should discontinue their quartodeciman use, *i.e.* the commemoration of the death of Christ on the day of the Jewish Passover.

When the spokesman of the Asiatics, bishop Polycrates of Ephesus, replied that their custom was in accordance with apostolic tradition, and found corroboration in pointing to the graves of the apostles in Asia Minor, Victor still persisted in his demand and threatened exclusion from the fellowship of the Church. But it then became clear that he no longer had the other districts of the Church upon his side. These were not willing to make the difference over Easter the occasion of a conflict that would break up the unity of the Church; and Irenaeus protested to his Roman colleague in strong terms against the overbearingness of his demand. Thus the Roman claim to extend its authority over the East as well was rejected; but the defeat had only a momentary significance. Nevertheless in this matter Rome had in fact been the representative of the general opinion of the Church and had intervened as such. Out of this situation sprang new possibilities for the future.

[1] The view of N. Zernov (*Church Quart. Rev.* CXVI, 1933, pp. 24 *sqq.*) that the controversy concerned only the community in Rome is not here adopted.

In what high esteem the Roman church was held in the West towards the close of the second century we see from the principal work of Irenaeus himself, who quotes the list of Roman bishops as exemplifying a line of tradition reaching back to the apostles, and from this draws the conclusion that undoubtedly the pure doctrine is to be found in Rome, with which in consequence all other communities that rest upon apostolic tradition must necessarily agree[1]. Rome was the principal centre of the West in the sense also that it was the scene of the theological conflicts that were brought to the West from the East, always more actively stirred by speculation. Not only the teaching of Marcion and the gnostics, but also various views on the nature of the divinity of Christ taught by representatives of Asia Minor, were put forward in Rome and for a time gained a not inconsiderable influence.

Those that made most impression were the so-called Monarchians[2], who would hear nothing of the learned speculations about Christ as the Logos. They refused to see in Christ, after the fashion of the theology of the Apologists, the incarnation of a second divine being begotten of the Father, the Logos, and accepted the statement that God was made man in its full and literal sense. There is only one God and no other divine being beside him, and this one God appeared on earth in human form as Jesus Christ, and died for us on the cross, and now works as holy Spirit in the Christian Church[3]. That was the popular theology, in the East no less than in the West, and in a certain sense it has remained so to the present day.

In Rome the bishops of the period about A.D. 200 were not disinclined to accept this interpretation. But in opposition to this the representatives of a more learned theology defended the Logos theology, sanctioned by the Gospel of St John, as the only possible doctrine; and the Roman presbyter Hippolytus was an impassioned champion of this point of view. He was opposed, not only by the Libyan theologian Sabellius, who had come to Rome, but still more strongly by Callistus, who became bishop on the death of Zephyrinus, whose supporter and practical administrator he had been. The antagonism rent the Roman community into two parts, and Hippolytus was elected bishop of the Roman circle that would have no association with the heterodox. The theological differences became more acute when Callistus, in his

---

[1] Irenaeus, *adv. Haer.* III, 3, 2–3.
[2] Tertullian, *adv. Prax.*; Hippolytus, *Refut.* VII, 35–6; IX, 2–3; IX, 7; IX, 10–12; X, 23–4; X, 27; *contra Noëtum*; Eusebius, *Hist. Eccl.* V, 28.
[3] Cf. Hippolytus, *Refut.* IX, 11, 3.

treatment of penitents who had been guilty of mortal sin, showed a leniency which departed definitely from the full rigour of the Primitive Church. Hippolytus and his party on their side regarded themselves as the guardians of Christian austerity.

Thus in Rome there were two communities, each of which regarded itself as, and called itself, the catholic church[1]; and the church of Hippolytus stood in opposition to that of Callistus and maintained this attitude even when Callistus was succeeded by Urban and Urban by Pontian in the episcopal see. But in the year 235 the Emperor Maximinus Thrax banished the heads of both communities, Hippolytus and Pontian, to Sardinia, and there under pressure of the grave situation a reconciliation seems to have taken place. Pontian laid down his office to enable the Romans to elect a successor, and Hippolytus in all probability did the same, but renounced his claim to a successor and recommended his community to join their former opponents. In return, he was recognized by the other side as possessing the ecclesiastical dignity of a presbyter. Anteros was elected bishop of the now united Roman community. Both his predecessors died in exile and their bodies were brought to Rome by Fabian (236–50) and there buried with all the honours proper to martyrs[2].

Of those who held office in the Roman community Hippolytus was the last to use the Greek language, and at the same time the last whose whole theological attitude was rooted in Greek ways of thought. He also had connections with Alexandria and drew inspiration from the work of the chronographer Julius Africanus (p. 477). With him he had in common a special interest in learned calculations of the duration of the world's history and of the date of the Day of Judgment and in employing these to close the door against over-hasty apocalyptic expectations. This motive, which in him was combined with a personal predilection for chronological calculations, produced his *Chronicle*; of this only fragments survive in the original Greek, but in Latin translations and adaptations it exercised a perceptible influence upon historical writing in the West. From this same favourite pursuit of Hippolytus issued his *Paschal Tables*, in which the first serious attempt was made to calculate the Easter full moon from astronomical data and so to become independent of the dates fixed by the Jewish Synagogue.

But just as in both these works the intention deserves more praise than the performance, so too in his exegetical works Hippolytus shows no evidence of a creative intelligence. For us

[1] Hippolytus, *Refut.* IX, 12, 25; cf. *Praef.* 6.
[2] *Liber Pontificalis*, XIX (Mommsen, p. 24 *sq.*); *Catalogus Liberianus* (*ib.*).

the most valuable of his surviving works in the theological field is
his *Refutation of the Heresies*, because it is based upon first-class
material and provides us with one of the most important sources
for the history of Gnosticism. To this must be added the *Church
Order*[1], preserved in numerous translations, in which Hippolytus,
as a defence against heretics and incompetent bishops—Callistus
is of course intended—draws a detailed picture of church order
according to apostolic tradition: for us, of course, this means a
description of the liturgical customs and ideas and usages of
church life in the community of Hippolytus in Rome about the
year 200. In later days the Roman church forgot Hippolytus
together with his writings and his *Church Order*. On the other
hand, his writings were read assiduously in the Egyptian church,
and his *Church Order* even came to be accepted as typical, so
much so that the translations of it into Coptic, Ethiopic, and even
Arabic, influenced decisively the life and order of the Eastern
churches concerned. The consequence was that in the third
century Egypt looked upon her traditional connection with Rome
as vouched for, not through Callistus, but through Hippolytus.

Under the pontificate of Fabian, the Roman see's growing
sense of its own importance begins to find expression in ways that
we can clearly trace. In the so-called Catacomb of Callistus an
artistically equipped burial chamber was constructed for the
Roman bishops. It was rediscovered in the nineteenth century
and contains the graves, identified by Greek inscriptions, of the
popes of the third century from Pontian (*ob.* 235) to Eutychian
(*ob.* 282). Under the same Fabian arose the custom of celebrating
the accession of the Roman bishops by an annual commemoration,
and the dates of their accession to office and the days of their
death began to be entered in official lists (see above, p. 531).
Under Fabian too the charitable activity of the clergy was re-
organized and the city of Rome divided into seven relief districts
(*regiones*) each of which was under one of the seven deacons, who
in turn was provided with a subdeacon as his assistant and presumptive successor[2]. Now too the other 'minor orders' begin to
appear in our sources: the 'acolytes' or attendants of the bishop,
the 'lectors,' who in the services read passages from holy scripture
in ceremonial style, and the 'exorcists' or those who exorcize
demons, in whom the primitive Christian gift of casting out
devils lived on in after days[3]. Carthage, which was closely

---

[1] See above, p. 524, n. 3.
[2] *Liber Pontificalis*, xxi (Mommsen, p. 27).
[3] Eusebius, *Hist. Eccl.* VI, 43, 11.

connected with Rome, adopted these offices at about the same time.

From all this we gain the impression that towards the middle of the third century the Roman community was steadily advancing in prosperity and solidarity. In this period the basis was laid for the development of the ecclesiastical 'parishes' in Rome and a number of the oldest 'Titular-churches' originated, which became the centres of the smaller parochial communities scattered throughout the capital. But the Roman community remained a unity of which the bishop was the head. When Fabian on 20 January 250 fell a victim to the Decian persecution, it was rightly held inexpedient at once to choose a successor, and for the time being the government of the community was left in the hands of the college of presbyters and deacons. To this period belongs a correspondence with the bishop of Carthage, which gives us the most valuable insight into the inner history of the Church in the West[1].

IV. ROME AND CARTHAGE

The African church was probably founded from Rome. We have no certain information on the question, but the conjecture of Roman origin is based upon its geographical situation and can be supported by a statement of Tertullian's that for Carthage Rome is vested with apostolic authority[2]. But in fact we have no knowledge of the early African church, and it is not until about 180 that the earliest expressions of Christian life in Africa become available. But as a compensation this church emerges into the light of history with a great personality, and through Tertullian[3] it attained a spiritual leadership which it held and increased until the day when Augustine's life drew to its close in his episcopal city of Hippo Regius, during its siege by the Vandals.

It must be admitted that the writings of this first of the Latin Fathers tell us little enough about the rise of the African church and of all that Christianity did and suffered about the year 200 in the spiritually most alive of the provinces of the West. But instead we become the more accurately acquainted with the movements of thought amidst which Tertullian lived, and with the theological dangers which he strove to avert from the church. We see clearly how all the controversial issues which disturbed the Roman church after the middle of the second century were also carried over to Africa. But the writings of Tertullian do not leave

[1] Cyprian, *Ep.* 8, 9, 20, 21, 22, 27, 28, 30, 31, 35, 36, 37.
[2] Tertullian, *de Praescr.* 36.
[3] On Tertullian, see also below, pp. 590 *sqq.*

the impression that the problems involved in the conflict of gnosticism, Marcionism, and Monarchianism with the Logos theology, problems which originated entirely in Greek thought, seriously disturbed the African church. Tertullian deals with all these questions in his own vehement fashion, but nowhere makes mention of any ecclesiastical counter-measures adopted by his countrymen. For him it is a purely theoretical conflict, which in his own fashion he brings to a victorious issue; and as its outcome he puts forth a series of simple formulations which, taken in conjunction with the baptismal confession as the *regula fidei*, contain the epitome of the faith. This method was evidently suited to the sentiments and to the comprehension of African churchmen, and his formulas of the one Substance and three Persons of the Trinity, and of the two Substances in Christ[1], did in fact anticipate the final issue of the dogmatic controversies of the fourth and fifth centuries.

The African church was more vitally affected by the Christian persecutions, and in his apologetic writings Tertullian not only combated paganism in theoretical debate but appealed with legal arguments to the conscience of the State officials and with moral arguments to his readers among the pagan public. He can write with flaming eloquence in defence of the standards of Christian life and can describe with wonderful effect the true sense of Christian fellowship. Because in his own experience the Christian religion had brought him deliverance from moral inferiority, he knew how to present this aspect of Christianity in all its force; but, on the other hand, he was passionately sensitive when he saw this aspect of it imperilled in the Church itself.

Thus he went over to Montanism at the time when it was winning adherents in Africa and became a fanatical protagonist of the new movement. This in the meantime had lost its original character and become a movement of reaction in favour of the ideals of the Primitive Church, combining a tradition of harsh austerity with the cultivation and recognition of spiritual prophetism in opposition to the new-formed officialdom of the Church. This brought him into sharp opposition to the native church of Africa, with its hierarchical organization, and to many customs of the community, which seemed to him illegitimate concessions to the world.

But in a vigorous pamphlet he also attacked the Roman bishop Callistus, on the ground that Callistus wished to allow the restoration of repentant sinners to the Church, even in cases of transgres-

[1] Tertullian, *adv. Prax.* 2, 6, 11.

sion of the sixth commandment[1]. It was the same far-sighted
forbearance that in Rome had aroused Hippolytus to battle (p. 534).
Tertullian's moral and enthusiastic radicalism answered to a
widespread temper of mind in Africa and had many adherents,
especially in the country districts and in the province of Numidia.
A century later it gave birth to the storm of Donatism, which
rent the African church for many generations afterwards.

As a figure of church history, the personality of Tertullian is
eclipsed by that of Cyprian, bishop of Carthage (see further
below, pp. 600 *sqq.*). He was elected in 248–9, but a year later had to
leave the community and remain in hiding in order to escape the
persecution of Decius. During this period he governed his community by letter and from his hiding-place continued faithfully to
fulfil his duty as a pastor of souls, as even those to whom his
departure had at first given offence had later to bear him witness.

While the persecution was still raging and the number of
those who had proved weak increased, the problem arose of how
the church was to care for the lapsed themselves. Were they, with
the strictness of the Primitive Church, to be abandoned as lost, or
was it possible to point the way to penance and to hold out to
them the hope of being again received into the Church? The
general temper of the community was in favour of leniency and so
these declared penance to be possible. Thereupon courageous
Christians, who were in prison for the confession they had made
and were awaiting death, began to pronounce absolution. They
felt that as martyrs they were endowed with and authorized by the
holy Spirit, and in virtue of this authority they issued to those of
the lapsed who seemed to them worthy a certificate (*libellus pacis*)
which secured admission to the fellowship of the Eucharist. And
there were not a few clergy who recognized these certificates
and re-admitted their holders to the Eucharist without special
examination and without the penance of the Church.

Cyprian heard with growing displeasure of this practice of the
confessors, which seemed to him an abuse of martyrdom and to be
undermining the discipline of the Church, which was the concern
of the bishop. Added to this, the confessors in giving their
certificates made no careful examination of individual cases, but
were very generous with their favour, and finally even issued open
certificates without specifying the individual names, and proclaimed a general pardon. In this they found support from a
group of Carthaginian presbyters who were hostile to Cyprian.
The bishop corresponded about this question with the Roman

[1] Tertullian, *de Pud.* 1.

college of presbyters, which, as we have seen, had the management
of affairs while the see was vacant. Agreement was reached without difficulty upon the principle that immediate admission to
communion could only be contemplated for those in danger of
dying. Otherwise, the lapsed were to receive pastoral care, but
they were not to be restored so long as the persecution lasted.
When peace returned, the question of forgiveness and admission to
communion might be settled by episcopal synods: that would then
be the place to examine carefully each individual case and to treat
it according to the gravity of the fault, and there too proper consideration could be given to the recommendations of the confessors.

This meant, of course, in reality a flat rejection of the claims of
these circles of martyrs. But Cyprian held his position with iron
resolution and was protected by his faithful clergy and supported
by Rome. The opposition then declared war upon him and refused obedience. When, after the death of Decius (A.D. 251), the
projected synods actually met, there too Cyprian was victorious.
His opponents, however, did not submit, but separated themselves
and proclaimed Fortunatus rival bishop of Carthage; we hear of
twenty-five African bishops who joined him, a number the correctness of which Cyprian vigorously disputed. In its actual effect,
the decision of the African synods proved to be more severe than
it had seemed beforehand. The examination of the gravity of the
cases was conducted in bitter earnest, and to those who had offered
sacrifice for any reason short of the direst compulsion restoration
was still denied. When, however, in the spring of A.D. 253 a
new persecution threatened, a judicious leniency was exercised,
and those who hitherto had still been excluded were received
again into the Church in order that the new conflict might be met
by a united Christendom. But the conflict did not come.

Meanwhile, in Rome too the problem of the treatment of the
lapsed had given rise to a serious difference of opinion. During
the vacancy of the see, the highly esteemed presbyter Novatian,
who had also won recognition as a theological writer, had been the
spiritual leader of the church[1]; when, however, the episcopal see
came to be filled, he was not elected, but instead the presbyter
Cornelius (March 251). The election did not meet with unanimous approval, and a section of the clergy under the leadership of
Novatian refused to recognize Cornelius: and these opponents
had a considerable section of the community behind them.
Cornelius showed a far-reaching leniency towards the lapsed.

[1] Cyprian, *Epp.* 30 and 36; cf. 55, 5. Novatian was the author of an
influential work *de Trinitate*. See below, p. 602 *sq.*

Perhaps he had been elected because such accommodation was expected from him. At all events, this question was exploited to deepen the opposition and make it one of principle, and Novatian placed himself as rival bishop at the head of a congregation which wished to remain a pure and holy church and not to be polluted by the membership of apostates from Christ.

Cyprian was painfully surprised by the quarrel over the election of the bishop in Rome, and delayed his recognition of Cornelius till he had made more precise enquiries. Then he ranged himself on the side of Cornelius, although the Novatianists were developing an active propaganda in Africa also, which was not without effect. In the East, where the Decian persecution apparently had less marked an effect on the stability of the communities, Novatian's action met with a powerful response, and it needed the mediating activity of Dionysius, bishop of Alexandria, to prevent a breach between the Eastern churches and Cornelius[1]. The Novatianist churches existed for centuries afterwards as separated societies and continued as the last survivals of the mentality of the Primitive Church.

But, as was natural, in the third century the first outburst of feeling which had often been further provoked by personal antagonism subsided, and many Christians regretted the step they had taken in the first moments of discontent and returned once more to the catholic church. Many of them had received baptism whilst members of the Novatianist community, and in various districts the problem then arose whether baptism thus administered outside the catholic church could be recognized as valid. In Africa, where the question had already been discussed at an earlier date[2], a negative answer was given. For Cyprian it was a matter of course that outside the catholic church there could be no salvation, and consequently no true sacraments, and in this view he was at one with the majority of the churches, and especially with those of the East. Pope Stephen of Rome (254–6) took the opposite point of view. The baptism of the Novatianists employed exactly the same forms as that of the catholic church, and no difference of doctrine was involved that made it necessary to declare this baptism invalid. The difference was not one of doctrine but of discipline, and as the Novatianists also recognized the catholic baptism—which in fact for the most part they had themselves received—there was no ground for rejecting their baptism. When the Africans, in full consciousness of this difference, brought their

[1] Eusebius, *Hist. Eccl.* VI, 45–6; VII, 5, 1.
[2] Cf. Tertullian, *de Bapt.* 15.

point of view, already confirmed by a council[1], to the notice of the bishop of Rome, they received from Stephen an unexpectedly sharp reply[2], and laid themselves open to the reproach, unwarranted though it was, of having introduced an innovation that was in conflict with tradition. Their protest had no effect upon Stephen's attitude; on the contrary, he proceeded to demand that all the churches should recognize the Roman practice, which could be traced back to the tradition of Peter. The primacy conferred upon Peter by Christ Himself involved as its necessary consequence the subordination of all churches to the Petrine tradition, which was guarded by Peter's successor[3].

The churches of the East, in which the anti-Roman feeling of the Novatianist conflict was still stirring, vehemently repudiated Stephen's arrogant claim, and their spokesman was Firmilian of Caesarea in Cappadocia, who wrote a sharp letter maintaining the apostolic tradition of the Eastern churches against the Roman thesis[4]. Cyprian, in confirmation of his point of view, could point to his doctrine of the Church, already fully developed some years before, which stressed the idea of unity in the strongest terms. But this unity was based upon the unity and equality of all bishops, all of whom alike were to be regarded as the successors of the apostles. When Christ declared the apostle Peter to be the foundation-stone of the Church, He intended the prominence thus given to the first apostle as a symbol of unity, and did not intend to confer on Peter or his successors any legal pre-eminence[5]. In face of the attitude of Stephen, the Africans were provoked into using Tertullian's ironical formula 'bishop of bishops,' a conception they entirely rejected.

This conflict over heretical baptism, like that over the question of Easter in earlier days, ended in the rejection of the Roman claims. Stephen died a martyr's death on 2 August 256, and Cyprian followed him on 14 September 258[6]. The dispute over heretical baptism lost its acuteness and was forgotten. Forgotten too in the storms of the period were the Roman claims to primacy. But the bishops of Rome preserved them faithfully, and awaited the time that would allow them to revive them once more with greater prospect of success.

---

[1] Cyprian, *Epp.* 70, 72. Cf. *Sententiae Episcoporum LXXXVII de Haer. Bapt.*, the minutes of the later Council of A.D. 256.　　[2] Cyprian, *Ep.* 74.
[3] Cyprian, *Epp.* 71, 3; 74, 1; 75, 17. Eusebius, *Hist. Eccl.* VII, 5, 4–9.
[4] Cyprian, *Ep.* 75.
[5] Cyprian, *de catholicae Ecclesiae Unitate*; *Epp.* 45, 3 (Hartel, p. 602, 18–19); 55, 24 (p. 642, 12–15).　　[6] Cyprian, *Ep.* 81; *Acta Cypriani.*

V. ROME AND ALEXANDRIA

When the relations of the West with the East during the period of the Early Church are surveyed as a whole, it is noticeable that the Alexandrian church stood throughout somewhat apart from the other provinces of the East, while on the other hand it throughout cultivated intimate relations, theologically and ecclesiastically, with the imperial city of Rome—until in the middle of the fifth century the policy of Dioscurus and his exorbitant claims to power severed the link.

Nothing indeed is known of the beginnings of Christianity in Egypt, and it is in connection with the gnostic movement that we first hear of notable leaders such as Basilides and Valentinus, who claimed to represent true Christianity in opposition to the catholic church. The recently expressed opinion[1] that in the earliest period Christianity in Egypt was predominantly gnostic and that it was in opposition to gnosticism that catholic communities first came into being has great probability (p. 478). It then at once becomes clear that none of the Eastern church provinces rendered this signal service to Egyptian orthodoxy, but that it was the Roman church that facilitated the formation of catholic communities among the Alexandrians and consecrated their first bishop. This supposition provides the simplest explanation of the close relationship that existed between Alexandria and Rome during the following centuries, and in particular of the attitude of respectful submission to Roman authority shown by the bishop of Alexandria, which from time to time unmistakably appears. Alexandria, towards the end of the second century, adopted the New Testament Canon of Rome, including the Roman apocalypse of Hermas, and in the succeeding period continued to hold the rival bishop of Rome, Hippolytus, together with his writings, in high regard, whilst the Roman church forgot both him and his work and retained only the remembrance of Hippolytus the martyr.

About the middle of the third century an instructive theological controversy between the two cities took place. Dionysius[2], the active bishop of Alexandria, who played an energetic part in many spheres, protested strongly and repeatedly against the propaganda which Sabellius was conducting in Libya and the Pentapolis on behalf of the Monarchian theology[3]. And opposition to Sabellius' denial of the individual personality of the Logos

---

[1] W. Bauer, *Rechtgläubigkeit und Ketzerei im ältesten Christenthum.*
[2] See above, p. 487.   [3] Eusebius, *Hist. Eccl.* VII, 6.

led him to maintain the sharply opposed thesis that the Logos was
to be regarded as a creature, and that the Father was related to him
no otherwise than as the husbandman to the vine and the boat-
builder to the boat. He was not co-eternal with the Father, but
first came into being with, and in, time. Persons of repute in
Alexandria took offence at this, and they significantly addressed
their complaints to his namesake, bishop Dionysius of Rome:
among their complaints was one that the Alexandrian pastor did
not ascribe to the Logos the predicate *homoousios*, a designation
which was evidently already widely current, though not yet
sufficiently thought out theologically[1].

The bishop of Rome summoned a council to deal with the
Alexandrian petition, and then addressed a treatise to the Alexandrian church in which he rejected alike Sabellianism and the
formulas employed by Dionysius of Alexandria, without indeed
mentioning his colleague by name. That he should have administered this correction shows clearly that the bishop of Rome
felt that he possessed a special authority in relation to the Egyptian
church, and the effect of his communication shows us that the
bishop of Alexandria also regarded it as a duty to submit himself
with respectful deference to the Roman decision. For he did not
reply, as did the later patriarchs, with vehement opposition, but
published an extensive work in his own defence, which to judge
from outward appearances signified the full withdrawal of his
earlier point of view and assent to the Roman thesis of the eternity
of the Son. In accordance with the Roman communication he
drew a distinction between begetting and creating, and in carefully
qualified sentences even accepted the term *homoousios*. The outcome of the affair was significant for Rome as a further step in the
advancement of her power, and for the Church as a whole as a
prelude to the Arian controversy, which in the fourth century was
to do such injury to Christendom. The legend, already found in
the fourth-century 'Monarchian' prologues to the Gospels[2], of
the founding of the Alexandrian see by Mark the disciple of
Peter (1 Peter v, 13) is the reflection of the actual relationship
between Alexandria and Rome.

[1] Eusebius, *Hist. Eccl.* VII, 26, 1. See C. L. Feltoe, *The Letters and
other Remains of Dionysius of Alexandria.*
[2] Lietzmann, *Kleine Texte*, 1, p. 16, 16.

CHAPTER XVI

THE TRANSITION TO LATE-CLASSICAL ART

I. FROM SEPTIMIUS SEVERUS TO ELAGABALUS

THE history of art between the accession of Septimius
Severus and the foundation of Constantinople does not appear
as a continuous chain made up of separate links, like that which
ran from the classicism of the Augustan age to the revival of the
Flavian style in the late Antonine era. In this later period, as in
the earlier, West and East, despite all parallelism and interaction,
preserved their own aspect. But the balance between the art-
techniques of the Greek East and the Roman-Celtic West[1] disappears once more. Stylistic fashions tend towards extremes and
provoke more hasty and violent reactions. Varying currents flow
side by side or cross and mingle. In the gradual dying fall of
classical antique art fresh themes may be heard which introduce
the late-classical[2] and are the prelude of medieval art. The
confusion of political events and of economic conditions is mirrored
to some extent in the art of the day, though this art in other
respects follows its own natural law. In one particular the history
of art shares the fate of contemporary political history: for the
middle part of this period the tradition is more broken than in the
earlier and later parts. It is a period arbitrarily bounded by
political events, but for the historian of art its opening and closing
years mark no epoch: rather they are organically linked with what
was past and what was to come.

The three first decades, including the reigns of Severus,
Caracalla, and Elagabalus, embrace both the zenith and the decline
of that nervous, excitable style which had matured in the late
Antonine age. A change of style, already foreshadowed under
Antoninus Pius, had taken place in the seventies of the second
century when the Roman sentiment, driven underground by
Hadrianic classicism, came to the surface anew. This was a
renaissance of the Flavian style in the strong expressiveness of
which we recognize the first indications of the 'late-classical.' The
column of Marcus Aurelius only reached completion during the
reign of Septimius Severus.

[1] Vol. XI, p. 804 *sq.*
[2] The term 'late-classical' is used in this chapter to represent the *terminus
technicus* 'spätantike.' See below, p. 561.

This emperor's portrait consciously and of deliberate purpose carries on the tradition of typical Antonine Imperial portraiture[1]. It does not present the military usurper with African blood in his veins, but rather the son, fictitious though the adoption was (p. 12), of Marcus Aurelius and brother of Commodus. We can, indeed, recognize individual traits, but they are subordinated to the traditional impression, which is apparent not only in the almost identical cut of beard and hair, but also in the air of calm, in the philosophic clearness of expression and in the character of the outlines. Private portrait busts doubtless followed the fashions of the court. Provincial variants of the Imperial portraiture appear on the Arch of Leptis, and in a head from Ephesus. Thus in Asia Minor a contemporary sculptor produced the head of a priest of the imperial cult, perhaps the Sophist Flavius Damianus of Ephesus, which has a force and expressiveness that heralds the style of a much later period, that of the fifth century.

A real break with the past in the presentation of the imperial portrait first becomes apparent with Caracalla[2], but this again is due to his personality. He wished to figure not as the philosopher regnant, but as the simple soldier. If, despite the complete change of style, portraits of Commodus and Severus retained some traces of Hadrianic and Hellenic elements, those of Caracalla, with their harsh and violent turn of the head and their emphasis on ugly and plebeian features, seem to stress anew a feeling that is Roman. One might regard the portrait of Caracalla either as the latest example of the Antonine style, or as the precursor of the 'impressionist' portraiture that the following period was to produce. Actually it stands between the two, separating them by an isolated and individual style, the peculiar character of which is not yet fully appreciated. The wealth of locks that framed the features of Marcus Aurelius and his successors was represented as a mass pictorially resolved into light and shade by deep-drilled hollows. But with the portrait of Severus Alexander there appears a totally different style, in which the smooth covering of close-fitting hair is only relieved by short chisel-marks. With Caracalla and his cousin Elagabalus came first a change of fashion. Caracalla's crisp curls are shorter than his father's: Elagabalus[3] has lanky hair. But what is more important is that the shape and definition of the distinctive plastic forms of hair and beard now come to their own once more. There were two utterly different 'pictorial' styles: one of the late Antonine age, the other of the period between

---

[1] Volume of Plates v, 168, a.   [2] Ib. 168, b.
[3] Ib. 168, c, d.

Severus Alexander and Gallienus. These styles were separated by a short intermediate phase more plastic than either of them.

Was there also in the field of statuary a movement similar to this temporary revival of sensitiveness to plastic form? The theory has been advanced[1] that by the beginning of the third century the production of copies of statues, other than portrait statues, had already ceased. But the wealth of sculptural decoration found, not only in the Baths of Caracalla, but also within the hall of the Palaestra attached to the eastern Thermae at Ephesus, suggest rather that interest in sculpture was still very much alive. It is improbable that this interest was merely satisfied by the re-installation of older works of art in new buildings. The colossal sculptures from the Baths of Caracalla like the Farnese Hercules[2] and the group of the Farnese Bull[3], are presumably products of this latest efflorescence of plastic art. It is only in the subsequent period that we meet with clear indications of the decline of plastic sensibility.

Roman historical reliefs could be traced back through a long period of development to two forms differing widely the one from the other. The one was the political and symbolical relief of monumental character, the style of which, despite all variations of details, had always been fundamentally classical. The other was the popular art of historical narrative, the real medium for which was painting but which had experienced a translation into a plastic medium on the sculptured bands of the columns of Trajan and Marcus Aurelius[4]. On the arches of Titus in Rome and of Trajan at Beneventum such popular subjects were relegated to the narrow friezes. But it can hardly be mere accident that on the Triumphal Arch of Septimius Severus[5] the monumental reliefs of classical type were replaced by popular descriptive carvings displayed on wide surfaces. There is little doubt that these carvings are based on the paintings which Severus after his Parthian campaign caused to be exhibited in Rome even before his return[6]. The division into several superimposed registers[7], the hard but lively characterization of personages, the composition of the scene in which the *imperator* harangues his troops—all these are in the tradition of the reliefs on the column of Marcus Aurelius, even though it is improbable that the same hands were at work on both

---

[1] By G. Lippold, *Kopien und Umbildungen griech. Statuen*, p. 83.
[2] Volume of Plates v, 170, *a*.　　　　[3] *Ib.* 170, *b*.
[4] Vol. xi, pp. 789, 796; Volume of Plates v, 36–40, 84, 106.
[5] Vol. of Plates v, 172.　　　　[6] Herodian iii, 9, 12.
[7] Vol. of Plates v, 174, *a*.

monuments. That Senate and People in setting up the arch should give the dominant position to these military scenes is clear evidence of the changed political conditions since the day when the Arch of Beneventum was built. On the Severan arch there was only room on the column-bases for reliefs of the high classical style[1]. Here there are groups of prisoners whose bearing and movements, flow of draperies, and carefully observed facial characteristics show that these figures are masterpieces which have not as yet received the appreciation they deserve either in text or picture. Great art and popular art are here to be seen side by side no less than in later times reliefs of different periods on the Arch of Constantine[2]. The popular art has something of the untamed quality but also of the strength of the barbarian. One might almost call it a provincial art within Rome itself.

Both these types of art had still a future before them: the large reliefs in the related art of third-century sarcophagi[3]; popular art in the pagan and Christian reliefs of the fourth century. The appearance of contemporary historical reliefs of the higher style is known from an example preserved in the Court of the Palazzo Sacchetti[4], which depicts a seated emperor making proclamations to the people against an architectural background. It has the lively excitement of the late Antonine style at its height, and can hardly be later than the time of Septimius Severus. In contrast with the reliefs of Marcus Aurelius on the *attica* of the Arch of Constantine there is here not only an increased restlessness filling the whole scene, but it even seems as though some elements of the popular style had invaded the theme.

It was in 203 that the Triumphal Arch was set up in the Roman Forum; and at about the same time in Septimius' birthplace, Leptis Magna, there was built and dedicated on the occasion of his visit to his African home the Tetrapylon, almost overloaded with reliefs, which is one of the finest discoveries of the Italian excavators[5]. A whole series of crowded scenes have been put together, depicting battles, cavalry in procession, and, above all, detailed representations of sacrifices, proclamations, and a triumphal procession. Comparison with the contemporary reliefs in Rome produces a problem which is interesting, controversial and as yet not capable of final solution. The differences between the two are so great that if one were ignorant of the historical context one would certainly assign different dates to the two monuments. It is not merely a matter of the translation of Imperial

[1] Volume of Plates v, 174, *b, c.*   [2] *Ib.* 218.   [3] *Ib.* 176, *a.*
[4] *Ib.* 176, *b.*   [5] *Ib.* 176, *c.*

Roman prototypes into a provincial style. Provincial styles may, in certain manifestations of the Primitive, precede the styles of the more cultured lands on the road to the 'late-classical' because, in the latter, development is arrested by the classical tradition. But here the whole artistic conception is something wholly different. The representative element outweighs the narrative to a far greater extent than on the column of Marcus Aurelius or on the Arch of Severus at Rome. Figures are forcibly twisted out of the plane of their action into a rigid frontality. The composition is here much closer to that of the late-classical period than it is on contemporary monuments in Rome.

There was no indigenous tradition of relief-carving in Tripoli. Are then the Leptis reliefs examples of the Italic-West Roman style freed from the constraint of classicism; or are they influenced by the East, where Parthian painting had already achieved a like solution of its problems? Formerly critics were too readily disposed to derive from the East all non-classical traits in Roman art. But in the past fifteen years we have come to see that numerous late-classical manifestations—expressionism, central composition and frontality—had roots of their own in Italian soil. Their growth was checked by the influence of classical Greek forms, but every now and again it came through. Nevertheless the reaction towards this view sometimes goes too far. In a given period parallelism of feeling also induces a readiness to welcome alien artistic stimuli. It is scarcely probable that Italic taste should have found a better scope for self-expression on the soil of Africa than in the popular art of Rome itself. On the other hand, it is very possible that the influence of Parthian painting should have passed, through the intermediary of some place like Doura, to North Africa. The fresco of the Tribune in Doura[1] which was painted at about the same time, or possibly rather earlier, supplies the closest parallel to the composition of the reliefs at Leptis. The stimulus may well have been brought direct by the Court of Septimius Severus and Julia Domna when they arrived from the East. It is to be noted, too, that contemporary art in Asia Minor about the turn of the century bears marked traces of the influence of Parthian hunting pictures.

The series of known historical reliefs breaks off with the two great Arches of Severus, beside which must be mentioned the artistically insignificant Arch of the Silversmiths erected in 204. It only revives again at the beginning of the fourth century. Consequently we now lose the sure guidance of that thread which

[1] Volume of Plates v, 28, b.

leads from the reliefs of the Ara Pacis through all the changes of styles up to the Arch of Septimius Severus. Did the production of historical reliefs really cease for a whole century, or are we merely misled by the lack of surviving monuments? It is, indeed, hard to believe that this proud tradition of official art should have been quite extinguished. On the other hand, it would certainly appear that third-century sarcophagi, by contrast with those of the second century, acquired a heightened importance as works of art, and that they to a certain extent took the place of historical reliefs. Once the evolution of the sarcophagus has been adequately studied, it may be that this form of art, together with portraiture, will provide the guiding clue for the history of art in the third century.

On the sarcophagi it is possible not only to observe the gradual change of style, but also the vanishing of older themes and the appearance of fresh ones. A good example of a traditional type reshaped to the sentiment of a new taste is supplied by the Taverna bridal-sarcophagus[1], the scenes on which are full of heightened intensity of feeling and of a lively restlessness permeating every detail. The figures are close-pressed, the gestures are more emotional. In shape the sarcophagus has grown in height.

A predominant subject on sarcophagi of the time of Septimius Severus is the battle-picture. An earlier generation had employed the Hellenistic motives of the fights between Greeks and Gauls; but now, under the influence of the reliefs that commemorated the victorious campaigns of Marcus Aurelius, a very different type of presentation depicting a contemporary battle appears, and it borrows no more than a few of the older motives. The earliest and most remarkable of these works is in the Terme Museum, a sarcophagus from the Via Appia probably made in the last years of Commodus or the first of Septimius Severus. Framed between groups of captives and underneath the trophy there is set a crowded, pictorial and stirring battle-scene, in which the barbarians collapse under the victorious onset of the Romans. Even though isolated fugitives or foes trying to ward off attack appear in the upper rows, yet the composition as a whole is partitioned into an upper world of the victors and a lower world of the vanquished.

A series of sarcophagi similar to this were made in the following decades. At the end of the period under discussion a new theme appeared which was destined to be more or less the predominant subject in the next period, the lion-hunt. Up to this

[1] Volume of Plates v, 176, a.

time, the Roman passion for the hunt—*Romana milities*—had been shown on sarcophagi in mythological guise by the hunters Hippolytus, Meleager, or Adonis, and these older themes were continued. But now there is a new creation in the composition of the lion-hunt which is perhaps dependent on the prototype of some Imperial monument, perhaps even the sarcophagus of Caracalla, who himself, as a new Alexander, 'contra leonem stetit[1].' A noble, clear composition appears on a sarcophagus in the Palazzo Mattei in Rome[2] with a few figures of large size which occupy the whole available space with their movements. Though the technique of the drill, common in the Severan period for working hair and mane, is still employed, yet we note in the treatment of the nude, in drapery, and in locks of hair clearly divided from one another a thorough tightening-up of plastic form. Here it is evident that the same change is in progress as that already observed in the portraits of Caracalla and of Elagabalus. The head of the effigy on the sarcophagus is still under the influence of Caracalla's Imperial portraiture, and thus this relief may have been carved about 220. It marks the turning-point towards a fresh development.

With the opening of the third century there begins the continuous evolution of painting in the Christian catacombs of Rome. This starts, as we should expect, with a pictorial style that corresponds to that of late Antonine and Severan reliefs. The earliest paintings are in the Lucina vault, the decorative scheme of which, having a certain architectural solidity, still holds a memory of the early Antonine style. After these a gradual loosening and deterioration is perceptible. The illusionistic manner seems to increase, but to be broken by reactions. As a rule the artistic quality of these paintings is rather low. Those in the vault of the Aurelii, probably still of the Severan style[3], are, however, more important. Here there are, besides landscapes and paintings with small figure subjects, some almost monumental figures, each over three feet high, of eleven apostles or prophets. During Caracalla's reign there was probably a break in purely illusionistic art in painting as well as in sculpture. Perhaps we possess a mere fragment of this intermediate phase in a small piece of fresco in the Baths of Caracalla which preserves a delicately and cleanly modelled head.

In architecture, as in the other arts, the first decades of the third century show a belated flowering after the wealth of the Hadrianic and Antonine periods. The impoverishment of the provinces and the consequences of social upheavals only began to take effect

---

[1] S.H.A. *Carac.* 5.   [2] Volume of Plates v, 178.
[3] *Ib.* 180, *a*, *b*.

gradually and in varying degrees in the several provinces. In Greece proper no building of importance appears to have been erected. The workshops of Athens were kept going by the manufacture of copies of statues and of sarcophagi for export. The flourishing life of Asia Minor was hit more violently by the ravages of the wars and their consequences. But in Ephesus in the reign of Severus there was still the wealthy sophist, Flavius Damianus, who could afford to build a large hall and to erect the new Palaestra of the Eastern Gymnasium and fill it with costly sculptures. Moreover, the Baths by the harbour carried on the Ephesian style of the gymnasium. After this period, however, building activity in Asia Minor almost ceased until the end of the century.

It is intelligible that in the provinces of Syria and Africa, which had suffered little from the wars, the zeal for building should continue from the second century. In Syria this period witnessed the new buildings of the temple of Juppiter Damascenus and the completion of the Propylaea at Heliopolis (Baalbek)[1]. This kind of activity was still greater in Africa, the province that was most closely bound to the dynasty. There is only need to mention the Capitolium (A.D. 208)[2] and the Arch of Severus at Lambaesis, the temple of Minerva at Tebessa, and the triumphal arches set up for Caracalla, one at Tebessa in 214, the other at Djemila. But as in Ephesus, so in Syria and Africa, there is an absence of all architectural novelty. Old plans are completed; new buildings are erected on traditional lines.

Rome itself, however, became the stage for an architectural achievement that marked a mighty advance on the work of the preceding epoch. In the year 191 a fire ravaged the city. Septimius Severus and Julia Domna did much to repair the damage. The Porticus Octavia, the temple of Vesta and the House of the Vestals were reconstructed, and the Pantheon was repaired. Severus built additions to the imperial palace on the Palatine including a new wing. And on the south-west slope of the Palatine looking towards the Via Appia he constructed the many-storeyed State building called the Septizonium, the columnar style of which may owe something to suggestions from Asia Minor. In the Forum Romanum there still stands the huge and impressive triumphal arch put up in the year 203 for the Emperor and his sons[3]. It is not always that we can, without forcing the evidence, draw stylistic parallels between architectural compositions and the arts of sculpture and painting. But the Arch of Severus does fit perfectly into the picture of the style of the late Antonine period.

---

[1] Volume of Plates v, 182, a.   [2] Ib. 182, b.   [3] Ib. 172.

In contrast to the classical lines and plastic simplicity of the much smaller Arch of Titus its architecture seems full of harshness and discord, and dependent on the picturesque contrasts of light and shade. A remarkable architect has here exercised his commanding power to derive new effects from old motives.

Caracalla's temple of Sarapis and the Sun-temple built by Elagabalus are entirely, or almost entirely, destroyed. But the Baths of Caracalla, which were only completed by his successors, have survived as one of the mightiest ruins in the world[1]. Their impressiveness has, incidentally, led to an overestimate of the achievement of the age. In actual fact they reproduce in all essentials the ground-plan and elevation of their classical prototype, the Baths of Trajan. The plan is distinguished by an almost ornamental scheme. The extent to which the wall-decorations may have supplied novelty, when contrasted with those of the older Baths, can no longer be known. There seem to have been some new and notable additions in the construction of ceilings and of the dome of the *calidarium*.

If we survey the portraiture, relief-sculpture, painting and architecture of this period, we get, in spite of certain contradictions and ups and downs, a consistent picture of a style, already moulded in previous decades, pursuing its course and moving to its conclusion. There is, then, a late Antonine-Severan style occupying roughly the half-century from A.D. 170 to 220.

II. FROM SEVERUS ALEXANDER TO THE ACCESSION OF DIOCLETIAN

Throughout the period of the crisis and disintegration of the Empire, there can be traced, if only in general outlines, a continuity of stylistic development. The City of Rome has a more central significance in the history of art in this period than in political history. In art the Roman national character had achieved a strength and activity which enabled it to assimilate to itself the foreign element that entered it, and to carry on a specifically Roman tradition into late-classical art.

Not more than six or eight years separate the portraits of Elagabalus from those of Severus Alexander[2]. A comparison of the likenesses of these two cousins reveals a complete change in the fashion of portraiture which dominates the decades that follow.

---

[1] See Plan 2 facing p. 570; Volume of Plates v, 184, *a, b*.
[2] Volume of Plates v, 168, *c, d*; 186, *a, b*.

It is marked most strongly by the technical representation of the hair. The impression made by an Antonine portrait depended primarily on the contrast between the shape of the face and the luxuriant mass of waving locks. The portrait of Elagabalus still had strands of hair plastically rounded and clearly distinguished. But now the hair flattens down into a cap barely separated from the face, only distinguished from it by its smoothness and colour. The firm plastic modelling of the features gives place to a soft modulation of the surface. We can trace a development of this style of portraiture from Maximinus and Gordian III[1] to Philip the Arabian. The slight plastic shaping of the hair that had at first been retained gradually disappears completely. The skull-cap of hair is broken by chisel-marks which at first follow the lines of the locks, though presently these too vanish. There is an attempt to recapture, in the manner of the ancient Roman traditional portrait, the momentary and personal element by holding and emphasizing characteristic forms, and there is success in expressing both the precocity in the features of the youthful Gordian and the barbarism in Maximinus and Philip. In classical art also impressionism and expressionism are but little apart. About the middle of the century the portrait of Decius[2] shows certain stylized mannerisms which would have led straight on to the portrait of Probus and 'late-classical' art, but for the fact that this tendency was thrust aside for several decades by a powerful reaction. But before we consider this we must glance at some of the surviving monuments of the first thirty years of this period.

The changes in coiffure and portraiture certainly represent a reaction against the Antonine and Severan concepts of a portrait, and in particular a reaction of the Roman spirit against the Hadrianic Hellenic traditions employed for the likenesses of the Antonine Emperors. The more homely and human character of the new style, which renounced all display of pomp, has occasionally led to the belief that this restrained art replaced the baroque art of the Severan age. But we should form an entirely false picture of our period were we to base our conclusions on portraiture alone.

Between about 225 and 230, judging from the portrait head upon it, the great Ludovisi battle-sarcophagus was made[3]. To this work the term baroque can be applied with more justification than to any other ancient work of art, though admittedly it is a style by no means identical with the baroque of more modern art. But it is at the same time a work in which there appear the complexity and the twofold tendencies of the day. As far as its artistic significance goes, it is a work of the first rank presenting the highest achievement of the time. When it is compared with the battle-sarcophagus from the Via Appia made a generation earlier (p. 549) a remarkable contrast is apparent. The composition taken over from the other has been clothed in entirely new forms. The first general impression of a baroque effect is produced by the larger size of sarcophagus and figures, by their close compression, and by the emotional expression that reaches in the faces of the mortally wounded an intensity surpassing anything previous in ancient art, for it recalls the work of the medieval and the baroque sculptor. But in contrast to the baroque this relief is kept firmly within the bounds of its frame and its front plane. The plastic sharpness of each single shape carries on the development of the art which we first met on the Mattei sarcophagus with the lion-hunt. But, though this plastic treatment is still purely classical, we seem to perceive in the pose and movement of each figure a certain lack of sure feeling for the organic growth and rhythm of the whole which attests a falling off in plastic sensibility.

The real difference between the battle-sarcophagi and their predecessors lies in composition. The number of figures is now small. Their relation to space and depth is altered. On both these sarcophagi the balance of the composition has been planned down to the smallest detail. But while on the older example groups are combined, figures recede in depth, and leave room between one another, there appears on the Ludovisi sarcophagus a whole crowd of figures filling the plane out evenly, for the figures that are behind stand out in the same relief as those in front or bend forward their heads to the front plane of the picture. Thus we get, despite the plasticity of the single figures, that carpet-like effect which A. Riegl has brought out in his analysis of a contemporary sarcophagus with Amazons[1]. Indeed, this effect must have been intensified when the gilding on the men's hair and horses' manes was visible. Emotion and rigidity are here combined in peculiar guise. The composition and construction of the design mark a definite step in the direction of the late-classical, while the modelling of individual figures harks back to classical art. In the intellectual conception of victory the sarcophagus also parts company with its prototype and tends towards the late-classical. The victorious general is no longer fighting but triumphant, and turns from the turmoil of battle towards the spectator, claiming worship. The subsidiary figures are noticeably smaller in size, an anticipa-

[1] In *Spätrömische Kunstindustrie* (1927 reprint), p. 139 *sq.*

tion of the later practice of representing personages in sizes that correspond to their relative importance.

The emotional temperament of the age showed a preference for hunting-scenes or fighting Amazons, and instilled an intense restlessness into other subjects like representations of the Thiasos or of sea-pieces. Quiet, simple portrait-busts are set in the midst of these reliefs on the sarcophagi to form a strange but quite intentional contrast with the movement, the very wildness of the reliefs. On the hunt-sarcophagi may be seen how the treatment of hair and garments became more full of movement between 230 and 250. Locks of hair wind about like snakes and end by looking like flickering flames. Just before the mid-century they again lose their plastic definition and become more pictorial. Facial expression grows even more exaggerated. The climax of this 'baroque' development is reached in works like the so-called sarcophagus of Balbinus in Copenhagen[1] which must be dated to about A.D. 250.

Was this baroque-like tendency confined to Rome, or did it also permeate the rest of the ancient world? We can recognize its presence on Attic sarcophagi in the evolution of what are misnamed Graeco-Roman examples. On one remarkable piece, the Achilles-sarcophagus of the Capitoline Museum[2] (c. 240 to 245), we encounter this baroque style with its wealth of tightly packed figures. Riegl recognized in this relief-work the true parallel to the sarcophagi made in the Capital[3]. But neither the violence of emotional expression nor the loosening of the plastic form go nearly as far as they do in Rome. Down to the very latest of their series the Attic sarcophagi retain something of the classical Attic manner. In conformity with this we find the portraits of the dead upon the lids also follow a Greek tradition. Nearer to a baroque style are the column-sarcophagi from Asia Minor, not only in their structure but also in the movement of their figures and the restlessness of their composition. The large Sidamara coffin in Istanbul is of this class and period[4]. The latest stage appears on the Mattei Muses-sarcophagus[5] in Rome which belongs to the second half of the third century. But sarcophagi from the Eastern provinces never approached the richness of those of Rome either in their wealth of subject matter or in their lively juxtaposition of varying and various styles. After the reign of Caracalla the East conspicuously lagged behind Rome in intensity of artistic creation.

---

[1] Volume of Plates v, 190, a, b, c.
[2] Ib. 192, a.
[3] Op. cit. p. 140.
[4] Volume of Plates v, 192, b.
[5] Ib. 192, c.

On the other hand we find at this time a highly original manifestation in the Celtic-Germanic Marches associated with the evolution of the grave-monuments of Trèves and its neighbourhood. The tombs with their multiplication of architectural motives and their excess of ornament take on fantastic shapes. The use of soft sandstone induced the employment of a pictorial treatment of the material. While in the East luminous surfaces and dark hollows were separated by ridges sharp as knives, here softly flowing transitions moved from convex high lights to deep shadows. Brilliant characterization distinguishes the types of peasants and boatmen[1]. No provincial art of the third century is equal to this in independence and creative power. Here is evidence of artistic gifts rooted in the unspoilt folk of the countryside. But the line of development ran parallel to the Roman and reached its climax about the mid-century or shortly after. So it fitted into the wide context that extended from Asia Minor to the Rhine frontier.

The advance of this pictorial baroque element to an extreme about the middle of the century makes the marked reaction of the 'Gallienic renaissance' comprehensible. This was first observed in portraiture, but manifests itself with equal distinctness in reliefs at Rome itself. Plotinus and Gallienus, the friendship between emperor and philosopher, these symbolize the spirit of the age. From the chaotic turmoils of the time the soul sought refuge in the peace of mystery religions and of Neoplatonism (p. 188). Art shows us that this longing finds its satisfaction not by ecstatic moods but by calm clarity.

In the portrait of Gallienus[2] there are apparent two elements both striving to recover something of the older classical spirit. The one, a Roman element, links itself to Augustan and Claudian prototypes; the other tries to recover the Greek portrait technique of the Hadrianic and Antonine period. The neo-Augustan style is also met with in certain Roman portraits of private personages. This reversal in style extends beyond the immediate circle of Gallienus, who was himself but the representative of a spiritual movement that touched the whole Roman Empire. Yet for all their parallelism each local circle of culture went on its way. Asia Minor and Greece had each its own special style for portraiture linked on to its own local prototypes. The finest gold coins of Postumus minted at Lugdunum show us, even more decisively than the bust of Gallienus, the ideal type of the period distinguished by philosopher's beard and Greek classic forms[3]. And the successors of Postumus down to Tetricus retained this fashion and form. It is

[1] Volume of Plates v, 194.   [2] *Ib.* 196, *a, b.*   [3] *Ib.* 214, *c*; 238, *o.*

no mere chance that the portrait of Postumus made in Gaul is founded on Greek rather than Roman models. In Rome itself, which was always ready to take up anything fresh, we find Roman and Greek styles side by side with a continuation of the portraiture fashionable in the forties of the third century.

In the list of subjects for sarcophagi lion-hunts and fighting Amazons no longer predominate, for preference is now given to scenes that depict the deceased, male or female, in the company of philosophers, or Muses, or both. The lion-hunt, however, remains a popular theme in the second half of the century, but only on works of inferior quality, and it sometimes, significantly enough, appears on the back panels of philosopher-sarcophagi. There is a sarcophagus in the Museo Torlonia[1] made c. 250–60 that depicts the dead man and his wife as seventh Sage and ninth Muse in a gathering of the Muses and Sages. Single motives like the centre group and the corresponding figures of seated philosophers are probably indebted to the Asia Minor style; but the composition as a whole follows the Roman tradition. In the restless ragged beards and locks there remains an after-effect of the restless style of the previous period. Otherwise, however, the tranquil shapes, the compact outlines of heads, the simplified folds fit in with the changed mood which seeks to replace the dramatic and the emotional by the solemn calm of an existence steeped in philosophy and art. This mental change of attitude corresponds to the altered situation of the whole age. And in like fashion the philosopher-sarcophagi of Rome itself, made between 250 and 270, represent in particular the impact on Rome of a flourishing philosophy—notably that of Plotinus and his disciples. In such circumstances the oldest Christian carved sarcophagi could come into existence, for they too could depict the dead man as sage and teacher amid symbolic figures. There are the Roman sarcophagus from the Via Salaria[2] and another from La Gayole, the latter made, like the portraits of Gallic emperors, under the influence of Greek forms. It is significant that the first Christian carved sarcophagi were made in the West, where their future was also to lie.

All trace of nervous unrest has vanished on the magnificent fragment of a philosopher-sarcophagus in the Lateran[3]. Here is a philosopher giving instruction from a scroll unrolled wide open and surrounded not only by two listening women, one of whom holds the scroll—symbol of learning—but by other philosophers who turn their heads to converse with other persons now missing. There is no proof that this was the coffin of Plotinus for it was

[1] Volume of Plates v, 198, a.   [2] Ib. 198, b.   [3] Ib. 200.

probably made in the sixties; but the master of Neoplatonism might well have been depicted in this atmosphere of elevated solemnity. The head of the central figure is inspired by this same lofty mood. The fashion of his hairdressing is in the style of the second quarter of the century.

Through all these contrasts subsisting between the sarcophagi of the lion-hunt period and of the philosopher period we can still trace a straight line of evolution leading in the direction of late-classical art; and we can see its negative no less than its positive sides. The feeling for the organic structure of the figure grows steadily weaker. Composition in relief, though occasionally chequered by reminiscences of the classical style, carries on the form typified by the great Ludovisi battle-sarcophagus. Centralized composition grows ever more popular. Along with this the tendency increases for a turning of figures and whole scenes toward frontality. A medallion of Severus Alexander shows a quadriga for the first time in frontal view, though the figures in the chariot still turn sideways. Coins of Postumus give the Imperial portrait almost full-face, and, what is still more important, the scene of an Imperial allocution in a centralized symmetrical composition[1]. A turning-point of the utmost significance for the history of art is marked by the frontal view of the reading philosopher of the Lateran sarcophagus. For in the motive of the seated figure we have here a dividing line between antiquity and the medieval.

In classical reliefs, as in those of the more ancient East, the ceremonial presentation of a figure enthroned in the foreground was avoided because it was out of harmony with the whole spirit of the relief of antiquity. But in Italy after the first century of the Principate we can observe a movement towards the presentation of a frontal view. For its realization, however, the true feeling for plastic form had to be so far extinguished that men were no longer disturbed by the contradiction between a foreshortened thigh and its actual appearance in light and shade. From this point onwards relief moves away from sculpture in the round and assimilates itself to drawing.

If the new dating given to a rock-carving at Shapur, assigning it to the reign of Shapur I, is correct, then it seems that a frontal enthroned figure of a ruler in the middle of a centralized composition appears for the first time in Mesopotamian art at about the same period. It is strange that we do not find it sooner in Parthian and Sassanian art, which is after all not plastic in character

[1] Volume of Plates v, 214, c, a.

but based on painting and relief work[1]. Have we here a case of parallel development or one of mutual influence? To what extent can the existence of artistic interrelations be proved? Recent research has been successful in tracing the origins of the late-classical in Classical art and the origins of Sassanian in Parthian art. A whole series of apparent correspondences, in which we were at one time inclined to see an orientalization of classical art, appear now rather as converging manifestations. But the closer these lines of development approach one another, the stronger grows the possibility that occasional sparks of inspiration leap from one to the other. The reliefs commemorating Shapur's victory and his capture of Valerian[2] are influenced by Roman victory-reliefs. On the other hand the concept of the ruler in the late-classical period and its outward manifestations have a strong Oriental tinge. Shapur's relief might have been influenced by a Valerian prototype. Yet the influence might equally have been in the opposite direction. The decisive step, so far as Rome was concerned, may well have been taken on some Imperial triumphal relief or sarcophagus.

More interesting even than the similarity in frontality between the reliefs of Shapur and the Lateran sarcophagus is the difference in their technique. In its counterpoise the form of seated figure of the Graeco-Roman philosopher is quite classical; in its symmetry of widespread legs and in the stiffness of its body the figure of the Sassanian king is thoroughly Oriental. The Roman proto-type continues almost unchanged through a series of imperial and divine figures into the Middle Ages, when it comes into conflict with the Oriental motive that has likewise been carried on by later Sassanian and then by Byzantine art.

A somewhat later Roman sarcophagus[3], made about 270 to 275, has in the centre the old-fashioned group of men clasping hands (*dextrarum iunctio*) and on the right and left of this group symbolical figures referring to the office of the deceased, who was an official of the *Annona*. Though it is still in high relief the unplastic hardening of the figures is here more exaggerated. All the more moving is the inner suffering which appears on the man's face and seems to portray the depth of his sensitiveness which still lives through the stiffening forms. In its general form this portrait head belongs to the end of the 'Gallienic renaissance.' And in heads which belong either to the end of this period or to the transition towards the next there now appears a definite tide of expressionism produced by stressing and exaggerating the charac-

[1] See above, p. 124.
[2] Volume of Plates v, 148.   [3] *Ib.* 202.

teristic features of the face. It was the current that had set in with the portrait of Decius, but had been stayed awhile by the classical reaction.

In the paintings of the Catacombs we may perhaps perceive about the middle of the century an increased use of the illusionistic manner in the production of figures and a loosening in decorative matter. Then comes a tendency to a firmer drawing of figure-subjects. But the style of the age of Gallienus is not as yet really to be grasped. Popular paintings of campaigns and hunting-scenes continued to be turned out, as we learn from a few chance references. After his German victories Maximinus not only sent a written report to the Senate and People, but had pictures painted 'ut erat bellum ipsum gestum,' and had them set up in front of the Curia 'ut facta eius pictura loqueretur[1].' Gordian organized a *silva*, a hunt for which the whole Circus was transformed into a forest, and this was depicted on a frieze on which no fewer than 1320 animals were painted. The baroque zeal for huge masses could find freer scope in painting than in carved reliefs. The painted records, to which texts refer, of the new-fashioned games given by Carus, Carinus, and Numerianus in the Circus must likewise have been large and packed with figures. From this popular painting the tradition of art in the City of Rome derives much of its power.

A peculiar contrast is provided by the aristocratic art of portraits in miniature, worked out in gold-leaf upon glass[2]. Its earliest examples belong to the period from A.D. 230 to 250. It can hardly be an accident that the art of miniatures reaches its height at the moment in which sculpture in the grand style declines. It is the way of art on the small scale to attain its zenith at just such times. These portraits in gold on glass initiate a development which slowly advances towards the end of the fourth century and leads to the efflorescence of late-classical illumination, ivory-carving and embossed metal-work.

We know least of all of the architecture of this period. This is certainly not due to the accident of destruction, but to the fact that economic decline has a greater effect on architecture than on other arts. There were now none of those private benefactors who played so large a part in encouraging building during the second century. Where there are large buildings, they are almost always associated with some emperor. In Africa, which still prospered at this period, there was built in A.D. 229 a temple at Djemila dedicated to the Gens Septimia. An inscription records the

[1] S.H.A. *Max. duo*, 12, 10. [2] Volume of Plates v, 204, *a*, *b*.

erection by Gordian III of a palace with adjoining baths at
Volubilis in Morocco. It was probably also at this time that the
huge amphitheatre of El Djem (Thysdrus), where Gordian I was
proclaimed emperor, was built[1]. If the circular temple at Heliopolis[2] is to be associated with Philip the Arabian, it would certainly
fit in with the baroque mood of the day. In and near Rome rose
some considerable imperial buildings, like the Villa of Gordian.
In these and certain circular tomb buildings we see that the problem of vaulting was what interested the architects of the time.
Only one building is comparatively well preserved, the so-called
temple of Minerva Medica[3], now held to be a Nymphaeum or part
of a block of Thermae of about A.D. 260. The dome rests on a
decagonal substructure, from the lower part of which apses curve
out between supporting piers, while the upper part is broken by
windows. Ideas attempted in Hadrian's Villa are here carried
through. It was not only the solution of the technical problem
that was bold and new, but also the widening and differentiating
of the interior spaces, and the complicated jointing of the exterior.
This single building proves that Roman architecture was still full
of ideas.

III. FROM DIOCLETIAN TO THE FOUNDING
OF CONSTANTINOPLE

In the history of art the term late-classical has been adopted
for the centuries that follow the true classical age. This term is
more comprehensive, and therefore more suitable, than 'late-
Roman' which Riegl employed in his work which laid the foundations for the study of this period. The late-classical is something
more than a phase in the transition from the ancient to the medieval
world. Not only on account of its long duration, but also by reason
of its own artistic achievement, it must be classed as a third phase
of ancient art following on the Greek and the Roman phases.
Where are we to place its beginning and its end? Is an essential
unity to be found amid the diversity of its manifestations?
That this phase is still a part of ancient art is clear from the fact
that its conclusion is more definitely detached from medieval art
than is its beginning from the preceding classical art. In Italy it
does not come to an end with the fall of the Western Empire in
A.D. 476, but with the great invasion of the Lombards in 568. The
Ostrogothic period in Italy is the age of the last bloom of late-

---

[1] Volume of Plates v, 206, a.   [2] Ib. 206, b.   [3] Ib. 206, c.

classical art. In the Eastern Empire the more gradual decline extends in part to the period of the Slavonic invasions during the second half of the sixth century, in part to that of the victories of the Arabs in the following century. In the Byzantine Empire a tradition was even retained up to the period of revival (ninth and tenth centuries). The flower of the art, however, came to an end in the East almost at the same time as in the West, after the death of Justinian. The part taken by national energy in the achievements of the three centuries is diverse. Up to the end of the fourth century the greater and more fruitful artistic production came from Italy, after that from Asia Minor and Byzantium. The part played by barbarian influence is not easy to estimate. We have now to reckon more than in previous periods with the activities of travelling artists and of workshops.

The beginning of late-classical art is fixed differently according to the different divisions of time favoured by the several studies that are concerned with it. Those scholars who write of 'L'art Byzantin'—a term more appropriate to the middle and late Byzantine epochs—mark the beginning by the foundation of Constantinople, which is for the art-historian of no significance as an epoch. Those concerned with Christian archaeology choose the date which is most momentous for Church history, either that of the Edict of Milan in 313, or the victory at the Milvian Bridge in 312. Both are too late and, indeed, the second is immediately followed by the earliest of those renaissance movements which are just as characteristic of the rhythm of the late-classical period as of the classical age, and are perhaps even more impressive. If we select the accession of Diocletian to mark the beginning of the late-classical, this is because it amounts to an acknowledgment that the spirit of the Dominus is the spirit permeating the art, in contrast to that of the classical ages. The date is no more than a symbol. In actual fact the change and the transition cover the period from A.D. 275 to 300.

An attempt to describe in brief the essence of late-classical art must confine itself to touching on its most important features. There appear side by side a change in pure artistic feeling and a change in the spiritual relationship between spectator and work of art. What is of the most decisive significance is the cessation of sculpture in the round, which had occupied the central point in Greek art, but which had been forced on the Romans by the power of Greek tradition, foreign though it actually was to their inner sentiment. It may be that the type of the commemorative statue, and especially of the figure of the emperor, was retained till the very end of the period. But statues of gods disappear, and the manufacture of copies of Greek masterpieces comes to an end. Relief work grows ever closer to painting. In the earliest classical age the statue of the god served the beholder for prayer, the portrait statue expressed veneration, while votive sculpture, reliefs and paintings stood for the participation of a spectator in a play. But prayers cease to be made to statues of the gods. Veneration of the portrait statue rises to virtual worship. The function of painting and relief is no longer to narrate but to preach; their appeal is no longer to a spectator but to a congregation of the faithful. This alteration of spiritual and emotional values leads to a form that gives expression to this new exaltation. This has frequently been defined by the word 'transcendentalism'; but it must be borne in mind that the uplifting reality in late-classical art is something fundamentally different from the other-worldliness of medieval art.

This transcendentalism, if we use the concept in this narrowed sense, or this expressionism, is the central factor of late-classical art, but it has to adjust itself to two other and quite different forces. One of these is a hard realism, which derives from unplumbed depths of popular feeling. In Rome itself new and vigorous sap flows from this realism into late-classical art. Another type of realism, nourished on different spiritual forces, was later on to influence Asiatic portraiture in the fifth century. The second force is the might of classical art standing, as it were, before the eyes of the late-classical in almost undiminished splendour. This was the cause of repeated renaissances which harked back to classical Greek or classicizing Roman prototypes. Out of the struggle of these three forces there grew the manifold tendencies, flowing, following, merging into one another in late-classical art.

The foundations of the late-classical manner may be recognized increasingly in the preceding centuries, and especially so in Italy on those monuments in which a Roman and unclassical feeling is expressed. Examples of this occur in Italian provincial art of the first century, and afterwards in historical reliefs of the second century, notably those of the Column of Marcus Aurelius. Then, with the period starting about 222, there begins, as we have seen, the immediate precursors of the late-classical.

Coins of the seventies of the third century[1] show that in portraiture the expressionist tendency—temporarily submerged by the classical phase of Gallienus' reign—has recovered. This had

---

[1] Volume of Plates v, 212, 214.

already appeared with the portraiture of Decius. The tendency to
frontality, begun under Severus Alexander and carried on under
Postumus, is continued on medallions of Probus, for it is there in
the frontal composition of the *adlocutio* scene. And it is the portraits of Probus[1], together with contemporary heads of private
personages[2], that carry along the features of late-classical art.
In the representation of the hair the tradition, never quite interrupted, of the second quarter of the century prevails again. In the
face there is emphasis on the harmony of those features that
determine the spiritual expression, like eyes, nose, and mouth, as
contrasted with the mere auxiliary features. In the time of Diocletian[3] and the Tetrarchy there appears in the face—now stylized
beyond any natural shape for the sake of expressive strength—
a kind of native primitiveness derived from the coarser popular
art which was developing at this time in Roman reliefs. The head
of the colossal figure of Constantine from the Basilica in the Forum[4],
with its new dynamic simplification that enhances the strength
of expression, and its new exaggeration of the features, marks
the creation of a new ideal of the Ruler. Despite several classicizing
interludes, this head had a marked influence on subsequent
Imperial portraiture.

The change of period is very clearly marked in the history
of the relief. In the East, Syria and Alexandria had never shown
much liking for this type of art. But Asia Minor and Greece
possessed in their monumental masons' yards a rich supply of
reliefs which, through the export of sarcophagi, were regularly
influencing the West. In the last decades of the third century this
trade died out. A few masons wandered over to Italy. In contrast
to Rome and the Western provinces, Asia Minor and Greece
were poor in reliefs during the 'late-classical' period. The few
sarcophagi with relief-decorations are isolated pieces. Economic
stress and disorganization of export trade certainly contributed to
this state of affairs, but were hardly its sole cause. There was here
afoot a change in taste that was perhaps already a presage of the
much stronger divergence to come between Eastern and Western
Europe in the Middle Ages.

Rome, North Italy, and Gaul were, up to the end of the fourth
century, the regions responsible for an abundant production of
sarcophagi ornamented with reliefs. In Ravenna and in Aquitania
this tradition carried through into the sixth century. The actual
transition happens in Rome itself. The old themes and subjects—

[1] Volume of Plates v, 208, *a*.   [2] *Ib.* 208, *b, d*.
[3] *Ib.* 208, *c*.   [4] *Ib.* 210.

mythological scenes and lion-hunts—so far as they can be assigned with tolerable certainty to this period—show a growing hardness of style and a falling-off in artistic merit. An example is the Adonis-sarcophagus in the Lateran, apparently made shortly before the reliefs of Constantine's Arch. To the last decades of the third century belongs the Borghese Phaeton-sarcophagus[1], on which the type of composition planned for the great Ludovisi battle-sarcophagus has degenerated into stiff schematization. On Roman-made sarcophagi the Asiatic type of figure on the lid now begins to appear more frequently. Perhaps this is due to the arrival from Asia Minor of masons, whose hands also seem to betray themselves in the composition and style of certain Hippolytus-sarcophagi in Split and in Rome.

Besides this dying classical style we are aware of the beginnings of a new movement that looks to the future. It is noteworthy that it appears in association with new themes. Subjects which at first only fit spaces on the lids of relief-sarcophagi presently begin to appear on the fronts. They are derived from observation of daily life, shepherds and flocks, feasts, a money-changer's office, or the payment of rent[2]. At the same time the Christian sarcophagi begin to appear with their single scenes, Jonah and the whale, the Good Shepherd, and the Eucharist, motives that were to acquire tremendous importance in the following century first in Rome and then in Gaul. Shortly before the Arch of Constantine there were produced the sarcophagi with only one row of figures that depict scenes from the life of Christ and Peter[3]. Some have ascribed this crude, popular, narrative, realistic art to an influx of provincials. But the provinces show no close antecedents. It is rather due to the fact that, as the pressure of the old classical tradition relaxes, the popular undercurrent, the provincial art of Rome itself, which has already been discerned in previous centuries, now comes to the surface. In painting its tradition had been uninterrupted since Republican days. The flower of Christian relief carving in the late-classical West is indebted for its rise to the union of the new, creative, Christian spirit with the related and still unexhausted Roman popular art. Its origins lie in Rome.

On reliefs of this character, made between 280 and 310, the use of the drill for the hair, eyes, nose, mouth, and drapery gradually becomes an extreme mannerism. It is therefore understandable that after the end of the third century there followed a revulsion from this style, causing the almost complete abandonment of the drill. It is, moreover, possible that this was helped

---

[1] Volume of Plates v, 216, a.   [2] Ib. 216, b, c.   [3] Ib. 216, d.

by the importation, about this time, from Alexandria of sculptures in porphyry, the almost peasant-like and provincial style of which was congenial to contemporary Roman sentiment. This change in technique is carried through within the popular realistic movement and almost reaches its completion with the contemporary sculptural decoration of the Arch of Constantine.

We can see both techniques side by side employed by two sculptors in the Roman Forum on the *Decennalia* base which is probably to be assigned to A.D. 303–4. This is simply a degenerate descendant of the politico-religious type of relief of an earlier day. The Arch of Galerius at Salonica with its wealth of ornament is of greater artistic significance. Though in the general building-up of its reliefs, as well as in some of the subject matter, there are perhaps Oriental influences derived from the répertoire of Sassanian art[1], the style as a whole is based on the popular historical relief, or on the historical painting of Rome. Moreover, the two opposing techniques, one employing, the other rejecting, the use of the drill, are again present side by side. But in certain details of the plastic work we can still perceive a last echo of Greek relief-work, perhaps introduced by assistant masons who still had some connection with the latest sarcophagus factories of Greece.

Popular Roman relief faced a task of historical importance in the decoration of the Arch of Constantine in 315[2]. This arch is a milestone in the history of art. The use of the drill has vanished from the narrow reliefs over the side arches, and its last traces may be observed in the reliefs of the column-bases. In the scenes of the triumphal procession, and especially in those of the siege of Rome and the victory on the Milvian Bridge there is all the rough forcefulness of popular art[3]. The Emperor over life-size, the merciless character of the scene of victory, these are Roman features the gradual growth of which can be watched from the beginning of the second century. Here are no worn-out motives deriving from a long tradition. The victorious soldiers are thrusting with convincing force, as do the hunters on some hunt-sarcophagi of a new type invented about this period. In contrast to these chronicle-like pictures are the static ceremonial scenes[4] with their centralized and frontal compositions corresponding to the increase of similar subjects and designs on medallions of the age of Constantine. In the East rows of identical figures were employed for such ceremonial subjects to increase the impressive effect; here in the West the symmetrical composition is enlivened by many new and freshly

---

[1] Volume of Plates v, 150, *b*.   [2] *Ib* 218.
[3] *Ib.* 220, *a, b*.   [4] *Ib.* 220, *c, d*.

observed touches of realism, episodes, national types, national costumes and the like. These reliefs are not masterpieces of great art, but they are instinct with a vigour that was to guarantee the Roman relief a long life when, after the foundation of Constantinople and the removal of the Court, a strong national consciousness grew up in Rome and Italy.

The architectural structure of the Arch of Constantine[1], in contrast to that of Septimius Severus in the Forum, is inspired by strong classical sentiment. It is the expression of a movement which may be termed 'Constantinian classicism.' It stands at the end of a powerful movement in architectural creation. The currents and undercurrents that reach the late-classical from the previous age can best be traced in portraits and reliefs; but high above these stands the great efflorescence of architecture, which above all marks out the true character of the period of the Tetrarchy and Constantine. In the buildings of the Tetrarchy Roman art rose once again, after the Flavian and Trajanic periods, to a great achievement which still impresses us to-day.

Besides Rome there now appear the new Imperial residences in Nicomedia, Thessalonica, Milan, and Trèves, and in addition to these the shifting Imperial courts and headquarters. It was not merely the 'infinita quaedam cupiditas aedificandi[2],' the 'building mania' of Diocletian himself that was here manifested. His co-regents and their followers also had great buildings to their credit. It is not their mere numbers, but rather the size and boldness of the architectural conceptions in these structures that is remarkable. Is this architectural climax under the Tetrarchy a kind of international manifestation with parallel developments in the several Western and Eastern parts of the Empire, or is it the product of one people, whether Roman, Greek, or barbarian? In the various Imperial residences there is inevitably visible an element of local tradition, displayed especially in technique and handicraft, but also on higher planes of work. Furthermore, there seem to have been travelling workshops with their decorators and masons, and we can apparently recognize influences from Asia Minor at work in the Balkans and in Rome. But the architects certainly travelled too; and the main architectural concepts are so definitely Roman, that we can undoubtedly treat the buildings of the Tetrarchy as the latest flowering of Roman Architecture.

The military tradition in which Diocletian was reared, and his national Roman sentiment, explain why his place of retirement

---

[1] Volume of Plates v, 218.
[2] Lactantius, de mort. pers. 7, 8.

at Split[1], as well as the palace at Palmyra[2] and perhaps also other residences, was built in the form of a Roman camp. We recall the derivation of the Forum Traianum from the Praetorium of a camp. The title *castra*, preserved in an inscription at Palmyra, applies, like the word *stratopedon*, not to a fortified defensive camp, but to the imperial court or headquarters camp. The masterly character of the planning which distinguished architecture under the Tetrarchy is apparent in the clever use of variation. At Palmyra, for example, by reason of the general lie of the landscape, the ceremonial rooms form the central point of the whole complex. At Split, on the other hand, these rooms face the sea, turning their back on the camp. The imperial Baths at Trèves[3] have a ground-plan which combines essential unity with movement. The numerous apses in which the inner rooms project outwards lend great variety to the plastic form of the exterior. By the side of this symphony of cross-vaults, domes and half-domes there stands a building serving quite another purpose; the plain, simple, large hall of the flat-roofed basilica[4].

The Baths of Diocletian in Rome followed the traditional ground-plan of the other great Roman Thermae. But there are differences too. With dominating sureness and simplicity the whole central complex is drawn together and becomes a unit, while the side-courts get a new main axis. The plan of Constantine's Baths was adapted to the configuration of the ground. It was a very bold idea, both technically and artistically, to isolate the kind of unit that had hitherto formed the cross-vaulted hall in Thermae, and to employ this design for building the detached Basilica of Maxentius[5], completed by Constantine. The latter altered it somewhat by adding a side-façade and a corresponding apse. The somewhat purposeless central hall, that had formerly been incorporated in the great Baths, now achieved, in the building of Maxentius, a kind of structural direction which terminated in an apse. The six large chambers, which lie between the piers that take the thrust, and which in the Thermae had served as passage ways or departments of the Baths, were now thrown open so as to form real spaces which are part of the main hall. They were not aisles flanking a nave, but they opened out like six gigantic side-chapels set at right angles to the hall[6]. Similar structures exist in the Liwans of Sassanian palaces. Mention must be made of Diocletian's reconstruction of the Curia in the Forum with its

[1] Plan 4, facing p. 570.
[2] Plan 3, facing p. 570.
[4] *Ib.* 222, *b.* [5] *Ib.* 224, *a.*
[3] Volume of Plates v, 222, *a.*
[6] Plan 5, facing p. 570.

cross-vaults springing straight out of the walls, of the cellae of the double-temple of Venus and Roma vaulted by Maxentius, of the gigantic structures of the Circus of Maxentius, as well as of further experiments with the problem of the circular building. This finally culminated in a new production exemplified by the tomb of S. Costanza, in which the dome rests upon a ring of double-columns which separate the central structure from a barrel-vaulted ambulatory.

The Basilica of Maxentius marks both the climax and the end of ancient Roman-classical development, which found no continuation. But early Constantinian architects created one monumental type of building which was to have a greater after-effect than any other. The Lateran Basilica[1] was probably the first large Christian ecclesiastical building, for the tradition holds that it is *mater et caput omnium ecclesiarum*. A fixed type for the Christian basilica had not previously existed save on a small scale. Of course certain basic principles like the separation of clergy and congregation, and the significant relation of the whole building to the altar, would already have been established in various early meeting rooms. The Christian Basilica with its flat wooden roof has been regarded as retrograde when compared with the Basilica of Maxentius. But it is just as deliberately built on a different plan as is the Basilica of Trèves on a plan differing from that of the neighbouring Thermae. The desire for the parallel movement of nave and aisles could not be realized in a cross-vaulted hall. Furthermore, a view obtained which was contrary to that prevalent since vaulting was adopted for romanesque architecture, and the vault was thought of as something secular contrasting with the sacred, horizontal, coffered ceiling of the temple. The monumental type of the Christian basilica was created by architects of genius to serve the needs of Christian worship. It is the peculiarity of the actual Roman basilica with transepts that the impressive flowing movement of nave and aisles is arrested by the transepts and turned to serenity. The creation of the Christian basilica is only properly appreciated when it is revealed as the most brilliant achievement of the last efflorescence of Roman architecture. A second climax was indeed reached by ancient architecture, but it was a unique achievement and it was final. This was Justinian's church of the Holy Wisdom in Constantinople, grounded on a long development that was rooted in the Hellenism of Asia Minor.

The victory of the Church resulted in a classicizing of Christian art. It coincided with a reaction in portraits and relief work

---

[1] Volume of Plates v, 224, *b*.

against the dry style of the Tetrarchy. After the year 315 there appear beside the expressionist portraits others that link on to an Augustan style[1]. With this classicism there is associated a return to a more plastic kind of modelling. There is pure Hellenistic inspiration, short-lived though it was, in the creation of Christian sculpture in the round. One splendid work of art made in Egypt for the Emperor, the porphyry sarcophagus destined to hold the remains of Helena, shows traces of a revolt against primitive expressionism and of a return to the classical forms of an earlier style[2]. From the time of the reliefs on the Arch of Constantine we can trace, both on the pagan and more especially on the Christian sarcophagi of Rome, a striving after more beauty of form and nobility of expression; and this attains an apex in the year 359 with the sarcophagus of Junius Bassus.

Thus in every branch of art the early years of Constantine marked the first beginnings of a tide that was to sweep beyond the year 330 in an unbroken flood.

[1] Volume of Plates v, 226, *a*, *b*.   [2] *Ib.* 228.

CHAPTER XVII

THE LATIN LITERATURE OF THE WEST FROM THE ANTONINES TO CONSTANTINE

I. INTRODUCTION

IN the age of the Antonines Latin literature enters a new period of its career. It is one, but only one, of the literatures of Rome. The other is Greek. From the time of the Punic Wars when, in Horace's words, Greece captive captured its rude victor, no eminent man of letters among the Romans had failed to be conversant with Greek literature, and a few now and then ventured to express themselves in the Greek language. Under Hadrian, the cosmopolitan, it became more natural for a writer to use either language as suited his needs. But it was not until the age of Hadrian's successors that this fusion of the two modes of literary expression became complete. The normal medium for Fronto was Latin, but Greek also slips freely from his pen. He writes to his Imperial master almost always in Latin, and to his master's mother, Domitia Lucilla, in Greek. Marcus Aurelius responds to his tutor in Latin, but expresses his deepest self in Greek. A half century later, if we may trust the *Historia Augusta*[1], the younger Maximin had as his tutor in Greek a scholar with the Latin name of Fabillus and as a tutor in Latin one with the Greek name of Philemon. The successors of Livy in this period—inferior successors—were Appian under the Antonines and Cassius Dio under the Severi; and both of them wrote in Greek. It was a bilingual world.

The unifying force in this hybrid culture was Rome. All the civilized Occident was Roman, the language and the birthplace of an author were matters of chance. Lucian and Athenaeus, writing in Greek, came the one from Syria, the other Egypt, but Aelian was born at Praeneste. Fronto and Apuleius, known mainly as Latin authors, were Africans. Whatever a writer's place of origin or his eventual domicile, the City is still the centre of attraction. Greek and Latin, to repeat, are but different *media* for the same literature—that of Rome. The treatment of Latin works in the present chapter is only part of the story.

---

[1] S.H.A. *Max. duo*, 27, 3–5.

Nor can the whole story be told without some consideration of the vital forces at work in this period. If we think of the glories of the age of Augustus, literature under the Antonines and their successors seems plainly on the retrograde. It accompanies the decline and fall of the Roman Empire. No surging, national impulse prompts writers to their best, as in the days of Virgil. For all that, the conception of a world running down does inadequate justice to the age that led from Hadrian to Constantine. Historians give various reasons for the breaking up of Rome, but the summation of the factors that they discuss—political, military, economic (and epidemic)—leaves something unexplained. It is more profitable, while following these various changes or catastrophes, to note the seeds of a new life that in spite of these, or along with these, was coming into being.

Here the fresh impulse comes from the East, and above all from Palestine. Greek and Roman religion had been hospitable long before to Oriental rites and ideas; under the Empire there came a second wave, spreading wider than the first. There was a conflict between the old and the new in pagan practice and there was a conflict between this modified paganism and Christianity. In the novelty of the Christian faith Celsus, Porphyry and Julian saw a menace to the Hellenistic civilization of their day and to the Empire of Rome. But the cleavage was not absolute. A reconciliation was in store, effected by the foundation of a new and Christian humanism in the fourth century. The period preceding, with which this chapter is concerned, was one of pregnant conflict.

Such is the background on which we may place the Latin literature of the second and third centuries of our era. Luckily no terms like 'Golden Age' or 'Silver Latinity' (or 'Leaden Latinity') have been applied to it by modern writers. We are free to identify its periods with the reigns of the different rulers or groups of these rulers. The Christian literature that demands our attention starts at the end of the second century. Though its founders are treated together in the account of the age of the Severi, Christians and pagans are not to be put in separate compartments. They were not in separate compartments when they wrote their works; they were citizens or subjects of the Roman Empire.

II. THE AGE OF THE ANTONINES

The Latin literature of the Age of the Antonines is not lacking in interest, variety or novelty. Fronto, the *arbiter litterarum* of the day, was not aware that ancient culture was going into a decline. He well sustained the lineage of those critics who, from Cicero on, had laid down the law to their generations or their princes. Fronto's theory of style, typified by the phrase *elocutio novella*, which is indeed his own, has been widely interpreted as an antiquarian attempt, something in the spirit of our Pre-Raphaelites, to go behind classic standards, to hunt out ancient words discarded by the purists, or popular words never accepted by them, and to make of those a quaint and novel style. A typical expression of this idea is given by Walter Pater in a passage of seductive beauty[1], though for just what *elocutio novella* means we go to Fronto.

MARCUS CORNELIUS FRONTO was born at Cirta in Numidia in the early years of the second century. He was presumably a Roman by descent, as his gentile name indicates, but his early training was in Greek literature rather than Roman. He probably studied at the famous schools of Alexandria, where rhetoric was the subject of his choice, and it remained the dominant influence in his career. He devoted himself, however, not to the profession of a *rhetor*, but, like Cicero, to a career in public life. He was a *triumvir capitalis* at Cirta, and always maintained an interest in the politics of his birthplace. Coming to Rome at the end of Hadrian's reign he was made a senator. He went through the regular *cursus honorum*, with a quaestorship—like Cicero's, again—in Sicily. Under Antoninus Pius he was *consul suffectus* in the same year, 143, that Herodes Atticus was *consul ordinarius*. If a philosopher was soon to become a king, Rhetoric at least controlled the consulate, as often in the past. Fronto was designated for a proconsulship in Asia, but the ailments from which he suffered prevented him from assuming that function. He remained in Rome, an ornament of the literary coteries of the day. His death occurred after 165 and probably before 169.

Such a career suggests in its outlines that of Cicero and prophesies that of Ausonius. Fronto's speeches won him an immediate and, in antiquity, an enduring fame, not revived in modern times until Cardinal Angelo Mai brought to light the fragments of his works contained in a famous palimpsest of Bobbio. This was an unhappy discovery, think some[2], for Fronto's reputation. Of late a more favourable view has rightly prevailed; for the *Letters* are among the treasures of Latin literature.

Shortly after Hadrian, in 138, had adopted Antoninus as his heir, with Marcus Aurelius and Lucius Verus to continue the line, Fronto was appointed tutor for the young princes. Most of the letters are written to Marcus, with some to Lucius, to the

---

[1] *Marius the Epicurean*, chap. v.   [2] Naber, Introd. p. iii.

Emperor Antoninus and to other friends of high standing. Some few are in Greek. Such a correspondence lacks the scope of either that of Cicero or that of Pliny, but it contains what neither of these do, the outpouring of a singularly warm friendship, the love of a master for the pupil whose genius he was moulding, and the love of the pupil, aware of his destiny and grateful to his guide. The young prince does not hesitate to lavish on Fronto epithets of a most romantic sound, while Fronto can declare that nothing is sweeter to him than his pupil's kiss. Such letters attest a high and noble element in the ancient affections of man for man; from its vice young Marcus, helped doubtless by his love of Fronto, had kept clear. He is spurred to his best because of him. 'Amo vitam propter te, amo litteras tecum.' He values him not so much for his mastery of rhetorical style as for his simplicity and his love of truth.

Thus the young philosopher cultivated rhetoric assiduously, for his master's sake. There are touches of humour and banter in the talkings to and fro. The lad breaks out in joy at his master's great consular speech and would give him a kiss for every section. He welcomes criticism and Fronto spares not the rhetorician's rod. But he can mix praise with blame, encourage to further effort, worry all night about his pupil's progress, and find at the last that in his twenty-second year Marcus has proved himself expert 'in omni genere dicendi,' conversant with all the liberal arts, and more important still, in the art of making friends. Rhetoric was not the whole of life for Fronto.

In his twenty-fifth year Marcus Aurelius declared open revolt against rhetoric[1]. Fronto faced the situation bravely, and wrote for his pupil a little discourse de eloquentia, a rhetorical Mirror of the Prince—for a prince who had turned philosopher. Marcus, though fixed in his resolve, was touched by his tutor's appeal and now worried about his health. He begged him to select for him the letters of Cicero that would best improve his style.

Fronto's theory of style is not the construction of a mosaic from rare words quarried from the primitives. He studies the primitives—among others—not for the rare word, but for the right word, exact and striking and luminous[2]. He spurns mere novelty for novelty's sake, for he knows that like the sublime it may descend swiftly to the ridiculous. The orator must search and

[1] ad M. Caes. IV, 13 (p. 75 N; I, p. 216 Loeb).
[2] ad Ant. Imp. I, 2, 5 (p. 98 N; II, p. 42 Loeb) verba non obvia sed optima; ad M. Caes. IV, 3, 3 (p. 63 N; I, p. 6 Loeb) insperata atque inopinata verba; ad M. Ant. de eloq. III (p. 150 N; II, p. 74 Loeb) verborum lumina.

study. Not all the ancients have the clarion-note; some of them bellow or shriek, for the change of even a syllable or a letter may spoil the beauty of a phrase. Such principles of style are not preciously archaistic. There is no proclamation of a quaint new mode of writing. The term *elocutio novella* heralds no novel quaintness, but refers to that freshness of expression for which Fronto was always on the watch[1]. Fronto's interest in the early writers is as wholesome as that of Cicero, whose mind was steeped in the poetry of Ennius and the oratory of Gracchus, and who can admire *verborum vetustas prisca*[2], new turns of phrase and luminous expression[3]. So Horace, though a modern of the moderns, bids the true poet hunt up in Cato or Cethegus words once bright but now caked with mould, and make them shine again[4]. Fronto is not one of the archaizers, found in any age, of whom the younger Seneca said that they talk the Twelve Tables[5].

Against this sentimental cult of the antique, Fronto's careful method seems like a deliberate protest. Hadrian, whom he could eulogize but not love, was guilty, as he puts it, of affecting a cloudy colouring of ancient eloquence[6]. For Fronto, the count of mighty poets was not made up with those of the early Republic. He calls Lucretius sublime, and Horace a 'memorable poet.' To Virgil he appeals as a master of nice distinctions in the use of words[7]. The historians favoured by him are not merely those of the earliest period. Julius Caesar evokes his admiration for his imperial style. Sallust is quoted many times, and his rhetoric is minutely and admiringly analysed. In oratory, besides Sallust, Cato commands the enthusiasm of both master and pupil. But Cicero, too, the orator supreme, is an indispensable model in Fronto's school. He may lack that patient search for the fitting word to which Fronto was devoted, but none excel him in the art of adorning his subject. Fronto declares in a phrase which the little Ciceronians of the Renaissance would have echoed with delight that Pompey deserved his title of 'The Great' not so much for his own achievements as for the speech on the Manilian Law. The orations of Cicero have the true clarion-call and nothing is more perfect than his letters[8].

---

[1] *ad. M. Ant. de eloq.* IV (p. 153 N; II, p. 80 Loeb).

[2] *de orat.* I, 43, 193; cf. on archaic art, *ib.* III, 25, 98.

[3] *de orat.* III, 6, 24.   [4] *Ep.* II, 2, 116–18.   [5] *Epist. Mor.* 114, 13 *sq.*

[6] *ad M. Caes.* II, I (p. 25 N; I, p. 110 Loeb); *ad Verum Imp.* II, I (p. 124 N; II, p. 138 Loeb) (E. Hauler, *Wien. Stud.* XXV, 1903, p. 163).

[7] Gellius, *N.A.* II, 26.

[8] *ad M. Ant. de eloq.* III (p. 149 N; II, p. 74 Loeb); *ad Ant. Imp.* II, 5 (p. 107 N; II, p. 158 Loeb).

But with Cicero Fronto's training of the young orator stops. No use is made of the Augustan authors—despite Fronto's reverence for Virgil—and those of the 'Silver Age' are mentioned only to be damned. Seneca, ironically called his master, is likened to a juggler, and Lucan is ridiculed for saying the same thing in seven different ways at the beginning of his poem on the Civil War. The rest with one exception[1] are passed over in silence.

This means nothing less than a quiet Republican revolution in letters. One may naturally think of the Neo-Attic movement in Greek literature. Fronto's first training was in Greek, and though the old Greek authors, with the exception of Homer, do not loom large in the *Letters*, he could not help knowing contemporary Greek writers associated with the court. Appian, the historian, was an intimate friend, to whom he writes in Greek, and Herodes Atticus, one of the leaders in the New Sophistic, was a fellow-tutor of young Marcus. But though his relations with Herodes were, on the whole, friendly, he would not have been disposed to adopt for the training of his imperial pupil in Latin style the method that his rival at court was exercising in Greek. In any case, his own doctrine reposed on a firmer basis than that of imitation. The influence of Neo-Atticism, which had started under Hadrian, may have affected him unawares, but Fronto's own purpose was not to create a Roman Neo-Attic style to match that in vogue among the Greeks. He ridicules the 'quarrelsome' style of Calvus, a professed Atticist, but calls that of Cicero 'triumphant.' Fronto's aim is to return to the best standards of the Republic after the degeneracy of Imperial oratory, particularly in the age that had preceded his own. He does not, like certain authors of the Silver Age, shed tears over the decay of culture and on the connection of that decay with tyranny. His spirit is rather the confidence of a humanist in the fore-front of a Renaissance than the wistfulness of a Pre-Raphaelite courting a primitive quaintness. With the ruler of the Empire as her pupil, Rhetoric will waken to a new life.

In Fronto's own style there is nothing bizarre or *recherché*, and nothing especially distinguished, in the fragments of his speeches. They are in the 'plain' style (*siccum*), according to Macrobius[2]. In some of his rhetorical exercises, particularly in the Fable of Sleep, which Pater deemed worthy of translation in his exquisite style[3], there is curiously a breath of something new

---

[1] Suetonius, quoted merely for an anatomical term: *ad amic.* I, 13 (p. 182 N; II, p. 174 Loeb).

[2] *Sat.* v, 1, 7. [3] *Marius the Epicurean*, chap. XIII.

and romantic, a harbinger of Apuleius—but this is a passing mood. In his letters, though the model may not be directly his much-admired Cicero, he at least achieves, with differences from Cicero in phrasing and cadence, a plain and unaffected manner. He modestly declares that in his search for fresh and vivid language he achieves merely an obsolete or a vulgar diction. In other words, he deplores as a failing what some have described as the guiding principle of his style. There is no denying the presence of archaisms in his vocabulary and his grammar, but his purpose, whatever his success in achieving it, was to cultivate a living Latin, not to dig up dead Latin from its grave.

Fronto's style befits his character—simple, kindly, conscient-ious, with touches of humour now and then. He speaks too profusely of his many ailments, but is just as solicitous about the health of his pupil. He is fond of his wife and of the 'little chicks' of Marcus; he is heart-broken when his own little grandson dies. He has a warm heart, possessing that virtue of *philostorgia*, the name and nature of which he had not found in Rome. He is devoted mind and soul to rhetoric and takes a natural pride in the training of his prince, but he has neither the little vanities of Pliny nor the large vanity of Cicero.

The age of the Antonines produced a number of learned men, some of them of the circle of Fronto. Among the grammarians were Aemilius Asper, a noted commentator on Virgil, Flavius Caper, and Statilius Maximus, who compared the rare expressions of Cato with those of Cicero—an undertaking quite in line with Fronto's Republican interests. Helenius Acro annotated Terence and also that *memorabilis poeta*, Horace. Probably in this era Juba wrote on metrics, and a writer borrowing the name of Hyginus compiled his sorry book of fables. Julius Titianus, perhaps towards the end of this period, compiled a geographical work on the Roman provinces, and made a collection of rhetorical themes drawn from Virgil. The foremost scholars of the day were, of course, the jurists.

One man of miscellaneous learning, who deserves a modest place among the jurists, too, is AULUS GELLIUS, a younger con-temporary of Fronto. Born we know not where or when, he studied at Rome under the grammarian Sulpicius Apollinaris, renowned in those days for his knowledge of Virgil and for his metrical *periochae* of Terence's plays. Gellius' teachers in rhetoric were Antonius Julianus and Titus Castricius. He writes pleasantly of the former master, who would sometimes hold his classes on the beach at Puteoli. Gellius would also call on Fronto, whose cultured conversations started him on the quest for the fitting word. He completed his studies by resorting to the philosophers of Athens. He also read widely in both the Greek and the Latin jurists, and held a minor judicial office. At Athens, he dined monthly with a little philosophical club and devoted his winter nights to making excerpts from a wide range of authors both Greek and Latin. In Fronto's spirit he hunted words and he hunted, besides, anecdotes and marvels and maxims and customs and questions of law and any good subject for comment. These excerpts and comments he put together in a work called fittingly *Attic Nights*. After his return he worked in odd moments at his pleasant task. Twenty books were published and garnerings in plenty remained. His death occurred probably about the middle of the reign of Marcus Aurelius.

Gellius is of the tribe of the anecdotists, like Favorinus and Aelian and Athenaeus, though his work lacks both the richness and the system of the *Deipnosophists* (p. 620). The anecdotes are jotted down with no attempt at orderly arrangement. He enlivens the treatment now and then with little dramatic dialogues, cast in some picturesque setting.

Gellius' reading in both Latin and Greek is more catholic, or less discriminating, than Fronto's. From Homer and Hesiod to Theocritus, from Parthenius to Plutarch and Appian, he sampled all that he could lay hands on. One might profitably arrange in chronological order the excerpts from the Latin authors; the value of his contribution to our knowledge of Latin literature would be set in striking relief. The quotations from Ennius alone make Gellius the rival of Cicero in preserving nearly all our significant fragments of the father of Latin poetry, and were it not for Gellius[1], our knowledge of the Romans' love-poetry before Catullus would be well-nigh a blank. He rivals Cicero again in his citations of the laws of the Twelve Tables. He quotes plentifully from Cato and gives us valuable information about the works of Varro. He sketches the contemporaneous developments of Greek and Roman civilization through the Punic Wars, and he discourses on the meaning of *humanitas* in a passage[2] with which all who write to-day on ancient humanism must reckon. Some of the anecdotes make the past suddenly alive with human interest[3].

Despite the breadth of Gellius' reading, we find on examining his quotations, that his interests in Latin literature were virtually those of Fronto. Of the writers of the Silver Age there appears

1 *N.A.* XIX, 9; II, 24, 8.   2 *N.A.* XVII, 21; XIII, 17 (16).
3 *E.g. N.A.* I, 23; XX, 1, 13.

the same neglect. He finds Valerius Maximus, Pliny the Elder and Suetonius useful for anecdotes and marvels. He pays tribute to the greatest scholar of the Empire, Valerius Probus. As a Virgilian he cites Annaeus Cornutus, and as a more ardent student of philosophy than Fronto, he speaks highly of Musonius Rufus and Epictetus. He weighs the pros and cons for Seneca with a certain tolerance, but concludes that he is a bad model for the young[1]. There is no word on Lucan or Persius, Juvenal or Tacitus: Gellius no less than Fronto champions a revival of Republican Rome in letters.

The prose of Gellius shows a quiet absence of style, as befits so learned a man. Like Fronto he is interested in ancient expressions and he consequently has certain seasonings of archaic phrases and constructions in his informal diction, but, like Fronto, he inveighs against those who either make a cult of antique usage or condescend to vulgarisms[2]. The African quality in the style of either Fronto or Gellius is no longer the subject of ardent debate. Doubtless the early Republican Latinity introduced into Africa in 146 B.C. had developed certain local peculiarities in its subsequent history, but its literary centres were not shut off from Augustan and post-Augustan influences. The quest of 'Africitas' in the writers of the second century after Christ is as tempting, and as satisfying, as that of Livy's 'Patavinity' or that of the spring of Bandusia on Horace's farm. For the moment, at least, the matter rests with a *non liquet*. Fronto, born in Africa, had Rome as his social, and Republican Latin literature as his intellectual, *milieu*. Gellius, whom nothing whatsoever connects with Africa, was domiciled in Athens, Rome and Praeneste; spiritually he dwelt with a multitude of Greek writers, with those of Republican Rome—and with Virgil.

The simple character of the writer is stamped upon his work. He is a modest scholar, a bit pedantic, but by no means inhuman. He liked good dinners and pleasant talk. He was born to be a Fellow of an Academy—not its president, but its *secrétaire perpétuel*.

The theories of Fronto in his search for a new and living Latin style found fruition in APULEIUS. This writer stands on the same peak with Lucian and Marcus Aurelius. These three and these three alone among the writers of the Antonine Age have the spark of genius; these three alone have moulded the thought and inspired the literary art of subsequent centuries; and they alone are widely read to-day.

[1] *N.A.* XII, 2. [2] *N.A.* I, 10; XI, 7, 1.

Apuleius was born of a well-to-do official at Madauros in Numidia about A.D. 124. He studied at Carthage and at Athens, quaffing the pleasant bowls, as he puts it, of the liberal arts, of poetry, of the natural sciences and of philosophy[1]. He was initiated into various religious rites. His restless and curious temperament prompted him to wander far and wide in search of mystic cults and strange adventures. He would have consorted well with Germany's Romantics, devoted to *Sturm und Drang* and *Wanderlust*. He could turn his ready wit to anything from a poem on tooth-powder to a scientific treatise on fishes or on magic. He came after his wanderings to the unescapable Rome and stayed there for a time. On his way back to his native region, he stopped at Oea in the Tripolitan district, where he married Aemilia Pudentilla the mother of his friend Pontianus, a lady of both more wealth and years than he. Jealous relatives brought suit against him for winning her affection by magical arts; and indeed he had a lively interest in magic,—*damnabilis curiositas* St Augustine calls it[2]. He conducted his own defence—his speech bears the title *Apologia*—before the proconsul Claudius Maximus at Sabrata. He then returned to Madauros, spending the rest of his days there or at Carthage. He enjoyed the fame of many an oratorical triumph, commemorated by statues erected in his honour at Carthage and elsewhere. But he also devoted his best energies to the interpretation of Plato. The battle between Rhetoric and Philosophy, decided in different ways by Fronto and Marcus Aurelius, was for him but the stirring of a nature hospitable to both[3]. A statue set up to him in his native place bore the title that he most prized, *Philosophus Platonicus*[4].

Were we not so uncertain as to the dates of the writings of Apuleius, both of those preserved and of the many that have not reached us—in Greek and in Latin, in poetry and in prose—it would be tempting to bisect his life, like that of Boccaccio and that of Marcus Aurelius, into a distraught, exuberant youth and a sober, philosophic maturity. The date of the trial at which his *Apologia*, full of autobiographical details, was presented, falls between A.D. 155 and 158. He probably, though not surely, composed his great Romance, the *Metamorphoses*, in Rome. That work, too, reflects his own experience, seen as in a glass, impressionistically, much as personal allegory shines through the *Eclogues* of Virgil. It were rash to take any detail in it as bio-

[1] *Flor.* 20.
[2] *Ep.* 138, 19.
[3] *de dogm. Plat.* II, 8; *Flor.* 9.
[4] P. Vallette, *Apol. Flor.* (Coll. Budé), Introd. p. vii.

graphical fact, but in essence it records the journeyings of a soul
through carnal adventures into a mystic peace. It is Apuleius of
Madauros who, in the person of his hero Lucius, becomes in the
end a *pastophoros* of Osiris. He had lived on at least through part
of the joint-reign of Marcus Aurelius and Lucius Verus. A century
or two later he would possibly have atoned for poetry and other
youthful sins by ending his days as a bishop, in the odour of
sanctity and the arms of the Church.

The *Apologia*, besides showing the speaker's mastery of law and
his ability to conduct a defence, bespeaks his wide acquaintance
with the writers, both Greek and Latin, of poetry and prose. His
range is as wide as that of Aulus Gellius and, though his quotations
may not number as many, his understanding, especially of poetry
and philosophy, is deeper. He is moved to cite the ancients by the
charges of his prosecutor Aemilianus, a man of little learning in
Latin and none in Greek, whom he smothers under a blanket of
urbane culture. His pungent wit recalls Cicero's treatment of
Caecilius, his dummy opponent in the trial of Verres. The
cultivated Claudius Maximus must have enjoyed himself at this
trial—and it was a warm day for Aemilianus.

The orator's favourites among the Latin authors, not to mention
his acquaintance with the whole stretch of Greek literature, are
not only the primitives, but Caesar, Catullus, Calvus, Ticidas,
Hortensius, Sallust, Varro, Nigidius Figulus, and Tibullus,
Propertius, Virgil. The Silver Age passes unnoticed, but the verse
of Hadrian and of his friend Vocontius appear. In short, this is
the Republican programme of Fronto, which Apuleius encountered at Rome.

The style of the *Apologia* shows Cicero's fluency as its arguments show his wit. Apuleius characterizes the different orators
much in the manner of Fronto. The *Apologia*, as a specimen of
the *genus iudiciale*, has fewer oratorical flights than appear in
the *Florida*, a collection of extracts from epideictic speeches,
which exhibit the manner of the wandering sophists of the period.
Whatever of Africa they may contain, the breath of Asia is surely
there.

In his last period may perhaps belong the works on Platonic
philosophy. That entitled *De Deo Socratis* treats of the demon of
Socrates in connection with the whole world of *daimones* that
appears in Plato's *Timaeus*. The ambitious subject of the work
De Platone et eius dogmate, is Plato's entire philosophy, considered
under three heads—natural science, dialectics and ethics. The
second part of these divisions is lost. What remains, taken with

remarks on Plato elsewhere[1], is nearer to Plato than is sometimes asserted: it all depends on the proper interpretation of the *Timaeus*, which from the time of Cicero onwards was taken literally, with but small allowance for the divine playfulness of its author. But of the Neoplatonic hierarchies, ecstasies and necromancies which one might expect to find, there is little trace. Apuleius was also devoted to Aristotle. By him may be a translation of the treatise *De Mundo* ascribed to Aristotle, and a translation of the *De Interpretatione*. Among the writings that have not come down to us are works on the liberal arts, which then as to Boethius and to medieval thinkers were indissolubly connected with the crown of them all, philosophy. Other works, on philosophical, scientific and historical subjects, along with love-poems and another romance have likewise perished. The style of the philosophical works preserved is appropriately simpler than that of the orations. Besides, various works by other writers eventually were attributed to him—for his name had acquired authority.

The philosophical programme of Apuleius was apparently that of Cicero before him and that of Boethius after him, to make the best of Greek philosophy accessible to Roman readers. And, whatever his defects as an expounder of the philosophy of Plato, we may grant him his coveted title of *Platonicus* for his remark that 'we of the household of Plato care for nothing that is not festal and joyous and solemn and high and celestial[2].'

The masterpiece of Apuleius, the *Metamorphoses*, is a composite of two literary forms. Into the frame of a romance, such as had been invented in Hellenistic times and popular under the Empire, he set a number of Milesian tales, spiced with ribaldry, sorceries, robberies and horrors. But the best of these stories, that of Cupid and Psyche, more of a medieval fairy tale than a Greek myth, is pure and sweet in tone. Its quality shines the brighter from the gruesome setting in which it is placed—an art that both Ovid and Boccaccio, an admirer of Apuleius, well understood. The story of a youth metamorphosed into an ass had been told by one Lucius of Patrae and perhaps by the great Lucian himself, of whose work a crude epitome still survives. Whatever the relation of Apuleius to his models, he has produced a structure of his own with touches of allegory and autobiography, as we have seen, that do not disturb the general design. Behind it is a mind not obsessed with romantic cravings, but master of itself, and of literary art, with careful

---

[1] *E.g. Apol.* 43, 49. The summary of Platonism may have been drawn from the same source as that of Albinus in Greek. See A. D. Nock, *Sallustius*, p. xxxvii.   [2] *Apol.* 64.

planning, dramatic suspense, *suasoriae*, parody—even of Virgil—
and delicate satire—even of the gods. Yet it is a kindly mind, with
sympathy for men and beasts. It enjoys good fun and a laugh at
its own expense[1]. It is a religious mind, that cleanses off its own
pollutions somewhat as Virgil's shepherds cease their ribaldries
when they begin their contest of song. The high mysticism, the
high purity, and the gorgeous liturgy in which the progress of the
soul culminates, sets forth in a sincere and alluring form the modes
of cult and devotion against which the faith of Christians had to
contend and over which it triumphed.

The style of this masterpiece is suited to the theme. The writer
apologizes—it is a mock apology—for the rude and exotic
Latinity, which he, a poor Grecian, had picked up in Rome[2]. No
learned parade of his reading is made. No authors except great
and typical figures, like Homer and Pythagoras, are mentioned.
Words and sentences are humble, caught from the lips of the
common people—of Africa, need we say? Diminutives abound,
as in the low Latin whence Italian is derived. But the language is
not really crude; it is fused with colour and with poetry. We may
adapt a phrase of his own to describe it—'pictura Babylonica
miris coloribus variegata[3].' Some of the expressions, not found
elsewhere, may well be the inventions of the author. Assonance
and rhyme abound. Stretches of such prose, like the prose of
George Meredith in his lyric moods, could be cut up into decent
free verse; the flow of the sentence sets itself many a time to music.
This is the manner that Fronto had imperfectly attempted in his
Fable of Sleep. It is wholly different from its author's oratorical
and philosophical styles and leagues away from Cato or anything
archaic. Nor is it a reflex of Neo-atticism, though Apuleius in his
literary feeling was half Greek. It is the proper diction for romance,
and Apuleius is its great perfecter.

One element in the spiritual make-up of this curious and many-
sided genius should not be forgotten. Apuleius was African by
birth, Athenian by training, Oriental by his contact with the
mystic cults, but also, by the magnetism of the City, an inhabitant
of Rome. His mind dwelt reverently, as the *Apologia* shows[4], in
various epochs of the Roman past. And the deity that comes to
Lucius in a vision gives him a blessing of which the old formula
'quod bonum felix faustumque sit' is a part[5]. But we are not
listening to a magistrate opening an assembly. A priest is ab-
solving a penitent's soul—'quod felix itaque ac faustum salu-

---

[1] *Met.* IX, 42.   [2] *Met.* I, I.   [3] *Flor.* 9.
[4] *E.g. Apol.* 18, 20, 66.   [5] *Met.* XI, 29.

tareque tibi sit.' A new world has entered with the simple change
of 'bonum' to 'salutare.'

The interests of the circle of Fronto found expression in poetry
as well as prose. The poets of the day, so far as the scanty fragments of their works permit a judgment, cultivated a simple vivid
style and the shorter forms of verse, in which some novelties
appear. As harbingers of the new movement we may regard the
Emperor Hadrian and his friend Florus, who exchanged trifles
of an Anacreontic nature that of a sudden could set forth true
pathos, as in the Emperor's address to his dying soul—'pallidula,
rigida, nudula.'

One of the Antonine poets is pleasantly pictured by Aulus
Gellius—Annianus. This gentleman possessed an estate in the
Faliscan territory in Etruria, where Gellius dined with him. The
poet could talk learnedly of the effect of the waning moon on
oysters, quoting Lucilius; he could cite Plautus and Terence on
the proper accentuation of certain words, and he admired Virgil—
here are traits that bespeak the age of Fronto[1]. He also wrote
Fescennine verse presumably of a salacious sort. It is cited by
Ausonius in his apology for his own indecent *Cento Nuptialis*.
Annianus also composed, apparently with his estate in mind, what
he called a *carmen Faliscum*[2], modelled on the work of Septimius
Serenus, the inventor of this form[3]. Since Serenus was a recent
writer for Terentianus Maurus, all three poets were contemporaries, or very nearly so, with Terentianus the last in the series.

Terentianus Maurus performed what at first would seem a
highly unpoetical task in writing a metrical treatise on metre
(*de Litteris, Syllabis, Metris*), with each metre described in specimens
of itself. But the poet, a master of his subject, is amazingly skilful
in turning technicalities into neat verse. He must have smiled
frequently at his success. He pursues the theory that the dactylic
hexameter and the iambic trimeter contain the other forms of
verse in embryo, and he deftly assists at their delivery. His chief
sources are Virgil, Horace, and Catullus, but he uses the primitives too, such as Livius Andronicus[4], and though generally
eschewing the authors of the Silver Age, does not disdain examples
from Pomponius Secundus, the tragedian of the time of Tiberius,

---

[1] Gellius, *N.A.* VI (VII), 7; IX, 10; XX, 8.

[2] Marius Victorinus, III, 14 (*Gramm. Lat.* VI, 122, 9 *sqq.* K).

[3] Terentianus Maurus, *de Lit. Syll. Metr.* 1991 and see Keil (*Gramm.
Lat.* VI, 323) on l. 1816 (anapaestic dimeters).

[4] *Ib.* ll. 1931 *sqq.*—a most important fragment, calmly assigned to
Laevius by some scholars.

and from Petronius. Interest in metre would lead Terentianus
farther afield than Fronto, but the scope of his reading in poetry
is virtually the same, and he seems to be speaking with Fronto's
voice in his encomiums of the 'striking'—*novitas inopina*[1].

The verse of SEPTIMIUS SERENUS that Annianus renamed
Faliscan consists of three dactyls followed by a pyrrhic or an
iambus—more easily read as a half of a dactylic hexameter (up to
the penthemimeral caesura) plus a proceleusmatic. The fragment
describes the proper mode of mating the vine and the elm:

> quando flagella iugas, ita iuga,
> vitis et ulmus uti simul eant:
> nam nisi sint paribus fruticibus,
> umbra necat teneras Amineas.   (2001–2004)

It looks as though Serenus had composed a new *Georgics* in a really
rustic verse. In fact we are told by Marius Victorinus that this
measure was called *calabrion* by the Greeks because it was used by
Calabrian peasants in their country songs[2]—all at once we have
a glimpse of the folk-poetry of Magna Graecia. Another fragment
in which the verse extends to the hephthemimeral caesura of the
dactylic hexameter—

> Inquit amicus ager domino—

is evidently from the same poem. For Maurus, who cites it as
one of his *exempla novella*, calls the work plainly a didactic poem
on the country[3]. Elsewhere in his 'dulcia opuscula' he uses three
choriambs plus a bacchius:

> Iane pater, Iane tuens, dive biceps, biformis.

Or the second choriamb in such a line may be replaced by two
iambi:

> cui reserata mugiunt aurea claustra mundi—

a graceful line of rapid movement. It is not certain that all these
bits and others in other metres amassed from other sources[4] are
from this new *Georgics* of Serenus, but it is clear that he experi-
mented with novel and light-moving forms of verse, some of which
were tried later by Boethius[5]. In fact Jerome can rank Serenus

---

[1] *Ib.* l. 1922. Cf. above, p. 574.   [2] *Gramm. Lat.* VI, 122, 9 K.
[3] Line 1975: *Septimius docuit quo ruris opuscula libro.*
[4] Baehrens, *Poetae Lat. Min.* VI, 384–8.
[5] In the *De Metris Boeti Libellus* compiled by Lupus Servatus, the metre
of *Cons. Phil.* III, m. 1 is called *faliscum* (ed. Peiper, 1871, p. xxvii). Some
good and ancient source was apparently followed by Lupus in this work.

with Pindar, Alcaeus, Horace and Catullus as the pagan lyric bards of whom King David the Psalmist is a Christian peer[1]. If this utterance of Jerome, no mean connoisseur of ancient letters, be given full credit, we have lost in Septimius Serenus a lyric poet worthy to be named with Horace and Catullus.

One more member of this circle of the moderns may be mentioned—ALFIUS AVITUS. He wrote not long before Maurus several books on *Excellentes*, 'Heroes,' in iambic dimeters[2]. Priscian[3] quotes from the second book of this work a fragment from the story of the faithless schoolmaster of Falerii who marched his pupils over to the Romans and whom, by order of Camillus, his pupils flogged back[4].

> Tum literatos creditos
> Ludo Faliscum liberos
> Causatus in campi patens
> Extraque muri ducere.
> Spatiando paulatim trahit
> Hostilis ad valli latus.

This poet, a modern with eyes on the past, seems to have anticipated Macaulay's plan of celebrating the heroes of his country—here Camillus—not in an epic but in lays of ancient Rome[5].

We may turn from these tantalizing fragments to a poem complete, or nearly so, and one of the most remarkable in the whole range of Latin verse, the *PERVIGILIUM VENERIS*. Not all would agree that it is a product of the Antonine Age, where Walter Pater and others have put it; in fact there has been something of a drift since Pater's time towards the assumption of a later date—but none of the later dates proposed has been definitely established. It may be said, with due caution, that nothing in the atmosphere, style or grammar of the poem jars with the age of Fronto and Apuleius or with the poetry just discussed.

But waiving all questions of date and authorship, we may centre our attention on the poem itself. It is included in an anthology of occasional verse contained in the famous Codex Salmasianus, which was put together at Carthage, about A.D. 532. That is not proof that the poem was written in Africa. In the Salmasianus the poem bears at the beginning the phrase 'sunt vero versus XXII,' which means not that the poem had twenty-two verses (it has ninety-three) or twenty-two strophes, but that there were

---

[1] *Ep.* 53, 8, 17.   [2] Terentianus Maurus, *op. cit.* l. 2448.
[3] *Gramm. Lat.* II, 426 K.   [4] Livy v, 27.
[5] The poem on the *Lupercalia* by Marianus (Baehrens, *Poetae Lat. Min.* VI, 384) may be of the same sort.

twenty-two poems in the division of the anthology that it heads. The presence of the frequent refrain:

cras amet qui numquam amavit quique amavit cras amet

would induce some omissions or transpositions, and a gap in the sense at line 58 makes some adjustment necessary. Some scholars assume that the original form presented a subtle series of strophes and antistrophes in the manner of a Greek ode, some would divide it into quatrains, a theory alluringly set forth by Dr Mackail, and some would note a series of irregular strophes which present an orderly succession of poetic ideas.

Assuming but a few changes in our present text, we have the following sequence: The poet announces the festival of Venus, which will take place on the morrow. He praises the spring, the season of love. To-morrow is the bridal of the earth and sky, when the sea gave birth to Venus. She is the universal spirit of generation. She is also the mother of the Romans, whose royal race she has preserved from Romulus to the present Caesar. She brightens the spring with roses, sprinkling their virgin buds with dew. On the morrow the rose will reveal its own crimson, and become a bride in pure and single wedlock. The goddess orders the Nymphs into the groves and Cupid escorts them. They are afraid of his arrows, so he goes naked and unarmed. Beware of him, however! Cupid when naked is armed *cap-à-pie*. Venus now sends the virgins to implore the virgin Diana to refrain from the chase during the festival. The appeal succeeds. One may now see for three nights joyous troops in the woods, making merry in their myrtle-trimmed huts. The goddess has her throne adorned with the flowers and holds her Court of Love. The spirit of Venus now spreads throughout the countryside. In the country her boy Cupid was born. All the beasts of the field, all the birds of the air feel her presence. The raucous cry of the swans is heard in the ponds, the nightingale sings joyously in the poplar's shade. But the poet has no joy, no love, no spring. He has only silence and the despite of the Muse. Amyclae was ruined for its silence, and silence has ruined the poet.

Loveless hearts shall love to-morrow, hearts that have loved shall love again.[1]

The poem with its supple verse, gorgeous colouring and mystic over-tones is fittingly called by Dr Mackail 'one of the finest flowers of Latin poetry.' It accords with Hadrian's interest in the

---

[1] Thus translated by F. L. Lucas in *The Decline and Fall of the Romantic Ideal*, p. 69.

cult of Venus; it is what a poet, growing old and sad, might well have written when Hadrian was about to pass off the scene, or a few years later. It is not liturgy, though there is perhaps a suggestion of liturgy mingled with reflection and seasoned with memories of Virgil, of Lucretius and possibly of Catullus. Its style in poetry suggests what Apuleius achieved in the prose of romance.

The Age of the Antonines, so far as Latin literature is concerned, means the reign of Antoninus Pius and the earlier part of that of Marcus Aurelius. They both were men of culture and patrons of learning, but Fronto's pupil, 'the only Emperor who had mastered the *schemata*,' renounced the pomps and vanities of rhetoric and applied himself with equal zeal to the business of State and the perfection of a Stoic character (see vol. XI, chap. IX). He rendered unto Caesar the things that are Caesar's and unto the Infinite the things that are the Infinite's, preparing his soul as conscientiously for its extinction as a Christian prepares his for its immortality. Had he lived a century or two later, he doubtless would have ended his days in a monastery; his spiritual experience was, unknown to himself, typical of the great revolution then slowly and surely at work in all society. The colleague and adoptive brother of Marcus Aurelius, Lucius Verus, had a good education and Fronto had made him, too, an orator, but his insignificant career ended in A.D. 169. Under Commodus there was little hope for the Muses. The descent from the philosopher-king to the king-gladiator, his son, one of the 'little chicks' of whom Fronto was fond, is one of the painful ironies of history.

III. THE AGE OF THE SEVERI AND THE RISE OF CHRISTIAN LATIN LITERATURE

The year before the accession of Septimius Severus saw the brief reigns of Pertinax and Didius Julianus. Had the former, a sturdy soldier and ex-schoolteacher—himself taught by Sulpicius Apollinaris—lived to establish the ancient discipline, as he desired, a revival of Roman integrity in literature as in the State might well have occurred, but his utter absence of tact led to his fall. Septimius Severus, a harsh, though firm and conscientious, ruler, was well-versed in both the Greek and the Latin authors, and in law. He had some interest in philosophy, which for him included astrology, and encouraged by his wife, the Syrian Julia Domna, displayed a strong and superstitious devotion to African and Oriental cults. He wrote an autobiography, now lost, which although he was

born in Leptis Magna, and spoke Latin with an African accent,
may not have been a monument of 'Africitas' in its style. For the
Emperor felt himself most Roman. He condemns Clodius
Albinus, another African and his rival for the throne, who had
'busied his senility with old-wives' tales and literary nonsense like
those Punic Milesian novels of his beloved Apuleius[1].' One may
possibly detect in the animadversions of the Roman Septimius a
note of revolt against the school of Fronto. At this time, or perhaps somewhat earlier, Julius Titianus[2] wrote imaginary letters
of illustrious women on the plan of Ovid's *Heroides*, but in prose.
His prose was so closely modelled on that of Cicero's *Letters* that
he gained from the Frontonians the title of the orator's ape[3].
Titianus may have belonged to a party of opposition—his return
to Ovid is significant.

The poetry of this period has nothing to show but mimes and
centos, nor did the reigns of terror under Caracalla and Elagabalus, separated by a brief respite under Macrinus, produce anything of note in letters.

In Severus Alexander a humanist, if not a philosopher, became
king. This monarch was well trained in the liberal arts and created
a literary circle about him—'amavit litteratos homines vehementer'
observes his biographer[4]. Among them was the Greek writer
Cassius Dio, who was at once administrator and historian. Latin
was the language of the eminent jurists, Aelius Gordianus, Paul
and Ulpian, the orators Claudius Venacus and Catilius Severus, and
the historian Encolpius. Severus himself was capable of metrical
quips in Greek, recalling, but not equalling, the *jeux d'esprit* of
Hadrian, and he wrote, we know not whether in Greek or in
Latin, verses on the lives of good emperors. A quotation from
Persius made by the Emperor[5] may indicate that the tide was
turning in the direction of the neglected 'Silver Age,' though there
is little additional evidence of this sort. Sammonicus Serenus in
his well-turned poem on medicine quotes Ennius, Plautus,
Titinius, Varro, Lucretius, Horace and Livy and his verse is
formed on that of Virgil. If this is a representative list, the
favourites of this poet are still within the circle of Fronto's
authors. Such is the meagre crop from the plentiful seeds of
liberal culture sown by Severus Alexander.

---

[1] S.H.A. *Clod. Alb.* 12, 12. The same writer tells us (11, 7) that Clodius
Albinus had also written *Georgica*.
[2] See above, p. 577.   [3] Sidonius Apoll. *Ep.* 1, 2.
[4] S.H.A. *Alex. Sev.* 3, 4.
[5] Persius, *Sat.* 2, 69 *ap.* S.H.A. *Alex. Sev.* 44, 9.

The Christian Church had no need of a literature for the first century or more of its existence. The new community pursued an underground existence until it came in conflict with the religion of the State. It throve in silence under persecution and at last found a voice to protest. The first apologies in the bilingual Roman world were in Greek. In the reigns of Hadrian and the Antonines at least a dozen of them appeared.

Africa is the cradle of Christian Latin literature and its father[1] is Q. Septimius Florens Tertullianus. Born a pagan at Carthage c. 150–160, trained in the same school of rhetoric as Apuleius, he was well-versed in Greek and Latin letters, in philosophy, and in law. A fiery, honest and original spirit, Tertullian reacted against ancient culture, married a Christian wife and is said to have become a priest of the Church. With Rome as his centre of authority he defended true doctrine against pagans, Jews and heretics. Disgusted at the laxness of Rome's bishop he embraced the hyperascetic *régime* of the followers of Montanus and the revelations of the Paraclete vouchsafed to them alone. He broke with this heresy and founded one of his own. For all his divagations he was recognized as the founder of Occidental theology. Jerome includes him in his history of the Eminent Men of the Church, omitting mention of his works, 'since everybody knows them[2].' He flourished in the reigns of Septimius Severus and Caracalla, and lived to a decrepit old age. In contrast with the pagan writers of that period, Tertullian had something to say.

Among Tertullian's earlier works there are defences of the faith against the pagans, consolations for martyrs, instructions on matters of Christian living, a general attack on heretics (*De Praescriptione Haereticorum*) and on Jews. Those that follow show his growing repugnance to the carnal-minded (*psychici*) and his hatred of heresy is directed against the sects of the day, save that into which he was drifting. The diverse errors of Hermogenes on the eternity of matter, of the gnostics (*Adversus Valentinianos*), of Marcion and of the Monarchianists (*Adversus Praxeam*) are all laid low. His *De Anima*, a startling defence of the corporeality of the soul, shows the lengths to which Tertullian's contempt of the gnostics' shadowy spirituality could go. Pendants to this scholarly treatise—of interest in the history of science as well as

---

[1] The long debate over the priority of Tertullian or Minucius Felix has apparently been settled in favour of Tertullian. See P. de Labriolle, *La réaction païenne*, p. 93. Yet note A. Amatucci in *Africa Romana*, p. 191.

[2] *de Vir. Ill.* 53. Every word in this brief biography is precious.

of religion—are the works *De Carne Christi* and the *De Resurrectione Carnis*. Some of the writings not extant were written in Greek, in which he might have written all his works, had he felt so inclined. Among these the loss of the seven books *De Ecstasi* is especially deplorable. They would have shown us how this foe of sentimentality had none the less an inner eye for visions, and why he could chide the Church for obtuseness when the Spirit would guide it into new truth.

Considered as literary products, the works of Tertullian suggest Cicero and Seneca as their chief models for both subject and form. *De Patientia*, like *De Clementia* or *De Amicitia*, is a philosophical essay, though the writer is a priest instructing catechumens, not a man of letters conducting a *conversazione*. The apologetic works are arguments for the defence, like those in Cicero's orations. *Ad Nationes*, written to the pagans at large, refutes their slanders and attacks their superstitions. The *Apologeticum*, written in the latter part of the year 197 to provincial magistrates who tried cases against Christians, is addressed to an imaginary court. The charge that Tertullian refutes is that the Christians are disloyal to the State and to the Emperor, its head. The answer is that they best render to Caesar the things that are Caesar's by invoking in his behalf the blessing of the one true God. The praise of the Emperor at the expense of the gods in this great and simple passage[1] is suggestive of the tone in which Richelieu addressed his monarch. With the same learning and the same mastery of the law that Apuleius had shown in his own *apologia*, he speaks out with an intensity prompted by the graver danger and the nobler cause. At the same time he has by no means renounced Rhetoric with other pomps of the world. He is as honest as she allows him to be. The Christian and the Sophist engage his spirit in a new *suasoria* and the Sophist too often wins the day.

The *Apologeticum* is of all Tertullian's works the most carefully composed and the best mirror of his mind, with its weaknesses and its strength. Despite his legal and rhetorical quibblings there is enough sound sense in the work to convert an intelligent pagan to the reality of Christian life, although the attack here and elsewhere on the pagan culture in which Tertullian had been reared is bitter and persistent. It was not the moment for a Christian humanism when smouldering animosities broke forth into active persecution. He would not court the sympathy of pagans by attempting a harmony between their poets and philosophers and the writers of Sacred Scripture[2]. Rather, in the words of St Paul,

[1] *Apol.* 30.　　　　[2] *de Test. Anim.* 1.

'the wisdom of this world is as foolishness with God[1],' and a professor of the classics a near neighbour to idolatry[2]. Yet once delivered of this epigram Tertullian draws the distinction between the teacher and the taught and wellnigh admits that the knowledge of literature is a necessary equipment for life. One bond there is between the ancient world and Christianity: it is that 'testimony of the naturally Christian soul' that common people, in calling on the name of God, have offered to His existence and His goodness[3]. But Tertullian holds out no hand to the past. His final argument, addressed to the proconsul Scapula in 212–213 and repeated later by Lactantius in his *De Mortibus Persecutorum*, is that the persecuting magistrates have drawn upon themselves the wrath of God and perished violently.

The authors whom Tertullian had read in the schools of Carthage are not completely indicated in his writings, for he quotes mainly to refute them or to gather from them evidence of the superstitions and immoralities of paganism or to show how much better were the men of old than their gods. It is evident at least that he was versed in Greek as well as in Latin literature, though some, perhaps many, of his references are at second hand. The names of Ovid, Tacitus, Suetonius and Pliny the Younger among his authors suggest that Fronto's boundary has been passed. The crucial instance is Seneca, who not only is quoted several times but called *saepe noster*[4].

The seekers of the *tumor Africus* have a happy hunting-ground in Tertullian. He is African by birth and temperament. He visited Rome, but eluded its attraction and broke with the Roman Church. His style should *a priori* reveal African traits. A plausible list of these has been assembled[5], yet the influence of his study of Greek and of the law and of the rhetorical tradition should not be forgotten. Despite his archaisms his oratorical model is not the simple Cato. His longer sentences are almost strophes with parallelisms, assonances, rhymes and metrical clausulae[6]. We must reckon also with his fondness for Seneca, and a trace of the gorgeously romantic colouring of Apuleius may perhaps be detected here and there, particularly in the *De Pallio*[7]. He has been

---

[1] *de Spect.* 18.   [2] *de Idol.* 10.
[3] *Apol.* 17; *de Test. Anim., passim.*   [4] *de Anima* 20.
[5] See particularly, H. Hoppe, *De Sermone Tertullianeo*, pp. 46–72.
[6] For examples see the beginning of the *de Pudicitia* and *de Patientia*; E. Norden, *Die antike Kunstprosa*, pp. 610 *sqq.*; Hoppe, *Syntax und Stil des Tertullian*, pp. 8–11, 154–68.
[7] Hoppe, *op. cit.* p. 23; Norden, *op. cit.* p. 614.

called in a clever epigram 'a barbarizing Tacitus[1],' but the phrase, like some epigrams, is faulty in both its parts. Tertullian was not a barbarian, and he certainly did not model his style on that of Tacitus, whom he called, in an epigram of his own, no tacit person but a mendacious chatter-box[2]. He started, like Tacitus, with the rhetoric of the schools, breaking through it, as Tacitus did in a different way, by the force of his native genius. At its best, his style is straightforward, strong and simple, the product of honest conviction and Christian humility. The Paraclete gave him at the right moment what he should say. He coins new words. His is a living and a growing language[3]. It contains in the germ those two antithetic styles, the ornate and the plain, which are displayed in the history of Christian Latin literature, sometimes in the work of the same writer, for instance Fortunatus, down into and through the Middle Ages.

Judged solely as a man of letters, Tertullian, like Jerome, deserves a high rank among the writers of satire. If he is not a barbarizing Tacitus he may well be entitled a Christian Juvenal. Like Juvenal, he did not hesitate to call a spade a spade. His invective is no less tart, as when he describes the theatre as the Devil's church, or the Bishop of Rome as *pastor moechorum*, or when he scolds the belles of Carthage—who, doubtless, loved to hear him scold—for dosing their hair with saffron like victims led to the altar, or when he ridicules the first families of Carthage for objecting to his use of the simple pallium—the national garb before their ancestors surrendered to Rome. Philosophers, professors and heretics all deal in shams, which Tertullian mercilessly blasts. Marcion, as a higher critic, 'emends Holy Scripture with the sword rather than the pen,' and Praxeas, the Patripassionist, doubly distasteful to Tertullian on account of his opposition to Montanism, 'exiled the Paraclete and crucified the Father.' Such are the thrusts of sarcasm and wit that enliven many a page in Tertullian.

If, further, we take 'satire' in the larger and ancient sense of the word, Tertullian presents little pictures of daily life both Christian and pagan that are of both human interest and historical importance[4]. What to the pagan onlooker seemed, like Lucretius' flock of sheep on the distant hill-side, a unified group—a group of subversive fanatics—becomes in the pages of Tertullian a little world of discords in faith and in practice no less pronounced than

---

[1] G. A. Simcox, *History of Latin Literature*, II, p. 275.   [2] *Apol.* 16, 3.
[3] P. Monceaux, *Hist. Litt. de l' Afrique Chrétienne*, I, p. 446.
[4] *E.g. Apol.* 39; *de Anima* 9.

those that exist to-day. Yet the discords resolve in a harmony of assurance. 'We are of yesterday, and yet we now fill the world[1].' It is a new world in religion and in morality, with, for instance, a conception of the sacrament of marriage, only adumbrated before, that makes a conjoint pagan and Christian household unthinkable.[2] Finally, though the satire of Tertullian, like the satire of Juvenal, is inspired by a *saeva indignatio*, it has its moments of tenderness and sympathy without which invective loses its force. For instance, he has nothing but praise for the real and simple Rome of old, or for the instinctively Christian soul that through the clouds of idolatry beheld a vision of God[3].

Tertullian is a character for tragedy. He, the scholarly de-fender of the Church against its enemies without and within, the founder of its theology and its language in the West, the apostle of a pure religion and undefiled, read himself out of the ranks by his very devotion to Christian revelation. With all his honesty, vigour and common sense, he could not escape the sophistic habit of mind. With all his devotion to tradition, his acceptance of the new prophecy transferred the seat of authority to the individual soul. The Church excluded Tertullian not for his Puritanism, but for his Protestantism. His confident reading of the Paraclete's messages engendered that self-will or *hybris* that brings a high-minded hero to his fall.

The simple style appropriate for Christian humility, attained by Tertullian in some moments, appears in a rare monument of his times, an account of the martyrdom of two Roman maidens, Perpetua and Felicitas, who suffered death with several of their friends in the persecution of A.D. 202–3. Perpetua had recorded the events up to the moment of her death, and some writer of Montanistic leanings, possibly Tertullian himself, published the little work, happily leaving its plainness unadorned. Perpetua deserves a place with the heroines of tragedy. When her father, a Roman of high station, asked her to recant, she said, 'Father, do you see that pitcher there?' 'Yes.' 'Can it be called by any other name than that which it has?' 'No.' 'Then I cannot call myself other than what I am, a Christian.' When the beasts attacked her in the amphitheatre, she pulled her torn garment about her, mindful of her modesty rather than her pain. When brought out again, she bound her scattered locks neatly, 'for it was not proper for a martyr to loosen her hair, lest she seem to mourn at the moment of her glory.' This is not the 'theatrical' death of Christians that offended Marcus Aurelius.

[1] *Apol.* 37, 4.　　　[2] *ad Uxorem*, II, 4, 9.　　　[3] *Apol.* 6; 17.

This brief document, as sincere as a Gospel, is the first of its kind in Christian Latin literature. It is the sort of record that lay before Prudentius when he composed the simpler of his poems—like that on St Eulalia—in honour of the *Martyrs' Crowns*.

MINUCIUS FELIX, no less eminent than Tertullian in the history of Christian Latin literature, reflects a different social entourage and most probably a different imperial régime. Like Tertullian he was a pagan at the start and probably a native of Africa. After an excellent education, wherever received, he settled in Rome, perhaps early in the third century, and acquired fame in the law.

Minucius' apology (the *Octavius*) takes the form of a dialogue, so artistically constructed that its apologetic contents seem incidental. The subject is the conversion, after the debate, of his friend Caecilius Natalis, who may be the M. Caecilius Natalis or his father Quintus who figure in an inscription of the early third century found at Cirta[1]. Cirta was Fronto's birthplace and Fronto's attack on the Christians is answered in the dialogue[2]. The work is named from the third speaker, Octavius Januarius. The debate, whether actual or imaginary, is placed in the past, as in some of the dialogues of Cicero. It is impossible, therefore, to find in the association with Fronto's speech an argument for the date of the work itself.

The setting of the dialogue is presented with no little charm. The three friends are strolling on the shore at Ostia. A reverential kiss blown by Caecilius to a statue of Serapis starts the debate, in which, with an admixture of Epicurean science and Neo-academic scepticism, he assaults the immoralities and credulities of the Christian sect. He then defends the old religion—in the new form that had welcomed Serapis—with that tenderness for traditions to which a sceptical mind sometimes resorts. Octavius, in reply, asserts the eternal Providence, which even the humble can know and which pagan poets and philosophers no less than the Holy Scriptures have attested. The absurd superstitions attributed falsely to Christians are more than matched by the myths about the gods, who all, as Euhemerus showed, were nothing but men of renown deified by their admirers. The real life of Christians, their true and simple worship, their bravery in affliction, their sure hope of a resurrection are presented with a quiet fervour that wins Caecilius. Minucius finds it unnecessary to play his part of arbiter, and the three friends go on their way rejoicing. The controversy ends in a smile, like Horace's satire and Cicero's debate on the training of the orator[3]—'laeti hilaresque discessimus.'

[1] Dessau 2933.   [2] *Octav.* 9, 6; 31, 2.   [3] *Sat.* II, 1, 86; *de orat.* I, 62, 265.

With the art that conceals art, Minucius has covered in this dialogue the range of ancient history and Greek philosophy. He knows his authors, especially the Romans, intimately, though he mentions or cites but few. In the phrase: 'sed quatenus indulgentes insano atque inepto labori ultra humilitatis nostrae terminos evagamur et in terram proiecti caelum ipsum et ipsa sidera audaci cupiditate transcendimus' (5, 6), a familiar echo of Virgil and two echoes of Horace catch the ear[1]. If the reader will turn to the edition of the learned Boenig, he will note reminiscences, or possible reminiscences, of virtually all the chief authors of Rome from Ennius to Tacitus and Juvenal. 'Quid gentilium litterarum dimisit intactum?' remarks Jerome. As in Tertullian, Fronto's literary prescriptions have no more weight. Seneca, unnamed, is present. The epigram 'Nobody can be as poor as when he was born' comes from him[2] and the chapter in which it occurs and that following are shot through with phrases of Seneca wisely conjoined with those of St Paul. The cultivated pagan reader who knew his Seneca might well be tempted to search the Christian scriptures.

Above all, the master of Minucius Felix is Cicero. The plan of the work is modelled on the *De Natura Deorum*; hardly a page fails to contain some glance at the arguments and the spirit of Cicero's works. The omission of Cicero's name, like that of Seneca's, is not an attempt to conceal the writer's borrowings, but an invitation to compare. With balanced periods and metrical clausulae his is a Ciceronian style, with some flavour of Seneca and Tertullian[3]. If Tertullian is the founder of Christian Latinity, Minucius is the first in the line of Christian Ciceros.

Pleased by the style of the *Octavius*, a pagan reader would also admire its dramatic character. The surrender of Caecilius is no foregone conclusion. He is allowed to argue with learned acumen and with an almost blasphemous satire at the expense of the Christian's transcendent God[4]. Indeed, Minucius goes so far in his tolerance towards the adversary that he has been accused himself either of an ignorance of Christian dogma or of the delicate scepticism of a Renan. But Minucius is not telling his readers the whole story. He is tempting them to enquire further. As St Paul cites 'certain of your own poets,' so Minucius[5] summons Virgil and the host of Greek philosophers to testify to the indwelling presence of the one God. That there is no mention of the name of

---

[1] *Aen.* VI, 135; *Od.* I, 22, 10 *sq.*; 3, 38 *sq.*
[2] *Octav.* 36, 5; cf. *de prov.* 6, 6.   [3] Monceaux, *op. cit.* I, p. 507.
[4] *Octav.* 10, 3–5.   [5] *Octav.* 19–20.

Christ nor any exposition of the inner articles of the Christian faith need surprise us no more than the failure to name Seneca or Cicero. He is not addressing some persecuting emperor or proconsul nor the *anima naturaliter Christiana* of humble folk, but presenting the new faith as worthy the attention of an *anima naturaliter philosophica*. There is finally, perhaps, an autobiographic element in the dialogue of Minucius. The debate between his two friends is one that at some time had gone on in his own mind.

The work of Minucius best suits the times and the entourage of the tolerant Severus Alexander[1]. Though the writer is apparently unacquainted with Clement of Alexandria, who was evidently unacquainted with him, the two are peers in their courteous treatment of the pagan past. Minucius may have borrowed from Tertullian much of his information about pagan rites and superstitions, abstaining from giving his source as he abstained from citing Cicero, Seneca and numerous other pagans, but the supposition of an earlier source, and that a Latin source, used independently by Tertullian and Minucius[2] has too quickly been ruled out of court.

The brief dialogue of Minucius was not awarded the influence that its merits deserved. It has come down to us in only one manuscript, in which it appears as a final book of the very different work of Arnobius—a torso, perhaps, of a collection of the Latin apologetes. Lactantius[3] and Jerome[4] recognized its importance, but with the works of these founders of Christian humanism on a grander scale at hand, the tiny masterpiece of Minucius passed from view. Boethius, too, in his *Consolatio Philosophiae* furnished the Middle Ages with a more sumptuous example of a philosophical approach to Christian revelation. For all that, the uniqueness of the *Octavius* remains.

IV. FROM THE SEVERI TO VALERIAN

In the age of varied turmoil that succeeded the momentary calm of the reign of Severus Alexander, polite letters did not wholly disappear. The *Historia Augusta* states that the Younger Maximinus, a beautiful barbarian, was well trained in the arts by his teachers, and the three Gordians (238–244) are represented as cultivated noblemen. The eldest of them converted the poems

---

[1] So J. J. De Jong, *Apologetiek en Christendom in den Octavius*, etc. p. 4 *sq.*   [2] W. Hartel, *Zeitschr. f. österr. Gym.* xx, 1869, p. 367.
[3] *Div. Inst.* v, 1, 22.   [4] *de Vir. Ill.* p. 58; *Ep.* 70, 5.

of Cicero—*Marius, Alcyonae, Uxorius, Nilus* and the translation of
Aratus—into modern style, and wrote a long epic with Antoninus
Pius and Marcus Aurelius for heroes. He also composed eulogies
in prose on all the Antonine Emperors, thus making his own
'mirror of the prince.' The ancient authors—Plato and Aristotle,
Cicero and Virgil—were the constant companions of his thought[1].
His son Gordian II, a capable administrator of elegant tastes but
loose living, wrote verse and prose that showed both talent and
decadence—the work of one who was 'abandoning his own
genius[2].' Gordian III, a merry and lovable youth, was also distinguished in letters, while the noble Balbinus was reputed
eminent in oratory and the first poet of his time—an easy compliment.

This sketch of the literary achievements of the Roman emperors
up to nearly the middle of the third century is taken from the much-
questioned *HISTORIA AUGUSTA*—generally damned and generally
used. It purports to be a collection of lives of the emperors
from Hadrian to Carus and his sons written by six authors—
Aelius Spartianus, Julius Capitolinus, Vulcacius Gallicanus, Aelius
Lampridius, Trebellius Pollio and Flavius Vopiscus. In some of
the lives Diocletian is addressed, in others Constantine. On the
face of it these writers lived in the age between Diocletian and
Constantine, or in some cases, perhaps, somewhat later. They
wrote partly, as it seems to the present writer, with the object
of constructing those 'mirrors of the prince' of which Roman
emperors were obviously fond. 'Te cupidum veterum imperatorum esse perspeximus,' says Capitolinus to Diocletian[3], and
Lampridius declares of Constantine that he adopted the virtues
of his imperial ancestors for his own[4]. A note of warning also
appears, in the fashion of Tertullian and Lactantius[5]. Whether
each author treated all the emperors it is impossible to say. Some
compiler, apparently, selected what he thought the best lives for
his purpose and published a collection of them, presumably with
additions, conflations and errors of his own. Various eminent
scholars, however, favour the theory that the whole affair is a
literary artifice used by a propagandist (whatever his propaganda
may have been) who invented the high-sounding names of the
putative authors and assigned them at random to the *Lives*[6]. Even

---

[1] S.H.A. *Gord. tres*, 7.   [2] *Ib.* 18–20.   [3] S.H.A. *Op. Macr.* 15, 4.
[4] *Hel.* 2, 4. See also 14, 1; 17, 7; 18, 4. See L. K. Born, *The Education
of a Christian Prince by Desiderius Erasmus*, pp. 83–4.
[5] *Hel.* 14, 1 (to Constantine); *Avid. Cass.* 8, 1 (to Diocletian).
[6] See the Appendix on Sources.

if this is so, the fiction is drawn, at least in part, from actual writings, both Greek and Latin, of the third century. We may be sure at least of an imperial chronicle[1] from Augustus to Diocletian and of the biographical works of Marius Maximus and Aelius Junius Cordus.

Marius Maximus is mentioned by Ammianus Marcellinus[2] and is, apparently, identical with that L. Marius Maximus Perpetuus Aurelianus who was consul under Severus Alexander. He wrote biographies of the emperors from Nerva to Elagabalus, thus bringing the work of Suetonius up to his own times. Suetonius was the natural model for the plan and style of his works, and for their uncritical information, plain and spicy, rumoured and true, in the manner of a modern journalist— 'mytho-historical volumes' is the apt designation in the *Historia Augusta*[3]. At the same time he must have held up the moral mirror to history now and then, since Constantine had read in him that it was better for a State to have a bad ruler surrounded by good advisers than a good one surrounded by bad[4].

Aelius Junius Cordus[5] is blamed for his excessive interest in scabrous tales, fabulous omens and petty statistics[6]. But the startling anecdote may still have its value. Although we may not be sure that the elder Maximinus wore his wife's bracelet for a ring, smashed horses' teeth with his fist or their legs with his heel, and consumed a keg of wine and sixty pounds of meat a day, yet from these stories we may perhaps with some confidence infer that this giant barbarian set people's tongues wagging.

In this third century Marius Maximus and Aelius Junius Cordus may not have stood alone; indeed if all the names cited in the *Historia Augusta* are those of genuine writers they lived in what was veritably an *aetas Suetoniana*. Gargilius Martialis is credited with biographies of Severus Alexander and other emperors[7]. Cassiodorus included in his select monastic library his work on gardens and the medicinal properties of plants, which is also mentioned by Servius. It is possible that this writer is to be identified with the man whose military career is attested by a fine inscription of A.D. 260[8].

[1] D. Magie, *The Scriptores Historiae Augustae* (Loeb), I, p. xxi; Schanz-Hosius-Krüger, *Gesch. d. röm. Litteratur*[3], III, § 545; N. H. Baynes, *The Historia Augusta, its Date and Purpose*, pp. 68–70.

[2] xxviii, 4, 14.   [3] S.H.A. *Quad. tyr.* (*Firmus*, etc.), I, 2.

[4] S.H.A. *Alex. Sev.* 65, 4.   [5] Schanz, *op. cit.* §§ 545, 547.

[6] S.H.A. *Clod. Alb.* 5, 10; *Op. Macr.* I, 3–5; *Max. duo* 29, 10; 31; *Gord. tres*, 21, 3–4.

[7] S.H.A. *Alex. Sev.* 37, 9; *Prob.* 2, 7.   [8] Dessau 2767.

Among the important scholars of that period is Censorinus, who in A.D. 238, lacking the money for a birthday present for his friend A. Caerellius, sent him instead, a learned treatise on birthdays, with their religious, educational, physiological, astrological and chronological implications. Helenius Acro comments on Terence, Persius (?) and Horace. The work preserved under Acro's name is spurious, but the helpful commentary of Porphyrio has come down in its genuine form. Grammarians of repute are C. Julius Romanus and Marius Plotius Sacerdos. C. Junius Solinus compiled, with large drafts on Suetonius and Pliny the Elder, an encyclopaedia of wondrous tales. Despite its second-hand character it became for the Middle Ages one of the great ancient books.

Another work profoundly esteemed in the Middle Ages is the *Disticha Catonis*, four books of moral admonitions in couplets. The author, whose name, whether by accident or intention, suggests the elder Cato and his *Carmen de Moribus*, is a pagan, but sound sense and pithy phrase are mated with Christian humility in its utterances. No wonder that the little work became a text-book in medieval schools. The pagan is betrayed in the maxims on woman, but the age of Chaucer and Jean de Meun would hardly count them heresy. There are numerous manuscripts of these books from the ninth century on; the work was turned into Latin prose and into the vernacular of all the important countries in Europe. Excerpts were made and numerous commentators spun its epigrams into sermons. It captivated the medieval mind from the beginning of its history to the end, as no other pagan work could do, save only Virgil.

If we return to Christian literature, the first figure is CYPRIAN. The outer life of Cyprian was full of turmoil in the age of intensified persecution under Decius and Valerian—within was a more than Stoic *placidissima pax*. He was born in Africa a pagan, and was well trained in rhetoric and the kindred arts. After his conversion he became a priest and (*c.* 248–9) bishop of Carthage. When the persecution of Decius began in 249, he left his flock for their best interests. He was active in promoting the unity of the Church, and in opposing the schism of Novatian (p. 540). He advocated firm yet lenient measures in the case of those who had fallen away from the faith and wished to be re-instated. Returning to his charge, he was sentenced and exiled during the new persecution under Valerian in 257. Brought back to Carthage, he was tried again and suffered martyrdom in 258.

Cyprian's writings are a mirror of the Church of his day. They all respond to the need of the moment. A work written to a friend before the persecution of Decius began (*Ad Donatum*) presents in a calm and pleasant tone, with many borrowings from Minucius Felix, the arguments that should turn a young man of good education to the new faith. When the storm breaks loose, we see in Cyprian's *Letters*, his tractates and his sermons the record of the wise bishop's concern for his churches and his ability to manage their affairs even when parted from them. He is also in touch with movements in Rome. His most characteristic work, *De Catholicae Ecclesiae Unitate*, whether or not he regards the Roman Pontiff as the head of Christendom, proclaims that principle of solidarity which has always been at the heart of the Catholic faith. In his apologetic works (*Ad Demetrianum* and *Quod idola dii non sint*) he answers the familiar charge that Christians were responsible for the calamities of the world. Highly characteristic are the three books of *Testimonia*, in which the Scriptures are searched for evidence bearing on Judaism, on the nature of Christ and on various points in Christian practice. He thus paves the way for Prosper of Aquitaine, Abelard, Peter Lombard and other medieval collectors of 'sentences.'

The number of manuscripts of Cyprian and of works wrongly attributed to him presents a situation unique in Christian Latin literature. Some of the pseudepigrapha may be contemporary. Some are in vulgar Latin. Naturally this *Corpus Cyprianum* has proved a paradise for investigators of '*Stylistik*.'

The style of Cyprian shows his training in rhetoric. He has metrical clausulae as strict as Cicero's. St Augustine, in his manual of a new Rhetoric, at once Christian and Ciceronian, cites only Cyprian and Ambrose for examples of the three styles—*genus submissum, temperatum, grande*[1]. But Cyprian does not indulge in display. Ciceronian art and Christian straightforwardness have become one in his clear and simple style. Holy Writ furnishes the source of his thought and the spirit, if not the form, of his diction.

Cyprian's two chief models in Christian literature are Minucius Felix and Tertullian. For the latter, despite his divagations, he had a hearty admiration. 'Hand me the master[2],' he would daily say to his servant. Tertullian, shorn of his heresy, furnishes the substance of many of Cyprian's observations and the plan of several of his discourses[3]. The charge of plagiarism would be

---

[1] *de Doctrina Christiana*, IV, 45–50.
[2] *Da magistrum* (Hieron. *de Vir. Ill.* 53).
[3] See L. Bayard, *Tertullien et S. Cyprien*, for extracts from both authors on the same subject.

absurd—arguments once delivered to the saints become common property. Cyprian's rewriting of Tertullian suggests the endeavours of Dryden and Pope to make Chaucer speak anew to their age. In both cases the tart vigour of the original is lost in the studied neatness of the reproduction. But there is more in Cyprian's adaptation than this. Let us take an example.

In his treatise *De cultu feminarum,* Tertullian starts promptly with a slap on the face for his fair hearer, daughter of Eve, the devil's gateway. Cyprian, imitating the work in his *De habitu Virginum,* praises the saintly maidens, who are the flower of the Church. But let them not dress too stylishly. For young men will gaze and sigh and conceive secret desires, '*so that even if you yourself are not ruined you will ruin others.*' After the exordium of Tertullian, a woman would feel indignant or amused, or both; after Cyprian's she would reverently obey the call of *noblesse oblige.* Cyprian has translated his master not only into an urbane Ciceronian diction, but into a wise urbanity of soul. Here speaks a great Christian teacher and father of his flock. Tertullian's disordered outbursts give place in Cyprian to a reasoned and effective art.

The Church did well in canonizing Cyprian, quite apart from his heroic death. He, like Tertullian, held open the Christian mind for revelations from the Paraclete, but the vision must come from within the united Church. Cyprian's greatness was recognized at once by the deacon Pontius, the author of his biography, and many others pay in their turn a homage that some writers to-day seem reluctant to apply. Lactantius emphasizes his eloquence, the happy gift for explanation and his powers of persuasion[1]. Jerome recommends the reading of Cyprian along with the Bible[2], and finds it unnecessary to speak of his works, 'cum sole clariora sint[3].' Prudentius finds the spirit of the prophets alive in him again and asserts that his fame shall endure as long as men and books survive. With a fine perception of the literary art of Cyprian, he weaves for his 'martyr's crown' not, as were also fitting, a simple ballad, but a stately Horatian ode[4].

NOVATIAN, the schismatic, a man of cultivation and the most celebrated of the Roman clergy of his day, wrote two letters to Cyprian[5], and also a discourse on the Trinity which has been preserved among the writings of Tertullian. In his work *De cibis Iudaicis,* which shows the symbolic character of the animals whose flesh the Jews refused to eat, Novatian paved the way for the wholesale allegorization of animals that prevailed in the Middle

---

[1] *Div. Inst.* v, 1, 25.   [2] *Ep.* 107, 12.
[3] *de Vir. Ill.* 67.   [4] *Peristeph.* 13.   [5] Cyprian, *Ep.* 30; 36.

Ages. He was the first Christian author who wrote exclusively
in Latin.

COMMODIAN, whose date seems now to have been definitely
placed in the third century, though perhaps later than he is here
treated[1], is the first to be recorded in the history of Christian
poetry, although his poetry seems curiously and wonderfully
made. The titles of his two works, *Instructiones* and *Carmen
Apologeticum*, bespeak that secondary inspiration of the Muse
which consists of the metaphrase of subjects long popular in prose.
The *Instructiones* consists of eighty short sections divided into two
books. Acrostics indicate the subjects of the several sections, the
last of which bears the mysterious title *Nomen Gasei*, which might
mean, 'The name of the inhabitant of Gaza.' The acrostic,
beginning at the last line and reading backwards, reveals the poet
as COMMODIANUS MENDICUS CHRISTI. The other poem, not
known till its discovery by Cardinal Pitra in 1852, bears no
ascription, but its style marks it as the product of the same author.
The words in its subscription—*Tractatus Sancti Episcopi*—may
indicate that the Beggar of Christ was also a Bishop.

Both poems are composed in what seems like rude hexameters
of thirteen to seventeen syllables which may always be divided
into six feet, but which ride rough-shod over quantity up to the
last two feet. Since some sixty fairly decent hexameters are found
in the course of the two poems,[2] Commodian might possibly have
employed throughout a more or less regular hexameter had he so
chosen. Though he censures the study of the pagan authors, he
himself had read some of them; Terence, Lucretius, Virgil,
Horace, and perhaps also Sallust, Cicero, Tibullus and Ovid, may
be traced in his verse. In the very passage that expresses his
condemnation of the pagans, he finds a phrase of Virgil useful[3].
His grammatical forms and syntax, however, are barbarous
enough. On the whole it would appear that Commodian is not
a person of cultivation who condescended to an ultra-humble style,
but one who, after a certain schooling, adopted a diction that
seemed natural to him. The same sort of limping hexameter is
found in African inscriptions of the period[4].

Moreover, as has recently been pointed out[5], it is better not to

---

[1] See A. Fr. van Katwijk, *Lexicon Commodianeum*, p. xxv.

[2] P. de Labriolle, *Hist. litt. lat. Chrét.* p. 244.

[3] *Carm. Apol.* 587 (ed. Dombart): *Insanumque forum* (*Georg.* II, 502).

[4] P. Monceaux, *Hist. lit. lat. Chrét.* p. 75.

[5] A. Amatucci, *Storia della letteratura latina cristiana*, p. 103; *Africa Romana*, p. 198.

calculate elaborately the relations of this verse of Commodian to the hexameter of Virgil, but while recognizing that relation in a general way, to see in his long line a combination of two short ones. The first has from five to seven syllables, the second from eight to ten, and their boundary line is in almost all cases what, if these were regular hexameters, would be the penthemimeral caesura. Elision is not observed, and word-accent, not metrical ictus, determines the rhythm. A line like

> Rex autem iniquus, qui obtinet illum ut audit

cannot be poured into the Virgilian mould. If one scans it with attention merely to word-accents, and scans the whole poem in the same way, the shackles fall from Commodian's verse. It is read no longer with torture, but with pleasure. Our poet is continuing the efforts for simplicity introduced by Septimius Serenus and the other experimenters with such metres as the Faliscan. He is returning, via Virgil, to something like the bipartite Saturnian of ancient times.

In both contents and spirit, the *Carmen Apologeticum* is the more interesting of the two poems. It is courteous in tone, presenting not an attack, but an invitation to come and see. He therefore sketches the history of Israel down to the Incarnation, adds that of the early Church, and portrays the struggle of Christ and anti-Christ in the last days. In the *Instructiones*, he pictures the pagan gods in sarcastic terms, impaling them neatly on his acrostics—a good mnemonic device—which fixes the revolting image on the believer's mind. The sections on the gods are followed by exhortations addressed to the unbelieving, and in the second book the varieties of Christians are described—the catechumen and priest, the true and the hypocrite, the sober and the drunken, the silent and the gossiping, martyrs divinely called and ill-advised aspirants for martyrdom.

Though our poet is heart and soul a believer, his theology falls into the Patripassionist heresy and revels in the fancies of the Chiliasts. In fact the theme that in both poems stirs his imagination is the end of the world, when the Thousand Years are over. He pictures[1] the last days in words of fire that burn through the stubble of his verse. The length of the passage makes it a little poem by itself of an essentially epic character. Commodian, not Juvencus, is the first of the Christian Latin poets to write epic.

The poems of Commodian, despite their crudities, had a vogue of some two hundred years. Gennadius, though admiring the

---

[1] *Carm. Apol.* 791 (ed. Dombart) to the end.

moral integrity of Commodian, found his perversion of Biblical prophecies a cause of amazement for those outside the fold and of despair for those within[1]. And the author of the *Decretum Gelasianum*[2], by putting the works on his index, showed the Beggar of Christ to the door.

V. FROM VALERIAN TO DIOCLETIAN

In the period of unutterable confusion that follows Valerian, Gallienus (260–8) stands out as a lover of *belles lettres* and everything Greek. He is an orator, a poet, and, with the possible exception of Helius Verus[3], the most interesting cynic in Roman history since Petronius[4]. He liked to make merry while the world was going to pieces. Yet, like Petronius, he could act with vigour on occasion, and his humbling of the Senate, which had become the chorus in the Roman tragedy, paved the way for Diocletian. The most enlightened act of Gallienus was his patronage of the philosopher Plotinus and his plans for founding a Platonic commonwealth in Campania.

A bit of the Emperor's poetry is given in his *Life* (11), a brief, impromptu epithalamium delivered at the marriage of his nephew. The smooth hexameters have a touch of humour, with another in an additional couplet preserved in one of the manuscripts of our present *Anthologia Latina*[5]. It may well be that many of the pieces preserved in the Codex Salmasianus go back to the third century. Here may belong the diverse rhetorical variations on themes from Virgil, the colourless *Epistula* of Dido to Aeneas, and the debate between cook and baker entitled *Vespa*[6]; this piece, the product of some strolling mountebank, has touches of parody of the pastoral and anticipates the medieval *conflictus* with its diverse themes. Definitely of the third century are the pieces assigned, if they are rightly assigned, as seems likely, to Nemesian[7].

M. Aurelius Olympicus Nemesianus of Carthage flourished during the reign of the Emperor Carus and his sons Numerianus and Carinus (282–4). Numerian was an orator of renown and reputedly the best poet of the day. He is said to have competed in prize contests even against Nemesian, and when an iambic poet,

---

[1] *de Vir. Ill.* 15.   [2] Migne, *Pat. Lat.* LIX, 163.
[3] See his life in the *Hist. Aug.* Oblivious of the tendencies that culminated in Fronto, he was fond of Apicius and Ovid, and called Martial his Virgil (5, 9).
[4] S.H.A. *Gall. Duo*, 11–18. See Gibbon, chap. x.
[5] Riese, *Anth. Lat.* I, 711.
[6] *Ib.* I, 199.   [7] *Ib.* I, 883–4.

Aurelius Apollinaris, presented a eulogy of his father, Numerian, we are told, totally eclipsed this performance with one of his own[1]. Nemesian perhaps aspired to be the Virgil of his day—at least we see signs of pastoral, didactic and epic poetry in his work. Epic exists as a mere promise. In his didactic poem on hunting[2] dedicated to the sons of Carus after his death in 283, he vows that he will next sing their praises. But the panegyric designed never came to fruition. In 284 Numerianus was murdered by his father-in-law, and Carinus at war with Diocletian was killed by his own troops. The extant fragment of the *Cynegetica* is true to the technique of Virgil, and is at least as attractive as its Augustan precursor, the *Cynegetica* of Grattius.

The eclogues of Nemesian were long attributed to Calpurnius, whose poems they adjoin in our manuscript source, but evidence both external and internal attest their separateness. Nemesian has little of the inventiveness of Calpurnius, but in spite of his close imitations of both Calpurnius and Virgil—mere mosaics of their phrases—he has virtues of his own. The first eclogue, in honour of his patron, is a stately bit of liturgy. The second portrays an unseemly pastoral passion. Like the fourth, on two shepherds who sharing 'equal frenzy for a different sex' are tricked by their darlings, it betrays a sad lack of humour.

The best is the third. Nyctilus, Mycon and Amyntas steal up as Pan sleeps, and try to play his pipe. Pan, awakening, promises a song. His theme is the birth of Bacchus and the invention of wine. Old Silenus holds in his arms the restless infant, who plucks his bristles, pats his snub nose and tweaks his pointed ears. The scene changes to his manhood, when he bids the satyrs tread the grapes. They drink the new liquor and the fun begins. They frolic and dance and chase the airy nymphs. This poem is Nemesian's one masterpiece. He has taken the framework of Virgil's sixth eclogue, relieved it of its allegory and panegyric, and told a merry tale vividly. Fontenelle thought he had surpassed his model.

VI. FROM DIOCLETIAN TO CONSTANTINE

The great Diocletian, though at least learned enough to quote Virgil[3], was not distinguished by a love of literature. In his reign pagan Latin literature was at its last gasp. Typical of its condition are the effusions of the Panegyrists (see below, p. 712). We turn

---

[1] S.H.A. *Carus*, 11.   [2] *Cynegetica*, 63–85.
[3] S.H.A. *Carus*, 13, 3.

rather to Christian Latin literature. The Persecutions under Diocletian in 303 led to the martyrdom of a curious writer, Bishop VICTORINUS OF PETTAU in Illyria, whose Commentary on the Apocalypse was re-edited by Jerome, shorn of heresies in thought and style. He revels in the mystic properties of numbers, the number one thousand included. For like Commodian, he was a Chiliast.

ARNOBIUS, the author of a novel apology, was born at Sicca Veneria in the province of Africa not far from the birthplace of Apuleius, Madauros, on the road to Carthage. He flourished under Diocletian and practised his profession of rhetorician illustriously in his native place. Until late in life a stalwart opponent of the new faith, he was suddenly converted by a dream, and like Saul of Tarsus, changed from an assailant to a champion. When his Bishop, suspicious of such an ally, demanded proof of his loyalty, he wrote his work *Adversus Nationes*.

Whether the Bishop was satisfied with the proof has been questioned more than once. Arnobius quotes the Scriptures rarely, proclaims that the soul must win its immortality by merit, and asserts that the pagan gods continue to exist though relegated to the rank of demons. He takes a sour view of human qualities, of the liberal arts and of the ability of the mind to arrive at truth. Morose, sceptical and ill-versed in Christian doctrine, he earned for his work a place among the *Catholicis vitanda* in the Gelasian list[1] and an unenviable estimate among most modern historians of Christian Latin literature. And yet, Jerome, while aware of the vagaries of Arnobius, calls the books of this treatise 'most splendid' ('luculentissimos') and implies that these 'hostages of piety' accomplished their purpose[2]. It is time to return to this verdict.

The work of Arnobius was written during the Persecution of Diocletian in A.D. 303. The first of the seven books starts with a vigorous disclaimer of the pagan assertion that the Christian faith is the cause of the woes of the world. On the contrary it has brought joy and peace to all mankind. In an ornate Ciceronian style, with metrical clausulae and a plethora of rhetorical questions, the writer presents a simple idea deeply felt by him—the truth and purity of Christ's life and works as seen on the background of pagan falsity.

But (Book II) some pagans still hate the Christian faith, though men of intellect are coming over to it in droves. They have learned

---

[1] Migne, *Pat. Lat.* LIX, 163.
[2] Jerome, *Chron.* p. 231, 14 *sqq.* (Helm).

to put a more moderate estimate on the mind. For despite the
great Plato, the soul is a humble organ. Its every passion is a
door to death[1]. It is of a medial and twofold substance—dwelling
all too near the fangs of destruction[2].

Here obviously is a refutation in the spirit of Lucretius, and
with a sprinkling of his phrases, of the Platonic proofs of the
immortality of the soul put forth by Cicero in the first book of his
Tusculan Disputations. But this is only half of the argument of
Arnobius. The soul has enough divinity to *win* its immortality by
the gift and grace of the Almighty Ruler. Arnobius has come into
Christianity through the science of Lucretius, but his deliverer is
not Epicurus, but Christ. He proposes to the pagans a new
reconciliation of science and religion. There are indeed gods, or
angels, or demons, but they are the creations of the one true God;
they are those *mediae naturae* whom Plato describes in his *Timaeus*.
Thus Plato plays a part in this reconciliation, though there can
be no truce with his idea of a divine soul in man; and Arnobius
proceeds to depict the littleness of the human soul with a vigour
that recalls Lucretius. His new solution, he says, does not pretend
to explain all moral and metaphysical difficulties. But what
philosopher has explained them? Yet one thing is certain, that
a new fountain of life has been opened[3]. Man has ever made progress in government and religion and the arts whereby life has
been built up and given polish—the phrase is from Lucretius[4] and
the passage gives Lucretius' fifth book in a nutshell. Thus has God
prepared the world for the coming of Christ. With brave words
on Christian martyrdom the book ends. This cursory summary
gives no idea of its wealth of illustrations, its pungent sarcasm and
its command of the science of the day.

The remaining books discuss the pagan cults with an assort-
ment of spicy legends from which even Ovid had refrained and
with a wealth of information that make Arnobius one of the happy
hunting-grounds for investigators of Roman religion. The work
ends with a question, Arnobius' favourite form of expressing an
idea. It contains a challenge to the imperialism of Rome.

These *luculentissimi libri* had no wide vogue. For the moment
when they were written they filled a need. How much the author

---

[1] II, 27: *Omnis enim passio leti atque interitus ianua est.* Cf. Lucretius I,
1112: *ianua leti.*
[2] II, 32: *non longe ab hiatibus mortis et faucibus.* Cf. Lucretius v, 373 *sqq.*:
leti...ianua...patet immani et vasto respectat hiatu.   [3] II, 64.
[4] II, 69: *artes quibus vita est exstructa et expolita communis.* Cf. Lucretius
v, 332: *artes expoliuntur.*

knew of the Christian scriptures or the doctrines of the Church is quite beside the point. He knows his ancient authors profoundly, Lucretius above all. He writes with a rich vocabulary partly classic, partly popular, completely African—for in Africa he lived —in a style as near to that of Cicero as he could come. His verbosities and interminable interrogations cannot spoil the brilliance of his performance. After the triumph of the Church under Constantine, the need of such an apology was no longer felt. Arnobius was superseded by his pupil Lactantius who, resuming the attitude of Minucius Felix towards pagan culture, laid the foundations of Christian humanism.

LACTANTIUS, likewise a pagan at the start, was given by Diocletian the chair of rhetoric at Nicomedia in Bithynia. When he, and Rome, became Christian, Constantine appointed him tutor of his son Crispus. The Christian orator needed no more to appeal for the Emperor's mercy; instead he became his spokesman in matters affecting the new culture, somewhat as Virgil and Horace proclaimed the higher policies of Augustus, which they themselves had taught him. His impetuous work *de mortibus persecutorum* is at once a kind of philosophy, or at least an apocalypse, of history, and like various works that we have discussed, a moral warning to the prince. If he wrote no epic on his master, he may somehow stand behind the famous *Oratio ad Sanctos*, in which Constantine gave his imperial sanction to the Christian interpretation of Virgil's Messianic eclogue.

Lactantius' greatest work, the *Divinae Institutiones*, is dedicated to Constantine, and intended by its author as a Christian counterpart of those 'Institutes' that lay down the principles of the Civil Law. In essence it is rather like Quintilian's 'Institution,' or training, of the orator. While dealing only indirectly with the seven liberal arts, Lactantius assumes at every turn by the quotation or the adaptation of the ancient authors that the study of them is a necessary precursor to the education of a Christian. While criticizing them vigorously at various points he does not reject but absorbs them. His great model is Cicero, whose style he comes near to reproducing and whose thoughts he translates into Christian. The writer feels himself another Cicero as he addresses the new age, which in the West in many respects is an *aetas Ciceroniana*.

The work falls into seven books. The first, *de Falsa Religione*, is like the reconciliations of science and religion of our day, save that religion is the true worship of the soul that underlies the superstition of mythology, and science the new Christian truth that clears the ancient fables away. The second, *de Origine Erroris*, deals with that primitive idolatry which nevertheless showed flashes of the vision of the one, true God. The third, *De Falsa Sapientia*, would be called to-day 'An Introduction to Philosophy' —written from a Catholic point of view. Master Cicero and the New Academy are much in evidence, yet Lucretius, whom he doubtless learned to admire from Arnobius, is treated, despite his patent falsities, with understanding and even courtesy. The fourth book, *De Vera Sapientia et Religione*, presents in an informal fashion the doctrines of the Christian faith. The fifth, *De Iustitia*, deals with personal ethics, and the principles of social justice. The sixth, *De Vero Cultu*, is not an exposition of liturgy (as one might hope) but a plea for the sincerity of worship. The seventh, *De Vita Beata*, is a new interpretation of Cicero's arguments on immortality in the *Tusculans*, set forth in Christian terms.

Despite slight imperfections in its theology, this 'Training of the Christian' at once became a standard work and a monument of the reign of Constantine. Jerome, Augustine, Cassiodorus and Isidore acclaimed it. A steady stream of manuscript copies flowed down through the Middle Ages to the Renaissance; it was among the first books printed in Italy.

The period in which we have been following the course of Latin literature from the age of the Antonines to that of Constantine, while barren of works of the first order, is not in itself a barren epoch, but one alive with new impulses and achievements. It begins with a unified Roman world in which there is one literature, in either Greek or Latin. It witnesses the decay of pagan letters, which had lost their meaning, and the rise of a Christian literature, full of a new meaning yet mainly dependent for its art on ancient models. At the end of the period there is a weakening of the bonds that held together East and West and of those that in literature as in government connected the provinces with Rome. But amid such dissolutions the elements of a new Roman unity may be discerned, later apprehended by St Augustine in his vision of the City of God.

CHAPTER XVIII

LITERATURE AND PHILOSOPHY IN THE EASTERN HALF OF THE EMPIRE

I. THE GREEK NOVEL AND RHETORIC

GREEK Literature at the beginning of the third century, apart from the Christian schools (see above, pp. 476 *sqq.*), has no outstanding name or striking personality, no work of any great note and very seldom one with even as much as a suggestion of poetry. It was not that any of the ancient forms were neglected. There was plenty of eagerness shown in the maintenance and restoration of theatres, Odeums and play-houses of various kinds; but they were chiefly for performances of mimes, and for farces such as parodies of Christian baptism, and though a tragedy of Euripides might sometimes still be seen holding the stage the real spirit of the theatre was dying. It is true enough, also, that while, as may be observed as a sign of the times, the *Georgics* of Virgil were translated into Greek hexameters, many didactic poems continued to be written. In one of these, *On Fishing* (*Halieutica*), the author, OPPIAN, admittedly shows very fair skill in his descriptions of the homes and habits of fish, and he won thereby the imperial favour of a coin of gold for each verse; but the other poem which has come down to us under his name, though it is not by him (the *Cynegetica*), would deserve very little attention did not the MSS. contain miniatures of the animals described and even a picture of Apamea, the author's birthplace.

In this age of prolific verse-making epic poems also swarmed[1]. Many a sand-heap in the Fayûm has been found full of scraps of papyrus covered with copies of a Soterichus, Pisander, Tryphiodorus, Zoticus or some other manufacturer of hexameters all of the same level. The craze for exertions of this kind went so far that a certain Nestor of Laranda sought to emulate Homer by producing an *Iliad* in words chosen in such a way that in none of the twenty-four books did there once occur its distinguishing letter of the alphabet. It may well be doubted whether at any time so many thousands of verses have been written with so little creative imagination; but it must be remembered contemporary taste

---

[1] A list of them will be found in Christ-Schmid, *Geschichte der griech. Literatur*, II, § 672.

required that all the poesy of which the age was capable should appear in prose in order to make it musical and florid.

With the Greek orators of this generation the art of speaking and writing concerned itself less and less with the mind, and speakers set themselves up more and more as 'melodists' and rivals of lyric poets. Even their delivery consisted of a rhythmical declamation of a very artificial kind. They followed a prosody which the living language of their day no longer obeyed, and by a form of virtuosity exploited the tone and modulations of their speech, in this way securing their effects on audiences by means which were largely musical. At a time when so much pleasure was taken in listening to various wind and string instruments, the lecturer was delighted if his singing and rhythmical eloquence was accompanied by the rapturous sounds of the flute. He was carried away by the music of his own voice, and cared little if his phrases were fine-sounding that they were almost devoid of meaning. An adequate idea of these speakers can be formed by perusing the *Lives of the Sophists* as told by their fellow-member and admirer Philostratus, an orator who was a native of Lemnos. One seldom finds an idea of any note or a flash of wit.

PHILOSTRATUS would have small claim to the space here given to him were it not for the fact that, in speaking of him, one cannot help touching on two people of an attractiveness widely different from his—the beautiful and spirited Julia Domna, the intelligent and self-willed Empress to whom the orator owed the subject of at least one of his chief works, and, with her, the Emperor Septimius Severus himself.

The grandson of an orator resident at Rome in the reign of Domitian, but born into a family which continued to speak Punic, the young Septimius Severus at the age of eighteen was capable of expressing himself in Greek with sufficient fluency to take part, in spite of his rustic accent[1], in public declamations at his native town of Leptis Magna. Having completed at Athens his equipment of literature and philosophy, Septimius arrived at Rome to make himself an orator and *advocatus fisci* before becoming a member of the Senate and commanding the legions of Pannonia who ultimately raised him to the rank of emperor. As part of the extraordinary industry of this hard-working man must be mentioned here the memoirs which he, like Marcus Aurelius, wrote in Greek, and the fragments of his letters addressed to the Senate, without any literary grace or charm, but concise, clear and

---

[1] His pronunciation of Latin is said to have remained faulty, see above, p. 24.

to the point. It is not surprising that one so well educated delighted to surround himself with men of letters and preferably with Greeks, while his wife, Julia Domna, the daughter of the High Priest of the Sun at Emesa, held a real literary salon upon the Palatine[1]. Besides her sister, Julia Maesa, and her two nieces, Soaemias and the half-Christian Mamaea, many famous writers and scholars were to be met at her house—the poet Oppian, who has already been mentioned; Aelian, the honey-tongued storyteller, engaged in collecting the anecdotes of his *Varia Historia*; Gordian, who was a poet before he was an emperor; the learned doctor Sammonicus Serenus, who owned a magnificent collection of books; sometimes Galen when his great age permitted him to be present; and many other intimates of the Palatine who figure in the *Deipnosophistae* of Athenaeus.

But Julia Domna, the impassioned Syrian, 'téméraire jusqu'à l'utopie' in Renan's phrase[2], must have had an almost classical literary taste. When the orator Hermogenes started a reaction against excessive regard for rhythm and musical effects in oratory (cf. p. 612), Julia Domna seems to have approved a return to a feeling for moderation and imitation of the ancient models; at all events, Philostratus in one of his letters clothes in the form of a learned treatise observations possibly intended to divert the Empress from an inclination towards an old-fashioned purism in literature, of which he disapproved.

As has often been pointed out, the advance of the new religions evoked an opposition from pagan intellectuals who sought to give new life to their old cults by allying them with philosophic creeds and especially with a theology of sun-worship which spread ever more widely in highly diverse forms, while in ethics they preached a Pythagorean asceticism. The Empress herself, who from youth up had been initiated in the hellenized beliefs of the great Semitic sanctuaries, and whose circle at Rome included thinkers from all parts of the Empire, was as it were predestined to become the high priestess of a syncretic polytheism. Realizing the need of finding a historical figure fitted to counter the propaganda of subversive gospels, she sought particularly to revive the memory of a hero of pagan hagiology, Apollonius of Tyana, who lived under the first two Flavians and had left behind him in Greek lands the reputation of a saint and wandering prophet drawing

---

[1] She was honoured in Greece as a second Demeter and a rival of the goddess Pallas.

[2] *Marc Aurèle*, p. 495: "Osant ce que jamais Romaine n'avait osé, ces syriennes 'rêvent de Sémiramis et de Nitocris.'" See Dio LXXVIII, 23.

multitudes to himself by his holy life and by so many beneficent miracles that the magicians of the East used to invoke his aid and issue the formulas of their incantations under his name. In time, he was looked upon as the greatest of all sorcerers. Chancing to come upon the memoirs of one who claimed to have been a confidant of this Apollonius—Damis a Babylonian—Julia Domna was impressed by the favourable light in which the charactet of the wise man was presented. Far from having practised sorcery this true follower of Pythagoras, according to his disciple, had taught the purest of religions, and in India especially, a country which long before Egypt and in different fashion had enjoyed the favour of divine wisdom, had found the evidence and inspiration to support his faith. As if to call attention to what Damis had recounted concerning India, some Brahmans and Samanians in the time of Julia Domna, taking advantage of the means of travel provided by a renewal of trade with Central Asia, came on a deputation to the religious propagandists in Syria, particularly to Bardaisan, and it can be seen from Porphyry that they succeeded in obtaining a hearing[1].

In any case the Empress, wishing to spread the knowledge of the model character of the life of Apollonius, the holy man of Tyana, and of the source of his wisdom in an Eastern country which worshipped the sun, entrusted the memoirs of Damis to Philostratus, one of the habitués of her parties whom we have already had occasion to mention. On the canvas provided the court hagiographer boldly embroidered his theme, borrowing extensively so as to unite in the eight books of his edifying biography the features best suited to bring out the importance and virtues of his hero: his love for his fellow-men, his profound pity for human suffering, his deeply-rooted religion which showed itself in the worship of all the gods and of the divine Sun in particular, and in his adoption of the Pythagorean prohibition of the sacrifice of living creatures.

However full it may be of fine-drawn speeches little to modern taste, the book was undeniably successful. Opponents of Christianity were not slow to see what use could be made of it in combating the propaganda of the new religion, if not in advancing a pagan syncretism. The story of Apollonius, accepted as true, could be set against the Gospel as a life noble, upright, godly, unselfish, and conspicuous for its miracles and good works: the

---

[1] At least Porphyry found in this connection the immediate confirmation of an 'epistle of Apollonius to the Brahmans' (frag. LXXVIII, Hercher); see Porphyry, Περὶ Στυγός quoted by Stobaeus, *Ecl.* i, 3, 56 and *de abstin.* iv, 17.

XVIII, 1] PHILOSTRATUS, HELIODORUS 615

apologists of Greek culture did not fail to exploit it, and the result
was that Philostratus, second-rate story-teller though he was,
became one of the most famous of the Greek novelists.

It may seem strange to connect with edifying work of this
nature the ten books of the *Loves of Theagenes and Chariclea* or
Aethiopica. Certainly at first sight there is nothing but agreeable diversion in the story of Chariclea, an Ethiopian princess
abandoned at birth by her mother, the queen Persina, then
carried off to Delphi to be brought up there by the Greek Callicles,
subsequently enamoured of the handsome Thessalian Theagenes
and by the unkindness of fate involved with him in the severest
trials of various kinds until she finally appears before the king
Hydaspes, her father. Then, on the point of being sacrificed to the
Sun with her faithful lover, she reveals herself, recovers her
rank and with it the right to marry the man she loves. But, on a
closer view, it will be seen that HELIODORUS, the author of this
seeming story of adventure, is almost as much concerned to
glorify the fierce chastity with which he endows his virgin heroine
as to demonstrate his skill in the art of tying and untying the
threads of an exciting plot. His descriptions of virtue often
become homilies, and, until the final words of his dénouement,
he exhibits a religious feeling which is too characteristic of his age
to be regarded as a traditional feature of his literary form[1].

Nothing is known about the author of *Daphnis and Chloe*, and,
this pastoral being unique of its kind, any attempt to determine
its own peculiar merits must be guess-work. As for LONGUS himself, although it is generally agreed that his work is to be included
with those of the orators of the time of Julia Domna, there is little
agreement about the type of society in which he wrote. Some are
impressed by the discovery in him of touches of a genuine and
almost rustic feeling for nature, while others insist that, from the
very opening scene, the balance of melodious antitheses betrays
the sophisticated pastoral of the salon with its bells and ribbons
affectedly bedecking the necks of lambkins, sleek and white
as snow. But, in speaking of *Daphnis and Chloe*, it is hardly
possible not to give oneself up to the pleasure of admiration
and leave on one side questions of date and other such problems.
It is, indeed, commonly admitted that this pearl of Greek romance

---

[1] R. M. Rattenbury, *Les Éthiopiques d'Héliodore*, 1, p. xxi, also observes
that in the *Aethiopica* the religion seems less artificial than elsewhere.
Compare the preface by the translator, J. Maillon, p. lxxxvi, who calls
attention to the same admiration for the gymnosophists and the same distinction
between magic and theurgy as in Philostratus.

is one of the most attractive works that have come down from antiquity. Translated by Amyot, admired by Goethe, and imitated by Bernardin de S. Pierre, the author of *Paul et Virginie*, this delightful source of inspiration may still be traced in our own day. After 'le petit berger avec sa flûte et ses chèvres' of a great painter, Corot, it has found expression in 'la symphonie chorégraphique' of an equally great musician, Ravel.

No summary need be given here of this story of the two young figures, Daphnis and Chloe, deserted by their parents and driven amid all kinds of abduction and romantic adventures to the discovery of natural love. In this pastoral the ordinary *motifs* of the *genre* make up only the frame of the plot, and the love of the country which pervades it certainly goes back to the poets of the Hellenistic age who first gave expression to the modern feeling for nature: for the rocks, meadows, fountains, streams, wooded hills, sea-shores, little chapels dedicated to Pan and the nymphs, which decorate his tale, it may be said that Longus had before him the Idylls of Theocritus, so strong is the bucolic tradition in his scenery. Here again, therefore, we end by being faced with what has been called by one scholar the 'Hellenistic sea,' the common source in whose vast waters were absorbed and mingled for a time the most varied currents and elements of the literatures of the world.

It has been already observed (vol. XI, p. 707) that 'the only literary form of the time which would show much power of development was the romance, which appeals largely through its opportunities of self-identification with hero or heroine.' Our picture would be seriously incomplete if we were to leave this field of romantic literature without noticing its productions outside scholarly circles. Everywhere in this age, even among the least educated sections of the population, tales were invented and wonders sought out. Among the Christians, too, edification was sought in the recital of adventures: travels of the Evangelists in the remotest countries, acts of the apostles (Andrew, John or Thomas) and even of the earliest evangelists, the life of Joseph the carpenter, stories of the childhood of Jesus, or Conversions or Confessions such as those of Cyprian of Antioch. The work of which Rufinus has left us a Latin translation with the title *S. Clementis Recognitiones* is one of the best examples of this type of composition. The title alone is almost enough to show the affinity of this edifying narrative with the romantic literature of the age.

In the third century delight in romantic fiction left its mark

even on works of the most profound theological speculation. Men
still continued to enjoy reading Plato, and this preserved a taste
for giving controversial writings the form of fictitious discussion.
Contemporary Christian apologetic especially may be said to have
caused a sort of revival of the philosophic dialogue. But there was
this difference, that fashionable adventure stories were introduced
into the setting. For instance, when METHODIUS, a cultured bishop
of Olympus in Lycia, wished to refute the very daring views of
Origen on the future life and the resurrection of the body (p. 483),
and had the idea of borrowing from the *Phaedo* the plan of a new
dialogue on the Immortality of the Soul, he did not stop at em-
bellishing his work with some touches from the *Protagoras*. He
also found room for some of the inventions which were then a
feature of adventure stories, and in this dialogue, entitled
Aglaophon, he relates how a friend of his, Theophilus, was cast up
by a storm on the Lycian coast, and how, when he sought for
him, he found him in the house of a doctor—the character who
gives his name to the dialogue—engaged in a discussion with him
on the subject of the resurrection. Aglaophon acts as the mouthpiece of Origen and accordingly maintains that, as the flesh is the
origin of evil, if the body is reborn, sin must necessarily at the
same time be reintroduced into the soul. A certain Memmian, in
the course of discussion, undertakes to refute this argument, and
the dialogue ends in the discomfiture of the rash doctor who had
claimed to eliminate from the future life the presence of the human
body, the most attractive of all forms, and to substitute for it, as
the support of the soul, the ethereal or astral vehicles of the
Platonists, with geometric shapes—sphere, polyhedron, cube
or pyramid—derived from the fancies of the *Timaeus*.

It was also in a dialogue that Methodius controverted the
doctrine of the eternity of the world—a doctrine assigned to a
fictitious follower of Origen of the name of Centaur—and in the
same form he discussed the problem of free-will. But he was
destined to go down to posterity more especially as the writer of
the long dialogue called the *Symposium of the Ten Virgins*. The pure
love-feasts of this *Symposium* are set in a delightful garden, a kind
of earthly paradise in the far East, which is poetically described by
the author with the aid of scraps from the *Phaedrus*, the *Theaetetus*
and the *Axiochus*. There also occurs a reminiscence of the untouched solitude which Euripides, in one of his plays, had taken as
the symbol of Modesty: Agatha, one of the wise virgins, exclaims
'there is the garland I offer to thee, woven with flowers picked
in the meadows of the Prophets, O Virtue, that I in my turn may

adorn thee[1].' Methodius knew that, if he substituted Chastity for the Eros of the *Symposium* of Plato, the best analogue for the purity of his heroines was the ideal of the *Hippolytus* of Euripides.

This type of romantic imagination, which is so noticeable a feature of the work of the bishop of Olympus, shows that Christian teaching, without losing too much of its seriousness, is already beginning to put off the heavy armour of its early polemics and is turning to seek the company of the Muses. It strikes out on new paths leading to the rhetorical schools, and secures the applause of the lecture-room. Somewhat in the manner of Methodius, Apollinarius of Laodicea a little later cast into Socratic dialogue the conversations of Jesus and the apostles. Subsequently the pagan emperor, Julian, vexed by the sight of Galileans at lectures on Greek literature, determined to put a stop to their coming and plundering the resources of the Greeks in order to use them against the civilization from which they had sprung[2].

Athens at this time was nothing more than a city of the past, the resort of tourists, of art-lovers and literary critics, a quiet town where men devoted themselves to disinterested study, literary pursuits and the contemplation of history. But this was not to endure. Soon the march of events tore Hellenism, in the most sacred of its retreats, from the joys of contemplation and swept it into the storms of political affairs, though, meanwhile, the Athenian rhetorical schools had, in LONGINUS, their last moment of splendour. A nephew through his mother of the sophist Fronto—a citizen of Emesa, like more than one of the friends of Julia Domna—Longinus, on coming into a legacy from his uncle, used his wealth in furthering his education by extensive travel, particularly to Alexandria, attended by Ammonius Saccas in a society in which we shall see his name reappear. He then settled at Athens, where he began by teaching rhetoric and philosophy. He was nicknamed the 'living library' and the 'walking museum,' but he was not lacking in shrewdness and taste. He soon became the leading figure in literary criticism. Some of his judgments are known to us, and they seem to deserve the esteem which they enjoyed. It was not long before pupils flocked to his school. Among them he singled out a man of an inexhaustible love of learning, one who, like himself, had come from Syria, the Tyrian Malchus, 'the king,' whose name he changed to its Greek equivalent, Porphyrius.

---

[1] *Symposium*, VI, 5, p. 70, 8 *sq.* Bonwetsch; cf. Euripides, *Hipp.* 73 *sqq.*
[2] Julian, *Epist.* 61 (ed. Bidez-Cumont) and Bidez, *La Vie de l'Empereur Julien*, pp. 263 *sqq.*

Longinus taught at the Academy, and, in loyalty to the traditions of the School, he piously observed the anniversary of its founder Plato. We have some detailed knowledge of one of these celebrations: at the commemorative symposium the conversation turned on learned questions. The thesis was put forward that Ephorus, Theopompus, Menander, Hellanicus, Herodotus and Euripides were plagiarists, and even the originality of the hero of the feast had to be defended. This scene is of a piece with what we know of contemporary teaching and reveals the learning and childishness of the talk of the scholars at Athens who were united in the veneration of Plato. The occasion was before Porphyry left for Rome about the year 262/3.

Five years later the Goths landed at the Piraeus. In Athens itself they would have made a bonfire of the books of one of the libraries, if one of their number, 'looked up to by his fellows for his wisdom,' had not pointed out to the barbarians that it would be better to leave the Greeks buried in the lumber room of old books, which made them easy to conquer, than to cause them to arm themselves with swords. About this time Zenobia, the queen of Palmyra, had invited her countryman Longinus to her court, and the master, hearkening to the voice of nature, decided it would be far better to win a new empire for Hellenism than to persist in the defence of the Acropolis. He therefore left Greece, entrusting the latter task to the historian Dexippus, and at Palmyra threw himself so whole-heartedly into his new work of adviser to an ambitious princess that not long afterwards, when Zenobia submitted to her conqueror Aurelian, he was condemned to death for high treason by the Roman emperor. After the bravely faced execution of the ill-starred champion of a lost cause, rhetoric at Athens was for a time brought to a standstill. On the other hand, Dexippus learnt from the grim fortunes of his times—like Cassius Dio, if not Herodian—the style and manner of Thucydides, the weightiest and most profound of the historical writers of antiquity.

II. ALEXANDRIA: PLOTINUS

After the assassination of Geta, and at the time of the massacres carried out at Alexandria by the merciless fratricide Caracalla (p. 49), the officials of the Museum at Alexandria were cruelly deprived of their revenues and allowances and suffered great hardship; those who were not natives of the country were even expelled. After this first alarm the reading-rooms of the city libraries recovered sufficient quiet for the Egyptian ATHENAEUS of Naucratis to be able to devote his leisure to the scrutiny of more than 1500 works and to draw from them the material for the essays in his *Deipnosophistae* in fifteen books on drinking, eating, seasoning, sauces, the delicacies of notable gourmets, the customs at banquets, and even on love, besides the dance, singing and games. These essays would have caused the guests at the banquet to die of boredom if the banquet had really been served. We to-day can find entertainment in the diverse episodes in the literary life of the past of which Athenaeus' compilation enables us to form a picture.

Literary pastimes such as those of Athenaeus were possible at Alexandria only for a short period. About the time when the Goths pillaged Athens, the troops of Zenobia (269–270) came and plundered the quarter of the public buildings and palaces (Brucheion) which had been erected in the capital of the Ptolemies near the tomb of Alexander. The Museum was not spared in the general destruction, and henceforth this great home of Greek culture, although it did not disappear completely, could hardly do more than maintain a shadow of what it had been in the past. As late as the time of Ammianus Marcellinus[1], the scientific genius of the old metropolis still pursued various branches of learning: 'geometry continued to make useful discoveries, music had its devotees, harmony its expounders, and, though astronomers were rarer, the movements of the stars were still observed; a study never ceased to be made of the science of numbers and especially of the art of foretelling the future.' There is no lack of names or examples for a commentary on this piece of evidence from Ammianus Marcellinus. It will be enough here to recall what was said in the last volume (p. 704) about the mathematician Diophantus, with whom may be placed the commentator Pappus and Theon his continuator. As for schools, Ammianus in speaking of Alexandria mentions also those of medicine which remained so celebrated that 'it was enough for a doctor to say that he had studied there, and no further recommendation was required of him.' But one thing Ammianus does not say, because he stood too close to perceive it. Even at Alexandria in the third century the times were unfavourable for scientific observation and research. The age of discovery had come to an end. One was content with making encyclopaedic compilations in order to adapt to the needs of the day what was essential in knowledge already

---

[1] XXII, 16, 17; cf. *Totius orbis descriptio* in Müller, *G.G.M.* II, p. 519, § 34 *sq.* etc.

acquired by science and technical achievement. Men no longer dreamed of probing into the secrets of nature; nature was regarded as the agent of wonders and to gain her service recourse was had to miracle-workers who expounded in oracles what they called the 'holy science' or 'the great art.'

Despite the establishment of official doctors, medicine itself so far declined that instead of being able to point to exact observations of clinical workers one has to cite a magical pharmacopoeia and the occultism of astrology, demonology and exorcism. In anatomy Galen, to give a single example, was one of the last to carry out dissection[1]. Moreover, with the growth of sick wards attached to Christian benevolent institutions the art of healing became in the end separated from university teaching. At the time of the great plague in the third century the Christians exhibited a devoted solicitude for the sick, while pagans were content to cast victims of the scourge into the street.

But to help us to form an idea of the new attitude taken up by those connected with the old-established Museum we have something more valuable than a series of facts of this kind; we can come to know a personality which by itself is worth more than a hundred others. His works will show us, among other things, that the art of healing which men sought more than anything else was a spiritual régime which would ensure the soul's happiness, not through the simple consciousness of belief (πίστις) and love, nor by the mystical and sacramental effect produced by initiation into the secrets of a 'gnosis,' but by the illumination of the intellect (νοῦς) enraptured and transported, as the result of a new conception of assimilation with God (ὁμοίωσις θεῷ), to the sublimities of the supreme Intelligence.

PLOTINUS was born at Lycopolis in A.D. 204 and was already twenty-eight when he came to Alexandria to learn philosophy. He studied under the most famous teachers, but instead of finding himself enlightened, he experienced a disillusion. In deep depression he confessed his disappointment to a friend, who at once introduced him to the very select circle of the mysterious Alexandrine, AMMONIUS SACCAS. Plotinus was accepted by Ammonius, and soon realized from talking with him that he had found exactly the sort of guide for whom he was looking.

It may be asked what precisely did Ammonius teach. As if it

---

[1] Dissection, that is to say, of animals. A papyrus, recently published by A. Wifstrand, 'Anatomischer Katechismus,' in *Bull. de la Société R. des Lettres de Lund*, 1934–5, pp. 64 *sqq.*, supplies a typical example of contemporary dogmatic instruction without the slightest attempt at observation.

were a mystery, all those who listened to him had to promise to
disclose nothing about it, and it is by the teaching of Plotinus
himself that we can best divine its nature. After eleven years
spent in philosophical discussion and meditation with this thinker,
Plotinus, when the Emperor Gordian opened the doors of the
temple of Janus at Rome to announce a great expedition against
the Sassanid kingdom, determined to make use of so fine an
opportunity to observe on the spot 'the philosophy practised by
the Persians,' as well as by the Indians, who likewise were at
that time exciting much interest (p. 614). He therefore joined the
army which was preparing to invade Mesopotamia. But some
months later Gordian was killed by riotous soldiers near Doura,
and Plotinus had to abandon his plan without having got even as
far as Ctesiphon. He returned to Antioch (February 244) after
having perhaps an opportunity at Apamea on the Orontes of
making himself familiar with the philosophy of Numenius (vol. xi,
p. 700), which had always filled his thoughts. Finally, from
Antioch he went to Rome, where he opened a school.

A visitor to it for the first time must have been deeply impressed.
Still stunned by the bustle of the great city, and only a step from
the streets in which was displayed, in a brilliant setting of public
buildings, the splendour of a life of pleasure such as we can
hardly imagine, he came upon a quiet circle of ascetics who turned
their backs upon the world and meditated on books of philosophy, practising a lofty disdain for external things. Leading
together a life of sanctity the initiates of this philosophic con-
venticle looked, first, for a moment of ecstasy on this earth and
ultimately for the deliverance of their soul through death and its
return to the bosom of the eternal Being. The existence in the
world-capital of this small cloistered brotherhood of 'pale folk'
is nothing of a surprise. It is one of those violent contrasts which
occur in the intense and hectic life of such a centre as that of
Imperial Rome.

When Porphyry, no doubt bearing a letter of introduction from
Longinus, presented himself to Plotinus, the master's teaching
had been fully thought out. His quiet and attractive manner,
his serious and simple nature, his distaste for fashionable rhetoric
and cheap success, the loftiness of his ideas and the strictness
with which he followed his philosophic principles, his knowledge of men and that intuitive understanding which sometimes
made him seem like a thought reader, the force and passion of his
words, his genuine enthusiasm and disinterestedness, won for
him an authority altogether different from that of the philosophers

who lived like private chaplains in the large houses of Rome and
were good fellows with whom master and servant enjoyed making
merry. Plotinus had transformed and exalted the part of the
philosopher. He had cast a halo round him by earning for himself so high a prestige in the eyes of the Romans. He was one of
those strong-willed geniuses who exercise a strange kind of
fascination. He still fascinates to-day. It is impossible to come
into contact with him without being overpowered. 'I have been
almost frightened,' Novalis wrote to a friend, 'by his resemblance
to Fichte and Kant. . . . In my heart I feel that he is worth more
than both of them.'

Plotinus' mode of life was simple. He showed an entire disregard for the care of the body and practised vegetarianism.
Sometimes he abstained even from bread. Although he was not
strong he disobeyed his doctors' orders, and he carried his scorn
for worldly things so far as to neglect them in all their forms,
from the sonorous style with which rhetoricians pleased the ear,
to the details of his own writing, which was by no means correct
and hardly readable. On the other hand, he gave himself up to
meditation with an intense concentration of which Porphyry has
left us an impressive account. He was consumed by the fire of an
intellectual passion which transfigured him. Four times while
Porphyry was staying with him, the wise hierophant 'went
beyond the choir of virtues as a man leaves behind him the statues
of the gods to enter the sanctuary' and reached ecstasy, or communion and identification with the Infinite.

One of the original features in the teaching of Plotinus is to be
seen in the part played by images and figurative expressions in the
exposition of his ideas. If it were not for the luminous and
brightly coloured touches which constantly help to make up for
the ineffectiveness of the reasoning, the *Enneads*, with their
laborious attempts to grasp the most elusive abstractions, would
not wholly succeed in conveying the writer's doctrine. In this
respect Plotinus followed the example of the wise men of his
country, who, as he tells us[1], instead of writing letters and words
on the walls of their temples, preferred to draw images and symbols. It will not be surprising to hear that speculation so little inspired by the method or even the spirit of the sciences called exact
showed itself as far removed as possible from a purely mechanistic
conception of the universe.

Nature, for Plotinus[2], knows not levers. That is why he
constantly emphasizes distant action; like an echo, which seems

[1] *Enneads*, v, 8, 6.   [2] *Ib.* III, 8, 2 *ad init.*

to come from a wall of rock, whereas in fact it is caused by the resonance of a far-off voice; like a softly spoken word which sets going something at vast distances; like the heavenly choirs and the harmony of the world whose agreement and rhythm are maintained across the intervening space simply by the attention of the executants[1]. Is it some material contact which causes a flower or stone to vibrate in accord with the astral powers? How can we explain the power of God in every branch of nature and the universal prayer which makes every being try to rise towards Him?

The more improbable materialistic mechanism appeared to Plotinus, the more universally he detected in the actions and interactions of beings the effects of a kind of magic power and recognized the reality of the universal sympathy made active in the mystical religions of his day. But Plotinus is not content with the principle of unity thus revealed in the interconnection of the members of a living organism. He needs a higher unity, and, drawing inspiration from the idealism of Plato, he finds it in the intelligence. For him the bond of dependence among beings becomes entirely intellectual. The intelligences are to the supreme Intelligence and to one another as the theorems of a particular science are to Science as a whole and to one another: each of them potentially includes the others however different from them it may be. Thus it is that one can contemplate in the unity of a science its whole content. On the other hand beings have no reality except in the Intelligence itself. They are neither before it, nor after it; the Intelligence is, as it were, alike their first legislator and their principle, or rather the very law of their being, and it is true to say that existence and thought are the same thing.

By synthesizing the 'rational-creative *Logoi*' of the Stoics with the Platonic Idea, and introducing them to the intelligible world whence these '*Logoi*' shape sensible beings and reflect themselves in them, Plotinus reached his famous doctrine of the creative activity of contemplation. It is by contemplating the one that the soul gives unity—and therefore being—to each of its productions[2].

To say that the one is the principle of being is for him the same as saying that the only true reality is contemplation. Not only is intelligence contemplation of its object, but nature also is contemplation, silent, unspeaking, unconscious contemplation of the intelligible pattern which it strives to imitate; an animal, a plant, any object has its form, in the Aristotelian sense, only in so

---

[1] *Enneads*, IV, 9, 3; VI *ad fin.*; etc.　　[2] *Ib.* III, 8, etc.

far as it contemplates the ideal pattern which is reflected in it. To maintain that contemplation is at the same time creation, is one of the most violent paradoxes ever propounded by philosophy. Plotinus develops it with a variety and abundance of arguments and images which are at times dazzling[1].

If anyone were to demand of Nature why it produces, it would answer, if it were willing to listen and speak: 'you should not ask questions, but like me understand in silence: for I am a silent one, and to talk is not my custom. What ought you to understand? This, that the created world is my silent contemplation, a contemplation produced by my nature: for being born myself of contemplation [the meditation of the Intellective Soul], I am naturally contemplative and that which contemplates in me produces an object of contemplation, *as geometers describe figures while contemplating.*' I, however, do not describe figures; but while I contemplate, the outlines of bodies take substance, as though they had fallen from my lap. I preserve the disposition of my mother [the universal soul] and of those who engendered me [the rational-creative *Logoi*]. They too were born of contemplation. So my birth in turn came about by no action of theirs[2]; from the self-contemplation of Principles that are greater than I, I was generated.

This passage contains a comparison which helps greatly towards understanding the paradox of creative contemplation: 'that which contemplates in me produces an object of contemplation, as geometers describe figures while contemplating.' If one turns to the *Timaeus* 53A–55C, it will be found there that, in the myth of creation, the four elements are produced with simple geometrical outlines, those of the four regular polyhedra—the cube in the case of earth, the icosahedron in that of water, the octahedron in that of air, the tetrahedron in that of fire; so, as with the geometer, the soul of the world has but to consider the design, as it were, of the constituent mathematical relations of the Intelligence, which is its model, and then, acted upon by Eros, the figures which the soul contemplates and whose beauty it admires and loves spontaneously project themselves into reality. This example alone is enough to show how deeply imbued with the spirit of Plato Plotinus was.

It will also have been noticed that the Mother of sensible beings, or Nature (Φύσις), who speaks thus, is the daughter of the universal soul (soul of the world or principle of life), and this soul

---

[1] *Enneads*, III, 8, 4 *sqq.*; E. Bréhier, *Histoire de la philosophie ancienne*, II, pp. 459 *sqq.*, and *Plotin*, pp. 53 *sqq.*

[2] '"*Praxis*", action, is contrasted with "*Theoria*", meditation, the other great form of energy; ...according to Plotinus, *Praxis* is *Theoria* in a weaker shape due to the intrusion of matter and therefore confined to the sensible universe.' E. R. Dodds, *Select passages illustrating Neoplatonism*, 1923, p. 35, n. 1.

is itself born of pure Intelligence, which is at once thought and being—the subject and object of modern philosophers—above which, to avoid plurality or, in other words, to escape from the influence of matter, one must go one step higher. Once arrived at the top of the slope by which the ascent has been made through the three chief stages—the famous system of 'the three hypostases' (the trinity of the soul, the spirit ($\nu o \tilde{\upsilon} s$) and the One)—a specially gifted man may experience, in a rapture, intuition of the Absolute. This Absolute, the father of beings, inconceivable except as pure goodness, cannot but bestow existence on all things, and while it keeps itself intact, unchanging, and indivisible throughout its constant production, on everything which emanates from it, it leaves its mark with a more or less vague or conscious desire to return to it. Here if a man wishes to understand he needs the help of comparisons and parallels.

Conceive a spring having no alien source; giving itself to all rivers, yet not exhausted therein, but itself abiding at rest; and the rivers that have gone out from it journeying a while together in one flood before they run their several courses, yet each as it were already conscious in what place its own waters shall find issue. Or conceive the life of a great plant pervading every part, whilst the source of that life itself endures undispersed, having its seat, as it were, in the root[1].

This, then, is the theme which this philosophy delights to return to and develop with every kind of variation: there proceeds from the Absolute in an unbroken continuity first the world of thought, secondly that of the pure ideas contained in it, thirdly that of souls and material bodies; then, under the impulse of desire, everything which has been born strives to return to the prime source of Being. The divine does not descend; however remote it may be, man must climb to the height of divinity, if he is to unite himself with the One above all multiplicity. The possibility of this union lies in the activity of pure thought, and, far beyond the human spirit, in the mysterious accord of the individual with the first Being, an accord beyond all reason. Only an imperfect idea of Plotinus can be gained without reading in their context some of the flashes of his 'quivering and vibrating' style, whereby is expressed the wealth of contradictory ideas and difficulties which come before him as soon as he tries to speak of this being in rapture with God in which consciousness of personality fades away[2].

[1] *Enneads*, III, 8, 10, trans. Dodds, *op. cit.* p. 54.
[2] Here may be quoted only one example, chosen because in it has been happily noticed the presence of an almost romantic lyricism which is ordi-

The teaching and vocation of this philosophy were renunciation of this world and detachment from all activity in it for the sake of a better. At the same time, this renunciation of the world did not at all imply condemnation of it, nor a horror or deep dislike or denial. In the eyes of Plotinus the world is beautiful, as should be the work and reflection of the divinity which is immanent in it. A last ray of the Greek spirit in its decline thus shines where the philosopher glorifies the splendour of the cosmos. On this theme he sometimes raises his voice in a way that can be explained only by the antipathy which his eyes observed in his own audience.

In Plotinus' day 'gnosis,' a religious philosophy of Oriental inspiration, was spreading everywhere in various forms (ch. XIII). It condemned a world created by the spirit of evil and given up to a cruel Destiny, and stressed the need of the worship of saving gods who would intervene in person here on earth and distribute their favours and mercy to gatherings of the faithful and elect. Dwelling on apocalypses and revelations, they set against Platonic cosmology, ruled by pure Intelligence, the dualism of the armies of Good and Evil. Compared with the immense antiquity of the traditions to which they appealed, whether they were Syrian, Chaldaean or Iranian, the seven centuries of Greek thought seemed nothing but the first phase of a philosophy still in its infancy. These 'gnostics' appeared to have everything in their favour. They went straight to men's souls in all they said. They set forth a fine display of theology and speculative fancies. They claimed that Plato himself was a pupil of their ancient wisdom and that Christ gave them the mystical benefit of his death and redemption. They forced their way into Plotinus' audiences and argued against him. Their persuasive tones shook the faith of his pupils, and Plotinus felt the need of breaking free from the hold which threatened to fetter him. Plato's position as the supreme director of thought was seriously menaced, and the dogma of the goodness of the world was openly flouted. Plotinus replied, and an echo of his vehement refutations may be heard in the *Enneads*[1]. Plotinus, in fact, refused to look upon the soul as a prisoner in a

narily alien to Plotinus' intellectualism (cf. G. Misch, *Gesch. der Autobiographie*, I, pp. 377 *sqq.*): 'Many times it has happened lifted out of the body into myself; becoming external to all other things and self-encentered; beholding a marvellous beauty; then, more than ever, assured of community with the loftiest order; enacting the noblest life, acquiring identity with the divine; stationing within It by having attained that activity; poised above whatsoever within the Intellectual is less than the Supreme,' *Enneads*, IV, 8, 1, transl. by Mackenna.   [1] II, 9, 5 *sqq.*

satanic gaol with no hope of salvation except by the supernatural intervention of a redeemer; for him, on the contrary, the soul, by itself and its own unaided powers, could free itself from the body, cleave to the pure Intelligence, regain its first dignity, and, at the end of its liberation, rise to God—not, of course, to the personal God of the gnostics, but to that state of ecstatic union with the One which it is the aim of philosophy to achieve. To find God Plotinus has no need to enter a temple or bow down before an image. His prayer is not a cry of despair, nor an avowal of repentance, nor an entreaty designed to move to pity a being who can help if he will. 'The gift of the intellect is not like a present which can be taken away.' After a divorce from unity the soul has only to turn again towards the lost communion and our fulness is re-established together with the desired equilibrium. Our destiny is entirely in the life within us; it depends on that, and on nothing else.

At Medinet Mâdi in the Fayûm a library has lately been discovered which proves that Manichaean writings could be read in Egypt in the time of Ammonius Saccas, and in order to explain the vigour of Plotinus' resistance to the invasion of gnosticism from the Near East his attempt to go and observe the philosophy of India on the spot has been called in evidence; writers have even tried to credit him with some of the understanding of Hindu asceticism which Mani had won in the course of his travels a century before and of which he took account in founding his cosmopolitan religion[1]. It is undeniable that there was some kind of contact between Plotinus and Indian thought. But it is another matter to say that without this contact Plotinus could not have conceived a type of idealism to which many independent thinkers since his time have approached. Rather may it be said that Plotinus' fundamental achievement was to bring to life in the heart of Platonism the activity of certain affinities with Asia as old as the first philosophic conversations in the gardens of the Academy. As far back as the time of Eudoxus of Cnidus Plato was sufficiently open-minded not to refuse to consider the ideas of the East[2]. Plotinus brought to his work as a Greek thinker the same readiness to learn.

[1] J. Przyluski, 'Mani et Plotin', *Bull. Acad. Belg., Classe des Lettres*, 1933, pp. 322 *sqq.*, and 'Les trois hypostases' etc., in *Mélanges Cumont*, pp. 926 *sqq.*

[2] J. Bidez, 'Platon, Eudoxe de Cnide et l'Orient,' *Bull. Acad. Belg., Classe des Lettres*, 1933, pp. 194 *sqq.*

III. PORPHYRY

In order to characterize the work of his pupil PORPHYRY it must be emphasized that Plotinus stands at the beginning of a new era. Men were ceasing to observe the external world and to try to understand it, utilize it or improve it. They were turning away from nature because they could no longer see in it anything but change, deterioration, corruption, materiality, coarseness and meanness. They were driven in upon themselves. In the inmost consciousness of life and the being of the soul they believed they were in touch with the eternal, the unchanging and the divine. Instead of deifying the world and uniting themselves with God by the heightening of the senses or by the contemplation of the stars, they began to draw fancies from their inner impulses or sought benefit in meditation. The idea of the beauty of the heavens and of the world went out of fashion and was replaced by that of the Infinite.

Plotinus was one of the chief authors of this revolution. He gave it theoretical justification. He clad the ascetic in the cloak of Platonic philosophy. He expressed the new teaching of the value of things by means of some of the most striking images which could appeal to men's minds. But there was nothing of the popularizer in the head of the Neoplatonic school, and a long initiation was necessary in order to penetrate his thought. He needed assistants capable of giving a kind of preliminary instruction. In this work Porphyry excelled. He trained the minds of his students in the *Organon* of Aristotle and in the study of formal logic. In time, by musing on the great principles of asceticism, he made himself the moralist of the teaching of which Plotinus was the metaphysician. In commenting on selected works of Aristotle and Plato on many points he developed, justified and clarified the ideas of his master and even found new applications of them. His untiring industry, his controversial ardour, and enthusiastic propaganda contributed greatly to the good management and early success of the school. It has been said that he became, as it were, the very soul of Hellenism and the protagonist of his party. The most striking conversions to the ideas of Plotinus were due to him; it was he who established the contact between Platonism and St Augustine, the builder of a new City of God.

Plotinus was an admirable improviser, but no composer on paper. He always disdained not only rhetorical artifice but also the trouble needed to secure a well-turned and exact phrase. He did not even re-read what he wrote. But he realized the value of a revision of his writings by a skilled hand, and entrusted the task of publishing them to Porphyry. His pupil accepted it, but did not carry it out at once. For a long time after the death of Plotinus he was content to expound his master's teachings orally. To those who like Longinus asked for the written word he sent indifferent copies. But he was urged ever more strongly to produce an accurate definitive text. There was inevitably a loud demand for such a publication on the part of the growing number of the admirers of Plotinus. Furthermore, in issuing the works of the last great pagan thinker, Porphyry was taking thought not only of the needs of the Platonic school but also for the Hellenism to which he was devoted. Plotinus was the true interpreter of Plato. His works supplemented those of the master of masters and were to supply men who were specially gifted and eager to learn with a selection of pious meditations which they needed. When Porphyry published his collection of Plotinus' lectures in six *Enneads* or divisions, each consisting of nine chapters, he added notes at the request of some friends who desired explanations. If to-day we may hope to restore to life the oral teaching of Plotinus, it is mainly due to the explanations that have by chance been handed down to us by the most understanding and attentive of his auditors[1]. Porphyry also provided his edition with summaries and arguments, and at the beginning of the work gave an account of the philosopher's life.

In the short work thus devoted to the biography of his master, Porphyry does not always speak in the tone or spirit that might be desired. In more than one place the philosopher is looked at through the idle fancies and hallucinations of silly imaginations obsessed by the marvellous, and many a story casts a halo round his head which he himself would not have permitted. But on the whole Porphyry succeeds in bringing his hero to life before us, in body and in soul. In his *Life of Plotinus* he is still practising the art of the older biographers, and there is a contrast between his way of showing forth the merits of an ascetic and the manner which is soon to distinguish the first products of Christian hagiography—for example the life of Antony the Hermit by Athanasius. The souls which Porphyry sets himself to win for his faith are not the simple souls of 'the poor in spirit.'

The fame of Porphyry is very largely due to his great work *Against the Christians*. During the reign of Severus Alexander and Gallienus the new religion had enjoyed toleration. After all, neither the observances of the believers nor their faith nor their

[1] P. Henry, 'Vers la reconstitution de l'enseignement oral de Plotin.' *Bull. Acad. Belg., Classe des Lettres,* 1937, pp. 310 *sqq.*

attitude to society were any longer a cause of trouble. Set beside the mystic frenzy of a strongly orientalized paganism, the Lord's Supper celebrated as a sacrifice, the water poured at baptism as in a rite of initiation, must have had the effect of attractive and easily understood symbols, and even the piety by which Christians were guided in invoking their Saviour God and asking salvation of him was still shared by many souls. In widely different circles the Gospel made steady progress. At Rome the number of those sealed of the faith was increasing rapidly, and during this period a strong and influential episcopacy was being organized in the principal churches. More and more, enlightened pagans had to take account of the seriousness of the situation. The time was coming when a systematic persecution was to be set on foot. It was these calamitous and troubled days that evoked the composition of Porphyry's treatise against the Christians.

There are in the *Enneads* moving hymns to the creative Soul, 'our beneficent sister who has the power to accomplish so much without effort.' As has been seen, she is the cause of the sympathy in all the parts of the universe, mankind and the stars, the sea, animals and plants. She gives nature its impressive beauty and its poignant sadness. Cybele drank the water of Lethe, but in her dreams, which follow one another like clouds racing across the sky, she seeks to recall God. She would not succeed in raising her eyes or in uttering the saving words if the human soul did not find them for her. For we are—as may be said, according to Plotinus—nature after its awakening, already speaking to God and ready to see Him face to face. How inexhaustible are such founts of a mysticism to which our poets will still so often go to seek ecstatic visions! How limitless the fruitfulness of a religion which could seem in fact dead, but which, even during its old age, still had so brilliant a hierophant! The Neoplatonist depicted it in such wonderful forms that the Christians felt compelled to avoid them. To avert the effect of its charms, they had to pronounce anathema upon it.

Among the more enlightened spirits the conflict was felt less keenly. With Plotinus certainly controversy never assumed an unduly personal colour, and it left unimpaired the dream of a common ideal and even of some measure of understanding. But the more men turned to the public at large, the greater the wish to extend the field of propaganda—the activity to which Porphyry devoted himself—and the more keenly felt and inevitable became the clashes. Faced by the common herd, men were soon drawn into a fighting attitude, and thus the Platonists undertook the justification of all the observances of the established cults, while the Christians thundered against the wickednesses of idolatry. There is, then, nothing surprising in the sight of a Porphyry who thus became at the same time popularizer of the teaching of Plotinus and adversary of the Church.

Nevertheless, the hostility of Porphyry is not to be explained entirely by the development of philosophy. Amelius, his fellow-student and collaborator, still invokes the testimony of the beginning of the gospel according to St John, and although, following the fashion of the school, he calls the disciple of Christ a 'barbarian,' there is nothing to show that he was hostile to the Church. Neoplatonism and Christianity were doubtless rivals destined sooner or later to meet in conflict, but, if we wish to explain the declaration of war, we must certainly take into account the personality of Porphyry himself. No Neoplatonist was more likely than he was to engage in hostilities. He had always concerned himself with Christian teaching and observances and with the error which they seemed to contain. In his earliest works, in his *Philosophy of the Oracles*, if he appears to bow before the sanctity of Christ, he looks upon the reverence shown to him as excessive. A little later, when he published his treatise *On the images of the gods*, he writes for the select, from whom the Christians are excluded, and it is the Christians whom he takes to task. It is clear that at every period of his literary activity and before he could have dreamed of putting his gifts at the service of the ideas of Plotinus, he looked on the new religion as a hostile force.

Porphyry's treatise against the Christians was a considerable work. It ran to fifteen books, wherein Porphyry made full use of his learning and intellectual skill. Trained, as he had been, by Longinus in critical scholarship, he soon saw how to set about revealing inventions, improbabilities and contradictions in the narratives of the Evangelists and other canonical books, and he laboured to shatter the authority of the evidence appealed to by true believers in support of their faith. Origen's allegorical interpretation, 'which cleverly read into the falsehoods of foreigners the beliefs of the Greeks,' did not find favour in his eyes.

Porphyry repeats, follows up and enlarges all that the ingenuity of Celsus had discovered by way of argument. He brings against the books of Daniel a proof of spuriousness that many modern scholars consider conclusive. He attacks the genealogy of Jesus. He claims to show by the contradictions of the synoptists that their narratives cannot claim to be believed. He criticizes many passages in the Acts of the Apostles. He finds that Peter is contradicted by Paul. Paul he attacks with special fury. The philhellene sees in him nothing but coarse rhetoric and intolerable incoherence. Porphyry's whole polemic is elaborated with an abundance of arguments in which contemporary controversialists might find many of their favourite themes. Whenever rationalism came into conflict with Christian revelation, it was enough to repeat what had been said by Porphyry.

Porphyry, like his predecessor Celsus, was particularly shocked to see among the Christians revolutionaries breaking with all their ancestral inheritance, even with the ordinances of the Old Testament, and threatening the established order of things. He puts them down as 'barbarians.' But, in spite of this, he seems less concerned than Celsus to defend the Roman State. His special originality comes out in the breadth of view with which he now and then comprehends the struggle. Since Celsus the horizon of Platonism had been widely extended. Porphyry has not the same contempt as Celsus either for the Jews or for Orientals. His humanity is such that he feels a measure of sympathy even with the person of Christ and some parts of his teaching. He keeps his wrath for the disciples of Jesus, for the distortions of which they were the originators and for the 'myths' of the Evangelists. As early as his day the canon of the writings of the New Testament had been determined. He knows it and directs his attacks at it, and it is this which gives his criticism a forcefulness and thrust which places it far above that of his predecessors. In him are found hardly any of the crude aspersions to which pagan polemic of the first centuries had recourse. Nor is he malevolent in tone like Julian. His controversy rarely sinks to the futile. He makes a careful study of the points at issue and tries to foresee objections. In the main he seems much less concerned with the effect he will have on the public than with the particular error which he is seeking to demonstrate.

Porphyry certainly endeavours to expose what he holds to be weaknesses in the arguments used to prove the divine origin of Christianity; but apart from this the work which he conceived is one of deep philosophy and not mere polemic. He speaks as a profoundly religious man. The need of revelation, redemption, asceticism and immortality inspires him with a faith like that of his opponents. In his desire to convince and to find what he calls a universal ('catholic') way of salvation[1], he goes so far as to jettison the theurgy and observances of pagan worship. He shows himself still filled with the lofty and conciliatory thought of Plotinus.

[1] See *de Regressu*, frag. 12 (Bidez, *Vie de Porphyre*, App. II, p. 42*sq*.).

In this respect, as in all others, he marks the transition between early Neoplatonism and that of the time of Iamblichus and Julian. Philosophy is already at war with Christianity; but, in spite of the outbreak of hostilities, there can always be suspected in him a hope of agreement.

This hope proved illusory. No settlement was possible. In the treatise which Porphyry wrote against them the Christians saw nothing but hostility, and they had good reason for feeling anxious about it. The sum-total of testimonies and doctrines on which the Church based its teaching had to meet the most formidable indictment which has ever been drawn up by Hellenism. Rejoinders succeeded one another. Methodius, Eusebius of Caesarea, Apollinarius of Laodicea and Philostorgius attempted refutations. But these refutations were not thought sufficient. As late as 448, by the orders of the Emperors Valentinian III and Theodosius II, the work was consigned to the flames, and the edict which prescribed this auto-da-fé mentions Porphyry alone, saying nothing of Celsus or of Hierocles or of Julian, as if of all the defences of paganism only his need cause disquiet. Jerome, for example, pours out on Porphyry all the abuse of which his nature was capable, and that is saying a good deal. He calls him a scoundrel, an impudent fellow, a vilifier, a sycophant, a lunatic and a mad dog.

It is as the collaborator of Plotinus that Porphyry has his chief claim to our gratitude; but, at the same time, he has rendered us services of a different kind. He was the author of a considerable number of commentaries and miscellaneous works of learning[1], and he is one of the chief scholars to whom we owe our knowledge of a host of writers of antiquity. A large part of the information to be found in the Homeric scholia, in the series of Neoplatonic commentaries and in many a Byzantine writer has come down to us through him. For example, in modern collections of the fragments of the pre-Socratics and Stoics, of the Orphic poems and many other works, it would be enough to put Porphyry's name at the head of the extracts which we really owe to him, to show that his contribution is one of the largest. In this respect he deserves a place beside Pliny, Galen, Ptolemy and the other men of letters of the Imperial age whose learned works enable us in some measure to make up for the loss of so many precious documents.

If Porphyry could return to the world of men, he would undoubtedly be not a little surprised at the fate which has befallen his work. Certainly the idea of the supreme importance of the spiritual life and the search for individual salvation to which he

[1] Bidez, *op. cit.* pp. 65* *sqq.*

gave a great part of his efforts, have worked wonders on this earth. For many centuries a large élite of mankind has withdrawn from the world and sought in the silence of the cloister forgetfulness of bondage to the flesh. But the triumph of idealism and mysticism has not fallen to the standards and to the leaders under whom the publisher of the *Enneads* took his place. The doctrines of the Neoplatonists have influenced men's minds in a Christian form. In the visions of Dante and in the outpourings of medieval piety Plotinus is forgotten, and in our own day also there are few indeed who have even a slight knowledge of the debt due to him.

IV. IAMBLICHUS

All that is known of the early education of the philosopher IAMBLICHUS can soon be told. Born about 250 at Chalcis in Coele-Syria, this Semite was at first, doubtless at Rome, the pupil of Porphyry and of the mathematician Anatolius; he then returned to Asia, and it is now known that, following the example of the Neoplatonist Amelius, he went to teach at Apamea[1]. Details concerning the life of Iamblichus are scanty, but of his works, which consisted of ponderous commentaries on Aristotle and Plato, a life of Alypius, an essay on the gods, and other writings, there remain considerable specimens and in particular long fragments from a collection of treatises dealing with the philosophy of Pythagoras: a *Life* of the master, an *Exhortation to Philosophy*, a treatise *On the science of mathematics*. All these make up a tedious collection, full of mystical remarks concerning the science of numbers and a mass of quotations drawn from every kind of writer and paraphrased from a moralistic standpoint, without any show of literary merit, but commonplace in form and diffuse in style, a nerveless and wearisome composition. Whoever has tried to read this writer, who far from having 'sacrificed to the graces of Hermes' seems to wish 'to repel with a phrase which grates upon the ears[2],' will ask himself how such a nincompoop could have been regarded by the most distinguished men of his time as a divine master and how he managed to arouse in them so passionate an enthusiasm.

For Plotinus, as has been seen, religion was a matter entirely for the inward man, and the means by which an attempt is made to impress the imagination in public worship were unworthy of a philosopher who wished to preserve his soul from all contact with

---

[1] Bidez, 'Le philosophe Jamblique et son école,' *Rev. des Études grecques* XXXII, 1919, p. 31 *sq.*   [2] Eunapius, *Vit. Soph.* p. 458, 9 *sq.* (Didot).

the external world. The master took little thought for the general public. It was enough for him if his mysticism was available to a chosen few. But as soon as Iamblichus took over the management of the school, at a time when paganism in its hour of danger was calling more and more urgently for all the forces of Hellenism to come to its help, the Neoplatonists threw themselves into the struggle and they soon found that Porphyry had been too yielding. In their desire to take more account of the needs of their time they ceased to concern themselves only with an élite and set to work to extend their field of propaganda. The system of Plotinus was too remote for many minds; hence, in order to give a less abstruse form to the speculations of his philosophy, Iamblichus and his successors thought it well to enable men to contemplate them through the showy and misty images of the mystery religions[1]. Sarapis, Isis, Hecate, Demeter, Dionysus and Cybele supplied them with a whole host of emblems which they put to ingenious use, and in future it was by symbolic visions that they claimed to prepare the return of the soul to God. The Neoplatonists thus turned themselves into 'hierophants' and initiated their pupils into the secret cults of their time. Multiplying the triads and hebdomads according to the needs of the cause, Iamblichus set the example by admitting as many as 360 divine entities with 21 lords of the world and 42 gods of nature. In this kind of barracks open for a general mobilization of polytheism, the mystic priest could find a place for anything which the established cults offered him, giving the place of honour naturally to the leader of the gods set in charge of Plotinus' intelligible world, the great king Helios, with his image the visible Sun, his doubles Zeus and Sarapis, his representatives Dionysus and Asclepius, his emanations Apollo and Athena (Providence and soul of the world), and lastly his companion Aphrodite.

To this Neoplatonist the real aim was to set up the great confraternity of all the doctrines and religious practices of Hellenism, a Hellenism which from now onwards let its flag fly over all the traditional beliefs of Greece and the Near East. The gods of every people are henceforth joined to form a pantheon which puts its sanctuaries and priesthoods at the disposal of all the devout, their religious blessings being, as it were, pooled. All difference of opinion must in future be abolished. Not only Plato, Aristotle and Pythagoras, but also Heraclitus, Democritus and

---

[1] This is already shown by Iamblichus' answer to the *Letter of Porphyrius to Anebo*, the *de mysteriis* that he published under the name of the Egyptian prophet, Abammon. See Bidez in *Mélanges Desrousseaux*, p. 12 *sq*.

the other philosophers—Epicurus and the Cynics alone being excepted—as well as the Orphics and the followers of Hermes Trismegistus and with them the Jews, gnostics and Chaldaeans, have all to be made to agree, and woe betide anyone who disturbs this united front! The 'queries' that Porphyry had submitted to the Egyptian priest Anebo will be regarded as blasphemous; Iamblichus will dispose of them and condemn them with equal severity and unction. The enlightened intellectualism of a Plotinus and a Porphyry drew its power and insight from the free effort of individual thought. Iamblichus is inspired by a mob fanaticism. Plotinus and Porphyry had rejected the help of saving gods: Iamblichus appeals to every form of redemption and revelation borne witness to by ancient tradition. Plotinus and Porphyry had laid great stress on silent prayer and banished living sacrifice from the worship of the gods. In his desire to found a pagan Catholic church Iamblichus is sensitive to the danger to which his plan would be exposed by the smallest concession to the revolutionary Evangelists: just as he pours scorn on the monks, so he persists in the search for clever sophistries to show that, religion being made for the people and the people having need of visible divinities to worship, like those which can be seen in the sky, the fire and smoke of sacrifice are symbols bearing, by their very antiquity, incomparable power to strengthen the prayers and raise towards the gods of the world the souls of the faithful gathered in the temples.

Egypt had long been for Greek religious feeling the Holy Land. But at the time when the Sassanids were making the voice of Zoroaster speak with a fresh accent, when the sacred books of the Hebrews, thanks to their hellenizing interpreters, were universally reverenced, when the prophet Mani claimed to renew the ancient predications of Buddha, Jesus and Zoroaster, it was impossible to put a comprehensive religious syncretism under the exclusive patronage of the old priesthoods of the country of the Pharaohs. In the Second Century two holy men called Julian, who styled themselves Chaldaeans, drew up the extraordinary series of oracles known as 'logia Chaldaica' in which re-appeared, with the very spirit of the *Timaeus* of Plato, the principles of the old Orphic-Pythagorean mysticism from which Plato himself had borrowed so much. To show the 'symphony' of the wise men of ancient Greece with the doctrines revealed to priesthoods many thousands of years old this doctrine of Oriental colour seemed like a godsend. Iamblichus at once said farewell to dialectic and the unsuccessful efforts of a rationality that had only shown into what fog and wild vagaries reason, suspended between myriads of errors, ends by sinking, and with all sail set sought shelter in the harbour of superhuman revelation[1]. Thus it is Iamblichus who was responsible for an alliance which was to make his successor, Proclus, observe that, if it were for him to decide, he would destroy all books, with two exceptions, the *Timaeus* and the *Logia*[2]. If any originality is to be attributed to Iamblichus, it would have to be found in his idea of combining so strangely the spirit of Plato with the most fanatical aberrations; the conjunction was certainly monstrous, but the influence which it produced spread rapidly, at all events in the East. In the crypt at Ephesus in which the Neoplatonist Maximus initiated the future Emperor Julian into the mysteries of paganism, the spells used by the wonder-worker were those which Iamblichus had borrowed from the theurgy of the oracles called Chaldaean. Writing from Gaul to the philosopher Priscus, one of his companions in Platonic mysticism, Julian asked him for a copy of 'everything that Iamblichus wrote on his namesake' (the theurge Julian). When he set down these words, Julian believed he was undergoing a supernatural experience and he apologizes for speaking with the rapture of an enthusiast and adds, 'for my part I idolize Iamblichus in philosophy and my namesake, the theurge] in theosophy, and, to speak in the manner of Apollodorus[3], compared with them in my eyes the others[4] do not count.' After this piece of evidence there is no reason for surprise at reading in Eunapius that pupils hurried in crowds all along the roads of Asia to the town of Apamea where Iamblichus taught and where his conversation— not the reading of his writings—charmed those present at his dinner parties so much that he seemed to fill them with nectar. Like one inspired, living in communion with the gods, when he made solemn sacrifice on the appointed dates, he caused spirits to appear on the waters of fountains, and, as he prayed, his garments changed to a beautiful golden hue, and, by a phenomenon like the levitation of spirits in modern times, his body soared aloft ten cubits from the ground[5].

---

[1] Iamblichus quoted in *Catalogue des mss. alchimiques*, VI, 163, 25 and 85 *sqq.*, and in *Mélanges Cumont*, p. 93, (Proclus) frag. II.

[2] Marinus, *Life of Proclus*, 38 *ad fin.*, and J. Bidez, *Revue belge de Philologie*, VII, 1928, p. 147 *sq.*, and above, vol. XI, p. 642 *sq.*

[3] The enthusiastic follower of Socrates; see Plato, *Symposium*, 173 D and Julian, *Ep.* 12, trans. Bidez, p. 19.   [4] Including even Plato!

[5] Eunapius, *Vit. Soph.* p. 458, 13 *sq.*; cf. similar stories by E. R. Dodds in *Greek Poetry and Life: Essays presented to Gilbert Murray*, p. 383.

V. CHRISTIAN APOLOGETICS: EUSEBIUS

The Phoenician Pamphilus was trained in the catechetical school of Alexandria under the direction of Pierius, the successor of Origen. On returning to his own country he settled at Caesarea in Palestine, the city already well-known through the Acts of the Apostles, where Origen had taught latterly and had left his books. To carry on the work of his master, Pamphilus founded a biblical school at Caesarea and as a second 'Demetrius of Phalerum' not only spent money freely on collecting the scattered remains of Origen's library, but also began to copy with his own hand the precious works which he was unable to acquire. Subsequently he had a whole staff of scribes, which was soon joined by Eusebius, working for him and with him so eagerly and efficiently that before long the school possessed a collection of books unrivalled in Christian circles. In friendly collaboration with Pamphilus, to whom he was so attached that he used his name like that of an adoptive father (ὁ Παμφίλου), Eusebius then occupied himself under his direction in transcribing, cataloguing and editing texts, in considering questions of authenticity, in drawing up chronological lists of writers and in collecting about them all kinds of information (ἱστορίαι) of literary history. With a mind and training less philosophic than Origen and a learning less profound than Porphyry he set himself, like them, to emulate the great librarians who had in an earlier day inaugurated the methods of historical and philological criticism in the Museum at Alexandria.

In 307 the persecution let loose by Galerius attacked the school at Caesarea, and Pamphilus was cast into prison. Eusebius relates the scenes of horror which he witnessed at that time. But none the less for two years—we do not know how—he managed to continue to work with his imprisoned master and together they wrote an elaborate *Apology for Origen*. Pamphilus was executed in 310, and his disciple took it on himself to complete their common work[1].

EUSEBIUS was an indefatigable worker and continued writing until a very advanced age. As has been said by the author of one of the best histories of the early Church, 'he knew everything, biblical history, pagan history, ancient literature, philosophy, geography, computation, exegesis. He commented on Isaiah, and the Psalms and on other books. He could explain the difficult question of the Passover which depended on exegesis, ritual and astronomy. Towards the end of his life men began to be

[1] Photius, *Cod.* 118.

interested in the Holy Places, and Eusebius, who had a thorough knowledge of Palestine and the Bible, explained the names of peoples and places mentioned in Scripture, described Judaea and reconstructed the ancient topography of the holy city. He excelled in formal orations; in particular he delivered the one which opened the discussions of the Council of Nicaea (325). It was to him that the Emperor Constantine turned when he needed well-written and accurate copies of the Bible: he once asked him for fifty all at once, for the churches of Constantinople[1].'

The vast activity of Eusebius reveals an impressive unity of inspiration. From start to finish of his literary career, the man who may be thought of as the first archivist historiographer of the Church set himself to rehabilitate the new religion in the eyes of educated men by securing for it a title to nobility of which the unbeliever Porphyry was ignorant. In the thought of this learned reviver of apologetic who gives a richness and entirely new splendour to the ideas of his predecessors, it is no longer a question of winning an indulgent toleration for an obscure and latter-day sect. Eusebius has the skill to draw from history a striking proof of Christianity, designed by God to enter upon the heritage of ancient civilizations. Taking up Origen's idea that with the accession of Augustus the reign of the *pax Romana* had smoothed the way for the mission of the Apostles and the preaching of the Gospel, he finds in it an argument to prove that the destiny of the Roman Empire was providentially bound up with that of Christianity[2], and in this way the *historia philologos* and *philosophos* of a Porphyry was, in the thought of his rival Eusebius, to serve as a preparation for what he calls 'ecclesiastical history.'

In the cause of Hellenism, or, as he put it, of 'philosophy,' in order to strengthen the consciousness that Greece ought to have of so many inherited virtues and benefits to mankind, Porphyry had composed a chronography[3]; Eusebius followed his example by beginning his work with the drawing up of a chronicle in the same way. But his subject led him to conceive of horizons differently set from those of his predecessor. To recall the origins of Greek thought it was naturally unnecessary to go farther back than Homer and the fall of Troy; but it was necessary to go very much farther back if one wished, as Eusebius did, to contrast with the traditions of the Greeks those of foreign nations. At the same time Eusebius does not lose himself in the obscurities of a past altogether

[1] Eusebius, *Vit. Const.* iv, 36; Duchesne, *Hist. de l'Église*, ii, 159 *sq.*
[2] Cf. E. Peterson, *Der Monotheismus als politisches Problem*, p. 75 *sq.*
[3] *F.H.G.* iii, p. 689 *sq.*, known by the borrowings made from it by Eusebius.

fabulous. Dismissing the apocalyptic fancies of his predecessor Julius Africanus who, in order to establish his messianic chiliasm, claimed to know how many years ago the world had been created, Eusebius had not to go beyond the time of the patriarch Abraham to prove his case. Even in its starting-point his chronology is the work of a careful and exact mind. In the first part (chronography) the author tried to fix the chronological order of the important events of his history, using for each people A.D. 325 as a terminal date; in the second (table of concordant dates) he abstracted from these different series of events a collection of synchronisms of which the most characteristic in his eyes was the simultaneousness of the birth of Jesus and the census of Quirinius. This work is the most considerable of its kind in antiquity, and one of the foundations on which still rests our knowledge of the dates in a large part of Greek and Roman history. It must be confessed that Eusebius does not display the complete independence of mind or the forceful originality of an Eratosthenes or Apollodorus, the creators of his type of research, but the Christian chronographer knew how to work according to their methods, and it may be allowed that, considering the evidence at his disposal, he was perfectly honest in thinking that he had established the priority of Moses to Homer and the primacy of the revelations of the Bible.

Christians were reproached by pagans with their novelty, and the criticism was damaging, for the word 'innovation' (νεωτερισμός) still bore the bad sense which the word 'revolutionary' has with us. But Eusebius held that the accusation was unjust, as he sets out to prove in his *Praeparatio* and *Demonstratio Evangelica*, starting invariably from the ideas of Origen. If the Christians gave up the beliefs of their ancestors (τὰ πάτρια) and went over to Judaism, that was because paganism with its obscene and shocking myths, with its idolatry and the bad customs which it fostered, was an indefensible aberration which had all too long perverted mankind. For centuries divine wisdom had vouch-safed a glimpse of the truth to the best of the Greek thinkers; in the teaching of a Plato Christians recognized opinions which were 'relations and friends' of their own. Having thus in the *Praeparatio* refuted pagan polytheism and shown the superiority of Hebraic monotheism, Eusebius in the *Demonstratio*, which formed the sequel, turned to the Jews to rebut their criticism that the Christians accepted Judaism only to alter it. He maintained that the legislation of Moses was only a temporary dispensation, intended to serve as a transition between the age of the patriarchs and the coming of Christ. Christianity with its doctrine of the Trinity—the Father, the Son (*Logos* or *Word*) and Holy Ghost—and of the salvation secured for men by free submission (or assimilation, ὁμοίωσις) to the divine will, was to him the natural development of Judaism and at the same time the clear revelation of the ideas and aspirations imperfectly expressed in the doctrines of the Platonic school. Nominally directed against the Jews, the *Demonstratio* quite as much as the *Praeparatio* is really aimed at Porphyry's treatise *Against the Christians*, which by sounding the alarm in the name of threatened traditions and philosophy, had reinforced among the conservative élite the dislike of the new religion. The innumerable quotations from various writers, biblical or profane, which form the staple of these two works of Eusebius, the *Praeparatio* and *Demonstratio Evangelica*, were put together and published first, with the title of 'introduction' (εἰσαγωγή), as collections of plain extracts, while an express and detailed refutation of Porphyry's treatise *Against the Christians* was given in a separate work now lost which had itself been preceded by a reply of the same kind to the pagan Hierocles, the author of a comparison intended to show that the merits of Apollonius of Tyana were quite as exemplary as those of Jesus. In this reply Eusebius made good use of his wide reading in overwhelming Hierocles with an exposure of his plagiarisms; on Eusebius' showing this sham writer had done nothing more than copy Celsus and a re-reading of Origen was enough to refute him. No doubt Porphyry was combated with a similar display of learning.

Having disabused the minds of his readers of all the prejudices fostered by pagan polemic and thrown light on the ancient origins of Christianity and on the orientation and course of universal history, Eusebius had only to deal with the period of its full bloom since the teaching of Jesus to complete his panegyric on the new religion. If he succeeded in demonstrating the constant loyalty of the Church to the teaching of its founder, men should recognize in it the realization of a work of salvation prepared and foretold in the most distant past. The sufferings of the Jews abandoned by God after the death of Christ and condemned to dispersion; all the power of the Faith borne witness to by the heroism of the martyrs and by the failure of persecutions; the permanence of the teaching of Christ assured by the unbroken tradition of the creed received from the holy apostles; finally the complete realization of divine promises with the victories, to begin with, of Constantine over Maxentius (first edition), later over Licinius (second edition) and with the coming of the kingdom of God in an Empire reconciled with the Church—these are the chief events whose connection he wished to make clear in his *Ecclesiastical History*. It was an indispensable work but one which no member of the Church had hitherto attempted although, in his eyes, a first sketch of it could be found in the corresponding part of his *Chronicle*[1]. By means of the translation of Rufinus the work soon spread throughout the Latin world, and made upon it a profound and lasting impression[2].

The relation of the method of Eusebius to that of the Alexandrine grammarians who were the first to try to put together a history of profane literature is now well understood[3]. General history in Eusebius comes out only through and by means of literary history. His practice is patiently to collect and revise texts, to date them and classify them, and finally to examine them pen in hand in order to extract passages containing exact evidence and proof; he draws up lists of succession (διαδοχαί) of bishops just as the grammarians drew up lists of succession for the heads of the great philosophical schools; for the martyrs he makes and reproduces a selection of the best authenticated records of their trials. Work of this kind is largely that of an archivist, and Eusebius did not always avoid the danger of letting his main idea disappear under a mass of documents. His literary skill and gift for composition are insufficient to overcome the difficulties of his task; for example, the periods represented by each of his chapters are unequally enlarged upon according to the greater or less abundance of the materials at his disposal. But, for all that, by means of clearly marked guide-posts he keeps a systematic arrangement where there seems only to be disorder; he brings out the stages of history, and leads us to his goal, not by phrases but by documents; and it is precisely this that gives an incomparable worth to what he insists is an 'ecclesiastical history,' and to the whole bulk of his writings, however slight their literary value may be.

It is hardly to be supposed that he did the work of an enquirer (ἴστωρ), that is to say of an enquirer irresistibly driven by curiosity to the search for the truth, as the title he chose (ἱστορία) might lead one to think. The time was really past even for the *historia* of Greek learning, and Porphyry had not succeeded in

---

[1] *Hist. Eccl.* I, 1, 5–6.
[2] E. Schwartz in P.W. *s.v.* Eusebios, col. 1406 *sq.*
[3] Cf. Schwartz, 'Über Kirchengeschichte,' *Nachr. d. K. Gesellsch. d. Wiss. zu Göttingen*, 1908, p. 111 especially, excellently summarized by A. Puech, *Histoire de la Litt. gr. chrét.* III, p. 181.

being more than an erudite compiler serving literary dilettanti. Much more than he Eusebius was incapable of going against the stream or recovering the lost spirit. It is not even as if his stimulus was a purely scientific curiosity. He labours to propagate a faith and his work is designed to further a particular cause. What he looks for is the material of an advocate. He concerns himself only with what suits him, and to suppress an irrelevant record seems to him part of his task. It is no less true that in his anxiety not to accept evidence or texts until they have been subjected to strong criticism he draws his inspiration from the old *historia*; and to form a proper idea of the very great merits of his work, as of that of Porphyry, whose rival he wished to be, it is enough to make a comparison and consider, for example, how much genuine understanding and breadth of view is to be found in the organizers of great modern encyclopaedias.

In the *Ecclesiastical History* of Eusebius there is one other feature to observe. This first picture of the Church's past, which was to give it a very real consciousness of itself and complete self-confidence, was not simply a work conceived and carried out in Greek, but was written from the point of view of the East. The Christian communities of the Western half of the Empire count for little; in the eyes of the historian the great unity of the *mare nostrum* is fading, or rather, as the vital centre of the organism grows weak, disintegration begins, and cracks appear foretelling a more complete schism. When, for example, Eusebius discusses heresies, the whole spectacle of the European part of the Mediterranean seems hidden from him. His knowledge of Tertullian's *Apologeticum* comes from a Greek translation, and he thinks Tertullian was a Roman[1]; he discovers at Caesarea the writings of Hippolytus of Rome, but carelessly enough locates somewhere or other what he calls his 'bishopric[2]'; he has no more regard for the writings of Cyprian[3]. Even concerning the church of Rome the conscientious archivist does not think it his duty to make himself well-informed; at least, for several pontificates his chronology seems to mix up years and months. But there is no reason for surprise. How could a scholar faithful to the spirit of the school at Alexandria give up his time to Latin? Besides, at the time when Eusebius concluded his *Ecclesiastical History*, men's minds were turned to the 'New Rome' of an Empire that had changed its centre, and in Greek ecclesiastical histories the Latins were soon to be referred to with a hint of contempt as Italians.

[1] *Hist. Eccl.* ii, 2, 4; Rufinus makes the correction.   [2] *Ib.* vi, 20, 2.
[3] *Ib.* vi, 43, 3; Rufinus touches up (p. 615 Mommsen).

The last part of Eusebius' work belongs to a new period on which we cannot enter. We may end by observing that in celebrating the Tricennalia of Constantine Eusebius glorifies an Empire which will not become Christian except with the aim of making the Church subordinate to it. The time is near when at the councils questions of dogma become questions of politics, and the choice of men in the succession (διαδοχή) of holy apostles is made according to the purpose and will of the Government. Further consideration cannot be given here to the relation of Eusebius' work to the great theological and political conflicts which threatened in his time, but this account of Eusebius may be fittingly closed with this quotation: certainly, the scholarship of the great disciple of Origen, Eusebius, 'was employed to fashion the political philosophy of the Byzantine world[1].'

When the sack of Rome by Alaric shattered the dreams of *Ecclesiastical History*, the two halves of the Mediterranean were already practically isolated from one another and shut up in two closed vessels, and the shock of the catastrophe reached the East only as an echo, as can be clearly seen by noticing how little space is given to the event in the parallel narratives of the three synoptic historians, Socrates, Sozomen and Theodoret, and, after their example, in the *Tripartita* composed by Cassiodorus for the West. Very soon after the death of Plotinus, his school is found roughly divided into two spheres of influence almost without inter-communication, that of Iamblichus in the countries which had long been hellenized, and that of Porphyry in the West which still remained younger. It is a sign of an incompatibility of temper, due, no doubt, to a difference in age, which begins to part the two areas of the world which Rome had hitherto united under its protection and which the pressure of nationalism was finally to sunder.

[1] N. H. Baynes, 'Eusebius and the Christian Empire' in *Ann. de l'Inst. de phil. et d'hist. Orient.* II, 1934, p. 18.

CHAPTER XIX

THE GREAT PERSECUTION

I. THE ATTITUDE OF PHILOSOPHERS TO CHRISTIANITY

THE histories of the countries surrounding the Mediterranean Sea from the standpoint of a spectator of a later day may be regarded as man's preparation of the *oikoumene* for the rule of Rome. The struggles of rival empires issue in the dominance of the only Empire which has ever held in sole supremacy all the shores of the inland sea. And the culture of this bilingual Mediterranean world is itself highly complex, and in that complexity is mirrored the fact that it is the legatee who has entered into possession of the goods of many predecessors. But before this culture of the Empire of Rome, the deposit of the pagan past, could become the culture of the Empire whose heart was Constantinople it needed yet a further contribution—the legacy of the Jew, the blood-bought treasure of the Christian. That final fusion of the elements which were to constitute the Byzantine inheritance came not through the tranquil process of a peaceful evolution: historically it was effected through the violent reaction of a pagan counter-reformation which failed and through the will of a Roman emperor who had put the God of the Christians to the test and had proved in his own experience that victory lay not with Juppiter Optimus Maximus but with the God whom through the centuries his worshippers had acknowledged as the Lord who was strong and mighty in battle—the Lord of Hosts.

We stand at one of the turning points in the history of Europe —at the moment when the old world of paganism is in travail, when against its will it gives birth to the Christian Empire. The

Note. The principal sources for the persecution are the *Church History* of Eusebius, Books VIII and IX and his monograph on the *Martyrs of Palestine*—a complete record of the persecution in his own province; for the rest of the empire we have no such evidence. The pamphlet of Lactantius—*De mortibus persecutorum*—was written, it is true, by a rhetorician maintaining a view of the divine government of the world, but the work is still of high value as a historical source. For the critical discussion of the authentic Acta and Passions see the Bibliography.

pagan world might refuse to acknowledge its offspring: the child might disclaim the links which bound it to a pagan past; but at length the pagan came to realize that his gods could be abandoned, that his literature, his philosophy and his art could outlive the deities with which they had been so intimately associated. This pagan culture, it was found, possessed a vitality which the Immortals could not command, and on his side the Christian could not forgo the inheritance of a world in which he had formerly felt himself an alien, as but a sojourner in another's city: the vessel of polytheism which had contained the treasure of the past could be broken and the treasure could still be preserved, the spoil of the Egyptians could become the pride of the despised Galilaeans. Thus in the fourth century of our era was brought about the final fusion which was to determine the faith and the achievement of the men of the later Empire. With the history of that momentous fusion this volume is not concerned: we have but to sketch the course of the crisis which made that fusion possible.

Roman State, Hellenistic culture, the Christian Church— these are the three forces in the crisis: how did they stand towards each other at the close of the third century? A brief retrospect can hardly be avoided. In the first century the new faith which had been born amongst the mongrel population of Galilee of the Gentiles, whose founder had been crucified as a common criminal, could hardly arouse the serious interest of the Roman world: it was but one more poisonous superstition from the East, the fruitful mother of queer and revolting cults. Scorn—or perhaps a scornful pity—for such delusion was all that could be expected. But in the second century some notice had perforce to be taken of the sect: a governor such as Pliny might be constrained to acknowledge that the superstition appeared morally guiltless; only the perverse obstinacy of the Christians offended the Roman's sense for discipline. The first writer seriously to attack the new faith was, so far as we know, Fronto, the tutor of the Emperor Marcus Aurelius; his work is lost, yet it probably furnished to Minucius much material for his statement of the pagans' case. But the world of culture still remained unconcerned, and when about 180 Celsus published his *True Discourse* against the Christians it may well have passed unnoticed[1]: pagan writers do not mention the treatise, and it was only seventy years later that the attention of Origen was called to the work; it is from his

---

[1] "Celse s'était adressé à des esprits trop peu alarmés." J. Bidez, *Vie de Porphyre*, p. 69.

elaborate reply that the greater part of Celsus' attack can be recovered. But the remarkable fact is that in its conception the *True Discourse* was something more than a criticism: in developing his argument Celsus may be led into sarcasm, ridicule and bitterness, but originally he had, it would seem, intended the *True Discourse* (ἀληθὴς λόγος) as an appeal for Christian cooperation: if men withdrew themselves from the service of the State, they were endangering the defence of the world of civilized life threatened by the chaos of encircling barbarism. The work ends with an invitation to share in the task of empire. The Platonist does not as yet demand the ruthless suppression of Christianity: his message is rather that of Macedonia to the early missionaries of the faith: 'Come over and help us.'

And in the opening years of the third century, when the school of Neoplatonism was being formed in Alexandria, it was a convert from Christianity, Ammonius Saccas, who was the leader of the movement, while Origen was the equal of his pagan contemporaries, and pagan and Christian could meet in a common search for truth[1].

That moment passed and it has been with plausibility suggested[2] that the hostility of Neoplatonism to Christianity begins with Plotinus: it is true that in the *Enneads* there is no direct attack upon Christianity, but the arguments marshalled by Plotinus against the gnostics might prove of equal service against the Christians. There were profound differences between the two faiths; in the thought of Plotinus, man needed no divine redeemer to secure his salvation, man's soul could by its own unaided powers regain its first dignity (see p. 628); the thought of Plotinus is indeed entirely pagan. Of this his affirmation of the eternity and incorruptibility of the world is sufficient proof, excluding as it did the Christian dogma of creation as well as Christian eschatology. The Cross remained for the Greek foolishness and the resurrection of the human body an absurdity. Neoplatonism and Christianity, it has been said, were rivals destined to fight each other. Under Gallienus persecution might be stayed: it was an unintelligent method of attack, but the intellectual battle must proceed. The forces of Hellenism must present a united front to a foe who was more dangerous than Epicurean or Sceptic precisely because Platonist and Christian held so much ground in

[1] Cf. R. Cadiou, *La jeunesse d'Origène*, Part 3.

[2] C. Schmidt, 'Plotins Stellung zum Gnosticismus und kirchlichen Christentum,' *Texte und Unters.* xx, Heft 4, 1900. Cf. P. de Labriolle, *La réaction païenne*, pp. 228 *sqq.* and Bidez, *op. cit.* pp. 69 *sqq.*

common. When Porphyry, the disciple of Plotinus, resumes the work of Celsus, he writes no longer an appeal for co-operation, but an uncompromising attack upon the Christian Church and upon its sacred books: he gave to that attack the title 'Against the Christians[1].' Porphyry, scholar and critic, trained at Athens in the school of Longinus, thus provided the arsenal from which all the later critics of Christianity drew their weapons. His hostility to the revolutionary sectaries who had deserted the traditions of their fathers continued to be the attitude of the Neoplatonist defenders of Hellenism.

But in the culture of the pagan world the Christians of the third century also claimed to share. Christian missionaries had naturally striven from the first to present their appeal to the Gentile world through the medium of conceptions with which it was already familiar. The Jewish Messiah thus became the *Logos* of the Supreme God. It was sought to reinforce the Christian message by showing that it was in conformity with Greek thought: the earliest extant apology addressed to the world of pagan culture called in evidence the words of 'certain of your own poets.' In the second century the Greek apologists present Christianity in so philosophic a form that at times it is no easy matter to recognize that they are seeking to recommend the same gospel as that proclaimed in the books of the New Testament[2]. There can have been few missionaries who rejected all Greek thought with the thoroughness of Tatian, who rejoiced in being a 'barbarian.' Yet it may be doubted whether these earlier defenders of the faith had many readers; it was in Alexandria through such teachers as Clement and Origen that pagan thought was adopted not merely as a missionary expedient, but was woven into the texture of Christian theology. The *De principiis* of Origen is a landmark, and from the influence of Origen, whether by attraction or repulsion, no later Christian writer could escape.

During the second half of the third century, while the Christian Church was consolidating its position after persecution and increasing its membership, pagan cults, it would seem, were suffering severely from the economic crisis: ephemeral emperors had neither time nor money for the endowment of religion, and the liberality of private citizens was paralysed. The evidence of

[1] de Labriolle, *op. cit.* pp. 223 *sqq.* The attitude of Porphyry to Jesus has been much discussed, see Bidez, *op. cit.* p. 77 and de Labriolle, *op. cit.* pp. 279 *sqq.* who gives references to the judgments of Harnack and Geffcken.

[2] An illuminating study of this aspect of the work of the early apologists is C. N. Moody's *The Mind of the Early Converts*, London, n.d. (1920).

inscriptions tells the same story both in the Eastern and Western provinces of the Empire[1]. This decline of paganism was the Church's opportunity: doctors, lawyers, rhetoricians—the representatives of the culture of the day—were joining the Christian community. Many were, however, still repelled by the prejudice of the educated against the vulgar simplicity of the style of the Christian scriptures[2]: in a world where literary form and verbal elaboration were so highly valued the Christians were regarded as 'barbarians,' 'ignorant folk' ($\dot{\alpha}\mu\alpha\theta\acute{\epsilon}\sigma\tau\alpha\tau\iota$)[3], completely lacking in the charms and graces of civilized life. It is for pagans such as these that Lactantius wrote his apologetic works. That which constitutes the permanent importance of the writings of Lactantius is that here one versed in the style and thought of Cicero makes his appeal to men of culture, and selects for his defence of Christianity the discussion of those problems with which his pagan contemporaries were wrestling. In the *De Opificio Dei* it is the problem of divine providence, maintained against Epicurean denials, which is illustrated in minutest—and sometimes humorous—detail by a consideration of man's body as the handiwork of God. In the *De Ira Dei* it is the impassibility of God—divine justice demands that He should be angry against the sinner: righteous anger is but an activity of divine providence.

It is this principle which inspires Lactantius' interpretation of history in the *De mortibus persecutorum*. Jurists had written Introductions (*Institutiones*) to the study of law, and now the time was ripe for an Introduction to Christianity in which the errors of paganism should be exposed and the true foundations of Christian worship and Christian ethics set forth. During the great persecution Lactantius produced his *Divine Institutes*. The early apologists had made use of the evidence of the Hebrew prophets: they were older than the oldest Greek scriptures, and by the fulfilment of their prophecies their authority even for pagans should be established. But Lactantius is writing for men of culture who recognized no such authority in the books of the Hebrew prophets, and thus his appeal is primarily to the works of pagan authors or to works such as the Sibylline oracles which he failed to recognize as coming from the hands of Jews or Christians. A man trained in a rhetorical school is addressing those of his own world. Modern critics of his work have complained that it

[1] Cf. J. Geffcken, *Der Ausgang des griechisch-römischen Heidentums*, ch. ii.

[2] Used as an argument in favour of Christianity by Arnobius, *Adv. Nationes*, I, 58.   [3] Cf. Bidez, *op. cit.* p. 21.

lacks originality, that his attacks upon the gods of paganism are composed of traditional material which could have had but little relevance for those schooled in the philosophic thought of the third century. It may be doubted whether such criticism is justified. We have perhaps laid too much stress upon the significance of the 'solar monotheism' of Aurelian: it is not easy to say how far the exclusiveness of that cult survived its founder's death. Philosophy does not proclaim a sole god: Plotinus is no monotheist[1]. The faith of philosophy is a divine monarchy, and the Summus Deus rules over lesser deities each with his own sphere of function. There was still reason to state the case for monotheism.

But that is not all: in face of the decline in the public cult of the gods, Porphyry sought in his later years to arouse the cultured pagan world from its religious lethargy by propounding startling questions (ἀπορίαι) which formed a challenge to its traditions (in his letter to Anebo). His *De abstinentia* went further: here the ascetic and religious enthusiast undermined the whole basis of the public worship of the gods: in his last work, his 'letter' to his wife Marcella, there are echoes of those Christian scriptures which he had closely studied. But paganism refused to accept so dangerous an ally from whose works Christians could draw such effective material for their criticism of the older faith. Before the peril of the Christian challenge this was no time to palter with a modernism which made the largest concessions to the foe: the one thing needed was a fundamentalism which admitted of no doubts, which re-affirmed the whole portentous inheritance—gods and statues, bloody sacrifices and libations, magic and theurgy. Iamblichus represents the spirit of one who writes after a pagan Church has issued its encyclical *Pascendi*. There were, it would seem, even those who thought that the Senate should perform the function of a pagan Holy Office and establish an Index of forbidden books. On this list should be placed such works as Cicero's *De natura deorum* and *De divinatione*—books 'quibus Christiana religio comprobetur et vetustatis opprimatur auctoritas[2].' It was to no solar monotheism that Diocletian professed allegiance: it was to many gods and to many local cults that he made his dedications. The pagan revival of Diocletian is essentially polytheistic. Lactantius knew what he was doing when he levelled his sarcasms against the gods and especially against Juppiter and Hercules— the patrons of the reigning Jovian and Herculian dynasties.

---

[1] Cf. Geffcken, *op. cit.* pp. 49–50.
[2] Arnobius, *Adv. Nationes*, III, 7. Cf. de Labriolle, *op. cit.* pp. 316–17.

The *Divine Institutes* have often been compared with earlier Christian apologies: it might be more fruitful to read the work of Lactantius alongside that of Porphyry's closing years, for Porphyry is not an original thinker, he does not stand solitary like Plotinus; despite the tide of obscurantism which at this time overwhelmed pagan thought there must have been not a few religious pagans with the scruples, the doubts and the aspirations of a Porphyry to whom Lactantius could address his apologia. Against the externalism of a religion of cultus and bodily acts Lactantius can assert that it matters not *how* man worships: the fundamental question is always *what* man worships. Over against *vetustatis auctoritas* Lactantius sets his majestic appeal[1] to human reason and the progress which can be made through man's intelligence and its criticism of tradition[2]. By their return to the past—in the interest of the faith—the pagans have only rendered a reasoned defence of that faith more difficult. Lactantius complains that the supporters of polytheism flee from argument, since they have no confidence in their own case: 'et idcirco disceptatione sublata, "pellitur e medio sapientia, vi geritur res[3]."' 'Cur enim tam crudeliter saeviant nisi quia metuunt, ne in dies invalescente iustitia cum diis suis cariosis relinquantur?[4]' Lactantius will meet violence with the argument of Christian certainty.

As Lactantius had studied Cicero, so Methodius had become familiar with Plato (see p. 617), while Africa produced in Arnobius another apologist from the schools of rhetoric. The *Adversus Nationes*, like the *Divine Institutes*, was written during the persecution, but between the work of Arnobius and that of Lactantius there is a vast difference. Indeed the fascination of the Christian literature produced before the Council of Nicaea lies largely in the fact that tradition and dogma did not confine men so closely as they did in later centuries.

To Lactantius the divine Providence is the centre of his faith: Arnobius denies that Providence. For Lactantius the wrath of God is a part of His justice; for Arnobius to attribute anger to God is blasphemy. Lactantius had devoted an entire monograph to the praise of man's body as the handiwork of God; to Arnobius man appears so miserable and abject that it would be an insult to Highest God to regard Him as the creator of this bag of ordure and of urine: some lesser power must have fashioned man's body. To Lactantius as to Origen the problem of evil can only

[1] *Div. Inst.* v, 20.   [2] Cf. Eusebius, *Praep. Evang.* IV, 20–21.
[3] *Div. Inst.* v, 1, 5.   [4] *Ib.* v, 12, 13.

be faced if we believe in the freedom of man's will: Eusebius redeems the weariness of the *Contra Hieroclem* by an impassioned assertion of man's freedom from inexorable fate[1]: to Arnobius the soul of man has been so contaminated by evil influences in its descent to earth that it possesses no freedom and thus before the coming of Christ it could commit no sin. Christ offered to the soul which in itself is not immortal the hope of immortality: the rejection of Christ's offer by the human soul brings sin to birth. Whence this poor thing, the human soul, came we cannot know and it is idle to enquire; what we can know is that its neutral character with its bare potentiality of survival can be gloriously changed by Christ into the fullness of a life which shall have no end. At the heart of Christianity there is a profound pessimism— 'without me ye can do nothing'—but never has that pessimism received more ruthless expression than in the *Adversus Nationes*. 'If I had not come, they would not have had sin': no one has taken this text to heart as did Arnobius.

The devout worshipper of pagan images and pagan relics[2] has appropriated the salvation brought by Christ from the Supreme God (*a deo principe*): he has received the gift of immortality unknown before[3]. This it seems was for Arnobius the decisive fact. His Saviour Christ Jesus had abolished death and brought life and immortality to light through the gospel. It is a strange Christianity which the African rhetorician expounds, but the triumph of a release from a great fear inspires the whole of his bitter attack upon the gods. Hierocles in an apology for paganism had sung the praises of the Summus Deus: we are the true worshippers of the Summus Deus, retorts Arnobius, 'magistro Christo.'

At a time when Pamphilus with his band of loyal disciples was labouring in selfless devotion to maintain the tradition of scholarship inherited from Origen, when pagan rhetoricians were deserting the schools to devote themselves to the service of the Church, the culture of the old world was finding a home amongst 'the barbarians': pagan and Christian shared a common appreciation of the legacy of the past: they were divided only by religion or by a philosophy which was itself essentially religious.

---

[1] Cf. Eusebius, *Praep. Evang.* VI, 6.
[2] I, 39.   [3] I, 65.

II. STATE AND CHURCH

What of the Roman State? Repression of a faith may clearly be either political or religious in its purpose: it may seek to avert a social peril or crush a belief which may endanger the safety of man's soul. The ancient world, it has been said, knew of religious cults, and of myths and legends, it had no dogmas which were necessary for man's salvation. Thus it could easily adopt the principle 'cuius regio eius religio.' Rome did not seek to suppress local cults, she rather endeavoured to affiliate them to her own national traditions. The idea of an exclusive individual faith which was not the traditional faith of a nation was foreign to Roman thought: it was natural to interpret such a faith as merely a veil for a deep-rooted hostility to State and Society. These sectaries were bent on turning the inhabited world upside down: here was a revolutionary transvaluation of all traditional values. To the modern student of the history of the Roman Empire it is the curious timidity of the Caesars which seems so remarkable—the queer anxiety lest in any way the hard-won peace and security of the Mediterranean world should be threatened: the establishment of the Pax Romana had been bought at so high a price that even a municipal fire-brigade in an Asian city was too perilous an association to receive imperial sanction. And in Christianity the Caesars were faced by no municipal association, but by a far-flung secret brotherhood. These 'Bolsheviks' must be suppressed. The Roman persecutions of the Christians, as has been pointed out[1], have been judged by their effects and treated as the prototype of religious intolerance. With regard to its motives the procedure of the Roman State can be censured only as an excess of political intolerance; in its results it constituted an undeniable violation of the Christian's liberty of conscience.

The persecutions of the Christians have been considered elsewhere in this volume in their effects upon the life of the Church (pp. 515 *sqq.*); in this place a brief retrospect is necessary in which that repression may be viewed from the standpoint of the Roman State. What was at first the precise legal basis for the persecution it is perhaps impossible for us to determine: was it founded upon successive decisions of Roman magistrates acting under their wide discretionary powers (*coercitio*), such decisions gradually hardening into a binding presumption of law?—or was

---

[1] F. Ruffini, *Religious Liberty*, pp. 21–2; cf. T. Lyon, *The Theory of Religious Liberty in England 1603–39*, Cambridge, 1937, p. 21 *sq.*

there, as the present writer thinks probable, a direct imperial pronouncement proscribing the sect? In any event, by the time of Trajan it had become established that the persistent avowal of Christianity carried as its consequence the penalty of death. From that position, in the view of the present writer, the Roman State never receded until A.D. 311—until that year the Christian Church was never granted express recognition as a lawful corporation (but see p. 207)[1]. Yet experience proved that Christians might be regarded as a peculiar brand of malefactors; against them the Roman magistrate was not under the obligation of proceeding on his own initiative—'conquirendi non sunt.' That initiative must be taken by the informer, and recantation of his faith secured for the Christian immunity from punishment. In fact the Roman State no longer believed that Christians constituted a danger to society, though repression of the sectaries might at times provide a useful outlet for popular discontent. Toleration in our modern world, it has been maintained, is the result of social development, it rests solely on the basis of empiricism; 'practically we are tolerant because no harm comes of our being so[2].' 'Toleration is one of the most valuable empirical maxims of modern politics[3].' When England in the early years of the nineteenth century discovered that Unitarians were not in any way dangerous to the peace and welfare of the kingdom but were 'very decent, well-behaved and well-to-do people' the penalties imposed by 9 William III, c. 35 were repealed for their benefit so far as concerned persons denying the doctrine of the Trinity[4]. Similarly Rome discovered that the early Christians were no menace to the State, but with traditional Roman conservatism the Empire did not pass any relieving act. Parliament admitted that it had been in error; the Caesars made no such direct admission.

[1] In the view of the present writer, the contention that Christianity was a *religio licita* as maintained by G. Krüger, *Die Rechtsstellung der vorkonstantinischen Kirchen*, Stuttgart, 1935, is untenable. Under what title (if any) the Christian church held its property in the pre-Constantinian period is still uncertain. To the references given in N. H. Baynes, 'Constantine and the Christian Church,' *Proc. of the British Academy*, xv, 71 *sq.* add L. Schnorr v. Carolsfeld, *Gesch. d. juristischen Person*, 1, especially iv Abschnitt, § 18; P. W. Duff, *Personality in Roman Private Law*, Cambridge, 1938, pp. 169 *sqq.*

& Sherwin-White, in *Journal of Theolog. Studies*, 1952.

[2] Cf. Mandell Creighton, *Persecution and Tolerance*, London, 1895, p. 114.

[3] A. J. Balfour, cited by Creighton.

[4] Cf. F. Pollock, *Essays in Jurisprudence and Ethics*, London, 1882, pp. 160 *sqq.*

Thus it was that even as late as the first half of the third century, when some disaster or natural catastrophe such as an earthquake suggested that the gods were angered with men, the populace might demand a persecution of the Christians in order to placate the wrath of an outraged Heaven, and then it is the attitude of the provincial governor which determines the severity of the repression: it is to the provincial governors that Tertullian addresses his apologia.

During the early decades of the third century national Roman feeling had been weakened; the Severi had favoured the provinces at the expense of Rome. When Caracalla had extended Roman citizenship to the provincial population, the Empire became a cosmopolis, and universalism could afford to be tolerant towards a faith which had from the first claimed the whole inhabited world for its Lord. Under a Syrian dynasty Origen could be summoned to the imperial court. It might have seemed that the reconciliation between the Roman State and the Christian Church would be realized through a peaceful evolution and mutual understanding. But the crisis of the third century brought other men and other ways of thought to the fore. In the rude soldiery of the Danube lands the Empire found its defenders, and on their side the Danubian soldiers adopted with the enthusiastic conviction of the newly converted the belief in the imperial traditions of Rome and its pagan past[1]. It is this new romanism of the Danube lands which revives the hostility of the Roman State towards those who had abandoned the worship of the Roman gods. The millenary celebration of the founding of Rome had recalled the pagan traditions forcibly to men's minds: Roman greatness had ever been dependent on the favour of the divine powers—on the maintenance of the *Pax Deorum*: now that the Empire was threatened with unexampled perils, how could success be more surely guaranteed than by a massive demonstration of an Empire's loyalty? It may be suggested that some such thought led the Pannonian Emperor Decius to issue his command that the entire population of the Roman world should by the act of sacrifice attest its devotion to the gods (see pp. 202, 521). The situation is changed: persecution becomes once more the policy of the Roman State, though that policy is now no longer sustained by any widespread hatred and animosity against the Christians. The initiative in repression has passed from the people to the central government.

---

[1] Cf. A. Alföldi, 'Die Vorherrschaft der Pannonier im Römerreiche etc.,' *Fünfundzwanzig Jahre Römisch-germanische Kommission.*

But even so it is not easy to say whether the order of Decius constituted in its motive a religious persecution of the Christians. Decius, for the welfare of a Roman world threatened with disaster, has resort to a religious act in which every inhabitant of that world should do uniform homage to the gods of Rome: is not this Act of Uniformity at least primarily a political measure? It would seem that Decius did not demand from the Christian any abjuration of his own faith—only that he should join in a 'supplicatio' such as Rome had traditionally employed in times of national crisis. It is by studying the persecution of another religious minority that we may best understand this measure of Decius. The hardships suffered by the Catholics in the early years of the reign of Elizabeth— are these to be regarded as a religious persecution? 'Burleigh was aiming at political power, and, for this, unity between Church and State was necessary[1].' Elizabeth writes[2] 'The Queen would not have any of their consciences unnecessarily sifted to know what affection they had to the old religion,' and if she has lately done so in the case of a few prisoners 'yet the cause thereof hath grown merely of themselves in that they have first manifestly broken the laws established for religion, in not coming at all to the church.' The first clause repels the accusation of oppressing people for their faith which is just what the second clause admits. Elizabeth's subjects are free to believe what they will, if in the interests of the State they join in the common worship.

Not dissimilar may have been the motive of the Emperor Decius: by these assurances of devotion the gods of Rome should be contented and render to the Romans the reward of their loyalty. The sudden command to sacrifice falling upon the Church after a long period of security caused wholesale apostasy, but for our present purpose it is more interesting to note that the Emperor's conviction could hardly have been generally held by those who were charged with the enforcement of the imperial order, otherwise it would not have been possible for Christians without compliance with that order to obtain so easily as they did the official certificate of sacrifice performed; further, as soon as the Emperor's attention was diverted to military operations, the proceedings against the Christians were suspended. The persecution begun in the winter of 249 was already at an end, at least in Carthage and in Rome, by the Easter of 251, although Decius did not meet his death until the following summer[3].

[1] A. O. Meyer, *England and the Catholic Church under Queen Elizabeth*, London, 1916, p. 89.   [2] *Ib.* p. 128.

[3] For another view of the Decian persecution see above, pp. 202 *sqq.*

The outworn calumnies against the Christians were discredited: pagans as well as their fellow-believers had been tended by the Christians during the great plague which devastated the empire in the middle years of the third century. Folk had come to know this peculiar people and pagans shared with Christians in the common life of the Roman cities. This change in popular sentiment is of the first significance for the understanding of the last great persecution. Outside of Egypt there were, it would seem, but few cities in the Roman East which emulated Gaza[1] in its popular enthusiasm for the older faith; in the Western provinces Maxentius, though himself a convinced worshipper of the gods, will find it prudent to adopt an attitude of tolerance.

The attempt of Valerian to break up the corporate life of the Church by striking at the bishops and the clergy and by forbidding all assemblies of Christians is interesting, since it would appear to have served as the model for those who instigated the last great persecution. Valerian's captivity in Persia, in the view of Dionysius of Alexandria, was the vengeance of the God of the Christians taken upon the oppressor of His people. Decius dead on the northern frontier, Valerian in the hands of the enemy, not a few pagans may have asked themselves: did such a result justify the effort to restore the *Pax Deorum*? It is certain that Gallienus handed back to Christian bishops the property which his father had confiscated, that the persecution was stayed, and that henceforth the Church was left in peace. The initiative of the Roman State had borne no fruit which could encourage an emperor to renew the challenge.

Between the Roman State and the Christian Church there had stood no greater obstacle to reconciliation than the worship of the emperor. The pagan could not understand the Christian objection to this tribute of respect to the ruler of the Roman world—the Christian refusal puzzled and irritated many a well-meaning Roman governor: it seemed to him, as to Marcus Aurelius, a perverse obstinacy. But what if the godhead of the emperor were after all a mistake?—what if the emperor were not God, but only God's vicegerent on earth? It was to this conviction, it would appear to the present writer, that Aurelian came: it was this view of his office that Diocletian held—he was not Juppiter, but Jovius, Juppiter's representative, his colleague was not Hercules, but Herculius. If this be true, the way to an understanding between

---

[1] Cf. B. Violet, 'Die Palästinischen Märtyrer des Eusebius von Cäsarea,' *Texte und Unters.* XIV, Heft 4, 1896, p. 17. See also above p. 447 and S. A. Cook, *The Religion of Ancient Palestine in the light of archaeology*, p. 186.

pagan ruler and Christian subject was open, for even the *pros-kynesis*—the prostration before the emperor—which had now become obligatory in court ceremonial—was not the worship of a god, but merely the outward symbol of homage to a human master. The cult of the emperors plays a very subordinate part in the last great persecution[1].

After the death of Valerian the Roman State had shown itself ready to trust the Christian and to welcome him to its service, and the individual Christian, whatever might be the official view of the Church, was clearly prepared to respond to these advances. The appeal with which Celsus had ended his *True Discourse* seemed in a fair way to be answered. It is no easy task to form any picture of the life of the ordinary Christian in the third century: how far did the views held by the leaders of Christian thought find expression in the contacts of believers with the pagan world about them? At this time when Christian exegetes could maintain that it wanted yet another two hundred years before the beginning of the 'last things,' the immediate expectation of the *parousia*, the second coming of Christ, had passed: what was the Christian's attitude to the Roman State, how far could he participate in its administration? Early canons had condemned military service. Origen is an intransigent pacifist; in the *Contra Celsum*, he had solemnly stated that Christians would not fight for the emperor even when called upon for service; the Christian's prayers are his *militia*. Similarly in the West the condemnation of the military profession is proclaimed with violent rhetoric by the rigorist Tertullian, and again at the beginning of the fourth century by another African, Lactantius[2]. Yet it is certain that such prohibitions can have had but little effect upon the general Christian practice. There were Christian soldiers in the Roman army under Marcus Aurelius[3]; in the persecution of Decius a small detachment of soldiers guarding a Christian prisoner declared itself to share the faith of the accused[4]. During the crisis of the third-century invasions the authorities doubtless asked no questions; they may have even been prepared discreetly to refuse

---

[1] Cf. H. Delehaye, 'La persécution dans l'Armée sous Dioclétien,' *Acad. royale de Belgique, Bulletin: Classe des Lettres etc.*, 1921, pp. 150–66.

[2] Note that Maximilian and Marcellus were both Africans (see below).

[3] There were soldiers of the XIIth legion stationed in Melitene, a district where Christianity early made many converts: cf. A. Harnack in *Sitz. Ber. Preuss. Akad.* 1894, p. 835.

[4] σύνταγμα στρατιωτικόν, Dionysius of Alexandria ap. Eusebius, *Hist. Eccl.* VI, 41, 22 *sq.*

to notice that at the military sacrifices the Christian protected himself from the demons by making the sign of the cross, just as the worshipper of Mithras was excused, it would seem, from wearing the festival crown, since his god was his crown. There must have been many Christians both in the civil and military service of the Empire when Diocletian came to the throne. And in the life of the municipalities Christians no longer sought to live apart from their pagan neighbours: they held office as municipal senators; apparently, to judge from the canons of the Council of Elvira, they were elected even to municipal priesthoods. Save in exceptional cases, as in the Tembris valley in Anatolia (see above, p. 458 *sq.*), the Christian did not desire to endanger his fellow-believers by any aggressive profession of his nonconformity: 'probably the same policy which placed on the gravestone an appeal to "the god," leaving the reader to understand in his own sense a term common to both Christians and Pagans, modified in similar slight ways many of the other forms of social and municipal life[1].' Alongside of the growth of asceticism and of a morality of ever-increasing strictness, there was admitted in practice amongst Christians a second ethic of the life in the world[2]. It might well have seemed that in the sphere of a common service of the State conciliation was slowly winning the day.

Indeed it is interesting to observe that at the very time when Christians were beginning freely to enter the service of the Empire, pagan philosophers were losing interest in political life. Plotinus sought to withdraw his friends from public office: 'a senator, Rogatianus, advanced to such detachment from political ambitions that he gave up all his property, dismissed all his slaves, renounced every dignity and on the point of taking up his praetorship, the lictors already at the door, refused to come out or to have anything to do with the office[3].' Celsus was profoundly concerned for the defence of the Empire, but there is no trace of such anxiety in the works of Porphyry[4].

And, further, there remained the fact that throughout all the persecutions no Christian had raised the standard of revolt[5]. From the time of the earliest apologists Christians had indeed constantly affirmed their loyalty to the emperor, for his power,

[1] Sir W. M. Ramsay, *Cities and Bishoprics*, II, p. 504.
[2] For this the eighth chapter of the first book of the *Demonstratio Evangelica* of Eusebius is evidence. Ed. Heikel, p. 39, ll. 26 *sqq.*
[3] Porphyry, *Life of Plotinus*, 7.
[4] Bidez, *op. cit.* pp. 67–8.
[5] Tertullian, *Apol.* 35.

however much he might abuse it, was God-given, and thus prayers for the emperor had always formed a part of a Christian's worship. Here surely was a foundation upon which wise statesmanship might build. To some far-seeing Christians such as Melito (see p. 461) there had already come the vision that Church and Empire were in the Providence of God ordained not to enmity, but to co-operation: Augustus and Christ were both the bringers of peace to a distracted world: in God's good time the alliance thus foreshadowed would be accomplished fact. There were many followers of Christ who were prepared to give their loyalty to a State which, while sustaining order and justice, would not demand of them apostasy from their faith. Lactantius is not only a Christian, he is a Roman who shrinks with terror from the thought that one day according to the scriptures of his religion the Empire of Rome would pass, as had already passed the empires of Babylon and of Alexander[1].

III. DIOCLETIAN'S POLICY

This is the background against which Diocletian undertakes his task of re-organization and reform: his effort is to unite all the forces of the Empire and to harness them to the work of imperial restoration. Why should he exclude those who are prepared to lend their aid? He seizes the opportunity: it should be made easy for Christians to play their part. Those who were willing to hold office were freed from the obligation of pagan sacrifice. For himself the Emperor chose the worship of Juppiter: he would re-affirm as the delegate of Jove the religious past of Rome: his colleague in the West should under the protection of Hercules labour, as had his divine patron, for mankind: 'c'était le reveil, dans le monde romain, de ce double culte de Jupiter maître du Capitole et d'Hercule héros du Palatin qui, depuis l'origine, avait fait l'orgueil et la sainteté de la Ville Éternelle[2].' The gods of paganism had not been, as was the Semitic Jehovah, jealous deities; there was room in the working-out of his task for the collaboration of the worshippers of the Christian God. Statesmanship could hardly come to any other conclusion.

---

[1] *Div. Inst.* VII, 15, 11.
[2] C. Jullian, *Histoire de la Gaule*, VII, p. 50. Diocletian was a Dalmatian; Juppiter and Hercules thus closely associated were specially worshipped in Dalmatia: cf. J. Toutain, *Les cultes païens dans l'empire romain*, I, pp. 405–7. For the Roman—and not Oriental—character of the cult of Juppiter and Hercules cf. G. Costa, *Religione e Politica nell'impero romano*, pp. 32–87.

Some modern scholars have argued that the new reign began with a persecution of the Christians: have we such evidence as would constrain us to adopt this view? To the present writer this appears to be a point of crucial import for the understanding of Diocletian's religious policy. Two considerations have to be borne in mind: the contemporary historians Lactantius and Eusebius have no knowledge of such persecution; Maximian, who was appointed by Diocletian to rule the Western provinces of the Empire, always followed faithfully the lead of the senior Augustus; he cannot be thought to have originated a course of action to which Diocletian was opposed. Nor is it likely, as some late accounts of Christian martyrdoms would imply, that Diocletian himself visited Rome shortly after his victory on the Margus and there began an attack upon the Christians at the beginning of his reign; for such a visit we have no independent evidence save a statement in Zonaras[1], and it would appear otherwise improbable. The martyrdom of the Quattuor Coronati has been placed at this time in Rome, but the Roman Passio deserves no credence; S. Genesius, the converted actor, whose martyrdom appears to be dated early in Diocletian's reign, is probably not a historical character: the S. Genesius whose cult was later celebrated in Rome may well have been S. Genesius of Arles, and the story of S. Genesius the actor is, it has been plausibly suggested, an adaptation of an Eastern legend. The Acta of S. Sebastian cannot be used as a historical source[2]. The presumption would thus appear to be unfavourable to the view that the new order was inaugurated by religious oppression. For a persecution conducted by Maximian in Gaul no reliance can be placed upon the stories of the exploits of the ubiquitous Rictiovarus[3]; he has all the appearance of being the creation of a hagiographer's imagination; it is possible that S. Maurice may have suffered martyrdom for some breach of military discipline, but until we can determine upon what sources the fifth-century account of the sufferings of the Christians in the Theban Legion is based, the historical student cannot use that document[4]. So far as the present

---

[1] Zonaras, XII, 31 (p. 614).

[2] Cf. H. Delehaye, *Étude sur le Légendier romain*, Index *s.v.* Sebastianus.

[3] On Rictiovar (or Reciofarus, the reading of the oldest MS.) cf. C. Jullian, 'Notes gallo-romaines, 100,' *Rev. ét. anc.* xxv, 1923, 367–78, who thinks it possible that there may have been such a person. For L. Duchesne, *Fastes épiscopaux de l'ancienne Gaule*, III, 1915, pp. 141–52, he is a 'personnage inconnu d'ailleurs et très évidemment imaginaire.'

[4] For the martyrdom of the Theban Legion see the Bibliography.

writer can judge, there is no adequate ground for the supposition
that at this time either Diocletian or Maximian broke the religious
truce which had been preserved since the accession of Gallienus[1].

We have seen that there were rigorists in the Church who
denied to the Christian the right to serve in the army, but that
this was not the general view[2]. In individual cases, it is true, the
old prejudice against the army was still alive. The father of the
young recruit Maximilian was a Christian veteran; he presented
his son for enrolment, but the son's conscience forbade him to
serve. For this breach of military discipline Maximilian was put
to death, but here there is no question of pagan religious observance: Maximilian was not called upon to sacrifice to the gods.
Similarly at a feast given on the Emperor's birthday Marcellus, a
centurion, stripped off his military belt, and declared that his
loyalty to Christ did not allow him to serve another master[3]. This
is not persecution by the Roman State: it is the tradition of
Tertullian's rigorism which thus suddenly awakened the scruples
of a Christian soldier.

The whole re-organization of the Empire was carried through,
the new Caesars were appointed, and still no religious difficulty
arose. And then, according to Lactantius, 'some time[4]' before
the general persecution, at a public sacrifice offered for the purpose of learning the will of Heaven by inspection of the livers of
the sacrificial animals, the Christians in the presence both of
Diocletian and Galerius[5] crossed themselves to ward off evil from

---

[1] For the legends of martyrdoms in France under Maximian in the early
days of the reign cf. the carefully guarded statement of the evidence in C. Jullian, *Histoire de la Gaule*, VII, pp. 67–72. He notes that '*aucun de ces martyrs
ne paraît appartenir à la cour ou à l'armée.*' It is of course possible that a provincial governor may have proceeded against some Gallic Christians during
these years.

[2] See above, p. 659.

[3] It is indeed stated in the Acta that this was done *apud signa legionis*, but
there is no statement that any cult of the *signa* influenced Marcellus. It
might be suggested that there was some connection with the new form of the
religion of the army of which Domaszewski found evidence during the reign
of Diocletian—the worship of the genii: thus by the side of the genius
castrorum (which even precedes Juppiter O.M. in *C.I.L.* III, 11111) we
find the genius legionis, the genius cohortium vigilum, the genius cohortium praetoriarum (*C.I.L.* VI, 216) while the genius Populi Romani of
the coinage would be, in Domaszewski's view, that of the *signa* of the Roman
army: cf. *Westdeutsche Zeitschr.* 14, 1895, pp. 113–14. For the Acta of
Maximilian and Marcellus see the Bibliography.

[4] *de mort. pers.* 11: *aliquanto tempore.*

[5] *Div. Inst.* IV, 27, 4, *sacrificantibus dominis.*

the demons. The augurs failed to find the customary marks on the livers and repeated the sacrifice without result until the chief augur Tagis pronounced that no answer had been obtained because of the presence at the rite of profane persons. Diocletian was furious and ordered that all in the palace should sacrifice and on refusal be beaten: letters were sent to the military commanders that the soldiers should sacrifice or be dismissed the service. It has sometimes been doubted whether so slight an incident could have had so far-reaching an effect. But it must be remembered that Christians and pagans alike believed in magic: it was one thing to tolerate Christians, another to allow them to disturb a solemn pagan rite. Dionysius under Valerian had written of the Christians that 'indeed they are and were capable by their presence and through being seen merely by their breath or word to scatter the designs of the baneful demons[1]' and in the *Divine Institutes* (not merely in the *De mortibus persecutorum*) Lactantius states that if a bystander makes the sign of the cross on the forehead, the pagan priest can obtain no answer from the gods[2]. This has, he continues, often been the principal reason why bad emperors have persecuted the Christians[3]. When account is taken of the beliefs of the time, we have every reason to trust Lactantius. But the trouble passed, and Diocletian took no further measures.

Galerius, it will have been noticed, had been present at this public sacrifice, and, according to Eusebius, it was Galerius who began the persecution: he forced the Christian officers[4] in his army either to sacrifice or to leave the service. This purification of the army was carried through by a *stratopedarches*—a master of the soldiery—acting, we must presume, under the orders of the Caesar. One or two Christians suffered the death penalty, but in what circumstances Eusebius does not tell us. If, as seems natural, the *stratopedarches* of the *Church History* (VIII, 4, 3) is to be identified with the *magister militiae* of Eusebius' *Chronicon*, these measures were taken between the years 298 and 301[5]. It may be suggested that Galerius was acting under the order of Diocletian reported by Lactantius. It is to be noted that in A.D. 298 Galerius had won his brilliant success over Persia and

[1] Eusebius, *Hist. Eccl.* VII, 10, 4.
[2] Cf. Arnobius, *Adv. Nationes*, I, 46, *s.f.*
[3] *Div. Inst.* IV, 27, 3 *sq.* This may indeed be a reference to the letter of Dionysius (preserved by Eusebius) attributing the persecution of the Christians by Valerian to the instigation of the magician Macrianus.
[4] Cf. Delehaye, *op. cit.* p. 5 on Eusebius *Hist. Eccl.* VIII, 4.
[5] Cf. A. Fliche and V. Martin (Edd.), *Histoire de l'Église*, II, p. 458.

this must have greatly strengthened his position. He hoped, Eusebius says, thus to pave the way for a general policy of repression.

In the winter of 302–3 Diocletian and his Caesar were both in Nicomedia, and here, according to Lactantius[1], Galerius pressed upon his Augustus the necessity for a rigorous persecution of the Christians; Diocletian continued to resist. Galerius was supported by a circle of Neoplatonist philosophers, among them Hierocles who was at this time consular governor (*consularis*) of Bithynia. Diocletian at length agreed to refer the question to the oracle of the Milesian Apollo, who answered 'ut divinae religionis inimicus.' This must be the same consultation of the oracle as that of which Constantine speaks[2] when the god replied that the just (οἱ δίκαιοι) upon the earth hindered him from declaring the truth and that this was the cause of false oracles issuing from the tripods[3]. To the insistence of his friends, the Caesar and the god, Diocletian yielded, but only on condition that blood should not be shed. In the opinion of the present writer— an opinion which would certainly not meet with general assent— both Eusebius and Lactantius consistently regarded Galerius as the author of the persecution, and in that view he would concur.

IV. THE PERSECUTION

We cannot recover the text of the fatal first edict which inaugurated the persecution—it is a curious fact that the text of no imperial edict has been cited in the historical *Acta* of the martyrs— but the principal provisions can be stated with some certainty: the Christian churches were to be destroyed, as well as, it would appear, such private houses as were regularly used for Christian services; all assemblages of Christians for worship were forbidden. The scriptures and liturgical books were to be surrendered and publicly burnt. Christians belonging to the higher classes were deprived of their privileges, e.g. immunity from torture in judicial process, and all Christians were placed outside the law, being forbidden to defend their rights in the courts. Lactantius closes his account of the edict with the words 'libertatem denique ac vocem non haberent.' Eusebius in the same position writes 'Those who were in "*oiketiai*," if they persisted in their profession

---

[1] *De mort. pers.* 10 *sq.*   [2] Eusebius, *Vita Const.* II, 50.
[3] The present writer is unable to follow H. Grégoire in his '*restauration un peu romancée peut-être*' of an inscription, *Mélanges Holleaux*, pp. 81–91.

of Christianity, were to be deprived of their freedom[1].' The words have been much discussed, and their meaning is uncertain. But the measures taken against the Christians by Valerian may have served as a precedent on this occasion[2]: in the former persecution Christians serving in the imperial bureaux, the Caesariani, were, if they persisted in their faith, reduced to slavery[3] and it may be suggested that this is the meaning of the phrase used by Eusebius[4].

It was decided that on the festival of the Terminalia (Feb. 23, 303) a term should be set to the Christian heresy: the imperial agents entered the cathedral at Nicomedia, and the work of destruction began. The following day the edict was placarded in the streets of the city: a Christian[5] straightway tore it down with the taunt 'More victories over Goths and Sarmatians.' He was arrested and burnt to death—'legitime coctus' as Lactantius writes[6].

There was to be no bloodshed Diocletian had determined, but that decision was abandoned when twice in succession fire broke out in the imperial palace. On the second occasion Galerius ostentatiously left the city—he was not going to be burnt alive by Christian incendiaries. A plot of Galerius against the Christians—so Lactantius: arson by the Christians—so Galerius: the palace struck by lightning according to the account of Constantine as quoted in the *Oratio ad Sanctos*—the cause of the fire must remain for us, as it was for contemporaries, a mystery. But a charge of arson, then as in later times, may have served political ends. Diocletian was furious, and, in the enquiry which followed, many of the imperial servants met their deaths: for a short time there seems to have been something like a reign of terror in Nicomedia. Then news came of revolts in Melitene and in Syria instigated, it was said, by the Christians. The Church must be deprived of its leaders. The clergy by a second edict were con-

---

[1] τοὺς δ' ἐν οἰκετίαις εἰ ἐπιμένοιεν τῇ τῶν χριστιανισμοῦ προθέσει ἐλευθερίας στερεῖσθαι Hist. Eccl. VIII, 2, 4 (ἐλευθερίας στερίσκεσθαι. De mart. Pal. Praef. 1).

[2] *E.g.* no meetings of Christians to be held.　　　[3] Cyprian, *Ep.* 80.

[4] The imperial chamberlains Dorotheus and Gorgonius are martyred ἅμα πλείοσιν τῆς βασιλικῆς οἰκετίας Hist. Eccl. VIII, 6, 5; ὅ τε γὰρ ἡγεμονικῆς οἰκετίας θεράπων. *De mart Pal.* 11 (long version), Greek text, Schwartz p. 923, 20. Theodulus τῆς ἡγεμονικῆς οἰκετίας πρώτης τιμῆς ἠξιωμένος *ib.* 11, 24.

[5] By name Euethius, it would seem. P.W. *s.v.* Eusebios, col. 1402 *s.f.*

[6] *De mort. pers.* 13.

demned to imprisonment: 'an unnumbered host was shut up in
every place and on every hand prisons built long ago for murderers
and violators of tombs were now filled with bishops and elders and
deacons, with readers and exorcists, so that no longer was any
space left in them for condemned criminals[1].' In the days of
Elizabeth the Catholics similarly filled the prisons of England.
'The prisons are so full of Catholics (1583) that there is no room
for thieves[2].' Just as the government of Elizabeth was troubled
by the problem of the cost of maintaining so many prisoners[3], so
must have been the Roman State. In the summer of A.D. 303
Diocletian left for the West to celebrate his Vicennalia in Rome.
On this festival the customary amnesty was granted to criminals:
these were released, but the administration was still faced with
the question of the incarcerated Christian clergy. By a third edict
it was ordered that they were to be constrained to sacrifice and
might then be set at liberty. Every effort was made to enforce the
order: 'For in one case a man's hands would be held and he would
be dragged to the altar; the foul and unholy sacrifice would be
thrust into his right hand and then he would be released as though
he had sacrificed. Another might never even have touched the
sacrifice, but when others declared that he had sacrificed, he would
go away in silence. Yet another was lifted up half dead and was
thrown down as though he were already a corpse; they freed him
from his fetters and counted him amongst those who had sacrificed.
While another was shouting and protesting that he would not yield,
he was struck on the mouth and silenced by a number of attendants appointed for the purpose; finally he was violently thrust
out of the prison, even though he had not sacrificed. So anxious
were they by any and every means to seem to have gained their
end[4].' Thus at length the prisons were emptied[5]. At Caesarea
three members of the lower ranks of the clergy suffered death for
lèse majesté, and on the same charge one at Antioch was martyred
while Galerius was present in the city.

During his visit to the West Diocletian fell dangerously ill,
and on his return to Nicomedia it appears that for a time he was
a mental wreck: it was reported that he was dead. On his recovery
he was so altered that men did not recognize him. During the
incapacity of the Augustus, Galerius seized his opportunity: he

---

[1] Eusebius, *Hist. Eccl.* VIII, 6, 9.　　[2] Meyer, *op. cit.* p. 166.
[3] *Ib.* pp. 166–8.　　[4] Eusebius, *de mart. Pal.* 1, 4.
[5] Not all students of Eusebius would agree with this interpretation. To
the present writer it would seem difficult to explain the texts otherwise than
in the way here adopted.

issued the bloody fourth edict commanding all—men, women and children—to sacrifice and make libation on penalty of death. The *dies traditionis*—the delivery of the sacred books—gave place to the *dies thurificationis*—the day of the offering of incense. The present writer has suggested that Galerius enforced the acceptance of this policy upon Maximian, the Western Augustus, by the threat of leading against him the troops which had recently defeated Persia. Galerius would present his Augustus with a *fait accompli*. And the answer of Diocletian to that challenge was the abdication both of himself and of his Western colleague[1].

This view is, it should be clearly understood, a hypothetical reconstruction of the course of events, and it is not the interpretation adopted by most of those who in recent years have studied the period[2]. For them, persecution of the Christians is the necessary and logical completion of Diocletian's reform: the ruler, they urge, who had placed himself under the protection of the Father of gods and men, the essentially Roman deity Juppiter Optimus Maximus, who stood for the old Roman faith to which the folk of his Balkan homeland had become enthusiastic converts—he must, if he were consistent, ruthlessly suppress the one serious rival creed which throughout the empire was daily gaining ground. They can point to his support of traditional views on the sanctity of marriage, and above all to the language of his violent edict against the Manichaeans (p. 339). Diocletian as the last of the Romans was fated to be the instigator of the most formidable of the Roman assaults upon the upstart faith. It is a strong case.

And yet to the present writer it would appear that against the weight of contemporary evidence it cannot be sustained: we have no adequate reason to believe that the reign began with persecution; rather, after his accession, Diocletian opened the way for Christians to enter the service of the State; once, as we have seen, in his presence at a solemn public ceremony the Christians by the magic of the sign of the cross defeated his desire to learn the will of his own gods. For the moment he was indignant—we may perhaps say, not without reason, but the momentary anger passed: for twenty years under an unquestioned absolutism a policy of toleration was maintained, and in his capital, Nicomedia, the Christian cathedral faced the imperial palace. At a time when the most formidable foe of the Empire was Persia, Diocletian attacked

---

[1] *Class. Quart.* XVIII, 1924, pp. 189 *sqq.* See, however, p. 340.
[2] Cf. *e.g.* K. Stade, *Der Politiker Diokletian und die letzte grosse Christenverfolgung.*

the Persian faith of the Manichaeans: those at least who have
lived through the Great War should recognise war-time propaganda when they meet with it in an earlier period. And contemporaries tell us that to the last Diocletian strenuously resisted the
introduction of a policy of repression, and yielded only on condition
that there should be no bloodshed. Surely the facts, so far as they
can be established, point irresistibly to the conclusion that with
Diocletian statesmanship had overruled religious fanaticism: he
would facilitate that process by which the sojourner in an alien
city should come to keep house together with the pagan and
through this 'synoikism' acknowledge his imperial citizenship
and shoulder the common burden of the defence of the Roman
world before the instant menace of barbarism. Constantine had
been Diocletian's companion at the Eastern court: Constantine as
a Christian completes the work of his pagan instructor, that work
which the bloody decade of persecution had interrupted. Diocletian had marked out the way of reconciliation between the faiths:
but Galerius did not share the outlook of his Augustus, and at
last, supported by Neoplatonist philosophers and by the oracle of
Apollo, Galerius carried the day.

Diocletian's abdication is the sequel to the victory of Galerius.
It was generally thought, we are told[1], that Constantine had been
selected by Diocletian for promotion to the rank of Caesar; but
the new policy demanded new men, and the choice was doubtless
left to Galerius who now became Augustus in the Eastern provinces. Severus was appointed Caesar under Constantius (now
senior Augustus) and Maximin Daia, the nephew of Galerius,
became the latter's subordinate in the East. It yet remained to be
seen whether Constantius would insist on his right to determine the
religious policy which his colleagues should pursue: Galerius and
his Caesar for a time were content to wait: thus for a whole year
there was not a single martyrdom in Palestine[2]. When Constantius had recalled Constantine to the West and made no move
to control the action of the Eastern Augustus, the policy of persecution was resumed. Maximin's new edict (early in A.D. 306),
as we learn from Eusebius, called upon the provincial governors
everywhere to enforce upon all—men, women and children—the
obligation to sacrifice to the gods. The brutal repression of the
Christians was continued with redoubled energy, and by his

---

[1] Lactantius, De mort. pers. 19.
[2] There may thus have been some shadow of plausibility in Maximin's
statement made in the letter to Sabinus, Eusebius, Hist. Eccl. IX, 9 a, 2.

presence both in Antioch and in Palestine Maximin stimulated the administration to greater excesses of cruelty.

No general history of the persecution can be written, for, so far as we know, the example of Eusebius in giving a detailed chrono-logical account of the sufferings of the martyrs and confessors of Palestine of which he had been an eye-witness was not followed in any other province of the empire. Crowds of renegades pressed to the pagan altars, and for a time it may well have appeared to Maximin that a policy of frightfulness would be crowned with success. But throughout the early history of the Church Christian leaders had never forgotten that their message was not addressed to men of intellect alone: *pistis*, the faith of the simple believer, and *gnosis*, the higher knowledge of the initiate, had each their place and justification in the Church. Through the writings alike of apologists and theologians the width and range of the gospel proclamation were maintained, and in the hour of crisis that loyalty of the Church to its catholic mission was splendidly re-warded. When bishops failed, women and girls, young men and uncultured folk endured the extremest torture which malignity could devise. 'For this is the love of God, that we keep his com-mandments. . . . For whatsoever is born of God overcometh the world: and this is the victory that overcometh the world, even our faith.' Against that faith the will of an emperor was powerless.

It would appear that after July 308 the persecution in Palestine was stayed for more than a year. Unfortunately the Syriac trans-lation of the longer version of the *Martyrs of Palestine* seems at this point to have an omission in the text. We read[1] that a heavy blow was sent down from God upon the tyrant Maximin, but what this was is not explained; there is no parallel phrase in the Greek of the shorter version, but here[2] Eusebius states that he who had received authority to persecute, as a result of some excite-ment (ἀνακίνησις), was again inflamed against the Christians with renewed passion[3]. But the meaning of the respite is apparent. In the autumn of A.D. 308 took place the meeting of Diocletian, Maximian and Galerius at Carnuntum (see p. 347); Maximin hoped as the result of that conference to receive recognition as Augustus from his colleagues. That hope was disappointed: at Carnuntum his claim to the title was ignored, and when he later sought to extort it from Galerius, his demand was refused. This must surely be the 'heavy blow' to which Eusebius refers. During

---

[1] Cf. B. Violet, *Die palästinischen Märtyrer*, etc., p. 66.
[2] *De mart. Pal.* 9, 1.
[3] The words ἐξ ὑπαρχῆς may imply 'he made a fresh start.'

the latter part of the year 308 Maximin's attention was diverted
from the persecution of the Christians, and it seems that there was
so little enthusiasm in Palestine for a policy of repression that
forthwith the persecuted ceased to be molested. Maximin's anger
and humiliation were reflected by the issue in A.D. 309 of a new
edict. The pagan temples were to be rebuilt and every one—even
babes at the breast—were to be present at the public sacrifices
and were to taste of the flesh of the victims: every article exposed
for sale in the market was to be defiled by libations and sprinkling
of the sacrificial blood. Even to the pagans this edict appeared
burdensome and excessive: it was they felt, 'out of place': they
had had more than enough of such oppressive measures[1]. Maximin perhaps felt that he was no longer supported by public
opinion: mutilation of resolute Christians and relegation to work
in the mines now generally take the place of the death penalty.
In Palestine the first martyrdom under the new edict is dated to
November 309, but already in March 310 the revival of persecution has spent itself and when in 311 the superintendent of the
copper mines desired to take action against the confessors there,
it is felt to be necessary to apply directly to Maximin for fresh
authority before making any move. Of these facts surely only one
interpretation is possible: the Roman East was sick of bloodshed.

It was in this year (311) that the unexpected happened:
Galerius, the author of the persecution, suffering from a horrible illness, issued an edict which was published in Nicomedia on 30 April.
By that edict the persecution was stayed and the Christians
were accorded legal recognition. Origen had written—we have
only the Latin translation of the homily[2]—'decreverunt [sc. principes Romani] legibus suis ut non sint Christiani': now for the
first time that principle is explicitly revoked: Galerius determines
'ut denuo Christiani sint'—the tolerance which Christianity had
in fact enjoyed in the early years of Diocletian's reign is restored
and is based upon direct imperial enactment. The Latin text of
the edict is preserved for us by Lactantius[3], while Eusebius[4] 'as
best he could' translated it into Greek. The modern student has
good cause to sympathize with Eusebius in the perplexities
of his task, for the edict presents many difficulties to an
interpreter. Those difficulties cannot be discussed in this place,

---

[1] ὡς ἂν περιττὴν ἤδη τὴν ἀτοπίαν καταμεμφομένων. Eusebius, *de mart.
Pal.* 9, 3.   [2] *In Lib. Jesu Nave, Homilia* IX, 10.
[3] *De mort. pers.* 34.   [4] Eusebius, *Hist. Eccl.* VIII, 17.

but of this 'palinode' of Galerius a translation must be attempted:

'Among other steps which we are always taking for the profit and advantage of the State we had formerly sought to set all things right according to the ancient laws and public order (disciplinam) of the Romans and further to provide that the Christians too who had abandoned the way of life (sectam) of their own fathers should return to sound reason (ad bonas mentes). For the said Christians had somehow become possessed by such obstinacy (read ⟨mala⟩ voluntas) and folly that, instead of following those institutions of the ancients which perchance their own ancestors had first established, they were at their own will and pleasure making laws for themselves and acting upon them and were assembling in different places people of different nationalities. After we had decreed that they should return to the institutions of the ancients, many were subjected to danger, many too were completely overthrown; and when very many (or 'most'—plurimi) persisted in their determination and we saw that they neither gave worship and due reverence to the gods nor practised the worship (observare) of the god of the Christians, considering our most gentle clemency and our immemorial custom by which we are wont to grant indulgence to all men, we have thought it right in their case too to extend the speediest indulgence to the effect that they may once more be free to live (sint) as Christians and may re-form their churches[1] (conventicula componant) always provided that they do nothing contrary to (public) order (disciplinam). Further by another letter we shall inform provincial governors (iudicibus) what conditions the Christians must observe. Wherefore in accordance with this our indulgence they will be bound to entreat their god for our well-being and for that of the State and for their own so that on every side the State may be preserved unharmed and that they themselves may live in their homes in security.'

This is an edict of toleration: that word 'pre-supposes the existence of a religious State, that is to say, of a State which believes it necessary for itself to make as a collective person profession of a certain religion just as if, like its individual members, it had a soul to be saved[2].' And the State compelled by necessity to admit other religions within its territory cannot but disapprove of them even when tolerating them: 'Toleration presumes an authority which has been and which again may become coercive: an authority which for subjective reasons is not brought to bear on the dissenting group. It implies...voluntary inaction on the part of the dominant group'[3], that group having waived in favour of a minority prerogatives which it regards as inalienable and absolute.

---

[1] An attempt to preserve the ambiguity of the Latin text.
[2] Ruffini, *op. cit.* p. 10.
[3] Cf. W. K. Jordan, *The Development of Religious Toleration in England*, 1, pp. 17 *sqq.*

Thus at the opening of the edict the language of earlier constitutions is recalled: the *anoia* (= <mala>voluntas), the *stultitia* of the Christians, the danger of their cosmopolitanism in breaking through the wall of partition which separated one national religion from another, while the grant itself is conditioned by an elastic proviso that nothing must be done 'contra disciplinam.' It has been doubted whether the recognition granted to Christians would carry with it the further right to make new converts from the pagan world: did the words 'conventicula componant' authorize the rebuilding of churches destroyed in the persecution? —what were the instructions contained in the letters sent to provincial governors—instructions which later seemed to Constantine and Licinius 'mischievous and alien from our clemency[1]'? It must further not be forgotten that there is no word in the edict of restitution of property of the Church which had been confiscated by the State or which had passed into private hands. The significance of the palinode must not be overrated; but at the same time it must be recognized as a momentous triumph for the Christian Church. Not only had individual freedom of conscience been won for the Christians, but also that further step on the ladder of religious liberty, the right of assembling themselves together[2] for common worship which Vinet once defined as the liberty of conscience of associations. The supreme effort of the pagan State had failed: Eusebius realized that it was a historic moment: with the text of the palinode issued by the author of the persecution he closed the first edition of his history.

Origen had said that a Christian's prayers were his service to the State—his 'militia': it was for the prayers of the Christians alike for Emperor and Empire that Galerius asked. But the prayers availed him nothing: a few days after the issue of the edict he was dead.

Lactantius and Eusebius agree that it was the fatal illness of Galerius—an illness which reminded Christian apologists of the sufferings of another persecutor, Herod of Judaea—which led to the issue of the edict. Modern students have not been content with that explanation. To one it has seemed that it must have been inspired by Licinius, another has maintained that Galerius yielded to the insistence of Constantine. It might not be easy to find any evidence in our authorities for either of these views. Is it not somewhat strange that both Lactantius and Eusebius should have

[1] Eusebius, *Hist. Eccl.* x, 5, 2–6.
[2] On liberty of worship cf. Ruffini, *op. cit.* p. 13.

missed so magnificent an opportunity and have failed to claim
credit for the issue of the edict on behalf of the two emperors who
were later to grant to the Roman world a yet wider liberty? If
Galerius in his mortal sickness sought anyone's advice it might
perhaps be suggested with greater plausibility that it was his wife
Valeria, who was known to be in close sympathy with the Christians,
who counselled him to placate the God of the persecuted.

With the palinode of Galerius a chapter closes. No history of
the great persecution, it must be repeated, can be written; it is idle
to attempt to estimate the number of those who gave their lives
for the faith. On one day in Egypt one hundred Christians were
martyred: in Palestine during all the years of the persecution not
one hundred were put to death. Of the extent of the repression in
Asia Minor where Christianity was strongest we can form no
impression. In Phrygia we are told a whole town was Christian:
in the persecution it was surrounded by soldiers who under orders
from the governor burned to death the entire population since
none would deny their faith[1]. It has been suggested that this
town may have been Eumeneia, for inscriptions found there cease
c. A.D. 300: 'the contrast between the rich intellectual and political
life of the Christians in the third century and the inarticulate
monotony of the many centuries that succeeded is painful; one
recognizes...the signs of a great misfortune...the destruction
of a vigorous and varied life[2].' Thus, it has been contended, the
persecution by exterminating the most progressive party in the
Eastern cities destroyed the last chance that the Empire had of
regaining vitality and health. 'Massacre then, as always, was
proved to be not merely a crime and a stupendous folly, but also
a terrible blow to the world, to civilization, and to humanity[3].'

But the student can hardly avoid the question whether both
Eusebius and Lactantius did not mention the disaster suffered by
this Phrygian town precisely because it was an exceptional
atrocity. We have not, so far as the present writer knows, any
descriptions from other provinces of such wholesale martyrdoms
as in Egypt, and here conditions were peculiar, and attention has
not always been paid to the evidence of Eusebius, who knew

[1] Eusebius, *Hist. Eccl.* VIII, 11. Lactantius, *Div. Inst.* V, 11, 10.
[2] Sir W. M. Ramsay, *Cities and Bishoprics of Phrygia*, II, pp. 502–9.
[3] "Christianity was the religion of an educated people and the last and
worst evil of the long struggle was that in Diocletian's persecution the more
cultured section of the Church was to a large extent killed out:....educa-
tion deteriorated and the quality of society in general was depreciated." Sir
W. M. Ramsay, *Pauline and other Studies*, p. 115.

Egypt and had been in that country during the persecution.
Here, he expressly states, Christians formed the majority of the
population[1]. Christ went down into Egypt because idolatry took
its rise there, and the Egyptians were formerly the most superstitious of peoples; because of Christ's visit the word of the gospel
teaching flourished amongst the Egyptians more than anywhere
else[2]. The spirit of idolatry which in Egypt is still active ($\epsilon i \sigma \epsilon \tau \iota$
$\nu \hat{\upsilon} \nu$) keeps the Egyptians in a ferment plotting against the Christians in order to extinguish Christianity and blot it out. Countless
times ($\mu \acute{\upsilon} \rho \iota \alpha \ \delta \epsilon \ \ddot{o} \sigma \alpha$) have they enquired of their gods against
us in oracles and prophecies and of the demons that lurk in the
statues and of the 'engastrimuthoi' who were once so powerful
amongst them, and yet have no profit from them. Believing in
these demons and being set in action by them, they raise persecution against the church of God[3]. In 'every place and town
and countryside' a Christian altar is to be found: nay more, every
town and every house is divided by a civil war waged between
Christians and idolaters[4]. These statements are made in proof of
the fulfilment of a prophecy of Isaiah[5], but they are too definite
not to be based upon facts which were known to Eusebius, and
they serve to explain the ferocity of the persecution in Egypt.

Elsewhere the reluctance of governors to impose the death
penalty is often striking. There is an instructive chapter in the
Divine Institutes[6]: governors would boast that they had not put
to death any Christians: they would resort to any torture in order
to break down the resistance of the Christian. 'I saw in Bithynia,'
writes Lactantius, 'the governor wonderfully elated as though
he had subdued some barbarian tribe, because one who had resisted for two years with great spirit appeared at the last to yield.'
It was the cruel persecutor who was most merciful because the
end came swiftly. Governors would try to make it easy for the
accused. A Christian when called upon to sacrifice to the gods
replied 'There is but one God only, the Creator.' Flavian, the
ruthless governor of Palestine, is prepared to assent: he changes

---

[1] Christ has ransomed the souls of the Egyptians so that $\tau o \grave{\upsilon} \varsigma \ \pi \lambda \epsilon \acute{\iota} o \upsilon \varsigma$
$\check{\eta} \delta \eta \ \tau \hat{\omega} \nu \ \kappa \alpha \tau' \ A \check{\iota} \gamma \upsilon \pi \tau o \nu \ \kappa \alpha \grave{\iota} \ \tau \alpha \acute{\upsilon} \tau \eta \varsigma \ \mathring{\alpha} \pi \eta \lambda \lambda \acute{\alpha} \chi \theta \alpha \iota \ \tau \hat{\eta} \varsigma \ \nu \acute{o} \sigma o \upsilon$. *Praep.*
Evang. III, 5 s.f.
[2] $\delta \iota \grave{o} \ \kappa \alpha \grave{\iota} \ \pi \acute{\alpha} \nu \tau \omega \nu \ \mathring{\alpha} \nu \theta \rho \acute{\omega} \pi \omega \nu \ \mu \hat{\alpha} \lambda \lambda o \nu \ \pi \alpha \rho' \ A \mathring{\iota} \gamma \upsilon \pi \tau \acute{\iota} o \iota \varsigma \ \check{\iota} \sigma \chi \upsilon \sigma \epsilon \nu \ \acute{o} \ \tau \hat{\eta} \varsigma$
$\epsilon \mathring{\upsilon} \alpha \gamma \gamma \epsilon \lambda \iota \kappa \hat{\eta} \varsigma \ \alpha \mathring{\upsilon} \tau o \hat{\upsilon} \ \delta \iota \delta \alpha \sigma \kappa \alpha \lambda \acute{\iota} \alpha \varsigma \ \lambda \acute{o} \gamma o \varsigma$. *Demonstr. Evang.* VI, 20, 9: cf. *ib.*
IX, 2, 4 and IX, 2, 6, $\mu \upsilon \rho \acute{\iota} \alpha \ \pi \lambda \acute{\eta} \theta \eta$ of the inhabitants deserting paganism
$\check{\epsilon} \tau \iota \ \kappa \alpha \grave{\iota} \ \nu \hat{\upsilon} \nu \ \tau \grave{o} \nu \ \tau \hat{\omega} \nu \ \acute{o} \lambda \omega \nu \ \acute{o} \mu o \lambda o \gamma \epsilon \hat{\iota} \ \mu \acute{o} \nu o \nu \ \epsilon \mathring{\iota} \delta \acute{\epsilon} \nu \alpha \iota \ \theta \epsilon \acute{o} \nu$.
[3] *Demonstr. Evang.* VI, 20, 16–19.
[4] *Demonstr. Evang.* VIII, 5. [5] Isaiah xix, 1–4. [6] V, 11.

the order 'Then sacrifice to the emperors[1].' Another governor
was ready to accept a sacrifice offered 'to the only God[2].' If we
may regard the *Passio* of Philip bishop of Heraclea[3] as historical,
it would appear that the governor, whose wife was a Christian, had
taken no steps to execute the early edicts: he acts only after the
issue of the fourth edict and enforces both the first and fourth
edicts at one and the same time. It is interesting to observe a
business-like and conscientious Roman official at his work in
Africa making an inventory of confiscated property. There is no
violence, simply the scrupulous performance of a tiresome duty[4].

And it must never be forgotten that Christians were at times
provocative. When Hierocles in Egypt had condemned a Christian virgin to confinement in a brothel, Aedesius knocked him
down and continued beating him as he lay on the ground. A careful study of *The Martyrs of Palestine* reveals a surprising number
of cases where Christians compelled the governor to take notice of
them, while their refusal to answer the formal questions concerning their place of origin must often have been exasperating[5]. On
one occasion several of the accused replied that their home city
lay in the East: it belonged to the Christians alone, and was called
Jerusalem[6]. The governor became alarmed and thought that the
sectaries were creating for themselves a centre hostile to Rome
where the disaffected could assemble and live as Christians, much
as Plotinus almost persuaded Gallienus to allow him to found a
state where men should dwell under Plato's laws[7]. Platonopolis
would have been situated in Campania: the Jerusalem of the
Christians, however, was in Heaven. During the persecution
governors were guilty of hideous brutalities, but it must be remembered that many of them must have found the task which the
government imposed on them a sorry duty. And some of the
simple stories of Christian confession under extreme torture are
still to the modern reader things of wonder and of beauty: to
extract a sentence or two is useless: those confessions must be

---

[1] Eusebius, *De mart. Pal.* c. 1 (Long version).

[2] *Passio of Phileas and Philoromus*, 1: cf. *De mart. Pal.* 10, 2: 11, 30.

[3] Ruinart, *Acta Martyrum*, edn of 1859, pp. 440 *sqq.* At least the speeches
are surely only literary: cf. J. Geffcken, *Zwei Griech. Apologeten*, p. 249.

[4] Proceedings before Zenophilus, Appendix to the work of Optatus
against the Donatists. Note that some excesses of Roman magistrates are
due to interpolations in otherwise historic *Acta*—a good example is to be
found in the Acta S. Crispinae, Ruinart, *op. cit.* pp. 477 *sqq.* See the study of
these Acta by Monceaux in *Mélanges Boissier*, pp. 383–9.

[5] Eusebius, *de mart. Pal.* 4, 12. [6] *De mart. Pal.* 11, 9–13.

[7] Porphyry, *Life of Plotinus*, 12.

read in their setting. Paul's prayer before his execution—for Christians and Jews, for Samaritans and the pagan world, for the judge who had condemned him and for the executioner—reduced the multitude of spectators to tears: when the martyred bodies of Christians were left for beasts to devour and none might bury them, the sympathies of the pagans of Caesarea were with the persecuted: in Alexandria pagans sheltered the Christians in their own homes. When Hierocles and another pagan apologist published attacks upon the Christians during the persecution, even pagan opinion disapproved. The government had outrun pagan animosity: it was no wonder that Lactantius thought that God had permitted the persecution in order to bring the pagans within the community of the Christian Church.

CHAPTER XX

CONSTANTINE

I. THE RISE OF CONSTANTINE

THE later Roman Empire was stamped with its own peculiar
character by the genius of two men—Constantine and Justinian—and both were sons of Balkan peasants. Theodora the
wife of Justinian was in her early days a prostitute; Helen the
mother of Constantine was, tradition said, a serving-maid in a
Balkan inn, and neither did dishonour to the proud position of an
imperial Augusta. The precise date of Constantine's birth we do
not know: but it was at Nish and probably about A.D. 280 that
Helen bore to the soldier Constantius the boy who was to become
the first Christian emperor. When Diocletian had appointed Constantius to be a Caesar of the Herculian dynasty with the task of
recovering Britain from Carausius, Constantine was sent to the
East where he became the companion of the senior Augustus: he
was with Diocletian in Egypt in 296–7. As a young man he
came to know the Christianity of the Asiatic provinces and he saw
the part which Christians were playing in the administration and
at the court of Diocletian. Men thought that in due time he would
be appointed Caesar: he would not be unprepared for the task. In
the East he saw the change of policy which was the work of
Galerius and the beginnings of the bloody persecution; after the
abdication of Diocletian he was kept in the East by Galerius as a
useful hostage. But Galerius could not refuse the demand of Constantius, now senior Augustus, that his son should join his father
in Gaul, and when Constantius died at York (July 306) Constantine was hailed as emperor by the soldiers. Constantine sought
the recognition of Galerius, and the latter acknowledged him as

Note. The principal sources for the reign of Constantine down to the
Council of Nicaea are the Anonymus Valesii, a fragment of a history
probably written by a contemporary; the Latin Panegyrici for the official
expression of the policy of the rulers of the Roman West: the bitter
pamphlet of Lactantius—*De mortibus persecutorum*—which is yet of great
historical value; the *Church History* of Eusebius and his *Vita Constantini*,
the latter a panegyric rather than a biography; the documents on the
Donatist Controversy preserved by Optatus are of outstanding importance.

Caesar in the West, while Severus was appointed to succeed Constantius as Augustus.

The history of the following five years has been told in another chapter (pp. 344 *sqq.*) and but little remains to be said here. Constantius had, it would seem, enforced the first edict of persecution so far as to destroy some Christian churches, but further than that he would not go[1]. The Donatists in Africa knew that in Gaul Christians had not been compelled to surrender their scriptures to the representatives of the Roman State: in the lands ruled by Constantius there had been no *traditores*. Constantius himself probably believed in the divine monarchy of a *summus deus*—a belief which might at times approach a pagan monotheism; officially he worshipped Hercules the divine patron of the dynasty. Severus, so far as we know, followed the lead of Constantius, and the Christians remained unmolested. Thus after the abdication of Diocletian persecution ceased in the Western provinces of the Empire. There can, indeed, have been no enthusiasm amongst the pagans for a policy of violent repression: even in Rome itself Maxentius, when he had seized imperial power, although a pagan, thought to win popularity through granting toleration to the Christians[2]. Pope Marcellinus died in A.D. 304: in 307 the Roman Christians could proceed to a new election. Marcellinus, it would seem probable, had betrayed the faith as *thurificatus* and *traditor*[3], he had surrendered Christian scriptures and burned incense on a pagan altar; in Rome, as in Africa, the problem of the treatment of the *lapsi* aroused bitter passions. Pope Marcellus, elected in 307, who was a rigorist, was opposed by a party which championed a more liberal treatment of the fallen, and the two sections of the church met in bloody conflicts in the streets of the capital. In defence of public order Marcellus was banished by Maxentius. On April 8, 308 Maxentius permitted the election of Pope Eusebius, but he, too, met with opposition and was banished to Sicily. On July 2, 311 Miltiades was consecrated as bishop, and

[1] See A. Riese, *Die Inschrift des Clematius und die kölnischen Martyrien*, Bonner Jahrbücher, CXVIII, 1909, p. 236. Even if, as W. Levison has contended (*Das Werden der Ursula-Legende, ib.* CXXXII, 1927, p. 1), the Clematius inscription is throughout genuine, it is impossible to tell in what persecution the virgins of Cologne were martyred, while it is only a guess which has dated the martyrdom of S. Alban to the great persecution: Gildas (*Chronicon* c. x), having reached the persecution of Diocletian, writes that S. Alban died 'supra dicto *ut conicimus* persecutionis tempore.'

[2] Eusebius, *Hist. Eccl.* VIII, 14, 1.

[3] For Marcellinus cf. J. Wilpert, *Röm. Quartalschr.* XXII, 1908, pp. 91 *sqq.*

now Maxentius went farther than Galerius had done in his edict of toleration issued in the spring of the same year (see p. 671) and restored to the Church the property which had been confiscated during the persecution. It is important to realize that Maxentius in banishing two bishops was but doing his duty in maintaining order within the City. When Constantine marched upon Rome it was not to free the Christians from religious persecution[1].

Constantine as Caesar naturally continued to acknowledge Hercules[2] as his official patron, especially when, on Maximian's flight from Italy to Gaul, Constantine married Fausta, Maximian's daughter, and received from his father-in-law the title of Augustus[3]. But with the treachery and death of Maximian, in A.D. 310, a Herculian title to imperial power became impossible: some new basis must be found for Constantine's *imperium*. Thus the panegyrist[4] forthwith explains, what had not been realized previously, that Constantine was connected with the family of the heroic third-century Emperor Claudius Gothicus. What the precise relationship may have been the orator discreetly does not seek to determine: the essential point to bring home to his hearers was that the derivation of Constantine's title from the grant of the discredited Maximian was nothing but an error. Already there had been two emperors in his family: Constantine was *born* an emperor. He alone of all his colleagues was one of a dynastic line.

The fiction prevailed: the dynasty of the Second Flavians was securely founded. With the change in the title to the throne was associated a change in the Emperor's religious allegiance. He now returns to the sun-worship of his Balkan ancestors, and henceforth Sol Invictus—Apollo—becomes his divine patron. Constantine's Herculian past is buried. This has been called Constantine's first conversion. The new imperial faith is duly celebrated in the panegyric delivered at Trèves after the death of Maximian. The orator gives free rein to his fancy and imagines[5] the appearance to the Emperor of Apollo in his temple to which Constantine has made his pilgrimage. At the side of the god stands the goddess Victoria. In Rome when Maximian had become *bis Augustus*—Augustus for the second time—the coinage had borne the wish that his third decade of rule might be prosperous (Vota

---

[1] On the extremely complex question of the succession of bishops at Rome cf. E. Schwartz, *Gött. Nach.* 1904, pp. 530 *sqq.*; H. Lietzmann, *Petrus und Paulus in Rom*[2], p. 9; E. Caspar, *Zeits. f. Kirchengesch.* XLVI, 1927, pp. 321 *sqq.*; *Gesch. des Papsttums*, I, pp. 97 *sqq.*

[2] *Paneg.* VIII (V), 4.

[3] *Ib.* VII (VI), 2.

[4] *Ib.* VI (VII), 2.

[5] *Ib.* VI (VII), 21.

xxx); men could desire for Constantine no less: Apollo bore wreaths each of which carried the promise of thirty years of rule[1]. No small importance has been attached to this vision by some scholars: it has been interpreted as the model on which the later Christian vision was fashioned. This is to do too much honour to the panegyrist's invention[2].

With the year 311 came the edict of toleration and the death of Galerius: Maximin seized his hour, anticipated Licinius and occupied Asia Minor. Henceforth the Hellespont divided the Emperors of the East. Licinius, deprived of the resources which possession of the Asiatic provinces would have given him, turned to Constantine for support. Already in 310 he had been betrothed to Constantine's sister, Constantia. In the summer of 311 Licinius is at Serdica where by granting special privileges to the soldiers he sought to secure their loyalty[3]. Maxentius in the West deified his murdered father and re-asserted his Herculian claim to rule. As Licinius becomes the ally of Constantine, so Maxentius and Maximin are drawn together. The revolt in Africa suppressed, his corn supplies secured, Maxentius can shelter behind the walls of Aurelian from which both Severus and Galerius had retired discomfited. In 312 Constantine, having re-established Roman authority on the Rhine, decided to march against the 'tyrant' who held the Western capital. There follows the lightning campaign which ended at the Milvian Bridge.

From Gaul Constantine struck across the Alps: he left behind him troops to guard the frontier of the Rhine, and, though we can form no precise numerical estimate of the strength of the army of invasion, it was less than 40,000 men. Maxentius, we are told, had in Italy some 100,000 soldiers, though many of these remained with the 'tyrant' in Rome; Constantine's march over the Mont Genèvre was unopposed, though the garrison of Susa had been reinforced. That fortress was stormed, and the discipline in Constantine's army was such that there was no plundering of the town. This rare moderation later bore its fruits: as Constantine advanced through Italy he was greeted with enthusiasm in other cities. The first important engagement was fought in the neigh-

---

[1] *Paneg.* vi (vii), 21, 4. *Vidisti...Apollinem tuum...coronas tibi laureas offerentem quae tricenum singulae ferunt omen annorum.*

[2] So Bidez. W. Seston has maintained the purely literary character of this vision, *Annuaire de l'Institut de Philologie et d'Histoire Orientales et Slaves* IV, 1936, pp. 373 *sqq.*

[3] E. Paulovics, *La Table de Privilèges de Brigetio* (=Archaeologia Hungarica xx), Budapest, 1936; W. Seston, *Byzantion*, XII, 1937, p. 477.

bourhood of Turin—perhaps between Alpignano and Rivoli:
Constantine's centre gave way before the mail-clad cavalry of
Maxentius, then the wings closed in upon the horsemen, and
clubmen brought down horse and rider[1]. Turin shut its gates
against the fugitives and then surrendered. A large force under
the command of Pompeianus Ruricius was concentrated at Verona.
After a short stay in Milan and an engagement at Brixia Constantine under cover of night crossed the Adige and began the
siege of Verona; Ruricius broke through Constantine's lines to
bring up reinforcements. Constantine did not hesitate: without
abandoning the siege he immediately advanced against the troops
with which Ruricius was returning. He himself led the attack;
the battle lasted far into the night. Ruricius fell; his men were
scattered. Aquileia was secured, Verona capitulated.

The march through central Italy continued; Modena after a
short siege surrendered; and the way to Rome lay open. But it
was precisely from the walls of Rome that Severus and Galerius
had retreated baffled and helpless: Constantine had prepared a
fleet with which to intercept the transport of grain to the Western
capital, but in vain, for the rebellion of Alexander had been
crushed in time, and Maxentius had drawn from the granary
of Africa copious supplies. Constantine's great fear was that
Maxentius would not quit Rome. It was the guardians of the
Sibylline books who achieved for Constantine that which he himself would have been powerless to enforce. Maxentius determined
to leave to his generals the command of his forces; his army advanced along the Via Flaminia as far as Saxa Rubra, where it
apparently came in contact with Constantine's troops. In the
first encounter the soldiers of Maxentius were victorious. Then
'Constantine moved all his forces nearer to the city and encamped
in the neighbourhood "regione" of the Milvian Bridge[2].' The real
difficulty of the battle, if we accept this statement of Lactantius,
is to understand how it was that, in face of the superior numbers
of Maxentius, Constantine was allowed to execute this flanking
movement unmolested. Are we to understand a previous retreat
and a wide détour? Just before dawn on October 28 'Constantine
was sleeping when he was bidden to mark ('notaret') on the
shields of his men the sublime sign of God and thus engage the
enemy. He did as he was bidden and marked on the shields the
letter X with a line drawn through it and turned round at the top,

[1] For a topographical discussion of this battle cf. M. A. Levi in *Boll.
storico-bibliografico subalpino* XXXVI, 1934, pp. 1–10 (with map).

[2] Lactantius, *de mort. pers.* 44, 3.

i.e. Christus[1].' Maxentius on the same day, the anniversary of his assumption of power, ordered that the Sibylline books should be consulted: the answer was given that on that day the enemy of the Romans would perish. The battle was already begun when Maxentius, assured of victory, joined his army. Constantine with like confidence threw his cavalry against the enemy, and his infantry followed. It was a bitterly contested struggle, but when the lines of Maxentius broke they could not retreat, for the Tiber ran close behind them. The bridge of boats by which they had crossed gave way under the press, and Maxentius perished with the fugitives.

Constantine as victor entered the Western capital. Against the advice of the augurs, in despite of his military counsellors, unsupported by the troops of Licinius, with incredible audacity Constantine had risked everything on a single hazard—and won. How shall that success be explained? Constantine himself knew well the reason for his victory: it had been won 'instinctu divinitatis[2],' by a 'virtus' which was no mere human valour, but was a mysterious force which had its origin in God. And as the ground of that conviction tradition has repeated the story of the Vision of the Cross athwart the afternoon sun—a vision which came to Constantine, it seems, while he was still in Gaul before he began his march into Italy. For that Vision of the Cross we have no contemporary evidence: indeed our only evidence is the assertion of Eusebius, made after Constantine's death in the *Vita Constantini*[3], that the Emperor had on his oath assured him of the fact. No mention of that vision occurs in any of the editions of the *Church History* of Eusebius: this of course proves nothing: Eusebius did not come into close contact with Constantine until A.D. 325 which is the probable date of the last edition of his *History*. It has been

---

[1] Lactantius, *de mort. pers.* 44, 5. The passage of Lactantius is of extreme difficulty; H. Grégoire proposes to read 'et [I] transversa X littera' or 'transversa X littera [I],' *Byzantion* 11, 1925, pp. 406 n. 2, 407. The question of the form of the monogram thus described by Lactantius is matter of dispute and cannot be fully discussed here (see N. H. Baynes, *Constantine the Great and the Christian Church*, pp. 60 *sqq.*); it may well have been that of the star with a knob on one of the radial arms ✳. This would explain the language used by Lactantius: the sign read as a monogram was not a XP in the ordinary form of the second letter, and therefore could not be so described. The present writer is not convinced that the sign in this form was regarded as an Apolline symbol (so Seston). Later the monogram ☧ became an essential part of the Christian standard, the Labarum.

[2] Dessau 694.   [3] I, 28.

contended[1] that the whole account is an interpolation of the
Theodosian period, but that contention is at present unproven.
In the year 351 Constantius was granted a vision of the Cross in
the heavens and it was then remarked that the son was more
blessed than the father: Constantine had but found in the earth
the true Cross: Constantius had seen it in the sky[2]. Does this
denote ignorance of the story of Eusebius[3] or a politic denial of
Eusebius' statement? Who shall say? The one thing which is
critically illegitimate is to treat the account given by Lactantius
of the dream of Constantine before the walls of Rome (see p. 682)
as though it described the same vision as that related by Eusebius.
In recent discussions the two quite distinct divine interventions
have at times been confused. But even though at present the
historical student may be forced to conclude any discussion of the
Eusebian report with a judgment of *non liquet*, to the present
writer it appears that the account of the church historian is at
least a true reflection of the Emperor's own thought—or at least
of his after-thought. Victory had been promised him by the God
of the Christians; he had challenged the Christian God to an
Ordeal by Battle and that God had kept his pledge. This belief
of Constantine remains of fundamental significance for the understanding of the policy of the reign.

II. CONSTANTINE AND CHRISTIANITY

Many are the scholars who have discussed Constantine's relation to Christianity and the Christian Church, and assuredly that
discussion is not ended, for no agreement has been reached. In
this place very little can be said, but at least it can be asserted that
until the authenticity of Constantine's letters written in connection
with the Donatist controversy has been successfully challenged,
it must be admitted that the Emperor long before his conquest
of the Roman East regarded himself as a Christian. Yet it must
never be forgotten that he was at the same time the ruler of subjects who were for the most part pagan, and that therefore his acts
and even his beliefs must, at least in these earlier years, be tolerant
of a pagan interpretation. Though Constantine might be assured

[1] By W. Seston, 'L'opinion païenne et la conversion de Constantin,'
Revue d'hist. et de philos. religieuses, XVI, 1936, pp. 250–264.

[2] Cyril of Jerusalem, Migne, *Patr. Gr.* XXXIII, 1168 B–1169 A.

[3] We shall be better able to estimate aright the account of Eusebius when
we can consult the promised monograph on the subject by Professor Bidez,
cf. *Byzantion* 10, 1935, pp 407 *sqq*. For the present cf. Seston, *op. cit.* (see
above, n. 1).

that the victory of the Milvian Bridge had been won through the aid of the Christian God, yet pagan rhetoricians must be allowed to express that conviction of divine aid through the medium of their own pagan interpretation of the fact.

The real content of Constantine's thought may well have been very different from that of its pagan interpreters. The language of the panegyrists indeed gives back the thought of Constantine reflected from a refracting mirror. And for Constantine, it may be suggested, an outworn past lives on because that past has been transformed into a symbol which has lost its original significance. The solar imagery of an earlier religious conviction is retained because Constantine is a member of a dynasty, and that solar imagery has become a part of a dynastic heraldry which proclaims an inherited title to imperial power[1]. The student must therefore be prepared to recognize a conscious ambiguity in the acts of Constantine—an ambiguity necessarily arising from the ambiguous position of a Christian emperor ruling a pagan empire, and bound to a pagan past. Thus the Senate may erect a statue in traditional form to its divinely guided sovereign and may have placed in the hand of the statue a traditional *vexillum*; as the ruler of a pagan world Constantine may have accepted this homage of his pagan subjects while for himself the *vexillum* was no mere traditional tribute: he may have seen in it the symbol of his personal faith, the Cross; it would thus have both for him and for the Christians its own novelty, its own peculiar character: 'in hoc *singulari* signo[2]' the victory had been won, and the interpretation given by Eusebius to the traditional imagery of the statue may after all have rightly interpreted the ambiguity of the inscription. It is through concessions to the past that Constantine mediated the transition to the Christian Empire of the future—that Empire which his sons educated in the Christian faith might one day behold as accomplished fact.

Discussion continues concerning the vision recounted by Lactantius; but whatever conclusions criticism may reach it is at least obvious that Lactantius is endeavouring to describe a definite form of the Christian monogram, and that description cannot be lightly dismissed. It must ultimately be explained, and not explained away. Certain it is that after the victory Constantine acts just as he might have been expected to act if the story in Lactantius were true. Created senior Augustus by the Senate, he writes to his Eastern colleague Maximin bidding him stay the

[1] Cf. Baynes, *op. cit.* pp. 95 *sqq.*
[2] Rufinus, translating Eusebius (cf. *Hist. Eccl.* ix, 9, 10–13).

persecution. If at this time, having abolished the *acta* of Maxentius, he formally published in Italy and Africa Galerius' Edict of Toleration, he immediately went far beyond that grudging recognition of Christian rights: not only did he order restoration of confiscated Church property, but instructions were given to the provincial finance officers to give to the Catholics—but not to the Donatists —such monies from the public funds as the Church might need. When early in 313 Constantine met his ally Licinius at Milan a policy of complete religious freedom was agreed upon. Technically it may be true that there was no Edict of Milan, but, in the view of the present writer, that is because Constantine had already accorded to all his subjects those rights which were granted to the provinces of Asia in the letter issued at Nicomedia by Licinius a few months later, which itself summarized Constantine's legislation promulgated by him as senior Augustus after the crowning mercy of the Battle of the Milvian Bridge. The facts for which the 'Edict of Milan' once stood are still facts, though the Edict itself has gone the way of many another symbolic representation of historical truth. But let it not be thought that Constantine was a passionless exponent of a philosophic doctrine of toleration. It has been contended[1] that when error prevails it is right to invoke liberty of conscience, when on the contrary truth predominates it is just to use coercion. Such doubtless was the view of Constantine: he was, it must be repeated, the ruler of a pagan world, and the Christian in Constantine must for the present yield to the statesman. To the Donatist schismatic and to the Christian heretic no such consideration need be shown. Constantine's ideal State would be hampered by no fetters of toleration.

Meanwhile in the Eastern provinces Maximin had unwillingly accepted the Edict issued just before his death by Galerius. The text of the Edict was not published by him, but he gave verbal instructions to his Praetorian Prefect, Sabinus, to write to the provincial governors: of that letter we possess a Greek translation: the authorities are directed that if any Christian be found following the religion of his nation he should be set free from molestation and from danger and should henceforth not be deemed punishable on this charge. The administration welcomed the permission to stay the persecution: the Christian prisoners were released: those relegated to the mines returned with joy, and the pagans themselves shared in the general rejoicing. But in Nicomedia men soon learned that the concession had been wrung from Maximin, and

---

[1] Cf. J. C. Bluntschli, *Ges. kleine Schriften*, i, 1879, p. 106.

that the city might look for imperial favour if the citizens would give the Emperor an excuse for a change of policy. A petition was presented asking that the Christians might be banished from Nicomedia. Before the year was out (October–November 311) persecution had begun afresh: on November 24[1] Peter Bishop of Alexandria was martyred; about the same time Silvanus, who had been bishop for forty years, suffered death at Emesa; on January 7, 312 Lucian was martyred at Nicomedia.

The example of Nicomedia was followed in Antioch where Theotecnus, curator of the city, instigated a similar demonstration, and the pagans in other cities likewise forwarded their petitions. These requests were graciously answered by Maximin in a rescript issued c. June 312; in return for their devotion to the gods the Emperor would forthwith grant any boon for which the cities might ask[2]. Maximin now developed a constructive policy and planned to create a pagan Church: priests of the gods were appointed in each city and those who had distinguished themselves in the public service were made provincial high-priests (*pontifices*); propaganda should support the pagan counter-reformation: to discredit the Christian faith forged Acts of Pilate were circulated throughout the Eastern provinces; they were to be studied in the schools and learnt by heart—'children in the schools had every day on their lips the names of Jesus and Pilate[3].' At Damascus a Roman general forced prostitutes under the threat of torture to state that they had formerly been Christians and that they had witnessed deeds of shame committed even in the Christian churches. These confessions were published at the Emperor's command. From an inscription we learn that in Pisidia members of the governor's civil staff were ordered to sacrifice, and the right to resign from the service was denied them[4]. Sheep and cattle were carried off from the fields for daily sacrifice: the soldiers, fed on sacrificial flesh, scorned their rations of bread. Attention has been called to traces in the epigraphy of Asia Minor of encouragement by the emperors of the pagan revival: this policy may be reflected in the association of the Tekmoreian Guest-Friends, a pagan society on the Imperial estates of Pisidian Antioch[5]. From

[1] Cf. *Class. Quart.* XVIII, 1924, p. 194.

[2] For the inscription of Arykanda see E. Preuschen, *Analecta*[2], Pt I (Tübingen, 1909), p. 100.

[3] Eusebius, *Hist. Eccl.* IX, 7, 1.

[4] On the inscription of Eugenius see the bibliography to this chapter, A, (2).

[5] Sir W. M. Ramsay, *Pauline and other Studies*, pp. 103–122.

an inscription the name of one of Maximin's priests has been recovered—Athanatos Epitynchanos; he was a priest in Phrygia who had been initiated by the high-priestess Ispatale; she had 'ransomed[1] many from evil torments,' probably those who through initiation had been rescued from the torments of the after-life, but possibly Christians saved from torture during the persecution[2].

But after Constantine's victory at the Milvian Bridge the plans of Maximin for a general revival of paganism in Roman Asia were rudely checked. He was told by Constantine that repression of the Christians must cease. That order he dared not disobey, and thus towards the end of A.D. 312[3] Maximin addressed another letter to Sabinus in which he explained that it was only fitting that he should grant the petitions of the cities, for their request had been pleasing to the gods; but he still desired that through persuasion his subjects should be brought fitly to reverence the gods: the Christians should not be constrained thereto by violence. The winter of 312–3 was indeed a disastrous time for Maximin: the harvest had failed, and famine and pestilence devastated the Eastern provinces. Maximin had sought to impose pagan worship upon the newly converted Armenians, and as a consequence war was declared. We know no details: the conflict must have been brief[4], for in the depth of winter, through rain and snow, while Licinius was still in Italy, Maximin by forced marches advanced from Syria to the Straits and invaded Europe. Licinius hastily left Milan to meet the invasion. The garrison of Byzantium capitulated after an investment of eleven days, and Heraclea and Perinthus similarly opened their gates. Licinius with a small force had now reached Adrianople, and, rapidly collecting as many troops as possible from the near neighbourhood, at the post-station of Tzirallum he faced with barely 30,000 men the 70,000 of Maximin's army. While Maximin vowed to Juppiter that, were victory granted him, he would extirpate the Christian name, an angel, so Lactantius tells us[5], dictated a prayer to Licinius: victory would be his, if he and his army would appeal to the Summus Deus.

---

[1] Cf. Titus II, 14.

[2] The inscription was set up in 313–14 after the victory of Licinius over Maximin, as H. Grégoire has shown, *Byzantion* VIII, 1933, p. 51.

[3] Cf. *Class. Quart. loc. cit.*

[4] Cf. O. Seeck, *Gesch. des Untergangs der antiken Welt*, Ed. 3. 1, pp. 148, 503.

[5] Lactantius, *de mort. pers.* 46.

It is a fine litany that, three times recited, inspired with confidence of divine succour the troops of Licinius[1]:

> Summe deus te rogamus
> Sancte deus te rogamus
> Omnem iustitiam tibi commendamus
> Salutem nostram tibi commendamus
> Imperium nostrum tibi commendamus
> Per te vivimus, per te victores et felices existimus:
> Summe, sancte deus, preces nostras exaudi:
> Bracchia nostra ad te tendimus:
> Exaudi, sancte, summe deus.

Maximin refused to consider terms of peace: he had hoped to win over the army of Licinius without a struggle, and then with united forces march against Constantine. But the angel's promise was kept: when the armies engaged, the soldiers of Maximin fled and with them their emperor (May 1, 313). His wrath fell heavily on the pagan priests who had promised him victory and at length he sought the support of the Christians: in Nicomedia (probably May 313) he not only issued an edict of toleration but even restored its confiscated property to the Church. But it was too late; before the advance of Licinius he retreated beyond the Taurus line, and in Tarsus he died, not in battle, but of a disease which blinded him and reduced him to a skeleton (c. August 313). In June 313 Licinius in Nicomedia published a letter granting complete freedom of belief in terms which we have every reason to think had been agreed upon with Constantine at the meeting in Milan[2]. A translation may be attempted:

> 'Since we saw that freedom of worship ought not to be denied, but that to each man's judgment and will the right should be given to care for sacred things according to each man's free choice, we have already some time ago bidden the Christians[3] to maintain the faith of their own sect and worship. But since in that edict by which such right was granted to the aforesaid Christians many and varied conditions (αἱρέσεις) clearly

---

[1] It has been pointed out by H. Grégoire that a similar prayer is attributed to Constantine by Eusebius (*Revue de l'Université de Bruxelles* XXXVI, 1931, 260), *Vita Constantini* IV, 20. When its language is compared with that of the letter of Licinius later published at Nicomedia it may be suggested that the text was agreed upon between Constantine and Licinius at their meeting in Milan.

[2] Latin text: Lactantius, *de mort. pers.* 48; Greek translation: Eusebius, *Eccl. Hist.* x, 5. On these texts cf. Baynes, *Constantine and the Christian Church*, pp. 69 *sqq.*

[3] τοῖς τε Χριστιανοῖς. It would appear that some words have dropped out here.

appeared to have been added, it may well perchance have come about that
after a short time many were repelled from practising their religion. Thus[1]
when I, Constantine Augustus, and I, Licinius Augustus, had met at
Mediolanum (Milan) and were discussing all those matters which relate
to the advantage and security of the State, amongst the other things which
we saw would benefit the majority of men we were convinced that first
of all those conditions by which reverence for the Divinity is secured should
be put in order by us to the end that we might give to the Christians and to
all men the right to follow freely whatever religion each had wished, so that
thereby whatever of Divinity there be[2] in the heavenly seat may be favourable and propitious to us and to all those who are placed under our authority.
And so by a salutary and most fitting line of reasoning we came to the conclusion that we should adopt this policy—namely our view should be that
to no one whatsoever should we deny liberty to follow either the religion
of the Christians or any other cult which of his own free choice he has
thought to be best adapted for himself, in order that the supreme Divinity[3],
to whose service we render our free obedience, may bestow upon us in all
things his wonted favour and benevolence. Wherefore we would that your
Devotion should know that it is our will that all those conditions should
be altogether removed which were contained in our former letters addressed
to you concerning the Christians [and which seemed to be entirely perverse
and alien from our clemency[4]]—these should be removed and now in freedom and without restriction let all those who desire to follow the aforesaid
religion of the Christians hasten to follow the same without any molestation or interference. We have felt that the fullest information should be
furnished on this matter to your Carefulness that you might be assured that
we have given to the aforesaid Christians complete and unrestricted liberty
to follow their religion. Further, when you see that this indulgence has
been granted by us to the aforesaid Christians, your Devotion will understand that to others also a similar free and unhindered liberty of religion
and cult has been granted, for such a grant is befitting to the peace of our
times, so that it may be open to every man to worship as he will. This has
been done by us so that we should not seem to have done dishonour to any
religion[5].'

The Emperors then proceed to order the return to the Christians of all confiscated churches[6], whether held by the imperial
Treasury, or by private persons; such restoration is to be made
'sine pecunia et sine ulla pretii petitione.' Similarly all other
properties formerly 'ad ius corporis eorum, id est ecclesiarum
non hominum singulorum pertinentia' are to be given back
'corpori et conventiculis eorum.' The Treasury will undertake to

---

[1] At this point the Latin text of Lactantius begins.
[2] *quicquid ⟨est⟩ divinitatis in sede caelesti.*
[3] Summa Divinitas.
[4] These words are only in the Greek text.
[5] The text in Lactantius is doubtful.
[6] loca ad quae antea convenire consuerant.

indemnify those who are thus deprived of land which they may have purchased. The aim of the imperial legislators is then re-affirmed: it is that 'the divine favour which we have experienced in a crisis of our fortunes may for all time prosper our undertakings and serve the public weal[1].'

III. CONSTANTINE AND LICINIUS

The Roman world was divided between the two victors. But, Italy won, Constantine showed no desire to transfer his court to Rome: he had for many years governed Gaul, and it seemed probable that Arles would become the capital of the Roman West. It was to Arles that the Christian bishops were summoned early in A.D. 314 (see below, p. 693). Italy might be ruled by another. Accordingly, Constantine suggested to Licinius that Bassianus, who had married Constantine's sister Anastasia, should be created Caesar. The brother of Bassianus, Senicio, was a partisan of Licinius, and it was agreed with the latter that Bassianus should attack Constantine. But the treacherous scheme was discovered. Already at Emona the statues of Constantine had been overthrown, and when Licinius refused to surrender Senicio, his complicity was declared[2]. Constantine on his coinage re-asserted his Claudian descent and dynastic claim, collected his forces in the north of Italy and at the head of 20,000 men advanced by way of Aquileia and Noviodunum to Siscia[3] (autumn 314). Near Cibalae (Vinkovce)[4] in Pannonia he was met by the army of Licinius 35,000 strong. That army was encamped in a wide plain; Constantine's march led through a defile, a hill on one side, a deep swamp on the other. But, undeterred, he forthwith attacked with his cavalry and thus won freedom for the advance of his infantry[5]. The battle was fiercely contested until nightfall, when the army of Licinius, deserting its baggage train, fled and did not halt until it

[1] Cf. L. Schnorr von Carolsfeld, *Gesch. der juristischen Person*, I, Munich, 1933, pp. 165 *sqq.*

[2] Our only account is that of Anon. Vales. 14 *sqq.*; Zosimus attributes to Constantine the responsibility for the breach, II, 18 *init.*

[3] J. Maurice, *Numismatique constantinienne*, I, p. xcvi.

[4] V. Nikolić has pointed out that the topographical description in Zosimus II, 18 fits not Cibalae, but Vukovar which lies some miles east of Vinkovce. The *palus Hiulca nomine* mentioned by [Aurelius Victor], *Epit.* XLI, 5 can be identified with the stream of the Vulka or Vuka which still flows through swamps. See Seeck, *op. cit.* Ed. 3, I, p. 505.

[5] The details of the account of the battle in Zosimus II, 18 appear obscure to the present writer.

reached Sirmium. Here the bridge over the Save was destroyed, and Licinius, having lost, it is said, 20,000 men in the battle at Cibalae, made for Thrace where he collected reinforcements. At Adrianople the frontier *dux* Valens was created Augustus[1], and then envoys were sent to Constantine, who was by this time in Philippopolis[2], to treat for peace. Constantine rejected the proposals, and at Campus Mardiensis[3], which probably lay somewhere between Philippopolis and Adrianople, a second battle was fought with great determination on both sides, but with indecisive result. After the battle Constantine lost touch with Licinius: thinking that the latter would make for Byzantium, he marched with all speed for that city only to find that Licinius was at Beroea and that his own lines of communication were thus broken, and reinforcements from the West could be intercepted. But by Constantine's march Licinius was similarly cut off from contact with his base in Asia, and thus it was Licinius who once more sought to negotiate a peace: he sent the *comes* Mestrianus[4] to Constantine and after diplomatic delays a new partition of the Roman world was agreed upon: Constantine gained the provinces of Pannonia, Illyricum, Macedonia, Greece and Moesia, while in Europe Licinius retained only Thrace. Licinius sacrificed his newly created Augustus Valens, and an attempt to secure the recognition of his own son as Caesar was defeated by Constantine[5].

When in the early spring of 313 Licinius had returned to the East to meet the invasion of Maximin, Constantine had been recalled from Milan to Gaul to repel Germans and Franks on the Rhine: at the end of the campaign Ludi Francici (15–20 July) celebrated his success. Henceforth the peace of Gaul was undisturbed: it was the religious divisions in Africa which claimed the Emperor's attention. The Donatists challenged Constantine's decision to exclude them from participation in the imperial benefactions: they prayed him to appoint bishops from Gaul to determine the issue between themselves and the Catholics: it was a step which was to have far-reaching consequences. It is unnecessary in this place to relate in detail the events which followed that appeal, but significant stages must be briefly noticed[6]. Constantine

[1] Maurice, *op. cit.* p. xcvi.
[2] Conjectured by Tillemont for the 'Philippi' of Anon. Vales. 17, cf. Leo Grammaticus (Bonn edn.), p. 85.
[3] Seeck, *op. cit.* I[3], p. 507, conjectures Campus Iarbiensis.
[4] Petrus Patricius, frag. 15 (*F.H.G.* IV, p. 189).
[5] Maurice, *op. cit.* p. xcvii.
[6] For the details see Baynes, *op. cit.* pp. 11–16.

on receipt of the petition referred the matter to Pope Miltiades and three Gallic bishops. Miltiades transformed this small committee into a Council in accordance with the traditional practice of the Church. From the adverse decision of this Roman synod the Donatists appealed: Constantine agreed to summon a more representative assembly. To Arles in 314 came bishops from all those parts of the empire ruled by Constantine: the Church raised no objection to this revision of the Roman judgment, which they independently confirmed. At the same time they took the opportunity to revise the canons issued a few years before by a Council held at Elvira: they expressly recognized that Christians could hold *civil* office without prejudice to their position in the Church[1]; in respect of service in the army, however, canon 3 is less explicit and has provoked discussion: 'Qui in pace arma proiiciunt excommunicentur': the words 'in pace' have been taken to mean 'now that persecution has ceased.' The present writer believes that the words should be given their natural sense: the Council condemns such conduct as that of Maximilian and Marcellus (see p. 663); it will not derogate from the rule that for a Christian the shedding of blood has once for all been condemned. But with the adverse decision of the Council of Arles the Donatists were not content: they appealed for Constantine's own judgment on their case: for a long time he hesitated, but at last in November 316 he yielded, and himself determined the issue: by an imperial constitution the Donatist churches were confiscated, the military repression of Donatism began, and the Donatist calendar of martyrs was formed. It was this experience which determined the action of Constantine when the Council of Nicaea had met in 325: there must be no Donatist schism in the Eastern provinces.

Constantine's plan for devolving upon another the government of Italy had failed. He spent the first half of the year 315 in the provinces which he had acquired from Licinius, and the second in Rome and Milan. In 316 he was in the Gaul which he knew so well. From Trèves by way of Vienne he went to Arles. And then there comes the change: Gaul which he had pacified held him no longer: he turned to his eastern provinces: at Serdica on March 1, 317[2] new Caesars were created—Constantine's two sons Crispus and Constantine and the younger Licinius, a bastard born

---

[1] Canon 7 only *cum coeperint contra disciplinam agere, tum demum a communione excludantur*—presumably this means 'when they have taken part in pagan ceremonies.'

[2] On the appearance in this year of the Christian standard borne by Constantine's bodyguard, the Labarum, see Baynes *op. cit.* p. 63.

of a slave. It is at Sirmium in the same year that Constantine's third son Constantius was born. Apart from a visit to Italy in the summer of 318 Constantine did not return to the West: from his constitutions he can be followed as he moves from Serdica to Sirmium and back again to Serdica: it must have been at this time that he thought of making Serdica his capital: 'My Rome is Serdica,' he said[1]. It was from these provinces that he was to march to the second and conclusive struggle with his colleague Licinius.

In the legislation of the years which preceded that civil war the influence of Christianity can be traced. Thus, for example, in 318 it is provided that even where the hearing of a case has begun before a civil judge, the matter shall at the wish of the parties be transferred to the bishop's court and the latter's decision shall be final[2]. In 321 it is enacted that manumissions, if granted in a church in presence of the clergy, shall be valid without the further formalities required by Roman law[3]. Despite the doubts of some scholars the constitutions dealing with the observance of the *Venerabilis dies solis*, though cast in a pagan form, were probably inspired by reverence for the Christian Sunday[4]. In the Eastern provinces Licinius, after the publication of his letter of 313, so far as we know, showed no further favour towards the Christians, and gradually drifted back into a policy of repression. This change seems to have been the result of the growing alienation between Constantine and his colleague. In 319 Constantine as senior Augustus announced himself and his son Constantine as consuls for 320; for 321 he nominated his sons Crispus and Constantine; the Caesar Licinius was passed over. That nomination was not recognized by Licinius. Hostility was thus openly declared.

It is from this time (320–321), it would seem, that the vexatious measures of Licinius against the Christians are first enforced. No Church Councils might in future be held, Christians must not meet in churches, but only in the open air outside the cities, and at their services men and women should not share in a common worship. Once more the imperial court was cleared of Christians, while civil servants lost their appointments if they refused to sacrifice[5]. Many governors went much further, and

---

[1] Anon. Dionis Continuator, frag. 15 (*F.H.G.* iv, p. 199).

[2] *Cod. Theod.* i, 27, 1.

[3] *Ib.* iv, 7, 1. Cf. *Cod. Just.* i, 13, 1.

[4] *Cod. Theod.* ii, 8, 1. *Cod. Just.* iii, 12, 2. Cf. A. Piganiol, *L'empereur Constantin*, pp. 128–9, who refers to *C.I.L.* iii, 4121.

[5] The evidence does not seem adequate to support the conclusion that there was a *general* persecution in the army.

some bishops were martyred—though we know no details. Thus at Amasia exceptional brutality was shown, and the account of the deaths of the Forty Martyrs of Sebastia *may* be rightly dated to the persecution of Licinius. It has been contended that the repressive policy of Licinius was intended to secure the support against Constantine of the pagans of the West: but Constantine's pagan subjects had no cause for complaint, and the Roman West had not shown any enthusiasm for repressive measures. There seems little reason to abandon the explanation of Eusebius: Licinius regarded the Christians of the Eastern provinces as partisans of Constantine and in consequence sought to weaken the Christian Church.

In the years after 320 it became increasingly clear that a civil war was imminent, and both rulers prepared for the struggle. Each realized that sea-power would be of importance for the control of the waterway between Europe and Asia, and for this reason built up large fleets. Constantine constructed a new harbour at Salonica. In 323 Constantine, while repelling a Gothic invasion, trespassed on the territory of Licinius, and thus gave the latter a ground for complaint. It now appears certain that the outbreak of war is to be dated not to A.D. 323, but to A.D. 324[1]. At Adrianople, situated at the confluence of the Maritza and the Tunja, Licinius in a fortified camp awaited Constantine's attack[2]. Advancing from Salonica the latter, after some days of inconsiderable skirmishes, distracted the attention of Licinius, crossed the river, and then under the cover of an attack by 5000 archers was joined by his army on the further bank. On July 3 there was a hotly fought general engagement. Licinius, leaving, we are told, 34,000 men dead on the field of battle, fled to Byzantium, where he was besieged by Constantine. Crispus, Constantine's seventeen-year-old son, now sailed from Salonica in nominal command of his father's fleet. The admiral of Licinius, Abantus, was posted at the mouth of the Dardanelles on the Asiatic side of the Straits. In the first day's engagement, owing to the narrowness of the channel, Crispus brought only eighty of his ships into action, and the result of the encounter was indecisive. Crispus withdrew to the shelter of Cape Helles. The following morning Constantine's whole fleet was engaged: the elements fought against Licinius: the northerly wind which had carried both fleets out to sea died down: and then a gale from the south spread panic amongst the

---

[1] E. Stein in *Zeits. für d. neutest. Wissenschaft*, xxx, 1931, pp. 177–85.

[2] The best study of the campaign is by E. Pears, *Eng. Hist. Rev.* xxiv, 1909, pp. 1–17.

crews of Licinius' ships: the galleys were dashed upon the rocks and islets south of the entrance to the Dardanelles. One hundred and thirty ships were lost. Crispus could sail to Byzantium unmolested. Before his arrival Licinius had crossed to the Asiatic shore. Constantine then collected as many light transports as he could find, and without raising the suspicions of Licinius by moving his fleet from Byzantium, he effected a landing on the Asiatic coast at a point 'near the mouth of the Pontus,' perhaps in the neighbourhood of the village of Riva. Hence he pressed on to Scutari (Chrysopolis) where Licinius had fixed his camp. Here on September 18, 324 the battle was fought which sealed the fate of Licinius. His wife Constantia appealed to the generosity of her brother: Constantine spared his rival and banished him to Salonica. The era of persecution was closed.

IV. CONSTANTINE AND THE CHURCH

This struggle between Licinius and Constantine is represented as a religious war, a trial of strength between the gods of paganism and the Christian God, and there is no reason to doubt the substantial truth of that interpretation. But it is also true that Constantine was now set upon realizing that vision of world-wide empire which long before had formed the theme of Gallic panegyrists. He claimed to be a descendant of Claudius Gothicus—once the sole ruler of the Roman world—and the title to that single *imperium* was his by right of birth. He had waited long, but the restoration of unity was the mission entrusted to him by the God of the Christians and that God had sustained him in all his ways. Lactantius had been right: the end of the persecutors had proven their sin. Diocletian's death had passed almost unnoticed, probably in A.D. 316; he had refused to be brought back to the tasks of government. The building of his palace at Salonae had filled his idle days, and after his abdication the only intimate view of him that has been preserved is his exasperation when the consciences of Christian stone-masons in Pannonia forbade them to fashion for that palace a statue of Aesculapius[1]. Galerius and Maximin had both died of loathsome diseases, and Licinius owed his life only to the victor's clemency. The Christian standard, the Labarum, had triumphed, and a Christian capital of the Roman world should form a majestic war memorial.

In November 324 the transformation of Byzantium into the City of Constantine was begun. It has been objected that it is an

---

[1] *Passio SS. Quattuor Coronatorum.* AA. SS. November, vol. III, pp. 748–84.

error to speak of Constantine's foundation as a Christian city: it is true that the pagan temples were not destroyed, that just as Rome had her Tyche—her Fortune—so naturally must the Eastern capital have her Tyche, her presiding spirit: this is traditional form; true also that pagan statues were collected from every side and housed in Constantinople as an adornment for the city, but when all this—and more—is admitted, the fact remains that the essential act in pagan worship was sacrifice, and pagan sacrifice, it is acknowledged, was banished from Constantine's city. That is the crucial fact, and because of that fact Constantinople stood as a *Christian* Rome[1]. From the first its destiny was determined. Some have sought to minimize the significance of Constantinople in the later history of the Empire: in the writer's view, that significance can hardly be overestimated. While Constantinople stood impregnable, the Empire stood, and it might without paradox be claimed that the foundation of the city which through the centuries bore his name was Constantine's most signal achievement.

But though imperial unity had been restored, there remained a further task for 'the man of God': he must restore unity within the Christian Church. The Council of Nicaea is in its own sphere the necessary complement to the victory at Chrysopolis. In the West the repression of the Donatists had proved a failure: on May 5, 321 a letter from Constantine granted to the schismatics a scornful tolerance. At a time when Licinius was beginning to persecute the Christians, Constantine would make no more martyrs. He left to God the punishment of the schismatics. Constantine had hoped to find in the provinces of the Roman East that religious unity which had been broken in the West: in place of unity he was faced with discord, with the Melitian schism— the Eastern parallel to Donatism—and the Arian heresy. To apply the remedy for such disunion was an urgent duty which admitted of no delay. At Nicaea Constantine's influence secured the adoption of a creed which should form the basis for the reconciliation of the conflicting parties. The Emperor asked only that the bishops should accept the creed: he declined to allow any official interpretation of its meaning: it was to be an eirenicon and not a source of further disagreements. To the creed of Nicaea Constantine remained loyal until his death, and at his death his policy had been so far successful that there was only one recalcitrant

[1] Whether Constantine gave the name of 'New Rome' to his city is disputed. Cf. F. Dölger, *Zeits. f. Kirchengesch.* LVI, 3. Folge, VI, 1937, pp. 1 *sqq.* That it was conceived by him as a Second Rome there is no doubt.

exile, Athanasius, and for him the see of Alexandria remained vacant. Athanasius had but to kiss the rod and the Emperor's triumph was complete.

In any attempt to recover and interpret the thought of Constantine it must never be forgotten that he is a Roman Emperor and a statesman. The emperor's ecclesiastical policy is a part of his imperial statesmanship, for that statesmanship was based upon the conviction of a mission in the service of the Christian God. Thus Christian theology may become a danger if it threatens to create disunion amongst the faithful. The dispute between Arius and his bishop is for Constantine an idle enquiry on points of the smallest consequence. Other Christian rulers have shared his outlook. We are reminded of the contempt of Elizabeth of England for the disputes of the German Protestants concerning the omnipresence of the body of Christ: to the Queen these were 'unprofitable discussions.' To Constantine, as to James I, unity was 'the mother of order' and it was thus but natural that James should hold that it was the duty of Christian Kings to govern their church 'by reforming of corruptions...by judging and cutting off all frivolous questions and schisms, as Constantine did[1].' Constantine's refusal to enquire curiously how bishops might interpret the creed of Nicaea provided only that they accepted it recalls Elizabeth's denial that she sought 'to make a window into men's souls,' and to a Tudor sovereign as to the Roman Emperor national prosperity was the seal which God had set upon the ruler's work: 'it is clear as daylight that God's blessing rests upon us, upon our people and realm with all the plainest signs of prosperity, peace, obedience, riches, power and increase of our subjects.' The words do but echo Constantine's thought. It is through comparison with other rulers who were faced with similar problems of ecclesiastical statesmanship that we may gain a fuller insight into the policy of the first Christian Emperor.

With the later years of the reign of Constantine this chapter has no concern: it is intended merely to form the bridge which leads to another history—the story of Europe's Middle Age. Eusebius had celebrated the issue of the first Edict of Toleration by publishing his *History of the Church*; after Constantine's victory over every rival the bishop of Caesarea formulated for the first time the theory of Christian sovereignty which was to remain the unquestioned foundation for the political thought of the East Roman world. But in that formulation there is no complete

---

[1] 'An Apologie for the Oath of Allegiance,' p. 108, in *Harvard Political Classics*, i, 1918.

breach with the past; many threads are gathered up and woven into the new pattern. The Iranian conception of kingly power as a trust from God had, since Aurelian's day, once more taken the place of an identification of the ruler with deity. And this view of the Emperor as deriving his authority from God had close parallels in Jewish and Christian thought: 'thou couldest have no power at all against me except it were given thee from above.' And when once the God-kingship had been abandoned, the rest of the Hellenistic theory of sovereignty could be adopted with hardly any change of language. The emperor's aim, for the Christian as for the pagan, is the imitation of God, just as the earthly State should be a copy of the heavenly order. Precisely as the Greek king has for guiding principle the divine Logos, so for the Christian emperor there is a divine Logos, the Word of God, to lead and counsel him. Thus the theory of Christian sovereignty as Eusebius set it forth is itself a symbol of the way in which the past of the ancient world was carried over into the Christian Empire. But though the transition is thus mediated there is none the less at this time a break and a turning-point in Roman history; the first Christian emperor was, indeed, as Ammianus described him, a 'turbator rerum,' a revolutionary. Constantine sitting amongst the Christian bishops at the oecumenical council of Nicaea is in his own person the beginning of Europe's Middle Age.

EPILOGUE

The third century of our era witnessed what must have seemed for a time to be the break-up of that strong system which for generations had held together the civilized world, a system in which the internationalism of the ancient world had culminated. What the Roman Empire made fact had, it is true, been preceded by partial approximations, and its debt to these is not to be underrated, hard though it often is to define it with certainty. The effect of the past is deeper and more extensive than is accounted for by tradition and memory, by institutions and conscious culture. Particularly among the ancient peoples of the Near East, who had largely come to be subjects of the Roman Empire, there were deep-seated instincts that reflected their life centuries before Rome was even a name to them. These peoples had seen the rise and fall of empires, the dignity of Egypt, the force of the Assyrians, the sophistication of Babylonia, and, as the archives of the fourteenth and thirteenth centuries show, the world of the Near East had known an age of precocious internationalism from the Aegean to Babylonia. The Iranian Empire of Persia had proved that a people, small in numbers but heirs of that internationalism, could dominate, if not wholly govern, a great range of countries, the power of the Great King radiating along roads which foreshadowed the achievements of the Romans. The politic wisdom of toleration, and that not in religion only, was known to the Persians, and some of their statecraft was taken over by their final conquerors and became part of the general heritage of imperial ideas.

Apart from experiments in the art of imperial government, the earliest period of known ancient history saw adventures in culture. Two thousand years before Rome became a city, ordered life in Crete had sheltered an art which was later matched by Greece of the Mycenaean age. And at the time when the labyrinthine palace of Cnossus was rising in secure splendour, a king in Babylon, Hammurabi, was elaborating a code in which men were subtly enmeshed in niceties of law, niceties which never entirely lost their hold. Masterful Pharaohs built their tombs to commemorate the past and to challenge the future. Whatever might be the disasters that broke upon the empires of the Tigris and the Nile, the idea may well have penetrated the minds of men that external grandeur and culture linked with power were to be defended as a possession or acquired as a prize. The ancient world was adept in taking its captors captive. Civilizations might appear to die, but civilization seemed to have in itself the seeds of immortality. In general, culture was bound up with authority. As time went on, art in Persia, for example, was the handmaid of an imperial sovereignty, the formal expression of a political fact.

In the meantime, in a small land that was of slight political importance, there was developed a new form of religion, authoritarian in its monotheism, which in Judaism by slow degrees raised up new values that outlived mundane vicissitudes, and ended by exalting the figure of the martyr rather than of the conqueror. Overlaid though it was by the racial and the legalistic, Jewish religion was destined to burn through to be a light from the East, so that from Judaism there was to proceed a religious movement which, in part by continuity and in part by conflict, was to become a power able to mould the Roman Empire itself. Nor was this the only contribution which the Eastern world was to make. Mithraism had its roots in ancient Persian belief, the religiosity of Egypt was long lived, the wisdom of the Babylonians continued to appeal to those who sought to rationalize, or at least dignify, fatalism.

But in all this something was still lacking, the claim of an unfettered intellectualism and of political ideas whereby nothing passed unchallenged. There grew up in Greek lands the city-state, in which culture belonged to the citizens, in which the citizen was the measure of all things human and almost all things divine. First in Ionia and then in Greece physical and ethical speculation, freed from the mythological elements of the past, led on to systems of philosophy which were to affect profoundly the culture of the ancient world. Despite comparatively transient autocracies, the Greek States were tenaciously republican, and when they had to accept the hegemony of a king, they retained institutions which continued to be theirs for centuries after they had become parts of the Roman Empire. Under Alexander the Great and his successors the Greek city-state spread over the Eastern world, and though the Greeks were too few to recreate the East in their own image, their culture and ways of thinking set standards to which a great Western power might appeal.

This power presently arose. On the banks of the Tiber another city grew to strength at the cost, or for the advantage, of its neighbours. The Italian peninsula, under Roman control, became the political centre of the Mediterranean world. Never wholly untouched by things Greek, Roman civilization acquired a Hellenic element which fitted the Republic to compound its instinctive statecraft with the more intellectualized practice of the Hellenistic monarchies which it supplanted. Destructive as Rome's power was to much that was finest in Greek life, relentless as was her advance to domination, yet she preserved Hellenic ideas and added to them her own. Policy and the chances of war brought the Western Mediterranean lands within the range of Roman control, and to the peoples of those lands Rome could bring a civilization that was Graeco-Roman and not Roman alone. All Italy became Roman, and the Italo-Roman people was able to set on the West a stamp still visible to-day.

In the Near East Rome had put an end to the wars of the rival Greek monarchies. The dream of the restoration of the single empire of Alexander the Great had now become accomplished fact. That which the Greeks had failed to effect had been achieved by Rome. And when the Hellenistic kingdoms had been overthrown, the conqueror was content to leave the Greek East to live its own life and think its own thoughts within a world secured by the 'immense majesty of the Roman peace.' The early Principate did not rudely impose upon all provinces alike a single administrative system; methods remained flexible, there was room for local adaptation and for the survival of cherished institutions. That is Rome's imperial secret: she was not in a hurry. In Western Europe she could trust to the attraction exercised by the civilization which was her gift. There was thus within the Empire diversity, but diversity in unity. From the first the subjects of Rome acquired the habit of looking to the *princeps* as to a human Providence: 'through him they lived, through him they sailed the seas, through him they enjoyed their liberty and their fortunes.' Under the protection of this Providence the countries of the Mediterranean world were bound together through peaceful commerce and intercourse, and through likeness, if not uniformity, of culture.

The early Empire was not always successful: it could not appease Jewish nationalism, it did nothing permanent to alleviate the lot of the Egyptian peasant. Apart, too, from any resistance it met, Graeco-Roman culture was not as vigorous and as secure as it seemed to be. Its ideals were too static, and the world did not stand still. Rome had contributed few vital and original ideas to form the content of the peace which she had established. The Greek world of thought was living on an inherited capital, and a rhetorical education made words of greater importance than the thoughts which they expressed. Imperial intervention in municipal affairs, however well-intentioned, tended to paralyse the generosity and patriotism of the city's benefactors, while the peasants, exploited by the city-dwellers, were also the victims of the greed and violence of an undisciplined soldiery. The opening decades of the third century saw in Persia the overthrow of Parthian rule and the establishment of the Sassanid dynasty supported by a newly awakened national sentiment. Antioch lay too near to enemy territory; Persian raiders crossed the Euphrates and sacked the capital of the Roman East. Throughout the length of the Empire's northern frontier—from the Rhine to the Black Sea— the barbarian world was on the move. Germanic tribes which lived by war saw before them an empire to plunder. An Empire organized on a peace footing, as Augustus had conceived it, could not stand the strain. The defensive system fixed by Hadrian and his successors was broken down. Small wonder that when the central government failed them provincial armies should seek to defend the land from which they had been recruited—that Postumus should found an empire of the Gauls, that Rome's ally the prince of Palmyra should seize the opportunity of the Empire's weakness to establish an independent kingdom, that on every hand generals made a bid for the purple and still further disorganized the Roman defence. It looked as though the unification of the Mediterranean world was at an end.

The third century is thus a period of crisis, of experiment and of transition. The military crisis brought economic chaos in its train. Every new emperor was forced to purchase the loyalty of his army; the world had, indeed, learned the art of spending, but not of saving. Any great emergency found little in the imperial treasury but hope, and the coming of the Golden Age of prosperity, so often proclaimed, was as often delayed, for the needs of the State had grown greatly and the power to meet them by ordinary taxation had declined. In both the military and economic spheres emperors tried expedient after expedient: in the army they resorted to special formations of picked troops, or to the introduction of new weapons or of defensive armour borrowed from their enemies: to meet growing expenditure they raised extraordinary contributions in kind from the provinces through which the armies marched, and debasement of the coinage was continuously carried to greater lengths. All, it seemed, to little effect.

Yet the threatened dissolution of the world which Rome had unified was in fact averted; and the restoration of the closing decades of the third century was essentially the work of the

Balkan soldiery and of the Illyrian emperors. Here in the Balkan peninsula pagan Rome had found her last great mission field and her converts were enthusiastic in defence of the Roman tradition as they conceived it. The history of the third century is for us a thing of shreds and patches; we can best understand it through studying the solutions which the emperors of the restoration brought to the problems that were its legacy. One of the most pressing of those problems was the safeguarding of the emperor's authority, for though there had been an increase in autocratic power there had also been an increase in the emperor's dependence upon his troops: by their will he was made and as readily unmade.

During the three centuries since Romanism had triumphed with the victory of Augustus at Actium the West of Europe had been romanized, but in the third century the pendulum was swinging back once more towards the East. In economics, in warfare, in religion and in literature the centre of gravity had shifted from Italy and the West. Diocletian fixing his capital at Nicomedia was in a Greek land, and for the folk of the Near East the absolutism of the successors of Alexander the Great had become second nature. Here the citizen Principate of Augustus had never been understood: from the first the emperor had been king, and consequently Lord and God. In the third century this conception had gained ground; the imperial house had become the *domus divina*: the emperor enjoyed the favour of the God who was his companion on the throne. Yet that favour was readily transferable and conferred no fixity of tenure: it might be a sail, but it was not an anchor. The Unconquered Sun had been unable to save Aurelian from assassination. Diocletian, by admitting and regularizing at his court a ceremonial which was appropriate to Greek conceptions of the imperial authority, was seeking to free the emperor from subjection to the passions of his soldiery. Here is the beginning of that 'imperial liturgy,' the strange mixture of civil and religious rites which was preserved with scrupulous care at the court of the Byzantine Caesars.

This instance is typical of Diocletian's work of restoration: it was based throughout upon previous experiment or contemporary practice. In finance the former extraordinary contributions in kind now formed the permanent basis of the Empire's system of taxation; the third century had already seen emperors ruling as colleagues, one in the East, the other in the West: of this the Tetrarchy of two Augusti and two Caesars is but an extension. By putting the undivided imperial office into commission Diocletian sought, as it were, to outnumber any usurper. Emperors had attempted to make good in some measure the lack of a mobile expeditionary force; in the *comitatenses* the Diocletio-Constantinian restoration created such an army. Diocletian's use of the *equites* as provincial governors, his separation of civil and military careers did but generalize previous usage. The Emperor's innovations are essentially a consistent adoption and elaboration of the tentative expedients through which his predecessors had sought escape from the crisis of the third century. Here and there the issue falsified his hopes—the Tetrarchy, for instance, broke down before rival ambitions—but, for good or evil, he set the Empire on its feet. It was given a new lease of life, though the Empire's subjects paid a high price for its survival.

But it is as a period of transition that the third century will always claim the interest of the student. The ancient magistracies, the constitutional executive which the Principate had inherited from the Republic, no longer play any part in the Empire's government, though they still carry with them high social distinction; the Senate as a body has similarly ceased to control policy of State. The emperor and the emperor's service alone remain. Thus Diocletian's restoration is itself part of the transition from the ancient world to the Middle Ages, for it is on the ruins of the Roman State as Diocletian planned it that the Teutonic kingdoms were built: its laws were taken up into their codes and so far as the invaders could they copied its administrative system. Neoplatonism is part also of that transition, for Neoplatonism, a philosophy which was also a religion, reinforced the faith of pagan thinkers, and it was Neoplatonism and not Mithraism which inspired the pagan leaders in their last attacks upon the 'Galileans,' while for many it may have proved to be, as it was for Augustine, but a stage on the road which led to Christianity.

In this period Italy steadily declines in importance: in literature the Italian peninsula is strangely unproductive. Gaul boasts her schools whence come the Latin panegyrists, while Africa leads the Latin West. It is once more a sign of the transition that literature, whether in Africa or the Near East, is, in large measure, the work of Christian writers. Men were being prepared for the culture of the Christian Empire: even the long lines of single uniform figures on the Arch of Constantine point forward to the art of Ravenna.

The universalism of the Empire—the desire for imperial unity —had sought expression through a religious cult, but neither Sol Invictus of Aurelian's worship nor Juppiter Optimus Maximus of Diocletian's allegiance could secure lasting unity. There was one

element, indeed, that actively opposed any such pagan universalism. The Christian Church was now a community as wide as
the Empire itself; its church order had given it the fixity of a
State, and it had survived the persecution under Decius and
Valerian with principles unprejudiced or modified only by a timely
concession that enabled it to reassemble its forces for another trial
of strength. Pagan and Christian were learning to live together:
the issue now lay between the State and the Church rather than
between Christian and pagan. If it is true that the Great Persecution under Diocletian was forced upon the Emperor by Galerius,
it would then appear rather an episode than the expression of an
irreconcilable antithesis.

It is worthy of note that in the last great attack upon the
Church the initiative has in general passed wholly into the hands
of the State. It is only in exceptional cases that popular hostility
is actively engaged. This fact serves to explain the unforced
association of pagan and Christian in the fourth century: the
martyrs and confessors after the middle of the third century had
suffered primarily from the intransigence of the Roman State, and
not from the animosity of their pagan fellow-citizens. But beyond
this striking conciliation in social life there is a further third-
century movement which bore its full fruit only in the later years of
the fourth century—the conciliation between the Christian Church
and the culture of the ancient world. The tradition initiated in the
school of Alexandria by Clement and Origen did not die with
them: even in prison during the persecution Pamphilus, the
master of Eusebius, continued his work of scholarship. Here
Lactantius is a significant figure, writing his *Divine Institutes*
especially for the cultured pagans of his day. Before the persecution many from the educated and professional classes were joining
the Church. It was becoming possible to separate pagan literature
from the pagan faith with which it had always been so intimately
associated. For Julian the Apostate such a separation was intolerable: one was not dealing merely with a literature, but with
sacred books—with scriptures. He who would expound the
scriptures must believe in their message. It is precisely Julian's
banishment of Christian teachers from the schools which arouses
furious exasperation in S. Gregory of Nazianzus: the masterpieces of the ancient world are a common possession to be shared
by pagan and by Christian. There were, indeed, those who, like
Chrysostom, found it difficult to overcome inherited scruples; in
unguarded moments they might condemn the whole of pagan
literature, but the Greek Fathers of the later fourth century had

been educated in the same school as their pagan contemporaries. Yet though in speech and writing both employ the same rhetorical style, there is yet a difference: the Christian has a vital message to proclaim, and from the pulpit he still addresses not only the scholar but also the simple believers—the throng of common folk. The pagan writer of the period is concerned not so much with the subject-matter of his oration, but rather with the form of its presentation and his audience is in general a narrow and highly cultured circle. To read a speech of Libanius and then to turn to a homily of Chrysostom is an instructive experience. A fact that is not always remembered is that it was this separation of the classical literature from the pagan faith which rendered it easy for the Church to appropriate the culture of the fourth-century world, and which among pagans opened the way for the victorious expansion of the Church.

When once the failure of the persecution had been avowed, a toleration granted by express enactment was the natural result of the situation thus created: what could not have been expected was the profession by a Roman emperor of the Christian faith. It was Constantine's action coming precisely when it did which led the Church to raise no questions, to accept without hesitation the gifts of imperial favour—the unilateral offer of an alliance. Had the conversion of the first Christian emperor come a century later, a far more powerful and more numerous Christian society might have imposed its own terms upon imperial authority: it might not, for instance, have so readily admitted the emperor's right to summon the Councils of the Church or to sanction by his approval the conciliar decisions: it might have insisted on a far-reaching revision of Roman Law. It is not merely the fact of Constantine's conversion, but that it took place immediately after the dark hour of the Great Persecution that gives it so permanent a significance in the history of the Church.

Of great importance in the Empire's history is the effect of Constantine's whole personality: here was the man chosen by the will of God to fulfil His purpose. This belief he impressed so deeply upon his contemporaries that it became an integral part of the political theology of the later Roman Empire. The emperor's title to rule comes to him from God ($\dot{\epsilon}\kappa\ \Theta\epsilon o\hat{v}$), and human electors do but ratify the judgment of Heaven. And similarly Constantine repeatedly asserted his conviction that the unity of the Church was the condition and guarantee of the prosperity of the Empire. It may well seem that for this principle of a united Church the Empire suffered and sacrificed much, but in the end the dream of

Constantine was realized, and a common religious belief became the cement which bound together the folk of East Rome. To the unquestioned acceptance of such beliefs as these the personal experience and the personality of Constantine must have contributed not a little.

The Near East had remained a Greek world: when Diocletian sought to encourage the spread of Latin in the Asiatic provinces, it proved to be too late in the day to inaugurate such a change, and the effort failed. But throughout the Empire Latin remained the language of Roman law, and Latin was in consequence studied in the Roman law schools, as at Berytus. Not only were both Diocletian and Constantine very active as legislators, but at this time a first beginning was made with the codification of the law of the Empire. There were two collections of the constitutions of the emperors, the *Codex Gregorianus* and the *Codex Hermogenianus*, the latter containing only constitutions issued during the reign of Diocletian. Both, however, were the work of private citizens and unofficial. It was long before the example thus set was followed by the State and imperial authority issued the codifications of Theodosius and Justinian. In the sphere of law, as elsewhere, Constantine was an innovator and it was he who first conferred upon the bishops judicial powers. The original extent of that grant has been disputed, but during the fourth century more and more of a bishop's time was occupied by what were really affairs of State. The Emperor had given his support to the Christian Church: the Church should in turn provide the State with a less corrupt administration of justice than that of its own lay judges. And because the Church had not remodelled the law of pagan Rome, it was forced to supplement imperial legislation; it had standards of conduct unrecognized by the law of the State and these it sought to enforce through ecclesiastical ordinance. The Church began in its Councils to fashion its own canon law.

The fourth century learned from the experiments of the third and systematized the latter's tentative solutions. Among the expedients to which the third century had had recourse were two convenient, but perilous principles—those of corporate liability and hereditary obligation. To these the fourth-century State resorted when, faced with the burden of the added pomp of the court and of the upkeep of an enlarged civil service and an increased army, it was compelled to secure its revenues. The result was that the initiative of the subject was stifled, that the aristocracy of the towns was ruined, and that in province after province the free peasants were successively reduced to the position of *coloni*, tied to the soil. The subject existed for the State, and the State was a ruthless taskmaster. Where powerful landed proprietors asserted themselves against the imperial claim it was at the expense of the common good and in selfish isolation. Under the strain of a burden unevenly borne the West of the Empire foundered in bankruptcy; the Eastern provinces, it was true, kept the barbarians at bay, but in the task of conciliating their own subjects the emperors of Constantinople failed. The Syrian and the Egyptian resented exploitation at the hands of 'the King's men,' and disaffection was ended only by the Arab Conquest.

But elsewhere the third century pointed the way to a masterstroke. The wars on the Eastern frontier had summoned emperors time and again to Antioch; Diocletian had fixed his court at Nicomedia. At first Serdica had been for Constantine his Rome, and before he finally chose Byzantium for his capital he had begun building on the site of Troy. The city to which Constantine gave his own name solved the third century's search for an Eastern capital: for a thousand years it stood as the fortress which guarded civilization, as the power-house of the Empire. With the sea at its gates, with the majestic harbour of the Golden Horn to shelter the imperial fleet, with its landward and seaward fortifications, it was indeed a peerless stronghold. Never until the fatal day when in 1204 the Crusaders captured the city did foreign arms break down the bulwark of the walls of New Rome. No small part of the significance of Constantine's foundation lay in the fact that Constantinople was from the first a Christian city and that its choice was directed by God. The God of the Christians, the Mother of God whose robe was later to be the city's Palladium—these would surely defend their own. Until 1204 that confidence was never disappointed. The foundation of New Rome, the Christian capital *in partibus Orientis*, may well be regarded as the symbolic act which brings to a close the history of the ancient world.

APPENDIX ON SOURCES

(1) LITERARY AUTHORITIES

CASSIUS DIO COCCEIANUS (see vol. XI, p. 855) had held important posts both in the provinces and in Rome; he was twice consul, the second time as colleague of Severus Alexander in 229. He spent ten years in collecting material and then wrote a complete 'annalistic' history of Rome down to the year 229 in eighty books (LXXIII, 23, 5)[1]. Of events after 180 he was himself a contemporary and eyewitness (LXXIII, 4, 2). After A.D. 46 (LX, 28, 3)— save for the incomplete texts of books 79 and 80 and for fragments preserved by Constantine Porphyrogenitus—we possess his history only in the compendium of Johannes Xiphilinus (eleventh century). For Dio's own view of the Imperial constitution in the third century the speech put into the mouth of Maecenas (LII, 14–40) is of the highest interest (see above, p. 59 sq.).

HERODIAN, a Syrian Greek, wrote in the third century a history of the years 180–238 in eight books. For the latter part of the period he speaks as a contemporary observer. He supplements the history of Dio, whose work he did not use. His style is rhetorical, and the lengthy speeches which he is fond of inserting are a weariness to the reader.

The HISTORIA AUGUSTA (see vol. XI, p. 856) is a collection of lives (written ostensibly by six authors) of the Roman emperors from Hadrian down to Numerianus, though the biographies from 244 to 253 are missing. The collection purports to be dated to the reigns of Diocletian and Constantine, and some scholars still accept this dating (see above, p. 598). But it is now generally held that the work in its present form is a product of the second half of the fourth century, whether of the reign of Julian the Apostate (see above, p. 58), or of the reign of Theodosius. It has also been proposed to date the collection to the early years of the fifth century, though the suggestion that it was compiled in Merovingian Gaul has won no wide support[2]. The date of composition is of significance, as far as the present volume is concerned, mainly for the reign of Severus Alexander of whom the *Historia Augusta* has a singular biography of otherwise unexampled length. If this is in reality an anachronistic picture of the imperial ideals of Julian the Apostate, this fact must necessarily influence the use made of the life in writing the history of the reign. In the same way if the main 'tendency' of the *Historia Augusta* is hostility to Christianity (p. 223), this will similarly affect the student's judgment of the historical value of not a few parts of the collection. These questions are still under discussion, and it is thus only natural that a difference of view is reflected in different chapters of the present volume.

[1] References from Dio are given according to Boissevain's edition, books being cited by the numbers on the left-hand pages of that work. Where any doubt can arise because of this notation, a reference is given to the page of Boissevain's edition.

[2] For representative works in the controversy about the character, value, date and purpose of the *Historia Augusta*, see below, p. 730.

Also the acceptance or rejection of details given in the work is bound to be governed by considerations of general probability and by the extent to which the sources that have been used can be controlled by their re-appearance in later historical writings (see below, p.   ).

In the poverty of our other sources for the history of the third century an increased importance attaches to the later brief epitomes of the history of the Empire. SEXTUS AURELIUS VICTOR, an African, wrote (c. 360) a *historia abbreviata*—the *Caesares*—which covered the period from Augustus to Constantius; another short history of the Empire (down to Theodosius) which purports to be an *Epitome* of the *Caesares* is really an independent work of which only the earliest part is in any way derived from Aurelius Victor. In the reign of Valens EUTROPIUS wrote his *Breviarium ab urbe condita*; one of the most important and hotly disputed literary problems of the fourth century is the question whether the writers or compiler of the *Historia Augusta* used the *Breviarium* of Eutropius, or whether Eutropius and the *Historia Augusta* both drew upon a (lost) common source. On the answer to this question depends in large measure the precise dating of the *Historia Augusta*.

RUFIUS FESTUS in his *Breviarium* (probably written after 369 and dedicated to the Emperor Valens) sketched the growth and expansion of Rome's Empire and then in the second part of his compendium gave an outline of the relations of Rome with the East. The Persian wars of the fourth century would naturally awake an interest in such a subject.

AMMIANUS MARCELLINUS, the last true historian of the ancient world, a soldier writing in Rome and, though a Greek, in the Latin language, composed, towards the close of the fourth century, a history of the Empire from Nerva down to A.D. 378. Unfortunately the thirteen books which brought the history down to the year 353 are lost, and for the period covered by the present volume it is only in chance references to earlier events that the work is of service. Our reconstruction of the course of the third-century development would be far more securely founded than it in fact is if we possessed the lost books of one who wrote with impartiality and with personal knowledge alike of the Roman West and the Roman East.

Of later works the *Historia Nova* of ZOSIMUS (written in Greek between 450 and 501) is of importance since, for his account of the movements of the Goths in the third century, he drew upon the *Scythica* of DEXIPPUS, an Athenian who played a leading part in the history of his city during the years 253 to 276 and had himself lived through the Gothic invasions. Further, Zosimus is of interest since he represents the pagan point of view, using as a source the lost history of Eunapius. But as a writer he is hurried and careless; his use of his sources is exasperating and the effort to obtain from his work any clear chronology appears at times to be a hopeless task. Similarly for Gothic history the work of JORDANES—*Getica*—published in A.D. 551 is significant, since it preserves extracts from the lost work on that subject of Cassiodorus, though here again the extracts are unskilfully put together.

But Greek historiography continued for many centuries, and some names must be mentioned however briefly. PETRUS PATRICIUS, born c. 500, was ambassador for Justinian to the Gothic court in Italy and to Persia, and thus his work, *de legationibus*, of which only fragments remain, was written with special knowledge. The universal history of Johannes Malalas (sixth century) in twelve books, despite woeful blunders, occasionally provides information upon Eastern affairs; Georgius Syncellus (early ninth century) compiled chronological tables of history from the Creation to the accession of Diocletian, incorporating material from Dexippus and Eusebius. John of Antioch, probably in the seventh century, compiled a Chronicle of World history from Adam to A.D. 610 of which we possess fragments and Leo Grammaticus in 1013 reissued with additions the earlier Chronicle of Symeon the Logothete which, beginning with Adam, was carried down to A.D. 948. We possess excerpts from the great *Encyclopaedia* of historical extracts which the Emperor Constantine Porphyrogenitus had drawn up in the tenth century, and probably to the same age belongs the *Lexicon* of Suidas, which includes articles on the emperors. In the eleventh century Johannes Xiphilinus compiled an *Epitome of the Roman History of Dio of Nicaea*, drawing on books XXXVI to LXXX of Dio; Georgius Cedrenus (between the eleventh and twelfth centuries) wrote a *Synopsis of Histories*; Johannes Zonaras (twelfth century) compiled an *Epitome of Histories*. All of these are of service in so far as they have incorporated material for third-century history which would otherwise have been lost to us (see below, p. 721).

There is singularly little historical writing to the credit of Latin authors of the later period of the Empire. St Jerome, probably at Constantinople in the year 381, translated into Latin the tables of world history which Eusebius had compiled and continued the work down to the year 378. Orosius, who in 414 fled before the Vandal invasion of his native Spain to Africa, under the inspiration of St Augustine wrote a world history *adversum Paganos* (in seven books), to prove that the miseries of the time were no greater than those of former pagan centuries.

Mention must also be made of a historical fragment, first published by H. Valois—the writer is in consequence generally known as the *Anonymus Valesii*—which covers the years 293–337. The author, probably a pagan, seems to have been a contemporary of Constantine, for whose reigns the fragment is a valuable historical source. It should be noted that the text has been interpolated by the insertion of extracts from Orosius.

When we turn from the historians and chroniclers, it is the writers of the Latin panegyrics who for the history of the early years of the fourth century are of special value. They reflect the policy and dynastic ambitions of the rulers of the Roman West and are particularly serviceable for any study of Constantine's political and religious development.

Of the Christian writers TERTULLIAN and ORIGEN illustrate Christian apologetic—in the *Apologeticum* and the *Contra Celsum*, while Tertullian's works provide not a little information on social life in North Africa. Cyprian's correspondence is a valuable source for any study of the renewed offensive of the Roman State against the Christian Church, while both Tertullian and Cyprian are important witnesses for the development of the authority claimed by the Bishops of Rome. But the outstanding historical work from the Christian side is the *Church History* of EUSEBIUS, Bishop of Caesarea in Palestine, which has preserved for us many original documents either in whole or in part; here the methods of Alexandrian scholarship are appropriated in the service of the Church by one who had been trained in the tradition of Origen. Further, Eusebius alone has left us a detailed history of the course of the Great Persecution within a single province of the Empire. In his *De martyribus Palaestinae* he gave a complete list of all the martyrs who died in Palestine; he hoped that others might imitate his example and make from their own personal knowledge similar local records; had they done so, we might to-day have been in a position to write an account of the Persecution as a whole.—It should be noted that from a study of the manuscript tradition E. Schwartz has distinguished the successive editions of the *Ecclesiastical History* which were issued between 311 and 325 (see his article in P.W. *s.v.* Eusebios).

The work which is commonly known under the Latin title *Vita Constantini* is in fact entitled εἰς τὸν βίον τοῦ μακαρίου Κωνσταντίνου βασιλέως: it does not profess to give a complete biographical record, but only deals with the Emperor's actions so far as they advanced the Christian religion— τὰ πρὸς τὸν θεοφιλῆ συντείνοντα βίον (i, 11). The critics of this panegyric written after Constantine's death have often failed to take account of the author's express object in writing the work.

There has been long dispute whether the philosophic and highly cultured student of Cicero, LACTANTIUS, who as a teacher was summoned from Africa to Nicomedia by Diocletian, could have been the author both of the *Divine Institutes* and of the bitter and impassioned pamphlet *On The Deaths of the Persecutors*. But the Lactantian authorship of the *De mortibus persecutorum* is now generally accepted. The account of the inception and course of the Persecution is vividly dramatic, but, though the story as Lactantius told it has often been questioned, there is, it would seem, no adequate reason to doubt its substantial truth. In his view that Galerius was the moving spirit in setting on foot the Great Persecution Lactantius is supported by Eusebius, and it is not easy to reject this agreement of the two contemporary writers (see above, p. 665).

For a period of history where our sources are so meagre the student must seek to base his chronology on all the available evidence whether of inscriptions, papyri, coins (see below) or the dating of imperial constitutions. In the economic crisis, however, of the third century there was little money to spend on such expensive memorials as inscriptions, and thus the constitutions cited in the Code of Justinian acquire an added importance. But there are difficulties: it is often uncertain whether the text of such constitutions in its present form can be trusted, while it is unfortunate that none of the imperial orders which introduced the Diocletio-Constantinian reforms have been preserved. (For the introduction into Egypt of the new system of taxation see the recently published papyrus cited on p. 338).

N. H. B.

(2) COINS

The ancient coin, like the modern, was primarily a means of exchange, and, in the absence of a developed system of banking, was even more important commercially than the modern. It was, at the same time, less efficient for its immediate purpose, inasmuch as it was less accurately struck and adjusted to weight, and frequently lacked date and mark of value. Unlike the modern, the ancient coin had often something of a medallic character—

that is to say, it referred directly to particular historical happenings of the time. Even apart from this, it was, in a far higher degree than the modern coin, an expression of the State in its religious and symbolical aspect. What is true of ancient coins as a whole is true in a pre-eminent degree of the coinage of the Roman Empire. It has a function quite distinct from the commercial. It supplies an almost continuous commentary on events and policies, keeps before the public the emperor, his features, titles, achievements, travels, and at the same time sketches in a background of thought and sentiment which helps to explain the events that fill the foreground. The Roman imperial coinage is, in fact, a series of medals, narrating the history and suggesting the atmosphere of political life, reign by reign.

A coinage of this character must obviously be considered seriously as a source for history. Even if the literary authorities were much more satisfactory and unbroken than they actually are, the coinage would still supply an invaluable check on accuracy and would add its own colour to the historical narrative. The accidental gaps in the tradition make numismatic evidence doubly valuable, as it may restore to us facts either completely lost or, at least, obscured in the literary tradition.

When we speak of 'Roman Imperial Coins' we usually mean the coinage, with Latin legends and in Roman denominations, issued by Roman authority, regularly in Rome, less regularly in the provinces as well. In the Early Empire Rome is the one great centre. The division of the coinage into the two branches, Imperial gold and silver and senatorial *aes*, affords a means of forming some conclusions of interest about the relations of *princeps* and Senate. Provincial mints arise, at first, from rebellions in the provinces and seldom from any other cause. In the second century of our era Rome seems to enjoy a monopoly of Imperial coinage that is almost complete. But in the third century there begins to appear a series of provincial mints, striking imperial denominations for military purposes, which finally develops into the system of Diocletian. Other coinage was struck, more or less directly by Roman authority, for certain provinces and, locally, by Roman permission, at a very great number of city-mints. These mints were always predominantly, after the Early Empire exclusively, Eastern. Any part of this coinage may occasionally yield material of value for history, and will some day yield more, when it has been collected and adequately annotated. For the time we are concerned primarily with the Imperial and senatorial mints of Rome and with mints of a similar character in the provinces. The greatest of all Greek mints, that of the second city of the Empire, Alexandria, will also give much help, particularly for chronology.

Before we can appraise the value of such a coinage for history, we must ask the question, what order of validity can it claim? Does it represent official opinion? Does it reflect public opinion in any vital sense? If it is official, does it represent the higher officialdom or merely some unimportant bureau, left to work without much direction from higher quarters? Was the coinage considered to be of sufficient importance to be treated seriously as an instrument of politics?

The first problem is, who controlled the mints? The imperial mint of Rome was run by imperial freedmen and slaves. But, from the reign of Trajan onwards, it is under a *procurator monetae*, answerable, if not to the emperor himself, at least to his chief financial officer, the *a rationibus*. The senatorial mint of Rome seems to have been, nominally and in part at least actually, distinct from the imperial. It was presumably under the supreme direction of the *praefecti aerario Saturni* answerable both to emperor and Senate, and the *tresviri a. a. a. f. f.*, who can be traced as late as the third century of our era, may still have found employment there. The mints in the provinces, when operating independently of Rome, must have been controlled by the financial officers on the spot. The third century presents a picture of transition. Even apart from the provincial 'empires,' the Empire was tending to break up into a number of great administrative districts. The mints of the third century represent this change. Perhaps subordinated in the first instance to the Roman, they must have become in practice more and more independent. The logical conclusion of the development is seen under Diocletian. Each mint is now under its own *procurator* or *rationalis*, who is answerable not to Rome, but to the financial chief of his district. So much for the Imperial coinage. The provincial and local coinage, as far as it bore on anything beyond local needs, was certainly under some kind of official check.

The answers to the questions that we have posed may now be given with some assurance. The coinage was under chiefs who could, if need be, secure access to high authority. The facts of the coinage themselves complete the answer. Had the coinage dealt only in a vague and general symbolism, it might have been possible to regard it as no more than the self-expression of a minor department of State. But this is definitely not the case. The coinage deals, not occasionally but consistently, with events of historical importance, with policies vital for the well-being of the Empire. It introduces to the attention of the public the assistants whom the emperor associates with himself in his task and restores the memory of those members of the Imperial House of the past whom the emperor delights to honour. The working-out of a programme in its details of type and legend may have been left to the technical advisers of the mint, but the general instructions must have been issued by high authority and the final draft must have been passed and approved by it. From the time of Trajan, there was a *procurator monetae*, and it is reasonable to assume that his task lay rather with these general questions of policy than with the technical work of the mint. Before Trajan there may have been less formality, at a time when the Imperial service was still run largely under the forms of a great private household. None the less, control, even if less formal, will have been just as real.

It is known that the emperors took pains to report news to the Roman public in the form of the *acta diurna*, officially edited by a special officer. In so far as the coins record definite events, we may think of them as very short, carefully selected extracts from those *acta*, illustrated with suitable types. But this does not exhaust their content. They deal also with hopes, aspirations, promises and prayers, and, to give due expression to these, a close acquaintance with the general thought and feeling of the age and with the symbolical expression of it was essential.

A few examples from history may be selected to illustrate these points. The coinage struck for Agrippa and Tiberius under Augustus, for Germanicus and Drusus under Tiberius, for Nero under Claudius, had in each case serious political significance and was certainly controlled and directed with due care. The 'constitutional' coinage of the first period of the reign of Nero gives place to a self-assertive, self-advertising coinage after the suppression of the conspiracy of Piso (vol. x, pp. 726 *sqq.*). There is an abrupt change in the tone of the coinage when Nerva succeeds Domitian, a scarcely less abrupt, and less to be expected change, when Trajan succeeds Nerva. In neither case can it be accidental. The adoption of Hadrian by Trajan is most carefully and judiciously brought to the notice of the public on the coins. Septimius Severus marks his acceptance of Albinus as Caesar by striking for him at the mints of Rome. When, in A.D. 195, Albinus breaks with Severus, this coinage at Rome ceases and is replaced by a little coinage for Albinus at Lugdunum, with the title of Augustus. The Palmyrene ascendency in the East, the Gallic and British empires in the West, find their full commemoration in the coinage. Many of the pretenders of the Great Anarchy have left a numismatic record of their short-lived efforts. The Sun-worship of Aurelian is written large on the coins of his reign, and the praise of the Jovian and Herculian dynasties fills a great part of the coinage of the reign of Diocletian.

These examples represent no more than an arbitrary selection from an almost inexhaustible stock. They fully justify the assertion that the coinage was very seriously regarded as one of the most effective means of publicity and propaganda. Knowing as much as we do of the close personal attention that a conscientious emperor might devote to the details of administration, we may be sure that not infrequently decisions on major points of coinage-policy were taken direct by him.

One or two objections may be raised. 'This view,' it may be urged, 'implies that the Roman regarded his coins with a close attention that seems hardly thinkable, when we reflect how casually we regard them to-day.' The answer to this is to be seen in a marked and notable difference between ancient and modern usage. The Roman studied his coins attentively, because he knew that he would find on them something worthy of his attention. There were also far fewer rival claims on that attention.

A more serious objection may be found in the rare instances in which coinage does not represent history as we know it from other sources. Take, for example, the reign of Gaius. The coinage faithfully represents his first phase of constitutionalism, based on the great inheritance of Augustus; it does not reflect his later phase of megalomania. The apparent exception only confirms the rule. Had Gaius lived longer, his vagaries might have spread to the coinage. As it was, his subordinates, realizing that he was unbalanced, succeeded in keeping his extravagances from finding official expression on the coins. A similar explanation may be advanced to explain the absence of coins for many of the pretenders of the third century. In some cases, coins may have been struck in such limited quantities that none have chanced to survive. Accident may still restore such issues to our knowledge. But, in others, the absence of coinage may be real and significant. The pretenders may never have laid claim to the rank of emperor, and the absence of coins is a warning not to take too readily at face-value such lists as that of the *Augustan History* with its 'Thirty Tyrants.'

This much agreed, what may we reasonably expect to learn from the Imperial coinage? From accidental error it will be as good as free. Where the same type and legend are attested by a number of dies, such error is automatically eliminated. In this respect the coin takes precedence of even the best single inscription. The coin may also be trusted, in general, to be true in point of fact. What purpose would there be in commemorating on the coinage a largesse that had not been given or an act of State that had not happened? How far the coin will be true in spirit and interpretation is a harder matter to decide. We must obviously expect to find the official point of view, with such deviations from absolute veracity as that must involve. But, for one thing, this official point of view is so inadequately represented in the literary tradition that the consistent expression of it on the coins has a value of its own. And, further, we have just seen reason to suppose that occasional extravagances of imperial government may have been evened out by the sane tradition of the imperial service. That a regard for public opinion formed a continuous check on the coinage may be assumed with confidence and, occasionally, demonstrated in detail. The frequent advertisement of 'libertas' and the 'optimus status rerum' under the 'optimus princeps' shows that the administration was conscious of having clients to consider, with definite tastes and requirements of their own. The provincial mints of the third century show, as might have been expected, traces of special needs and wishes. One great advantage of the coinage, particularly in the third century, is that it is continuous, where the literary tradition is so broken. It is, in fact, the only surviving continuous source for the period. In considering its historical use, it is the third century that is here most in point, and it may be considered under the following headings: (1) Chronology. (2) Current events at home and abroad. (3) The emperor and his subjects. (4) Religion. (5) The background of thought and sentiment in the empire.

(1) *Chronology.* Imperial coinage is often dated by the tribunician power, the consulships, the titles of honour and the imperatorial acclamations of the emperor. In some reigns, as those of Antoninus Pius to Commodus, or of Septimius Severus to Maximinus Thrax the record is almost unbroken. But, even where dated coins are rare, the undated can usually be placed within a year or so of their true date by comparison with the dated material. In many instances this exact chronology is still to be attained, but it is already certain that it may reasonably be hoped for in the future. Thus for almost all questions of dates numismatic evidence is of cardinal importance. It can be used in conjunction with our other authorities to establish a true chronology; when the coins and the other authorities disagree, it is to the coins that we must give the preference. A few examples will suffice. The coins show, that Valerian reckoned the beginning of his reign from a date before the end of August A.D. 253. They provide the true limits of date for the Gallic Empire, A.D. 258–9 to 274 and the true order of the Gallic emperors, Postumus, Laelianus, Marius, Victorinus, Tetricus. They prove that Victorinus was never adopted as co-regent by Postumus (see p. 188, n. 1). The high tribunician numbers of Aurelian, TR. P. VI and VII, with COS. II, seem to point to a reckoning continued from that of Claudius II. Finally, they enable us to fix the death of Carus with some precision in July 283, and show that Maximian can only have been Caesar for a very short time.

(2) *Current events at home and abroad.* The content of the Imperial coinage varied appreciably from age to age, and the period of maximum historical interest was already past by the third century. General references

to victories, vows, largesses, arrivals and departures still occur, but they begin to assume a less particular form than in the earlier reigns. Claudius for example celebrates a 'victoria Gothica,' Aurelian his victories over Zenobia and Tetricus, but it is mainly with such simple types as Victory or trophy and captives, not with such elaborate pictorial designs as the 'Imperator' types or the REX PARTHIS DATVS of Trajan.

Even so, the coins have something to add to history. The coinage of Postumus at the mint of Milan, at the very moment when that city was in the hands of Aureolus, reveals a fact otherwise unrecorded, that Aureolus was acting in the name of Postumus (p. 189). It throws a new light both on the activities of Aureolus and on the relations of the Gallic Empire with Rome. The coins of Carausius supply valuable evidence for the character of the peace which he won from Rome (see p. 333).

The absence of coinage can be as significant as its presence. The fact that Aurelian strikes no coins for Vaballathus at any of his own mints is strongly against the theory that he ever recognized him as his co-ruler in the East. The absence of coins of Carausius in mints of the Empire defines clearly the limits of the 'peace' with the Empire achieved by that hardy rebel. As has already been suggested, the fact that so many of the 'Thirty Tyrants' have left no coinage suggests grave doubts of the reality of their usurpations. On the other hand, the discovery of coins of Domitianus and Saturninus in recent years is a warning that gaps may be accidental and that, where issues are in their very nature rare, chance may have played a large part in survival or the reverse. The rare gold coins of Uranius Antoninus add a curious little chapter to the history of the East in the early third century (p. 70).

(3) *The emperor and his subjects.* The emperor is the centre of the coinage, senatorial as well as Imperial. His portrait replaces the original deity or city-type of the obverse. His family relationships, his marriages, his children, his heirs, his vows and largesses, his comings and goings still fill up a large part of the canvas. The decline of the Senate is shown in the disappearance of its mark, S. C., from the coinage and in the general fall of the *aes* coinage as a whole. In the references to the emperor, as elsewhere, the general tends to replace the particular. Vows and largesses are no longer chronicled with so much detail and such a type as ADVENTVS AVGVSTI seems to assume a wider symbolical significance, not so much the entry of the emperor into his capital city in actual presence, as the 'advent' of the saviour to his waiting world.

In one respect the coins have a quite exceptional importance. They outrun the legal facts and theories and show the actual process by which the *princeps* passed into the *dominus et deus* of the Late Empire. Whatever the constitutional theory, the emperor on coins continually appeared with attributes, borrowed from the gods, and with suggestions of Eastern royalty. The gradual invasion of the coinage by such forms has recently been demonstrated in a remarkable paper[1]. By the reign of Aurelian they are becoming explicit, so much so, in fact, that Diocletian seems rather to impose some slight check on them than to promote their further development. The extraordinary demonstrations of fervour and loyalty at the mint of Serdica show clearly that coinage could faithfully mirror local feeling.

---

[1] A. Alföldi in *Röm. Mitt.* L, 1935, pp. 1 *sqq.*

(4) *Religion*. The religious note is never long silent in any part of the coinage. The references to the emperor and his virtues, for example, have their religious aspect. For this section, however, we reserve more specifically religious demonstrations. Elagabalus crowded the Roman coinage with the honours of his local Syrian Baal. Decius chose the figures of the Illyrian peoples (Dacia, Pannoniae, Genius Exercitus Illyriciani) rather than the figures of the gods to symbolize the revival of old Roman ways and beliefs that he wished by their aid to achieve. It is his series of coins of the deified emperors, the 'Divi,' that represents the spirit that prompted the first general persecution of the Christian Church. The 'ubique pax' of Gallienus refers more to the internal peace in his domains, the peace with the Church included, than to the peace that was not secured in the Empire as a whole[1]. Aurelian celebrates Sol, his divine helper, 'Sol dominus imperi Romani.' Coins of the end of his reign, continuing down to Probus, show Sol as bestower of empire through the 'loyal' army. Diocletian advertises widely the dynasties of the 'Jovian' and 'Herculian' emperors and then enters on his war with the Christian Church under the sign of Genius, 'Genius Populi Romani,' 'Genius Augusti' (see above, pp. 414 *sqq*.).

(5) *General background*. Finally, the coinage performs the valuable function of suggesting the unspoken beliefs that governed the minds of men.

Perhaps the most important suggestion of all is what may be called the theme of the 'optimus status rerum,' defined by the protection of the gods and the virtues, immanent and operative in the emperor. The picture varies from time to time and from mint to mint, and it will be possible to attach fuller meaning to the variations, when the significance of the individual signs of this pictorial alphabet is known more accurately than at present. Prominent always are the thoughts of the divine protection, of the victory and valour of the emperor, of his peace—his quality as peace-bearer—of his power as lord of material wealth and plenty, as author of concord and even of liberty.

Closely connected with this theme is that of the Golden Age. The modern man dreams of progress, of steady advance along new paths into a richer and fuller life; the ancient dreamed vaguely of a return to ideal conditions, dimly placed in the remote past, of the restoration of a magical, almost unbelievable profusion of well-being, material and moral. This theme haunts the coinage: the old hope revives again and again, undaunted by constant disappointment. A similar theme, but with more reference to the future, is that of the 'Aeternitas Imperii' or the 'Aeternitas Augusti' or, again, of 'Roma Aeterna,' in which the stress falls on the divine mission of Rome and her emperors. A touch of mysticism seems here to fall on the material world. The eternal overshadows the temporal and men find consolation, amid scenes of change, in contemplating the permanent assurance of happiness and peace. Yet another theme is that of 'Concordia,' in the Imperial House, in the State, above all, in the army. Here the 'Concordia' types have at times a peculiar and sinister significance of their own. They are the comment of the mint on the terrible facts of the military anarchy, an instance of what is now called wish-fulfilment.

---

[1] See however, p. 194.

Thus the coinage provides a continuous exposition of the policy of the Empire, as it presented it before the bar of public opinion. One-sided of course it is; how can an 'apologia pro vita sua' be otherwise? But it enables us to fill in the background which the literary authorities so often leave empty, and to realize the mood in which Rome of the third century faced and surmounted the strange vicissitudes of the times. So much the coins can already give. They will have more to give in future: for we can already see before us an ideal, realizable, if only partly realized—an exact chronology and attribution to mints and a complete annotation, based on comparison with the whole of the evidence for the Empire.

But, apart from the evidence of the coins as medals, they have, naturally, their own significance for economic history. The great inflation and collapse of the third century, the reform of Aurelian and the more drastic reform of Diocletian represent important chapters in economic history (chaps. VII, IX). We can already make some use of them, and shall be able to make more when numismatists can agree better on their facts and interpretations. Already the coins suggest interesting conclusions about the policy of the emperors in face of the army and the civil population, about the causes of discontent, particularly in the West from Aurelian to Carausius, and, perhaps, about the inner meaning of the great rise in prices that called forth the *Edictum de maximis pretiis* of Diocletian.

Finally, there is the evidence of coin-finds, whether in hoards or in chance deposits on sites. For frontier districts such evidence, when complete, should be decisive for the date of the Roman abandonment. It can already be used to control the date of the Roman abandonment of Dacia (p. 301, n. 1). At present, however, the evidence is not fully available and there is doubt in places of its exact bearing. Do the multitudinous hoards of Tetricus and his fellows mark the course of barbarian invasions or do they rather show the refusal of the Western provincial to give up his old coins for the money of the reform of Aurelian?

Here, as at many other points, numismatic evidence must be used with due caution. But it is beyond doubt that in the coins lies a treasure, partly won, partly awaiting further study as a condition of its full exploitation; a treasure which, failing new discoveries of inscriptions or manuscripts, offers almost our only chance of penetrating the thick darkness that still envelops so much of the history of the third century.

H. M.

NOTES

1. THE SOURCES FOR THE GOTHIC INVASIONS OF THE YEARS 260–270

The statements of ancient authors about the Gothic wars under Valerian and Gallienus show an unprecedented state of confusion, for the reasons that follow. First, the late compendia and, with special exaggeration, the *Historia Augusta* have represented Gallienus, according to a literary convention, as a tyrant sinking ever lower and lower, and thus have made it seem as if the heaviest disasters fell at the end of his reign. Next the compiler of the *Historia Augusta* has divided up piece-meal the several accounts of the Gothic wars and scattered them throughout his text, often with repetitions; and he did not flinch from seeking to enhance the credibility of his procedure by repeated arbitrary insertions of datings by consuls. The result is that scholars have been so far misled that modern accounts are full of Gothic wars which never happened. Fortunately, it is possible to show that the compiler drew his material from the very compendia which served as sources for the Byzantine authors whose works have been preserved.[1]

These authors, then, must supply the clue to a judgment of the source-material, as also for the chronological order of events. For the Gothic wars of Gallienus and Claudius II the decisive evidence is the fact that the statements of the *Vita Gallieni* coincide with the narrative in Syncellus and so must be arranged and reconstructed according to the order given by the latter, whereas in the *Vita Claudii* the source followed by Syncellus is exchanged for that followed by Zosimus. All other statements—or almost all—can be grouped round this two-fold core; and by this process three, and only three, invasions between 260 and 270 can be distinguished.[2] These are as follows.

A. The expedition to Asia Minor, reported by Syncellus, p. 716, 16 *sqq.* (Bonn) is contained in the following passage of the *Vita Gallieni*: 4, 7–8; 6, 2; 11, 1; 12, 6. Besides these, the same account is to be found in Jordanes, *Get.* xx, 107–8 M. The date is given by the death of Odenathus in the spring of 267, which followed immediately upon the expedition.

B. After this Syncellus p. 717, 9 *sqq.* gives the account of the next great German expedition to western Asia Minor, Greece and the Balkan countries, of which a brief paraphrase is also to be found in Zosimus 1, 39, 1 and 40, 1. The account in the *Vita Gallieni* 13, 6–10, together with the notices 5, 6–6, 1, agrees with the source of Syncellus. Jordanes also (*Get.* xx, 108) clearly separates the expedition from the preceding one: 'post Asiae ergo tale excidium Thracia eorum experta est feritatem.' Some additional details are to be found in Dexippus, frag. 28 (Jacoby, *F.G.H.* ii, p. 472) and in Jordanes, *Get.* xx, 108 M; cf. Ammianus Marcellinus xxxi, 5, 16, S.H.A.

[1] See for a good instance the analysis of the war against Postumus in *Zeitschr. für Num.* xl, 1930, pp. 11 *sqq.*

[2] This process renders obsolete the present writer's arguments in 'A gót mozgalom és Dácia feladása' in *Egyetemes Philologiai Közlöny*, 1930.

Claud. 12, 4, etc. The date of the war can be deduced from the interruption due to the complications with Aureolus and the death of Gallienus on his hasty return to Italy.

C. Syncellus (p. 720) mentions the fact that in the next year (under Claudius in 269) the Heruli once more made an expedition by sea, which, however, had little success. The compiler of the *Historia Augusta* had apparently before him a correspondingly short mention in the source of Syncellus and regarded it as too meagre to suit his preconceived purpose of glorifying Claudius. For this reason, he changed over to the use of the source of Zosimus 1, 41 *sqq.* With this coincides, in particular, the account of the Gothic war of Claudius in the *Vita Claudii*, 18, 1; 6, 1–2; 6, 5; 8, 1, 2, 4; 9, 3–4; 9, 7–8; 11, 3–8; 12, 1. Short notices in Zonaras XII, 26 (p. 604 *sq.*), Ammianus Marcellinus *loc. cit.*, Petrus Patricius frag. 169 (Cassius Dio, ed. Boissevain, III, p. 745), Cedrenus, I, p. 454, 12 *sqq.* etc. coincide with this account. The surprising fact then emerges that the first, larger half of his narrative coincides with the account of the expedition of 268 given in Syncellus p. 717 and the sources that correspond with it (see B above). The points of likeness are too numerous to be accidental, as will be seen from the table which follows.

B (Invasion of Goths and Heruli in the last year of Gallienus)	*C* (Invasion of Goths and Heruli under Claudius II)
1. The barbarian fleet takes Byzantium and Chrysopolis; it is here defeated in a naval engagement (Syncellus 717 *sqq.*; S.H.A. *Gall. duo* 13, 6–7).	Naval battle off Byzantium (S.H.A. *Claud.* 9, 7).
2. Cleodamus 'and Athenaeus' as admirals (S.H.A. *Gall. duo* 13, 6).	The Athenian Cleodemus comes with a fleet to Greece, and drives out the barbarians (Zonaras XII, 26 [p. 605]).
3. Capture of Athens by the Germans (Syncellus, *loc. cit.*; Zosimus I, 39, 1).	Capture of Athens by the Germans (Zonaras *loc. cit.*; Petrus Patricius frag. 169, Cedrenus, I, p. 454, 12 etc.).
4. Unsuccessful attack on Cyzicus (Syncellus *loc. cit.*; cf. S.H.A. *Gall. duo* 13, 8).	Failure before Cyzicus (Zosimus I, 43, 1).
5. Siege of Thessalonica, and its abandonment because of the approach of the Emperor (Gallienus) (Syncellus, *loc. cit.*; Zosimus I, 39, 1; S.H.A. *Gall. duo* 5, 6).	Siege of Thessalonica and the approach of the Emperor (Claudius) (S.H.A. *Claud.* 9, 8; Zosimus I, 43, 1; Zonaras XII, 26 [p. 604 *sq.*]; Eusebius frag. 1 (Jacoby, *F.G.H.* II, p. 480)).

B (Invasion of Goths and Heruli in the last year of Gallienus)	C (Invasion of Goths and Heruli under Claudius II)
6. The imperial army destroys 3000 barbarians at 'Nessus' (Syncellus, *loc. cit.*); Gallienus wins a victory in Illyricum (S.H.A. *Gall. duo* 13, 9; cf. Zonaras XII, 24 [p. 596]).	The Dalmatian cavalry of the Emperor (Claudius) annihilates 3000 Germans (Zosimus 1, 43, 2). The Emperor wins a victory at 'Naïssus' (Zosimus 1, 43, 2).
7. The defeated Germans retreat to the mountain Gessax and defend themselves with a laager (S.H.A. *Gall. duo* 13, 9).	The laager of the defeated Germans mentioned in Zosimus 1, 45, 1, and in S.H.A. *Claud.* 6, 1–2; 11, 3.
8. Marcianus takes over the command (S.H.A. *Gall. duo* 13, 10).	The successes of Marcianus (S.H.A. *Claud.* 6, 1).
9. The remnant of the defeated barbarians urge the other barbarians to invasion (S.H.A. *Gall. duo* 13, 10).	The identical, verbally coincident statement in S.H.A. *Claud.* 6, 1–2; cf. Zosimus (1, 45, 1), who also mentions the 'remnant of the barbarians'.

In view of this close connection of the two accounts, it is beyond doubt that the same German offensive is the theme of both, and that the battle at the Nessus and at Naïssus is the same battle. It is also readily intelligible that the operations, begun under Gallienus and consummated under Claudius, against the Germans who made their invasion in 268 and were not destroyed until 269 should have been epitomized from the *Scythica* of Dexippus by one late-classical author under the earlier emperor, and by a second author under that emperor's successor; that this double entry was not observed by the undiscerning and superficial late-classical compilers is not at all unusual.

What is important is that the continuation of the account of this war in Zosimus 1, 45–6 and the corresponding passages of the *Vita Claudii* (11, 3–4; 11, 6–8; 12, 1; 9, 4) which treats of new conflicts and the ending of the war by Claudius are organically continuous with the preceding events, a fact which makes it certain that they belong to the year 269. What Syncellus (p. 720) has to say of the new naval expedition, and what Zosimus and the *Vita Claudii* tell us of an expedition by new hordes of Germans against the (Danube) provinces in 269 can easily be brought into harmony with this.

A. A.

2. HERODIANUS, KING OF PALMYRA

H. Seyrig in *Syria*, XVIII, 1937, pp. 1 *sqq.* has shown that there was also a son Herodianus, king of Palmyra. He has the title 'King of Kings' which he could hardly have borne during the lifetime of his father Odenathus (as his colleague). He is credited with a victory over the Persians, but this was not an honour limited to the eldest brother, since Vaballathus also, after him, could be called Persicus Maximus (*Ann. épig.* 1904, no. 60). It seems, therefore, that this Herodianus cannot be identified with the Herodes who met his death in 267. A further argument is that the woman, represented with him on a lead seal (Seyrig, *op. cit.* Pl. VI, 1–2), can be none other than Zenobia with the laurel-wreath of the Empress (*Augusta*) (cf. A. Alföldi in *Röm. Mitt.* L, 1935, p. 124) and she did not enjoy that position until after the death of her husband. Herodianus, then, seems to be the correct name of the Herennianus of the *Historia Augusta* (*Trig. tyr.* 27). If Herodianus did not survive long, then the third son, Vaballathus, may be the *Timolaus* of S.H.A. *Trig. tyr.* 28.

A. A.

3. INFLATION IN THE SECOND AND THIRD CENTURIES

(*a*) *From Nero to Marcus Aurelius.* Nero had, so it seems, reduced the weight of the aureus like that of the denarius, the one by about 6·5 per cent., the other by about 12·6 per cent., and lowered its content in precious metal at the same time to about 95–90 per cent. Trajan carried this reduction to 85, Marcus Aurelius to 75 per cent. The earlier view was that this was done in order to improve the State finances, but recently scholars (F. Heichelheim, P. L. Strack, G. Mickwitz and W. Giesecke) have inclined to see in it, so far as the second century is concerned, no more than an adjustment of the currency to the market price of the metals (gold becoming cheaper, silver becoming dearer). This they regard as a consequence of the highly mobile non-monometallic Roman imperial currency and of the reckoning of the coins by their intrinsic value. This hypothesis also, in the view of the present writer, overshoots the mark. First, a reduction of weight is combined with a reduction of purity of content; second, the temporary fall in the value of gold of about 4 per cent. in the time of Trajan so far as P. Bad. 37 yields any moderately assured evidence[1], and the debasing of the silver, which under Trajan as compared with Nero is of 11 per cent., do not all certainly correspond; third, account has to be taken of the fact that the gap between coined and uncoined gold may be considerable (G. Mickwitz, *Geld und Wirtschaft im röm. Reiche des 4. Jahrhunderts n. Chr.* p. 44) so that a certain tariffing downwards of the latter is

---

[1] The text says: the aureus ($\chi\rho\upsilon\sigma o\hat{\upsilon}\varsigma$) was dealt in at eleven instead of fifteen drachmae. Segrè's interpretation (at 111 instead of 115 drachmae in copper), despite all, remains, in the view of the present writer, more probable than that proposed by W. K. Prentice and A. C. Johnson in *Amer. Journ. of Arch.* XXXVIII, 1934, p. 52 (that gold stood to silver in the relation of 11 : 1 instead of 15 : 1).

possible; fourth, the character of the coins as issued by the State influences their nominal value (W. Giesecke, *Antikes Geldwesen*, p. 248) so long at least as the State remains powerful and can command confidence. A decrease in the value of money, which happens by very small stages and which is taken in hand by a powerful state concurrently with a prudent increase in the money in circulation, does not, therefore, of necessity result in any immediate rise in prices[1].

Very far-reaching conclusions have been drawn concerning the fall of prices in the second century from P. Bad. 79 (probably of the time of Antoninus Pius) because it was taken to give a price for wheat of 6 drachmas an *artabe*, but the difficulties of interpretation which the text offers are such that the papyrus cannot for the present be used with profit.

(b) *From Commodus to A.D. 256.* Under Commodus the alloy of the denarius reached 30 per cent. and more, under Septimius Severus about 50 per cent., by A.D. 256 about 60 per cent. In accordance with this, instead of 25 denarii being equivalent to an aureus in the reign of Antoninus Pius, 50 denarii in the time of Severus Alexander and about 60 in A.D. 244/5 became equivalent to an aureus, which itself, as it seems, now was issued in an irregularly smaller weight. Cf. Mickwitz, *op. cit.* p. 35; F. Heichelheim in *Klio* XXVI, 1933, p. 102. For the same reason the legionary pay rose from 300 denarii (under Domitian) to 375 (under Commodus), to 500 (under Septimius Severus), to 750 (under Caracalla); the price of bread at Ephesus doubled between the time of Trajan and the beginning of the third century; and the price of corn in Egypt rose to double or two-and-a-half times. Heichelheim, *op. cit.* p. 102 *sq.*, Mickwitz, *op. cit.* pp. 36 *sqq.*, 48.

For the great inflation after A.D. 256 see above, p. 266.

FR. O.

[1] On the slowness of this process see Heichelheim himself now in *Econ. Hist.* III, 10 Feb. 1935, p. 10.

LIST OF ABBREVIATIONS

[See also General Bibliography, Parts II and IV.]

Abh. Arch.-epig.	Abhandlungen d. archäol.-epigraph. Seminars d. Univ. Wien.
Aeg.	Aegyptus. Rivista italiana di egittologia e di papirologia.
A.J.A.	American Journal of Archaeology.
A.J. Ph.	American Journal of Philology.
Ann. épig.	L'Année épigraphique.
Arch. Anz.	Archäologischer Anzeiger (in J.D.A.I.).
Arch. Pap.	Archiv für Papyrusforschung.
Arch. Relig.	Archiv für Religionswissenschaft.
Ath. Mitt.	Mitteilungen des deutschen arch. Inst. Athenische Abteilung.
Atti Acc. Torino	Atti della reale Accademia di scienze di Torino.
Bay. Abh.	Abhandlungen d. bayerischen Akad. d. Wissenschaften.
Bay. S.B.	Sitzungsberichte d. bayerischen Akad. d. Wissenschaften.
B.C.H.	Bulletin de Correspondance hellénique.
Berl. Abh.	Abhandlungen d. preuss. Akad. d. Wissenschaften zu Berlin.
Berl. S.B.	Sitzungsberichte d. preuss. Akad. d. Wissenschaften zu Berlin.
B.J.	Bonner Jahrbücher.
B.M. Cat.	British Museum Catalogue.
B.S.A.	Annual of the British School at Athens.
B.S.R.	Papers of the British School at Rome.
Bull. Comm. Arch.	Bullettino della Commissione archeol. comunale.
Bursian	Bursian's Jahresbericht.
C.I.L.	Corpus Inscriptionum Latinarum.
C.J.	Classical Journal.
C.P.	Classical Philology.
C.Q.	Classical Quarterly.
C.R.	Classical Review.
C.R. Ac. Inscr.	Comptes rendus de l'Académie des Inscriptions et Belles-Lettres.
Dessau	Dessau, Inscriptiones Latinae Selectae.
Ditt.[3]	Dittenberger, Sylloge Inscriptionum Graecarum. Ed. 3.
Eph. Ep.	Ephemeris Epigraphica.
F.Gr. Hist.	F. Jacoby's Fragmente der griechischen Historiker.
F.H.G.	C. Müller's Fragmenta Historicorum Graecorum.
Germ.	Germania.
G.G.A.	Göttingische Gelehrte Anzeigen.
Gött. Abh.	Abhandlungen d. Gesellschaft d. Wissenschaften zu Göttingen.
Gött. Nach.	Nachrichten von der Gesellschaft der Wissenschaften zu Göttingen. Phil.-hist. Klasse.
Harv. St.	Harvard Studies in Classical Philology.
H.Z.	Historische Zeitschrift.
I.G.	Inscriptiones Graecae.
I.G.R.R.	Inscriptiones Graecae ad res Romanas pertinentes.
Jahreshefte	Jahreshefte d. österreichischen archäologischen Instituts in Wien.
J.D.A.I.	Jahrbuch des deutschen archäologischen Instituts.
J. d. Sav.	Journal des Savants.
J.E.A.	Journal of Egyptian Archaeology.
J.H.S.	Journal of Hellenic Studies.

LIST OF ABBREVIATIONS

J.R.S.	Journal of Roman Studies.
Mém. Ac. Inscr.	Mémoires de l'Académie des Inscriptions et Belles-Lettres.
Mem. Acc. Lincei	Memorie della reale Accademia nazionale dei Lincei.
Mem. Acc. Torino	Memorie della reale Accademia di scienze di Torino.
Mnem.	Mnemosyne.
Mon. Linc.	Monumenti antichi pubblicati per cura della reale Accademia nazionale dei Lincei.
Mus. B.	Musée belge.
N. J. f. Wiss.	Neue Jahrbücher für Wissenschaft und Jugendbildung.
N. J. Kl. Alt.	Neue Jahrbücher für das klassische Altertum.
N.J.P.	Neue Jahrbücher für Philologie.
Not. arch.	Notiziario archeologico del Ministero delle Colonie.
N.S.A.	Notizie degli Scavi di Antichità.
Num. Chr.	Numismatic Chronicle.
Num. Z.	Numismatische Zeitschrift.
O.G.I.S.	Orientis Graeci Inscriptiones Selectae.
Phil.	Philologus.
Phil. Woch.	Philologische Wochenschrift.
P.I.R.	Prosopographia Imperii Romani.
P.W.	Pauly-Wissowa-Kroll's Real-Encyclopädie der classischen Altertumswissenschaft.
Rend. Linc.	Rendiconti della reale Accademia dei Lincei.
Rev. Arch.	Revue archéologique.
Rev. Belge	Revue Belge de philosophie et d'histoire.
Rev. E. A.	Revue des études anciennes.
Rev. E. G.	Revue des études grecques.
Rev. E. L.	Revue des études latines.
Rev. H.	Revue historique.
Rev. Hist. Rel.	Revue de l'histoire des religions.
Rev. N.	Revue numismatique.
Rev. Phil.	Revue de philologie, de littérature et d'histoire anciennes.
R.-G. K. Ber.	Berichte der Römisch-Germanischen Kommission.
Rh. Mus.	Rheinisches Museum für Philologie.
Riv. Fil.	Rivista di filologia.
Riv. stor. ant.	Rivista di storia antica.
Röm. Mitt.	Mitteilungen des deutschen arch. Inst. Römische Abteilung.
Sächs. Abh.	Abhandlungen d. sächs. Akad. d. Wissenschaften zu Leipzig.
S.B.	Sitzungsberichte.
S.E.G.	Supplementum Epigraphicum Graecum.
Suppl.	Supplementband.
Symb. Osl.	Symbolae Osloenses.
Wien Anz.	Anzeiger d. Akad. d. Wissenschaften in Wien.
Wien S.B.	Sitzungsberichte d. Akad. d. Wissenschaften in Wien.
Wien. St.	Wiener Studien.
Z. D. Pal.-V.	Zeitschrift des Deutschen Palästina-Vereins.
Z. d. Sav.-Stift.	Zeitschrift d. Savigny-Stiftung f. Rechtsgeschichte, Romanistische Abteilung.
Z.N.	Zeitschrift für Numismatik.

For Papyri see the list of titles and abbreviations given in Vol. x, pp. 922 *sqq.*

BIBLIOGRAPHIES

These bibliographies do not aim at completeness. They include modern and standard works and, in particular, books utilized in the writings of the chapters. Some technical monographs, especially in journals, are omitted, but the works that are registered below will put the reader on their track. The first page only of articles in journals is given.

GENERAL BIBLIOGRAPHY

I. GENERAL HISTORIES

Albertini, E. *L'Empire romain.* (Vol. iv in the *Peuples et Civilisations* Series directed by L. Halphen and P. Sagnac.) Paris, 1929.

Barbagallo, C. *Roma Antica,* ii. *L'Impero romano.* (Vol. ii of *Storia universale.*) Turin, 1932.

Besnier, M. *L'Empire romain de l'avènement des Sévères au concile de Nicée.* (Vol. iv. i, of *Histoire romaine* in the *Histoire générale* directed by G. Glotz.) Paris, 1937.

Boak, A. E. R. *A History of Rome to* A.D. 565. Ed. 2. New York, 1929.

Chapot, V. *Le monde romain.* Paris, 1927.

von Domaszewski, A. *Geschichte der römischen Kaiser.* 2 vols. Ed. 3. Leipzig, 1922.

Frank, T. *A History of Rome.* London, n.d. [1923].

—— *An Economic History of Rome.* Ed. 2. Baltimore, 1927.

Gibbon, E. *The History of the Decline and Fall of the Roman Empire,* edited by J. B. Bury. London, vol. i, 1896.

Kornemann, E. and J. Vogt, *Römische Geschichte* in Gercke-Norden, *Einleitung in die Altertumswissenschaft.* Ed. 3, iii, 2. Leipzig-Berlin, 1933.

Lot, F. *La Fin du Monde antique et le Début du Moyen Age.* Paris, 1927.

Miller, S. N. *The Roman Empire in the first three centuries.* In *European Civilization: its origin and development* (ed. E. Eyre), ii. London, 1935, pp. 279–522.

Mommsen, Th. *The Provinces of the Roman Empire from Caesar to Diocletian.* (English Translation by W. P. Dickson in 1886, reprinted with corrections in 1909.) London, 1909.

Niese, B. *Grundriss der römischen Geschichte nebst Quellenkunde.* 5te Auflage neubearbeitet von E. Hohl. (Müller's *Handbuch der klassischen Altertumswissenschaft,* Band iii, Abt. 5.) Munich, 1923.

Parker, H. M. D. *A History of the Roman World from A.D. 138 to 337.* London, 1935.

Rostovtzeff, M. *The Social and Economic History of the Roman Empire.* 1926. Ed. 2, *Gesellschaft und Wirtschaft im römischen Kaiserreich.* Leipzig, n.d. [1930]: ed. 3, *Storia economica e sociale dell' impero Romano.* Florence, 1933.

—— *A history of the Ancient World.* Vol. ii, *Rome.* Oxford, 1927.

Seeck, O. *Geschichte des Untergangs der antiken Welt.* 2 vols., Stuttgart, 1921.

Stein, E. *Geschichte des spätrömischen Reiches.* Vol. i, Vienna, 1928.

Stevenson, G. H. *The Roman Empire.* London, 1930.

Stuart Jones, H. *The Roman Empire,* B.C. 29–A.D. 476. 3rd Impression, London, 1916.

II. Works of Reference, Dictionaries, etc.

Abbott, F. F. and A. C. Johnson. *Municipal Administration in the Roman Empire.* Princeton, N.J., 1926.

Daremberg, Ch. and E. Saglio. *Dictionnaire des antiquités grecques et romaines d'après les textes et les monuments.* Paris, 1877–1919. (D.S.)

De Ruggiero, G. *Dizionario Epigrafico di Antichità romane.* Rome. 1895– . (Diz. Epig.)

Friedländer, L. and G. Wissowa. *Darstellungen aus der Sittengeschichte Roms.* Edd. 9 and 10. Leipzig, 1919–21.

Gercke, A. and E. Norden. *Einleitung in die Altertumswissenschaft.* Ed. 2, Leipzig-Berlin, 1914. Ed. 3 in course of publication.

Hirschfeld, O. *Die kaiserlichen Verwaltungsbeamten bis auf Diocletian.* Ed. 2. Berlin, 1905.

Klebs, E., H. Dessau and P. von Rohden. *Prosopographia Imperii Romani Saec. I, II, III.* Berlin. Vol. i, ed. E. Klebs, 1897; vol. ii, ed. H. Dessau, 1897; vol. iii, edd. P. de Rohden et H. Dessau, 1898. Vol. i of the 2nd edition, edd. E. Groag et A. Stein, Berlin-Leipzig, 1933; vol. ii, 1936. (P.I.R.)

Lübker, Friedrich. *Reallexikon des klassischen Altertums für Gymnasien.* Ed. 8 (by J. Geffcken and E. Ziebarth). Leipzig, 1914. (Lübker.)

Marquardt, J. *Römische Staatsverwaltung.* Leipzig. Ed. 2. Vol. i, 1881; vol. ii, 1884; vol. iii, 1885.

Mommsen, Th. *Römisches Staatsrecht.* Leipzig. Vol. i (ed. 3), 1887; vol. ii, 1 (ed. 3), 1887; vol. ii, 2 (ed. 3), 1887; vol. iii, 1, 1887; vol. iii, 2, 1888.

von Müller, Iwan. *Handbuch der Altertumswissenschaft.* (In course of revision under editorship of W. Otto.) Munich, 1886– (Müllers Handbuch.)

Platner, S. B. *A Topographical Dictionary of Ancient Rome.* (Completed and revised by T. Ashby.) Oxford, 1929.

Sandys, Sir J. E. *A Companion to Latin Studies.* Ed. 3. Cambridge, 1929.

Stuart Jones, H. *A Companion to Roman History.* Oxford, 1912.

Wissowa, G. *Pauly's Real-Encyclopädie der classischen Altertumswissenschaft.* Neue Bearbeitung. (Under editorship of W. Kroll.) Stuttgart, 1894– . (P.W.)

III. Chronology

Bickermann, E. *Chronologie,* in Gercke-Norden, Band iii, Heft 5. Leipzig-Berlin, 1933.

Griffin, M. H. and G. A. Harrer. *Fasti Consulares.* A.J.A. xxxiv, 1930, pp. 360 *sqq.*

Kubitschek, W. *Grundriss der antiken Zeitrechnung,* in Müllers Handbuch, i, 7. Munich, 1928.

Leuze, O. *Bericht über die Literatur zur Chronologie (Kalendar und Jahrzählung) in die Jahren* 1921–1928. Bursian, ccxxvii, 1930, pp. 97–139.

Liebenam, W. *Fasti Consulares imperii Romani von* 30 v. Chr. bis 565 n. Chr. Bonn, 1909.

IV. Numismatics

Bernhart, M. *Handbuch zur Münzkunde der römischen Kaiserzeit.* Halle a.S., 1926.

Cohen, H. *Description historique des monnaies frappées sous l'empire romain.* Ed. 2. Paris, 1880–92.

Mattingly, H. and E. A. Sydenham. *The Roman Imperial Coinage*. London, vol. IV, part i (Pertinax to Geta), 1936; vol. v, by P. H. Webb, part i (Valerian to Florian), 1927, part ii (Probus to Diocletian), 1933. (M.-S.)

Milne, J. G. *Catalogue of Alexandrian Coins in the Ashmolean Museum*. Oxford, 1932.

Schulz, O. Th. *Die Rechtstitel und Regierungsprogramme auf römischen Kaisermünzen, von Caesar bis Severus*. (Studien zur Geschichte und Kultur des Altertums, XIII, 4.) Paderborn, 1925.

Vogt, J. *Die alexandrinischen Münzen: Grundlegung einer alexandrinischen Kaisergeschichte*. Part I, Text; Part II, Münzverzeichnis. Stuttgart, 1924.

V. Source Criticism

A. General

Leo, F. *Die griechisch-römische Biographie nach ihrer litterarischen Form*. Leipzig, 1901.

Peter, H. *Die geschichtliche Literatur über die römische Kaiserzeit bis Theodosius I und ihre Quellen*. Leipzig, 1897. 2 vols.

Rosenberg, A. *Einleitung und Quellenkunde zur römischen Geschichte*. Berlin, 1921.

Wachsmuth, C. *Einleitung in das Studium der alten Geschichte*. Leipzig, 1895.

B. Special

(For treatment of particular portions of the Sources see the bibliographies to the relevant chapters.)

Schultz, H. Art. in P.W. *s.v.* Herodianus (3).

Schwartz, E. Art. in P.W. *s.v.* Cassius (40) Dio Cocceianus.

(Items 3–13, on the *Historia Augusta*, are in chronological order to show the progress of the discussion.)

Enmann, A. *Eine verlorene Geschichte der römischen Kaiser*. Phil. Suppl. IV, 1884, p. 337.

Dessau, H. *Über Zeit und Persönlichkeit der Scriptores Historiae Augustae*. Hermes, XXIV, 1889, p. 337. Cf. ib. XXVII, 1892, p. 561.

De Sanctis, G. *Gli Scriptores Historiae Augustae*. Riv. stor. ant. I, 1896, p. 90.

Tropea, G. *Studi sugli Scriptores Historiae Augustae*. Messina, 1899.

Lécrivain, C. *Études sur l'Histoire Auguste*. Paris, 1904.

Seeck, O. *Politische Tendenzgeschichte im 5 Jahrhundert*. Rh. Mus. LXVII, 1912, p. 591.

Mommsen, Th. *Die Scriptores historiae Augustae*. Ges.Schrift. VII, 1909, pp. 302–52.

Hohl, E. *Das Problem der Historia Augusta*. N.J. Kl. Alt. XXXIII, 1914, p. 698.

von Domaszewski, A. *Die Personennamen bei den Scriptores Historiae Augustae*. Heid. S.B. 1918, 13 Abh.

Baynes, N. *The Historia Augusta, its date and purpose*. (With Bibliography.) Oxford, 1926.

Hohl, E. *Bericht über die Literatur zu den Scriptores Historiae Augustae für die Jahre 1924–1935*. Bursian, Band CCLVI, 1937, pp. 127–156.

CHAPTER I

THE ARMY AND THE IMPERIAL HOUSE

A. Ancient Sources

(1) *Texts*

Codex Justinianus, rec. P. Krueger, ed. 9, Berlin, 1915.
Digesta, rec. Th. Mommsen, ed. 14, Berlin, 1922.
Dio LXXIV–LXXX (LXXIX, 2, 2–LXXX, 8, 3, in the original text, mutilated; the rest
    in the abridgement of Xiphilinus, supplemented by citations of Dio in the
    Excerpta Constantiniana and elsewhere), ed. U. P. Boissevain, vol. III, Berlin,
    1901.
Herodian II–V, ed. K. Stavenhagen, Leipzig, 1922.
Scriptores Historiae Augustae, ed. E. Hohl, I, Leipzig, 1927.

Philostratus and Tertullian offer an occasional item for the general history of the
period. See also Aurelius Victor, the Chronographer of 354, the *Chronicle* of Jerome
and the *Chronicon Paschale*, the *Epitome de Caesaribus*, Eutropius, Festus, Orosius,
and Zosimus.

For the later (Greek) tradition see the *Excerpta Constantiniana*, F.H.G. IV,
Malalas, Suidas, Georgius Syncellus, and Zonaras.

(2) *Coins*

In addition to the relevant pages in the works of Cohen, Mattingly-Sydenham, and
Vogt, cited in the General Bibliography (IV), see also
British Museum Catalogues of the Greek Coins. London, 1873–1927.
Dattari, G. *Numi Augg. Alexandrini*. I, Cairo, 1901.
Hasebroek, J. *Untersuchungen zur Geschichte des Kaisers Septimius Severus*.
    Heidelberg, 1921, pp. 152–72. (Numismatic material for the reign of Severus:
    cf. W. Kubitschek in Num.Z. XIV, 1921, p. 184.)
Mattingly, H. *The Coinage of Septimius Severus and his Times*. Num.Chr. 5th ser.,
    XII, 1932, p. 177.

(3) *Inscriptions*

The more important inscriptions will be found in Dessau, Ditt.[3], I.G.R.R., and
O.G.I.S., supplemented by Ann. épig., Eph. Ep., and S.E.G. See also
Hasebroek, J. *Op. cit.* pp. 174–94. (Epigraphic material for the reign of Severus.)
de Ruggiero, E. *Dizionario epigrafico di Antichità romane*, Rome, 1895–, *s.vv.*
    Caracalla, Elagabalus (the god), Geta, Heliogabalus, etc.

(4) *Ostraca*

Wilcken, U. *Griechische Ostraka aus Aegypten und Nubien*. Leipzig, 1899, I,
    pp. 802–5.

(5) *Papyri*

See especially B.G.U. 902; Mitteis-Wilcken, *Grundzüge und Chrestomathie*, I, ii,
22, 96, 171, 245, 407, 408, 461, 490; II, ii, 375, 377 (= P. Giessen 40[1]), 378;
P. Lond. 351; P. Oxy. 1100, 1405, 1406, 1408, 1905; P.S.I. 101, 102, 105, 249,
683; Preisigke, *Sammelbuch*, 8, 4284; Rostovtzeff, C.R. Ac. Inscr. 1933, p. 316 =
Ann. épig. 1933, no. 107 (from Doura). See also, for chronology, B.G.U. 326;

Mitteis-Wilcken, *op. cit.* I, ii, 96; P. Grenf. 60; P. Oxy. 719, 1725; and, for the date of the Egyptian journey of Severus, the imperial rescripts published at Alexandria in 199–200 (J. Hasebroek, *op. cit.* p. 119).

For the literature on P. Giessen 40[1] see below under B (*d*) the 'Constitutio Antoniniana.'

B. Modern Works

(*a*) *Criticism of the Sources*

In addition to the works of Baynes, Leo, Peter and Rosenberg cited in the General Bibliography (p. 730), see

Baaz, E. *De Herodiani fontibus et auctoritate.* Diss. Berlin, 1909.

Hasebroek, J. *Die Fälschung der Vita Nigri und Vita Albini in den S.H.A.* Diss. Heidelberg, Leipzig/Berlin, 1916.

Hönn, K. *Quellenuntersuchungen zu den Viten des Heliogabalus und des Severus Alexander im Corpus der S.H.A.* Berlin, 1911.

Reusch, W. *Der historische Wert der Caracallavita in den Scriptores Historiae Augustae.* Klio, Beiheft XXIV, 1931.

Roos, A. G. *Herodian's Method of Composition.* J.R.S. V, 1915, p. 191.

Schulz, H. Art. in P.W. *s.v.* Herodianus (3).

Schulz, O. Th. *Beiträge zur Kritik unserer literarischen Überlieferung für die Zeit vom Commodus' Sturze bis auf den Tod des M. Aurelius Antoninus* (Caracalla). Diss. Leipzig, 1903.

Schwartz, E. Art. in P.W. *s.v.* Cassius (40) Dio Cocceianus.

Van Sickle, C. E. *The Headings of Rescripts of the Severi in the Justinian Code.* C.P. XXIII, 1928, p. 270.

Smits, J. S. P. *De fontibus e quibus res a Heliogabalo et Alexandro Severo gestae colliguntur.* Diss. Amsterdam, 1908.

Werner, R. *Der historische Wert der Pertinaxvita in den Scriptores Historiae Augustae.* Klio, XXVI, 1933, p. 283. (But cf. G. Barbieri's criticisms in *Stud. ital. di fil. class.* XIII, 1936, p. 183.)

(*b*) *General*

See also the relevant pages of works in the General Bibliography (pp. 728–30) not included in this list. In the works cited here, and in the footnotes to the chapter, references will be found to monographs and articles dealing with special topics.

Basset, H. J. *Macrinus and Diadumenianus.* Diss. Michigan, 1920.

Bihlmeyer, K. *Die 'syrischen' Kaiser zu Rom* (211–235) *und das Christentum.* Rottenburg, 1916.

Butler, O. F. *Studies in the Life of Elagabalus.* Univ. of Michigan Studies, New York, 1910.

de Ceuleneer, A. *Essai sur la vie et le règne de Septime Sévère.* Brussels, 1880.

Cumont, F. Art. in P.W. *s.v.* Elagabalus (the god).

Fluss, M. Arts. in P.W. *s.vv.* Helvius (15 a) Pertinax (Supp. III, 1918, coll. 895–904); Septimius (32) Geta; Severus (13).

Harrer, G. A. *The Chronology of the Revolt of Pescennius Niger.* J.R.S. X, 1920, p. 155. (Cf. J. Hasebroek in Phil. Woch. XLIII, 1923, coll. 397–9.)

Hasebroek, J. *Untersuchungen zur Geschichte des Kaisers Septimius Severus.* Heidelberg, 1921.

Herzog, G. Arts. in P.W. *s.vv.* Iulius 566 (Domna), 579 (Maesa), 596 (Soaemias).

Holzapfel, L. *Römische Kaiserdaten.* Klio, XVIII, 1923, pp. 99–103 (Pertinax); 253–6 (Didius Julianus and Septimius Severus).

Homo, L. *Les privilèges administratifs du Sénat romain sous l'Empire et leur disparition graduelle au cours du IIIe siècle*. Rev. H. CXXXVII, 1921, p. 161; CXXXVIII, 1921, p. 1.

Keyes, C. W. *The Rise of the Equites in the Third Century of the Roman Empire*. Princeton, N.J. 1915.

Lambrechts, P. *La composition du Sénat romain de Septime Sévère à Dioclétien*. Diss. Pann. Ser. I, fasc. 8, Budapest, 1937.

Macchioro, V. *L'Impero romano nell' età dei Severi*. Riv. stor. ant. x, 1905–6, p. 201; XI, 1906–7, pp. 285, 341.

Platnauer, M. *On the date of the defeat of C. Pescennius Niger at Issus*. J.R.S. VIII, 1918, p. 146.

—— *The Life and Reign of the Emperor Lucius Septimius Severus*. Oxford, 1918.

Reusch, W. Art. in P.W. *s.v.* Pescennius (2) Niger.

Réville, J. *La Religion à Rome sous les Sévères*. Paris, 1886.

von Rohden, P. Art. in P.W. *s.v.* Aurelius 46 (Caracalla).

Schulz, O. Th. *Der römische Kaiser Caracalla: Genie, Wahnsinn oder Verbrechen*. Leipzig, 1909.

—— *Vom Prinzipat zum Dominat*. Paderborn, 1919.

Stein, A. *Der römische Ritterstand*. Munich, 1927.

Williams, M. G. *Studies in the lives of Roman empresses: 1. Julia Domna*. A.J.A. 2nd ser. VI, 1902, p. 259.

von Wotava, A. Arts. in P.W. *s.vv.* Clodius (17) Albinus, Didius (8) Iulianus.

(c) Britain

References to the more important texts and inscriptions and to the coin evidence will be found in the footnotes to section IV of the chapter. The following bibliography relates especially to the archaeological evidence.

For evidence of destruction at the legionary headquarters at York and Chester in the late second century, and of a subsequent restoration, see S. N. Miller in *J.R.S.* xv, 1925, p. 176; XVIII, 1928, p. 61, and J. P. Droop and R. Newstead in *Liverpool Ann. of Arch.* XVIII, 1931, p. 7 and XXIII, 1936, pp. 5–6 (cf. the fragmentary inscription, *J.R.S.* XVII, 1927, p. 212, no. 3).

For Wales see V. E. Nash-Williams in *Archaeologia Cambrensis*, 1931, p. 157 (cf. id., *Catalogue of the Roman inscribed and sculptured stones found at Caerleon*, Cardiff, 1935, p. 5, no. 2 = *C.I.L.* VII, 106); R. E. M. Wheeler, *Prehistoric and Roman Wales*, Oxford, 1925, pp. 232–3; *Segontium and the Roman Occupation of Wales*, London, 1924, pp. 46–66 (cf. *C.I.L.* VII, 142); *The Roman amphitheatre at Caerleon*, Archaeologia, LXXVIII, 1928, pp. 153–4; and *The Roman Fort near Brecon*, Y Cymmrodor, XXXVII, 1926, pp. 79–83.

For the system of the Wall as the evidence stood in 1920, see R. G. Collingwood, *Hadrian's Wall: a history of the problem*, J.R.S. XI, 1921, p. 49. For the progress of the investigation of the Wall and its outposts since 1920 see the reports of excavations by F. G. Simpson, I. A. Richmond, and E. B. Birley in *Archaeologia Aeliana*, and *Transactions of the Cumberland and Westmorland Antiq. and Arch. Society*.

For evidence of a Severan reoccupation of Birrens, in Dumfriesshire, see E. B. Birley, in the *Proc. of the Soc. of Antiq. of Scotland*, LXXII, 1937–8.

For Scotland in general, in relation to the campaigns of Severus, see besides Birley, *op. cit.* F. Haverfield, *Roman Scotland*, Edinburgh Review, CCXIII, 1911, p. 487; F. Haverfield and Sir G. Macdonald, *The Roman Occupation of Britain*, Oxford, 1924, p. 123; Sir G. Macdonald, *Roman Coins found in Scotland*, Proc. of the Soc. of Antiq. of Scotland, LII, 1917–18, pp. 252–3, 274–6, and *The Roman Wall in Scotland*, ed. 2, Oxford, 1934, pp. 13–19.

(*d*) *The* 'Constitutio Antoniniana'

For a review of the literature on the Constitutio which appeared between the publication of P. Giessen 40, in 1910, and 1934 see

Jones, A. H. M. *Another Interpretation of the 'Constitutio Antoniniana.'* J.R.S. xxvi, 1936, pp. 223–7.

For views of the Constitutio since 1934 see, besides Jones, *op. cit.* pp. 227–35,

Albertario, E. *Introduzione storica allo studio del diritto Romano Giustiniano,* i. Rome, 1935, p. 3.

Kreller, H. *Römische Rechtsgeschichte* in *Grundrisse des Deutschen Rechtes.* Herausg. von H. Stoll und H. Lange. Tübingen, 1936, p. 33.

Kübler, B. Art. in P.W. *s.v.* Peregrinus, coll. 641–3.

Kunkel, W. *Römisches Privatrecht auf Grund des Werkes von Paul Jörs.* Ed. 2, Berlin, 1935, p. 57, n. 10.

Schönbauer, E. *Reichsrecht, Volksrecht und Provinzialrecht. Studien über die Bedeutung der Constitutio Antoniniana für die römische Rechtsentwicklung.* Z.d. Sav.-Stift. lvii, 1937, p. 309.

Schulz, F. *Principles of Roman Law.* Oxford, 1936, esp. p. 123, n. 3.

Weiss, E. *Grundzüge der römischen Rechtsgeschichte.* Reichenberg, 1936, p. 104.

CHAPTER II

THE SENATE AND THE ARMY

A. ANCIENT SOURCES

(1) *Inscriptions*

For inscriptions compare the selection in Dessau, III, Index iii, pp. 293–7, Ditt.[3] 888, and O.G.I.S. 519, 578, 640, with the references given in the footnotes to the chapter. Besides these see also the books and articles by K. Hönn, A. Jardé, P. W. Townsend, W. Thiele, and M. G. Williams (under Modern Works).

(2) *Coins*

In addition to the works of Cohen, Mattingly-Sydenham, and Vogt cited in the General Bibliography (IV) see

Bosch, Cl. *Die kleinasiatischen Münzen der römischen Kaiserzeit.* Teil II, Bd. 1: Bithynien, 1. Hälfte, Stuttgart, 1935, pp. 52–7, 205–6.

Elmer, G. *Die Münzprägung von Viminacium und die Zeitrechnung der Provinz Ober-Moesien.* Num. Z. (N.F.), XXVIII, 1935, p. 35.

Pink, K. *Der Aufbau der römischen Münzprägung in der Kaiserzeit.* III, *Von Alexander Severus bis Philippus.* Ib. p. 12.

(3) *Papyri*

P. Berl. Bibl. 1, with U. Wilcken's revision in R. Deissmann, *Licht vom Osten,* Stuttgart, 1909, p. 277. P. Par. 69: cf. U. Wilcken, *Phil.* LIII, 1894, p. 81 = *Chrestomathie,* I, 2, no. 41. Yale Coll. of Papyri, no. 156 = P. W. Townsend, *A.J.Ph.* LI, 1930, p. 62. C. C. Torrey, *A Syriac Parchment from Edessa of the year 243 A.D.,* Zeits. f. Semitistik und verwandte Gebiete, X, 1935, p. 33: cf. A. R. Bellinger and C. B. Welles, *A Third-Century Contract of Sale from Edessa in Osrhoene,* Yale Class. Stud. V, 1935, p. 93. Compare F. Hohmann, *Zur Chronologie der Papyrusurkunden (Römische Kaiserzeit),* Greifswald, 1911, pp. 15–17, and O. W. Reinmuth, *The Prefect of Egypt from Augustus to Diocletian,* Klio, Beiheft XXXIV, 1935, p. 138.

(4) *Texts*

Codex Justinianus, rec. P. Krueger, ed. 9, Berlin, 1915: index pp. 491–3.

Corpus legum ab imperatoribus Romanis ante Justinianum latarum, von G. Haenel, Leipzig, 1857.

Digesta, rec. Th. Mommsen, ed. 14, Berlin, 1922. (The references will be found in the footnotes to the chapter.)

Dio LXXVIII, 30, 3: LXXIX, 17, 2 *sq.*; 19 *sq.*: LXXX, 1–5, ed. U. P. Boissevain, vol. III, Berlin, 1901.

εἰς βασιλέα = Ps.-Aristides, or. 9 (ed. L. Dindorf), = or. 35 (ed. B. Keil). See E. Groag, *Studien zur röm. Kaisergeschichte,* II, Linz, 1918, p. 13, and M. Rostovtzeff, *The Soc. and Econ. History of the Rom. Emp.* Oxford, 1926, p. 397 (and cf. p. 614, note 15).

Eusebius, *Hist. eccl.* (ed. E. Schwartz), VI, 21–3; 28 *sq.*; 34; 39.

Herodian V–VIII, ed. K. Stavenhagen, Leipzig, 1922.

Jordanes, *Getica* 83–90; *Romana* 280–3 (ed. Th. Mommsen).

Orosius, *Historiae adversus Paganos*, VII, 18, 6–21, 2 (ed. C. Zangemeister, Leipzig, 1889).

Scriptores Historiae Augustae, ed. E. Hohl, Leipzig, 1927. *Alexander Severus: Maximini duo: Gordiani tres: Maximus et Balbinus.* For fuller references see the index to Hohl, vol. II, pp. 251, 258, 273, 283, and 284, and for the Philippi, p. 289.

Zosimus I, 11–22; III, 14, 2, and 32, 4, ed. L. Mendelssohn, Leipzig, 1887.

For some other items see Ammianus Marcellinus XIV, 1, 8, XXIII, 5, 7, 17, and XXVI, 6, 20; Anonymus Valesianus (ed. V. Gardthausen), § 33, and Julian, *Convivium* (Caesares), 313 A. For the later Latin tradition see Aurelius Victor, the *Epitome de Caesaribus*, and Eutropius: for the later Greek tradition see John of Antioch, Malalas, Georgius Syncellus, and Zonaras.

B. Modern Works

(a) *Works embracing the whole period*

von Domaszewski, A. *Die Daten der scriptores historiae Augustae von Severus Alexander bis Carus.* S.B. Heidelberger Akad. 1917, Abh. 1.

Herzog, E. *Geschichte und System der römischen Staatsverfassung.* Vol. II, i, Leipzig, 1887, pp. 487–519.

Manaresi, A. *L' Impero Romano e il Cristianesimo.* Turin, 1914, pp. 298–323.

Neumann, K. J. *Der römische Staat und die allgemeine Kirche.* Vol. I, Leipzig, 1890, pp. 207–54.

Schulz, O. Th. *Vom Prinzipat zum Dominat.* Paderborn, 1919, pp. 21–76, 196–203.

(b) *Severus Alexander*

Baynes, N. H. *The Historia Augusta, its Date and Purpose.* Oxford, 1926.

Bihlmeyer, K. *Die 'syrischen' Kaiser zu Rom (211–235) und das Christentum.* Rottenburg, 1916, pp. 68–166.

Hönn, K. *Quellenuntersuchungen zu den Viten des Heliogabalus und des Severus Alexander im Corpus der S. H. A.* Leipzig/Berlin, 1911.

Homo, L. *Les privilèges administratifs du sénat romain sous l'Empire et leur disparition graduelle au cours du IIIe siècle.* Rev. H. CXXXVII, 1921, p. 161; CXXXVIII, 1921, p. 1.

Hopkins, R. V. N. *The Life of Alexander Severus.* Cambridge Historical Essays, no. xiv, 1907.

Jardé, A. *Études critiques sur la vie et le règne de Sévère Alexandre.* Paris, 1925; cf. W. Schur, *G.G.A.* 1929, p. 504.

Jullian, C. *Histoire de la Gaule.* Vol. IV, Paris, 1924, pp. 534–7.

Macchioro, V. *L' Impero romano nell' età dei Severi.* Riv. stor. ant. x, 1905–6, p. 201; XI, 1906–7, pp. 285 and 341.

Meyer, P. M. *Die Epistula Severi Alexandri Dig. XLIX, i,* 25 (= P. Oxy. XVII, 2104). Studi in onore di P. Bonfante, II, 1929, p. 341.

Thiele, W. *De Severo Alexandro Imperatore.* Berlin, 1909.

Van Sickle, C. E. *The terminal dates of the reign of Alexander Severus.* C.P. XXII, 1927, p. 315.

Williams, M. G. *Studies in the Lives of Roman Empresses: Julia Mamaea.* University of Michigan Studies, Human. Ser., vol. I, 1904, p. 67.

Arts. in P.W. *s.vv.* Aurelius (221) Severus Alexander (Groebe); Iulius-Iulia (558) Avita Mamaea and Iulia (579) Maesa (Herzog); Gessius (6) Marcianus, Sallustius (4) (A. Stein), and Seius-Seia (22) (Fluss).

(c) Maximinus Thrax, the Gordians, Pupienus and Balbinus

Bersanetti, G. M. *Massimino il Trace e la reta stradale dell' impero romano.* Atti III Congr. nazionale di Studi Romani, I, 1934, p. 590.

—— *Studi in Massimino il Trace. I rapporti fra Massimino e il Senato.* Rivista-Indo-Greco-Italica, XVIII, 1934, p. 89.

Brusin, G. *Gli Scavi di Aquileia.* Udine, 1934, pp. 73–6.

Calderini, A. *Aquileia Romana.* Milan, 1930, pp. 52–61.

Carcopino, J. *Le 'Limes' de Numidie et sa garde Syrienne.* Syria, VI, 1925, pp. 30–57: 118–149.

Costa, G. Art *s.v.* Gordianus in Diz. Epig.

Lehmann, K. F. *Kaiser Gordian III.* Berlin, 1911.

Löhrer, J. *De C. Iulio Vero Maximino.* Diss. Münster, 1883.

Seeck, O. *Der erste Barbar auf dem römischen Kaiserthrone.* Preuss. Jahrb. LVI, 1885, p. 267 (= Populäre Schriften, Berlin, 1898, p. 191).

Townsend, P. W. *Chronology of the Year* 238 A.D. Yale Class. Stud. I, 1928, p. 231.

—— *The Administration of Gordian III.* Ib. IV, 1934, p. 59.

Uhlhorn, G. Art. s.v. *Maximinus Thrax* in Realencyklop. für protest. Theologie, vol. XII³, p. 456.

Van Sickle, C. E. *A hypothetical chronology for the year of the Gordians.* C.P. XXII, 1927, p. 416.

—— *Some further observations on the chronology of the year* 238 A.D. Ib. XXIV, 1929, p. 285.

Arts. in P.W. *s.vv.* Antonius (60–62) Gordianus (von Rohden): Caecilia Paulina (Caecilius 138), Caelius (20) Calvinus Balbinus, Clodius (50) Pupienus Maximus, and Furius (89) Sabinius Aquila Timesitheus (A. Stein): Iulius (526) Verus Maximinus and Iulius (527) Verus Maximus (Hohl): and Magnus (1) (Fluss).

(d) Philip the Arabian

Stein, E. Art. in P.W. s.v. *Iulius* (386/7) *Philippus.*

Uhlhorn, G. and F. Görres. Art. s.v. *Philippus Arabs* in Realencyklop. für protest. Theologie, vol. XV³, p. 331.

See also the various articles in the two new volumes of the second edition of P.I.R. by E. Groag and A. Stein.

CHAPTER III

THE BARBARIAN BACKGROUND

I. General Works

(a) The geographical background: F. Grenard, *La Haute Asie* (vol. VIII, pp. 235–379, of *Géographie universelle*, edited by P. Vidal de la Blache and L. Gallois), Paris, 1929; A. Stein, *Geography as a factor in history*, Geogr. Journal, LXV, 1925, p. 377.

(b) The historical background: L. Cahun, *Introduction à l'histoire de l'Asie*, Paris, 1896 (to be used with caution); L. Halphen, *Les Barbares, des grandes invasions aux conquêtes turques du XIe siècle* (vol. V of *Peuples et Civilisations*), Paris, 1926; ed. 3, revised and enlarged, 1936; E. H. Parker, *A thousand years of the Tartars*, ed. 2, London, 1924; P. Pelliot, *La Haute Asie*, Paris, 1931.

II. Archaeology

(a) General

Andersson, J. G. *Der Weg über die Steppen.* Museum of Far Eastern Antiquities, Stockholm, I, 1929, p. 152.

Borovka, G. *Scythian Art* (trans. by V. G. Childe). London, 1928.

Janse, O. *L'empire des steppes.* Rev. des arts asiatiques, IX, 1935, p. 9.

Rostovtzeff, M. *L'art gréco-sarmate et l'art chinois de l'époque des Han.* Aréthuse, April, 1924, p. 81.

—— *The animal style in South Russia and China.* Princeton, N.J., 1929.

—— *Le centre de l'Asie, la Russie, la Chine et le style animal.* Semin. Konda-kovianum, Prague, 1929.

(b) Russia

Ebert, M. *Südrussland in Altertum.* Bonn—Leipzig, 1921.

Minns, E. H. *Scythians and Greeks.* Cambridge, 1913.

Rostovtzeff, M. *Iranians and Greeks in South Russia.* Oxford, 1922.

—— *Une trouvaille de l'époque gréco-sarmate de Kertch.* Mon. et Mém. Piot, XXVI, 1923, pp. 99 *sqq.*

—— *Skythien und der Bosporus.* I, Berlin, 1931.

Schmidt, A. V. *Kačka. Beiträge zur Erforschung der Kulturen Ostrusslands in der Zeit der Völkerwanderung* (III–V Jahrh.). Eurasia septentrionalis antiqua, I, 1927, p. 18.

Tallgren, A. M. *Études archéologiques sur la Russie orientale durant l'ancien âge du fer.* Ib. VII, 1932, p. 7.

—— *Collection Zaoussaïlov au Musée de Finlande à Helsingfors.* Helsingfors, vol. I (Catalogue raisonné de la collection de l'âge du bronze), 1916; vol. II (Monographies de la section du l'âge du fer de l'époque de Bolgary), 1918.

Tolstoi, J., Kondakov, N. and S. Reinach. *Antiquités de la Russie méridionale.* Paris, 1891.

(c) Siberia

Adrianov, A. *Das Martjanovsche Staatmuseum in Minussinsk.* (Text in Russian.) Minusinsk, 1924.

Heikel, A. *Antiquités de la Sibérie occidentale.* Helsingfors, 1894.

Martin, T. R. *L'âge du bronze au Musée de Minoussinsk.* Stockholm, 1893.

von Merhart, G. *Bronzezeit am Jenissei.* Vienna, 1926.
Radloff, W. *Siberian antiquities.* Materials for the archaeology of Russia, vols. III,
	v, xv and xxvII, St Petersburg, 1888, 1891, 1894 and 1902.
Salmony, A. *Sino-Siberian Art in the Collection of C. T. Loo.* Paris, 1923.
Tallgren, A. M. *Collection Tovostine. Antiquités préhistoriques de Minoussinsk.*
	Helsingfors, 1917.
—— *Inner-Asiatic and Siberian rock pictures.* Eur. septent. ant. vIII, 1933, p. 175.

(d) Mongolia

Borovka, G. *Compte-rendu pour l'exploration du nord de la Mongolie.* (Text in Russian.)
	Leningrad, 1925.
Heikel, A. *Altertümer aus dem Thale des Talas im Turkestan.* Société finno-ougrienne,
	Travaux ethnographiques, IV, Helsingfors, 1918.
von Takacs, Z. *Chinesisch-hunnische Kunstformen.* Sofia, 1925.
—— *Francis Hop memorial exhibition* 1933: *the art of Greater Asia.* Budapest, 1933.
Werner, J. *Zur Stellung der Ordosbronzen.* Eur. septent. ant. IX (Minns volume),
	1934, p. 259.

III. The Huns and their Relations with China

Brockelmann, C. *Volkskundliches aus Altturkestan.* Asia Major, II, 1925, p. 110.
Chavannes, E. *Documents sur les T'ou-Kiue (Turcs) occidentaux.* St Petersburg,
	1903.
—— *Notes additionnelles sur les T'ou-Kiue occidentaux.* T'oung Pao, v, 1904,
	pp. 1–110.
—— *Les pays d'Occident d'après le Wei lio.* Ib. vI, 1905, pp. 519–571.
—— *Trois généraux chinois de la dynastie des Han.* Ib. vII, 1906, pp. 210–269.
—— *Les pays d'Occident d'après le* Heou Han Chou. Ib. vIII, 1907, pp. 149–234.
Chih Louh Kouoh Kiang Yuh Tchi. Histoire géographique des xvI *royaumes fondés
	en Chine par les Tartares.* (French trans. by A. Des Michels.) Paris, 1891.
De Groot, J. J. M. *Die Hunnen der vorchristlichen Zeiten. Chinesische Urkunden zur
	Geschichte Asiens.* I, Berlin—Leipzig, 1921. (Compare a review by M. O.
	Franke in *Ostasiatische Zeits.* 1920–21, p. 144, and an article by E. von Zach,
	Einige Verbesserungen zu De Groot, Asia Major, I, 1924, p. 125.)
—— *Die Westlande Chinas in der vorchristlichen Zeiten. Chinesische Urkunden,*
	II, 1926.
Franke, M. O. *Beiträge aus chinesischen Quellen zur Kenntniss der Türkenvölker
	und Skythen Zentralasiens.* Berlin, 1904.
Herrmann, A. *Die Gobi im Zeitalter der Hunen-Herrschaft.* Geografiska Annalen
	(Sven Hedin volume), 1935, Stockholm, pp. 130–143.
—— *Die Hephthaliten und ihre Beziehungen zu China.* Asia Major, II, 1925,
	pp. 564–580.
Inostranzev, K. A. *Hunnu and Huns: analysis of the theories of the origin of the
	Hunnu people of Chinese annals and of the European Huns.* London, 1926.
Jamsheji Modi. *Early history of the Huns and their inroads in India and Persia.*
	Journal Bombay Branch Roy. Asiatic Soc. 1917, p. 539.
Marquart, J. *Ērānšahr nach der Geographie des Ps.-Moses Xorenac'i.* Berlin, 1901.
—— *Osteuropäische und ostasiatische Streifzüge.* Leipzig, 1903.
Pelliot, P. *L'origine de T'ou-kiue.* T'oung Pao, xvI, 1915, pp. 687–689.
Radloff, W. *Alttürkische Inschriften der Mongolei.* St Petersburg, 1894–99.
Shiratori, K. *Ueber den Wusunstamm in Centralasien.* Keleti Szemle, III, Budapest,
	1902.

Shiratori, K. *Sur l'origine des Hiong-nou.* Journ. Asiatique, ccii, 1923, p. 71.
—— *On the titles Khan and Kaghan.* Proc. of the Imp. Acad. (of Japan), Tokyo, ii, 1926, pp. 241–4.
—— *On the territory of the Hsiung-nu prince Hsiu-t'u-wang and his metal statues for heaven worship.* Mem. of the Research Department of the Toyo Bunko, v, Tokyo, 1930.
Thomsen, V. *Les inscriptions de l'Orkhon déchiffrées.* Mém. de la Soc. finno-ougrienne, v, Helsingfors, 1896.
Torii, R. and K. *Populations primitives de la Mongolie orientale.* Journal Coll. Science, Imp. Univ. of Tokyo, xxxvi, 1913–15, art. 4.

IV. The Tarim Basin

Grousset, R. *L'Iran extérieur. Son art.* Cahiers de la Soc. d. Ét. Iraniennes de Paris, Cahier no. 2, Paris, 1931.
Herrmann, A. *Die alten Seidenstrassen zwischen China und Syrien.* Berlin, 1910 (Quellen und Forschungen zur alten Gesch. u. Geogr., Heft 21).
—— *Die Verkehrswege zwischen China, Indien und Rom um* 100 *n. Chr. Geb.* Leipzig, 1922.
von Le Coq, A. *Bilderatlas zur Kunst- und Kulturgeschichte Mittelasiens.* Berlin, 1925.
—— *Buried treasures of Chinese Turkestan.* London, 1928.
—— *Die Buddhistische Spätantike in Mittelasien.* 7 vols. Berlin, 1922–31.
Levi, S. *Le tokharien B, langue de Koutcha.* Journ. Asiatique, ii (11th Ser.), 1913, p. 311.
—— *Fragments de textes koutchéens.* (Cahiers de la Société asiatique.) Paris, 1933.
Pelliot, P. *Tokharien et koutchéen.* Journ. Asiatique, ccxxiv, 1934, p. 23.
Sieg, E. and W. Siegling. *Tocharische Grammatik.* Göttingen, 1931.
Stein, (Sir) A. *Sand-buried ruins of Khotan.* 2 vols. Oxford, 1907.
—— *Serindia.* 5 vols. Oxford, 1921.
—— *Innermost Asia.* 2 vols. Oxford, 1932.
—— *On ancient Central-Asian tracks.* London, 1933.
Waldschmidt, E. *Gandhâra, Kutscha, Turfan.* Leipzig, 1925.

V. China and its Relations with the Huns

Franke, O. M. *Geschichte des chinesischen Reiches.* Berlin, i (to the end of the Han), 1930; ii (from the end of the Han to the end of the T'ang), 1936.
Grousset, R. *Histoire de l'Extrême-Orient.* 2 vols. Paris, 1929.
Wieger, le Rév. Père. *Textes historiques.* Ed. 3, vol. i, Shanghai, 1936.

CHAPTER IV

SASSANID PERSIA

SECTIONS I–V

I. ANCIENT SOURCES

A. *Greek and Roman*

The notices in classical authors such as Dio Cassius, Herodian, Dexippus, Trebellius Pollio, Lactantius, Vopiscus, Eusebius, Rufinus, and Aurelius Victor deal mainly with the political contacts of Iran with Rome. Ammianus Marcellinus supplies some information about the military and administrative organization of the Sassanid Empire. A summary of the history of the Sassanid dynasty is to be found in Agathias, book II.

For religion see especially C. Clemen, *Fontes Historiae Religionis Persicae*, Bonn, 1920.

B. *Syrian*

THE CHRONICLE OF ARBELA. For editions and commentaries see the Bibliography to chapter III of volume XI, p. 877.

ACTS OF THE PERSIAN MARTYRS. *Acta Sanctorum Martyrum*, ed. St. Assemanus, vol. I, Rome, 1748; P. Bédjan, *Acta Martyrum et Sanctorum*, vols. II and IV, Paris, 1891, 1894; G. Hoffmann, *Auszüge aus syrischen Akten persischer Märtyrer*, Leipzig, 1880. (Abh. f. die Kunde des Morgenlandes, VII, 3.)

C. *Armenian*

FAUSTUS OF BYZANTIUM. Ed. Ch. Patkanian, St Petersburg, 1883; French trans. in V. Langlois, *Collection des historiens anciens et modernes de l'Arménie*, vol. I, Paris, 1867, pp. 209 *sqq.*; *Des Faustus von Byzanz Geschichte Armeniens*, übers. von M. Lauer, Cologne, 1879.

For religious history:

EZNIK OF KOLB. The Venice edition, reprint of 1914; French trans. by Le Vaillant de Florival, Paris, 1853; V. Langlois, *op. cit.* II, pp. 375 *sqq.*; Eznik, *Wider die Sekten*, übers. von J. M. Schmid, Vienna, 1900; L. Mariès, *Le De Deo d'Eznik de Kolb*, Paris, 1924.

ELISAEUS VARDAPET. Ed. by X. Hovhaniseanç, Moscow, 1892; Michael P'orthugal, Venice, 1903; V. Langlois, *op. cit.* II, pp. 177 *sqq.*; P. Nerses Akinian, *Elisäus Vardapet und seine Geschichte des Armenischen Krieges*, I–II, Vienna, 1932–6 (in Armenian, with German résumé).

LAZARUS OF PHARP. Critical edition by G. Ter-Mkrtitschian and S. Malchassian, Tiflis, 1904; V. Langlois, *op. cit.* II, pp. 259 *sqq.*

D. *The Iranian Tradition*

Both the Pahlavi *Khvadhāynāmagh* ('Book of Kings'), composed towards the end of the Sassanian era, and the Arabic translations and adaptations, of which the most famous was the work of Ibn-el-Moqaffaʻ (died *c.* A.D. 760), have perished. But these Arabic translations formed the chief source for the summaries of ancient Iranian history that are still to be found in the Arab chronicles (such as those of Ya'qūbī, Ibn Quteiba, Eutychius, Dīnawarī, Tabari, Hamza of Ispahan, Mas'udi, Ta'alibi, and Biruni) and in the Persian (the Shāhnāmeh of Firdausī, the Fārsnāmeh, and the Mujmilu't-tawārīkh). A short Pahlavi historical romance, of which the text survives, the Kārnāmagh ('Book of Great Deeds') of Ardashir Pabhagan, is a mixture of historical fact and older legends, among which several features of the legendary history of Cyrus the Great are recognizable. Nearly all the details of the political and organizing work of Ardashir supplied by our Persian and Arab sources derive from Pahlavi works of the sixth century; these really describe institutions in the time of Chosroes I, but try to enhance their credit by attributing them to the founder of the dynasty; see A. Christensen, *Les gestes des rois dans les traditions de l'Iran antique*, Paris, 1936, chap. III.

E. *Inscriptions: Coins: Seals*

(a) *Inscriptions*

Some of the investiture-reliefs (*e.g.* those of Ardashir I, of Shapur I, and that of Vahram I which Narses annexed) bear inscriptions indicating only the name, the titles, and the genealogy of the king.

Inscriptions cited in the chapter:

SH. SHAP. A bilingual inscription (in Sassanid Pahlavi and Arsacid Pahlavi) on a monument erected at Shapur in honour of Shapur I, found by R. Ghirshman in the French excavations of 1935–6. It furnishes important chronological details, fixing the date of the accession of Ardashir I to the throne of Persis, that of his coronation as Great King of Iran, and that of the coronation of Shapur I. A description of it by R. Ghirshman, with some remarks by A. Christensen, will be found in the *Rev. des arts asiat.* x, 1936, pp. 123–9.

HJB. A bilingual inscription of Shapur I at Hajiabad. It gives an account of how the Great King shot an arrow in front of a solemn gathering of the notables of the empire. It was first published on pages 83–4 of Westergaard's edition of the Bundahishn (*Bundehesh, liber pehlevicus*), Havniae, 1851; text and translation in E. Herzfeld, *Paikuli*, pp. 87–9.

KB. Z. An inscription containing 34 long lines in Sassanid Pahlavi, carved at the foot of the building called the 'Ka'ba of Zoroaster,' which lies in front of the cliffs of Naqsh-e-Rostam in Persis. It was discovered, deep in the sand, by the expedition sent out by the Chicago Oriental Institute, in 1936, headed by Erich F. Schmidt. The first part of it, which is unfortunately seriously damaged, contains a catalogue of towns and districts, above all in the western region of the empire. The remainder gives an account of the institution of fires and the presentation of offerings for the souls of a large number of royal personages, princes and others, of both sexes; they are named with their titles, beginning with Prince Sassan, Kings Pabhagh and Shapur of Persis, and the King of Kings Ardashir I. M. Sprengling, of the University of Chicago, who has published a preliminary report together with a provisional translation (*Amer. Journ. of Sem. Lang. and Lit.* LIII, no. 2, January, 1937), is inclined to date the composition of it to the reign of Narses. In the opinion of the present writer, it should be attributed to Shapur I; but any discussion of this topic would exceed the bounds of this bibliography.

N. RJB. KRT. and N. RST. KRT. Two inscriptions, at Naqsh-e-Rajab and Naqsh-e-Rostam respectively, in which the *Mobadh Karter* Hormizd gives an account of his pious life and career of service to the empire under the reigns of Shapur I, Hormizd I, Vahram I and Vahram II. Text and provisional translation in Herzfeld, *Paikuli*, pp. 89–93.

Paik. The lengthy inscription of Narses at Paikuli, to the North of Qasr-e-Shirin in Kurdistan, was engraved on the stones of a square tower; this collapsed, and the stones which remain were scattered on the ground. Herzfeld has tried to arrange the fragments of this inscription in order; it contains the names and the titles of client-kings and great nobles, and gives us a rough idea of the extent and the boundaries of the empire at this period. Text, transcription, a provisional translation into English, and vocabulary will be found in Herzfeld's *Paikuli*, I, pp. 84–102; photographs in Vol. II.

(*b*) *Coins.* (The items are set out in chronological order.)

Mordtmann, A. D. A series of articles on Sassanid coins in the *Zeits. d. deutsch. morgenl. Ges.* vols. VIII, XII, XIX and XXXIII.

Dorn, B. *Collection de monnaies sassanides de feu le Lieutenant-Général J. de Bartholomæi.* St Petersburg, 1873.

Drouin, É. *Observations sur les monnaies à légendes en pehlvi.* Rev. Arch. 1884 and 1885.

—— *Les légendes des monnaies sassanides.* Ib. 1898.

Paruck Furdonjee, D. J. *Sāsānian Coins.* Bombay, 1924. (Including 23 photographic plates, and a reproduction of 32 plates from Dorn's book.)

Vasmer, R. *Sassanian Coins in the Ermitage.* Num. Chr. 1928, p. 249.

Herzfeld, E. *Kushano-Sasanian Coins.* Mem. of the Arch. Survey of India, no. 38, 1930; see also *Paikuli*, I, p. 35.

(*c*) *Seals*

Herzfeld, E. *Paikuli*, I, Berlin, 1924, pp. 74–82.

Horn, P. and G. Steindorff, *Sassanidische Siegelsteine.* Berlin, 1891 (Königl. Museen zu Berlin. Mitt. aus den orient. Sammlung, IV).

Justi, F. *Beiträge zur Erklärung der Pehlewi-Siegelinschriften.* Zeitschr. d. deutsch. morgenl. Ges. XLVI, pp. 280–90.

II. Modern Books and Monographs

Christensen, A. *L'Iran sous les Sassanides.* Copenhagen–Paris, 1936. (Includes political and social history, religion, laws, art and archaeology. All subjects dealt with in the same author's *L'empire des Sassanides*, 1907, will be found here in a revised and up-to-date form.)

A. *Political History*

von Gutschmid, A. *Geschichte Irans und seiner Nachbarländer von Alexander dem Grossen bis zum Untergang der Arsaciden.* Tübingen, 1888.

Herzfeld, E. *Paikuli.* I, Berlin, 1924, pp. 35–51.

Justi, F. *Geschichte Irans.* Grundriss d. iran. Philologie, II, Strassburg, 1896–1904.

Marquart (Markwart), J. *Erānšahr nach der Geographie des Ps.-Moses Xorenac̣i.* Berlin, 1901. Gött. Abh. 1901, no. 2.

—— *A Catalogue of the Provincial Capitals of Eranshahr.* Analecta Orientalia, ed. by G. Messina, III, Rome, 1931.

Nöldeke, Th. Ṭabarî. *Geschichte der Perser und Araber zur Zeit der Sasaniden.* Aus der arab. Chronik des Ṭabarî übersetzt, Leyden, 1879.

Taqizadeh, S. H. *Some Chronological Data relating to the Sasanian Period.* Bull. of the School of Orient. Stud. IX, 1, 1937, pp. 125–39.

B. *Organisation: Social and Economic Conditions*

Benveniste, E. *Les classes sociales dans la tradition avestique.* Journ. Asiatique, CCXXI, ii, 1932, p. 117.

Herrmann, A. *Die alten Seidenstrassen zwischen China und Syrien.* Berlin, 1910. (Quellen u. Forschungen zur alten Gesch. u. Geogr., Heft 21.)

Herzfeld, E. *Paikuli.* Berlin, 1924. (Glossary, *passim.*)

—— *Old-Iranian 'Peership.'* Bull. of the School of Orient. Stud. VIII, 1936, p. 937.

Inostrantzev, K. A. *Sassanian Studies.* (Сасанидскіе этюды.) St Petersburg, 1909.

Reinaud, M. *Relations politiques et commerciales de l'empire romain avec l'Asie orientale.* Paris, 1863.

Schaeder, H. H. *Iranica.* Gött. Abh. 1934, no. 10.

—— *Ein parthischer Titel im Sogdischen.* Bull. of the School of Orient. Stud. VIII, 1936, p. 737.

Streck, M. *Seleucia und Ktesiphon.* (Der alte Orient, XVI, 3–4.) Leipzig, 1917.

Tavadia, J. C. *Sūr saxvan. A Dinner Speech in Middle Persian.* Journ. of the K. R. Cama Orient. Inst. XXIX, 1935.

The Pahlavi book of law, which has been the subject of studies by Chr. Bartholomae and by M. A. Pagliaro, is concerned with the latest period of Sassanian history.

C. *Religions*

Benveniste, E. *Le témoignage de Théodore bar Kōnay sur le zoroastrisme.* Le Monde orient. XXV, 1932, p. 170.

Christensen, A. *Études sur le zoroastrisme de la Perse antique.* (Det Kgl. danske Videnskabernes Selskabs filol.-hist. Meddelelser, XV, 2.)

—— *Abarsām et Tansar.* Acta Orientalia, VIII, 1924, p. 81.

—— *A-t-il existé une religion zurvānite?* Le Monde orient. XXV, 1932, p. 69.

Clemen, C. *Die griechischen und lateinischen Nachrichten über die persische Religion.* Giessen, 1920.

Hoffmann, G. *Auszüge aus syrischen Akten persischer Märtyrer.* Leipzig, 1880.

Jackson, A. V. Williams. *Zoroastrian Studies.* New York, 1928.

Labourt, J. *Le christianisme dans l'empire perse sous la dynastie sassanide.* Paris, 1904.

Nöldeke, Th. *Syrische Polemik gegen die persische Religion.* Festgruss an R. v. Roth, Stuttgart, 1893, pp. 34 *sqq.*

Nyberg, H. S. *Questions de cosmogonie et de cosmologie mazdéennes.* Journ. asiatique, CCXIV, ii, 1931, pp. 1–134, 193–244.

Pagliaro, A. *Notes on the History of the Sacred Fires of Zoroastrianism.* Orient. Studies in Honour of C. E. Pavry, London, 1933, pp. 373 *sqq.*

von Wesendonk, O. G. *Das Weltbild der Iranier.* Munich, 1933.

For literature on Manicheeism see the Bibliography to chaps. XIII–XV, section *g*, p. 773.

D. *Art and Archaeology*

Dieulafoy, M. *L'art antique de la Perse.* Vols. I–V. Paris, 1884–9.

Erdmann, K. *Die sasanidischen Jagdschalen.* Jahrb. der preuss. Kunstsammlungen, LVII, pp. 193 *sqq.*

Flandin, E. and P. Coste. *Voyage en Perse.* Plates, vols. I–II. Paris, 1843.

Herzfeld, E. *Am Tor von Asien.* Berlin, 1920.

—— *Archäologische Mitteilungen aus Iran.* I–VIII, Berlin, 1929–36.

—— *Archaeological History of Iran.* London, 1935.

Jackson, A. V. Williams. *Persia Past and Present.* New York, 1906.

de Morgan, J. *Mission scientifique en Perse.* Recherches archéologiques, Paris, 1900–11.

Morgenstern, L. *Esthétiques d'Orient et d'Occident.* Paris, 1937.

Pope, A. U. *A Survey of Persian Art.* London–New York, 1938.

Rostovtzeff, M. *Caravan Cities*. Oxford, 1932.
Sarre, Fr. *Die Kunst des alten Persien*. Berlin, 1922.
Sarre, Fr. and E. Herzfeld. *Iranische Felsreliefs*. Berlin, 1910.
—— *Archäologische Reise im Euphrat- und Tigrisgebiet*. II, Berlin, 1920.

For excavations at Seleuceia-Ctesiphon see Ed. Meyer, in the *Mitt. d. deutschen Orient-Gesellschaft*, no. 67, 1929; O. Reuther, *Die deutsche Ktesiphon-Expedition 1928/29*, Berlin, 1930; J. M. Upton in the *Bulletin of the Metropolitan Museum*, 1932, pp. 188 *sqq.*; E. Kühnel and O. Wachtsmuth, *Die Ktesiphon-Expedition 1931–2*, Berlin, 1933; J. Heinrich Schmidt, *L'expédition de Ctésiphon en 1931–2*, Syria, xv, 1934, p. 1.

SECTION VI. The Persian Wars with Rome

I. Ancient Sources

(A) *Texts*

Apart from the relevant passages in the continuous histories of Aurelius Victor, the *Epitome de Caesaribus*, Eusebius, Eutropius, Malalas, Orosius, the *Scriptores Historiae Augustae*, Georgius Syncellus, Zonaras and Zosimus, detailed reference may be made here to more special sources:

Agathangelus. Chapters I–III (Fr. trans. by V. Langlois) in *F.H.G.* vol. v, 2, pp. 110–22: 26/7: IV, 23/4: pp. 121 *sq.*: pp. 256 *sqq.*
Agathias. II (ed. B. G. Niebuhr, Bonn, 1828): Hist. Graeci Min. (ed. L. Dindorf), II, pp. 224 *sqq.* and 330 *sqq.*
Ammianus Marcellinus. XXIII, 5, 3 (ed. C. U. Clark).
Anonymus continuator Dionis. Frags. 1, 3 (*F.H.G.* IV, pp. 192–3).
Michael Syrus. French trans. by V. Langlois, Venice, 1868, pp. 109–10.
Moses of Chorene. II, 56, 67, 71, 76, 81. (Ital. trans. by the Armenian Mechitarist monks of San Lazzaro, ed. 2, Venice, 1850.)
Oracula Sibyllina. xiii *passim* (ed. J. Geffcken).
Petrus Patricius. Frags. 8, 9, 11. *F.H.G.* IV, pp. 186–8: Hist. Graeci Min. I, pp. 429–31.
Ṭabarî. In Nöldeke's translation, pp. 1–42. (See II A above.)

(B) *Inscription*

Dessau 8879. Cf. *ib.* 8878, note 1 = *C.I.G.* 1253, and *O.G.I.S.* 640.

II. Modern Works

Asdourian, P. *Die politischen Beziehungen zwischen Armenien und Rom von 190 v. Chr. bis 428 n. Chr.* Venice, 1911, pp. 120–9.
Christensen, A. *L'Iran sous les Sassanides*. Copenhagen–Paris, 1936, pp. 79–91; 213–20.
Ensslin, W. *Die weltgeschichtliche Bedeutung der Kämpfe zwischen Rom und Persien.* N.J. f. Wiss. IV, 1928, p. 399.
Fluss, M. Art. in P.W. *s.v.* Sapor I.
von Gutschmid, A. *Geschichte Irans.* Tübingen, 1888, pp. 156–64.
Mommsen, Th. *Römische Geschichte.* Vol. v, pp. 419–33.
Nöldeke, Th. *Aufsätze zur Persischen Geschichte.* Leipzig, 1887, pp. 86–94.
—— Art. in P.W. *s.v.* Artaxerxes (Ardaschir) I.
Sykes, (Sir) P. *A History of Persia.* Vol. I, ed. 2, London, 1921, pp. 391–402.
Wickert, L. Art. in P.W. *s.v.* Licinius (173) Valerianus.

CHAPTERS V AND VI

THE INVASIONS OF PEOPLES FROM THE RHINE AND THE BLACK SEA: THE CRISIS OF THE EMPIRE (A.D. 249–270)

A. ANCIENT SOURCES

(1) *Texts*

In addition to the continuous narrative histories other authors should be consulted: among Roman writers Lactantius, Jordanes, and Orosius, the Chronographer of 354, the *Chronicle* of Jerome, and the *Chronicon* of Cassiodorus; among Byzantine writers the *Anonymus* (ed. Sathas), Cedrenus, Malalas, Leo Grammaticus, and John of Antioch. Special reference is made to the following:

Codex Justinianus, rec. P. Krueger, ed. 9, Berlin, 1915.

Cyprian, *Opera*, ed. G. Hartel (Corpus Script. Eccl. Lat. III, 1–3), Vienna, 1868–71.

Dexippus, fragments in *F. Gr. Hist.* II, pp. 304 *sqq.*

Dionysius of Alexandria, fragments in Eusebius, *Hist. eccl.* (ed. Schwartz), VI, VII.

Petrus Patricius, fragments in Cassius Dio (ed. Boissevain), vol. III, pp. 731 *sqq.* and in *F.H.G.* IV, pp. 187 *sqq.*

For the Christian literature see the Bibliography for chaps. XIII, XIV and XV.

(2) *Criticism of the Sources*

In addition to the works mentioned in the General Bibliography, V, A (p. 730) the following should be consulted:

Alföldi, A. *Das Problem des 'verweiblichten' Kaisers Gallienus.* Z.N. XXXVIII, 1928, p. 156.

—— *Der Rechtsstreit zwischen der römischen Kirche und dem Verein der Popinarii.* Klio, XXXI, 1938, p. 249.

Hartke, W. *De saeculi quarti exeuntis historiarum scriptoribus quaestiones.* Diss. Berlin, 1932.

Peter, H. *Die römischen sogenannten dreissig Tyrannen.* Sächs. Abh. XXVII, no. 6, 1909.

Reitzenstein, R. *Die Nachrichten über den Tod Cyprians.* S.B. der Heidelberger Akad. Phil.-hist. Kl. 1913, no. 14 (cf. G.G.A. 1919, p. 205).

Schenk, A. (Graf von Stauffenberg). *Die römische Kaisergeschichte bei Malalas.* Stuttgart, 1931.

(3) *Coins, Inscriptions, Papyri*

Alföldi, A. *Zur Entstehungszeit der staatlichen Munzstätte in Viminacium.* Numizm. Közlöny, XXXIV/v, 1938, p. 66.

—— *Siscia.* Budapest, vol. I, 1931, vol. II, 1938.

Blanchet, A. *Les trésors de monnaies romaines et les invasions germaniques en Gaule.* Paris, 1900.

—— *Les rapports entre les dépôts monétaires et les événements militaires, politiques et économiques.* Paris, 1936.

Cantineau, J. *Inventaire des inscriptions de Palmyre.* Beyrouth, 1930–33.

Elmer, G. *Die Prägungen der gallischen Sonderkaiser.* B.J. 143, 1938.

Fiebiger, O. and L. Schmidt. *Inschriftensammlung zur Geschichte der Ostgermanen.* Wien. S.B. Phil.-hist. Kl. 1917.

Kubitschek, W. *Die Münzen Regalians und Dryantillas.* Jahreshefte, II, 1901, pp. 210 *sqq.* (cf. ib. Beibl. p. 101 and Num. Z. 1908, p. 127).

Markl, A. *Die Reichsmünzstätten des Claudius II.* Num. Z. XVI, 1884, p. 1.

—— *Das Provinzialcourant unter Claudius II Gothicus.* Ib. XXXI, 1899, p. 319.

—— *Die Reichsmünzstätten unter der Regierung des Quintillus.* Ib. XXII, 1890, p. 11.

Mattingly, H. *The Reign of Aemilian. A Chronological Note.* J.R.S. XXV, 1935, p. 55.

Mouchmoff, M. *Le Trésor des monnaies de Réka-Devnia.* Sofia, 1934.

Pick, B. *Die antiken Münzen Nordgriechenlands.* Vol. I (Dacien und Moesien). Berlin, 1899.

Pink, B. *Der Aufbau der römischen Münzprägung in der Kaiserzeit.* IV. Von Decius bis Aemilianus. Num. Z. LXIX, 1936, p. 10.

Stein, A. *Zu den Kaiserdaten in der Mitte des III. Jahrhunderts.* Laureae Aquincenses, Budapest, 1938.

Voetter, O. *Die Münzen des Kaisers Gallienus und seiner Familie.* Num. Z. XXXII, 1900, p. 117; XXXIII, 1901, p. 73.

B. Modern Works

(a) The Invasions

Alföldi, A. *Die Gotenbewegungen und die Aufgabe der Provinz Dacien.* A contribution to 'Die Römer in Ungarn,' to be published at Frankfurt in 1939.

Bang, M. *Die Germanen im römischen Dienst bis zum Regierungsantritt Constantius I.* Berlin, 1906.

Manley, I. J. *Effects of the Germanic invasions on Gaul 234–284 A.D.* Univ. of Calif. Publ. in History, XVII, no. 2, 1934, p. 25.

Norden, E. *Alt-Germanien. Völker- und namengeschichtliche Untersuchungen.* Leipzig-Berlin, 1934.

Rappaport, Br. *Die Einfälle der Goten in das römische Reich.* Leipzig, 1899.

Schmidt, L. *Geschichte der deutschen Stämme bis zum Ausgang der Völkerwanderung.* I. Die Ostgermanen, ed. 2, Munich, 1934; II. Die Westgermanen, Pt. I, ed. 2, Munich, 1938.

Art. in P.W. *s.v.* Carpi (Patsch).

(b) Emperors and Usurpers, from Decius to Quintillus

Apart from the relevant pages of the general histories see also:

Alföldi, A. *Die Besiegung eines Gegenkaisers im J.* 263. Z.N. XL, 1930, p. 1.

—— *The Numbering of the Victories of Gallienus and of the Loyalty of his Legions.* Num. Chr. 1929, p. 218.

—— *Die Hauptereignisse im römischen Osten zwischen 253 und 260 im Spiegel der Münzprägungen.* Berytus, IV, 1937 (1938), p. 53.

(A continuation of this study, to A.D. 270, is to appear in this periodical.)

Bernhardt, Th. *Politische Geschichte des römischen Reiches von Valerian bis zu Diocletians Regierungsantritt.* Berlin, 1867.

Clermont-Ganneau, Ch. *Odeinat et Vaballat.* Rev. biblique, XXIX, 1920, p. 382.

Damerau, P. *Kaiser Claudius II Goticus (268–270 n. Chr.).* Klio, Beih. XXXIII, 1934.

von Domaszewski, A. *Die Rede des Aristides* εἰς βασιλέα. Phil. LXV, 1906, p. 344.

Février, J. G. *Essai sur l'histoire politique et économique de Palmyre.* Paris, 1931.

Homo, L. *De Claudio Gothico Romanorum imperatore.* Paris, 1903.
—— *L'empereur Gallien et la crise de l'empire romain au IIIe siècle.* Rev. H. CXIII, 1913, pp. 1 and 225.
Arts. in P.I.R.² vol. I, no. 430 (Aemilianus); vol. II, no. 466 (Postumus), and no. 1499 (Salonina), all by A. Stein.
Art. in Diz. Epig. *s.v.* Decius (Costa).
Arts. in P.W. *s.vv.* Fulvius (82) Macrianus (A. Stein), Licinius (173) Valerianus (Wickert), Messius (10) Quintus Traianus Decius (Wittig), Regalianus (A. Stein), and Sulpicia (117) Dryantilla (Fluss).

(c) The Decian Persecution

(Texts are given first, and then modern works.)

Knipfing, J. R. *The Libelli of the Decian Persecution.* Harv. Theol. Rev. XVI, 1923, p. 345. (Edition of Greek text with English transl.)
Roasenda, P. *Decio e i libellatici.* Didaskaleion, N.S. V, 1927, p. 31. (Edits the libelli.)
Bludau, A. *Die ägyptischen Libelli und die Christenverfolgung des Kaisers Decius.* Röm. Quartalschrift, Supplementheft XXVII. Freiburg i/B. 1931. (German translation of Libelli.)
Bihlmeyer, K. *Die Christenverfolgung des Kaisers Decius.* Theol. Quartalschrift, XCII, 1910, p. 19.
De Regibus, L. *Decio e la crisi dell' impero romano nel III Secolo.* Didaskaleion, N.S. III, 1925, Fasc. 3, p. 1.
Faulhaber, L. *Die Libelli in der Christenverfolgung des Kaisers Decius.* Zeits. f. kath. Theologie, XLIII, 1919, pp. 439, 617.
Foucart, P. *Les certificats de sacrifice pendant la persécution de Décius (250).* J.d. Sav. 1908, p. 169.
Franchi de' Cavalieri, P. Studi e Testi, XIX, p. 45; XXII, 1909, p. 77 with Appendices ii and iii.
Liesering, E. *Untersuchungen zur Christenverfolgung des Kaisers Decius.* Diss. Würzburg, 1933.
Schoenaich, G. *Die Libelli und ihre Bedeutung für die Christenverfolgung des Kaisers Decius.* Wiss. Beiträge zum Jahresbericht des Kön. Friedrichs-Gymnasiums zu Breslau für 1910. Breslau, 1910.
—— *Die Christenverfolgung des Kaisers Decius.* Jauer, 1907.

(d) The Army

Alföldi, A. *Der Usurpator Aureolus und die Kavalleriereform des Kaisers Gallienus.* Z.N. XXXVII, 1927, p. 198, and XXXVIII, 1928, p. 200.
van Berchem, D. *L'annone militaire dans l'Empire romain au IIIe siècle.* Mém. de la Soc. nat. des Antiquaires de France, LXXX, 1937, p. 117.
Blümlein, C. *Bericht über die Literatur zu den röm. Kriegsaltertümen.* Bursian, CCXVIII, p. 69, and CCXLVIII, p. 148.
Cagnat, R. *L'armée romain d'Afrique.* Ed. 2, Paris, 1913.
Cantacuzène, G. *Le recrutement de quelques cohortes Syriennes.* Mus.B. XXXI, 1927, p. 157.
—— *Un papyrus relatif à la défense du Bas Danube.* Aeg. IX, 1928, p. 63.
Cheesman, G. L. *The Auxilia of the Roman Imperial Army.* Oxford, 1914.
Christescu, V. *Istoria militară a Daciei Romane.* Bucarest, 1937.
Couissin, P. *Les armes romains.* Paris, 1926.

von Domaszewski, A. *Die Rangordnung des römischen Heeres.* B.J. 117, 1908, p. 1.
—— *Der Truppensold der Kaiserzeit.* Neue Heidelb. Jahrb. x, 1900, p. 218.
Fabricius, E. *Das römische Heer in Obergermanien und Raetien.* H.Z. xcviii, 1907, p. 1.
Grosse, R. *Römische Militärgeschichte von Gallienus bis zum Beginn der byzantinischen Themenverfassung.* Berlin, 1920.
Kornemann, E. *Die unsichtbaren Grenzen des römischen Kaiserreiches.* In 'Staaten, Völker, Männer,' Leipzig, 1934, pp. 96–116.
Lesquier, J. *L'armée romaine d'Égypte.* Cairo, 1918.
Macdonald, Sir G. *The Roman Wall in Scotland.* Ed. 2, Oxford, 1934.
Mommsen, Th. *Die Conscriptionsordnung der Kaiserzeit.* Ges. Schriften, vi, pp. 20 *sqq.*
—— *Das römische Militärwesen seit Diocletian.* Ib. vi, pp. 206 *sqq.*
Ritterling, E. *Das Kastell Niederbieber.* B.J. 120, 1911, p. 259.
—— *Zum römischen Heerwesen des ausgehenden III. Jahrhunderts.* Festschrift Hirschfeld, 1903, pp. 345 *sqq.*
—— *Zwei Münzfunde aus Niederbieber.* B.J. 107, 1901, p. 95.
Seyrig, H. *Armes et costumes iraniens de Palmyre.* Syria, xviii, 1937, p. 4.
Stein, E. *Die kaiserlichen Beamten und Truppenkörper im römischen Deutschland unter dem Prinzipat.* Vienna, 1932.
van de Weerd, H. and P. Lambrechts. *Note sur les corps d'archers au Haut-Empire.* Laureae Aquincenses, Budapest, 1938.
Arts. in P.W. *s.vv.* ala, cohors (Cichorius), exercitus (Liebenam), exploratores (Fiebiger), legio (Ritterling), limes (Fabricius) and numerus (Rowell).

(e) Special Topics

Alföldi, A. *Die Ausgestaltung des monarchischen Zeremoniells am römischen Kaiserhofe.* Röm. Mitt. xlix, 1934, p. 3.
—— *Insignien und Tracht der römischen Kaiser.* Ib. l, 1935, p. 3.
—— *Die Vorherrschaft der Pannonier im Römerreiche und die Reaktion des Hellenentums unter Gallienus.* 25. Jahre Röm.-Germ. Kommission, 1930, p. 11.
—— *Augustus als Vorbild des Gallienus.* Z.N. xxxviii, 1928, p. 197.
—— *The Year-Reckoning of the Reigns of Valerianus and Gallienus.* J.R.S. xxxix, 1939.
—— *Die Christenverfolgungen in der Mitte des III. Jahrh.* Klio, xxxi, 1938, p. 323.
—— *La grande crise du monde romain au IIIᵉ siècle.* L'Antiquité Classique, vii, 1938, p. 5.
Baynes, N. H. *The Effect of the Edict of Gallienus.* J.R.S. xv, 1925, p. 195.
von Domaszewski, A. *Die Pompa an den Decennalien des Gallienus.* Rh. Mus. lvii, 1902, p. 575.
Lambrechts, P. *La composition du Sénat romain de Septime Sévère à Dioclétien.* Diss. Pann. Ser. I, fasc. 8, Budapest, 1937.
Seyrig, H. *Note sur Hérodien, prince de Palmyre.* Syria, xviii, 1937, p. 1.
Stein, A. *Tenagino Probus.* Klio, xxix, 1936, p. 237.
Stein, E. *Kleine Beiträge zur römischen Geschichte.* Hermes, lii, 1917, p. 57.

CHAPTER VII

THE ECONOMIC LIFE OF THE EMPIRE

I. Ancient Sources

The literary sources now are secondary to the documentary, but among them Aristides' speech Εἰς Ῥώμην (xxvi, Keil), of A.D. 156, with Dio Chrysostom's speeches (as e.g. vii, Εὐβοϊκός) are important for the early and middle second century, Herodian, book vii, for the beginning of the third century, and pseudo-Aristides' speech Εἰς Βασιλέα (xxxv, Keil), of A.D. 247 (cf. E. Groag, Wien. Stud. xl, 1918, p. 37) for the period after Severus Alexander, while sources of the fourth or early fifth century, such as the *Expositio Totius Mundi* (Geogr. lat. min. ed. Riese, pp. 104 *sqq.*) and the *Notitia dignitatum* (ed. Seeck, 1876), Libanius' speeches and Ausonius, can be brought in to supplement them. In addition there is a mass of scattered notices in Arrian (*Periplus Ponti Euxini*), Aristides, the geographer Ptolemy, Dio Cassius and so on down to the Church Fathers, to Zosimus and Malalas. Nor can we neglect the numerous observations in the *Historia Augusta*, in spite of their doubtful value. Even foreign sources, such as the *Chinese Annals* published by F. Hirth (*China and the Roman Orient*, Leipzig-Munich, 1885), are of importance.

Far more valuable, however, is the immense and still not fully exploited documentary material: here we have sources from Roman law, *e.g.* book L of the Digest, but above all Roman and Greek inscriptions: these contain not only documents of unique value, such as the *Edictum Diocletiani de pretiis* (ed. Mommsen and Blümner, Berlin, 1893), but also such records as the Spanish Mine-Law of Vipasca (Dessau, 6891), the African *saltus* inscriptions (Bruns⁷, 61 and 86), the Customs-tables of Coptos (O.G.I.S. 674) and Palmyra (*ib.* 629), the huge mass of the Gallic inscriptions, and so on.

Equally important are the Egyptian papyri, which supply an immense amount of information precisely for the economic history of the second and third centuries and for the economic crisis of the third century (*e.g.* minutes of the town-council of Oxyrhynchus): and to these can now be added the parchments and papyri of Dura-Europus (see below II B, 3). Coins, too, by their differences in weight and purity, mirror similar changes in economic life, while the widely-scattered coin-finds outside the Empire illustrate the great extent of commerce. Last, but not least, there is an immense wealth of archaeological material: this wealth,—whether it be African or German mosaics, the monuments of Trèves, villas in Gaul, Germany, and Britain, the magnificent new discoveries at Dura, Gallo-German sculptures, remains of buildings throughout the whole empire, whether it be artistic or commercial products, found within or beyond the boundaries of the empire,—in its totality gives a clear impression of the economic standards of the time.

Generally, see T. Frank, *An Economic Survey of ancient Rome*, section II B, 3.

II. Modern Works

This Bibliography is supplementary to that for Chapter XIII of Vol. x, given on pp. 944–5 of that volume.

A. General

Apart from the relevant pages of the general histories cited in the General Bibliography, I, such as Besnier, Gibbon, Lot, Mommsen, and above all the works of Friedländer-Wissowa and Rostovtzeff (*Social and Economic History*), the following works, additional to those given in Volume x, should be noted:

1. *Political and Social Conditions*

Abbott, F. F. and A. C. Johnson. *Municipal administration in the Roman Empire.* Princeton, N.J. 1926.

Bücher, K. *Die Diokletianische Taxordnung vom Jahre* 301. Zeits. f. d. ges. Staatswiss. 1894, pp. 189 and 672. (= Beiträge zur Wirtschaftsgeschichte, pp. 179 *sqq.* Tübingen, 1922.)

Buckler, W. H. *Labour disputes in the Province of Asia Minor.* Anatolian Studies presented to Sir William Ramsay, Manchester, 1923, pp. 27 *sqq.*

Ciccotti, E. *La civiltà del mondo antico.* 2 vols. Udine, 1935. (The last chapter, "*Il crollo dell' Impero e della civiltà antica,*" has been printed in Nuova Rivista Storica, xix, 1935, p. 305.)

Delbrück, H. *Geschichte der Kriegskunst.* Vol. ii, ed. 2. Berlin, 1921.

Gelzer, M. *Studien zur byzantinischen Verwaltung Ägyptens.* Diss. Leipzig, 1909.

—— *Altertumswissenschaft und Spätantike.* H.Z. cxxxv, 1926, p. 173.

Groag, E. *Collegien und Zwangsgenossenschaften im 3. Jahrhundert.* Vierteljahrschr. f. Soz.- u. Wirtsch.-Gesch. 1904, p. 481.

Grosse, R. *Römische Militärgeschichte von Gallienus bis zum Beginn der byzantinischen Themenverfassung.* Berlin, 1920.

Hartmann, L. M. *Der Untergang der antiken Welt.* Weltgeschichte in gemeinverständlicher Darstellung, Vol. iii, ed. 2, Gotha, 1921, pp. 201 *sqq.*

Hasebroek, J. *Untersuchungen zur Geschichte des Kaisers Septimius Severus.* Heidelberg, 1921.

Heitland, W. E. *Last words on the Roman municipalities.* Cambridge, 1928.

Hirschfeld, O. *Die kaiserlichen Verwaltungsbeamten.* Ed. 2, Berlin, 1905.

—— *Die Sicherheitspolizei im römischen Kaiserreich.* Kleine Schriften, Berlin, 1913, pp. 576 *sqq.*

—— *Die ägyptische Polizei der römischen Kaiserzeit nach Papyrusurkunden.* Ib. pp. 613 *sqq.*

—— *Die agentes in rebus.* Ib. pp. 624 sqq.

Kornemann, E. *Staat und Wirtschaft im Altertum.* Schriften der Industrie- u. Handelskammer, Breslau, Heft 13, 1929.

—— *Das Problem des Untergangs der antiken Welt.* Vergangenheit u. Gegenwart, xii, 1922, pp. 193 and 241.

Kreller, H. *Lex Rhodia. Untersuchungen zur Quellengeschichte des römischen Seerechtes.* Zeits. f. d. ges. Handels-Recht u. Konkursrecht, lxxxv, 1921, p. 257.

Laum, B. *Stiftungen in der griechischen und römischen Antike.* 2 vols, Leipzig, 1914.

Liebenam, W. *Städteverwaltung im römischen Kaiserreiche.* Leipzig, 1900.

Martroye, F. *Les patronages d'agriculteurs et de vici au IVᵉ et au Vᵉ siècles.* Rev. hist. de droit franç. et étranger, ivᵉ Sér., vii, 1928, p. 201.

Oertel, F. *Die Liturgie. Studien zur ptolemäischen und kaiserlichen Verwaltung Ägyptens.* Leipzig, 1917. (Cf. J. Partsch, Arch. Pap. vii, p. 264.)

Rostovtzeff, M. *Studien zur Geschichte des römischen Kolonates.* Leipzig, 1910.

—— *Geschichte der Staatspacht in der römischen Kaiserzeit bis Diokletian.* Leipzig, 1902.

Schönbauer, E. *Reichsrecht gegen Volksrecht? Studien über die Bedeutung der Const. Anton. für die römische Rechtsentwicklung.* Z. d. Sav.-Stift. li, 1931, p. 277.

Stade, K. *Der Politiker Diokletian und die letzte grosse Christenverfolgung.* Diss. Frankfurt a.M., Wiesbaden, 1926.

Vinogradoff, P. *Social and economic conditions of the Roman Empire in the fourth century.* Cambridge Medieval History, i, 1911, pp. 543 *sqq.* (with bibliography, pp. 688 *sqq.*).

Numerous articles in P.W. e.g. *s.vv.* Bauernstand (Kornemann), Berufsvereine (Stöckle), collegium (Kornemann), colonatus (Seeck), curatores (Kornemann), Domitius (36) L. Aurelianus=Aurelian, fiscus (Rostovtzeff), frumentarii (Fiebiger), legio (Ritterling-Kubitschek), res privata (Liebenam), Severus (13)=Septimius Severus, Sklaverei (Westermann), and Art. *s.v.* fiscus in Diz. Epig. (Rostovtzeff).

2. *General Economic History*

Brentano, L. *Das Wirtschaftsleben der antiken Welt.* Vorlesungen, Jena, 1929.

Ciccotti, E. *Il problema economico nel mondo antico.* Nuova Rivista Storica, xvi, 1932, pp. 1–51, 145–187.

Dopsch, A. *Naturalwirtschaft und Geldwirtschaft in der Weltgeschichte.* Vienna, 1930.

Heichelheim, F. *Welthistorische Gesichtspunkte zu den vormittelalterlichen Wirtschaftsepochen.* Schmollers Jahrb. lvi, 1933, p. 994.

Heitland, W. E. *Agricola.* Cambridge, 1921.

Rostovtzeff, M. *The decay of the ancient world and its economic explanation.* Econ. Hist. Review, ii, 1930, p. 197.

Salvioli, G. *Il capitalismo antico.* Bari, 1929.

Weber, M. *Die sozialen Gründe des Untergangs der antiken Kultur.* "Die Wahrheit," 1. Maiheft, 1896 (= Gesammelte Aufsätze z. Soz.- und Wirtschafts-Geschichte, Tübingen, 1924, pp. 289 *sqq.*).

—— *Agrarverhältnisse im Altertum.* Handwörterbuch der Staatswissenschaften, i, ed. 3, 1909 = Ges. Aufs. pp. 1 *sqq.*

West, L. C. *The economic collapse of the Roman Empire.* C.J. 1932/33, p. 96.

Numerous articles in P.W. e.g. *s.vv.* Kapitalismus (Sigwart), Karten (Kubitschek), Landwirtschaft (Orth), navicularii (Stöckle), Industrie und Handel (Gummerus).

B. Special Topics

1. *Ramifications of Agriculture, Industry, Trade and Commerce*

Bolin, St. *Fynden av romerska mynt i det fria Germanien.* Lund, 1926.

—— *Die Funde römischer und byzantinischer Münzen im freien Germanien.* Röm.-German. Kommission 1929 (1930), p. 86.

Brogan, O. *Trade between the Roman Empire and the free Germans.* J.R.S. xxvi, 1936, p. 195.

Ekholm, G. *Zur Geschichte des römisch-germanischen Handels.* Acta archaeol. vi, 1935, p. 49.

—— *Die Einfuhr von Bronzeschüsseln der römischen und frühmerowingischen Zeit nach Skandinavien.* Altschlesien, v, 1934, p. 247.

(On Ekholm's work see H. J. Eggers, *Germania,* xx, 1936, p. 146.)

Gummerus, H. *Der römische Gutsbetrieb als wirtschaftlicher Organismus nach den Werken des Cato, Varro und Columella.* Leipzig, 1906.

Herrmann, A. *Die Seidenstrassen vom alten China nach dem römischen Reich.* Mitt. der Geogr. Ges. in Wien, lviii, 1915, p. 472.

—— *Die Verkehrswege zwischen China, Indien und Rom um* 100 *n. Chr. Geb.* Leipzig, 1922.

Kortenbeutel, H. *Der ägyptische Süd- und Osthandel in der Politik der Ptolemäer und römischen Kaiser.* Diss. Berlin, 1931.

Persson, A. W. *Staat und Manufaktur im römischen Reiche.* Lund, 1923.

Rostovtzeff, M. *Caravan Cities.* Oxford, 1932. (Contains a good bibliography.)

Schaal, H. *Flussschiffahrt und Flusshandel im Altertum*. Festschr. 400 Jahr-Feier Alt. Gymn. Bremen, 1928, p. 370.

Schönbauer, E. *Beiträge zur Geschichte des Bergbaurechts*. Münchener Beitr. z. Pap.-Forschg. u. ant. Rechtsgesch., 12. Heft, Munich, 1929.

Westermann, W. L. *On inland transportation and communication in Antiquity*. Polit. Sc. Quart. XLIII, 1928, p. 364.

Numerous articles in P.W. e.g. *s.vv.* Domänen (Kornemann), fabricenses (Seeck), frumentum (Rostovtzeff).

2. *Monetary Policy. Prices*

Babelon, E., *Traité des monnaies grecques et romaines*. Vol. I, Paris, 1901.

Bernhart, M. *Handbuch zur Münzkunde der römischen Kaiserzeit*. Halle, 1926.

Giesecke, W. *Antikes Geldwesen*. Leipzig, 1938.

Heichelheim, F. *Zu Pap. Bad. 37, ein Beitrag zur römischen Geldgeschichte unter Trajan*. Klio, XXV, 1932, p. 124.

—— *Zur Währungskrisis des römischen Imperiums im 3. Jahrhundert n. Chr.* Klio, XXVI, 1933, p. 96.

—— *New light on currency and inflation in Hellenistic-Roman times*. Economic History, III, 10, February 1935.

Johnson, A. C. *Notes on Egyptian coins*. A.J.A. XXXVIII, 1934, p. 49.

Kubitschek, W. *Der Übergang von der vordiokletianischen Währung ins 4. Jahrhundert*. Randbemerkungen zu Schriften von G. Mickwitz. Byzant. Zeits. XXXV, 1935, p. 340.

Mattingly, H. *Roman Coins*. London, 1928 (with bibliography). Book II (The Empire: Augustus to Diocletian) and Book III (The Empire: Diocletian to Romulus Augustulus). And see bibliography to Chap. IX.

Mickwitz, G. *Geld und Wirtschaft im römischen Reich des 4. Jahrhunderts n. Chr.* Soc. scient. Fennica. Comment. human. litt. IV, 2, Helsingfors, 1932.

—— *Ein Goldwertindex der römisch-byzantinischen Zeit*. Aeg. XIII, 1933, p. 95.

—— *Le problème de l'or dans le monde antique*. Ann. d'hist. écon. et soc. VI, 1934, pp. 239 *sqq.*

—— *Die Systeme des römischen Silbergeldes im 4. Jahrh. n. Chr.* Soc. scient. Fennica. Comment. human. litt. VI, 2, Helsingfors, 1935.

Regling, K. *Münzkunde*. In *Einleitung in die Altertumswissenschaft*, hrsg. von A. Gercke und E. Norden, Bd. II, ii, ed. 4. Leipzig, 1930.

Segrè, A. Καινὸν νόμισμα. Atti Acc. Linc. XVI, 1920, p. 4.

—— *Circolazione monetaria e prezzi nel mondo antico ed in particolare in Egitto*. Rome, 1922.

—— *Metrologia e circolazione monetaria degli antichi*. Bologna, 1928.

—— *Circolazione e inflazione nel mondo antico*. Historia, 1929, p. 369.

Numerous articles in P.W. e.g. *s.vv.* follis (Seeck), Münzkunde (Regling)

3. *Particular areas*

(Supplementary to those given in Vol. X, p. 945.) For the relevant works for the several provinces in the period of that Volume, see the Bibliographies to chapters XII–XVI of Vol. XI, pp. 903 *sqq.* (including a reference back, for Egypt, to Vol. X, pp. 922 *sqq.*). To these may be added the great work edited by Tenney Frank, *An economic survey of ancient Rome*. Vol. II: Johnson, A. C., *Roman Egypt* (with Bibliography), Baltimore, 1936. Vol. III: Collingwood, R. G., *Roman Britain* (and see Bibliography to Chap. VIII). van Nostrand, J. J., *Roman Spain* (with Bibliography). Scramuzza, V. M., *Roman Sicily* (with Bibliography). Grenier, A., *La Gaule*

Romaine. Baltimore, 1937. Vol. IV: Haywood, R. M., *Roman Africa*. Heichelheim, F., *Roman Syria* (with Bibliography). Larsen, J. A. O., *Roman Greece* (with Bibliography). Broughton, T. R. S., *Roman Asia*. Baltimore, 1938.—See also:

Aubin, H. *Die wirtschaftliche Entwickelung des römischen Deutschlands*. H.Z. 141, 1930, p. 1.

Bell, H. I. *The byzantine servile state in Egypt*. J.E.A. IV, 1917, p. 86.

Blümlein, C. *Römer und Germanen*. Bilder aus dem römisch-germanischen Kulturleben. Munich, 1926.

Colin, J. *Les antiquités romaines de la Rhénanie*. Paris, 1927.

Daicovici, C. *La Transylvanie dans l'antiquité*. Bucarest, 1938.

DURA. For the excavations at Dura see F. Cumont, *Fouilles de Doura-Europos* (1922–1923), Paris, 1926, and the six *Preliminary Reports* on the excavations from 1928 to 1933, edited by Baur, Bellinger, Hopkins, Rostovtzeff and Welles: Vol. VI, New Haven, Conn. 1936.

Frank, T. *The people of Ostia*. C.J. XXIX, 1933/34, p. 481.

Gnirs, A. *Forschungen über antiken Villenbau in Südistrien*. Jahresh. XVIII, 1915, Beiblatt, p. 101.

Hertlein, Fr., O. Paret and P. Goessler. *Die Römer in Württemberg*. 3 vols. Stuttgart, 1928–32.

Jullian, C. *Histoire de la Gaule*. Vol. VII, Paris, 1926; vol. VIII, Paris, 1926.

Kromayer, J. *Die wirtschaftliche Entwickelung Italiens im 2. und 1. Jahrhundert v. Chr.* N.J.Kl.Alt. XXXIII, 1914, p. 145.

Ledroit, J. *Die römische Schiffahrt im Stromgebiet des Rheines*. Kulturgeschichtl. Wegweiser durch das röm.-germ. Zentralmuseum Nr. 12, Mainz, 1930.

Martin, V. *Les papyrus et l'histoire administrative de l'Égypte gréco-romaine*. Papyri und Altertumswissenschaft, Munich, 1934, pp. 102 *sqq.*

—— *La fiscalité romaine en Égypte aux trois premiers siècles de l'Empire*. Discours Genève 1925. Geneva, 1926.

Oelmann, F. *Römische Villen im Rheinland*. J.D.A.I. XLIII, 1928, p. 228.

Oertel, F. *Der Niedergang der hellenistischen Kultur in Ägypten*. N.J.Kl.Alt. XLV, 1920, p. 361.

Rostovtzeff, M. *Iranians and Greeks in South Russia*. Oxford, 1922.

Schumacher, K. *Siedelungs- und Kulturgeschichte der Rheinlande*. Vol. II, Die römische Periode. Mainz, 1923.

Stähelin, F. *Die Schweiz in römischer Zeit*. Ed. 2, Basel, 1931.

Wagner, F. *Die Römer in Bayern*. Ed. 4, Munich, 1928.

Wenger, L. *Volk und Staat in Ägypten am Ausgang der Römerherrschaft*. Festrede München, 1922.

West, L. C. (besides Roman Gaul, Imperial Roman Spain; cf. C.A.H. XI). *Roman Britain. The objects of trade*. Oxford, 1931.

—— *Phases of commercial life in Roman Egypt*. J.R.S. VII, 1917, p. 45.

CHAPTER VIII

BRITAIN

A. Ancient Sources

The evidence from the literary sources is not large: it has been collected in *Monumenta Historica Britannica*, vol. i (all published), 1848.

The inscriptions were collected by E. Hübner in vol. vii of *C.I.L.* Supplements and additions to this were published by Hübner in *Eph. Epig.* vols. iii and iv, and by F. Haverfield, *ib.* vols. vii and ix. A new Corpus of the inscriptions, edited by R. G. Collingwood, is in preparation. Since 1921 an annual report upon Roman Britain, summarizing the results of excavations and publishing the new inscriptions, has been given in *J.R.S.* by R. G. Collingwood and Miss M. V. Taylor. For a survey of the results attained between 1914 and 1928 see Sir G. Macdonald, *Roman Britain 1914–1928*, British Academy Proceedings, n.d. [1931].

B. Modern Works

I. *General*

Collingwood, R. G. *Roman Britain*. Ed. 3. Oxford, 1934.
—— *The Archaeology of Roman Britain*. London, 1930. (Ed. 2 in preparation.)
Collingwood, R. G. and J. N. L. Myres. *Roman Britain and the English Settlements*. Oxford, 1936.
Haverfield, F. *The Romanization of Roman Britain*. Ed. 4 (revised by George Macdonald). Oxford, 1924.
—— *The Roman Occupation of Britain*. (Revised by George Macdonald.) Oxford, 1924.

II. *Special Topics*

The topics discussed in this chapter are all treated at greater length by the writer in *Roman Britain and the English Settlements*, and (so far as they concern economic matters) in the section upon Britain in Tenney Frank's *An Economic Survey of Ancient Rome*, vol. iii, 1937, pp. 1–118.

The History of towns: R. E. M. Wheeler, *Report on Excavations at Verulamium* (Soc. of Antiquaries, 1936); Sir G. Macdonald, *Roman Britain 1914–1928*, ch. viii.

Villas: for generalities, Haverfield-Macdonald, *Roman Occupation...*, pp. 219–32; Collingwood, *Archaeology of Rom. Brit.* ch. vii; T. D. Kendrick and C. Hawkes, *Archaeology in England and Wales 1914–1931*, London, 1932, pp. 260–67.

Villages and peasantry: Haverfield-Macdonald, *op. cit.* pp. 233–4; Haverfield, *Romanization of Rom. Brit.* pp. 45–7; Collingwood, *Archaeology...*, ch. x; Kendrick-Hawkes, *op. cit.* pp. 267–70.

Mines: O. Davies, *Roman Mines in Europe*, Oxford, 1935, ch. v; G. C. Whittick, *Roman Mining in Britain* (Trans. Newcomen Society, xii, 1931–32).

Pottery: the Nene valley: *Victoria County Hist. Hunts.* i, 1926, pp. 225–52; E. T. Artis, *The Durobrivae of Antoninus identified and illustrated...*, London, 1828; the New Forest: Heywood Sumner, *Excavations in New Forest pottery sites*, 1927.

Fulling in villas: G. E. Fox, *Archaeologia*, lix, 1905, p. 207.

The Celtic revival in art: E. T. Leeds, *Celtic Ornament*, 1933, ch. vi.

CHAPTER IX

THE IMPERIAL RECOVERY

A. ANCIENT SOURCES

(1) *Inscriptions*

For inscriptions see the selection in Dessau, III, Index iii, pp. 301–8, and O.G.I.S. 569, 612, 718 and 719, and Appendix III in L. Homo's *Essai sur le règne de l'empereur Aurélien (270–275)*, pp. 350 *sqq.* (see B. I, 1) and the references given in the footnotes to the chapter.

(2) *Coins*

Besides the relevant parts of Cohen, *Description historique*, Mattingly, *Handbook of Roman Coins*, Mattingly and Sydenham, *The Roman Imperial Coinage* (vols. v, i and v, ii by P. H. Webb), and J. Vogt, *Alexandrinische Münzen*, see also:

Babelon, J. *Médaillons d'or du trésor d'Arras*. Aréthuse, I, 1924, p. 45.
Blanchet, A. *Études de numismatique*. Paris, vol. II, 1901, pp. 212 *sqq.*
Brett, A. B. *Aurei and Solidi of the Arras Hoard*. Num. Chr. 1933, p. 268.
Evans, (Sir) Arthur. *Some Notes on the Arras Hoard*. Num. Chr. 1930, p. 221.
Giesecke, W. *Antikes Geldwesen*. Leipzig, 1938.
Lépaulle, E. *La monnaie romaine à la fin du haut Empire*. Rev. N. 1888, p. 391; 1889, p. 115.
Oman, (Sir) C. *The Legionary Coins of Victorinus, Carausius and Allectus*. Num. Chr. 1924, p. 53.
Pink, K. *The Minting of Gold in the Period of Diocletian and the Arras Hoard*. Num. Chr. 1934, p. 106.
von Sallet, A. *Die Daten der Alexandrinischen Münzen*. Berlin, 1870.

(3) *Texts*

Anonymus continuator Dionis. Frags. 10–15 (F.H.G. IV, pp. 197–9).
Aurelius Victor, *Caesares*, ed. F. Pichlmayr, Leipzig, 1911, XXXV–XL.
Dexippus. Frag. 24 (F.H.G. III, pp. 682–686). A better text in *F. Gr. Hist.* (Jacoby), II, p. 460.
Eutropius (ed. F. Ruehl, Leipzig, 1887), IX, 13–X, 5.
Lactantius, *de mortibus persecutorum*, ed. J. Pesenti, Turin, 1923.
Orosius, *Historiae adversum Paganos* (ed. C. Zangemeister, Leipzig, 1889), VII, 23, 3–28, 22.
XII *Panegyrici Latini* (iterum rec. Guil. Baehrens, Leipzig, 1911), VI (VII), VIII (V), X (II), and XI (III).
Petrus Patricius. Frags. 12–15. (F.H.G. IV, pp. 188–90.)
Scriptores Historiae Augustae (ed. E. Hohl, II, Leipzig, 1927), *Aurelianus, Tacitus, Probus, Quadrigae tyrannorum (Firmus, Saturninus, Proculus et Bonosus)* and *Carus, Numerianus, Carinus*.
Zonaras, XII, 26–XIII, 1.
Zosimus (ed. L. Mendelssohn, Leipzig, 1887), I, 47–II, 17.

Occasional items may be gathered from Jordanes, *Romana* and *Getica*: for the later Greek tradition see Eunapius, John of Antioch, and Malalas.

B. Modern Works

In addition to the relevant parts of works cited in the General Bibliography, the following should be consulted:

I. The Emperors

1. *Aurelian*

Brambach, W. *Beiträge zur römischen Münzgeschichte.* I. *Sestertius.* Frankfurter Münzzeitung, no. 232, 1920, p. 197.

Clermont-Ganneau, Ch. *Odeinat et Vaballat.* Rev. biblique, xxix, 1920, p. 382.

Dorligny, A. S. *Aurélien et la guerre des monnayeurs.* Rev. N. ix (Sér. 3), 1891, p. 105.

Février, J. C. *Essai sur l'histoire politique et économique de Palmyre.* Paris, 1931.

Fisher, W. H. *The Augustan 'Vita Aureliani.'* J.R.S. xix, 1929, p. 125.

Giesecke, W. *Die Münzreformen der Kaiser Caracalla, Aurelianus und Diocletianus.* Frankfurter Münzzeitung, no. 41 (N.F.), 1933, p. 65 and p. 99.

Homo, L. *Essai sur le règne de l'empereur Aurélien* (270–275). Paris, 1904.

Jorga, N. *Le problème de l'abandon de la Dacie.* Rev. hist. du Sud-Est Européen, i, 1924, p. 37.

Mattingly, H. *Sestertius and Denarius under Aurelian.* Num. Chr. 1927, p. 219.

Pridik, E. *Zur Münzreform des Kaisers Aurelianus.* Numismatik (Munich), xxxiv, 1933, p. 160.

Richmond, I. A. *The City-Wall of Imperial Rome.* Oxford, 1930.

Schnabel, P. *Die Chronologie Aurelians.* Klio, xx, 1926, p. 363.

Stein, A. *Zeitbestimmungen von Gallienus bis Aurelian.* Klio, xxi, 1927, p. 197.

Sydenham, E. A. *The Roman Monetary System.* Num. Chr. 1919, p. 140.

Waltzing, J. P. *Étude historique sur les corporations professionnelles chez les Romains depuis les origines jusqu'à la chute de l'Empire de l'Occident.* 4 vols. Louvain, 1895–1900.

Webb, P. H. *The Reform of Aurelian.* Num. Chr. 1919, p. 235; 1927, p. 304.

Arts. in P.W. *s.vv.* Domitius (36) L. Aurelianus (E. Groag), Aurelius (84) Quintillus (Henze).

2. *Tacitus*

Baynes, N. H. *Three Notes on the Reforms of Diocletian and Constantine.* 1. *The Effect of the Edict of Gallienus.* J.R.S. xv, 1925, p. 195.

Hohl, E. *Vopiscus und die Biographie des Kaisers Tacitus.* Klio, xi, 1911, p. 178 and p. 284.

Art. in P.W. *s.v.* Claudius (361) M. Tacitus (Stein).

3. *Probus*

Alföldi, A. *Die* tribunicia potestas *des Kaisers Probus.* Blätter f. Münzfreunde, 1923, p. 352.

Babelon, E. *Le tyran Saturninus.* Rev. N. 1896, p. 133.

Crees, J. H. E. *The Reign of the Emperor Probus.* London, 1911.

Dannhäuser, E. *Untersuchungen zur Geschichte des Kaisers Probus* (276–282). Jena, 1909.

Lépaulle, E. *Étude historique sur M. Aurelius Probus d'après la numismatique du règne de cet empereur.* Lyons, 1884.

Stein, A. *Tenagino Probus.* Klio, xxix, 1936, p. 237.

Westermann, W. L. *The Papyri and the Chronology of the Reign of the Emperor Probus.* Aeg. i, 1920, p. 297.

Art. in P.W. *s.v* Aurelius (194) M. Probus (Henze).

4. *Carus and his sons*

Elmer, G. *Der Feldzug des Kaisers Carinus gegen die Quadi.* Der Münzensammler, 1935, p. 11.

Arts. in P.W. *s.vv.* Aurelius (75) M. Carinus, Aurelius (77) M. Carus, Aurelius (174) Numerius Numerianus (Henze).

5. *Diocletian and his Colleagues*

Babelon, J. *Constance Chlore et la Tétrarchie; un médaillon d'or inédit.* Gazette des Beaux Arts, 1933, p. 11.

Bulič, Fr. *L'imperatore Diocleziano.* Spalato, 1916.

Cantarelli, L. *Per la storia dell' imperatore Costanzo Cloro.* Atti d. Pont. Accad. romana di archeologia, I, i (Ser. 3), 1923, p. 31.

Costa, G. *C. Valerius Diocletianus.* Estratto dal Diz. Epig. Vol. II, pp. 1793–1908, Spoleto, 1912.

Janssens, E. *Carausius, premier souverain national de la Grande Bretagne.* Latomos, 1937, p. 269.

Kinch, K. F. *L'arc de triomphe de Salonique.* Paris, 1890.

Kubitschek, W. *Zur Geschichte des Usurpators Achilleus.* Wien S.B. 1928, p. 2081.

Mattingly, H. *The Roman "Virtues".* Harv. Theol. Rev. xxx, 1937, p. 103.

Seeck, O. *Neue und alte Daten zur Geschichte Diocletians und Constantins.* Rh. Mus. LXII, 1907, p. 488.

Stade, K. *Der Politiker Diokletian und die letzte grosse Christenverfolgung.* Diss. Frankfurt a.M., Wiesbaden, 1926.

Webb, P. H. *The coinage of Allectus.* Num. Chr. 1906, p. 127.

—— *The reign and coinage of Carausius.* London, 1908.

Wilcken, U. *Zur Geschichte des Usurpators Achilleus.* Berl. S.B. xxv, 1927, p. 270.

6. *The Successors of Diocletian*

Antoniades, C. *Kaiser Licinius.* Munich, 1884.

Baynes, N. H. *Constantine the Great and the Christian Church.* Proceedings of the British Academy, xv, 1929.

Kubitschek, W. *Domitius Domitianus und Alexander Tyrannus.* Mitt. d. Num. Gesellschaft in Wien, xvi, 1929, p. 1.

Laffranchi, L. *L'xi Anno Imperatorio di Costantino Magno.* Atti d. Pont. Accad. romana di archeologia, 1921, p. 413.

Maurice, J. *Numismatique Constantinienne.* 3 vols. Paris, 1908–12.

Stückelberg, E. A. *La parenté de Maxence et de Constance I d'après les monnaies.* Riv. Ital. d. Numismatica, 1899, p. 377.

Voetter, O. *Ahnenmünzen Kaiser Constantins des Grossen.* Mitt. d. Clubs der Münz- und Medaillon-Freunde in Wien, 1895, p. 76.

Westphalen, Count. *La date de l'avènement au trône de Constantin le Grand.* Rev. N. 1887, p. 26.

Arts. in P.W. *s.vv.* Constantinus (2) (Benjamin), Constantius (1) (Seeck), Licinius (31a) (Seeck), Maxentius (Groag), Maximianus (1) Herculius, (2) Galerius (Ensslin).

II. Special Topics

1. *Chronology*

Stein, A. *Zur Chronologie der römischen Kaiser von Decius bis Diocletian.* Arch. Pap. VII, 1924, p. 30 (and see VIII, 1927, p. 11).

2. *Ceremonial*

Alföldi, A. *Die Ausgestaltung des monarchischen Zeremoniells am römischen Kaiserhofe.* Röm. Mitt. XLIX, 1934, p. 3.
—— *Insignien und Tracht der römischen Kaiser.* Ib. L, 1935, p. 3.

3. *The Gallic Empire*

Blanchet, A. *Note sur la Legio V Macedonica sous Gallien et Victorin.* Mus. B. XXVII, 1923, p. 169.
Erman, A. *Marius und Victorinus.* Z.N. VII, 1880, p. 347.
Jullian, C. *Histoire de la Gaule.* Paris, vol. V (ed. 2, 1921), pp. 570–615.
Mattingly, H. *The Legionary Coins of Victorinus.* Trans. of the International Numismatic Congress, June 30–July 3, 1936, London, 1938, pp. 214–18.

4. *The Goths*

Bang, M. *Die Germanen im römischen Dienst bis zum Regierungsantritt Constantins I.* Berlin, 1906.
Bury, J. B. *The Invasion of Europe by the Barbarians.* London, 1928, pp. 21–51.
Rappaport, B. *Die Einfälle der Goten in das römische Reich bis auf Constantin.* Leipzig, 1899.

5. *Persia and the East*

Chapot, V. *La frontière de l'Euphrate.* Paris, 1907.
Christensen, A. *L'Iran sous les Sassanides.* Copenhagen–Paris, 1936.
Ensslin, W. *Die weltgeschichtliche Bedeutung der Kämpfe zwischen Rom und Persien.* N.J.f. Wiss. IV, 1928, p. 399.
Nöldeke, Th. ṬABARÎ. *Geschichte der Perser und Araber zur Zeit der Sasaniden.* Aus der arab. Chronik des Ṭabarî übersetzt, Leyden, 1879.
—— *Aufsätze zur Persischen Geschichte.* Leipzig, 1887.

CHAPTER X

THE END OF THE PRINCIPATE

Reference to the more important passages in the Ancient Sources is given from time to time in the footnotes. The list of works here cited must be supplemented by the bibliographies to other Chapters (e.g. I, II, V, VI, and IX), and the writer has included here those that seemed to him of special worth. Also, to avoid repetition, works which contain matter upon the reforms of Diocletian are mentioned here only.

Alföldi, A. *Die Ausgestaltung des monarchischen Zeremoniells am römischen Kaiserhofe.* Röm. Mitt. XLIX, 1934, p. 3.
—— *Insignien und Tracht der römischen Kaiser.* Röm. Mitt. L, 1935, p. 1.
—— *Zur Kenntnis der Zeit der römischen Soldatenkaiser.* Z.N. XXXVII, 1927, p. 197 (also XXXVIII, 1928, p. 156).
—— *La grande crise du monde romain au IIIe siècle.* L'Antiquité Classique, VII, 1938, p. 5.
—— *Die Vorherrschaft der Pannonier im Römerreiche und die Reaktion des Hellenentums unter Gallienus.* 25 Jahre Röm.-Germ. Kommission, 1930, p. 11.
Anderson, J. G. C. *The Genesis of Diocletian's Provincial Re-organisation.* J.R.S. XXII, 1932, p. 24.
Babut, E. Ch. *Recherches sur la Garde Impériale et sur le Corps d'Officiers de l'Armée Romaine.* Rev. H. CXIV, 1913, p. 225 and CXVI, 1914, p. 225.
Baynes, N. H. *Three Notes on the Reforms of Diocletian and Constantine. I. The Effect of the Edict of Gallienus.* J.R.S. XV, 1925, p. 195.
Besnier, M. *Histoire Romaine.* Paris, 1937, pp. 109–17; 187–91; 244–63.
Charlesworth, M. P. *Some Observations on Ruler-Cult especially in Rome.* Harv. Theol. Rev. XXVIII, 1935, p. 5.
—— *Providentia and Aeternitas.* Harv. Theol. Rev. XXIX, 1936, p. 107.
Cheesman, G. L. *The Auxilia of the Roman Imperial Army.* Oxford, 1914.
Costa, G. *Religione e Politica nell' Impero Romano.* Turin, 1923, pp. 32–87; 271–87.
Delbrueck, R. *Der spätrömische Kaiserornat.* Antike, VIII, 1932, p. 1.
Ferrero, G. *The Ruin of the Ancient Civilisation and the Triumph of Christianity.* Translated by the Hon. Lady Whitehead, New York, 1921.
Gmelin, U. *Auctoritas. Römischer Princeps und päpstlicher Primat.* In *Geistige Grundlagen römischer Kirchenpolitik*: Forschungen zur Kirchen- und Geistesgeschichte, XI, Stuttgart, 1937, pp. 58–79.
Grosse, R. *Römische Militärgeschichte von Gallienus bis zum Beginn der byzantinischen Themenverfassung.* Berlin, 1920.
Hahn, L. *Das Kaisertum.* Leipzig, 1913.
Herzog, E. *Geschichte und System der römischen Staatsverfassung. II. Die Kaiserzeit von der Diktatur Cäsars bis zum Regierungsantritt Diocletians.* 1. *Geschichtliche Übersicht.* 2. *System der Verfassung der Kaiserzeit.* Leipzig, 1887–1891.
Hirschfeld, O. *Die kaiserlichen Verwaltungsbeamten.* Ed. 2, Berlin, 1905.
—— *Die Rangtitel der römischen Kaiserzeit.* Berl. S.B. 1901, p. 579 (= Kleine Schriften, Berlin, 1913, p. 646).
—— *Die römische Staatszeitung und die Akklamationen im Senat.* Berl. S.B. 1905, p. 930 (= Kleine Schriften, Berlin, 1913, p. 682).

Jäntere, K. *Die römische Weltreichsidee und die Entstehung der weltlichen Macht des Papstes.* Annales Universitatis Turkuensis, Ser. B, vol. XXI, Turku, 1936.

Karlowa, O. *Römische Rechtsgeschichte.* Vol. I, *Staatsrecht und Rechtsquellen.* Leipzig, 1885.

Keyes, C. W. *The Rise of the Equites in the Third Century of the Roman Empire.* Princeton, N.J. 1915.

Kornemann, E. *Doppelprinzipat und Reichsteilung im Imperium Romanum.* Leipzig–Berlin, 1930, pp. 78–123.

—— *Vom antiken Staat.* In Staaten, Völker, Männer. Leipzig, 1934, pp. 12–16.

Kruse, H. *Studien zur offiziellen Geltung des Kaiserbildes im römischen Reiche.* Paderborn, 1934.

Lambrechts, P. *La Composition du Sénat romain de Septime Sévère à Dioclétien* (193–284). Diss. Pann. Ser. I, fasc. 8, Budapest, 1937.

Mattingly, H. *Roman Coins.* London, 1928.

Mitteis, L. *Reichsrecht und Volksrecht in den östlichen Provinzen des römischen Kaiserreiches.* Leipzig, 1891.

Mommsen, Th. *Römisches Staatsrecht.* II, 2³; III, 2. Leipzig, 1887–1888.

Pippidi, D. M. *Le 'Numen Augusti,' observations sur une forme occidentale du culte impériale.* Rev. E.L. XI, 1931, p. 83.

Ritterling, E. *Zum römischen Heerwesen des ausgehenden dritten Jahrhunderts.* Festschrift für Otto Hirschfeld, Berlin, 1903, p. 345.

—— Art. *s.v.* legio in P.W. coll. 1329–62.

Rostovtzeff, M. *The Social and Economic History of the Roman Empire.* Chs. IX–XII. Oxford, 1926.

(Later additions are to be found in the German and Italian editions given in the General Bibliography.)

Schulz, O. Th. *Vom Prinzipat zum Dominat.* Paderborn, 1919.

Stein, A. *Der römische Ritterstand. Ein Beitrag zur Sozial- und Personengeschichte des römischen Reiches.* Munich, 1927.

—— *Stellvertreter der Praefecti Praetorio.* Hermes, LX, 1925, p. 94.

Stein, E. *Geschichte des spätrömischen Reiches.* Vol. I, *Vom römischen zum byzantinischen Staate.* Vienna, 1928, pp. 1–93.

—— *Zum Gebrauch des prokonsularischen Titels seitens der römischen Kaiser.* Klio, XII, 1912, p. 392.

—— *Die kaiserlichen Beamten und Truppenkörper im römischen Deutschland unter dem Prinzipat.* Vienna, 1932.

Vogelstein, M. *Kaiseridee-Romidee und das Verhältnis von Staat und Kirche seit Constantin.* Teil 1: *Von Augustus bis Diocletian.* Breslau, 1930, pp. 4–49.

Weber, M. *Römische Kaisergeschichte und Kirchengeschichte.* Stuttgart, 1929.

—— *Die Vereinheitlichung der religiösen Welt.* In R. Laqueur, H. Koch and W. Weber, *Probleme der Spätantike.* Stuttgart, 1930, pp. 67 *sqq.*

Numerous articles in P.W. *s.vv.* a cognitionibus (v. Premerstein), ab epistolis (Rostowzew), a libellis (v. Premerstein), a memoria (Fluss), a rationibus (Liebenam), res privata (Liebenam), officium (Boak), perfectissimus (Ensslin), senatus (O'Brien Moore, in Suppl. VI), a studiis (Kübler); and in D.-S. *s.vv.* consilium principis (Humbert), praefectus praetorio and praefectus urbi (Cagnat).

CHAPTER XI

THE REFORMS OF DIOCLETIAN

This bibliography is to be read in conjunction with that to Chapter x, *The End of the Principate*: for that reason several works, listed there already, are not repeated here.

Baynes, N. H. *Three Notes on the Reforms of Diocletian and Constantine.* 2. *The Army reforms of Diocletian and Constantine.* J.R.S. xv, 1925, p. 201.

Besnier, M. *Histoire Romaine.* Paris, 1937, pp. 297–317.

Bott, H. *Die Grundzüge der diokletianischen Steuerverfassung.* Diss.-Frankfurt, Darmstadt, 1928. (But see the review by G. Ostrogorsky in Deutsche Literaturzeitung, L, 1929, col. 1349 *sqq.*)

Bücher, K. *Die diokletianische Taxordnung vom Jahre* 301. Zeitschrift für die gesamte Staatswissenschaft, L, 1894, pp. 189–672 (= Beiträge zur Wirtschaftsgeschichte, Tübingen, 1922, pp. 179–242.)

Bury, J. B. *The Provincial List of Verona.* J.R.S. xiii, 1923, p. 127.

Costa, G. *C. Valerius Diocletianus.* Estratto dal Diz. Epig. Vol. ii, pp. 1793–1908, Spoleto, 1912.

Lot, F. *L'impôt foncier et la capitation personnelle sous le bas-empire et à l'époque franque.* Paris, 1928.

Mickwitz, G. *Geld und Wirtschaft im römischen Reich des 4. Jahrhunderts n. Chr.* Helsingfors, 1932.

Mommsen, Th. *Das römische Militärwesen seit Diocletian.* Hermes, xxiv, 1889, p. 195 (= Gesammelte Schriften, vol. vi, 1910, p. 284).

—— *Die diocletianische Reichspraefectur.* Hermes, xxxi, 1901, p. 201 (= Gesammelte Schriften, vol. vi, 1910, p. 201).

—— *Dux.* Gesammelte Schriften, vol. vi, 1910, p. 204.

—— *Verzeichniss der römischen Provinzen aufgesetzt um* 297. Berl. Abh. 1862, p. 489 (= Gesammelte Schriften, vol. v, 1908, p. 561).

Mommsen, Th. and H. Blümner. *Der Maximaltarif des Diocletian.* Berlin, 1893.

Nischer, E. C. *The Army Reforms of Diocletian and Constantine and their Modifications up to the Time of the Notitia Dignitatum.* J.R.S. xiii, 1923, p. 1.

—— *Die Quellen für das spätrömische Heerwesen.* A.J.Ph. liii, 1932, pp. 21–97.

—— in J. Kromayer and G. Veith, *Heerwesen und Kriegführung*, Müllers Handbuch, Abt. 4, Teil 3, Band 2, Munich, 1928, pp. 481 *sqq.* (But see some corrections and modifications of Nischer's conclusions by N. H. Baynes (*supra*), by E. Stein in *Byz. Zeitschr.* xxv, 1925, p. 387, n. 3, and by W. Kubitschek in P.W. *s.v.* legio, col. 1832 *sqq.*).

Parker, H. M. D. *A History of the Roman World from* A.D. 138 *to* 337. Chaps. iv and v: *The Reforms of Diocletian and Constantine.* London, 1935, pp. 262–290.

—— *The Legions of Diocletian and Constantine.* J.R.S. xxiii, 1933, p. 175.

Piganiol, A. *L'Impôt de Capitation sous le Bas-Empire Romain.* Chambéry, 1916.

Pink, K. *Die Silberprägung der diocletianischen Tetrarchie.* N.Z. lxiii (N.F. xxiii), 1930, p. 9.

—— *Die Goldprägung des Diocletian und seiner Mitregenten.* N.Z. lxiv (N.F. xxiv), 1931, p. 1.

Seeck, O. *Geschichte des Untergangs der antiken Welt.* Book iii, *Die Verwaltung des Reiches.* Vol. ii², Stuttgart, 1921.

Van Sickle, C. E. *Conservatism and philosophical influence in the reign of Diocletian.* C.P. XXVII, 1932, p. 51.

Stade, K. *Der Politiker Diokletian und die letzte grosse Christenverfolgung.* Diss. Frankfurt a.M., Wiesbaden, 1926.

Stein, E. *Geschichte des spätrömischen Reiches.* Vol. I, Vienna, 1928, pp. 98–114.

—— *Untersuchungen über das Officium der Prätorianerpräfektur seit Diokletian.* Vienna, 1922.

Taubenschlag, R. *Das römische Privatrecht zur Zeit Diokletians.* Bull. Acad. Polon. des Sciences et Lettres, Cracow, 1923, p. 141.

Numerous articles in P.W. *s.vv.* corrector (v. Premerstein), comitatenses, comitatus, consistorium, dux, scrinium (Seeck), consularis (Kübler); and in D.-S. *s.vv.* vicarius (Lécrivain).

CHAPTER XII

THE DEVELOPMENT OF PAGANISM IN THE ROMAN EMPIRE

The ancient sources are listed in the bibliographies to the earlier chapters. Attention may be called to the selection of relevant inscriptions in Dessau 2957–5050a, 9230–9339.

For detailed surveys of the modern literature, see the reports in Bursian (latest by Fr. Pfister, *Supp.* ccxxix, 1930: published separately as *Die Religion der Griechen und Römer.* Leipzig, 1930); Arch. Relig. (latest by O. Weinreich, xxxiii, 1936, and xxxiv, 1937); Year's Work in Classical Studies (by H. J. Rose); J. E. A. (1927–1936 by A. D. Nock, from 1937 by H. J. Rose, in the collaborative bibliography of Graeco-Roman Egypt); Jahrbuch für Liturgiewissenschaft (by O. Casel and collaborators).

Alföldi, A. *Die Ausgestaltung des monarchischen Zeremoniells am römischen Kaiserhofe.* Röm. Mitt. xlix, 1934, p. 3.
—— *Insignien und Tracht der römischen Kaiser.* Ib. l, 1935, p. 3.
—— *A Festival of Isis in Rome under the Christian Emperors of the IVth Century.* Diss. Pann. Ser. ii, fasc. 7, Budapest, 1937.
Behn, F. *Das Mithrasheiligtum zu Dieburg.* Römisch-germanische Forschungen, 1, Berlin, 1928. (See the review by A. D. Nock in Gnomon, vi, 1930, p. 30.)
Bidez, J. *La vie de l'Empereur Julien.* Paris, 1930.
—— *Vie de Porphyre.* Ghent, 1913.
Blinkenberg, Chr. *Archäologische Studien.* Copenhagen, 1904.
Boissier, G. *La fin du paganisme.* 2 vols. Paris, 1891.
Bonner, C. *Some Phases of Religious Feeling in Later Paganism.* Harv. Theol. Rev. xxx, 1937, p. 119.
Bosch, Cl. *Die kleinasiatischen Münzen der römischen Kaiserzeit.* Teil ii, Einzeluntersuchungen. Bd. 1: Bithynien, 1 Hälfte. Stuttgart, 1935.
Boulanger, A. *Orphée.* Paris, 1925.
Brelich, A. *Aspetti della morte nelle iscrizioni sepolcrali dell' Impero romano.* Diss. Pann. Ser. 1, fasc. 7, Budapest, 1937.
Calder, W. M. *Notes on Anatolian religion.* Journ. Manchester Egyptian and Oriental Society, xi, 1924, p. 19.
Chapouthier, F. *Les Dioscures au service d'une déesse.* Paris, 1935.
Clemen, C. *Religionsgeschichtliche Erklärung des Neuen Testaments.* Ed. 2, Giessen, 1924.
Cook, S. A. *The Religions of Ancient Palestine in the Light of Archaeology.* London, 1930. Chap. iii, The Graeco-Roman Age, pp. 153–230.
Cumont, F. *Textes et monuments figurés relatifs aux mystères de Mithra.* 2 vols. Brussels, 1894–1900.
—— *Les mystères de Mithra.* Ed. 3, Brussels, 1913.
—— *Mithra en Étrurie.* In *Scritti in onore di Bartolomeo Nogara*, Città del Vaticano, 1937, p. 95.
—— *Les religions orientales dans le paganisme romain.* Ed. 4, Paris, 1929.
—— *After Life in Roman Paganism.* New Haven, 1922.
—— *Astrology and Religion among the Greeks and Romans.* New York, 1912.
    For a list of his other publications see *Mélanges Franz Cumont* (Brussels, 1936), p. vii.

Deissmann, A. *Licht vom Osten*. Ed. 4, Tübingen, 1923. (Eng. trans. by R. L. M. Strachan, London, 1927.)

Dieterich, A. *Eine Mithrasliturgie*. Ed. 3, rev. by O. Weinreich, Leipzig, 1923.

—— *Kleine Schriften*. Leipzig, 1911.

Dölger, F. J. *Antike und Christentum: Kultur- und religionsgeschichtliche Studien*. 1–Münster, 1929–.

—— *Sol Salutis*. Ed. 2, Münster, 1925.

—— ΙΧΘΥΣ. Münster: vol. 1, 1910 (ed. 2, 1928); 11 and 111, 1922; 1v, 1927; v, in preparation.

von Domaszewski, A. *Die Religion des römischen Heeres*. Westdeutsche Zeitschrift, xiv, 1895, p. 1.

—— *Abhandlungen zur römischen Religion*. Leipzig, 1909.

Eitrem, S. *Aus "Papyrologie und Religionsgeschichte": die magischen Papyri*. Münchener Beitr. z. Papyrusforschung u. ant. Rechtsgeschichte, xix, 1934, p. 243.

Festugière, A.-J. *L'Idéal religieux des Grecs et l'Évangile*. Ed. 2, Paris, 1931.

Festugière, A.-J. and P. Fabre, *Le monde gréco-romain au temps de Notre Seigneur*. 2 vols. Paris, 1935.

Geffcken, J. *Der Ausgang des griechisch-römischen Heidentums*. Heidelberg, 1920, and *Nachtrag*, 1929 (included in reprint).

Gernet, L. and A. Boulanger. *Le génie grec dans la religion*. Paris, 1932.

Gordon, A. E. *The cults of Africa*. Univ. of Calif. Publ. in Class. Arch. 11, no. 1, Berkeley, Cal. 1934.

Graillot, H. *Le Culte de Cybèle*. Paris, 1912.

Halliday, W. R. *The Pagan Background of early Christianity*. Liverpool, 1925.

Haussleiter, J. *Der Vegetarismus in der Antike*. Religionsgeschichtliche Versuche und Vorarbeiten, xxiv, Berlin, 1935.

Hepding, H. *Attis, seine Mythen und sein Kult*. Ib. 1, Giessen, 1903.

Herter, H. *De Priapo*. Ib. xxiii, Giessen, 1932.

Hill, Sir G. F. *Some Palestinian Cults in the Graeco-Roman Age*. Proc. Brit. Acad. v, 1912.

Hopfner, Th. *Griechisch-ägyptischer Offenbarungszauber*. Stud. z. Palaeographie u. Papyruskunde, ed. C. Wessely, xxi, xxiii. Leipzig, 1922–24.

Jones, L. W. *The Cults of Dacia*. Univ. of Calif. Publ. in Class. Phil. ix, 1929, no. 8. Berkeley, Cal. 1929.

Kan, A. H. *De Iovis Dolicheni cultu....* Groningen, 1901.

Kazarow, G. *Neue Mithrasdenkmäler aus Bulgarien*. Germ. xix, 1935, p. 24.

—— *Mithrasdenkmäler aus Bulgarien*. Ann. Mus. Nat. Bulg. vi, 1932–34, p. 39.

Keil, J. *Die Kulte Lydiens*. In *Anatolian Studies presented to Sir William Mitchell Ramsay*, Manchester, 1923, p. 239.

Kittel, G. (ed.). *Theologisches Wörterbuch zum Neuen Testament*. Stuttgart, 1932–.

Kroll, J. *Die Lehren des Hermes Trismegistos*. Münster, 1914.

Kroll, W. *De oraculis Chaldaicis*. Breslauer phil. Abh. vii, i, Breslau, 1894.

Lafaye, G. *Histoire du culte des divinités d'Alexandrie*. Paris, 1884.

Lagrange, M.-J. *Introduction à l'Étude du Nouveau Testament*: Quatrième Partie: *Critique historique*. 1, *Les Mystères: l'Orphisme*. Paris, 1937.

La Piana, G. *Foreign groups in Rome during the first centuries of the Empire*. Harv. Theol. Rev. xx, 1927, p. 183.

Latte, K. Art. *s.v.* Synkretismus in *Die Religion in Geschichte und Gegenwart*, ed. 2.

Lietzmann, H. *Geschichte der alten Kirche*. Berlin, vol. 1, 1932 (Eng. trans. by B. L. Wolff, London, 1936); vol. 11, 1936.

—— *Die Umwelt des jungen Christentums*. Die Antike, viii, 1932, p. 254.

Macchioro, V. *Il sincretismo religioso e l' epigrafia*. Rev. Arch. 4ᵉ Sér. ix, 1907, pp. 141 and 253.

Manteuffel, G. *De opusculis Graecis Aegypti e papyris, ostracis lapidibusque collectis*. Trav. de la Soc. des Sciences et des Lettres de Varsovie, Classe 1 (1930), No. 12, Warsaw, 1930.

Milne, J. G. Art. *s.v.* Graeco-Egyptian Religion in *Encyclopaedia of Religion and Ethics*, ed. J. Hastings.

Moore, C. H. *The Distribution of Oriental Cults in the Gauls and Germanies*. Trans. Am. Phil. Ass. xxxviii, 1907, p. 109.

Nilsson, M. P. *En marge de la grande inscription bacchique du Metropolitan Museum*. Studi e Materiali di Storia delle Religioni, x, 1934, p. 1.

—— *Wesensverschiedenheiten der römischen und der griechischen Religion*. Röm. Mitt. xlviii, 1933, p. 245.

Nock, A. D. *Conversion*. Oxford, 1933.

—— *Early Gentile Christianity and its Hellenistic Background*. In *Essays on the Trinity and the Incarnation*, ed. A. E. J. Rawlinson, London, 1928.

—— *St Paul*. London, 1938.

Norden, E. *Agnostos Theos*. Ed. 2, Leipzig, 1923 (one page added to ed. 1).

Perdrizet, P. *Les terres cuites grecques d'Égypte de la collection Fouquet*. 2 vols. Nancy, 1921.

Peterson, E. ΕΙΣ ΘΕΟΣ. Göttingen, 1926.

Picard, Ch. *Éphèse et Claros*. Paris, 1922.

Preisendanz, K. *Papyri graecae magicae. Die griechischen Zauberpapyri*. 1– Leipzig, 1928–.

Quandt, G. *De Baccho ab Alexandri aetate in Asia minore culto*. Diss. phil. Hal. xxi, pars 2, Halle, 1913.

Reitzenstein, R. *Die hellenistischen Mysterienreligionen*. Ed. 3, Leipzig, 1927. (For other works, cf. bibliography in *Festschrift Richard Reitzenstein*, Leipzig, 1931.)

Roscher, W. H. (ed.). *Ausführliches Lexikon der griechischen und römischen Mythologie*. Leipzig, 1884–1937.

Saxl, F. *Mithras. Typengeschichtliche Untersuchungen*. Berlin, 1931. (See reviews by M. P. Nilsson, *Deutsche Lit.-Z.* 1933, col. 250; L. Deubner, *Gnomon*, ix, 1933, p. 372; E. Loewy, *Orient. Lit.-Z.* xxxvii, 1934, col. 485.)

Scott, W. and A. S. Ferguson. *Hermetica*. 4 vols. Oxford, 1925–36.

Seyrig, H. *La triade héliopolitaine et les temples de Baalbek*. Syria, x, 1929, p. 314 (and many other articles in the same periodical).

Swoboda, E. *Die Schlange im Mithraskult*. Jahreshefte, xxx, 1936, p. 1.

Taylor, L. R. *The Cults of Ostia*. Bryn Mawr, Penn. 1912.

Todoroff, Y. *The Pagan Cults in Moesia Inferior*. Sofia, 1928.

Toutain, J. *Les cultes païens dans l'empire romain*. 1–, Paris, 1907–.

Usener, H. *Das Weihnachtsfest*. 1, ed. 2, Bonn, 1911.

Volkmann, H. *Studien zum Nemesiskult*. Arch. Relig. xxvi, 1928, p. 296.

—— *Neue Beiträge zum Nemesiskult*. Ib. xxxi, 1934, p. 57.

Weber, W. *Die ägyptisch-griechischen Terrakotten*. (Königl. Museen zu Berlin. Mitt. aus der ägypt. Sammlung.) 2 vols. Berlin, 1914.

Weber, W. In R. Laqueur, H. Koch, and W. Weber, *Probleme der Spätantike*. Stuttgart, 1930. pp. 67 *sqq.*

Weinreich, O. *Neue Urkunden zur Sarapis-Religion*. Tübingen, 1919.

Wendland, P. *Die hellenistisch-römische Kultur in ihren Beziehungen zu Judentum und Christentum*. Eds. 2 and 3. Tübingen, 1912.

Westholm, A. *The Temples of Soli. Studies on Cypriote art during Hellenistic and Roman periods*. Stockholm, 1936.

Wissowa, G. *Religion und Kultus der Römer*. Ed. 2, Munich, 1912.

CHAPTERS XIII, XIV, AND XV

PAGAN PHILOSOPHY AND THE CHRISTIAN CHURCH: THE CHRISTIAN CHURCH IN THE EAST: THE CHRISTIAN CHURCH IN THE WEST

Section I, General, and Section II (*i*) are due to Professors Creed and Lietzmann, Section II (*a*) to (*f*) is by Professor Creed, Section II (*g*) is by Mr C. R. C. Allberry, Fellow of Christ's College, and Section II (*h*) is by Mr J. Stevenson of St John's College, Cambridge.

In this bibliography the following abbreviations are used:

C.S.E.L. Corpus Scriptorum Ecclesiasticorum Latinorum. Vienna.
Gr. Chr. Schr. Griechische Christliche Schriftsteller. Leipzig.
T.U. Texte und Untersuchungen. Berlin.

Texts and translations are placed first, and then modern works.

I. General

Eusebius, *Historia Ecclesiastica*. The best edition is published in Gr. Chr. Schr. together with the Latin translation of Rufinus. Edd. E. Schwartz and Th. Mommsen. Vol. ix, i and ii, Text; iii, Introduction, Indices, etc. Leipzig, 1903–1909. The text is conveniently reproduced in an Editio Minor: *Eusebius Kirchengeschichte*, ed. E. Schwartz (Leipzig, 1908).

Lawlor, H. J. and J. E. L. Oulton, *The Ecclesiastical History and the Martyrs of Palestine*. 2 vols. London, 1927. Vol. i, Translation; vol. ii, Introduction and Notes.

McGiffert, A. C. English translation, introduction and notes in vol. i of the 2nd Series of *Nicene and Post-Nicene Fathers*. Oxford, 1890.

Lake, K. and J. E. L. Oulton, Text and Translation, 2 vols. (Loeb). London, 1926, 1932.

Apostolic Fathers. Funk, F. X. *Patres Apostolici*. 2 vols. Tübingen, 1901. 3rd ed. of vol. ii, ed. F. Diekamp. Tübingen, 1913.

Bihlmeyer, K. *Die Apostolischen Väter*. Neubearbeitung der Funkschen Ausgabe. I Teil (Didache, Barnabas, Clemens I, II, Ignatius, Polycarp, Quadratus, Diognetus). Tübingen, 1924.

J. B. Lightfoot. *The Apostolic Fathers*. Pt I, vols. 1 and 2, *S. Clement of Rome*. London, 1890; Pt II, vols. 1–3, *S. Ignatius and S. Polycarp*. 2nd ed. London, 1889. A posthumous work edited by J. R. Harmer, London, 1891, gives text and translation of Clement, Ignatius, Polycarp, the Didache, Barnabas, Hermas, Diognetus, Papias.

Die apostolischen Väter in *Handbuch zum neuen Testament*, ed. H. Lietzmann. Ergänzungsband. 4 Pts. Tübingen, 1920–1923.

English translation by F. Crombie and others in *The Ante-Nicene Christian Library*, vol. i, Edinburgh, 1868.

Lake, K. *The Apostolic Fathers*: text and translation. 2 vols. (Loeb). London, 1912, 1913.

English translations: The Epistles of St Ignatius, by J. H. Srawley. London, 1919; The Doctrine of the Twelve Apostles, by L. B. Radford, revised edition by A. J. Maclean. London, 1922; The First Epistle of Clement to the Corinthians, by W. K. L. Clarke. London, 1937.

DIONYSIUS OF ALEXANDRIA. Feltoe, C. L. ΔΙΟΝΥΣΙΟΥ ΛΕΙΨΑΝΑ. *The Letters and other Remains of Dionysius of Alexandria.* Cambridge, 1904: he has also published an English translation of the Letters and Treatises. London, n.d. (?1918).

An English translation by S. D. F. Salmond is published in *The Ante-Nicene Christian Library*, vol. xx. Edinburgh, 1871.

EPIPHANIUS, ed. K. Holl, in Gr. Chr. Schr. vol. xxv (1915), Ancoratus and Panarion Haer. 1–33; vol. xxxi (1922) Panarion Haer. 34–64; vol. xxxvii (1933) Panarion Haer. 65–80. De fide.

HIPPOLYTUS in Gr. Chr. Schr. vol. i (1897), edd. G. N. Bonwetsch and H. Achelis (Commentary on Daniel and Song of Solomon, etc.); vol. xxvi (1916), ed. P. Wendland (Refutatio omnium Haeresium); vol. xxxvi (1929), edd. A. Bauer and R. Helm (The Chronicle). Translation by J. H. MacMahon and S. D. F. Salmond in *The Ante-Nicene Christian Library*, vols. vi and ix. Edinburgh, 1868–1869. For an English translation of the *Refutation of all Heresies*: F. Legge, *Philosophumena*. 2 vols. London, 1921.

IRENAEUS. *Sancti Irenaei episcopi Lugdunensis libros quinque adversus haereses*, ed. W. W. Harvey. 2 vols. Cambridge, 1857.

The Armenian translation of Books iv and v was published by E. Ter-Minassiantz in T.U. xxxv, 1910.

English translations by J. Keble in *A Library of Fathers of the Holy Catholic Church*, Oxford, 1872, and by A. Roberts and W. H. Rambaut in *The Ante-Nicene Christian Library*, vols. v and ix, Edinburgh, 1868, 1869. An English translation of the principal passages by F. R. Montgomery Hitchcock appeared in the series *Early Church Classics*. 2 vols. London, 1916.

Εἰς ἐπίδειξιν τοῦ ἀποστολικοῦ κηρύγματος. The Armenian translation was published by K. Ter-Měkěrttschian and E. Ter-Minassiantz in T.U. xxxi, 1907 (with German translation). Latin translation by S. Weber, Freiburg im B., 1917. Republished with English and French translations in *Patrologia Orientalis*, xii, Fasc. 5, Paris, 1919. Translated (with introduction)—*The Demonstration of the Apostolic Preaching*—by J. Armitage Robinson, London, 1920. (On the sources of Irenaeus cf. F. Loofs, T.U. xlvi, Heft 2, 1930 with F. R. Montgomery Hitchcock, J.T.S. xxxviii, 1937, p. 130, p. 255.)

JULIUS AFRICANUS. Fragmenta: M. J. Routh, *Reliquiae Sacrae*. Ed. altera, vol. ii, pp. 221–309, 312–509. Oxford, 1846.

MARCION. A. von Harnack, *Marcion: das Evangelium vom fremden Gott*. T.U. xlv, 1921; 2nd ed. 1924; *Neue Studien zu Marcion*. T.U. xliv, Heft 4, 1923.

METHODIUS in Gr. Chr. Schr. vol. xxvii (1917), ed. G. N. Bonwetsch. Translation in vol. xiv of *The Ante-Nicene Christian Library*, Edinburgh, 1869.

Achelis, H. *Das Christentum in den ersten drei Jahrhunderten*. 2 vols. Leipzig, 1912. (The second edition of 1925 contains no notes.)

Altaner, B. *Patrologie*. Freiburg im B., 1938 (with bibliography of recent work).

Bardenhewer, O. *Patrologie*. 3rd ed. Freiburg im B., 1910. English translation from 2nd ed. by J. J. Strahan, St Louis, Mo., 1908.

—— *Geschichte der altkirchlichen Literatur*. Vol. 2. 2nd ed. Freiburg im B., 1914.

Bauer, W. *Rechtgläubigkeit und Ketzerei im ältesten Christentum*. Tübingen, 1934.

Bethune-Baker, J. F. *An Introduction to the early history of Christian Doctrine*. Ed. 5. London, 1933.

Bihlmeyer, K. *Kirchengeschichte* auf Grund des Lehrbuches von F. X. von Funk. I Teil. *Das christliche Altertum*. Paderborn, 1936. (Useful bibliographies.)

von Campenhausen, H. *Die Idee des Martyriums in der alten Kirche*. Göttingen, 1936.

Caspar, E. *Geschichte des Papsttums*. Vol. I. Tübingen, 1930.

Duchesne, L. *Histoire ancienne de l'Église*. Vol. I. Paris, 1906. English translation, vol. I, *Early History of the Christian Church*. London, 1909.

Ehrhard, A. *Die Kirche der Märtyrer*. Munich, 1932.

—— *Urkirche und Frühkatholizismus*. Bonn, 1935.

Fliche, A. and V. Martin, *Histoire de l'Église*. Vol. II, by J. Lebreton and J. Zeiller, *De la fin du 2ᵉ siècle à la paix constantinienne*. Paris, 1935.

Gwatkin, H. M. *Early Church History to A.D. 313*. 2 vols. London, 1912.

Haller, J. *Das Papsttum*. Vol. I, Stuttgart, 1934.

von Harnack, A. *Die Mission und Ausbreitung des Christentums in den ersten drei Jahrhunderten*. 4th ed., 2 vols. Leipzig, 1924. English translation of the 2nd edition by J. Moffatt, *The Mission and Expansion of Christianity in the first three centuries*. London, 1908.

—— *Geschichte der altchristlichen Literatur bis Eusebius*. 3 vols. Leipzig, 1893–1904.

Harrison, P. N. *The Problem of the Pastoral Epistles*. London, 1921.

—— *Polycarp's Two Epistles to the Philippians*. Cambridge, 1936.

Jackson, F. and K. Lake, *The Beginnings of Christianity*. Part I, vol. v. London, 1933.

Kidd, B. J. *A History of the Church to A.D. 461*. Vol. I, Oxford, 1922.

de Labriolle, P. *Histoire de la littérature latine chrétienne*. Ed. 2, Paris, 1924.

—— *La réaction païenne. Étude sur la polémique antichrétienne du Iᵉʳ au VIᵉ siècle*. Paris, 1934.

Lawlor, H. J. *Eusebiana. Essays on the Ecclesiastical History*. Oxford, 1912.

Lietzmann, H. *Geschichte der alten Kirche*. Vol. II, *Ecclesia catholica*. Berlin, 1936.

—— *Petrus und Paulus in Rom*. Ed. 2. Berlin–Leipzig, 1927.

Loofs, F. *Leitfaden zum Studium der Dogmengeschichte*. Ed. 4. Halle, 1906.

Montgomery Hitchcock, F. R. *Irenaeus of Lugdunum*. Cambridge, 1914.

Müller, K. *Kirchengeschichte*. Vol. I, ed. 2, Tübingen, 1924–1929.

Philotesia, P. Kleinert zum LXX Geburtstag dargebracht von Ad. Harnack, H. Diels, K. Holl, etc. Berlin, 1907.

Preuschen, E. and G. Krüger, *Handbuch der Kirchengeschichte*. I. Teil, *Das Altertum*. Ed. 2, Tübingen, 1923.

Puech, A. *Histoire de la littérature grecque chrétienne*. Vol. II. Paris, 1928.

Ramsay, W. M. *The Cities and Bishoprics of Phrygia*. Part I. 2 vols., Oxford, 1895, 1897.

Roberts, C. H. *An unpublished Fragment of the Fourth Gospel*. Manchester, 1935.

Sanday, W. *The Gospels in the Second Century*. London, 1876.

Schwartz, E. *Kaiser Constantin und die christliche Kirche*. Ed. 2, Leipzig, 1936.

—— Art. in P.W. *s.v.* Eusebius.

Tixeront, J. *Histoire des Dogmes*. Vol. I, ed. 11, Paris, 1930.

Turner, C. H. *Studia Biblica et Ecclesiastica*, II, 1890, p. 105.

II. Special Topics

(a) The New Testament Canon: New Testament Apocrypha: Worship and Organization

Hippolytus. *Church Order*. (1) Latin Version, ed. E. Hauler, *Didascaliae Apostolorum fragmenta Veronensia Latina, accedunt Canonum qui dicuntur Apostolorum et Aegyptiorum reliquiae*. Leipzig, 1900. (2) Ethiopic, Arabic and Coptic Versions, ed. G. Horner, *The Statutes of the Apostles* (with Eng. trans.). London, 1904.

Connolly, R. H. *The so-called Egyptian Church Order and derived documents*. (Texts and Studies, VIII, 4), Cambridge, 1916.

—— *Didascalia Apostolorum*. Trans. with Introduction and Notes. Oxford, 1929.

Dix, G. Ἀποστολικὴ Παράδοσις. *The Treatise on the Apostolic Tradition of St Hippolytus of Rome*. Vol. I. Historical Introduction, Textual Materials and Translation. London, 1937.

Easton, B. S. *The Apostolic Tradition of Hippolytus translated into English with introduction and notes*. Cambridge, 1934.

Funk, F. X. *Didascalia et Constitutiones Apostolorum*. 2 vols., Paderborn, 1905–1906.

Hennecke, E. *Neutestamentliche Apokryphen*. Ed. 2, Tübingen, 1923–1924.

James, M. R. (Editor.) *Apocrypha Anecdota*. 2nd series (Texts and Studies, V), Cambridge, 1897.

—— *The Apocryphal New Testament*. Oxford, 1924.

Schmidt, C. ΠΡΑΞΕΙΣ ΠΑΥΛΟΥ (nach dem Papyrus der Hamburger Staats- und Universitäts-Bibliothek unter Mitarbeit von W. Schubart). Glückstadt, 1936.

—— [*Epistula Apostolorum*.] *Gespräche Jesu mit seinen Jüngern nach der Auferstehung*. (T.U. vol. XLIII.) Leipzig, 1919.

---

von Harnack, A. *Die Briefsammlung des Apostels Paulus*. Leipzig, 1926.

Jülicher, A. and E. Fascher, *Einleitung in das Neue Testament*. 2ter Teil. *Die Geschichte des NTlichen Kanons*, pp. 450–558. Ed. 7, Tübingen, 1931.

Leipoldt, J. *Geschichte des neutestamentlichen Kanons*. 1er Teil. Leipzig, 1907.

Lietzmann, H. *Messe und Herrenmahl*. Bonn, 1926.

Schermann, T. *Die allgemeine Kirchenordnung*. Paderborn, 1914.

Schwartz, E. *Über die pseudoapostolischen Kirchenordnungen*. (Schrift. der wiss. Gesell. in Strassburg.) Strassburg, 1910.

Streeter, B. H. *The Primitive Church*. London, 1929.

Turner, C. H. *Apostolic Succession*. In *Essays on the Early History of the Church and the Ministry*, ed. H. B. Swete. London, 1918.

(b) The Early Greek Apologists

The Apologists.

Goodspeed, E J. *Die ältesten Apologeten*. (The most convenient text. Includes all the second-century Apologists, except Theophilus.) Göttingen, 1915.

Corpus Apologetarum Christianorum saeculi secundi. Ed. J. C. Th. Otto. Vols. 1–5 (genuine works of S. Justin and works attributed to him). Vol. i, Jena, 1842; 3rd ed. 1876; vol. ii, 3rd ed. 1877; vol. iii, 3rd ed. 1879; vol. iv, 3rd ed. 1880; vol. v, 3rd ed. 1881; vol. vi, Tatian, 1851; vol. vii, Athenagoras, 1857; vol. viii, Theophilus of Antioch, 1861; vol. ix, Hermias, Aristides, Aristo, Miltiades, Melito, Apollinaris, 1872.

Separate editions:

Justin Martyr: *The Apologies of Justin Martyr.* Ed. A. W. F. Blunt. Cambridge, 1911.

Aristides: *The Apology of Aristides.* Ed. and translated by J. Rendel Harris (Texts and Studies, I, i). Cambridge, 1891.

Seeberg, R. *Der Apologet Aristides.* Erlangen–Leipzig, 1894.

Geffcken, J. in *Zwei griechische Apologeten* (see below).

Athenagoras: *Athenagorae Libellus pro Christianis.* Rec. E. Schwartz. Leipzig, 1891 (T.U. IV, Heft 2).

Geffcken, J. in *Zwei griechische Apologeten* (see below).

Tatian: *Tatiani Oratio ad Graecos.* Rec. E. Schwartz. Leipzig, 1888 (T.U. IV, Heft 1).

An English translation of Justin Martyr and Athenagoras by M. Dods, G. Reith and B. P. Pratten is published in *The Ante-Nicene Christian Library,* vol. II, Edinburgh, 1867, and of Tatian and Theophilus in vol. III of the same library, 1867. There is a French translation (with Greek text and introduction) of St Justin's Apologies by L. Pautigny in the series of *Textes et Documents,* edited by H. Hemmer and P. Lejay, Paris, 1904, and there are German translations of the Apologists in the *Bibliothek der Kirchenväter,* vols. XII, XIV and XXXIII. Munich, 1913–1917.

English translation of Justin Martyr: *The Dialogue with Trypho* by A. Lukyn Williams. London, 1930.

Bardy, G. on *Justin,* Dict. théol. cath. 8 (1925), 2228–2277.

Bonwetsch, G. N. *Justin der Märtyrer* in Realencyclopädie für protest. Theologie und Kirche, ed. 3, IX, pp. 641–650.

Geffcken, J. *Zwei griechische Apologeten.* (In addition to a full commentary on Aristides and Athenagoras includes very valuable chapters on the Apologetic literature as a whole.) Leipzig–Berlin, 1907.

Goodenough, E. R. *The Theology of Justin Martyr.* Jena, 1923.

Lagrange, M.-J. *Saint Justin.* Ed. 3, Paris, 1914.

Moody, C. N. *The Mind of the early Converts.* London, [? 1920].

Puech, A. *Les Apologistes grecs du IIe siècle de notre ère.* Paris, 1912.

(c) The School of Alexandria

CLEMENT OF ALEXANDRIA. All the extant works ed. by Otto Stählin in Gr. Chr. Schr. 3 vols. Leipzig, 1905–9, with Index (vol. IV), 1936.

English translation by W. Wilson in *The Ante-Nicene Christian Library,* vols. IV, XII, XXII. Edinburgh, 1868–1871.

G. W. Butterworth has translated the *Protreptikos,* the *Quis dives salvetur* and *Fragment of an Address to the Newly Baptised* in the Loeb Classical Library. London, 1919.

The translation by O. Stählin in the *Bibl. d. Kirchenväter,* 2te Reihe, vols. VII (1934), VIII (1934), XVII (1936) and XX (1938), is important since it is based on his own critical text.

ORIGEN. *Origenis Opera omnia,* ed. C. H. E. Lommatzsch. Berlin, 1831–1848. 25 vols. This edition is now superseded for some of the most important works by 11 vols. in Gr. Chr. Schr., especially the volumes edited by P. Koetschau: I and II (including Εἰς μαρτύριον προτρεπτικός, the eight books of Κατὰ Κέλσου and Περὶ Εὐχῆς); and V, De Principiis (Περὶ Ἀρχῶν). Vols. III, VI, VII, VIII, IX contain Homilies; vol. IV, Commentary on John; vols. X, XI, Commentary on Matthew.

The Philocalia of Origen, ed. J. Armitage Robinson. Cambridge, 1893.

The Commentary of Origen on S. John's Gospel, ed A. E. Brooke. 2 vols., Cambridge, 1896.

Celsi ΑΛΗΘΗΣ ΛΟΓΟΣ, excussit et restituere conatus est O. Glöckner. Bonn, 1924.

English translations: *Contra Celsum* in *The Ante-Nicene Christian Library*, vols. 10 and 23. Edinburgh, 1869, 1872; *De Principiis* based on Koetschau's critical text by G. W. Butterworth, London, 1936; *Philocalia* by G. Lewis, Edinburgh, 1911; selections from the Commentaries and Homilies by R. B. Tollinton, London, 1929.

Cadiou, R. *Introduction au Système d'Origène*. Paris, 1932.

—— *La jeunesse d'Origène: histoire de l'école d'Alexandrie au début du III*e *siècle*. Paris, 1935.

Faye, E. de. *Clément d'Alexandrie. Étude sur les rapports du christianisme et de la philosophie grecque au II*e *siècle*. Paris, 1898.

—— *Origène: sa vie, son œuvre, sa pensée*. 3 vols., Paris, 1923–8.

Koch, H. *Pronoia und Paideusis. Studien über Origenes und sein Verhältnis zum Platonismus*. Berlin–Leipzig, 1932.

Miura-Stange, A. *Celsus und Origenes. Das Gemeinsame ihrer Weltanschauung*. Giessen, 1926.

Molland, E. *The Conception of the Gospel in the Alexandrinian theology*. Oslo, 1938.

Rougier, L. *Celse ou le conflit de la civilisation antique et du christianisme primitif*. Paris, 1925.

Tollinton, R. B. *Clement of Alexandria. A study in Christian Liberalism*. 2 vols., London, 1914.

Völker, W. *Das Vollkommenheitsideal des Origenes*. Tübingen, 1931.

(d) Montanism

Anderson, J. G. C. *Paganism and Christianity in the Upper Tembris Valley* in *Studies in the History and Art of the Eastern Provinces of the Roman Empire*. Aberdeen, 1906.

Bonwetsch, G. N. *Texte zur Geschichte des Montanismus*. Bonn, 1914.

Calder, W. M. *Philadelphia and Montanism*. Bull. John Ryl. Lib. VII, 1923, p. 309.

—— *The Epigraphy of the Anatolian Heresies*. Anatolian Studies, p. 59. Manchester, 1923.

—— *The New Jerusalem of the Montanists*. Byzantion, VI, 1931, p. 421.

—— *The Messenger Lectures* (Cornell University) (to be published shortly).

Grégoire, H. *Du nouveau sur la hiérarchie de la secte montaniste d'après une inscription grecque trouvée près de Philadelphie en Lydie*. Byzantion, II, 1925, p. 329.

—— *Notes épigraphiques*, ib. VIII, 1933, p. 49.

de Labriolle, P. *La crise montaniste*. Paris, 1913.

—— *Les sources de l'histoire du Montanisme*. Fribourg (Suisse), Paris, 1913.

Schepelern, W. *Der Montanismus und die phrygischen Kulte*. Tübingen, 1929.

(e) Gnosticism and the Church

For Irenaeus and Hippolytus: see above.

Schmidt, C. *Pistis Sophia*. (Critical edition of the Coptic text.) Hauniae, 1925.

—— *Koptisch Gnostische Schriften*. (Includes *Pistis Sophia*, the two Books of Jeû and an anonymous work from the Askew MS in the B.M. and the Bruce MS in the Bodleian.) Leipzig, 1905.

Bousset, W. *Hauptprobleme der Gnosis*. Göttingen, 1907.

Burkitt, F. C. *The Church and Gnosis.* Cambridge, 1931.

Faye, E. de. *Gnostiques et gnosticisme. Étude critique des documents du Gnosticisme chrétien aux IIᵉ et IIIᵉ siècles.* Ed. 2, Paris, 1925.

von Harnack, A. *Marcion:* see above, p. 768.

Horner, G. *Pistis Sophia literally translated from the Coptic.* London, 1924.

Schmidt, C. *Plotins Stellung zum Gnosticismus und kirchlichen Christentum.* (T.U. vol. xx.) Leipzig, 1901.

Völker, W. *Quellen zur Geschichte der christlichen Gnosis.* Tübingen, 1932.

(f) Syriac-speaking Christianity

ADDAI. *The Doctrine of Addai the Apostle.* Syriac Text with English translation and notes by G. Phillips. London, 1876.

APHRAATES. Ed. W. Wright. *The Homilies of Aphraates, the Persian Sage.* Vol. I (all published), The Syriac Text. London–Edinburgh, 1869. Ed. J. Parisot, *Patrologia Syriaca,* Pars I, Tomus I (Syriac text and French trans.), Paris, 1894, Tomus II, pp. 1–489 (containing Hom. 23 and Indexes), 1907.

BARDESANES. Ed. F. Nau. *Patrologia Syriaca,* Pars I, Tomus II, pp. 490–658. Paris, 1907.

EPHRAEM SYRUS. *Prose Refutations of Mani, Marcion and Bardaisan.* 2 vols. ed. C. W. Mitchell (completed by A. A. Bevan and F. C. Burkitt). London, 1912–1921.

Overbeck, J. J. *S. Ephraemi Syri, Rabulae Episcopi Edesseni, Balaei aliorumque opera selecta.* Oxford, 1865.

Kraeling, C. H. *A Greek Fragment of Tatian's Diatessaron from Dura edited with facsimile, transcription and introduction.* Studies and Documents, edd. K. Lake and S. Lake, No. III. London, 1935.

Baumstark, A. *Geschichte der syrischen Literatur.* Bonn, 1922.

Burkitt, F. C. *Early Eastern Christianity.* London, 1904.

—— *Evangelion da-Mepharreshe.* 2 vols. Cambridge, 1904.

—— *Euphemia and the Goth.* Text and Translation Society. London, 1913.

—— *St. Ephraim's Quotations from the Gospel.* Texts and Studies, VII, No. 2. 1901.

Cureton, W. *Ancient Syriac Documents.* London, 1864.

(g) Mani and the Manichees

(i) Editions of Original Texts

(a) Central Asian.

Andreas, F. C. and W. Henning. *Mitteliranische Manichaica aus Chinesisch-Turkestan, I–III.* Berl. S.B. 1932–4.

Bang, W. *Manichäische Erzähler.* Muséon, XLIV, 1931, p. 1.

—— *Manichäische Laien-Beichtspiegel.* Ib. XXXVI, 1923, p. 137.

—— *Manichäische Hymnen.* Ib. XXXVIII, 1925, p. 1.

Bang, W. and A. von Gabain. *Türkische Turfan-Texten.* Berl. S.B. 1929, p. 411.

Chavannes, E. and P. Pelliot. *Un traité manichéen retrouvé en Chine.* Journ. Asiatique (Série 10), XVIII, 1911, p. 499; (Série 11), I, 1913, p. 261.

Henning, W. *Ein manichäischer kosmogonischer Hymnus.* Gött. Nach. 1932, p. 214.

—— *Geburt und Entsendung des manichäischen Urmenschen.* Ib. 1933, p. 306.

—— *Ein manichäisches Henochbuch.* Berl. S.B. 1934, p. 3.

—— *Ein manichäisches Bet- und Beichtbuch.* Berl. Abh. 1937, No. 10.

von Le Coq, A. *Türkische Manichaica aus Chotscho I–III.* Berl. Abh. 1912, 1919, 1922.

—— *Ein manichäisches Buch-Fragment aus Chotscho.* Festschrift V. Thomsen... dargebracht. Leipzig, 1912, p. 145.

—— *Ein christliches und ein manichäisches Manuscriptfragment in türkischer Sprache aus Turfan.* Berl. S.B. 1909, p. 1202.

—— *Koktürkisches aus Turfan.* Berl. S.B. 1909, p. 1047.

Muller, F. W. K. *Handschriften-Reste aus Turfan I–II.* Berl. S.B. and Abh. 1904.

—— *Ein Doppelblatt aus einem manichäischen Hymnenbuch (Mahrnamâg).* Berl. Abh. 1913, p. 3.

—— *Eine Hermas Stelle in manichäischer Version.* Berl. S.B. 1905, p. 1077.

—— *Der Hofstaat eines Iuguren-Königs.* Festschrift V. Thomsen...dargebracht. Leipzig, 1912, p. 207.

Salemann, C. *Ein Bruchstük (sic) manichäischen Schrifttums im Asiatischen Museum.* Mémoires de l'Acad. Imp. des Sciences de St Pétersbourg, 1904.

—— *Manichaica, I, III, IV.* Bull. de l'Acad. Imp. des Sciences de St Pétersbourg, 1907, p. 175; 1912, p. 1.

—— *Manichäische Studien I.* Mémoires de l'Acad. Imp. des Sciences de St Pétersbourg, 1908.

Waldschmidt, E. and W. Lentz. *Die Stellung Jesu im Manichäismus.* Berl. Abh. 1926, p. 3.

—— *Manichäische Dogmatik aus chinesischen und iranischen Texten.* Berl. S.B. 1933, p. 480.

(*b*) *Coptic.*

Allberry, C. R. C. *A Manichaean Psalm-Book,* Pt II. Stuttgart, 1938.

Budge, Sir E. A. W. *Coptic Martyrdoms in the Dialect of Upper Egypt.* London, 1914.

Polotsky, H. J. *Manichäische Homilien.* Stuttgart, 1934.

Schmidt, C. and H. J. Polotsky. *Ein Mani-Fund in Aegypten.* Berl. S.B. 1933, p. 4.

Schmidt, C., H. J. Polotsky and A. Böhlig. *Kephalaia,* Lieferungen 1–8. Stuttgart, 1935–7.

(ii) *Ancient Authorities*

Beeson, C. H. *Hegemonius, Acta Archelai.* Leipzig, 1906.

Brinkmann, A. *Alexander Lycopolitanus contra Manichaeos.* Leipzig, 1895.

Casey, R. P. *Serapion of Thmuis, Against the Manichees.* (Harvard Theological Studies, xv.) Cambridge (Mass.), 1931.

Flügel, G. *Mani, seine Lehre und seine Schriften, aus dem Fihrist.* Leipzig, 1862.

Holl, K. *Epiphanius, Bd. III* in Gr. Chr. Schr. (see above). Panarion 66.

de Lagarde, P. A. *Titus Bostrenus contra Manichaeos,* graece, *id.* syriace, Berlin, 1859 (reprint 1924).

Mitchell, C. W. *St Ephraim's Prose Refutations of Mani, Marcion, and Bardaisan.* Vol. I, London, 1912. Vol. II (completed by F. C. Burkitt and A. A. Bevan), London, 1921.

Pognon, H. *Inscriptions mandaïtes des Coupes de Khouabir.* Paris, 1898. Appendix II: Extraits du Livre des Scholies de Theodore bar Khouni, p. 125.

Sachau, E. *Al-Biruni: Chronology of Ancient Nations.* London, 1879.

Zycha, J. *Augustinus, Scripta contra Manichaeos* (Opera, sect. 6, pars 1 et 2), in C.S.E.L. xxv, 1891–2.

For the formulas of abjuration cf. *Appendix Monumentorum ad Recognitiones Clementinas.* Migne, P.G. 1, col. 1461 and Methodius, περὶ τῶν ἀπ' ἀρνήσεως. Migne, P.G. c, col. 1321.

(iii) *General*

Alfaric, P. *Les Écritures manichéennes.* 2 vols. Paris, 1918.
Bardy, G. *Manichéisme.* Dictionnaire de Théologie Catholique, vol. 9, p. 1841. Paris, 1926.
Baur, F. C. *Das manichäische Religionssystem.* Tübingen, 1831; reprinted Göttingen, 1928.
de Beausobre, I. *Histoire critique de Manichée et du Manichéisme.* Vol. I, Amsterdam, 1734: vol. II, Amsterdam, 1739.
Burkitt, F. C. *The Religion of the Manichees.* Cambridge, 1925.
Christensen, A. *L'Iran sous les Sassanides.* Paris, 1936. Chapter IV.
Cumont, F. *Recherches sur le Manichéisme.* Paris, vol. I, 1908; vols. II, III, 1912.
Kessler, K. *Mani. Forschungen über die manichäische Religion.* Berlin, 1889.
von Le Coq, A. *Chotscho.* Berlin, 1911.
—— *Die buddhistische Spätantike in Mittelasien.* Pt. II, Die manichäischer Miniaturen. Berlin, 1923.
Nyberg, H. S. *Forschungen über den Manichäismus.* Zeitschr. f. d. neutestamentl. Wissensch. XXXIV, 1935, p. 70.
Polotsky, H. J. *Manichäismus.* P.W. Supplementband VI, p. 241.
Reitzenstein, R. and H. H. Schaeder. *Studien zum antiken Synkretismus aus Iran und Griechenland.* Leipzig, 1926.
Schaeder, H. H. Review of C. Schmidt and H. J. Polotsky, *Ein Mani-Fund* (see above). Gnomon, IX, 1933, p. 337.
—— *Manichäismus.* Die Religion in Geschichte und Gegenwart, III, Tübingen, 1929, p. 1959.
—— *Urform und Fortbildungen des manichäischen Systems.* Leipzig, 1927.
von Wesendonk, O. G. *Die Lehre des Mani.* Leipzig, 1922.
Williams Jackson, A. V. *Researches in Manichaeism.* New York, 1932.

(*h*) *Christianity and the Roman State*

(See also Bibliography to chap. XIX.)

von Gebhardt, O. *Ausgewählte Märtyreracten und andere Urkunden aus der Verfolgungszeit der christlichen Kirche.* Leipzig, 1902.
Knopf, R. *Ausgewählte Märtyrerakten.* Ed. 3 by G. Krüger. Tübingen, 1929.
Owen, E. C. E. *Some authentic Acts of the early Martyrs translated with notes and introductions.* Oxford, 1927.
Preuschen, E. *Analecta. Kürzere Texte zur Geschichte der alten Kirche und des Kanons,* 2nd ed. I. Teil. *Staat und Christentum bis auf Konstantin.* Tübingen, 1909.
Ruinart, T. *Acta Martyrum.* 1690. Later edition, Ratisbon, 1859.
Allard, P. *Histoire des Persécutions pendant les deux premiers siècles.* Ed. 3, Paris, 1903.
—— *Histoire des Persécutions pendant la première moitié du troisième siècle.* Ed. 2, Paris, 1894.
—— *Les dernières Persécutions du troisième siècle.* Ed. 2, Paris, 1898.
—— *Le Christianisme et l'Empire romain de Néron à Théodose.* Ed. 9, Paris, 1925.
Bouché-Leclercq, A. *L'intolérance religieuse et la politique.* Paris, 1917.
Cadoux, C. J. *The Early Church and the World.* Edinburgh, 1925.
Callewaert, C. *Les premiers Chrétiens furent-ils persécutés par édits généraux ou par mesures de police?* Rev. hist. ecclés. II (1901), p. 771; III (1902), pp. 5, 324, 601 [and see ib. XII (1911), pp. 5, 633; *Rev. quest. hist.* LXXIV (1903), p. 28; ib. LXXVI (1904), p. 5; *ib.* LXXXII (1907), p. 5].
Canfield, L. H. *The early Persecutions of the Christians.* Columbia University Studies in History, Economics and Public Law, vol. LV, No. 2. New York, 1913.

Conrat, M. *Die Christenverfolgungen im römischen Reiche vom Standpunkte des Juristen.* Leipzig, 1897.

Costa, G. *Religione e politica nell' impero romano.* Turin, 1923 (cf. p. 794).

Fracassini, U. *L' impero e il cristianesimo da Nerone a Costantino.* Perugia, 1913.

Guérin, L. *Étude sur le fondement juridique des persécutions dirigées contre les chrétiens pendant les deux premiers siècles de notre ère.* Nouvelle Rev. hist. du droit français et étranger, xix, 1895, pp. 601, 714.

Hardy, E. G. *Christianity and the Roman Government.* London, 1894. Ed. 2. 1906. Reprint of 1st ed. 1925.

Last, H. *The Study of the 'Persecutions.'* J.R.S. xxvii, 1937, p. 80.

Leclercq, H. *Droit persécuteur.* Dict. d'arch. chrét. et de liturgie, iv, 2ᵐᵉ partie, 1921, coll. 1565–1648 (with full bibliography).

Linsenmayer, A. *Die Bekämpfung des Christentums durch den römischen Staat, etc.* Munich, 1905.

Manaresi, A. *L' impero romano e il cristianesimo.* Turin, 1914.

Meyer, E. *Ursprung und Anfänge des Christentums,* vol. iii, pp. 510 *sqq.* Stuttgart–Berlin, 1923.

Mommsen, T. *Der Religionsfrevel nach römischem Recht.* H.Z. lxiv (N.F. xxviii) 1890, p. 389 [=*Gesammelte Schriften,* iii, p. 389].

Neumann, K. J. *Der römische Staat und die allgemeine Kirche.* Vol. i, Leipzig, 1890.

Ramsay, W. M. *The Church in the Roman Empire before* A.D. 170. Ed. 7, London, 1903.

Walzing, J. P. *Le crime rituel reproché aux chrétiens du IIe siècle.* Brussels, 1925.

(i) The West

TERTULLIAN. *Quae supersunt omnia,* ed. F. Oehler. 3 vols., Leipzig, vol. i, 1853; vol. ii, 1854; vol. iii, 1851.

In C.S.E.L. vol. xx (1890). Edd. A. Reifferscheid and G. Wissowa (*De spect. De idol. Ad nat. De test. anim. Scorpiace. De orat. De Bapt. De Pudic. De jejun. De anima*) and vol. xlvii (1906), ed. A. Kroymann (*De Pat. De carnis res. Adv. Herm. Adv. Valent. Adv. omnes haer. Adv. Praxean. Adv. Marci.*).

Separate editions: *De Paenitentia and de Pudicitia,* ed. G. Rauschen, *Florilegium Patristicum,* Fasc. x, Bonn, 1915; *De Baptismo,* in same series Fasc. xi, Bonn, 1916, and by J. M. Lupton, Cambridge, 1908; *De Praescriptione Haer.* in *Florilegium Patristicum,* Fasc. iv, by J. Martin, Bonn, 1930; *De Testimonio Animae,* by W. A. J. C. Scholte, Amsterdam, 1934.

For the *Apologeticum:* the latest edn is by J. Martin, *Florilegium Patristicum,* Fasc. vi, Bonn, 1933. See also the edition of J. E. B. Mayor with English translation by A. Souter, Cambridge, 1917, and text and Eng. trans. by T. R. Glover (Loeb), 1931. Cf. J. P. Waltzing, *Texte établi d'après le Codex Fuldensis* in Bibl. de la Fac. de philos. et lettres de l'Université de Liége, Fasc. xxii, 1914; *Texte établi d'après la double tradition manuscrite* (with literal translation), ib. Fasc. xxiii, 1919. He has also published (with A. Severyns) a text and French trans. (Budé), 1929, and a *Commentaire analytique, grammatical et historique.* Paris, 1931. R. Heinze, *Tertullians Apologeticum.* Berichte über die Verhandl. d. Kön. Sächs. Gesell. d. Wiss. zu Leipzig, Phil.-Hist. Kl. lxii, 1910, p. 281.

There is an Eng. trans. of Tertullian by P. Holmes in *The Ante-Nicene Christian Library,* vols. vii (1868), xi (1869), xv (1870) and xviii (1870), and there are valuable recent translations by A. Souter of *Concerning the Resurrection of the Flesh,* London, 1922; of *Against Praxeas,* London, 1919; *Concerning Prayer and Concerning Baptism,* London, 1919. T. H. Bindley has translated *On the Testimony of the Soul* and *On the 'Prescription' of Heretics,* London, 1914.

CYPRIANUS. *Opera Omnia*, ed. G. Hartel. C.S.E.L. vol. III in 3 parts. Vienna, 1868–1871.

There are separate editions of the *De Lapsis*, rec. J. Martin, *Florilegium Patristicum*, Fasc. XXI, Bonn, 1930, and of the *De unitate ecclesiae*, rec. E. H. Blakeney, London, 1928.

There is an English translation of the letters in *A Library of Fathers of the Holy Catholic Church*, Oxford, 1844 and of the treatises in the same Library, Oxford, 1839: R. E. Wallis translated the letters and treatises in *The Ante-Nicene Christian Library*, vols. VIII and XIII, Edinburgh, 1868, 1869. Canon Bayard has translated the letters into French, 2 vols., Paris, 1925, and T. A. Lacey has published, in English, *Select Epistles of St Cyprian treating of the Episcopate.* London, n.d.

LIBER PONTIFICALIS, ed. Th. Mommsen. Pars I. Berlin, 1898 (containing St. Peter to Pope Constantinus †715).

MINUCIUS FELIX. *Octavius*, ed. by C. Halm in C.S.E.L. vol. II, 1867.

Text: J. P. Waltzing, Leipzig, 1912: his edition and commentary, Bruges, 1909. English translation by G. H. Rendall in Loeb Classical Library, London, 1931, and by J. H. Freese, London, n.d.

NOVATIAN. *On the Trinity*, ed. W. Yorke Fausset, Cambridge, 1909. English translation by H. Moore, London, 1919.

———

Benson, E. W. *Cyprian: his life, his times, his work.* London, 1897.

Buonaiuti, E. *Il cristianesimo nell' Africa romana.* Bari, 1928.

von Harnack, A. *Das Leben Cyprians von Pontius. Die erste christliche Biographie.* T.U. XXXIX. Leipzig, 1913.

Koch, H. *Cyprianische Untersuchungen.* Bonn, 1926.

Langen, J. *Geschichte der römischen Kirche bis zum Pontifikate Leo's I.* Bonn, 1881.

Lortz, J. *Tertullian als Apologet.* 2 vols., Münster, 1927–8.

Monceaux, P. *Histoire littéraire de l' Afrique chrétienne.* Vol. I (Tertullian), vol. II (Cyprian). Paris, 1901, 1902.

Moricca, U. *Storia della Letteratura latina cristiana.* Vol. I, Turin, 1925.

CHAPTER XVI

THE TRANSITION TO LATE CLASSICAL ART

I. General

The reader should consult the Bibliography to Chapter xx in Vol. xi, pp. 942–44.

Rivoira, G. T. *Roman architecture.* Oxford, 1925.

Robertson, D. S. *A Handbook of Greek and Roman architecture.* Cambridge, 1929.

Strong, E. *La Scultura Romana.* 2 vols. Florence, 1923–26.

—— *Art in Ancient Rome.* 2 vols. London, 1929.

II. Special Periods

(a) From Septimius Severus to Elagabalus

Bartoccini, R. *L' arco quadrifronte dei Severi a Lepcis.* Africa ital. iv, 1931, p. 32.

Bendinelli, G. *Il monumento sepolcrale degli Aureli.* Mon. Ant. xxviii, 1922–23, p. 289.

von Gerkan, A. *Die Entwicklung des grossen Tempels von Baalbek.* Corolla für L. Curtius, Stuttgart, 1937, p. 55.

Rodenwaldt, G. *Säulensarkophage.* Röm. Mitt. xxxviii–ix, 1923–24, p. 1.

Watzinger, C. and K. Wulzinger. *Damaskus, die antike Stadt.* Berlin, 1922.

Weigand, E. *Baalbek, Datierung und kunstgeschichtliche Stellung seiner Bauten.* Jahrb. f. Kunstwissenschaft, 1924, pp. 79 *sqq.* and 165 *sqq.*

Wirth, F. *Römische Wandmalerei.* Berlin, 1934.

(b) From Alexander Severus to the Accession of Diocletian

Albizzati, C. *Vetri dorati del terzo secolo d. Cr.* Röm. Mitt. xxix, 1914, p. 240.

Alföldi, A. *Die Vorherrschaft der Pannonier in Römerreiche.* 25 Jahre Röm.-Germ. Kommission, Berlin, 1930, p. 11.

—— *Die Ausgestaltung des monarchischen Zeremoniells am römischen Kaiserhofe.* Röm. Mitt. xlix, 1934, p. 3.

Garger, E. *Untersuchungen zur römischen Bildkomposition.* Jahrb. d. Kunsthist. Wien, ix, 1935, p. 1.

Herzfeld, E. *Am Tor von Asien.* Berlin, 1920.

L'orange, H. P. *Studien zur Geschichte des spätantiken Porträts.* Oslo, 1933.

Rodenwaldt, G. *Ara Pacis und S. Vitale.* B.J. 133, 1928, p. 228.

—— *Der ludovisische Schlachtsarkophag.* Antike Denkmäler, iv, 1929, pp. 61 *sqq.* (Tafel 41).

—— *Porträts auf spätrömischen Sarkophagen.* Zeits. f. bild. Kunst, xxxiii, 1923, p. 119.

—— *Zur Kunstgeschichte der Jahre 220–270.* J.D.A.I. li, 1936, pp. 82 *sqq.*

Rostovtzeff, M. *Dura and the problem of Parthian Art.* Yale Class. Stud. v, 1935, pp. 155–301.

Strong, E. *Apotheosis and After-life.* London, 1915.

(c) From Diocletian to Constantine

Cecchelli, C. *Studi e scoperte italiane sull' archeologia e l' arte del tardo Impero.* Istit. di Studi Romani. Rome, 1938.

Delbrück, R. *Antike Porphyrwerke.* Berlin, 1932.

—— *Spätantike Kaiserporträts.* Berlin, 1933.

Egger, R. *Studi e scoperte austriache sull' archeologia e l' arte del tardo Impero.* Istit. di Studi Romani. Rome, 1938.

Gerke, F. *Petrus und Paulus.* Riv. d. arch. crist. x, 1933, p. 307.

—— *Die christlichen Sarkophage der vorkonstantinischen Zeit.* Studien z. spätant. Kunstgesch. herausgeg. von Lietzmann und Rodenwaldt, x, Berlin, 1938.

—— *Studien zur Sarkophagplastik der theodosianischen Renaissance,* 1. Röm. Quartalsschrift, xlii, 1934, p. 1.

Hinks, R. *Carolingian Art.* London, 1935.

—— *Raum und Fläche im spätantiken Relief.* Arch. Anz. 1936, p. 238.

de Jerphanion, P. G. *Studi e scoperte francese sull' archeologia e l' arte del tardo Impero.* Istit. di Studi Romani. Rome, 1938.

Kähler, H. *Zwei Sockel eines Triumphbogens in Boboligarten in Florenz.* Berlin, 1936.

Kaschnitz-Weinberg, G. *Spätrömische Porträts.* Die Antike, ii, 1926, p. 361.

Kinch, K. F. *L'arc de triomphe de Salonique.* Paris, 1890.

Krencker, D. and E. Krüger. *Die Trierer Kaiserthermen.* Augsburg, 1929.

—— *Das römische Trier.* Berlin, 1923.

Laqueur, R., H. Koch and W. Weber. *Probleme der Spätantike.* Stuttgart, 1930.

Lawrence, M. *Studi americani sull' archeologia e l' arte del tardo Impero.* Istit. di Studi Romani. Rome, 1938.

Lietzmann, H. *Das Problem der Spätantike.* Berl. S.B. 1927, p. 342.

L'orange, H. P. *Zum Porträt des Kaisers Diocletian.* Röm. Mitt. xliv, 1929, p. 180.

—— *Zum römischen Porträt frühkonstantinischer Zeit.* Serta Rudbergiana, Oslo, 1931, p. 36.

—— *Maurische Auxilien im Fries des Konstantinsbogens.* Symb. Osl. xiii, 1934, p. 105.

—— *Sol invictus imperator.* Symb. Osl. xiv, 1935, p. 86.

Niemann, G. *Der Palast Diokletians in Spalato.* Vienna, 1910.

Riegl, A. *Die spätrömische Kunstindustrie.* Vienna, 1927. (New impression of the original edition of 1901.)

Rodenwaldt, G. *Eine spätantike Kunstströmung in Rom.* Röm. Mitt. xxxvi–vii, 1921–22, p. 58.

—— *Der Belgrader Cameo.* J.D.A.I. xxxvii, 1922, p. 17.

—— *Studi e scoperte germaniche sull' archeologia e l' arte del tardo Impero.* Istit. di Studi Romani. Rome, 1937.

von Schlosser, J. *Praeludien.* Berlin, 1928.

von Schönebeck, I. *Ein christlicher Sarkophag aus St Guilhem.* J.D.A.I. xlvii, 1932, p. 97.

—— *Der Mailander Sarkophag und seine Nachfolge.* Studi di arch. crist. x, 1935.

—— *Die christliche Sarkophagplastik unter Konstantin.* Röm. Mitt. li, 1936, p. 238.

Weigand, Ed. *Ist die frühchristliche Kirchenanlage hellenistisch oder römisch?* Forsch. u. Fortschr. ix, 1933, p. 458.

Wiegand, Th. *Palmyra.* Berlin, 1932.

Wilpert, G. *I sarcofagi cristiani antichi.* 2 vols. Rome, 1029–1932.

CHAPTER XVII

THE LATIN LITERATURE OF THE WEST FROM THE ANTONINES TO CONSTANTINE

I. General Works on Latin Literature (Pagan and Christian)

Full bibliographies of editions and works on the various authors discussed in this chapter are given in the large general literary histories of Schanz and Teuffel, and in the *Histoire* of de Labriolle mentioned below. With a few exceptions only works not mentioned there are given here. For texts of the Christian Latin writers see (besides those mentioned below) Migne, *Patrologia Latina*, and the *Corpus Scriptorum Ecclesiasticorum Latinorum*; for the lives of the writers see St Jerome, *Liber de viris inlustribus*: Gennadius, *Liber de viris inlustribus*: ed. by E. C. Richardson, Leipzig, 1896.

Amatucci, A. G. (and others). *Africa Romana*. Milan, 1935.
—— *Storia della letteratura latina cristiana*. Bari, 1929.
Duff, J. Wight. *A Literary History of Rome in the Silver Age from Tiberius to Hadrian*. London and New York, 1927.
Jordan, H. *Geschichte der altchristlichen Literatur*. Leipzig, 1911.
Krüger, G. *History of Early Christian Literature in the First Three Centuries* (trans. by C. R. Gillett). New York, 1897.
de Labriolle, P. *Histoire de la littérature latine chrétienne*. Ed. 2, Paris, 1924.
—— *La réaction païenne*. Paris, 1934.
Leclercq, H. *Manuel d'archéologie chrétienne depuis les origines jusqu'au viiie siècle*. Paris, 1907.
Löfstedt, E. *Syntactica*. Lund, i, 1928, ii, 1933.
—— *Vermischte Studien zur lateinischen Sprachkunde und Syntax*. Lund, 1936.
[Löfstedt's works are an invaluable guide to the Latinity of the period. See the index for most of the authors treated in this chapter, and the bibliography for the author's special discussions of Tertullian.]
Monceaux, P. *Histoire de la littérature latine chrétienne*. Paris, 1924.
—— *Histoire littéraire de l'Afrique chrétienne depuis les origines jusqu'à l'invasion arabe*. Vols. i–vii, Paris, 1901–1923.
Norden, E. *Die antike Kunstprosa*. Ed. 2, Leipzig, 1909.
Raby, F. J. E. *A History of Christian Latin Poetry from the Beginning to the Close of the Middle Ages*. Oxford, 1921.
—— *A History of Secular Latin Poetry in the Middle Ages*. Oxford, 1934.
Terzaghi, N. *Storia della Letteratura Latina da Tiberio a Giustiniano*. Milan, 1934.

II. The Age of the Antonines

Fronto

For texts see the editions of the Correspondence by S. A. Naber, Leipzig, 1867, C. R. Haines (Loeb), London and New York, 1919, and E. Hauler (in progress).
Brock, M. D. *Studies in Fronto and his Age*. Cambridge, 1911.
Hanslik, R. *Die Anordnung der Briefsammlung Frontos*. Comment. Vindobon. i, 1935, pp. 41–7.
Hawes, A. B. *Citizens of Long Ago*. New York, 1934, pp. 47–73.
Pater, W. *Marius the Epicurean*. London, 1885.
Schmitt, A. *Das Bild als Stilmittel Frontos*. Munich, 1934

Aulus Gellius

See the Teubner text by C. Hosius, 2 vols. 1903; *The Attic Nights of Aulus Gellius*, John C. Rolfe (Loeb), 3 vols. 1927–28; *Aulu Gelle, Les Nuits Attiques*, translation, introduction, and notes by Maurice Mignon, 2 vols. Paris, 1934; *A. Gellius. Noctium Atticarum Book I*, ed. with introduction and notes by H. M. Hornsby, New York, 1937.

Foster, W. E. *Studies in Archaism in Aulus Gellius.* New York, 1912.

Africitas

Sister Wilfrid. *Is there an Africitas?* Class. Weekly, xxii (Dec. 17, 1928), pp. 73–8 (with a bibliography). See also Brock, *op. cit.* pp. 161–261, 338–341.

Apuleius

For texts see the edition of the *Metamorphoses* by R. Helm, Leipzig, 1913; *Apuleius the Golden Ass, being the Metamorphoses of Lucius Apuleius*, with an English translation by W. Adlington (1566) revised by S. Gaselee (Loeb), 1919; *The Story of Cupid and Psyche as related by Apuleius*, ed. L. C. Purser, London, 1910; and *Apulée— Apologie, Florides*, texte établi et traduit par Paul Vallette (*Collection des universités de France, Les Belles Lettres*). Paris, 1924.

Haight, E. H. *Apuleius and his Influence* (with bibliography). New York, 1927.

Nock, A. D. *Conversion.* Oxford, 1933. Chap. ix, 'The Conversion of Lucius,' pp. 138–55.

Oldfather, Canter and Perry. *Index Apuleianus.* (*Amer. Phil. Assoc. Monographs*, iii.) Middletown, Conn., 1934.

Poetry

Baehrens, E. *Poetae Latini Minores*, vi. (*Fragmenta Poetarum Romanorum*.) Leipzig, 1886.

Anthologia Latina, ed. A. Riese. 2 vols. ed. 2, Leipzig, 1894–1906; *Supplementum*, cur. E. Lommatzsch, 1926.

Terentianus Maurus, ed. Heinrich Keil. *Grammatici Latini*, vi. Leipzig, 1874.

Pervigilium Veneris

For texts see *Anthologia Latina* (ed. A. Riese), No. 200; J. W. Mackail in *Catullus* (Loeb), 1912; *The Pervigilium Veneris*, edited with introduction and notes by Sir Cecil Clementi, ed. 3, Oxford, 1936 (with an excellent bibliography); *Pervigilium Veneris*, edited by J. A. Fort, with a preface by J. W. Mackail, Oxford, 1922, and G. B. A. Fletcher, *Notes and Additions to Clementi's Pervigilium Veneris*, C.P. xxviii, 1933, pp. 209–16.

Martin, G. *Transposition of Verses in the Pervigilium Veneris.* C.P. xxx, 1935, pp. 255–9.

Rand, E. K. *Sur le Pervigilium Veneris.* Rev. E.L. xii, 1934, pp. 85–95.

—— *Spirit and Plan of the Pervigilium Veneris.* Trans. Amer. Phil. Assoc. lxv, 1934, pp. 1–12.

III. The Age of the Severi and the Rise of Christian Latin Literature

(See also section (*i*) of the bibliography to Chapters XIII–XV.)

Tertullian

Tertullian, Apology and De Spectaculis, edited and translated into English by T. R. Glover (Loeb), 1931.

De praescriptione haereticorum, texte latin, traduction française, introduction et index, par P. de Labriolle. Paris, 1907.

Tertulliani Apologeticum, recensuit J. Martin. Bonn, 1933.

Tertulliani de testimonio animae liber cum praefatione, translatione, adnotationibus, ed. W. A. J. C. Scholte, Amsterdam, 1934.

Hoppe, H. *De Sermone Tertullianeo Quaestiones Selectae*. Marburg, 1897.

—— *Syntax und Stil des Tertullian*. Leipzig, 1903.

Schrijnen, J. *Le latin chrétien devenu langue commune*. Rev. E. L. XII, 1934, p. 96.

Shortt, C. de L. *The Influence of Philosophy on the Mind of Tertullian*. London, 1933.

Perpetua and Felicitas

Robinson, J. A. *Texts and Studies*, I, No. 2, London, 1891.

Van Beek, C. I. M. I. *Passio sanctarum Perpetuae et Felicitatis*. Nimwegen, 1936.

Minucius Felix

Minucius Felix, with an English translation by G. H. Rendall, based on an unprinted version by W. C. A. Ker (Loeb), 1931.

M. Minucii Felicis Octavius, recensuit et praefatus est Herm. Boenig. Leipzig, 1903.

——, ed. P. Waltzing. Ed. 2, Leipzig, 1926.

De Jong, J. J. *Apologetiek en Christendom in den Octavius van Minucius Felix*. With a summary in English. Maastricht, 1935.

Schmidt, G. *Minucius Felix oder Tertullian*. Leipzig, 1932.

IV. From the Severi to Valerian

Disticha Catonis

Cf. the various writings of M. Boas, e.g. *Die Epistola Catonis*, Verhandel. der kon. Akademie te Amsterdam, Letterkunde, Nieuwe Reeks, XXXIII, 1. Amsterdam, 1934. For text see J. W. Duff and A. M. Duff, *Poetae Latini Minores* (Loeb), 1934.

St Cyprian

Bayard, L. *Tertullianus et St Cyprien*. Paris, 1930.

Monceaux, P. *St Cyprien, Évêque de Carthage*. Paris, 1914.

Commodian

Frank, T. *Latin Quantitative Speech*. A.J.Ph. XLIV, 1924, p. 169.

Katwijk, A. Fr. van. *Lexicon Commodianeum, cum Introductione de Commodiani vita, temporibus, sermone*. Amsterdam, 1934 (with excellent bibliography).

Sturtevant, E. H. *Commodian and Medieval Rhythmic Verse*. Language, II, 4 (December, 1926).

V. From Valerian to Diocletian

Nemesian

Anthologia Latina, edidit A. Riese. Vol. II, nos. 883–4.

Calpurnii Siculi et Nemesiani Bucolica, edidit C. Giarratano. Rome, 1910.

VI. FROM DIOCLETIAN TO CONSTANTINE

Arnobius

Arnobii adversus nationes libri VII, rec. C. Marchesi. Turin, 1934.
Gabarrou, F. *Arnobe, son œuvre*. Paris, 1921.
—— *Le latin d'Arnobe*. Paris, 1921.
Guinagh, K. *Bibliography of Arnobiana*. Class. Weekly, xxix, 9 (January 6, 1936),
pp. 69–70.

Lactantius

Pichon, R. *Lactance*. Paris, 1901.
Rand, E. K. *Founders of the Middle Ages*. Harvard Univ. Press, 1929, pp. 49–64.

(See also the bibliography to chap. xix, p. 789.)

The Historia Augusta

Scriptores Historiae Augustae, ed. E. Hohl, 2 vols., Leipzig, 1927.
Historiae Augustae Scriptores, edited and translated by David Magie (Loeb), 3 vols.
1922–1932.
Baynes, Norman. *The Historia Augusta, its date and purpose*. Oxford, 1926.

A most judicious review of the question is by Magie, vol. II (1924), pp. vii–xliv
(with bibliography), with additions to the bibliography in vol. III (1932), pp. vii–x.
Baynes (1926) gives a brilliant exposition of his theory, also with an excellent bibliography. An important utterance is that of de Labriolle (*Réaction*, p. 338), who rejects
the sceptical view of Dessau, though recommending a proper caution in the use of
the *S.H.A.* Similarly Terzaghi, *op. cit.* pp. 452–54. For other works on the
S.H.A. see the General Bibliography, v, B.

CHAPTER XVIII

LITERATURE, SCIENCE AND PHILOSOPHY IN THE EASTERN HALF OF THE EMPIRE

I. GENERAL WORKS

(a) Literature and Culture

Geffcken, J. *Der Ausgang des griechisch-römischen Heidentums.* Heidelberg, 1920 (a reprint of ed. 1).

Harnack, A. *The expansion of Christianity in the first three centuries* (Eng. trans. by J. Moffatt). 2 vols. London–New York, 1904–5.

Hatch, E. *The influence of Greek Ideas and Usages upon the Christian Church.* London, 1907.

Hirzel, R. *Der Dialog.* Vol. II, Leipzig, 1895, pp. 334 *sqq.*

de Labriolle, P. *La réaction païenne.* Paris, 1934.

Misch, G. *Geschichte der Autobiographie.* Band I, *Das Altertum*, pp. 290 *sqq. Die religiöse Selbstdarstellung und die Seelengeschichte.* Leipzig-Berlin, [1907].

Norden, E. *Die antike Kunstprosa.* Vol. II, ed. 2, Leipzig, 1900.

Puech, A. *Histoire de la littérature grecque chrétienne.* Vol. II, Paris, 1928.

Richtsteig, E. *Bericht über die Literatur zur sogenannten zweiten Sophistik aus den Jahren* 1926–1930. Bursian, CCXXXIV, 1932 and CCXXXVIII, 1933.

Rohde, E. *Der griechische Roman.* Ed. 2, Leipzig, 1900.

Schmid, W. and O. Stählin. *Geschichte der griechischen Litteratur.* II. Teil, 2. Band, ed. 6, Munich, 1934.

von Wilamowitz-Moellendorff, U. *Die griechische Litteratur des Altertums.* Leipzig, 1912, pp. 188 *sqq.*

—— *Der Glaube der Hellenen.* Vol. II, Berlin, 1932.

(b) Philosophy

Bidez, J. *Vie de Porphyre.* Ghent, 1918.

Bigg, C. *Neoplatonism.* London, 1895.

—— *The Christian Platonists of Alexandria.* London, 1913.

Bréhier, E. *Histoire de la Philosophie.* Vol. I, ii, Paris, 1931, pp. 449 *sqq.*

Dodds, E. R. *Select passages illustrative of Neoplatonism.* London, 1923 (trans.) and 1924 (Greek texts).

Praechter, K. *Richtungen und Schulen im Neuplatonismus* (Robert's Genethliakon, pp. 105 *sqq.*). Berlin, 1910.

—— *Überwegs Geschichte der Philosophie.* Vol. I, ed. 12, Berlin, 1926.

Schissel, O. *Das Ende des Platonismus im Altertum.* Fulda, 1929.

Theiler, W. *Die Vorbereitung des Neuplatonismus* (Problemata, I). Berlin, 1930.

Whittaker, T. *The Neo-platonists.* Cambridge, 1901.

Zeller, E. *Die Philosophie der Griechen.* Vol. III, ed. 5 (a reprint of ed. 4), edited by E. Wellmann, Leipzig, 1923.

Arts. in P.W. *s.vv.* Gnosis (Schulthess), Gnosis and Gnostiker (Bousset), Hermes Trismegistos (Kroll).

(c) Science

Diels, H. *Antike Technik* (pp. 121 *sqq.*: 'Antike Chemie'). Ed. 2, Leipzig, 1920.

Duhem, P. *Le système du monde: histoire des doctrines cosmologiques de Platon à Copernic.* Vol. II, Paris, 1914.

Heiberg, J. L. *Naturwissenschaften, Mathematik und Medizin im klassischen Altertum.* Leipzig, 1920.

Kantor, M. *Vorlesungen über Geschichte der Mathematik.* Vol. 1, ed. 3, Leipzig, 1907.

von Lippmann, E. *Entstehung und Ausbreitung der Alchemie.* Berlin, 1919; Band 11, *Ein lese- und nachschlage-Buch.* Berlin, 1931.

Neuburger, M. *Geschichte der Medizin.* Vol. 11: *Die Medizin in der Verfallszeit der Antike.* Stuttgart, 1911.

Zeuthen, H. G. *Geschichte der Mathematik im Altertum,* etc. Copenhagen, 1896.

Art. in P.W. *s.v.* Alchemie (Riess).

II. INDIVIDUAL AUTHORS

(a) Poetry

Soterichus, Pisander, Tryphiodorus, Zoticus, Nestor of Laranda, and the other epic poets of this period are known only by unimportant fragments.

OPPIAN. *Halieutica* (with the *Cynegetica*, which is not by Oppian); ed. F. S. Lehrs in *Poetae Bucolici et Didactici*, Paris (Didot), 1862; ed. P. Boudreaux, Paris, 1908. Text, trans. and notes by A. W. Mair (Loeb). For some new views on Pseudo-Oppian see W. Lameere, *Apamée de Syrie et les Cynégétiques du Ps.-Oppien*, in *Bull. Institut. hist. belge de Rome*, 1938.

(b) Literary Criticism and Rhetoric

HERMOGENES. *Opera*, ed. H. Rabe, in *Rhetores Graeci*, vol. VI (Teubner), 1913; Syrianus' commentaries on Hermogenes, ib. vol. XVI, 1892–3; see Bursian, CXLII, 1909, pp. 226 *sqq.* and art. *s.v.* Hermogenes in P.W. (L. Radermacher).

APSINES of Gadara. *De arte rhetorica*, ed. C. Hammer, in *Rhetores Graeci*, vol. I, i, 1894, pp. 217 *sqq.*

LONGINUS. *De arte rhetorica*, ed. C. Hammer, ib. pp. 179 *sqq.*

(c) The Sophistic Movement

PHILOSTRATUS. *Opera*, ed. A. Westermann, Paris, 1849; ed. C. L. Kayser, Leipzig, 1870–1; edd. O. Benndorf and C. Schenkl (Teubner), 1893–1902. *Imagines*, rec. Semin. Vindob. sodales, Leipzig, 1893; text and trans., A. Fairbanks (Loeb); *Life of Apollonius of Tyana*, text and trans., F. C. Conybeare, 2 vols. (Loeb); *Lives of the Sophists*, text and trans., W. C. Wright (Loeb).

See also E. Richtsteig in Bursian, CCXXXIV, 1932, pp. 76 *sqq.*; S. Eitrem, *Zu Philostrats Heroikos*, Symb. Osl. VIII, 1929, p. 1, claims that it belongs to the 'edifying literature' of the Pythagoreans. *Epistles*: ed. J. F. Boissonade, Paris, 1842; ed. R. Hercher, in *Epistolographi Graeci*, Paris (Didot), 1873.

On the life of Apollonius see especially P. Batiffol, *La Paix Constantinienne*, Paris, 1914, pp. 29 *sqq.*; A. D. Nock, *Conversion*, Oxford, 1933, pp. 195 *sqq.*

(d) The Greek Novel

HELIODORUS. *Aethiopica* (Theagenes and Charicleia), ed. G. H. Hirschig, in *Erotici Scriptores*, Paris (Didot), 1856; text edd. R. M. Rattenbury and T. W. Lumb, French trans. by J. Maillon, Paris (Budé), i, 1935, and ii, 1938. There are several early English translations (e.g. by Abraham Fraunce into hexameters, 1622, 1638, etc.), while the French trans. by Jacques Amyot is 'peut-être le chef-d'œuvre de l'admirable écrivain.'

LONGUS. *Pastoralia* (Daphnis and Chloe), ed. P. L. Courier with the help of L. de Sinner, Paris, 1829; ed. G. H. Hirschig in *Erotici Scriptores*; ed. A. Kaïris, Athens, 1932; ed. with French trans., introduction, etc., G. Dalmeyda, Paris,

1934. G. Thornley's trans. of 1733 revised by J. M. Edmonds (Loeb). See S. L. Wolff, *The Greek romances in Elizabethan prose fiction*, Diss. New York, 1912. Famous French trans. by Amyot, 1559, 1712, etc.—'corrigée, complétée, etc. par Paul Louis Courier,' ed. 5, Paris, 1812.

Clementinae Recognitiones, ed. E. G. Gersdorff, *et Homiliae*, ed. J. B. Cotelerius, reprinted in Migne, Patrol. Graeca, i, col. 1201 *sqq.* and ii, col. 25 *sqq.* *Clementina*, ed. P. de Lagarde, Leipzig, 1865. See H. Waitz, *Die Pseudo-klementinen*, W. Heintze, *Der Clemensroman und seine griechische Quellen*, and W. Frankenberg, *Die syrischen Clementinen mit griech. Paralleltext*, in Texte und Untersuchungen zur Gesch. d. altchristl. Lit. xxv, 4, 1904, xl, 2, 1914, and xlviii, 1937, and J. Bidez and F. Cumont, *Les Mages hellénisés*, Paris, 1938, vol. i, pp. 55 *sqq.*

The Apocryphal Gospels, etc. Text and French trans. by Ch. Michel and P. Peeters, vol. i (Protevang. and History of Joseph), Paris, 1911. Eng. trans. by M. R. James, *The Apocryphal New Testament*, Oxford, 1924 (with good short bibliography).

Acta Apostolorum Apocrypha; Acta Martyrum, etc. For texts of these see the principal textbooks, such as O. Bardenhewer, *Patrologie*. See articles in Herzog-Hauck, in Realencycl. f. protest. Theologie, *s.vv.* Apokryphen, Acta Martyrum, etc.

METHODIUS. *Symposium, De autexusio, De vita, Aglaophon sive de resurrectione*, etc. Ed. R. Bonwetsch, Leipzig, 1917. See P. Heseler, *Zum Symposion des Methodius*, Byz. Neugr. Jahrb. vi, pp. 95 *sqq.* and x, pp. 325 *sqq.*

(e) Philosophy

NUMENIUS. Text (a new collection of the fragments) ed. E. A. Leemans, Brussels, 1937.

ORIGEN. (The alleged pagan philosopher.) See R. Cadiou, *La jeunesse d'Origène* (ch. vii, pp. 231 *sqq.*), Paris, 1935, and N. H. Baynes in *J.H.S.* lvii, 1937, p. 110 *sq.*

PLOTINUS. *The Enneads*. Text, ed. H. F. Mueller, 2 vols., Berlin, 1878–80; text, with French trans., introduction and notes, by E. Bréhier, 6 vols., Paris, 1924–36; German trans. by R. Harder, Leipzig, vol. i, 1930, ii, 1936; English trans. by St. MacKenna and B. S. Page, 5 vols. 1926–30 (cf. J. H. Stocks in *J.H.S.* li, 1931, pp. 313 *sqq.*).

The following is a selection from the considerable literature that has gathered around the great work of Plotinus:

Arnou, R., *Le désir de Dieu dans la philosophie de Plotin*, Paris, 1931; Müller, H. F., *Orientalisches bei Plotinos?* Hermes, xlix, 1914, pp. 70 *sqq.*; Bréhier, E., *La philosophie de Plotin*, Paris, 1928; Inge, R., *The Philosophy of Plotinus*, ed. 3, London, 1929; Oppermann, H., *Plotins Leben*, Heidelberg, 1929; R. E. Witt, *Plotinus*, etc., in C.Q. xxiv, pp. 198 *sqq.*, and xxv, pp. 103 *sqq.* (other recent publications, analysed by P. Henry, *Bulletin Revue Théolog.*, Sept.–Dec. 1932); De Corte, M., *Aristote et Plotin*, Paris, 1935; Przyluski, J., *Les trois hypostases dans l'Inde et à Alexandrie*, Mélanges Cumont, 1936, ii, pp. 925; Henry, P., *Plotin et l'Occident*, Louvain, 1934, and *Recherches sur . . . l'éd. perdue de Plotin publiée par Eustochius*, Paris, 1935; the same writer's recent paper, *Vers la reconstitution de l'enseignement oral de Plotin*, Bulletin Acad. R. Belg., Classe des Lettres, 1937, pp. 310 *sqq.* makes new approaches to the problem; see also his forthcoming work, *Les états du texte de Plotin*.

PORPHYRIUS. *Histor. philos. fragm., Vita Pythagorae, De antro nympharum, De abstin., et Ad Marcellam*; text, ed. 2, A. Nauck, Leipzig, 1886.—*De philosophia ex oraculis haurienda*, ed. G. Wolff, Berlin, 1866.—*Isagoge, et In categorias*

Aristot., ed. A. Busse, Berlin, 1887.—*Vita Plotini* (prefixed to the text of *Ennead* I), ed. E. Bréhier, Paris, 1924.—*Quaestiones Homericae*, ed. H. Schrader, Leipzig, 1880–2 and 1890.—Ἀφορμαί, ed. B. Mommert, Leipzig, 1907.—*Contra Christianos*, fr. coll. A. von Harnack, Berl. Abh. 1916, and new fragments in Berl. S.B. 1921.—Περὶ ἀγαλμάτων et *De regressu animae*, ed. J. Bidez, Ghent, 1913, as appendix to the *Vie de Porphyre*, with a bibliography of all his works (pp. 65 *sqq.*) amounting to 77 titles, of which only 10 or 11 survive.

IAMBLICHUS. *De Mysteriis*, ed. G. Parthey, Berlin, 1857.—*Protrepticus, De communi mathem. scientia, In Nicomachi arithm. introd.* Text, edd. E. Pistelli and N. Festa (Teubner), 1888, 1891–4.—*De vita Pythagorica.* Text, ed. L. Deubner, Leipzig, 1937.

(*f*) *Science*

(1) Mathematics.

ANATOLIUS (an Alexandrian who became bishop of Laodicea in Syria; a polymath with a preference for music). Some fragments of his mathematical works in the *Theologoumena Arithmeticae*, ed. V. De Falco (Teubner), 1922.

DIOPHANTUS. *Arithmetica.* Text, P. Tannery (Teubner), 1893.—Sir T. L. Heath, *Diophantus of Alexandria*, ed. 2, Cambridge, 1910.

PAPPUS. *La collection mathématique.* French trans. with introd. and notes, by P. Von Eecke, 2 vols. Paris–Bruges, 1933.

(2) Music.

PORPHYRIUS. *Kommentar zur Harmonielehre des Ptolemaios.* Text, I. Düring, Göteborg, 1932.

ALYPIUS. *Introductio in Musicam.* Text, C. E. Ruelle, Paris, 1895.

ARISTIDES QUINTILIANUS. *De musica libri.* III. Text, A. Iahnius, Berlin, 1882.

(3) Geography.

DIONYSIUS of Byzantium. *Anaplus Bospori Thracii.* Text by C. Müller, *Geographi graeci minores*, II, p. 2 *sq.*—C. Wescher, Paris, 1874.

(4) Chemistry, Alchemy, the occult sciences.

Ps.-DEMOCRITUS. *Physica et Mystica.* Text, Berthelot-Ruelle, *Alchimistes grecs*, vol. II, p. 41 *sq.* (text) and vol. III, p. 43 *sq.* (trans.): *Les mages hellénisés*, vol. II, texts edd. J. Bidez and Fr. Cumont, Brussels, 1938.

ZOSIMUS of Panopolis. Large fragments in Berthelot-Ruelle, ib., *passim*; cf. R. Reitzenstein, *Poimandres, passim*, etc.

JULIUS AFRICANUS. *Cesti* (Κεστοί). A large treatise of a miscellaneous character, embracing natural history, alchemy, medicine, agriculture, etc. Cf. art. in P.W. *s.v.* Iulius (47) (Kroll).

(*g*) *History, chronology, apologetics*

HERODIAN. *Historiae.* Text, L. Mendelssohn, Leipzig, 1883.—K. Stavenhagen, (Teubner), 1922.

DEXIPPUS. *Historiarum fragmenta.* Text, L. Dindorf, in *Historici graeci minores.* Vol. I, Leipzig, 1870, pp. 165 *sqq.*

DIO CASSIUS. *Historia Romana.* Text, J. Melber, Leipzig, 3 vols., 1890–1928.—U. P. Boissevain, Berlin, 1895–1901. Text and trans., E. Cary, 9 vols., London; see art. in P.W. *s.v.* Cassius (40), Schwartz.

JULIUS AFRICANUS. See H. Gelzer, *Sextus Julius Africanus und die byzantinische Chronographie.* Leipzig, 2 vols., 1880–98.

HIPPOLYTUS. *Die Chronik.* Ed. R. Helm-Marquardt, Leipzig, 1929.

PORPHYRIUS. *Chronica* (a source used by Eusebius). Fragm. ed. C. Müller, in F.H.G., vol. III, pp. 688 *sqq.*

EUSEBIUS. All his principal works (save the *Praeparatio Evangelica*, of which K. Mras is preparing an edition) have already been published in the great Berlin Corpus, *Griech. Christl. Schriftsteller*, which supersedes all previous editions: *Demonstratio evangelica*, ed. Heikel, 1913; *Chronica*, ed. Karst, 1911; *Contra Marcellum*, ed. Klostermann, 1906; *Theophania*, ed. Gramman, 1904; *Onomasticon*, ed. Klostermann, 1904; the *Ecclesiastical History*, ed. Schwartz, with the Latin translation of Rufinus (ed. Mommsen) on the opposite page, 3 vols., 1903–9; an English trans. by Kirsopp Lake and J. E. L. Oulton, 2 vols. (Loeb). Finally the *Vita Constantini* and related treatises, ed. Heikel, 1902 (cf. art. *s.v.* Eusebius in P.W. by Schwartz), still retain their value, even after the flood of modern literature upon them (see, for example, R. Laqueur, *Eusebius als Historiker seiner Zeit*, Berlin, 1929, and E. Peterson, *Der Monotheismus als politisches Problem*, Leipzig, 1935, pp. 71 *sqq.*); no attempt can be made here to give any review of this literature, and in any event the career of Eusebius passes beyond the date of this history. It should be added that upon the works of Origen and Eusebius the reader will find in the relevant chapters of H. Lietzmann's admirable *Geschichte der alten Kirche*, vols. II and III, masterly and lucid appreciations.

Such are the surviving works; to give some idea of what is missing, we may mention the complete loss of the works of the head of the theological and exegetical school of Antioch, Lucian, the teacher of Arius, and especially of the *apologia* for Christianity that he presented to the emperor Maximin. On his importance see A. Harnack, *Lucian der Märtyrer*, in Herzog-Hauck, *Realencycl. f. protest. Theologie*, XI, pp. 654 *sqq.*, and the recent study by G. Bardy, *Recherches sur S. Lucien d'Antioche*, Rev. E.A. XXXVIII, 1936, p. 481. See also H. Lietzmann, *Geschichte der alten Kirche*, vol. III, 1938, pp. 154 *sqq.* (for Eusebius).

(h) Miscellaneous

DIOGENES LAERTIUS. *De philosophorum vitis.* Text ed. Cobet, Paris, 1878. No new edition has yet replaced this faulty text, but considerable portions have been published with critical apparatus, notably in H. Diels' *Vorsokratiker*. See too *La Vie de Pythagore*, A. Delatte, Brussels, 1922; *Epicuri Epistulae*, ed. P. vonder Muehll, Leipzig, 1922. There is an Eng. trans. by R. D. Hicks, 2 vols. (Loeb).

AELIAN. *Variae historiae et Historia animalium*, ed. Hercher (Teubner), 1864 and 1867; *Epistolae* in Epistolographi Graeci, ed. Hercher, Paris (Didot), 1873.

ATHENAEUS. *Deipnosophistae.* Text, ed. Kaibel, 3 vols. (Teubner), 1887–90; Eng. trans. by C. Burton Gulick, vols. I–V (Loeb). See *Animadversiones in Athenaeum*, J. Schweighaeuser, 9 vols. Strassburg, 1801–7.

CHAPTER XIX

THE GREAT PERSECUTION

This Bibliography is supplementary to the Bibliographies for Chapters VI, IX, and XIII–XV; see too the Bibliographical notes in N. H. Baynes, *Constantine the Great and the Christian Church*, British Academy: Proceedings, vol. XV, 1929. As in the Bibliography to Chapters XIII–XV the following abbreviations are used:

C.S.E.L.=*Corpus Scriptorum Ecclesiasticorum Latinorum.*
Gr. Chr. Schr.=*Griechische Christliche Schriftsteller.*
T.U.=*Texte und Untersuchungen.*

A. Ancient Sources

(a) Texts

For collections of Acts and Passions of the Martyrs see Bibl. to Chapters XIII–V, § II(*h*).

Arnobius. *Adversus Nationes*, ed. C. Marchesi. Turin, 1934.

Eusebius. *Ecclesiastical History.* See Bibliography, above, p. 767. *De Martyribus Palaestinae*: printed with the *Ecclesiastical History* (in vol. 2 of the edition by E. Schwartz).

For the longer edition of the *Martyrs of Palestine* preserved in Syriac see B. Violet, *Die palästinischen Märtyrer des Eusebius von Cäsarea*, T.U. XIV, Heft 4, Leipzig, 1896 (with German translation).

Of the Greek text of this longer—second—edition of the *Martyrs of Palestine* H. Delehaye published some fragments in An. Boll. XVI, 1897, p. 113. These fragments contain the Passion of St Pamphilus and of this text 'une nouvelle rédaction abrégée' was published by H. Delehaye from Brit. Mus. Add. 36,589, An. Boll. XXV, 1906, p. 499. This redaction is not included in Schwartz's text, cf. An Boll. XXVII, 1908, p. 203.

—— The *Praeparatio Evangelica.* Ed. E. H. Gifford. 4 vols. Oxford, 1903.

—— The *Demonstratio Evangelica.* Ed. I. A. Heikel. Gr. Chr. Schr., vol. XXIII.

Translations: The Praeparatio Evangelica, by E. H. Gifford, Vol. III of his edition: in two parts. Oxford, 1903.

—— The Demonstratio Evangelica, by W. J. Ferrar. 2 vols. London, 1920.

Lactantius. *Opera.* Ed. S. Brandt. 2 vols. C.S.E.L. Vienna, 1890–1893.

—— *De mortibus persecutorum.* Ed. J. Pesenti. Turin, 1922.

—— Translation by W. Fletcher. Ante-Nicene Christian Library, vols. XXI–XXII. Edinburgh, 1871.

Optatus. Ed. C. Ziwsa. C.S.E.L. vol. XXVI. Vienna, 1893.

—— Translation by O. R. Vassall-Phillips. London, 1917.

Urkunden zur Entstehungsgeschichte des Donatismus. Ed. H. von Soden. Bonn, 1913.

Peter, Bp. of Alexandria. Fragments in M. J. Routh, *Reliquiae Sacrae*[2], vol. IV. Oxford, 1846.

Melitian Schism: the early years.

(i) Canonical Letter of S. Peter of Alexandria. M. J. Routh, *Reliquiae Sacrae*[2], vol. IV, Oxford, 1846, pp. 23 sqq.; A. P. de Lagarde, *Reliquiae iuris ecclesiastici antiquissimae. Graece edidit* A. P. de L. Leipzig, 1856, pp. 63 sqq
A Syriac version with additions in *Reliquiae iuris ecclesiastici antiquissimae*

Syriace edidit A. P. de Lagarde, Leipzig, 1856: Greek translation of these additions in E. Schwartz, *Zur Gesch. des Athanasius*. Gött. Nach. 1905, p. 164.

(ii) Documents appended to the Historia Acephala of Athanasius. Cf. P. Batiffol, in Byz. Zeits. x, 1901, p. 128.

(iii) Epiphanius, *Opera*. Ed. G. Dindorf. 5 vols. Leipzig, 1859–63; or in Gr. Chr. Schr., ed. K. Holl. Vol. iii, 1931. *Haer.* § 68.

(iv) Epistola ad Meletium. Routh, *Reliquiae Sacrae*². Oxford, 1846, vol. 4, p. 91.

(v) Bell, H. I. *Jews and Christians in Egypt*. London, 1924.

Grégoire, H. *Recueil des Inscriptions grecques chrétiennes d'Asie Mineure*. Fasc. 1, Paris, 1922.

Iurisprudentiae anteiustinianae reliquias, ed. E. Seckel and B. Kuebler, ed. 6, vol. 2, Fasc. 2. Leipzig, 1927 (Manichaean Edict, p. 381). For discussion of date of the edict cf. L. Poinssot in *Nouvelles Archives des Missions scientifiques et littéraires*, N.S. vol. xxi, Fasc. 8, 1913, at pp. 170–171.

(The Letter of Theonas is a forgery. Cf. P. Batiffol, Bull. crit. vii, 1886, p. 155; A. Harnack, Theol. Literaturzeitung, xi, 1886, col. 319.)

(b) Works on the Sources

Arnobius.

Marchesi, C. *Questioni Arnobiane*. Atti R. Ist. Veneto, vol. lxxxviii, Parte 2nda, 1929, p. 1009.

—— *Il Pessimismo di un apologista cristiano*. Pègaso, vol. ii, Parte 1 (Florence), 1930, p. 536.

On the construction and composition of the apology cf. S. Colombo, *Arnobio Afro e i suoi sette libri Adversus Nationes*. Didaskaleion, N.S. ix, 1930, Fasc. 3, p. 1.

Eusebius.

Lawlor, H. J. *Eusebiana*. Oxford, 1912.

Puech, A. *Histoire de la littérature grecque chrétienne*. Vol. iii, Paris, 1930.

Schwartz, E. Art. in P.W. *s.v.* Eusebios.

Lactantius.

Brandt, S. *Über die dualistischen Zusätze und die Kaiseranreden bei Lactantius. Nebst einer Untersuchung über das Leben des Lactantius und die Entstehungsverhältnisse seiner Prosaschriften*. Wien S.B. Phil.-hist. Kl. cxviii, 1889 (1892), Abh. 8; *ib.* cxix, 1889, Abh. 1; *ib.* cxx, 1890, Abh. 5; *ib.* cxxv, 1891 (1892), Abh. 6 (with altered title).

Pichon, R. *Lactance*. Paris, 1901. After reading this book Brandt admitted the Lactantian authorship of the *De mort. pers.* (Cf. J. G. P. Borleffs, Mnem. (N.S.) lviii, 1930, p. 223.)

Piganiol, A. *Dates constantiniennes*. Revue d'hist. et de philos. religieuses, xii, 1932, p. 360.

(c) The Passions and Acta

For a discussion of early Martyria see A. Harnack, *Gesch. d. altchristl. Litteratur bis Eusebius*. Teil ii, Band ii, Leipzig, 1904, pp. 463–482. For the publications of texts of Passions and Acta of the Martyrs it will suffice to refer to the bibliographies in (i) *Bibliotheca hagiographica Latina*. 2 vols. Brussels, 1898–1901. Supplement, ed. 2, Brussels, 1911. (ii) *Bibliotheca hagiographica Graeca*. Ed. 2, Brussels, 1909. (iii) *Bibliotheca hagiographica Orientalis*. Brussels, 1910.

[In what follows no reference is made to martyrs who have merely hypothetically been assigned to the period of the great persecution by modern scholars.]

For general studies of martyrs and confessors of particular areas see for the Danubian provinces, J. Zeiller (see below); for Dalmatia, J. Zeiller (see below); H. Delehaye, *Saints d'Istrie et de Dalmatie*. An. Boll. XVIII, 1899, p. 369 (for Salonae, An. Boll. XXIII, 1904, p. 5; XXXIII, 1914–1919, p. 265; XLVII, 1929, p. 77); id. Saints of Thrace and Moesia. An. Boll. XXXI, 1912, p. 161; id. *Les martyrs d'Égypte*. An. Boll. XL, 1922, p. 5, p. 299; id. Saints of Cyprus. An. Boll. XXVI, 1907, p. 161. For Africa: P. Monceaux, *Histoire littéraire de l'Afrique chrétienne*, vol. 3, ch. 2. Paris, 1905.

Abitinae, Martyrs of (A.D. 304). See below *s.v.* Saturninus.

SS. Agape, Chione and Irene. Text: P. Franchi de' Cavalieri, Studi e Testi IX, 1902, p. 15. Discussion: ib. pp. 3, 67; G. Borghezio, Didaskaleion IV, 1915, p. 245; and see Delehaye, *Les Passions des Martyrs*, etc. pp. 141–143.

S. Barlaam. A reference to this martyr in a rhetorical plural in Eusebius, *Hist. eccl.* VIII, 12, 2 (cf. Delehaye, An. Boll. XL, 1922, p. 309). Text and discussion, (Delehaye) An. Boll. XXII, 1903, p. 129.

SS. Claudius, Asterius and Neon. Date (23 August, 285) of martyrdom must be false. Discussion of Latin versions of lost Greek text: Franchi de' Cavalieri, Nuovo Bull. di arch. crist. X, 1904, p. 17; Studi e Testi, XXVII, 1915, p. 107.

S. Crispina. Text by Franchi de' Cavalieri, Studi e Testi, IX, 1902, p. 23; variant readings Nuovo Bull. di arch. crist. XI, 1905, p. 255 n. (and cf. ib. X, 1904, p. 19). Critical discussion of the Acta by P. Monceaux in *Mél. Boissier*, Paris, 1903, p. 383 and *Histoire*... III, pp. 159–161 (cf. Fliche et Martin, *Histoire de l'Église* II, p. 467 n. 6); Delehaye, *Les Passions*, pp. 110–114.

S. Dasius. Text by F. Cumont, An. Boll. XVI, 1897, p. 11; discussion, ib. p. 5. See further Parmentier and Cumont, Rev. Phil. XXI, 1897, p. 143; P. Wendland, Hermes, XXXIII, 1898, p. 176. For criticism of this curious Passion see Delehaye, An. Boll. XXVII, 1908, p. 217; XXXI, 1912, p. 265; *Les Passions*, pp. 321–328. For the martyr's tomb at Durostorum cf. Cumont, An. Boll. XXVII, 1908, p. 369 (sarcophagus at Ancona: ? brought from Durostorum at Avar sack of the town in A.D. 579).

S. Dioscoros. The Greek original is lost: text in two redactions An. Boll. XXIV, 1905, 321; discussion, H. Quentin, ib. p. 330. Fragments of a Syriac version (with Latin translation by Mgr Tisserant), An. Boll. XXXIX, 1921, p. 333. For discussion of the Passio: P. Allard in *Mél. G. Kurth*, Liège, 1908 (inaccessible to the writer); Franchi de' Cavalieri, Nuovo Bull. di arch. crist. XI, 1905, p. 251 n. Variant readings in a Bodleian MS. (Fell 3): see Delehaye, An. Boll. XL, 1922, pp. 324, 352.

S. Domnio. On the martyr of Salonae of this name see Delehaye, An. Boll. XVIII, 1899, p. 399; ib. XXIII, 1904, p. 11; F. Bulić, Bull. di arch. e storia dalmata, XXI, 1898, p. 113; ib. XXIII, 1900, p. 213. The acta are without historical value: on a possible confused memory of the name of a *praeses* of Dalmatia (M. Aurelius Julius A.D. 299) cf. Delehaye, An. Boll. XVIII, 1889, p. 403; ib. XXVII, 1908, p. 75. For the discovery of the sarcophagus of Primus, Domnio's grandson, in the basilica at Monastirine cf. Bulić, Nuovo Bull. di arch. crist. VI, 1900, p. 275.

S. Euplus. Texts: Franchi de' Cavalieri, Studi e Testi XLIX, 1928, p. 47, 239. Discussion: ib. p. 1.

S. Fabius. Text: An. Boll. IX, 1890, p. 123 (and see at p. 109). Discussion: Franchi de' Cavalieri, Studi e Testi, LXV, 1935, p. 101 (cf. Delehaye, An. Boll. LIV, 1936, p. 300) and see Monceaux, *Histoire*... III, p. 122.

S. Felix of Thibiuca. Text: An. Boll. XXXIX, 1921, p. 247. Discussion: ib. pp. 241, 259. (Cf. ib. XVI, 1897, p. 19.) Monceaux, *La Passio Felicis. Étude critique*

sur les documents relatifs au martyre de Félix, évêque de Thibiuca, Rev. Arch.
Ser. 4, vol. v, 1905, p. 335 (cf. id. *Histoire*... iii, p. 136).

Forty Martyrs of Sebastia. Though the Passio may not be authentic, it seems that the
Testament of the martyrs is genuine. See N. Bonwetsch, Neue kirchliche Zeits.
iii, 1892, p. 705; Hausleiter, ib. p. 978; N. Bonwetsch and R. Seeberg, Studien
zur Gesch. d. Theologie und Kirche, i, i, 1897 (cf. An. Boll. xvii, 1898, p. 467);
Franchi de' Cavalieri, Studi e Testi, xxii, 1909, p. 64; ib. xlix, 1928, p. 155.
On the Syrian legend W. Weyh in Byz. Zeits. xxi, 1912, p. 76 and on a Coptic
text D. P. Buckle, Bull. John Rylands Library, vi, 1921, p. 352 (cf. An. Boll.
xli, 1923, p. 176). On Sarin (in the Testament): Cumont, An. Boll. xxv, 1906,
p. 241 and on Zimara ib. xxiii, 1904, p. 448.

S. Genesius. On the Genesius legend cf. Bertha von der Lage, *Studien zur Genesius-
legende*, 2 pts., Berlin, 1898 and 1899. Beilage zum Jahresbericht der
Charlottenschule (cf. An. Boll. xviii, 1899, p. 186); P. Roasenda, Didaskaleion
N.S. vii, 1929, Fasc. 2, p. 93. With the Genesius legend cf. the Passion of
S. Porphyry the Mime: An. Boll. xxix, 1910, p. 258. For possible confusion
with S. Genesius of Arles cf. Franchi de' Cavalieri, Studi e Testi, lxv, 1935,
p. 203. For the name of the martyr at Rome cf. Bull. d. Commiss. arch. com. di
Roma, xxxii, 1904, p. 325, but this may be S. Genesius of Arles.

S. Marcellus. For text and discussion see Delehaye, An. Boll. xli, 1923, p. 257 (cf.
A. Bonilauri, Didaskaleion, N.S. ix, 1930, Fasc. i, p. i). A variant text was
published by M. Denicolai in Didaskaleion, v, 1916, p. 141 (martyrdom dated
to A.D. 298). The Passio of Cassian is a pure plagiarism and valueless; An. Boll.
xli, p. 276.

[The Passio SS. Marcelli, Petri, etc., defended as authentic by H. Achelis, *Die
Martyrologien*, Berlin, 1900, pp. 173–177, is regarded as "un racconto in-
ventato da cima a fondo" by Franchi de' Cavalieri, Nuovo Bull. di arch. crist.
xi, 1905, p. 237 at p. 267.]

SS. Maxima, Secunda and Donatilla. Text: An. Boll. ix, 1890, p. 110. Discussion:
Franchi de' Cavalieri, Studi e Testi, lxv, 1935, p. 75; cf. Delehaye, An. Boll.
liv, 1936, p. 296.

S. Maximilian. Text: Harnack in his *Militia Christi* and Knopf only repeat the text
of Ruinart: "Le texte laisse à désirer et devrait être revue sur les manuscrits."
Delehaye. Discussion: Delehaye, *Les Passions*, pp. 104–110; Monceaux,
Histoire... iii, pp. 114–118.

SS. Phileas and Philoromus. Discussion: Delehaye, An. Boll. xl, 1922, p. 299. But
dating on p. 312 is to be corrected: the praefecture of Culcianus extended to
May 306: see papyrus reff. in O. W. Reinmuth, *The Prefect of Egypt*, Klio
Beiheft 34, Leipzig, 1935, p. 139.

S. Philippus (of Heraclea). It appears that a Greek original has been misunderstood
by the translator of the Passion. Discussion: Franchi de' Cavalieri, Studi e Testi,
xix, 1908, p. 124; ib. xxvii, 1915, p. 97; Delehaye, An. Boll. xxxi, 1912,
p. 243; J. Geffcken, *Zwei griechische Apologeten*, Leipzig, 1907, p. 249.

[The Epistle of Psenosiris: this papyrus was thought to have reference to the great
persecution. See A. Deissmann, *The Epistle of Psenosiris*, London, 1907 (cf.
Franchi de' Cavalieri, Nuovo Bull. di arch. crist. viii, 1902, p. 15); but it should
probably be otherwise interpreted: see W. Crönert, De critici arte in papyris
exercenda § 22 in *Raccolta di Scritti in onore di Giacomo Lumbroso*, Milan,
1925, pp. 514–528. Reference due to Dr H. I. Bell.]

S. Psotius. Text: An. Boll. xl, 1922, p. 343. Discussion: Delehaye, ib. p. 314.

Quattuor Coronati. For earlier literature see Zeiller, *Les origines chrétiennes dans les
provinces danubiennes* etc. pp. 88 *sqq.* For text and full discussion Delehaye, in
AA.SS. Novembris, vol. iii, Brussels, 1910, pp. 748 *sqq.*, and *Les Passions,*

pp. 328–344, and cf. L. Duchesne, *Mél. d'arch. et d'hist.* XXXI, 1911, p. 231;
Franchi de' Cavalieri, Studi e Testi, XXIV, 1912, p. 57; Delehaye, *Le Culte des
Quatre Couronnés à Rome*, An. Boll. XXXII, 1913, p. 63. For topography cf. F.
Bulić in Bull. di arch. e storia dalmata, XXXI, 1908, p. 111 (see An. Boll. XXIX,
1910, p. 205). N. Vulić in Riv. di arch. crist. XI, 1934, p. 156. J. P. Kirsch in
Hist. Jahrbuch, XXXVIII, 1917, p. 72 denies the authenticity or value of the
Pannonian Passion, but this is an indefensible view: cf. Delehaye, *Le Légendier
romain*, pp. 64 *sqq.*

SS. Saturninus, Dativus and companions. Text: Franchi de' Cavalieri, Studi e Testi,
LXV, 1935, p. 49. Discussion: ib. p. 3. Cf. Delehaye, *Les Passions*, pp. 114–116
and An. Boll. LIV, 1936, p. 293.

S. Sebastian. See Delehaye, *Le Légendier romain*: Index *s.v.*

S. Theagenes (under Licinius). Greek text: Franchi de' Cavalieri, Studi e Testi, XXIV,
1912, p. 179. On the Passion see Franchi de' Cavalieri, Studi e Testi, XXII,
1909, p. 101; ib. XXIV, 1912, p. 161; ib. XXVII, 1915, p. 116 and A. Ehrhard,
Byz. Zeits. XXII, 1913, p. 500.

S. Theodotus of Ancyra. The Passion until recently was regarded as a valuable
historical source: as such it was discussed at length by Franchi de' Cavalieri,
Studi e Testi, VI, 1901, p. 9; two texts printed p. 61; addenda p. 183. Delehaye
in An. Boll. XXII, 1903, p. 320 treated the whole Passio as a romance; Franchi
de' Cavalieri replied, Nuovo Bull. di arch. crist. X, 1904, p. 27, but later he
himself published a shorter text, Studi e Testi, XXXIII, 1920, p. 105, and on the
basis of that text came to the conclusion that the Passio was a homily and Theodotus
unhistorical. An attempt to distinguish a historical core in the Passio has since
been made by M. Astori in Didaskaleion, N.S. X, 1931, Fasc. 2–3, p. 53.

S. Tipasius. Text: An. Boll. IX, 1890, p. 116 (and see p. 109). On the legendary
elements in the Passio cf. Monceaux, in Rev. Arch., 4me Série, IV, 1904, p. 267.

THE PERSECUTION IN GAUL AND BRITAIN

(i) The Theban Legion. Text ed. Krusch in Mon. Germ. Hist., Scriptores Rerum
Merovingicarum III, 1896, pp. 32–40. The modern literature is considerable:
it will suffice to refer to F. Stolle, *Das Martyrium der thebäischen Legion*,
Breslau, 1891 (Bibl. of earlier work at p. 111); R. Berg, *Der heilige Mauricius
und die thebäische Legion*, Halle, 1895; P. Bourban, *Saint Maurice d'Agaune
en Suisse et ses fouilles*, Nuovo Bull. di arch. crist. IV, 1898, p. 194; ib. V, 1899,
pp. 71, 177; ib. XXII, 1916, p. 105; M. Besson, *Monasterium Acauense*,
Fribourg, 1913; C. Jullian, *Notes gallo-romaines*, 85, Rev. E.A. XXII, 1920,
p. 41; Delehaye, *Les origines du culte des Martyrs*, Ed. 2, Brussels, 1933,
pp. 86, 355. For a study of modern views cf. A. Hirschmann, Hist. Jahrb. XIII,
1892, p. 783.

(ii) The Legend of St Ursula and the Virgins of Cologne. For the inscription of
Clematius see F. X. Kraus, *Die christlichen Inschriften der Rheinlande*, I, 1890,
pp. 143 *sqq.* References to earlier literature in J. Klinkenberg, *Studien zur
Geschichte der Kölner Märterinnen*, B.J. 88, 1889, p. 79; ib. 89, 1890, p. 105;
ib. 93, 1892, p. 130; A. Riese, *Die Inschrift des Clematius und die kölnischen
Martyrien*, ib. 118, 1909, p. 236; H. Friedrich, *Die Anfänge des Christentums
etc. im Gebiet des Nieder- und Mittelrheins und der Mosel*, ib. 131, 1926, p. 10
(see, in particular, pp. 32–33), and cf. ib. pp. 323–324 (cf. M. Coens, An.
Boll. XLVII, 1929, p. 89); W. Levison, *Das Werden der Ursula Legende*, ib.
132, 1927, p. 1.

(iii) St Alban. W. Meyer, *Die Legende des h. Albanus*. Abh. Gött. Phil.-hist. Kl.
N.F. VIII, No. 1, Berlin, 1904.

B. Modern Works

Allard, P. *La persécution de Dioclétien et le triomphe de l'église.* 2 vols., ed. 4, Paris, 1908. (Uncritical.)

Andreotti, R. *Costanzo Cloro.* Didaskaleion, N.S. ix, 1930, Fasc. 1, p. 157; Fasc. 2, p. 1.

Augar, F. *Die Frau im römischen Christenprocess.* T.U. xxviii, Heft 4, 1905. (Cf. Franchi de' Cavalieri, Studi e Testi, lxv, 1935, at p. 238.)

Bardy, G. *Les objections d'un philosophe païen d'après l'Apocriticus de Macaire de Magnésie.* Bull. d'Anc. litt. et d'archéol. chrét. iii, 1913, p. 95.

Batiffol, P. *Les premiers chrétiens et la guerre.* In *L'Église et le Droit de Guerre.* Ed. 2, Paris, 1920.

Baynes, N. H. *Two Notes on the Great Persecution.* C.Q. xviii, 1924, p. 189. (On the Fourth Edict and on the chronology of Book ix of the Church History of Eusebius; and see Lawlor below.)

Belser, J. *Zur diokletianischen Christenverfolgung.* University of Tübingen Einladung Programm of March 6, 1891. (The attempt to date several martyrdoms to the beginning of Diocletian's reign has not convinced the present writer.)

Bigelmair, A. *Die Beteiligung der Christen am öffentlichen Leben in vorconstantinischer Zeit.* Munich, 1902.

Bihlmeyer, K. *Das Toleranzedikt des Galerius von* 311 (*Lactantius, De mort. pers.* c. 34). Theol. Quartalschrift, xciv, 1912, pp. 411, 527.

—— *Das angebliche Toleranzedikt Konstantins von 312. Mit Beiträgen zur Mailänder Konstitution* (313). Ib. xcvi, 1914, pp. 65, 198.

Buonaiuti, E. *La politica religiosa di Massimino e l'epitafio del vescovo Eugenio.* In *Saggi sul cristianesimo primitivo,* Città di Castello, 1923.

Cadoux, C. J. *The Early Christian Attitude to War.* London, 1919.

Caspar, E. *Kleine Beiträge zur älteren Papstgeschichte.* Zeits. f. Kirchengesch. xlvi (N.F. ix), 1927–8, p. 321.

Costa, G. Articles in Bilychnis, iii, 1914, p. 85; iv, 1914, p. 292; v, 1915, p. 437; vi, 1915, p. 18; xiv, 1919, pp. 2, 95. For the most part reproduced in abbreviated form without notes in *Religione e Politica nell' Impero romano.* Ed. 2, Turin, 1923.

De Jong, K. H. E. *Dienstweigering bij de Oude Christenen.* Leiden, 1905.

Delehaye, H. *Les origines du Culte des Martyrs.* Ed. 2, Brussels, 1933.

—— *Les légendes hagiographiques.* Ed. 3, Brussels, 1927.

—— *Cinq leçons sur la méthode hagiographique.* Brussels, 1934.

—— *Les passions des martyrs et les genres littéraires.* Brussels, 1921.

—— *Le témoignage des martyrologes.* An. Boll. xxvi, 1907, p. 78.

—— *Les légendes grecques des saints militaires.* Paris, 1909.

—— *Étude sur le Légendier romain. Les Saints de Novembre et de Décembre.* Brussels, 1936.

—— *La Persécution dans l'Armée sous Dioclétien.* Acad. Royale de Belgique, Bull. de la Classe des Lettres etc. 1921, p. 150. (An answer to E. Babut: *L'adoration des empereurs et l'origine de la persécution de Dioclétien.* Rev. H. cxxiii, 1916, p. 222.)

—— *Contributions récentes à l'hagiographie de Rome et d'Afrique.* An. Boll. liv, 1936, p. 265.

De Regibus, L. *Storia e diritto romano negli Acta Martyrum.* Didaskaleion, N.S. iv, 1926, Fasc. 2, p. 127.

Dölger, F. *Rom in der Gedankenwelt der Byzantiner.* Zeits. f. Kirchengesch. lvi, 3 Folge, vi, 1937, p. 1.

Duchesne, L. *Histoire ancienne de l'Église.* Ed. 4, vol. ii, Paris, 1908.

Dufourcq, A. *Étude sur les Gesta Martyrum romains.* Vol. i, Paris. 1900.

Fliche, A. and V. Martin, edd. *Histoire de l'Église.* Vols. ii, iii. Paris, 1935, 1936.

Florin, H. *Untersuchungen zur diocletianischen Christenverfolgung.* Diss. Giessen, 1928.

Franchi de' Cavalieri, P. *Osservazioni sopra alcuni Atti di martiri da Settimio Severo a Massimino Daza.* Nuovo Bull. di arch. crist. x, 1904, p. 5.

Gelzer, M. *Der Urheber der Christenverfolgung von 303.* In Festschrift für Eberhard Vischer: *Vom Wesen und Wandel der Kirche.* Basel, 1935, pp. 35–44.

Grégoire, H. *Les chrétiens et l'oracle de Didymes.* Mélanges Holleaux. Paris, 1913, pp. 81–91.

Haller, J. *Das Papsttum.* Vol. i. Stuttgart-Berlin, 1934.

Harnack, A. *Militia Christi.* Tübingen, 1905.

—— *Kritik des Neuen Testaments von einem griechischen Philosophen des 3 Jahrhunderts (die im Apocriticus des Macarius Magnes enthaltene Streitschrift).* T.U. xxxvii, Heft 4, 1911.

Healy, P. J. *The Valerian Persecution.* London, 1905.

Hulen, A. B. *Porphyry's Work against the Christians. An interpretation.* Yale Studies in Religion, i, 1933.

Hülle, H. *Die Toleranzerlasse römischen Kaiser für das Christentum bis zum Jahre 313.* Diss. Greifswald, Berlin, 1895.

Hunziker, O. *Zur Regierung und Christenverfolgung des Kaisers Diocletianus und seiner Nachfolger 303–313.* Leipzig, 1868.

Jullian, C. *Histoire de la Gaule.* Vols. vii, viii, Paris, 1926.

Knipfing, J. R. *The Edict of Galerius* (311 A.D.) *re-considered.* Rev. belge de philol. et d'hist. i, 1922, p. 693.

Lawlor, H. J., N. H. Baynes and G. W. Richardson. *The Chronology of Eusebius.* C.Q. xix, 1925, p. 94.

Maassen, F. *Über die Gründe des Kampfes zwischen dem heidnisch-röm. Staat und dem Christentum.* Vienna, 1882.

Mason, A. J. *The Persecution of Diocletian.* Cambridge, 1876.

Moricca, U. *Storia della Letteratura latina cristiana.* Vol. i, Turin, 1925.

Neumann, K. J. *Hippolytus von Rom in seiner Stellung zu Staat und Welt.* Leipzig, 1902.

Phillips, C. S. *The New Commandment. An inquiry into the Social Precept and Practice of the Ancient Church.* London, 1930.

Quentin, H. *Les Martyrologes historiques du Moyen Age. Étude sur la formation du Martyrologe romain.* Paris, 1908.

Schnorr von Carolsfeld, L. *Geschichte der juristischen Person.* Vol. i, Munich, 1933.

Schoenaich, G. *Die Kämpfe zwischen Römertum und Christentum in ihrer geschichtlichen Entwicklung von Nero bis auf Konstantin den Grossen.* Breslau, 1927.

Schwartz, E. *Zur Geschichte des Athanasius.* Gött. Nach. 1904, Heft 4 and 5; 1905, Heft 2 and 3; 1908, Heft 3 and 1911, Heft 4. (These are masterly and fundamental studies.)

Stade, K. *Der Politiker Diokletian und die letzte grosse Christenverfolgung.* Diss. Frankfurt a. Main, Wiesbaden, 1926.

Teuffel, W. S. *Geschichte der römischen Literatur.* Ed. 6, Vol. iii, Leipzig, 1913.

Toutain, J. *Les cultes païens dans l'empire romain.* 3 vols. Paris, 1907–1920.

Wendland, P. *Christentum und Hellenismus in ihren litterarischen Beziehungen.* (From N. J. Klass. Alt. 1902.) Leipzig, 1902.

Zeiller, J. *Les origines chrétiennes dans les provinces danubiennes de l'empire romain.* Paris, 1918.

—— *Les origines chrétiennes dans la province romaine de Dalmatie.* Paris, 1906.

Zimmern, A. *Porphyry the Philosopher to his wife Marcella* (English transl.). London, 1910.

CHAPTER XX

CONSTANTINE

This bibliography is, in the main, complementary to the bibliography on chapter XIX and the bibliographies to the other chapters there mentioned. For a fuller (critical) bibliography see N. H. Baynes, *Constantine the Great and the Christian Church* [see below, B, (*b*)].

A. Ancient Sources

(1) *Texts*

Eusebius, *Hist. eccl.* ix, x. See Bibliography to chapters XIII–XV.
—— *Vita Constantini, Oratio ad Sanctos, Speech at Tricennalia*, ed. I. A. Heikel in Gr. Chr. Schr. vol. 7, 1902. On the *Vita Constantini*, cf. Baynes, *op. cit.* pp. 31, 40 *sqq.* English transl. in vol. 1 of *Library of Nicene and Post-Nicene Fathers* (Eusebius), Oxford, 1890.
Lactantius, *De mortibus persecutorum*. See Bibliography to chap. XIX.
Anonymus Valesii, Pars I, or *Origo Constantini Imperatoris*, ed. T. Mommsen, Chronica Minora, vol. 1, pp. 7 *sqq.* in Monumenta Germaniae Historica.
Westerhuis, D. J. A. Diss. Groningen, Campis, 1906 (Text with commentary).
XII Panegyrici Latini, ed. G. Baehrens, Leipzig, 1911.
Zosimus, *Historia Nova*, ed. L. Mendelssohn, Leipzig, 1887.

(2) *Inscriptions*

For imperial support of the pagan counter-reformation which, it has been thought, is attested by the inscriptions see
Sir W. M. Ramsay, *Pauline and Other Studies*. London, 1906, ch. iv.
—— *The Letters to the Seven Churches of Asia*. London, n.d. ch. ix.
—— *The Tekmoreian Guest-Friends* in Studies in the History and Art of the Eastern Roman Provinces, London, 1906, pp. 305 *sqq.* (cf. ib. pp. 128, 200).
For the Epitynchanos Inscription see: Sir W. M. Ramsay, *Cities and Bishoprics of Phrygia*, ii, Oxford, 1897, pp. 566–7, 790; É. de Stoop, *Revue de l'Instruction publique en Belgique*, LII, 1909, p. 293; F. Cumont, *Catalogue des sculptures et inscriptions antiques (monuments lapidaires) des Musées royaux du Cinquantenaire.* Ed. 2, Brussels, 1913, pp. 158 *sqq.*; H. Grégoire, *Byzantion*, VIII, 1933, p. 49 (cf. W. M. Calder, *J.R.S.* II, 1912, p. 244).
Inscription of Eugenius: Text ed. W. M. Calder, *J.R.S.* x, 1920, p. 42; Bibliography, ib. p. 42, n. 2; E. Buonaiuti, *La politica religiosa di Massimino* in Saggi sul cristianesimo primitivo, Città di Castello, 1923, pp. 220 *sqq.*; W. M. Calder, *Some Monuments of the Great Persecution*, Bull. John Rylands Library, VIII, 1924, p. 345. There are difficulties in identifying this Eugenius with the bishop of the same name whose epitaph has been published by Calder (from Laodicea Combusta): *J.R.S.* x, 1920, p. 47; cf. P. Franchi de' Cavalieri in *Studi e Testi*, XLIX, 1928, pp. 101 *sqq.*
Paulovics, É. *La Table de Privilèges de Brigetio*. Archaeologia Hungarica, xx, 1936.

B. Modern Works

(a) Criticism of the Sources

Ohnesorge, W. *Der Anonymus Valesii de Constantino.* Diss. Kiel, 1885.

Pichon, R. *Les derniers écrivains profanes.* Paris, 1906. (For the Latin Panegyrici.)

Schwartz, E. *Zur Geschichte des Athanasius.* See Bibliography to Chapter XIX, p. 795.

Seeck, O. *Regesten der Kaiser und Päpste.* Part I. Stuttgart, n.d. [?1919].

(b) General

Batiffol, P. *La Paix Constantinienne et le Catholicisme.* Paris, 1914. (Note *Excursus B* on *Summus Deus*.)

Baynes, N. H. *Constantine the Great and the Christian Church.* Proceedings of the British Academy, XV, 1929.

—— *Eusebius and the Christian Empire.* Annuaire de l'Institut de Philol. et d'Hist. Orientales II, 1933–34 (Mélanges Bidez), Brussels, p. 13.

Burckhardt, J. *Die Zeit Konstantins des Grossen.* Ed. 2, Leipzig, 1880. In Gesamtausgabe of Burckhardt's works, vol. II, Berlin and Leipzig, 1929, with Preface by F. Stähelin; illustrated edition Vienna [?1935].

Dölger, F. J. (Editor). *Konstantin der Grosse und seine Zeit.* (Collection of papers.) Röm. Quartalschrift, Supplementband XIX. Freiburg i.B., 1913.

Fliche, A. and V. Martin, edd. *Histoire de l'Église.* Vol. III, Paris, 1936.

Gerland, E. *Konstantin der Grosse in Geschichte und Sage.* Beiheft XXIII to Byzantinisch-neugriech. Jahrbücher, Athens [1937]. (For bibliography.)

Hefele, J. *Histoire des Conciles.* (French transl. by H. Leclercq.) I, Paris, 1907.

Koch, H. *Konstantin der Grosse und das Christentum.* Munich, 1913.

Laqueur, R., H. Koch, and W. Weber. *Probleme der Spätantike.* Stuttgart, 1930.

Lietzmann, H. *Der Glaube Konstantins des Grossen.* Berl. S.B. Phil.-hist. Kl., 1937, p. 263.

—— *Geschichte der alten Kirche.* Vol. III, Berlin, 1938.

Lot, F. *La Fin du Monde antique et le Début du Moyen Age.* Paris, 1927. Eng. trans. London, 1931.

Manaresi, A. *L' Impero romano e il Cristianesimo.* Turin, 1914.

Müller, K. *Konstantin der Grosse und die christliche Kirche.* H.Z. CXL, 1929, p. 261.

Palanque, J.-R. *Constantin* in *Hommes d'État,* Vol. I. Paris, 1936.

Piganiol, A. *L'empereur Constantin.* Paris, 1932. (See J. Bidez in *L'Antiquité classique,* I, 1932, p. 1.)

Pincherle, A. *La politica ecclesiastica di Massenzio.* Studi ital. di fil. class. N.S. VII, 1929, p. 131.

Salvatorelli, L. *Costantino il Grande* in the series *Profili,* no. 103. Rome, 1928.

—— *La politica religiosa degl' imperatori romani e la vittoria del cristianesimo sotto Costantino.* Saggi di storia e politica religiosa. Città di Castello, 1914, p. 101.

Schwartz, E. *Kaiser Konstantin und die christliche Kirche.* Ed. 2. Leipzig, 1936.

Seeck, O. *Geschichte des Untergangs der antiken Welt.* Ed. 3. Vol. I, Berlin, 1910.

Şesan, V. *Kirche und Staat im römisch-byzantinischen Reiche* etc. Vol. I, Czernowitz, 1911.

Stähelin, F. *Constantin der Grosse und das Christentum.* Zeits. f. Schweiz. Gesch. XVII, 1937, p. 385.

C. Special Topics

(a) Constantine's Conversion

[*Vision of the Cross*: for a parallel vision on 17 Dec. 1826 cf. *La Vie intellectuelle* (Juvisy) V, 10 June, 1933, p. 182.]

798 BIBLIOGRAPHY

Alföldi, A. *The Helmet of Constantine with the Christian Monogram.* J.R.S. xxii, 1932, p. 9.
—— *Eine spätrömische Helmform und ihre Schicksale im Germanisch-Romanischen Mittelalter.* Acta Archaeologica, v, 1934, p. 99.
Batiffol, P. *Les étapes de la conversion de Constantin.* Bull. d'ancienne litt. et d'arch. chrétiennes, iii, 1913, pp. 178, 241.
Gagé, J. *La Virtus de Constantin, à propos d'une inscription discutée.* Rev. E.L. xii, 1934, p. 398.
Grégoire, H. *La "conversion" de Constantin.* Rev. de l'Université de Bruxelles, xxxvi, 1930–31, p. 231.
—— *La statue de Constantin et le Signe de la Croix.* L'Antiq. class. i, 1932, p. 135.
Pichon, R. *La politique de Constantin d'après les panegyrici latini.* C.R. Ac. Inscr. 1906, p. 289 (cf. Maurice, J., *Numismatique constantinienne,* ii, pp. xi–xlviii).
Schrörs, H. *Die Bekehrung Konstantins des Grossen in der Überlieferung.* Zeits. f. kath. Theol. xl, 1916, p. 238.
—— *Konstantins des Grossen Kreuzerscheinung.* Bonn, 1913.
Seston, W. *L'opinion païenne et la conversion de Constantin.* Rev. d'hist. et de philos. religieuses, xvi, 1936, p. 250.
—— *La vision païenne de 310 et les origines du chrisme constantinien.* Annuaire de l'Inst. de Philol. et d'Hist. Orientales et Slaves, iv, 1936, p. 373.
Wrzoł, L. *Konstantins des Grossen persönliche Stellung zum Christentum.* Weidenauer Studien, i, 1906, p. 229.

(b) Military

Costa, G. *La Battaglia di Costantino a Ponte Milvio.* Bilychnis, ii, 1913, p. 197.
Gagé, J. Σταυρὸς νικοποιός. *La victoire impériale dans l'empire chrétien.* Rev. d'hist. et de philos. religieuses, xiii, 1933, p. 370.
Grégoire, H. *On the etymology of the word Labarum.* Byzantion, iv, 1927–8, p. 477; xii, 1937, p. 277.
Grossi-Gondi, F. *La grande vittoria di Costantino.* Letture Costantiniane, Rome, 1914, p. 61.
Levi, M. A. *La campagna di Costantino nell' Italia Settentrionale (A. 312).* Bollettino storico-bibliografico subalpino, xxxvi, 1934, p. 1.
Monaci, A. *La Battaglia ad "Saxa Rubra" e il bassorilievo Costantiniano.* Dissertazioni della Pontif. Accad. Romana di Arch. Serie 2, viii, 1903, Rome, p. 105.
—— *La campagna di Costantino in Italia nel 312.* Nuovo Bull. di arch. crist. xix, 1913, p. 43.
Pears, Sir E. *The Campaign against Paganism,* a.d. 324. Eng. Hist. Review, xxiv, 1909, p. 1.
Toebelmann, F. *Der Bogen von Malborghetto.* Abh. Heidelberg Akad. d. Wiss. Phil.-hist. Kl. Abh. 2, 1915.

(c) The 'Edict of Milan'

For a comparison and discussion of the Eusebian and Lactantian texts cf. I. A. Heikel, *De Constantini Imperatoris scriptis edendis.* Inbjudning-Skrift of the University of Helsingfors dated 29 March, 1916, pp. 17 *sqq.* and note E. Schwartz, *Gött. Nach.* 1904, p. 534 n. 1.

Batiffol, P. *Le seizième Centenaire de l'Édit de Milan. L'Édit et les origines de la liberté religieuse.* Le Correspondant, 10 Mars, 1913, p. 839.
Knipfing, J. R. *Das angebliche "Mailänder Edikt" v.J. 313 im Lichte der neueren Forschung.* Zeits. f. Kirchengeschichte xl (N.F. iii), 1922, p. 206.

Laqueur, R. *Die beiden Fassungen des sogenannten Toleranzedikts von Mailand.* In Έπιτύμβιον *H. Swoboda dargebracht.* Reichenberg, 1927, p. 132.

Palanque, J.-R. *À propos du prétendu Édit de Milan.* Byzantion, x, 1935, p. 607.

Perugi, G. L. *La fonte giuridica dell' Editto di Milano.* Roma e l' Oriente, Anno iii, vol. vi, 1913, p. 13 (= p. 273 of volume).

Pichon, R. *La Liberté de Conscience dans l'ancienne Rome.* Rev. des deux Mondes, 15 July 1913, p. 314.

Schnyder, W. *Die Anerkennung der christlichen Kirche von seiten des röm. Staates unter Konstantin dem Grossen.* Jahres-Bericht der kant. höheren Lehranstalten etc. in Luzern für das Schuljahr 1912/13. Lucerne, 1913, p. 71.

Seeck, O. *Das sogenannte Edikt von Mailand.* Zeits. f. Kirchengeschichte, xii, 1891, p. 381.

(d) Constantinople

Bréhier, L. *Constantin et la fondation de Constantinople.* Rev. H. cxix, 1915, p. 241.

Dölger, F. *Rom in der Gedankenwelt der Byzantiner.* Zeits. f. Kirchengeschichte, lvi (3 Folge, vi), 1937, p. 1.

Lathoud, D. *La consécration et la dédicace de Constantinople.* Échos d'Orient, xxvii, 1924, p. 289.

Maurice, J. *Les origines de Constantinople.* Société nat. des Antiq. de France. Centenaire, 1804–1904. Recueil de Mémoires. Paris, 1904, p. 287.

(e) The Council of Nicaea

d'Alès, A. *Le Dogme de Nicée.* Paris, 1926.

Burn, A. E. *The Council of Nicaea.* London, 1925.

(f) Coinage

Maurice, J. *Numismatique Constantinienne.* 3 vols. Paris, 1908–12.

Schultze, V. *Die christlichen Münzprägungen unter den Konstantinern.* Zeits. f. Kirchengesch. xliv (N.F. vii), 1925, p. 321.

(g) Chronology

Kase, E. H. *A Papyrus Roll in the Princeton Collection.* Baltimore, 1933.

Kluge, E. *Beiträge zur Chronologie der Geschichte Constantins des Grossen.* Hist. Jahrbuch, xlii, 1922, p. 89.

Piganiol, A. *Dates Constantiniennes.* Rev. d'hist. et de phil. religieuses, xii, 1932, p. 360.

Seston, W. *Recherches sur la chronologie du règne de Constantin le Grand.* Rev. E.A. xxxix, 1937, p. 197.

—— *Sur les deux dates de la Table de Privilèges de Brigetio.* Byzantion, xii, 1937, p. 477.

Stein, E. *Konstantin d. Gr. gelangte 324 zur Alleinherrschaft.* Zeits. f. d. neutest. Wiss. xxx, 1931, p. 177.

(h) Miscellaneous

Franchi de' Cavalieri, P. *Della furca e della sua sostituzione alla croce nel diritto penale romano.* Nuovo Bull. di arch. crist. xiii, 1907, p. 63.

Hartmann, W. *Konstantin der Grosse als Christ und Philosoph in seinen Briefen und Erlassen.* Beilage zum Programm des städtischen Gymnasiums zur Fürsten-walde. Fürstenwalde, Spree, 1902.

Pfättisch, J. M. *Die Kirche in den Schriften Konstantins des Grossen.* Historisch-politische Blätter, cli, 1913, p. 753.

Seuffert, L. *Konstantins Gesetze und das Christentum.* Würzburg, 1891.

GENERAL INDEX

When the mention of a name does not record a fact of historical importance, the name is usually omitted. Romans are indexed under the most familiar part of their name, whether *praenomen, nomen* or *cognomen*. If there is doubt, a cross-reference is given. References to Roman Britain (Sites, etc.) are given under Britain.

Aaron of Caerleon, martyr, 296
Abantus, admiral of Licinius, 695
Abellius, 'vicarius' of the City Prefect, killed, 345
Abgar, dynasty of Osrhoëne, 10
— IX, 17; friend of Bardaisan, 496
— X, 87, 130
— the Black, in Syriac tradition, 493
Abrittus (Aptaat-Kalessi), in the Dobrudja, Decius killed at, 145, 167
Academy, the, Longinus and, 619
Achaea, province of, 392
Achilles sarcophagus, in Capitoline Museum, 555
Achilleus (Domitius Domitianus), revolt of, 277, 335; coinage of, 335
Acmoneia in Phrygia, cult of the 'immortal gods' at, 437
Acta Martyrum, nature of, 518; historical value of, 202, 207; imperial edicts not cited in, 665; interpolations in, 676 *n.*
Addai, *see also under* Tatian; *Acts of,* 500; *Doctrine of,* 502
Adhur-Anahid, wife of Ardashir, 110
Adiabene, 9, 49, 126; Christianity in, 496
Adige, R., 682
admissio, 362
Adonaea, area at Rome, 427
Adonis, 410
Adonis sarcophagus, in the Lateran, 565
adoratio, to the likeness of the Emperor, 356, 363; form of, 388
Adraha, fortification of, 175
Adrianople, 692; victory of Licinius near, 688; victory of Constantine at, 695
Adulis, 271
Aedesius, Christian, 676
Aelian, author, 613
Aelius Gordianus, jurist, 589
Aelius Junius Cordus, biographer, 599
Aemilia Pudentilla, wife of Apuleius, 570
Aemilianus, prosecutor of Apuleius, 581
— Aemilius, governor of Lower Moesia, defeats Goths, 147; proclaimed emperor, 147, 168, 229; defeats Gallus, 168; murdered, 169
— L. Mussius, Prefect of Egypt, revolt of, 173 *sq.,* 186
Aemilius Asper, grammarian, 577

aerarium, 373 *sq.*
aeternitas, on coins, 357 *sq.,* 386, 417, 719, interpretation of, 719
Aethiopica of Heliodorus, 615
Afinia Gemina Baebiana, wife of Gallus, 167; on coins, 167 *n.*
Africa, Septimius Severus and, 6, 21, 24; division of, 27; army in, 6; disturbances in, 76; Gordian proclaimed emperor in, 76 *sq.*; revolts in, 84 *sq.,* 349 *sq.,* 681 *sq.*; government of, under Diocletian, 392; joins Maxentius, 345; desert tribes in, 20; Christianity in, 536 *sqq.,* 676; martyrs in, 518, 520; religious divisions in, 692 *sqq.*; taxation units in, 400; roads in, 33 *n.*; economic progress of, 240; imperial domains in, 249; agriculture in, 278; buildings in, in early third century, 551; 'Africitas,' 579, 583, 589, 592, 609; African senators, 25, 375
Africanus, Julius, assists at building of library at Rome, 66, 477; life and works of, 477 *sq.*; and Origen, 485, 488; Eusebius and, 641
Agathonice, martyr at Pergamum, 518
agentes in rebus, 390
Agriculture, in Africa, 278; in Britain, 284 *sqq.*; in Egypt, 252, 273, 276; in Italy, 238 *sq.,* 254, 260 *sq.,* 276; in the provinces, 240 *sqq.*; importance of, 251, 254; decline of, 260, 268, 276
agri decumates, overrun by barbarians, 156, 158, 308
Agrippa, in Cassius Dio, 59 *sq.*
Ahriman, 118 *sq.,* 430
Ahura Mazda, 430; *see also under* Mazdean
Aitilāhā (Theodore), Bishop of Edessa, 500
Akiba, Rabbi, 484
ala, Ulpia contariorum civium Romanorum, 210; *I Gallorum et Pannoniorum catafractata,* 210; of camelry, 210; *alae,* increase of, under Diocletian, 397
Alans, 100
Alban of Verulam, martyr, 296, 679 *n.*
Albano, legion at, 24, 26, 43, 155, 376
Albinus, philosopher, 582 *n.*
Albinus, D. Clodius, governor of Britain, 15, 22, 27, 36, 589; becomes Caesar, 5, 6 and *n.*; war of, with Septimius

INDEX OF MAPS

Maps have each their own index, and reference is here made only to the number of the map. The alphabetical arrangement ignores the usual prefixes (lake, etc.)

INDEX OF PASSAGES REFERRED TO

(Texts p. 837; inscriptions p. 847; papyri p. 848. References to pages
include the notes at the foot of the page)

CAMBRIDGE: PRINTED BY
WALTER LEWIS, M.A.,
AT THE UNIVERSITY PRESS